macroeconomics

THE MCGRAW HILL SERIES: ECONOMICS

ESSENTIALS OF ECONOMICS

Brue, McConnell, and Flynn
Essentials of Economics
Fifth Edition

Mandel
M: Economics, The Basics
Fourth Edition

McConnell, Brue, and Flynn
**Economics: Brief Edition.
Macroeconomics: Brief Edition, and
Macroeconomics: Brief Edition**
Third Edition

Schiller and Gebhardt
Essentials of Economics
Twelfth Edition

PRINCIPLES OF ECONOMICS

Asarta and Butters
**Connect Master: Principles of
Economics**

Colander
**Economics, Microeconomics, and
Macroeconomics**
Twelfth Edition

Frank, Bernanke, Antonovics, and Heffetz
**Principles of Economics, Principles
of Microeconomics, Principles of
Macroeconomics**
Eighth Edition

Frank, Bernanke, Antonovics, and Heffetz
**Streamlined Editions: Principles
of Economics, Principles of
Microeconomics, Principles of
Macroeconomics**
Fourth Edition

Karlan and Morduch
**Economics, Microeconomics, and
Macroeconomics**
Third Edition

McConnell, Brue, and Flynn
**Economics, Microeconomics, and
Macroeconomics**
Twenty-Third Edition

Schiller and Gebhardt
**The Economy Today, The Micro Economy
Today, and The Macro
Economy Today**
Sixteenth Edition

Slavin
**Economics, Microeconomics, and
Macroeconomics**
Twelfth Edition

ECONOMICS OF SOCIAL ISSUES

Guell
Issues in Economics Today
Tenth Edition

Register and Grimes
Economics of Social Issues
Twenty-First Edition

DATA ANALYTICS FOR ECONOMICS

Jaggia, Kelly, Lertwachara, and Chen
**Business Analytics: Communicating
with Numbers**
Second Edition

Prince
**Predictive Analytics for Business
Strategy**
First Edition

Richardson and Weidenmier-Watson
Introduction to Business Analytics
First Edition

Taddy, Hendrix, and Harding
Modern Business Analytics
First Edition

MANAGERIAL ECONOMICS

Baye and Prince
**Managerial Economics and Business
Strategy**
Tenth Edition

Brickley, Smith, and Zimmerman
**Managerial Economics and
Organizational Architecture**
Seventh Edition

Thomas and Maurice
Managerial Economics
Thirteenth Edition

INTERMEDIATE ECONOMICS

Bernheim and Whinston
Microeconomics
Second Edition

Dornbusch, Fischer, and Startz
Macroeconomics
Thirteenth Edition

Frank
Microeconomics and Behavior
Tenth Edition

ADVANCED ECONOMICS

Romer
Advanced Macroeconomics
Fifth Edition

MONEY AND BANKING

Cecchetti and Schoenholtz
Money, Banking, and Financial Markets
Sixth Edition

URBAN ECONOMICS

O'Sullivan
Urban Economics
Nineth Edition

LABOR ECONOMICS

Borjas
Labor Economics
Nineth Edition

McConnell, Brue, and Macpherson
Contemporary Labor Economics
Twelfth Edition

PUBLIC FINANCE

Rosen and Gayer
Public Finance
Tenth Edition

ENVIRONMENTAL ECONOMICS

Field and Field
**Environmental Economics:
An Introduction**
Eighth Edition

INTERNATIONAL ECONOMICS

Appleyard and Field
International Economics
Ninth Edition

Pugel
International Economics
Eighteenth Edition

THE FOUR VERSIONS OF MCCONNELL, BRUE, FLYNN

Economics 23e Chapter Title	Economics 23e	Microeconomics 23e	Macroeconomics 23e	Essentials of Economics 5e
Limits, Alternatives, and Choices	x	x	x	x
The Market System and the Circular Flow	x	x	x	x
Demand, Supply, and Market Equilibrium	x	x	x	x
Market Failures Caused by Externalities & Asymmetric Information	x	x	x	x
Public Goods, Public Choice, and Government Failure	x	x	x	x
Elasticity	x	x		x
Utility Maximization	x	x		x
Behavioral Economics	x	x		
Businesses and the Costs of Production	x	x		x
Pure Competition	x	x		x
Pure Monopoly	x	x		x
Monopolistic Competition	x	x		x
Oligopoly and Strategic Behavior	x	x		x
Internet Oligopoly: Networks and Platforms	x	x		
Technology, R&D, and Efficiency	x	x		
The Demand for Resources	x	x		
Wage Determination	x	x		
Rent, Interest, and Profit	x	x		
Environmental Economics	x	x		
Public Finance: Expenditures and Taxes	x	x		
Antitrust Policy and Regulation	x	x		
Agriculture: Economics and Policy	x	x		x
Income Inequality, Poverty, and Discrimination	x	x		
Health Care	x	x		
Immigration	x	x		
An Introduction to Macroeconomics	x		x	x
Measuring Domestic Output and National Income	x		x	x
Economic Growth	x		x	x
Business Cycles, Unemployment, and Inflation	x		x	x
Basic Macroeconomic Relationships	x		x	x
The Aggregate Expenditures Model	x		x	x
Aggregate Demand and Aggregate Supply	x		x	x
Fiscal Policy, Deficits, and Debt	x		x	x
Money, the Federal Reserve, and Interest Rates	x		x	x
Monetary Policy, GDP, and the Price Level	x		x	
Financial Economics	x		x	
Extending the Analysis of Aggregate Supply	x		x	x
Current Issues in Macro Theory and Policy	x		x	
International Trade	x	x	x	x
The Balance of Payments, Exchange Rates, and Trade Deficits	x	x	x	x
The Economics of Developing Countries	x	x	x	

A red "X" indicates chapters that combine or consolidate content from two or more *Economics* chapters.

macroeconomics

Twenty-Third Edition

Campbell R. McConnell
University of Nebraska

Stanley L. Brue
Pacific Lutheran University

Sean M. Flynn
Scripps College

Mc
Graw
Hill

MACROECONOMICS, TWENTY-THIRD EDITION

Published by McGraw Hill LLC, 1325 Avenue of the Americas, New York, NY 10019. Copyright ©2024 by McGraw Hill LLC. All rights reserved. Printed in the United States of America. Previous editions ©2021, 2018, and 2015. No part of this publication may be reproduced or distributed in any form or by any means, or stored in a database or retrieval system, without the prior written consent of McGraw Hill LLC, including, but not limited to, in any network or other electronic storage or transmission, or broadcast for distance learning.

Some ancillaries, including electronic and print components, may not be available to customers outside the United States.

This book is printed on acid-free paper.

1 2 3 4 5 6 7 8 9 LWI 28 27 26 25 24 23

ISBN 978-1-265-30699-1 (bound edition)
MHID 1-265-30699-0 (bound edition)
ISBN 978-1-265-30831-5 (loose-leaf edition)
MHID 1-265-30831-4 (loose-leaf edition)

Director: *Anke Weekes*
Lead Product Developer: *Kelly I. Pekelder*
Marketing Manager: *Carla Damrose*
Content Project Managers: *Harvey Yep (Core)/Emily Windelborn (Assessment)*
Buyer: *Laura Fuller*
Design: *Aptara®, Inc.*
Content Licensing Specialist: *Lorraine Buczek*
Cover Image: *vchal/Shutterstock*
Compositor: *Aptara®, Inc.*

All credits appearing on page or at the end of the book are considered to be an extension of the copyright page.

Library of Congress Cataloging-in-Publication Data

Names: McConnell, Campbell R., author. | Brue, Stanley L., 1945- author. |
    Flynn, Sean Masaki, author.
Title: Macroeconomics / Campbell R. McConnell, University of Nebraska,
    Stanley L. Brue, Pacific Lutheran University, Sean M. Flynn, Scripps College.
Description: Twenty-third edition. | New York, NY : McGraw Hill LLC, [2024] |
    Series: The McGraw Hill series: economics | Includes index.
Identifiers: LCCN 2022033527 (print) | LCCN 2022033528 (ebook) | ISBN
    9781265306991 (hardcover) | ISBN 9781265308315 (spiral bound) | ISBN
    9781265271411 (ebook) | ISBN 9781265307745 (ebook other)
Subjects: LCSH: Macroeconomics.
Classification: LCC HB172.5 .M3743 2024 (print) | LCC HB172.5 (ebook) | DDC
    339—dc23/eng/20220715
LC record available at https://lccn.loc.gov/2022033527
LC ebook record available at https://lccn.loc.gov/2022033528

The Internet addresses listed in the text were accurate at the time of publication. The inclusion of a website does not indicate an endorsement by the authors or McGraw Hill LLC, and McGraw Hill LLC does not guarantee the accuracy of the information presented at these sites.

To Mac and Mem, Terri and Craig, and past instructors.

Campbell R. McConnell/McGraw Hill

CAMPBELL R. MCCONNELL earned his Ph.D. at the University of Iowa after receiving degrees from Cornell College and the University of Illinois. He taught at the University of Nebraska–Lincoln from 1953 until his retirement in 1990. He was also coauthor of *Contemporary Labor Economics* and *Essentials of Economics.* He was a recipient of both the University of Nebraska Distinguished Teaching Award and the James A. Lake Academic Freedom Award and served as president of the Midwest Economics Association. Professor McConnell was awarded an honorary Doctor of Laws degree from Cornell College in 1973 and received its Distinguished Achievement Award in 1994. He was also a jazz expert and aficionado until his passing in 2019.

Stanley L. Brue/McGraw Hill

STANLEY L. BRUE did his undergraduate work at Augustana College (South Dakota) and received its Distinguished Achievement Award in 1991. He received his Ph.D. from the University of Nebraska–Lincoln. He is retired from a long career at Pacific Lutheran University, where he was honored as a recipient of the Burlington Northern Faculty Achievement Award. Professor Brue has also received the national Leavey Award for excellence in economics education. He has served as national president and chair of the Board of Trustees of Omicron Delta Epsilon International Economics Honorary. He is coauthor of *Economic Scenes,* fifth edition (Prentice-Hall); *Contemporary Labor Economics,* twelfth edition; *Essentials of Economics,* fourth edition; and *The Evolution of Economic Thought,* eighth edition (Cengage Learning). For relaxation, he enjoys international travel, attending sporting events, and going on fishing trips.

Sean M. Flynn/McGraw Hill

SEAN M. FLYNN did his undergraduate work at the University of Southern California before completing his Ph.D. at U.C. Berkeley, where he served as the Head Graduate Student Instructor for the Department of Economics after receiving the Outstanding Graduate Student Instructor Award. He teaches at Scripps College (of the Claremont Colleges) and is the author of *Economics for Dummies,* third edition (Wiley); *Essentials of Economics,* fourth edition; and *The Cure That Works: How to Have the World's Best Healthcare—at a Quarter of the Price* (Regnery). His research interests include behavioral finance, behavioral economics, and health care economics. An accomplished martial artist, Sean has coached five of his students to national championships and is the author of *Understanding Shodokan Aikido.* Other hobbies include running, traveling, and cooking.

Welcome to the 23rd edition of *Macroeconomics*, America's most innovative—and popular—economics learning resource.

We are pleased to present faculty and students with comprehensive revisions, insightful new content, and significant improvements to both our online learning system and our industry-leading ancillary materials.

From real-life examples to cutting-edge learning resources, our modern approach makes learning and applying economics easier for both students and instructors.

- For students, *Macroeconomics* **offers a student-centered learning environment that presents the subject matter in new and engaging ways.**

- For instructors, **a full and supportive teaching package does the heavy lifting with regard to basic concepts and ideas so that instructors can focus their attention on helping students achieve the highest levels of Bloom's taxonomy of learning,** including being able to analyze, apply, and create based on economics concepts and ideas.

Optimize your outcomes
MORE Student-Centered

McConnell has always put students at the center of every revision and the new edition is no exception. Extensive market feedback and a keen focus on optimizing student outcomes drove this revision. Nearly every element—from the work itself to the digital tools and resources—has been updated and optimized for today's learners.

- **An all-new chapter, "Internet Oligopoly: Networks and Platforms,"** provides an intuitive presentation of the Nobel Prize-winning economic theories that explain why Internet industries are highly concentrated due to network effects but at the same time often deliver their main products for free, as though the firms in those industries had no pricing power at all. This innovative chapter also explains why Internet platforms that bring together different groups of users typically charge one those groups nothing while charging other groups (like advertisers) heavily. We have found that this material is highly popular with both students and instructors.

- **We have consolidated our previous two chapters on pure competition into a single chapter** in response to extensive faculty feedback that there is too much material to cover in the principles course and to give more room for other material, like the new chapter on Internet Oligopoly.

- **We have updated and enhanced SmartBook,** making our adaptive reading experience more personal, more accessible, and more productive, in addition to making it fully mobile across devices for students who, for example, begin a SmartBook assignment on their laptop but then want to finish it on their smartphone.

- **We have created additional Concept Overview and Guided Examples videos** to help students with challenging concepts and to offer immediate feedback and assistance as students work through difficult problems.

- **We have developed additional Application-Based Activities (ABAs)** that immerse students in real-time interactive role playing scenarios in order to hone problem-solving skills and sharpen economics intuition.

- **We have updated our Adaptive Econ Prep: Math and Graphing tool** that gives students just-in-time math remediation as well as experience with the graphing fundamentals that are a prerequisite to success in principles of economics courses.

- **We have extended our ongoing efforts to accommodate the fast-paced, nonlinear learning style of contemporary students** by streamlining paragraphs, highlighting key examples, and introducing additional Key Graphs. These changes will help digital natives quickly scan for key concepts and core material. Scores of newly added headers, Quick Review boxes, and bullet points will assist them in rapidly identifying the most important ideas and information.

MORE Accessible

We are proud that our publisher, McGraw Hill, is fully committed to Accessibility, as is made clear by McGraw Hill's Accessibility Statement:

> At McGraw Hill, we're committed to unlocking the potential of all learners. We believe that the best learning materials should be accessible to students of all abilities, and are building an inclusive culture that considers the needs of every learner from the outset. We achieve this through a comprehensive strategy that starts with planning and research. We seek to create learning materials that are accessible to all learners. McGraw Hill is making every effort to ensure that all new educational content and technology follows the WCAG (Web Content Accessibility Guidelines) version 2.1 AA guidelines and best practices. To achieve this and continuously improve the accessibility of our products, our internal product teams regularly engage with external experts and solicit user feedback.

One aspect of Accessibility is the ability of students from all backgrounds to instantly and immediately open, use, and benefit from every learning tool available to them no matter what device they are using to access the Internet and our content.

- **We are consequently very happy to announce that** *Macroeconomics* **takes full advantage of McGraw Hill's free ReadAnywhere app.** Available for both iOS and Android smartphones and tablets, ReadAnywhere gives students access to all of the McGraw Hill learning tools, including SmartBook 2.0, Recharge, and our Adaptive Learning Assignments. Students using ReadAnywhere can even take notes, highlight key material, and complete assignments *offline* knowing that all of their work will sync the next time they connect to the Internet.

Another key aspect of Accessibility is affordability. Our goal is an "education of value" for each and every student regardless of background or circumstance. **Therefore, we are very appreciative of McGraw Hill's commitment to improving access by providing institutions and instructors with a wide range of options to lower costs and thereby clear more paths that can help to achieve equity across campuses and learners.**

MORE Current

- *Incorporating the Pandemic* For the current generation of traditional-aged college students, the COVID-19 pandemic has been the most extreme and long-lasting economic event of their lives. We have thus striven in this edition to use examples from the pandemic to illustrate economics principles and to explain the economic logic behind various government efforts to moderate the harm caused by the pandemic. To that end, the new edition features extensive coverage of the effects that the pandemic had on everything from labor markets to chip shortages. We also detail the government's various fiscal and monetary policy responses, many of which directly affected our students, their families, and their employers.

- *Consolidating our Presentation of Monetary Policy* We have consolidated what were formerly three chapters on central banking, monetary policy, and money creation into two succinct chapters on the Federal Reserve, interest rates, and monetary policy. This major consolidation was a response both to faculty surveys and to the Fed's elimination of reserve requirements, which rendered concepts like the monetary multiplier irrelevant to the conduct of monetary policy.

- *Enhancing our Discussion of the Fed's Policy Tools* We have fully revised our discussion of the Fed's current set of monetary policy tools so as to emphasize (1) the Fed's use of the so-called administered rates—especially the IORB and ON RRP rates—to control short-term interest rates in every segment of the money market, including the federal funds market; (2) the Fed's ability to use open-market purchases and sales of longer-term bonds to influence medium- and long-term interest rates through quantitative easing or tightening; and (3) the Fed's ability to use forward guidance to shape expectations. This presentation is pithy, intuitive, and has been met with very positive responses from both students and faculty.

MORE Examples

The 23rd edition abounds with new examples on many topics, including pandemic-induced labor shortages, the supply-chain problems caused by the COVID-19 pandemic, economies of scale in cloud computing, how firms in various industries implemented the short-run shutdown condition during the pandemic, the strategies employed by pharmaceutical companies when attempting to extend their patents past the normal 20-year expiration date, nonprice competition among oligopoly credit-card issuers, and the various ways that governments are seeking to regulate oligopoly Internet firms that enjoy network effects and platform externalities.

We have also added seventeen new "Consider This" and "Last Word" boxed features. These short, stand-alone essays convey key ideas in an accessible, student-oriented manner. New additions include, "The COVID Inflation," "The Great Resignation," and "A New Inflationary Era?"

MORE Faculty Tools, Resources, and Support

Faculty time is precious. To preserve as much of it as possible for faculty adopting *Macroeconomics*, we went sentence-by-sentence and section-by-section, pulling out extraneous examples, eliminating unnecessary paragraphs, and—in some cases—removing entire sections that faculty reported they didn't have time to teach.

These changes have been reviewed positively by faculty and **we are excited that our streamlined presentation frees up faculty time for more advanced classroom activities,** including experiments, debates, simulations, and various forms of peer instruction and team-based learning. (Instructors can find more information about our Guided Peer Instruction resources below and, if interested, should reach out to their reps for access.)

Accelerating Student Achievement via Adaptive Learning and Innovative Ancillary Materials

Would you as a faculty member enjoy spending less time on definitions and more time on theory, applications, and enrichment material? Most faculty say YES!—which is why we **continue to make large annual improvements to what is already the most effective digital learning platform in higher education: Connect Economics.**

Before Class

You can use Connect Economics and its built-in adaptive reading technology, SmartBook, to ensure that students know all the basics before class starts. Simply assign your selected chapter readings in SmartBook and have students complete related problems and questions before lecture. The Connect Economics platform will automatically probe for misunderstandings and then fix them with instant feedback and remediation.

To further enhance the ability of instructors to "get students up to speed" before class, **we also offer adaptive economics preparedness tutorials for math and graphing as well as a large bank of custom-made videos covering real-world examples.** All are assignable within Connect Economics, and each includes assessment questions that offer instant feedback whenever students give incorrect answers.

During Class

You can then proceed, during class, to higher-level learning activities that build correct intuitions and the ability to apply models, theories, and concepts to new situations that have not already been covered in your class.

Creating higher-level classroom activities is no easy task, and we know from personal experience that faculty often find themselves with too little time left over at the end of a long day of teaching, service, and research to create the high-quality enrichment materials that they would like to use in class.

To that end, we have gone out of our way to develop three major in-class enrichment tools that instructors can use to "flip the classroom" and engage students at a higher level.

Guided Peer Instruction

With the help of Todd Fitch of U.C. Berkeley, we have authored and field-tested hundreds of in-class questions and answers that can be used to facilitate the peer-instruction teaching method pioneered by Eric Mazur of Harvard University. Our version, which we call Guided Peer Instruction, is a student-focused, interactive teaching method that has been shown to more than double student understanding relative to lecture-based presentation formats like "chalk and talk." We are proud to be the first to offer Guided Peer Instruction.

Interactive Graphs

Easier to use than going directly to the St. Louis Fed's FRED site, our Interactive Graphs provide instructors with quick access to visual displays of real-world data that can be used to immediately illustrate important economic concepts and relationships. These Interactive Graphs are also available for students to play with and learn from. To that end, each Interactive Graph is accompanied by assignable assessment questions as well as feedback and tutorials to guide students through the experience of learning to read and interpret graphs and data.

ECON Everyday

Our ECON Everyday Blog saves instructors time by bringing current, student-centered content into their courses all semester long. Short articles written for principles-level students are tagged by topic to make them easily searchable. We also provide discussion questions to help instructors drive the conversation forward. Visit www.econeveryday.com and subscribe for updates.

After Class

Our Application-Based Activities (ABAs) are immersive decision-making simulations that put students into the role of everyday economists. Students practice their economics thinking and problem-solving skills as they apply course concepts to interactive digital scenarios that are delivered within Connect Economics. Each simulation was designed as a 15-minute experience that instructors can set to be replayed repeatedly.

Hundreds of problems with algorithmic variations provide ample opportunities for students to practice quantitative skills outside the classroom, while scores of graphing exercises give students the opportunity to draw, interact with, and analyze graphs even when studying alone.

Remote Proctoring & Browser-Locking Capabilities

Remote proctoring and browser-locking capabilities, curated by Proctorio, provide faculty with control of the assessment environment by enabling security options and verifying the identity of each student. Seamlessly integrated within Connect, these services allow instructors to control the assessment experience by verifying identification, restricting browser activity, and monitoring student actions. Instant and detailed reporting gives instructors an at-a-glance view of potential academic integrity concerns, thereby avoiding personal bias and supporting evidence-based claims.

High-Quality Instruction and Assessment through Preconfigured, OLC-Aligned Courseware

In consultation with the Online Learning Consortium (OLC) and our Certified Faculty Consultants, McGraw Hill has created preconfigured courseware using the OLC's quality scorecard to align with best practices in online course delivery. This turnkey courseware contains a combination of formative assessments, summative assessments, homework, and application activities, and can easily be customized to meet an individual instructor's needs and desired course outcomes. For more information, visit https://www.mheducation.com/highered/olc.

Support at Every Step

To ensure that it will continue providing the best faculty support services in higher education, McGraw Hill interviewed hundreds of faculty, who helped to identify the most common and problematic pain points with respect to the successful implementation and use of digital courseware.

Based on that information, McGraw Hill teamed up with faculty consultants to design and build higher-education's leading faculty support portal, Support at Every Step.

From initial training to implementing new tools, Support at Every Step is ready to help. If you're looking for a prebuilt course, or a tool to help design your own course, or you just want to talk to another McConnell user, please visit www.supportateverystep.com.

Reflecting the Diverse World around Us

McGraw Hill believes in unlocking the potential of every learner at every stage of life. To accomplish that, we are dedicated to creating products that reflect, and are accessible to, all the diverse global customers that McGraw Hill serves. Within McGraw Hill, we foster a culture of belonging, and we work with partners who share our commitment to equity, inclusion, and diversity in all forms. This includes, but is not limited to:

- Refreshing and implementing inclusive content guidelines around topics including generalizations and stereotypes, gender, abilities/disabilities, race/ethnicity, sexual orientation, diversity of names, and age.
- Enhancing best practices in assessment creation to eliminate cultural, cognitive, and affective biases.
- Maintaining and continually updating a robust photo library of diverse images that reflect our student populations.
- Including more diverse voices in the development and review of our content.
- Strengthening art guidelines to improve accessibility both by ensuring meaningful text and by ensuring that images are distinguishable and perceivable by users with limited color vision as well as by users with moderately low vision.

A 23rd Edition for the 21st Century

Macroeconomics has maintained its position as the world's best-selling economics textbook for over six decades by continually updating its coverage and its pedagogy. We weren't just the first with adaptive learning and instant remediation, but first also with everything from student study guides to computerized test banks.

McConnell Is/Was/and Will Remain the Innovation Champion:

- The first with a student study guide.
- The first with test banks.
- The first with multi-color graphs.
- The first with televised economics lectures.
- The first with overhead projector slides.
- The first with an instructors' manual.
- The first with a computerized test bank.
- The first with PowerPoint slides.
- The first with algorithmic problem sets.

- The first with an adaptive-learning system.
- The first optimized for smartphones.

It is our sincere hope that our 23rd edition will continue to promote rapid learning and deep understanding as the 21st century approaches its 25th birthday. We have worked hard to ensure that *Macroeconomics* and all of its ancillary materials are comprehensive, analytical, and challenging—yet fully accessible to a wide range of students. **Where needed, an extra sentence of explanation is provided. Brevity at the expense of clarity is false economy.**

Sean M. Flynn
Stanley L. Brue

Chapter-by-Chapter Changes

Each chapter of *Macroeconomics,* 23rd edition, contains data updates and numerous revised examples that will be fresh and relevant for today's students. Chapter-specific updates include new boxed pieces, additional Key Graphs, and substantial revisions to the core content. The content and examples were also revised with a keen eye toward diversity, equity and inclusion.

A new consolidated, intuitive, and state-of-the-art presentation of monetary policy as the Fed now conducts it is summarized in Chapters 14 and 15. Other changes include the following:

Chapter 1: Limits, Alternatives, and Choices features updated examples and a revised presentation of capital (and, thus, investment) that highlights the fact that "capital" includes intangible intellectual capital as well as physical capital. By popular demand, we have also brought back the Last Word about faulty economic reasoning that appeared in several earlier editions.

Chapter 2: The Market System and the Circular Flow contains two new Key Words (*coordination problem* and *incentive problem*), revised examples, increased clarity on the benefits of property rights, and a streamlined presentation of the circular flow model.

Chapter 3: Demand, Supply, and Market Equilibrium includes several new examples, new material on how network and congestion effects shift demand curves, a new Key Word (*rent control*), and a new Last Word on how rapid shifts in supply and demand prompted dramatic price changes as well as shortages during the COVID-19 pandemic.

Chapter 4: Market Failures Caused by Externalities and Asymmetric Information contains two new Key Words (*deadweight loss* and *private information*) as well as several updates in both the text and in figures to emphasize the concepts of maximum willingness to pay (demand curve) and minimum willingness to accept (supply curve), thereby enhancing student understanding of both consumer and producer surplus as well as the efficiency losses that result from over- and under-production.

Chapter 5: Public Goods, Public Choice, and Government Failure contains data updates as well as revisions that clarify the necessity that a good or service be excludable if private firms are going to be willing to provide it; the fact that the collective demand schedule used for valuing public goods is a collective willingness-to-pay curve; and the strength and generalizability of the median voter theorem. We also introduce a new Key Word (*collective demand for a public good*).

Chapter 6: An Introduction to Macroeconomics features a new Consider This boxed piece about the COVID-19 recession, a more efficient summary section, and various updates and wording improvements.

Chapter 7: Measuring Domestic Output and National Income benefits from data updates, revisions to our presentation of the income and allocation approaches to totaling up GDP, and a revised presentation of why financial transactions are excluded from GDP.

Chapter 8: Economic Growth contains numerous data updates and several wording improvements for clarity. (As an aside, we would like to mention the recently available extensions to Angus Maddison's historical tables of long-run economic growth that are now being maintained by the Maddison Project at the University of Groningen. Kudos to them for extending Professor Maddison's groundbreaking data tables after his passing.)

Chapter 9: Business Cycles, Unemployment, and Inflation has extensive data updates, new material that relates the chapter's key concepts to the COVID-19 recession, and a new Last Word on the highly unusual behavior of labor markets and unemployment over the course of the pandemic.

Chapter 10: Basic Macroeconomic Relationships features a revised Consider This, a new example about 3-D printers, and a revised Discussion Question.

Chapter 11: The Aggregate Expenditures Model contains new material that relates the aggregate expenditure model to the COVID-19 recession, as well as several small but meaningful wording improvements.

Chapter 12: Aggregate Demand and Aggregate Supply contains improved definitions of two Key Words (*short-run aggregate supply* and *long-run aggregate supply*) as well as substantial new material relating the AD-AS model to the COVID-19 recession, including a new Last Word explaining how unusual it was to have a recession and then a recovery in which inflation rose due to *simultaneous* shifts of AD (to the right, due to stimulus funds) and AS (to the left, due to supply chain disruptions and labor shortages).

Chapter 13: Fiscal Policy, Deficits, and Debt incorporates several discussions of fiscal policy before and during the COVID-19 pandemic, especially with respect to the sheer magnitude of the stimulus but also with respect to other things, like how unusual the stimulus was in not having any recognition lag and, compared with typical recessions, hardly any administrative or operational lag, either.

Chapter 14: Money, the Federal Reserve, and Interest Rates is the first of two monetary policy chapters that respond to faculty feedback that we should consolidate what had previously been three monetary policy chapters into two. Much of the consolidation was also necessitated by the Federal Reserve's decision to eliminate reserve requirements for banks, thereby rendering irrelevant for policy purposes concepts like the monetary multiplier. This chapter contains much of the material that was previously in our chapter titled "Money, Banking, and Financial Institutions" (which was Chapter 14 in the previous edition). We have added to it the material on interest rate determination (that appeared in the previous edition's Chapter 16, "Interest Rates and Monetary Policy") in addition to adding discussions of debit cards as a means of accessing checkable deposits, electronic cash-transfer systems like PayPal and Venmo, and a new Last Word about cryptocurrencies, including Bitcoin and central-bank digital currencies. Please also note the subtle but profound revisions that were necessitated by the Fed's changing the definitions of the $M1$ and $M2$ measures of the money supply such that noncheckable savings deposits are now part of $M1$ rather than $M2$. That definitional adjustment has produced the strange result that $M2$ is now only about 5 percent larger than $M1$ (whereas, previously, $M2$ had always been at least triple the size of $M1$).

Chapter 15: Monetary Policy, GDP, and Price Level is the second of our two monetary policy chapters that respond to faculty feedback that we should consolidate what had previously been three monetary policy chapters into two. In making those consolidations, we completely eliminated the previous edition's Chapter 15 ("Money Creation") both in response to faculty feedback and in response to the Federal Reserve's decision to eliminate bank reserve requirements in March 2020. The Fed is now opting to control bank lending (and thus bank money creation) through other channels, especially its ability to modulate the interest rate on reserve balances (IORB). Much of the material in this chapter is brand new, including an innovative presentation of the Fed's current set of monetary policy tools. Along those lines, we explain how the modern Fed uses IORB and the overnight reverse repo rate (ON RRP) to control short-run interest rates, including the effective federal funds rate, independently of longer-run rates, which it can manipulate with quantitative easing and quantitative tightening. Other new topics include the Fed's ability, through the payment of IORB to banks and ON RRP to nonbanks, to use the banking and financial system as a giant anti-inflationary "money sponge" that can be used to help offset the massive increases in the money supply that have been generated by the Fed's massive quantitative-easing asset purchases. The Dual-Mandate Bullseye Chart has also been expanded into a Key Graph with an embedded Quick Quiz.

Chapter 16: Financial Economics contains data updates; a new Key Word (*securities*); improved presentations of present value and the inverse relationship between asset prices and rates of return; and a discussion of how time-varying risk premiums can explain the initial stock market crash at the very start of the COVID-19 pandemic as well as the subsequent recovery in stock prices over the following six months.

Chapter 17: Extending the Analysis of Aggregate Supply delivers data updates, several new or revised Key Words (*short run, long run, short-run downward sloping Phillips Curve*), and a new Consider This on how the COVID-19 supply shocks contributed to rising inflation.

Chapter 18: Current Issues in Macro Theory and Policy includes data updates, new examples, and a brief summary of the successful policy actions that the Fed took between March and June 2020 in order to prevent the COVID-19 pandemic from causing a major financial crisis.

Chapter 19: International Trade contains extensive data updates, a new Key Word (*trade*), a streamlined Summary, and a highly revised and substantially more intuitive presentation of absolute and comparative advantage.

Chapter 20: The Balance of Payments, Exchange Rates, and Trade Deficits offers extensive data updates, various edits for concision and clarity, and a new Last Word describing the Exchange Rate Trilemma.

Chapter 21: The Economics of Developing Countries includes data updates, a new Global Perspective on the high cost of legally registering a new business in many developing countries, and an integration of the concepts of *state capacity* and *failed states* into our discussion of the economic factors that can hinder or help economic development. *State capacity* and *failed states* have also been made into Key Words, with glossary and margin entries.

Historical Data We have added four rows to the macroeconomic historical data that appears after the final chapter of both *Economics* and *Macroeconomics*. The new rows show historical data for, respectively, (1) real GDP per capita, (2) the annual percentage growth rate of real GDP per capita, (3) the federal budget deficit or surplus, and (4) the federal budget deficit or surplus as a percentage of GDP. By contrast, the microeconomic historical data that appears after the final chapter of *Microeconomics* remains unchanged.

Acknowledgments

We give special thanks to Peggy Dalton and Peter Staples for their hard work updating and accuracy checking the questions and problems in *Connect,* as well as the material they created for the additional Connect Problems.

A big thank you to Stephanie Campbell and Randy Grant for all of their efforts updating and accuracy checking the test bank.

We thank Tom Barbiero (the coauthor of our Canadian edition) for helpful ideas and insights.

We are greatly indebted to an all-star group of professionals at McGraw Hill—in particular, Kelly Pekelder, Anke Weekes, Bobby Pearson, Harvey Yep, and Jackie Higgason—for their publishing and marketing expertise. We would also like to thank the talented McGraw Hill Learning Technology Representatives and Implementation Teams.

The 23rd edition has also greatly benefited from a number of perceptive faculty reviews. The reviewers, listed in the next section, were a rich source of suggestions for this revision. To each of you, and to any others we may have inadvertently overlooked, thank you for your considerable help in improving *Macroeconomics*.

Instructors
Student Success Starts with You

Tools to enhance your unique voice

Want to build your own course? No problem. Prefer to use an OLC-aligned, prebuilt course? Easy. Want to make changes throughout the semester? Sure. And you'll save time with Connect's auto-grading, too.

65%
Less Time Grading

Laptop: Getty Images; Woman/dog: George Doyle/Getty Images

A unique path for each student

In Connect, instructors can assign an adaptive reading experience with SmartBook® 2.0. Rooted in advanced learning science principles, SmartBook 2.0 delivers each student a personalized experience, focusing students on their learning gaps, ensuring that the time they spend studying is time well-spent.
mheducation.com/highered/connect/smartbook

Affordable solutions, added value

Make technology work for you with LMS integration for single sign-on access, mobile access to the digital textbook, and reports to quickly show you how each of your students is doing. And with our Inclusive Access program, you can provide all these tools at the lowest available market price to your students. Ask your McGraw Hill representative for more information.

Solutions for your challenges

A product isn't a solution. Real solutions are affordable, reliable, and come with training and ongoing support when you need it and how you want it. Visit **supportateverystep.com** for videos and resources both you and your students can use throughout the term.

Students
Get Learning that Fits You

Effective tools for efficient studying

Connect is designed to help you be more productive with simple, flexible, intuitive tools that maximize your study time and meet your individual learning needs. Get learning that works for you with Connect.

Study anytime, anywhere

Download the free ReadAnywhere® app and access your online eBook, SmartBook® 2.0, or Adaptive Learning Assignments when it's convenient, even if you're offline. And since the app automatically syncs with your Connect account, all of your work is available every time you open it. Find out more at **mheducation.com/readanywhere**

"I really liked this app—it made it easy to study when you don't have your text-book in front of you."

- Jordan Cunningham, Eastern Washington University

iPhone: Getty Images

Everything you need in one place

Your Connect course has everything you need—whether reading your digital eBook or completing assignments for class, Connect makes it easy to get your work done.

Learning for everyone

McGraw Hill works directly with Accessibility Services Departments and faculty to meet the learning needs of all students. Please contact your Accessibility Services Office and ask them to email accessibility@mheducation.com, or visit **mheducation.com/about/accessibility** for more information.

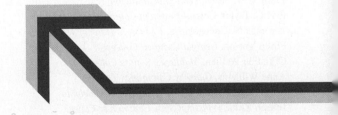

REVIEWERS

REVIEWERS SUPPORTING THE 23RD EDITION:

Carlos Aguilar, *El Paso Community College*
Barbara Baer, *Palomar College*
Kuntal Banerjee, *Florida Atlantic University*
Jill M. Beccaris-Pescatore, *Montgomery County Community College*
Lee A. Bertman, *Indian River State College*
Roberta Biby, *Grand Valley State University*
Melissa Blankenship, *North Central Texas College*
Stephanie Lyn Blowe, *Lone Star College*
Andrea Borchard, *Hillsborough Community College*
Greg Burge, *University of Oklahoma*
Mark L. Burkey, *North Carolina A&T State University*
William Byrd, *Troy University*
Joab Corey, *University of California-Riverside*
Norman Cure, *Macomb Community College*
Sonia Dalmia, *Grand Valley State University*
Maria S. Davis, *Indian River State College*
Irani DeAraujo, *Pace University*
Carter Doyle, *University of Virginia*
Sheryl Dusek, *Nashville State Community College*
Lynne Elkes, *Loyola University Maryland*
Tammie Fischer, *University of Nebraska-Lincoln*
Robert J. Foran, *Miami Dade College-Wolfson Campus*
Michael G. Goode, *Central Piedmont Community College*
Joseph Guider, *Essex County College*
Gabriela Hamilton, *Hillsborough Community College*
Christiana Hilmer, *San Diego State University*
Michael Hilmer, *San Diego State University*
Daniel Hoffman, *University of Nebraska-Lincoln*
Liang Hu, *Wayne State University*
Zagros Madjd-Sadjadi, *Winston-Salem State University*
Laura Maghoney, *Solano Community College*
Marilyn Markel, *Western Michigan University*
Erika Martinez, *University of South Florida*
Jesse D. Melvin, *Rowan University*
Victoria Miller, *Piedmont Technical College*
Phillip Mixon, *Troy University*
Alex Obiya, *San Diego City College*
Larry Olanrewaju, *John Tyler Community College*
Andre Luis Oliveira, *Utah Valley University*
Samuel Olowu, *Lone Star College*
Grace Onodipe, *Georgia Gwinnett College*
Louis A. Palombit, *Macomb Community College*
Marina Rubenkov, *Milwaukee Area Technical College*
Dustin J. Rumbaugh, *Belmont University*
Thomas Sahajdack, *Kent State University*
Mark Scanlan, *Stephen F. Austin State University*
Anne Shugars, *Harford Community College*
Thomas W. Stone, *Penn State Abington*
Eric C. Taylor, *Central Piedmont Community College*
Veronica N. Udeogalanya, *Fashion Institute of Technology*
Philip Vinson, *Georgia Gwinnett College*
Christine Wathen, *Middlesex County College*
Anne Williams, *Gateway Community College*
Karen Yancey, *Community College of Philadelphia*
Joseph Zitka, *Pellissippi State Community College*

REVIEWERS SUPPORTING PREVIOUS EDITIONS:

Alison J. Adderley, *Valencia College*
Richard Agesa, *Marshall University*
Carlos Aguilar, *El Paso Community College*
Yamin Ahmad, *University of Wisconsin-Whitewater*
Eun Ahn, *University of Hawaii-West Oahu*
Miki Anderson, *Pikes Peak Community College*
Giuliana Andreopoulos, *William Paterson University*
Thomas Andrews, *West Chester University of Pennsylvania*
Fatma Antar, *Manchester Community College*
Len Anyanwu, *Union County College*
Kathleen Arano, *Indiana University Southeast*
Emmanuel Asigbee, *Kirkwood Community College*
John Atkins, *Pensacola State College*
Moses Ayiku, *Essex County College*
Barbara Baer, *Palomar College*
Wendy Bailey, *Troy University*
Dean Baim, *Pepperdine University*
Herman Baine, *Broward College*
Kuntal Banerjee, *Florida Atlantic University*
Tyra Barrett, *Pellissippi State Community College*
David Barrus, *Brigham Young University-Idaho*
Leon Battista, *CUNY Bronx Community College*
Jill M. Beccaris-Pescatore, *Montgomery County Community College*
Kevin Beckwith, *Salem State University*
Christian Beer, *Cape Fear Community College*
Robert Belsterling, *Pennsylvania State University-Altoona*
Lee A. Bertman, *Indian River State College*
Laura Jean Bhadra, *Northern Virginia Community College-Manassas*
Roberta Biby, *Grand Valley State University*
David Black, *University of Toledo*
Melissa Blankenship, *North Central Texas College*
Priscilla Block, *Broward College*
Stephanie Lyn Blowe, *Lone Star College*
Augustine Boakye, *Essex County College*
Andrea Borchard, *Hillsborough Community College*
Greg Burge, *University of Oklahoma*
Mark L. Burkey, *North Carolina A&T State University*
William Byrd, *Troy University*
Stephanie Campbell, *Mineral Area College*
Bruce Carpenter, *Mansfield University*
Tom Cate, *Northern Kentucky University*
Semih Emre Çekin, *Texas Tech University*
Suparna Chakraborty, *University of San Francisco*
Claude Chang, *Johnson & Wales University*
Amy Chataginer, *Mississippi Gulf Coast Community College-Gautier*
Shuo Chen, *State University of New York-Geneseo*
Jon Chesbro, *Montana Tech of the University of Montana*
Amod Choudhary, *Lehman College*
Constantinos Christofides, *East Stroudsburg University*
Kathy Clark, *Edison College-Fort Myers*
Wes Clark, *Midlands Technical College*
Jane Clary, *College of Charleston*
Jane Cline, *Forsyth Technical Community College*
Joab Corey, *University of California-Riverside*
Ana Carolina Corrales, *Miami Dade College-Wolfson Campus*

Norman Cure, *Macomb Community College*
Patricia Daigle, *Mount Wachusett Community College*
Sonia Dalmia, *Grand Valley State University*
Anthony Daniele, *St. Petersburg College-Gibbs*
Rosa Lee Danielson, *College of DuPage*
Ribhi Daoud, *Sinclair Community College*
Maria S. Davis, *Indian River State College*
William L. Davis, *University of Tennessee-Martin*
Irani DeAraujo, *Pace University*
Richard Dixon, *Thomas Nelson Community College*
Tanya Downing, *Cuesta College*
Carter Doyle, *University of Virginia*
Scott Dressler, *Villanova University*
Brad Duerson, *Des Moines Area Community College*
Sheryl Dusek, *Nashville State Community College*
Lynne Elkes, *Loyola University Maryland*
Mark J. Eschenfelder, *Robert Morris University*
Maxwell Eseonu, *Virginia State University*
Michael Fenick, *Broward College*
Tyrone Ferdnance, *Hampton University*
Tammie Fischer, *University of Nebraska-Lincoln*
Mary Flannery, *University of Notre Dame*
Robert J. Foran, *Miami Dade College-Wolfson Campus*
Jeffrey Forrest, *St. Louis Community College-Florissant Valley*
Richard Fowles, *University of Utah, Salt Lake City*
Mark Frascatore, *Clarkson University*
Shelby Frost, *Georgia State University*
Connel Fullenkamp, *Duke University*
Sudip Ghosh, *Penn State University-Berks*
Alex Gialanella, *Fordham University*
Daniel Giedeman, *Grand Valley State University*
Scott Gilbert, *Southern Illinois University*
James Giordano, *Villanova University*
Susan Glanz, *St. John's University*
Lowell Glenn, *Utah Valley University*
Randy Glover, *Brevard Community College-Melbourne*
Terri Gonzales, *Delgado Community College*
Michael G. Goode, *Central Piedmont Community College*
Paul Graf, *Indiana University-Bloomington*
Joseph Guider, *Essex County College*
Cole Gustafson, *North Dakota State University-Fargo*
Sheryl Hadley, *Johnson County Community College*
Gabriela Hamilton, *Hillsborough Community College*
Moonsu Han, *North Shore Community College*
Charlie Harrington, *Nova Southeastern University-Main*
Virden Harrison, *Modesto Junior College*
Darcy Hartman, *Ohio State University*
Richard R. Hawkins, *University of West Florida*
Kim Hawtrey, *Hope College*
Glenn Haynes, *Western Illinois University*
Mark Healy, *Harper College*
Dennis Heiner, *College of Southern Idaho*
Michael Heslop, *Northern Virginia Community College-Annandale*
Jesse Hoyt Hill, *Tarrant County College*
Christiana Hilmer, *San Diego State University*
Michael Hilmer, *San Diego State University*
Daniel Hoffman, *University of Nebraska-Lincoln*
Calvin Hoy, *County College of Morris*
Liang Hu, *Wayne State University*

Jim Hubert, *Seattle Central Community College*
Greg W. Hunter, *California State Polytechnic University-Pomona*
Christos Ioannou, *University of Minnesota-Minneapolis*
Faridul Islam, *Utah Valley University*
Mahshid Jalilvand, *University of Wisconsin-Stout*
Ricot Jean, *Valencia Community College-Osceola*
Jonatan Jelen, *City College of New York*
Stephen Kaifa, *County College of Morris*
Brad Kamp, *University of South Florida, Sarasota-Manatee*
Robert Kao, *Park University*
Gus Karam, *Pace University-Pleasantville*
Kevin Kelley, *Northwest Vista College*
Chris Klein, *Middle Tennessee State University*
Barry Kotlove, *Edmonds Community College*
Richard Kramer, *New England College*
Felix Kwan, *Maryville University*
Ted Labay, *Bishop State Community College*
Alex Lancaster, *Tallahassee Community College*
Tina Lance, *Germanna Community College-Fredericksburg*
Sarah Leahy, *Brookdale Community College*
Yu-Feng Lee, *New Mexico State University-Las Cruces*
Jim Lee, *Texas A&M University-Corpus Christi*
Adam Y. C. Lei, *Midwestern State University*
Phillip Letting, *Harrisburg Area Community College*
Hank Lewis, *Lone Star College*
Brian Lynch, *Lake Land College*
Zagros Madjd-Sadjadi, *Winston-Salem State University*
Laura Maghoney, *Solano Community College*
Svitlana Maksymenko, *University of Pittsburgh*
Christine Lucy Malakar, *Lorain County Community College*
Vincent Mangum, *Grambling State University*
Marilyn Markel, *Western Michigan University*
Erika Martinez, *University of South Florida*
Benjamin Matta, *New Mexico State University-Las Cruces*
Pete Mavrokordatos, *Tarrant County College-Northeast Campus*
Frederick May, *Trident Technical College*
Katherine McClain, *University of Georgia*
Michael McIntyre, *Copiah-Lincoln Community College*
Robert McKizzie, *Tarrant County College-Southeast Campus*
Kevin McWoodson, *Moraine Valley Community College*
Jesse D. Melvin, *Rowan University*
Edwin Mensah, *University of North Carolina at Pembroke*
Randy Methenitis, *Richland College*
Victoria Miller, *Piedmont Technical College*
Ida Mirzaie, *The Ohio State University*
David Mitch, *University of Maryland-Baltimore County*
Phillip Mixon, *Troy University*
Ramesh Mohan, *Bryant University*
Daniel Morvey, *Piedmont Technical College*
Tina Mosleh, *Ohlone College*
Shahriar Mostashari, *Campbell University*
Richard Mount, *Monmouth University*
Stefan Mullinax, *College of Lake County*
Ted Muzio, *St. John's University*
Pattabiraman Neelakantan, *East Stroudsburg University of Pennsylvania*
John A. Neri, *University of Maryland*
Cliff Nowell, *Weber State University*
Alex Obiya, *San Diego City College*
Constantin Ogloblin, *Georgia Southern University*

Albert Okunade, *University of Memphis*
Larry Olanrewaju, *John Tyler Community College*
Andre Luis Oliveira, *Utah Valley University*
Samuel Olowu, *Lone Star College*
Grace Onodipe, *Georgia Gwinnett College*
Mary Ellen Overbay, *Seton Hall University*
Louis A. Palombit, *Macomb Community College*
Tammy Parker, *University of Louisiana at Monroe*
Alberto Alexander Perez, *Harford Community College*
David Petersen, *American River College*
Mary Anne Pettit, *Southern Illinois University-Edwardsville*
Jeff Phillips, *Morrisville State College*
William Piper, *Piedmont College*
Robert Poulton, *Graceland University*
Dezzie Prewitt, *Rio Hondo College*
Joe Prinzinger, *Lynchburg College*
Jaishankar Raman, *Valparaiso University*
Gregory Randolph, *Southern New Hampshire University*
Natalie Reaves, *Rowan University*
Virginia Reilly, *Ocean County College*
Tim Reynolds, *Alvin Community College*
Jose Rafael Rodriguez-Solis, *Nova Community College-Annandale*
John Romps, *Saint Anselm College*
Marina Rubenkov, *Milwaukee Area Technical College*
Melissa Rueterbusch, *Mott Community College*
Dustin J. Rumbaugh, *Belmont University*
Thomas Sahajdack, *Kent State University*
Mark Scanlan, *Stephen F. Austin State University*
Tom Scheiding, *Elizabethtown College*
Amy Schmidt, *Saint Anselm College*
Ron Schuelke, *Santa Rosa Junior College*
Richard Alan Seals, Jr., *Auburn University*
James K. Self, *Indiana University-Bloomington Campus*
Sangheon Shin, *Alabama State University*
Alexandra Shiu, *McLennan Community College*
Anne Shugars, *Harford Community College*
Dorothy Siden, *Salem State University*

Robert Simonson, *Minnesota State University-Mankato*
Timothy Simpson, *Central New Mexico Community College*
Jonathan Sleeper, *Indian River State College*
Jose Rodriguez Solis, *Northern Virginia Community College*
Camille Soltau-Nelson, *Oregon State University*
Robert Sonora, *Fort Lewis College*
Maritza Sotomayor, *Utah Valley University-Orem*
Nick Spangenberg, *Ozarks Technical Community College*
Dennis Spector, *Naugatuck Valley Community College*
Thomas Stevens, *University of Massachusetts-Amherst*
Tamika Steward, *Tarrant County College-Southeast*
Thomas W. Stone, *Penn State Abington*
Robin Sturik, *Cuyahoga Community College Western-Parma*
Regina Tawah, *Bowie State University*
Eric C. Taylor, *Central Piedmont Community College*
Travis Taylor, *Christopher Newport University*
Ross Thomas, *Central New Mexico Community College*
Mark Thompson, *Augusta State University*
Owen Thompson, *University of Wisconsin-Milwaukee*
Deborah Thorsen, *Palm Beach State College*
Michael Toma, *Armstrong Atlantic State University*
Dosse Toulaboe, *Fort Hays State University*
Veronica N. Udeogalanya, *Fashion Institute of Technology*
Adriana Vamosiu, *University of San Diego*
Jeff Vance, *Sinclair Community College*
Philip Vinson, *Georgia Gwinnett College*
Cheryl Wachenheim, *North Dakota State University-Fargo*
Brandon Walcutt, *Mohawk Valley Community College*
Christine Wathen, *Middlesex County College*
Anne Williams, *Gateway Community College*
Scott Williams, *Winston-Salem State University*
Wendy Wysocki, *Monroe County Community College*
Karen Yancey, *Community College of Philadelphia*
Edward Zajicek, *Winston-Salem State University*
Sourushe Zandvakili, *University of Cincinnati*
Joseph Zitka, *Pellissippi State Community College*

BRIEF CONTENTS

Blue: Core Chapter
Black: Topics Chapter

CONTENTS

PART ONE
Introduction to Economics and the Economy

PART TWO
Price, Quantity, and Efficiency

PART FOUR
Macroeconomic Models and Fiscal Policy

Chapter 10
Basic Macroeconomic Relationships

Chapter 11
The Aggregate Expenditures Model

Chapter 12
Aggregate Demand and Aggregate Supply

Chapter 13
Fiscal Policy, Deficits, and Debt

Roschetzky Photography/Shutterstock

Limits, Alternatives, and Choices

>> LEARNING OBJECTIVES

LO1.1   Define economics and explain the economic perspective.

LO1.2   Describe the role of economic theory in economics.

LO1.3   Distinguish microeconomics from macroeconomics and positive economics from normative economics.

LO1.4   Explain the individual's economizing problem and illustrate trade-offs, opportunity costs, and attainable combinations with budget lines.

LO1.5   List the categories of scarce resources and explain society's economizing problem.

LO1.6   Apply production possibilities analysis.

LO1.7   Explain how economic growth and international trade increase consumption possibilities.

LO1.8   (Appendix) Understand graphs, curves, and slopes as they relate to economics.

People's wants are numerous and varied. Biologically, people need only air, water, food, clothing, and shelter. But in modern societies, people also desire goods and services that provide a more comfortable or affluent standard of living. We want bottled water, soft drinks, and fruit juices, not just water from the creek. We want salads, burgers, and pizzas, not just berries and nuts. We also want flat-panel TVs, Internet service, education, national defense, smartphones, health care, and much more.

Fortunately, society possesses productive resources, such as labor and managerial talent, tools and machinery, and land and mineral deposits. These resources, employed in the economic system (or simply the economy), help us produce goods and services that satisfy many of our economic wants. But in reality, our economic wants far exceed the productive capacity of our scarce (limited) resources. We are forced to make choices. This unyielding truth underlies the definition of **economics** as the social science concerned with how individuals, institutions, and society make optimal (best) choices under conditions of scarcity.

economics The social science concerned with how individuals, institutions, and society make optimal (best) choices under conditions of scarcity.

The Economic Perspective

>> **LO1.1** Define economics and explain the economic perspective.

Economists view things from a unique perspective. This **economic perspective** has several critical and closely interrelated features.

economic perspective A viewpoint that envisions individuals and institutions making rational decisions by comparing the *marginal benefits* and *marginal costs* associated with their actions.

scarcity The limits placed on the amounts and types of *goods* and *services* available for consumption as the result of there being only limited *economic resources* from which to produce output; the fundamental economic constraint that creates *opportunity costs* and that necessitates the use of *marginal analysis* (*cost-benefit analysis*) to make optimal choices.

opportunity cost The amount of other products that must be forgone or sacrificed to produce a unit of a given product.

utility The want-satisfying power of a *good* or *service;* the satisfaction or pleasure a consumer obtains from the consumption of a good or service (or from the consumption of a collection of *goods* and *services*).

Scarcity and Choice

The economic resources needed to make goods and services are in limited supply. This **scarcity** restricts options and demands choices. Because we "can't have it all," we must decide what we will have and what we must forgo.

At the core of economics is the idea that "there is no free lunch." You may be treated to lunch, making it "free" from your perspective, but someone must bear the cost. The scarce inputs involved in creating the lunch include land, equipment, and farm labor. Because society could have used these resources to produce other things, it sacrifices those other goods and services in making the lunch available. Economists call such sacrifices **opportunity costs:** To obtain more of one thing, society sacrifices the opportunity of getting the next best thing that could have been created with those resources.

The nearby Consider This story about Facebook discusses yet another example of a "free" product that is anything but.

Purposeful Behavior

Economics assumes that human behavior reflects "rational self-interest." Individuals and institutions look for and pursue opportunities to increase their **utility**—the pleasure, happiness, or satisfaction obtained from consuming goods and services. They allocate their time, energy, and money to maximize their satisfaction. Because they weigh costs and benefits, their economic decisions are purposeful or rational, not random or chaotic.

"Purposeful behavior" does not assume that people and institutions are immune from faulty logic and therefore are perfect decision makers. They sometimes make mistakes. Nor does it mean that people's decisions are unaffected by emotion or the decisions of those around them. Indeed, economists acknowledge that people are sometimes impulsive or irrational. "Purposeful behavior" simply means that people make decisions with some desired outcome in mind.

Please note that rational self-interest is not the same as selfishness. To begin with, increasing one's own wage, rent, interest, or profit normally requires identifying and satisfying somebody else's wants! In addition, self-interested people routinely make personal sacrifices for others. They, for example, contribute time and money to charities because they derive pleasure from doing so. And parents help pay for their children's education for the same reason. These self-interested, but unselfish, acts help maximize the givers' satisfaction as much as any personal purchase of goods or services.

Marginal Analysis: Comparing Benefits and Costs

The economic perspective focuses largely on **marginal analysis**—comparisons of marginal benefits and marginal costs, usually for decision making. To economists, "marginal" means "extra," "additional," or "a change in." Most choices or decisions involve changes in the existing state of affairs.

CONSIDER THIS . . .

Is Facebook Free?

Facebook spends over $50 billion every year updating its platform, running server farms, and paying its employees. It also gives away its product for free to more than 3 billion users. Has Facebook figured out a way to overcome scarcity?

No, it hasn't. Scarcity is permanent. But Facebook *has* figured out a way to more than cover its costs without charging its users a penny. Facebook's trick is to charge advertisers instead. They pay Facebook over

rvlsoft/Shutterstock

$100 billion per year to boost content and target ads to specific individuals.

Lesson One: If you are consuming a good or service and not paying for it, the cost is being borne by someone else.

Lesson Two: Companies don't usually give freebies to be nice; they do it as part of their business model. Facebook grants users free access to its platform to make sure that it has as many "eyeballs" as possible to sell to advertisers.

Should you attend school for another year? Should you study an extra hour for an exam? Should a business expand or reduce its output? Should government increase or decrease its funding for a missile defense system?

Each option involves marginal benefits and marginal costs. In making choices rationally, the decision maker must compare those two amounts. Example: You and your significant other are shopping for an engagement ring. Should you buy a $\frac{1}{2}$-carat diamond or a 1-carat diamond? The marginal cost of the larger diamond is the added expense beyond the cost of the smaller diamond. The marginal benefit is the perceived lifetime pleasure (utility) from the larger stone. If the marginal benefit of the larger diamond exceeds its marginal cost (and you can afford it), buy the larger stone. But if the marginal cost is more than the marginal benefit, you should buy the smaller diamond instead—even if you can afford the larger stone!

In a world of scarcity, the decision to obtain the marginal benefit associated with some specific option always includes the marginal cost of giving up something else. The money spent on the larger diamond means forgoing some other product. An opportunity cost—the value of the next best thing given up—is always present whenever a choice is made.

marginal analysis The comparison of *marginal* ("extra" or "additional") *benefits* and *marginal costs,* usually for decision making.

Theories, Principles, and Models

Like the other sciences, economics relies on the **scientific method** to transform specific observations of real-world activity into general explanations of how the world works. That procedure consists of several elements:

>> **LO1.2** Describe the role of economic theory in economics.

- Observing real-world behavior and outcomes.
- Based on those observations, formulating a possible explanation (hypothesis) of cause and effect.
- Testing this explanation by comparing the outcomes of specific events to the outcome predicted by the hypothesis.
- Accepting, rejecting, and modifying the hypothesis, based on these comparisons.
- Continuing to test the hypothesis against the facts. If favorable results accumulate, the hypothesis evolves into a theory. A very well-tested and widely accepted theory is called an economic law or an **economic principle**—a statement about economic behavior or the economy that enables prediction of the probable effects of certain actions. Combinations of such laws or principles are incorporated into models, which are simplified representations of how something works, such as a market or segment of the economy.

scientific method The procedure for the systematic pursuit of knowledge involving the observation of facts and the formulation and testing of hypotheses to obtain theories, principles, and laws.

economic principle A widely accepted generalization about the economic behavior of individuals or institutions.

Theories, principles, and models are "purposeful simplifications." The full scope of economic reality itself is too complex to be fully understood. In developing theories, principles, and models, economists remove the clutter and simplify. Despite their simplifications, good theories do a good job of explaining and predicting how individuals and institutions actually behave in producing, exchanging, and consuming goods and services.

There are some other things you should know about economic principles.

- *Generalizations* Economic principles are generalizations. Economic principles are expressed as the tendencies of typical or average consumers, workers, or business firms. For example, economists say that consumers buy more of a particular product when its price falls. Economists recognize that some consumers may increase their purchases by a large amount, others by a small amount, and a few not at all. This "price-quantity" principle, however, holds for the typical consumer and for consumers as a group.
- *Other-things-equal assumption* In constructing theories, economists use the *ceteris paribus* or **other-things-equal assumption**—the assumption that factors other than those being considered do not change. They assume that all variables except those under immediate consideration are held constant for a particular analysis. For example, when considering the relationship between the price of Pepsi and the amount of Pepsi purchased, economists ignore all of the other factors that might influence the amount of Pepsi purchased (for example, the price of Coca-Cola and consumer incomes and preferences). Holding all of those other things equal is helpful because the economist can then focus on the relationship between the price of Pepsi and purchases of Pepsi without being confused by changes in other variables.
- *Graphical expression* Many economic models are expressed graphically. Be sure to read the appendix at the end of this chapter as a review of graphs.

other-things-equal assumption The assumption that factors other than those being considered are held constant. Also known as the *ceteris paribus* assumption.

Microeconomics and Macroeconomics

Economists develop economic principles and models at two levels.

>> **LO1.3** Distinguish microeconomics from macroeconomics and positive economics from normative economics.

Microeconomics

Microeconomics is concerned with decision making by individual customers, workers, households, and business firms. At this level of analysis, we observe the details of their behavior under a figurative microscope. We measure the price of a specific product, the revenue or income of a particular firm or household, or the expenditures of a specific firm, government entity, or family.

microeconomics The part of economics concerned with (1) decision making by individual units such as a *household,* a *firm,* or an *industry* and (2) individual markets, specific *goods* and *services,* and product and resource *prices.*

Macroeconomics

Macroeconomics examines the performance and behavior of the economy as a whole. It focuses on economic growth, the business cycle, interest rates, inflation, and the behavior of major economic aggregates such as the government, household, and business sectors. An **aggregate** is a collection of specific economic units treated as if they were one unit. Therefore, we might lump together the millions of consumers in the U.S. economy and treat them as one huge unit called "consumers."

In using aggregates, macroeconomics seeks to obtain an overview of the economy and the relationships of its major aggregates. Macroeconomics speaks of such economic measures as total output, total employment, total income, aggregate expenditures, and the general level of prices. Very little attention is given to the specific units making up the various aggregates.

The micro–macro distinction does not mean that economics is so highly compartmentalized that every topic can be readily labeled as either micro or macro; many topics and subdivisions of economics are rooted in both. Example: While unemployment is usually treated as a macroeconomic topic (because unemployment relates to aggregate production), economists recognize that the decisions made by *individual* workers and the way *specific* labor markets encourage or impede hiring are also critical in determining the unemployment rate.

macroeconomics The part of *economics* concerned with the performance and behavior of the economy as a whole. Focuses on *economic growth,* the *business cycle, interest rates, inflation,* and the behavior of major economic *aggregates* such as the household, business, and government sectors.

aggregate A collection of specific economic units treated as if they were one unit.

Positive and Normative Economics

Positive economics focuses on facts and cause-and-effect relationships. It avoids value judgments and tries to establish scientific statements about economic behavior. Such scientific analysis is critical to good policy analysis.

In contrast, **normative economics** incorporates value judgments about what the economy should be like or what policy actions should be recommended. Normative economics underlies expressions of support for, or opposition to, particular economic policies.

Positive economics concerns *what is,* whereas normative economics embodies subjective feelings about *what ought to be.* Examples: Positive statement: "The unemployment rate in France is higher than that in the United States." Normative statement: "France ought to undertake policies to make its labor market more flexible to reduce unemployment rates." Whenever words such as "ought" or "should" appear in a sentence, you are likely encountering a normative statement. Most of the disagreement among economists involves normative, value-based policy questions.

positive economics The analysis of facts or data to establish scientific generalizations about economic behavior.

normative economics The part of economics involving value judgments about what the economy should be like; focused on which economic goals and policies should be implemented; policy economics.

QUICK REVIEW

1.1

▶ Economics examines how individuals, institutions, and society make choices under conditions of scarcity.

▶ The economic perspective stresses (a) resource scarcity and the necessity of making choices, (b) the assumption of purposeful (or rational) behavior, and (c) comparisons of marginal benefit and marginal cost.

▶ In choosing the best option, people incur an opportunity cost—the value of the next-best option.

▶ Economists use the scientific method to establish economic theories—cause-effect generalizations about the economic behavior of individuals and institutions.

▶ Microeconomics focuses on specific decision-making units within the economy. Macroeconomics examines the economy as a whole.

▶ Positive economics deals with factual statements ("what is"); normative economics involves value judgments ("what ought to be").

Individual's Economizing Problem

A close examination of the **economizing problem**—the need to make choices because economic wants exceed economic means—will enhance your understanding of economic models and the difference between microeconomics and macroeconomics.

To that end, let's first build a microeconomic model of the economizing problem faced by an individual. We will then, later in this chapter, build a macroeconomic model of the economizing problem faced by an entire nation or society.

>> **LO1.4** Explain the individual's economizing problem and illustrate trade-offs, opportunity costs, and attainable combinations with budget lines.

Limited Income

We all have a finite amount of income, even the wealthiest among us. Even Jeff Bezos must decide how to spend his money! Our income comes in the form of wages, interest, rent, and profit, although we may also receive money from government programs or family members. As Global Perspective 1.1 shows, the average income of Americans in 2020 was $65,280 after adjusting for international differences in the cost of living. In the poorest nations, it was less than $500.

economizing problem The choices necessitated because society's economic wants for *goods* and *services* are unlimited but the resources available to satisfy these wants are limited (scarce).

Unlimited Wants

Most people have virtually unlimited wants. Our wants extend over a wide range of products, from *necessities* (food, shelter, clothing) to *luxuries* (perfumes, yachts, sports cars).

Over time, as new and improved products are introduced, economic wants tend to change and multiply. Only recently have people wanted wi-fi connections, tablet computers, and flying drones—products that did not exist a generation ago. Also, the satisfaction of certain wants may trigger others: The acquisition of a Chevy Spark or a Nissan Versa has been known to whet the appetite for a Lexus or a Mercedes.

Like goods, services also satisfy our wants. Car repair work, legal and accounting advice, and haircuts all satisfy human wants. Actually, we buy many goods, such as automobiles and washing machines, for the services they render.

Most people's desires for goods and services cannot be fully satisfied, though our desires for a particular good or service can be satisfied; over a short period of time, we can surely get enough toothpaste or pasta. But our broader desire for more goods and services and higher-quality goods and services seems to be another story.

Because we have only limited income (usually through our work) but seemingly insatiable wants, it is in our self-interest to economize: to pick and choose goods and services that maximize our satisfaction given the limitations we face.

GLOBAL PERSPECTIVE 1.1

AVERAGE INCOME PER PERSON, SELECTED NATIONS

Average income per capita, and therefore typical individual budget constraints, vary greatly from one country to another, even after adjusting for international differences in the cost of living.

Country	Country Per Capita Income, 2020 (PPP-adjusted international dollars)
Switzerland	$70,277
Norway	67,979
United States	65,280
Germany	55,891
Canada	50,511
Japan	42,338
Poland	34,131
Mexico	20,447
China	16,847
Guatemala	8,983
India	6,994
Burundi	783
Zimbabwe	411

Source: The World Bank, data.worldbank.org. Cost of living adjustments are based on purchasing power parity (PPP).

A Budget Line

budget line A line that shows the different combinations of two products a consumer can purchase with a specific money income, given the products' *prices*.

We can clarify the economizing problem facing consumers by visualizing a **budget line** or *budget constraint*, which is a schedule or curve that shows various combinations of two products a consumer can purchase with a specific income. Although we assume two products, the analysis generalizes to the full range of products available to consumers.

To understand what a budget line shows, suppose that you receive an Amazon gift card as a birthday present. The $120 card will soon expire. You go to Amazon.com and confine your purchase decisions to two alternatives: t-shirts and paperback books. T-shirts are $20 each and paperback books are $10 each. The table in Figure 1.1 shows your purchase options.

At one extreme, you might spend all of your $120 "income" on 6 t-shirts at $20 each and have nothing left to spend on books. Or, by giving up 2 t-shirts and thereby gaining $40, you can buy 4 t-shirts at $20 each and 4 books at $10 each. At the other extreme, you could buy 12 books at $10 each, spending your entire gift card on books with nothing left to spend on t-shirts.

The graph in Figure 1.1 shows the budget line. Every point on the graph represents a possible combination of t-shirts and books, including fractional quantities. The slope of the graphed budget line measures the ratio of the price of books (P_b) to the price of t-shirts (P_t); more precisely, the slope is $P_b/P_t = \$-10/\$+20 = -\frac{1}{2}$. So you must forgo 1 t-shirt (measured on the vertical axis) to buy 2 books (measured on the horizontal axis). This yields a slope of $-\frac{1}{2}$ or $-.5$.

The budget line illustrates several ideas.

Attainable and Unattainable Combinations All the combinations of t-shirts and books on or inside the budget line are *attainable* with $120 of income. You can afford to buy, for example, 3 t-shirts at $20 each and 6 books at $10 each. You also can afford to buy 2 t-shirts and 5 books, thereby using up only $90 of the $120 available on your gift card. But to achieve maximum utility, you will want to spend the full $120. The budget line shows all of the combinations that cost exactly the full $120.

In contrast, all combinations beyond the budget line are *unattainable*. The $120 limit simply does not allow you to purchase, for example, 5 t-shirts at $20 each and 5 books at $10 each. That $150 expenditure would clearly exceed the $120 limit.

Trade-Offs and Opportunity Costs The budget line in Figure 1.1 illustrates the idea of trade-offs arising from limited income. To obtain more t-shirts, you have to give up some books. For example, to obtain the first t-shirt, you trade off 2 books. So the opportunity cost of the first t-shirt is 2 books. To obtain the second t-shirt, the opportunity cost is also 2 books. The straight-line budget constraint, with its constant slope, indicates constant opportunity cost. That is, the opportunity cost of 1 extra t-shirt remains the same (= 2 books) as you purchase more t-shirts. Likewise, the opportunity cost of 1 extra book does not change (= $\frac{1}{2}$ t-shirt) as you purchase more books.

FIGURE 1.1 A consumer's budget line.

A consumer's budget line (or budget constraint) shows all the combinations of any two products that can be purchased, given the prices of the products and the consumer's income.

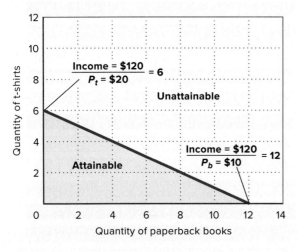

The Budget Line: Whole-Unit Combinations of T-shirts and Paperback Books Attainable with an Income of $120		
Units of T-shirts (Price = $20)	**Units of Books (Price = $10)**	**Total Expenditure**
6	0	$120 (= $120 + $0)
5	2	$120 (= $100 + $20)
4	4	$120 (= $80 + $40)
3	6	$120 (= $60 + $60)
2	8	$120 (= $40 + $80)
1	10	$120 (= $20 + $100)
0	12	$120 (= $0 + $120)

Did Zuckerberg, Durant, and Grande Make Bad Choices?

Opportunity costs come into play in decisions well beyond simple buying decisions. Consider the different choices people make with respect to college. The average salaries earned by college graduates are nearly twice as high as those earned by persons with just high school diplomas. For most capable students, "Go to college, stay in college, and earn a degree" is very sound advice.

Yet Facebook founder Mark Zuckerberg and basketball superstar Kevin Durant both dropped out of college, while pop singer Ariana Grande never even bothered to start classes. What were they thinking?

Unlike most students, Zuckerberg faced enormous opportunity costs for staying in college. He had a vision for

Swen Pförtner/dpa/Alamy Stock Photo

his company, and dropping out helped to ensure Facebook's success.

Durant was the college basketball player of the year as a freshman. So it was a natural for him to head to the NBA the next year and begin earning millions of dollars rather than stay in school for zero pay.

Grande knew that staying on top in the world of pop takes unceasing work. So after her first album became a massive hit, it made sense for her to skip college in order to relentlessly pursue continuing success.

Zuckerberg, Durant, and Grande understood opportunity costs and made their choices accordingly. They knew that size matters when it comes to opportunity costs and individual decisions.

Choice Limited income forces people to choose what to buy and what to forgo. You will select the combination of t-shirts and paperback books that you think is "best." That is, you will evaluate your marginal benefits and marginal costs (here, product price) to make choices that maximize your satisfaction. Other people, with the same $120 gift card, would undoubtedly make different choices.

Income Changes The budget line varies with income. An increase in income shifts the budget line to the right; a decrease in income shifts it to the left. To verify this, recalculate the table in Figure 1.1, assuming the card value (income) is (a) $240 and (b) $60, and plot the new budget lines in the graph. No wonder people like to have more income: It shifts their budget lines outward and enables them to buy more goods and services. But even with more income, people still face spending trade-offs, choices, and opportunity costs.

▶ Because wants exceed incomes, individuals face an economizing problem; they must decide what to buy and what to forgo.

▶ A budget line (budget constraint) shows the various combinations of two goods that a consumer can purchase with a specific income.

▶ Straight-line budget constraints imply constant opportunity costs for both goods.

Society's Economizing Problem

Society also faces an economizing problem. Should it devote more of its limited resources to the criminal justice system (police, courts, and prisons) or to education (teachers, books, and schools)? If it decides to devote more resources to both, what other goods and services does it forgo?

>> **LO1.5** List the categories of scarce resources and explain society's economizing problem.

Scarce Resources

Society has limited or scarce **economic resources,** meaning all natural, human, and manufactured resources that go into the production of goods and services.

Resource Categories

Economists classify economic resources into four general categories.

economic resources The *land, labor, capital,* and *entrepreneurial ability* that are used to produce *goods* and *services*. Also known as the *factors of production*.

land In addition to the part of the earth's surface not covered by water, this term refers to any and all natural resources ("free gifts of nature") that are used to produce *goods* and *services.* Thus, it includes the oceans, sunshine, coal deposits, forests, the electromagnetic spectrum, and *fisheries.* Note that land is one of the four *economic resources.*

labor Any mental or physical exertion on the part of a human being that is used in the production of a *good* or *service.* One of the four *economic resources.*

capital Man-made physical objects (factories, roads) and intangible ideas (the recipe for cement) that do not directly satisfy human wants but which help to produce *goods* and *services* that do satisfy human wants. One of the four *economic resources.*

consumer goods Products and *services* that satisfy human wants directly.

investment Expenditures that increase the volume of physical *capital* (roads, factories, wireless networks) and intangible ideas (formulas, processes, algorithms) that help to produce goods and services. Also known as *economic investment.* Not to be confused with *financial investment.*

entrepreneurial ability The human resource that combines the other *economic resources* of *land, labor,* and *capital* to produce new products or make innovations in the production of existing products; provided by *entrepreneurs.*

>> **LO1.6** Apply production possibilities analysis.

Land **Land** includes all natural resources used in the production process. These include forests, mineral and oil deposits, water resources, wind power, sunlight, and arable land.

Labor The **labor** resource consists of the physical actions and mental activities that people contribute to the production of goods and services. The work-related activities of a retail clerk, teacher, professional football player, and nuclear physicist all fall under the general heading "labor."

Capital For economists, **capital** includes all human-produced physical objects and intangible ideas used to produce consumer goods and services.

- The physical objects, or *capital goods*, include all factory, storage, transportation, and distribution facilities, as well as tools and machinery, electrical grids, and communication satellites.
- The intangible ideas, or intellectual property, include inventions, recipes, designs, blueprints, instructions, and software.

Note that while **consumer goods** satisfy wants directly, *capital* does so indirectly by aiding in the production of consumer goods. For example, a large commercial baking oven (a capital good) combined with a particular recipe (an intangible idea) helps make loaves of bread (a consumer good).

Also understand that the term "capital" as used by economists does *not* refer to money. Because money produces nothing, economists do not consider it an economic resource.

Finally, please also note that while the words *capital* and *investment* are related, economists have a very restrictive definition of the word **investment.** When an economist uses the word investment, she is referring to spending that pays for the production of *new* physical or intangible capital. Thus Bill Gates spending a billion dollars to invent a cure for malaria is investment (since it pays for the creation of a *new* vaccine recipe) but his purchasing an old factory is not (because that capital good already existed and thus no new capital is created as a result of his purchase).

Entrepreneurial Ability Finally, there is the very special human resource, distinct from labor, that is known as entrepreneurial ability. **Entrepreneurial ability** combines the other economic resources of land, labor, and capital to produce new products or make *innovations* in the production of existing products.

Entrepreneurial ability is supplied by **entrepreneurs,** who perform several important economic functions that are not performed by ordinary labor, which engages in routine functions and does not innovate.

The unique contributions of entrepreneurs include:

- Taking the initiative in combining resources to produce a good or a service—entrepreneurs are the creative force behind production.
- Making the strategic business decisions that set the course of an enterprise.
- Innovating by commercializing new products, new production techniques, and new forms of business organization.
- Bearing risk. Because innovation is risky, progress would cease without entrepreneurs willing to bear risk by devoting their time, effort, and ability—as well as their own money and the money of others—to commercializing new products and ideas.

In closing, note that because land, labor, capital, and entrepreneurial ability are combined to produce goods and services, they are called the **factors of production,** or simply "inputs."

Production Possibilities Model

Society uses its scarce resources to produce goods and services. The alternatives it faces can best be understood through a macroeconomic model of production possibilities. To keep things simple, let's initially assume:

- *Full employment* The economy is employing all of its available resources.
- *Fixed resources* The quantity and quality of the factors of production are fixed.
- *Fixed technology* The state of technology (the methods used to produce output) is constant.

TABLE 1.1 **Production Possibilities of Pizzas and Industrial Robots**

Type of Product	Production Alternatives				
	A	B	C	D	E
Pizzas (in hundred thousands)	0	1	2	3	4
Robots (in thousands)	10	9	7	4	0

- *Two goods* The economy is producing only two goods: pizzas and industrial robots. Pizzas symbolize **consumer goods,** products that satisfy our wants directly; industrial robots (for example, the kind used to weld automobile frames) symbolize *capital*, physical objects or intangible ideas that satisfy our wants indirectly by making possible more efficient production of consumer goods.

Production Possibilities Table

A production possibilities table lists the different combinations of two products that can be produced with a specific set of resources, assuming full employment. Table 1.1 presents a simple hypothetical economy that is producing pizzas and industrial robots. At alternative A, this economy would be devoting all its resources to the production of industrial robots (capital). At alternative E, all resources would go to pizza production (consumer goods). Those alternatives are unrealistic extremes; an economy typically produces both capital goods and consumer goods, as in B, C, and D. As we move from alternative A to E, we increase the production of pizzas at the expense of the production of industrial robots.

Because consumer goods satisfy our wants directly, any movement toward E looks tempting. In producing more pizzas, society increases the satisfaction of its current wants. But there is a cost: More pizzas mean fewer industrial robots. This shift to consumer goods catches up with society over time because the stock of capital expands more slowly, thereby reducing potential future production. By moving toward alternative E, society chooses "more now" at the expense of "much more later."

In contrast, by moving toward A, society chooses to forgo current consumption, thereby freeing up resources to increase the production of capital. By choosing to build up its stock of capital, society will have greater future production and, therefore, greater future consumption. By moving toward A, society is choosing "more later" at the cost of "less now."

Generalization: At any point in time, a fully employed economy must sacrifice some of one good to obtain more of another good. Scarce resources prohibit a fully employed economy from having more of both goods. Having more of one thing means having less of something else.

Production Possibilities Curve

The data presented in a production possibilities table are shown graphically as a **production possibilities curve.** This curve displays the different combinations of goods and services that society can produce in a fully employed economy, assuming a fixed availability of supplies of resources and fixed technology.

In **Figure 1.2 (Key Graph),** each point on the production possibilities curve represents a maximum output combination of the two products. Consequently, the entire length of the curve can be thought of as a "constraint" because it shows the limit of attainable outputs given current resources and technology.

- Points on the curve are attainable as long as the economy uses all its available resources and technology.
- Points inside the curve are also attainable, but are associated with less than full employment of resources and technology. These inside points reflect less total output than points on the curve and are therefore not as desirable as points on the curve.
- Points lying beyond the production possibilities curve, like *W*, represent a greater output than the output at any point on the curve. Such points, however, are unattainable with current resources and technology.

entrepreneurs Individuals who provide *entrepreneurial ability* to *firms* by setting strategy, advancing innovations, and bearing the financial risk if their firms do poorly.

factors of production The four *economic resources: land, labor, capital,* and *entrepreneurial ability.*

consumer goods Products and services that satisfy human wants directly.

production possibilities curve A curve showing the different combinations of two goods or *services* that can be produced in a *full-employment, full-production* economy where the available supplies of *resources* and technology are fixed.

..Il KEY GRAPH

FIGURE 1.2 The production possibilities curve.

Each point on the production possibilities curve represents some maximum combination of two products that can be produced if resources are fully employed. When an economy is operating on the curve, more industrial robots means fewer pizzas, and vice versa. Limited resources and a fixed technology make any combination of industrial robots and pizzas lying outside the curve (such as at *W*) unattainable. Points inside the curve are attainable, but they indicate that full employment is not being realized.

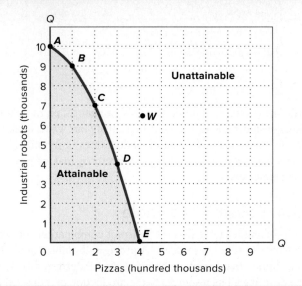

QUICK QUIZ FOR FIGURE 1.2

1. **Production possibilities curve *ABCDE* is bowed out from the origin because:**
   a. the marginal benefit of pizzas declines as more pizzas are consumed.
   b. the curve gets steeper as we move from *E* to *A*.
   c. it reflects the law of increasing opportunity costs.
   d. resources are scarce.

2. **The marginal opportunity cost of the second unit of pizza is:**
   a. 2 units of robots.
   b. 3 units of robots.
   c. 7 units of robots.
   d. 9 units of robots.

3. **The total opportunity cost of 7 units of robots is:**
   a. 1 unit of pizza.
   b. 2 units of pizza.
   c. 3 units of pizza.
   d. 4 units of pizza.

4. **All points on this production possibilities curve necessarily represent:**
   a. society's optimal choice.
   b. less than full use of resources.
   c. unattainable levels of output.
   d. full employment.

Answers: 1. c; 2. a; 3. b; 4. d

Law of Increasing Opportunity Costs

Figure 1.2 clearly shows that more pizzas mean fewer industrial robots. The number of industrial robots that must be given up to obtain another pizza is the opportunity cost of pizza.

In moving from alternative *A* to alternative *B* in Table 1.1, the cost of 1 additional pizza is 1 fewer robot. As we move from *B* to *C*, *C* to *D*, and *D* to *E*, an important economic principle is revealed: For society, the opportunity cost of each additional pizza is greater than the opportunity cost of the preceding pizza. When we move from *A* to *B*, just 1 industrial robot is sacrificed for 1 more pizza; but in going from *B* to *C*, we sacrifice 2 industrial robots for 1 more pizza; then 3 industrial robots for 1 more pizza; and finally 4 for 1. Conversely, confirm that as we move from *E* to *A*, the cost of an additional industrial robot (on average) is $\frac{1}{4}$, $\frac{1}{3}$, $\frac{1}{2}$, and 1 pizzas, respectively, for the four successive moves.

law of increasing opportunity costs The principle that as the production of a good increases, the *opportunity cost* of producing an additional unit rises.

Our example illustrates the **law of increasing opportunity costs.** As we increase the production of a particular good, the opportunity cost of producing an additional unit rises.

Shape of the Curve The law of increasing opportunity costs is reflected in the shape of the production possibilities curve: The curve is bowed out from the origin of the graph. As Figure 1.2 shows, when the economy moves from *A* to *E*, it must give up successively larger amounts of industrial robots (1, 2, 3, and 4) to acquire equal increments of pizzas (1, 1, 1, and 1). Thus the slope of the production possibilities curve becomes steeper as we move from *A* to *E*.

Economic Rationale   The economic rationale for the law of increasing opportunity costs is that economic resources are not completely adaptable to alternative uses. Many resources are better at producing one type of good than at producing others. Some land, for example, is highly suited to growing the ingredients necessary for pizza production, but as pizza production expands, society has to start using land that is less bountiful for farming. Other land, by contrast, is rich in mineral deposits and therefore well-suited to producing the materials needed to make industrial robots. As society steps up the production of robots, it must use land that is less and less adaptable to making their components.

If we start at *A* and move to *B* in Figure 1.2, we can shift resources whose productivity is relatively high in pizza production and low in industrial robots. But as we move from *B* to *C*, *C* to *D*, and so on, resources highly productive of pizzas become increasingly scarce. To get more pizzas, resources whose productivity in industrial robots is relatively great will be needed. Increasingly more of such resources, and hence greater sacrifices of industrial robots, will be needed to achieve each 1-unit increase in pizzas. This lack of perfect flexibility, or interchangeability, on the part of resources is the cause of increasing opportunity costs for society.

Optimal Allocation

Of all the attainable combinations of pizzas and industrial robots along the production possibilities curve in Figure 1.2, which one is optimal (best)? That is, which quantities of pizzas and industrial robots will maximize satisfaction?

Recall that economic decisions center on comparisons of marginal benefit (MB) and marginal cost (MC): Any economic activity should be expanded as long as marginal benefit exceeds marginal cost; and any economic activity should be reduced as long as marginal cost exceeds marginal benefit. The optimal amount of the activity occurs where MB = MC.

The Optimum Quantity of Pizza   Society can use the same logic to decide which output combination to produce among all the output combinations available along the production possibilities curve in Figure 1.2.

Consider pizzas. We know from the law of increasing opportunity costs that the marginal cost of additional pizzas will rise as more pizzas are produced. At the same time, we need to recognize that the extra, or marginal, benefits that come from consuming pizza decline with each additional pizza because as consumers eat more and more pizza, they begin to get fed up with it and, as they do, the value they place on each additional pizza decreases. Consequently, each additional pizza brings both increasing marginal costs and decreasing marginal benefits.

The optimal quantity of pizza production—200,000 pizzas—is indicated in Figure 1.3 by point *e* at the intersection of the MB and MC curves.

Why is 200,000 pizzas the optimal quantity?

- If only 100,000 pizzas were produced, the marginal benefit of an extra pizza (point *a*) would exceed its marginal cost (point *b*). In money terms, MB is $15, while MC is only $5. When society gains something worth $15 at a marginal cost of only $5, it is better off. In Figure 1.3, net gains continue to be realized until pizza production has been increased to 200,000 pizzas.

- In contrast, the production of 300,000 pizzas is excessive. At that quantity, the MC of an added pizza is $15 (point *c*) and its MB is only $5 (point *d*). This is a losing proposition for society, as would be any output level above 200,000 pizzas.

You can see from this analysis that the optimal (utility maximizing) amount of this society's limited resources will be allocated to pizza production when

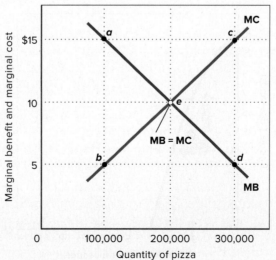

FIGURE 1.3
Optimal output: MB = MC.

Achieving the optimal output requires the expansion of a good's output until its marginal benefit (MB) and marginal cost (MC) are equal. No resources beyond that point should be allocated to the product. Here, optimal output occurs at point *e*, where 200,000 pizzas are produced.

exactly 200,000 pizzas are produced. The remainder of society's resources will then flow toward the production of industrial robots. That would put us at point *C* on the production possibilities curve in Figure 1.2, with 200,000 pizzas and 7,000 robots being produced simultaneously by fully employing all of this society's limited supplies of land, labor, capital, and entrepreneurial ability.

QUICK REVIEW

1.3

▶ Economists categorize economic resources as land, labor, capital, and entrepreneurial ability.

▶ The production possibilities curve illustrates several ideas: (a) scarcity of resources is implied by the area of unattainable combinations of output lying outside the production possibilities curve; (b) choice among outputs is reflected in the variety of attainable combinations of goods lying along

the curve; (c) opportunity cost is illustrated by the downward slope of the curve; (d) the law of increasing opportunity costs is reflected in the bowed-outward shape of the curve.

▶ A comparison of marginal benefits and marginal costs is needed to determine the best or optimal output mix on a production possibilities curve.

Unemployment, Growth, and the Future

>> **LO1.7** Explain how economic growth and international trade increase consumption possibilities.

In the depths of the Great Depression of the 1930s, one-quarter of U.S. workers were unemployed and one-third of U.S. production capacity was idle. Subsequent downturns have been much less severe. During the brief but sharp COVID-19 recession of 2020, for instance, 1 in 7 workers was without a job while production fell by a comparably small 10 percent.

Almost all nations have experienced widespread unemployment and unused production capacity from business downturns. Since 2020, for example, Brazil, Italy, Russia, Japan, and France have had economic downturns and elevated unemployment. How do these realities relate to the production possibilities model?

Our analysis and conclusions change if we relax the assumption that all available resources are fully employed. The five alternatives in Table 1.1 represent maximum outputs; they illustrate the combinations of pizzas and industrial robots that can be produced when the economy is operating at full employment. With unemployment, this economy would produce less than each alternative shown in the table.

Graphically, we represent situations of unemployment by points inside the original production possibilities curve (reproduced here in Figure 1.4). Point *U* is one such point. At point *U*, the economy is falling short of the various maximum combinations of pizzas and industrial robots represented by the points on the production possibilities curve. Movement toward full employment would yield a greater output of one or both products.

A Growing Economy

When we drop the assumption that the quantity and quality of resources and technology are fixed, the production possibilities curve shifts positions, and the economy's potential maximum output changes.

FIGURE 1.4
Unemployment and the production possibilities curve.

Any point inside the production possibilities curve, such as *U*, represents unemployment or a failure to achieve full employment. The arrows indicate that by realizing full employment, the economy could operate on the curve. This means it could produce more of one or both products than it is producing at point *U*.

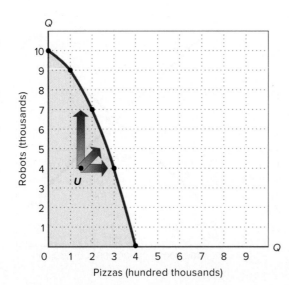

Increases in Resource Supplies Although resource supplies are fixed at any specific moment, they change over time. For example, a nation's growing population increases the supplies of labor and entrepreneurial ability. Also, labor quality usually improves over time via more education and training. And although some of our energy and mineral resources are being depleted, new sources are also being discovered. The development of irrigation systems, for example, adds to the supply of arable land.

The net result of these increases in the factors of production is society's ability to produce more consumer goods and more capital goods. The new production possibilities might look like those in the table in

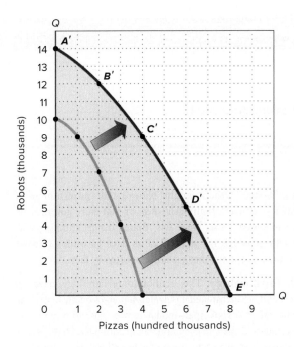

FIGURE 1.5 Economic growth and the production possibilities curve.

The increase in supplies of resources, improvements in resource quality, and technological advances that occur in a dynamic economy move the production possibilities curve outward and to the right, allowing the economy to have larger quantities of both types of goods.

	Production Alternatives				
Type of Product	A′	B′	C′	D′	E′
Pizzas (in hundred thousands)	0	2	4	6	8
Robots (in thousands)	14	12	9	5	0

Figure 1.5. The greater abundance of resources will result in a greater potential output of one or both products. The economy will have achieved economic growth in the form of expanded potential output. Graphically, the production possibilities curve shifts outward and to the right, as illustrated in Figure 1.5 by the move from the original, inner, curve to curve A′B′C′D′E′. This shift represents increased productive capacity, which, if used, will result in **economic growth** and a larger total output.

economic growth (1) An outward shift in the *production possibilities curve* that results from an increase in resource supplies or quality or an improvement in *technology*; (2) an increase of real output (*gross domestic product*) or real output per capita.

Advances in Technology Improvements in technology bring both new and better goods and improved ways of producing them. For now, let's focus on one type of technological advance: improvements in the methods of production—for example, the introduction of computerized artificial intelligence (AI) systems to manage inventories and schedule production. These advances allow society to produce more goods with available resources. They make possible the production of more industrial robots *and* more pizzas.

Conclusion: Economic growth is the result of (1) increases in supplies of resources, (2) improvements in resource quality, and (3) technological advances. Whereas static, no-growth economies must sacrifice some of one good to obtain more of another, dynamic, growing economies can produce larger quantities of both goods.

Present Choices and Future Possibilities

An economy's current choice of its position on its production possibilities curve helps determine the curve's future location. Let's designate the two axes of the production possibilities curve as "goods for the future" and "goods for the present," as in Figure 1.6. Goods for the future include capital goods, research, education, and preventive medicine; they are the ingredients of economic growth. Goods for the present are consumer goods such as food, clothing, and entertainment.

Now suppose there are two hypothetical economies, Presentville and Futureville, that are initially identical in every respect except one: Presentville's current choice of positions on its production possibilities curve (point P in Figure 1.6a) strongly favors present goods over future goods. Futureville, in contrast, makes a current choice that stresses larger amounts of future goods and smaller amounts of present goods, as shown by point F in Figure 1.6b.

Now, other things equal, we can expect Futureville's future production possibilities curve to be farther to the right than Presentville's. By currently choosing an output more favorable to technological advances and to increases in the quantity and quality of resources, Futureville will achieve greater economic growth than Presentville. In terms of capital goods, Futureville is choosing to make larger current additions to its "national factory" by devoting more of its current output to capital than Presentville. The payoff for Futureville is greater future production capacity and economic growth. The opportunity cost is fewer consumer goods in the present.

Pitfalls to Sound Economic Reasoning

Because They Affect Us So Personally, We Often Have Trouble Thinking Accurately and Objectively about Economic Issues.

LEON NEAL/AFP/GettyImages

Here are some common pitfalls to avoid in successfully applying the economic perspective.

Biases Most people bring a bundle of biases and preconceptions to the field of economics. For example, some might think that corporate profits are excessive or that lending money is always superior to borrowing money. Others might believe that government is necessarily less efficient than businesses, or that more government regulation is always better than less. Biases distort thinking and interfere with objective analysis. All of us must be willing to shed biases and preconceptions that are not supported by facts.

Loaded Terminology The economic terminology used in newspapers and broadcast media is sometimes emotionally biased, or loaded. The writer or spokesperson may have a cause to promote or an ax to grind, and may slant comments accordingly. High profits may be labeled "obscene," low wages may be called "exploitative," or self-interested behavior may be "greed." Government workers may be referred to as "mindless bureaucrats" and those favoring stronger government regulations may be called "socialists." To objectively analyze economic issues, you must be prepared to reject or discount such terminology.

Fallacy of Composition Another pitfall in economic thinking is the assumption that what is true for one individual or part of a whole is necessarily true for a group of individuals or the whole. This is a logical fallacy called the *fallacy of composition*; the assumption is not correct. A statement that is valid for an individual or part is not necessarily valid for the larger group or whole.

FIGURE 1.6 Present choices and future locations of production possibilities curves.

(a) Presentville's current choice to produce more "present goods" and fewer "future goods," as represented by point *P,* will result in a modest outward shift of the production possibilities curve in the future. (b) Futureville's current choice of producing fewer "present goods" and more "future goods," as depicted by point *F,* will lead to a greater outward shift of the production possibilities curve in the future.

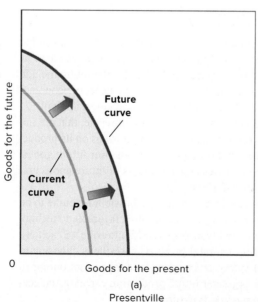

(a)
Presentville

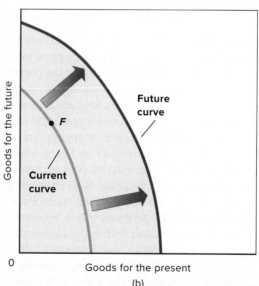

(b)
Futureville

Noneconomic example:

- You may see the action better if you leap to your feet to see an outstanding play at a football game. But if all the spectators leap to their feet at the same time, nobody—including you—will have a better view than when all remained seated.

Economic examples:

- An individual stockholder can sell shares of, say, Tesla stock without affecting the price of the stock. The individual's sale will not noticeably reduce the share price because the sale is a negligible fraction of the total shares of Tesla being bought and sold. But if all the Tesla shareholders decide to sell their shares the same day, the market will be flooded with shares and the stock price will fall precipitously.
- A single cattle ranch can increase its revenue by expanding the size of its livestock herd. The extra cattle will not affect the price of cattle when they are brought to market. But if all ranchers as a group expand their herds, the total output of cattle will increase so much that the price of cattle will decline when the cattle are sold. If the price reduction is relatively large, ranchers as a group might find that their income has fallen despite their having sold a greater number of cattle because the fall in price overwhelms the increase in quantity.

Post Hoc Fallacy You must think very carefully before concluding that because event A precedes event B, A is the cause of B. This kind of faulty reasoning is known as the *post hoc, ergo propter hoc,* or "after this, therefore because of this," fallacy.

Noneconomic example:

- A professional football team hires a new coach and the team's record improves. Is the new coach the cause? Maybe. Perhaps the presence of more experienced and talented players or an easier schedule is the true cause. The rooster crows before dawn, but does not cause the sunrise.

Economic example:

- Many people blamed the Great Depression of the 1930s on the stock market crash of 1929. But the crash did not cause the Great Depression. The same severe weaknesses in the economy that caused the crash caused the Great Depression. The depression would have occurred even without the preceding stock market crash.

Correlation but Not Causation Do not confuse correlation, or connection, with causation. Correlation between two events or two sets of data indicates only that they are associated in some systematic and dependable way. For example, we may find that when variable X increases, Y also increases. But this correlation does not necessarily mean that there is causation—that increases in X cause increases in Y. The relationship could be purely coincidental or dependent on some other factor, Z, not included in the analysis.

Here is an example: Economists have found a positive correlation between education and income. In general, people with more education earn higher incomes than those with less education. Common sense suggests education is the cause and higher incomes are the effect; more education implies a more knowledgeable and productive worker, and such workers receive larger salaries.

But might the relationship be explainable in other ways? Are education and income correlated because the characteristics required for succeeding in education—ability and motivation—are the same ones required to be a productive and highly paid worker? If so, then people with those traits will probably both obtain more education and earn higher incomes. But greater education will not be the sole cause of the higher income.

Is Futureville's choice necessarily "better" than Presentville's? We cannot say. The different outcomes simply reflect different preferences and priorities in the two countries.

Global Perspective 1.2 indicates that nations differ substantially in how large a fraction of their respective *national incomes* they choose to devote to investments in capital ("goods for the future") as opposed to expenditures on consumer goods ("goods for the present").

A Qualification: International Trade

Production possibilities analysis implies that an individual nation is limited to the combinations of output indicated by its production possibilities curve. But we must modify this principle when international specialization and trade exist.

You will see in later chapters that an economy can circumvent, through international specialization and trade, the output limits imposed by its domestic production possibilities curve. With international specialization and trade, each nation specializes in the production of those items for which it has the lowest opportunity costs. Countries then engage in trade, with each country exchanging the items that it can produce at the lowest opportunity costs for the items that other countries can produce at their lowest opportunity costs.

International specialization and trade allow a nation to get more of a desired good at less sacrifice of some other good. Rather than sacrifice three units of domestically produced robots to get a third domestically produced pizza, as in Table 1.1, a nation that engages in specialization and trade might be able to do much better. If it specializes in robots while another country specializes in pizza, then it may be able to obtain the third unit of pizza by trading only two domestically

15

GLOBAL PERSPECTIVE 1.2

GROSS FIXED CAPITAL FORMATION AS A PERCENTAGE OF NATIONAL INCOME, SELECTED NATIONS, 2020

Countries vary widely in the percentage of their respective national incomes that they devote to investments in capital goods ("gross fixed capital formation") rather than on purchases of consumer goods. Only the former generates increases in future production capacity.

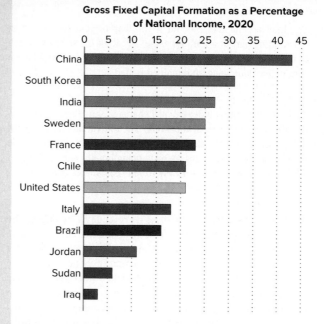

Gross Fixed Capital Formation as a Percentage of National Income, 2020

Source: The World Bank, www.worldbank.org.

produced robots for one foreign-produced pizza. Specialization and trade have the same effect as having more and better resources or discovering improved production techniques; both increase the quantities of capital and consumer goods available to society. Expansion of domestic production possibilities and international trade are two separate routes for obtaining greater output.

QUICK REVIEW

1.4

▶ Unemployment causes an economy to operate at a point inside its production possibilities curve.

▶ Increases in resource supplies, improvements in resource quality, and technological advance cause economic growth, which shifts the production possibilities curve outward.

▶ An economy's present choice of capital and consumer goods helps determine its future production possibilities curve.

▶ International specialization and trade enable a nation to obtain more goods than its production possibilities curve indicates.

Summary

LO1.1 Define economics and explain the economic perspective.

Economics is the social science that examines how individuals, institutions, and society make optimal choices under conditions of scarcity. Central to economics is the idea of opportunity cost: the value of the next-best good or service forgone to obtain something.

The economic perspective includes three elements: scarcity and choice, purposeful behavior, and marginal analysis. It sees individuals and institutions as making rational decisions based on comparisons of marginal costs and marginal benefits.

LO1.2 Describe the role of economic theory in economics.

Economists employ the scientific method, in which they form and test hypotheses of cause-and-effect relationships to generate theories, laws, and principles. Economists often combine theories into representations called models.

LO1.3 Distinguish microeconomics from macroeconomics and positive economics from normative economics.

Microeconomics examines the decision making of specific economic units or institutions. Macroeconomics looks at the economy as a whole or its major aggregates.

Positive economic analysis deals with facts; normative economics reflects value judgments.

LO1.4 Explain the individual's economizing problem and illustrate trade-offs, opportunity costs, and attainable combinations with budget lines.

Individuals face an economizing problem. Because their wants exceed their incomes, they must decide what to purchase and what to forgo. Society also faces an economizing problem. Societal wants exceed the available resources necessary to fulfill them. Society therefore must decide what to produce and what to forgo.

Graphically, a budget line (or budget constraint) illustrates the economizing problem for individuals. The line shows the various combinations of two products that a consumer can purchase with a specific money income, given the prices of the two products.

LO1.5 List the categories of scarce resources and explain society's economizing problem.
Economic resources are inputs into the production process and can be classified as land, labor, capital, or entrepreneurial ability. Economic resources are also known as factors of production or inputs.

Economists illustrate society's economizing problem through production possibilities analysis. Production possibilities tables and curves show the different combinations of goods and services that can be produced in a fully employed economy, assuming that resource quantity, resource quality, and technology are fixed.

LO1.6 Apply production possibilities analysis.
An economy that is fully employed and thus operating on its production possibilities curve must sacrifice the output of some types of goods and services to increase the production of others. The gain of one type of good or service is always accompanied by an opportunity cost in the form of the loss of some of the other type of good or service.

Because resources are not equally productive in all possible uses, shifting resources from one use to another creates increasing opportunity costs. The production of additional units of one product requires the sacrifice of increasing amounts of the other product.

The optimal (best) point on the production possibilities curve represents the most desirable mix of goods. It requires the expanded production of each good until its marginal benefit (MB) equals its marginal cost (MC).

LO1.7 Explain how economic growth and international trade increase consumption possibilities.
Over time, technological advances and increases in the quantity and quality of resources enable the economy to produce more of all goods and services—that is, to experience economic growth. Society's choice regarding the mix of consumer goods and capital goods in current output determines the future location of the production possibilities curve and the extent of economic growth.

International trade enables a nation to obtain more goods from its limited resources than its production possibilities curve indicates.

Terms and Concepts

economics	macroeconomics	investment
economic perspective	aggregate	consumer goods
scarcity	positive economics	entrepreneurial ability
opportunity cost	normative economics	entrepreneurs
utility	economizing problem	factors of production
marginal analysis	budget line	production possibilities curve
scientific method	economic resources	law of increasing opportunity costs
economic principle	land	economic growth
other-things-equal assumption	labor	
microeconomics	capital	

Discussion Questions

1. What is an opportunity cost? How does the idea relate to the definition of economics? Which of the following decisions would entail the greater opportunity cost: allocating a square block in the heart of New York City for a surface parking lot or allocating a square block at the edge of a typical suburb for such a lot? Explain. **LO1.1**
2. Cite three examples of recent decisions that you made in which you, at least implicitly, weighed marginal cost and marginal benefit. **LO1.1**
3. What is "utility" and how does it relate to purposeful behavior? **LO1.1**
4. What are the key elements of the scientific method, and how does this method relate to economic principles and laws? **LO1.2**
5. Make (a) a positive economic statement of your choice, and then (b) a normative economic statement relating to your first statement. **LO1.3**
6. How does the slope of a budget line illustrate opportunity costs and trade-offs? How does a budget line illustrate scarcity and the effect of limited incomes? **LO1.4**
7. What are economic resources? What categories do economists use to classify them? Why are resources also called factors of production? Why are they called inputs? **LO1.5**
8. Why is money not considered to be a capital resource in economics? Why is entrepreneurial ability considered a category of economic resource, distinct from labor? What roles do entrepreneurs play in the economy? **LO1.5**
9. Explain the typical shapes of marginal-benefit and marginal-cost curves. How are these curves used to determine the optimal allocation of resources to a particular product? If current output is such that marginal cost exceeds marginal benefit, should more or fewer resources be allocated to this product? Explain. **LO1.6**

10. Suppose that, on the basis of a nation's production possibilities curve, an economy must sacrifice 10,000 pizzas domestically to get the 1 additional industrial robot it desires, but it can get the robot from another country in exchange for 9,000 pizzas. Relate this information to the following statement: "Through international specialization and trade, a nation can reduce its opportunity cost of obtaining goods and thus move outside its production possibilities curve." LO1.7

11. **LAST WORD** Studies indicate that married men on average earn more income than unmarried men of the same age and education level. Why must we be cautious in concluding that marriage is the cause and higher income is the effect?

Review Questions

1. Match each term with the correct definition. LO1.1
   economics
   opportunity cost
   marginal analysis
   utility
   a. The next-best thing that must be forgone in order to produce one more unit of a given product.
   b. The pleasure, happiness, or satisfaction obtained from consuming a good or service.
   c. The social science concerned with how individuals, institutions, and society make optimal (best) choices under conditions of scarcity.
   d. Making choices based on comparing marginal benefits with marginal costs.

2. Indicate whether each of the following statements applies to microeconomics or macroeconomics: LO1.3
   a. The unemployment rate in the United States was 5.2 percent in August 2021.
   b. A U.S. software firm laid off 15 workers last month and transferred the work to India.
   c. An unexpected freeze in central Florida reduced the citrus crop and caused the price of oranges to rise.
   d. U.S. output, adjusted for inflation, decreased by 3.5 percent in 2020.
   e. Last week Wells Fargo Bank lowered its interest rate on business loans by one-half of 1 percentage point.
   f. The consumer price index rose by 0.3 percent from July 2021 to August 2021.

3. Suppose that you initially have $100 to spend on books or movie tickets. The books start off costing $25 each and the movie tickets start off costing $10 each. For each of the following situations, would the attainable set of combinations that you can afford increase or decrease? LO1.4
   a. Your budget increases from $100 to $150 while the prices stay the same.
   b. Your budget remains $100, and the price of books remains $25, but the price of movie tickets rises to $20.
   c. Your budget remains $100, and the price of movie tickets remains $10, but the price of a book falls to $15.

4. Suppose that you are given a $100 budget at work that can be spent only on two items: staplers and pens. If staplers cost $10 each and pens cost $2.50 each, then the opportunity cost of purchasing one stapler is: LO1.4
   a. 10 pens.
   b. 5 pens.
   c. zero pens.
   d. 4 pens.

5. As economists use the terms, investment is related to capital in the same way that: LO1.5
   a. MB is to MC.
   b. practice is to acquiring skill.
   c. color is to sound.
   d. positive economics is to normative economics.

6. For each of the following situations involving marginal cost (MC) and marginal benefit (MB), indicate whether it would be best to produce more, fewer, or the current number of units. LO1.6
   a. 3,000 units at which MC = $10 and MB = $13.
   b. 11 units at which MC = $4 and MB = $3.
   c. 43,277 units at which MC = $99 and MB = $99.
   d. 82 units at which MC < MB.
   e. 5 units at which MB < MC.

7. Explain how (if at all) each of the following events affects the location of a country's production possibilities curve. LO1.6
   a. The quality of education increases.
   b. The number of unemployed workers increases.
   c. A new technique improves the efficiency of extracting copper from ore.
   d. A devastating earthquake destroys numerous production facilities.

8. What are the two major ways in which an economy can grow and push out its production possibilities curve? LO1.7
   a. Better weather and nicer cars
   b. Higher taxes and lower spending
   c. Increases in resource supplies and advances in technology
   d. Decreases in scarcity and advances in auditing

9. To obtain greater output, a nation can: LO1.7
   a. invest in more goods for the future (capital).
   b. increase the quantity and quality of its resources.
   c. engage in international specialization and trade.
   d. all of the above.

Problems

1. Potatoes cost Janice $1 per pound, and she has $5.00 that she could possibly spend on potatoes or other items. If she feels that the first pound of potatoes is worth $1.50, the second pound is worth $1.14, the third pound is worth $1.05, and all subsequent pounds are worth $0.30 per pound, how many pounds of potatoes will she purchase? How many pounds will she purchase if she has only $2 to spend? LO1.1

2. Pham can work as many or as few hours as she wants at the college bookstore for $12 per hour. But due to her hectic schedule, she has just 15 hours per week that she can spend working at either the bookstore or other potential jobs. One potential job, at a café, will pay her $15 per hour for up to 6 hours per week. She has another job offer at a garage that will pay her $13 an hour for up to 5 hours per week. And she has a potential job at a daycare center that will pay her $11.50 per hour for as many hours as she can work. If her goal is to maximize the amount of money she can make each week, how many hours will she work at the bookstore? LO1.1

3. Suppose you won $15 on a lotto ticket at the local 7-Eleven and decided to spend all the winnings on candy bars and bags of peanuts. Candy bars cost $0.75 each while bags of peanuts cost $1.50 each. **LO1.4**
   a. Construct a table showing the alternative combinations of the two products that are available.
   b. Plot the data in your table as a budget line in a graph. What is the slope of the budget line? What is the opportunity cost of one more candy bar? Of one more bag of peanuts? Do these opportunity costs rise, fall, or remain constant as additional units are purchased?
   c. Does the budget line tell you which of the available combinations of candy bars and bags of peanuts to buy?
   d. Suppose that you had won $30 on your ticket, not $15. Show the $30 budget line in your diagram. Has the number of available combinations increased or decreased?

4. Suppose that you are on a desert island and possess exactly 20 coconuts. Your neighbor, Friday, is a fisherman, and he is willing to trade 2 fish for every 1 coconut that you are willing to give him. Another neighbor, Kwame, is also a fisherman, and he is willing to trade 3 fish for every 1 coconut. **LO1.5**
   a. On a single figure, draw budget lines for trading with Friday and for trading with Kwame. (Put coconuts on the vertical axis.)
   b. What is the slope of the budget line from trading with Friday?
   c. What is the slope of the budget line from trading with Kwame?
   d. Which budget line features a larger set of attainable combinations of coconuts and fish?
   e. If you are going to trade coconuts for fish, would you rather trade with Friday or Kwame? Why?

5. Refer to the following production possibilities table for consumer goods (automobiles) and capital goods (forklifts): **LO1.6**
   a. Show these data graphically. Upon what specific assumptions is this production possibilities curve based?
   b. If the economy is at point C, what is the cost of one more automobile? Of one more forklift? Which characteristic of the production possibilities curve reflects the law of increasing opportunity costs: its shape or its length?

   c. If the economy characterized by this production possibilities table and curve is producing 3 automobiles and 20 forklifts, what could you conclude about its use of its available resources?
   d. Is production at a point outside the production possibilities curve currently possible? Could a future advance in technology allow production beyond the current production possibilities curve? Could international trade allow a country to consume beyond its current production possibilities curve?

Type of Production	Production Alternatives				
	A	B	C	D	E
Automobiles	0	2	4	6	8
Forklifts	30	27	21	12	0

6. Refer to Figure 1.3. Suppose that the cost of cheese falls, so that the marginal cost of producing pizza decreases. Will the MC curve shift up or down? Will the optimal amount of pizza increase or decrease? Explain. **LO1.6**

7. Referring to the table in problem 5, suppose improvement occurs in the technology of producing forklifts but not in the technology of producing automobiles. Draw the new production possibilities curve. Now assume that a technological advance occurs in producing automobiles but not in producing forklifts. Draw the new production possibilities curve. Now draw a production possibilities curve that reflects technological improvement in the production of both goods. **LO1.7**

8. Because investment and capital goods are paid for with savings, higher savings rates reflect a decision to consume fewer goods in the present so as to invest in more goods for the future. Households in China save about 35 percent of their annual incomes each year, whereas U.S. households save only around 7 percent. At the same time, production possibilities are growing at roughly 6 percent per year in China but only about 2 percent per year in the United States. Use graphical analysis of "present goods" versus "future goods" to explain the difference between China's growth rate and the U.S. growth rate. **LO1.7**

Graphs and Their Meanings

LO1.8 Understand graphs, curves, and slopes as they relate to economics.

Economists often use graphs to illustrate economic models. By understanding these "pictures," you will more readily comprehend economic relationships.

Constructing a Graph

A *graph* is a visual representation of the relationship between two economic quantities, or variables. The table in Figure 1 is a hypothetical illustration showing the relationship between income and consumption for the economy as a whole. We logically expect that people will buy more goods and services when their incomes go up. Thus, it is not surprising to find in the table that total consumption in the economy increases as total income increases.

The information in the table is expressed graphically in Figure 1. Here is how it is done: We want to show visually how consumption changes as income changes. We therefore represent income on the **horizontal axis** of the graph and consumption on the **vertical axis.**

FIGURE 1 **Graphing the direct relationship between consumption and income.**

Two sets of data that are positively or directly related, such as consumption and income, graph as an upward sloping line.

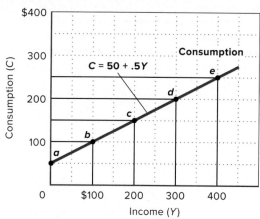

Income per Week	Consumption per Week	Point
$ 0	$ 50	a
100	100	b
200	150	c
300	200	d
400	250	e

horizontal axis The "left-right" or "west-east" measurement line on a graph or grid.

vertical axis The "up-down" or "north-south" measurement line on a graph or grid.

Now we arrange the vertical and horizontal scales of the graph to reflect the ranges of values for consumption and income and mark the scales in convenient increments. As you can see, the values marked on the graph cover all the values in the table. The increments on both scales are $100.

Because the graph has two dimensions, each point within it represents an income value and its associated consumption value. To find a point that represents one of the five income-consumption combinations in the table in Figure 1, we draw straight lines from the appropriate values on the vertical and horizontal axes. For example, to plot point *c* (the $200 income–$150 consumption point), we draw straight lines up from the horizontal (income) axis at $200 and across from the vertical (consumption) axis at $150. These lines intersect at point *c*, which represents this particular income-consumption combination. You should verify that the other income-consumption combinations shown in the table are properly located in the graph in Figure 1. Finally, by assuming that the same general relationship between income and consumption prevails for all other incomes, we draw a line or smooth curve to connect these points. That line or curve represents the income-consumption relationship.

If the curve is a straight line, as in Figure 1, we say the relationship is *linear.* (It is permissible, and even customary, to refer to straight lines in graphs as "curves.")

Direct and Inverse Relationships

The line in Figure 1 slopes upward to the right, so it depicts a direct (or positive) relationship between income and consumption. When two variables (in this case, consumption and income) have a **direct relationship** (or positive relationship), they change in the *same* direction. An increase in consumption is associated with an increase in income; a decrease in consumption accompanies a decrease in income. When two sets of data are directly (or positively) related, they always graph as an *upward sloping* line, as in Figure 1.

In contrast, two sets of data may be inversely (or negatively) related. Consider the table in Figure 2, which shows the relationship between the price of basketball tickets and game attendance at Gigantic State University (GSU). Here we have an **inverse relationship** (or negative relationship) because the two variables change in *opposite* directions. When ticket prices decrease, attendance increases. When ticket prices increase, attendance decreases. The six data points in the table in Figure 2 are plotted in the graph. An inverse (or negative) relationship always graphs as a *downward sloping* line.

direct relationship The relationship between two variables that change in the same direction, for example, product *price* and quantity supplied; a positive relationship.

inverse relationship The relationship between two variables that change in opposite directions, for example, product *price* and quantity demanded; a negative relationship.

FIGURE 2 Graphing the inverse relationship between ticket prices and game attendance.
Two sets of data that are negatively or inversely related, such as ticket price and the attendance at basketball games, graph as a downward sloping line.

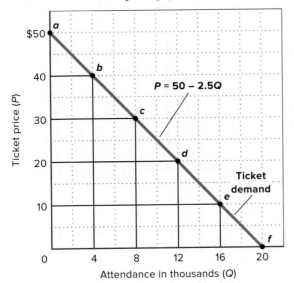

Ticket Price	Attendance, Thousands	Point
$50	0	a
40	4	b
30	8	c
20	12	d
10	16	e
0	20	f

Dependent and Independent Variables

Economists often seek to determine which variable is the "cause" and which is the "effect." The **independent variable** is the cause or source; it is the variable that changes first. The **dependent variable** is the effect or outcome; it is the variable that changes as a result of the change in the independent variable. In our income-consumption example, income is the independent variable while consumption is the dependent variable. Income causes consumption to be what it is rather than the other way around. Similarly, ticket prices (set in advance of the season and printed on the ticket) determine attendance at GSU basketball games; attendance at games does not determine the printed ticket prices for those games. Ticket price is the independent variable and the quantity of tickets purchased is the dependent variable.

independent variable The variable causing a change in some other (dependent) variable.

dependent variable A variable that changes as a consequence of a change in some other (independent) variable; the "effect" or outcome.

Axis Placement of Dependent and Independent Variables

Your may recall from your high school math courses that mathematicians are in the habit of putting the independent variable (cause) on the horizontal axis and the dependent variable (effect) on the vertical axis. Economists are less tidy; their graphing of independent and dependent variables is more arbitrary. For example, economists' graphing of the income-consumption relationship is consistent with mathematical convention, but, contrariwise, economists put price and cost data (which are both cause variables) on the vertical axis, as we did in Figure 2.

This does not present any sort of fundamental difficulty, but we want you to be aware of this fact to avoid any possible confusion. Independent variables are the "cause" variables and dependent variables are the "effect" variables. But their axis placement varies in economics.

Other Things Equal

Our simple two-variable graphs purposely ignore many other factors that might affect the amount of consumption occurring at each income level or the number of people who attend GSU basketball games at each possible ticket price. When economists plot the relationship between any two variables, they employ the *ceteris paribus* (other-things-equal) assumption. Thus, in Figure 1 all factors other than income that might affect the amount of consumption are presumed to be constant or unchanged. Similarly, in Figure 2 all factors other than ticket price that might influence attendance at GSU basketball games are assumed constant. In reality, "other things" are not equal; they often change, and when they do, the relationship represented in our two tables and graphs will change. Specifically, the lines we have plotted would *shift* to new locations.

Consider a stock market "crash." The dramatic drop in the value of stocks might make people less willing to consume at each level of income. The result might be a downward shift of the consumption line. To see this, you should plot a new consumption line in Figure 1, assuming that consumption is, say, $20 less at each income level. Note that the relationship remains direct; the line merely shifts downward to reflect less consumption spending at each income level.

Similarly, factors other than ticket prices might affect GSU game attendance. If GSU loses most of its games, attendance at GSU games might be less at each ticket price. To see this, redraw Figure 2 assuming that 2,000 fewer fans attend GSU games at each ticket price.

Slope of a Line

Lines can be described in terms of their slopes. The **slope of a straight line** is the ratio of the vertical change (the rise or

slope of a straight line The ratio of the vertical change (the rise or fall) to the horizontal change (the run) between any two points on a straight line. The slope of an upward-sloping line is positive, reflecting a direct relationship between two variables; the slope of a downward-sloping line is negative, reflecting an inverse relationship between two variables.

drop) to the horizontal change (the run) between any two points on the line.

Positive Slope

Between point b and point c in Figure 1, the rise or vertical change (the change in consumption) is +$50 and the run or horizontal change (the change in income) is +$100. Therefore:

$$\text{slope} = \frac{\text{vertical change}}{\text{horizontal change}} = \frac{+50}{+100} = \frac{1}{2} = .5$$

Note that our slope of .5 is positive because consumption and income change in the same direction; that is, consumption and income are directly or positively related.

The slope of .5 tells us there will be a $0.50 increase in consumption for every $1 increase in income. Similarly, there will be a $0.50 decrease in consumption for every $1 decrease in income.

Negative Slope

Between any two of the identified points in Figure 2, say, point c and point d, the vertical change is −10 (the drop) and the horizontal change is +4 (the run).

Therefore:

$$\text{slope} = \frac{\text{vertical change}}{\text{horizontal change}} = \frac{-10}{+4} = -2\frac{1}{2} = -2.5$$

This slope is negative because ticket price and attendance have an inverse relationship.

Note that the values on the horizontal axis are stated in thousands of people. So the slope of −10 / +4 or −2.5 means that lowering the price by $10 will increase attendance by 4,000 people. That ratio also implies that a $2.50 price reduction will increase attendance by 1,000 persons.

Slopes and Measurement Units

The slope of a line will be affected by the choice of units for either variable. In our ticket-price illustration, if we had chosen to measure attendance in individual people rather than in thousands of people, our horizontal change would have been 4,000 and the slope would have been

$$\text{slope} = \frac{-10}{+4,000} = \frac{-1}{+400} = -.0025$$

Slopes and Marginal Analysis

The concept of slope is important in economics because it reflects marginal changes—those involving 1 more (or 1 fewer) unit. For example, in Figure 1 the .5 slope shows that $0.50 of extra or marginal consumption is associated with each $1 change in income. In that example, people collectively will consume $0.50 of any $1 increase in their incomes and reduce their consumption by $0.50 for each $1 decline in income.

Infinite and Zero Slopes

Many variables are unrelated (or "independent") of one another. For example, the quantity of wristwatches purchased is not related to the price of bananas. Figure 3a represents the

FIGURE 3 Infinite and zero slopes.

(a) A line parallel to the vertical axis has an infinite slope. Here, purchases of watches remain the same no matter what happens to the price of bananas. (b) A line parallel to the horizontal axis has a slope of zero. In this case, consumption remains the same no matter what happens to the divorce rate. In both (a) and (b), the two variables are totally unrelated to each other.

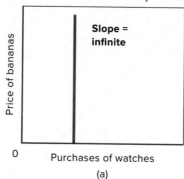

(a)

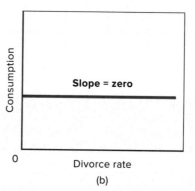

(b)

price of bananas on the vertical axis and the quantity of watches demanded on the horizontal axis. The graph of their relationship is the line parallel to the vertical axis. The line's vertical slope indicates that the same quantity of watches is purchased no matter what the price of bananas. The slope of vertical lines is *infinite*.

Similarly, aggregate consumption is completely unrelated to the nation's divorce rate. Figure 3b places consumption on the vertical axis and the divorce rate on the horizontal axis. The line parallel to the horizontal axis represents this lack of relatedness because the amount of consumption remains the same no matter what happens to the divorce rate. The slope of horizontal lines is *zero*.

Absolute Value of Slopes

The demand curves and production possibilities curves that you will encounter in subsequent chapters will typically have negative slopes because they plot inverse relationships. But it is sometimes useful to drop the negative sign and speak only of the **absolute value** of the slope. Thus a slope of −8/2 would equal 8/2 = 4 once you took its absolute value and dispensed with the negative sign.

---

absolute value The magnitude of a number without regard to its sign. For any number x, the absolute value of x is denoted $|x|$, and $|x| = +x$ no matter whether x itself is a positive or negative number. Thus, $|-3| = +3$ and $|+3| = +3$.

Vertical Intercept

Any line can be positioned on a graph (without plotting points) if we know just two things: its slope and its vertical intercept. We have already discussed slope. The **vertical intercept** of a line is the point where the line meets the vertical axis. In Figure 1 the vertical intercept is $50. This intercept means that if current income were zero, consumers would still spend $50. They might do this by borrowing or by selling some of their assets. Similarly, the $50 vertical intercept in Figure 2 shows that at a $50 ticket price, GSU's basketball team would be playing in an empty arena.

Equation of a Linear Relationship

If we know the vertical intercept and slope, we can describe a line in equation form. When the independent variable is on the horizontal axis, the equation of a straight line is

$$y = a + bx$$

where y = dependent variable
a = vertical intercept
b = slope of line
x = independent variable

For our income-consumption example, if C represents consumption (the dependent variable) and Y represents income (the independent variable), we can write $C = a + bY$. By substituting the known values of the intercept and the slope, we get

$$C = 50 + .5Y$$

This equation also allows us to determine the amount of consumption C at any specific level of income. You should use it to confirm that at the $250 income level, consumption is $175.

When economists put the independent variable on the vertical axis and the dependent variable on the horizontal axis, then y stands for the independent variable. Look again at our GSU ticket price–attendance data. If P represents the ticket price (independent variable) and Q represents attendance (dependent variable), their relationship is given by

$$P = 50 - 2.5Q$$

where the vertical intercept is 50 and the negative slope is $-2\frac{1}{2}$, or -2.5. Knowing the value of P lets us solve for Q, our

vertical intercept The point at which a line meets the vertical axis of a graph.

dependent variable. You should use this equation to predict GSU ticket sales when the ticket price is $15.

Slope of a Nonlinear Curve

We now move from the simple world of linear relationships (straight lines) to the more complex world of nonlinear relationships (curved lines). The slope of a straight line is the same at all its points. The slope of a line representing a nonlinear relationship changes from one point to another. Such lines are always called *curves*.

Consider the downward sloping curve in Figure 4. Its slope is negative throughout, but the curve flattens as we move down along it. Thus, its slope constantly changes; the curve has a different slope at each point.

To measure the slope at a specific point, we draw a straight line tangent to the curve at that point. A straight line is *tangent* at a point if it touches, but does not intersect, the curve at that point. Thus, line *aa* is tangent to the curve in Figure 4 at point *A*. The slope of the curve at that point is equal to the slope of the tangent line. Specifically, the total vertical change (drop) in the tangent line *aa* is -20 and the total horizontal change (run) is $+5$. Because the slope of the tangent line *aa* is $-20/+5$, or -4, the slope of the curve at point *A* is also -4.

Line *bb* in Figure 4 is tangent to the curve at point *B*. Following the same procedure, we find the slope at *B* to be $-5/+15$, or $-\frac{1}{3}$. Thus, in this flatter part of the curve, the slope is less negative.

FIGURE 4 **Determining the slopes of curves.**
The slope of a nonlinear curve changes from point to point on the curve. The slope at any point (say, *B*) can be determined by drawing a straight line that is tangent to that point (line *bb*) and calculating the slope of that line.

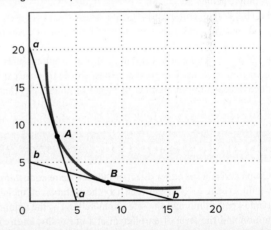

Appendix Summary

LO1.8 Understand graphs, curves, and slopes as they relate to economics.
Graphs are a convenient and revealing way to represent economic relationships.

Two variables are positively (or directly) related when their values change in the same direction. The line or curve representing two directly related variables slopes upward.

Two variables are negatively (or inversely) related when their values change in opposite directions. The line or curve representing two inversely related variables slopes downward.

The value of the dependent variable (the "effect") is determined by the value of the independent variable (the "cause").

When the "other factors" that might affect a two-variable relationship are allowed to change, the graph of the relationship will likely shift to a new location.

The slope of a straight line is the ratio of the vertical change to the horizontal change between any two points. The slope of an upward sloping line is positive; the slope of a downward sloping line is negative.

The slope of a line or curve depends on the units used in measuring the variables. The slope is especially relevant for economics because it measures marginal changes.

The slope of a horizontal line is zero; the slope of a vertical line is infinite.

Together, the vertical intercept and slope of a line determine its location; they are used in expressing the line—and the relationship between the two variables—as an equation.

The slope of a curve at any point is determined by calculating the slope of a straight line tangent to the curve at that point.

Appendix Terms and Concepts

horizontal axis	inverse (negative) relationship	slope of a straight line
vertical axis	independent variable	absolute value
direct (positive) relationship	dependent variable	vertical intercept

Appendix Discussion Questions

1. What is an inverse relationship? How does it graph? What is a direct relationship? How does it graph? **LO1.8**
2. Describe the graphical relationship between ticket prices and the number of people choosing to visit amusement parks. Is that relationship consistent with the fact that, historically, park attendance and ticket prices have both risen? Explain. **LO1.8**
3. Look back at Figure 2, which shows the inverse relationship between ticket prices and game attendance at Gigantic State University. (a) Interpret the meaning of both the slope and the intercept. (b) If the slope of the line were steeper, what would that say about the amount by which ticket sales respond to increases in ticket prices? (c) If the slope of the line stayed the same but the intercept increased, what could you say about the amount by which ticket sales respond to increases in ticket prices? **LO1.8**

Appendix Review Questions

1. Indicate whether each of the following relationships is usually a direct relationship or an inverse relationship. **LO1.8**
   a. A sports team's winning percentage and attendance at its home games
   b. Higher temperatures and sweater sales
   c. A person's income and how often he or she shops at discount stores
   d. Higher gasoline prices and miles driven in automobiles
2. Erin grows pecans. The number of bushels (B) that she can produce depends on the number of inches of rainfall (R) that her orchards get. The relationship is given by the following equation: $B = 3,000 + 800R$. Match each part of this equation with the correct term. **LO1.8**

B	slope
3,000	dependent variable
800	vertical intercept
R	independent variable

Appendix Problems

1. Graph and label as either direct or indirect the relationships you would expect to find between (a) the number of inches of rainfall per month and the sale of umbrellas, (b) the amount of tuition and the level of enrollment at a university, and (c) the popularity of an entertainer and the price of her concert tickets. **LO1.8**
2. Indicate how each of the following might affect the data shown in the table and graph in Figure 2 of this appendix: **LO1.8**
   a. GSU's athletic director schedules higher-quality opponents.
   b. An NBA team locates in the city where GSU plays.
   c. GSU contracts to have all its home games televised.
3. The table at the top of the next page contains data on the relationship between saving and income. Rearrange these data into a meaningful order and graph them on the grid displayed for this problem. What is the slope of the line? The vertical intercept? Write the equation that represents this line. What would you predict saving to be at the $12,500 level of income? **LO1.8**

Graph for Problem 3

(Graph: vertical axis "Saving" ranging from −500 to $1,500; horizontal axis "Income (thousands)" marked at $5, 10, 15, 20)

Income per Year	Saving per Year
$15,000	$1,000
0	−500
10,000	500
5,000	0
20,000	1,500

4. Construct a table from the data shown in the accompanying graph. Which is the dependent variable and which is the independent variable? Summarize the data in equation form. **LO1.8**

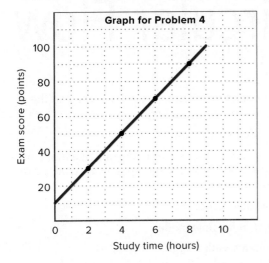

Graph for Problem 4

(y-axis: Exam score (points), x-axis: Study time (hours))

5. Suppose that when the interest rate on loans is 16 percent, businesses find it unprofitable to invest in machinery and equipment. However, when the interest rate is 14 percent, $5 billion worth of investment is profitable. At 12 percent interest, a total of $10 billion of investment is profitable. Similarly, total investment increases by $5 billion for each successive 2-percentage-point decline in the interest rate. Describe the relevant relationship between the interest rate and investment in a table, on a graph, and as an equation. Put the interest rate on the vertical axis and investment on the horizontal axis. In your equation use the form $i = a + bI$, where i is the interest rate, a is the vertical intercept, b is the slope of the line (which is negative), and I is the level of investment. **LO1.8**

6. Suppose that $C = a + bY$, where C = consumption, a = consumption at zero income, b = slope, and Y = income. **LO1.8**
   a. Are C and Y positively related, or are they negatively related?
   b. If graphed, would the curve for this equation slope upward or slope downward?

c. Are the variables C and Y inversely related or directly related?
d. What is the value of C if $a = 10$, $b = 0.50$, and $Y = 200$?
e. What is the value of Y if $C = 100$, $a = 10$, and $b = 0.25$?

7. The accompanying graph shows curve XX' and tangents at points A, B, and C. Calculate the slope of the curve at these three points. **LO1.8**

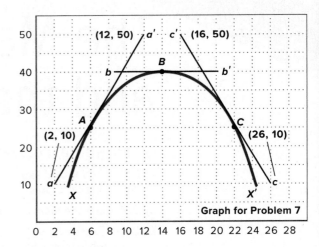

Graph for Problem 7

8. In the accompanying graph, is the slope of curve AA' positive or negative? Does the slope increase or decrease as we move along the curve from A to A'? Answer the same two questions for curve BB'. **LO1.8**

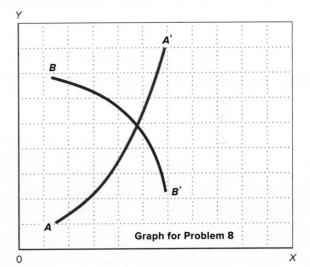

Graph for Problem 8

CHAPTER

2

The Market System and the Circular Flow

>> LEARNING OBJECTIVES

LO2.1   Define and explain laissez-faire capitalism, the command system, and the market system.

LO2.2   List the main characteristics of the market system.

LO2.3   Explain how the market system answers the five fundamental questions of what to produce, how to produce, who obtains the output, how to adjust to change, and how to promote technological progress.

LO2.4   Explain the operation of the "invisible hand."

LO2.5   Describe the mechanics of the circular flow model.

LO2.6   Explain how the market system deals with risk.

Frustrated with shopping online, you decide to go to the local mall, where you can touch and feel products before deciding what to buy. There are fewer products at the mall than online, but suppose you tried to compile a list of all the individual goods and services available at the mall. That task would be daunting, but your list could prompt some fundamental questions about the economy, such as:

- Who decides which goods and services should be produced?
- How do the producers determine which technologies and resources to use in producing these goods?
- Who will obtain these products?
- What accounts for new and improved products?

This chapter answers all of these questions.

>> **LO2.1** Define and explain laissez-faire capitalism, the command system, and the market system.

economic system A particular set of institutional arrangements and a coordinating mechanism for solving the *economizing problem;* a method of organizing an economy, of which the *market system* and the *command system* are the two general types.

Economic Systems

Every society needs to develop an **economic system**—a particular set of institutional arrangements and a coordinating mechanism—to respond to the economizing problem. The economic system determines what goods are produced, how they are produced, who gets them, how to accommodate change, and how to promote technological progress.

Economic systems differ as to (1) who owns the factors of production and (2) the methods used to motivate, coordinate, and direct economic activity.

Economics systems can be classified by their degree of centralized or decentralized decision making. At one extreme lies *laissez-faire capitalism*, in which government intervention is minimal and markets and prices direct nearly all economic activity. At the other extreme lie *command systems*, in which governments have total control over all economic activity. The vast majority of national economies lie somewhere in the middle. These economies have *market systems* or *mixed economies*.

Laissez-Faire Capitalism

In **laissez-faire capitalism**—or "pure capitalism"—the government's role is limited to protecting private property and establishing a legal environment in which contracts are enforced and people interact in markets to buy and sell goods, services, and resources.

The term "laissez-faire" is French for "let it be," meaning that the government should leave entrepreneurs and businesspeople unmolested so that they can make their own decisions about what to produce and how to produce it. Proponents of laissez-faire believe that any interference in the economy on the part of government reduces human welfare. They maintain that governments are corrupted by special interests that use the government's economic influence to benefit themselves rather than society at large.

To prevent that from happening, the proponents of laissez-faire argue that government's only role should be preventing individuals and firms from coercing each other, thus ensuring that only mutually beneficial economic transactions are negotiated and completed. The result should be the highest possible level of human satisfaction because, after all, who knows better what people want than the people themselves?

In reality, no society has ever employed a pure laissez-faire system. In fact, no government has *ever* limited its economic actions to the short list of functions permitted under laissez-faire. Instead, every government in history has undertaken a wider range of economic activities, including industrial safety regulations, taxes and subsidies, occupational licensing requirements, and income redistribution.

laissez-faire capitalism
A hypothetical *economic system* in which the government's economic role is limited to protecting private property and establishing a legal environment appropriate to the operation of *markets* in which only mutually agreeable transactions take place between buyers and sellers; sometimes referred to as "pure capitalism."

The Command System

The polar opposite of laissez-faire capitalism is the **command system,** in which government owns most property resources, and economic decision making is set by a central economic plan created and enforced by the government. The command system has been utilized by several countries with socialist or communist governments, including the Soviet Union, Cuba, and China.

Under the command system, the government owns most of the business firms, which produce according to government directives. A central planning board determines production goals for each enterprise and specifies the amount of resources allocated to each enterprise so that it can reach its production goals. The division of output between capital and consumer goods is centrally decided, and capital goods are allocated among industries based on the central planning board's long-term priorities.

A pure command economy would rely exclusively on a central plan. But, in reality, even the preeminent command economy—the Soviet Union—tolerated some private ownership before its collapse in 1992. Subsequent reforms in Russia and most of the eastern European nations have, to one degree or another, transformed their command economies to capitalistic, market-oriented systems. China's reforms have not gone as far, but they have greatly reduced China's reliance on central planning. Although government ownership of resources and capital in China is still extensive, the nation has increasingly relied on markets to organize and coordinate its economy. North Korea and Cuba are the last prominent remaining examples of largely centrally planned economies. Other countries using mainly the command system include Turkmenistan, Laos, Belarus, Myanmar, Venezuela, and Iran.

command system A method of organizing an economy in which property resources are publicly owned and government uses *central economic planning* to direct and coordinate economic activities; *socialism; communism.* Compare with *market system.*

The Market System

The vast majority of the world's economies utilize the **market system,** also known as *capitalism,* the *mixed economy,* or the market economy.

The market system is characterized by a mixture of centralized government economic initiatives and decentralized actions taken by individuals and firms. The precise mixture varies by country, but in each case the system features the private ownership of resources and the use of markets and prices to coordinate and direct economic activity.

In the market system, individuals and businesses seek to achieve their economic goals through their own decisions regarding work, consumption, or production. The system allows for the private ownership of capital, communicates through prices, and coordinates economic activity through **markets**—places where buyers and sellers come together to buy and sell goods, services, and resources.

market system (1) An *economic system* in which individuals own most *economic resources* and in which *markets* and *prices* serve as the dominant coordinating mechanism used to allocate those resources; *capitalism.* Compare with *command system.* (2) All the product and resource markets of a *market economy* and the relationships among them.

market Any institution or mechanism that brings together buyers (demanders) and sellers (suppliers) of a particular *good* or *service.*

Participants pursue their own self-interest, and goods and services are produced and resources are supplied by whoever is willing and able to do so. The result is competition among independently acting buyers and sellers and an economic system in which decision making is widely dispersed.

The market system offers high potential monetary rewards that create powerful incentives for existing firms to innovate and for entrepreneurs to pioneer new products and processes.

It is true, however, that in the capitalism practiced in the United States and most other countries, the government plays a substantial role in the economy. It not only sets the rules for economic activity but also promotes economic stability and growth, provides certain goods and services that would otherwise be underproduced or not produced at all, and modifies the distribution of income. The government, however, is not the dominant economic force in deciding what to produce, how to produce it, and who will get it. That force is the market and the individuals participating in it.

Characteristics of the Market System

>> **LO2.2** List the main characteristics of the market system.

Let's examine the key features of the market system.

Private Property

In addition to providing individuals with the freedom to engage in the economic activities of their choice, the market system is characterized by the private ownership of most property resources, including capital. That extensive private ownership of capital is what gives capitalism its name.

private property The right of private persons and *firms* to obtain, own, control, employ, dispose of, and bequeath *land, capital,* and other property.

More broadly speaking, the legal right to **private property,** coupled with the freedom to negotiate binding legal contracts, enables individuals and businesses to obtain, use, and dispose of property resources as they see fit.

Property rights encourage people to cooperate by helping to ensure that only *mutually agreeable* economic transactions take place. To understand why this is true, imagine a world without legally enforceable property rights. In that world, the strong could simply take whatever they wanted from the weak without compensating them. But in a world with legally enforceable property rights, any person who wants something must pay for it. If a person really wants something you have, they must offer you something that you value in return. That is, the person must offer you a mutually agreeable economic transaction—one that benefits both of you. Thus property rights facilitate exchange.

Property rights also:

- Encourage investment, innovation, and economic growth. Nobody would stock a store, build a factory, or clear land for farming if someone else, or the government itself, could take away that property at any moment.

- Encourage owners to maintain or improve their property so as to preserve or increase its value.

- Enable people to spend their time and resources increasing the production of goods and services, rather than having to devote money and time to protecting and retaining the property they already possess.

freedom of enterprise The freedom of *firms* to obtain economic resources, to use those resources to produce products of the firms' own choosing, and to sell their products in markets of their choice.

- Protect intellectual property through patents, copyrights, and trademarks. Such long-term protection encourages people to write books, compose music, create social media platforms, and invent new products and production processes.

Freedom of Enterprise and Choice

Closely related to private property is freedom of enterprise and freedom of choice.

- **Freedom of enterprise** ensures that entrepreneurs and private businesses are free to obtain and use economic resources to produce their choice of goods and services and to sell them in their chosen markets.

freedom of choice The freedom of owners of property resources to employ or dispose of them as they see fit, of workers to enter any line of work for which they are qualified, and of consumers to spend their incomes in the manner that they prefer.

- **Freedom of choice** allows owners to employ or dispose of their property and money as they see fit. It also allows workers to try to enter any line of work for which they are qualified. Finally, it ensures that consumers are free to buy the goods and services that best satisfy their wants and that their budgets allow.

These choices are free only within legal limitations, however. Illegal choices such as human trafficking and drug trafficking are punished through fines or imprisonment. (As Global Perspective 2.1 shows, the degree of economic freedom varies greatly from country to country.)

GLOBAL PERSPECTIVE 2.1

INDEX OF ECONOMIC FREEDOM, SELECTED ECONOMIES, 2021

The Index of Economic Freedom measures economic freedom using 10 major groupings such as trade policy, property rights, and government intervention, with each category containing more than 50 specific criteria. The index then ranks 178 economies according to their degree of economic freedom. Those freedom rankings are used to place each country into one of five categories: Free, Mostly Free, Moderately Free, Mostly Unfree, and Repressed. We present three countries from each category as well as their respective overall ranks (from 1, most free, to 178, least free).

Source: The Heritage Foundation, www.heritage.org.

FREE
- 1 Singapore
- 2 New Zealand
- 3 Australia

MOSTLY FREE
- 14 United Arab Emirates
- 20 United States
- 29 Germany

MODERATELY FREE
- 39 Spain
- 68 Italy
- 92 Russia

MOSTLY UNFREE
- 105 Nigeria
- 121 India
- 143 Brazil

REPRESSED
- 168 Iran
- 177 Venezuela
- 178 North Korea

Self-Interest

In the market system, **self-interest** is the motivating force. Self-interest simply means that each economic unit tries to achieve its own particular goal. Entrepreneurs try to maximize profit or minimize loss. Property owners try to get the highest price for the sale or rent of their resources. Workers try to maximize their utility (satisfaction) by finding jobs that offer the best combination of wages, hours, benefits, and working conditions. Consumers try to obtain products at the lowest possible price. Self-interest provides direction and consistency to what might otherwise be a chaotic economy.

> **self-interest** That which each *firm*, property owner, worker, and consumer believes is best for itself and seeks to obtain.

Competition

The market system depends on **competition** among economic units. Very broadly defined, competition requires

- Two or more buyers and two or more sellers acting independently in a particular product or resource market. (Usually there are many more than two buyers and two sellers.)
- Freedom of sellers and buyers to enter or leave (exit) markets, on the basis of their economic self-interest.

> **competition** The effort and striving between two or more independent rivals to secure the business of one or more third parties by offering the best possible terms.

Competition among buyers and sellers diffuses economic power throughout the economy. When many buyers and many sellers act independently of each other in a market, no single buyer or seller can dictate the price of the product or resource because other buyers and sellers can undercut that price.

In a competitive system, producers can enter or leave an industry; no insurmountable barriers prevent an industry from expanding or contracting. This freedom to expand or contract provides the economy with the flexibility needed to remain efficient over time. Freedom of entry and exit enables the economy to adjust to changes in consumer tastes, technology, and resource availability.

The diffusion of economic power inherent in competition limits the potential abuse of that power. A producer that charges more than the competitive market price will lose sales to other producers. An employer who pays less than the competitive market wage rate will lose workers to other employers. Competition is the key regulatory force in the market system.

Markets and Prices

You may wonder why an economy based on self-interest does not collapse into chaos. If consumers want breakfast cereal, but businesses choose to produce running shoes, the economy could become deadlocked by the inconsistencies between what consumers and producers desire.

In reality, the billions of decisions made by households and businesses each day are highly coordinated by markets, prices, and profits. The preferences of buyers and the production costs of sellers are brought together in markets, where prices rise and fall in response to changing demands by consumers and the changing resource and opportunity costs facing producers.

Those changes guide resource owners, entrepreneurs, and consumers as they make and revise their choices and pursue their self-interest. Businesses, in particular, react strongly to how changes in prices affect their profitability and thus whether they should continue doing what they have been doing or make changes and adjustments.

Just as competition is the regulatory mechanism of the market system, the system of markets and prices is the coordinating mechanism. It is an elaborate communication network through which innumerable individual choices are recorded, summarized, and balanced. Those who respond to market signals are rewarded with greater profit or increased *utility* (satisfaction). Those who ignore or do not respond to those signals are penalized with losses or decreased utility.

QUICK REVIEW
2.1

▶ The market system rests on the private ownership of property and on freedom of enterprise and freedom of choice.

▶ Property rights encourage people to cooperate and make mutually agreeable economic transactions.

▶ The market system permits consumers, resource suppliers, and businesses to pursue their self-interest.

▶ Competition diffuses economic power and limits the actions of any single seller or buyer.

▶ The coordinating mechanism of capitalism is a system of markets and prices.

Technology and Capital Goods

In the market system, the monetary rewards for creating new products or production techniques accrue directly to the innovator. The market system therefore encourages extensive use and rapid development of complex capital goods, including wireless networks, the Global Positioning System (GPS), highly automated warehouse distribution centers, and the software necessary to run nuclear power plants and self-driving cars.

Advanced technology and capital goods are important because the most direct methods of production are often the least efficient. The only way to avoid that inefficiency is to rely on capital goods. It would be ridiculous for a farmer to go at production with bare hands. Huge benefits can be derived from creating and using even simple capital equipment such as horse-drawn plows, let alone modern farm equipment like self-driving tractors and AI-guided pollination drones. More efficient production means much more output.

Specialization

specialization The use of the *resources* of an individual, a *firm*, a region, or a nation to concentrate production on one or a small number of *goods* and *services*.

division of labor The separation of the work required to produce a product into a number of different tasks that are performed by different workers; *specialization* of workers.

Market economies rely on specialization. **Specialization** means using the resources of an individual, firm, region, or nation to produce one or a few goods or services rather than the entire range of desired goods and services. The economic unit then exchanges those goods and services for a wide range of desired products. The majority of consumers produce virtually none of the goods and services they consume, and they consume little or nothing of the items they produce. The person working nine to five installing windows in commercial aircraft may rarely fly. Some dairy farmers sell their milk to the local or regional dairy cooperative and then buy energy drinks at the local grocery store.

Division of Labor   Human specialization—called the **division of labor**—contributes to society's output in several ways:

- *Human specialization makes use of differences in ability.* Human specialization enables individuals to take advantage of the differences in their abilities and skills. If LeBron is good at shooting a basketball and Beyoncé can sing and dance, their talents are most efficiently used if LeBron plays professional basketball while Beyoncé records songs and gives concerts.

- *Human specialization fosters learning by doing.* Even if two people have identical abilities, specialization may still be advantageous. By devoting time to a single task, people are more likely to develop the skills required and to improve their techniques. You learn to be a good lawyer by studying, practicing, and specializing in law.

- *Human specialization saves time.* By devoting time to a single task, a person avoids the loss of time incurred in shifting from one job to another. Also, time is saved by not "fumbling around" with tasks that one is not trained to do.

For all these reasons, human specialization increases the total output society derives from limited resources.

Geographic Specialization Specialization also works on a regional and international basis. Oranges could be grown in Nebraska, but because of the unsuitability of the land, rainfall, and temperature, the cost would be very high. And wheat could be grown in Florida, but it would be costly for similar geographical reasons. So Nebraskans produce the wheat for which their resources are best suited, and Floridians produce oranges. By specializing, both economies produce more than is needed locally. Then, very sensibly, Nebraskans and Floridians swap some of their surpluses—wheat for oranges, oranges for wheat.

Similarly, on an international scale, the United States specializes in producing such items as commercial aircraft and software, which it sells abroad in exchange for machinery from Mexico, mobile phones from China, and footwear from Vietnam. Both human specialization and geographic specialization increase efficiency in the use of our limited resources.

Use of Money

Any economic system makes extensive use of money. Money performs several functions, but first and foremost it is a **medium of exchange.** It makes trade easier.

Specialization requires exchange. Exchange can, and sometimes does, occur through **barter**—swapping goods for goods, say, wheat for oranges. But barter poses serious problems because it requires a *coincidence of wants* between the buyer and the seller. In our example, we assumed that Nebraskans had excess wheat to trade and wanted oranges. And we assumed that Floridians had excess oranges to trade and wanted wheat. So an exchange occurred. But if this coincidence of wants is missing, trade is stymied.

Suppose that Nebraska has no interest in Florida's oranges but wants potatoes from Idaho. And suppose that Idaho wants Florida's oranges but not Nebraska's wheat. And, to complicate matters, suppose that Florida wants some of Nebraska's wheat but none of Idaho's potatoes. Figure 2.1 summarizes the situation.

In none of the cases shown in the figure is there a coincidence of wants. Trade by barter clearly would be difficult. Instead, people in each state use **money,** which is simply a convenient social invention to facilitate the exchange of goods and services. To serve as money, an item needs to pass only one test: Sellers must be willing to accept it as payment for their goods and services.

medium of exchange Any item sellers generally accept and buyers generally use to pay for a *good* or *service; money;* a convenient means of exchanging goods and *services* without engaging in *barter.*

barter The direct exchange of one *good* or *service* for another good or service.

money Any item that is generally acceptable to sellers in exchange for *goods* and *services.*

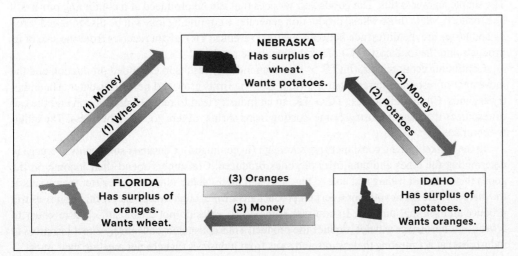

FIGURE 2.1
Money facilitates trade when wants do not coincide.

The use of money as a medium of exchange permits trade to be accomplished despite a noncoincidence of wants. (1) Nebraska trades the wheat that Florida wants for money from Floridians; (2) Nebraska trades the money it receives from Florida for the potatoes it wants from Idaho; (3) Idaho trades the money it receives from Nebraska for the oranges it wants from Florida.

Money is socially defined; whatever society accepts as a medium of exchange *is* money. Today, most economies use pieces of paper as money in addition to checking account balances and, recently, electronic "cryptocurrencies" like Bitcoin.

On a global basis, specialization and exchange are complicated by the fact that different nations have different currencies. But markets in which currencies are bought and sold make it possible for people living in different countries to exchange goods and services without resorting to barter.

Active, but Limited, Government

An active, but limited, government is the final characteristic of modern market systems. Although a market system promotes a high degree of efficiency in the use of its resources, it has certain inherent shortcomings, called "market failures." We will discover in later chapters that governments can often increase the overall effectiveness of a market system. That said, governments have their own set of shortcomings that can cause substantial misallocations of resources. Consequently, we will also investigate several types of "government failure."

QUICK REVIEW 2.2

▶ The market systems of modern industrial economies are characterized by extensive use of technologically advanced capital goods. Such goods help these economies achieve greater efficiency in production.

▶ Specialization is extensive in market systems; it enhances efficiency and output by enabling individuals, regions, and nations to produce the goods and services for which their resources are best suited.

▶ The use of money in market systems facilitates the exchange of goods and services that specialization requires.

Five Fundamental Questions

>> **LO2.3** Explain how the market system answers the five fundamental questions of what to produce, how to produce, who obtains the output, how to adjust to change, and how to promote technological progress.

The key features of the market system help explain how market economies respond to five fundamental questions:

- What goods and services will be produced?
- How will the goods and services be produced?
- Who will get the output?
- How will the system accommodate change?
- How will the system promote technological progress?

These five questions highlight the economic choices underlying the production possibilities curve discussed in Chapter 1. They reflect the constraints that scarce resources impose on a world of unlimited wants.

What Will Be Produced?

consumer sovereignty The determination by consumers of the types and quantities of *goods* and *services* that will be produced with the scarce resources of the economy; consumers' direction of production through their *dollar votes*.

dollar votes The "votes" that consumers cast for the production of preferred products when they purchase those products rather than the alternatives that were also available.

How does a market system decide on the specific types and quantities of goods to be produced? The simple answer is this: The goods and services that can be produced at a continuing profit will be produced, while those whose production generates a continuing loss will be discontinued. Profits and losses are the difference between the total revenue (TR) a firm receives from the sale of its products and the total cost (TC) of producing those products.

Continuing economic profit (TR > TC) in an industry results in expanded production and the movement of resources toward that industry. Existing firms grow and new firms enter. The industry expands. Continuing losses (TC > TR) in an industry lead to reduced production and the exit of resources from that industry. Some existing firms shrink; others go out of business. The industry contracts.

In the market system, consumers are sovereign (in command). **Consumer sovereignty** is crucial in determining the types and quantities of goods produced. Consumers spend their income on the goods they are most willing and able to buy. Through these "**dollar votes**," they register their wants in the market. If the dollar votes for a certain product are great enough to create a profit, businesses will produce and sell that product. In contrast, if the dollar votes do not create sufficient revenues to cover costs, businesses will not produce the product. Thus consumers collectively direct resources to industries that are meeting their wants and away from industries that are not meeting their wants.

CONSIDER THIS . . .

Bitcoin and Cheap Electrons

Bitcoin is an electronic "cryptocurrency" accepted as payment for goods and services by millions of people around the world. It has several novel characteristics, including not being issued by any government and existing and transacting entirely in cyberspace.

The creation of additional Bitcoins (units of Bitcoin currency) is also done entirely electronically, with anyone in the world able to download a free piece of software and start "mining" for Bitcoins by having their computers solve some of the difficult mathematical

Valery Bond/123RF

calculations required to maintain the Bitcoin payments system.

Since computers operate on electricity, mining Bitcoins is at its most profitable when Bitcoin miners utilize the least costly electricity. So it should be no surprise that large-scale Bitcoin mining operations have tended to cluster around low-cost sources of electricity, including hydroelectric dams in the United States and geothermal electricity plants in Iceland.

Market forces encourage low-cost production, even for intangible items like Bitcoin.

How Will the Goods and Services Be Produced?

What combinations of resources and technologies will be used to produce goods and services? How will the production be organized? The answer: in combinations and ways that minimize the cost per unit of output. Inefficiency drives up costs and lowers profits. As a result, any firm wishing to maximize its profits will make great efforts to minimize production costs. These efforts include using the right mix of labor and capital. They also mean locating production facilities optimally to hold down production and transportation expenses (as in the nearby Consider This story about Bitcoin mining).

These efforts will be intensified if the firm faces competition, as consumers strongly prefer low prices and will shift their purchases to the firms that can produce and sell a quality product for the lowest possible price. Any firm foolish enough to use higher-cost production methods will go bankrupt as it is undersold by more efficient competitors who can still make a profit when selling at a lower price. Simply stated: Competition eliminates high-cost producers.

To see how competition favors the lowest-cost combination of resources to produce a given product, suppose there are three possible techniques for producing $15 worth of bars of soap. Table 2.1 shows the quantity of each resource required by each production technique and the prices of those resources. By multiplying the required quantities of each resource by its price in each of the three techniques, we can determine the total cost of producing $15 worth of soap by means of each technique.

Technique 2 is economically the most efficient because it is the least costly. It enables society to obtain $15 worth of output by using a smaller amount of resources—$13 worth—than the $15 worth required by the two other techniques. Competition will dictate that producers use technique 2. Thus, the question of how goods will be produced is answered: They will be produced in the least-costly way.

A change in either technology or resource prices may cause a firm to shift from the technology it is using. Firms will find they can lower their costs by shifting to a technology that uses more of the resource whose price has fallen. For example, if the price of labor falls to $0.50, technique 1 becomes more desirable than technique 2.

TABLE 2.1 Three Techniques for Producing $15 Worth of Bar Soap

Resource	Price per Unit of Resource	Technique 1		Technique 2		Technique 3	
		Units	Cost	Units	Cost	Units	Cost
Labor	$2	4	$ 8	2	$ 4	1	$ 2
Land	1	1	1	3	3	4	4
Capital	3	1	3	1	3	2	6
Entrepreneurial ability	3	1	3	1	3	1	3
Total cost of $15 worth of bar soap			$15		$13		$15

Who Will Get the Output?

In a market economy, a good or service is distributed to consumers on the basis of their ability and willingness to pay the market price. If the price of some product (say, a small sailboat) is $3,000, then buyers who are willing and able to pay that price will "sail, sail away." Consumers who are unwilling or unable to pay the price will be "sitting on the dock of the bay."

The ability to pay the market price for sailboats and other products depends for the most part on the amount of income that consumers have at their disposal. The amount of income they possess depends, in turn, on (1) the quantities of the property resources (land and capital) and human resources (labor and entrepreneurship) that they supply and (2) the prices that those resources command in the resource markets. The more income a consumer can generate from selling resources, the more output they will be able to purchase and consume.

How Will the System Accommodate Change?

Market systems are dynamic: Consumer preferences, technologies, and resource supplies all change. Thus the allocation of resources that is now the most efficient for a specific pattern of consumer tastes, range of technological alternatives, and amount of available resources will become inefficient as consumer preferences change, new production techniques are discovered, and resource supplies change. Can a market economy adjust to such changes?

Suppose consumer tastes change. For instance, assume that consumers decide they want more fruit juice and less milk than the economy currently provides. They communicate these changes in consumer tastes to producers by spending more on fruit juice and less on milk. Other things equal, prices and profits in the fruit-juice industry will rise, and those in the milk industry will fall. Self-interest will induce existing fruit-juice producers to expand output and entice new competitors to enter the prosperous fruit-juice industry. At the same time, firms in the milk industry will scale down, or exit the industry entirely.

The higher prices and greater economic profit in the fruit-juice industry will not only cause that industry to expand but also give it the revenue needed to obtain the resources essential to its growth. Higher prices and profits will permit fruit producers to attract more resources from less-urgent alternative uses. The reverse occurs in the milk industry, where fewer workers and other resources are employed. These adjustments in the economy are appropriate responses to the changes in consumer tastes. This is consumer sovereignty at work.

This directing or guiding function of prices and profits is a core element of the market system. Without such a system, a government planning board or some other administrative agency would have to direct businesses and resources into the appropriate industries.

How Will the System Promote Technological Progress?

Society desires economic growth (greater output) and higher standards of living (greater output per person). How does the market system promote technological improvements and capital accumulation, which both contribute to a higher standard of living?

Technological Advance The market system provides a strong incentive for technological advance. Better products and processes supplant inferior ones. An entrepreneur or firm that introduces a popular new product will gain revenue and economic profit at the expense of rivals. Technological advance also includes new and improved methods that reduce production or distribution costs. By passing part of its cost reduction to the consumer through a lower product price, a firm can increase sales and obtain economic profit at the expense of rival firms.

Moreover, the market system promotes the rapid spread of technological advance throughout an industry. Rival firms must follow the lead of the most innovative firm or else suffer immediate losses and eventual failure. In some cases, the result is **creative destruction:** The creation of new products and production methods completely destroys the market positions of firms that are wedded to existing products and older ways of doing business. Example: Compact discs demolished vinyl records in the 1980s, while online streaming displaced compact discs in the 2000s. In recent years, smartphones have subsumed many functions previously performed by stand-alone products, including wristwatches, compasses, printed maps, flashlights, video cameras, alarm clocks, GPS systems, document scanners, voice recorders, guitar tuners, newspapers, and books.

creative destruction The hypothesis that the creation of new products and production methods destroys the market power of firms committed to existing products and older ways of doing business.

Capital Accumulation Most technological advances require additional capital goods. The market system provides the resources necessary to produce additional capital goods through increased dollar votes for those goods. That is, the market system acknowledges dollar voting for capital goods as well as for consumer goods.

Who counts the dollar votes for capital goods? Answer: Entrepreneurs and business owners. They often use some of their profits to purchase capital goods. They do so because their additional capital may generate even greater profits in the future if the technological innovation that required the additional capital is successful.

▶ The output mix of the market system is determined by profits, which in turn depend heavily on consumer preferences. Economic profits cause industries to expand; losses cause industries to contract.

▶ Competition forces industries to use the least costly production methods.

▶ Competitive markets reallocate resources in response to changes in consumer tastes, technological advances, and changes in availability of resources.

▶ In a market economy, consumer income and product prices determine how output will be distributed.

▶ Competitive markets create incentives for technological advance and capital accumulation, both of which contribute to increases in standards of living.

QUICK REVIEW
2.3

The "Invisible Hand"

In his 1776 book *The Wealth of Nations*, Adam Smith noted that the operation of a market system creates a curious unity between private interests and social interests. Firms and resource suppliers, seeking to further their own self-interests and operating within the framework of a highly competitive market system, will simultaneously, as though guided by an **"invisible hand,"** promote the public interest.

For example, we have seen that in a competitive environment, businesses seek to build new and improved products to increase profits. Those enhanced products increase society's well-being. Businesses also use the least costly combination of resources to produce a specific output because doing so is in their self-interest. But least-cost production is also clearly in the social interest because it "frees up" resources that can be used to produce other products or reduce the strain on the environment.

Firms and resource suppliers have their own interests in mind. But competition forces them to take other people's interests to heart. The invisible hand of competition ensures that when firms maximize their own profits and resource suppliers maximize their own incomes, they also help to maximize *society's* output and income.

Of the various virtues of the market system, three stand out:

- *Efficiency* The market system promotes the efficient use of resources by guiding them into the production of the goods and services most wanted by society. It also encourages the development and adoption of new and more efficient production techniques.

- *Incentives* The market system encourages skill acquisition, hard work, innovation, and entrepreneurship. Greater work skills and effort mean greater production and higher incomes, which usually translate into a higher standard of living. Successful innovations generate economic rewards. Lower-cost production raises profits while freeing up resources to be used elsewhere.

- *Freedom* The major noneconomic argument for the market system is its emphasis on personal freedom. Unlike central planning, the market system coordinates economic activity without coercion. The market system permits—indeed, it thrives on—freedom of enterprise and choice. Entrepreneurs and workers are free to further their own self-interest, subject to the rewards and penalties imposed by the market system itself.

Of course, no economic system, including the market system, is flawless. In Chapters 4 and 5, we discuss several well-known shortcomings of the market system and examine the government policies that try to remedy them.

The Demise of the Command Systems

Our discussion of how a market system answers the five fundamental questions provides insights into why the command systems of the Soviet Union, eastern Europe, and China (prior to its market reforms) failed. Those systems encountered two insurmountable problems.

The Coordination Problem The first difficulty was the **coordination problem.** The central planners had to coordinate the millions of individual decisions by consumers, resource suppliers, and businesses. Consider the setting up of a factory to produce tractors. The central planners had to

>> **LO2.4** Explain the operation of the "invisible hand."

invisible hand The tendency of *competition* to cause individuals and firms to unintentionally but quite effectively promote the interests of society even when each individual or firm is only attempting to pursue its own interests.

coordination problem The chronic failure of command economies to harmonize the economic activities of producers so as to efficiently satisfy consumer demands; caused by command economies eschewing economic coordination via markets, prices, and profits in favor of central planning.

establish a realistic annual production target, for example, 1,000 tractors. They then had to make available all the necessary inputs—labor, machinery, electric power, steel, tires, glass, paint, transportation—for the production and delivery of those tractors.

Because the outputs of many industries serve as inputs to other industries, the failure of any single industry to achieve its output target caused a chain reaction of repercussions. For example, if iron mines, for want of machinery or labor or transportation, did not supply the steel industry with the required inputs of iron ore, the steel mills were unable to fulfill the input needs of the many industries that depended on steel. Those steel-using industries (such as tractor, automobile, and transportation) were unable to fulfill their planned production goals. Eventually the chain reaction spread to all firms that used steel as an input and from there to other input buyers or final consumers.

The coordination problem became more difficult as the economies expanded. Products and production processes grew more sophisticated and the number of industries requiring planning increased. Planning techniques that worked for a simpler economy proved highly inadequate and inefficient for a more complicated economy. Bottlenecks and production stoppages became the norm, not the exception. In trying to cope, planners suppressed product variety, focusing on one or two products in each product category. What little got produced all looked the same.

A lack of a reliable success indicator added to the coordination problem in the Soviet Union before its demise and in China prior to its market reforms. We have seen that market economies rely on profit as a success indicator. Profit depends on consumer demand, production efficiency, and product quality. In contrast, the major success indicator for the command economies usually was a quantitative production target that the central planners assigned. Production costs, product quality, and product mix were secondary considerations. Managers and workers often sacrificed product quality and variety because they were being awarded bonuses for meeting quantitative, not qualitative, targets. If meeting production goals meant sloppy assembly work and little product variety, so be it.

It was also extremely difficult for planners to assign quantitative production targets without unintentionally producing distortions in output. If the plan specified a production target for producing nails in terms of *weight* (tons of nails), the enterprise made only large nails. But if it specified the target as a *quantity* (thousands of nails), the firm made only small nails, and lots of them!

incentive problem The difficulty common to command economies wherein the numerical production targets set by central planning boards cause managers to produce substandard or unwanted output.

The Incentive Problem The command economies also faced an **incentive problem.** Central planners determined the output mix. When they misjudged how many automobiles, shoes, shirts, and chickens were wanted at the government-set prices, persistent shortages and surpluses of those products arose. But as long as the managers who oversaw the production of those goods were rewarded for meeting their assigned production goals, they had no incentive to adjust production in response to the shortages and surpluses. And there were no fluctuations in prices and profitability to signal that more or less of certain products was desired. Thus, many products were unavailable or in short supply, while other products were overproduced and sat for months or years in warehouses.

The Consider This story discusses the economic differences between North Korea and South Korea—many of them directly attributable to North Korea's nearly complete reliance on the command system and, thus, on dealing poorly with the coordination and incentive problems.

CONSIDER THIS . . .

Korea by Night

After the Second World War, the Korean peninsula was divided into North Korea and South Korea.

North Korea, under the influence of the Soviet Union, established a command economy that emphasized government ownership and central government planning. South Korea, protected by the United States, established a market economy based upon private ownership and the profit motive.

Today, South Korea is far more prosperous, with South Koreans enjoying an average annual income (adjusted for

Vladi333/Shutterstock

international differences in the cost of living) of $42,765 per year versus $1,700 in North Korea, or over 25 times higher. That differential is especially startling when you find out that North Korea was richer and more highly industrialized when the countries were separated in 1953.

South Korea's much greater prosperity shows up dramatically in the accompanying satellite photo of the Korean peninsula at night. The highly electrified South is a web of light while the North is as dark as the surrounding oceans save for its capital city, Pyongyang.

The Circular Flow Model

The dynamic market economy creates continuous, repetitive flows of goods and services, resources, and money. The **circular flow diagram,** shown in **Figure 2.2 (Key Graph),** illustrates those flows for a simplified economy in which there is no government. The figure groups the economy's decision makers into *businesses* and *households.* Additionally, we divide this economy's markets into the *resource market* and the *product market.*

Households

The blue rectangle on the right side of the circular flow diagram in Figure 2.2 represents **households,** defined as one or more persons occupying a housing unit. There are currently about 123 million households in the U.S. economy. Households buy the goods and services that businesses make available in the product market. Households obtain the income needed to buy those products by selling resources in the resource market.

All the resources in our no-government economy are ultimately owned or provided by households. For instance, the members of one household or another directly provide all of the labor and entrepreneurial ability in the economy. Households also own all of the land and all of the capital in the economy either directly, as personal property, or indirectly, as a consequence of owning all of the businesses in the economy (and thereby controlling all of the land and capital

>> **LO2.5** Describe the mechanics of the circular flow model.

circular flow diagram An illustration showing the flow of *resources* from *households* to *firms* and of products from firms to households. These flows are accompanied by reverse flows of *money* from firms to households and from households to firms.

households Economic entities (of one or more persons occupying a housing unit) that provide *resources* to the economy and use the *income* received to purchase *goods* and *services* that satisfy economic wants.

..ıl KEY GRAPH

FIGURE 2.2 **The circular flow diagram.**

Resources flow from households to businesses through the resource market, and products flow from businesses to households through the product market. Opposite these real flows are monetary flows. Households receive income from businesses (their costs) through the resource market, and businesses receive revenue from households (their expenditures) through the product market.

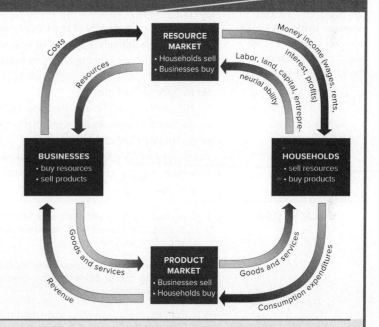

QUICK QUIZ FOR FIGURE 2.2

1. **The resource market is the place where:**
   a. households sell products and businesses buy products.
   b. businesses sell resources and households sell products.
   c. households sell resources and businesses buy resources (or the services of resources).
   d. businesses sell resources and households buy resources (or the services of resources).

2. **Which of the following would be determined in the product market?**
   a. manager's salary
   b. the price of equipment used in a bottling plant
   c. the price of 80 acres of farmland
   d. the price of a new pair of athletic shoes

3. **In this circular flow diagram:**
   a. money flows counterclockwise.
   b. resources flow counterclockwise.
   c. goods and services flow clockwise.
   d. households are on the selling side of the product market.

4. **In the circular flow diagram:**
   a. households spend income in the product market.
   b. firms sell resources to households.
   c. households receive income through the product market.
   d. households produce goods.

Answers: 1. c; 2. d; 3. b; 4. a

owned by businesses). Thus, all of the income in the economy—all wages, rents, interest, and profits—flows to households because they provide the economy's labor, land, capital, and entrepreneurial ability.

Businesses

businesses Economic entities (*firms*) that purchase resources and provide *goods* and *services* to the economy.

The blue rectangle on the left side of the circular flow diagram represents **businesses,** which are commercial establishments that attempt to earn profits for their owners by offering goods and services for sale.

Businesses sell goods and services in the product market in order to obtain revenue, and they incur costs in the resource market when they purchase the labor, land, capital, and entrepreneurial ability that they need to produce their goods and services.

There currently are about 30 million businesses in the United States, ranging from enormous corporations like Walmart, with 2020 sales of $559 billion and 2.2 million employees worldwide, to single-person sole proprietorships with sales of less than $100 per day.

Product Market

product market A market in which products are sold by *firms* and bought by *households*.

The red rectangle at the bottom of the diagram represents the **product market** in which households purchase the goods and services produced by businesses. Households use the income they receive from the sale of resources to buy goods and services. The money that they spend on goods and services flows to businesses as revenue.

Resource Market

resource market A market in which *households* sell and *firms* buy *resources* or the services of resources.

Finally, the red rectangle at the top of the circular flow diagram represents the **resource market** in which households sell resources to businesses. The households sell resources to generate income, and the businesses buy resources to produce goods and services. Productive resources flow from households to businesses, while money flows from businesses to households in the form of wages, rents, interest, and profits.

To summarize: The circular flow model depicts a complex web of economic activity in which businesses and households are both buyers and sellers. Businesses buy resources and sell products. Households buy products and sell resources. The counterclockwise flow of economic resources and finished products, which is illustrated by the red arrows in Figure 2.2, is paid for by the clockwise flow of money income and consumption expenditures illustrated by the blue arrows.

QUICK REVIEW
2.4

▶ Competition leads individuals and firms to promote the social interest, as if they were guided by a benevolent "invisible hand."

▶ Command systems fail economically because central planning cannot solve the coordination and incentive problems.

▶ The circular flow model illustrates how resources flow from households to businesses and how payments for those resources flow from businesses to households.

How the Market System Deals with Risk

>> LO2.6 Explain how the market system deals with risk.

Producing goods and services is risky. Input shortages can suddenly arise. Consumer preferences can quickly change. Natural disasters can destroy factories and cripple supply chains.

For an economic system to maximize its potential, it must develop methods for assessing and managing risk. The market system does so by confronting business owners with the financial consequences of their decisions. If they manage risks well, they may prosper. If they manage risks poorly, they may lose everything.

The Profit System

As explained in Chapter 1, entrepreneurial ability is the economic resource that organizes and directs the other three resources of land, labor, and capital toward productive uses. The owners of a firm may supply the entrepreneurial ability themselves, or they can hire professional managers to supply the necessary leadership and decision making. Either way, it falls to those acting as the firm's entrepreneurs to deal with risk.

The firm's managers are guided toward sensible decisions by the profit system. This system is actually a profit-and-loss system because entrepreneurs gain profits if they choose wisely but suffer losses if they choose poorly. Entrepreneurs therefore have a large financial incentive to avoid unnecessary risks and make prudent decisions.

Shielding Employees and Suppliers from Business Risk

Under the market system, only a firm's owners are subject to business risk and the possibility of losing money. In contrast, the firm's employees and suppliers are shielded from business risk because they are legally entitled to receive their contracted wages and payments on time and in full regardless of whether the firm is earning a profit or generating a loss.

Consider a new pizza parlor that is opening in a small town. Its investors put up $50,000 to get it going. They rent a storefront, lease ovens, purchase computers, and set some money aside as a reserve.

The firm then has to attract employees. To do so, it will offer wage contracts that promise to pay employees every two weeks without regard to whether the firm is making a profit or generating a loss. This guarantee shields the firm's employees from the risks of owning and operating the business. They will get paid even if the pizza parlor is losing money.

In the same way, the contracts that the firm signs with its suppliers and with anyone who loans the firm money (for instance, the local bank) will also specify that they will be paid on time and in full no matter how the firm is doing in terms of profitability.

Because everyone else is legally entitled to get paid before the firm's owners, the firm's owners are called **residual claimants.** That is, the owners are the legal recipients (claimants) of whatever profit or loss remains (is residual) after all other parties have been paid. The possibility of a profit after everyone else has been paid is the owner's compensation for bearing business risk.

Dealing with Losses So what happens if the firm starts losing money? The owners will take the financial hit. Suppose that the pizza parlor loses $1,500 during the month of October because it runs up $11,500 in costs but generates only $10,000 in revenue. In that situation, the investors' wealth will shrink by $1,500 as the firm is forced to dip into its reserve to cover the loss. If the firm continues to lose money in subsequent months and exhausts the reserve, the owners will then have to decide whether they want to close the shop or put in additional money in the hope that things will turn around.

But throughout all those months of losses, the suppliers and employees are safeguarded. Because they are paid on time and in full, they are shielded from the firm's business risks and whether it is generating a profit or a loss. However, they are not legally entitled to share in the profits if the firm ends up being profitable. That privilege is reserved under the market system for the firm's owners; it is their reward for bearing business risk.

The nearby Consider This story discusses how insurance subsidies affect risk management.

residual claimant In a market system, the economic agent who receives (is claimant to) whatever profit or loss remains (is residual) at a firm after all other *input* providers have been paid. The residual is compensation for providing the economic input of *entrepreneurial ability* and flows to the firm's owners.

CONSIDER THIS . . .

Built on Sand

Insurance policies can help guide people toward better decisions by putting a price on risk. Consider fire insurance and its effect on building decisions. Anyone wanting to build a new home or business in a fire-prone area like Southern California will face substantially higher fire insurance costs than they would if they built in a drizzly locale like coastal Washington. Other things equal, Southern California will see less construction.

Those risk assessments go awry when the government subsidizes insurance premiums. Look at flood insurance. Millions of people who would have otherwise chosen to live

Robert J. Bennett/Pixtal/age fotostock

and work on higher ground live and work in floodplains because the federal government subsidizes flood insurance by about 50 percent.

If those people had been confronted with unsubsidized rates for flood insurance, they would have chosen to live and work on higher ground. But as things now stand, they will be flooded out repeatedly, with taxpayers picking up the tab for flood damages and reconstruction costs.

That's bad for both residents and taxpayers. But it's a predictable consequence of making the financial costs of risky behavior look artificially low.

LAST WORD

Hasta La Vista, Venezuela

Venezuela, Once Prosperous, Starved. What Terminated Its Economy?

How can a modern, technologically sophisticated nation in possession of the world's largest oil reserves end up collapsing its economy so badly that there are no medicines in hospitals, toilet paper is unavailable, gasoline has to be rationed, and food gets so expensive that its citizens lost an average of 24 pounds of body weight in 2017?

The country in question is Venezuela, and all those problems began with the election of Hugo Chavez in 1998. He attained the presidency on a promise to alleviate poverty and ensure that everyone in Venezuela had a chance to participate in the country's prosperity, which included supersonic Concord flights to Paris, South America's best arts and entertainment scene, and a highly profitable oil industry that brought massive tax revenues to the government.

Several of Chavez's initial policy efforts were beneficial, including mass literacy programs and the construction of rural health clinics. Unfortunately, Chavez's early anti-poverty programs were just the start of a comprehensive campaign to totally transform Venezuela's economy and society.

As you know from this chapter, most economies are *mixed economies* in which the government sets broad rules but in which businesses have substantial autonomy over what to produce, how to produce it, and what to charge for it. That autonomy was slowly eliminated by Chavez and his successor, Nicolas Maduro, who both pursued an economic policy that they termed Bolivarian Socialism.

Industries were nationalized, meaning that they were taken over by the government without compensation to their owners. That included the oil industry, which pumped 3.4 million barrels per day when Chavez took over in 1998 but just 1.4 million barrels per day 20 years later.

Chavez and Maduro ruined the industry by putting "friends" in charge of the oil rigs. These cronies were thoroughly corrupt, directing into their own pockets the money needed for equipment repairs. The result was leaking pipelines, broken drills, and ever declining production.

The reduced production put a severe strain on the government's finances. By 2013, the government could no longer raise enough tax revenue to pay its bills. Instead of making the tough choices necessary to balance its budget, the government resorted to printing money to pay its bills.

Rapid money printing always and everywhere results in a *hyperinflation*, or a super-fast increase in the overall level of prices in the economy. Double the money supply and prices will double; triple the money supply and prices will triple; and so on.

Venezuela's inflation rate skyrocketed from 25 percent per year in 2012 to 2,600 percent per year in 2017. But oil production continued to fall and the government's deficit situation grew worse.

Maduro's solution? *Print even faster!* The result? Inflation accelerated to 1.3 *million* percent per year in 2018.

Román Camacho/SOPA Images/LightRocket/Getty Images

Maduro could not admit that his government's money printing was responsible for the hyperinflation. He blamed foreigners and rebels intent on overthrowing his government. To "fight" them, he imposed price controls on consumer goods.

Price controls are legal limits on how much sellers can charge for a product. For example, the government might make it illegal to charge more than $5 for a haircut. That *price ceiling* will be attractive to consumers, but it will quickly bankrupt producers because the prices that they have to pay for inputs like labor will keep increasing due to the hyperinflation. The cost of production soon blows past the legal selling price. The only avenues of escape are selling illegally at higher prices or going out of business.

With Maduro's troops imprisoning anybody who dared to sell at higher prices, many firms went bankrupt and closed permanently. As they did, shortages of every imaginable product arose. People began to starve and over 3 million Venezuelans fled to other countries.

So as you consider the pluses and minuses of the market economy and its limited level of government intervention, be sure to remember what became of a once prosperous country brought low by an incompetent, unresponsive, and corrupt government that tried to control every aspect of economic life.

Chavez and Maduro claimed to be saviors. But their socialist economic policies wrought nearly as much damage as the genocidal robots of the *Terminator* movies.

A few rays of hope began to shine by 2021, however, as Maduro decided to relax government control over some areas of the economy, thereby encouraging some brave businesspeople to start operating again. Whether this return to normalcy will continue remains to be seen, though. And unless things improve rapidly, we may have to continue to say *Hasta La Vista, Baby,* to Venezuela's once prosperous economy.

Benefits of Restricting Business Risk to Owners

Two major benefits arise from the market system's restriction of business risk to owners and investors.

Attracting Inputs   Many people deeply dislike risk and would not be willing to participate in a business venture if they were exposed to the possibility of losing money. Many workers just want to do their jobs and get paid twice a month without having to worry about whether their employer is doing well or not. The same is true for most suppliers, whose only concern is receiving full and prompt payment for the inputs they supply to businesses.

For both groups, the concentration of business risk on owners is very welcome because they can supply their resources to a firm without worrying about the firm's profitability. That sense of security makes it much easier for firms to attract labor and other inputs, which in turn helps the economy innovate and grow.

Focusing Attention   The profit system helps to achieve prudent risk management by focusing owners on the responsibility and the rewards for successfully managing risk. Owners can provide the risk-managing input of entrepreneurial ability themselves or hire it by paying a skilled manager. But either way, some individual's full-time job includes the specialized task of managing business risk.

▶ The market system incentivizes the prudent management of business risk by concentrating any profit or loss on a firm's owners and investors.

▶ The market system shields employees, suppliers, and lenders from business risks, but in exchange for that protection, they do not share any profit that might be earned.

▶ By focusing risk on owners and investors, the market system (a) creates an incentive for owners and investors to hire managerial and entrepreneurial specialists to prudently manage business risks and (b) encourages the participation of workers, suppliers, and lenders who dislike risk.

QUICK REVIEW

2.5

Summary

LO2.1 Define and explain laissez-faire capitalism, the command system, and the market system.
Laissez-faire capitalism is a hypothetical economic system in which government's role would be restricted to protecting private property and enforcing contracts. All real-world economic systems feature a larger role for government. Governments in command systems own nearly all property and resources and make nearly all decisions about what to produce, how to produce it, and who gets the output. Most countries today, including the United States, have market systems in which the government does play a large role, but in which most property and resources are privately owned and markets are the major force in determining what to produce, how to produce it, and who gets it.

LO2.2 List the main characteristics of the market system.
The market system is characterized by the private ownership of resources, including capital, and the freedom of individuals to engage in economic activities of their choice to advance their well-being. Self-interest is the driving force of such an economy, and competition functions as a regulatory or control mechanism.

In the market system, markets, prices, and profits organize and coordinate the many millions of individual economic decisions that occur daily.

Specialization, the use of advanced technology, and the extensive use of capital goods are common features of market systems. By functioning as a medium of exchange, money eliminates the problems of bartering and permits easy trade and greater specialization, both domestically and internationally.

LO2.3 Explain how the market system answers the five fundamental questions of what to produce, how to produce, who obtains the output, how to adjust to change, and how to promote technological progress.
Every economy faces five fundamental questions: (a) What goods and services will be produced? (b) How will the goods and services be produced? (c) Who will get the output? (d) How will the system accommodate change? (e) How will the system promote technological progress?

The market system produces products whose production and sale yield total revenue sufficient to cover total cost. It does not produce products for which total revenue continuously falls short of total cost. Competition forces firms to use the lowest-cost production techniques.

Economic profit (total revenue minus total cost) indicates that an industry is prosperous and promotes its expansion. Losses signify that an industry is not prosperous and hasten its contraction.

Consumer sovereignty means that both businesses and resource suppliers are subject to consumers' wants. Through their dollar votes, consumers decide on the composition of output.

The prices that a household receives for the resources it supplies to the economy determine that household's income. This income determines the household's claim on the economy's output.

By communicating changes in consumer tastes to entrepreneurs and resource suppliers, the market system prompts appropriate adjustments in the allocation of the economy's resources. The market system also encourages technological advance and capital accumulation, both of which raise a nation's standard of living.

LO2.4 Explain the operation of the "invisible hand."
Competition, the primary mechanism of control in the market economy, promotes a unity of self-interest and social interests. As if directed by an invisible hand, competition harnesses the self-interested motives of businesses and resource suppliers to further the social interest.

The command systems of the Soviet Union and pre-reform China met their demise because central planning could not solve the coordination problem and because the numerical targets given to managers created an incentive problem.

LO2.5 Describe the mechanics of the circular flow model.
The circular flow model illustrates the flows of resources and products from households to businesses and from businesses to households, along with the corresponding monetary flows. Businesses are on the buying side of the resource market and the selling side of the product market. Households are on the selling side of the resource market and the buying side of the product market.

LO2.6 Explain how the market system deals with risk.
By focusing business risks onto owners, the market system encourages the participation of workers and suppliers who dislike risk while at the same time creating a strong incentive for owners to manage business risks prudently.

Terms and Concepts

economic system
laissez-faire capitalism
command system
market system
market
private property
freedom of enterprise
freedom of choice
self-interest

competition
specialization
division of labor
medium of exchange
barter
money
consumer sovereignty
dollar votes
creative destruction

invisible hand
coordination problem
incentive problem
circular flow diagram
households
businesses
product market
resource market
residual claimant

Discussion Questions

1. Contrast how a market system and a command economy try to cope with economic scarcity. **LO2.1**
2. How does self-interest help achieve society's economic goals? Why is there such a wide variety of desired goods and services in a market system? In what way are entrepreneurs and businesses at the helm of the economy but commanded by consumers? **LO2.2**
3. Why are private property, and the protection of property rights, so critical to the success of the market system? How do property rights encourage cooperation? **LO2.2**
4. What are the advantages of using capital in the production process? What is meant by the term "division of labor"? What are the advantages of specialization in the use of human and material resources? Explain why exchange is the necessary consequence of specialization. **LO2.2**
5. What problem does barter entail? Indicate the economic significance of money as a medium of exchange. What is meant by the statement "We want money only to part with it"? **LO2.2**
6. Evaluate and explain the following statements: **LO2.2**
   a. The market system is a profit-and-loss system.
   b. Competition is the disciplinarian of the market economy.
7. Some large hardware stores, such as Home Depot, boast of carrying as many as 20,000 different products in each store. What motivated the producers of those individual products to make them and offer them for sale? How did the producers decide on the best combinations of resources to use? Who made those resources available, and why? Who decides whether these particular hardware products should continue to be produced and offered for sale? **LO2.3**
8. What is meant by the term "creative destruction"? How does the emergence of self-driving cars relate to this idea? **LO2.3**
9. In a sentence, describe the meaning of the phrase "invisible hand." **LO2.4**
10. In market economies, firms rarely worry about the availability of inputs to produce their products, whereas in command economies input availability is a constant concern. Why the difference? **LO2.4**
11. Distinguish between the resource market and the product market in the circular flow model. In what way are businesses and households both sellers and buyers in this model? What are the flows in the circular flow model? **LO2.5**
12. How does shielding employees and suppliers from business risk help to improve economic outcomes? Who is responsible for managing business risks in the market system? **LO2.6**
13. **LAST WORD** Why are price ceilings during a hyperinflation problematic? What generalizations do you draw from Venezuela's economic collapse? Would a Venezuelan-style economic collapse be less likely in the United States? Explain.

Review Questions

Mc Graw Hill connect

1. Decide whether each of the following descriptions most closely corresponds to being part of a command system, a market system, or a laissez-faire system. **LO2.1**
   a. A woman who wants to start a flower shop finds she cannot do so unless the central government has already decided to allow a flower shop in her area.
   b. Shops stock and sell the goods their customers want, but the government levies a sales tax on each transaction in order to fund elementary schools, public libraries, and welfare programs for the poor.
   c. The only taxes levied by the government are to pay for national defense, law enforcement, and a legal system designed to enforce contracts between private citizens.

2. Match each term with the correct definition. **LO2.2**
   private property
   freedom of enterprise
   mutually agreeable
   freedom of choice
   self-interest
   competition
   market
   a. An institution that brings buyers and sellers together
   b. The right of private persons and firms to obtain, control, employ, dispose of, and bequeath land, capital, and other property
   c. The presence in a market of independent buyers and sellers who compete with one another and who are free to enter and exit the market as each sees fit
   d. The freedom of firms to obtain economic resources, decide what products to produce with those resources, and sell those products in markets of their choice
   e. What each individual or firm believes is best for itself and seeks to obtain
   f. Economic transactions willingly undertaken by both the buyer and the seller because each feels that the transaction will make them better off
   g. The freedom of resource owners to dispose of their resources as they think best; of workers to enter any line of work for which they are qualified; and of consumers to spend their incomes in whatever way they feel is most appropriate

3. True or False: Money must be issued by a government for people to accept it. **LO2.2**

4. Assume that a business firm finds that its profit is greatest when it produces $40 worth of product A. Suppose also that each of the three techniques shown in the following table will produce the desired output. **LO2.3**
   a. With the resource prices shown, which technique will the firm choose? Why? Will production using that technique result in profit or loss? What will be the amount of that profit or loss? Will the industry expand or contract? When will that expansion or contraction end?
   b. Assume now that a new technique, technique 4, is developed. It combines 2 units of labor, 2 of land, 6 of capital, and 3 of entrepreneurial ability. With the resources priced as shown in the table, will the firm adopt the new technique? Explain.
   c. Suppose that an increase in the labor supply causes the price of labor to fall to $1.50 per unit, all other resource prices

remaining unchanged. Which technique will the producer now choose? Explain.
   d. "The market system causes the economy to conserve most in the use of resources that are particularly scarce in supply. Resources that are scarcest relative to the demand for them have the highest prices. As a result, producers use these resources as sparingly as is possible." Evaluate this statement. Does your answer to part c, above, bear out this contention? Explain.

Resource	Price per Unit of Resource	Resource Units Required		
		Technique 1	Technique 2	Technique 3
Labor	$3	5	2	3
Land	4	2	4	2
Capital	2	2	4	5
Entrepreneurial ability	2	4	2	4

5. Identify each of the following quotes as being associated with either the concept of the invisible hand or the concept of creative destruction. **LO2.4**
   a. "If you compare a list of today's most powerful and profitable companies with a similar list from 30 years ago, you will see lots of new entries."
   b. "Managers in the old Soviet Union often sacrificed product quality and variety because they were being awarded bonuses for quantitative, not qualitative, targets."
   c. "Each day, central planners in the old Soviet Union were tasked with setting 27 million prices—correctly."
   d. "It is not from the benevolence of the butcher, the brewer, or the baker that we expect our dinner, but from their regard to their own interest."

6. True or False: Households sell finished products to businesses. **LO2.6**

7. Aaliyah, Madison, Mia, and Maya have decided to pool their financial resources and business skills to open and run a new coffee shop. They will share any profits or losses that the business generates and will be personally responsible for making good on any debt that their business undertakes. Their business is a: **LO2.6**
   a. corporation.
   b. sole proprietorship.
   c. partnership.
   d. none of the above.

8. Ted and Fred are the owners of a gas station. They invested $150,000 each and pay an employee named Lawrence $35,000 per year. This year's revenues are $900,000, while costs are $940,000. Who is legally responsible for bearing the $40,000 loss? **LO2.6**
   a. Lawrence
   b. Ted
   c. Fred
   d. Ted and Fred
   e. Lawrence, Ted, and Fred

Problems

1. Table 2.1 contains information on three techniques for producing $15 worth of bar soap. Assume that we specified "$15 worth of bar soap" because soap costs $3 per bar and all three techniques produce 5 bars of soap ($15 = $3 per bar × 5 bars). So you know each technique produces 5 bars of soap. **LO2.3**

   a. What technique will you want to use if the price of a bar of soap falls to $2.75? Which technique will you use if the price of a bar of soap rises to $4? To $5?

   b. How many bars of soap will you want to produce if the price of a bar of soap falls to $2.00?

   c. Suppose that the price of soap is again $3 per bar but that the prices of all four resources are now $1 per unit. Which is now the least-profitable technique?

   d. If the resource prices return to their original levels (those shown in the table) but a new technique is invented that can produce 3 bars of soap (yes, 3 bars, not 5 bars!) using 1 unit of each of the four resources, will firms prefer the new technique? Why or why not?

2. Suppose Natasha currently makes $50,000 per year working as a manager at a cable TV company. She then develops two possible entrepreneurial business opportunities. In one, she will quit her job to start an organic soap company. In the other, she will try to develop an Internet-based competitor to the local cable company. For the soap-making opportunity, she anticipates annual revenue of $465,000. She estimates the costs for the necessary land, labor, and capital to be $395,000 per year. For the Internet opportunity, she anticipates costs for land, labor, and capital of $3,250,000 per year and revenues of $3,275,000 per year. (a) Should she quit her current job to become an entrepreneur? (b) If she does quit her current job, which opportunity would she pursue? **LO2.3**

3. With current technology, suppose a firm is producing 400 loaves of banana bread daily. Also assume that the least-cost combination of resources for producing those loaves is 5 units of labor, 7 units of land, 2 units of capital, and 1 unit of entrepreneurial ability, selling at prices of $40, $60, $60, and $20, respectively. If the firm can sell these 400 loaves at $2 per unit, what is its total revenue? Its total cost? Its profit or loss? Will it continue to produce banana bread? If this firm's situation is typical for the other makers of banana bread, will resources flow toward or away from this bakery good? **LO2.3**

4. Let's put dollar amounts on the flows in the circular flow diagram of Figure 2.2. **LO2.5**

   a. Suppose that businesses buy a total of $100 billion of the four resources (labor, land, capital, and entrepreneurial ability) from households. If households receive $60 billion in wages, $10 billion in rent, and $20 billion in interest, how much are households paid for providing entrepreneurial ability?

   b. If households spend $55 billion on goods and $45 billion on services, how much in revenues do businesses receive in the product market?

Demand, Supply, and Market Equilibrium

>> LEARNING OBJECTIVES

LO3.1 Characterize and give examples of markets.

LO3.2 Describe *demand* and explain how it can change.

LO3.3 Describe *supply* and explain how it can change.

LO3.4 Explain how supply and demand interact to determine market equilibrium.

LO3.5 Explain how changes in supply and demand affect equilibrium prices and quantities.

LO3.6 Define government-set prices and explain how they can cause surpluses and shortages.

LO3.7 (Appendix) Use supply-and-demand analysis to analyze specific real-world situations.

The model of supply and demand is the economics profession's greatest contribution to human understanding. It explains the operation of the markets on which we depend for nearly every-thing that we eat, drink, and consume. It is also the economic model most often used to explain and analyze economic decision making. The model is so powerful and so widely used that to many people supply and demand *is* economics.

This chapter explains how the model works and how you can use it to predict the *prices* and *quantities* of goods and services bought and sold in markets.

Markets

Markets bring together buyers ("demanders") and sellers ("suppliers"). Everyday consumer markets include the corner gas station, Amazon.com, and the local bakery shop. The New York Stock Exchange and the Chicago Board of Trade are markets in which buyers and sellers from all over the world exchange bonds, stocks, and commodities. In labor markets, new college graduates "sell" and employers "buy" specific labor services. Ride-sharing apps like Uber and Lyft match people who want to buy rides with people who want to sell rides.

Some markets are local; others are national or international. Some are highly personal, involving face-to-face contact between demander and supplier; others are faceless, with buyer and seller never seeing or knowing each other.

To keep things simple, we will focus on markets in which large numbers of independently acting buyers and sellers come together to buy and sell standardized products. Markets with these characteristics are the economy's most highly competitive markets. They include the wheat market, the stock market, and the market for foreign currencies. All such markets involve demand,

>> **LO3.1** Characterize and give examples of markets.

supply, price, and quantity. As you will soon see, the price is "discovered" through the interacting decisions of buyers and sellers.

Demand

>> **LO3.2** Describe *demand* and explain how it can change.

demand A schedule or curve that shows the various amounts of a product that consumers are willing and able to purchase at each of a series of possible *prices* during a specified period of time.

demand schedule A table of numbers showing the amounts of a *good* or *service* buyers are willing and able to purchase at various *prices* over a specified period of time.

Demand is a schedule (table of numbers) or a curve that shows the various amounts of a product that consumers are willing and able to purchase at each of a series of possible prices during a specified period of time, *other things equal*. The table in Figure 3.1 is a hypothetical **demand schedule** for a *single consumer* purchasing gallons of gasoline.

The table reveals the relationship between the various prices of gasoline and the quantity (amount) of gasoline a particular consumer is willing and able to purchase at each price. We say "willing and able" because willingness alone is not effective in the market. You may be willing to buy an ultra-high-definition 4K television set, but if that willingness is not backed by the necessary dollars, it will not be reflected in the market. In the table in Figure 3.1, if the price of gasoline is $5 per gallon, our consumer is willing and able to buy 10 gallons per week; if the price is $4, the consumer is willing and able to buy 20 gallons per week; and so forth.

The table does not tell us which of the five possible prices will actually exist in the gasoline market. The price depends on the interaction between demand and supply. Demand is simply a statement of a buyer's plans, or intentions, with respect to purchasing a product.

To be meaningful, the quantities demanded at each price must relate to a specific period—a day, a week, a month. Saying "A consumer will buy 10 gallons of gas at $5 per gallon" is meaningless. Saying "A consumer will buy 10 gallons of gas *per week* at $5 per gallon" is meaningful. Unless a specific time period is stated, we do not know whether the demand for a product is large or small.

law of demand The principle that, other things equal, an increase in a product's *price* will reduce the quantity of it demanded, and conversely for a decrease in price.

Law of Demand

Other things equal, as price falls, the quantity demanded rises, and as price rises, the quantity demanded falls. In short, there is a *negative* or inverse relationship between price and quantity demanded. Economists call this inverse relationship the **law of demand.**

The other-things-equal assumption is critical here. Many factors other than the price of the product being considered affect the amount purchased. For example, the quantity of Nikes

FIGURE 3.1 **An individual buyer's demand for gasoline.**

Because price and quantity demanded are inversely related, an individual's demand schedule graphs as a downward sloping curve such as *D*. Other things equal, consumers will buy more of a product as its price declines and less of the product as its price rises. (Here and in later figures, *P* stands for price and *Q* stands for quantity demanded or supplied.)

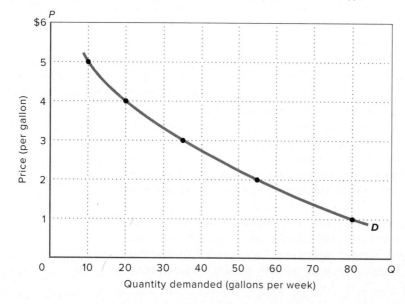

Demand for Gasoline	
Price per Gallon	Quantity (Amount) Demanded per Week
$5	10
4	20
3	35
2	55
1	80

purchased will depend not only on the price of Nikes but also on the prices of shoes produced by Adidas, Reebok, and New Balance. The law of demand in this case says that fewer Nikes will be purchased if the price of Nikes rises while the prices of Adidas, Reeboks, and New Balances remain constant. In short, if the *relative price* of Nikes rises, fewer Nikes will be bought. However, if the price of Nikes and the prices of all other competing shoes increase by some amount—say $5—consumers may buy more, fewer, or the same number of Nikes. To isolate the demand for Nikes, you have to hold other things equal.

Why is there an inverse relationship between price and quantity demanded? Let's look at three explanations, beginning with the simplest one:

- The law of demand is consistent with common sense. People ordinarily do buy more of a product at a low price than at a high price. Price is an obstacle that deters consumers. The higher that obstacle, the less of a product they will buy; the lower the price obstacle, the more they will buy. The fact that businesses conduct "clearance sales" to liquidate unsold items firmly supports the law of demand.

- In any specific time period, each buyer of a product will derive less satisfaction (or benefit, or utility) from each successive unit of the product consumed. The second Big Mac will yield less satisfaction than the first, and the third less than the second. That is, consumption is subject to **diminishing marginal utility.** And because successive units of a particular product yield less and less marginal utility, consumers will buy additional units only if the price of those units is progressively reduced.

- We can also explain the law of demand in terms of income and substitution effects. The **income effect** indicates that a lower price increases the purchasing power of a buyer's money income, enabling the buyer to purchase more of a product than before. A higher price has the opposite effect. The **substitution effect** suggests that buyers have an incentive to substitute a product whose price has fallen for other products whose prices have remained the same. The substitution occurs because the product whose price has fallen is now "a better deal" relative to the other products, whose prices remain unchanged.

For example, a decline in the price of chicken will increase the purchasing power of consumer incomes, enabling people to buy more chicken (the income effect). At a lower price, chicken is relatively more attractive and consumers tend to substitute it for pork, beef, and fish (the substitution effect). The income and substitution effects combine to make consumers able and willing to buy more of a product at a lower price than at a higher price.

The Demand Curve

The inverse relationship between price and quantity demanded for any product can be represented on a simple graph with quantity demanded on the horizontal axis and price on the vertical axis. The graph in Figure 3.1 plots the five price-quantity data points listed in the accompanying table and connects the points with a smooth curve, labeled *D*. This curve is called a **demand curve.** Its downward slope reflects the law of demand—people buy more of a product, service, or resource as its price falls, other things equal.

Market Demand

So far, we have concentrated on just one consumer. But competition requires more than one buyer in each market. By adding the quantities demanded by all consumers at each possible price, we can get from *individual* demand to *market* demand. If there are just three buyers in the market, as represented in the table in Figure 3.2, it is relatively easy to determine the total quantity demanded at each price. Figure 3.2 shows the graphical summing procedure: At each price we sum horizontally the quantities demanded by Joe, Jen, and Jay to obtain the total quantity demanded at that price. We then plot the price and the total quantity demanded as one point on the market demand curve. At the price of $3, for example, the three individual curves yield a total quantity demanded of 100 gallons (= 35 + 39 + 26).

diminishing marginal utility The principle that as a consumer increases the consumption of a *good* or *service*, the *marginal utility* obtained from each additional unit of the good or service decreases.

income effect A change in the quantity demanded of a product that results from the change in *real income* (*purchasing power*) caused by a change in the product's *price*.

substitution effect (1) A change in the quantity demanded of a *consumer good* that results from a change in its relative expensiveness caused by a change in the good's own *price*. (2) The reduction in the *quantity demanded* of the second of a pair of *substitute resources* that occurs when the price of the first resource falls and causes *firms* that employ both resources to switch to using more of the first resource (whose price has fallen) and less of the second resource (whose price has remained the same).

demand curve A curve that illustrates the *demand* for a product by showing how each possible *price* (on the *vertical axis*) is associated with a specific *quantity demanded* (on the *horizontal axis*).

FIGURE 3.2 Market demand for gasoline, three buyers.

The market demand curve D is the horizontal summation of the individual demand curves (D_1, D_2, and D_3) of all the consumers in the market. At the price of $3, for example, the three individual curves yield a total quantity demanded of 100 gallons (= 35 + 39 + 26).

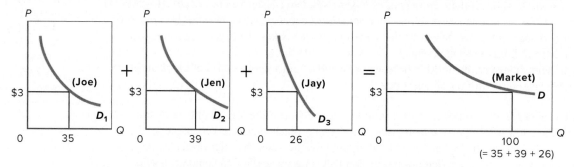

	Market Demand for Gasoline, Three Buyers			
	Quantity Demanded			**Total Quantity**
Price per Gallon	**Joe**	**Jen**	**Jay**	**Demanded per Week**
$5	10 +	12 +	8 =	30
4	20 +	23 +	17 =	60
3	35 +	39 +	26 =	100
2	55 +	60 +	39 =	154
1	80 +	87 +	54 =	221

Competition, of course, ordinarily entails many more than three buyers of a product. For simplicity, we suppose that all the buyers in a market are willing and able to buy the same amounts at each possible price. Then we just multiply those amounts by the number of buyers to obtain the market demand. That is how we arrive at the demand schedule and demand curve D_1 in Figure 3.3 for a market of 200 gasoline buyers, each with the quantity demanded in the table in Figure 3.1.

FIGURE 3.3 Changes in the demand for gasoline.

A change in one or more of the determinants of demand causes a change in demand. An increase in demand is shown as a shift of the demand curve to the right, as from D_1 to D_2. A decrease in demand is shown as a shift of the demand curve to the left, as from D_1 to D_3. These changes in demand are to be distinguished from a change in quantity demanded, which is caused by a change in the price of the product, as shown by a movement from, say, point a to point b on fixed demand curve D_1.

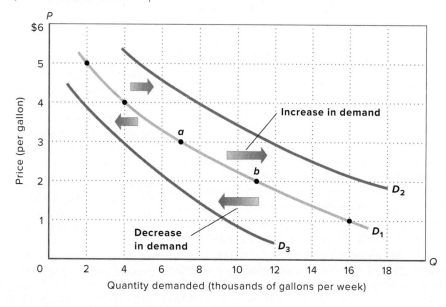

Market Demand for Gasoline, 200 Buyers, (D_1)	
	(2)
(1)	**Total Quantity**
Price per	**Demanded**
Gallon	**per Week**
$5	2,000
4	4,000
3	7,000
2	11,000
1	16,000

In constructing a demand curve such as D_1 in Figure 3.3, economists assume that price is the most important influence on the amount of any product purchased. But other factors can and do affect purchases. These factors, called **determinants of demand,** are assumed to be constant when a demand curve like D_1 is drawn. When any of these determinants change, the demand curve will shift to the right or left. For this reason, determinants of demand are sometimes called *demand shifters*.

The basic determinants of demand are (1) consumers' tastes (preferences), (2) the number of buyers in the market, (3) consumers' incomes, (4) the prices of related goods, and (5) consumer expectations.

determinants of demand Factors other than *price* that determine the quantities demanded of a *good* or *service*. Also referred to as "demand shifters" because changes in the determinants of demand will cause the *demand curve* to shift either right or left.

Changes in Demand

A change in one or more of the determinants of demand will change the demand data (the demand schedule) in the table accompanying Figure 3.3 and therefore the location of the demand curve. A change in the demand schedule or, graphically, a shift in the demand curve, is called a *change in demand*.

If consumers collectively desire to buy more gasoline at each possible price than is reflected in column 2 in the table in Figure 3.3, that *increase in demand* shifts the demand curve to the right, say, from D_1 to D_2. Conversely, a *decrease in demand* occurs when consumers buy less gas at each possible price than is indicated in column 2. The leftward shift of the demand curve from D_1 to D_3 in Figure 3.3 shows that situation.

Now let's see how changes in each determinant affect demand.

Tastes A favorable change in consumer tastes (preferences) for a product—a change that makes the product more desirable—means that more of it will be demanded at each price. Demand will increase; the demand curve will shift rightward. An unfavorable change in consumer preferences will decrease demand, shifting the demand curve to the left.

New products may affect consumer tastes; for example, the introduction of Instagram and Snapchat greatly decreased the demand for Facebook among teens. Consumer concerns over obesity have increased the demand for broccoli, low-calorie beverages, and fresh fruit while decreasing the demand for beef, eggs, and whole milk. Over the past decade, the demand for vegan food and electric vehicles has increased rapidly, driven by a change in tastes.

Number of Buyers An increase in the number of buyers in a market is likely to increase demand; a decrease in the number of buyers will probably decrease demand.

The most obvious way that changes in the number of consumers can affect demand is by changing the number of potential consumers.

- The rising number of older persons in the United States, for example, has increased the demand for motor homes, medical care, and retirement communities.

- In contrast, out-migration from many small rural communities has reduced their populations and thus the demand for housing, home appliances, and auto repair in those towns.

A more subtle way in which changes in the number of buyers can affect demand is through network effects and congestion effects.

- A *network effect* happens when the value of a product increases as more people use it. This is true for things like cell phones and social apps. Having a cell phone or an Instagram account would not be of any value if you were the only person using a cell phone network or Instagram. There would be nobody to connect to! But the more people who join either of those networks, the more valuable they become and thus the greater the number of people who wish to use them. The result is an increase in demand and a rightward shift of the demand curve.

- A *congestion effect* happens when the value of a product decreases as more people use it. This is true, for instance, for driving on highways or streaming data on a wi-fi network that has limited bandwidth. The more people there are crowded onto a highway or trying to simultaneously stream data on a wi-fi network with finite capacity, the worse the user experience as congestion takes hold and things slow to a crawl. In these situations, quality declines, fewer people wish to use the product, and demand shifts to the left.

normal good A *good* or *service* whose consumption increases when *income* increases and falls when income decreases, other things equal.

inferior good A *good* or *service* whose consumption declines as *income* rises, other things equal.

substitute goods Products or *services* that can be used in place of each other. When the *price* of one falls, the *demand* for the other product falls; conversely, when the price of one product rises, the demand for the other product rises.

complementary goods Products and *services* that are used together. When the *price* of one falls, the demand for the other increases (and conversely).

Income For most products, a rise in income causes an increase in demand. Consumers typically buy more steaks, furniture, and electronic equipment as their incomes increase. Conversely, the demand for such products declines as their incomes fall. Products whose demand varies directly with money income are called *superior goods,* or **normal goods.**

Although most products are normal goods, there are some exceptions. As incomes increase beyond some point, the demand for used clothing, retread tires, and third-hand automobiles may decrease because the higher incomes enable consumers to buy new versions of those products. Similarly, rising incomes may cause the demand for charcoal grills to decline as wealthier consumers switch to gas grills. Goods whose demand varies inversely with money income are called **inferior goods.**

Prices of Related Goods A change in the price of a related good may either increase or decrease the demand for a product, depending on whether the related good is a substitute or a complement:

- A **substitute good** is one that can be used in place of another good.
- A **complementary good** is one that is used together with another good.

Substitutes Häagen-Dazs ice cream and Ben & Jerry's ice cream are substitute goods or, simply, *substitutes.* When two products are substitutes, an increase in the price of one will increase the demand for the other. Conversely, a decrease in the price of one will decrease the demand for the other. For example, when the price of Häagen-Dazs ice cream rises, consumers will buy less of it and increase their demand for Ben & Jerry's ice cream. The two brands are *substitutes in consumption.*

Complements Because complementary goods (or, simply, *complements*) are used together, they are typically demanded jointly. Examples include computers and software, smartphones and cellular service, and snowboards and lift tickets. If the price of a complement (for example, lettuce) goes up, the demand for the related good (salad dressing) will decline. Conversely, if the price of a complement (for example, tuition) falls, the demand for a related good (textbooks) will increase.

Unrelated Goods The vast majority of goods are not related to one another and are called *independent goods.* Examples are butter and golf balls, potatoes and automobiles, and bananas and wristwatches. A change in the price of one has little or no effect on the demand for the other.

Consumer Expectations Changes in consumer expectations may shift demand. A newly formed expectation of higher future prices may cause consumers to buy now in order to "beat" the anticipated price hike, thus increasing current demand. That is often what happens in "hot" real-estate markets. Buyers rush in because they think the price of homes will continue to escalate rapidly. Some buyers fear being "priced out of the market" and therefore not obtaining the home they desire. Other buyers—speculators—believe they will be able to sell the houses later at a higher price. Whatever their motivation, these expectation-driven buyers increase the current demand for houses.

Similarly, a change in expectations concerning future income may prompt consumers to change their current spending. For example, first-round NFL draft choices may splurge on new luxury cars in anticipation of lucrative professional football contracts. Or workers who become fearful of losing their jobs may reduce their demand for, say, vacation travel.

In summary, an *increase* in demand—the decision by consumers to buy larger quantities of a product at each possible price—may be caused by:

- A favorable change in consumer tastes.
- An increase in the number of buyers.
- Rising incomes if the product is a normal good.
- Falling incomes if the product is an inferior good.
- An increase in the price of a substitute good.
- A decrease in the price of a complementary good.
- A new consumer expectation that either prices or income will be higher in the future.

You should "reverse" these generalizations to explain a *decrease* in demand. Table 3.1 provides additional illustrations of the determinants of demand.

Determinant	Examples
Change in buyer tastes	Physical fitness rises in popularity, increasing the demand for jogging shoes and bicycles; smartphone use rises, reducing the demand for desktop and laptop computers; vegetarianism increases in popularity, raising the demand for non-meat "impossible" burgers.
Change in number of buyers	A decline in the birthrate reduces the demand for children's toys; an additional 600 million people on WhatsApp makes it a more attractive communications network; the migration of Californians to Colorado increases the demand for housing in Denver.
Change in income	A rise in incomes increases the demand for normal goods such as restaurant meals, sports tickets, and smartphones while reducing the demand for inferior goods such as turnips, bus passes, and cheap wine.
Change in the prices of related goods	A reduction in airfares reduces the demand for train transportation (substitute goods); a decline in the price of printers increases the demand for ink cartridges (complementary goods).
Change in consumer expectations	Inclement weather in South America creates an expectation of higher future coffee bean prices, thereby increasing today's demand for coffee beans. The expectation that other consumers will rush to buy toilet paper next week as a hurricane approaches causes many consumers to increase their purchases of toilet paper this week.

TABLE 3.1
Determinants of Demand: Factors That Shift the Demand Curve

Changes in Quantity Demanded

A *change in demand* must not be confused with a *change in quantity demanded.*

Recall that "demand" is a schedule or a curve. So a **change in demand** implies a change in the schedule and a corresponding shift of the curve.

A change in demand occurs when a consumer's state of mind about purchasing a product has changed in response to a change in one or more of the determinants of demand. Graphically, a change in demand is a shift of the demand curve to the right (an increase in demand) or to the left (a decrease in demand).

In contrast, a **change in quantity demanded** is a movement from one point to another point—from one price-quantity combination to another—along a fixed demand curve or schedule. The cause of such a change is an increase or decrease in the price of the product under consideration. In the table in Figure 3.3, for example, a decline in the price of gasoline from $5 to $4 will increase the quantity demanded from 2,000 to 4,000 gallons. Make sure you can identify the corresponding movement between those two points along fixed demand curve D_1 in Figure 3.3.

Let's review. In Figure 3.3 the shift of the demand curve D_1 to either D_2 or D_3 is a "change in demand." But the movement from point *a* to point *b* on curve D_1 represents a "change in quantity demanded." In this latter case, demand has not changed; it is the entire curve D_1, which remains fixed in place as we move from point *a* to point *b*.

change in demand A movement of an entire *demand curve* (or of the numerical entries in a demand schedule) such that the *quantity demanded* changes at every particular *price;* caused by a change in one or more of the *determinants of demand.*

change in quantity demanded A change in the *quantity demanded* along a fixed *demand curve* (or within a fixed demand schedule) as a result of a change in the *price* of the product.

▸ Demand is a schedule or a curve showing the amount of a product that buyers are willing and able to purchase, in a particular time period, at each possible price in a series of prices, holding other things equal.

▸ The law of demand states that, other things equal, the quantity of a good purchased varies inversely with its price.

▸ The demand curve shifts because of changes in: (a) consumer tastes; (b) the number of buyers in the market; (c) consumer income; (d) the prices of substitute or complementary goods; and (e) consumer expectations.

▸ A change in demand is a shift of the demand curve; a change in quantity demanded is a movement from one point to another on a fixed demand curve.

**QUICK REVIEW
3.1**

Supply

Supply is a schedule or curve showing the various amounts of a product that producers are willing and able to make available for sale at each of a series of possible prices during a specific period, other things equal. The table in Figure 3.4 is a hypothetical **supply schedule** for a single supplier (producer) of gasoline. It shows the quantities of gasoline that are supplied at various prices, other things equal.

>> **LO3.3** Describe *supply* and explain how it can change.

FIGURE 3.4 **An individual supplier's supply of gasoline.**

Because price and quantity supplied are directly related, the supply curve for an individual supplier graphs as an upsloping curve. Other things equal, suppliers (producers) will offer more of a product for sale as its price rises and less of the product for sale as its price falls.

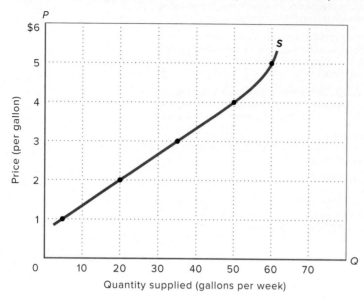

Supply of Gasoline	
Price per Gallon	Quantity (Amount) Supplied per Week
$5	60
4	50
3	35
2	20
1	5

Law of Supply

The table in Figure 3.4 shows that a positive or direct relationship prevails between price and quantity supplied. As price rises, the quantity supplied rises; as price falls, the quantity supplied falls. This relationship is called the **law of supply.** Other things equal, firms will produce and offer for sale more of their product at a high price than at a low price.

Price is an obstacle from the standpoint of the consumer, who is on the paying end. The higher the price, the less the consumer will buy. The supplier, though, is on the receiving end of the product's price. To a supplier, price represents *revenue,* which serves as an incentive to produce and sell a product. The higher the price, the greater this incentive and the greater the quantity supplied. This, again, is basically common sense.

Consider oil producers and refiners who are deciding how much gasoline to supply. As the price of gasoline rises, as shown in the table in Figure 3.4, they will find it profitable to increase production since the higher price will allow them to cover the higher costs associated with more rapid production, including having to drill deeper wells, having to hire additional workers, and having to pay for more shipping and distribution. The result is more gasoline as the price of gasoline rises.

Now consider manufacturers more generally. Beyond some quantity of production, manufacturers usually encounter increases in *marginal cost*—the added cost of producing one more unit of output. Certain productive resources—in particular, the firm's plant and machinery—cannot be expanded quickly, so the firm uses more of other resources, such as labor, to produce more output. But as labor becomes more abundant relative to the fixed plant and equipment, the additional workers have relatively less space and access to equipment. For example, the added workers may have to wait to gain access to machines. As a result, each added worker produces less added output, and the marginal cost of successive units of output rises accordingly. The firm will not produce the more costly units unless it receives a higher price for them. Again, price and quantity supplied are directly related; they increase together along a supply curve or schedule.

The Supply Curve

As with demand, it is convenient to represent individual supply graphically. In Figure 3.4, curve *S* is the **supply curve** that corresponds with the price-quantity data supplied in the accompanying table. The upward slope of the curve reflects the law of supply—producers offer more of a good, service, or resource for sale as its price rises.

supply A schedule or curve that shows the various amounts of a product that producers are willing and able to make available for sale at each of a series of possible *prices* during a specified period of time.

supply schedule A table of numbers showing the amounts of a *good* or *service* producers are willing and able to make available for sale at each of a series of possible *prices* during a specified period of time.

law of supply The principle that, other things equal, an increase in the *price* of a product will increase the quantity of it supplied, and conversely for a price decrease.

supply curve A curve that illustrates the *supply* for a product by showing how each possible *price* (on the *vertical axis*) is associated with a specific *quantity supplied* (on the *horizontal axis*).

FIGURE 3.5 Changes in the supply of gasoline.

A change in one or more of the determinants of supply causes a change in supply. An increase in supply is shown as a rightward shift of the supply curve, as from S_1 to S_2. A decrease in supply is depicted as a leftward shift of the curve, as from S_1 to S_3. In contrast, a change in the *quantity supplied* is caused by a change in the product's price and is shown by a movement from one point to another, as from *b* to *a* on fixed supply curve S_1.

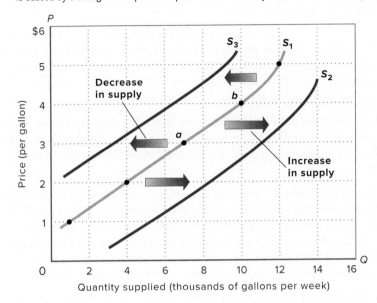

Market Supply of Gasoline, 200 Producers, (S_1)	
(1) Price per Gallon	(2) Total Quantity Supplied per Week
$5	12,000
4	10,000
3	7,000
2	4,000
1	1,000

Market Supply

To derive market supply from individual supply, we sum the quantities supplied by each producer at each price. That is, we "horizontally add" the supply curves of the individual producers. The price–quantity data supplied in the table accompanying Figure 3.5 are for an assumed 200 identical producers in the market, each willing to supply gasoline according to the supply schedule shown in Figure 3.4. Curve S_1 in Figure 3.5 is a graph of the market supply data. Note that the values of the axes in Figure 3.5 are the same as those used in our graph of market demand (Figure 3.3). The only difference is that we change the label on the horizontal axis from "quantity demanded" to "quantity supplied."

Determinants of Supply

In constructing a supply curve, we assume that price is the most significant influence on the quantity supplied of any product. But other factors can and do affect supply. The supply curve is drawn on the assumption that these other factors do not change. If one of them does change, a *change in supply* will occur, and the entire supply curve will shift.

The basic **determinants of supply** are (1) resource prices, (2) technology, (3) taxes and subsidies, (4) prices of other goods, (5) producer expectations, and (6) the number of sellers in the market. A change in any one or more of these determinants of supply, or *supply shifters,* will shift the supply curve for a product either right or left. A shift to the *right,* as from S_1 to S_2 in Figure 3.5, signifies an *increase* in supply: Producers supply larger quantities of the product at each possible price. A shift to the *left,* as from S_1 to S_3, indicates a *decrease* in supply: Producers offer less output at each price.

determinants of supply
Factors other than *price* that determine the quantities supplied of a *good* or *service.* Also referred to as "supply shifters" because changes in the determinants of supply will cause the *supply curve* to shift either right or left.

Changes in Supply

Let's consider how changes in each of the determinants affect supply. The key idea is that costs are a major factor underlying supply curves; anything that affects costs usually shifts the supply curve.

Resource Prices The prices of the resources used in the production process help determine a firm's costs of production. Higher *resource* prices raise production costs and, assuming a particular product price, squeeze profits. That reduction in profits reduces firms' incentive to supply output at each product price. For example, an increase in the price of sand, crushed rock, or Portland cement will increase the cost of producing concrete and reduce its supply.

In contrast, lower *resource* prices reduce production costs and increase profits. So when resource prices fall, firms supply greater output at each product price. For example, a decrease in the price of iron ore will decrease the price of steel.

Technology Improvements in technology (techniques of production) enable firms to produce units of output with fewer resources. Because resources are costly, using fewer of them lowers production costs and increases supply. Example: Technological advances in producing computer monitors have greatly reduced their cost. Thus, manufacturers now offer more monitors than previously at the various prices; the supply of monitors has increased.

Taxes and Subsidies Businesses treat most taxes as costs. An increase in sales or property taxes will increase production costs and reduce supply. In contrast, subsidies are "taxes in reverse." If the government subsidizes the production of a good, the subsidy in effect lowers the producers' costs and increases supply.

Prices of Other Goods Firms that produce a particular product, say soccer balls, can sometimes use their plant and equipment to produce alternative goods, say basketballs or volleyballs. If the prices of those other goods increase, soccer ball producers may switch production to those other goods in order to increase profits. This *substitution in production* would decrease the supply of soccer balls. Alternatively, when the prices of basketballs and volleyballs decline relative to the price of soccer balls, producers of those goods may decide to produce more soccer balls instead.

Producer Expectations Changes in expectations about the future price of a product may affect the producer's current willingness to supply that product. Farmers anticipating a higher wheat price in the future might withhold some of their current wheat harvest from the market, thereby causing a decrease in the current supply of wheat. In contrast, in many manufacturing industries, the expectation that selling prices will increase in a few months may induce firms to add another shift of workers or to expand their production facilities, causing current supply to increase.

Number of Sellers Other things equal, the larger the number of suppliers, the greater the market supply. As more firms enter an industry, the supply curve shifts to the right. Conversely, the smaller the number of firms in the industry, the less the market supply. As firms leave an industry, the supply curve shifts to the left. Example: Before Uber, Lyft, and other ride-sharing apps, cities restricted the number of taxi licenses, thereby restricting the number of drivers who could legally provide rides. When Uber and other ride-sharing services made their debut, millions of additional drivers and their cars became available worldwide, massively increasing the supply of rides.

Table 3.2 is a checklist of the determinants of supply, along with additional illustrations.

TABLE 3.2
Determinants of Supply: Factors That Shift the Supply Curve

Determinant	Examples
Change in resource prices	A decrease in the price of microchips increases the supply of computers; an increase in the price of crude oil reduces the supply of gasoline.
Change in technology	The development of lower-cost space-launch technology increases the supply of satellite broadband; improvements in artificial intelligence increase the supply of customer-service chatbots.
Changes in taxes or subsidies	An increase in the excise tax on cigarettes reduces the supply of cigarettes; a decline in subsidies to state universities reduces the supply of higher education; tax credits (subsidies) for child care increase the number of daycare centers; a tax on indoor tanning reduces the number of tanning salons.
Change in prices of other goods	An increase in the price of cucumbers decreases the supply of watermelons; an increase in the price of alcohol-based hand sanitizers causes a decrease in the supply of gin.
Change in producer expectations	An expectation of a substantial rise in future lumber prices decreases the supply of logs today; the belief that gasoline prices will fall next year increases the supply of oil this year.
Change in number of suppliers	An increase in the number of tattoo parlors increases the supply of tattoos; the formation of women's professional basketball leagues increases the supply of women's professional basketball games.

Changes in Quantity Supplied

The difference between a change in supply and a change in quantity supplied parallels the difference between a change in demand and a change in quantity demanded. Because supply is a schedule or curve, a **change in supply** means a change in the schedule and a shift of the curve. An increase in supply shifts the curve to the right; a decrease in supply shifts it to the left. The cause of a change in supply is a change in one or more of the determinants of supply.

In contrast, a **change in quantity supplied** is a movement from one point to another along a fixed supply curve. The cause of this movement is a change in the price of the specific product being considered.

Consider supply curve S_1 in Figure 3.5. A decline in the price of gasoline from \$4 to \$3 decreases the quantity of gasoline supplied per week from 10,000 to 7,000 gallons. This movement from point b to point a along S_1 is a change in quantity supplied, not a change in supply. Supply is the full schedule of prices and quantities shown, and this schedule does not change when the price of gasoline changes.

change in supply A movement of an entire *supply curve* (or of the numerical entries in a schedule) such that the *quantity supplied* changes at every particular *price;* caused by a change in one or more of the *determinants of supply*.

change in quantity supplied A change in the *quantity supplied* of a product along a fixed *supply curve* (or within a fixed *supply schedule*) as a result of a change in the product's *price*.

> ► A supply schedule or curve shows that, other things equal, the quantity of a good supplied varies directly with its price.
>
> ► The supply curve shifts because of changes in (a) resource prices, (b) technology, (c) taxes or subsidies, (d) prices of other goods, (e) expectations of future prices, and (f) the number of suppliers.
>
> ► A change in supply is a shift of the supply curve; a change in quantity supplied is a movement from one point to another along a fixed supply curve.

QUICK REVIEW
3.2

Market Equilibrium

With our understanding of demand and supply, we can now show how the decisions of buyers of gasoline and sellers of gasoline interact to determine the equilibrium price and quantity of gasoline. In the table in Figure 3.6, columns 1 and 2 repeat the market supply of gasoline (from the table in Figure 3.5), and columns 2 and 3 repeat the market demand for gasoline (from the table in Figure 3.3). We assume this is a competitive market so that neither buyers nor sellers can unilaterally influence the price.

>> **LO3.4** Explain how supply and demand interact to determine market equilibrium.

Equilibrium Price and Quantity

The **equilibrium price** (or *market-clearing price*) is the price where the intentions of buyers and sellers match. It is the price where quantity demanded equals quantity supplied. The table in Figure 3.6 reveals that at \$3, *and only at that price,* the number of gallons of gasoline that sellers wish to sell (7,000) is identical to the number of gallons of gasoline that consumers want to buy (also 7,000). At \$3 and 7,000 gallons of gasoline, there is neither a shortage nor a surplus of gasoline. So 7,000 gallons of gasoline is the **equilibrium quantity:** the quantity at which the intentions of buyers and sellers match, so that the quantity demanded equals quantity supplied.

Graphically, the equilibrium price is indicated by the intersection of the supply curve and the demand curve in **Figure 3.6 (Key Graph).** (The horizontal axis now measures both quantity demanded and quantity supplied.) With neither a shortage nor a surplus at \$3 per gallon, the market is *in equilibrium,* meaning "in balance" or "at rest."

Competition among buyers and among sellers drives the price to the equilibrium price; once there, it will remain there unless it is subsequently disturbed by changes in demand or supply (shifts of the curves).

To better understand the equilibrium price, let's consider other prices.

- **At any above-equilibrium price, quantity supplied exceeds quantity demanded.** For example, at \$4, sellers will offer 10,000 gallons of gasoline, but buyers will purchase only 4,000. The \$4 price encourages sellers to offer lots of gasoline, but discourages many consumers from buying it. The result is a **surplus** (or *excess supply*) of 6,000 gallons that will go unsold.
- **Surpluses drive prices down.** Even if the \$4 price existed temporarily, it could not persist. Competition among the sellers would prompt them to lower the price to encourage buyers to take the surplus off their hands. As the price fell, the incentive for suppliers to produce

equilibrium price The *price* in a competitive market at which the *quantity demanded* and the *quantity supplied* are equal, there is neither a shortage nor a surplus, and there is no tendency for price to rise or fall.

equilibrium quantity (1) The quantity at which the intentions of buyers and sellers in a particular market match at a particular *price* such that the *quantity demanded* and the *quantity supplied* are equal; (2) the profit-maximizing output of a *firm*.

surplus The amount by which the *quantity supplied* of a product exceeds the *quantity demanded* at a specific (above-equilibrium) *price*.

..ıl KEY GRAPH

FIGURE 3.6 Equilibrium price and quantity.

The intersection of the downsloping demand curve *D* and the upsloping supply curve *S* indicates the equilibrium price and quantity, here $3 and 7,000 gallons of gasoline. The shortages of gasoline at below-equilibrium prices (for example, 7,000 gallons at $2) push price up. The rising prices increase the quantity supplied and reduce the quantity demanded until equilibrium is achieved. The surpluses caused by above-equilibrium prices (for example, 6,000 gallons at $4) push price down. As price drops, the quantity demanded rises and the quantity supplied falls until equilibrium is established. At the equilibrium price and quantity, there are neither shortages nor surpluses of gasoline and, consequently, no pressure for prices to rise or fall.

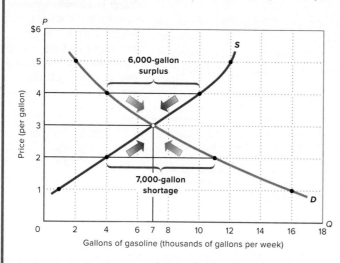

Market Supply of and Demand for Gasoline			
(1) Total Quantity Supplied per Week	(2) Price per Gallon	(3) Total Quantity Demanded per Week	(4) Surplus (+) or Shortage (−)*
12,000	$5	2,000	+10,000 ↓
10,000	4	4,000	+6,000 ↓
7,000	3	7,000	0
4,000	2	11,000	−7,000 ↑
1,000	1	16,000	−15,000 ↑

*Arrows indicate the effect on price.

QUICK QUIZ FOR FIGURE 3.6

1. **Demand curve *D* is downsloping because:**
   a. producers offer less of a product for sale as the price of the product falls.
   b. lower prices of a product create income and substitution effects that lead consumers to purchase more of it.
   c. the larger the number of buyers in a market, the lower the product price.
   d. price and quantity demanded are directly (positively) related.

2. **Supply curve *S*:**
   a. reflects an inverse (negative) relationship between price and quantity supplied.
   b. reflects a direct (positive) relationship between price and quantity supplied.

   c. depicts the collective behavior of buyers in this market.
   d. shows that producers will offer more of a product for sale at a low product price than at a high product price.

3. **At the $3 price:**
   a. quantity supplied exceeds quantity demanded.
   b. quantity demanded exceeds quantity supplied.
   c. the product is abundant and a surplus exists.
   d. there is no pressure on price to rise or fall.

4. **At price $5 in this market:**
   a. there will be a shortage of 10,000 units.
   b. there will be a surplus of 10,000 units.
   c. quantity demanded will be 12,000 units.
   d. quantity demanded will equal quantity supplied.

Answers: 1. b; 2. b; 3. d; 4. b.

gasoline would decline and consumers' incentive to buy gasoline would increase. As Figure 3.6 shows, the market will move to its equilibrium at $3.

- **At any below-equilibrium price, quantity demanded exceeds quantity supplied.** Consider a $2 price, for example. We see both from column 2 of the table and from the demand curve in Figure 3.6 that quantity demanded exceeds quantity supplied at that price. The result is a **shortage** (or *excess demand*) of 7,000 gallons of gasoline.

- **Shortages drive prices up.** The $2 price cannot persist because many consumers who want to buy gasoline at this price will not obtain it. They will express a willingness to pay more than $2 to get a gallon of gasoline and competition among these buyers will drive up the price, eventually to the $3 equilibrium level.

shortage The amount by which the *quantity demanded* of a product exceeds the *quantity supplied* at a particular (below-equilibrium) *price*.

Unless disrupted by changes in supply or demand, the $3 equilibrium price of gasoline will prevail indefinitely.

CONSIDER THIS . . .

Emergent Equilibria

Market equilibrium is a surprising phenomenon. Buyers' demand curves show a *negative* relationship between price and quantity, while sellers' supply curves show a *positive* relationship. Given that contradiction, you would never expect the interaction of demand and supply to lead to the perfectly synchronized outcome of quantity supplied exactly equaling quantity demanded.

But that is precisely what happens billions of times per day in markets all over the world. Market equilibrium and market rationing emerge spontaneously from the interactions of buyers and sellers who are simply pursuing their own interests and who are not in any way attempting to coordinate.

Lee Prince/Shutterstock

Adam Smith tried to explain this miraculous result as the work of an "invisible hand" that guided people's interactions toward a coordinated, socially beneficial outcome.

Nowadays, some economists classify market equilibrium as an "emergent property," or a behavior demonstrated by an entire system that is not found in any of its constituent parts. In the same way that a human brain as a whole is capable of consciousness but its individual neurons are not, so too markets synchronize the actions of individual buyers and sellers without any of them intending to harmonize their activities. Market equilibrium emerges, as if by magic, from a stew of uncoordinated individual intentions.

Rationing Function of Prices

The *rationing function of prices* refers to the ability of the forces of supply and demand to establish a price at which selling and buying decisions are consistent. In our example, the equilibrium price of $3 clears the market, leaving no burdensome surplus for sellers and no inconvenient shortage for buyers. And it is the combination of freely made individual decisions that sets this market-clearing price. In effect, the market outcome says that all buyers who are willing and able to pay $3 for a gallon of gasoline will obtain it; all buyers who cannot or will not pay $3 will go without gasoline. Similarly, all producers who are willing and able to offer gasoline for sale at $3 a gallon will sell it; all producers who cannot or will not sell for $3 per gallon will not sell their product.

Efficient Allocation

A competitive market not only rations goods to consumers but also allocates society's resources efficiently to the particular product. Competition among gasoline producers forces them to use the best technology and right mix of productive resources. If they didn't, their costs would be too high relative to the market price, and they would be unprofitable. The result is **productive efficiency:** the production of any particular good in the least costly way.

When society produces gasoline at the lowest achievable per-unit cost, it is expending the least-valued combination of resources to produce that product and therefore is making available more-valued resources to produce other desired goods. Suppose society has only $100 worth of resources available. If it can produce a gallon of gasoline for $3, then it will have $97 remaining to produce other goods. This situation is clearly better than producing the gasoline for $5 and having only $95 available for the alternative uses.

Competitive markets also produce **allocative efficiency:** the *particular mix* of goods and services most highly valued by society (minimum-cost production assumed). For example, society wants engineers with suitable backgrounds working on improving the gasoline supply and reducing its environmental impact, not helping to improve cupcake recipes. It wants diamonds to be used for jewelry, not crushed up and used as an additive to give concrete more sparkle. It wants streaming online music, not cassette players, compact discs, or phonographs. Moreover, society does not want to devote all its resources to gasoline, diamonds, and streaming music. It wants to assign resources to other uses, too, like medical research and professional sports leagues. Competitive markets make those assignments in an allocatively efficient manner.

productive efficiency The production of a *good* in the least costly way; occurs when production takes place at the output level at which per-unit production costs are minimized.

allocative efficiency The apportionment of resources among *firms* and industries to obtain the production of the products most wanted by society (consumers); the output of each product at which its *marginal cost* and *marginal benefit* are equal, and at which the sum of *consumer surplus* and *producer surplus* is maximized.

▶ In competitive markets, prices adjust to the equilibrium level at which quantity demanded equals quantity supplied.

▶ The equilibrium price and quantity are those indicated by the intersection of the supply and demand curves for any product or resource.

▶ The market equilibrium generates both productive efficiency (lowest cost production) as well as allocative efficiency (producing the right amount of the product relative to other products).

Changes in Supply, Demand, and Equilibrium

>> **LO3.5** Explain how changes in supply and demand affect equilibrium prices and quantities.

What effects do changes in supply and demand have on equilibrium price and quantity?

Changes in Demand

Suppose that the supply of some good (for example, health care) is constant and demand increases, as shown in Figure 3.7a. As a result, the new intersection of the supply and demand curves is at higher values on both the price and the quantity axes. Clearly, an increase in demand raises both equilibrium price and equilibrium quantity. Conversely, a decrease in demand such as that shown in Figure 3.7b reduces both equilibrium price and equilibrium quantity. (The value of

FIGURE 3.7 **Changes in demand and supply and the effects on price and quantity.**

The increase in demand from D_1 to D_2 in (a) increases both equilibrium price and equilibrium quantity. The decrease in demand from D_3 to D_4 in (b) decreases both equilibrium price and equilibrium quantity. The increase in supply from S_1 to S_2 in (c) decreases equilibrium price and increases equilibrium quantity. The decline in supply from S_3 to S_4 in (d) increases equilibrium price and decreases equilibrium quantity. The boxes in the top right corners summarize the respective changes and outcomes. The upward arrows in the boxes signify increases in equilibrium price (P) and equilibrium quantity (Q); the downward arrows signify decreases in these items.

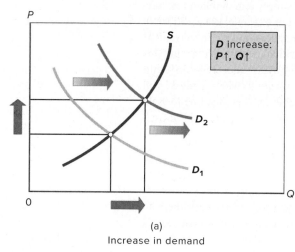

(a)
Increase in demand

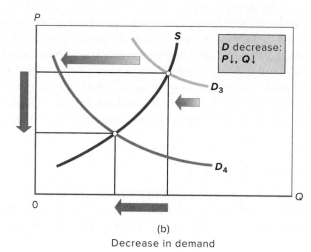

(b)
Decrease in demand

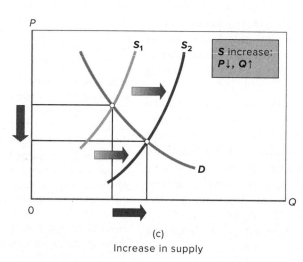

(c)
Increase in supply

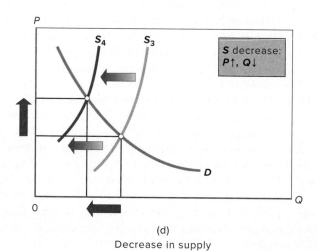

(d)
Decrease in supply

graphical analysis is now apparent: We need not fumble with columns of figures to determine the outcomes; we need only compare the new and the old points of intersection on the graph.)

Changes in Supply

What happens if the demand for some good (for example, automobiles) is constant but supply increases, as in Figure 3.7c? The new intersection of supply and demand is located at a lower equilibrium price but at a higher equilibrium quantity. An increase in supply reduces equilibrium price but increases equilibrium quantity. In contrast, if supply decreases, as in Figure 3.7d, equilibrium price rises while equilibrium quantity declines.

Complex Cases

When both supply and demand change, the final effect is a combination of the individual effects.

Supply Increase; Demand Decrease What effect will a supply increase and a demand decrease for some good (for example, apples) have on equilibrium price? Both changes decrease price, so the net result is a price drop greater than that resulting from either change alone.

What happens to equilibrium quantity? Here the effects of the changes in supply and demand are opposed: The increase in supply increases equilibrium quantity, but the decrease in demand reduces it. The direction of the change in equilibrium quantity depends on the relative sizes of the changes in supply and demand. If the increase in supply is larger than the decrease in demand, the equilibrium quantity will increase. But if the decrease in demand is greater than the increase in supply, the equilibrium quantity will decrease.

Supply Decrease; Demand Increase A decrease in supply and an increase in demand for some good (for example, gasoline) both increase price. Their combined effect is an increase in equilibrium price greater than that caused by either change separately. But their effect on the equilibrium quantity is indeterminate and depends on the relative sizes of the changes in supply and demand. If the decrease in supply is larger than the increase in demand, the equilibrium quantity will decrease. In contrast, if the increase in demand is greater than the decrease in supply, the equilibrium quantity will increase.

Supply Increase; Demand Increase What if supply and demand both increase for some good (for example, smartphones)? A supply increase drops equilibrium price, while a demand increase boosts it. If the increase in supply is greater than the increase in demand, the equilibrium price will fall. If the opposite holds, the equilibrium price will rise.

The effect on equilibrium quantity is certain: The increases in supply and demand both raise the equilibrium quantity. Therefore, the equilibrium quantity will increase by an amount greater than that caused by either change alone.

Supply Decrease; Demand Decrease What about decreases in both supply and demand for some good (for example, new homes)? If the decrease in supply is greater than the decrease in demand, equilibrium price will rise. If the reverse is true, equilibrium price will fall. Because the decreases in supply and demand each reduce equilibrium quantity, we can be sure that equilibrium quantity will fall.

Table 3.3 summarizes these four cases. To understand them fully, you should draw supply and demand diagrams for each case to confirm the effects listed in this table.

	Change in Supply	Change in Demand	Effect on Equilibrium Price	Effect on Equilibrium Quantity
1	Increase	Decrease	Decrease	Indeterminate
2	Decrease	Increase	Increase	Indeterminate
3	Increase	Increase	Indeterminate	Increase
4	Decrease	Decrease	Indeterminate	Decrease

TABLE 3.3
Effects of Changes in Both Supply and Demand

🌐 GLOBAL PERSPECTIVE 3.1

AVERAGE PRICE OF A LOAF OF WHITE BREAD, SELECTED NATIONS, 2020

The market equilibrium price of a 500 gram (1.1 pound) loaf of white bread differs substantially across countries, reflecting local differences in supply and demand, as well as government interventions like subsidies and price ceilings. Foreign prices were converted to U.S. dollars using current exchange rates.

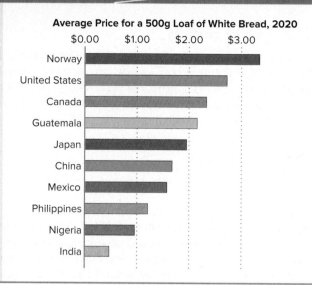

Average Price for a 500g Loaf of White Bread, 2020

Source: Numbeo, www.numbeo.com.

CONSIDER THIS . . .

Salsa and Coffee Beans

If you forget the other-things-equal assumption, you can encounter situations that *seem* to be in conflict with the laws of demand and supply. For example, suppose salsa manufacturers sell 1 million bottles of salsa at $4 a bottle in one year; 2 million bottles at $5 in the next year; and 3 million at $6 in the year thereafter. Price and quantity purchased vary directly, and these data seem to be at odds with the law of demand.

But there is no conflict here; the data do not refute the law of demand. The catch is that the law of demand's other-things-equal assumption has been violated over the three years in the example. Specifically, because of changing tastes and rising incomes, the demand for salsa has increased sharply, as in

Nancy R. Cohen/Photodisc/
Getty Images

Figure 3.7a. The result is higher prices *and* larger quantities purchased.

Another example: The price of coffee beans occasionally shoots upward at the same time that the quantity of coffee beans harvested declines. These events seemingly contradict the direct relationship between price and quantity denoted by supply. The catch again is that the other-things-equal assumption underlying the upsloping supply curve is violated. Poor coffee harvests decrease supply, as in Figure 3.7d, increasing the equilibrium price of coffee and reducing the equilibrium quantity.

The laws of demand and supply are not refuted by observations of price and quantity made over periods of time in which either demand or supply curves shift.

Special cases arise when a decrease in demand and a decrease in supply, or an increase in demand and an increase in supply, exactly cancel out. In both cases, the net effect on equilibrium price will be zero; price will not change.

Global Perspective 3.1 shows that the price of a standard loaf of white bread varies considerably from country to country, reflecting substantial differences in local demand and supply.

Application: Government-Set Prices

>>**LO3.6** Define government-set prices and explain how they can cause surpluses and shortages.

Prices in most markets are free to rise or fall to their equilibrium levels, no matter how high or low those levels might be. However, government sometimes concludes that supply and demand will produce prices that are unfairly high for buyers or unfairly low for sellers. So government may place legal limits on how high or low a price may go. Is that a good idea?

Price Ceilings on Gasoline

A **price ceiling** sets the maximum legal price a seller may charge for a product or service. A price at or below the ceiling is legal; a price above it is not. The rationale for establishing price ceilings (or *ceiling prices*) on specific products is that they purportedly enable consumers to obtain some "essential" good or service that they could not afford at the equilibrium price. Examples are rent controls and usury laws, which specify maximum "prices" for rent and interest rates, respectively.

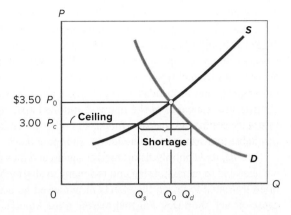

FIGURE 3.8
A price ceiling.

A price ceiling is a maximum legal price such as P_c. When the ceiling price is below the equilibrium price, a persistent product shortage results. Here that shortage is shown by the horizontal distance between Q_d and Q_s.

Graphical Analysis We can show the effects of price ceilings graphically. Suppose that rapidly rising world income boosts sales of automobiles and shifts the demand for gasoline to the right so that the market equilibrium price reaches $3.50 per gallon, shown as P_0 in Figure 3.8. The rapidly rising price of gasoline greatly burdens low- and moderate-income households, which pressure government to "do something." To keep gasoline prices down, the government imposes a ceiling price P_c of $3 per gallon. To affect the market, a price ceiling must be below the equilibrium price. A ceiling price of $4, for example, would have had no effect on the price of gasoline in the current situation.

What are the effects of this $3 ceiling price? The rationing ability of the free market is rendered ineffective. Because the ceiling price P_c is below the market-clearing price P_0, there is a lasting shortage of gasoline. The quantity of gasoline demanded at P_c is Q_d and the quantity supplied is only Q_s; a persistent shortage of amount $Q_d - Q_s$ occurs.

The price ceiling P_c prevents the usual market adjustment in which competition among buyers bids up price, inducing more production and rationing some buyers out of the market. That process would normally continue until the shortage disappeared at the equilibrium price and quantity, P_0 and Q_0.

By preventing these market adjustments from occurring, the price ceiling creates two related problems.

Rationing Problem How will the available supply Q_s be apportioned among buyers who want the greater amount Q_d? Should gasoline be distributed on a first-come, first-served basis—that is, to those willing and able to get in line the soonest or stay in line the longest? Or should gas stations decide how to distribute it? Because an unregulated shortage does not lead to an equitable distribution of gasoline, the government must establish some formal system for rationing it to consumers. One option is to issue ration coupons, which authorize bearers to purchase a fixed amount of gasoline per month. The rationing system might entail first the printing of coupons that permit the purchase of a certain amount of gasoline and then the equal distribution of the coupons so that every household receives the same number of coupons.

Black Markets Ration coupons will not prevent a second problem from arising. The demand curve in Figure 3.8 reveals that many buyers are willing to pay more than the ceiling price P_c. And, of course, it is more profitable for gas stations to sell at prices above the ceiling. Thus, despite the laws imposed by the price controls, *black markets* arise in which gasoline is illegally bought and sold at prices above the legal limits. Counterfeiting of ration coupons will also be a problem. And since the price of gasoline is now "set by the government," the government may face political pressure to set the price even lower.

Rent Controls

About 200 cities in the United States, including New York City, Boston, and San Francisco, have at one time or another enacted **rent controls:** maximum rents established by law (or, more recently, maximum rent increases for existing tenants). Such laws are intended to protect low-income families from escalating rents and to make housing more affordable to the poor.

What have been the actual economic effects? On the demand side, the below-equilibrium rents attract a larger number of renters. Some are locals seeking to move into their own apartments after

price ceiling A legally established maximum *price* for a *good*, or service. Normally set at a price below the *equilibrium price*.

rent control A law that sets a maximum price on the rents that a landlord can legally charge tenants for renting an apartment or a house.

sharing housing with friends or family. Others are outsiders attracted into the area by the artificially lower rents. But a large problem occurs on the supply side. Price controls make it less attractive for landlords to offer housing on the rental market. Many owners may decide to get out of the rental business altogether, opting either to sell their rental units or convert them to condominiums (which are generally exempt from rent-control laws). And for those owners who choose to continue renting out property, low rents make it unprofitable for them to repair or renovate their rental units. (Rent controls are one cause of the many abandoned apartment buildings found in larger cities.) Also, insurance companies, pension funds, and other potential new investors in housing will find it more profitable to invest in office buildings, shopping malls, or motels, where rents are not controlled.

In brief, rent controls distort market signals and thus resources are misallocated: Too few resources are allocated to rental housing and too many to alternative uses. Ironically, although rent controls are often legislated to lessen the effects of perceived housing shortages, controls in fact are a primary cause of such shortages. For that reason, most American cities that have ever had rent control laws have either abandoned them or are currently in the process of dismantling or weakening them.

Price Floors on Wheat

price floor A legally established minimum *price* for a *good*, or service. Normally set at a price above the *equilibrium price*.

A **price floor** is a minimum price fixed by the government. A price at or above the price floor is legal; a price below it is not. Price floors above equilibrium prices are usually invoked when society feels that the market system has not provided a sufficient income for certain groups of resource suppliers or producers. Supported prices for agricultural products and minimum wage laws are two examples of price (or wage) floors. Let's look at the former.

Suppose that many farmers have extremely low incomes when the price of wheat is at its equilibrium value of $2 per bushel. The government decides to help out by establishing a legal price floor (or *price support*) of $3 per bushel.

What will be the effects? At any price above the equilibrium price, quantity supplied will exceed quantity demanded—that is, there will be a persistent excess supply or surplus of the product. Farmers will be willing to produce and offer for sale more than private buyers are willing to purchase. Like a price ceiling, a price floor disrupts the rationing ability of the free market.

Graphical Analysis Figure 3.9 illustrates the effect of a price floor graphically. Suppose that S and D are the supply and demand curves for wheat. Equilibrium price and quantity are P_0 and Q_0, respectively. If the government imposes a price floor of P_f, farmers will produce Q_s but private buyers will purchase only Q_d. The surplus is the excess of Q_s over Q_d.

The government may cope with the surplus resulting from a price floor in two ways:

- It can restrict supply (for example, by instituting acreage allotments by which farmers agree to take a certain amount of land out of production) or increase demand (for example, by researching new uses for the product involved). These actions may reduce the difference between the equilibrium price and the price floor and thereby reduce the size of the surplus.

- If these efforts are not successful, then the government must purchase the surplus output at the $3 price (thereby subsidizing farmers) and store or otherwise dispose of it.

FIGURE 3.9
A price floor.

A price floor is a minimum legal price such as P_f. When the price floor is above the equilibrium price, a persistent product surplus results. Here that surplus is shown by the horizontal distance between Q_s and Q_d.

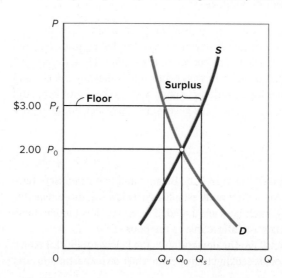

Additional Consequences Price floors such as P_f in Figure 3.9 not only disrupt prices' rationing ability but also distort resource allocation. Without the price floor, the $2 equilibrium price of wheat would cause financial losses and force high-cost wheat producers to plant other crops or abandon farming altogether. But the $3 price floor allows them to continue to grow wheat and remain farmers. So society devotes too many of its scarce resources to wheat production and too few to producing other, more valuable, goods and services. It fails to achieve allocative efficiency.

That's not all. Consumers of wheat-based products pay higher prices because

Pandemic Prices

Dramatic Shifts in Supply and Demand Explain Much of the Economics of the COVID-19 Pandemic, Including Shortages of Consumer Goods and Vacillating Prices for Housing and Used Cars.

The COVID-19 pandemic that began in late 2019 became gravely serious in March 2020, when local and national governments began strict lockdowns that kept the large majority of workers and consumers at home except for occasional trips out for grocery shopping or crucial medical appointments. The strictest of the lockdowns ended in the United States within a few weeks, but the economic dislocations continued well into 2023 (when this edition went to print).

The most obvious economic effect of the pandemic, initially, was the empty store shelves caused by panic buying. Uncertain about how long the lockdowns might last, nervous consumers rushed to stores to stock up on items like toilet paper, hand sanitizer, and canned food that they feared would soon be in short supply. That massive increase in demand generated a self-fulfilling prophecy as stores could not restock quickly enough to keep up with the panic buying. Store managers were also reluctant to raise prices as demand increased, lest they be accused of price gouging. Thus, retail prices remained largely fixed (similar to a government-imposed price ceiling) as demand shifted massively rightward, with the result being huge shortages as quantity demanded far exceeded quantity supplied at the traditional, unchanged prices.

The supply and demand model also explains the brief crash in the stock market that was observed in the spring of 2020. Stocks are ownership shares in companies, and stocks derive their value from investors' expectations about how profitable companies will be in the future. When it became obvious that the pandemic would be severe, expectations about future profits fell, since it was assumed that the lockdowns and other anti-pandemic efforts would greatly hinder economic activity. As a result, the demand for stocks decreased precipitously, causing the equilibrium price of stocks to decline by nearly one-third. Fortunately, when it subsequently became clear that the pandemic would not be as awful as was initially feared, the demand for stocks rebounded and so did stock prices.

With both international and domestic travel heavily restricted around the world, hotel chains, rental car companies, and even individuals renting apartments on Airbnb experienced a dramatic decrease in the demand for their services. Things got so bad for rental car companies like Hertz and Avis that they began selling off their rental car fleets to try to generate enough cash to survive until the demand for rental cars rebounded. But when it did rebound, about a year later, the rental car companies were again caught by surprise, with their much reduced fleets being unable to keep up with renewed demand as consumers and businesspeople began traveling again in large numbers. The result of robust demand meeting limited supply was much higher rental car prices.

The decision of rental car companies to sell off their fleets in 2020 drove the price of used cars down nearly 20 percent that spring

F Armstrong Photography/Shutterstock

as the supply of used cars massively increased. But over the next 18 months, the price of used cars (as measured by the Manheim Index) nearly doubled because supply-chain disruptions caused a worldwide shortage of computer chips that in turn led to major carmakers like Honda and Ford being forced to dramatically decrease the production of new cars. Since new cars compete with used cars among car buyers, the reduced supply of new cars ended up increasing the demand for used cars, thereby causing their prices to soar. The reduced supply of new cars also drove up the price of new cars, but not nearly as dramatically since carmakers put pressure on new car dealers to resist price increases in order to avoid being accused of price gouging.

Working from home using Zoom and other digital tools became much more common during the pandemic, as many businesses sent workers home for the initial lockdowns and then kept them working remotely over the next two years as various virus mutations came and went. This newfound ability to work from home caused millions of formerly city-dwelling workers to temporarily and then in many cases permanently move to new locations, many of them suburban or rural. Their relocation increased the demand for housing in suburban and rural areas at the same time as their departure put downward pressure on housing prices in crowded urban areas.

The pandemic also witnessed widespread labor shortages due to unprecedentedly generous government unemployment benefits that delivered to tens of millions of workers a higher income than they would have earned if they had returned to work. Many of those workers chose to stay unemployed (so as to collect the high unemployment benefits) even when jobs were available. That decrease in labor supply drove up the equilibrium wage. But not all firms could afford to pay the higher equilibrium wage. The result was widespread labor shortages in industries such as transportation, hospitality, and child care services.

of the price floor. Taxpayers pay higher taxes to finance the government's purchase of the surplus. And the price floor may cause environmental damage by encouraging wheat farmers to bring hilly, erosion-prone "marginal land" into production.

　　With all price ceilings and price floors, good intentions lead to bad economic outcomes. Government-controlled prices cause shortages or surpluses, distort resource allocation, and produce negative side effects.

QUICK REVIEW

3.4

▶ An increase in demand increases equilibrium price and quantity; a decrease in demand decreases equilibrium price and quantity.

▶ An increase in supply reduces equilibrium price but increases equilibrium quantity; a decrease in supply increases equilibrium price but reduces equilibrium quantity.

▶ Over time, equilibrium price and quantity may change in directions that seem at odds with the laws of demand and supply because the other-things-equal assumption is violated.

▶ Government-controlled prices in the form of ceilings and floors stifle the rationing function of prices, distort resource allocations, and cause negative side effects.

Summary

LO3.1 Characterize and give examples of markets.

Markets bring buyers and sellers together. Some markets are local, others international. Some have physical locations, while others are online. In highly competitive markets, large numbers of buyers and sellers come together to buy and sell standardized products. All such markets involve demand, supply, price, and quantity, with price being "discovered" through the interacting decisions of buyers and sellers.

LO3.2 Describe *demand* and explain how it can change.

Demand is a schedule or curve representing buyers' willingness and ability to purchase a particular product at each of various prices in a specific period. The law of demand states that consumers will buy more of a product at a low price than at a high price. So, other things equal, the relationship between price and quantity demanded is negative or inverse; it graphs as a downward sloping curve.

　　Market demand curves are found by adding horizontally the demand curves of the many individual consumers in the market.

　　A change in demand is different from a change in quantity demanded.

　　A *change in demand* occurs when there is a change in one or more of the determinants of demand: consumer tastes; the number of buyers in the market; the money incomes of consumers; the prices of related goods; and consumer expectations. A change in demand will shift the market demand curve either right or left. A shift to the right is an increase in demand; a shift to the left is a decrease in demand.

　　A *change in quantity demanded* is a movement from one point to another point on a fixed demand curve caused by a change in a product's price, holding all other factors constant.

LO3.3 Describe *supply* and explain how it can change.

Supply is a schedule or curve showing the amounts of a product that producers are willing to offer in the market at each possible price during a specific period of time. The law of supply states that, other things equal, producers will offer more of a product at a high price than at a low price. Thus, the relationship between price and quantity supplied is positive or direct; it graphs as an upward sloping curve.

　　The market supply curve is the horizontal summation of the supply curves of the individual producers of the product.

　　A *change in supply* occurs when there is a change in one or more of the determinants of supply (resource prices, production techniques, taxes or subsidies, the prices of other goods, producer expectations, or the number of sellers in the market). A change in supply shifts a product's supply curve. A shift to the right is an increase in supply; a shift to the left is a decrease in supply.

　　In contrast, a change in the price of the product being considered causes a *change in the quantity supplied*, which is shown as a movement from one point to another point along a fixed supply curve.

LO3.4 Explain how supply and demand interact to determine market equilibrium.

The equilibrium price and quantity are established at the intersection of the supply and demand curves. The interaction of market demand and market supply adjusts the price to the point at which the quantities demanded and supplied are equal. This is the equilibrium price. The corresponding quantity is the equilibrium quantity.

　　The ability of market forces to synchronize selling and buying decisions to eliminate potential surpluses and shortages is known as the rationing function of prices. The equilibrium quantity in competitive markets reflects both productive efficiency (least-cost production) and allocative efficiency (producing the right amount of the product relative to other products).

LO3.5 Explain how changes in supply and demand affect equilibrium prices and quantities.

A change in either demand or supply changes the equilibrium price and quantity. Increases in demand raise both equilibrium price and equilibrium quantity; decreases in demand lower both equilibrium price and equilibrium quantity. Increases in supply lower equilibrium price and raise equilibrium quantity. Decreases in supply raise equilibrium price and lower equilibrium quantity.

　　Simultaneous changes in demand and supply affect equilibrium price and quantity in various ways, depending on their direction and relative magnitudes (see Table 3.3).

LO3.6 Define government-set prices and explain how they can cause surpluses and shortages.

A price ceiling is a maximum price set by government and is designed to help consumers. Effective price ceilings produce persistent product shortages, and if an equitable distribution of the product is sought, government must ration the product to consumers.

A price floor is a minimum price set by government and is designed to aid producers. Effective price floors lead to persistent product surpluses; the government must either purchase the product or eliminate the surplus by imposing restrictions on production or increasing private demand.

Legally fixed prices stifle the rationing function of prices and distort the allocation of resources.

Terms and Concepts

demand

demand schedule

law of demand

diminishing marginal utility

income effect

substitution effect

demand curve

determinants of demand

normal good

inferior good

substitute goods

complementary goods

change in demand

change in quantity demanded

supply

supply schedule

law of supply

supply curve

determinants of supply

change in supply

change in quantity supplied

equilibrium price

equilibrium quantity

surplus

shortage

productive efficiency

allocative efficiency

price ceiling

rent control

price floor

Discussion Questions

1. Explain the law of demand. Why does a demand curve slope downward? How is a market demand curve derived from individual demand curves? **LO3.2**
2. What are the determinants of demand? What happens to the demand curve when any of these determinants change? Distinguish between a change in demand and a movement along a fixed demand curve, noting the cause(s) of each. **LO3.2**
3. Suppose that Rhonda has a TikTok account. If all of her TikTok friends switch to Snapchat, in which direction will Rhonda's demand for TikTok shift? What will likely happen to Rhonda's demand for Snapchat? **LO3.2**
4. Explain the law of supply. Why does the supply curve slope upward? How is the market supply curve derived from the supply curves of individual producers? **LO3.3**
5. What are the determinants of supply? What happens to the supply curve when any of these determinants change? Distinguish between a change in supply and a change in the quantity supplied, noting the cause(s) of each. **LO3.3**

6. Between 2018 and 2021, an outbreak of African Swine Fever that spread to dozens of countries led to the slaughter of nearly one-quarter of all of the world's domesticated pigs. What impact would you expect that to have had on the supply of pig leather as well as on other pork byproducts such as drumheads, violin strings, and pig-bristle paint brushes? Explain. **LO3.5**
7. For each stock in the stock market, the number of shares sold daily equals the number of shares purchased. That is, the quantity of each firm's shares demanded equals the quantity supplied. Why, then, do the prices of stock shares change? **LO3.5**
8. What do economists mean when they say "Price floors and ceilings stifle the rationing function of prices and distort resource allocation"? **LO3.6**
9. **LAST WORD** What caused used car prices to fall near the start of the pandemic and then soar over the next two years? What government policy helped to generate labor shortages in several industries? Expectations about what in particular caused the stock market to crash near the start of the pandemic?

Review Questions

1. What effect will each of the following have on the demand for small cars such as the Mini Cooper and Fiat 500? **LO3.2**
   a. Small cars become more fashionable.
   b. The price of large cars rises (with the price of small cars remaining the same).
   c. Income declines and small cars are an inferior good.
   d. Consumers anticipate that the price of small cars will decrease substantially in the near future.
   e. The price of gasoline substantially drops.

2. True or False: A "change in quantity demanded" is a shift of the entire demand curve to the right or to the left. **LO3.2**
3. Yogi Berra was once asked about a popular New York restaurant. He said, "Nobody ever goes there anymore—it's too crowded." All joking aside, he was referring to: **LO3.2**
   a. a shortage.
   b. a network effect.
   c. a surplus.
   d. a congestion effect.

4. What effect will each of the following have on the supply of auto tires? **LO3.3**
   a. A technological advance in the methods of producing tires
   b. A decline in the number of firms in the tire industry
   c. An increase in the price of rubber used in the production of tires
   d. The expectation that the equilibrium price of auto tires will be lower in the future than it is now
   e. A decline in the price of the large tires used for semi trucks and earth-hauling rigs (with no change in the price of auto tires)
   f. The levying of a per-unit tax on each auto tire sold
   g. The granting of a 50-cent-per-unit subsidy for each auto tire produced

5. "In the corn market, demand often exceeds supply, and supply sometimes exceeds demand." "The price of corn rises and falls in response to changes in supply and demand." In which of these two statements are the terms "supply" and "demand" used correctly? Explain. **LO3.4**

6. Suppose that in the market for computer memory chips, the equilibrium price is $50 per chip. If the current price is $55 per chip, then there will be a(an) _____ of memory chips. **LO3.4**
   a. shortage
   b. surplus
   c. equilibrium quantity
   d. none of the above

7. Critically evaluate: "In comparing the two equilibrium positions in Figure 3.7b, I note that a smaller amount is actually demanded at a lower price. This observation refutes the law of demand." **LO3.5**

8. Label each of the following scenarios with the set of symbols that best indicates the price change and quantity change that occur in each scenario. In some scenarios, it may not be possible from the information given to determine the direction of a particular price change or a particular quantity change. We will symbolize those cases as, respectively, "P?" and "Q?" The four possible combinations of price and quantity changes are: **LO3.5**
   P↓Q?   P?Q↓
   P↑Q?   P?Q↑

   a. On a hot day, both the demand for lemonade and the supply of lemonade increase.
   b. On a cold day, both the demand for ice cream and the supply of ice cream decrease.
   c. When Hawaii's Mt. Kilauea erupts violently, tourists' demand for sightseeing flights increases, but the supply of pilots willing to provide these dangerous flights decreases.
   d. In a hot area of Arizona where a lot of electricity is generated with wind turbines, the demand for electricity falls on windy days as people switch off their air conditioners and enjoy the breeze. But at the same time, the amount of electricity supplied increases as the wind turbines spin faster.

9. Suppose the total demand for wheat and the total supply of wheat per month in the Kansas City grain market are as shown in the following table. Suppose that the government establishes a price ceiling of $3.70 for wheat. What might prompt the government to establish this price ceiling? Explain carefully the main effects. Demonstrate your answer graphically. Next, suppose that the government establishes a price floor of $4.60 for wheat. What will be the main effects of this price floor? Demonstrate your answer graphically. **LO3.6**

Thousands of Bushels Demanded	Price per Bushel	Thousands of Bushels Supplied
85	$3.40	72
80	3.70	73
75	4.00	75
70	4.30	77
65	4.60	79
60	4.90	81

10. A price ceiling will result in a shortage only if the ceiling price is _____ the equilibrium price. **LO3.6**
    a. less than
    b. equal to
    c. greater than

Problems

1. Suppose there are three buyers of candy in a market: Tex, Dex, and Rex. The market demand and the individual demands of Tex, Dex, and Rex are shown in the following table. **LO3.2**
   a. Fill in the missing values.
   b. Which buyer demands the least at a price of $5? The most at a price of $7?
   c. Which buyer's quantity demanded increases the most when the price decreases from $7 to $6?
   d. In which direction would the market demand curve shift if Tex withdrew from the market? What would happen to the market demand curve if Dex doubled his purchases at each possible price?
   e. Suppose that at a price of $6, the total quantity demanded increases from 19 to 38. Is this a "change in the quantity demanded" or a "change in demand"? Explain.

Price per Candy	Tex		Dex		Rex		Total Quantity Demanded
$8	3	+	1	+	0	=	___
7	8	+	2	+	___	=	12
6	___	+	3	+	4	=	19
5	17	+	___	+	6	=	27
4	23	+	5	+	8	=	___

2. The figure below shows the supply curve for tennis balls, S_1, for Drop Volley Tennis, a producer of tennis equipment. Use the figure and the table below to give your answers to the following questions. **LO3.3**

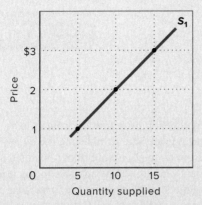

a. Use the figure to fill in the quantity supplied on supply curve S_1 for each price in the following table.

Price	S_1 Quantity Supplied	S_2 Quantity Supplied	Change in Quantity Supplied
$3	_____	4	_____
2	_____	2	_____
1	_____	0	_____

b. If production costs were to increase, the quantities supplied at each price would be as shown by the third column of the table ("S_2 Quantity Supplied"). Use those data to draw supply curve S_2 on the same graph as supply curve S_1.

c. In the fourth column of the table, enter the amount by which the quantity supplied at each price changes due to the increase in product costs. (Use positive numbers for increases and negative numbers for decreases.)

d. Did the increase in production costs cause a "decrease in supply" or a "decrease in quantity supplied"? Explain.

3. Refer to the following expanded table from review question 9. **LO3.4**

a. What is the equilibrium price? At what price is there neither a shortage nor a surplus? Fill in the surplus-shortage column and use it to confirm your answers.

b. Graph the demand for wheat and the supply of wheat. Be sure to label the axes of your graph correctly. Label equilibrium price P and equilibrium quantity Q.

c. How big is the surplus or shortage at $3.40? At $4.90? How big a surplus or shortage results if the price is 60 cents higher than the equilibrium price? 30 cents lower than the equilibrium price?

Thousands of Bushels Demanded	Price per Bushel	Thousands of Bushels Supplied	Surplus (+) or Shortage (−)
85	$3.40	72	_____
80	3.70	73	_____
75	4.00	75	_____
70	4.30	77	_____
65	4.60	79	_____
60	4.90	81	_____

4. How will each of the following changes in demand and/or supply affect equilibrium price and equilibrium quantity in a competitive market? That is, do price and quantity rise, fall, or remain unchanged, or are the answers indeterminate because they depend on the magnitudes of the shifts? **LO3.5**

a. Supply decreases and demand is constant.
b. Demand decreases and supply is constant.
c. Supply increases and demand is constant.
d. Demand increases and supply increases.
e. Demand increases and supply is constant.
f. Supply increases and demand decreases.
g. Demand increases and supply decreases.
h. Demand decreases and supply decreases.

5. Use two market diagrams to explain how an increase in state subsidies to public colleges might affect tuition and enrollments in both public and private colleges. **LO3.5**

6. **ADVANCED ANALYSIS** Assume that demand for a commodity is represented by the equation $P = 10 - .2Q_d$ and supply by the equation $P = 2 + .2Q_s$, where Q_d and Q_s are quantity demanded and quantity supplied, respectively, and P is price. Using the equilibrium condition $Q_s = Q_d$, solve the equations to determine equilibrium price and equilibrium quantity. **LO3.5**

7. Suppose that the demand and supply schedules for rental apartments in the city of Gotham are as given in the following table. **LO3.6**

Monthly Rent	Apartments Demanded	Apartments Supplied
$2,500	10,000	15,000
2,000	12,500	12,500
1,500	15,000	10,000
1,000	17,500	7,500
500	20,000	5,000

a. What is the market equilibrium rental price per month and the market equilibrium number of apartments demanded and supplied?

b. If the local government can enforce a rent-control law that sets the maximum monthly rent at $1,500, will there be a surplus or a shortage? Of how many units? How many units will actually be rented each month?

c. Suppose that a new government is elected that wants to keep out the poor. It declares that the minimum rent that landlords can charge is $2,500 per month. If the government can enforce that price floor, will there be a surplus or a shortage? Of how many units? And how many units will actually be rented each month?

d. Suppose that the government wishes to decrease the market equilibrium monthly rent by increasing the supply of housing. Assuming that demand remains unchanged, how many additional units of housing would the government need to supply to get the market equilibrium rental price to fall to $1,500 per month? To $1,000 per month? To $500 per month?

Additional Examples of Supply and Demand

LO3.7 Use supply-and-demand analysis to analyze specific real-world situations.

Supply-and-demand analysis is a powerful tool for understanding equilibrium prices and quantities. The information provided in this chapter is fully sufficient for moving forward in the book, but you may find that additional examples of supply and demand are helpful. This appendix provides several concrete illustrations of changes in supply and demand.

Changes in Supply and Demand

As Figure 3.7 demonstrates, changes in supply and demand cause changes in equilibrium price, quantity, or both. The following applications illustrate this fact in several real-world markets. The simplest situations are those in which either supply changes while demand remains constant or demand changes while supply remains constant. Let's consider a simple case first, before looking at more complex applications.

Lettuce

Every now and then, extreme weather severely reduces the size of some crop. Suppose, for example, that a severe freeze destroys a sizable portion of the lettuce crop. This unfortunate situation implies a significant decline in supply, which we represent as a leftward shift of the supply curve from S_1 to S_2 in Figure 1. At each price, consumers desire as much lettuce as before, so the freeze does not affect the demand for lettuce. That is, demand curve D_1 does not shift.

What are the consequences of the reduced supply of lettuce? As Figure 1 shows, the leftward shift of the supply curve disrupts the previous equilibrium in the lettuce market and

drives the equilibrium price upward from P_1 to P_2. Consumers respond to that price hike by reducing the quantity of lettuce demanded from Q_1 to Q_2. Equilibrium is restored at P_2 and Q_2.

Consumers who are willing and able to pay price P_2 obtain lettuce; consumers unwilling or unable to pay that price do not. Some consumers continue to buy as much lettuce as before, even at the higher price. Others buy some lettuce but not as much as before, and still others opt out of the market completely.

The latter two groups use the money they would have spent on lettuce to obtain other products—carrots, for example. (Because of our other-things-equal assumption, the prices of other products have not changed.)

Pink Salmon

Now let's see what happens when both supply and demand change at the same time. Several decades ago, people who caught salmon earned as much as $1 for each pound of pink salmon—the type of salmon most commonly used for canning. In Figure 2 that price is represented as P_1, at the intersection of supply curve S_1 and demand curve D_1. The corresponding quantity of pink salmon is shown as Q_1 pounds.

As time passed, supply and demand changed in the market for pink salmon. On the supply side, improved technology in the form of larger, more efficient fishing boats greatly increased the catch and lowered the cost of obtaining it. Also, high profits at price P_1 encouraged many new fishers to enter the industry. As a result of these changes, the supply of pink salmon greatly increased and the supply curve shifted to the right, as from S_1 to S_2 in Figure 2.

FIGURE 1 **The market for lettuce.**
The decrease in the supply of lettuce, shown here by the shift from S_1 to S_2, increases the equilibrium price of lettuce from P_1 to P_2 and reduces the equilibrium quantity from Q_1 to Q_2.

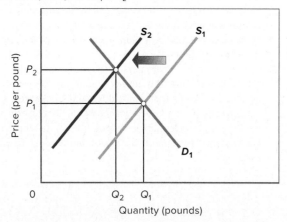

FIGURE 2 **The market for pink salmon.**
In the last several decades, the supply of pink salmon has increased and the demand for pink salmon has decreased. As a result, the price of pink salmon has declined, as from P_1 to P_2. Because supply has increased by more than demand has decreased, the equilibrium quantity of pink salmon has increased, as from Q_1 to Q_2.

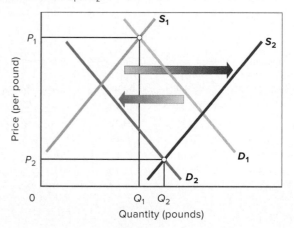

Over the same years, the demand for pink salmon declined, as represented by the leftward shift from D_1 to D_2 in Figure 2. That decrease was caused by increases in consumer income and reductions in the price of substitute products. As buyers' incomes rose, consumers shifted demand away from canned fish and toward higher-quality fresh or frozen fish, including more-valued chinook, sockeye, and coho salmon. Moreover, the emergence of fish farming, in which salmon are raised in ocean net pens, lowered the prices of these other species, thus reducing the demand for pink salmon.

The altered supply and demand reduced the price of pink salmon to as low as $0.10 per pound, as represented by the drop in price from P_1 to P_2 in Figure 2. Both the supply increase and the demand decrease helped reduce the equilibrium price. However, in this particular case, the equilibrium quantity of pink salmon increased, as represented by the move from Q_1 to Q_2. Both shifts reduced the equilibrium price, but equilibrium quantity increased because the increase in supply exceeded the decrease in demand.

Gasoline

The price of gasoline in the United States has increased rapidly several times during the past several years. For example, the average price of a gallon of gasoline rose from around $1.88 in April 2020 during the lowest point of the COVID-19 recession to $3.22 in July 2021. What caused this 71 percent increase in the price of gasoline? How would we graph this increase?

We begin in Figure 3 with the price of a gallon of gasoline at P_1, representing the $1.88 price. Simultaneous supply and demand factors disturbed this equilibrium. Supply uncertainties

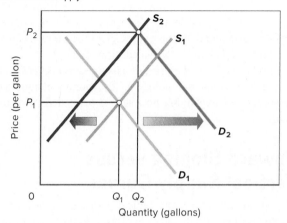

FIGURE 3 **The market for gasoline.**
An increase in the demand for gasoline, as shown by the shift from D_1 to D_2, coupled with a decrease in supply, as shown by the shift from S_1 to S_2, boosts equilibrium price (here from P_1 to P_2). In this case, equilibrium quantity increases from Q_1 to Q_2 because the increase in demand outweighs the decrease in supply.

relating to Middle East politics and expanded demand for oil by fast-growing countries such as China pushed up the price of oil from just under $17 per barrel in April 2020 to a bit over $73 per barrel in July 2021. Oil is the main input for producing gasoline, so any sustained rise in its price boosts the per-unit cost of producing gasoline. Such increases in cost decrease the supply of gasoline, as represented by the leftward shift of the supply curve from S_1 to S_2 in Figure 3.

While the supply of gasoline declined between April 2020 and July 2021, the demand for gasoline increased, as depicted by the rightward shift of the demand curve from D_1 to D_2.

CONSIDER THIS . . .

Uber and Dynamic Pricing

The ride-sharing service known as Uber rose to prominence in 2013 by offering consumers an alternative to government-regulated taxi companies. Uber works via the Internet, matching people who need a ride with people who are willing to use their own vehicles to provide rides. Both parties can find each other easily and instantly via a smartphone app and Uber makes its money by taking a percentage of the fare.

Uber is innovative in many ways, including empowering anybody to become a paid driver, breaking up local taxi monopolies, and making it effortless to arrange a quick pickup. But Uber's most interesting feature is dynamic pricing, under which Uber sets equilibrium prices in real time, constantly adjusting fares so as to equalize quantity demanded and quality supplied. The result is extremely short waiting times for both riders and drivers as

Uber Manila Tips

Uber will, for instance, set a substantially higher "surge price" in a given location if demand suddenly increases due to, say, a bunch of people leaving a concert all at once and wanting rides. The higher fare encourages more Uber drivers to converge on the area, thereby minimizing waiting times for both drivers and passengers.

The short wait times created by Uber's use of dynamic pricing stand in sharp contrast to taxi fares, which are fixed by law and therefore unable to adjust to ongoing changes in supply and demand. On days when demand is high relative to supply, taxi shortages arise. On days when demand is low relative to supply, drivers sit idle for long stretches of time. All of that inefficiency and inconvenience is eliminated by Uber's use of market equilibrium prices to equalize the quantity demanded of rides with the quantity supplied of rides.

Incomes in general were rising over this period because the U.S. economy was expanding out of the COVID-19 recession. Rising incomes increase the demand for all normal goods, including gasoline.

The combined decline in gasoline supply and increase in gasoline demand boosted the price of gasoline from $1.88 to $3.22, as represented by the rise from P_1 to P_2 in Figure 3. Because the demand increase outweighed the supply decrease, the equilibrium quantity expanded, from Q_1 to Q_2.

In other periods, the price of gasoline has *declined* as the demand for gasoline has increased. Test your understanding of the analysis by explaining how such a price decrease could occur.

Upward Sloping versus Vertical Supply Curves

As you already know, the typical good or service has an upward sloping supply curve because a higher market price causes producers to increase the quantity supplied. There are, however, some goods and services whose quantities supplied are fixed and totally unresponsive to changes in price. Examples include the amount of land in a given area, the number of seats in a stadium, and the limited part of the electromagnetic spectrum that is reserved for cellular telephone transmissions. These goods and services have vertical supply curves because the same fixed amount is available no matter what price is offered to suppliers.

Reactions to Demand Shifts

Markets react very differently to a shift in demand depending upon whether they have upward sloping or vertical supply curves.

Upward Sloping Supply Curves When a market has an upward sloping supply curve, any shift in demand will cause both the equilibrium price *and* the equilibrium quantity to adjust. As we saw in Figure 3.7(a), price and quantity both change.

Vertical Supply Curves When a market has a vertical supply curve, any shift in demand will cause only the equilibrium price to change; the equilibrium quantity remains the same because the quantity supplied is fixed and cannot adjust.

Consider Figure 4, in which the supply of land in San Francisco is fixed at quantity Q_0. If demand increases from D_1 to D_2, the movement from the initial equilibrium at point *a* to the final equilibrium at point *b* is accomplished solely by a rise in the equilibrium price from P_1 to P_2. Because the quantity of land is fixed, the increase in demand cannot cause any change in the equilibrium quantity supplied. The entire adjustment from the initial equilibrium to the final equilibrium has to come in the form of a higher equilibrium price.

This fact explains why real estate prices are so high in San Francisco and other major cities. With the quantity of land in fixed supply, any increase in the demand for land leads to an increase in the price of land.

FIGURE 4 The market for land in San Francisco.

Because the quantity of land in San Francisco is fixed at Q_0, the supply curve is vertical above Q_0 in order to indicate that the same quantity of land will be supplied no matter what the price is. As demand increases from D_1 to D_2, the equilibrium price rises from P_1 to P_2. Because the quantity of land is fixed at Q_0, the movement from equilibrium *a* to equilibrium *b* involves only a change in the equilibrium price; the equilibrium quantity remains at Q_0 due to land being in fixed supply.

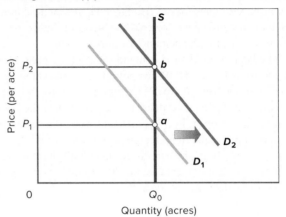

Preset Prices

In this chapter, we saw that an effective government-imposed price ceiling (legal maximum price) causes quantity demanded to exceed quantity supplied—a shortage. By contrast, an effective government-imposed price floor (legal minimum price) causes quantity supplied to exceed quantity demanded—a surplus.

We now want to establish that shortages and surpluses can occur in markets other than those in which government imposes price floors and ceilings. Such market imbalances happen when sellers set prices in advance of sales and those prices turn out to be below or above equilibrium prices. Consider the following two examples.

Olympic Figure Skating Finals

Tickets for the women's figure skating championship at the Olympics are among the world's "hottest tickets." The popularity of this event and the high incomes of buyers translate into tremendous ticket demand. The Olympic officials set the price for the tickets in advance. Invariably, the price, although high, is considerably below the equilibrium price that would equate quantity demanded and quantity supplied. A severe shortage of tickets therefore occurs in the *primary market*—that is, the market involving the official ticket office.

The shortage, in turn, creates a *secondary market* in which buyers bid for tickets held by initial purchasers rather than the original seller. Scalping tickets—selling them above the original ticket price—may be legal or illegal, depending on local laws.

Figure 5 shows how the shortage in the primary ticket market looks in terms of supply and demand analysis. Demand curve *D* represents the demand for tickets and supply curve *S* represents the supply of tickets. The supply curve is vertical because a fixed number of tickets are printed to match the

FIGURE 5 The market for tickets to the Olympic women's figure skating finals.
The demand curve *D* and supply curve *S* for the Olympic women's figure skating finals produce an equilibrium price that is above the P_1 price printed on the ticket. At price P_1 the quantity of tickets demanded, Q_2, greatly exceeds the quantity of tickets available, Q_1. The resulting shortage of $ab (= Q_2 - Q_1)$ gives rise to a legal or illegal secondary market.

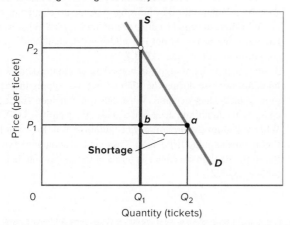

FIGURE 6 The market for tickets to the Olympic curling preliminaries.
The demand curve *D* and supply curve *S* for the Olympic curling preliminaries produce an equilibrium price below the P_1 price printed on the ticket. At price P_1 the quantity of tickets demanded is less than the quantity of tickets available. The resulting surplus of $ba (= Q_1 - Q_2)$ means the event is not sold out.

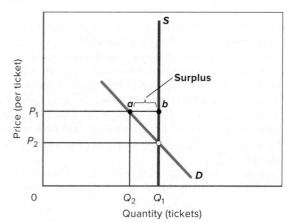

arena's capacity. At the printed ticket price of P_1, the quantity of tickets demanded, Q_2, exceeds the quantity supplied, Q_1. The result is a shortage of ab—the horizontal distance between Q_2 and Q_1 in the primary market.

Olympic Curling Preliminaries

Contrast the shortage of tickets for the women's figure skating finals at the Olympics to the surplus of tickets for one of the preliminary curling matches. For the uninitiated, curling is a sport in which participants slide a heavy round object called a "stone" down a lane painted on an ice rink toward a target while teammates called "sweepers" use brooms to alter the course of the stone.

Curling is a popular spectator sport in a few nations, including Canada, but it does not draw many fans in most countries. So the demand for tickets to most of the preliminary

curling events is not very strong. We demonstrate this weak demand as *D* in Figure 6. As in our previous example, the supply of tickets is fixed by the size of the arena and is shown as vertical line *S*.

We represent the printed ticket price as P_1 in Figure 6. In this case, the printed price is much higher than the equilibrium price of P_2. At the printed ticket price, quantity supplied is Q_1 and quantity demanded is Q_2. So a surplus of tickets of $ba (= Q_1 - Q_2)$ occurs. No ticket scalping occurs and there are numerous empty seats. Only if the Olympic officials had priced the tickets at the lower price P_2 would the event have been a sellout. (Actually, Olympic officials try to adjust to demand realities for curling contests by holding them in smaller arenas and by charging less for tickets. Nevertheless, the stands are rarely full for the preliminary contests, which compete against final events in other winter Olympic sports.)

Appendix Summary

LO3.7 Use supply-and-demand analysis to analyze specific real-world situations.
A decrease in the supply of a product increases its equilibrium price and reduces its equilibrium quantity. In contrast, an increase in the demand for a product boosts both its equilibrium price and its equilibrium quantity.

Simultaneous changes in supply and demand affect equilibrium price and quantity in various ways, depending on the relative magnitudes of the changes in supply and demand. Equal increases in supply and demand, for example, leave equilibrium price unchanged.

Products (such as land) whose quantities supplied do not vary with price have vertical supply curves. For these products, any shift in demand will lead to a change in the equilibrium price but no change in the equilibrium quantity.

Sellers set prices of some items such as tickets in advance of the event. These items are sold in a primary market that involves the original sellers and buyers. If preset prices turn out to be below equilibrium prices, shortages occur, and scalping in legal or illegal secondary markets arises. The prices in the secondary market then rise above the preset prices. In contrast, surpluses occur when the preset prices end up exceeding the equilibrium prices.

Appendix Discussion Questions

1. Why are shortages or surpluses more likely with preset prices (such as those on tickets) than with flexible prices (such as those on gasoline)? **LO3.7**

2. Most scalping laws make it illegal to sell—but not to buy—tickets at prices above those printed on the tickets. Assuming the existence of such laws, use supply-and-demand analysis to explain why the equilibrium ticket price in an illegal secondary market tends to be higher than in a legal secondary market. **LO3.7**

3. Go to the website of the Energy Information Administration, www.eia.gov, and follow the links to find the current retail price of gasoline. How does the current price of regular gasoline compare with the price a year ago? What must have happened to supply, demand, or both to explain the observed price change? **LO3.7**

4. Suppose the supply of apples sharply increases because of perfect weather conditions throughout the growing season. Assuming no change in demand, explain the effect on the equilibrium price and quantity of apples. Explain why quantity demanded increases even though demand does not change. **LO3.7**

5. Assume the demand for lumber suddenly rises because of rapid growth in demand for new housing. Assume no change in supply. Why does the equilibrium price of lumber rise? What would happen if the price did not rise under the demand and supply circumstances described? **LO3.7**

6. Assume that both the supply of bottled water and the demand for bottled water rise during the summer but that supply increases more rapidly than demand. What can you conclude about the changes in equilibrium price and equilibrium quantity? **LO3.7**

7. When asked for investment advice, humorist Will Rogers joked that people should "[b]uy land. They ain't making any more of the stuff." Explain his advice in terms of the supply-and-demand model. **LO3.7**

Appendix Review Questions

1. Will the equilibrium price of orange juice increase or decrease in each of the following situations? **LO3.7**
   a. A medical study reporting that orange juice reduces cancer is released at the same time that a freak storm destroys half of the orange crop in Florida.
   b. The prices of all beverages except orange juice fall by half, while unexpectedly perfect weather in Florida results in an orange crop that is 20 percent larger than normal.

2. Consider the market for coffee beans. Suppose that the prices of all other caffeinated beverages go up 30 percent while at the same time a new fertilizer boosts production at coffee plantations dramatically. What is likely to happen to the equilibrium price and quantity of coffee beans? **LO3.7**

3. True or False. A price ceiling will result in a shortage only if the ceiling price is greater than the equilibrium price. **LO3.7**

4. Suppose that you are the economic advisor to a local government that has to deal with a politically embarrassing surplus that was caused by a price floor that the government recently imposed. Your first suggestion is to get rid of the price floor, but the politicians don't want to do that. Instead, they present you with the following list of options that they hope will get rid of the surplus while keeping the price floor. Identify each one as either *could work* or *can't work*. **LO3.7**
   a. Restricting supply
   b. Decreasing demand
   c. Purchasing the surplus at the floor price

5. Suppose both the demand for olives and the supply of olives decline by equal amounts over some time period. Use graphical analysis to show the effect on equilibrium price and quantity. **LO3.7**

6. Governments can use subsidies to increase demand. For instance, a government can pay farmers to use organic fertilizers rather than traditional fertilizers. That subsidy increases the demand for organic fertilizer. Consider two industries, one in which supply is nearly vertical and the other in which supply is nearly horizontal. Assume that firms in both industries would prefer a higher market equilibrium price, which would mean higher profits. Which industry would probably spend more resources lobbying the government to increase the demand for its output? (Assume that both industries have similarly sloped demand curves.) **LO3.7**
   a. The industry with a nearly flat supply curve
   b. The industry with a nearly vertical supply curve

Appendix Problems

1. Demand and supply often shift in the retail market for gasoline. Below are two demand curves and two supply curves for gallons of gasoline in the month of May in a small town in Maine. Some of the data are missing. **LO3.7**

Price	Quantities Demanded		Quantities Supplied	
	D_1	D_2	S_1	S_2
$4.00	5,000	7,500	9,000	9,500
____	6,000	8,000	8,000	9,000
2.00	____	8,500	____	8,500
____	____	9,000	5,000	____

   a. Use the following facts to fill in the missing data in the table. If demand is D_1 and supply is S_1, the equilibrium quantity is 7,000 gallons per month. When demand is D_2 and supply is S_1, the equilibrium price is $3.00 per gallon. When demand is D_2 and supply is S_1, there is an excess demand of 4,000 gallons per month at a price of $1.00 per gallon. If demand is D_1 and supply is S_2, the equilibrium quantity is 8,000 gallons per month.
   b. Compare two equilibriums. In the first, demand is D_1 and supply is S_1. In the second, demand is D_1 and supply is S_2. By how much does the equilibrium quantity change? By how much does the equilibrium price change?

c. If supply falls from S_2 to S_1 while demand declines from D_2 to D_1, does the equilibrium price rise, fall, or stay the same? What happens if only supply falls? What happens if only demand falls?

d. Suppose that supply is fixed at S_1 and that demand starts at D_1. By how many gallons per month would demand have to increase at each price such that the equilibrium price per gallon would be $3.00? $4.00?

2. The following table shows two demand schedules for a given style of men's shoe—that is, how many pairs per month will be demanded at various prices at Stromnord, a men's clothing store.

Price	D_1 Quantity Demanded	D_2 Quantity Demanded
$75	53	13
70	60	15
65	68	18
60	77	22
55	87	27

Suppose that Stromnord has exactly 65 pairs of this style of shoe in inventory at the start of the month of July and will not receive any more pairs of this style until at least August 1. **LO3.7**

a. If demand is D_1, what is the lowest price that Stromnord can charge so that it will not run out of this model of shoe in the month of July? What if demand is D_2?

b. If the price of shoes is set at $75 for both July and August and demand will be D_2 in July and D_1 in August, how many pairs of shoes should Stromnord order if it wants to end the month of August with exactly zero pairs of shoes in its inventory? How many pairs of shoes should it order if the price is set at $55 for both months?

3. Use the following table to answer the questions that follow: **LO3.7**

a. If this table reflects the supply of and demand for tickets to a particular World Cup soccer game, what is the stadium capacity?

b. If the preset ticket price is $45, would we expect to see a secondary market for tickets? Why or why not? Would the price of a ticket in the secondary market be higher than, the same as, or lower than the price in the primary (original) market?

c. Suppose for some other World Cup game the quantity of tickets demanded is 20,000 lower at each ticket price than shown in the table. If the ticket price remains $45, would the event be a sellout?

Quantity Demanded, Thousands	Price	Quantity Supplied, Thousands
80	$25	60
75	35	60
70	45	60
65	55	60
60	65	60
55	75	60
50	85	60

Market Failures Caused by Externalities and Asymmetric Information

>> LEARNING OBJECTIVES

LO4.1 Explain consumer surplus, producer surplus, and how properly functioning markets maximize total surplus and allocate resources optimally.

LO4.2 Explain how positive and negative externalities cause under- and overallocations of resources.

LO4.3 Explain why society is usually unwilling to pay the costs of completely eliminating negative externalities, such as air pollution.

LO4.4 Understand why asymmetric information may justify government intervention in some markets.

We begin this chapter by demonstrating how properly functioning markets allocate resources efficiently. We then explore *externalities* and *asymmetric information*, which are two major causes of *market failure*, or situations in which markets underproduce, overproduce, or fail to produce goods and services. When a market failure occurs, an economic role for government may arise, with interventions like pollution taxes helping to restore allocative and productive efficiency.

Efficiently Functioning Markets

>> **LO4.1** Explain consumer surplus, producer surplus, and how properly functioning markets maximize total surplus and allocate resources optimally.

In Chapter 3, we saw that competitive markets usually produce an assignment of resources that is "right" from an economic perspective. We now want to focus on the word "usually" and discuss exceptions. We must do so because robust competition involving many buyers and many sellers may not, by itself, be enough to guarantee that a market will allocate resources correctly. Under certain circumstances, markets may fail to deliver the highest possible amount of net benefits from the limited amount of resources available to society.

The best way to understand these instances of **market failure** is to first understand how properly functioning competitive markets achieve economic efficiency. We touched on this subject in Chapter 3, but we now want to expand and deepen that analysis.

Two conditions must hold for a competitive market to produce efficient outcomes:

- The market demand curve must reflect the full willingness to pay of every person receiving benefits from the product being sold in the market.

- The market supply curve must reflect all of the costs of production, including those that may fall onto persons not directly involved with the production of the product being sold in the market.

If these conditions hold, then the market will produce only units for which benefits are at least equal to costs. It will also maximize the **total surplus,** or social surplus, that is shared between consumers and producers. This is important because the *total surplus* measures the net benefits accruing to society from the conversion of scarce resource inputs into various forms of output. When the total surplus is maximized, society is getting as much benefit as possible from its limited supply of resources.

The fact that total surplus is shared between consumers and producers can be expressed in equation form as,

$$\text{Total Surplus} = \text{Consumer Surplus} + \text{Producer Surplus}$$

Let's now dig in more deeply with respect to what, exactly, economists mean by "consumer surplus" and "producer surplus."

Consumer Surplus

The share of the total surplus that is received by a consumer or consumers in a market is called **consumer surplus.** It is defined as the difference between the maximum price a consumer is (or consumers are) willing to pay for a product and the actual price that they do pay.

The maximum price that a person is willing to pay is equal to the marginal benefit that they receive, which in turn depends on the opportunity cost of that person's consumption alternatives. Suppose that Ted is offered the chance to purchase an apple. He would like to have it for free, but the maximum amount he is willing to pay depends on the alternative uses to which he can put his money. If his maximum willingness to pay for an apple is $1.25, then we know that he is willing to forgo up to—but not more than—$1.25 of other goods and services. Paying even one cent more would entail giving up too much of other goods and services. Paying even one cent more would exceed the marginal benefit that he would receive from purchasing and consuming the apple.

However, if Ted pays any market price less than $1.25, he will receive a consumer surplus equal to the difference between the $1.25 maximum price that he was willing to pay and the lower market price. For instance, if the market price is $0.50 per apple, Ted will receive a consumer surplus of $0.75 per apple (= $1.25 − $0.50). In nearly all markets, consumers individually and collectively gain more total utility or satisfaction in dollar terms from their purchases than the amount of their expenditures (= product price × quantity). This utility surplus arises because each consumer who buys the product pays only the market equilibrium price even though many were willing to pay *more* than the equilibrium price to obtain the product.

The concept of maximum willingness to pay also gives us another way to understand demand curves. You learned in previous chapters that demand curves are equivalent to MB (marginal benefit) curves. It is also the case that they are equivalent to maximum willingness to pay curves. Consider Table 4.1, where the first two columns show the maximum amounts that six consumers would each be willing to pay for a bag of oranges. Bashir, for instance, is willing to pay a maximum of $13, while Blessing is willing to pay a maximum of $8.

Notice that the maximum prices that these individuals are willing to pay represent points on a demand curve because the lower the market price, the more bags of oranges will be demanded. At a price of $12.50, for instance, Bashir will be the only person listed in the table who will purchase a bag. But at a price of $11.50, both Bashir and Barb will want to purchase a bag. And at a price of $10.50, Bashir, Barb, and Bill will each want to purchase a bag. The lower the price, the greater the total quantity demanded.

market failure The inability of a *market* to bring about the allocation of *resources* that best satisfies the wants of society; in particular, the overallocation or underallocation of resources to the production of a particular *good* or *service* because of *externalities* or *asymmetric information,* or because markets fail to provide desired *public goods.*

total surplus The sum of consumer surplus and producer surplus; a measure of social welfare; also known as social surplus.

consumer surplus The difference between the maximum *price* a consumer is (or consumers are) willing to pay for an additional unit of a product and its market price; the triangular area below the demand curve and above the market price.

TABLE 4.1
Consumer Surplus

(1) Person	(2) Maximum Price Willing to Pay (= MB)	(3) Actual Price (Equilibrium Price)	(4) Consumer Surplus
Bashir	$13	$8	$5 (= $13 − $8)
Barb	12	8	4 (= $12 − $8)
Bill	11	8	3 (= $11 − $8)
Beeja	10	8	2 (= $10 − $8)
Brent	9	8	1 (= $9 − $8)
Blessing	8	8	0 (= $8 − $8)

Lower prices also imply larger consumer surpluses. When the price is $12.50, Bashir gets only $0.50 in consumer surplus because his maximum willingness to pay of $13 is only $0.50 higher than the market price of $12.50. But if the market price falls to $8, then his consumer surplus would be $5(= $13 − $8). The third and fourth columns of Table 4.1 show how much consumer surplus each consumer will receive if the market price of a bag of oranges is $8. Only Blessing receives no consumer surplus because her maximum willingness to pay exactly matches the $8 equilibrium price.

Graphing Consumer Surplus It is easy to show on a graph both the individual consumer surplus received by each particular buyer in a market as well as the collective consumer surplus received by all the buyers in a market. Consider Figure 4.1, which shows the market equilibrium price $P_1 = $8 as well as the downward sloping demand curve D for bags of oranges.

Demand curve D includes not only the six consumers in Table 4.1 but also every other consumer of oranges in the market. The consumer surplus of each individual who is willing to buy at the $8 market price is simply the vertical distance from the horizontal line that marks the $8 market price up to that buyer's maximum willingness to pay. The collective consumer surplus obtained by all of our named and unnamed buyers is found by adding together each of their individual consumer surpluses.

To obtain the Q_1 bags of oranges represented in Figure 4.1, consumers are collectively *willing* to pay the total amount that is equal to the sum of the amounts represented by the green triangle and yellow rectangle, which both lie under the demand curve and to the left of Q_1. But consumers only *have* to pay the amount represented by the yellow rectangle (= $P_1 \times Q_1$). So the green triangle is the consumer surplus in this market. It is the sum of the vertical distances between the demand curve and the $8 equilibrium price at each quantity up to Q_1. Alternatively, it is the sum of the gaps between maximum willingness to pay and actual price, such as those we calculated in Table 4.1. Thus, consumer surplus can also be defined as the area that lies below the demand curve and above the price line that extends horizontally from P_1.

Consumer surplus and price are inversely (negatively) related. Given the demand curve, higher prices reduce consumer surplus; lower prices increase it. To test this generalization, draw in an equilibrium price above $8 in Figure 4.1 and observe the reduced size of the triangle representing consumer surplus. Next, draw in an equilibrium price below $8 and see that consumer surplus increases.

producer surplus The difference between the actual *price* a producer receives (or producers receive) and the minimum acceptable price; the triangular area above the *supply curve* and below the market price.

FIGURE 4.1
Consumer surplus.

Consumer surplus—shown as the green triangle—is the difference between the maximum prices consumers are willing to pay for a product and the lower equilibrium price, here assumed to be $8. For quantity Q_1, consumers are willing to pay the sum of the amounts represented by the green triangle and the yellow rectangle. Because they need to pay only the amount shown as the yellow rectangle, the green triangle shows consumer surplus.

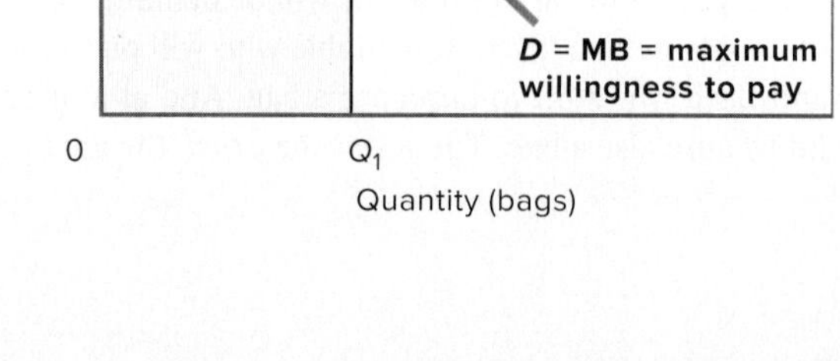

Producer Surplus

Like consumers, producers also receive a share of the total surplus generated by a market equilibrium. This **producer surplus** is the difference between the actual price a producer receives (or producers receive) and the minimum price that a consumer would have to pay the producer to make a particular unit of output available.

TABLE 4.2
Producer Surplus

(1) Person	(2) Minimum Acceptable Price (= MC)	(3) Actual Price (Equilibrium Price)	(4) Producer Surplus
Chander	$3	$8	$5 (= $8 − $3)
Chaaya	4	8	4 (= $8 − $4)
Chuck	5	8	3 (= $8 − $5)
Chazen	6	8	2 (= $8 − $6)
Chuma	7	8	1 (= $8 − $7)
Chad	8	8	0 (= $8 − $8)

A producer's minimum acceptable price for a particular unit will equal the producer's marginal cost of producing that unit. That marginal cost will be the sum of the rent, wages, interest, and profit that the producer will need to pay in order to obtain the land, labor, capital, and entrepreneurship required to produce that unit. In this section, we are assuming that the marginal cost of producing a unit includes *all* of the costs of production, including those that may fall onto individuals not directly involved in production.

A producer's minimum acceptable price, which equals the marginal cost, can also be interpreted as the opportunity cost of bidding resources away from the production of other products. To see why, suppose that Leah is an apple grower. The resources necessary for her to produce one apple could be used to produce other things. To get them directed toward producing an apple, it is necessary to pay Leah what it will cost her to bid the necessary resources away from other entrepreneurs who would like to use them to produce other products. Leah would, naturally, like to get paid as much as possible to produce the apple for you. But her minimum acceptable price is the lowest price you could pay her such that she can just break even after bidding away resources from other uses.

The size of the producer surplus earned on any particular unit is the difference between the market price that the producer actually receives and the producer's minimum acceptable price. Consider Table 4.2, which shows the minimum acceptable prices of six different orange growers. With a market price of $8, Chander, for instance, has a producer surplus of $5, which is equal to the market price of $8 minus his minimum acceptable price of $3. Chad, by contrast, receives no producer surplus because his minimum acceptable price of $8 just equals the market equilibrium price of $8.

Chander's minimum acceptable price is lower than Chad's minimum acceptable price because Chander is a more efficient producer than Chad, by which we mean that Chander produces oranges using a less-costly combination of resources than Chad uses. The differences in efficiency between Chander and Chad are likely due to differences in the type and quality of resources available to them. Chander, for instance, may own land perfectly suited to growing oranges, while Chad has land in the desert that requires costly irrigation if it is to be used to grow oranges. Thus, Chad has a higher marginal cost of producing oranges.

The minimum acceptable prices that producers are willing to accept form points on a supply curve because the higher the price, the more bags of oranges will be supplied. At a price of $3.50, for instance, only Chander is willing to supply a bag of oranges. But at a price of $5.50, Chander, Chaaya, and Chuck are all willing to supply a bag of oranges.

Please note that in previous chapters you learned that supply curves are equivalent to MC (marginal cost curves). You now know that supply curves are also equivalent to minimum-acceptable-price curves since the minimum prices that producers are willing to accept are equal to their marginal costs of production.

Graphing Producer Surplus The supply curve in Figure 4.2 includes not only the six producers named in Table 4.2 but also every other producer of oranges in

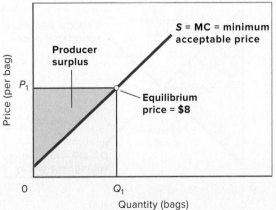

FIGURE 4.2
Producer surplus.

Producer surplus—shown as the blue triangle—is the difference between the actual price producers receive for a product (here $8) and the lower minimum payments they are willing to accept. For quantity Q_1, producers receive the sum of the amounts represented by the blue triangle plus the yellow area. Because we would only need to pay them the amount shown by the yellow area to get them to produce Q_1, the blue triangle represents producer surplus.

the market. At the market price of $8 per bag, Q_1 bags are produced because only those producers whose minimum acceptable prices are less than $8 per bag will choose to produce oranges with their resources. Those lower acceptable prices for each of the units up to Q_1 are shown by the portion of the supply curve lying to the left of and below the assumed $8 market price.

The individual producer surplus of each seller is thus the vertical distance from the seller's minimum acceptable price on the supply curve up to the $8 market price. Their collective producer surplus is shown by the blue triangle in Figure 4.2. In that figure, producers collect revenues of $P_1 \times Q_1$, which is the sum of the blue triangle and the yellow area. But producers would only need to receive the yellow area in order to make them just willing to supply Q_1 bags of oranges. The sellers therefore receive a producer surplus shown by the blue triangle. That surplus is the sum of the vertical distances between the supply curve and the $8 equilibrium price at each of the quantities to the left of Q_1.

There is a direct (positive) relationship between equilibrium price and the amount of producer surplus. Given the supply curve, lower prices reduce producer surplus; higher prices increase it. If you pencil in a lower equilibrium price than $8, you will see that the producer surplus triangle gets smaller. If you pencil in an equilibrium price above $8, the size of the producer surplus triangle increases.

▸ Consumer surplus is the difference between the maximum price that a consumer is willing to pay for a product and the lower price actually paid.

▸ Producer surplus is the difference between the minimum price that a producer is willing to accept for a product and the higher price actually received.

▸ In a graph of demand and supply, consumer surplus is represented by the area below the demand curve and above the market price; producer surplus by the area above the supply curve and below the market price.

productive efficiency The production of a *good* in the least costly way; occurs when production takes place at the output level at which per-unit production costs are minimized.

allocative efficiency The apportionment of resources among *firms* and industries to obtain the production of the products most wanted by society (consumers); the output of each product at which its *marginal cost* and *marginal benefit* are equal, and at which the sum of *consumer surplus* and *producer surplus* is maximized.

FIGURE 4.3

Efficiency: maximum combined consumer and producer surplus.

At quantity Q_1 the combined amount of consumer surplus, shown as the green triangle, and producer surplus, shown as the blue triangle, is maximized. Efficiency occurs at Q_1 because maximum willingness to pay, indicated by the points on the demand curve, equals minimum acceptable price, shown by the points on the supply curve. All units prior to Q_1 generate net benefits because maximum willingness to pay exceeds minimum acceptable price for each of those units.

Total Surplus and Efficiency

In Figure 4.3 we bring together the demand and supply curves of Figures 4.1 and 4.2 to show the equilibrium price and quantity and the previously described regions of consumer and producer surplus. All markets that have downward sloping demand curves and upward sloping supply curves yield consumer and producer surplus.

Because we are assuming in Figure 4.3 that the demand curve reflects buyers' full willingness to pay and the supply curve reflects all of the costs facing sellers, the equilibrium quantity in Figure 4.3 reflects economic efficiency, which consists of productive efficiency (lowest-cost production) and allocative efficiency (directing scarce resources toward their highest-valued use).

- **Productive efficiency** is achieved because competition forces orange growers to use the best technologies and combinations of resources available. Doing so minimizes the per-unit cost of the output produced.

- **Allocative efficiency** is achieved because the correct quantity of oranges—Q_1—is produced relative to other goods and services. Scarce resources are allocated to orange production only as long as the marginal benefit of additional orange production exceeds the opportunity cost of redirecting resources away from the production of other products.

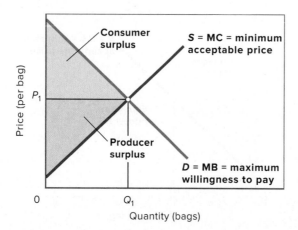

Three Equivalent Conditions for Allocative Efficiency

There are three equally valid ways to understand why the market equilibrium quantity Q_1 is the correct (allocatively efficient) quantity of oranges.

Marginal Benefit = Marginal Cost Recall from Chapter 1 that the correct amount of society's scarce resources is efficiently allocated to a particular good or service when that product is produced at the output level at which MB = MC (see Figure 1.3). In this chapter, we have emphasized that demand curves are MB curves and supply curves are MC curves. In particular, the points on the demand curve in Figure 4.3 measure the marginal benefit of oranges at each level of output, while the points on the supply curve measure the marginal cost of oranges at each level of output. As a result, MB = MC where the demand and supply curves intersect—which means that the market equilibrium quantity Q_1 must be allocatively efficient.

Maximum Willingness to Pay = Minimum Acceptable Price The second way to understand why the market equilibrium quantity Q_1 is allocatively efficient is to take advantage of the fact that demand and supply curves can also be interpreted as, respectively, maximum-willingness-to-pay and minimum-acceptable-price curves.

In Figure 4.3, the maximum willingness to pay on the demand curve for each bag of oranges up to Q_1 exceeds the corresponding minimum acceptable price on the supply curve. So people gain more utility from producing and consuming those units than they would if they produced and consumed anything else that could be made with the resources that went into making those units.

Only at the equilibrium quantity Q_1—where the maximum willingness to pay exactly equals the minimum acceptable price—does society exhaust all opportunities to produce units for which marginal benefits exceed marginal costs (including opportunity costs). Producing Q_1 units therefore achieves allocative efficiency.

Total Surplus is Maximized The third way to understand why the market equilibrium quantity Q_1 is allocatively efficient relies on the fact that producing Q_1 units maximizes total surplus (= the combined area of consumer and producer surplus) in Figure 4.3. If any other amount were produced, the total surplus would be less than it is at Q_1 units, implying that either consumers or producers (or both!) will end up receiving a smaller amount of surplus than they do when exactly Q_1 units are produced. The market equilibrium quantity is, consequently, allocatively efficient because it represents the only allocation of resources to this product that will maximize the sum of consumer and producer surplus (= the full areas of the blue and green triangles in Figure 4.3).

Recap and Implications Let's briefly summarize what we have learned about the efficiency of the market equilibrium.

- When demand curves reflect buyers' full willingness to pay and when supply curves reflect all of the costs facing sellers, competitive markets produce equilibrium quantities that maximize the sum of consumer and producer surplus.

- Allocative efficiency occurs at the market equilibrium quantity, where three conditions exist simultaneously:
  1. MB = MC (see Figure 1.3).
  2. Maximum willingness to pay = minimum acceptable price.
  3. Total surplus (= sum of consumer and producer surplus) is at a maximum.

Economists are enamored of markets because properly functioning markets automatically achieve allocative efficiency. Other methods of allocating resources—such as government central planning—do exist. But because other methods cannot do any better than properly functioning markets—and in many cases, do much worse—economists usually prefer to see resources allocated through markets.

QUICK REVIEW 4.2

▶ When demand curves reflect buyers' full willingness to pay and supply curves reflect all of the costs facing sellers, the market equilibrium quantity will be both productively and allocatively efficient.

▶ Total surplus (= sum of consumer surplus and producer surplus) represents the net benefits (social surplus) received by members of society from the production and consumption of the market equilibrium quantity of output.

▶ At the equilibrium price and quantity in a competitive market, MB = MC, maximum willingness to pay equals minimum acceptable price, and total surplus is maximized. Each of these conditions implies allocative efficiency.

Externalities and Efficiency Losses

Figures 4.4a and 4.4b demonstrate that both underproduction and overproduction cause reductions in the size of the total surplus. These reductions are known as **efficiency losses,** or deadweight losses.

>> **LO4.2** Explain how positive and negative externalities cause under- and overallocations of resources.

FIGURE 4.4 Efficiency losses (or deadweight losses).

Quantity levels either less than or greater than the efficient quantity Q_1 create efficiency losses. (a) Triangle *dbe* shows the efficiency loss associated with underproduction at output Q_2. (b) Triangle *bfg* illustrates the efficiency loss associated with overproduction at output level Q_3.

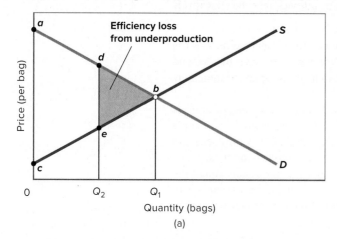
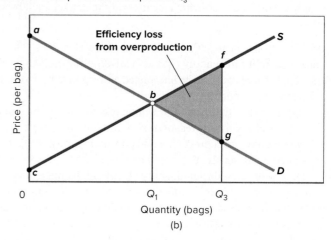

(a)

(b)

efficiency loss Reductions in combined consumer and producer surplus caused by an underallocation or over-allocation of resources to the production of a *good* or *service*. Also called *deadweight loss*.

deadweight loss A reduction in the total net benefit that society can obtain from its limited supply of resources. Caused by an underalloca-tion or overallocation of resources to the production of a particular *good* or *service*. Also called *efficiency loss*.

Deadweight Losses from Underproduction

First consider Figure 4.4a, which analyzes the case of underproduction by considering what hap-pens if output falls from the efficient level Q_1 to the smaller amount Q_2. When that happens, the sum of consumer and producer surplus, previously *abc,* falls to *adec*. Thus total surplus declines by the amount of the gray triangle to the left of Q_1. That triangle (*dbe*) represents an efficiency loss to buyers and sellers. And because buyers and sellers are members of society, it represents a **deadweight loss** to society as a whole.

For output levels from Q_2 to Q_1, consumers' maximum willingness to pay (as reflected by points on the demand curve) exceeds producers' minimum acceptable price (as reflected by points on the supply curve). By failing to produce these units for which a consumer is willing to pay more than a producer is willing to accept, society suffers a loss of net benefits. As a concrete example, consider a particular unit for which a consumer is willing to pay $10 and a producer is willing to accept $6. The $4 difference between those values is a net benefit that will not be realized if this unit is not produced. In addition, the resources that should have gone to producing this unit will go instead to producing other products that will generate a smaller net benefit.

Deadweight Losses from Overproduction

Next, consider the case of overproduction shown in Figure 4.4b, in which the number of oranges produced is Q_3 rather than the efficient level Q_1. In Figure 4.4b the total surplus declines by *bfg*— the gray triangle to the right of Q_1. This triangle subtracts from the total consumer and producer surplus of *abc* that would occur if the quantity had been Q_1. That is, for all units from 0 to Q_1, benefits exceed costs, so that those units generate the economic surplus shown by triangle *abc*. But the units from Q_1 to Q_3 are such that costs exceed benefits. Thus, they generate a loss of total surplus shown by triangle *bfg*. The total economic surplus for all units from 0 to Q_3 is therefore the economic surplus given by *abc* for the units from 0 to Q_1 *minus* the loss of surplus indicated by *bfg* for the units from Q_1 to Q_3.

Producing any unit beyond Q_1 generates an efficiency loss because consumers' willingness to pay for such units is less than producers' minimum acceptable price to produce such units. As a concrete example, note that producing an item for which the maximum willingness to pay is $7 and the minimum acceptable price is $10 subtracts $3 from society's net benefits. Such produc-tion is uneconomical and creates an efficiency loss (or deadweight loss) for society.

In summary: When demand reflects consumers' full willingness to pay and when supply reflects all costs, the market equilibrium quantity will automatically equal the allocatively efficient output level and there will be neither efficiency losses from underproduction nor effi-ciency losses from overproduction. But if for any reason more or less than the market equilib-rium quantity is produced, deadweight losses will result, either from underproduction or overproduction.

Externalities

An **externality** occurs when some of the costs or benefits of a good or service are passed onto or "spill over to" someone other than the immediate buyer or seller. These spillovers are called "externalities" because they accrue to some third party that is external to the market transaction.

Externalities can be positive or negative. An example of a negative externality is the cost of breathing polluted air; an example of a positive externality is the benefit of having everyone else inoculated against some disease. As you will see, both types of externality generate allocative inefficiency and deadweight losses.

Negative Externalities **Negative externalities** occur when producers or suppliers impose costs on third parties who are not directly involved in a market transaction. Consider the costs of breathing polluted air that are imposed on third parties living downwind of smoke-spewing factories. Because polluting firms do not take account of such costs, they oversupply the products they make, producing units for which total costs (including those that fall on third parties) exceed total benefits. The same is true when airlines fail to account for the costs that noisy jet engines impose on people living near airports.

Overproduction In terms of supply and demand, this failure to account for all costs—including the costs of negative externalities—shifts firms' supply curves to the right of (below) where they would be if firms properly accounted for all costs. This can be seen in **Figure 4.5a (Key Graph)**, which illustrates how negative externalities affect the allocation of resources.

When producers shift some of their costs onto the community as external costs, producers' marginal costs are lower than they would be if they had to pay those costs themselves. Thus their supply curves do not include or "capture" all the costs legitimately associated with the production

externality A cost or benefit from production or consumption that accrues to someone other than the immediate buyers and sellers of the product being produced or consumed (see *negative externality* and *positive externality*).

negative externality A cost imposed without compensation on third parties by the production or consumption of sellers or buyers. Example: A manufacturer dumps toxic chemicals into a river, killing fish prized by sports fishers. Also known as an external cost or a spillover cost.

..ıl KEY GRAPH

FIGURE 4.5 Negative and positive externalities.

(a) With negative externalities borne by society, the producers' supply curve *S* is to the right of (below) the total-cost supply curve *S₁*. Consequently, the equilibrium output Q_e is greater than the optimal output Q_o, and the efficiency loss is *abc*.
(b) When positive externalities accrue to society, the market demand curve *D* is to the left of (below) the total-benefit demand curve D_t. As a result, the equilibrium output Q_e is less than the optimal output Q_o and the efficiency loss is *xyz*.

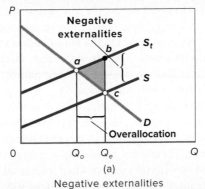

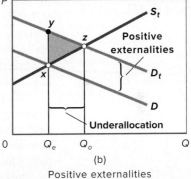

(a)
Negative externalities

(b)
Positive externalities

QUICK QUIZ FOR FIGURE 4.5

1. In Figure 4.5a, the supply curve S_t lies to the left of (above) supply curve *S* because:
   a. marginal costs are rising faster for S_t than *S*.
   b. *S* reflects more efficient, lower-cost production methods.
   c. only S_t reflects the costs that fall on people other than buyers and sellers.
   d. only S_t reflects the law of increasing opportunity costs.

2. In Figure 4.5a, the market equilibrium will be located at:
   a. point *a*.
   b. point *b*.
   c. point *c*.
   d. Q_o.

3. In Figure 4.5b, there is an underallocation of resources to the production of this product because:
   a. low prices are depressing the quantity demanded.
   b. the vertical distance from point *x* to point *y* fails to reflect net benefits.
   c. demand curve D_t externalizes consumers' opportunity costs.
   d. equilibrium reflects the absence from the market of the consumers who benefit from this product without having to pay for it.

4. In Figure 4.5b, the market equilibrium price will be:
   a. less than the price at point *x*.
   b. equal to the vertical distance between D_t and *D*.
   c. less than the price at point *z*.
   d. equal to the price at point *y*.

Answers: 1. c; 2. c; 3. d; 4. c

of their products. A polluting producer's supply curve such as S in Figure 4.5a therefore understates the total cost of production. The polluter's supply curve S lies to the right of (below) the total-cost supply curve S_t, which includes the spillover costs. Through polluting and thus transferring costs to society, the firm enjoys lower production costs than it would if it had to pay for those negative externalities. By dumping those costs onto others, it produces more at each possible price than it would if it had to account for all costs. That is why supply curve S lies to the right of (below) supply curve S_t.

Efficiency Losses from Overproduction The market outcome is shown in Figure 4.5a. Equilibrium output Q_e (which is determined by the intersection of supply curve S and demand curve D) is larger than the optimal output Q_o. Resources are overallocated to the production of this commodity; too many units of it are produced. In fact, there is a net loss to society for every unit from Q_o to Q_e. That net loss occurs because, for each of those units, the total MC to society (including the costs of the negative externality) exceeds the MB to society. You can see this clearly by noting that for all the units between Q_o and Q_e, the supply curve that accounts for all costs, S_t, lies above the demand curve D that accounts for benefits. Therefore, MC exceeds MB for those units.

   The negative externality results in a deadweight efficiency loss represented by triangle abc. The resources that went into producing the units between Q_o and Q_e should have been used elsewhere in the economy to produce other things.

positive externality A benefit obtained without compensation by third parties from the production or consumption of sellers or buyers. Example: A beekeeper benefits when a neighboring farmer plants clover. Also known as an *external benefit* or a spillover benefit.

Positive Externalities **Positive externalities** occur when people who are not directly involved in a market transaction receive benefits from the market transaction without having to pay for them. An example would be people living near Disneyland who enjoy the park's nightly fireworks display even though they did not purchase admission to the park. These people receive something beneficial (positive) despite being outside of (external to) the market transaction between Disneyland and its paying customers. These nonpaying beneficiaries are sometimes referred to as "free riders," after the scofflaws who ride public transportation without paying for a ticket.

Underproduction When positive externalities are present, market demand curves fail to include the willingness to pay of the people who receive the positive externality. This failure to account for all benefits—including those received by people not directly involved in the market transaction—shifts market demand curves to the left of (below) where they would be if they included all benefits and total willingness to pay. In such cases, markets fail to produce all units for which benefits (including those that are received by third parties) exceed costs. As a result, products featuring positive externalities are underproduced.

   Vaccinations are a good example of how positive externalities reduce demand. When John gets vaccinated against a disease, he benefits not only himself (because he can no longer contract the disease) but also everyone else around him (because they know that in the future he will never be able to infect them). These other people would presumably be willing to pay some positive amount of money for the benefits they receive when John is vaccinated. But there is no way to make them pay.

   Thus, the market demand for vaccinations will include John's personal willingness to pay for the benefits that he personally receives from the vaccination, but it will fail to include the benefits that others receive. As a result, demand will be too low and vaccinations will be underproduced.

Efficiency Losses from Underproduction Figure 4.5b shows the impact of positive externalities on resource allocation. When external benefits occur, the market demand curve D lies to the left of (below) the total-benefits demand curve, D_t. At any particular price, fewer units of output are demanded along D than along D_t. That's because D includes only the benefits received by people paying for the product, while D_t includes not only those paid-for benefits but also the external benefits received by free riders. D_t is the demand curve that would exist if everybody receiving benefits had to pay for them.

   With D lying to the left of (below) D_t, the market equilibrium output Q_e (which is determined by the intersection of demand curve D and supply curve S_t) is less than the optimal output Q_o. The market fails to produce enough output and resources are underallocated to this product. The underproduction implies that society is missing out on a significant amount of potential net benefits. For every unit from Q_e to Q_o, the demand curve that accounts for all benefits, D_t, lies above the supply curve S that accounts for all costs—including the opportunity cost of producing other products with the resources that were used to produce these units. Because D_t includes all benefits while S includes all costs, we see that MB > MC for each of these units. We conclude that society should redeploy some of its resources away from the production of other items and toward the production of these units for which net benefits are positive.

In terms of our previous analysis, the positive externality results in a deadweight efficiency loss represented by triangle *xyz*. Shifting the demand curve from *D* to *D*, eliminates that deadweight loss. The underallocation of resources to this product disappears as the market equilibrium shifts from *x* to *z*.

> ▸ Quantities less than or greater than the allocatively efficient level of output create efficiency losses, often called deadweight losses.
>
> ▸ An externality occurs when a benefit or cost of a market transaction falls on parties other than the immediate buyers and sellers interacting in the market.
>
> ▸ Negative externalities lead to overproduction and overallocation, while positive externalities lead to underproduction and underallocation.

Government Intervention

Government intervention may achieve economic efficiency when externalities affect large numbers of people or when community interests are at stake. Governments can counter the overproduction caused by negative externalities with direct controls or Pigovian taxes. And governments can counter the underproduction caused by positive externalities with subsidies or government provision.

Direct Controls The most direct way of reducing negative externalities arising from a certain activity is to pass legislation limiting that activity. Such **direct controls** force the offending firms to incur the actual costs of the offending activity. Historically, direct controls in the form of uniform emission standards—limits on allowable pollution—have dominated U.S. air pollution policy. Similarly, clean-water legislation limits the amount of heavy metals, detergents, and other pollutants that firms can discharge into rivers and bays. And toxic-waste laws dictate special procedures and dump sites for disposing of contaminated soil and solvents. Violating these laws means fines and, in some cases, imprisonment.

Direct controls raise the marginal cost of production because polluting firms must operate and maintain pollution-control equipment. Raising the marginal cost of production shifts the supply curve leftward (or upward). For example, in Figure 4.6b, the supply curve *S*, which does not reflect external costs, shifts leftward (upward) to the total-cost supply curve, S_t. The equilibrium price increases, equilibrium output falls from Q_e to the socially optimal amount Q_o, and the initial overallocation of resources shown in Figure 4.6a is corrected. Observe that the efficiency loss shown by triangle *abc* in Figure 4.6a disappears after the overallocation is corrected in Figure 4.6b.

Pigovian Taxes Another way to approach negative externalities is for government to levy taxes or charges on the related good. These targeted tax assessments are often called **Pigovian taxes** in honor of Arthur Pigou, the first economist to study externalities. Example: The U.S. government

direct controls Government policies that directly constrain activities that generate *negative externalities*. Examples include maximum emissions limits for factory smokestacks and laws mandating the proper disposal of toxic wastes.

Pigovian tax A *tax* or charge levied on the production of a product that generates *negative externalities*. If set correctly, the tax will precisely offset the overallocation (overproduction) generated by the negative externality.

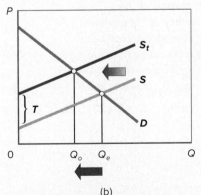

(a) Negative externalities
Negative externalities

(b) Correcting the overallocation of resources via direct controls or via a tax

FIGURE 4.6 Correcting for negative externalities.

(a) Negative externalities result in an overallocation of resources. (b) Government can correct this overallocation in two ways: (1) using direct controls, which would shift the supply curve from *S* to S_t and reduce equilibrium output from Q_e to Q_o, or (2) imposing a specific tax *T*, which would also shift the supply curve from *S* to S_t, eliminating the overallocation of resources and thus the efficiency loss.

CONSIDER THIS . . .

The Fable of the Bees

Economist Ronald Coase received the Nobel Prize for his so-called **Coase theorem,** which pointed out that private individuals could often use private bargaining to negotiate their own mutually agreeable solutions to externality problems without the need for government interventions like pollution taxes.

LilKar/Shutterstock

This is a very important insight because it means that we shouldn't automatically call for government intervention every time we see an externality problem. Consider the positive externalities that bees provide by pollinating farmers' crops. Should we assume that beekeeping will be underprovided unless the government intervenes with, for instance, subsidies to encourage more hives and hence more pollination?

As it turns out, no. Research has shown that farmers and beekeepers long ago used private bargaining to develop customs and payment systems that avoid free riding by farmers and encourage beekeepers to keep the optimal number of hives. Free riding is avoided by the custom that all farmers in an area simultaneously hire beekeepers to provide bees to pollinate their crops. And farmers always pay the beekeepers for their pollination services because if they didn't, then no beekeeper would ever work with them in the future—a situation that would lead to massively reduced crop yields due to a lack of pollination.

The "Fable of the Bees" is a good reminder that it is a fallacy to assume that the government must always get involved to remedy externalities. In many cases, the private sector can solve both positive and negative externality problems on its own.

Coase theorem The idea, first stated by economist Ronald Coase, that some *externalities* can be resolved through private negotiations among the affected parties.

has placed a tax on CFCs, which deplete the stratospheric ozone layer protecting Earth from excessive solar ultraviolet radiation. Facing this tax, manufacturers must decide whether to pay the tax or expend additional funds to purchase or develop substitute products. In either case, the tax raises the marginal cost of producing CFCs, shifting the supply curve for this product leftward (upward).

In Figure 4.6b, a tax equal to T per unit increases the firm's marginal cost, shifting the supply curve from S to S_t. The equilibrium price rises, and the equilibrium output declines from Q_e to the economically efficient level Q_o. The tax eliminates the initial overallocation of resources and the associated efficiency loss.

Many governments have imposed Pigovian pollution taxes on carbon dioxide (CO_2) in order to raise the marginal cost of burning fossil fuels and thereby offset the negative externalities imposed by carbon dioxide emissions. Global Perspective 4.1 shows the percentage of carbon-dioxide emissions that are taxed at a rate of $70 per ton or higher in each of ten countries.

GLOBAL PERSPECTIVE 4.1

PERCENTAGE OF CO_2 EMISSIONS TAXED, SELECTED NATIONS, 2018

Countries vary widely in the percentage of their total carbon dioxide (CO_2) emissions that they tax at a price of $70 per ton or higher. The percentages vary across countries due to both differences in the tax rate per ton and differences in which industries (agricultural, industrial, transportation, etc.) are subject to CO_2 taxes in each country.

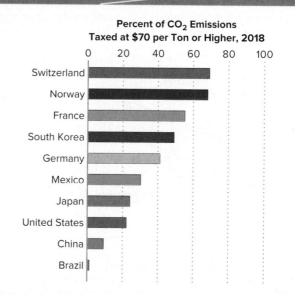

Percent of CO_2 Emissions
Taxed at $70 per Ton or Higher, 2018

Source: Effective Carbon Rates 2021, Organization for Economic Co-operation and Development (OECD), oecd.org.

FIGURE 4.7 Correcting for positive externalities.

(a) Positive externalities result in an underallocation of resources. (b) This underallocation can be corrected through a subsidy to consumers, which shifts market demand from D to D_t and increases output from Q_e to Q_o. (c) Alternatively, the underallocation can be eliminated by providing producers with a subsidy of U, which shifts their supply curve from S_t to S_t', increasing output from Q_e to Q_o and eliminating the underallocation, and thus the efficiency loss, shown in graph a.

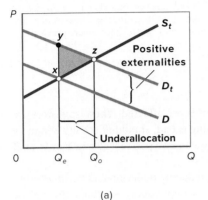

(a)
Positive externalities

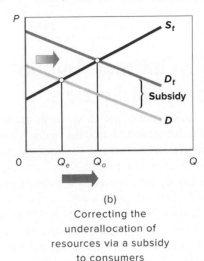

(b)
Correcting the
underallocation of
resources via a subsidy
to consumers

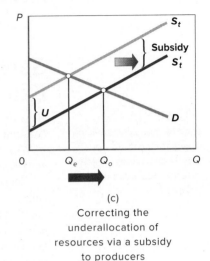

(c)
Correcting the
underallocation of
resources via a subsidy
to producers

Subsidies and Government Provision Where spillover benefits (positive externalities) are large and diffuse, government has three options for correcting the underallocation of resources:

- *Subsidies to buyers* Figure 4.7a replicates the supply-demand situation for positive externalities that you first encountered in Figure 4.5b. Government could correct the underallocation of resources to inoculations by subsidizing consumers of the product. It could give each new parent in the United States a discount coupon to be used for a series of inoculations for their child. The coupon would reduce the "price" to the mother by, say, 50 percent. As Figure 4.7b shows, this program would shift the demand curve for inoculations from too-low D to the appropriate D_t. The number of inoculations would rise from Q_e to the economically optimal Q_o, eliminating the underallocation of resources and the associated efficiency loss.

- *Subsidies to producers* A subsidy to producers is a tax in reverse. Taxes are payments *to* the government that increase producers' costs. Subsidies are payments *from* the government that decrease producers' costs. As Figure 4.7c shows, a subsidy of U per inoculation to physicians and medical clinics would reduce their marginal costs and shift their supply curve rightward (upward) from S_t to S_t'. The output of inoculations would increase from Q_e to the optimal level Q_o, correcting the underallocation of resources and the associated efficiency loss.

- *Government provision* Finally, where positive externalities are extremely large, the government may decide to provide the product for free to everyone. The U.S. government largely eradicated the crippling disease polio by administering free vaccines to all children. India ended smallpox by paying people in rural areas to come to public clinics to have their children vaccinated.

Table 4.3 lists several methods for correcting externalities, including those we have discussed thus far. The nearby Consider This box also relates how one of those methods—private bargaining—can help to correct for externalities privately, without government intervention.

TABLE 4.3
Methods for Dealing with Externalities

Problem	Resource Allocation Outcome	Ways to Correct
Negative externalities (spillover costs)	Overproduction of output and therefore overallocation of resources	1. Private bargaining 2. Liability rules and lawsuits 3. Taxes on producers 4. Direct controls 5. Markets for externality rights
Positive externalities (spillover benefits)	Underproduction of output and therefore underallocation of resources	1. Private bargaining 2. Subsidies to consumers 3. Subsidies to producers 4. Government provision

▶ Governments can attempt to counter the overproduction caused by negative externalities and the underproduction caused by positive externalities.

▶ Government policies for coping with the overallocation of resources, and therefore efficiency losses, caused by negative externalities include (a) private bargaining, (b) liability rules and lawsuits,

(c) direct controls, (d) Pigovian taxes, and (e) markets for externality rights.

▶ Government policies for correcting the underallocation of resources, and therefore efficiency losses, associated with positive externalities include (a) private bargaining, (b) subsidies to producers, (c) subsidies to consumers, and (d) government provision.

Society's Optimal Amount of Externality Reduction

>> **LO4.3** Explain why society is usually unwilling to pay the costs of completely eliminating negative externalities, such as air pollution.

Negative externalities such as pollution reduce the utility of those affected. These spillovers are not economic goods but rather economic "bads." If something is bad, shouldn't society eliminate it? Why should society allow firms to discharge *any* impure waste into public waterways or to emit *any* pollution whatsoever into the air?

Economists answer these questions by pointing out that reducing pollution and negative externalities is not free. There are costs as well as benefits to reducing pollution. As a result, the correct question to ask is not, "Do we pollute a lot or pollute zero?" That is an all-or-nothing question that ignores marginal costs and marginal benefits. Instead, the correct question is, "What is the optimal amount to clean up—that is, the amount that equalizes the marginal cost of cleaning up with the marginal benefit of a cleaner environment?"

If we ask that question, we see that reducing a negative externality has a "price." Society must decide how much of a reduction it wants to "buy." High costs may mean that totally eliminating pollution might not be desirable, even if it is technologically feasible. Because of the *law of increasing opportunity costs*, cleaning up the second 10 percent of pollutants from an industrial smokestack normally is more costly than cleaning up the first 10 percent. Eliminating the third 10 percent is more costly than cleaning up the second 10 percent, and so on. Therefore, cleaning up the last 10 percent of pollutants is the most costly reduction of all.

The marginal cost (MC) to the firm and hence to society—the opportunity cost of the extra resources used—rises as pollution is reduced more and more. At some point, MC may rise so high that it exceeds society's marginal benefit (MB) of further pollution reduction. Additional actions to reduce pollution will therefore lower society's well-being; total cost will rise more than total benefit.

optimal reduction of an externality The reduction of a *negative externality* such as pollution to the level at which the *marginal benefit* and *marginal cost* of reduction (abatement) are equal.

MC, MB, and Optimal Abatement

Figure 4.8 shows both the upward sloping marginal-cost curve MC for pollution abatement (reduction) as well as the downward sloping marginal-benefit curve MB for pollution abatement.

- MB slopes downward because of the *law of diminishing marginal utility:* The more pollution society reduces, the lower the utility (benefit) of the next unit of pollution reduction.

FIGURE 4.8 Society's optimal amount of pollution abatement.

The optimal amount of externality reduction—in this case, pollution abatement—occurs at Q_1, where society's marginal cost MC and marginal benefit MB of reducing the spillover are equal.

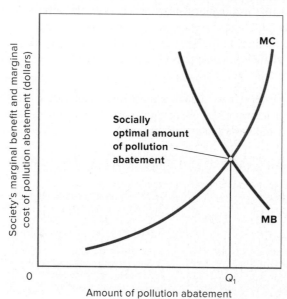

- MC slopes upward because of the *law of increasing opportunity costs:* the more pollution society reduces, the higher the cost of each additional unit of pollution reduction.

The **optimal reduction of an externality** occurs when society's marginal cost and marginal benefit of reducing that externality are equal (MC = MB). In Figure 4.8 the optimal amount of pollution abatement is Q_1 units. When MB exceeds MC, additional abatement moves society toward economic efficiency; the added benefit of cleaner air or water exceeds the benefit forgone of any alternative use of the required resources. When MC exceeds MB, additional abatement reduces economic efficiency; there would be greater benefits from using resources in some other way than to further reduce pollution.

In reality, it is difficult to measure the marginal costs and benefits of pollution control. Nevertheless, Figure 4.8 demonstrates that a positive level of pollution may be economically efficient. This efficiency occurs not because pollution is desirable but because beyond some level, further abatement may reduce society's net well-being. For example, it would cost the government billions of dollars to clean up every last piece of litter in America. Thus, it is better to tolerate some trash blowing around if the money saved by not trying to pick up every last piece will yield larger net benefits when spent elsewhere.

Shifts of the Abatement MB and MC Curves

The locations of the MC and MB curves in Figure 4.8 are not forever fixed. They can, and probably do, shift over time. For example, suppose that the technology of pollution-control equipment improved noticeably. We would expect the cost of pollution abatement to fall, society's MC curve to shift rightward, and the optimal level of abatement to rise. Or suppose that society decides that it wants cleaner air and water because of new information about the adverse health effects of pollution. The MB curve in Figure 4.8 will shift rightward, and the optimal level of pollution control would increase beyond Q_1. Test your understanding of these statements by drawing the new MC and MB curves in Figure 4.8.

Government's Role When Externalities Are Present

Correcting for market failures is neither easy nor straightforward. For starters, government officials must correctly identify both the existence and the cause of any particular market failure. That process may be difficult, time consuming, and costly. Then, even after a market failure is correctly identified and diagnosed, political pressures may hamper or block remedial action due to the fact that the main personal objective of many politicians is to get elected and stay elected. Only in some cases will voting to correct a market failure serve that purpose. In others, it may even be the case that political pressures incline politicians to vote for laws that make the market failure worse, not better.

Political pressures can, as a result, lead to overregulation in some cases, and underregulation in others. Some government taxes and subsidies are imposed not because their benefits exceed their costs but because their benefits accrue to firms located in states represented by powerful elected officials. Sometimes direct controls are imposed at the behest of large corporations who know that their smaller competitors will not be able to afford them. Policies to correct negative externalities can be blocked in the legislature by the entities that are producing the spillovers.

In short, the economic role of government, although critical to a well-functioning economy, is not always perfectly carried out. Economists use the term *government failure* to describe economically inefficient outcomes caused by shortcomings in the public sector. You can read more about government failure in the next chapter.

CONSIDER THIS . . .

Congestion Pricing

Driving is costly. The private costs include paying for gas and the opportunity cost of the time drivers spend in traffic getting to their destinations. But there are external costs, too.

If you are the only person driving down a highway, there is no way for you to impose a negative externality on other drivers. But if traffic is moderate or heavy, your entering a roadway imposes an additional amount of congestion on other drivers. That additional crowding slows traffic down, raising time and gasoline costs for you and everyone else. And the problem is mutual, because the presence of the other drivers imposes a negative congestion externality on you, too.

One solution is to charge people for using the roadway, as with toll roads and the paid express lanes now found in many major cities. The fees that are assessed raise the

Stefano Carnevali/Shutterstock

direct private cost of driving to you and other drivers. But that higher private cost will discourage some people from driving, especially at peak hours. If the tolls are set correctly, drivers will collectively save more in reduced congestion costs than they pay in tolling fees. In the case of highways that have paid express lanes running in parallel with free lanes, drivers will sort themselves according to their opportunity costs and their willingness and ability to pay. Those with low opportunity costs for time will prefer to endure heavier traffic in the free lanes even if they have the ability to pay for the express lanes. But those who have a high opportunity cost for time will prefer to pay for the express lanes whenever they can afford to do so.

▶ Negative-externality reduction comes at a cost, and the marginal cost of each additional reduction is higher than for the previous reduction.

▶ The optimal amount of negative-externality reduction occurs where society's marginal cost and

marginal benefit of reducing the externality are equal.

▶ Political pressures often cause governments to respond inefficiently when attempting to correct for market failures.

Asymmetric Information

>> **LO4.4** Understand why asymmetric information may justify government intervention in some markets.

asymmetric information A situation where one party to a market transaction has more information about a product or service than the other. The result may be an under- or overallocation of resources.

private information Facts known by one party to a market transaction but hidden from others; results in *asymmetric information.*

We have already discussed the two most prominent sources of market failure: negative and positive externalities. But there is also another, subtler, type of market failure that is caused by **asymmetric information,** or the situation that occurs when one party to a market transaction possesses **private information** that is not readily available to the other party at a low cost.

This asymmetry (inequality) of information makes it difficult to distinguish trustworthy sellers from untrustworthy sellers or trustworthy buyers from untrustworthy buyers. When information is asymmetric, society's scarce resources may be allocated inefficiently, thus implying that the government should intervene. The government may, for example, take steps to equalize the information available to market participants. Under rare circumstances, the government may even supply a good or service whose private sector production has been hobbled by asymmetric information.

When Sellers Possess Private Information

Situations in which sellers possess *private information* that is not available to buyers at a low cost can result in market failure and an underallocation of resources to the production of a good or service. Two examples of this information asymmetry will help you understand the problem.

Example: Gasoline Market Assume an absurd situation: Suppose there is no system of weights and measures established by law, no government inspection of gasoline pumps, and no law against false advertising. Each gas station can use whatever measure it chooses; it can define a gallon of gas as it pleases. A station can advertise that its gas is 87 octane, when in fact it is only 75. It can rig its pumps to indicate that it is providing more gas than the amount being delivered.

Obviously, the consumer's cost of obtaining reliable information under such chaotic conditions is exceptionally high, if not prohibitive. Customers or their representatives would have to buy samples of gas from various gas stations, have them tested for octane level, and test the accuracy of calibrations at the pump. And these activities would have to be repeated regularly, since a station owner could alter the product quality and the accuracy of the pump at will.

Because of the high cost of obtaining information about the seller, many consumers would opt out of this chaotic market. One tankful of a 50 percent mixture of gasoline and water would be enough to discourage most motorists from further driving. More realistically, the conditions in this market would encourage consumers to vote for political candidates who promise to provide a government solution. The oil companies and honest gasoline stations would most likely welcome government intervention. They would realize that accurate information, by enabling this market to work, would expand their total sales and profits.

The government has in fact intervened in the market for gasoline and other markets with similar potential information difficulties. It has established a system of weights and measures, employed inspectors to check the accuracy of gasoline pumps, and passed laws against fraudulent claims and misleading advertising. Clearly, these government activities have produced net benefits for society.

Example: Licensing of Surgeons Suppose that anyone can hang out a shingle and claim to be a surgeon, much as anyone can become a house painter. The market would eventually sort the true surgeons from the frauds. As people died from botched surgeries, lawsuits for malpractice would eventually identify and eliminate most of the medical impostors. And people needing surgery for themselves or their loved ones would seek out information about physician quality from newspaper reports, websites, or people who have undergone similar operations.

But this process of obtaining information will take considerable time and impose unacceptably high human and economic costs. There is a fundamental difference between getting an amateurish paint job on one's house and being on the receiving end of a heart surgery performed by a bogus physician. The marginal cost of obtaining information about sellers in the surgery market will be excessively high. That will make the risk of proceeding to surgery too high for many consumers. The result will be too few surgeries being performed and an underallocation of resources to surgery.

The government has remedied this market failure through a system of qualifying tests and licensing. The licensing provides consumers with inexpensive information about a service—surgery—that they only rarely purchase.

The government has pursued similar policies in several other areas of the economy that are afflicted by asymmetric information. For example, it approves new medicines, regulates the securities industry, and requires warnings on containers of potentially hazardous substances. It also requires warning labels on cigarette packages and disseminates information about communicable diseases. And it issues warnings about unsafe toys and inspects restaurants for health-related violations. Each of these efforts provides either increased certainty about product quality or sufficient warning about a risk that would otherwise remain obscure.

When Buyers Possess Private Information

Situations in which buyers possess *private information* not available to sellers at a low cost can also result in market failure and an underallocation of resources to the production of a good or service. The buyers may be consumers purchasing consumer goods or firms bidding for resources. In either case, the private information held by buyers may put them in a position to take advantage of the sellers. The sellers, knowing that this could be a problem, are naturally reluctant to interact with buyers. The result is reduced—or even zero—market activity.

Moral Hazard The **moral hazard problem** arises when a person behaves more recklessly after obtaining a contract that shifts the costs of bad outcomes onto another party, such as an insurance company or the government. Examples: A truck driver starts speeding and passing aggressively after obtaining auto insurance because he knows that if he wrecks, the insurance company will be stuck with the bill. Lenders start making loans to shady, high-risk firms after obtaining government loan guarantees because they know that the government will have to pay back the loans if the firms go bankrupt.

You might hope that people would not manifest this behavior, but the financial temptation and the ethical dilemma (moral hazard) are too much for many people. They begin to take on more risks because they know that someone else will have to bear the consequences if anything goes wrong.

Private markets may underallocate resources to a good or service that is affected by the moral hazard problem because the sellers of the product will not be able to tell which specific buyers may be affected by moral hazard, the degree to which that moral hazard may lead them to engage in costly behavior, and whether such buyers are very common or few and far between. All that information about buyer behavior is private information held by the buyers, who of course know their own inclinations and can costlessly observe their own actions.

To see why this information asymmetry will tend to repel sellers, suppose a firm offers an insurance policy that pays a set amount of money per month to people who get divorced. Such insurance would spread the economic risk of divorce across thousands of people, thereby helping to protect spouses and children from the economic hardship that divorce often brings.

Unfortunately, the moral hazard problem reduces the likelihood that insurance companies can profitably provide this type of insurance. After purchasing divorce insurance, policyholders can look forward to fewer hardships should a divorce occur. But that reduction in future risk will cause some policyholders to fear divorce less. They will begin to take fewer steps to avert divorce and thereby raise the likelihood of getting divorced. For example, married couples would have less incentive to get along or to iron out marital difficulties if they obtain divorce insurance. At the extreme, some couples might be motivated to obtain a divorce, collect the insurance, and then continue to live together. Such insurance could even promote divorce, the very outcome that it is intended to protect against. The moral hazard problem would force the insurer to charge such a high premium that few policies would be bought.

If the insurer could identify in advance those people most prone to alter their behavior, the firm could exclude them from buying the insurance. But the firm's marginal cost of getting such information is too high compared with the marginal benefit. The result is a failed market.

moral hazard problem The possibility that individuals or institutions will behave more recklessly after they obtain insurance or similar contracts that shift the financial burden of bad outcomes onto others. Example: A bank whose deposits are insured against losses may make riskier loans and investments.

Although divorce insurance will not be available, society recognizes the benefits of protecting people against the hardships of divorce. It has corrected for this underallocation of "hardship insurance" through child-support laws that dictate payments to the spouse who retains the children.

The moral hazard problem also arises in the following situations:

- Medical malpractice insurance may increase the amount of malpractice.
- Unemployment compensation may lead some workers to shirk.
- Guaranteed contracts for professional athletes may reduce the quality of their performance.

adverse selection problem
A problem arising when information known to one party to a contract or agreement is not known to the other party, causing the latter to incur major costs. Example: Individuals who have the poorest health are most likely to buy health insurance.

Adverse Selection   The **adverse selection problem** manifests itself in insurance markets whenever the people who are most likely to need insurance payouts are the people most likely to buy insurance. For example, those in poorest health will be the most likely to purchase health insurance. Or, at the extreme, a person planning to hire an arsonist to "torch" her failing business will have a much stronger incentive to buy fire insurance than a person not planning to incinerate her business.

The adverse selection problem tends to eliminate the unbiased pooling of low and high risks, which is the basis of profitable insurance. With the insurance pool dominated by high risks, premiums must shoot up. And as they do, people with low risks will decide not to buy insurance. The sorting (selection) of people purchasing insurance will become biased toward those with high risks and therefore disadvantageous (adverse) to the insurance company. Insurance rates must then be set so high that few people would want to (or be able to) buy such insurance.

In theory, one solution to the adverse selection problem would be for insurance companies to charge different rates to high-risk and low-risk customers. That is not possible in practice, however, because the information necessary to distinguish between high-risk and low-risk applicants is private information held by buyers. There is, consequently, virtually nothing that a private insurance company can do to prevent adverse selection when buyers hold tightly to their private information.

Governments, by contrast, do have a way of overcoming the adverse selection problem: they can require that every potential customer purchase insurance. That way the insurance pool will include both the low-risk customers as well as the high-risk customers, thereby eliminating the possibility of adverse selection. This is, for example, the strategy followed by the 48 states that require every licensed driver to purchase automobile insurance. It is also the strategy applied by the Social Security system in the United States, which provides insurance against poverty during old age. By mandating nearly universal participation, the people who are most likely to need the minimum benefits that Social Security provides are automatically participants in the program. So, too, are those not likely to need the benefits. With both groups participating at equal rates, adverse selection is averted.

Qualification

We should not leave you with the incorrect impression that every information asymmetry requires a government intervention. In many cases, households and businesses have invented ingenious methods that can overcome information asymmetries without the need for government involvement.

For example, many firms offer product warranties to overcome the lack of information about themselves and their products. Franchising also helps overcome this problem. When you visit a Wendy's or a Marriott, you know what you are going to get, as opposed to stopping at Slim's Hamburger Shop or the Triple Eight Motel.

Also, some private firms and organizations specialize in providing information to buyers and sellers. *Consumer Reports, Mobil Travel Guide,* and numerous Internet sites provide product information; labor unions collect and disseminate information about job safety; and credit bureaus provide information about credit histories and past bankruptcies to lending institutions and insurance companies. Brokers, bonding agencies, and intermediaries also provide information to clients.

However, economists agree that the private sector cannot remedy all information problems. In some situations, government intervention is desirable to promote an efficient allocation of society's scarce resources.

Visible Pollution, Hidden Costs

How Can Governments Reduce Air Pollution at the Lowest Possible Cost If Only the Polluters Themselves Know the Costs of Abatement?

Governments around the world are interested in reducing the emission of gases like carbon dioxide (CO_2) and methane that are released when fossil fuels are burned. Such gasses are believed to be prime drivers of *global warming* and *climate change,* but the costs of reducing the emissions of such gasses can vary widely depending on what policy a government chooses to pursue. An outright ban on burning fossil fuels, for instance, would be extremely costly as it would shut down tens of thousands of existing businesses, plunging their employees into unemployment.

Thus, governments have pursued less draconian methods of reducing air pollution. If implemented correctly, these alternatives, such as carbon taxes and emissions limits, can generate major reductions at a reasonable cost, thereby avoiding the severe economic dislocation that would come with a sudden outright ban on the burning of fossil fuels.

Sensible pollution-abatement policies account for marginal benefits and marginal costs. Society will want as much of an activity like burning gasoline to power ambulances as is associated with the allocatively efficient output level that takes into account all costs (including negative externalities) as well as all benefits. A draconian policy that bans gasoline would go too far; we need ambulances and are willing to tolerate some air pollution in order to transport sick and injured people rapidly and affordably to hospitals.

The trick for government, then, is to figure out how to achieve the allocatively efficient output level at the lowest possible cost. As you know from this chapter, that can be accomplished by figuring out the marginal cost of pollution abatement for each source of pollution and comparing it with the marginal benefit associated with mitigating that source of pollution. The government should then eliminate all of the polluting activities for which the marginal benefit of abatement exceeds the marginal cost of abatement.

That's a great strategy, but can the government implement it? The answer is yes, but the government needs to overcome an important obstacle. The costs of pollution abatement are not obvious. Would it, for instance, be less costly to eliminate 1 million tons per year of CO_2 emissions by shutting down a small factory in Memphis or by paying to retire highly inefficient older vehicles in Denver? To the extent those costs are known, they are often known to the emitters themselves, but not to the government.

The government therefore encounters an asymmetric information problem. How can it reduce pollution at the lowest cost when it is the polluters themselves that are the only ones likely to know what those costs are? One way is to compel the information. Mandatory vehicle smog checks are a good example. Ninety percent of auto emissions are generated by just 25 percent of vehicles, so it is worthwhile for governments to impose the inspection costs needed to identify the high emitters.

Nordroden/123RF

Tradeable emissions permits ("cap and trade") are another way to overcome the asymmetric information problem. These work by giving polluters a financial incentive to reveal their emission reduction costs and, better yet, follow through on emissions reductions. Suppose the U.S. government knows that the allocatively optimal amount of CO_2 emissions is 4 billion tons per year, but that 5 billion tons are currently being emitted. The government will cap the total amount of emissions by printing up and handing out to polluters only 4 billion tons' worth of tradable emissions permits. Each permit may be for, say, 1 ton of CO_2 emissions, and emitting that amount of CO_2 is legal only if you have a permit.

The government will have to hand out the permits without knowing whether they are going to the emitters that have the lowest costs of abatement. But that turns out not to matter if the government makes the permits tradeable, so that they can be bought and sold freely. An emissions-trading market will pop up and what you'll find is that the firms with the highest costs of emissions reduction will purchase permits away from the firms with the lowest costs of emission reduction.

The high-cost firms benefit because it is less expensive for them to buy permits to keep on polluting than it is to reduce their own pollution. And the low-cost firms benefit because they can make more money selling their permits than it will cost them to reduce their emissions (which they must do after they sell away their permits). Both sides win, the externality is reduced at the lowest cost, and society achieves the allocatively efficient level of pollution by setting up a market and allowing the invisible hand to work its magic.

Tradeable pollution permits have worked successfully in several regions for several different types of emissions. They are an economically sophisticated way of overcoming the asymmetric information problem in pollution abatement in order to reduce emissions at the lowest possible cost.

QUICK REVIEW

4.6

▶ Asymmetric information—which occurs when either buyers or sellers have private information that is not available to other market participants— can lead to mistrust that results in market failure and a misallocation of resources.

▶ The moral hazard problem is the tendency of one party to a contract or agreement to alter its behavior in ways that are costly to the other party; for example, a person who obtains insurance may intentionally incur additional risk.

▶ Adverse selection occurs in an insurance market when policies are purchased predominantly by buyers with higher risk profiles, thereby making the provision of insurance prohibitively expensive.

▶ While governments have in specific cases intervened to overcome market failures caused by asymmetric information, the private sector has in many other cases developed ingenious ways to solve asymmetric information problems.

Summary

LO4.1 Explain consumer surplus, producer surplus, and how properly functioning markets maximize total surplus and allocate resources optimally.

Consumer surplus is the difference between the maximum price that a consumer is willing to pay for a product and the lower price actually paid; producer surplus is the difference between the minimum price that a producer is willing to accept for a product and the higher price actually received.

Graphically, consumer surplus is represented by the triangle under the demand curve and above the actual price. Producer surplus is shown by the triangle above the supply curve and below the actual price.

The combined amount of producer and consumer surplus, or total surplus, is represented graphically by the triangle to the left of the intersection of the supply and demand curves that is below the demand curve and above the supply curve.

At the equilibrium price and quantity in a competitive market, marginal benefit equals marginal cost, maximum willingness to pay equals minimum acceptable price, and total surplus is maximized.

Output levels that are either less than or greater than the equilibrium output create efficiency losses, also called deadweight losses. These losses are reductions in total surplus. Underproduction creates efficiency losses because output is not being produced for which maximum willingness to pay exceeds minimum acceptable price. Overproduction creates efficiency losses because output is being produced for which minimum acceptable price exceeds maximum willingness to pay.

LO4.2 Explain how positive and negative externalities cause under- and overallocations of resources.

Externalities, or spillovers, are costs or benefits that accrue to someone other than the immediate buyer or seller. Such costs or benefits are not captured in market demand or supply curves and therefore cause the output of certain goods to vary from society's optimal output. Negative externalities (or spillover costs or external costs) result in an overallocation of resources to a particular product. Positive externalities (or spillover benefits or external benefits) result in an underallocation of resources to a particular product.

Direct controls and specifically targeted Pigovian taxes can improve resource allocation in situations where negative externalities affect many people and community resources. Both direct controls (for example, smokestack emission standards) and Pigovian taxes (for example, taxes on the production of toxic chemicals) increase production costs and hence product price. As product price rises, the

externality, overallocation of resources, and efficiency loss are reduced because less output is produced.

Government can correct the underallocation of resources and efficiency losses either by subsidizing consumers (which increases market demand) or by subsidizing producers (which increases market supply). Such subsidies increase the equilibrium output, reducing or eliminating the positive externality, the underallocation of resources, and the efficiency loss.

The Coase theorem suggests that under the right circumstances private bargaining can solve externality problems. Thus, government intervention is not always needed to deal with externality problems.

LO4.3 Explain why society is usually unwilling to pay the costs of completely eliminating negative externalities, such as air pollution.

The socially optimal amount of externality abatement occurs where society's marginal cost and marginal benefit of reducing an externality are equal. With pollution, for example, the optimal amount of pollution abatement is likely to be less than a 100 percent reduction.

Market failures present government with opportunities to improve the allocation of resources and thereby enhance society's total well-being, but political pressures may make it difficult or impossible to implement an effective solution.

LO4.4 Understand why asymmetric information may justify government intervention in some markets.

Asymmetric information can cause a market to fail if the party with less information decides to withdraw from the market because it fears being exploited by the party with more information. If the party with less information reduces its participation in a market, the reduction in the size of the market may cause an underallocation of resources to the production of the product sold in the market.

The moral hazard problem is the tendency of one party to a contract or agreement to alter their behavior in ways that are costly to the other party. For example, a person who buys insurance may willingly incur added risk.

The adverse selection problem arises when one party to a contract or agreement has less information than the other party and incurs a cost because of that asymmetrical information. For example, an insurance company offering "no medical exam required" life insurance policies may attract customers who have life-threatening diseases.

Terms and Concepts

market failure	deadweight loss	optimal reduction of an externality
total surplus	externality	asymmetric information
consumer surplus	negative externality	private information
producer surplus	positive externality	moral hazard problem
productive efficiency	direct controls	adverse selection problem
allocative efficiency	Coase theorem	
efficiency loss	Pigovian tax	

Discussion Questions

1. Use the ideas of consumer surplus and producer surplus to explain why economists say competitive markets are efficient. Why are below- or above-equilibrium levels of output inefficient, according to these two ideas? **LO4.1**

2. What divergences arise between equilibrium output and efficient output when (a) negative externalities and (b) positive externalities are present? How might government correct these divergences? Cite an example (other than the text examples) of an external cost and an external benefit. **LO4.2**

3. Why are spillover costs and spillover benefits also called negative and positive externalities? Show graphically how a tax can correct for a negative externality and how a subsidy to producers can correct for a positive externality. How does a subsidy to consumers differ from a subsidy to producers in correcting a positive externality? **LO4.2**

4. An apple grower's orchard provides nectar to a neighbor's bees, while the beekeeper's bees help the apple grower by pollinating his apple blossoms. Use Figure 4.5b to explain why this situation of dual positive externalities might lead to an underallocation of resources to both apple growing and beekeeping. How might this underallocation get resolved via the means suggested by the Coase theorem? **LO4.2**

5. The LoJack car recovery system allows the police to track stolen cars. As a result, they not only recover 90 percent of LoJack-equipped cars that are stolen but also arrest many auto thieves and shut down many "chop shops" that rip apart stolen vehicles to get their parts. Thus, LoJack provides both private benefits and positive externalities. Should the government consider subsidizing LoJack purchases? **LO4.2**

6. Explain why zoning laws, which allow certain land uses only in specific locations, might be justified in dealing with negative externalities. Explain why in areas where buildings sit close together, tax breaks to property owners for installing extra fire-prevention equipment might be justified due to positive externalities. **LO4.2**

7. Because medical records are private, individuals applying for health insurance will know more about their own health conditions than will the insurance companies to which they are applying for coverage. Is this information asymmetry likely to increase or decrease the insurance premium? Why? **LO4.4**

8. Why is it in the interest of people purchasing new homes as well as the builders of new homes to have government building codes and building inspectors? **LO4.4**

9. Which of the following are moral hazard problems? Which are adverse selection problems? **LO4.4**
   a. A person with a terminal illness buys several life insurance policies through the mail.
   b. A person drives carelessly because she has automobile insurance.
   c. A person who intends to torch his warehouse takes out a large fire insurance policy.
   d. A professional athlete who has a guaranteed contract fails to stay in shape during the off season.
   e. A person who anticipates having a large family takes a job with a firm that offers exceptional child care benefits.

10. **LAST WORD** What information does a government need if it wants to attempt to reduce a widespread negative externality like air pollution? Who, typically, is actually in possession of that information? How do markets in tradeable emissions permits solve the asymmetric information problem affecting pollution abatement efforts?

Review Questions

1. Draw a supply and demand graph and identify the areas of consumer surplus and producer surplus. Given the demand curve, how will an increase in supply affect the amount of consumer surplus shown in your diagram? Explain. **LO4.1**

2. Assume that candle wax is traded in a perfectly competitive market in which the demand curve captures buyers' full willingness to pay while the supply curve reflects all production costs. For each of the following situations, indicate whether the total output should be increased, decreased, or kept the same in order to achieve allocative and productive efficiency. **LO4.1**
   a. Maximum willingness to pay exceeds minimum acceptable price.
   b. MC > MB.
   c. Total surplus is at a maximum.
   d. The current quantity produced exceeds the market equilibrium quantity.

3. Efficiency losses _____. **LO4.1**
   a. are not possible if suppliers are willing to produce and sell a product.
   b. can result only from underproduction.
   c. can result only from overproduction.
   d. none of the above.
4. Match each of the following characteristics or scenarios with either the term *negative externality* or the term *positive externality*. **LO4.2**
   a. Resources are overallocated.
   b. Xochitl installs a very nice front garden, raising the property values of all the other houses on her block.
   c. Market demand curves are too far to the left (too low).
   d. Resources are underallocated.
   e. Water pollution from a factory forces neighbors to buy water purifiers.
5. Use marginal cost–marginal benefit analysis to determine if the following statement is true or false: "The optimal amount

of pollution abatement for some substances, say, dirty water from storm drains, is very low; the optimal amount of abatement for other substances, say, cyanide poison, is close to 100 percent." **LO4.3**
6. People drive faster when they have auto insurance. This example illustrates: **LO4.4**
   a. adverse selection.
   b. asymmetric information.
   c. moral hazard.
7. Government inspectors who check on the quality of services provided by retailers and government requirements for licensing in various professions are both attempts to resolve: **LO4.4**
   a. the moral hazard problem.
   b. the asymmetric information problem.
8. True or False: A market may collapse and have relatively few transactions between buyers and sellers if buyers have more information than sellers. **LO4.4**

Problems

1. Refer to Table 4.1. If the six people listed in the table are the only consumers in the market, and the equilibrium price is $11 (not the $8 shown), how much consumer surplus will the market generate? **LO4.1**
2. Refer to Table 4.2. If the six people listed in the table are the only producers in the market, and the equilibrium price is $6 (not the $8 shown), how much producer surplus will the market generate? **LO4.1**
3. Look at Tables 4.1 and 4.2 together. What is the total surplus if Bashir buys a unit from Chander? If Barb buys a unit from Chaaya? If Bashir buys a unit from Chad? If you match up pairs of buyers and sellers so as to maximize the total surplus of all transactions, what is the largest total surplus that can be achieved? **LO4.1**
4. **ADVANCED ANALYSIS** Assume the following values for Figures 4.4a and 4.4b: $Q_1 = 20$ bags. $Q_2 = 15$ bags. $Q_3 = 27$ bags. The market equilibrium price is $45 per bag. The price at a is $85 per bag. The price at c is $5 per bag. The price at f is $59 per bag. The price at g is $31 per bag. Apply the formula for the area of a triangle (Area = $1/2 \times$ Base $\times$ Height) to answer the following questions. **LO4.1**
   a. What is the dollar value of the total surplus (= producer surplus + consumer surplus) when the allocatively efficient output level is produced? What is the dollar value of the consumer surplus at that output level?
   b. What is the dollar value of the deadweight loss when output level Q_2 is produced? What is the total surplus when output level Q_2 is produced?
   c. What is the dollar value of the deadweight loss when output level Q_3 is produced? What is the dollar value of the total surplus when output level Q_3 is produced?
5. Refer to Tables 4.1 and 4.2, which show, respectively, the willingness to pay and the willingness to accept of buyers and sellers of bags of oranges. For the following questions, assume that the equilibrium price and quantity depend on the following changes in supply and demand. Also assume that the only

market participants are those listed by name in the two tables. **LO4.2**
   a. What are the equilibrium price and quantity for the data displayed in the two tables?
   b. Instead of bags of oranges, assume that the data in the two tables deal with a good (such as fireworks displays) that can be enjoyed by free riders who do not pay for it. If all the buyers in the two tables free ride, what quantity will private sellers supply?
   c. Assume that we are back to talking about bags of oranges (a private good), but the government has decided that tossed orange peels impose a negative externality on the public that must be rectified by imposing a $2-per-bag tax on sellers. What is the new equilibrium price and quantity? If the new equilibrium quantity is the optimal quantity, by how many bags were oranges overproduced before?
6. Consider a used-car market with asymmetric information. The owners of used cars know what their vehicles are worth but have no way of credibly demonstrating those values to potential buyers. Thus, potential buyers must always worry that the used car they are being offered may be a low-quality "lemon." **LO4.4**
   a. Suppose that there are equal numbers of good and bad used cars in the market. Good used cars are worth $13,000, and bad used cars are worth $5,000. What is the average value of a used car?
   b. By how much does the average value exceed the value of a bad used car? By how much does the value of a good used car exceed the average value?
   c. Would a potential seller of a good used car be willing to accept the average value as payment for the vehicle?
   d. If a buyer negotiates with a seller to purchase the seller's used car for a price equal to the average value, is the car more likely to be good or bad?
   e. Will the used-car market come to feature mostly—if not exclusively—lemons? Explain. How much will used cars end up costing if all the good cars are withdrawn from the market?

Public Goods, Public Choice, and Government Failure

>> LEARNING OBJECTIVES

LO5.1 Describe free riding and public goods, and illustrate why private firms cannot normally produce public goods.

LO5.2 Explain the difficulties of conveying economic preferences through majority voting.

LO5.3 Define government failure and explain its causes.

In the previous chapter, we discussed *externalities* and *asymmetric information*, two types of *market failure* that can cause markets to either overproduce or underproduce relative to the social optimum.

This chapter takes as its starting point *public goods*, which can be afflicted by a more extreme variety of market failure in which production drops all the way to zero. In these situations, government often steps forward to produce the missing public good. But that leads to an interesting economic problem: How much should the government provide? What quantity of a public good is allocatively efficient?

We also study why governments often fail to intervene in the economy in socially optimal ways. Causes include corruption, special interest lobbying, and the voting paradoxes that can make it nearly impossible for government officials to discern the "will of the people." Our study of these problems—collectively known as *government failure*—balances our analysis of *market failure*. Markets can go haywire, but so can government. Vigilance is warranted with respect to both.

Public Goods

Demand-side market failures arise when demand curves underreport how much consumers are willing and able to pay for a product. When that happens, demand curves shift left and equilibrium output is below the social optimum. That was the case with the positive externalities studied in the previous chapter.

The underreporting of demand reaches its most extreme form in the case of public goods. Markets may fail to produce *any* of a public good because its demand curve may reflect *none* of its potential consumers' willingness to pay. But to understand public goods, we first need to understand the characteristics that define private goods.

>> **LO5.1** Describe free riding and public goods, and illustrate why private firms cannot normally produce public goods.

demand-side market failures Underallocations of resources that occur when private demand curves understate consumers' full willingness to pay for a *good* or *service*.

private good A *good* or *service* that is individually consumed and that can be profitably provided by privately owned *firms* because they can exclude nonpayers from receiving the benefits.

rivalry The characteristic displayed by certain goods and services that consumption by one person precludes consumption by others.

excludability The characteristic displayed by those goods and services for which sellers are able to prevent nonbuyers from obtaining benefits.

public good A *good* or *service* that is characterized by *non*rivalry and *non*excludability. These characteristics typically imply that no private *firm* can break even when attempting to provide such products. As a result, they are often provided by governments, who pay for them using general *tax* revenues.

nonrivalry The idea that one person's benefit from a certain *good* does not reduce the benefit available to others; a characteristic of a *public good*.

nonexcludability The inability to keep nonpayers (free riders) from obtaining benefits from a certain good; a characteristic of a *public good*.

free-rider problem The inability of potential providers of an economically desirable *good* or *service* to obtain payment from those who benefit, because of *nonexcludability*.

Characteristics of Private Goods

The vast majority of goods and services consumed by people on a daily basis are private goods produced by private, for-profit companies.

Private goods are distinguished by rivalry and excludability.

- **Rivalry** (in consumption) means that when one person consumes a product, it is not available for another person to consume. When Garcia purchases and drinks a bottle of mineral water, it is not available for Johnson to purchase and consume.

- **Excludability** means that sellers can prevent people who do not pay for a product from obtaining its benefits. Only people who are willing and able to pay the market price for bottles of water can obtain these drinks and the benefits they confer.

Excludability is the key feature when it comes to understanding why for-profit companies are happy to produce private goods for consumers. Indeed, it is only because private goods are excludable that private producers are willing to produce them. Excludability means that private producers can "put a fence around" private goods and require payment by consumers. That is crucial because if private firms were not able to charge customers for their products, they would not be able to cover their production costs and would soon go bankrupt.

Consumers fully express their personal demands for private goods in the market. If Garcia likes bottled mineral water, that fact will be known by her desire to purchase the product. Other things equal, the higher the price of bottled water, the fewer bottles she will buy. This is simply *individual* demand, as described in Chapter 3.

The *market* demand for a private good is the horizontal summation of the individual demand schedules (review Figure 3.2). Suppose just two consumers comprise the market for bottled water and the price is $1 per bottle. If Garcia will purchase 3 bottles and Johnson will buy 2, the market demand reflects consumers' demand for 5 bottles at the $1 price. Similar summations of quantities demanded at other prices will generate the market demand schedule and curve.

Suppose the equilibrium price of bottled water is $1. Garcia and Johnson will buy a total of 5 bottles, and the sellers will obtain total revenue of $5 (= $1 × 5). If the sellers' cost per bottle is $0.80, their total cost will be $4 (= $0.80 × 5). So sellers charging $1 per bottle will obtain $5 of total revenue, incur $4 of total cost, and earn $1 of profit on the 5 bottles sold.

Because firms can charge for private goods, they are able to "tap market demand." Consumers willing to pay the market price obtain the goods; nonpayers go without. A competitive market not only makes private goods available to consumers but also allocates society's resources efficiently to the particular product. There is neither underproduction nor overproduction of the product.

Public Goods Characteristics

Public goods are the opposite of private goods in terms of rivalry and excludability. In fact, public goods are distinguished by *non*rivalry and *non*excludability.

- **Nonrivalry** (in consumption) means that one person's consumption of a good does not preclude consumption of the good by others. Everyone can simultaneously obtain the benefit from a public good such as national defense, street lighting, or a global positioning system.

- **Nonexcludability** means there is no effective way of excluding individuals from the benefit of the good once it comes into existence. You cannot exclude someone from benefiting from national defense, street lighting, or a global positioning system.

These two characteristics create a **free-rider problem.** Once a producer has provided a public good, everyone, including nonpayers, can obtain the benefit.

Because most people do not voluntarily pay for something that they can obtain for free, most people become free riders. These free riders like the public good and would be willing to pay for it if producers could somehow force them to pay—but nonexcludability means that there is no way for producers to withhold the good from the free riders, whose willingness to pay is, consequently, not expressed in the market. From the producers' viewpoint, free riding reduces demand. The more free riding, the less demand. And if all consumers free ride, demand will collapse to zero.

The low or zero demand caused by free riding makes it virtually impossible for private firms to profitably provide public goods. With little or no demand, firms cannot effectively "tap market demand" for revenues and profits. As a result, they will not produce public goods. Society will

CONSIDER THIS . . .

Street Entertainers

Street entertainers are often found in tourist areas of major cities. These entertainers illuminate the concepts of free riders and public goods.

Most street entertainers have a hard time earning a living from their activities (unless event organizers pay them) because they have no way of excluding non-payers from the benefits of their entertainment. They essentially are providing public, not private, goods and must rely on voluntary payments.

The result is a significant free-rider problem. Only a few in the audience put money in the container or instrument case, and many who do so contribute only token amounts. The rest are free riders who obtain the benefits of the street entertainment and retain their money for purchases that they themselves initiate.

500px/Alamy Stock Photo

Street entertainers are acutely aware of the free-rider problem, and some have found creative ways to lessen it. For example, some entertainers involve the audience directly in the act. This usually creates a greater sense of audience willingness (or obligation) to contribute money at the end of the performance.

"Pay for performance" is another creative approach to lessening the free-rider problem. A good example is the street entertainer painted up to look like a statue. When people drop coins into the container, the "statue" makes a slight movement. The greater the contributions, the greater the movement. But these human "statues" still face a free-rider problem: Nonpayers also get to enjoy the acts.

therefore suffer efficiency losses because goods for which marginal benefits exceed marginal costs are not produced. Thus, if society wants a public good to be produced, it must turn to nonmarket provision by entities that do not have to worry about profitability.

One option is private philanthropy. But many public goods—such as national defense and universal public education—are too expensive for private philanthropy. So society often looks to government to provide public goods.

Those government-provided public goods will still be nonexcludable; so the government won't have any better luck preventing free riding. But the government doesn't have to worry about profitability because it can finance the provision of public goods through taxation. It can therefore provide public goods when private firms and philanthropic organizations can't.

Examples of public goods include national defense, outdoor fireworks displays, the light beams projected by lighthouses, public art displays, and public concerts. All of these goods or services show both nonrivalry and nonexcludability.

In a few special cases, private firms can provide public goods because the production costs of these public goods can be covered by the profits generated by closely related private goods. For instance, private companies can make a profit providing broadcast TV—which is a nonrival, nonexcludable public good—because they control who gets to air TV commercials, which are rival and excludable private goods. The money that broadcasters make from selling airtime for ads allows them to turn a profit despite having to provide their main product, broadcast TV, for free.

For the large majority of public goods, however, private provision is unprofitable. As a result, they must be furnished, if at all, by either private philanthropy or the government. For many less expensive or less important public goods like fireworks displays or public art, society may feel comfortable relying on private philanthropy. But when it comes to public goods like national defense, people normally look to the government.

This leads to an important question: Once a government decides to produce a particular public good, how can it determine the optimal amount that it should provide? How can it avoid either underallocating or overallocating society's scarce resources to the production of the public good?

Optimal Quantity of a Public Good

If consumers need not reveal their true demand for a public good in the marketplace, how can society determine the optimal amount of that good? The answer is that the government must try to estimate the demand for the public good through surveys or public votes. It can then compare the marginal benefit (MB) of an added unit of the good against the government's marginal cost (MC) of providing it. Adhering to the MB = MC rule, government can provide the "right," or "efficient," amount of the public good.

▶ Private goods are characterized by rivalry (one person's consumption precludes anyone else's consumption) and excludability (nonpayers can be excluded from consumption).

▶ Public goods are characterized by nonrivalry (consumption by one person does not diminish anyone else's consumption) and nonexcludability (nonpayers cannot be excluded from consumption).

▶ The socially optimal amount of a public good is the amount at which the marginal cost and marginal benefit of the good are equal: MB = MC.

Demand for Public Goods

The demand for a public good is somewhat unusual. Suppose Garcia and Johnson are the only two people in the society, and their marginal willingness to pay for a public good, national defense, is as shown in Table 5.1. Economists might have discovered these schedules through a survey asking questions about how much each citizen is willing to pay for various types and amounts of public goods rather than go without them.

Notice that the schedules in Table 5.1 are price-quantity schedules, implying that they are demand schedules. Rather than depicting demand in the usual way—the quantity of a product someone is willing to buy at each possible price—these schedules show the price someone is willing to pay for an extra unit at each possible quantity. That is, Garcia is willing to pay $4 for the first unit of the public good, $3 for the second, $2 for the third, and so on.

Suppose the government produces 1 unit of this public good. Because of nonrivalry, Garcia's consumption of the good does not preclude Johnson from also consuming it, and vice versa. So both consume the good, and neither volunteers to pay for it. But from Table 5.1 we can find the amount these two people would be willing to pay, together, rather than do without this 1 unit of the good. Columns 1 and 2 show that Garcia would be willing to pay $4 for the first unit of the public good; columns 1 and 3 show that Johnson would be willing to pay $5 for it. So the two people are jointly willing to pay $9 (= $4 + $5) for this first unit.

For the second unit of the public good, the collective price they are willing to pay is $7 (= $3 from Garcia + $4 from Johnson); for the third unit they would pay $5 (= $2 + $3); and so on. By finding the collective willingness to pay for each additional unit (column 4), we can construct a schedule of the **collective demand for a public good** (= collective willingness-to-pay for the public good). Here we are *not* adding the quantities demanded at each possible price, as we do when we determine the market demand for a private good. Instead, we are adding the prices that people are willing to pay for the last unit of the public good at each possible quantity demanded.

Figure 5.1 shows the same adding procedure graphically, using the data from Table 5.1. Note that we sum Garcia's and Johnson's willingness-to-pay curves *vertically* to derive the collective willingness-to-pay curve (demand curve). The summing procedure is downward from the top graph to the middle graph to the bottom (total) graph. For example, the height of the collective demand curve D_c at 2 units of output in the bottom graph is $7, the sum of the amounts that Garcia and Johnson are each willing to pay for the second unit (= $3 + $4). Likewise, the height of the collective demand curve at 4 units of the public good is $3 (= $1 + $2).

Please note that each of these demand curves is not only a willingness-to-pay curve but also a marginal-benefit (MB) curve. Consequently, we can interpret the collective demand curve for a public good as capturing both the collective willingness to pay for each possible unit of a public good as well as the collective marginal benefit of each unit of the public good.

collective demand for a public good A schedule or a curve showing the collective willingness to pay of consumers for a public good. Can be found by vertically adding individual demand curves, which is equivalent to adding the respective maximum prices that individual consumers are willing to pay for the last unit of the public good at each possible quantity demanded.

TABLE 5.1   Demand for a Public Good, Two Individuals

(1) Quantity of Public Good	(2) Garcia's Willingness to Pay (Price)		(3) Johnson's Willingness to Pay (Price)		(4) Collective Willingness to Pay (Price)
1	$4	+	$5	=	$9
2	3	+	4	=	7
3	2	+	3	=	5
4	1	+	2	=	3
5	0	+	1	=	1

Comparing MB and MC

We can now determine the optimal quantity of the public good. The collective demand curve D_c in Figure 5.1c measures society's marginal benefit of each unit of this particular good. The supply curve S measures society's marginal cost of each unit. The optimal quantity of this public good occurs where marginal benefit equals marginal cost, or where the two curves intersect. In Figure 5.1c that point is 3 units of the public good, where the collective willingness to pay for the last (third) unit—the marginal benefit—just matches that unit's marginal cost ($5 = $5). As we saw in Chapter 1, equating marginal benefit and marginal cost efficiently allocates society's scarce resources.

Cost-Benefit Analysis

The above example suggests a practical means, called **cost-benefit analysis,** for deciding whether to provide a particular public good and how much of it to provide. Let's go through an extended example that applies cost-benefit analysis to an infrastructure project.

Concept Suppose the federal government is contemplating several different plans for a highway construction project. Because the economy's resources are limited, any decision to use more resources in the public sector will mean fewer resources for the private sector. There will be an opportunity cost, as well as a benefit. The cost is the loss of satisfaction resulting from the accompanying decline in the production of private goods; the benefit is the extra satisfaction resulting from the output of more public goods. Should the needed resources be shifted from the private to the public sector? The answer is yes if the benefit from the new highways exceeds the cost of having fewer private goods. The answer is no if the cost of the forgone private goods is greater than the benefit associated with the new highways.

Illustration Roads and highways can be run privately, as excludability is possible with toll booths. However, the U.S. federal highway system is almost entirely nonexclusive because anyone with a car can get on and off most federal highways without restriction. Federal highways therefore satisfy one characteristic of a public good, nonexcludability. Highways are also nonrival; unless a highway is already extremely crowded, one person's driving on the highway does not preclude another person's driving on the highway. Thus, the federal highway system is effectively a public good. We can now turn to two important questions: Should the federal government expand the federal highway system? If so, what is the proper size or scope for the overall project?

Table 5.2 lists four increasingly ambitious and increasingly costly highway improvement plans: widening existing two-lane highways; building new two-lane highways; building new four-lane highways; and building new six-lane highways. The extent to which government should undertake highway construction depends on the costs and benefits. The costs are largely the costs of constructing and maintaining the highways; the benefits are improved flows of people and goods throughout the country.

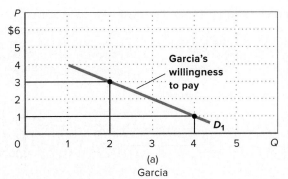
(a)
Garcia

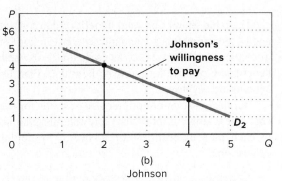
(b)
Johnson

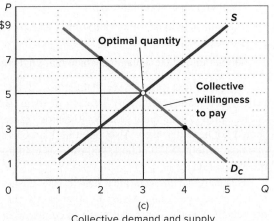
(c)
Collective demand and supply

FIGURE 5.1
The optimal amount of a public good.

Two people—Garcia and Johnson—are the only members of a hypothetical economy. (a) D_1 shows Garcia's willingness to pay for various quantities of a particular public good. (b) D_2 shows Johnson's willingness to pay for these same quantities of this public good. (c) The collective demand for this public good is shown by D_c and is found by summing vertically Garcia's and Johnson's individual willingness-to-pay curves. The supply S of the public good is upward sloping, reflecting rising marginal costs. The optimal amount of the public good is 3 units, determined by the intersection of D_c and S. At that output, marginal benefit (reflected in the collective demand curve D_c) equals marginal cost (reflected in the supply curve S).

cost-benefit analysis
A method for deciding whether or not to provide a public good that involves a comparison of the total cost of providing that public good with its collective benefit (measured by collective willingness to pay).

TABLE 5.2 Cost-Benefit Analysis for a National Highway Construction Project (in Billions)

(1) Plan	(2) Total Cost of Project	(3) Marginal Cost	(4) Total Benefit	(5) Marginal Benefit	(6) Net Benefit (4) − (2)
No new construction	$ 0		$ 0		$ 0
A: Widen existing highways	50	$ 50	200	$200	150
B: New 2-lane highways	140	90	350	150	210
C: New 4-lane highways	240	100	470	120	230
D: New 6-lane highways	620	380	580	110	−40

The table shows that total benefit (column 4) exceeds total cost (column 2) for plans A, B, and C, indicating that some highway construction is economically justifiable. We see this directly in column 6, where total costs (column 2) are subtracted from total benefits (column 4). Net benefits are positive for plans A, B, and C. Plan D is not economically justifiable because net benefits are negative.

But the question of optimal size or scope for this project remains. Comparing the marginal cost (the change in total cost) and the marginal benefit (the change in total benefit) relating to each plan determines the answer. The guideline is well known to you from previous discussions:

- Increase an activity, project, or output as long as the marginal benefit (column 5) exceeds the marginal cost (column 3).

- Stop the activity at, or as close as possible to, the point at which the marginal benefit equals the marginal cost.

- Do not undertake a plan for which marginal cost exceeds marginal benefit.

Applying those rules, we see that plans A, B, and C should all be undertaken because marginal benefit exceeds marginal cost for each of them. But the federal government should stop there because plan D's marginal cost ($380 billion) exceeds its marginal benefit ($110 billion). Plan D should not be undertaken. Also note that Plan C is closest to the theoretical optimum because its marginal benefit ($120 billion) still exceeds marginal cost ($100 billion) while coming closest to the MB = MC ideal.

marginal cost-marginal benefit rule As it applies to *cost-benefit analysis,* the tenet that a government project or program should be expanded to the point where the *marginal cost* and *marginal benefit* of additional expenditures are equal.

This **marginal cost–marginal benefit rule** tells us which plan provides the maximum excess of total benefits over total costs or, in other words, the plan that provides society with the maximum net benefit. You can confirm directly in column 6 that the maximum net benefit (= $230 billion) is associated with plan C.

Cost-benefit analysis shatters the myth that "economy in government" and "reduced government spending" are synonymous. "Economy" is concerned with using scarce resources efficiently. If the marginal cost of a proposed government program exceeds its marginal benefit, then the proposed public program should not be undertaken. But if the marginal benefit exceeds the marginal cost, then it would be uneconomical or "wasteful" not to spend on that government program. Economy in government does not mean minimization of public spending. It means allocating resources between the private and public sectors and among public goods to achieve maximum net benefit.

Quasi-Public Goods

quasi-public good A *good* or *service* to which *excludability* could apply but that has such a large *positive externality* that government sponsors its production to prevent an underallocation of resources.

Government provides many goods that fit the economist's definition of a public good. However, it also provides other goods and services that could be produced and delivered in such a way that exclusion would be possible. Such goods, called **quasi-public goods,** include education, streets and highways, police and fire protection, libraries and museums, preventive medicine, and sewage disposal. They could all be priced and provided by private firms through the market system. But because the benefits of these goods flow well beyond the benefit to individual buyers, the market system would underproduce these goods. Therefore, government often provides them to avoid the underallocation of resources that would otherwise occur if these goods with large positive externalities were produced solely by the private sector.

The Reallocation Process

How are resources reallocated from the production of private goods to the production of public and quasi-public goods? If the economy's resources are fully employed, government must free up resources from the production of private goods and make them available for producing public and quasi-public goods. It does so by reducing the private demand for resources. And it does that by levying taxes on households and businesses, taking some of their income out of the circular flow (see Figure 2.2). With lower incomes and hence less purchasing power, households and businesses must curtail their consumption and investment spending. As a result, the private demand for goods and services declines, as does the private demand for resources. So, by diverting purchasing power from private spenders to government, taxes remove resources from private use.

Government then spends the tax proceeds to provide public and quasi-public goods and services. Taxation releases resources from the production of private consumer goods (food, clothing, television sets) and private investment goods (wi-fi networks, software for flying taxis, distribution centers). Government shifts those resources to the production of public and quasi-public goods (post offices, submarines, parks), changing the composition of the economy's total output.

Public Choice Theory and Voting Paradoxes
Public Choice Theory

Market failures, such as public goods and externalities, impede economic efficiency and justify government intervention in the economy. But the government's response to market failures is not without its own problems and pitfalls. In fact, government may sometimes fail as badly or even worse than markets.

That is why it is important to study **public choice theory**—the economic analysis of government decision making, politics, and elections. We are going to find that the intricacies and limitations of democratic voting can make it impossible for government officials to determine the public will and thus what government actions they should take in order to ensure allocative efficiency in the economy.

Revealing Preferences through Majority Voting

Through some process, society must decide which public goods it wants and in what amounts. It also must determine the extent to which it wants government to intervene in private markets to correct externalities. Decisions must be made about the extent and type of business regulation, income redistribution, policies to mitigate *asymmetric information* problems, and so on. Furthermore, society must collect taxes for financing government. How should government apportion (divide) the total tax burden among the public?

Decisions such as these are made collectively in the United States through a democratic process that relies heavily on majority voting. Candidates for office offer alternative policy packages, and citizens elect people who they think will make the best decisions on their collective behalf. Voters "retire" officials who do not adequately represent their collective wishes. Also, at the state and local levels, citizens sometimes vote directly on public expenditures or new legislation.

Although the democratic process does a reasonably good job of revealing society's preferences, it is imperfect. Public choice theory demonstrates that majority voting can produce inefficiencies and inconsistencies.

Inefficient Voting Outcomes Society's well-being is enhanced when government provides a public good whose total benefit exceeds its total cost. Unfortunately, traditional one-person-one-vote majority voting does not always deliver that outcome.

FIGURE 5.2
Inefficient voting outcomes.

Majority voting can produce inefficient decisions. (a) Majority voting leads to rejection of a public good that would entail a greater total benefit than total cost. (b) Majority voting results in acceptance of a public good that has a higher total cost than total benefit.

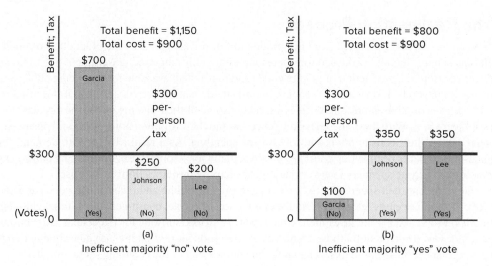

(a)
Inefficient majority "no" vote

(b)
Inefficient majority "yes" vote

Illustration: Inefficient "No" Vote   Assume that the government can provide a public good (say, national defense) at a total expense of $900. Also assume that the society is composed of only three individuals—Garcia, Johnson, and Lee—and that they will share the $900 tax expense equally, each being taxed $300 if the proposed public good is provided. And assume, as Figure 5.2a illustrates, that Garcia would receive $700 worth of benefits from having this public good; Johnson, $250; and Lee, $200.

What will be the result if a majority vote determines whether or not this public good is provided? Although people do not always vote strictly according to their own economic interest, it is likely Johnson and Lee will vote "no" because they will incur tax costs of $300 each while gaining benefits of only $250 and $200, respectively. Garcia will vote "yes." So the majority vote will defeat the proposal even though the total benefit of $1,150 (= $700 for Garcia + $250 for Johnson + $200 for Lee) exceeds the total cost of $900. Resources should be devoted to this good, but they will not be. Too little of this public good will be produced.

Illustration: Inefficient "Yes" Vote   Now consider a situation in which the majority favors a public good even though its total cost exceeds its total benefit. Figure 5.2b shows the details. Again, Garcia, Johnson, and Lee will equally share the $900 cost of the public good; each will be taxed $300. But because Garcia's benefit now is only $100 from the public good, she will vote against it. Meanwhile, Johnson and Lee will benefit by $350 each. They will vote for the public good because the benefit ($350) exceeds their tax payments ($300). The majority vote will provide a public good costing $900 that produces total benefits of only $800 (= $100 for Garcia + $350 for Johnson + $350 for Lee). Society's resources will be inefficiently allocated to this public good. Too much of it will be produced.

Implications   The point is that an inefficient outcome may occur as an overproduction or an underproduction of a specific public good, and therefore as an overallocation or underallocation of resources for that particular use. Earlier in this chapter, we saw that government can improve economic efficiency by providing public goods that the market system will not make available. Now we have extended that analysis to reveal that inefficient voting outcomes may cause a government to either underprovide or overprovide public goods.

In our examples, each person has only a single vote, no matter how much they might gain or lose from a public good. In the first example (inefficient "no" vote), Garcia would be willing to purchase a vote from either Johnson or Lee if buying votes were legal. That way, Garcia could be assured of obtaining the national defense she so highly values. But because buying votes is illegal, many people with strong preferences for certain public goods may have to go without them.

Because majority voting fails to incorporate the intensity of individual voters' preferences, it may produce economically inefficient outcomes.

Interest Groups and Logrolling   Some, but not all, of the inefficiencies of majority voting get resolved through the political process. Two examples follow.

Interest Groups People who share strong preferences for a particular public good may band together into interest groups and use advertisements, mailings, and direct persuasion to convince others of the merits of the public good in question. Garcia might try to persuade Johnson and Lee that it is in their best interest to vote for national defense–that national defense is much more valuable to them than their respective $250 and $200 valuations. Such appeals are common in democratic politics. Sometimes they are successful; sometimes they are not.

Political Logrolling Perhaps surprisingly, **logrolling**–the trading of votes to secure desired outcomes–can also turn an inefficient outcome into an efficient one. In our first example (Figure 5.2a), suppose that Johnson has a strong preference for a different public good–for example, a new road–which Garcia and Lee do not think is worth the tax expense. The stage is set for Garcia and Johnson to trade votes to ensure provision of both national defense and the new road. That is, Garcia and Johnson would each vote "yes" on both measures. Garcia would get the national defense and Johnson would get the road. Without the logrolling, both public goods would have been rejected. This logrolling will add to society's well-being if, as was true for national defense, the road creates a greater overall benefit than cost.

But logrolling need not increase economic efficiency. Even if national defense and the road each cost more than the total benefit each produces, both might still be provided if there is vote trading. Garcia and Johnson might still engage in logrolling if each expects to secure a sufficient net gain from her or his favored public good, even though the gains would come at Lee's expense.

Paradox of Voting

Another difficulty with majority voting is the **paradox of voting,** a situation in which society may not be able to rank its preferences consistently through paired-choice majority voting.

Preferences Consider Table 5.3, in which we again assume a community of three voters: Garcia, Johnson, and Lee. Suppose the community has three alternative public goods from which to choose: national defense, a road, and a weather warning system. Each member of the community prefers the three alternatives in a certain order. For example, one person might prefer national defense to a road and a road to a weather warning system. We can attempt to determine the community's preferences through paired-choice majority voting. Specifically, a vote can be held between any two of the public goods, and the winner of that vote can then be matched against the third public good in another vote.

The three goods and the three voters' individual preferences are listed in the top part of Table 5.3. Garcia prefers national defense to the road and the road to the weather warning system. By implication, Garcia prefers national defense to the weather warning system. Johnson values the road more than the weather warning system and the warning system more than national defense. Lee's order of preference is weather warning system, national defense, and road.

Voting Outcomes The lower part of Table 5.3 shows the outcomes of three hypothetical elections decided through majority vote. In the first, national defense wins against the road because a majority of voters (Garcia and Lee) prefer national defense to the road. In the second election, to see whether this community wants a road or a weather warning system, a majority of voters (Garcia and Johnson) prefer the road.

logrolling The trading of votes by legislators to secure favorable outcomes on decisions concerning the provision of *public goods* and *quasi-public goods.*

paradox of voting A situation where paired-choice voting by majority rule fails to provide a consistent ranking of society's preferences for *public goods* or *public services.*

TABLE 5.3 Paradox of Voting

	Preferences		
Public Good	**Garcia**	**Johnson**	**Lee**
National defense	1st choice	3d choice	2d choice
Road	2d choice	1st choice	3d choice
Weather warning system	3d choice	2d choice	1st choice
Election	**Voting Outcomes: Winner**		
1. National defense vs. road	National defense (preferred by Garcia and Lee)		
2. Road vs. weather warning system	Road (preferred by Garcia and Johnson)		
3. National defense vs. weather warning system	Weather warning system (preferred by Johnson and Lee)		

We have determined that the majority of people in this community prefer national defense to a road and prefer a road to a weather warning system. It seems logical to conclude that the community prefers national defense to a weather warning system. But it does not!

To demonstrate this conclusion, we hold a direct election between national defense and the weather warning system. Row 3 shows that a majority of voters (Johnson and Lee) prefer the weather warning system to national defense. As listed in Table 5.3, then, the three paired-choice majority votes imply that this community is irrational: It seems to prefer national defense to a road and a road to a weather warning system, but it would rather have a weather warning system than national defense.

The problem is not irrational community preferences but rather a flawed procedure for determining those preferences. We see that the outcome from paired-choice majority voting may depend on the order in which the votes are taken. Different sequences can lead to different outcomes, many of which may fail to reflect the electorate's underlying preferences. As a consequence, government may find it difficult to provide the "correct" public goods by acting in accordance with majority voting.

Important note: This critique is not meant to suggest that majority voting has no place in making decisions about public goods or that it is among the least-good ways of making such decisions. Majority voting is, for instance, *much* more likely to reflect community preferences than decisions made by a dictator or an aristocracy. As British Prime Minister Winston Churchill astutely joked, "Democracy is the worst form of government—except for all the others."

Median-Voter Model

median-voter model The theory that under majority rule the median (middle) voter will be in the dominant position to determine the outcome of an election.

Another aspect of majority voting reveals further insights into real-world phenomena. The **median-voter model** suggests that, under majority rule and consistent voting preferences, the median voter will in a sense determine the outcomes of elections. The median voter is the person holding the middle position on an issue: Half the other voters have stronger preferences for a public good, amount of taxation, or degree of government regulation, while half have weaker or negative preferences. The extreme voters on each side of an issue prefer the median choice rather than the other extreme position, so the median voter's choice predominates.

Example Suppose that a society composed of Garcia, Johnson, and Lee has agreed that it needs a weather warning system but that there is disagreement about how expensive a system to set up.

To start the process of figuring out how expensive a system to build, each person independently submits a total dollar amount that they think should be spent on the warning system, assuming each will be taxed one-third of that amount. Two successive elections will then be needed to determine the size of the system. That's because each person can be expected to vote for their own proposal—so that no majority will occur if all the proposals are placed on the ballot at the same time. Thus, the group decides to hold two sequential paired-choice votes: They will first vote between two of the proposals and then match the winner of that vote against the remaining proposal.

The three proposals are as follows: Garcia desires a $400 system; Johnson wants an $800 system; Lee opts for a $300 system. Which proposal will win? The median-voter model suggests the winner will be the $400 proposal submitted by the median voter, Garcia. Half the other voters favor a more costly system; half favor a less costly system. To understand why the $400 system will be the outcome, let's conduct two sequential paired-choice votes.

1. First, suppose that the $400 proposal is matched against the $800 proposal. Garcia naturally votes for her $400 proposal, and Johnson votes for his own $800 proposal. Lee, who proposed the $300 expenditure for the warning system, votes for the $400 proposal because it is closer to her own proposal. So Garcia's $400 proposal is selected by a 2-to-1 majority vote.

2. Next, we match the $400 proposal against the $300 proposal. Again the $400 proposal wins. It gets a vote from Garcia and a vote from Johnson, who proposed the $800 expenditure and for that reason prefers a $400 expenditure to a $300 expenditure. Garcia, the median voter in this case, is in a sense the person who has decided the level of expenditure on the weather warning system.

Real-World Applicability Although our illustration is simple, it explains a great deal. We do note a tendency for public choices to match most closely the median view. Political candidates, for example, take one set of positions to win the nomination of their political parties; in so doing, they tend to appeal to the median voter within the party to get the nomination. They then shift their views more closely to the political center when they square off against opponents from the opposite political party. In effect, they redirect their appeal toward the median voter within the total population. They conduct polls and adjust their positions on issues accordingly.

Implications The median-voter model has two important implications:

- At any point in time, many people will be dissatisfied by the extent of government involvement in the economy. The size of government will largely be determined by the median preference, leaving many people desiring a much larger, or a much smaller, public sector.

- Some people may "vote with their feet" by moving into political jurisdictions where the median voter's preferences are closer to their own. They may move from the city to a suburb where the level of government services, and therefore taxes, is lower. Or they may move into an area known for its excellent, but expensive, school system. Some may move to other states; a few may even move to other countries.

Because our personal preferences for publicly provided goods and services are not static, the median preference shifts over time. Moreover, information about people's preferences is imperfect, leaving much room for politicians to misjudge the true median position. When they do, they may have a difficult time getting elected or reelected.

▶ Majority voting can produce voting outcomes that are inefficient; projects having greater total benefits than total costs may be defeated, and projects having greater total costs than total benefits may be approved.

▶ The paradox of voting occurs when voting by majority rule does not provide a consistent ranking of society's preferences for public goods and services.

▶ The median-voter model suggests that under majority rule and consistent voting preferences, the voter who has the middle preference will determine the outcome of an election.

Alternative Voting Mechanisms

Because majority voting can lead to inefficient voting outcomes, economists have proposed several alternative voting mechanisms. Instead of the traditional one-person-one-vote (1p1v) system in which each voter gets one vote and a simple majority wins, these alternative voting systems allow for people to cast multiple votes as a way of accounting for the strength of their respective preferences. By doing so, alternative voting mechanisms are more likely than 1p1v to avoid inefficient voting outcomes and thereby approve only those public goods for which total benefit exceeds total cost.

Quadratic Voting **Quadratic voting** is an alternative voting mechanism that leads to fewer inefficient voting outcomes than 1p1v. Under quadratic voting, the winning side of an election (Yes or No) is still determined by the "50 percent plus 1" majority voting rule that you are familiar with. But under a quadratic voting system, each voter can purchase and then cast as many votes as she desires. Naturally, voters with strong preferences will wish to buy more votes because the outcome matters more for them than for people with weak preferences. The question then becomes: how many votes will each voter want to purchase?

The answer, as you might have guessed, is that each voter will purchase votes up to the point where the marginal benefit from purchasing additional votes equals the marginal cost of purchasing additional votes. Under quadratic voting, the cost of purchasing votes is quadratic, meaning that it increases exponentially with the square of the number of votes purchased. If a voter desires

quadratic voting system
A majority voting system in which voters can express strength of preference by purchasing as many votes as they like at a price equal to the square of the number of votes purchased. Quadratic voting is more likely (but not guaranteed) to result in economically efficient decisions than traditional one-person-one-vote (1p1v) majority voting systems.

TABLE 5.4 Desired Number of Votes and their Cost under Quadratic Voting

Desired Number of Votes (v)	Cost to Purchase Desired Number of Votes (= v²)
0	$ 0
1	1
2	4
3	9
4	16
5	25
6	36
7	49
8	64
9	81
10	100
11	121
12	144
13	169
14	196
15	225
16	256
17	289
18	324
19	361
20	400

to purchase v votes, the cost will be v^2 dollars. Table 5.4 shows this relationship for purchases of up to 20 votes. In the first row of the table, you can see that the cost to purchase zero votes is the square of zero, or $0 (= 0^2)$. The second row shows that the cost to purchase 1 vote is the square of 1, or $1 (= 1^2)$. The third row shows that the cost to purchase two votes is the square of 2, or $4 (= 2^2)$. Continuing down the table you can see that the cost of purchasing 12 votes is the square of 12, or $144 (= 12^2)$. The final row shows that the cost of purchasing 20 votes is $400 (= 20^2)$.

Note that the quadratic cost of purchasing votes implies that the marginal cost of vote buying is increasing with each additional vote purchased. As an example, the marginal cost of a fifth vote is $9 (= $25 cost of 5 votes minus $16 cost of 4 votes) while the marginal cost of a sixth vote is $11 (= $36 cost of 6 votes minus $25 cost of 5 votes).

Example As you saw in Figure 5.2a, ordinary 1p1v majority voting can fail because it cannot account for the strength of voters' preferences. As we went over before, Garcia stands to realize a large net benefit of $400 (= $700 personal benefit minus $300 cost of tax) if Yes passes. So she will vote Yes. Meanwhile, Johnson and Lee would realize modest net losses of, respectively, $50 and $75 if Yes were to pass. So they will both vote No. When all the votes are counted, we end up with an inefficient majority No vote (two against, one in favor) despite total benefit exceeding total cost by $250 (= $1,150 total benefit minus $900 total cost).

The vote goes the wrong way because 1p1v does not allow Garcia to express how strongly she favors a Yes vote and her potential gain of $400. Neither is there any way for 1p1v to capture the fact that Johnson and Lee are only mildly opposed, since they will lose only $50 and $75, respectively, if Yes wins. By contrast, quadratic voting *does* account for differences in strength of preference. By doing so, quadratic voting makes it more likely that projects with positive net benefits will be approved by voters.

To see that process in action, consider again the example in Figure 5.2a, but this time assume that we are going to conduct the election using a quadratic voting system. Garcia, Johnson, and Lee can purchase as many votes as they like. Let's first figure out how many each will purchase and then total up the votes in favor versus the votes against. We assume that each of them will rationally purchase votes up to the point where MB = MC.

- Garcia will want to purchase 20 votes and use them all to vote Yes. To see why she will purchase 20 votes, note that if the public good is approved, Garcia will personally gain $400 (= $700 benefit to Garcia minus $300 tax payment by Garcia). Thus, she will want to spend up to $400 buying votes. Looking at Table 5.4, we see that Garcia can purchase 20 votes for $400. So she will purchase 20 votes and vote Yes with each of them.

- Johnson will purchase 7 votes and use them all to vote No. To see why he will purchase 7 votes, note that if the public good is approved, Johnson will personally lose $50 (= $250 benefit to Johnson minus $300 tax payment by Johnson). Thus he would be willing to spend up to $50 buying votes so as to prevent that $50 loss. Looking at Table 5.4, we see that Johnson can purchase 7 votes for $49. So he will purchase 7 votes and vote No with each of them. (He would not purchase 8 votes because that would cost him $64, which would be a bigger loss of money than the $50 he would lose if the public good gets approved.)

- Lee will purchase 10 votes and use them all to vote No. To see why she will purchase 10 votes, note that if the public good is approved, Lee will personally lose $100 (= $200 benefit to Lee minus $300 tax payment by Lee). Thus she would be willing to spend up to $100 buying votes to prevent that $100 loss. Looking at Table 5.4, we see that Lee can purchase 10 votes for $100. So she will purchase 10 votes and vote No with each of them. (She would not purchase 11 votes because that would cost her $121, or more than the $100 she would lose if the public good got approved.)

Looking over the vote buying decision of Garcia, Johnson, and Lee, we see that there are 20 Yes votes (all from Garcia) against 17 No votes (7 from Johnson plus 10 from Lee). Thus, Yes will win by a vote of 20 to 17, and this public good with positive net benefits will be approved. So quadratic voting achieves the socially optimal outcome in this example, whereas traditional one-person-one-vote (1p1v) majority voting fails to do so.

Discussion This example is not unique. Economists have found that in many situations quadratic voting is more likely to yield economically efficient outcomes than the traditional 1p1v voting system. But no voting system is perfect and it is easy to construct examples in which quadratic voting and other alternative voting systems fail as badly as 1p1v in achieving the economically efficient outcome.

Another consideration that weighs against quadratic voting is the fact that we have a long tradition in our society of employing 1p1v majority voting. It is straightforward to explain and the public is used to it. 1p1v majority voting also allows for strength of preference to be expressed in other ways, including logrolling and lobbying (which are studied in the next section). So while quadratic voting has found some support among experts, it is not likely to displace traditional 1p1v majority voting any time soon!

One final point. In our example above, we had Garcia, Johnson, and Lee purchasing votes with cash. Such a system would obviously favor the wealthy and those with high incomes. Proponents of quadratic voting overcome this problem by handing out an equal number of pieces of "currency" to each voter. For instance, each voter might be given 1,000 "voice credits" as their budget for purchasing votes in several upcoming elections. Under quadratic voting, 1 vote in one of those elections would cost 1 voice credit, 2 votes would cost 4 voice credits, 3 votes would cost 9 voice credits, and so on. With each person endowed with an equal number of voice credits, we could utilize a voting system that accounts for strength of preference without having to worry about the rich outvoting the poor.

Mechanism Design Alternative voting mechanisms like quadratic voting are studied by economists interested in the field of **mechanism design.** In *economics* and *game theory,* a coordination mechanism, or simply a mechanism, is a procedure or set of rules for organizing how people interact to get something accomplished. The field of mechanism design studies how to set up the best procedures, or mechanisms, for any given situation—including auctions, on-line dating, and kidney donations.

The people who design mechanisms are called mechanism designers. With respect to democratic voting, their goal is to design a set of voting rules that will make the likelihood of inefficient votes as small as possible. But will the voting mechanism that works best for a small committee in Washington, D.C., be the same as for a statewide ballot measure in Texas? Probably not. So we need to be cautious about specific voting mechanisms like quadratic voting; they may work great in some contexts but fail miserably in others.

mechanism design The part of *game theory* concerned with designing the rules of a *game* so as to maximize the likelihood of players reaching a socially optimal outcome.

Government Failure

The term **government failure** refers to economically inefficient outcomes caused by shortcomings in the public sector. The *voting paradoxes* studied in the previous section were one source of government failure. They caused problems by making it difficult for government officials to discern voter preferences. Here, we deal with several other causes of government failure that all share an interesting common feature: they occur even when government officials know exactly what citizens want.

Representative Democracy and the Principal-Agent Problem

The U.S. system of representative democracy has the advantage of allowing us to elect full-time representatives who can specialize in understanding the pros and cons of different potential laws. But the system also suffers from principal-agent problems.

>> **LO5.3** Define government failure and explain its causes.

government failure Inefficiencies in resource allocation caused by problems in the operation of the *public sector* (government). Specific examples include the *principal-agent problem,* the *special-interest effect,* the *collective-action problem, rent seeking,* and *political corruption.*

principal-agent problem
(1) At a *firm,* a conflict of interest that occurs when agents (workers or managers) pursue their own objectives to the detriment of the principals' (stockholders') goals. (2) In *public choice theory,* a conflict of interest that arises when elected officials (who are the agents of the people) pursue policies that are in their own interests rather than policies that would be in the better interests of the public (the principals).

Principal-agent problems are conflicts that arise when tasks are delegated by one group of people (principals) to another group of people (agents). The conflicts arise because the agents' interests may not be the same as the principals' interests, in which case the agents may end up taking actions that are harmful to the principals for whom they work.

In the business world, principal-agent problems often arise when a company's managers (the agents) take actions that are not in the best interests of the company's shareholders (the principals). Examples include the managers spending huge amounts of company money on executive jets and lavish offices or holding meetings at expensive resorts. Those perks are very nice for managers, but extremely costly for shareholders. Yet managers may make many such decisions when they are free to pursue their own interests rather than those of the shareholders.

In a representative democracy, principal-agent problems often arise because politicians' goals, such as reelection, may be inconsistent with pursuing their constituents' best interests. Indeed, "sound economics" and "good politics" often differ. Sound economics calls for the public sector to pursue programs as long as marginal benefits exceed marginal costs. Good politics, however, suggests that politicians support programs and policies that maximize their chances of getting reelected. Economic inefficiency is the likely outcome.

special-interest effect Any political outcome in which a small group ("special interest") gains substantially at the expense of a much larger number of persons who each individually suffers a small loss.

Special-Interest Effect   Efficient public decision making is often impaired by the **special-interest effect,** which occurs when a small group that shares a particular goal, or special interest, is able to get the government to grant them a personally advantageous program or policy even though doing so defies the will of the majority.

The small group of potential beneficiaries is usually well informed and highly vocal on the issue in question, and they court politicians by making campaign contributions and by hiring well-connected professional advocates known as "lobbyists" to aggressively press their case.

Normally, you would think that politicians would never vote for a policy that only a small group wants. Democracy, after all, favors the majority over the minority. But things go awry because benefits are concentrated but costs are diffuse. Because the special interest is small, any success it achieves will be highly concentrated and worth a lot to each member of the group. So members will lobby hard and be very vocal. By contrast, the cost of the program will be spread across hundreds of millions of taxpayers, so that individual taxpayers won't have much of a financial incentive to organize any resistance. Only one side will be heard and the special interest will likely get its way.

collective-action problem
The difficulty of getting a large group of voters to organize against a policy when the costs of that policy are widely dispersed (so that none of them individually has much of a personal incentive to take action).

Example: A $10 million subsidy to a group of six dronemakers would amount to less than 3 cents per person when spread out over the entire U.S. population. So the dronemakers will be happy to spend up to $10 million lobbying in favor of the subsidy while individual taxpayers won't have much of an incentive at all to tell their political representatives to vote no. The result? Politicians doing the bidding of a special-interest group rather than what would be allocatively efficient based on cost-benefit analysis.

See the Consider This story for a notorious example of the special-interest effect in action.

CONSIDER THIS . . .

Getting Fleeced

Each year the federal government provides millions of dollars in subsidized loans to Angora goat farmers in Texas, Arizona, and New Mexico. The federal government began the subsidy in the late 1940s to ensure a large supply of insulation for the jackets needed to keep pilots warm in the unheated military aircraft of that era.

The mohair subsidy should have ended in the 1950s when heated cabins became standard, but it survives because it costs taxpayers only a few cents each. This means

Hein Von Horsten/Gallo Images/Getty Images

that it would cost them more to organize and defeat the mohair subsidy than they would save by having the subsidy terminated.

As with other examples of the special-interest effect, the mohair subsidy is characterized by "concentrated benefits and diffuse costs." Concentrated benefits make proponents easy to organize, while diffuse costs make opponents difficult to organize. The outcome? A **collective-action problem** that explains why taxpayers are still getting fleeced, seven decades on.

Pork Barrel Politics The special-interest effect is evident in so-called *pork-barrel politics,* which are government projects that yield benefits mainly to a single political district and its political representative. In this case, the special-interest group comprises local constituents, while the larger group consists of relatively uninformed taxpayers scattered across a much larger geographic area. Politicians have a strong incentive to secure government projects ("pork") for their local constituents. Such projects win political favor because constituents value them highly. Meanwhile, the costs are borne mainly by taxpayers located elsewhere.

At the federal level, pork-barrel politics often consists of congressional members inserting specific provisions that authorize spending for local projects (that will benefit only local constituents) into comprehensive legislation (that is supposed to be about making laws for the entire country). Such narrow, specifically designated authorizations of expenditure are called **earmarks.** In 2021, legislation contained 285 earmarks totaling $16.8 billion. Although some of the earmarked projects deliver marginal benefits that exceed marginal costs, many others are questionable at best. These latter expenditures very likely reallocate some of society's scarce resources from higher-valued uses to lower-valued uses. "Vote for my special local project and I will vote for yours" becomes part of the overall strategy for securing "pork" and remaining elected.

Rent-Seeking Behavior The appeal to government for special benefits at someone else's expense is called **rent seeking.** The term "rent" in "rent seeking" is used loosely to refer to any payment in excess of the minimum amount that is needed to keep a resource employed in its current use. Those engaged in "rent seeking" attempt to use government influence to help them get paid more for providing a good or service than the *minimum* amount someone would have to pay them to provide that good or service.

Rent seeking goes beyond the usual profit seeking by which firms try to increase their profits by adjusting their output levels, improving their products, and incorporating cost-saving technologies. Rent seeking looks to obtain extra profit or income by influencing government policies. Corporations, trade associations, labor unions, and professional organizations employ vast resources to secure favorable government policies that result in rent—higher profit or income than would otherwise occur. The government is able to dispense such rent directly or indirectly through laws, rules, hiring, and purchases. Elected officials are willing to provide such rent because they want to be responsive to the key constituents who can help them remain in office.

Some examples of "rent-providing" legislation or policies are tariffs on foreign products that limit competition and raise prices to consumers, tax breaks that benefit specific corporations, government construction projects that create union jobs but cost more than the benefits they yield, occupational licensing that goes beyond what is needed to protect consumers, and large subsidies to farmers. None of these result in economic efficiency.

earmarks Narrow, specially designated spending authorizations placed in broad legislation by senators and representatives for the purpose of providing benefits to *firms* and organizations within their constituencies. Earmarked projects are exempt from competitive bidding and normal evaluation procedures.

rent-seeking behavior Attempts by individuals, firms, or unions to use political influence to receive payments in excess of the minimum amount they would normally be willing to accept to provide a particular good or service.

▶ Principal-agent problems are conflicts that occur when the agents who are supposed to be acting in the best interests of their principals instead take actions that help themselves but hurt their principals.

▶ Because larger groups are more difficult to organize and motivate than smaller groups, special

interests can often obtain what they want politically even when what they want is opposed by a majority of voters.

▶ Rent seeking involves influencing government policies so that one can get paid more for providing a good or service than it costs to produce.

QUICK REVIEW
5.5

Limited and Bundled Choice

Economic theory points out that the political process forces citizens and their elected representatives to be less selective in choosing public goods and services than they are in choosing private goods and services.

In the marketplace, the citizen as a consumer can exactly satisfy personal preferences by buying certain goods and not buying others. However, in the public sector the citizen as a voter is confronted with, say, only two or three candidates for an office, each representing a different "bundle" of programs (public goods and services). None of these bundles of public goods is likely to fit exactly the preferences of any particular voter. Yet the voter must choose one of them. The candidate who comes closest to voter Smith's preference may endorse national health insurance, increases in Social Security benefits, subsidies to tobacco farmers, and tariffs on imported goods. Smith is likely to vote for that candidate even though Smith strongly opposes tobacco subsidies.

CONSIDER THIS . . .

Government, Scofflaw

An interesting example of government failure occurs when companies that are completely owned and operated by the government violate health and safety laws at higher rates than private companies.

A study of 1,000 hospitals, 3,000 power plants, and 4,200 water utilities found that public providers were substantially more likely than private companies to violate health and safety laws. Public hospitals and public power plants had 20 percent more high-priority violations of the Clean Air Act, while public water companies had 14 percent more health violations as well as 29 percent more monitoring violations of the Safe Drinking Water Act.

Jerry McBride/The Durango Herald/ Polaris/Newscom

One explanation is that public companies may have difficulty getting taxpayers and politicians to approve the funding that would be needed to improve their facilities by enough to comply with the law. But the law also appears to be applied much more leniently against public companies. As just one example, public power plants and public hospitals are 20 percent less likely to be fined when found to be in violation of the Clean Air Act. In addition, there is evidence that public violators are allowed to delay or avoid paying fines even when they are assessed. So they appear to be under substantially less pressure than private firms to comply with the law.

In other words, the voter must take the bad with the good. In the public sector, people are forced to "buy" goods and services they do not want. It is as if, in going to a sporting-goods store, you were forced to buy an unwanted pool cue to get a wanted pair of running shoes. This is a situation where resources are not being used efficiently to satisfy consumer wants. In this sense, the provision of public goods and services is inherently inefficient.

Congress is confronted with a similar limited-choice, bundled-goods problem. Appropriations legislation combines hundreds, even thousands, of spending items into a single bill. Many of these spending items may be completely unrelated to the main purpose of the legislation. Yet congressional representatives must vote on the entire package—yea or nay. Unlike consumers in the marketplace, they cannot be selective.

Bureaucracy and Inefficiency

Some economists contend that public agencies are generally less efficient than private businesses. The reason is not that lazy and incompetent workers somehow end up in the public sector while ambitious and capable people gravitate to the private sector. Rather, the market system creates incentives for internal efficiency that are absent from the public sector. Private enterprises have a clear goal—profit. Efficient management means lower costs and higher profit. The higher profit not only benefits the firm's owners but also enhances the promotion prospects of the firm's managers. Moreover, part of the managers' pay may be tied to profit via profit-sharing plans, bonuses, and stock options. There is no similar gain to government agencies and their managers—no counterpart to profit—to create a strong incentive to achieve efficiency.

The market system imposes a very obvious test of performance on private firms: the test of profit and loss. An efficient firm is profitable and therefore successful; it survives, prospers, and grows. An inefficient firm is unprofitable and unsuccessful; it declines and in time goes out of business. But there is no similar, clear-cut test for assessing the efficiency or inefficiency of public agencies. How can anyone determine whether a public hydroelectricity provider, a state university, a local fire department, or the Bureau of Indian Affairs is operating efficiently?

Furthermore, economists assert that government employees, together with the special-interest groups they serve, often gain sufficient political clout to block attempts to pare down or eliminate their agencies. Politicians who attempt to reduce the size of huge federal bureaucracies (such as those relating to agriculture, education, health, and national defense) incur sizable political risk because bureaucrats and special-interest groups will team up to defeat them.

Finally, critics point out that government bureaucrats tend to justify their continued employment by looking for and eventually finding new problems to solve. It is not surprising that social "problems," as defined by government, persist or even expand.

Inefficient Regulation and Intervention

Governments regulate many aspects of the market economy. Examples include health and safety regulations, environmental laws, banking supervision, and the imposition of wage and price controls. These interventions are designed to improve economic outcomes, but several forms of regulation and intervention have generated outcomes that are less beneficial than intended.

Regulatory Capture A government agency that is supposed to supervise a particular industry suffers from **regulatory capture** if its regulatory and monitoring activities come to be heavily influenced by the industry that it is supposed to be regulating.

Regulatory capture is often facilitated by the fact that nearly everyone who knows anything about the details of a regulated industry works in the industry. So when it comes time for the regulatory agency to find qualified people to help write intelligent regulations, it ends up hiring a lot of people from regulated firms. Those individuals bring their old opinions and sympathies with them when they become bureaucrats. As a result, many regulations end up favoring the interests of regulated firms.

Complaints about regulatory capture at the federal level have been voiced about the Food and Drug Administration's supervision of the pharmaceutical industry, the Securities and Exchange Commission's supervision of Wall Street financial firms, and the Bureau of Land Management's policies with respect to leasing federal lands for oil drilling, mining, and forestry.

regulatory capture The situation that occurs when a governmental *regulatory agency* ends up being controlled by the industry that it is supposed to be regulating.

Deregulation as an Alternative One potential solution to regulatory capture is for the government to engage in **deregulation** and intentionally remove most or even all of the regulations governing an industry.

Deregulation solves the problem of regulatory capture because there is no regulatory agency left to capture. But it works well in terms of economic efficiency only if the deregulated industry becomes competitive and is automatically guided toward allocative and productive efficiency by competitive forces and the invisible hand. If the deregulated industry instead tends toward monopoly or ends up generating substantial negative externalities, continued regulation might be the better option.

Proponents of deregulation often cite the deregulation of interstate trucking, railroads, and airlines in the 1970s and 1980s as an example of competition successfully replacing regulation. They do so because after regulation was removed, robust competition led to lower prices, increased output, and higher levels of productivity and efficiency.

But for government agencies tasked with environmental protection, human safety, and financial regulation, there is substantially less confidence as to whether competitive pressures might be able to replace regulation. Regulation may always be necessary. If so, the possibility of regulatory capture will have to be monitored closely because regulated firms will always have an incentive to capture their regulators.

deregulation The removal of most or even all of the government regulation and laws designed to supervise an industry. Sometimes undertaken to combat *regulatory capture.*

Corruption

Political corruption is the unlawful misdirection of governmental resources that occurs when government officials abuse their entrusted powers for personal gain. For instance, a police supervisor engages in political corruption if she accepts a bribe in exchange for illegally freeing a thief who had been lawfully arrested by another officer. Similarly, a government bureaucrat engages in political corruption if he refuses to issue a building permit to a homebuilder who is in full compliance with the law unless the homebuilder makes a "voluntary contribution" to the bureaucrat's favorite charity.

While relatively uncommon in the United States, political corruption is "business as usual" in many parts of the world. But it may be hard to tell in some cases if a particular activity is corrupt or not. For example, if a political candidate accepts campaign contributions from a special-interest group and then shows subsequent support for that group's legislative goals, has a subtle form of political corruption taken place? While there are strong opinions on both sides of the issue, it is often hard to tell in any particular case whether a special interest's campaign contribution amounts to a bribe. On the one hand, the special interest may indeed be trying to influence the politician's vote. On the other hand, the special interest may simply be trying to support and elect a person who already sees things their way.

political corruption The unlawful misdirection of government resources, or actions that occur when government officials abuse their entrusted powers for personal gain. (Also see *corruption.*)

Should Governments Subsidize Corporate Relocations?

Local and State Governments Spend an Estimated $45 Billion Each Year Trying to Tempt Established Businesses to Move to Their Locations. Is That a Good Deal?

In late 2017, Seattle-based Internet giant Amazon announced that it would be building a second headquarters, or HQ2. Its need for a second headquarters was not surprising; after two decades of relentless expansion, Amazon was well on its way to becoming the world's most valuable company and needed more office space to house its rapidly increasing managerial and executive staff.

SeaRick1/Shutterstock

But Amazon threw in an unexpected twist when it made the announcement. HQ2 would *not* be located in Amazon's home base of Seattle, where its first HQ was located. Amazon announced that it wanted to place its second headquarters elsewhere within the United States. It also announced that it wanted cities and states to apply for that opportunity and pitch Amazon on why it would be best for Amazon to put its HQ2 in their location. This application process set off a frenzy of subsidy offers, as local governments competed with each other to offer Amazon tax breaks, wage subsidies, free land, and a host of other taxpayer-paid inducements to get Amazon to build in their location.

Naturally, you could see why each local government might want HQ2 for its own. To begin with, Amazon announced that the project would bring with it 50,000 high paying jobs . The spending of those employees (average salary: $150,000) would greatly boost the economic prospects of established local businesses. The presence of HQ2 would also bring with it the chance to establish a local tech hub, attracting many Internet-economy startups to the area, thereby creating more jobs and even more opportunities for local residents.

Applications were submitted by 238 locales. Amazon looked them over before issuing yet another surprise. HQ2 would be split in two, with half being built in Queens, New York, and the other half being built in the Arlington, Virginia, area.

Now, you might think that those locations won the bidding war because of their generous offers. But New York and Arlington were the most natural locations for Amazon from the very start due to their proximity to major population centers and the airports and other distribution infrastructure that Amazon needs as the western hemisphere's largest Internet retailer. This made many people suspect that Amazon would have put HQ2 in NYC and Arlington no matter what. Thus, there would have been no need for either city to give away billions in taxpayer subsidies; they would have gotten HQ2 anyways.

This situation is not unique. Research indicates that location subsidies are largely a waste of money. Seventy-five percent of businesses considering a new location end up going with their original first choice anyway. For those companies, the subsidies are just a nice unearned windfall.

For cities and governments, the subsidies represent a tremendous waste of taxpayer money. As just one example, the State of Virginia discovered that its film incentive program (to get Hollywood producers to shoot scenes in Virginia rather than elsewhere) returned only 20 cents to the Virginia economy for every $1 in subsidies given to movie producers. Many economists suspect that the economic returns to other location subsidy programs are just as bad if not worse.

So why do these deals persist? The answer appears to be politics. Politicians love to be seen at ribbon-cutting ceremonies, looking as though they, personally, are responsible for bringing new businesses, new jobs, and economic growth to their area. That's an illusion, of course, but one that serves the political goal of getting reelected. The subsidies are, consequently, an example of government failure induced by the principal-agent problem that exists between the voters who must pay for subsidies and the politicians whose main goal is staying in office.

The HQ2 episode had an unexpected ending. In early 2019, Amazon reversed its decision to build half of HQ2 in Queens after meeting with political resistance from a variety of local groups, including those concerned about location subsidies being a waste of money.

That said, the impression of impropriety lingers, and so laws have been passed in the United States limiting the amount of money that individuals can donate to specific candidates and making it illegal for certain groups to donate money directly to individual politicians (as distinct from directing funds toward supporting specific issues or advocacy groups—which is both legal and unrestricted). Proponents of these laws hope that the limitations strike a good balance—allowing individuals and groups to meaningfully support candidates they agree with but keeping contributions small enough that no one individual or group can singlehandedly donate enough money to sway a politician's vote.

Imperfect Institutions

It is possible to argue that the wide variety of criticisms of public-sector inefficiency discussed in this chapter are exaggerated and cynical. Perhaps they are. Nevertheless, they do tend to shatter the concept of a benevolent government that responds with precision and efficiency to its citizens' wants. The market system of the private sector is far from perfectly efficient, and government's economic function is mainly to correct that system's shortcomings. But the public sector is subject to deficiencies in fulfilling its economic function. "The relevant comparison is not between perfect markets and imperfect governments, nor between faulty markets and all-knowing, rational, benevolent governments, but between inevitably imperfect institutions."[1]

Because markets and governments are both imperfect, it is sometimes difficult to determine whether a particular activity can be performed more successfully in the private sector or in the public sector. It is easy to reach agreement on opposite extremes: National defense must lie with the public sector, while automobile production is best accomplished by the private sector. But what about health insurance? Fire protection? Housing? Education? It is hard to assess every good or service and to say absolutely that it should be assigned to either the public sector or the private sector. Evidence: All the goods and services just mentioned are provided in part by both private enterprises and public agencies.

▶ Unlike the private sector—where the profit motive helps to ensure efficiency and variety—government lacks a strong incentive to be efficient and typically offers only limited and bundled choices.

▶ Regulatory capture occurs when a regulated industry can control its government regulator

and get it to implement policies that favor the industry.

▶ Political corruption occurs when government officials abuse their powers for personal gain.

QUICK REVIEW
5.6

---

[1]Otto Eckstein, *Public Finance,* 3rd ed. (Englewood Cliffs, NJ: Prentice Hall, 1973), p. 17.

Summary

LO5.1 Describe free riding and public goods, and illustrate why private firms cannot normally produce public goods.
Private goods are characterized by rivalry (in consumption) and excludability. One person's purchase and consumption of a private good precludes others from also buying and consuming it. Producers can exclude nonpayers (free riders) from receiving the benefits. In contrast, public goods are characterized by nonrivalry (in consumption) and nonexcludability. Public goods are not profitable to private firms because nonpayers (free riders) can obtain and consume those goods without paying. Government can, however, provide desirable public goods, financing them through taxation.

The collective demand schedule for a particular public good is found by summing the prices that each individual is willing to pay for an additional unit. Graphically, that demand curve is found by summing vertically the individual demand curves for that good. The resulting total demand curve indicates the collective willingness to pay for (or marginal benefit of) any given amount of the public good.

The optimal quantity of a public good occurs where the society's willingness to pay for the last unit—the marginal benefit of the good—equals the marginal cost of the good.

LO5.2 Explain the difficulties of conveying economic preferences through majority voting.
Public choice theory suggests that government failures may result when majority voting fails to correctly indicate voter preferences.

Majority voting creates the possibility of (a) underallocations or overallocations of resources to particular public goods and (b) inconsistent voting outcomes that make it impossible for a democratic political system to definitively determine the will of the people.

The median-voter model predicts that, under majority rule, the person holding the middle position on an issue will determine the outcome of an election involving that issue.

Researchers have compared traditional 1-person-one-vote (1p1v) majority-voting systems with a variety of alternative voting systems, including quadratic voting. Quadratic voting is more likely than 1p1v to provide economically efficient outcomes because it accounts for the strength of voter preferences. Voters can purchase as many votes v as they like for a price equal to the number of votes squared v^2. Whichever side has the most votes wins.

Mechanism design is the branch of economics that studies how to design a set of rules, or coordinating mechanism, such that the people interacting in a given situation will be most likely to achieve economically efficient outcomes. Quadratic voting and 1p1v voting are two different coordinating mechanisms for collective decision making. In some situations, quadratic voting is more likely than 1p1v to achieve allocative efficiency.

LO5.3 Define government failure and explain its causes.
Politicians and other government officials may sometimes manifest a principal-agent problem, pursuing actions that serve their own interests (such as reelection) rather than those that would serve the public.

The special-interest effect implies that groups with shared goals can perpetuate unpopular policies as long as diffuse costs make opponents difficult to organize.

Rent seeking occurs whenever a special interest group attempts to get government policy altered in a way that would award the special interest with above-normal profits or compensation.

Economic theorists cite several reasons why government might be inefficient in providing public goods. (a) Citizens as voters face limited and bundled choices regarding candidates and public goods, whereas consumers in the private sector can be highly selective in their choices. (b) Government bureaucracies have less incentive to operate efficiently than do private businesses. (c) Regulated industries may sometimes capture their government regulatory agencies and mold government policies toward their own best interests.

Deregulation is one way to prevent industries from capturing their regulators. But deregulation works well in terms of economic efficiency only if the deregulated industry becomes competitive.

Neither governments nor markets are perfect economic institutions. Each has its own set of shortcomings, and citizens should be aware of where each is likely to fail and where each is likely to succeed.

Terms and Concepts

demand-side market failures

private good

rivalry

excludability

public good

nonrivalry

nonexcludability

free-rider problem

collective demand for a public good

cost-benefit analysis

marginal cost–marginal benefit rule

quasi-public good

public choice theory

logrolling

paradox of voting

median-voter model

quadratic voting

mechanism design

government failure

principal-agent problem

special-interest effect

collective-action problem

earmarks

rent seeking

regulatory capture

deregulation

political corruption

Discussion Questions

1. What are the two characteristics of public goods? Explain the significance of each for public provision as opposed to private provision. What is the free-rider problem as it relates to public goods? Is U.S. border patrol a public good or a private good? Why? What type of good is satellite TV? Explain. **LO5.1**
2. Explain how affirmative and negative majority votes can sometimes lead to inefficient allocations of resources to public goods. Use Figures 5.2a and 5.2b to show how society might be better off if Garcia were allowed to buy votes. **LO5.2**
3. "Majority voting ensures that government will produce only those public goods for which benefits exceed costs." Discuss. **LO5.2**
4. "The problem with our democratic institutions is that they don't correctly reflect the will of the people! If the people—rather than self-interested politicians or lobbyists—had control, we wouldn't have to worry about government taking actions that don't maximize allocative and productive efficiency." Critique. **LO5.2**
5. Does traditional one-person-one-vote (1p1v) majority voting allow voters to directly express differences in strengths of preference? Does quadratic voting do any better? Discuss the differences and then explain which system you prefer, and why. **LO5.2**
6. Jean-Baptiste Colbert was the Minister of Finance under King Louis XIV of France. He famously observed, "The art of taxation consists in so plucking the goose as to obtain the largest

possible amount of feathers with the smallest possible amount of hissing." How does his comment relate to the special-interest effect? **LO5.3**
7. What is rent seeking, and how does it differ from the kinds of profit maximization and profit seeking that we discussed in previous chapters? Provide an actual or hypothetical example of rent seeking by firms in an industry, by a union, or by a professional association (for example, physicians, school teachers, or lawyers). Why do elected officials often accommodate rent-seeking behavior, particularly by special-interest groups located in their home states? **LO5.3**
8. How does the problem of limited and bundled choice in the public sector relate to economic efficiency? Why are public bureaucracies possibly less efficient than business firms? **LO5.3**
9. Explain: "Politicians would make more rational economic decisions if they weren't running for reelection every few years." **LO5.3**
10. Critique: "Thank goodness we have so many government regulatory agencies. They keep Big Business in check." **LO5.3**
11. **LAST WORD** What are the pluses and minuses of corporate location subsidies? Why do politicians like them so much? Would you be surprised to know that many of the 238 cities bidding for Amazon's HQ2 offered much larger location subsidies than did New York City and Alexandria, Virginia? Explain.

Review Questions

1. Draw a production possibilities curve with public goods on the vertical axis and private goods on the horizontal axis. Assuming the economy is initially operating on the curve, indicate how the production of public goods might be increased. How might the output of public goods be increased if the economy is initially operating at a point inside the curve? **LO5.1**
2. Use the distinction between the characteristics of private goods and public goods to determine whether the following should be produced through the market system or provided by government: (a) French fries, (b) airport screening, (c) court systems, (d) mail delivery, and (e) medical care. Explain your answers. **LO5.1**

3. We can apply voting paradoxes to the highway construction example of Table 5.2. Suppose there are only five people in a society, and each favors one of the five highway construction options listed in Table 5.2 ("No new construction" is one of the five options). Explain which of these highway options will be selected using a majority paired-choice vote. Will this option be the optimal size of the project from an economic perspective? **LO5.2**

4. True or False: The median-voter model explains why politicians so often stake out fringe positions that appeal only to a small segment of the electorate. **LO5.2**

5. In Figure 5.2b, we saw that traditional one-person-one-vote (1p1v) majority voting results in an inefficient majority Yes vote (two in favor, one opposed). Let's see whether the outcome is better under quadratic voting. **LO5.2**
   a. How much will Garcia be willing to spend on votes?
   b. How much each will Johnson and Lee be willing to spend on votes?
   c. How many votes will Garcia purchase? How many will Johnson and Lee each purchase?
   d. What is the total number of votes cast for No? For Yes?

e. Approval of this project requires a 50-percent-plus-1 majority. Will the project be approved?
f. Does quadratic voting lead to the economically efficient outcome here?

6. Suppose that total costs (TC) double for each project listed in Table 5.2. Which project(s) is (are) now economically viable? **LO5.3**
   a. Plan A only
   b. Plans C and D only
   c. Plans B and C
   d. Plans A and B only

7. Explain the paradox of voting through reference to the accompanying table, which shows the ranking of three public goods by voters Gbowee, Ebadi, and Yousafzai: **LO5.3**

	Rankings		
Public Good	**Gbowee**	**Ebadi**	**Yousafzai**
Courthouse	2nd choice	1st choice	3rd choice
School	3rd choice	2nd choice	1st choice
Park	1st choice	3rd choice	2nd choice

Problems

1. On the basis of the three individual demand schedules in the following table, and assuming these are the only three people in the society, determine (a) the market demand schedule on the assumption that the good is a private good and (b) the collective demand schedule on the assumption that the good is a public good. **LO5.1**

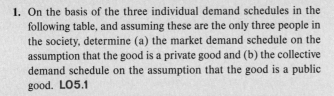

P	$Q_d (D_1)$	$Q_d (D_2)$	$Q_d (D_3)$
$8	0	1	0
7	0	2	0
6	0	3	1
5	1	4	2
4	2	5	3
3	3	6	4
2	4	7	5
1	5	8	6

2. Use your demand schedule for a public good, determined in problem 1, and the following supply schedule to ascertain the optimal quantity of this public good. **LO5.1**

P	Q_s
$19	10
16	8
13	6
10	4
7	2
4	1

3. Look back at Figures 5.2a and 5.2b, which show the costs and benefits to voters Garcia, Johnson, and Lee of two different public goods that the government will produce if a majority of voters support them. Suppose that Garcia, Johnson, and Lee have decided to have one single vote at which the funding for both of those public goods will be decided simultaneously. **LO5.2**

a. Given the $300 cost per person of each public good, what are Garcia's net benefits for each public good individually and for the two combined? Will she vote yes or no on the proposal to fund both projects simultaneously?
b. What are Lee's net benefits for each public good individually and for the two combined? Will she vote yes or no on the proposal to fund both projects simultaneously?
c. What are Johnson's net benefits for each public good individually and for the two combined? Will he vote yes or no on the proposal to fund both projects simultaneously—or will he be indifferent?
d. Who is the median voter here? Whom will the two other voters be attempting to persuade?

4. Political advertising is often directed at winning over so-called swing voters, whose votes might go either way. Suppose that two political parties—the Freedom Party and the Liberty Party—disagree on whether to build a new road. Polling shows that of 1,000 total voters, 450 are firmly for the new road and 450 are firmly against the new road. Thus, each party will try to win over a majority of the 100 remaining swing voters. **LO5.2**

a. Suppose that each party spends $5,000 on untargeted TV, radio, and newspaper ads that are equally likely to reach any and all voters. How much per voter will be spent by both parties combined?
b. Suppose that, instead, each party could direct all of its spending toward just the swing voters by using targeted social media ads. If all of the two parties' combined spending is targeted at just swing voters, how much will be spent per swing voter?
c. Suppose that only the Freedom Party knows how to target voters using social media. How much per swing voter will it be spending? If at the same time the Liberty Party is still using only untargeted TV, radio, and newspaper ads, what portion of its total spending is likely to be reaching the 100 swing voters? How much per swing voter does that portion amount to?

d. Looking at your answers to part *c*, how much more per swing voter will the Freedom Party be spending than the Liberty Party? If spending per swing voter influences elections, which party is more likely to win?

5. Let's see whether quadratic voting can avoid the paradox of voting that arose in Table 5.3 when using 1p1v in a series of paired-choice majority votes. To reexamine this situation using quadratic voting, the following table presents the maximum willingness to pay of Garcia, Johnson, and Lee for each of the three public goods. Notice that each person's numbers for willingness to pay match her or his ordering of preferences (1st choice, 2nd choice, 3rd choice) presented in Table 5.3. Thus, Garcia is willing to spend more on her 1st choice of national defense ($400) than on her second choice of a road ($100) or her third choice of a weather warning system ($0). **LO5.2**

Public Good	Willingness to Pay		
	Garcia	Johnson	Lee
National defense	$400	$ 50	$150
Road	100	300	100
Weather warning system	0	150	250

a. Assume that voting will be done using a quadratic voting system and that Garcia, Johnson, and Lee are each given $500 that can only be spent on purchasing votes (i.e., any unspent money has to be returned). How many votes will Garcia purchase to support national defense? How many for the road? Place those values into the appropriate blanks in the table below and then do the same for the blanks for Johnson and Lee.

Public Good	Votes Purchased		
	Garcia	Johnson	Lee
National defense	____	____	12
Road	____	17	____
Weather warning system	0	____	____

b. Across all three voters, how many votes are there in favor of national defense? The road? The weather warning system?
c. If a paired-choice vote is taken of national defense versus the road, which one wins?
d. If a paired-choice vote is taken of the road versus the weather warning system, which one wins?
e. If a paired-choice vote is taken of national defense versus the weather warning system, which one wins?
f. Review your answers to parts *c, d,* and *e*. Has quadratic voting eliminated the paradox of voting that we found when using 1p1v?

6. Consider a specific example of the special-interest effect and the collective-action problem. In 2021, it was estimated that the total value of all corn-production subsidies in the United States was about $3 billion. The population of the United States was approximately 300 million people that year. **LO5.3**

a. On average, how much did corn subsidies cost per person in the United States in 2021? (Hint: A billion is a 1 followed by nine zeros. A million is a 1 followed by six zeros.)
b. If each person in the United States is willing to spend only $0.50 to support efforts to overturn the corn subsidy, and if antisubsidy advocates can only raise funds from 10 percent of the population, how much money will they be able to raise for their lobbying efforts?
c. If the recipients of corn subsidies donate just 1 percent of the total amount that they receive in subsidies, how much could they raise to support lobbying efforts to continue the corn subsidy?
d. By how many dollars does the amount raised by the recipients of the corn subsidy exceed the amount raised by the opponents of the corn subsidy?

7. Consider a corrupt provincial government in which each housing inspector examines two newly built structures each week. All the builders in the province are unethical and want to increase their profits by using substandard construction materials, but they can't do that unless they can bribe a housing inspector into approving a substandard building **LO5.3**

a. If bribes cost $1,000 each, how much will a housing inspector make each year in bribes? (Assume that inspectors work 52 weeks a year and get bribed for every house that they inspect.)
b. There is a provincial construction supervisor who gets to hire all of the housing inspectors. He himself is corrupt and expects his housing inspectors to share their bribes with him. Suppose that 20 inspectors work for him and that each passes along half the bribes collected from builders. How much will the construction supervisor collect each year?
c. Corrupt officials may have an incentive to reduce the provision of government services to help line their own pockets. Suppose that the provincial construction supervisor decides to cut the total number of housing inspectors from 20 to 10 in order to decrease the supply of new housing permits. This decrease in the supply of permits raises the equilibrium bribe from $1,000 to $2,500. How much per year will the construction supervisor now receive if he is still getting half of all the bribes collected by the 10 inspectors? How much more is the construction supervisor getting now than when he had 20 inspectors working in part *b*? Will he personally be happy with the reduction in government services?
d. What would happen if reducing the number of inspectors from 20 to 10 only increased the equilibrium bribe from $1,000 to $1,500? In this case, how much per year would the construction supervisor collect from his 10 inspectors? How much less is the construction supervisor getting than when he had 20 inspectors working in part *b*? In this case, will the construction supervisor be happy with the reduction in government services? Will he want to go back to using 20 inspectors?

An Introduction to Macroeconomics

>> LEARNING OBJECTIVES

LO6.1 Explain why economists use GDP, inflation, and unemployment to assess the economy's health.

LO6.2 Discuss why sustained increases in living standards are historically recent.

LO6.3 Identify why saving and investment promote higher living standards.

LO6.4 Explain why shocks and sticky prices are responsible for short-run fluctuations in output and employment.

LO6.5 Characterize the degree to which various prices are sticky.

LO6.6 Explain why economists use different macroeconomic models for different time horizons.

Macroeconomics focuses on national economies while seeking answers to large-scale economic questions, including: Why are some countries really rich while others are deeply impoverished? Why do all countries—even the richest—go through alternating boom and bust periods? Can governments do anything to improve living standards or fight recessions?

Because this chapter is an introduction, it will answer these questions only in brief. Subsequent chapters provide the highly interesting details.

Performance and Policy

Macroeconomics studies the behavior of the economy as a whole. It is primarily concerned with two topics: long-run economic growth and the short-run fluctuations in output and employment that comprise the **business cycle.** These phenomena are closely related. Most economies enjoy a distinct growth trend that leads to higher output and higher standards of living in the long run. But the rate of growth is not constant. Sometimes it proceeds rapidly, sometimes slowly, and sometimes it even turns negative for while, a situation known as a *recession*.

To understand how economies operate and how to improve their performance, economists collect and analyze economic data, including the amount of new construction taking place each month, how many ships laden with cargo arrive at U.S. ports each year, and how many new inventions have been patented in the last few weeks. That said, macroeconomists tend to focus on three key statistics when assessing an economy's health and development.

Real GDP

Real GDP, or **real gross domestic product,** measures the value of the final goods and services produced within a country's borders during a specific period of time, typically a year. This statistic is very

>> **LO6.1** Explain why economists use GDP, inflation, and unemployment to assess the economy's health.

business cycle Recurring increases and decreases in the level of economic activity over periods of years; consists of peak, recession, trough, and expansion phases.

real gross domestic product (GDP) *Gross domestic product* adjusted for *inflation;* gross domestic product in a year divided by the GDP *price index* for that year, the index expressed as a decimal. Compare with *nominal GDP.*

useful because it tells us whether an economy's output is growing. For instance, if U.S. real GDP in one year is larger than in the previous year, we know that U.S. output increased from the first year to the second.

nominal gross domestic product (GDP) *GDP* measured in terms of *the price level* at the time of measurement; *GDP* not adjusted for *inflation*. Compare with *real gross domestic product* (*real GDP*).

To calculate the value of real GDP, government statisticians first calculate **nominal GDP,** which is the dollar value of all goods and services produced within a country's borders using their prices during the year they were produced. Nominal GDP suffers from a major problem: It can increase from one year to the next even if there is no increase in output. To see how, consider a commercial blacksmith who produced 10 iron spiral staircases last year and 10 identical staircases this year. Clearly, the blacksmith's output did not change. But if the market price of a staircase rose from $10,000 last year to $20,000 this year, nominal GDP will have increased from $100,000 (= 10 × $10,000) to $200,000 (= 10 × $20,000). Without knowing about the price increase, we might incorrectly conclude that the output of staircases had doubled.

Real GDP avoids this problem by accounting for price changes. As a result, we can compare real GDP numbers from one year to the next and really know if there is a change in output (rather than a change in prices).

Because more output means more consumption possibilities—including not only fun things like more movies and more vacations, but also serious things like better health care and safer roads—economists and policymakers are deeply committed to encouraging a large and growing real GDP.

Unemployment

unemployment The failure to use all available *economic resources* to produce desired *goods* and *services;* the failure of the economy to fully employ its *labor force.*

Unemployment occurs when a person cannot get a job despite being willing to work and actively seeking work. High unemployment rates are undesirable because they indicate that a nation is not using a large portion of its most important resource—the talents and skills of its people. Unemployment is wasteful because we lose all the goods and services that unemployed workers could have produced if they had been working. Researchers have also drawn links between higher unemployment rates and major social problems such as higher crime rates, greater political unrest, and higher rates of depression and heart disease among unemployed people.

Inflation

inflation A rise in the general level of *prices* in an economy; an increase in an economy's *price level.*

Inflation is an increase in the overall level of prices. As an example, consider all the goods and services that a typical family buys over the course of one year. If the economy is experiencing inflation, the family will spend more money to buy those goods and services this year than it spent on those same goods and services last year. This can be troublesome for several reasons. First, if the family's income does not rise as fast as prices do, the family won't be able to purchase as much as it used to, and its standard of living will fall. In addition, a surprise jump in inflation reduces the purchasing power of people's savings. Their savings will buy less than expected due to the higher-than-expected prices.

Preview

Because real GDP, unemployment, and inflation are the standards by which economists keep track of long-run growth and short-run fluctuations, we spend a substantial amount of time in the next few chapters examining how these statistics are computed, how they affect people's well-being, and how they vary both across countries and over time.

We then build on that understanding by developing macroeconomic models of both long-run growth and short-run fluctuations to help you understand how policymakers attempt to maximize growth while minimizing unemployment and inflation.

QUICK REVIEW

6.1

▶ Macroeconomics studies long-run economic growth and short-run economic fluctuations.

▶ Macroeconomists focus their attention on three key economic statistics: real GDP, unemployment, and inflation.

▶ Macroeconomic models help to clarify many important questions about government economic policy.

The Miracle of Modern Economic Growth

Rapid and sustained economic growth is a modern phenomenon. Before the Industrial Revolution began in the late 1700s in England, standards of living showed virtually no growth over hundreds or even thousands of years. For instance, the standard of living of the average Roman peasant was virtually the same at the start of the Roman Empire around the year 500 B.C. as it was at the end of the Roman Empire 1,000 years later. Similarly, historians have estimated that the average Chinese peasant's standard of living was essentially the same in the year A.D. 1800 as it was in the year A.D. 100.

That is not to say that the Roman and Chinese economies did not expand over time. They did. In fact, their total output of goods and services increased many times over. However, as their output increased, their populations increased by similar proportions so that the amount of output *per person* remained virtually unchanged.

This pattern continued until the start of the Industrial Revolution, which ushered in not only factory production and automation but also constantly improving production technologies thanks to an emphasis on research and development. As a result, output began to grow faster than population, so that living standards rose as the amount of output per person increased.

In countries experiencing **modern economic growth,** output per person rises. Under modern economic growth, the annual increase in output per person is often not large, perhaps 2 percent per year in countries such as England that were the first to industrialize. But when compounded over time, an annual growth rate of 2 percent adds up rapidly. Indeed, it implies that the standard of living will double every 35 years. Thus, if the average citizen of a country enjoying 2 percent growth begins this year with an income of $10,000, in 35 years that person will have an income of $20,000. Then, 35 years after that, income will double again, so that her income 70 years from now will be $40,000. And 35 years after that, the average citizen's income will double again, to $80,000. Such high rates of growth are amazing when compared to the period before modern economic growth when standards of living remained unchanged for centuries.

Today, the citizens of the world's richest nations enjoy material standards of living that are on average more than 50 times higher than those experienced by citizens of the world's lowest-income nations, as shown in Global Perspective 6.1, which compares GDP per capita (per person) for

>> **LO6.2** Discuss why sustained increases in living standards are historically recent.

modern economic growth The historically recent phenomenon in which nations for the first time have experienced sustained increases in *real GDP per capita.*

🌐 GLOBAL PERSPECTIVE 6.1

GDP PER PERSON, SELECTED COUNTRIES

Average income per person—which by definition equals gross domestic product (GDP) per person—varies massively from country to country, even after adjusting for differences in the cost of living. This is best seen by comparing the average income per person in one of the world's richest countries, Switzerland, with that in one of the world's poorest, Burundi. In 2020, Switzerland's GDP per person of $71,352 was 93 times larger than Burundi's $771 per person.

Country	GDP per Person, 2020 (U.S. dollars based on purchasing power parity)
Switzerland	$71,352
United States	63,544
Germany	53,694
Canada	48,072
Saudi Arabia	46,763
United Kingdom	44,916
Japan	42,197
Russia	28,213
Mexico	18,333
China	17,312
India	6,454
Nigeria	5,187
Afghanistan	2,088
Somalia	875
Burundi	771

Source: The World Bank Group, data.worldbank.org.

the world's wealthiest and poorest countries. Those vast differences in living standards are almost entirely the result of the fact that different countries began modern economic growth at different dates. The countries that have been at it the longest have ended up far richer than those that began modern economic growth only recently.

QUICK REVIEW

6.2

▶ Before the Industrial Revolution, living standards did not show any sustained increases over time because any increase in output was usually offset by an equally large increase in population.

▶ Since the Industrial Revolution, many nations have experienced *modern economic growth* in which output grows faster than population—so that living standards rise over time.

>> **LO6.3** Identify why saving and investment promote higher living standards.

saving The flow of money that is generated when *personal consumption expenditures* are less than *disposable income.* Compare with *savings.*

investment Expenditures that increase the volume of physical *capital* (roads, factories, wireless networks) and intangible ideas (formulas, processes, algorithms) that help to produce goods and services. Also known as *economic investment.* Not to be confused with *financial investment.*

financial investment The purchase of a financial asset (such as a *stock, bond,* or *mutual fund*) or real asset (such as a house, land, or factories) in the expectation of financial gain. Compare with economic investment.

Saving, Investment, and Choosing between Present and Future Consumption

To raise living standards over time, an economy must devote at least some part of its current output to increasing future output. This process requires both saving and investment.

- **Saving** occurs when current consumption is less than current income; the difference between them is savings.

- **Investment** happens when resources are directed toward increasing future output—either by paying for research to develop more efficient production technologies or by paying for the production of newly created capital goods (such as machinery, tools, and infrastructure) that will increase future output.

When thinking about why saving and investment are so important for economic growth, the key point is that the amount of investment is ultimately limited by the amount of saving. The only way that more output can be directed at investment activities is if saving increases. But that, in turn, implies that individuals and society as a whole must make trade-offs between current and future consumption. This is true because the only way to pay for more investment—and the higher levels of future consumption that more investment can generate—is to increase present saving. But increased saving can only come at the price of reduced current consumption. Individuals and society as a whole must therefore wrestle with a choice between present consumption and future consumption. They must decide how to balance the reductions in current consumption required to fund current investment against the increases in future consumption that the added current investment will make possible.

The nearby Consider This story explains the crucial difference between economic investment and financial investment. When economists say "investment," they mean economic investment.

CONSIDER THIS . . .

Economic versus Financial Investment

Economics students often are confused by the word "investment" because the ordinary usage of the word refers to a *financial investment* whereas economists use the word to refer to *economic investment,* which is an entirely different concept.

Financial investment captures what ordinary people mean when they say investment, namely, the purchase of assets like stocks, bonds, and real estate in the hope of reaping a financial gain. By contrast, when economists say "investment," they are referring to **economic investment,** which relates to the expansion of the economy's

Stephen Brashear/Getty Images

productive capacity. So economic investment includes, for example, spending that pays for the production of newly created capital goods like factories and wireless networks as well as the costs of developing new technologies like solar-powered helicopters or a cure for cancer.

For economists, purely financial transactions, such as swapping cash for a stock or a bond, are not "investment." Neither are the purchases of capital goods built in previous years. These transactions simply transfer the ownership of existing assets from one party to another. They do not increase the economy's productive capacity. And so they are not considered "investments" by economists.

Banks and Other Financial Institutions

Households are the principal source of savings, but businesses are the main economic investors. So how does the pool of savings generated by households get transferred to businesses? Banks and other financial institutions (such as mutual funds, pension plans, and insurance companies) act as intermediaries between households and businesses. These institutions collect households' savings, rewarding savers with interest, dividends, or capital gains (increases in asset values). They then lend the funds to businesses, which invest in equipment, factories, and other capital goods as well as research and development.

Macroeconomics devotes considerable attention to money, banking, and financial institutions because a well-functioning financial system promotes economic growth and stability by encouraging saving and by directing that saving into the most productive possible investments. In contrast, a poorly functioning financial system can create serious problems for an economy.

economic investment
Spending for the production and accumulation of *capital*, additions to *inventories*, or the research and development of new goods or services, including funds spent on the creation of new works of music, literature, or software. Compare with *financial investment*.

▶ An economy can only grow if it invests, and it can only invest if it saves some of its current output. Thus, saving is crucial to increasing investment and, consequently, future output.

▶ Banks and other financial institutions channel household savings toward businesses, which invest in equipment, factories, and other capital goods as well as in the development of new productive technologies.

**QUICK REVIEW
6.3**

Uncertainty, Expectations, and Shocks

Decisions about savings and investment are complicated by the fact that the future is uncertain. Investment projects sometimes produce disappointing results or fail totally. As a result, firms spend considerable time trying to predict future trends so that they invest only in projects that are likely to succeed. For this reason, macroeconomics must take into account **expectations** about the future.

>> **LO6.4** Explain why shocks and sticky prices are responsible for short-run fluctuations in output and employment.

The Importance of Expectations and Shocks

Expectations are important for two reasons. The more obvious reason involves the effects of changing expectations on current behavior. If firms grow more pessimistic about the future returns that they expect from current investments, they will invest less today than they would if they were more optimistic. Expectations therefore have a large effect on economic growth because increased pessimism leads to less current investment and, subsequently, less future consumption.

The less-obvious reason that expectations are so important concerns what happens when expectations are unmet. Firms are often forced to cope with **shocks**—situations in which they were expecting one thing to happen but something else happened instead. For instance, consider a situation in which a firm decides to build a high-speed railroad that will shuttle passengers between Los Angeles and Las Vegas. The firm expects it to be very popular and make a handsome profit. But what if the railroad turns out to be unpopular and loses money? The firm will need to figure out how to respond to the unexpected bad news. Should it go out of business completely? Should it try to turn a profit by hauling cargo instead of passengers? Should it borrow $30 million to pay for a massive advertising campaign? These sorts of decisions are necessitated by the shock and surprise of having to deal with an unexpected situation.

Economies experience both demand shocks and supply shocks. **Demand shocks** are unexpected changes in the demand for goods and services. **Supply shocks** are unexpected changes in the supply of goods and services. Note that the word *shock* reveals only that something unexpected has happened. It does not tell us whether what has happened is unexpectedly good or unexpectedly bad. For this reason, economists use more specific terms. For instance, a *positive demand shock* refers to a situation in which actual demand is higher than expected, while a *negative demand shock* refers to a situation in which actual demand is lower than expected.

expectations The anticipations of consumers, *firms*, and others about future economic conditions.

shocks Sudden, unexpected changes in *demand* (or *aggregate demand*) or supply (or *aggregate supply*).

demand shocks Sudden, unexpected changes in demand.

supply shocks Sudden, unexpected changes in *aggregate supply.*

Demand Shocks and Sticky Prices

Economists believe that most short-run fluctuations in GDP and the business cycle are the result of demand shocks. Supply shocks do happen in some cases and are very important when they do occur. But we will focus most of our initial attention in this chapter and subsequent chapters on demand shocks, how they affect the economy, and how government policy may be able to help the economy adjust to them.

But why are demand shocks such a big problem? Why would we have to consider calling in the government to help deal with them? And why can't firms deal with demand shocks on their own?

The answer to these questions is that the prices of many goods and services are inflexible (slow to change, or "sticky") in the short run. As we will explain, this implies that price changes do not quickly equalize the quantities demanded of such goods and services with their respective quantities supplied. Instead, because prices are inflexible, the economy is forced to respond in the short run to demand shocks primarily through changes in output and employment rather than through changes in prices.

Example: A Single Firm Dealing with Demand Shocks and Sticky Prices

Although an entire economy is vastly more complex than a single firm, an analogy that uses a single car factory is helpful in explaining why demand shocks and inflexible prices help to explain most short-run fluctuations in output and employment. Consider a car manufacturing company named Buzzer Auto. Like most companies, Buzzer Auto is in business to make a profit. Part of turning a profit involves developing accurate expectations about future market conditions. Consequently, Buzzer constantly conducts market research to estimate future demand conditions so that it will design and build cars that people want to buy.

Setting Expectations After extensive market research, Buzzer concludes that it can earn a modest profit if it builds and staffs an appropriately sized factory to build an environmentally friendly SUV, which it decides to call the Proton. Buzzer's marketing economists collaborate with Buzzer's engineers and conclude that expected profits will be maximized if the firm builds a factory whose optimal (least cost) output rate is 900 cars per week. If the factory operates at this rate, it can produce a Proton for only $36,500 per vehicle. This cost per vehicle is good news because the firm's estimates for demand indicate that a supply of 900 vehicles per week can be sold at a price of $37,000 per vehicle. So, if everything goes according to plan, Buzzer Auto should make an accounting profit of $500 on each Proton that it produces and sells. Expecting these future conditions, Buzzer decides to build the factory, staff it, and begin making Protons.

Examine **Figure 6.1 (Key Graph)**, which shows the market for Protons when the vertical supply curve for Protons is fixed at the factory's optimal output rate of 900 cars per week. Notice that we have drawn in three possible demand curves. D_L corresponds to low demand for Protons, D_M corresponds to the medium level of demand that Buzzer's marketing economists expect to materialize, and D_H corresponds to high demand for Protons.

Figure 6.1a can be used to illustrate what will happen if everything goes according to the firm's expectations: If all goes according to plan and the actual demand that materializes is D_M, the equilibrium price will in fact be $37,000 per Proton, and the equilibrium quantity demanded will be 900 cars per week. Thus, if all goes according to expectations, the factory will have exactly the right capacity to meet the expected quantity demanded at the sales price of $37,000 per vehicle. In addition, the firm's books will show a profit of $500 per vehicle on each of the 900 vehicles that it builds and expects to sell each week at that price.

Full Employment with No Shocks If its expectations are always fulfilled, Buzzer Auto will never contribute to any of the short-run fluctuations in output and unemployment that affect real-world economies. First, if everything always goes according to plan and Buzzer Auto's expectations always come true, then the factory will always produce and sell at its optimal output rate of 900 cars per week. Thus, it would never experience any fluctuations in output—either in the short run or in the long run. At the same time, because producing a constant output of 900 cars each week will always require the same number of workers, the factory's labor demand and employment should never vary. So, if everything always goes according to plan, Buzzer Auto will never have any effect on unemployment because it will always hire a constant number of workers.

These facts imply that the short-run fluctuations in output and unemployment that we see in the real world must be the result of shocks—of things *not* going according to plan. In particular, business cycle fluctuations typically arise because actual demand ends up being either lower or higher than what businesses were expecting. In those cases, some adjustments are necessary to bring quantity demanded and quantity supplied back into alignment.

Price Changes If There Are Demand Shocks *and* Flexible Prices Figure 6.1a can also be used to illustrate how the market for Protons will adjust to unexpected changes in demand if prices are

..ıl KEY GRAPH

FIGURE 6.1 **The effect of demand shocks under flexible and fixed prices.**

(a) If prices are flexible, then no matter what demand turns out to be, Buzzer Auto can continue to sell its optimal (least cost) output of 900 cars per week since the equilibrium price will adjust to equalize the quantity demanded with the quantity supplied. (b) By contrast, if Buzzer Auto sticks with a fixed-price policy, then the quantity demanded will vary with the level of demand. At the fixed price of $37,000 per vehicle, the quantity demanded will be 700 cars per week if demand is D_L, 900 cars per week if demand is D_M, and 1,150 cars per week if demand is D_H.

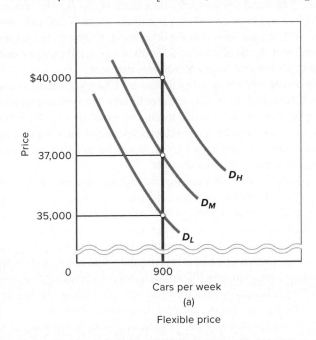

(a)
Flexible price

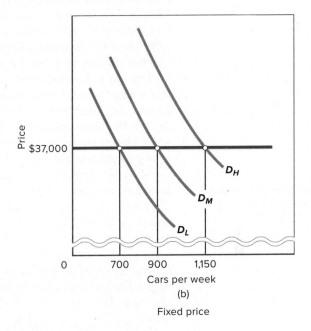

(b)
Fixed price

QUICK QUIZ FOR FIGURE 6.1

1. **Comparing what happens in Figures 6.1a and 6.1b, the equilibrium price, if demand D_H happens, will be higher if:**
   a. the price per vehicle is fixed.
   b. the price per vehicle is free to vary.
   c. the automaker's optimal output rate increases from 900 cars per week to 1,150 cars per week.
   d. demand shifts back down to D_M.

2. **In Figure 6.1a, increased demand:**
   a. raises price.
   b. lowers price.
   c. stabilizes price.
   d. none of the above.

3. **In Figure 6.1b, increased demand:**
   a. increases price.
   b. increases output.
   c. decreases price.
   d. decreases output.

4. **At what level of demand will the same number of cars be sold regardless of whether price per vehicle is fixed or flexible?**
   a. D_L
   b. D_M
   c. D_H
   d. all of the above

Answers: 1. b; 2. a; 3. b; 4. b

---

flexible. If demand is unexpectedly low at D_L, the market price will adjust downward to $35,000 per vehicle so that the quantity demanded at that price still equals the factory's optimal output rate of 900 cars per week. However, if demand is unexpectedly high at D_H, the market price will adjust upward to $40,000 per vehicle so that the quantity demanded still equals the factory's optimal output rate of 900 cars per week. These adjustments imply that if the price of Protons is free to quickly adjust in response to unexpected changes in demand, the factory can always operate at its optimal output rate of 900 cars per week. Only the amount of profit or loss will vary with demand.

Applying this logic to the economy as a whole, if the prices of goods and services can always adjust quickly to unexpected changes in demand, then the economy can always produce at its optimal capacity because prices will adjust to ensure that the quantity demanded of each good and service always equals the quantity supplied. If prices are fully flexible, there will be no short-run fluctuations in output. Production levels will remain constant, and unemployment levels will not change because firms will always need the same number of workers to produce the same amount of output.

Output Changes If There Are Demand Shocks *and* Sticky Prices In reality, many prices in the economy are inflexible and do not change rapidly when demand changes unexpectedly. Consider the extreme case shown in Figure 6.1b, in which the price of Protons is totally inflexible, fixed at $37,000 per Proton. Here, if demand unexpectedly falls from D_M to D_L, the quantity demanded at the fixed price of $37,000 will be only 700 cars per week, which is 200 cars fewer than the factory's optimal output of 900 cars per week. On the other hand, if demand is unexpectedly high at D_H, the quantity demanded at the fixed price of $37,000 will be 1,150 cars per week, which is 250 cars more than the factory's optimal output of 900 cars per week.

One way to deal with these unexpected shifts in quantity demanded is to try to adjust the factory's output to match them. That is, during weeks of low demand, Buzzer Auto could attempt to produce only 700 Protons, while during weeks of high demand it could try to produce 1,150 Protons. But this flexible output strategy is very expensive because factories operate at their lowest costs when they are producing constantly at their optimal output levels. Operating at either a higher or a lower production rate results in higher per-unit production costs.

inventories Goods that have been produced but remain unsold.

Manufacturing firms typically attempt to deal with unexpected changes in demand by maintaining an **inventory,** which is a stock of output that has been produced but not yet sold. Inventories are useful because companies can allow them to grow or decline in periods when demand is unexpectedly low or high—thereby allowing production to proceed smoothly and constantly at the optimal output level even when demand is variable. In our example, Buzzer Auto would maintain an inventory of unsold Protons. In weeks when demand is unexpectedly low, the inventory will increase by 200 Protons as the quantity demanded falls 200 vehicles short of the factory's optimal output. During weeks when demand is unexpectedly high, the inventory will decrease as the quantity demanded exceeds the factory's optimal output by 250 cars. By allowing inventory levels to fluctuate, Buzzer Auto can respond to unexpected shifts in demand by adjusting inventory levels rather than output levels. With any luck, the overall inventory level will stay roughly constant over time as unexpected increases and decreases in demand cancel each other out.

But consider what will happen if the firm experiences many successive weeks of unexpectedly low demand. Each week, the firm's inventory of unsold Protons will increase by 200 cars. If inventory continues to increase for many weeks, then Buzzer's managers will be forced to cut production because, among other things, there will simply be no place to park so many unsold vehicles. More importantly, holding large numbers of unsold cars in inventory is unprofitable: While the company incurs costs to build an unsold car, an unsold car obviously brings in no revenue. Constantly rising inventories hurt profits, and management will want to reduce output if it sees inventories rising week after week due to unexpectedly low demand. As output falls, the firm will have to lay off workers, and unemployment will increase.

Generalizing from a Single Firm to the Entire Economy

This simplified story about a single car company explains why economists believe that a combination of unexpected changes in demand and inflexible prices are the key to understanding the short-run fluctuations that affect real-world economies. Generalizing this story to the economy as a whole, if demand falls off for many goods and services across the entire economy for an extended period of time, then the firms that make those goods and services will be forced to cut production. As both manufacturing and service output decline, real GDP will fall and unemployment will rise.

On the other hand, if demand is unexpectedly high for a prolonged period of time, the economy will boom and unemployment will fall. In the case of our Proton example, for each week that demand is unexpectedly high, inventories will fall by 250 cars. If inventories continue to decrease week after week, they will eventually fall to zero. Buzzer will have to react by increasing production to more than the optimal output rate of 900 cars per week so that orders do not go unfilled. GDP will increase as more cars per week are produced, and unemployment will fall because the factory will need to hire more workers to produce the larger number of cars. (The nearby Consider This applies the lessons of Buzzer Auto to the COVID-19 recession of 2020, which involved both a demand shock *and* a supply shock.)

CONSIDER THIS . . .

Double Whammy!

The COVID-19 recession of 2020 was incredibly interesting from a macroeconomic perspective because it led to both a demand shock and a supply shock *simultaneously*.

The U.S. economy had been doing very well in the late 2010s, with low unemployment, subdued inflation, steadily rising wages, and a booming stock market. But then the pandemic arrived and governments around the world imposed "lockdowns" during which most businesses were forced to close and virtually all workers were ordered to stay at home to try to slow the spread of the coronavirus.

MOLPIX/Shutterstock

That unexpected turn of events was a shock. But it was one that generated both a decrease in the demand for goods and services (a negative demand shock) as well as a decrease in the supply of goods and services (a negative supply shock) because workers stuck at home not getting paid spent less on goods and services while firms shut down by the government could not produce any output.

That "double whammy" was one of the reasons that governments responded to the pandemic very aggressively, with the largest economic relief programs in history. We'll detail those policies and how they worked in coming chapters.

- Economic shocks occur when events unfold in ways that people or businesses are not expecting.

- Demand and supply shocks take place when demand or supply ends up being either higher or lower than expected.

- Real-world prices are often inflexible or "sticky" in the short run.

- When prices are sticky, the economy adjusts to demand shocks mostly through changes in output and employment (rather than through changes in prices).

QUICK REVIEW
6.4

How Sticky Are Prices?

We have just shown that **inflexible prices**—or "*sticky prices*" as economists often call them—help to explain how unexpected changes in demand lead to the fluctuations in GDP and employment that occur over the course of the business cycle. But not all prices are sticky. Indeed, the markets for many commodities and raw materials such as corn, oil, and natural gas feature extremely **flexible prices** that react within seconds to changes in supply and demand. By contrast, the prices of most consumer products are rather sticky, with the average good or service going 4.3 months between price changes.

To better appreciate how price stickiness varies by product or service, look at Table 6.1, which gives the average number of months between price changes in various industries, including manufacturing and retail. Service industry prices go nearly a year on average between updates while prices in the retail sector are updated on average every 4.6 months. The prices of specific products can change much more rapidly, including gasoline (two to three weeks) and airline tickets (hourly). By contrast, haircuts and newspapers average more than two years between price changes.

In later chapters, we identify and discuss several factors that cause short-run price stickiness. To keep the current discussion brief, let's focus on just two factors here. First, companies selling consumer products know that consumers prefer stable, predictable prices that do not fluctuate rapidly with changes in demand. Consumers would be annoyed if the same bottle of soda or shampoo cost one price one day, a different price the next day, and yet another price a week later. Volatile prices make planning more difficult. In addition, consumers who come in to buy the product on a day when the price happens to be high will likely feel that they are being taken advantage of. Thus, most retailers try to maintain stable prices as much as they can. Such firms do hold sales from time to time, but on the whole they try to keep prices stable and predictable—the result being price inflexibility.

>> **LO6.5** Characterize the degree to which various prices are sticky.

inflexible prices Product *prices* that remain in place (at least for a while) even though *supply* or *demand* has changed; stuck prices or sticky prices.

flexible prices Product *prices* that freely move upward or downward when product demand or supply changes.

Industry	Months
Services	11.3
Manufacturing	8.1
Finance	7.1
Utilities	4.7
Retail	4.6
Agriculture	3.2

TABLE 6.1
Average Number of Months between Price Changes in Selected Industries

Source: Yuriy Gorodnichenko and Michael Weber, "Are Sticky Prices Costly? Evidence from the Stock Market," *American Economic Review,* January 2016, pp. 165–99.

Second, in certain situations, a firm may fear that cutting its price will be counterproductive because its rivals might simply match the price cut—a situation often referred to as a "price war." This possibility is common among firms that have only one or two major rivals. Consider Coca-Cola and Pepsi. If Coca-Cola faces unexpectedly low demand for its product, it might be tempted to reduce its price in the hope that it can steal business away from Pepsi. But such a strategy will work only if Pepsi leaves its price alone when Coca-Cola cuts its price. In reality, if Coca-Cola cuts its price, Pepsi will very likely cut its price in retaliation, doing its best to make sure that Coca-Cola doesn't steal away its customers. If Pepsi retaliates, Coca-Cola will be made worse off by its decision to cut its price: It will not pick up much more business (because Pepsi also cut its price), and it will also be receiving less money for each bottle of Coke that it sells. Thus, firms that face the possibility of price wars often have sticky prices.

Categorizing Macroeconomic Models Using Price Stickiness

>> **LO6.6** Explain why economists use different macroeconomic models for different time horizons.

Price stickiness moderates over time. Firms that choose to use a fixed-price policy in the short run do not have to stick with that policy permanently. If unexpected changes in demand begin to look permanent, many firms will allow their prices to change so that price changes (in addition to quantity changes) can help to equalize quantities supplied with quantities demanded.

For this reason, economists speak of "sticky prices" rather than "stuck prices." Only in the very short run are prices totally inflexible. As time passes and prices are revised, the world looks much more like Figure 6.1a, in which prices are fully flexible, than Figure 6.1b, in which prices are totally inflexible. Indeed, the totally inflexible case shown in Figure 6.1b can be viewed as the extremely short-run response to an unexpected change in demand, while the fully flexible case shown in Figure 6.1a can be viewed as the long-run response that will take place as prices become fully flexible.

This insight is very useful in categorizing and understanding the differences between the various macroeconomic models that we will be presenting in subsequent chapters. For instance, the aggregate expenditures model presented in Chapter 11 is a short-run model that assumes perfectly inflexible prices. By contrast, the aggregate demand–aggregate supply model presented in Chapter 12 allows for flexible prices and is therefore useful for understanding how the economy behaves over longer periods of time.

As you study these various models, keep in mind that we need different models precisely because the economy behaves so differently depending on how much time has passed after a demand shock. The differences in behavior result from the fact that prices go from completely stuck immediately after a shock to fully flexible in the long run. Using different models for different stages in this process gives us much better insights into not only how economies actually behave but also how various government and central bank policies may have different effects in the short run (when prices are fixed) versus the long run (when prices are flexible).

Where will we go from here? In the remainder of Part 3, we examine how economists measure GDP and why GDP has expanded over time. Then, we discuss the terminology of business cycles and explore the measurement and types of unemployment and inflation. At that point you will be well prepared to examine the economic models, monetary considerations, and stabilization policies that lie at the heart of macroeconomics.

QUICK REVIEW
6.5

▸ Many commodity prices are extremely flexible and change constantly, but other prices in the economy change only infrequently.

▸ Some prices are inflexible in order to please retail customers, others because rival firms are afraid that price changes may trigger a price war.

▸ Prices tend to become more flexible over time, so that as time passes, the economy can react to demand shocks with price changes as well as with output and employment changes.

▸ Different macroeconomics models are required for the short run, during which prices are inflexible (so that demand shocks lead almost exclusively to output and employment changes), and for longer periods, during which prices become increasingly flexible (so that demand shocks lead more to price changes than output and employment changes).

The Behavioral Economics of Sticky Prices

Employee Psychology Appears to Play a Key Role in Price Stickiness.

This chapter discussed two reasons for sticky output prices: consumers preferring predictable prices and businesses fearing price wars. Another major cause of sticky output prices is the stickiness of a particular input price—the price of labor, that is, wages and salaries.

To understand why "sticky wages" can have such a large impact on the stickiness of output prices, we have to begin with the fact that wages and salaries make up about 70 percent of the average firm's costs. This means that firms will have difficulty cutting their per-unit output prices unless they can figure out a way to slash per-unit labor costs. Substantial efficiencies may be possible with respect to other production costs—such as rent and raw materials—but with labor costs comprising 70 percent of all costs, firms will be hard pressed to cut their per-unit selling prices by any substantial percentage unless they can figure out a way to cut their per-unit labor costs substantially.

As it turns out, reductions in per-unit labor costs are typically self-defeating due to psychological and cultural factors that constrain the relationship between a company and its employees. These factors are best explained by applying insights from behavioral economics, which is the subfield of economics that incorporates psychology and culture into the study of economic behavior. The key insight is that workers tend to get quite upset if their wages or salaries are cut. A firm that is facing reduced demand due to a recession may explain to its workers that it would like to cut costs in order to reduce its selling price and thereby recoup some of its lost sales. But workers whose pay is cut will feel that they are being taken advantage of by their employer since they are being asked to do the same amount of work for less money.

This resentment is counterproductive for firms because workers typically retaliate when their wages or salaries are reduced. Business people who have imposed pay cuts report that employee retaliation can take many forms. Workers may stop showing up on time. They often put in less effort while at work and also call in sick much more often. They begin to organize unions. And they may even go so far as to start stealing supplies or even vandalizing equipment. Taking these factors into account, firms have found that pay cuts often *increase* per-unit production costs.

Knowing that workers react so poorly to wage and salary cuts, most managers are loath to even propose such cuts. But at the same time, a reduction in demand that is caused by a recession means that either (1) per-unit costs must be cut in order to lower selling prices and thereby revive sales, or (2) a firm's output level must be reduced at the original price level in order to bring quantity supplied into alignment with the reduced level of quantity demand. Faced with this dilemma, most firms resort to layoffs that

VGstockstudio/Shutterstock

reduce total employment and thus total production (option 2) rather than pay cuts that keep everyone working but at a lower wage (option 1).

As an example, consider a typical firm, one whose labor costs constitute 70 percent of all of its costs. If a recession reduces the firm's sales by 20 percent, it may pursue option 2 by laying off 20 percent of its workforce but keeping wages and salaries unchanged for the 80 percent of workers who remain employed at the firm. The workers who were laid off will likely be resentful. But their negative feelings will not translate into higher costs or lower productivity for the firm. What is important for management is to avoid pay cuts for the workers who remain. By keeping their wages and salaries fixed, the firm will not engender any retaliation. Morale and productivity may even rise because the workers who remain employed may be grateful to still have paying jobs while many millions of workers across the economy are plunged into unemployment as a result of the recession.

A key point to understand, though, is that the layoffs will not change the firm's per-unit production costs. The firm's workforce will become 20 percent smaller, and thus its total labor bill will fall by 20 percent. But at the same time, a 20-percent smaller labor force will produce 20 percent less output, other things equal. This implies that the firm's labor cost per unit of output will remain unchanged. As a result, the firm will find it difficult to cut its price per unit. Unless the firm can find ways of making deep cuts in its nonlabor costs, its output price will tend to be sticky if not stuck. In this way, the stickiness of wages and salaries translates into price stickiness.

There are of course other causes of price stickiness in the economy, but this story of workers reacting badly to pay cuts is considered to be a leading contributor by most macroeconomists. When recessions hit, firms cut labor costs by firing workers rather than lowering wages and salaries.

Summary

LO6.1 Explain why economists use GDP, inflation, and unemployment to assess the economy's health.
Macroeconomics studies long-run economic growth and short-run economic fluctuations.

Macroeconomists focus their attention on three key economic statistics: real GDP, unemployment, and inflation. Real GDP measures the value of all final goods and services produced in a country during a specific period of time. The unemployment rate measures the percentage of all workers who are not able to find paid employment despite being willing and able to work at currently available wages. The inflation rate measures the extent to which the overall level of prices is rising in the economy.

LO6.2 Discuss why sustained increases in living standards are historically recent.
Before the Industrial Revolution, living standards did not show any sustained increases over time. Economies grew, but any increase in output was offset by an equally large increase in the population, so that the amount of output per person did not rise. By contrast, since the Industrial Revolution began in the late 1700s, many nations have experienced modern economic growth in which output grows faster than population—so that standards of living rise over time.

LO6.3 Identify why saving and investment promote higher living standards.
A key to modern economic growth is the promotion of saving and investment. Investment activities (such as funding research or increasing the amount of physical capital) increase the economy's future potential output level. But investment must be funded by savings, which accumulate only if people are willing to reduce current consumption below current income. Consequently, individuals and society face a trade-off between current consumption and future consumption.

Banks and other financial institutions help to convert saving into investment by lending the savings generated by households to businesses that wish to make investments.

LO6.4 Explain why shocks and sticky prices are responsible for short-run fluctuations in output and employment.
Expectations have an important effect on the economy because if people and businesses are more positive about the future, they will save and invest more. However, expectations are not always fulfilled. Individuals and firms must sometimes adjust to shocks—situations in which the future does not turn out as expected.

If prices are inflexible, or "sticky," shocks to demand or supply can result in disequilibrium situations in which quantity demanded does not equal quantity supplied. In such situations, the only way for the economy to adjust in the short run (the time horizon over which prices remain sticky) is through changes in output, employment, and inventories.

LO6.5 Characterize the degree to which various prices are sticky.
Prices are inflexible in the short run for various reasons. One reason is that firms often attempt to maintain stable prices to please consumers, who tend to prefer predictable prices. Second, a firm with just a few competitors may be reluctant to cut its price due to the fear of starting a price war.

LO6.6 Explain why economists use different macroeconomic models for different time horizons.
Price stickiness moderates over time. As a result, economists have found it sensible to build separate economic models for different time horizons. For instance, some models reflect the high degree of price inflexibility that occurs in the immediate short run, while other models reflect the high degree of price flexibility that occurs in the long run.

Terms and Concepts

business cycle	saving	demand shocks
real GDP (real gross domestic product)	investment	supply shocks
nominal GDP	financial investment	inventory
unemployment	economic investment	inflexible prices ("sticky prices")
inflation	expectations	flexible prices
modern economic growth	shocks	

Discussion Questions

1. Why do you think macroeconomists focus on just a few key statistics when trying to understand the health and trajectory of an economy? Would it be better to try to examine all possible data? Why or why not? **LO6.1**

2. Consider a nation in which the volume of goods and services is growing by 5 percent per year. What is the likely impact of this high rate of growth on the power and influence of its government relative to other countries experiencing slower rates of growth? How will this 5 percent growth rate likely affect the nation's living standards? Will the standard of living grow by 5 percent per year, given population growth? Why or why not? **LO6.2**

3. Has economic output always grown faster than the population? When did modern economic growth begin? Have all of the world's nations experienced the same extent of modern economic growth? **LO6.2**

4. Why is there a trade-off between the amount of consumption that people can enjoy today and the amount of consumption that they can enjoy in the future? Why can't people enjoy more of both? How does saving relate to investment and thus to economic growth? What role do banks and other financial institutions play in aiding the economic growth process? **LO6.3**

5. How does investment as defined by economists differ from investment as defined by the general public? What would happen

to the amount of economic investment made today if firms expect the future returns to such investment to be very low? What would happen to the amount of economic investment today if firms expect future returns to be very high? **LO6.4**

6. Why, in general, do shocks force people to make changes? Give at least two examples from your own experience. **LO6.4**

7. Catalog companies are committed to selling at the prices printed in their catalogs. If a catalog company finds its inventory of sweaters rising, what does that tell you about the demand for sweaters? Was it unexpectedly high, unexpectedly low, or as expected? If the company could change the price of sweaters, would it raise the price, lower the price, or keep the price the same? Given that the company cannot change the price of sweaters, however, consider the number of sweaters it orders each month from the company that manufactures the sweaters.

If inventories become very high, will the catalog company increase orders, decrease orders, or keep orders the same? Given what the catalog company does with its orders, what is likely to happen to employment and output at the sweater manufacturer? **LO6.4**

8. Are all prices in the economy equally inflexible? Which ones show large amounts of short-run flexibility? Which ones show a great deal of inflexibility over months or years? **LO6.5**

9. Why do many firms strive to maintain stable prices? **LO6.5**

10. Do prices tend to become more flexible or less flexible as time passes? Explain. **LO6.6**

11. **LAST WORD** Are labor costs a major fraction of the typical firm's overall production costs? How does wage stickiness cause price stickiness? Discuss why firms are averse to cutting wages and salaries during a business downturn.

Review Questions

1. An increase in _____ GDP guarantees that more goods and services are being produced by an economy. **LO6.1**
   a. nominal
   b. real

2. True or False: The term *economic investment* includes purchases of stocks, bonds, and real estate. **LO6.3**

3. If an economy has sticky prices, and demand unexpectedly increases, you would expect the economy's real GDP to: **LO6.4**
   a. increase.
   b. decrease.
   c. remain the same.

4. If an economy has fully flexible prices and demand unexpectedly increases, you would expect the economy's real GDP to: **LO6.4**

   a. increase.
   b. decrease.
   c. remain the same.

5. If the demand for a firm's output unexpectedly decreases, you would expect its inventory to: **LO6.4**
   a. increase.
   b. decrease.
   c. remain the same.
   d. increase or remain the same, depending on whether or not prices are sticky.

6. True or False: Because price stickiness matters only in the short run, economists are comfortable using just one macroeconomic model for all situations. **LO6.6**

Problems

1. Suppose that the annual rates of growth of real GDP in Econoland over a five-year period were sequentially as follows: 3 percent, 1 percent, −2 percent, 4 percent, and 5 percent. What was the average of these growth rates in Econoland over these five years? What term would economists use to describe what happened in year 3? If the growth rate in year 3 had been a positive 2 percent rather than a negative 2 percent, what would have been Econoland's average growth rate over the five years? **LO6.1**

2. Suppose that Glitter Gulch, a gold mining firm, increased its sales revenues on newly mined gold from $100 million to $200 million between one year and the next. Assuming that the price of gold increased by 100 percent over the same period, by what numerical amount did Glitter Gulch's real output change? If the price of gold had not changed, what would have been the change in Glitter Gulch's real output? **LO6.1**

3. A mathematical approximation called the rule of 70 tells us how long it will take for something to double in size if it grows at a constant rate. The doubling time is approximately equal to the number 70 divided by the percentage rate of growth. Thus, if Oman's real GDP per person is growing at 7 percent per year, it will take about 10 years (= 70/7) to double. Apply the rule of 70 to solve the following problem: Real GDP per person in Oman in 2020 was about $15,000 per person, while it was about

$60,000 per person in the United States. If real GDP per person in Oman grows at the rate of 5 percent per year, about how long will it take Oman's real GDP per person to reach the level that the United States enjoyed in 2020? (Hint: How many times would Oman's 2020 real GDP per person have to double to reach the United States' 2020 real GDP per person?) **LO6.2**

4. Assume that a national restaurant chain called BBQ builds 10 new restaurants at a cost of $1 million per restaurant. It outfits each restaurant with an additional $200,000 of equipment and furnishings. To help partially defray the cost of this expansion, BBQ issues and sells 200,000 shares of stock at $30 per share. What is the amount of economic investment that has resulted from BBQ's actions? How much purely financial investment took place? **LO6.3**

5. Refer to Figure 6.1b and assume that price is fixed at $37,000 and that Buzzer Auto needs 5 workers for every 1 automobile produced. If demand is D_M and Buzzer wants to perfectly match its output and sales, how many cars will Buzzer produce, and how many workers will it hire? If, instead, demand unexpectedly falls from D_M to D_L, how many fewer cars will Buzzer sell? How many fewer workers will it need if it decides to match production to these lower sales? **LO6.4**

CHAPTER

7

Measuring Domestic Output and National Income

>> LEARNING OBJECTIVES

LO7.1 Define and measure gross domestic product (GDP).

LO7.2 Determine GDP by summing all expenditures on final goods and services.

LO7.3 Determine GDP by summing all incomes received for providing resources.

LO7.4 Describe the relationships among GDP, net domestic product, national income, personal income, and disposable income.

LO7.5 Distinguish between nominal GDP and real GDP.

LO7.6 Explain some limitations of the GDP measure.

"Disposable Income Flat." "Personal Consumption Surges." "GDP Up 4 Percent." These headlines, typical of cable TV news reports or *The Wall Street Journal,* give knowledgeable readers valuable information on the state of the economy. This chapter will help you interpret such headlines and understand the stories reported under them. More specifically, you will become familiar with the vocabulary and methods of national income accounting.

Assessing the Economy's Performance

>> **LO7.1** Define and measure gross domestic product (GDP).

national income accounting The techniques used to measure the overall production of a country's economy as well as other related variables.

gross domestic product (GDP) The total market value of all *final goods* and *services* produced annually within the boundaries of a nation.

National income accounting measures the economy's overall performance. The Bureau of Economic Analysis (BEA), an agency of the U.S. Commerce Department, compiles the National Income and Product Accounts (NIPA) for the U.S. economy. This accounting helps economists and policymakers:

- Assess the economy's health by monitoring production and employment levels.
- Track the economy's long-run growth trajectory.
- Adjust economic policies to safeguard and improve the economy's health.

Gross Domestic Product

The primary measure of an economy's performance is its *aggregate output*, or total output, of goods and services. There are several ways to measure aggregate output. The one favored by the Bureau of Economic Analysis is **gross domestic product (GDP),** or the dollar value of all final goods and services produced within a country's borders during a specific period of time, typically a year or a quarter.

Final Products Only Note that GDP only counts the value of **final goods and services,** that is, products that are purchased by their end (final) users. GDP excludes **intermediate goods and services** that are purchased for resale or as inputs used to produce other products. Thus, a loaf of bread that is purchased by a family for a camping trip is counted in GDP (because the family is the end user) while an identical loaf that is purchased by a sandwich shop is not counted in GDP (because the sandwich shop will be using the loaf of bread as an input to the production of its final product, sandwiches).

final goods and services Products that have been purchased for final use (rather than for resale or further processing or manufacturing).

Domestic Output Only GDP includes only the value of final goods and services produced within a nation's boundaries. Thus, the value of the cars produced at a Japanese-owned Toyota factory in Ohio would count as part of U.S. GDP (because the factory is located in the United States) but the value of the trucks produced at an American-owned Ford factory in Canada would not (because the factory lies outside the borders of the United States). What matters for GDP is where the final output is produced, not who makes it or who consumes it.

intermediate goods and services Products that are purchased for resale or further processing or manufacturing.

A Monetary Measure There's an old expression that says, "You can't add apples and oranges." That expression is true because apples and oranges are measured in different units. Apples are measured as 1 apple, 2 apples, 3 apples, 4 apples, and so forth. Oranges are measured as 1 orange, 2 oranges, 3 oranges, 4 oranges, etc. Thus it would make no sense to ask, "What is 2 apples plus 4 oranges?" You would get nowhere because the correct answer is "2 apples plus 4 oranges," which simply restates the question.

To add dissimilar items like apples and oranges together, they must share a common unit of measurement. When it comes to apples and oranges, one way to do this is by adding together pounds of apples and pounds of oranges. That can be done because both items (pounds of apples and pounds of oranges) now share a common unit of measurement (pounds).

Another strategy is to add together the dollar values of apples and oranges—and, by extension, the dollar values of any group of items. This is the method used to calculate GDP. Statisticians sum up the *monetary values* of all the final goods and services produced in the economy.

Consider the example presented in Table 7.1, where the economy produces three sofas and two computers in year 1 and two sofas and three computers in year 2. Because sofas and computers lack a common unit of measurement, there is no way to add them together. But we *can* add together the number of dollars of sofas and the number of dollars of computers. At $500 per sofa and $2,000 per computer, the market value (dollar value) of the economy's output in year 1 is $5,500 while the monetary value of the economy's output in year 2 is $7,000. It is consequently clear that aggregate output has increased by $1,500.

The higher valuation for aggregate output in year 2 is not at all obvious if you are merely told the numbers of sofas and computers produced in each year. Only by measuring individual outputs in the common unit of dollars can you understand that aggregate output has in fact increased.

Using dollars as the common unit of measurement for calculating GDP has an additional benefit. Because people put higher dollar values on things they like, we can infer that higher levels of GDP imply higher levels of satisfaction, all other things equal. It is for this reason that policymakers are deeply concerned with how to increase GDP.

Value Added

GDP counts only final goods and services. But final goods and services are the result of a long chain of intermediate production steps. As an example, consider Table 7.2 and the multiple stages of production needed to manufacture a wool coat and get it to a final consumer. Firm A, a sheep ranch, sells $120 worth of raw wool to firm B, a wool processor. Firm B takes that raw wool and combines it with land, labor, capital, and entrepreneurship to produce $180 of processed wool that it sells to Firm C, a coat manufacturer. Firm C, the manufacturer, sells the coat to firm D, a wholesaler, which sells it to firm E, a retailer. Finally, a consumer, the final user, buys the coat for $350 from the retailer.

TABLE 7.1 Comparing Heterogeneous Output by Using Money Prices

Year	Annual Output	Market Value
1	3 sofas and 2 computers	3 at $500 + 2 at $2,000 = $5,500
2	2 sofas and 3 computers	2 at $500 + 3 at $2,000 = $7,000

TABLE 7.2 Value Added in a Five-Stage Production Process

(1) Stage of Production	(2) Sales Value of Materials or Product	(3) Value Added
	$ 0	
Firm A, sheep ranch	120	$120 (= $120 − $ 0)
Firm B, wool processor	180	60 (= 180 − 120)
Firm C, coat manufacturer	220	40 (= 220 − 180)
Firm D, clothing wholesaler	270	50 (= 270 − 220)
Firm E, retail clothier	**350**	80 (= 350 − 270)
Total sales values	$1,140	
Value added (total income)		**$350**

Because GDP counts only final goods and services, GDP in this example must be $350, the price that the final consumer pays Firm E for the final product (the wool coat). But there is another way to calculate the $350 dollar value of GDP that shines some light on the intermediate stages of production. It involves measuring and cumulating the *value added* at each stage of production.

value added The value of a product sold by a *firm* less the value of the products (materials) purchased and used by the firm to produce that product.

Value added is the market value of a firm's output *less* the value of the inputs the firm has bought. As Column 3 of Table 7.2 indicates, the value added by firm B is $60, the difference between the $180 value of its output, processed wool, and the $120 it paid to firm A for raw wool. Similarly, the value added by firm C is $40, or the difference between the $220 market value of its output, a finished coat, and the $180 it paid to firm B for processed wool.

Note that if you add together all of the value-added numbers in Column 3, they sum to $350, which is the same as the value of GDP that we calculated by looking only at the $350 market price paid by the final user. This is no coincidence. A final product's GDP value can always be calculated *either* as the market value paid by the final user *or* as the sum of the values added at each stage of the production process.

Gross Output and Multiple Counting

gross output (GO) The dollar value of the economic activity taking place at every stage of production and distribution. By contrast, *gross domestic product* (GDP) only accounts for the value of final output.

Gross output (GO) sums together the sales values received by firms at each stage of production. In Table 7.2, gross output is $1,140, or the sum of the sales values received by firms A through E.

Note that gross output is always larger than GDP because it includes not only the value of the final product but also the values of all of the earlier "business to business" transactions involving intermediate goods. Thus, in Table 7.2, we see that the GO of $1,140 is much larger than the GDP of $350.

multiple counting Wrongly including the value of *intermediate goods* in the *gross domestic product*; counting the same *good* or *service* more than once.

That large difference points out why we must do our best to avoid *multiple counting* when calculating GDP. **Multiple counting** is the mistake of including the sales values of intermediate goods in GDP. That is a mistake because GDP should only include the sales value of final products.

The most direct way of avoiding multiple counting is by making sure that you are adding together the sales values of final products only. The other is to calculate GDP by summing together values added. That method avoids multiple counting because the value added that is calculated at each stage of production subtracts off the input costs incurred at earlier stages of production. By subtracting them off, they do not get counted multiple times. The only thing that gets counted is each firm's unique contribution to the value of the final product.

GDP Excludes Nonproduction Transactions

Although many monetary transactions in the economy involve final goods and services, many others do not. These nonproduction transactions must be excluded from GDP because they have nothing to do with the production of final goods.

There are two types of *nonproduction transactions* that must be excluded from GDP: purely financial transactions and secondhand sales.

Financial Transactions Purely financial transactions include the following:

- *Public transfer payments* These are the social security payments, welfare payments, and veterans' payments that the government makes directly to households. Because the recipients contribute nothing to current production in return, including such payments in GDP would overstate the year's output.

- *Private transfer payments* These payments include, for example, allowance money given by parents to children and cash gifts given during the holidays. They produce no output. They simply transfer funds from one private individual to another and consequently do not enter into GDP.

- *Financial asset transactions* The buying and selling of stocks, bonds, and other financial assets is just a matter of transferring the ownership of existing financial assets from one person to another. Such transactions create nothing in the way of current production and are not included in GDP. Payments for the services provided by a stockbroker are included, however, because their services are currently provided and are thus a part of the economy's current output of goods and services.

Secondhand Sales Secondhand sales contribute nothing to current production and are therefore excluded from GDP. Suppose you sell your 2015 Ford Mustang to a friend. That transaction will not be counted in this year's GDP because it generates no current production.

Two Ways of Looking at GDP: Spending and Income

Let's look again at how the market value of total output—or of any single unit of total output—is measured. Given the data listed in Table 7.2, how can we measure the market value of a coat?

The first approach is to see how much the final user paid for it. That will tell us the market value of the final product. Or we can add up the entire wage, rent, interest, and profit incomes that were created in producing the coat. The second approach is the value-added method demonstrated in Table 7.2.

The final-product approach and the value-added approach are two ways of looking at the same thing. What is spent on making a product is income to those who helped make it. If $350 is spent on manufacturing a coat, then $350 is the total income derived from its production.

We can look at GDP in the same two ways. We can view GDP as the sum of all the money spent in buying it. That is the *output approach*, or **expenditures approach.** Or we can view GDP in terms of the income derived or created from producing it. That is the *earnings, allocations,* or **income approach.**

As illustrated in Figure 7.1, we can determine GDP for a particular year either by adding up all the money that was spent to buy total output *or* by adding up all the money that was derived as income from its production. Buying (spending money) and selling (receiving income) are two aspects of the same transaction. On the expenditures side of GDP, all final goods produced by the economy are bought either by the three domestic sectors (households, businesses, and

expenditures approach The method that adds all expenditures made for *final goods* and final *services* to measure the *gross domestic product.*

income approach The method that adds all the *income* generated by the production of *final goods* and final *services* to measure the *gross domestic product.*

FIGURE 7.1 The expenditures and income approaches to GDP.

There are two general approaches to measuring gross domestic product. We can determine GDP as the value of output by summing all expenditures on that output. Alternatively, with some modifications, we can determine GDP by adding up all the components of income arising from the production of that output.

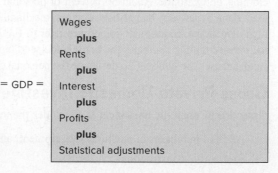

Expenditures, or output, approach		Income, or allocations, approach
Consumption expenditures by households		Wages
plus		plus
Investment expenditures by businesses		Rents
plus	= GDP =	plus
Government purchases of goods and services		Interest
plus		plus
Expenditures by foreigners		Profits
		plus
		Statistical adjustments

TABLE 7.3 Accounting Statement for the U.S. Economy Using the Expenditures (Output) Approach, 2021 (in Billions)

	Billions
Sum of:	
Personal consumption expenditures (*C*)	$15,742
Gross private domestic investment (*I*$_g$)	4,120
Government purchases (*G*)	4,053
Net exports (*X*$_n$)	−918
Equals:	
Gross domestic product	**$22,996**

Source: U.S. Bureau of Economic Analysis.

TABLE 7.4 Accounting Statement for the U.S. Economy Using the Income (Allocations) Approach, 2021 (in Billions)*

	Billions
Sum of:	
Compensation of employees	$ 12,581
Rents	726
Interest	686
Proprietors' income	1,822
Corporate profits	2,806
Taxes on production and imports	1,299
Equals:	
National income	**$19,920**
Less: Net foreign factor income	252
Plus: Consumption of fixed capital	3,848
Plus: Statistical discrepancy	−520
Equals:	
Gross domestic product	**$22,996**

*Some of the items in this table combine related categories that appear in the more detailed accounts. All data are subject to government revision.

Source: U.S. Bureau of Economic Analysis.

government) or by foreign buyers. On the income side (once certain statistical adjustments are made), the total receipts acquired from the sale of that total output are allocated to the suppliers of resources as wages, rents, interest, and profit.

Table 7.3 shows U.S. GDP for 2021 totaled up using the expenditures approach. Table 7.4 shows U.S. GDP for 2021 totaled up using the income approach. Both methods lead to the same result: U.S. GDP in 2021 was $22,996 billion.

QUICK REVIEW

7.1

▸ Gross domestic product (GDP) is a measure of the total market value of all final goods and services produced domestically in a specific quarter or year.

▸ GDP can be obtained by adding together the market selling prices of all final goods and services or by adding up the values added at each stage of production.

▸ GDP can be calculated as either the sum of all the money spent purchasing final goods and services (expenditures approach) or as the sum of all the incomes earned from providing the resources that went into producing those final goods and services (income approach).

The Expenditures Approach

>> **LO7.2** Determine GDP by summing all expenditures on final goods and services.

To determine GDP using the expenditures approach, we add up all the spending on final goods and services that has taken place throughout the year. National income accountants have developed precise definitions for each of the types of spending listed on the left side of Figure 7.1.

Personal Consumption Expenditures (*C*)

personal consumption expenditures (*C*) The expenditures of *households* for both durable and nondurable *consumer goods*.

durable good A consumer good with an expected life (use) of three or more years.

nondurable good A *consumer good* with an expected life (use) of less than three years.

service An (intangible) act or use for which a consumer, *firm*, or government is willing to pay.

What we have called "consumption expenditures by households" is what the national income accountants call **personal consumption expenditures (*C*).** This category covers all expenditures by households on goods and services. In a typical year, roughly 10 percent of personal consumption expenditures are on **durable goods**—products that have expected lives of 3 years or more. Such goods include new automobiles, furniture, and refrigerators. **Nondurable goods**—products with less than 3 years of expected life—make up 30 percent of personal consumption expenditures. Included in this category are food, clothing, and gasoline. About 60 percent of personal consumption expenditures is for **services**—the work done by lawyers, hair stylists, doctors, mechanics, and other service providers. Because of this high percentage, economists sometimes refer to the U.S. economy as a *service economy*. National income accounting combines the household spending on durable goods, nondurable goods, and services and uses the symbol *C* to designate the personal consumption expenditures component of GDP.

Gross Private Domestic Investment (*I*$_g$)

Gross private domestic investment (*I*$_g$) includes the following items:

- All final purchases of machinery, equipment, and tools used by business enterprises.
- Residential construction.

- Expenditures on the research and development (R&D) of new productive technologies.
- Money spent on the creation of new works of art, music, writing, film, and software.
- Changes in inventories.

Investment—or, more correctly, *economic investment*—refers to activities that increase the nation's stock of capital, which is the collection of human-made resources that help to produce goods and services. Those human-created resources can be divided into two broad categories that we can informally refer to as "tools" and "recipes."

Tools are tangible physical objects that help to produce goods and services. Recipes are the intangible methods, techniques, and management practices necessary to produce goods and services. A well-stocked kitchen requires both cooking equipment (tools) and an understanding of how to cook (recipes). A productive economy requires both tangible physical capital (factories, wireless networks, infrastructure) and intangible intellectual capital (knowing when to plant a crop, understanding how to fly a plane, comprehending the best way to organize a factory).

The first two items fall into the tools category. Final purchases of plant, machinery, and equipment increase the amount of physical capital available to produce future output. In a similar fashion, residential construction generates a future flow of output—housing services—that will keep people productive by keeping them healthy and sheltered.

The next two items fall into the recipes category. Spending on R&D increases the intangible stock of methods and techniques that we can use to produce output. Spending that funds the creation of new works of art, music, writing, and film increases the flow of entertainment and educational services, while spending that pays for new or improved software increases the productivity of everything from cell phones to self-driving cars.

Finally, please note that increases in inventories (unsold goods) are considered investments because they represent, in effect, "unconsumed output," or output that will increase the future supply of final goods and services when it is sold out of inventory and consumed in future periods. For economists, all new output that is not consumed is, by definition, capital. So an increase in inventories is registered as an addition (although perhaps temporary) to the economy's stock of capital goods (i.e., physical objects that increase future consumption).

Positive and Negative Changes in Inventories We need to look at changes in inventories more closely. Inventories can either increase or decrease over some period. Suppose they increased by $10 billion between December 31, 2026, and December 31, 2027. Therefore, in 2027, the economy produced $10 billion more output than people purchased. We want to count all output produced in 2027 as part of that year's GDP, even though some of it remained unsold at the end of the year. We do so by including the $10 billion increase in inventories as part of year 2027's investment. That way, the expenditures in 2027 correctly measure the output produced that year.

Alternatively, suppose that inventories decreased by $10 billion in 2027. This "drawing down of inventories" means that the economy sold $10 billion more of output in 2027 than it produced that year. It did so by selling goods produced in prior years—goods already counted as GDP in those years. Unless corrected, expenditures in 2027 will overstate GDP for 2027. So in 2027 we consider the $10 billion decline in inventories as "negative investment" and subtract it from total investment that year.

Excluding Financial Investment Please note that economists and NIPA accountants are careful to distinguish between *economic investment* and *financial investment*.

- Economic investment involves the creation of new productive capital, either new tools (plant, equipment, infrastructure) or new recipes (methods, systems, applications). As far as the national income and product accounts are concerned, economic investment is the only investment that matters and the only investment that should be included in the NIPA tables.

- By contrast, financial investment, like purchasing stocks or buying a bond, merely transfers the ownership of existing assets; it does not produce new capital goods. Thus, financial investment is *not* included in GDP.

So be careful to remember that while ordinary people in daily life do not distinguish between economic investment and financial investment, the only "investment" that is reported in the national income and product accounts is economic investment—the creation of new capital assets.

gross private domestic investment (I_g) Expenditures that increase the nation's stock of capital, which is the collection of physical objects and intangible ideas that help to produce goods and services. Includes spending on final purchases of plant, machinery, and equipment by business enterprises; residential construction; changes in *inventories*; expenditures on the *research and development (R&D)* of new productive technologies; and money spent on the creation of new works of art, music, writing, film, and software.

FIGURE 7.2

Gross investment, depreciation, net investment, and the stock of capital.

When gross investment exceeds depreciation during a year, net investment occurs. This net investment expands the stock of private capital from the beginning of the year to the end of the year by the amount of the net investment. Other things equal, the economy's production capacity expands.

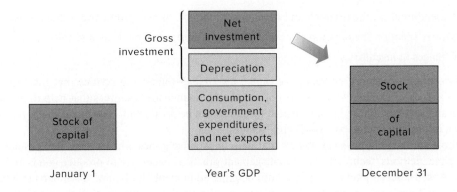

Gross Investment versus Net Investment When we speak of *gross private domestic investment*, the words "private" and "domestic" mean that we are speaking of investment spending by private businesses, not by government, and that the investment is taking place inside the country, not abroad.

The word "gross" means that we are referring to *all* investment goods—both those that replace machinery, equipment, and buildings that were used up (worn out or made obsolete) in producing the current year's output *as well as* any net additions to the economy's capital stock.

Net private domestic investment measures only the *net* additions to the economy's total stock of capital. It is calculated by taking the economy's gross amount of investment and subtracting off the amount of capital that is used up over the course of a year, a quantity that is referred to as *depreciation:*

net private domestic investment *Gross private domestic investment* less *consumption of fixed capital;* the addition to the nation's stock of *capital* during a year.

$$\text{Net investment} = \text{gross investment} - \text{depreciation}$$

In typical years, gross investment exceeds depreciation. Thus net investment is positive and the nation's capital stock rises by the amount of net investment. As Figure 7.2, illustrates, the capital stock at the end of a typical year exceeds the capital stock at the beginning of the year by the amount of net investment.

Gross investment does not always exceed depreciation, however. When gross investment and depreciation are *equal*, net investment is zero and there is no change in the size of the capital stock. When gross investment is *less* than depreciation, net investment is negative. In that case, the economy is *disinvesting*—using up more capital than it is producing—and the nation's stock of capital shrinks, which is exactly what happened during the Great Depression of the 1930s.

National income accountants use the symbol I for private domestic investment spending. To differentiate between gross investment and net investment, they add either the subscript g or the subscript n. But it is gross investment, I_g, that they use when tallying up GDP—not net investment (I_n).

Government Purchases (G)

government purchases (G) Expenditures by government for *goods* and *services* that government consumes in providing public services as well as expenditures for publicly owned capital that has a long lifetime; the expenditures of all governments in the economy for those *final goods* and final *services*.

The third category of expenditures in the national income accounts is **government purchases,** officially labeled "government consumption expenditures and gross investment." These expenditures have three components: (1) expenditures for goods and services that the government consumes in providing public services; (2) expenditures for *publicly owned capital* such as schools and highways, which have long lifetimes; and (3) government expenditures on R&D and other activities that increase the economy's stock of know-how.

These purchases include all government expenditures (federal, state, and local) on final goods as well as all direct purchases of resources, including labor. They do *not* include government transfer payments because, as we have seen, such payments merely transfer money to certain households and generate no production. National income accountants use the symbol G to signify government purchases.

Net Exports (X_n)

International trade transactions are a significant item in national income accounting. But when calculating U.S. GDP, we must keep in mind that we want to total up only those expenditures that are used to purchase goods and services produced *within the borders of the United States.*

Thus, we must add in the value of exports, X, because the money that people in other countries spend purchasing U.S. exports is by definition spending on goods and services produced within the United States.

Don't be confused by the fact that it is foreigners who buy our exports. The definition of GDP does not specify *who* is buying U.S.-made goods and services—only that the goods and services that they buy are made within U.S. borders. Thus, foreign spending on U.S. exports *must* be included in U.S. GDP.

At this point, you might incorrectly think that GDP should equal the sum of $C + I_g + G + X$. But C, I_g, and G include not only expenditures on domestically produced goods and services but also goods and services produced outside the United States. So to correctly calculate gross domestic product, we must subtract off the spending that goes to imports, M. That subtraction yields the correct formula for calculating gross domestic product: $GDP = C + I_g + G + X - M$.

Accountants simplify this formula for GDP by defining **net exports**, X_n, to be equal to exports minus imports:

net exports (X_n) *Exports minus imports.*

$$\text{Net exports}(X_n) = \text{exports}(X) - \text{imports}(M)$$

Using this definition of net exports, gross domestic product can be defined as the sum of household consumption expenditures, gross private domestic investment, government purchases, and net exports. In algebra:

$$GDP = C + I_g + G + X_n$$

Table 7.3 shows that in 2021 Americans spent $918 billion more on imports than foreigners spent on U.S. exports. That is, net exports in 2021 were a *minus* $918 billion.

Putting It All Together: GDP $= C + I_g + G + X_n$

Taken together, the four categories of expenditures provide a measure of the market value of a specific year's total output—its GDP. Table 7.3 indicates that 2021 U.S. GDP (in billions) totaled:

$$GDP = \$15{,}742 + \$4{,}120 + \$4{,}053 - \$918$$

Global Perspective 7.1 lists the GDPs of several countries in U.S. dollars.

GLOBAL PERSPECTIVE 7.1

COMPARATIVE GDPs IN TRILLIONS OF U.S. DOLLARS, SELECTED NATIONS, 2020

The United States, China, and Japan have the world's highest GDPs when local, domestic-currency GDPs are converted into U.S. dollars using international exchange rates. That method of comparing national incomes does not account for differences between countries in the cost of living. But it does demonstrate how countries compare in terms of being able to purchase and sell on international markets, which is a major concern for international trade and economic development.

GDP in Trillions of U.S. Dollars

0 2 4 6 8 10 12 14 16 18 20 22

United States
China
Japan
Germany
United Kingdom
India
Italy
Canada
South Korea
Russia
Brazil
Spain
Mexico
Nigeria
Egypt

Source: The World Bank Group, data.worldbank.org.

>> LO7.3 Determine GDP by summing all incomes received for providing resources.

The Income Approach

Table 7.4 shows how 2021's expenditures of $22,996 billion were allocated as income to those responsible for producing that year's output. It would be convenient if we could say that the entire amount of expenditures flowed back to them in the form of wages, rent, interest, and profit. But some expenditures flow to other recipients (such as the government) or to other uses (such as paying to replace the capital goods that have worn out while producing this year's GDP). These items must be taken into account in order for the income approach and the expenditures approach to arrive at the same value for GDP. We will begin by looking at the items that make up *national income* in Table 7.4.

Compensation of Employees

By far the largest share of national income—$12,581 billion in 2021—was paid as wages and salaries by business and government to their employees. That figure also includes wage and salary supplements, including payments by employers into social insurance and into a variety of private pension, health, and welfare funds for workers.

Rents

Rents consist of the income received by the households and businesses that supply property resources. They include the monthly payments tenants make to landlords and the lease payments corporations pay for the use of office space. The figure used in the national accounts is *net* rent—gross rental income minus depreciation of the rental property.

Interest

Interest consists of the money paid by private businesses to the suppliers of loans used to purchase capital. It also includes the interest that households receive on savings deposits, certificates of deposit (CDs), and corporate bonds.

Proprietors' Income

The national income accounts divide "profits" into two accounts: *proprietors' income*, which consists of the net income of sole proprietorships, partnerships, and other unincorporated businesses; and *corporate profits*.

Corporate Profits

Corporate profits are the earnings of corporations. National income accountants subdivide corporate profits into three categories:

- *Corporate income taxes* These taxes are levied on corporations' profits. They flow to the government.
- *Dividends* Dividends are the part of after-tax profits that corporations choose to pay out, or distribute, to their stockholders. They thus flow to households, which are the ultimate owners of all corporations.
- *Undistributed corporate profits* Any after-tax profits that are not distributed to shareholders are saved, or retained, by corporations to pay for subsequent investment. Undistributed corporate profits are also called *retained earnings*.

taxes on production and imports A *national income accounting* category that includes such taxes as *sales, excise,* business property taxes, and *tariffs* that *firms* treat as costs of producing a product and pass on (in whole or in part) to buyers by charging a higher *price*.

Taxes on Production and Imports

The account called **taxes on production and imports** includes general sales taxes, excise taxes, business property taxes, license fees, and customs duties. Why do national income accountants add these indirect business taxes to wages, rent, interest, and profits in determining national income? The answer is: "to account for expenditures that are diverted to the government." Consider an item that would otherwise sell for $1 but costs $1.05 because the government has imposed a

5 percent sales tax. When this item is purchased, consumers spend $1.05 to buy it. But only $1 will go to the seller (who then distributes it as income in the form of wages, rent, interest, and profit). The remaining 5 cents flow as revenue to the government. The GDP accountants place the extra 5 cents into the category called "Taxes on Production and Imports" and loosely consider these taxes to be "income" to government.

From National Income to GDP

Expenditures on final goods and services flow either as income to private citizens or as "income" to government. As a result, **national income** is the total of all sources of private income (employee compensation, rents, interest, proprietors' income, and corporate profits) plus government revenue from taxes on production and imports. National income is all the income that flows to U.S.-supplied resources, whether here or abroad, plus taxes on production and imports.

Notice that the figure for national income shown in Table 7.4—$19,920 billion—is less than GDP as determined by the expenditures approach in Table 7.3. The two versions of the national accounting statement—the expenditures version and the income version—are brought into balance by subtracting one item from national income and adding two others.

national income Total *income* earned by *resource* suppliers for their contributions to *gross domestic product* plus *taxes on production and imports;* the sum of wages and salaries, rent, interest, profit, proprietors' income, and such taxes.

Net Foreign Factor Income   First, we need to make a slight adjustment to account for the difference between "national income" and "domestic income." National income includes the total income of Americans, whether it was earned in the United States or abroad. But GDP is a measure of *domestic* output—total output produced within the United States regardless of the nationality of those who provide the resources. So, in moving from national income to GDP, we must take out the income Americans gain from supplying resources abroad and add in the income that people living in other countries gain by supplying resources in the United States. That process yields *net foreign factor income*.

In 2021, net foreign factor income was $252 billion, meaning that American-owned resources earned $252 billion more in other countries than foreign-owned resources earned in the United States. Because this $252 billion reflects the earnings of Americans, it is included in U.S. national income. But this income is not part of U.S. domestic income because it reflects earnings from output produced in other nations. It is part of those nations' domestic income, derived from the production of their domestic output. Thus, we subtract net foreign factor income from U.S. national income to determine the value of U.S. *domestic output* (output produced within U.S. borders).

Consumption of Fixed Capital   Next, we must recognize that the useful lives of private capital equipment (such as cell phone towers or automobile assembly lines) extend far beyond the year in which they were produced. To avoid understating profit and income in the year of purchase and to avoid overstating profit and income in succeeding years, the cost of such capital must be allocated over its lifetime. The amount allocated is an estimate of how much of the capital is being used up, or depreciated, each year.

The economywide amount of depreciation is called **consumption of fixed capital** because it accounts for capital that has been "consumed" in producing the year's GDP. It is the portion of GDP that is set aside to pay for the ultimate replacement of the capital goods that have suffered depreciation and is consequently *not* available to flow to households as income. For that reason, it is not counted as part of national income.

On the other hand, depreciation *is* a cost of production and thus must be included in the gross value of output. We must therefore add the amount set aside for the consumption of fixed capital to national income in Table 7.4 to correctly calculate the economy's expenditures on output.

consumption of fixed capital An estimate of the amount of *capital* worn out or used up (consumed) in producing the *gross domestic product;* also called depreciation.

Statistical Discrepancy   As you know, it should be possible to calculate GDP either by totaling up expenditures or by summing up incomes. Either method should give the same result.

In practice, however, it is not possible for NIPA accountants to measure every amount with total precision. Difficulties arise due to a wide range of factors, including people misreporting their incomes on tax returns and the difficulty involved with accurately estimating depreciation.

As a result, the GDP number produced by the income method always differs by a small percentage from the GDP number produced by the expenditures method.

To account for this difference, NIPA accountants add a statistical discrepancy to national income. The addition of that number equalizes the GDP totals produced by the two methods. As Table 7.4 shows, in 2021 the discrepancy value was negative $520 billion, or about 2.3 percent of GDP.

QUICK REVIEW

7.2

▶ The expenditures approach to GDP sums the total spending on final goods and services: GDP = $C + I_g + G + X_n$.

▶ The economy's stock of private capital expands when net investment is positive; stays constant when net investment is zero; and declines when net investment is negative.

▶ The income approach to GDP sums compensation to employees, rent, interest, proprietors' income, corporate profits, and taxes on production and imports to obtain national income, and then subtracts net foreign factor income and adds consumption of fixed capital and a statistical discrepancy to obtain GDP.

Other National Accounts

>> **LO7.4** Describe the relationships among GDP, net domestic product, national income, personal income, and disposable income.

Several other national accounts provide additional useful information about the economy's performance.

Net Domestic Product

net domestic product (NDP) *Gross domestic product less the part of the year's output that is needed to replace the capital goods worn out in producing the output; the nation's total output available for consumption or additions to the capital stock.*

Because GDP is a measure of total output, it does not make allowances for replacing the capital goods used up in each year's production. As a result, it does not tell us how much output is available (for either consumption or *net* additions to the capital stock) after we set aside funds to pay for depreciation. To determine that amount, we must subtract consumption of fixed capital (depreciation) from GDP. The result is called **net domestic product (NDP)**:

$$NDP = GDP - \text{consumption of fixed capital (depreciation)}$$

For the United States in 2021:

	Billions
Gross domestic product	$22,996
Less: Consumption of fixed capital	3,848
Equals: Net domestic product	$19,148

NDP is simply GDP adjusted for depreciation. It measures the total annual output that the entire economy—households, businesses, government, and foreigners—can consume without impairing its capacity to produce in ensuing years.

National Income

Recall that U.S. *national income* (NI) includes all income earned through the use of American-owned resources, whether they are located at home or abroad. It also includes taxes on production and imports.

To derive NI from NDP, we must subtract the statistical discrepancy from NDP and add net foreign factor income, because the latter is income earned by Americans overseas minus income earned by foreigners in the United States.

For the United States in 2021:

	Billions
Net domestic product	$19,148
Less: Statistical discrepancy	−520
Plus: Net foreign factor income	252
Equals: National income	$19,920

An alternative but equally valid method for adding up national income is to apply the income approach and sum together employee compensation, rent, interest, proprietors' income, corporate profit, and taxes on production and imports. That's what we did in the top half of Table 7.4.

Personal Income

Personal income (PI) includes all income received by households, whether earned or unearned. The starting point for calculating personal income is national income, which accounts for all the income *earned* by households for providing resources. But then, to calculate the total amount of income that was actually *received* by households, we must subtract off the value of business taxes, payroll taxes, and retained corporate profits before adding in the value of transfer payments.

We need to subtract off business taxes, payroll taxes, and retained corporate profits because households do not receive all of the income that they earn by providing resources. Taxes on production and imports, Social Security taxes (payroll taxes), corporate income taxes, and undistributed corporate profits flow either to the government or are retained by firms. They do not flow to households as personal income.

On the other hand, households receive trillions of dollars of government transfer payments that they collect, unearned, without having to provide any resources. These transfer payments include Social Security payments, unemployment compensation payments, welfare payments, disability and education payments to veterans, and private pension payments. To arrive at a correct value for personal income, we must add in the value of these transfer payments.

Thus, in moving from national income to personal income, we must subtract the income that is earned but not received and add the income that is received but not earned. For the United States in 2021:

personal income (PI) The earned and unearned *income* available to resource suppliers and others before the payment of personal *taxes.*

	Billions
National income	$19,920
Less: Taxes on production and imports	1,148
Less: Corporate income taxes	381
Less: Social Security contributions	1,591
Less: Undistributed corporate profits	1,006
Plus: Transfer payments	5,284*
Equals: Personal income	$21,077

*Includes statistical discrepancy, rounding error, and items that appear in more detailed accounts.

Disposable Income

Disposable income (DI) is the amount of income that households are free to dispose of (spend or save) after meeting all their legal tax obligations. Disposable income is equal to personal income less personal taxes, including personal income taxes, personal property taxes, and inheritance taxes. Households are free to divide their disposable income between consumption (C) and saving (S) as they see fit. Algebraically:

disposable income (DI) *Personal income* less personal taxes; income available for *personal consumption expenditures* and *personal saving.*

$$DI = C + S$$

For the United States in 2021:

	Billions
Personal income	$21,077
Less: Personal taxes	2,583
Equals: Disposable income	$18,495

Table 7.5 summarizes the relationship among GDP, NDP, NI, PI, and DI.

TABLE 7.5 The Relationships among GDP, NDP, NI, PI, and DI in the United States, 2021*

	Billions
Gross domestic product (GDP)	$22,996
Less: Consumption of fixed capital	3,848
Equals: Net domestic product	$19,148
Net domestic product (NDP)	$19,148
Less: Statistical discrepancy	−520
Plus: Net foreign factor income	252
Equals: National income (NI)	$19,920
National income (NI)	$19,920
Less: Taxes on production and imports	1,148
Less: Corporate income taxes	381
Less: Social Security contributions	1,591
Less: Undistributed corporate profits	1,006
Plus: Transfer payments	5,284*
Equals: Personal income (PI)	$21,077
Personal income (PI)	$21,077
Less: Personal taxes	2,583
Equals: Disposable income (DI)	$18,495

*Some of the items combine categories that appear in the more detailed accounts.

Source: Bureau of Economic Analysis, www.bea.gov.

The Circular Flow Revisited

Figure 7.3 is an elaborate flow diagram that shows the economy's four main sectors (households, businesses, government, and foreign) along with the flows of expenditures and allocations that determine GDP, NDP, NI, and PI. The orange arrows represent the spending flows—$C + I_g + G + X_n$—that together measure gross domestic product. To the right of the GDP rectangle are green arrows that show first the allocations of GDP and then the adjustments needed to derive NDP, NI, PI, and DI.

The diagram illustrates the adjustments necessary to determine each of the national income accounts. For example, net domestic product is smaller than GDP because consumption of fixed capital flows away from GDP in determining NDP. Also, disposable income is smaller than personal income because personal taxes flow away from PI (to government).

Note the three domestic sectors of the economy: households, government, and businesses. The household sector has an inflow of disposable income and outflows of consumption spending and savings. The government sector has an inflow of revenue from various types of taxes and an outflow of disbursements in the form of purchases and transfers. The business sector has inflows from three major sources of funds for business investment and an outflow of investment expenditures.

Also, take a look at the foreign sector (all other countries) in the flow diagram. Spending by foreigners on U.S. exports adds to U.S. GDP, but some of U.S. consumption, government, and investment expenditures buys imported products. The flow from the foreign sector shows that we handle this complication by calculating net exports (U.S. exports minus U.S. imports). The net export flow may be a positive or negative amount, adding to or subtracting from U.S. GDP.

Finally, you need to be aware that the flows shown in Figure 7.3 are dynamic entities and generally expand in size over time as the economy grows. But not always! Case in point: The COVID-19 recession of 2020—which is described in a Consider This story in Chapter 26—produced a pronounced slowing of the main spending and income flows. Specifically, U.S. businesses greatly reduced investment expenditures while households modestly reduced personal consumption expenditures. Consequently, GDP, NDP, NI, and PI all significantly declined.

FIGURE 7.3 U.S. domestic output and the flows of expenditure and income. This figure is an elaborate circular flow diagram that fits the expenditures and allocations sides of GDP to one another. The expenditures flows are shown in orange; the allocations or income flows are shown in green. You should trace through the income and expenditures flows, relating them to the five basic national income accounting measures.

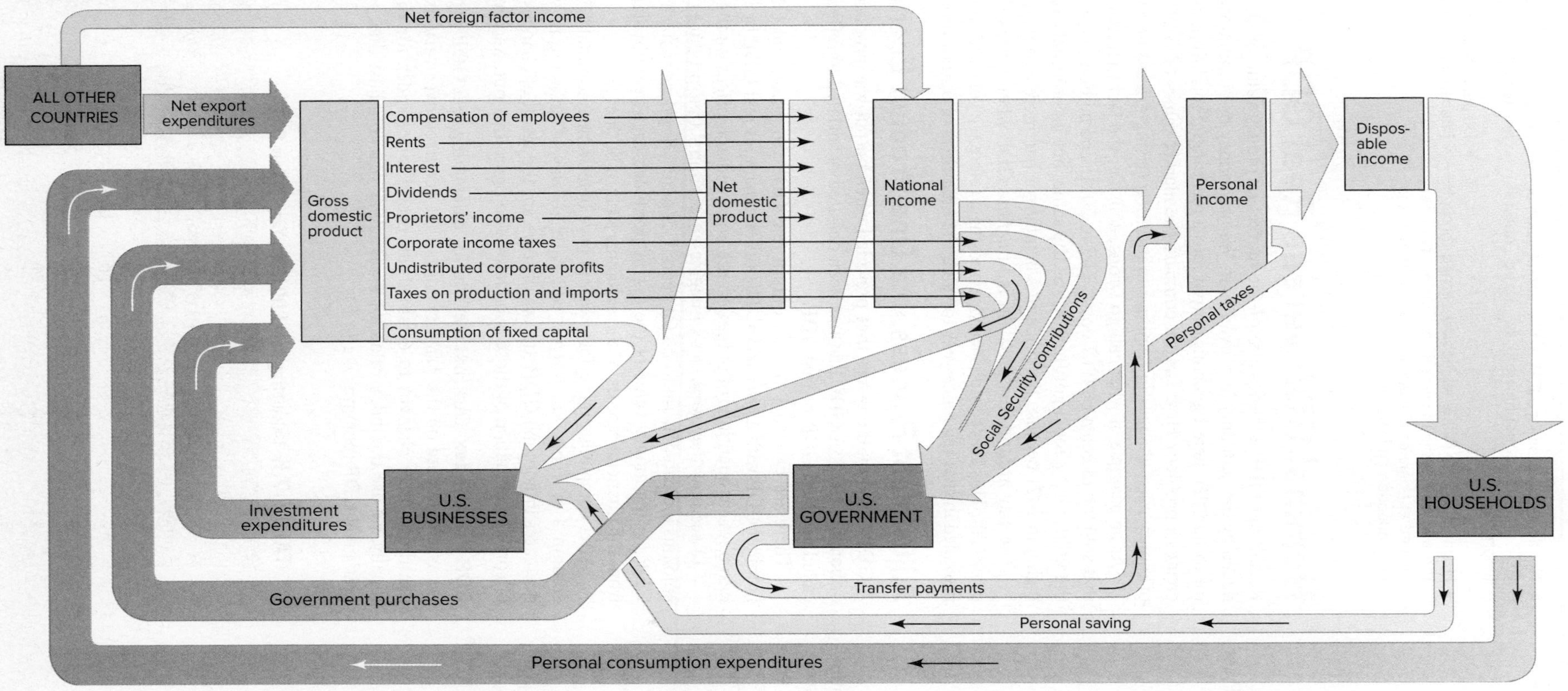

143

▶ Net domestic product (NDP) is the market value of GDP minus consumption of fixed capital (depreciation).

▶ National income (NI) is all income earned through the use of American-owned resources, whether located at home or abroad. NI also includes taxes on production and imports.

▶ Personal income (PI) is all income received by households, whether earned or not.

▶ Disposable income (DI) is all income received by households minus personal taxes.

Nominal GDP versus Real GDP

>> **LO7.5** Distinguish between nominal GDP and real GDP.

Recall that GDP is a measure of the market or money value of all final goods and services produced by the economy in a given year. We use money or nominal values as a common denominator to sum that heterogeneous output into a meaningful total. But, as alluded to in Chapter 6, that creates a problem: How can we compare the market values of GDP from year to year if the value of money itself changes in response to inflation (rising prices) or deflation (falling prices)?

As an example of what can go wrong, consider the fact that the same McDonald's hamburger that sold for 18 cents in 1967 cost $1.69 in 2021. The hamburger was the same in both years and the utility that people got from it was the same, but its nominal GDP value was over nine times higher in 2021 because the price of a hamburger had increased from 18 cents to $1.69.

The way around this problem is to *deflate* GDP when prices rise and to *inflate* GDP when prices fall. This is accomplished by choosing a reference year and then using the output prices that prevailed in that reference year to value the quantities of output produced in other years.

Adjustment Process in a One-Product Economy

nominal gross domestic product (GDP) *GDP* measured in terms of the *price level* at the time of measurement; *GDP* not adjusted for *inflation*. Compare with *real gross domestic product* (*real GDP*).

real GDP *Gross domestic product* adjusted for *inflation*; gross domestic product in a year divided by the GDP *price index* for that year, the index expressed as a decimal. Compare with *nominal GDP*.

A GDP based on the prices that prevailed when output was produced is called unadjusted GDP, or **nominal GDP**. A GDP that has been deflated or inflated to reflect changes in the price level is called adjusted GDP, or **real GDP**.

There are two ways we can obtain real GDP from nominal GDP. One involves combining nominal GDP with a *price index*. The other calculates real GDP by breaking down nominal GDP into physical quantities of output on the one hand and prices on the other.

To see how they work, let's imagine an economy that produces only one good, pizza, in the amounts indicated in Table 7.6 for years 1, 2, and 3. Suppose that we measure each year's nominal GDP (= the money value of the pizzas produced each year) by gathering revenue data directly from the financial reports of the economy's pizza businesses.

After completing our effort, we will have determined nominal GDP for each year, as shown in column 4 of Table 7.6. But we will have no way of knowing to what extent the increases or decreases in nominal GDP that we observe are the result of changes in prices, changes in output, or some combination of those two factors. To figure that out, we need to calculate real GDP.

GDP Price Index Our first method for calculating real GDP proceeds in three stages. First, we assemble data on the price changes that occurred over various years (column 2). Then we use those price changes to establish an overall price index for the entire period (column 3). Finally, we use the index value for a particular year to adjust that year's nominal GDP into that year's real GDP (columns 4 and 5).

TABLE 7.6 Calculating Real GDP (Base Year = Year 1)

Year	(1) Units of Output	(2) Price of Pizza per Unit	(3) Price Index (Year 1 = 100)	(4) Unadjusted, or Nominal, GDP, (1) × (2)	(5) Adjusted, or Real, GDP
1	5	$10	100	$ 50	$50
2	7	20	200	140	70
3	8	25	250	200	80
4	10	30	____	____	____
5	11	28	____	____	____

A **price index** is a measure of the price of a specified collection of goods and services, called a "market basket," in a given year as compared to the price of an identical (or highly similar) collection of goods and services in a reference year. That point of reference, or benchmark, is known as the base period, **base year,** or, simply, the reference year. More formally,

$$\text{Price index in given year} = \frac{\text{price of market basket in specific year}}{\text{price of same market basket in base year}} \times 100 \qquad (1)$$

By convention, the price ratio between a given year and the base year is multiplied by 100 to facilitate computation. For example, a price ratio of 2/1 (= 2) is expressed as a price index of 200. A price ratio of 1/3 (= 0.33) is expressed as a price index of 33.

In our pizza-only example, our market basket consists of only one product. Column 2 of Table 7.6 reveals that the price of pizza was $10 in year 1, $20 in year 2, and $25 in year 3. Let's select year 1 as our base year. Now we can express the prices of our market basket in years 2 and 3 relative to the price of the market basket in year 1:

$$\text{Price index, year 2} = \frac{\$20}{\$10} \times 100 = 200$$

$$\text{Price index, year 3} = \frac{\$25}{\$10} \times 100 = 250$$

For year 1 the index has to be 100, because that year and the base year are identical.

The index numbers tell us that the price of pizza rose from year 1 to year 2 by 100 percent $\{= [(200 - 100)/100] \times 100\}$ and from year 1 to year 3 by 150 percent $\{= [(250 - 100)/100] \times 100\}$.

Dividing Nominal GDP by the Price Index We can now use the index numbers shown in column 3 to deflate the nominal GDP figures in column 4. The simplest and most direct method of deflating is to divide nominal GDP by the corresponding index number expressed in hundredths (decimal form). Doing so gives us real GDP:

$$\text{Real GDP} = \frac{\text{nominal GDP}}{\text{price index (in hundredths)}} \qquad (2)$$

Column 5 shows the results. These figures for real GDP measure the market value of the output of pizza in years 1, 2, and 3 as if the price of pizza had been a constant $10 throughout the 3-year period. In short, real GDP reveals the market value of each year's output measured in terms of dollars that have the same purchasing power that dollars had in the base year.

To test your understanding, extend Table 7.6 to years 4 and 5, using equations 1 and 2. Then run through the entire deflating procedure, using year 3 as the base period. (Hint: You will have to inflate some of the nominal GDP data. Use the same procedure as we used in the examples.)

An Alternative Method

The second method for calculating real GDP involves gathering data on physical outputs (as in column 1 of Table 7.6) and their prices (as in column 2). With those values in hand, we can calculate what the market value of output would have been in successive years if the base-year price ($10) had prevailed every year. In year 2, for instance, the 7 units of pizza would have had a value of $70 (= 7 units × $10). As column 5 confirms, that $70 worth of output is year 2's real GDP. Similarly, we could determine the real GDP for year 3 by multiplying the 8 units of output that year by the $10 price in the base year.

Once we have determined real GDP through this method, we can identify the price index for a given year by dividing the nominal GDP by the real GDP for that year:

$$\text{Price index (in hundredths)} = \frac{\text{nominal GDP}}{\text{real GDP}} \qquad (3)$$

Example: In year 2 we get a price index of 200—or, in hundredths, 2.00—which equals the nominal GDP of $140 divided by the real GDP of $70.

Note that equation 3 is simply a rearrangement of equation 2.

price index An index number that shows how the weighted-average *price* of a "market basket" of goods changes over time relative to its price in a specific *base year.*

TABLE 7.7 Steps for Deriving Real GDP from Nominal GDP

Method 1

1. Find nominal GDP for each year.

2. Compute a GDP price index.

3. Divide each year's nominal GDP by that year's price index (in hundredths) to determine real GDP.

Method 2

1. Break down nominal GDP into physical quantities of output and prices for each year.

2. Find real GDP for each year by determining the dollar amount that each year's physical output would have sold for if base-year prices had prevailed. (The GDP price index can then be found by dividing nominal GDP by real GDP.)

Table 7.7 summarizes the two methods of determining real GDP in our single-good economy.

Real-World Considerations and Data

In the real world of *many* goods and services, determining GDP and constructing a reliable price index are far more complex matters than in our pizza-only economy. The government accountants must assign a "weight" to each of several categories of goods and services based on the relative proportion of each category in total output. They update the weights annually as expenditure patterns change and roll the base year forward year by year using a moving average of expenditure patterns. The GDP price index used in the United States is called the *chain-type annual-weights price index*—which hints at its complexity. We spare you the details.

Table 7.8 shows some of the relationships among nominal GDP, real GDP, and the GDP price index for the U.S. economy. Here the base year is 2012, where the value of the index is set at 100. Because the U.S. price level has been rising over the long run, the pre-2012 values of real GDP (column 3) are higher than the nominal values of GDP for those years (column 2). This upward adjustment acknowledges that prices were lower in the years before 2012, and thus nominal GDP understates the real output of those years when they are measured in terms of year 2012 prices. Since these pre-2012 values understate real GDP relative to 2012, they must be inflated to show the correct relationship to other years.

Conversely, the rising price level of the post-2012 years caused nominal GDP figures for those years to overstate real output relative to 2012 prices. So the statisticians deflate those figures to determine what real GDP would have been in other years if 2012 prices had prevailed. Doing so reveals that real GDP has been less than nominal GDP since 2012.

By inflating the nominal pre-2012 GDP data and deflating the post-2012 data, government accountants determine each year's real GDP, which can then be compared with the real GDP of any other year in the series. Consequently, the real GDP values in column 3 are directly comparable with one another.

Once we have determined nominal GDP and real GDP, we can compute the price index. And once we have determined nominal GDP and the price index, we can calculate real GDP. Example: Nominal GDP in 2015 was $18,206.0 billion and real GDP was $17,390.3 billion. So the price level in 2015 was 104.7 (= [$18,206.0/$17,390.3] × 100), or 4.7 percent higher than in 2012. If we knew the nominal GDP and the price level only, we could find the real GDP for 2015 by dividing the nominal GDP of $18,206.0 by the 2015 price index, expressed in hundredths (1.047).

To test your understanding of the relationships between nominal GDP, real GDP, and the price level, determine the values of the price index for 2000 in Table 7.8 and determine real GDP for 2005 and 2012. We have left those figures out on purpose.

TABLE 7.8 Nominal GDP, Real GDP, and GDP Price Index for the United States, Selected Years

Source: U.S. Bureau of Economic Analysis. All data subject to government revision.

(1) Year	(2) Nominal GDP, Billions of $	(3) Real GDP, Billions of $	(4) GDP Price Index (2012 = 100)
2000	10,251.0	13,138.0	____
2005	13,039.2	____	87.5
2010	15,049.0	15,649.0	96.2
2012	16,254.0	____	100.0
2015	18,206.0	17,390.3	104.7
2020	20,893.7	18,384.7	113.6

QUICK REVIEW
7.4

▸ Nominal GDP is output valued at current prices. Real GDP is output valued at constant base-year prices.

▸ The GDP price index compares the price (market value) of all the goods and services included in

GDP in a given year to the price of the same market basket in a reference year.

▸ Nominal GDP can be transformed into real GDP by dividing nominal GDP by the GDP price index expressed in hundredths.

Shortcomings of GDP

GDP is a reasonably accurate and highly useful measure of how well or how poorly the economy is performing. But it has several shortcomings as a measure of both total output and well-being (utility).

>> **LO7.6** Explain some limitations of the GDP measure.

Nonmarket Activities

Certain productive activities do not take place in any market—the services of stay-at-home parents, for example, and the labor of carpenters who repair their own homes. Such activities do not show up in GDP because government accountants receive data only on economic transactions involving *market activities*—that is, transactions in which output or resources are traded for money. Consequently, GDP understates a nation's total output because it does not count *unpaid work*. There is one exception: The portion of farmers' output that farmers consume themselves is estimated and included in GDP.

Leisure and Psychic Income

The average workweek (excluding overtime) in the United States has declined since the beginning of the 1900s—from about 53 hours to about 35 hours. Moreover, workers today have more paid vacations, holidays, and leave time. This increase in leisure time has clearly had a positive effect on overall well-being. But our system of national income accounting understates well-being by ignoring leisure's value. Nor does the system accommodate the satisfaction—the "psychic income"—that many people derive from their work.

Improved Product Quality

Because GDP is quantitative rather than qualitative, it fails to capture the full value of improvements in product quality. For example, an $800 smartphone purchased today is of much higher quality than a smartphone that cost $800 a decade ago.

Quality improvement obviously has a great effect on economic well-being, an effect that goes above and beyond any increase in the quantity of output. Although the BEA adjusts GDP for the quality improvements of selected items, the vast majority of quality improvements are not yet reflected in GDP. (See this chapter's Last Word for more on this subject.)

The Underground Economy

Embedded in our economy is a flourishing, productive underground sector. Some of the people who conduct business there are bookies, smugglers, "fences" of stolen goods, and drug dealers. They have good reason to conceal their incomes.

Most participants in the underground economy, however, engage in perfectly legal activities but choose illegally not to report their full incomes to the Internal Revenue Service (IRS). A barista at a coffee shop may report just a portion of the tips received from customers. Storekeepers may report only a portion of their sales receipts. Workers who want to hold onto their unemployment compensation benefits may take an "off-the-books" or "cash-only" job. A brick mason may agree to rebuild a neighbor's fireplace in exchange for the neighbor's repairing his boat engine. None of these transactions show up in GDP.

Global Perspective 7.2 presents estimates of how big the underground economy is in various countries. Since underground transactions amount to about 7 percent of U.S. GDP, we can estimate that U.S. GDP was understated by about $1.6 trillion in 2021.

GDP and the Environment

The growth of GDP is sometimes accompanied by an increase in "gross domestic by-products," including dirty air and polluted water, toxic waste, congestion, and noise. The social costs of the

GLOBAL PERSPECTIVE 7.2

THE UNDERGROUND ECONOMY AS A PERCENTAGE OF GDP, SELECTED NATIONS

Underground economies vary in size worldwide. Three factors that help explain the variation are (1) the extent and complexity of regulation, (2) the type and degree of taxation, and (3) the effectiveness of law enforcement.

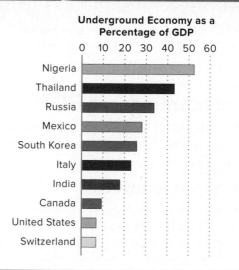

Underground Economy as a Percentage of GDP

Source: Leandro Medina and Friedrich Schneider, *Shadow Economies Around the World: What Did We Learn Over the Last 20 Years?* International Monetary Fund (IMF), 2018.

negative by-products reduce our economic well-being. Because those costs are not deducted from total output, GDP overstates our national well-being. Ironically, when money is spent to clean up pollution and reduce congestion, those expenses *are* added to GDP!

Composition and Distribution of Output

The composition of output is undoubtedly important for well-being, but GDP does not tell us whether the currently produced mix of goods and services is enriching or potentially detrimental to society. GDP assigns equal weight to an assault rifle and a laptop computer, as long as both sell for the same price. Moreover, GDP reveals nothing about the distribution of output. Does 90 percent of the output go to 10 percent of the households, for example, or is output more evenly distributed? The distribution of output may make a big difference for society's overall well-being.

Noneconomic Sources of Well-Being

Finally, just as a household's income does not measure its total happiness, a nation's GDP does not measure its total well-being. Many things could make a society better off without necessarily raising GDP: a reduction of crime and violence, peaceful relations with other countries, people's greater civility toward one another, better understanding between parents and children, or a reduction of drug and alcohol abuse.

The Importance of Intermediate Output

Because GDP focuses on final output, it ignores all of the business-to-business economic activity that takes place in the economy at earlier stages of production and distribution. That omission is worrisome because many people's jobs and many firms' profitability depend on economic activity at earlier stages.

We can get a sense of what is going on at those earlier stages by examining *gross output* (GO), which sums together the sales values received by firms at *every* stage of production. As you learned earlier in this chapter, GO is always larger than GDP because GO includes every stage of production while GDP only accounts for the final stage of production. In 2021, GO was $41.2 trillion in the United States while GDP was $23.0 trillion.

GO is particularly useful when attempting to gauge the magnitude of business cycle fluctuations. During the 2007–2009 recession, real GDP fell by 4.2 percent, while real GO fell by 8.6 percent. Thus, total economic activity fell by more than twice as much as final output. That substantial difference goes some way toward explaining why employment fell so dramatically during the Great Recession.

LAST WORD

Measuring Quality to Price the Priceless

The Bureau of Economic Analysis (BEA) Faces a Difficult Task as It Attempts to Measure GDP and Inflation in the Digital Age.

GDP attempts to measure the value of an economy's output by summing together the dollar values of all final goods and services. That strategy for measuring the value of an economy's output has become significantly more challenging over the past twenty years. There are two basic problems. First, it is difficult to properly account for quality improvements, which are rapid for Digital Age products like electronics, software, and video games. Second, many Internet products—for instance, Google searches and driving directions—are provided free of charge.

Suppose that the price of an iPhone is the same now as it was last year, even though this year's iPhone is better than last year's iPhone. With the price fixed, the contribution of an iPhone to GDP will remain unchanged, even though the utility (satisfaction) that people get from purchasing an iPhone has increased. GDP will miss that increase in value. Similarly, if a service like Google is priced at zero, GDP will miss the value that users receive from Google searches.

Rapid quality improvements have also made inflation calculations more difficult. If this year's most popular video game delivered twice as much entertainment as last year's top-selling video game but their prices were both $60, how much of a contribution did those games make toward the economy's overall level of inflation? Viewed from a perspective of "the price of a top video game remained constant at $60," the contribution was zero. Viewed from a perspective of "how much money does it cost to purchase one unit of entertainment?" the contribution was negative 50 percent since the same dollar expenditure delivers twice as much enjoyment today as it did last year.

The statisticians at the BEA who compile the National Income and Product Accounts have decided to look at things from the latter perspective. Quality improvements matter and should be accounted for in GDP and inflation to the extent possible. The procedure for doing so is called hedonic adjustment (hedonic means "relating to pleasure"). It involves looking at a product as a collection of separate characteristics or services for which people are willing to pay money. Viewed this way, an iPhone is not a single item but a collection of, among other things, a camera, a web browser, a video game platform, a telephone, a compass, a map, a flashlight, and a way of accessing social media platforms.

Once an iPhone is thought of as a collection of attributes or services, inflation in the economy will depend not on the price of iPhones themselves, but on how the prices of the underlying attributes or services vary over time. For example, if this year's iPhone is identical in all ways to last year's iPhone but costs 3 percent less, then the value of one or more of the underlying characteristics or services must have gone down. It's up to national income accountants to figure out which ones changed, and by how much. Once they complete the fancy math, they can get a better handle on inflation.

Alex Potemkin/E+/Getty Images

By one estimate, properly accounting for hedonic adjustments reduces reported inflation by about 0.6 percent, which is a big deal since inflation is usually around 2 to 3 percent.

A different approach has to be taken when trying to account for the value of free products like Facebook and Google. When a product's price is zero, how do you account for the value that consumers receive from the product? One suggestion has been to value free services by putting a dollar value on the time that users spend using the service. If Safiyya spends 3.5 hours on Facebook each day and we estimate the value of her time to be worth $10 per hour, then we can place a value of $35 (= 3.5 hours × $10 per hour) on the services that she receives from Facebook.

The need to place a value on free services also matters because consumers have been transitioning from paid versions to free versions of various products. Consider maps. People used to pay for printed road maps. But now they can get electronic maps for free on their mobile devices. The money spent on printed maps was counted in GDP. But there is nothing to count with respect to digital maps. So, GDP will decline if we fail to capture the value that people receive from digital maps. The same is true for free music and video streamed over the Internet, storage space for photo albums, stock and bond prices, news and weather reports, and so on. These products are still valuable, so we would like to include them in GDP.

QUICK REVIEW
7.5

▶ GDP is a reasonably accurate and very useful indicator of a nation's economic performance but should not be interpreted as a comprehensive measure of well-being.

▶ The major limitations of GDP as an indicator of well-being are that it fails to account for nonmarket and illegal transactions, changes in leisure and in product quality, the composition and distribution of output, the environmental effects of pollution, and economic activity at earlier stages of production and distribution.

Summary

LO7.1 Define and measure gross domestic product (GDP).

Gross domestic product (GDP), a basic measure of an economy's economic performance, is the market value of all final goods and services produced within a nation's borders in a year.

Final goods are those purchased by end users, whereas intermediate goods are those purchased for resale or for further processing or manufacturing. Intermediate goods, nonproduction transactions, and secondhand sales are excluded in calculating GDP.

LO7.2 Determine GDP by summing all expenditures on final goods and services.

GDP may be calculated by summing total expenditures on all final output or by summing the income derived from the production of that output.

By the expenditures approach, GDP is determined by adding consumer purchases of goods and services, gross investment spending by businesses, government purchases, and net exports: $GDP = C + I_g + G + X_n$.

Personal consumption expenditures consist of expenditures on goods (durable goods and nondurable goods) and services. About 60 percent of consumer expenditures in the United States are on services, leading economists to refer to the U.S. economy as a *service economy*.

Gross investment is divided into (*a*) replacement investment (required to maintain the nation's stock of capital at its existing level) and (*b*) net investment (the net increase in the stock of capital). In most years, net investment is positive, and therefore the economy's stock of capital and production capacity increase.

LO7.3 Determine GDP by summing all incomes received for providing resources.

By the income, or allocations, approach, GDP is calculated as the sum of compensation to employees, rents, interest, proprietors' income, corporate profits, and taxes on production and imports, *minus* net foreign factor income, *plus* consumption of fixed capital and a statistical discrepancy.

LO7.4 Describe the relationships among GDP, net domestic product, national income, personal income, and disposable income.

Net domestic product (NDP) is GDP minus the consumption of fixed capital. National income (NI) is total income earned by a nation's resource suppliers plus taxes on production and imports; it is found by subtracting a statistical discrepancy from NDP and adding net foreign factor income to NDP. Personal income (PI) is the total income paid to households before they pay personal taxes. Disposable income (DI) is personal income after households have paid personal taxes. DI measures the amount of income available to households to consume or save.

LO7.5 Distinguish between nominal GDP and real GDP.

Nominal (current-dollar) GDP measures each year's output valued in terms of the prices prevailing in that year. Real (constant-dollar) GDP measures each year's output in terms of the prevailing prices in a selected base year. Because real GDP is adjusted for price-level changes, differences in real GDP are due only to differences in production activity. Economists use a GDP price index to convert nominal GDP to real GDP.

LO7.6 Explain some limitations of the GDP measure.

GDP is a reasonably accurate and very useful indicator of a nation's economic performance, but it has its limitations. It fails to account for nonmarket and illegal transactions, changes in leisure and in product quality, the composition and distribution of output, the environmental effects of pollution, noneconomic sources of well-being, and economic activity at earlier stages of production and distribution.

Terms and Concepts

national income accounting

gross domestic product (GDP)

final goods and services

intermediate goods and services

value added

gross output (GO)

multiple counting

expenditures approach

income approach

personal consumption expenditures (*C*)

durable good

nondurable good

service

gross private domestic investment (I_g)

net private domestic investment

government purchases (*G*)

net exports (X_n)

taxes on production and imports

national income

consumption of fixed capital

net domestic product (NDP)

personal income (PI)

disposable income (DI)

nominal GDP

real GDP

price index

base year

Discussion Questions

1. In what ways are national income statistics useful? **LO7.1**
2. Why do national income accountants compare the market value of the total outputs in various years rather than actual physical volumes of production? What problem is posed by any comparison over time of the market values of various total outputs? How is this problem resolved? **LO7.1**
3. Which of the following goods are usually intermediate goods and which are usually final goods: running shoes, cotton fibers, watches, textbooks, coal, sunscreen lotion, lumber? **LO7.1**
4. Why do economists include only final goods and services when measuring GDP? Why don't they include the value of the stocks and bonds bought and sold? Why don't they include the value of the used furniture bought and sold? **LO7.1**
5. Explain why an economy's output, in essence, is also its income. **LO7.1**
6. Provide three examples of each: consumer durable goods, consumer nondurable goods, and services. **LO7.2**
7. Why are changes in inventories included as part of investment spending? Suppose inventories decline by $1 billion during 2025. How would this $1 billion decrease affect the size of gross private domestic investment and gross domestic product in 2025? Explain. **LO7.2**
8. What is the difference between gross private domestic investment and net private domestic investment? If you were to determine net domestic product (NDP) through the expenditures approach, which of these two measures of investment spending would be appropriate? Explain. **LO7.2**
9. Use the concepts of gross investment and net investment to distinguish between an economy that has a rising capital stock and one that has a falling capital stock. Explain: "Though net investment can be positive, negative, or zero, it is impossible for gross investment to be less than zero." **LO7.2**
10. Define net exports. How are net exports determined? Explain why net exports might be a negative amount. **LO7.2**
11. Contrast nominal GDP and real GDP. Why is one more reliable than the other for comparing changes in the standard of living over a series of years? What is the GDP price index, and what is its role in differentiating nominal GDP and real GDP? **LO7.5**
12. Which of the following are included in this year's GDP? Which are excluded? Explain your answers. **LO7.6**
    a. Interest received on an AT&T corporate bond.
    b. Social Security payments received by a retired factory worker.
    c. Unpaid services of a family member who painted the family home.
    d. Income of a dentist from the dental services she provided.
    e. A monthly allowance that a college student receives from home.
    f. Money received by Josh when he resells his nearly brand-new Honda automobile to Kim.
    g. The publication and sale of a new college textbook.
    h. An increase in leisure resulting from a 2-hour decrease in the length of the workweek, with no reduction in pay.
    i. A $2 billion increase in business inventories.
    j. The purchase of 100 shares of Alphabet (the parent company of Google) stock.
13. Why is gross output a better measure of overall economic activity than GDP is? How could you construct a new statistic that focuses only on nonfinal economic activity? Given what you know about the behavior of GO and GDP during the Great Recession, would you expect your new statistic to show more or less volatility than GO and GDP? Why? How would you rank the three in terms of volatility? **LO7.6**
14. **LAST WORD** How do "free" products make the calculation of GDP more difficult? What are hedonic adjustments and why are they necessary? Will inflation tend to be overstated or understated if quality improvements are not accounted for? Explain.

Review Questions

1. Satoshi walks into Vitalik's sporting goods store and buys a punching bag for $100. That $100 payment counts as _____ for Satoshi and _____ for Vitalik. **LO7.1**
   a. income; expenditure
   b. value added; multiple counting
   c. expenditure; income
   d. rents; profits
2. Which of the following transactions are counted in GDP? **LO7.1**
   Select one or more answers from the choices shown.
   a. Kerry buys a new sweater to wear this winter.
   b. Patricia receives a Social Security check.
   c. Roberto gives his daughter $50 for her birthday.
   d. Nayana sells $1,000 of General Electric stock.
   e. Nick buys a new car.
   f. Patrick buys a used car.
3. A small economy starts the year with $1 million in capital. During the course of the year, gross investment is $150,000 and depreciation is $50,000. What is the economy's capital stock at the end of the year? **LO7.2**
   a. $1,150,000
   b. $1,100,000
   c. $1,000,000
   d. $850,000
   e. $800,000
4. Suppose that this year a small country has a GDP of $100 billion. Also assume that I_g = $30 billion, C = $60 billion, and X_n = − $10 billion. What is the value of G? **LO7.3**
   a. $0
   b. $10 billion
   c. $20 billion
   d. $30 billion

5. Suppose that California imposes a sales tax of 10 percent on all goods and services. A Californian named Ralph then goes into a home improvement store in the state capital of Sacramento and buys a leaf blower that is priced at $200. With the 10 percent sales tax, his total comes to $220. How much of the $220 paid by Ralph is in the national income and product accounts as private income (employee compensation, rents, interest, proprietor's income, and corporate profits)? **LO7.3**
   a. $220
   b. $200
   c. $180
   d. none of the above

6. Suppose GDP is $16 trillion, with $10 trillion coming from consumption, $2 trillion coming from gross investment, $3.5 trillion coming from government expenditures, and $500 billion coming from net exports. Also suppose that across the whole economy, depreciation (consumption of fixed capital) totals $1 trillion. From these figures, we see that net domestic product equals: **LO7.4**
   a. $17.0 trillion.
   b. $16.0 trillion.
   c. $15.5 trillion.
   d. none of the above.

7. Suppose GDP is $15 trillion, with $8 trillion coming from consumption, $2.5 trillion coming from gross investment, $3.5 trillion coming from government expenditures, and $1 trillion coming from net exports. Also suppose that across the whole economy, personal income is $12 trillion. If the government collects $1.5 trillion in personal taxes, then disposable income is: **LO7.4**
   a. $13.5 trillion.
   b. $12.0 trillion.

   c. $10.5 trillion.
   d. none of the above.

8. Suppose that this year's nominal GDP is $16 trillion. To account for the effects of inflation, we construct a price-level index in which an index value of 100 represents the price level 5 years ago. Using that index, we find that this year's real GDP is $15 trillion. Given those numbers, we can conclude that the current value of the index is: **LO7.5**
   a. higher than 100.
   b. lower than 100.
   c. still 100.

9. Which of the following items are included in official U.S. GDP statistics? **LO7.6**
   *Select **one or more** answers from the choices shown.*
   a. Revenue generated by illegal marijuana growers.
   b. Money spent to clean up a toxic waste site in Ohio.
   c. Revenue generated by legal medical marijuana sales in California.
   d. The dollar value of the annoyance felt by local citizens living near a noisy airport in Georgia.
   e. Andre paying Ted for a haircut in Chicago.
   f. Emily and Aliya trading an hour of dance lessons for a haircut in Dallas.

10. Suppose GDP is $5.0 trillion, depreciation is $1 trillion, and gross output (GO) is $17.25 trillion. **LO7.6**
    a. What is the value of all stages of production and distribution *except for* final sales of goods and services?
    b. What is the dollar value of the economic activity taking place at every stage of production and distribution?

Problems

1. Suppose that annual output in year 1 in a three-good economy is 3 quarts of ice cream, 1 bottle of shampoo, and 3 jars of peanut butter. In year 2, the output mix changes to 5 quarts of ice cream, 2 bottles of shampoo, and 2 jars of peanut butter. If the prices in both years are $4 per quart for ice cream, $3 per bottle of shampoo, and $2 per jar of peanut butter, what was the economy's GDP in year 1? What was its GDP in year 2? **LO7.1**

2. Assume that a grower of flower bulbs sells its annual output of bulbs to an Internet retailer for $70,000. The retailer, in turn, brings in $160,000 from selling the bulbs directly to final customers. What amount would these two transactions add to personal consumption expenditures and thus to GDP during the year? **LO7.1**

3. If in some country personal consumption expenditures in a specific year are $50 billion, purchases of stocks and bonds are $30 billion, net exports are −$10 billion, government purchases are $20 billion, sales of secondhand items are $8 billion, and gross investment is $25 billion, what is the country's GDP for the year? **LO7.2**

4. The nearby table contains a list of domestic output and national income figures for a certain year. All figures are in billions. The questions that follow ask you to determine the major national income measures by both the expenditures and income approaches. The results you obtain with the different methods should be the same. **LO7.4**

Personal consumption expenditures	$245
Net foreign factor income	4
Transfer payments	12
Rents	14
Consumption of fixed capital (depreciation)	27
Statistical discrepancy	8
Social Security contributions	20
Interest	13
Proprietors' income	33
Net exports	11
Dividends	16
Compensation of employees	223
Taxes on production and imports	18
Undistributed corporate profits	21
Personal taxes	26
Corporate income taxes	19
Corporate profits	56
Government purchases	72
Net private domestic investment	33
Personal saving	20

a. Using the above data, determine GDP by both the expenditures approach and the income approach. Then determine NDP.

b. Now determine NI in two ways: first, by making the required additions or subtractions from NDP; and second, by adding up the types of income and taxes that make up NI.

c. Adjust NI (from part *b*) as required to obtain PI.

d. Adjust PI (from part *c*) as required to obtain DI.

5. Using the following national income accounting data, compute (*a*) GDP, (*b*) NDP, and (*c*) NI. All figures are in billions. **LO7.4**

Compensation of employees	$194.2
U.S. exports of goods and services	17.8
Consumption of fixed capital	11.8
Government purchases	59.4
Taxes on production and imports	14.4
Net private domestic investment	52.1
Transfer payments	13.9
U.S. imports of goods and services	16.5
Personal taxes	40.5
Net foreign factor income	2.2
Personal consumption expenditures	219.1
Statistical discrepancy	0.0

6. Suppose that in 2014 the total output in a single-good economy was 7,000 buckets of chicken. Also suppose that in 2014 each bucket of chicken was priced at $10. Finally, assume that in 2025 the price per bucket of chicken was $16 and that 22,000 buckets were produced. Determine the GDP price index for 2014, using 2025 as the base year. By what percentage did the price level, as measured by this index, rise between 2014 and 2025? What were the amounts of real GDP in 2014 and 2025? **LO7.5**

7. The following table shows nominal GDP and an appropriate price index for a group of selected years. Compute real GDP. Indicate in each calculation whether you are inflating or deflating the nominal GDP data. **LO7.5**

Year	Nominal GDP, Billions	Price Index 2005 = 100	Real GDP, Billions
1978	2,293.8	40.40	$_____
1988	5,100.4	66.98	$_____
1998	8,793.5	85.51	$_____
2008	14,441.4	108.48	$_____
2018	20,501.0	128.59	$_____

8. Assume that the total value of the following items is $600 billion in a specific year for Upper Mongoose: net exports = $50 billion; value of new goods and services produced in the underground economy = $75 billion; personal consumption expenditures = $300 billion; value of the services of stay-at-home parents = $25 billion; gross domestic investment = $100 billion; government purchases = $50 billion. What is Upper Mongoose's GDP for the year? What is the size of the underground economy as a percentage of GDP? By what percentage would GDP increase if the value of the services of stay-at-home spouses were included in GDP? **LO7.6**

CHAPTER

8

Economic Growth

>> LEARNING OBJECTIVES

LO8.1 Explain two ways to measure economic growth.

LO8.2 Describe the institutional structures necessary for modern economic growth.

LO8.3 Identify the supply, demand, and efficiency forces that lead to economic growth.

LO8.4 Describe the specific factors accounting for U.S. economic growth.

LO8.5 Explain how U.S. productivity growth has fluctuated since 1973.

LO8.6 Discuss whether economic growth is desirable and sustainable.

Economic growth is arguably the most revolutionary and powerful force in world history. Until a couple of hundred years ago, poverty, disease, and starvation were the normal lot of people throughout the world. As just one example, France during the 17th century suffered a famine about once every five or six years, with the severe famine of 1693 killing 7 percent of the population just by itself.

Today, by contrast, much of the world's population lives with luxuries that were unknown to our ancestors—hot running water, sewers, automobiles, televisions, antibiotics, wi-fi, fast food, air conditioning, and free public schools. Famine is rare. Life expectancy at birth has increased from 30 years to nearly 73 worldwide. And measured in constant 1990 dollars, the average annual income per capita worldwide has increased from about $600 five hundred years ago to about $10,600 today.

But not every part of the world has enjoyed economic growth; many places are still extremely poor. So economists feel compelled to investigate the causes of economic growth, the institutional structures that appear to promote economic growth, and the controversies surrounding the benefits and costs of economic growth.

>> **LO8.1** Explain two ways to measure economic growth.

economic growth (1) An outward shift in the *production possibilities curve* that results from an increase in resource supplies or quality or an improvement in *technology*; (2) an increase of real output (*gross domestic product*) or real output per capita.

Economic Growth

Economists define **economic growth** as either:

- An increase in *real GDP* over some time period.
- An increase in *real GDP per capita* over some time period.

With either definition, economic growth is calculated as a percentage rate of growth per quarter (3-month period) or per year. For the first definition, for example, real GDP in the United States (measured in constant 2012 dollars) was $18,384.7 billion in 2020 and $19,427.3 in 2021. So the real (inflation-adjusted) U.S. economic growth rate for 2021 was 5.7 percent [= [(19,427.3 billion − $18,384.7 billion)/$18,384.7 billion] × 100]. Growth rates are usually, but not always, positive. In recession year 2009, for instance, the U.S. rate of economic growth was *minus* 2.4 percent. Also note that the growth rate for 2021 was unusually high, due to the U.S. economy snapping back sharply after the short but extremely severe 2020 recession that was caused by the COVID-19 pandemic. Since 1970, the annual U.S. growth rate for real GDP has only exceeded 5 percent per year six times and the 2021 growth rate was the highest observed since real GDP grew at a 7.2 percent annual rate in 1984.

The second definition of economic growth takes into consideration the size of the population. **Real GDP per capita** (or *per capita output*) is the amount of real output per person in a country. It is calculated as follows:

$$\text{Real GDP per capita} = \frac{\text{Real GDP}}{\text{Population}}$$

real GDP per capita
Inflation-adjusted output per person; *real GDP/ population.*

For example, in 2020, real GDP in the United States was $18,384.7 billion and the population was 331.8 million. Therefore, real GDP per capita in that year was $55,409 (= $18,384.7 billion divided by 331.8 million). In 2021, real GDP per capita increased to $58,481 (= $19,427.3 billion divided by 2018's population of 332.2 million). So the growth rate of real GDP per capita in 2021 was 5.4 percent {= [($58,418 − $55,409)/$55,409] × 100}. By way of comparison, real GDP per capita fell by 3.5 percent in recession year 2009.

For measuring the expansion of military potential or political prominence, the growth of real GDP is more useful than the growth of real GDP per capita. Unless specified otherwise, the growth rates reported in the news and by international agencies refer to the growth rates of real GDP rather than real GDP per capita. For comparing living standards, however, the growth rate of real GDP per capita is superior. While China's GDP in 2020 was $14,722 billion compared with Denmark's $356 billion, Denmark's GDP per capita was $61,063 compared with China's strikingly lower $10,435.

In some cases, real GDP growth statistics can be misleading. For example, the African nation of Eritrea had real GDP growth of 1.3 percent per year from 2000 to 2008. But over the same period its annual population growth rate was 3.8 percent per year, resulting in a 2.5 percent per year decline in real GDP per capita.

Growth as a Goal

Growth is a widely held economic goal. The expansion of total output relative to population results in rising real wages and incomes and thus higher standards of living. An economy that is experiencing economic growth is better able to meet people's wants and resolve socioeconomic problems. Rising real wages and income provide more opportunities to individuals and families—a vacation trip, a personal computer, tuition—without sacrificing other opportunities and pleasures. A growing economy can undertake new programs to alleviate poverty, cultivate the arts, and protect the environment without impairing existing levels of consumption, investment, and public goods production.

In short, *growth lessens the burden of scarcity*. Unlike a static economy, a growing economy can consume more today while increasing its capacity to produce more in the future. By easing the burden of scarcity—by relaxing society's constraints on production—economic growth helps a nation attain its economic goals and undertake new endeavors.

Arithmetic of Growth

Economists pay so much attention to small changes in the rate of economic growth because those small changes in growth rates have large effects on the volume of output. For the United States, with a current nominal GDP of about $23 trillion, the difference between a 3 percent and a 4 percent growth rate is about $230 billion of output each year. For a poor country, a difference of one-half of a percentage point in the growth rate may mean the difference between hunger and starvation.

The mathematical approximation called the **rule of 70** helps us understand the effect of economic growth. According to the rule of 70, we can find the number of years it will take for some measure to double by dividing the number 70 by the measure's annual percentage rate of growth. For real GDP:

$$\text{Approximate number of years required to double real GDP} = \frac{70}{\text{annual percentage rate of growth}}$$

rule of 70 A method for determining the number of years it will take for some measure to double, given its annual percentage increase. Example: To determine the number of years it will take for the *price level* to double, divide 70 by the annual rate of *inflation*.

TABLE 8.1 U.S. Real GDP and Real GDP per Capita, Selected Years, 1950–2021

(1) Year	(2) Real GDP, Billions of 2012 $	(3) Population, Millions	(4) Real GDP, per Capita, 2012 $ (2) ÷ (3)
1950	$ 2,291	151.7	$15,102
1960	3,262	180.8	18,042
1970	4,954	205.1	24,154
1980	6,764	227.7	29,706
1990	9,372	250.2	37,458
2000	13,138	282.4	46,523
2010	15,649	309.8	50,513
2020	18,385	331.8	55,410
2021	19,427	332.2	58,480

Source: U.S. Bureau of Economic Analysis and U.S. Census Bureau.

Examples: A 3 percent annual growth rate will double real GDP in about 23 (= 70 ÷ 3) years. Growth of 8 percent per year will double real GDP in about 9 (= 70 ÷ 8) years. When compounded over many years, an apparently small difference in the growth rate thus becomes highly significant. Suppose China and Italy start with identical GDPs, but then China grows at 8 percent yearly, while Italy grows at 2 percent. China's GDP would double in about 9 years, while Italy's GDP would double in 35 years.

Growth in the United States

Table 8.1 gives an overview of economic growth in the United States since 1950. Column 2 reveals strong growth as measured by increases in real GDP. Note that between 1950 and 2021, real GDP increased more than eightfold.

The U.S. population also increased over that time period. Nevertheless, column 4 shows that real GDP per capita rose nearly fourfold over these years.

How quickly has U.S. GDP grown since 1950? Real GDP grew at an average annual rate of about 3.0 percent per year while real GDP per capita increased on average at roughly 1.9 percent per year. Those are very respectable growth rates, but we must qualify how we interpret them:

- *Improved products and services* Because the numbers in Table 8.1 do not fully account for improvements in products and services, they understate the growth of economic well-being. Such purely quantitative data do not fully compare an era of vacuum tube computers and low-efficiency V8 hot rods with an era of digital cell phone networks and fuel-sipping, hybrid-drive vehicles.

- *Added leisure* The increases in real GDP and per capita GDP in Table 8.1 were accomplished despite increases in leisure. The average workweek, once 50 hours, is now about 35 hours (excluding overtime hours). Again the raw growth numbers understate the gain in economic well-being.

- *Other impacts* These measures of growth do not account for the effects of growth on the environment and the quality of life. If growth debases the physical environment, excessively warms the planet, and creates a stressful work environment, the bare growth numbers will overstate the gains in well-being that result from growth. In contrast, if growth leads to stronger environmental protections or a more secure and stress-free lifestyle, GDP growth statistics will understate the gains in well-being.

QUICK REVIEW

8.1

- ▶ Economists measure economic growth as either (a) an increase in real GDP over time or (b) an increase in real GDP per capita over time.

- ▶ Real GDP in the United States has grown by about 3.0 percent annually since 1950, while real GDP per capita has grown by roughly 1.9 percent annually over the same period.

- ▶ Real GDP fails to fully account for quality improvements, excludes the dollar value of leisure activities, and does not account for the effects of growth on the environment.

Modern Economic Growth

Before the Industrial Revolution of the late 1700s, living standards were virtually constant over long periods of time. Greek peasants living in the year 300 B.C. had, for example, about the same material standard of living as Greek peasants living in the year A.D. 1500. By contrast, our current era of **modern economic growth** is characterized by sustained and ongoing increases in material prosperity that yield dramatic increases in the standard of living within less than a single human lifetime.

Economic historians informally date the start of the Industrial Revolution to the year 1776, when the Scottish inventor James Watt perfected an efficient steam engine that could power not only steamships and steam locomotives, but also factory equipment. Nearly all manufacturing shifted from items produced by hand by local craftsmen to items mass-produced in distant factories. New steamships and steam locomotives meant that resources flowed easily to factories and that factory output could be shipped to distant consumers at low cost. The result was a huge increase in long-distance trade and a major population shift as people left farms to work in the towns and cities where the new industrial factories were concentrated.

Many more inventions followed Watt's steam engine. These included electric power, railroads, motorized vehicles, telephones, airplanes, container ships, computers, and the Internet. The key point is that the last 250 years of history have been fundamentally different from anything that went before.

Modern economic growth has deeply affected cultural, social, and political arrangements.

- Culturally, the vast increases in wealth and living standards have given ordinary people significant time for leisure activities and the arts.

- Socially, countries experiencing modern economic growth have abolished feudalism, instituted universal public education, and largely eliminated ancient social norms and legal restrictions against women and minorities doing certain jobs or holding certain positions.

- Politically, countries experiencing modern economic growth have tended to move toward democracy, a form of government that was extremely rare before the Industrial Revolution.

In addition, the average human lifespan has more than doubled, from less than 30 years before modern economic growth began in the late 1700s to a worldwide average of over 72 years today. These and other changes speak to the truly revolutionary power of economic growth and naturally lead economists to consider the causes of economic growth and what policies can be pursued to sustain and promote it. Their desire is intensified by the reality that economic growth has been distributed so unevenly around the globe.

The Uneven Distribution of Growth

Modern economic growth spread slowly from its British birthplace. It first advanced to France, Germany, and other parts of Western Europe in the early 1800s before spreading to the United States, Canada, and Australia by the mid-1800s. Japan began to industrialize in the 1870s, but the rest of Asia did not follow until the early to mid-1900s. At that time, large parts of Central America, South America, and the Middle East also began to experience modern economic growth. Most recent has been Africa, which for the most part did not begin to experience modern economic growth until the last half-century.

The different starting dates for modern economic growth in various parts of the world are the main cause of the vast differences in today's per capita GDP levels. Figure 8.1 shows how GDP per capita has evolved since 1820 in the United States, Western Europe, Latin America, Asia, and Africa.

To make the comparisons easier in Figure 8.1, income levels in all places and at all times have been converted into 2011 U.S. dollars. Thus, it is clear that in 1820 per capita incomes in all areas were quite similar. The richest area in the world in 1820, Western Europe, had an average per capita income of $2,307, while the poorest area of the world at that time, Africa, had an average per capita income of $800. Thus, in 1820, average incomes in the richest area in the world were only about three times larger than those in the poorest area.

But because Western Europe and the United States started experiencing modern economic growth earlier than other areas, they are now vastly richer than most other areas. As just one example, per capita GDP in 2021 was $58,480 in the United States but only about $3,532 in

>> **LO8.2** Describe the institutional structures necessary for modern economic growth.

modern economic growth
The historically recent phenomenon in which nations for the first time have experienced sustained increases in *real GDP per capita*.

FIGURE 8.1
The great divergence in standards of living.

Income levels around the world were very similar in 1820. But they are now very different because certain areas, including the United States and Western Europe, began experiencing modern economic growth much earlier than other areas.

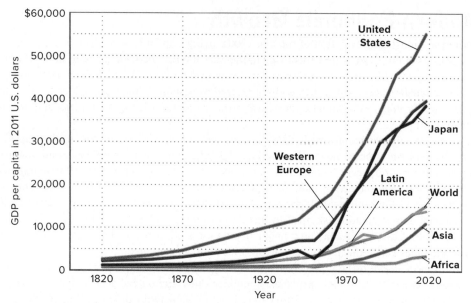

Source: *Maddison Historical Statistics,* The Maddison Project, University of Groningen.

Africa. Because modern economic growth has occurred for so much longer in the United States, U.S. living standards are nearly 17 times higher than those in Africa, on average.

Catching Up Is Possible

The countries that began modern economic growth more recently are not doomed to be permanently poorer than the countries that began modern economic growth earlier. Why? Because people can adopt technology more quickly than they can invent it.

The world's richest countries are rich mostly because they employ the most advanced productive technology. But because they already utilize the most advanced technology, they must invent new technology to get even richer. Because inventing and implementing new technology is slow and costly, real GDP per capita in the richest **leader countries** like the United States and Japan typically grows by just 2 to 3 percent per year.

By contrast, poorer **follower countries** can grow much faster because they can adopt, rather than reinvent, existing technologies. For instance, in many countries in Africa, the first telephones that most people ever used were mobile phones. These countries did not bother to install the copper wires necessary for land-line telephones, which use nineteenth-century technology. Instead, they chose to jump directly to Internet-capable mobile networks, which employ twenty-first-century technology. In doing so, these countries skipped past many stages of technology that the United States and other leader countries took over a century to invent and implement.

By skipping directly to the most advanced modern technology, follower countries can experience extremely rapid **catch-up growth.** South Korea, for example, averaged 8.8 percent annual growth in real GDP between 1960 and 2020–a pace of growth that transformed South Korea from one of the poorest countries in the world into a rich leader country that is on the cutting edge of technology in several areas, including electronics and automobiles.

China grew even more rapidly after it undertook market-oriented economic reforms starting in the late 1970s. Between 1980 and 2020, China's real GDP grew at an average annual rate of 9.9 percent per year. That rate of growth lifted hundreds of millions out of abject poverty and raised China to great power status in political and military relations.

China is now, however, near the "technological frontier" at which it will no longer be able to grow rapidly simply by borrowing established technologies from other countries. As with other countries that have pulled close to the technological frontier, its growth rate is slowing rapidly since it must now invest significant resources into invention and innovation. Once it becomes a leader country across all types of technology, its growth rate can be expected to decrease down to the 2 to 3 percent rate typical of established technological leader countries like Japan and the United States.

leader countries As it relates to *economic growth,* countries that develop and use the most advanced technologies, which then become available to *follower countries.*

follower countries As it relates to *economic growth,* countries that adopt advanced technologies that previously were developed and used by *leader countries.*

catch-up growth The rapid increases in real GDP per capita that can be achieved when a poor *follower country* adopts, rather than reinvents, cutting edge technologies that took *leader countries* decades to invent and implement.

Institutional Structures That Promote Modern Economic Growth

How does a country start the process of modern economic growth? And once it has started modern economic growth, how does it keep the process going?

Economic historians have identified several institutional structures that promote and sustain modern economic growth. Some institutions increase the savings and investment that are needed to fund the construction and maintenance of the factories and infrastructure required to run modern economies. Other institutions promote the development of new technologies. Still others ensure that resources flow efficiently to their most productive uses. These growth-promoting institutional structures include:

- *Strong property rights* Strong property rights are essential for promoting rapid and sustained economic growth. People will not invest if they believe that thieves, bandits, or a rapacious and tyrannical government will steal their investments or their expected returns.

- *Patents and copyrights* Before patents and copyrights were first issued and enforced, inventors and authors usually saw their ideas stolen before they could profit from them. By giving inventors and authors the exclusive right to market and sell their creations, patents and copyrights provide a strong financial incentive to invent and create (as is discussed in the nearby Consider This story about drug prices).

- *Efficient financial institutions* These institutions channel household savings toward the businesses, entrepreneurs, and inventors that do most of society's investing and inventing. Banks, along with stock and bond markets, appear to be crucial to modern economic growth.

- *Literacy and widespread education* Without highly educated scientists and inventors, new technologies do not get developed. And without a highly educated workforce, it is impossible to put those technologies to productive use.

- *Free trade* Free trade promotes economic growth by allowing countries to specialize. With specialization, various types of output are produced in the countries where they can be made at the lowest opportunity cost. Free trade also promotes the rapid spread of new ideas so that innovations made in one country quickly spread to other countries.

CONSIDER THIS . . .

Patents and Innovation

It costs U.S. and European drug companies about $1 billion to research, patent, and safety-test a new drug because literally thousands of candidate drugs fail for each drug that succeeds. The only way to recover these costs is by relying on patent protections that give a drug's developer the exclusive monopoly right to market and sell the new drug for 20 years. The revenues over that time period will hopefully be enough to cover the drug's development costs and—if the drug is popular—generate a profit for the drug company.

Photodisc Collection/EyeWire/Getty Images

Leader and follower countries have gotten into heated disputes over patented drugs, however, because the follower countries have often refused to recognize the patents granted to pharmaceutical companies in rich countries. India, for instance, has allowed local drug companies to copy and sell drugs that were developed by U.S.

companies and are still under patent protection in the United States.

That policy benefits Indian consumers because competition among the local drug companies drives down the price to below the monopoly price that would be charged by the patent owner. But the weak patent protections in India have a side effect. They make it completely unprofitable for local drug producers to try to develop innovative new drugs. Local rivals would simply copy the new drugs and sell them at very low prices. So India has recently moved to strengthen its patent protections to try to provide financial incentives to transform its local drug companies from copycats into innovators.

But note that the innovative new drugs that may result from the increased patent protections will not arrive without an opportunity cost. As patent protections in India are improved, inexpensive local drugs copied from the leader countries will no longer be available to Indian consumers.

- *A competitive market system* Under a market system, prices and profits serve as the signals that tell firms what and how much to make. Rich leader countries vary substantially in terms of how much government regulation they impose on markets, but in all cases, firms have substantial autonomy to follow market signals in determining their production and investment decisions.

Several other difficult-to-measure factors also influence a nation's capacity for economic growth. The overall social-cultural-political environment of the United States, for example, has encouraged economic growth. The United States has a stable political system characterized by democratic principles, internal order, the right of property ownership, the legal status of enterprise, and the enforcement of contracts. Economic freedom and political freedom have been "growth friendly."

In addition, there are virtually no social or moral taboos on production and material progress in the United States. The nation's social philosophy has embraced wealth creation as an attainable and desirable goal, and the inventor, the innovator, and the businessperson are given high degrees of prestige and respect. Finally, Americans have a positive attitude toward work and risk taking, resulting in an ample supply of willing workers and innovative entrepreneurs. A flow of enterprising immigrants has greatly augmented that supply.

The nearby Consider This shows how follower countries sometimes alter their institutional structures as they draw closer to the technological frontier.

QUICK REVIEW
8.2

▶ Large differences in standards of living exist today because technological leader countries like the United States have experienced up to 250 years of modern economic growth while technological follower countries have enjoyed modern economic growth for only a few decades.

▶ Poor follower countries can catch up to the living standards of rich leader countries by adopting the

cutting-edge technologies and institutions already developed by rich leader countries.

▶ Institutional structures that promote growth include strong property rights, patents, efficient financial institutions, education, and a competitive market system.

Determinants of Growth

>> LO8.3 Identify the supply, demand, and efficiency forces that lead to economic growth.

We now focus on six factors that directly affect the rate and quality of economic growth. These determinants of economic growth can be grouped into four supply factors, one demand factor, and one efficiency factor.

Supply Factors

supply factors (in growth)
The four determinants of an economy's physical ability to achieve *economic growth* by increasing *potential output* and shifting out the *production possibilities curve*. The four determinants are improvements in technology plus increases in the quantity and quality of natural resources, human resources, and the stock of capital goods.

The first four determinants of economic growth relate to relaxing the physical and technical limits that constrain economic expansion. They are:

- Increases in the quantity and quality of natural resources
- Increases in the quantity and quality of human resources
- Increases in the supply (stock) of capital goods
- Improvements in technology

Any increases or improvements in these **supply factors** will increase the *potential* size of an economy's GDP. The remaining two factors (that is, the demand factor and the efficiency factor) are necessary for that potential to be fulfilled.

Demand Factor

demand factor (in growth)
The requirement that *aggregate demand* increase as fast as *potential output* if *economic growth* is to proceed as quickly as possible.

The fifth determinant of economic growth is the **demand factor:**

- To achieve the higher production potential created when the supply factors increase or improve, households, businesses, and the government must also expand their purchases of goods and services so as to provide a market for all the new output that can potentially be produced.

When this demand condition is met, there will be no unplanned increases in inventories, and resources will remain fully employed. The demand factor acknowledges that economic growth requires increases in total spending to realize the output gains made possible by increased production capacity.

Efficiency Factor

The first five determinants affect the quantity of economic output. The sixth determinant, the **efficiency factor,** deals with the quality of economic output:

- An economy must achieve economic efficiency in addition to full employment if it is to maximize the amount of satisfaction or utility that can be derived from its scarce resources.

To maximize well-being, the economy must use its resources in the least costly way (productive efficiency) to produce the specific mix of goods and services that maximizes people's utility (allocative efficiency). The ability to expand production, together with the full use of available resources, is not sufficient for achieving welfare-maximizing growth. To maximize well-being, those resources must be employed efficiently, as well.

The supply, demand, and efficiency factors in economic growth are related. Unemployment caused by insufficient total spending (the demand factor) may lower the rate of new capital accumulation (a supply factor) and delay expenditures on research (also a supply factor). Conversely, low spending on investment (a supply factor) may cause insufficient spending (the demand factor) and unemployment. Widespread inefficiency in the use of resources (the efficiency factor) may translate into higher costs of goods and services and thus lower profits, which in turn may slow innovation and reduce the accumulation of capital (supply factors).

Production Possibilities Analysis

To put the six factors affecting the rate of economic growth into better perspective, let's apply the production possibilities analysis introduced in Chapter 1.

Growth and Production Possibilities Recall that a curve like *AB* in Figure 8.2 is a production possibilities curve. It indicates the various *maximum* combinations of products an economy can produce with its fixed quantity and quality of natural, human, and capital resources and its current stock of technological knowledge. An improvement in any of the supply factors will push the production possibilities curve outward, as from *AB* to *CD*.

But the demand factor reminds us that the economy needs an increase in total spending to move from a point like *a* on curve *AB* to any of the points on the higher curve *CD*. And the efficiency factor reminds us that we need least-cost production and an optimal location on *CD* for the resources to make their maximum possible contribution to total output and human welfare. Recall from Chapter 1 that this "best allocation" is determined by expanding the production of each good until its marginal benefit equals its marginal cost. Here, we assume that this optimal combination of capital and consumer goods occurs at point *b*. If the efficiency factor is in full effect, then the economy will produce at point *b* rather than at any other point along curve *CD*.

Example: The net increase in the size of the U.S. labor force in recent decades has been 1 to 1.5 million workers per year. That increase raises the economy's production capacity. But obtaining the extra output that these added workers can produce depends on their success in finding jobs. It also depends on whether jobs are available in firms and industries where the workers' talents are fully and optimally used. Society does not want new labor-force entrants to be unemployed. Nor does it want pediatricians working as plumbers or pediatricians producing pediatric services for which marginal costs exceed marginal benefits.

Normally, increases in total spending match increases in production capacity, and the economy moves from a point on the previous production possibilities curve to a point on the expanded curve. Moreover, the

efficiency factor (in growth) The capacity of an economy to achieve *allocative* and *productive efficiency* and thereby fulfill the potential for growth that the *supply factors (of growth)* make possible; the capacity of an economy to achieve *economic efficiency* and thereby reach the optimal point on its *production possibilities curve*.

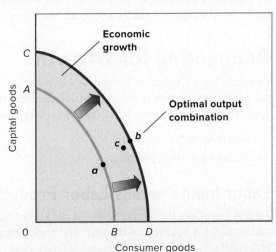

FIGURE 8.2
Economic growth and the production possibilities curve.

Economic growth is made possible by the four supply factors that shift the production possibilities curve outward, as from *AB* to *CD*. Economic growth is realized when the demand factor and the efficiency factor move the economy from points such as *a* and *c* that are inside *CD* to the optimal output point, which is assumed to be point *b* in this figure.

FIGURE 8.3
The supply determinants of real output.

Real GDP is usefully viewed as the product of the quantity of labor inputs (hours of work) multiplied by labor productivity.

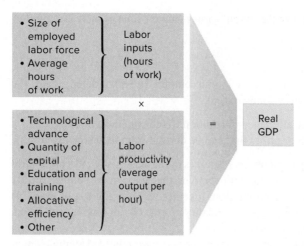

competitive market system tends to drive the economy toward productive and allocative efficiency. Occasionally, however, the economy ends up at some point such as *c* in Figure 8.2. That outcome occurred in the United States during the COVID-19 recession of 2020. Real output fell substantially below the amount of output that the economy could have produced if it had achieved full employment and operated on its production possibilities curve.

Labor and Productivity Society can increase its real output and income in two fundamental ways: (1) by increasing its inputs of resources and (2) by raising the productivity of those inputs. Figure 8.3 concentrates on the input of *labor* and provides a useful framework for discussing the role of supply factors in growth. A nation's real GDP in any year depends on the input of labor (measured in hours of work) multiplied by **labor productivity** (measured as real output per hour of work):

$$\text{Real GDP} = \text{hours of work} \times \text{labor productivity}$$

labor productivity Total output (GDP) divided by the quantity of labor (hours of work) employed to produce it; the *average product* of labor, or output per hour of work.

From this perspective, a nation's economic growth from one year to the next depends on its increase in labor inputs (if any) and its increase in labor productivity (if any).

Illustration: Assume that the hypothetical economy of Ziam has 10 workers in year 1, each working 2,000 hours per year (= 50 weeks at 40 hours per week). The total input of labor therefore is 20,000 hours. If productivity (average real output per hour of work) is $20, then real GDP in Ziam will be $400,000 (= 20,000 × $20). If work hours rise to 20,200 and labor productivity rises to $21 per hour, Ziam's real GDP will increase to $424,200 in year 2. Ziam's rate of economic growth will be about 6 percent [= ($424,200 − $400,000)/$400,000] for the year.

Hours of Work What determines the number of hours worked each year? As Figure 8.3 shows, the hours of labor input depend on the size of the employed labor force and the length of the average workweek. Labor-force size depends on the size of the working-age population and the **labor-force participation rate**–the percentage of the working-age population actually in the labor force. The length of the average workweek is governed by legal and institutional considerations and by collective bargaining agreements negotiated between unions and employers.

labor-force participation rate The percentage of the working-age population that is actually in the *labor force.*

Labor Productivity Figure 8.3 tells us that labor productivity is determined by technological progress, the quantity of capital goods available to workers, the quality of labor inputs, and the efficiency with which inputs are allocated, combined, and managed. Productivity rises when the health, training, education, and motivation of workers improve; when workers have more and better machinery and natural resources to work with; when production is better organized and managed; and when labor is reallocated from less-efficient industries to more-efficient industries.

Accounting for Growth

>> LO8.4 Describe the specific factors accounting for U.S. economic growth.

The President's Council of Economic Advisers uses a system called **growth accounting** to assess the relative importance of the supply-side elements that contribute to changes in real GDP. This system groups these elements into two main categories:

growth accounting The bookkeeping of the supply-side elements such as productivity and labor inputs that contribute to changes in *real GDP* over some specific time period.

- Increases in hours of work
- Increases in labor productivity

Labor Inputs versus Labor Productivity

Table 8.2 provides the relevant data for the United States for five periods. The symbol "Q" in the table stands for "quarter" of the year. The beginning points for the first four periods are business-cycle peaks, and the last period includes future projections by the Council of Economic Advisers.

TABLE 8.2 Accounting for the Growth of U.S. Real GDP, 1953–2019, plus Projection from 2019 to 2032 (Average Annual Percentage Changes)

Item	Actual				Projected
	1953 Q2 to 1973 Q4	1973 Q4 to 1995 Q2	1995 Q2 to 2007 Q4	2007 Q4 to 2019 Q4	2019 Q4 to 2032 Q4
Increase in real GDP	3.6	2.8	3.2	1.7	2.2
Increase in quantity of labor	1.1	1.3	0.5	0.3	0.4
Increase in labor productivity	2.5	1.5	2.7	1.4	1.8

Source: *Economic Report of the President,* 2008 and 2019; U.S. Bureau of Economic Analysis; and U.S. Bureau of Labor Statistics.

The table clearly shows that increases in the quantity of labor and increases in labor productivity are both important sources of economic growth.

- Between 1953 and 2021, the labor force increased from 63.1 million to 161.2 million workers. Over that period, the average length of the workweek remained relatively stable. Falling birthrates slowed the growth of the native population, but increased immigration partly offset that slowdown. Of particular significance was a surge of women's participation in the labor force. Partly as a result, U.S. labor-force growth averaged about 1.4 million workers per year over those 71 years.

- The growth of labor productivity has also been important to economic growth. In fact, productivity growth has usually been more significant than labor force growth. For example, between 2007 and 2019, labor inputs increased by just 0.3 percent per year. As a result, 82 percent of the 1.7 percent average annual growth rate of GDP over that period was due to increases in labor productivity. The final column of Table 8.2 indicates that this trend is expected to continue; productivity growth is projected to account for 82 percent of the growth of real GDP between 2019 and 2032.

Because increases in labor productivity are so important to economic growth, economists investigate and assess the relative importance of the factors that contribute to productivity growth. There are five factors that appear to explain changes in productivity growth rates: technological advance, the amount of capital per worker, education and training, economies of scale, and resource allocation. We will examine each factor in turn, noting how much each factor contributes to productivity growth.

Technological Advance

The largest contributor to productivity growth is technological advance, which is thought to account for about 40 percent of productivity growth. As Nobel Laureate Paul Romer stated, "Human history teaches us that economic growth springs from better recipes, not just from more cooking."

Technological advance includes not only innovative production techniques but also new managerial methods and new forms of business organization that improve the production process. Technological advance is generated by the discovery of new knowledge, which allows resources to be combined in improved ways that increase output. Once discovered and implemented, new knowledge soon becomes available to entrepreneurs and firms at relatively low cost. Technological advance therefore eventually spreads through the entire economy, boosting productivity and economic growth.

Technological advance and capital formation (investment) are closely related, because technological advance usually promotes investment in new machinery and equipment. In fact, technological advance is often *embodied* within new capital (for example, new computers and autonomous drones).

Technological advance has been both rapid and profound. Gas and diesel engines, conveyor belts, and assembly lines are significant developments of the past. So, too, are fuel-efficient commercial aircraft, integrated microcircuits, personal computers, and containerized shipping. More recently, technological advance has exploded, particularly in the areas of computers, wireless communications, artificial intelligence, and the Internet. Other fertile areas of recent innovation are medicine and biotechnology.

Quantity of Capital per Worker

A second major contributor to productivity growth is increased capital, which explains roughly 30 percent of productivity growth. More and better plant and equipment make workers more productive. A nation acquires more capital by saving some of its income and using that savings to invest in plant and equipment.

Although some capital substitutes for labor, most capital is complementary to labor—it makes labor more productive. A key determinant of labor productivity is the amount of capital goods available *per worker*. If both the aggregate stock of capital goods and the size of the labor force increase over a given period, the individual worker is not necessarily better equipped, and productivity will not necessarily rise. Fortunately, the quantity of capital (machinery and buildings) available per U.S. worker has increased greatly over time. (In 2020 it was about $255,870 per worker.)

infrastructure The interconnected network of large-scale *capital goods* (such as roads, sewers, electrical grids, railways, ports, and the Internet) needed to operate a technologically advanced economy.

U.S. public investment in **infrastructure** (highways and bridges, public transit systems, wastewater treatment facilities, airports, educational facilities, and so on) has also grown over the years. This publicly owned capital complements private capital. Public investments in new highways, for instance, can promote private investments in new factories and retail stores along their routes.

Private investment in infrastructure also plays a large role in economic growth. One example is the tremendous growth of private capital relating to communications systems over the years.

Education and Training

human capital The knowledge and skills that make a person productive.

Ben Franklin once said, "He that hath a trade hath an estate," meaning that education and training contribute to a worker's stock of **human capital**—the knowledge and skills that make a worker productive. Investment in human capital includes not only formal education but also on-the-job training. Like investment in physical capital, investment in human capital is an important means of increasing labor productivity and earnings. An estimated 15 percent of productivity growth derives from investments in people's education and skills.

One measure of a nation's quality of labor is its level of educational attainment. Figure 8.4 shows large gains in education attainment over the past several decades. In 1960, only 44 percent of the U.S. population age 25 or older had at least a high school education, and only 8 percent had a college or post-college education. By 2020, those numbers had increased to 91 percent and 38 percent, respectively. More people are receiving more education than ever before.

But all is not upbeat with education in the United States. Many observers think that the quality of education in the United States has declined. For example, U.S. students perform poorly on science and math tests relative to students in many other nations, as can be seen in Global Perspective 8.1. And the United States has been producing fewer engineers and scientists, a problem that may trace back to inadequate training in math and science in elementary school, middle school, and high school. For these reasons, much recent public policy discussion and legislation has focused on improving the quality of the U.S. education and training system.

FIGURE 8.4
Changes in the educational attainment of the U.S. adult population.

The percentage of the U.S. adult population, age 25 or older, completing high school and college has been rising over recent decades.

Source: U.S. Census Bureau.

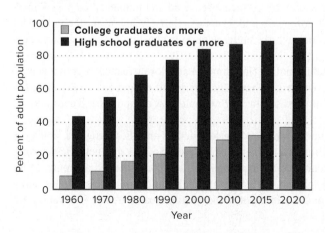

Economies of Scale and Resource Allocation

Economies of scale and improved resource allocation are the fourth and fifth sources of productivity growth; together, they explain about 15 percent of all productivity growth.

Economies of Scale Reductions in per-unit production costs that

GLOBAL PERSPECTIVE 8.1

AVERAGE TEST SCORES OF EIGHTH-GRADE STUDENTS IN MATH AND SCIENCE, TOP 12 TEST-TAKING COUNTRIES

The average performance of U.S. eighth-grade students did not compare favorably with that of eighth-graders in several other nations in the Seventh International Math and Science Study (2019).

Mathematics Rank	Score	Science Rank	Score
1 Singapore	616	1 Singapore	608
2 Taiwan	612	2 Taiwan	574
3 South Korea	607	3 Japan	570
4 Japan	594	4 South Korea	561
5 Hong Kong	578	5 Russia	543
6 Russia	543	6 Finland	542
7 Ireland	524	7 Lithuania	534
8 Lithuania	520	8 Hungary	530
9 Israel	519	9 Australia	528
10 Australia	517	10 Ireland	523
11 Hungary	517	11 United States	522
12 United States	515	12 Sweden	521

Source: National Science Foundation.

result from increases in output levels are called **economies of scale.** Markets have grown over time, allowing firms to increase output levels and thereby achieve production advantages associated with greater size. As firms expand their size and output, they are able to use larger, more productive equipment and employ methods of manufacturing and delivery that increase productivity. They also are better able to recoup substantial investments in developing new products and production methods.

Examples: A large manufacturer of autos can use elaborate assembly lines with computerization and robotics, while smaller producers must compensate for less-advanced technologies by using more labor inputs. Large pharmaceutical firms greatly reduce the average amount of labor (researchers, production workers) needed to produce each pill as they increase the number of pills produced. Accordingly, economies of scale generate more real output and thus contribute to economic growth. Economies of scale account for about 7 percent of all productivity growth.

Improved Resource Allocation Thanks to improved resource allocation, workers have moved from low-productivity employment to high-productivity employment. Historically, many workers shifted from agriculture, where labor productivity is low, to manufacturing, where it is high. More recently, labor has shifted away from some manufacturing industries to even higher-productivity industries such as computer software, business consulting, and pharmaceuticals. As a result of such shifts, the average productivity of U.S. workers has increased.

Also, discrimination in education and the labor market has historically deterred some women and minorities from entering high-productivity jobs. With the decline of such discrimination over time, many members of those groups have shifted from lower-productivity jobs to higher-productivity jobs. The result has been higher overall labor productivity and higher real GDP.

Finally, tariffs, import quotas, and other barriers to international trade tend to relegate resources to relatively unproductive pursuits. The long-run movement toward liberalized international trade through international agreements has improved the allocation of resources, increased

economies of scale The situation when a firm's *average total cost* of producing a product decreases in the *long run* as the firm increases the size of its *plant* (and, hence, its output).

labor productivity, and expanded real output, both here and abroad. Improved resource allocation accounts for about 8 percent of all productivity growth.

To solidify your memory, make a pie chart of the percentage contributions made by each of the five factors that contribute to productivity growth (technological advance, the amount of capital per worker, education and training, economies of scale, and resource allocation).

**QUICK REVIEW
8.3**

▶ The determinants of economic growth include four supply factors (increases in the quantity and quality of natural resources, increases in the quantity and quality of human resources, increases in the stock of capital goods, and improvements in technology), one demand factor (increases in total spending), and one efficiency factor (allocative and productive efficiency).

▶ Improved technology, more capital per worker, greater education and training, economies of scale, and better resource allocation have been the main contributors to U.S. productivity growth and thus to U.S. economic growth.

Recent Fluctuations in Average Productivity Growth

>> **LO8.5** Explain how U.S. productivity growth has fluctuated since 1973.

Figure 8.5 shows the growth of labor productivity (as measured by changes in the index of labor productivity) in the United States from 1973 to 2021, along with separate trend lines for 1973–1995, 1995–2010, and 2010–2021. Labor productivity in the business sector grew by an average of 1.5 percent per year over the 1973–1995 period. But productivity growth nearly doubled to 2.8 percent per year between 1995 and 2010 before decelerating to just 1.2 percent per year between 2010 and 2021.

Robust productivity growth is important because real output, real income, and real wages are linked to labor productivity. To see why, suppose that you are alone on an uninhabited island. The number of fish you can catch or coconuts you can pick per hour—your productivity—is your real wage (or real income) per hour. By *increasing your* productivity, you can improve your standard of living because you can gather more fish or more coconuts (goods) for each hour of work.

So it is for the economy as a whole: Over long periods, the economy's labor productivity determines its average real hourly wage. Thus, productivity growth is the economy's main route for improving living standards.

FIGURE 8.5 **Growth of labor productivity in the United States, 1973–2021.**

U.S. labor productivity (here, for the business sector) increased at an average annual rate of 1.5 percent from 1973 to 1995. But between 1995 and 2010, it rose at an annual rate of 2.8 percent before slowing to just 1.2 percent per year between 2010 and 2021.

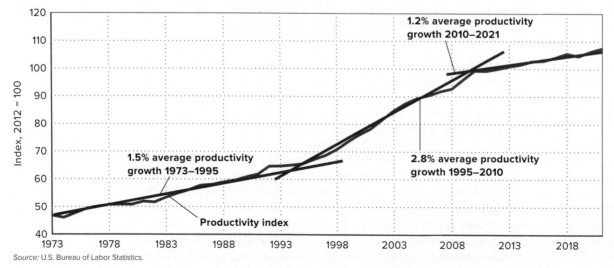

Source: U.S. Bureau of Labor Statistics.

Reasons for the Rise in Average Productivity Growth Between 1995 and 2010

Why did productivity growth increase rapidly between 1995 and 2010?

The Microchip and Information Technology The core element of the productivity speedup between 1995 and 2010 was an explosion of entrepreneurship and innovation based on the microprocessor, or *microchip*, which bundles transistors on a piece of silicon. Some observers liken the invention of the microchip to that of electricity, the automobile, air travel, the telephone, and television in importance and scope.

The microchip has found its way into thousands of applications. It has helped create a wide array of new products and services and new ways of doing business. Its immediate results were the pocket calculator, the bar-code scanner, the personal computer, and more powerful business computers. The miniaturization of electronic circuits also advanced the development of many other products, including cell phones, the global positioning system, Doppler radar, and gene sequencing equipment.

Perhaps of greatest significance, the widespread availability of personal and laptop computers stimulated the desire to tie them together. That desire promoted the rapid development of the Internet and its many manifestations, such as business-to-household and business-to-business electronic commerce (e-commerce). The combination of the computer, fiber-optic cable, wireless technology, and the Internet constitutes a spectacular advance in **information technology,** which now connects almost all parts of the world.

information technology New and more efficient methods of delivering and receiving information through the use of computers, wi-fi networks, wireless phones, and the Internet.

Start-ups Hundreds of new **start-up firms** advanced various aspects of the new information technology. Many of these firms created more "hype" than goods and services and quickly fell by the wayside. But a number of firms flourished, including Intel (microchips); Apple and Dell (personal computers); Microsoft and Oracle (computer software); Cisco Systems (Internet switching systems); Yahoo and Google (Internet search); and eBay, PayPal, and Amazon.com (electronic commerce). There are scores more! Most of these firms were either nonexistent or just a small blip on the radar 30 years ago. Today each of them has a large annual revenue and employs thousands of workers.

start-up firm A new *firm* focused on creating and introducing a particular new product or employing a specific new production or distribution method.

Increasing Returns Many of the successful information technology start-ups enjoyed **increasing returns,** which is what happens when a given percentage increase in the amount of inputs used by a firm leads to a larger percentage increase in the amount of output produced by the firm.

increasing returns An increase in a *firm*'s output by a larger percentage than the percentage increase in its inputs.

As an illustration, suppose that a company called Techco decides to double the size of its operations to meet the growing demand for its services.

- After doubling its plant and equipment and doubling its workforce, say, from 100 workers to 200 workers, it finds that its total output has tripled, from 8,000 units to 24,000 units.
- Techco has experienced increasing returns; its output has increased by 200 percent, while its inputs have increased by only 100 percent.
- Techco's labor productivity has also gone up from 80 units per worker (= 8,000 units/ 100 workers) to 120 units per worker (= 24,000 units/200 workers).

Increasing returns boost labor productivity and reduce per-unit production costs. Because these cost reductions result from increased output levels, increasing returns are an example of *economies of scale,* which occur when a firm's per-unit production cost declines as its output volume increases.

Both emerging firms and established firms were able to exploit several different sources of increasing returns and economies of scale during the so-called tech boom:

- *More specialized inputs* Firms were able to use more specialized and thus more productive capital and workers as they expanded their operations. A growing e-commerce business located in Silicon Valley, for example, could purchase highly specialized inventory management systems and hire specialized personnel such as accountants, marketing managers, and system maintenance experts.
- *Spreading of development costs* Firms were able to spread high product development costs over greater output. For example, suppose that a new software product cost $100,000 to

develop but only $2 per unit to manufacture and sell. If the firm sold 1,000 units of the software, its per-unit cost was $102.00 [= ($100,000 + $2,000)/1,000], but if it sold 500,000 units, that cost dropped to only $2.20 [= ($100,000 + $1 million)/500,000].

- *Simultaneous consumption* Many technology products were able to satisfy large numbers of customers at the same time. Unlike a gallon of gas that needs to be produced for each buyer, a software program needs to be produced only once. It can then be made available at very low expense to thousands or even millions of buyers. The same was true of books delivered to electronic reading devices, movies distributed through streaming services, and information disseminated through the Internet.

network effects Increases in the value of a product to each user, including existing users, as the total number of users rises.

- *Network effects* The domestic and global expansion of the Internet, wireless networks, and social media produced enormous network effects that magnified the value of output well beyond the cost of inputs. **Network effects** occur when a product's value to each user increases as more users use it. To see the power of network effects, imagine that you are the only one in the world with an Instagram account. That would be pretty pointless as the whole point is to share content and connect with people. But if there were a few thousand people also using Instagram, you would suddenly be able to derive significant benefits from your Instagram account. And if the number of users continued to increase, your benefit would continue to grow as there would be even more people to interact with. The larger the network of people using the service, the more beneficial it becomes to each individual user. Since the Internet is the largest network ever created, it's not surprising that it has generated the largest network effects ever seen and, along with them, extremely large economies of scale. You only have to build Instagram once. As the network grows, the cost per user falls, fast.

learning by doing Achieving greater *productivity* and lower *average total cost* through gains in knowledge and skill that accompany repetition of a task; a source of *economies of scale*.

- *Learning by doing* Finally, the start-ups that produced new products or pioneered new ways of doing business were often able to experience increasing returns through **learning by doing.** Tasks that initially may have taken firms hours may take them only minutes once the methods are perfected. The more they produce, the more efficient they become.

Whatever the particular source of increasing returns, the result was higher productivity, which tended to reduce the per-unit cost of producing and delivering technology products during the 1995 to 2010 period.

Global Competition As with today's economy, the economy between 1995 and 2010 was characterized not only by information technology and increasing returns but also by heightened global competition. The market liberalization in China and the collapse of the socialist economies in the early 1990s led to a reawakening of capitalism throughout the world. New information technologies "shrank the globe" and made it imperative for all firms to lower their costs and innovate in order to remain competitive. Free-trade zones such as NAFTA and the European Union (EU), along with trade liberalization through the World Trade Organization (WTO), increased international competition by removing trade barriers. The larger geographic markets, in turn, enabled firms to expand beyond their national borders. Countries had to compete if they wanted to grow. (The nearby Global Perspective lists the 10 highest-ranked countries in terms of international economic competitiveness.)

Implications for Economic Growth

Other things equal, stronger productivity growth and heightened global competition allowed the economy to achieve a higher rate of economic growth during the 1995 to 2010 period. A glance back at Figure 8.2 will help make this point. Suppose that the shift of the production possibilities curve from *AB* to *CD* reflects annual changes in potential output before the increase in growth rates observed during the 1995 to 2010 period. Then the higher growth rates of that period would be depicted by a *larger* outward shift of the economy's production possibilities from *AB* to a curve beyond *CD*. When coupled with economic efficiency and increased total spending, the economy's real GDP was able to rise by even more than what is shown.

The Recent Productivity Slowdown

It is not clear whether the dramatic slowdown in productivity growth that took place after the Great Recession is permanent or transitory. Some economists have argued that the high

GLOBAL PERSPECTIVE 8.2

WORLD COMPETITIVENESS RANKINGS

The World Competitiveness Ranking, published annually by the International Institute for Management Development in Switzerland, measures each country's potential for economic growth. The index uses various factors—such as innovativeness, the capability to transfer technology among sectors, the efficiency of the financial system, rates of investment, and the degree of economic integration with the rest of the world—to measure a country's ability to achieve economic growth over time.

Country	Global Competitiveness Ranking, 2021
Switzerland	1
Sweden	2
Denmark	3
Netherlands	4
Singapore	5
Norway	6
Hong Kong	7
Taiwan	8
United Arab Emirates	9
United States	10

Source: IMD World Competitiveness Yearbook 2021, International Institute for Management Development.

productivity growth rates of 1995–2010 were a one-time anomaly due to the information technology revolution. But even if information technology caused an unusual burst of growth for 15 years, it is still surprising that post-2010 productivity growth rates have been so very low, much lower in fact than the rates observed before the information technology revolution.

Several possible explanations have been put forward to explain why productivity growth rates have fallen so low. One possible culprit is the high debt levels that accumulated before the Great Recession. Under this hypothesis, individuals and firms were too busy paying down debts after the Financial Crisis of 2007–2009 to make a lot of productive investments. At the same time, entrepreneurs who might have been able to improve productivity were perhaps unable to obtain loans because banks became reluctant to lend after having made so many bad loans prior to the Great Recession.

Overcapacity may be another explanation for the productivity slowdown. During the boom that preceded the Great Recession, worldwide productive capacity increased massively as many new factories were built. But the additional capacity may have been excessive relative to consumer demand. If so, firms would have been reluctant to install newer, more productive equipment or build newer, more productive factories because they already had more than enough production capacity. Under this hypothesis, productivity stagnated because producers continued to rely on aging machinery and equipment.

Another possible explanation points to the fact that many recent products—especially Internet apps—do not generate much of a measurable effect on GDP. Consider Facebook, YouTube, and Instagram. They are for the most part totally free to consumers. So measured output will hardly increase even if billions of people are using them. That being said, measured output isn't everything. The new products are undoubtedly generating a huge amount of consumer satisfaction; we just can't see those benefits in the GDP and productivity statistics.

Finally, it is possible that technological progress itself may have stalled. Under this hypothesis, productivity growth will remain slow until invention and innovation speed up again. Time will tell.

- ▶ Over long time periods, labor productivity growth determines an economy's growth of real wages and its standard of living.

- ▶ U.S. labor productivity grew at an average annual rate of 1.5 percent from 1973 to 1995, 2.8 percent from 1995 to 2010, and 1.2 percent from 2010 to 2021.

- ▶ The high labor productivity growth rate observed between 1995 and 2010 is attributed to the information technology revolution, start-ups, increasing returns, and heightened global competition.

- ▶ Possible explanations for the low productivity growth rate after 2010 include high debt levels, overcapacity, the rise of "free" Internet products, and a slowdown in technological progress.

QUICK REVIEW

8.4

Is Growth Desirable and Sustainable?

>> LO8.6 Discuss whether economic growth is desirable and sustainable.

Economists usually take for granted that economic growth is desirable and sustainable. But not everyone agrees.

The Antigrowth View

Critics of growth say industrialization and growth result in pollution, climate change, species extinction, and other environmental problems. These adverse negative externalities occur because inputs in the production process reenter the environment as some form of waste. The more rapid our growth and the higher our standard of living, the more waste the environment must absorb—or attempt to absorb. In an already wealthy society, further growth usually means satisfying increasingly trivial wants at the cost of mounting threats to the ecological system.

Critics of growth also argue that there is little compelling evidence that economic growth has solved social problems such as poverty, homelessness, and discrimination. Consider poverty: In the antigrowth view, U.S. poverty is a problem of distribution, not production. Solving the problem requires a firm commitment to redistribute wealth and income, not further increases in output.

Antigrowth sentiment also says that while growth may permit us to "make a better living," it does not give us "the good life." We may be producing more and enjoying less, focused too much on materialism and not enough on families, friendship, and community. Growth means zero work-life balance, employee burnout, and worker alienation. In addition, the changing technology at the core of growth poses new anxieties and new sources of insecurity for workers. Both high-level and low-level workers face the prospect of having their hard-earned skills and experience rendered obsolete by onrushing technology. High-growth economies are high-stress economies, which may impair our physical and mental health.

Finally, critics of high rates of growth doubt that they are sustainable. The earth has finite amounts of natural resources, and they are being consumed at alarming rates. Higher rates of economic growth simply speed up the degradation and depletion of the earth's resources. In this view, slower, environmentally sustainable economic growth is preferable to faster growth.

In Defense of Economic Growth

Those who support economic growth believe that it is the path to the greater material abundance and higher living standards desired by the vast majority of people. Growth also enables society to improve the nation's infrastructure, enhance the care of the sick and elderly, provide greater access for the disabled, and provide more police and fire protection.

Economic growth may also be the only realistic way to reduce poverty, because there is only limited political support for greater redistribution of income. The proponents of growth argue that the best way to improve the economic position of the poor is to increase household incomes through higher productivity and faster economic growth. Also, a no-growth policy among industrial nations might severely limit growth in poor nations. Foreign investment and development assistance in those nations would fall, keeping the world's poor in poverty longer.

Economic growth has not made labor more unpleasant or hazardous, as critics suggest. In fact, growth advocates say, new machinery is usually less taxing and less dangerous than the machinery it replaces. Air-conditioned workplaces are more pleasant than steamy workshops. Furthermore, there is no guarantee that an end to economic growth will reduce materialism or worker alienation. The loudest protests against materialism are heard in those nations that now enjoy the highest levels of material abundance! The high standard of living that growth provides has increased our leisure and given us more time for reflection and self-fulfillment.

Economic growth need not threaten the environment, say growth proponents. Pollution is not so much a by-product of growth as it is a "problem of the commons." Much of the environment—streams, lakes, oceans, the air—is treated as common property, with insufficient or no restrictions on its use. The commons have become our dumping grounds; we have overused and debased them. Environmental pollution is a case of negative externalities, and correcting this problem involves regulatory legislation, pollution taxes, or market-based

Ladies First

The Substantial Rise in the Number of Women in the Paid Workforce in the United States Has Been One of the Major Labor Market Trends of the Past Six Decades.

In 1960, about 40 percent of American women worked full-time or part-time in paid jobs. Today, that number is about 60 percent. What's more, almost half of the U.S. workforce is now female. Let's examine some of the causes and consequences of this historically unprecedented increase in labor force participation.

American women have greatly increased their productivity in the workplace by becoming better educated and professionally trained. Women have earned the majority of bachelor's degrees since 1982, the majority of master's degrees since 1987, and the majority of doctoral degrees since 2008.

This decades-long dominance in educational attainment means that as of 2020, women constituted 53 percent of American workers with a bachelor's degree or higher. Since 1982, women have cumulatively earned 13 million more bachelor's, master's, and doctoral degrees than men. That translates to 131 female degrees for every 100 male degrees.

That superiority in educational attainment appears set to continue for at least another couple of generations. In 2018, women earned 141 bachelor's, master's, and doctoral degrees for every 100 earned by men. And, looking forward, the U.S. Department of Education projects that in 2027 women will earn 151 bachelor's, master's, or doctoral degrees for every 100 earned by men. This implies that the large majority of highly educated workers will be women for at least the next few decades.

Rising productivity has also increased women's wage rates. Those higher wages have, in turn, raised the opportunity costs—the forgone wage earnings—of staying at home. Women have therefore substituted employment in the labor market for what were once traditional home activities. This substitution has been particularly pronounced among married women. (Single women have always had substantial labor-force participation rates.)

Furthermore, changing lifestyles and the widespread availability of birth control have freed up time for greater labor-force participation by women. Women not only have fewer children, but those children are spaced closer together in age. Thus women who leave their jobs during their children's early years return to the labor force sooner.

Greater access to jobs by women has also raised their labor-force participation. Service industries—teaching, nursing, and office work, for

Jacob Lund/Shutterstock

instance—that traditionally have employed many women have expanded rapidly in the past several decades. Also, the population in general has shifted from farms and rural regions to urban areas, where jobs for women are more abundant and more geographically accessible. Additionally, discrimination and other occupational barriers to professions have greatly eroded, resulting in many more women becoming business managers, lawyers, professors, physicians, and entrepreneurs.

Concerns about discrimination persist. While there are relatively few examples of male and female colleagues with equal experience, tenure, and training being paid differently for doing the same job, women continue to enter lower-paid professions like education and home health care in larger numbers than men. They also tend to opt for more part-time as opposed to full-time work, and to fall behind equally educated male peers because women take more and longer career breaks to engage in child rearing.

When it comes to earnings, these factors offset the educational advantage held by women. Across all jobs and all earnings, women take home about 78 cents for every dollar earned by men. This has prompted calls for laws mandating paid maternity leave and legal guarantees that women who take time off from their careers to raise children not be demoted when they return to paid employment.

incentives. In addition, economic growth has allowed economies to preserve wilderness, create national parks and monuments, and clean up hazardous waste, while still enabling rising household incomes.

Is growth sustainable? Yes, say the proponents of growth. If we were depleting natural resources faster than we discover them, we would see the prices of those resources rise. That has not been the case for most natural resources; in fact, the prices of most of them have declined. And if one natural resource becomes too expensive, another resource will be substituted for it.

Moreover, say growth advocates, economic growth has to do with the expansion and application of human knowledge and information, not extractable natural resources. In this view, economic growth is limited only by human imagination.

8.5

▶ Critics of growth argue that it degrades the environment, increases human stress, and exhausts the earth's finite supply of natural resources.

▶ Defenders of growth say that it is the primary path to higher living standards, that it need not debase the environment, and that there are no indications that we are running out of resources.

▶ Defenders of growth argue that growth is sustainable because it is based on the expansion and application of human knowledge, which is limited only by human imagination.

Summary

LO8.1 Explain two ways to measure economic growth.
A nation's economic growth is measured either as an increase in real GDP over time or as an increase in real GDP per capita over time. Real GDP in the United States has grown at an average annual rate of about 3.0 percent since 1950; real GDP per capita has grown at roughly 1.9 percent annually over that same period.

LO8.2 Describe the institutional structures necessary for modern economic growth.
Sustained increases in real GDP per capita did not happen until the past two or so centuries, when England and then other countries began to experience modern economic growth, which is characterized by institutional structures that encourage savings, investment, and the development of new technologies. Institutional structures that promote growth include strong property rights, patents, efficient financial institutions, education, and a competitive market system.

Because technological leader countries have enjoyed up to two and a half centuries of modern economic growth, they now have much high standards of living compared with technological follower countries that have only recently begun to experience modern economic growth.

To continue raising living standards, rich leader countries must invent and apply new technologies; that limits their per-capita growth rates to about 2 percent per year. By contrast, poor follower countries can experience much faster catch-up growth by adopting, rather than reinventing, the institutions and cutting-edge technologies already developed by technological leader countries.

LO8.3 Identify the supply, demand, and efficiency forces that lead to economic growth.
The determinants of economic growth include four supply factors (changes in the quantity and quality of natural resources, changes in the quantity and quality of human resources, changes in the stock of capital goods, and improvements in technology), one demand factor (changes in total spending), and one efficiency factor (changes in how well an economy achieves allocative and productive efficiency).

The growth of a nation's capacity to produce output can be illustrated graphically by an outward shift of its production possibilities curve.

LO8.4 Describe the specific factors accounting for U.S. economic growth.
Growth accounting attributes increases in real GDP either to increases in the amount of labor being employed or to increases in the productivity of the labor being employed.

U.S. real GDP growth has been driven by increases in the productivity of labor. Those increases in labor productivity can be attributed to technological progress, increases in the quantity of capital per worker, improvements in the education and training of workers, the exploitation of economies of scale, and improvements in the allocation of labor across different industries.

LO8.5 Explain how U.S. productivity growth has fluctuated since 1973.
Over long time periods, the growth of labor productivity underlies an economy's growth of real wages and its standard of living. U.S. productivity rose by 1.5 percent annually between 1973 and 1995, 2.8 percent annually between 1995 and 2010, and just 1.2 percent annually from 2010 to 2021.

The 1995 to 2010 increase in the average rate of productivity growth was based on (a) rapid technological change in the form of the microchip and information technology, (b) new firms, increasing returns, and lower per-unit costs, and (c) heightened global competition that holds down prices.

The main sources of increasing returns are (a) the use of more specialized inputs as firms grow, (b) the spreading of development costs, (c) simultaneous consumption by consumers, (d) network effects, and (e) learning by doing. Increasing returns mean higher productivity and lower per-unit production costs.

Possible explanations for the slow productivity growth rate after the Great Recession of 2007–2009 include high debt levels, overcapacity, the rise of "free" Internet products, and a slowdown in technological innovation.

LO8.6 Discuss whether economic growth is desirable and sustainable.
Critics of rapid growth say that it degrades the environment, increases human stress, and depletes the earth's finite supply of natural resources. Defenders of rapid growth say that it is the primary path to the high and rising material standard of living that most people desire, that it need not debase the environment, and that there are no indications that we are running out of resources. Defenders argue that there are no natural limits to sustainable, environmentally friendly growth because growth is based on the expansion and application of human knowledge, which is limited only by human imagination.

Terms and Concepts

economic growth

real GDP per capita

rule of 70

modern economic growth

leader countries

follower countries

catch-up growth

supply factors (in growth)

demand factor (in growth)

efficiency factor (in growth)

labor productivity

labor-force participation rate

growth accounting

infrastructure

human capital

economies of scale

information technology

start-up firms

increasing returns

network effects

learning by doing

Discussion Questions

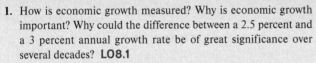

1. How is economic growth measured? Why is economic growth important? Why could the difference between a 2.5 percent and a 3 percent annual growth rate be of great significance over several decades? **LO8.1**
2. When and where did modern economic growth first happen? What are the major institutional factors that form the foundation for modern economic growth? What do they have in common? **LO8.2**
3. Why are some countries today much poorer than other countries? Are today's poor countries destined to always be poorer than today's rich countries? If so, explain why. If not, explain how today's poor countries can catch up to or even pass today's rich countries. **LO8.2**
4. What are the four supply factors of economic growth? What is the demand factor? What is the efficiency factor? Illustrate these factors in terms of the production possibilities curve. **LO8.3**
5. Suppose that Alpha and Omega have identically sized working-age populations but that total annual hours of work are much greater in Alpha than in Omega. Provide two possible reasons for this difference. **LO8.3**
6. What is growth accounting? To what extent have increases in U.S. real GDP resulted from more labor inputs? From greater labor productivity? Rearrange the following contributors to the growth of productivity in order of their quantitative importance: economies of scale, quantity of capital per worker, improved

resource allocation, education and training, and technological advance. **LO8.4**
7. True or False. If false, explain why: **LO8.4**
   a. Technological advance, which to date has played a relatively small role in U.S. economic growth, is destined to play a more important role in the future.
   b. Many public capital goods are complementary to private capital goods.
   c. Immigration has slowed economic growth in the United States.
8. Explain why there is such a close relationship between changes in a nation's rate of productivity growth and changes in its average real hourly wage. **LO8.5**
9. Relate each of the following to the 1995–2010 increase in the trend rate of productivity growth: **LO8.5**
   a. information technology
   b. increasing returns
   c. network effects
   d. global competition
10. What, if any, are the benefits and costs of economic growth, particularly as measured by real GDP per capita? **LO8.6**
11. **LAST WORD** Has female labor force participation increased or decreased in recent decades? What is the distribution of higher education degrees like across genders? Aside from discrimination, what are the reasons that women earn less than men on average, despite having higher levels of educational attainment?

Review Questions

1. If real GDP grows at 7 percent per year, then real GDP will double in approximately _____ years. **LO8.1**
   a. 70
   b. 14
   c. 10
   d. 7
2. In 1820, living standards in various places around the globe were _____ they are today. **LO8.2**
   a. more widely varying than
   b. just as widely varying as
   c. less widely varying than
3. True or False: Countries that currently have a low real GDP per capita are destined to always have lower living standards

than countries that currently have a high real GDP per capita. **LO8.2**
4. Identify each of the following situations as something that either promotes growth or inhibits growth. **LO8.2**
   a. Increasing corruption allows government officials to steal people's homes.
   b. A nation introduces patent laws for the first time.
   c. A court order shuts down all banks permanently.
   d. A poor country extends free public schooling from 8 years to 12 years.
   e. A nation adopts a free-trade policy.
   f. A formerly communist country adopts free markets.

5. Real GDP equals _____ times _____. **LO8.4**
   a. average hours of work; quantity of capital
   b. average hours of work; allocative efficiency
   c. labor input; labor productivity
   d. natural resources; improvements in technology

6. Suppose that just by doubling the amount of output that it produces each year, a firm's per-unit production costs fall by 30 percent. This result is an example of: **LO8.4**
   a. economies of scale.
   b. improved resource allocation.
   c. technological advance.
   d. the demand factor.

7. True or False: Computers and increased global competition have inhibited economic growth in recent decades. **LO8.5**

8. Identify the following arguments about economic growth as either antigrowth or pro-growth. **LO8.6**
   a. Growth means worker burnout and frantic schedules.
   b. Rising incomes allow people to buy more education, medical care, and recreation.
   c. Earth has only finite amounts of natural resources.
   d. Even the richest countries still have poverty, homelessness, and discrimination.
   e. Richer countries spend more money protecting the environment.
   f. Natural resource prices have fallen rather than increased over time.

Problems

1. Suppose an economy's real GDP is $30,000 in year 1 and $31,200 in year 2. What is the growth rate of its real GDP? Assume that the population is 100 in year 1 and 102 in year 2. What is the growth rate of real GDP per capita? **LO8.1**

2. What annual growth rate is needed for a country to double its output in 7 years? In 35 years? In 70 years? In 140 years? **LO8.1**

3. Assume that a leader country has real GDP per capita of $40,000, whereas a follower country has real GDP per capita of $20,000. Next suppose that the growth of real GDP per capita falls to zero percent in the leader country and rises to 7 percent in the follower country. If these rates continue for long periods of time, how many years will it take for the follower country to catch up to the living standard of the leader country? **LO8.2**

4. Refer to Figure 8.2 and assume that the values for points *a*, *b*, and *c* are $10 billion, $20 billion, and $18 billion, respectively. If the economy moves from point *a* to point *b* over a 10-year period, what must have been its annual rate of economic growth? If, instead, the economy was at point *c* at the end of the 10-year period, by what percentage did it fall short of its production capacity? **LO8.3**

5. Suppose that work hours in New Zombie are 200 in year 1, and productivity is $8 per hour worked. What is New Zombie's real GDP? If work hours increase to 210 in year 2 and productivity rises to $10 per hour, what is New Zombie's rate of economic growth? **LO8.4**

6. The per-unit cost of an item is its average total cost (= total cost/quantity). Suppose that a new smartphone app costs $100,000 to develop and only $0.50 per unit to deliver to each smartphone customer. What will be the per-unit cost of the app if it sells 100 units? 1,000 units? 1 million units? **LO8.5**

Business Cycles, Unemployment, and Inflation

>> LEARNING OBJECTIVES

LO9.1 Describe the phases of the business cycle.

LO9.2 Measure unemployment and explain the different types of unemployment.

LO9.3 Measure inflation and distinguish between cost-push inflation and demand-pull inflation.

LO9.4 Explain how unanticipated inflation can redistribute real income.

LO9.5 Describe how inflation may affect the economy's level of real output.

The United States has experienced remarkable economic growth over time. But this growth has not been smooth, steady, and predictable from year to year. At various times the United States has experienced recessions, high unemployment, and high inflation. For example, U.S. unemployment rose by 17 million workers and the unemployment rate increased from 3.5 percent to 14.8 percent at the start of the COVID-19 pandemic in 2020. Other nations have also suffered from high unemployment or substantial inflation in recent years. For example, the Greek unemployment rate exceeded 17 percent in 2019 and Venezuela's inflation rate soared to 1.4 *million* percent in 2018 before slowing to a relatively small 2,000 percent in 2022.

In this chapter, we examine the concepts, terminology, and facts relating to macroeconomic instability. Specifically, we discuss the business cycle, unemployment, and inflation.

The Business Cycle

In the United States, real GDP grows by about 3 percent per year, *on average*. So the long-run trend is up, as illustrated by the upsloping line labeled "Growth Trend" in Figure 9.1. There is, however, a lot of variation around the average growth trend. That's because the U.S. economy demonstrates a pattern of alternating rises and declines in the rate of economic activity.

Economists refer to this cyclical pattern as the **business cycle.** Individual cycles (one "up" followed by one "down") vary substantially in duration and intensity. So while each cycle has similar stages, no two are identical.

>> **LO9.1** Describe the phases of the business cycle.

business cycle Recurring increases and decreases in the level of economic activity over periods of years; consists of peak, recession, trough, and expansion phases.

FIGURE 9.1
The business cycle.

Economists distinguish four phases of the business cycle; the duration and strength of each phase may vary.

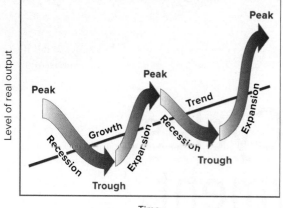

Phases of the Business Cycle

Figure 9.1 shows the four phases of a generalized business cycle:

- At a **peak,** business activity has reached a temporary maximum. Here the economy is near or at full employment, and the level of real output is at or very close to the economy's capacity. The price level is likely to rise during this phase.

- A **recession** is a period of decline in total output, income, and

peak The point in a *business cycle* at which business activity has reached a temporary maximum; the point at which an *expansion* ends and a *recession* begins. At the peak, the economy is near or at *full employment* and the level of real output is at or very close to the economy's capacity.

recession A period of declining *real GDP*, accompanied by lower *real income* and higher *unemployment*.

employment that lasts at least six months. Recessions generate a widespread contraction of business activity in many sectors of the economy. Along with a decline in real GDP, unemployment increases significantly. Table 9.1 documents the duration and intensity of the 11 recessions that the United States experienced between 1950 and 2020.

- In the **trough** of the recession or depression, output and employment "bottom out" at their lowest levels. The trough phase may be either short-lived or quite long.

- A recession is usually followed by a recovery and **expansion,** a period in which real GDP, income, and employment rise. At some point, the economy again approaches full employment. If spending then expands faster than production capacity, the prices of nearly all goods and services will rise, thereby generating a bout of inflation.

Although all business cycles pass through the same phases, they vary greatly in duration and intensity. Many economists prefer to talk of business fluctuations rather than business cycles because the word cycles implies regularity while the term fluctuations does not.

The Great Depression of the 1930s resulted in a 27 percent decline in U.S. real GDP over a 3-year period and seriously impaired business activity for a decade. By comparison, the more recent recessions detailed in Table 9.1 were less severe in both intensity and duration.

The Business Cycle Dating Committee of the National Bureau of Economic Research (NBER) declares the start and end of recessions in the United States. Citing evidence of declining real output and falling employment, the NBER officially declared that the pandemic recession of 2020—the shortest and sharpest on record—lasted from February to April of 2020, when the COVID-19 lockdowns shuttered businesses, causing output and employment to plummet.

Recessions occur in other countries, too. Nearly all industrial nations and many developing nations suffer recessions in any given decade. In addition, it should be pointed out that the worldwide COVID-19 pandemic was highly unusual in that it put all of the world's economies into recession simultaneously. Normally, recessions are only loosely correlated across countries, with many countries showing growth even as some others enter or exit recessions.

TABLE 9.1
U.S. Recessions between 1950 and 2020

Period	Duration, Months	Depth (Decline in Real Output)
1953–54	10	−2.6%
1957–58	8	−3.7
1960–61	10	−1.1
1969–70	11	−0.2
1973–75	16	−3.2
1980	6	−2.2
1981–82	16	−2.9
1990–91	8	−1.4
2001	8	−0.4
2007–09	18	−4.3
2020	2	−10.1

Source: National Bureau of Economic Research (NBER).

Causation: A First Glance

A key question in macroeconomics is why the economy experiences business cycle fluctuations rather than slow, smooth growth. In terms of Figure 9.1, why does output move up and down rather than just staying on the smooth trend line?

The most prominent theory is that business cycle fluctuations are the result of sticky prices interacting with economic shocks. As discussed in Chapter 26, economic shocks are events that unexpectedly shift demand or supply. If prices were fully flexible, markets could always adjust very quickly to unexpected shifts in demand or supply because market prices would rapidly adjust to equalize the quantities demanded and quantities supplied of every product in the economy. But the prices of many goods and services are, in fact, sticky (barely able to adjust) or stuck (completely unable to adjust) in the weeks and months after a shock occurs. As a result, the economy is forced to respond to shocks primarily through changes in output and employment rather than through changes in prices.

With these factors in mind, economists cite several sources for the demand and supply shocks that cause most business cycles.

- *Political events* Unexpected political events, such as peace treaties, new wars, or terrorist attacks, can create economic opportunities or strains. In adjusting to these shocks, the economy may experience upswings or downswings.

- *Financial instability* Unexpected financial bubbles (rapid asset price increases) or bursts (abrupt asset price decreases) can spill over to the general economy. They may expand or contract lending, and they may boost or erode the confidence of consumers and businesses. Booms and busts in the rest of the economy may follow.

- *Irregular innovation* Significant new products or production methods, such as those associated with railroads, automobiles, computers, and the Internet, can rapidly spread through the economy, sparking sizable increases in investment, consumption, output, and employment. After the economy has largely absorbed the new innovation, the economy may for a time slow down or even decline. Because such innovations occur irregularly and unexpectedly, they may contribute to the variability of economic activity.

- *Productivity changes* When productivity—output per unit of input—unexpectedly increases, the economy booms; when productivity unexpectedly decreases, the economy recedes. These changes in productivity can result from unexpected changes in resource availability (of, say, oil or agricultural commodities) or from unexpected changes in the general rate of technological advance.

- *Monetary factors* Some economists see business cycles as purely monetary phenomena. When a nation's central bank shocks the economy by creating more money than people were expecting, an inflationary boom in output occurs. By contrast, printing less money than people were expecting triggers an output decline and, eventually, a decrease in the price level.

The COVID-19 recession of 2020 was very unusual in that it was caused by a public health crisis rather than by a shock to one of the above factors. But do note that the onset of the pandemic was itself a shock since both the U.S. economy and much of the world economy had been growing handsomely during the prior few years and were expected to continue growing robustly before the pandemic struck.

Whatever the source of economic shocks, most economists agree that unexpected changes in the level of total spending cause the majority of cyclical fluctuations. If total spending unexpectedly sinks and firms cannot lower prices, firms sell fewer units of output (because with prices fixed, lower spending implies fewer items purchased). Slower sales cause firms to cut back on production. As they do, GDP falls. And because fewer workers are needed to produce less output, employment also falls. The economy contracts and enters a recession.

By contrast, if the level of spending unexpectedly rises, then output, employment, and incomes rise. With prices sticky, the increased spending means that consumers buy more goods and services (because, with prices fixed, more spending means more items purchased). Firms respond by increasing output, which increases GDP. And because firms need to hire more workers to produce the larger volume of output, employment also increases. The economy booms and enjoys an expansion. Eventually, as time passes and prices become more flexible, prices also rise due to the increased spending.

Cyclical Impact: Durables and Nondurables

Although the business cycle is felt throughout the economy, it affects different sectors in different ways and to different degrees.

Firms and industries producing *capital goods* (for example, housing, communications satellites, and heavy equipment) and *consumer durables* (for example, automobiles, personal computers, and refrigerators) are affected most by the business cycle. Within limits, firms can postpone the purchase

trough The point in a *business cycle* at which business activity has reached a temporary minimum; the point at which a *recession* ends and an *expansion* (recovery) begins. At the trough, the economy experiences substantial *unemployment* and *real GDP* is less than *potential output*.

expansion The phase of the *business cycle* in which *real GDP, income,* and employment rise.

of capital goods. When a recession strikes, firms patch up their old equipment and make do rather than replace the old equipment. As a result, investment in capital goods declines sharply. The pattern is much the same for consumer durables such as cars and refrigerators. When recession occurs and households must trim their budgets, they often defer their purchases of these goods. Families repair their old cars and appliances rather than buy new ones, and the firms producing these products suffer. (However, producers of capital goods and consumer durables also benefit most from expansions.)

In contrast, *service* industries and industries that produce *nondurable consumer goods* are somewhat insulated from the recession's most severe effects. People find it difficult to cut back on needed medical and legal services, for example. And a recession actually helps some service firms, such as pawnbrokers and law firms that specialize in bankruptcy. Nor are the purchases of many nondurable goods, such as food and clothing, easy to postpone. As a result, the quantity and quality of the nondurable goods that are purchased will decline, but not by as much as the quantity and quality of the capital goods and consumer durables that are purchased.

QUICK REVIEW 9.1

▸ The typical business cycle goes through four phases: peak, recession, trough, and expansion.

▸ Fluctuations in output and employment are caused by economic shocks combined with sticky prices.

▸ Sources of shocks include irregular innovation, productivity changes, monetary factors, political events, financial instability, and major public health emergencies (like the COVID-19 pandemic).

▸ During a recession, industries that produce capital goods and consumer durables normally suffer greater output and employment declines than industries that produce services or nondurable consumer goods.

Unemployment

>> LO9.2 Measure unemployment and explain the different types of unemployment.

Two problems that arise over the course of the business cycle are unemployment and inflation. Let's look at unemployment first.

Measurement of Unemployment

The U.S. Bureau of Labor Statistics (BLS) conducts a nationwide random survey of some 60,000 households each month to determine who is employed and who is not. It asks which members of the household are working, unemployed and looking for work, not looking for work, and so on. From the answers, it determines the nation's unemployment rate for the month.

Figure 9.2 explains the mathematics.

To construct Figure 9.2, the BLS divides the total U.S. population into four groups:

FIGURE 9.2
The U.S. labor force, employment and unemployment, 2021.

The labor force consists of persons 16 years of age or older who are not in institutions and who are (1) employed or (2) unemployed but seeking employment.

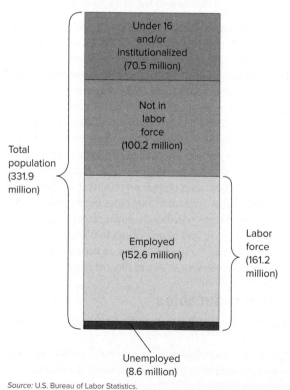

Source: U.S. Bureau of Labor Statistics.

- *Under 16 and/or institutionalized* is composed of people under 16 years of age, active duty military personnel, and individuals who are living in psychological hospitals, correctional institutions, or skilled nursing facilities. These people are assumed to be unemployable in the private sector either because of child labor laws, military obligations, or the circumstances that accompany institutionalization.

- *Not in labor force* is composed of noninstitutionalized people 16 years of age or older who are neither employed nor seeking work. They include stay-at-home parents, full-time students, and retirees.

- *Employed* consists of noninstitutionalized people age 16 and older who have jobs. These are people who both want to work *and* have a job.

- *Unemployed* consists of every noninstitutionalized person age 16 or older who is not employed but who wants to work and is actively seeking employment. (Please note that to be classified as unemployed, a person has to not only want a job but also be *actively seeking employment*. A person who claims to want a job but who isn't bothering to look for work is classified as "not in labor force.")

The **labor force** consists of the latter two groups—the employed plus the unemployed. The labor force includes anyone who has a job plus anyone lacking a job who is actively seeking employment.

The **unemployment rate** is the percentage of the labor force that is unemployed:

$$\text{Unemployment rate} = \frac{\text{unemployed}}{\text{labor force}} \times 100$$

The statistics underlying the rounded numbers in Figure 9.2 show that in 2021 the unemployment rate averaged

$$\frac{8,600,000}{161,200,000} \times 100 = 5.3\%$$

Despite the use of scientific sampling and interviewing techniques, the data collected by the monthly BLS surveys are subject to the following criticisms:

- *Part-time employment* The BLS lists all part-time workers as fully employed. In 2021 about 28 million people worked part-time as a result of personal choice. But another 5 million part-time workers either (1) wanted to work full-time and could not find a full-time job or (2) worked fewer part-time hours than desired. By counting them as fully employed, critics say, the BLS understates the unemployment rate.

- *Discouraged workers* You must be actively seeking work to be counted as unemployed. But many jobless people who actively search for employment become discouraged after a period of unsuccessful efforts. They stop actively searching for employment and get reclassified as "not in the labor force." According to critics, that reclassification understates the unemployment problem. The discouraged workers still want jobs, but are missing entirely in the official unemployment statistics. The number of such **discouraged workers** was roughly 463,000 in 2021, down from 657,000 in 2020.

Types of Unemployment

There are three types of unemployment: frictional, structural, and cyclical.

Frictional Unemployment At any given time some workers are "between jobs." Some of them are moving voluntarily from one job to another. Others have been fired and are seeking reemployment. Still others have been laid off because they work seasonal jobs and the season just changed. In addition to those between jobs, there are always many young workers searching for their first job.

As these unemployed people find jobs or are called back from temporary layoffs, other job seekers and laid-off workers replace them in the "unemployment pool." While the pool itself persists because newly unemployed workers are always flowing into it, most workers do not stay in the unemployment pool for very long. Indeed, when the economy is strong, most unemployed workers find new jobs within a couple of months. We should be careful not to confuse the permanence of the pool itself with the false idea that the pool's membership is permanent, too. That being said, there are workers who do remain unemployed and in the unemployment pool for many months or even several years.

Economists use the term **frictional unemployment,** or search unemployment, for workers who are unemployed as they actively search for a job. The word "frictional" reflects the fact that the labor market does not operate perfectly and instantaneously (without friction) in matching workers and jobs.

Frictional unemployment is inevitable and, at least in part, desirable. Many workers who are voluntarily between jobs are moving from low-paying, low-productivity jobs to higher-paying, higher-productivity positions. Their new jobs mean greater income for the workers, a better allocation of labor resources, and a larger real GDP for the economy.

Structural Unemployment Frictional unemployment blurs into **structural unemployment.** Changes over time in consumer demand and in technology alter the "structure" of the total demand for labor, both occupationally and geographically.

labor force Persons 16 years of age and older who are not in institutions and who are employed or are unemployed and seeking work.

unemployment rate The percentage of the *labor force* unemployed at any time.

discouraged workers Employees who have left the *labor force* because they have not been able to find employment.

frictional unemployment A type of unemployment caused by workers voluntarily changing jobs and by temporary layoffs; unemployed workers between jobs.

structural unemployment *Unemployment* of workers whose skills are not demanded by employers, who lack sufficient skill to obtain employment, or who cannot easily move to locations where jobs are available.

Occupationally, the demand for certain skills (for example, sewing clothes or working on farms) may decline or even vanish. The demand for other skills (for example, designing software or maintaining computer networks) will intensify. Structural unemployment occurs because the composition of the labor force does not respond immediately or completely to the new structure of job opportunities. Workers whose skills and experience have become obsolete or unneeded thus find that they have no marketable talents. They are structurally unemployed until they develop skills that employers want.

Geographically, the demand for labor also changes over time. An example is the migration of industry and thus of employment opportunities from the Snowbelt to the Sunbelt over the past few decades. Another example is the *offshoring* of jobs that occurs when the demand for a particular type of labor shifts from domestic firms to foreign firms. As job opportunities shift from one place to another, some workers become structurally unemployed.

The distinction between frictional and structural unemployment is hazy. The key difference is that *frictionally* unemployed workers have marketable skills and either live in areas where jobs exist or are able to move to areas that have job opportunities. *Structurally* unemployed workers find it hard to obtain new jobs without retraining, additional education, or moving to a new area. Frictional unemployment is short-term; structural unemployment is more likely to be long-term and consequently more serious.

Cyclical Unemployment Unemployment that is caused by a decline in total spending is called **cyclical unemployment.** It typically begins in the recession phase of the business cycle. As the demand for goods and services decreases, employment falls and unemployment rises. Cyclical unemployment results from insufficient demand for goods and services and is exacerbated by the downward stickiness of wages in the economy, as discussed in the nearby Consider This story. The 25 percent unemployment rate in the depth of the Great Depression in 1933 reflected mainly cyclical unemployment.

We will say more about the high costs of cyclical unemployment later, but first we need to define "full employment."

cyclical unemployment A type of *unemployment* caused by insufficient total spending (insufficient *aggregate demand*) and which typically begins in the *recession* phase of the *business cycle*.

CONSIDER THIS . . .

Downwardly Sticky Wages and Unemployment

Labor markets have an important quirk that helps to explain why unemployment goes up so much during a recession.

The quirk is that wages are flexible upward but sticky downward.

On the one hand, workers are perfectly happy to accept wage increases. So when the economy is booming and firms start bidding for the limited supply of labor, wages rise—often quite rapidly.

On the other hand, workers deeply resent pay cuts. So if the economy goes into a recession and firms need to reduce labor costs, managers almost never cut wages because doing so would only lead to disgruntled employees, low productivity, and—in extreme cases—workers stealing supplies or actively sabotaging their own firms.

Instead, managers usually opt for layoffs. The workers who are let go obviously don't like being unemployed. But those who remain get to keep their old wages. As a result, they keep on being as productive and cooperative as they were before.

The preference that managers show for layoffs over wage cuts results in downwardly sticky wages and an informal price floor that help to explain why unemployment goes up so much during a recession. The problem is that when the demand for labor falls during a recession, the informal

Jamie Grill/JGI/Blend Images/Getty Images

price floor prevents wages from falling. As a result, there is no way for falling wages to help entice at least some firms to hire a few more workers. Thus, when a recession hits, employment falls more precipitously than it would have if wages had been downwardly flexible.

Definition of Full Employment

Because frictional and structural unemployment are largely unavoidable in a dynamic economy, *full employment* is something less than 100 percent employment of the labor force. Economists say that the economy is "fully employed" when it is experiencing only frictional and structural unemployment. That is, full employment occurs when there is no cyclical unemployment.

Economists label the unemployment rate that is consistent with full employment as the **full-employment rate of unemployment,** or the **natural rate of unemployment (NRU).** At the NRU, the economy is said to be producing its **potential output,** the real GDP that occurs when the labor force and other inputs are "fully employed."

Note that a fully employed economy does not mean zero unemployment. Even when the economy is fully employed, the NRU is some positive percentage because it takes time for frictionally unemployed job seekers to find jobs. Also, it takes time for the structurally unemployed to achieve the skills needed for reemployment.

"Natural" does not mean that the economy will always operate at the NRU and thus realize its potential output. When cyclical unemployment occurs, the economy has much more unemployment than it would at the NRU. Moreover, the economy can operate for a while at an unemployment rate *below* the NRU. At times, the demand for labor may be so great that firms take a stronger initiative to hire and train the structurally unemployed. Also, some parents, teenagers, college students, and retirees who were casually looking for just the right part-time or full-time jobs may quickly find them. Thus the unemployment rate temporarily falls below the natural rate.

Also note that the NRU can vary over time as demographic factors, job-search methods, and public policies change. In the 1980s, the NRU was about 6 percent. Today, it is estimated to be between 3 and 4 percent.

Economic Cost of Unemployment

High unemployment involves heavy economic and social costs.

The GDP Gap The basic economic cost of unemployment is forgone output. When the economy fails to create enough jobs for all who are able and willing to work, potential production is irretrievably lost. Unemployment above the natural rate means that society is operating at some point inside its production possibilities curve. Economists call this sacrifice of output a **GDP gap**—the difference between actual and potential GDP. That is:

$$GDP\ gap = actual\ GDP - potential\ GDP$$

The GDP gap can be either negative or positive:

- When unemployment is above the natural rate of unemployment, the GDP gap will be negative (actual GDP < potential GDP) because only a smaller amount of output can be produced when employing a smaller amount of labor.

- By contrast, when unemployment is below the natural rate, the GDP gap will be positive (actual GDP > potential GDP) because the large quantity of labor being utilized allows the economy to produce more than the full-employment level of output.

To calculate potential GDP at any point in time, the BLS estimates what the economy's output would be at that instant if the actual unemployment rate equaled the natural rate of unemployment. Figure 9.3a shows the U.S. GDP gap for recent years while Figure 9.3b shows the actual unemployment rate over the same time period. Please note the close correlation between the actual unemployment rate (Figure 9.3b) and the GDP gap (Figure 9.3a). The higher the unemployment rate, the larger the GDP gap.

Okun's Law Arthur Okun was the first macroeconomist to quantify the inverse relationship between the actual unemployment rate and the GDP gap. He noticed that, on average:

$$GDP\ gap = -2.0 \times (actual\ unemployment\ rate - natural\ unemployment\ rate)$$

This relationship came to be known as **Okun's law.** With respect to recessions, it implies that for every 1 percentage point by which the actual unemployment rate exceeds the natural rate, a GDP gap of about negative 2.0 percent will occur.

full-employment rate of unemployment The *unemployment rate* at which there is no *cyclical unemployment* of the *labor force;* equal to around 4 percent (rather than zero percent) in the United States because *frictional* and *structural unemployment* are unavoidable.

natural rate of unemployment (NRU) The *full-employment rate of unemployment;* the *unemployment rate* occurring when there is no cyclical unemployment and the economy is achieving its *potential output;* the unemployment rate at which actual *inflation* equals expected inflation.

potential output The real output (*GDP*) an economy can produce when it fully employs its available resources.

GDP gap Actual *gross domestic product* minus *potential output;* may be either a positive amount (a *positive GDP gap*) or a negative amount (a *negative GDP gap*).

Okun's law The generalization that any 1-percentage-point rise in the *unemployment rate* above the *full-employment rate of unemployment* is associated with a rise in the *negative GDP gap* by 2 percent of *potential output* (potential *GDP*).

FIGURE 9.3 **Actual and potential real GDP and the unemployment rate.**

(a) The difference between actual and potential GDP is the GDP gap. A negative GDP gap measures the output the economy sacrifices when actual GDP falls short of potential GDP. A positive GDP gap indicates that actual GDP is above potential GDP. (b) A high unemployment rate means a large GDP gap (negative), and a low unemployment rate means a small or even positive GDP gap.

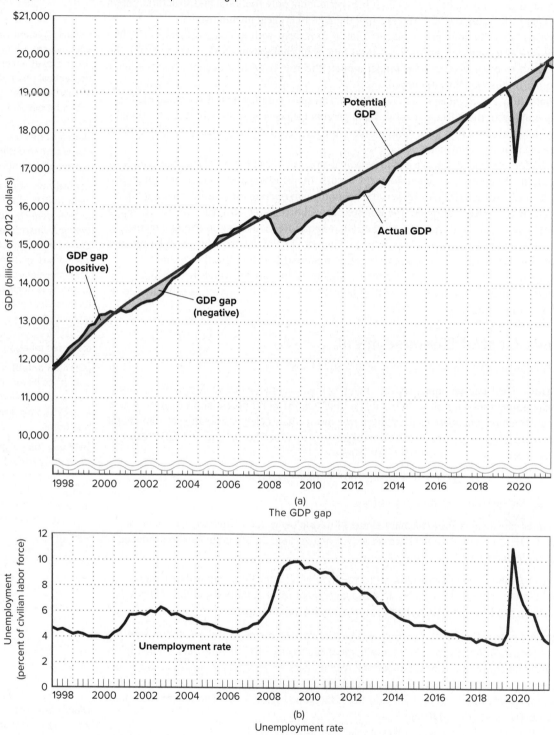

Sources: Congressional Budget Office; Bureau of Economic Analysis; and Bureau of Labor Statistics.

By applying Okun's law, we can calculate the absolute loss of output associated with any above-natural unemployment rate. For example, in 2020 the average monthly unemployment rate was 8.1 percent, or 4.6 percentage points above that period's 3.5 percent natural rate of unemployment. Multiplying this 4.6 percent by Okun's negative 2.0 indicates that 2020's GDP gap was approximately negative 9.2 percent of potential GDP (in real terms). Applying this 9.2 percent loss of output to 2020's potential GDP of $19,344 billion, we find that the economy sacrificed $1,780 billion of real output.

As Figure 9.3 shows, sometimes the economy's actual output exceeds its potential or full-employment output. An unusually strong economic expansion in 1999 and 2000, for example, caused actual GDP to exceed potential GDP, thereby generating a positive GDP gap for those two years. You should note, though, that while actual GDP can exceed potential GDP for a time, positive GDP gaps create strong demand-pull inflationary pressures and cannot be sustained indefinitely.

Unequal Burdens An increase in the unemployment rate from, say, 5 percent to 9 or 10 percent might be more tolerable to society if every worker's hours and income were reduced proportionally. But this is not the case. The burden of unemployment is unequally distributed. Some workers retain their hours and income, while others become unemployed and earn nothing.

Table 9.2 examines unemployment rates for both the overall labor force and various demographic subgroups. We look at the years 2019 and 2020 as a way of investigating how unemployment varies over the course of the business cycle. In 2019, for example, the business cycle reached a peak, with the unemployment rate averaging 3.7 percent over the year. The economy then receded quickly in the spring of 2020 when the COVID-19 lockdowns began. The unemployment rate increased, with the average monthly unemployment rate equaling 8.1 percent during 2020.

TABLE 9.2
Unemployment Rates by Demographic Group: Full Employment (2019) and Recession (2020)*

Demographic Group	Unemployment Rate 2019	Unemployment Rate 2020
Overall	3.7%	8.1%
Occupation:		
Management and professional occupations	2.0	4.5
Production occupations	3.9	9.0
Age:		
16–19	12.7	17.9
African American, 16–19	20.8	24.8
White, 16–19	11.5	17.0
Female, 20+	3.3	8.0
Male, 20+	3.4	7.4
Race and ethnicity:		
African American	6.1	11.4
Hispanic	4.3	10.4
Asian	2.7	8.7
White	3.3	7.3
Gender:		
Women	3.6	8.4
Men	3.7	7.8
Education:[†]		
Less than high school diploma	5.4	11.7
High school diploma only	3.7	9.0
College degree or more	2.1	4.8
Duration:		
15 or more weeks	2.8	4.2

*Civilian labor force data.
†People age 25 or over.

Sources: *Economic Report of the President 2019*, Bureau of Labor Statistics, Census Bureau.

By observing the large differences in unemployment rates in 2019 and 2020 for different demographic subgroups, we can generalize as follows:

- *Occupation* Workers in lower-skilled occupations (for example, laborers) have higher unemployment rates than workers in higher-skilled occupations (for example, professionals). Lower-skilled workers have more and longer spells of structural unemployment than higher-skilled workers. They also are less likely to be self-employed than are higher-skilled workers. Manufacturing, construction, and mining workers tend to be particularly hard-hit, but businesses generally retain most of their higher-skilled workers, in whom they have invested the expense of training.

- *Age* Teenagers have much higher unemployment rates than adults. Teenagers have lower skill levels, quit their jobs more frequently, are more frequently fired, and have less geographic mobility than adults. Many unemployed teenagers are new in the labor market, searching for their first jobs. Male African American teenagers, in particular, have very high unemployment rates. The unemployment rate for all teenagers rises during recessions.

- *Race and ethnicity* The unemployment rates of African Americans and Hispanics exceed the white unemployment rate at all stages of the business cycle. The causes include lower rates of educational attainment, greater concentration in lower-skilled occupations, and discrimination in the labor market. In general, the unemployment rate for African Americans is about twice that of whites and rises by about twice as many percentage points during most recessions.

- *Gender* The unemployment rates for men and women normally are very similar. But during the 2020 recession, the unemployment rate of women exceeded that of men, a fact attributable at least in part to women leaving the labor force in greater numbers than men to either care for sick family members or to provide at-home supervision for children whose schools switched from in-person instruction to distance learning during the pandemic.

- *Education* Less-educated workers, on average, have higher unemployment rates than workers with more education. Less education is usually associated with lower-skilled, less-permanent jobs; more time between jobs; and jobs that are more vulnerable to cyclical layoff.

- *Duration* The number of persons unemployed for long periods—15 weeks or more—as a percentage of the labor force is much lower than the overall unemployment rate. But that percentage rises significantly during recessions. Notice that it rose from 2.8 percent of the labor force in 2019 to 4.2 percent in 2020.

Noneconomic Costs

Policymakers are deeply concerned with unemployment rates and how to minimize the length and depth of business cycle downturns as a way of moderating the harm caused by unemployment. Their attention is warranted because severe cyclical unemployment is more than an economic malady; it is a social catastrophe.

- At the individual level, research links high unemployment to increases in suicide, homicide, heart attacks, strokes, and mental illness. The unemployed lose skills and self-respect. Morale plummets and families disintegrate. Widespread joblessness increases poverty, reduces hope for material advancement, and heightens ethnic tensions.

- At the social level, severe unemployment can lead to rapid and sometimes violent political upheaval. Witness Adolph Hitler's ascent to power against a background of unemployment in Germany.

QUICK REVIEW 9.2

- There are three types of unemployment: frictional, structural, and cyclical.
- The natural rate of unemployment (frictional plus structural) is presently around 3.5 percent in the United States.
- A positive GDP gap occurs when actual GDP exceeds potential GDP; a negative GDP gap occurs when actual GDP falls short of potential GDP.
- According to Okun's law, for each 1 percentage point of unemployment above the natural rate, the U.S. economy suffers an additional 2 percent decline in real GDP below potential GDP.
- Lower-skilled workers, teenagers, African Americans and Hispanics, and less-educated workers bear a disproportionate burden of unemployment.

Inflation

Inflation is a rise in the general level of prices. When inflation occurs, each dollar of income buys fewer goods and services than before. Inflation reduces the "purchasing power" of money. But inflation does not mean that all prices are rising. Even during periods of rapid inflation, some prices may be relatively constant, while others may even fall. For example, although the United States experienced high rates of inflation in the 1970s and early 1980s, the prices of video recorders, digital watches, and personal computers declined.

Measurement of Inflation

The **Consumer Price Index (CPI)** is the main measure of inflation in the United States. The government uses this index to report inflation rates each month and each year. It also uses the CPI to adjust Social Security benefits and income tax brackets for inflation. The CPI reports the price of a "market basket" of some 300 consumer goods and services that are purchased by typical urban consumers.

The composition of the market basket for the CPI is based on spending patterns of urban consumers in a specific period, presently 2013–2014. The BLS updates the composition of the market basket every few years so that it reflects the most recent patterns of consumer purchases and captures current inflation.

The BLS arbitrarily sets the CPI equal to 100 for 1982–1984. So the CPI for any particular year is calculated as follows:

$$CPI = \frac{\text{price of the most recent market basket in the particular year}}{\text{price estimate of the market basket in 1982–1984}} \times 100$$

The inflation rate is equal to the percentage growth of CPI from one year to the next. For example, the CPI was 278.8 in 2021, up from 260.5 in 2020. So the rate of inflation for 2021 is calculated as follows:

$$\text{Rate of inflation} = \frac{278.8 - 260.5}{260.5} \times 100 = 7.0\%$$

In rare cases, the CPI declines from one year to the next. For example, the CPI fell from 215.3 in 2008 to 214.5 in 2009. So the rate of inflation for 2009 was −0.4 percent. A decline in the price level is called **deflation.**

In Chapter 28, we discussed the *rule of 70,* which tells us that we can find the number of years it will take for some measure to double, assuming that it grows at a constant annual percentage rate. To do so, we divide the number 70 by the annual percentage growth rate. Inflation is the growth rate of the price level. So a 3 percent annual rate of inflation will double the price level in about 23 (= 70 ÷ 3) years. Inflation of 8 percent per year will double the price level in about 9 (= 70 ÷ 8) years.

Facts of Inflation

Figure 9.4 shows December-to-December rates of annual inflation in the United States between 1960 and 2021. Observe that inflation reached double-digit rates in the 1970s and early 1980s

>> **LO9.3** Measure inflation and distinguish between cost-push inflation and demand-pull inflation.

inflation A rise in the general level of *prices* in an economy; an increase in an economy's *price level*.

Consumer Price Index (CPI) An index that measures the prices of a fixed "market basket" of some 300 goods and services bought by a "typical" consumer.

deflation A decline in the general level of *prices* in an economy; a decline in an economy's *price level*.

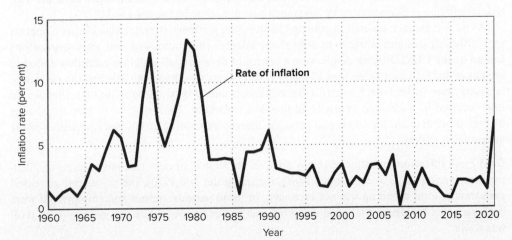

FIGURE 9.4
Annual inflation rates in the United States, 1960–2021 (December-to-December changes in the CPI).

Since 1960, the major periods of rapid inflation in the United States were in the 1970s, early 1980s, and in the wake of the COVID-19 pandemic.

Source: U.S. Bureau of Labor Statistics.

GLOBAL PERSPECTIVE 9.1

INFLATION RATES IN FIVE INDUSTRIAL NATIONS, 2010–2021

Inflation rates in the United States in recent years were neither extraordinarily high nor extraordinarily low relative to rates in other industrial nations, but did spike higher than the inflation rates of many other countries when the COVID 10 pandemic struck in 2020.

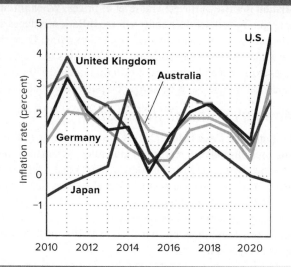

Source: International Monetary Fund.

Note: These are annual average inflation rates, which do not align directly with the December-to-December inflation rates shown in Figure 9.4 for the United States.

before declining. It remained muted during the decade or so following the Great Recession of 2007–2009 but then popped up to 7.0 percent in 2021 as the result of the COVID-19 pandemic, the ensuing supply chain disruptions, and how the federal government responded to the crisis in terms of generously distributing anti-recessionary stimulus funds.

Although the U.S. inflation rate spiked upward toward 10 percent after the COVID-19 pandemic, it was still the case that the U.S. inflation rate has been neither unusually high nor unusually low relative to the inflation rates typical of industrial nations, which saw a similar spike in inflation after the COVID-19 pandemic (see Global Perspective 9.1). By contrast, some other nations (not shown) have had extremely high annual rates of inflation in recent years independent of the COVID-19 pandemic. In 2020, for example, the annual inflation rate in Zimbabwe was 557 percent; Venezuela, 255 percent; Lebanon, 155 percent; and Sudan, 150 percent.

Types of Inflation

Nearly all prices in the economy are set by supply and demand. So if the overall price level is rising, we need to look for an explanation in terms of supply and demand.

Demand-Pull Inflation Usually, increases in the price level are caused by an excess of total spending beyond the economy's capacity to produce. Where inflation is rapid and sustained for long periods, the cause is invariably an overissuance of money by the central bank (the Federal Reserve in the United States) that leads to excessive spending and demand. When resources are already fully employed, the business sector cannot respond to that excess demand by expanding output. The excess demand bids up the prices of the limited output, producing **demand-pull inflation.** This type of inflation is characterized by "too much spending chasing too few goods."

> **demand-pull inflation**
> Increases in the *price level* (*inflation*) resulting from increases in *aggregate demand*.

As we will explain in detail in coming chapters, the generous stimulus checks that Congress sent to businesses and workers to help them weather the shutdowns and work disruptions caused by the COVID-19 pandemic were a source of demand-pull inflation until they ended in the fall of 2021. In particular, tens of millions of workers who had been idled by the pandemic received more income each month from enhanced unemployment benefits than they would have received in wages and salaries had they been working. That increase in spending power increased the demand for goods and services, thereby generating inflationary pressures of the demand-pull variety.

Cost-Push Inflation Inflation also may arise on the supply, or cost, side of the economy. During some periods in U.S. economic history, including the mid-1970s, the price level increased even though total spending was not excessive. In these periods, output and employment were both *declining* (evidence that total spending was not excessive) while the general price level was *rising*.

The theory of **cost-push inflation** explains rising output prices in terms of factors that raise **per-unit production costs** at each level of spending. Rising per-unit production costs squeeze profits and reduce the amount of output firms are willing to supply at the existing price level. As a result, the economy's supply of goods and services declines, and the price level rises.

$$\text{Per-unit production cost} = \frac{\text{total input cost}}{\text{units of output}}$$

In this scenario, costs are *pushing* the price level upward, whereas in demand-pull inflation demand is *pulling* it upward.

The major source of cost-push inflation has been *supply shocks*. Specifically, abrupt increases in the costs of productive inputs have occasionally driven up per-unit production costs and thus product prices. The rocketing prices of imported oil in 1973–1974 and again in 1979–1980 are good illustrations. As energy prices surged upward during these periods, the costs of producing and transporting virtually every product in the economy rose. Cost-push inflation ensued.

The COVID-19 pandemic caused supply shocks in the form of disruptions to the *supply chain* by which raw materials get transformed into finished products that must then be distributed to consumers. With employees locked down at home in various countries for various lengths of time, the economy's normal flow of production and distribution was disrupted. Shortages of labor and other inputs increased per-unit production costs. Inflation erupted in economies around the world in 2021 as cost-push inflation (caused by supply chain disruptions) reinforced demand-pull inflation (generated by stimulus spending).

Core Inflation

The inflation statistics calculated by the BLS are supposed to reflect the general trend in overall prices. That general trend can be obscured, though, by the rapid up and down price movements typical of energy and food products like wheat, gasoline, corn, and natural gas.

To avoid being misled by these rapid but temporary price changes, BLS employees calculate a measure of inflation called **core inflation** that excludes food and energy items.

If core inflation is low and stable, policymakers may be satisfied with current policy even though changes in the overall CPI index may be suggesting a rising inflation rate. But policymakers become greatly concerned when core inflation is high and rising, and they take deliberate measures to try to halt it.

We discuss these policy actions in detail in later chapters, but at this point it is important to add that the Federal Reserve (the U.S. central bank) has set a 2-percent inflation target since 2012, with the promise that it will adjust monetary policy as necessary to keep the U.S. inflation rate at or near 2 percent per year.

> **cost-push inflation**
> Increases in the *price level* (*inflation*) resulting from an increase in resource costs (for example, raw-material prices) and hence in *per-unit production costs*; inflation caused by reductions in *aggregate supply*.

> **per-unit production cost** The average production cost of a particular level of output; total input cost divided by units of output.

> **core inflation** The underlying increases in the *price level* after volatile food and energy *prices* are removed.

QUICK REVIEW
9.3

- ▶ Inflation is a rising general level of prices and is measured as a percentage change in a price index such as the CPI; deflation is a decline in the general level of prices.

- ▶ Demand-pull inflation occurs when total spending exceeds the economy's ability to provide goods and services at the existing price level; total spending *pulls* the price level upward.

- ▶ Cost-push inflation occurs when factors such as rapid increases in the prices of imported raw materials drive up per-unit production costs; higher costs *push* the price level upward.

- ▶ Core inflation is the underlying inflation rate after volatile food and energy prices have been removed.

Redistribution Effects of Inflation

Inflation redistributes real income. This redistribution helps some people, hurts other people, and leaves yet others largely unaffected. Who gets hurt? Who benefits? Who is unaffected? Before we can answer those questions, we need some terminology.

Nominal and Real Income

There is a difference between money (nominal) income and real income. **Nominal income** is the number of dollars received as wages, rent, interest, or profit. **Real income** measures the amount of

> **>> LO9.4** Explain how unanticipated inflation can redistribute real income.

> **nominal income** The number of dollars received by an individual or group for its *resources* during some period of time.

real income The amount of *goods* and *services* that can be purchased with *nominal income* during some period of time; nominal income adjusted for *inflation*.

goods and services that nominal income can buy; it is the purchasing power of nominal income, or income adjusted for inflation, and it is calculated as follows:

$$\text{Real income} = \frac{\text{nominal income}}{\text{price index (in hundredths)}}$$

Inflation need not alter an economy's overall real income—its total purchasing power. The above equation makes it clear that real income will remain the same when nominal income rises at the same percentage rate as the price index.

But when inflation occurs, not everyone's nominal income rises at the same pace as the price level. Therein lies the potential for a redistribution of real income. If the change in the price level differs from the change in a person's nominal income, his or her real income will be affected. The following approximation (shown by the ≅ sign) tells us roughly how much real income will change:

Percentage		percentage		percentage
change in	≅	change in	−	change in
real income		nominal income		price level

For example, suppose that the price level rises by 6 percent. If Bob's nominal income rises by 6 percent, his real income will *remain unchanged*. But if his nominal income instead rises by 10 percent, his real income will increase by about 4 percent. If Bob's nominal income rises by only 2 percent, his real income will *decline* by about 4 percent.

Anticipations

The redistribution effects of inflation depend on whether or not it is expected:

unanticipated inflation An increase of the *price level* (*inflation*) at a rate greater than expected.

anticipated inflation Increases in the *price level* (*inflation*) that occur at the expected rate.

- We will first discuss situations involving **unanticipated inflation,** which causes real income and wealth to be redistributed, harming some and benefiting others.

- We will then discuss situations involving **anticipated inflation,** in which people see an inflation coming. With the ability to plan ahead, people are able to avoid or lessen the redistribution effects of inflation.

Who Is Hurt by Inflation?

Unanticipated inflation hurts fixed-income recipients, savers, and creditors. It redistributes real income away from them and toward others.

Fixed-Income Receivers People whose incomes are fixed see their real incomes fall when unanticipated inflation occurs. The classic case is the elderly couple living on a private pension or annuity that provides a fixed amount of nominal income each month. They may have retired in, say, 2004 on what appeared to be an adequate pension. However, by 2022, they would have discovered that inflation had cut the annual purchasing power of that pension—their real income—by one-third.

Similarly, landlords who receive lease payments of fixed dollar amounts are hurt by inflation as they receive dollars of declining value over time. Likewise, public sector workers whose incomes are based on fixed pay schedules may see a decrease in their purchasing power. The fixed "steps" (the upward yearly increases) in their pay schedules may not keep up with inflation. Minimum-wage workers and families living on fixed welfare incomes are also hurt by inflation.

Savers Unanticipated inflation hurts savers. As prices rise, the real value (purchasing power) of accumulated savings deteriorates. Paper assets such as savings accounts, insurance policies, and annuities that were once adequate to meet rainy-day contingencies or provide for a comfortable retirement decline in real value. The simplest case is the person who hoards cash. A $1,000 cash balance lost about 20 percent of its real value between 2012 and 2022. Of course, most forms of savings earn interest. But the value of savings will still decline if the inflation rate exceeds the interest rate.

Creditors Unanticipated inflation harms creditors (lenders). Suppose Chase Bank lends Bob $1,000, to be repaid in two years. If in that time the price level doubles, the $1,000 that Bob repays will possess only half the purchasing power of the $1,000 he borrowed. As prices go up, the purchasing power of the dollar goes down. So the borrower pays back less-valuable dollars than those received from the lender. The owners of Chase Bank suffer a loss of real income.

Who Is Unaffected or Helped by Inflation?

Not everyone is hurt by unanticipated inflation.

Flexible-Income Receivers People who have flexible incomes may escape inflation's harm or even benefit from it. For example, individuals who derive their incomes solely from Social Security are largely unaffected by inflation because Social Security payments are *indexed* to the CPI. Nominal benefits automatically increase when the CPI increases, thus preventing inflation from eroding their purchasing power. Some union workers also get automatic **cost-of-living adjustments (COLAs)** in their pay when the CPI rises, although such increases rarely equal the full percentage rise in inflation.

In addition, some flexible-income receivers are helped by unanticipated inflation. The strong product demand and labor shortages implied by rapid demand-pull inflation may cause some nominal incomes to spurt ahead of the price level, thereby enhancing real incomes. For some, the 3 percent increase in nominal income that occurs when inflation is 2 percent may become a 7 percent increase when inflation is 5 percent. As an example, property owners faced with an inflation-induced real estate boom may be able to boost rents by more than the inflation rate. Also, some business owners may benefit from inflation. If product prices rise faster than resource prices, business revenues will increase more rapidly than costs.

Debtors Unanticipated inflation benefits debtors (borrowers). In our earlier example, Chase Bank's loss of real income from inflation is Bob's gain of real income. Debtor Bob borrows "dear" dollars but, because of inflation, pays back the principal and interest with "cheap" dollars whose purchasing power has been eroded by inflation. Real income is redistributed away from the owners of Chase Bank toward borrowers such as Bob.

The federal government, which had amassed over $29 trillion of public debt through 2021, has also benefited from inflation. Historically, the federal government has regularly paid off loans by taking out new loans. Inflation allows the Treasury to pay off loans with dollars of less purchasing power than the dollars originally borrowed. Nominal national income and therefore tax collections rise with inflation; the amount of public debt owed does not. Thus, inflation reduces the real burden of the public debt.

Anticipated Inflation

The redistribution effects of inflation are less severe or eliminated altogether if people anticipate inflation and can adjust their future nominal incomes to reflect expected increases in the price level. The prolonged inflation that began in the late 1960s prompted many labor unions in the 1970s to insist on labor contracts that provided cost-of-living adjustments.

Similarly, if inflation is anticipated, the redistribution of income from lender to borrower may be altered. Suppose a lender (perhaps a commercial bank) and a borrower (a household) both agree that 5 percent is a fair rate of interest on a 1-year loan provided the price level is constant. But assume that inflation has been occurring and is expected to be 6 percent over the next year. If the bank lends the household $100 at 5 percent interest, the borrower will pay the bank $105 at the end of the year. But if 6 percent inflation occurs during that year, the purchasing power of the $105 will have been reduced to about $99. The lender will, in effect, have paid the borrower $1 for the use of the lender's money for a year.

The lender can avoid this subsidy by charging an *inflation premium*—that is, by raising the interest rate by 6 percent, the amount of the anticipated inflation. By charging 11 percent interest, the lender will receive back $111 at the end of the year. Adjusted for the 6 percent inflation, that amount will have roughly the same purchasing power as $105 worth of today's money. The result then will be a mutually agreeable transfer of purchasing power from borrower to lender of $5, or 5 percent, for the use of $100 for one year.

Our example reveals the difference between the real interest rate and the nominal interest rate. The **real interest rate** is the percentage increase in *purchasing power* that the borrower pays the

cost-of-living adjustment (COLA) An automatic increase in the incomes (*wages*) of workers when *inflation* occurs; often included in *collective bargaining* agreements between *firms* and *unions*. Cost-of-living adjustments are also guaranteed by law for *Social Security* benefits and certain other government *transfer payments*.

real interest rate The *interest rate* expressed in dollars of constant value (adjusted for *inflation*) and equal to the *nominal interest rate* less the expected rate of inflation.

FIGURE 9.5
The inflation premium and nominal and real interest rates.

The inflation premium—the expected rate of inflation—gets built into the nominal interest rate. Here, the nominal interest rate of 11 percent comprises the real interest rate of 5 percent plus the inflation premium of 6 percent.

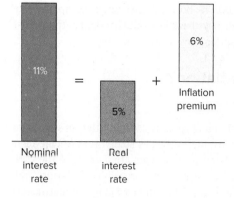

lender. In our example, the real interest rate is 5 percent. The **nominal interest rate** is the percentage increase in *money* that the borrower pays the lender, including that resulting from the built-in expectation of inflation, if any. In equation form:

$$\text{Nominal interest rate} = \text{real interest rate} + \text{inflation premium}$$
$$\text{(the expected rate of inflation)}$$

As Figure 9.5 shows, the nominal interest rate in our example is 11 percent.

nominal interest rate The *interest rate* expressed in terms of annual amounts currently charged for *interest* and not adjusted for *inflation*.

Other Redistribution Issues

We end our discussion of the redistribution effects of inflation by making three final points:

- *Deflation* The effects of unanticipated deflation—declines in the price level—are the reverse of those of inflation. People with fixed nominal incomes will find their real incomes enhanced. Creditors will benefit at the expense of debtors. And savers will discover that the purchasing power of their savings has grown because of the falling prices.

- *Mixed effects* A person who is simultaneously an income earner, a holder of financial assets, and a debtor will probably find that the redistribution impact of unanticipated inflation is cushioned. If the person owns fixed-value monetary assets (savings accounts, bonds, and insurance policies), inflation will lessen their real value. But that same inflation may produce an increase in the person's nominal wage. Also, if the person holds a fixed-interest-rate mortgage, the real burden of that debt will decline. In short, many individuals are simultaneously hurt and helped by inflation. All these effects must be considered before we can conclude that any particular person's net position is better or worse because of inflation.

- *Arbitrariness* The redistribution effects of inflation occur regardless of society's goals and values. Inflation lacks a social conscience. It takes from some and gives to others, whether they are rich, poor, young, old, healthy, or infirm.

QUICK REVIEW 9.4

▶ Inflation harms those who receive relatively fixed nominal incomes and either leaves unaffected or helps those who receive flexible nominal incomes.

▶ Unanticipated inflation hurts savers and creditors while benefiting debtors.

▶ The nominal interest rate equals the real interest rate plus the inflation premium (the expected inflation rate).

Does Inflation Affect Output?

>> **LO9.5** Describe how inflation may affect the economy's level of real output.

Thus far, our discussion has focused on how inflation redistributes a specific level of total real income. But inflation also may affect an economy's level of real output (and thus its level of real income).

Cost-Push Inflation and Real Output

Recall that abrupt and unexpected increases in the prices of key resources such as oil can drive up overall production costs and generate cost-push inflation. As prices rise, the quantity demanded of goods and services falls. Firms respond by producing less output, and unemployment goes up.

Economic events of the 1970s provide an example of how inflation can reduce real output. In late 1973, the Organization of Petroleum Exporting Countries (OPEC) managed to quadruple the price of oil by unexpectedly restricting supply. The resulting cost-push inflation generated rapid price-level increases in the 1973–1975 period. At the same time, the U.S. unemployment rate rose from slightly less than 5 percent in 1973 to 8.5 percent in 1975. Similar outcomes occurred in 1979–1980 in response to a second OPEC oil supply shock.

Like other forms of unexpected inflation, cost-push inflation redistributes income and output. But cost-push inflation is unique in that it reduces the overall quantity of real output that gets divided. Prices rose for everybody during the 1973–1975 period, but OPEC members experienced higher incomes while unemployed workers in oil importing countries like the United States lost their incomes entirely.

Demand-Pull Inflation and Real Output

Economists do not fully agree on the effects of mild inflation (less than 3 percent) on real output.

The Case for Zero Inflation Some economists believe that even low levels of inflation reduce real output because inflation diverts time and effort toward activities designed to hedge against inflation. For example:

- Businesses incur the cost of changing millions of prices on their shelves and in their computers simply to keep up with inflation.

- Households and businesses spend considerable time and effort obtaining the information they need to distinguish between real and nominal prices, wages, and interest rates.

These economists argue that without inflation, more time and effort would be spent producing valuable goods and services. Proponents of "zero inflation" bolster their case by pointing to cross-country studies indicating that lower inflation rates are associated with higher rates of economic growth. Even mild inflation, say these economists, is detrimental to economic growth.

The Case for Mild Inflation Other economists note that full employment and economic growth depend on strong levels of total spending.

- They argue that strong spending creates high profits, a strong demand for labor, and a powerful incentive for firms to expand their plants and equipment. In this view, the mild inflation that is a by-product of strong spending is a small price to pay for full employment and continued economic growth.

- A low but steady rate of inflation also makes it easier for firms to adjust real wages downward when the level of total spending declines. That is helpful to the overall economy because if real wages can be cut during a recession, firms can afford to hire more workers. To see why having some inflation matters, note that with mild inflation, firms can reduce real wages by holding nominal wages steady. That is a good strategy for firms because workers tend to focus on what happens to nominal, rather than real, wages. Their real wages will in fact be falling because of the inflation, but they will continue to work just as hard because their nominal wages remain unchanged. By contrast, if inflation were zero, the only way to reduce real wages would be by cutting nominal wages and thereby angering employees, who would likely retaliate by putting in less effort and agitating for higher pay.

The defenders of mild inflation argue that it is much better for an economy to err on the side of strong spending, full employment, economic growth, and mild inflation than on the side of weak spending, unemployment, recession, and deflation.

Hyperinflation

A **hyperinflation** occurs when a country's inflation rate exceeds 50 percent per month. Compounded over a year, that is equivalent to an annual rate of about 13,000 percent.

Adverse Effects Unlike mild inflation, which has its fans, hyperinflation is roundly condemned by all economists because it has devastating impacts on real output and employment.

- As prices shoot up during a hyperinflation, normal economic relationships are disrupted. Business owners do not know what to charge for their products. Consumers do not know what to pay.

- Production declines because businesses, anticipating further price increases, find that it makes more financial sense to hoard (rather than use) materials, and to stockpile (rather than sell) finished products. Why sell today when the same product will fetch more money tomorrow?

hyperinflation An extremely high rate of *inflation*, usually defined as an inflation rate in excess of 50 percent per month.

The Great Resignation

The First Two Years of the COVID Pandemic Generated a Wide Variety of Firsts in U.S. Labor Markets—Everything from Mass Unemployment to Mass Resignations.

When the COVID-19 pandemic spread worldwide in the first months of 2020, most governments opted for lockdowns to slow the spread of the disease. In the United States, essential businesses such as grocery stores and hospitals were allowed to remain open, but the vast majority of firms had to shut their doors and send their employees home.

Since most businesses cannot operate using remote labor, output fell toward zero at the majority of businesses, which implied little or no money to pay workers. The situation was especially grave because it was not clear in the early spring of 2020 how long the lockdowns would last.

As thing turned out, most states ended their lockdowns within a couple of months, so that most businesses started recalling employees back to work by the late spring of 2020. But before that occurred, congress had already voted unprecedentedly generous unemployment benefits that would end up being available in most states through the summer of 2021.

What ensued was a historically unprecedented situation in which massive labor shortages arose largely because the enhanced unemployment benefits were so generous that 68 percent of the workers eligible to receive them could get more money collecting unemployment benefits than they could earn if they returned to work.

Given those options, millions of workers chose to remain unemployed even after jobs became plentiful again. The resulting shortage of workers was acute in many industries, including restaurants and food service, which had been hurt badly by the lockdowns and subsequent restrictions on indoor dining, but then, just a few months later, faced a situation in which they could not get enough workers even after most of their customers had returned.

Other huge labor market changes were also afoot as a result of the pandemic. Millions of white collar workers who had been allowed to work remotely using Zoom and other tools were reluctant to go back to offices even after offices had reopened. Managers had to scramble to see if they could accommodate those employees, some of whom were afraid to return to the office due to health concerns (especially before vaccines became widely available in the spring of 2021) but also because they had found that they liked working at home and not having to commute.

Many firms began to respond to the new situation by considering remote work to be a permanent feature of operations, some firms going so far as to cancel leases of office space because they were planning on having much, or even all, of their workforce working remotely from then on.

At the same time, the ongoing labor shortages gave employees leverage to ask for everything from wage increases to different work schedules. By the summer of 2021, numerous news articles reported the labor shortages and speculated on how long they would last. A

Michael Siluk/Alamy Stock Photo

common assumption was that things might go back to normal after the enhanced unemployment benefits ended in September 2021.

But then another surprising thing happened. Even after the generous unemployment benefits ended and even though there were still firms begging for workers and even though average wages had risen by 10 percent, the number of people working either full time or part time in the fall of 2021 was still 4 million fewer than before the pandemic.

By early 2022, the unemployment rate had fallen to under 4 percent, about where it had been before the pandemic. But the size of the labor force (which, as a reminder, includes both people who have jobs as well as unemployed people who are actively seeking work) was 3 million less than it was before the pandemic—meaning that even if everyone who in early 2022 was unemployed and seeking work joined those who were already working, the economy would have to get by with 3 million fewer workers than before the pandemic.

Once consequence of that dearth of workers was that anyone who *was* working had unprecedented opportunities to quit jobs that they didn't like and immediately get hired for jobs they liked better. This phenomenon became known as the Great Resignation, and by early 2022, nearly 5 million people a month were voluntarily quitting one job for another, by far the highest rate ever recorded.

But what had happened to the millions of people who had not come back to work by early 2022 despite what was arguably the best job market ever? More than half were probably older people near retirement age who had decided to retire a bit earlier than they had previously planned, assisted by retirement accounts rising rapidly due to a booming stock market. Others included younger people who had decided to live off of savings and not work for a while, and couples who had decided that they could get by on one income rather than two.

- Investment also declines as savers refuse to extend loans to businesses, knowing that the loans will be repaid with rapidly depreciating money.

- Many people give up on money altogether and revert to barter, causing production and exchange to drop further as people spend literally hours every day trading and bartering instead of working and producing.

- The net result is economic collapse and, often, political chaos.

Examples Examples of hyperinflation include Germany after the First World War and Japan after the Second World War. In Germany, "prices increased so rapidly that waiters changed the prices on the menu several times during the course of a lunch. Sometimes customers had to pay double the price listed on the menu when they ordered."[1] In postwar Japan in 1947, "fishermen and farmers . . . used scales to weigh currency and change, rather than bothering to count it."[2]

Causation Hyperinflations are *always* caused by governments instituting highly imprudent expansions of the money supply. The rocketing money supply produces frenzied total spending and severe demand-pull inflation. Zimbabwe's 14.9 billion percent inflation rate in 2008 is the worst example. Venezuela in 2018 and several dozen other countries over the last century have caused inflation rates of 1 million percent per year or more.

Motivation Because hyperinflation causes so much harm, you may be asking why governments are sometimes willing to engage in the reckless money printing that invariably generates hyperinflation. The answer is that governments sometimes find themselves in a situation in which they cannot obtain enough revenue through either taxation or borrowing to cover the government's desired level of spending.

This is often the case during or immediately after a war, when government expenses skyrocket but tax revenues stagnate or even decline due to a depressed wartime or postwar economy. Unwilling or unable to slash spending down to a level that could be paid for by taxes plus borrowing, the government resorts to the printing press and prints up whatever amount of money is needed to cover its funding gap. The by-product is hyperinflation. The government maintains its rate of spending, but crashes the economy as a side effect.

Termination Hyperinflations end when governments cut their spending down to or below the amount of revenue that they can obtain through taxes and borrowing. Because the collateral damage is so great, most bouts of hyperinflation last 12 months or less. On the other hand, Greece in the 1940s and Nicaragua in the late 1980s each experienced over four years of continuous hyperinflation.

▶ Cost-push inflation reduces real output and employment.

▶ Economists argue about the effects of demand-pull inflation. Some argue that even mild demand-pull inflation (1 to 3 percent) reduces the economy's real output. Other say that mild inflation may be a

necessary by-product of the high and growing spending that produces high levels of output, full employment, and economic growth.

▶ Hyperinflation, caused by highly imprudent expansions of the money supply, may undermine the monetary system and severely decrease real output.

QUICK REVIEW 9.5

---

[1] Theodore Morgan, *Income and Employment,* 2nd ed. (Englewood Cliffs, NJ: Prentice Hall, 1952), p. 361.
[2] Rayburn M. Williams, *Inflation! Money, Jobs, and Politicians* (Arlington Heights, IL: AHM Publishing, 1980), p. 2.

Summary

LO9.1 Describe the phases of the business cycle.
The United States and other industrial economies have gone through periods of fluctuations in real GDP, employment, and the price level. Although they have certain phases in common—peak, recession, trough, expansion—business cycles vary greatly in duration and intensity.

Although economists explain the business cycle in terms of underlying causal factors such as major innovations, productivity shocks, money creation, and financial crises, they generally agree that changes in the level of total spending are the immediate causes of fluctuating real output and employment.

The business cycle affects all sectors of the economy, though in varying ways and degrees. The cycle has greater effects on output and employment in the capital goods and durable consumer goods industries than in the services and nondurable goods industries.

LO9.2 Measure unemployment and explain the different types of unemployment.

Economists distinguish among frictional, structural, and cyclical unemployment. The full-employment or natural rate of unemployment, which is composed of frictional and structural unemployment, is currently between 3 and 4 percent. The presence of part-time and discouraged workers makes it difficult to measure unemployment accurately.

The GDP gap, which can be either a positive or a negative value, is found by subtracting potential GDP from actual GDP. The economic cost of unemployment, as measured by the GDP gap, consists of the goods and services forgone by society when its resources are involuntarily idle. Okun's law suggests that every 1-percentage-point increase in the actual unemployment rate above the natural rate of unemployment causes an additional 2 percent negative GDP gap.

LO9.3 Measure inflation and distinguish between cost-push inflation and demand-pull inflation.

Inflation is a rise in the general price level and is measured in the United States by the Consumer Price Index (CPI). When inflation occurs, each dollar of income buys fewer goods and services than before. That is, inflation reduces the purchasing power of money. Deflation is a decline in the general price level.

Economists identify both demand-pull and cost-push (supply-side) inflation. Demand-pull inflation results from an excess of total spending relative to the economy's capacity to produce. The main source of cost-push inflation is abrupt and rapid increases in the prices of key resources. These supply shocks push up per-unit production costs and ultimately raise the prices of consumer goods.

LO9.4 Explain how unanticipated inflation can redistribute real income.

Unanticipated inflation arbitrarily redistributes real income at the expense of fixed-income receivers, creditors, and savers. If inflation is anticipated, individuals and businesses may be able to take steps to lessen or eliminate adverse redistribution effects.

When inflation is anticipated, lenders add an inflation premium to the interest rate charged on loans. The nominal interest rate thus reflects the real interest rate plus the inflation premium (the expected inflation rate).

LO9.5 Describe how inflation may affect the economy's level of real output.

Cost-push inflation reduces real output and employment. Proponents of zero inflation argue that even mild demand-pull inflation (1 to 3 percent) reduces the economy's real output. Other economists say that mild inflation may be a necessary by-product of the high and growing spending that produces high levels of output, full employment, and economic growth. A mild inflation also makes it easier for firms to adjust real wages downward when the level of total spending declines. They can do so by keeping nominal wages fixed while inflation reduces the purchasing power of every dollar received by employees.

Hyperinflation, caused by highly imprudent expansions of the money supply, may undermine the monetary system and severely decrease real output.

Terms and Concepts

business cycle	full-employment rate of unemployment	core inflation
peak	natural rate of unemployment (NRU)	nominal income
recession	potential output	real income
trough	GDP gap	unanticipated inflation
expansion	Okun's law	anticipated inflation
labor force	inflation	cost-of-living adjustments (COLAs)
unemployment rate	Consumer Price Index (CPI)	real interest rate
discouraged workers	deflation	nominal interest rate
frictional unemployment	demand-pull inflation	hyperinflation
structural unemployment	cost-push inflation	
cyclical unemployment	per-unit production costs	

Discussion Questions

1. What are the four phases of the business cycle? How long do business cycles last? Why does the business cycle affect output and employment in capital goods industries and consumer durable goods industries more severely than in industries producing consumer nondurables? **LO9.1**

2. How can a financial crisis lead to a recession? How can a major new invention lead to an expansion? **LO9.1**

3. How is the labor force defined, and who measures it? How is the unemployment rate calculated? Does an increase in the unemployment rate necessarily mean a decline in the size of the labor

force? Why is a positive unemployment rate—more than zero percent—fully compatible with full employment? **LO9.2**

4. How do unemployment rates vary by race and ethnicity, gender, occupation, and education? Why does the average length of time people are unemployed rise during a recession? **LO9.2**

5. Why is it difficult to distinguish among frictional, structural, and cyclical unemployment? Why is unemployment an economic problem? What are the consequences of a negative GDP gap? What are the noneconomic effects of unemployment? **LO9.2**

6. Even though the United States has an unemployment compensation program that provides income for those out of work, why should we worry about unemployment? **LO9.2**

7. What is the Consumer Price Index (CPI), and how is it determined each month? How does the Bureau of Labor Statistics calculate the inflation rate from one year to the next? How does inflation affect the purchasing power of a dollar? How does it explain differences between nominal and real interest rates? How does deflation differ from inflation? **LO9.3**

8. Distinguish between demand-pull inflation and cost-push inflation. Which of the two types is more likely to be associated with a negative GDP gap? Which is more likely to be associated with a positive GDP gap, in which actual GDP exceeds potential GDP? What is core inflation? Why is it calculated? **LO9.3**

9. Explain how an increase in your nominal income and a decrease in your real income might occur simultaneously. Who loses from inflation? Who gains? **LO9.4**

10. Explain how hyperinflation might lead to a severe decline in total output. **LO9.5**

11. **LAST WORD** How did the enhanced unemployment benefits approved by congress in the early days of the pandemic affect paid employment over the following year and a half? Why did some firms cancel leases? What role did older people play in the reduced size of the labor force?

Review Questions

1. Place the phases of the business cycle in order, starting with the highest level of GDP: recession, trough, peak, expansion. **LO9.1**

2. Most economists agree that the immediate cause of most cyclical changes in real output and employment is an unexpected change in _____. **LO9.1**
   a. the level of total spending
   b. the value of the stock market
   c. the value of the trade deficit
   d. the unemployment rate

3. Suppose that a country has 9 million people working full-time. It also has 1 million people who are actively seeking work but are currently unemployed, along with 2 million discouraged workers who have given up looking for work and are currently unemployed. What is this country's unemployment rate? **LO9.2**
   a. 10 percent
   b. 15 percent
   c. 20 percent
   d. 25 percent

4. Label each of the following scenarios as either frictional unemployment, structural unemployment, or cyclical unemployment. **LO9.2**
   a. Mariam just graduated from college and is looking for a job.
   b. A recession causes a local factory to lay off 30 workers.
   c. Thousands of bus and truck drivers permanently lose their jobs to self-driving vehicles.
   d. Hundreds of New York legal jobs permanently disappear when a lot of legal work gets outsourced to lawyers in India.

5. The unemployment rate that is consistent with full employment is _____. **LO9.2**
   a. the natural rate of unemployment
   b. the unnatural rate of unemployment
   c. the status quo rate of unemployment
   d. cyclical unemployment
   e. Okun's rate of unemployment

6. A country's current unemployment rate is 11 percent. Economists estimate that its natural rate of unemployment is 6 percent. About how large is this economy's negative GDP gap? **LO9.2**
   a. 1 percent
   b. 3 percent
   c. 6 percent
   d. 10 percent

7. Cost-push inflation occurs in the presence of _____. **LO9.3**
   a. excess inventory
   b. a trade deficit
   c. rising per-unit production costs
   d. excess demand for goods and services

8. Zion's nominal income will go up by 10 percent next year. Inflation is expected to be −2 percent next year. By approximately how much will Zion's real income change next year? **LO9.3**
   a. −2 percent
   b. 8 percent
   c. 10 percent
   d. 12 percent

9. Kaitlin has $10,000 of savings that she may deposit with her local bank. Kaitlin wants to earn a real rate of return of at least 4 percent, and she is expecting inflation to be exactly 3 percent. What is the lowest nominal interest rate that Kaitlin would be willing to accept from her local bank? **LO9.4**
   a. 4 percent
   b. 5 percent
   c. 6 percent
   d. 7 percent

10. True or False: Lenders are helped by unanticipated inflation. **LO9.4**

11. Economists agree that _____ inflation reduces real output. **LO9.5**
    a. cost-push
    b. demand-pull
    c. push-pull

Problems

1. Suppose that a country's annual growth rates were 5, 3, 4, −1, −2, 2, 3, 4, 6, and 3 percent in yearly sequence over a 10-year period. What was the country's trend rate of growth over this period? Which set of years most clearly demonstrates an expansionary phase of the business cycle? Which set of years best illustrates a recessionary phase of the business cycle? **LO9.1**

2. Assume the following data for a country: total population, 500; population under 16 years of age or institutionalized, 120; not in the labor force, 150; unemployed, 23; part-time workers looking for full-time jobs, 10. What is the size of the labor force? What is the official unemployment rate? **LO9.2**

3. Suppose that the natural rate of unemployment in a particular year is 5 percent and the actual unemployment rate is 9 percent. Use Okun's law to determine the size of the GDP gap in percentage-point terms. If potential GDP is $500 billion in that year, how much output is forgone because of cyclical unemployment? **LO9.2**

4. If the CPI was 110 last year and is 121 this year, what is this year's inflation rate? In contrast, suppose that the CPI was 110 last year and is 108 this year. What is this year's inflation rate? What term do economists use to describe this second outcome? **LO9.3**

5. How long would it take for the price level to double if inflation persisted at (*a*) 2 percent per year, (*b*) 5 percent per year, and (*c*) 10 percent per year? **LO9.3**

6. If your nominal income rises by 5.3 percent and the price level rises by 3.8 percent in some year, by what percentage will your real income (approximately) increase? If your nominal income rises by 2.8 percent and your real income rises by 1.1 percent in some year, what is the (approximate) inflation rate? **LO9.4**

7. Suppose that the nominal inflation rate is 4 percent and the inflation premium is 2 percent. What is the real interest rate? Alternatively, assume that the real interest rate is 1 percent and the nominal interest rate is 6 percent. What is the inflation premium? **LO9.4**

8. If the inflation premium is 2 percent and the nominal interest rate is 1 percent, what is the real interest rate? What is the real interest rate if the inflation premium is 3 percent while the nominal interest rate is 0.5 percent? **LO9.4**

PART 4

Pavel Bobrovskiy/Shutterstock

Basic Macroeconomic Relationships*

>> LEARNING OBJECTIVES

LO10.1 Describe how changes in income affect consumption and saving.

LO10.2 List and explain factors other than income that can affect consumption.

LO10.3 Explain how changes in real interest rates affect investment.

LO10.4 Identify and explain factors other than the real interest rate that can affect investment.

LO10.5 Illustrate how changes in investment and the other components of total spending can multiply real GDP.

This chapter examines the basic relationships between three different pairs of economic aggregates. (Recall that "aggregate" means "total" or "combined.") Specifically, this chapter looks at the relationships between:

- Income and consumption (and income and saving).
- The interest rate and investment.
- Changes in spending and changes in output.

The Income-Consumption and Income-Saving Relationships

The direct (positive) relationship between income and consumption is one of the best-established relationships in macroeconomics. In examining this other-things-equal relationship, we are also exploring the relationship between income and saving. Recall that economists define *personal saving* as "not spending" or as "that part of disposable (after-tax) income not consumed." Saving (S) equals disposable income (DI) *minus* consumption (C).

Many factors determine a nation's levels of consumption and saving, but the most significant is disposable income. Consider some recent historical data for the United States. In Figure 10.1 each dot represents consumption and disposable income for one year since 2002. The line C that loosely fits these points shows that consumption is, normally, directly (positively) related to disposable income. Moreover, households spend most of their disposable income.

The **45°(degree) line** is a reference line. Because it bisects the 90° angle formed by the two axes of the graph, each point on it is equidistant from the two axes. At each point on the 45° line, consumption equals disposable income, or C = DI. Therefore, the vertical distance between the

>> **LO10.1** Describe how changes in income affect consumption and saving.

45° (degree) line The reference line in a two-dimensional graph that shows equality between the variable measured on the *horizontal axis* and the variable measured on the *vertical axis*. In the *aggregate expenditures model*, the line along which the value of output (measured horizontally) is equal to the value of *aggregate expenditures* (measured vertically).

---

*Note to the Instructor: If you wish to bypass the aggregate expenditures model (Keynesian cross model) covered in full in Chapter 11, assigning the present chapter will provide a seamless transition to the AD–AS model of Chapter 12 and the chapters beyond. If you want to cover the aggregate expenditures model, this present chapter provides the necessary building blocks.

FIGURE 10.1
Consumption and disposable income, 2002–2021.

Each dot in this figure shows consumption and disposable income in a specific year. The line *C*, which generalizes the relationship between consumption and disposable income, indicates a direct relationship and shows that households consume most of their after-tax incomes.

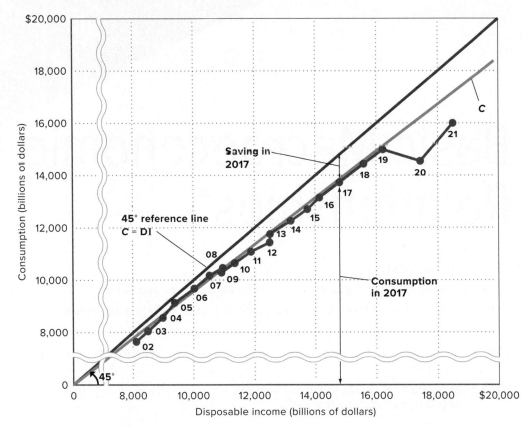

Source: Bureau of Economic Analysis.

45° line and any point on the horizontal axis measures either consumption or disposable income. If we use it to measure disposable income, then the vertical distance between it and the consumption line labeled *C* represents the amount of saving (*S*) in that year.

Saving is the amount by which actual consumption in any year falls short of the 45° line (*S* = DI − *C*). In 2017, for instance, disposable income was $14,801 billion and consumption was $13,725 billion, so saving was $1,076 billion (= $14,801 billion − $13,725 billion). Observe that the vertical distance between the 45° line and line *C* increases as we move rightward along the horizontal axis and decreases as we move leftward. Like consumption, saving typically varies directly with disposable income.

Consumption, Savings, and Disposable Income During the COVID-19 Pandemic

As you examine Figure 10.1, notice that the dots for 2002 through 2019 lie nearly atop line *C*, reflecting that, for each of those successive years, increases in disposable income (measured on the horizontal axis) were accompanied by increases in consumption (measured on the vertical axis). By contrast, if you compare the dots for 2019 and 2020, you will notice that while disposable income increased by $1,213 billion between 2019 and 2020, consumption *fell* by $437 billion between those two years. That is, an increase in disposable income between 2019 and 2020 resulted in a *decrease* in consumption between 2019 and 2020.

What accounts for that highly unusual anomaly in which consumption varied inversely, rather than directly, with disposable income? The answer will probably not surprise you. The anomaly was caused by the COVID-19 pandemic and how the public reacted to the various government stimulus programs which were enacted to fight the pandemic.

As mentioned in earlier chapters, the U.S. government began issuing massive stimulus payments during the spring of 2020 to fight the economic downturn caused by the pandemic. Those payments dramatically increased U.S. disposable income in 2020 and 2021. But Americans were very worried about the future even after those payments started to arrive because nobody could be sure just how long the pandemic might last or how large a toll it might take on the world economy and human health. As a result, people were not eager to spend down the large increase in disposable income that was generated by the stimulus payments. Fearing for the future, much of the windfall was saved, so much so that the personal savings rate increased from 7.6 percent of disposable income in late 2019 to 33.8 percent during the spring of 2020, immediately after lockdowns began.[1] That increase in savings more than offset the increase in disposable income, with the result being that consumption spending fell between 2019 and 2020 despite the sharp increase in disposable income.

If you compare the dots for 2020 and 2021, you will see that the inverse relationship between consumption and disposable income lasted only one year (between 2019 and 2020). Things were back to normal between 2020 and 2021, with higher disposable income (on the horizontal axis) being associated with higher consumption spending (on the vertical axis). That return to normalcy reflected growing confidence in the future as vaccines became available and the pandemic turned out to be less bad than initially feared. As that confidence increased, so did the willingness of individuals to consume, rather than save, out of disposable income.

The Consumption Schedule

The dots in Figure 10.1 represent historical data—the actual amounts of DI, C, and S in the United States over a period of years. But because we want to understand how the economy would behave under different possible scenarios, we need a hypothetical schedule showing the various amounts that households plan to consume at each level of disposable income that might prevail at some specific time. Columns 1 and 2 of Table 10.1, represented in **Figure 10.2a (Key Graph),** show the hypothetical consumption schedule. This **consumption schedule** (or "consumption function") reflects the direct consumption–disposable income relationship suggested by the data in Figure 10.1. It is consistent with many household budget studies. In the aggregate, households increase their spending as their disposable income rises, and they spend a larger proportion of a small disposable income than of a large disposable income.

consumption schedule A table of numbers showing the amounts *households* plan to spend for *consumer goods* at different levels of *disposable income.*

The Saving Schedule

It is relatively easy to derive a **saving schedule** (or "saving function"). Because saving equals disposable income less consumption ($S = DI - C$), we need only subtract consumption (Table 10.1, column 2) from disposable income (column 1) to find the amount saved (column 3) at each DI. Thus, columns 1 and 3 in Table 10.1 are the saving schedule, represented in Figure 10.2b. The

saving schedule A table of numbers that shows the amounts *households* plan to save (plan not to spend for *consumer goods*), at different levels of *disposable income.*

TABLE 10.1 Consumption and Saving Schedules (in Billions) and Propensities to Consume and Save

(1) Level of Output and Income (GDP = DI)	(2) Consumption (C)	(3) Saving (S), (1) − (2)	(4) Average Propensity to Consume (APC), (2)/(1)	(5) Average Propensity to Save (APS), (3)/(1)	(6) Marginal Propensity to Consume (MPC), Δ(2)/Δ(1)*	(7) Marginal Propensity to Save (MPS), Δ(3)/Δ(1)*
(1) $370	$375	$−5	1.01	−.01		
					.75	.25
(2) 390	390	0	1.00	.00		
					.75	.25
(3) 410	405	5	.99	.01		
					.75	.25
(4) 430	420	10	.98	.02		
					.75	.25
(5) 450	435	15	.97	.03		
					.75	.25
(6) 470	450	20	.96	.04		
					.75	.25
(7) 490	465	25	.95	.05		
					.75	.25
(8) 510	480	30	.94	.06		
					.75	.25
(9) 530	495	35	.93	.07		
					.75	.25
(10) 550	510	40	.93	.07		

*The Greek letter Δ, delta, means "the change in."

---

[1]By comparison, the previous all-time high for the savings rate was 17.3 percent (in May of 1975).

ᴵᴵᴵ KEY GRAPH

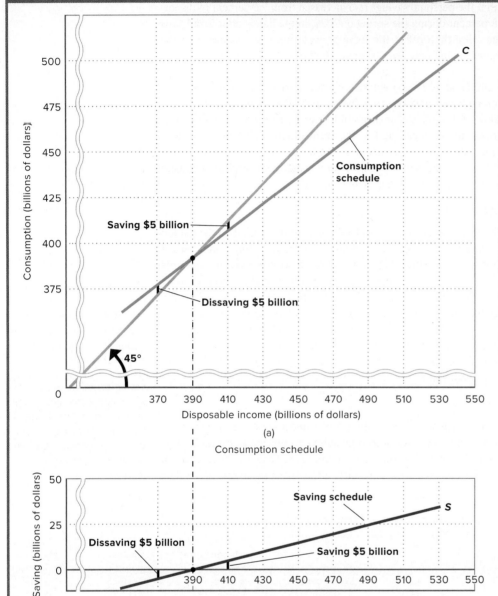

FIGURE 10.2 **Consumption and saving schedules.**

The two parts of this figure show the income-consumption and income-saving relationships in Table 10.1 graphically. (a) Consumption rises as income increases. Saving is negative (dissaving occurs) when the consumption schedule is above the 45° line, and saving is positive when the consumption schedule is below the 45° line. (b) Like consumption, saving increases as income goes up. The saving schedule is found by subtracting the consumption schedule in the top graph vertically from the 45° line. For these hypothetical data, saving is −$5 billion at $370 billion of income, zero at $390 billion of income, and $5 billion at $410 billion of income. Saving is zero where consumption equals disposable income.

QUICK QUIZ FOR FIGURE 10.2

1. **The slope of the consumption schedule in this figure is 0.75. Thus, the:**
   a. slope of the saving schedule is 1.33.
   b. marginal propensity to consume is 0.75.
   c. average propensity to consume is 0.25.
   d. slope of the saving schedule is also 0.75.

2. **In this figure, when consumption is a positive amount, saving:**
   a. must be a negative amount.
   b. must also be a positive amount.
   c. can be either a positive or a negative amount.
   d. is zero.

3. **In this figure:**
   a. the marginal propensity to consume is constant at all levels of income.
   b. the marginal propensity to save rises as disposable income rises.
   c. consumption is inversely (negatively) related to disposable income.
   d. saving is inversely (negatively) related to disposable income.

4. **When consumption equals disposable income:**
   a. the marginal propensity to consume is zero.
   b. the average propensity to consume is zero.
   c. consumption and saving must be equal.
   d. saving must be zero.

graph shows the direct relationship between saving and DI. It also shows that saving is a smaller proportion of a small DI than of a large DI. If households consume a smaller and smaller proportion of DI as DI increases, then they must be saving a larger and larger proportion of DI.

Remembering that at each point on the 45° line consumption equals DI, we see that *dissaving* (consuming in excess of after-tax income) will occur at relatively low DIs. For example, at $370 billion (row 1, Table 10.1), consumption is $375 billion. Households can consume more than their current incomes by liquidating (selling for cash) accumulated wealth or by borrowing. Graphically, dissaving is shown as the vertical distance of the consumption schedule above the 45° line or as the vertical distance of the saving schedule below the horizontal axis. We have marked the dissaving at the $370 billion level of income in Figures 10.2a and 10.2b. Both vertical distances measure the $5 billion of dissaving that occurs at $370 billion of income.

In our example, the **break-even income** is $390 billion (row 2, Table 10.1). At this income level, households plan to consume their entire incomes ($C = \text{DI}$). Graphically, the consumption schedule cuts the 45° line, and the saving schedule cuts the horizontal axis (saving is zero) at the break-even income level.

At all higher incomes, households plan to save part of their incomes. Graphically, the vertical distance between the consumption schedule and the 45° line measures this saving (see Figure 10.2a), as does the vertical distance between the saving schedule and the horizontal axis (see Figure 10.2b). For example, at the $410 billion level of income (row 3, Table 10.1), both these distances indicate $5 billion of saving.

Average and Marginal Propensities

Columns 4 to 7 in Table 10.1 show additional characteristics of the consumption and saving schedules.

APC and APS The fraction, or percentage, of total income that is consumed is the **average propensity to consume (APC)**. The fraction of total income that is saved is the **average propensity to save (APS)**:

$$APC = \frac{\text{consumption}}{\text{income}}$$

and

$$APS = \frac{\text{saving}}{\text{income}}$$

For example, at $470 billion of income (row 6, Table 10.1), the APC is $\frac{450}{470} = \frac{45}{47}$, or about 0.96 (= 96 percent), while the APS is $\frac{20}{470} = \frac{2}{47}$, or about 0.04 (= 4 percent). Columns 4 and 5 in Table 10.1 show the APC and APS at each of the 10 levels of DI. The APC falls as DI increases, while the APS rises as DI goes up.

Because disposable income is either consumed or saved, the fraction of any DI consumed plus the fraction saved (not consumed) must exhaust that income. Mathematically, APC + APS = 1 at any level of disposable income, as columns 4 and 5 in Table 10.1 illustrate. So if 0.96 of the $470 billion of income in row 6 is consumed, 0.04 must be saved. That is why APC + APS = 1.

Global Perspective 10.1 shows APCs for several countries.

MPC and MPS The fact that households consume a certain proportion of a particular total income, for example, $\frac{45}{47}$ of a $470 billion disposable income, does not guarantee they will consume the same proportion of any *change* in income they might receive. The proportion, or fraction, of any change in income consumed is called the **marginal propensity to consume (MPC)**, "marginal" meaning "extra" or "a change in." Equivalently, the MPC is the ratio of a change in consumption to a change in the income that caused the consumption change:

$$MPC = \frac{\text{change in consumption}}{\text{change in income}}$$

The fraction of any change in income saved is the **marginal propensity to save (MPS)**. The MPS is the ratio of a change in saving to the change in income that brought it about:

$$MPS = \frac{\text{change in saving}}{\text{change in income}}$$

break-even income The level of *disposable income* at which *households* plan to consume (spend) all their income and to save none of it.

average propensity to consume (APC) Fraction (or percentage) of *disposable income* that *households* spend on *consumer goods;* consumption divided by *disposable income.*

average propensity to save (APS) Fraction (or percentage) of *disposable income* that *households* save; *saving* divided by *disposable income.*

marginal propensity to consume (MPC) The fraction of any change in *disposable income* spent for *consumer goods;* equal to the change in consumption divided by the change in disposable income.

marginal propensity to save (MPS) The fraction of any change in *disposable income* that *households* save; equal to the change in *saving* divided by the change in disposable income.

GLOBAL PERSPECTIVE 10.1

AVERAGE PROPENSITIES TO CONSUME, SELECTED NATIONS

There are surprisingly large differences in average propensities to consume (APCs) among nations. In 2020, Greece had an APC higher than 100 percent, indicating dissaving (negative saving). Most countries have APCs between 80 and 95 percent of disposable income. By contrast, China has a very high savings rate, leading to an APC of only 65 percent.

Source: Bureau of Economic Analysis.

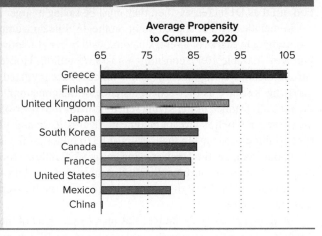

Average Propensity to Consume, 2020

If disposable income starts at $470 billion (row 6 horizontally in Table 10.1) and then rises by $20 billion to $490 billion (row 7), households will consume $\frac{15}{20}$, or $\frac{3}{4}$, and save $\frac{5}{20}$, or $\frac{1}{4}$, of that increase in income. In other words, the MPC is $\frac{3}{4}$ or 0.75, and the MPS is $\frac{1}{4}$ or 0.25, as shown in columns 6 and 7.

The sum of the MPC and the MPS for any change in disposable income must always be 1. Consuming or saving out of extra income is an either-or proposition; the fraction of any change in income not consumed is, by definition, saved. If 0.75 of extra disposable income is consumed, 0.25 must be saved. The fraction consumed (MPC) plus the fraction saved (MPS) must exhaust the whole change in income:

$$MPC + MPS = 1$$

FIGURE 10.3
The marginal propensity to consume and the marginal propensity to save.

In the two parts of this figure, the Greek letter delta (Δ) means "the change in." (a) The MPC is the slope (ΔC/ΔDI) of the consumption schedule. (b) The MPS is the slope (ΔS/ΔDI) of the saving schedule.

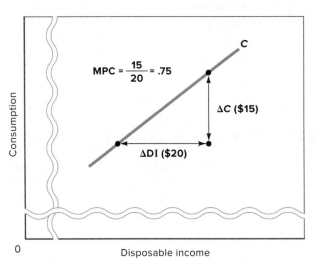

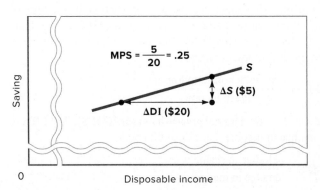

In our example, 0.75 plus 0.25 equals 1.

MPC and MPS as Slopes The MPC is the numerical value of the slope of the consumption schedule, and the MPS is the numerical value of the slope of the saving schedule. We know from the appendix to Chapter 1 that the slope of any line is the ratio of the vertical change to the horizontal change occasioned in moving from one point to another on that line.

Figure 10.3 measures the slopes of the consumption and saving lines, using enlarged portions of Figures 10.2a and 10.2b. Observe that consumption changes by $15 billion (the vertical change) for each $20 billion change in disposable income (the horizontal change). The slope of the consumption line is thus 0.75 (= $15/$20), which is the value of the MPC. Saving changes by $5 billion (shown as the vertical change) for every $20 billion change in disposable income (shown as the horizontal change). The slope of the saving line therefore is 0.25 (= $5/$20), which is the value of the MPS.

▶ Both consumption spending and saving rise when disposable income increases; both fall when disposable income decreases.

▶ The average propensity to consume (APC) is the fraction of any specific level of disposable income that is spent on consumer goods; the average propensity to save (APS) is the fraction of any specific level of disposable income that is saved. As disposable income increases, the APC falls and the APS rises.

▶ The marginal propensity to consume (MPC) is the fraction of a change in disposable income that is consumed, and it is the slope of the consumption schedule. The marginal propensity to save (MPS) is the fraction of a change in disposable income that is saved, and it is the slope of the saving schedule.

Nonincome Determinants of Consumption and Saving

Disposable income is the primary determinant of the amounts households will consume and save. But other determinants might prompt households to consume more or less at each possible level of income. Those other determinants are wealth, borrowing, expectations, and interest rates.

>> LO10.2 List and explain factors other than income that can affect consumption.

- *Wealth* A household's wealth is the dollar amount of all the assets that it owns minus the dollar amount of its liabilities (its total debt). Households build wealth by saving money out of current income. The point of building wealth is to increase consumption possibilities. The larger a household's stock of wealth, the larger its present and future consumption possibilities.

    When events suddenly boost the value of existing wealth, households tend to increase their spending and reduce their saving. This **wealth effect** shifts the consumption schedule upward and the saving schedule downward. The schedules move in response to households taking advantage of the increased consumption possibilities granted by the sudden wealth increase. Examples: In the late 1990s, skyrocketing U.S. stock values expanded the value of household wealth by increasing the value of household assets. Predictably, households spent more and saved less. In contrast, a strong "reverse wealth effect" occurred in 2008. Plunging real estate and stock market prices joined to erase $11.2 trillion (yes, trillion) of household wealth. Consumers quickly reacted by reducing their consumption spending. The consumption schedule shifted downward.

wealth effect The tendency for people to increase their consumption spending when the value of their financial and real *assets* rises and to decrease their consumption spending when the value of those assets falls.

- *Borrowing* When a household borrows, it can increase current consumption beyond its disposable income. By allowing households to spend more, borrowing shifts the current consumption schedule upward.

    But note that there is no "free lunch." While borrowing in the present allows for higher consumption now, it necessitates lower consumption in the future when the debt must be repaid. Stated differently, increased borrowing increases debt (liabilities), which in turn reduces household wealth (because wealth = assets − liabilities). This reduction in wealth reduces future consumption possibilities.

- *Expectations* Household expectations about future prices and income may affect current spending and saving. For example, the expectation of higher prices tomorrow may cause households to buy more today while prices are still low. Thus, the current consumption schedule shifts up and the current saving schedule shifts down. In contrast, expectations of a recession and thus lower income in the future may lead households to reduce consumption and save more today. Greater present saving will help households build wealth that will help them ride out the expected bad times. The consumption schedule therefore shifts down and the saving schedule shifts up.

- *Real interest rates* When real interest rates (those adjusted for inflation) fall, households tend to borrow more, consume more, and save less. A lower real interest rate, for example, decreases monthly loan payments and induces consumers to purchase automobiles and other goods bought on credit. A lower real interest rate also diminishes the incentive to save because of the reduced interest "payment" to the saver. These effects on consumption and saving, however, are very modest. They mainly shift consumption toward some products (those bought on credit) and away from others. At best, lower real interest rates shift the consumption schedule slightly upward and the saving schedule slightly downward. Higher real interest rates do the opposite.

Other Important Considerations

We must make several additional important points regarding the consumption and saving schedules:

- *Switching to real GDP* When developing macroeconomic models, economists change their focus from the relationship between consumption (and saving) and *disposable income* to the relationship between consumption (and saving) and *real domestic output (real GDP)*. This modification is reflected in Figures 10.4a and 10.4b, where the horizontal axes measure real GDP.

- *Changes along schedules* The movement from one point to another on a consumption schedule (for example, from *a* to *b* on C_0 in Figure 10.4a) is a *change in the amount consumed* and is caused solely by a change in real GDP. On the other hand, an upward or downward shift of the entire schedule, for example, a shift from C_0 to C_1 or C_2 in Figure 10.4a, is a *shift of the consumption schedule* and is caused by changes in any one or more of the *nonincome* determinants of consumption just discussed.

  Similar terminology applies to the saving schedule in Figure 10.4b.

- *Simultaneous shifts* Changes in wealth, expectations, interest rates, and household debt shift the consumption schedule in one direction and the saving schedule in the opposite direction. If households decide to consume more at each possible level of real GDP, they must save less, and vice versa. (Even when they spend more by borrowing, they are, in effect, reducing their current saving by the amount borrowed because borrowing is, effectively, "negative saving.") Graphically, if the consumption schedule shifts upward from C_0 to C_1 in Figure 10.4a, the saving schedule shifts downward, from S_0 to S_1 in Figure 10.4b. Similarly, a downward shift of the consumption schedule from C_0 to C_2 means an upward shift of the saving schedule from S_0 to S_2.

- *Taxation* A change in taxes shifts the consumption and saving schedules in the same direction. Taxes are paid partly at the expense of consumption and partly at the expense of saving. So an increase in taxes reduces consumption *and* saving, thereby shifting downward both the consumption schedule in Figure 10.4a and the saving schedule in Figure 10.4b. Conversely, households partly consume and partly save any decrease in taxes. Both the consumption schedule and saving schedule shift upward.

- *Stability* The consumption and saving schedules usually are relatively stable unless altered by major tax increases or decreases. Their stability may come from the fact that consumption–saving decisions are strongly influenced by long-term considerations such as saving to meet emergencies or saving for retirement. In addition, changes in the nonincome determinants frequently work in opposite directions and therefore may be self-canceling.

FIGURE 10.4
Shifts of the (a) consumption and (b) saving schedules.

Normally, if households consume more at each level of real GDP, they are necessarily saving less. Graphically this means that an upward shift of the consumption schedule (C_0 to C_1) entails a downward shift of the saving schedule (S_0 to S_1). If households consume less at each level of real GDP, they are saving more. A downward shift of the consumption schedule (C_0 to C_2) is reflected in an upward shift of the saving schedule (S_0 to S_2). This pattern breaks down, however, when taxes change; then the consumption and saving schedules move in the *same* direction—opposite to the direction of the tax change.

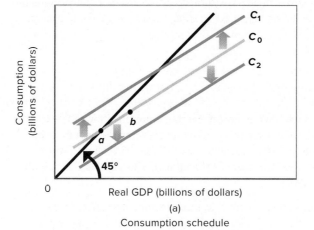

Real GDP (billions of dollars)

(a)
Consumption schedule

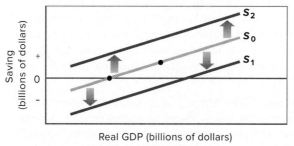

Real GDP (billions of dollars)

(b)
Saving schedule

CONSIDER THIS . . .

The Pandemic Recession and the Paradox of Thrift

The Pandemic Recession of 2020 altered the prior consumption and saving behavior in the economy. Concerned about reduced wealth, high debt, and potential job losses, households increased their saving and reduced their consumption at each level of after-tax income (or each level of GDP). In Figure 10.4, this outcome is illustrated as the downward *shift* of the consumption schedule in the top graph and the upward *shift* of the saving schedule in the lower graph.

This change of behavior illustrates the so-called **paradox of thrift,** which refers to the possibility that a recession can be made worse when households become more thrifty and save in response to the downturn. The paradox of thrift rests on two major ironies. One irony is that saving more is *good* for the economy in the long run, as noted in Chapter 1 and Chapter 6. It finances investment and therefore fuels subsequent economic

Digital Vision/Getty Images

growth. But saving more can be *bad* for the economy during a recession. Because firms are pessimistic about future sales, the increased saving is not likely to be matched by an equal amount of added investment. The extra saving simply reduces spending on currently produced goods and services. That means that even more businesses suffer, more layoffs occur, and people's incomes decline even more.

The paradox of thrift has a second irony related to the so-called *fallacy of composition:* Households as a group may inadvertently end up saving less when each individual household tries to save more during a recession. This is because each household's attempt to save more implies that it is also attempting to spend less. Across all households, that collective reduction in total spending in the economy creates additional job losses and further drives down total income. The decline in total income reduces the ability of households as a group to save as much as they did before their spending reduction and subsequent income decline.

The Interest-Rate–Investment Relationship

Recall that investment consists of expenditures on new plants, capital equipment, machinery, inventories, and so on. The investment decision is a marginal-benefit–marginal-cost decision: The marginal benefit from investment is the expected rate of return businesses hope to realize. The marginal cost is the interest rate that businesses must pay to borrow money. Businesses will invest in all projects for which the expected rate of return exceeds the real interest rate. Expected returns (profits) and the real interest rate therefore determine investment spending.

Expected Rate of Return

Investment spending is guided by the profit motive; businesses buy capital goods only when they think such purchases will be profitable. Suppose the owner of a small auto parts business is considering whether to invest in a new 3-D printer that costs $1,000 and has a useful life of only 1 year. The new machine will increase the firm's output and sales revenue. Suppose the net expected revenue from the machine (that is, revenue after subtracting operating costs such as electricity, labor, and certain taxes) is $1,100. After subtracting the $1,000 cost of the machine from the net expected revenue of $1,100, the firm will have an expected profit of $100. Dividing this $100 profit by the $1,000 cost of the machine, we find that the machine's **expected rate of return,** r, is 10 percent ($= \$100/\$1,000$). It is important to note that this rate of return is *expected*, not *guaranteed*. The investment may or may not generate as much revenue or as much profit as anticipated. Investment involves risk.

The Real Interest Rate

In our example, the interest cost of an investment is computed by multiplying the interest rate, i, by the $1,000 borrowed to buy the machine. If the interest rate is, say, 7 percent, the total interest cost will be $70. This amount compares favorably with the net expected return of $100, which equals a 10 percent expected rate of return. If the investment works out as expected, it will add $30 to the firm's profit.

>> **LO10.3** Explain how changes in real interest rates affect investment.

paradox of thrift The possibility that households trying to protect themselves against a recession by saving more may inadvertently worsen the recession and hurt themselves by reducing overall consumption and economic activity.

expected rate of return The increase in profit a *firm* anticipates it will obtain by purchasing capital or engaging in research and development (*R&D*); expressed as a percentage of the total cost of the investment (or R&D) activity.

We can generalize as follows: If the expected rate of return (10 percent) exceeds the interest rate (here, 7 percent), the investment should be undertaken. The firm expects the investment to be profitable. But if the interest rate (say, 12 percent) exceeds the expected rate of return (10 percent), the investment should not be undertaken because the firm expects the investment to be unprofitable.

The firm should undertake every investment project that it expects to be profitable. In other words, the firm should array its prospective investment projects from the highest expected rate of return, r, downward and then invest in all projects for which r exceeds i. The firm should invest to the point where r = i because then it will have undertaken all investments for which r is greater than i.

The *real interest* rate, rather than the *nominal* rate, is crucial in making investment decisions. Recall from Chapter 9 that the nominal interest rate is expressed in dollars of current value, while the real interest rate is stated in constant or inflation-adjusted dollars. Also recall that the real interest rate is the nominal rate minus the inflation rate. In our 3-D printer illustration, our implicit assumption of a constant price level ensures that all our data, including the interest rate, are in real terms.

But what if inflation is occurring? Suppose a $1,000 investment is expected to yield a real (inflation-adjusted) return of 10 percent and the nominal interest rate is 15 percent. At first glance, we would say the investment would be unprofitable. But assume there is ongoing inflation of 10 percent per year. In that case, the investing firm will pay back dollars with approximately 10 percent less in purchasing power. While the nominal interest rate is 15 percent, the real rate is only 5 percent (= 15 percent − 10 percent). By comparing this 5 percent real interest rate with the 10 percent expected real rate of return, we find that the investment is potentially profitable and should be undertaken.

Investment Demand Curve

We now move from a single firm's investment decision to total demand for investment goods by the entire business sector. Assume that every firm has estimated the expected rates of return from all investment projects and has recorded those data. We can sum these data by asking: How many dollars' worth of investment projects have an expected rate of return of, say, 16 percent or more? How many have 14 percent or more? How many have 12 percent or more? And so on.

Suppose no prospective investments yield an expected return of 16 percent or more. But there are $5 billion of investment opportunities with expected rates of return between 14 and 16 percent; an additional $5 billion yielding between 12 and 14 percent; an additional $5 billion yielding between 10 and 12 percent; and an additional $5 billion in each successive 2 percent range of yield down to and including the 0 to 2 percent range.

To sum these figures for each rate of return, r, we add the amounts of investment that will yield each particular rate of return r or higher. Doing so provides the data table and the graph in **Figure 10.5 (Key Graph).** In the table, the number opposite 12 percent, for example, means there are $10 billion of investment opportunities that will yield an expected rate of return of 12 percent or more. The $10 billion includes the $5 billion of investment expected to yield a return of 14 percent or more plus the $5 billion expected to yield between 12 and 14 percent.

Our example of the 3-D printer tells us that a firm will undertake an investment project whose expected rate of return, r, exceeds the real interest rate, i. Let's first suppose i is 12 percent. Businesses will undertake all investments for which r exceeds 12 percent. That is, they will invest until the 12 percent rate of return equals the 12 percent interest rate. Figure 10.5 reveals that $10 billion of investment spending will be undertaken at a 12 percent interest rate. In other words, $10 billion of investment projects have an expected rate of return of 12 percent or more.

Put another way: When the "price" of borrowing is 12 percent, firms will demand $10 billion of investment goods. If the interest rate is lower, say, 8 percent, the amount of investment for which r equals or exceeds i is $20 billion. Thus, firms will demand $20 billion of investment goods at an 8 percent real interest rate. At 6 percent, they will demand $25 billion of investment goods.

By applying the marginal-benefit–marginal-cost rule that firms should undertake investment projects up to the point where r = i, we see that we can add the real interest rate to the vertical axis in Figure 10.5. That is, the curve in Figure 10.5 not only shows rates of return; it also shows the quantity of investment demanded at each "price" i (interest rate) of investment. The vertical axis in Figure 10.5 shows the various possible real interest rates, and the horizontal axis shows the corresponding quantities of investment demanded. The inverse (downward sloping) relationship

..Ill KEY GRAPH

FIGURE 10.5 The investment demand curve.

The investment demand curve is constructed by arraying all potential investment projects in descending order of their expected rates of return. The curve slopes downward, reflecting an inverse relationship between the real interest rate (the financial "price" of each dollar of investing) and the quantity of investment demanded.

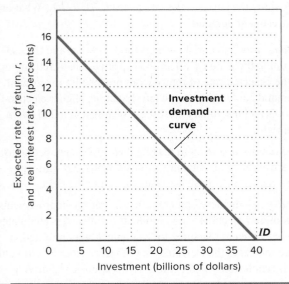

Real Interest Rate (i) and Expected Rate of Return (r)	Cumulative Amount of Investment Having this Rate of Return or Higher, Billions per Year
16%	$ 0
14	5
12	10
10	15
8	20
6	25
4	30
2	35
0	40

QUICK QUIZ FOR FIGURE 10.5

1. **The investment demand curve:**
   a. reflects a direct (positive) relationship between the real interest rate and investment.
   b. reflects an inverse (negative) relationship between the real interest rate and investment.
   c. shifts to the right when the real interest rate rises.
   d. shifts to the left when the real interest rate rises.

2. **In this figure:**
   a. greater cumulative amounts of investment are associated with lower real interest rates.
   b. lesser cumulative amounts of investment are associated with lower expected rates of return on investment.
   c. higher interest rates are associated with higher expected rates of return on investment, and therefore greater amounts of investment.
   d. interest rates and investment move in the same direction.

3. **In this figure, if the real interest rate falls from 6 to 4 percent:**
   a. investment will increase from 0 to $30 billion.
   b. investment will decrease by $5 billion.
   c. the expected rate of return will rise by $5 billion.
   d. investment will increase from $25 billion to $30 billion.

4. **In this figure, investment will be:**
   a. zero if the real interest rate is zero.
   b. $40 billion if the real interest rate is 16 percent.
   c. $30 billion if the real interest rate is 4 percent.
   d. $20 billion if the real interest rate is 12 percent.

Answers: 1. b; 2. a; 3. d; 4. c

---

between the interest rate (price) and the dollar quantity of investment demanded conforms to the law of demand discussed in Chapter 3. The curve *ID* in Figure 10.5 is the economy's **investment demand curve.** It shows the amount of investment at each real interest rate. The level of investment depends on the expected rate of return and the real interest rate.

investment demand curve
A curve that shows the amounts of *investment* demanded by an economy at a series of *real interest rates.*

▶ Changes in consumer wealth, consumer expectations, interest rates, household debt, and taxes can shift the consumption and saving schedules (as they relate to real GDP).

▶ A specific investment will be undertaken if the expected rate of return, *r*, equals or exceeds the real interest rate, *i*.

▶ The investment demand curve shows the total monetary amounts that will be invested by an economy at various possible real interest rates.

**QUICK REVIEW
10.2**

Shifts of the Investment Demand Curve

Figure 10.5 shows the relationship between the real interest rate and the amount of investment demanded, other things equal. When other things change, the investment demand curve shifts. In general, any factor that leads businesses collectively to expect greater rates of return on their investments increases investment demand. That factor shifts the investment demand curve to the right, as from ID_0 to ID_1 in Figure 10.6. Any factor that leads businesses collectively to expect lower rates of return on their investments shifts the curve to the left, as from ID_0 to ID_2. What are those non-interest-rate determinants of investment demand?

- *Acquisition, maintenance, and operating costs* The initial costs of capital goods, and the estimated costs of operating and maintaining those items, affect the expected rate of return on investment. When these costs rise, the expected rate of return from prospective investment projects falls, and the investment demand curve shifts to the left. Example: Higher electricity costs associated with operating tools and machinery shift the investment demand curve to the left. Lower costs shift it to the right.

- *Business taxes* Firms look to expected returns *after taxes* in making their investment decisions. An increase in business taxes lowers the expected profitability of investments and shifts the investment demand curve to the left; a reduction of business taxes shifts it to the right.

- *Technological change* Technological progress—the development of new products, improvements in existing products, and the creation of new machinery and production processes—stimulates investment. The development of a more efficient machine, for example, lowers production costs or improves product quality and increases the expected rate of return from investing in the machine. Profitable new products (cholesterol medications, flying drones, self-driving cars, and so on) induce a flurry of investment as businesses tool up for expanded production. A rapid rate of technological progress shifts the investment demand curve to the right.

- *Stock of capital goods on hand* The stock of capital goods on hand, relative to output and sales, influences firms' investment decisions. When the economy is overstocked with production facilities and when firms have excessive inventories of finished goods, the expected rate of return on new investment declines. Firms with excess production capacity have little incentive to invest in new capital. Therefore, less investment is forthcoming at each real interest rate; the investment demand curve shifts leftward.

  When the economy is understocked with production facilities and when firms are selling their output as fast as they can produce it, the expected rate of return on new investment increases, and the investment demand curve shifts rightward.

- *Planned inventory changes* Recall from Chapter 7 that the definition of investment includes changes in inventories of unsold goods. An increase in inventories is a positive investment while a decrease in inventories is a negative investment. It is important to remember that some inventory changes are planned, while others are unplanned. Because the investment demand curve shows only planned investment, it is affected only by planned changes in firms' inventory levels. If firms plan to increase their inventories, the investment demand curve shifts to the right. If firms plan to decrease their inventories, the investment demand curve shifts to the left.

  Firms make planned changes to their inventory levels mostly because they expect either faster or slower sales. A firm that expects its sales to double next year will want to keep more inventory in stock, thereby increasing its investment demand. By contrast, a firm that is expecting slower sales will plan to reduce its inventory, thereby reducing its overall

FIGURE 10.6
Shifts of the investment demand curve.

Increases in investment demand are shown as rightward shifts of the investment demand curve; decreases in investment demand are shown as leftward shifts of the investment demand curve.

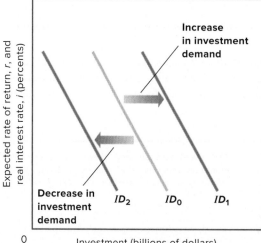

investment demand. But because life often does not turn out as expected, firms often find that the actual amount of inventory investment that they end up making is either more or less than what they had planned. The size of the gap is the dollar amount of unplanned inventory changes.

- *Expectations* Most capital goods are durable, with a life expectancy of 10 or 20 years. Thus, the expected rate of return on capital investment depends on the firm's expectations of future sales, future operating costs, and future profitability of the product that the capital helps produce. These expectations are based on forecasts of future business conditions as well as on difficult-to-predict factors, such as changes in the domestic political climate, international relations, population growth, and consumer tastes. If executives become more optimistic about future sales, costs, and profits, the investment demand curve will shift to the right; a pessimistic outlook will shift the curve to the left.

Instability of Investment

Unlike consumption, investment is unstable; it rises and falls quite often. In fact, investment is the most volatile component of total spending—so much so that most fluctuations in output and employment result from demand shocks relating to unexpected increases and decreases in investment. Several interrelated factors explain the variability of investment.

- *Variability of expectations* Business expectations can change quickly when some event suggests a significant possible change in future business conditions. Changes in exchange rates, trade barriers, legislative actions, stock market prices, government economic policies, the outlook for war or peace, court decisions in key labor or antitrust cases, and a host of other considerations may substantially shift business expectations.

- *Durability* Within limits, purchases of capital goods are discretionary and therefore can be postponed. Firms can scrap or replace older equipment and buildings, or they can patch them up and use them for a few more years. Optimism about the future may prompt firms to replace their older facilities, and such modernizing will call for a high level of investment. A less optimistic view, however, may lead to smaller amounts of investment as firms repair older facilities and keep them in use.

- *Irregularity of innovation* New products and processes stimulate investment. Major innovations such as electricity, airplanes, automobiles, computers, and artificial intelligence induce vast upsurges or "waves" of investment spending that in time recede. But such innovations occur quite irregularly, adding to the volatility of investment.

- *Variability of profits* High current profits often generate optimism about the future profitability of new investments, whereas low current profits or losses spawn considerable doubt about the wisdom of new investments. Additionally, firms often save a portion of current profits as retained earnings and use these funds (as well as borrowed funds) to finance new investments. So current profits affect both the incentive and ability to invest. But profits themselves are highly variable from year to year, contributing to the volatility of investment.

The volatility of investment causes occasional and substantial unexpected shifts of the investment demand curve (as in Figure 10.6), which in turn generate significant changes in investment spending. These demand shocks can contribute to cyclical instability.

▶ The investment demand curve shifts when changes occur in (a) the costs of acquiring, operating, and maintaining capital goods, (b) business taxes, (c) technology, (d) the stock of capital goods on hand, and (e) business expectations.

▶ Investment is the most volatile component of total spending and most fluctuations in output and employment result from investment demand shocks.

▶ Investment volatility is driven by (a) changing expectations, (b) the flexibility that firms have to delay capital purchases, (c) the irregularity of innovation, and (d) fluctuations in profits, which affect the enthusiasm for investment and the money available to fund it.

QUICK REVIEW

10.3

The Multiplier Effect*

>> **LO10.5** Illustrate how changes in investment and the other components of total spending can multiply real GDP.

Assuming that the economy has room to expand—so that increases in spending do not lead to increases in prices—there is a direct (positive) relationship between changes in spending and changes in real GDP. More spending results in a higher real GDP; less spending results in a lower real GDP.

But there is much more to the relationship between these two aggregates. As an example, note that an initial change in investment spending can change output and income by a larger amount (that is, by an amount larger than the initial change in investment spending). That surprising result is called the multiplier effect: any initial change in a component of total spending can lead to a larger change in GDP.

The number known as the **multiplier** determines how much larger that change will be; it is the ratio of the change in GDP to the initial change in spending (in this case, investment). Stated algebraically,

multiplier The ratio of a change in *equilibrium GDP* to the change in *investment* or in any other component of *aggregate expenditures* or *aggregate demand;* the number by which a change in any such component must be multiplied to find the resulting change in equilibrium GDP.

$$\text{Multiplier} = \frac{\text{change in real GDP}}{\text{initial change in spending}}$$

By rearranging this equation, we can also say that the change in real GDP = multiplier × initial change in spending.

So if investment in an economy rises by \$30 billion and GDP increases by \$90 billion as a result, we know from the first version of that equation that the multiplier is 3 (= \$90/\$30).

Note these three points about the multiplier:

- The "initial change in spending" is usually associated with investment spending. But changes in consumption (unrelated to changes in income), net exports, and government purchases can also generate multiplier effects.

- The "initial change in spending" associated with investment spending results from a change in the real interest rate and/or a shift of the investment demand curve.

- The multiplier works in both directions. An initial increase in spending will create a "multiplied" increase in GDP, while an initial decrease in spending will create a "multiplied" decrease in GDP.

Rationale

The multiplier effect follows from two facts:

- First, the economy supports a continuous flow of expenditures and income through which dollars spent by Lee are received as income by Okafor and then spent by Okafor and received as income by Mendoza, and so on. (This chapter's Last Word presents this idea in a humorous way.)

- Second, any change in income changes both consumption and saving in the same direction as, and by a constant fraction of, the change in income.

It follows that an initial change in spending will start a "spending chain" throughout the economy—a chain in which each successive link is fractionally smaller than the previous link. That chain of spending will multiply the initial change in GDP. As a result, any initial change in spending will produce a magnified change in output and income.

The table in **Figure 10.7 (Key Graph)** illustrates the rationale underlying the multiplier effect. Suppose that a \$5.00 billion increase in investment spending occurs. We assume that the MPC is 0.75, the MPS is 0.25, and prices remain constant. That is, neither the initial increase in spending nor any of the subsequent increases in spending cause prices to rise.

The initial \$5.00 billion increase in investment spending generates an equal amount of wage, rent, interest, and profit income that will flow to households because spending and receiving

---

*Instructors who cover the full aggregate expenditures (AE) model (Chapter 11) rather than moving directly to aggregate demand and aggregate supply (Chapter 12) may choose to defer this discussion until after the analysis of equilibrium real GDP.

..ıl KEY GRAPH

FIGURE 10.7 **The multiplier process (MPC = 0.75).**

An initial change in investment spending of $5.00 billion creates an equal $5.00 billion of new income in round 1. Under our assumption that households have a marginal propensity to consume (MPC) equal to 0.75, households will spend $3.75 (= 0.75 × $5.00) billion of this new income, creating $3.75 billion of added income in round 2. Of this $3.75 billion of new income, households will spend $2.81 (= 0.75 × $3.75) billion, and income will rise by that amount in round 3. Such income increments over the entire process get successively smaller but eventually produce a total change in income and GDP of $20 billion. The multiplier therefore is 4 (= $20 billion/$5 billion).

	(1) Change in Income	(2) Change in Consumption (MPC = 0.75)	(3) Change in Saving (MPS = 0.25)
Increase in investment of **$5.00**	$5.00	$ 3.75	$1.25
Second round	3.75	2.81	0.94
Third round	2.81	2.11	0.70
Fourth round	2.11	1.58	0.53
Fifth round	1.58	1.19	0.39
All other rounds	4.75	3.56	1.19
Total	**$20.00**	$15.00	$5.00

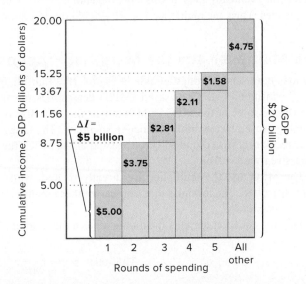

QUICK QUIZ FOR FIGURE 10.7

1. If the multiplier process stopped after two rounds, the cumulative change in income would be:
a. $3.75.
b. $5.00.
c. $8.75.
d. $20.00.

2. If the marginal propensity to consume (MPC) were larger than 0.75:
a. the total change in income after all rounds would be less than $20.
b. the marginal propensity to save would also increase.
c. the total change in income after all rounds would still be $20.
d. the multiplier would be larger than 4.

3. If the marginal propensity to save (MPS) were 0.40, the multiplier would be:
a. less than 4.
b. equal to 4.
c. greater than 4.
d. depends on what MPC equaled.

4. For the multiplier to be equal to 1, it would have to be the case that:
a. MPC = 1.
b. MPS = 1.
c. MPS = 0.
d. MPC = MPS = 1.

Answers: 1. c; 2. d; 3. a; 4. b

income are two sides of the same transaction. What businesses spend on investment, households will receive as income.

The $5.00 billion increase in household income will prompt an initial increase in consumption. How large will that initial increase in consumption be? We find the answer by applying the marginal propensity to consume of 0.75 to this change in income. The $5.00 billion increase in household income raises consumption by $3.75 (= 0.75 × $5) billion and saving by $1.25 (= 0.25 × $5) billion, as shown in columns 2 and 3 in the table.

Other households receive as income (second round) the $3.75 billion of consumption spending. Those households consume 0.75 of this $3.75 billion, or $2.81 billion, and save 0.25 of it, or $0.94 billion. The $2.81 billion that is consumed flows to still other households as income to be spent or saved (third round). And the process continues, with the added consumption and income becoming less in each round. The process ends when there is no more additional income to spend.

The bar chart in Figure 10.7 shows several rounds of this multiplier process, each bar corresponding to a row in the table. As shown by rounds 1 to 5 in the bar chart, each round adds a smaller and smaller blue block to national income and GDP. The process continues beyond the five rounds shown (for convenience we have simply cumulated the subsequent declining blocks into a single block labeled "All other"). The accumulation of the additional income in each round—the sum of the blue blocks—is the total change in income or GDP resulting from the initial $5.00 billion change in spending. Because the spending and respending effects of the increase in investment diminish with each successive round of spending, the cumulative increase in output and income eventually ends. In this case, the ending occurs when $20 billion of additional income accumulates. Thus, the multiplier is 4 (= $20 billion/$5 billion).

The Multiplier and the Marginal Propensities

You may have sensed from the table in Figure 10.7 that the fraction of any increase in income that is consumed (MPC) or saved (MPS) determines the size of the multiplier. That is true because the value of the MPC or MPS determines the size of each of the successive rounds of spending caused by any initial change in spending. The larger the MPC (smaller the MPS), the larger each successive round will be. The smaller the MPC (the larger the MPS), the smaller each successive round will be.

The MPC and the multiplier are directly related, while the MPS and the multiplier are inversely related. The formulas that summarize these multiplier relationships are presented in the next two equations.

The first equation presents the multiplier as a function of MPC:

$$\text{Multiplier} = \frac{1}{1 - \text{MPC}}$$

To understand the second equation, which presents the multiplier as a function of MPS, recall that MPC + MPS = 1. Therefore MPS = 1 − MPC, which means we can also write the multiplier formula as

$$\text{Multiplier} = \frac{1}{\text{MPS}}$$

This version of the multiplier formula indicates that the multiplier varies inversely with the MPS, so that a larger MPS implies a smaller multiplier, and vice versa. You can verify this inverse relationship for yourself by substituting particular MPS values into the formula. For instance, when the MPS is 0.25, as in our example, the multiplier is 4. If the MPS were 0.2, the multiplier would be 5. If the MPS were 0.33, the multiplier would be 3.

The intuition behind this inverse relationship between MPS and the multiplier has to do with how changes in the MPS affect the size of each round of the multiplier process. As we will demonstrate, the smaller the fraction of any change in income saved (that is, the smaller the MPS), the greater the amount of respending at each round and, therefore, the greater the multiplier.

To see why that is true, suppose that there is again a $5 billion increase in investment but this time assume that the MPS is 0.2 rather than 0.25. That lower MPS value of 0.2 implies a higher MPC value of 0.8 (since MPC = 1 − MPS). Taking that higher MPC of 0.8 into account, the first round of the table in Figure 10.7 will have consumption increasing by $4 billion (= MPC of 0.8 × $5 billion) rather than by $3.75 billion because saving will increase by $1 billion (= MPS of 0.2 × $5 billion) rather than $1.25 billion. The larger rise in consumption in round 1 will produce a larger increase in income in round 2. The same will be true for all successive rounds. If we worked through all of the following rounds, we would find that the process ends when income has cumulatively increased by $25 billion, not the $20 billion shown in the table. When the MPS is 0.2 rather than 0.25, the multiplier is 5 (= $25 billion/$5 billion) as opposed to 4 (= $20 billion/$5 billion). The smaller MPS has caused a larger multiplier.

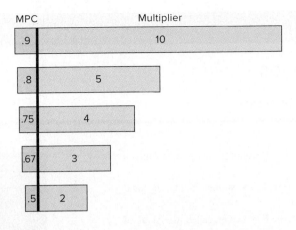

FIGURE 10.8
The MPC and the multiplier.

The larger the MPC, the greater the size of the multiplier.

By contrast, consider what happens if the MPS is increased to a larger value, say 0.33 rather than 0.25. That increase in the MPS to 0.33 implies a decrease in the MPC to 0.67 (since MPC = 1 − MPS). That smaller MPC of 0.67 means that each round's increase in consumption and income would be less than those in the table in Figure 10.7. Consequently, the multiplier process would end with a $15 billion increase in income rather than the $20 billion shown. When the MPS is 0.33 rather than 0.25, the multiplier is 3 (= $15 billion/$5 billion) as opposed to 4 (= $20 billion/$5 billion). The larger MPS has caused a smaller multiplier.

We can summarize these results in terms of MPC. A large MPC (small MPS) means the succeeding rounds of consumption spending shown in Figure 10.7 diminish slowly and thereby cumulate to a large total change in income. Conversely, a small MPC (a large MPS) causes the increases in consumption to decline quickly, so the cumulative change in income is small.

Figure 10.8 summarizes the direct (positive) relationship between the MPC and the multiplier; they get bigger together. To test your understanding, see if you can draw a similar graph that summarizes the inverse (negative) relationship between the MPS and the multiplier; when one gets bigger, the other gets smaller.

How Large Is the Actual Multiplier?

The multiplier that we have just described is based on simplifying assumptions. We have, for example, ignored taxes and imports. They matter because they reduce the amount by which the consumption of domestic output increases in each round of the multiplier process. When taxes and imports apply, households use some of the extra income that they receive in each round to purchase additional goods from abroad (imports) and to pay additional taxes. Buying imports and paying taxes drains off some of the additional consumption spending (on domestic output) created by each round's increase in income. So the multiplier effect is reduced, and the 1/MPS formula for the multiplier overstates the actual outcome. To correct this problem, we would need to change the multiplier equation to read "1 divided by the fraction of the change in income that is not spent on domestic output."

Also, an increase in spending may be partly dissipated as inflation rather than realized fully as an increase in real GDP. The multiplier process still happens, but it induces a much smaller change in real output because, at higher prices, any given amount of spending buys less real output.

Economists disagree on the size of the actual multiplier in the United States. Estimates range from as high as 2.5 to as low as zero. As you read subsequent chapters, keep in mind that the actual multiplier is much lower than the multipliers that we used here in this chapter for our simple explanatory examples of how the multiplier process works.

Toppling Dominoes

A Humorous Look at the Multiplier

CLEVELAND—Yesterday, the local economy was plunged into a recession in less than 6 hours.

Many people are trying to explain the sudden change in local prospects. Here's one conjecture.

At precisely 9 a.m., Humbug, the Ford dealer, called Mr. Ajani, of Ajani's Men's Wear. "It's a great day, Mr. Ajani! The new models are in. Per your request, I've put in an order for you."

Agitated, Mr. Ajani responded, "That's not going to work Mr. Humbug. I just got hit with an unexpected tax bill. It's huge and I can't afford a new car right now. Sorry."

Humbug hung up. Two minutes later, his cell phone rang.

"This is Tanaka the landscaper. When do you want us to start working on your yard?"

"I'm sorry, Tanaka, but I can't do that right now," said Humbug.

Perplexed, Tanaka responded, "You were so excited about your new yard. What happened?"

"It's one of my customers. He canceled an order because he got hit with an unexpected tax bill."

Two hours later, Tanaka received a call from his wife, Samantha. "I'm so excited! Goldman's Electronics just received our new TV. They said they can install it tomorrow."

"We're going to have to send it back."

"Why?"

"Because Humbug isn't going to have that yard put in now that his customer Ajani can't buy a new car due to an unexpected tax assessment."

Ten minutes later, Samantha called Goldman's Electronics. "We don't need the TV."

Goldman frowned. He immediately called his travel agent, Gonzales. "Remember that trip to Spain that you scheduled for me?"

"Yes, everything is ready to go. We just need to run your credit card."

"It's impossible now. Mrs. Tanaka just canceled a TV order because Humbug didn't sell a car to Ajani because Ajani can't figure out how to pay his taxes."

Gonzalez got online and canceled Goldman's trip to Spain. He also went over to his local bank to talk to the lending officer, Tommy

Everything is stock/Shutterstock

Tightfist. "I can't make this month's loan payment because Goldman canceled his trip to Spain."

Tightfist got upset but knew that nothing could be done.

When Ms. Kozysic the baker came into the bank a bit later to ask for a loan, Tightfist shouted "No! How can I loan you money, Ms. Kozysic, when Gonzalez can't repay what he owes me?"

Dejected, Kozysic phoned up her general contractor, Bill Johnson, and said she couldn't remodel her storefront. Johnson laid off seven workers. It was a tough thing to tell them right after lunch.

At 2 p.m., Ford announced that it would be offering big rebates on all its new models.

Humbug phoned Ajani immediately, "I have great news. Unless that unexpected tax bill is massive, you are still going to be able to afford the car you wanted!"

"I don't have an expected tax bill," Ajani said. "My accountant made an error. It was all a mistake."

"Excellent!" exclaimed Humbug. "Now you can afford that lovely new car."

"Not possible," replied Ajani in a grim tone. "Business has been lousy."

"I'm sorry to hear that. What's going on?"

"I haven't seen Tanaka, Goldman, Gonzalez, Tightfist, or Kozysic for over a month. How can I survive if they don't patronize my shop?"

Source: Adopted from Art Buchwald, "Squaring the Economic Circle," *Cleveland Plain Dealer*, February 22, 1975.

QUICK REVIEW

10.4

▶ The multiplier effect reveals that an initial change in spending can cause a larger change in domestic income and output. The multiplier is the factor by which the initial change is magnified: multiplier = change in real GDP/initial change in spending.

▶ The higher the marginal propensity to consume (the lower the marginal propensity to save), the larger the multiplier [= 1/(1 − MPC) or 1/MPS].

▶ Economists disagree on the size of the actual multiplier in the U.S. economy; estimates range all the way from zero to 2.5.

Summary

LO10.1 Describe how changes in income affect consumption and saving.
Other things equal, a direct (positive) relationship exists between income and consumption and between income and saving. The consumption and saving schedules show the various amounts that households intend to consume and save at the various income and output levels, assuming a fixed price level.

The *average* propensities to consume and save show the fractions of any total income that are consumed and saved; APC + APS = 1. The *marginal* propensities to consume and save show the fractions of any change in total income that are consumed and saved; MPC + MPS = 1.

LO10.2 List and explain factors other than income that can affect consumption.
Consumption and saving schedules (as they relate to real GDP) are determined by (*a*) the amount of wealth owned by households, (*b*) borrowing, (*c*) expectations of future prices and incomes, and (*d*) real interest rates and taxes. The consumption and saving schedules are relatively stable.

LO10.3 Explain how changes in real interest rates affect investment.
The immediate determinants of investment are (*a*) the expected rate of return and (*b*) the real interest rate. The economy's investment demand curve is found by cumulating investment projects, arraying them in descending order according to their expected rates of return, graphing the result, and applying the rule that firms should undertake investment up to the point at which the real interest rate, *i*, equals the expected rate of return, *r*. The investment demand curve reveals an inverse (negative) relationship between the real interest rate and the level of aggregate investment.

Either changes in real interest rates or shifts of the investment demand curve can change the level of investment.

LO10.4 Identify and explain factors other than the real interest rate that can affect investment.
Shifts of the investment demand curve can occur as the result of changes in (*a*) the acquisition, maintenance, and operating costs of capital goods; (*b*) business taxes; (*c*) technology; (*d*) the stocks of capital goods on hand; (*e*) planned inventory changes, and (*f*) expectations. Factors that contribute to the instability of investment spending include varying expectations, the durability of capital goods, the irregular occurrence of major innovations, and profit volatility.

LO10.5 Illustrate how changes in investment and the other components of total spending can multiply GDP.
Through the multiplier effect, an increase in investment spending (or consumption spending, government purchases, or net export spending) ripples through the economy, ultimately creating a magnified increase in real GDP. The multiplier equals the ultimate change in GDP divided by the initiating change in investment (or other component of spending).

The multiplier is equal to the reciprocal of the marginal propensity to save: The greater is the marginal propensity to save, the smaller is the multiplier. Also, the greater is the marginal propensity to consume, the larger is the multiplier.

Economists disagree on the size of the multiplier in the United States, with estimates ranging from 2.5 to 0. But all estimates of actual-economy multipliers are less than the multiplier in our purposefully simplified text illustrations.

Terms and Concepts

45° (degree) line	average propensity to save (APS)	expected rate of return
consumption schedule	marginal propensity to consume (MPC)	investment demand curve
saving schedule	marginal propensity to save (MPS)	multiplier
break-even income	wealth effect	
average propensity to consume (APC)	paradox of thrift	

Discussion Questions

connect

1. Precisely how do the MPC and the APC differ? How does the MPC differ from the MPS? Why must the sum of the MPC and the MPS equal 1? **LO10.1**
2. Why does a downshift of the consumption schedule typically involve an equal upshift of the saving schedule? What is the exception to this relationship? **LO10.2**
3. Why will a reduction in the real interest rate increase investment spending, other things equal? **LO10.3**
4. In what direction will each of the following occurrences shift the investment demand curve, other things equal? **LO10.4**
   a. An increase in unused production capacity occurs.
   b. Business taxes decline.
   c. The cost of acquiring equipment falls.
   d. Widespread pessimism arises about future business conditions and sales revenues.
   e. A major new technological breakthrough creates prospects for a wide range of profitable new products.
5. How is it possible for investment spending to increase even in a period in which the real interest rate rises? **LO10.4**
6. Why is investment spending unstable? **LO10.4**
7. Is the relationship between changes in spending and changes in real GDP in the multiplier effect a direct (positive) relationship,

or is it an inverse (negative) relationship? How does the size of the multiplier relate to the size of the MPC? The MPS? What is the logic of the multiplier-MPC relationship? **LO10.5**

8. Why is the actual multiplier in the U.S. economy less than the multiplier in this chapter's example? **LO10.5**

9. **LAST WORD** What is the central economic idea humorously illustrated in the Last Word "Toppling Dominoes"? How does the central idea relate to economic recessions, on the one hand, and vigorous economic expansions, on the other?

Review Questions

1. What are the variables (the items measured on the axes) in a graph of the (a) consumption schedule and (b) saving schedule? Are the variables inversely (negatively) related, or are they directly (positively) related? What is the fundamental reason that the levels of consumption and saving in the United States are each higher today than they were a decade ago? **LO10.1**

2. In year 1, Anita earns $1,000 and saves $100. In year 2, Anita gets a $500 raise so that she earns a total of $1,500. Out of that $1,500, she saves $200. What is Anita's MPC out of her $500 raise? **LO10.1**
   a. 0.50
   b. 0.75
   c. 0.80
   d. 1.00

3. If the MPS rises, then the MPC will: **LO10.1**
   a. fall.
   b. rise.
   c. stay the same.

4. In what direction will each of the following occurrences shift the consumption and saving schedules, other things equal? **LO10.2**
   a. A large decrease in real estate values, including private homes.
   b. A sharp, sustained increase in stock prices.
   c. A 5-year increase in the minimum age for collecting Social Security benefits.
   d. An economywide expectation that a recession is over and that a robust expansion will occur.

   e. A substantial increase in household borrowing to finance auto purchases.

5. Irving owns several frozen yogurt shops. He is considering whether he should build a new location downtown. The expected rate of return is 15 percent per year. He can borrow money at a 12 percent interest rate to finance the project. Should Irving proceed with this project? **LO10.3**
   a. Yes
   b. No

6. Which of the following scenarios will shift the investment demand curve right? *Select **one or more** answers from the choices shown.* **LO10.4**
   a. Business taxes increase.
   b. The expected return on capital increases.
   c. Firms have a lot of unused production capacity.
   d. Firms are planning on increasing their inventories.

7. True or False: Real GDP is more volatile (variable) than gross investment. **LO10.4**

8. If a $50 billion initial increase in spending leads to a $250 billion change in real GDP, how big is the multiplier? **LO10.5**
   a. 1.0
   b. 2.5
   c. 4.0
   d. 5.0

9. True or False: Larger MPCs imply larger multipliers. **LO10.5**

Problems

1. Refer to the table below. **LO10.1**
   a. Fill in the missing numbers in the table.
   b. What is the break-even level of income in the table? What is the term that economists use for the saving situation shown at the $240 level of income?

   c. For each of the following items, indicate whether the value in the table is either constant or variable as income changes: the MPS, the APC, the MPC, the APS.

Level of Output and Income (GDP = DI)	Consumption	Saving	APC	APS	MPC	MPS
$240	$_____	$ −4	___	___		
260	_____	0	___	___	___	___
280	_____	4	___	___	___	___
300	_____	8	___	___	___	___
320	_____	12	___	___	___	___
340	_____	16	___	___	___	___
360	_____	20	___	___	___	___
380	_____	24	___	___	___	___
400	_____	28	___	___	___	___

2. Suppose that disposable income, consumption, and saving in some country are $200 billion, $150 billion, and $50 billion, respectively. Next, assume that disposable income increases by $20 billion, consumption rises by $18 billion, and saving goes up by $2 billion. What is the economy's MPC? Its MPS? What was the APC before the increase in disposable income? After the increase? **LO10.1**

3. **ADVANCED ANALYSIS** Suppose that the linear equation for consumption in a hypothetical economy is $C = 40 + 0.8Y$. Also suppose that income (Y) is $400. Determine (a) the marginal propensity to consume, (b) the marginal propensity to save, (c) the level of consumption, (d) the average propensity to consume, (e) the level of saving, and (f) the average propensity to save. **LO10.1**

4. **ADVANCED ANALYSIS** Linear equations for the consumption and saving schedules take the general form $C = a + bY$ and $S = -a + (1 - b)Y$, where C, S, and Y are consumption, saving, and national income, respectively. The constant a represents the vertical intercept, and b represents the slope of the consumption schedule. **LO10.1, LO10.2**

   a. Use the following data to substitute numerical values for a and b in the consumption and saving equations.

National Income (Y)	Consumption (C)
$ 0	$ 80
100	140
200	200
300	260
400	320

   b. What is the economic meaning of b? Of $(1 - b)$?
   c. Suppose that the amount of saving that occurs at each level of national income falls by $20 but that the values of b and $(1 - b)$ remain unchanged. Restate the saving and consumption equations inserting the new numerical values, and cite a factor that might have caused the change.

5. Use your completed table for problem 1 to solve this problem. Suppose the wealth effect is such that $10 changes in wealth produce $1 changes in consumption at each level of income. If real estate prices tumble such that wealth declines by $80, what will be the new level of consumption and saving at the $340 billion level of disposable income? The new level of saving? **LO10.2**

6. Suppose a handbill publisher can buy a new duplicating machine for $500 and the duplicator has a 1-year life. The machine is expected to contribute $550 to the year's net revenue. What is the expected rate of return? If the real interest rate at which funds can be borrowed to purchase the machine is 8 percent, will the publisher choose to invest in the machine? Will it invest in the machine if the real interest rate is 9 percent? If it is 11 percent? **LO10.3**

7. Assume there are no investment projects in the economy that yield an expected rate of return of 25 percent or more. But suppose there are $10 billion of investment projects yielding expected returns of between 20 and 25 percent; another $10 billion yielding between 15 and 20 percent; another $10 billion between 10 and 15 percent; and so forth. Cumulate these data and present them graphically, putting the expected rate of return (and the real interest rate) on the vertical axis and the amount of investment on the horizontal axis. What will be the equilibrium level of aggregate investment if the real interest rate is (a) 15 percent, (b) 10 percent, and (c) 5 percent? **LO10.3**

8. Refer to the table in Figure 10.5 and suppose that the real interest rate is 6 percent. Next, assume that some factor changes such that the expected rate of return declines by 2 percentage points at each prospective level of investment. Assuming no change in the real interest rate, by how much and in what direction will investment change? Which of the following might cause this change: (a) a decision to increase inventories; (b) an increase in excess production capacity? **LO10.4**

9. What will the multiplier be when the MPS is 0, 0.4, 0.6, and 1? What will it be when the MPC is 1, 0.90, 0.67, 0.50, and 0? How much of a change in GDP will result if firms increase their level of investment by $8 billion and the MPC is 0.80? If the MPC instead is 0.67? **LO10.5**

10. Suppose that an initial $10 billion increase in investment spending expands GDP by $10 billion in the first round of the multiplier process. If GDP and consumption both rise by $6 billion in the second round of the process, what is the MPC in this economy? What is the size of the multiplier? If, instead, GDP and consumption both rose by $8 billion in the second round, what would have been the size of the multiplier? **LO10.5**

CHAPTER 11

The Aggregate Expenditures Model

>> LEARNING OBJECTIVES

LO11.1 Explain the role of sticky prices in the aggregate expenditures model.

LO11.2 Derive an economy's investment schedule from the investment demand curve and an interest rate.

LO11.3 Combine consumption and investment to create an aggregate expenditures schedule for a private, closed economy and determine the economy's equilibrium level of output.

LO11.4 Discuss two alternate ways to characterize the equilibrium level of real GDP in a private closed economy.

LO11.5 Explain how the multiplier affects equilibrium real GDP.

LO11.6 Integrate the international sector into the aggregate expenditures model.

LO11.7 Integrate the public sector into the aggregate expenditures model.

LO11.8 Define equilibrium GDP, full-employment GDP, recessionary expenditure gaps, and inflationary expenditure gaps.

What determines a country's GDP, given its production capacity? What causes real GDP to rise in one period and to fall in another? To more thoroughly answer these two questions, we construct the aggregate expenditures model, which originated in the 1936 writings of British economist John Maynard Keynes (pronounced "Canes"). The basic premise of the aggregate expenditures model—also known as the "Keynesian cross" model—is that the amount of goods and services produced and the level of employment depend directly on the level of aggregate expenditures (total spending). Businesses will produce only a level of output that they think they can profitably sell. They will idle their workers and machinery when there are no markets for their goods and services.

Assumptions and Simplifications

>> **LO11.1** Explain the role of sticky prices in the aggregate expenditures model.

Keynes created the aggregate expenditures model in the middle of the Great Depression, hoping to explain both why the Great Depression had happened and how it might be ended.

A "Stuck Price" Model

The simplifying assumptions underpinning the aggregate expenditures model reflect the economic conditions that prevailed during the Great Depression. The most important assumption is that prices are fixed. The aggregate expenditures model is an extreme version of a sticky price model (Chapter 6). In fact, it is a stuck-price model because the price level cannot change at all.

Keynes made this simplifying assumption because he had observed that prices had not declined sufficiently during the Great Depression to boost spending and maintain output and employment at their pre-Depression levels. Macroeconomic theories popular before the Great Depression had predicted that prices would fall to equate quantity supplied and quantity demanded. But actual prices did not fall sufficiently during the Great Depression, and the economy sank far below its potential output. U.S. real GDP declined by 27 percent from 1929 to 1933, and the unemployment rate rose to 25 percent. Thousands of factories sat idle, gathering dust and producing nothing because there was insufficient demand for their output.

Unplanned Inventory Adjustments

To Keynes, the Great Depression's massive unemployment of labor and capital was caused by firms reacting in a predictable way to unplanned increases in inventory levels. Recall that inventory consists of goods that have been produced but which have not yet been sold. Firms may stock up on inventory in anticipation of rapid future sales. They may also intentionally decrease inventory levels if they believe that demand will decline in the future. But sometimes life does not go as planned. Sometimes inventories either rise or fall more than intended because demand is either unexpectedly high or unexpectedly low.

The Great Depression took everyone by surprise. Households and businesses unexpectedly reduced their spending, which caused inventories of unsold goods to unexpectedly surge. Unable or unwilling to slash their prices, firms could not sell output fast enough to prevent inventories from continuing to pile up. So they greatly reduced their rates of production, in some cases shutting down factories completely until inventory levels declined. Reduced production brought with it discharged workers, idle factory lines, and, in some cases, shuttered factories gathering dust. Keynes thought that economics needed a new model to explain these events. So he created the aggregate expenditures model that we study in this chapter.

The model's other key assumption—the one that allows it to achieve equilibrium—is that production decisions are made in response to unexpected changes in inventory levels. If inventories are unexpectedly rising (because sales unexpectedly lag production) firms will cut back on production so as to balance production with sales and prevent inventory levels from exceeding warehouse capacity. If inventories are unexpectedly falling (because sales unexpectedly exceed production) firms will increase production so as to take advantage of an unexpectedly good selling environment.

Current Relevance

The Keynesian aggregate expenditures model remains relevant today because many prices in the modern economy are inflexible downward over relatively short periods of time, as we discussed in Chapter 6. The aggregate expenditures model therefore helps us understand how the modern economy is likely to adjust to various economic shocks over shorter periods of time. For example, it provides insight into several aspects of the COVID-19 recession and recovery, including why unexpected initial declines in spending caused even larger declines in real GDP. It also illuminates the thinking underlying the various government stimulus programs—including tax cuts, government spending increases, and lower interest rates—that were implemented in response to the pandemic.

A Preview

We will build up the aggregate expenditures model in stages. As a first step, we examine aggregate expenditures and equilibrium GDP in a *private closed economy* that lacks both international trade and government. Then we will open the closed economy to exports and imports. We will also convert our "private" economy that has only private actors (businesses and households) into a more realistic "mixed" economy that includes the government sector. Doing so will allow us to analyze the effects of government expenditures and taxes.

Until we introduce taxes, we will assume that real GDP equals disposable income (DI). For instance, if $500 billion of output is produced as GDP, households will receive exactly $500 billion of disposable income that they can then consume or save.

Finally, unless specified otherwise, we will assume (as Keynes did) that the presence of excess production capacity and unemployed labor implies that an increase in aggregate expenditures will increase real output and employment without raising the price level.

Consumption and Investment Schedules

>> LO11.2 Derive an economy's investment schedule from the investment demand curve and an interest rate.

planned investment The amount that *firms* plan or intend to invest.

In the private closed economy, the two components of aggregate expenditures are consumption, *C*, and gross investment, I_g. Because we examined the *consumption schedule* (Figure 10.2a) in the previous chapter, there is no need to repeat that analysis here. But to add the investment decisions of businesses to the consumption plans of households, we need to construct an investment schedule showing the amounts business firms collectively intend to invest—their **planned investment**—at each possible level of GDP. Such a schedule represents the investment plans of businesses in the same way the consumption schedule represents the consumption plans of households. In developing the investment schedule, we will assume that planned investment is independent of the level of current disposable income or real output.

TABLE 11.1
The Investment Schedule (in Billions)

investment schedule A curve or schedule that shows the amounts that firms plan to invest at various possible values of *real gross domestic product* (real GDP).

(1) Level of Real Output and Income	(2) Investment (I_g)
$370	$20
390	20
410	20
430	20
450	20
470	20
490	20
510	20
530	20
550	20

Suppose the investment demand curve, *ID*, is as shown in Figure 11.1a and the current real interest rate is 8 percent. This means that firms will spend $20 billion on investment goods at both low and high levels of GDP. The line I_g in Figure 11.1b shows this graphically; it is the economy's **investment schedule.** You should not confuse this investment schedule I_g with the investment demand curve *ID* in Figure 11.1a. The investment schedule shows the amount of investment forthcoming at each level of GDP. As indicated in Figure 11.1b, the interest rate and investment demand curve together determine this amount ($20 billion). Table 11.1 shows the investment schedule in tabular form. Note that investment (I_g) in column 2 is $20 billion at all levels of real GDP.

FIGURE 11.1
(a) The investment demand curve and (b) the investment schedule.

(a) The level of investment spending (here, $20 billion) is determined by the real interest rate (here, 8 percent) together with the investment demand curve *ID*. (b) The investment schedule I_g relates the amount of investment ($20 billion) determined in (a) to the various levels of GDP. In this example, the amount of investment ($20 billion) is the same at all levels of GDP.

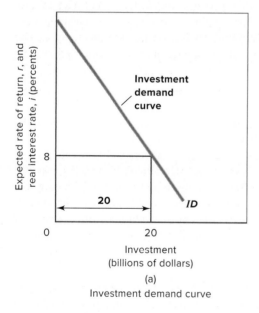

(a)
Investment demand curve

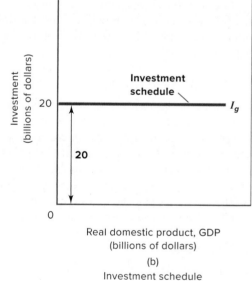

(b)
Investment schedule

QUICK REVIEW
11.1

▶ The aggregate expenditures model is a stuck-price model in which the amount of real output depends directly on the amount of total spending in the economy.

▶ Firms decide how much real output to produce in response to unexpected changes in inventory levels.

▶ If total spending is unexpectedly low in the economy, inventories will unexpectedly rise, causing firms to cut back on production. If total spending is unexpectedly high, inventories will unexpectedly fall, causing firms to increase production.

▶ The investment schedule I_g shows the amount of investment forthcoming at each level of GDP; I_g is different from the investment demand curve, *ID*, which shows how much investment firms plan to make at each interest rate.

Equilibrium GDP: $C + I_g = $ GDP

Now let's combine the consumption schedule of Chapter 10 with the investment schedule of the previous section to explain the equilibrium levels of output, income, and employment in the private closed economy.

Tabular Analysis

Columns 2 through 5 in Table 11.2 repeat the consumption and saving schedules of Table 30.1 and the investment schedule of Table 11.1.

Real Domestic Output Column 2 in Table 11.2 lists the various possible levels of total output—of real GDP—that the private sector might produce. Firms are willing to produce any one of these 10 levels of output just as long as the revenue that they receive from selling any particular amount of output equals or exceeds the costs of producing it. Those costs are the factor payments needed to obtain the required amounts of land, labor, capital, and entrepreneurship. For example, firms are willing to produce $370 billion of output if the costs of production (wages, rents, interest, and the normal profit needed to attract entrepreneurship) do not exceed the $370 billion in revenue that they will get from selling the output.

Aggregate Expenditures In the private closed economy of Table 11.2, aggregate expenditures consist of consumption (column 3) plus investment (column 5). Their sum is shown in column 6, which along with column 2 makes up the **aggregate expenditures schedule** for the private closed economy. This schedule shows the amount $(C + I_g)$ that will be spent at each possible output or income level.

At this point we are working with *planned investment*—the data in column 5 of Table 11.2. These data show the amounts that firms plan or intend to invest, not the amounts they actually will invest if there are unplanned changes in inventories. More about that shortly.

Equilibrium GDP Of the 10 possible levels of GDP in Table 11.2, which is the equilibrium level? Which total output is the economy capable of sustaining?

The equilibrium output is the output whose production creates total spending just sufficient to purchase that output. In other words, the **equilibrium GDP** occurs where the total quantity of goods produced (GDP) equals the total quantity of goods purchased $(C + I_g)$:

$$C + I_g = \text{GDP}$$

>> **LO11.3** Combine consumption and investment to create an aggregate expenditures schedule for a private, closed economy and determine the economy's equilibrium level of output.

aggregate expenditures schedule A table of numbers showing the total amount spent on *final goods* and final *services* at different levels of *real gross domestic product (real GDP)*.

equilibrium GDP The gross domestic product at which the total quantity of final goods and final services purchased (aggregate expenditures) is equal to the total quantity of final goods and services produced (the real domestic output); the real domestic output at which the aggregate demand curve intersects the aggregate supply curve. Also known as *equilibrium real output*.

TABLE 11.2 Determination of the Equilibrium Levels of Employment, Output, and Income: A Private Closed Economy

(1) Possible Levels of Employment, Millions	(2) Real Domestic Output (and Income) (GDP = DI)* Billions	(3) Consumption (C), Billions	(4) Saving (S), Billions	(5) Investment (I_g), Billions	(6) Aggregate Expenditures $(C + I_g)$, Billions	(7) Unplanned Changes in Inventories, (+ or −)	(8) Tendency of Employment, Output, and Income
(1) 40	$370	$375	$−5	$20	$395	$−25	Increase
(2) 45	390	390	0	20	410	−20	Increase
(3) 50	410	405	5	20	425	−15	Increase
(4) 55	430	420	10	20	440	−10	Increase
(5) 60	450	435	15	20	455	−5	Increase
(6) 65	470	450	20	20	470	0	Equilibrium
(7) 70	490	465	25	20	485	+5	Decrease
(8) 75	510	480	30	20	500	+10	Decrease
(9) 80	530	495	35	20	515	+15	Decrease
(10) 85	550	510	40	20	530	+20	Decrease

*If we assume that depreciation and net foreign factor income are zero, government is ignored, and all saving occurs in the household sector of the economy, then GDP as a measure of domestic output is equal to NI, PI, and DI. This means that households receive a DI equal to the value of total output, real GDP.

If you look at the domestic output levels in column 2 and the aggregate expenditures levels in column 6, you will see that this equality exists only at $470 billion of GDP (row 6). That is the only output at which economywide spending precisely equals the amount needed to move that output off the shelves. At $470 billion of GDP, annual production and spending are in balance. There is no overproduction, which would result in excess inventories and consequently cutbacks in production. Nor is there an excess of total spending, which would draw down inventories of goods and prompt increases in production. In short, there is no reason for businesses to alter this rate of production; $470 billion is the equilibrium GDP.

Disequilibrium No level of GDP other than the equilibrium level of GDP can be sustained. At levels of GDP *less than* equilibrium, spending always exceeds GDP. If, for example, firms produced $410 billion of GDP (row 3 in Table 11.2), they would find it would yield $405 billion in consumer spending. Supplemented by $20 billion of planned investment, aggregate expenditures $(C + I_g)$ would be $425 billion, as shown in column 6. The economy would provide an annual rate of spending more than sufficient to purchase the $410 billion of annual production. Because buyers would be taking goods off the shelves faster than firms could produce them, an unplanned decline in business inventories of $15 billion would occur (column 7) if this situation continued. But businesses can adjust to such an imbalance between aggregate expenditures and real output by stepping up production. Greater output will increase employment and total income. This process will continue until the equilibrium level of GDP is reached ($470 billion).

The reverse is true at all levels of GDP *greater than* the $470 billion equilibrium level. Businesses will find that these total outputs fail to generate the spending needed to clear the shelves of goods. Being unable to recover their costs, businesses will cut back on production. To illustrate: At the $510 billion output (row 8), business managers would find spending is insufficient to permit the sale of all that output. Of the $510 billion of income that this output creates, $480 billion would be received back by businesses as consumption spending. Though supplemented by $20 billion of planned investment spending, total expenditures ($500 billion) would still be $10 billion below the $510 billion quantity produced. If this imbalance persisted, $10 billion of inventories would pile up (column 7). But businesses can adjust to this unintended accumulation of unsold goods by cutting back on the rate of production. The resulting decline in output would mean fewer jobs and a decline in total income.

Graphical Analysis

We can demonstrate our analysis graphically. In **Figure 11.2 (Key Graph)** the 45° line we developed in Chapter 10 takes on increased significance. At any point on this line, the value of what is measured on the horizontal axis (here, GDP) equals the value of what is measured on the vertical axis (here, aggregate expenditures, or $C + I_g$). Having discovered in our tabular analysis that the equilibrium level of domestic output occurs where $C + I_g$ equals GDP, we can say that the 45° line in Figure 11.2 is a graphical representation of that equilibrium condition.

Now we must graph the aggregate expenditures schedule onto Figure 11.2. To do so, we duplicate the consumption schedule C in Figure 10.2a and add to it vertically the constant $20 billion amount of investment I_g from Figure 11.1b. This $20 billion is the amount that firms plan to invest at all levels of GDP. Or, more directly, we can plot the $C + I_g$ data in column 6, Table 11.2.

In Figure 11.2, the aggregate expenditures line $C + I_g$ shows that total spending rises with income and output (GDP), but not as much as income rises. That condition holds true because the marginal propensity to consume—the slope of line C—is less than 1. A part of any increase in income will be saved rather than spent. And because the aggregate expenditures line $C + I_g$ is parallel to the consumption line C, the slope of the aggregate expenditures line also equals the MPC for the economy and is less than 1. For our particular data, aggregate expenditures rise by $15 billion for every $20 billion increase in real output and income because $5 billion of each $20 billion increment is saved. Therefore, the slope of the aggregate expenditures line is 0.75 (= $15/$20).

The equilibrium level of GDP occurs at the intersection of the aggregate expenditures schedule and the 45° line. This intersection locates the only point at which aggregate expenditures (on the vertical axis) are equal to GDP (on the horizontal axis). Because Figure 11.2 is based on the

..ıl KEY GRAPH

FIGURE 11.2 Equilibrium GDP in a private closed economy.

The aggregate expenditures schedule, $C + I_g$, is determined by adding the investment schedule I_g to the upsloping consumption schedule C. Since investment is assumed to be the same at each level of GDP, the vertical distances between C and $C + I_g$ do not change. Equilibrium GDP is determined where the aggregate expenditures schedule intersects the 45° line, in this case at $470 billion.

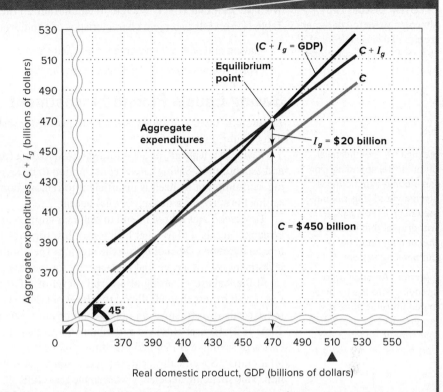

QUICK QUIZ FOR FIGURE 11.2

1. In this figure, the slope of the aggregate expenditures schedule $C + I_g$:
    a. increases as real GDP increases.
    b. falls as real GDP increases.
    c. is constant and equals the MPC.
    d. is constant and equals the MPS.

2. At all points on the 45° line:
    a. equilibrium GDP is possible.
    b. aggregate expenditures exceed real GDP.
    c. consumption exceeds investment.
    d. aggregate expenditures are less than real GDP.

3. The $490 billion level of real GDP is not an equilibrium because:
    a. investment exceeds consumption.
    b. consumption exceeds investment.
    c. planned $C + I_g$ exceeds real GDP.
    d. planned $C + I_g$ is less than real GDP.

4. The $430 billion level of real GDP is not an equilibrium because:
    a. investment exceeds consumption.
    b. consumption exceeds investment.
    c. planned $C + I_g$ exceeds real GDP.
    d. planned $C + I_g$ is less than real GDP.

Answers: 1. c; 2. a; 3. d; 4. c

data in Table 11.2, we once again find that equilibrium output is $470 billion. Observe that consumption at this output is $450 billion, and investment is $20 billion.

It is evident from Figure 11.2 that no levels of GDP *above* the equilibrium level are sustainable because at those levels $C + I_g$ falls short of GDP. In those situations, the aggregate expenditures schedule lies below the 45° line. At the $510 billion GDP level, for example, $C + I_g$ is only $500 billion. This underspending causes inventories to rise, prompting firms to adjust production downward, toward the $470 billion output level.

Conversely, at levels of GDP *below* $470 billion, the economy wants to spend in excess of what businesses are producing. Therefore, $C + I_g$ exceeds total output. Graphically, the aggregate expenditures schedule lies above the 45° line. At the $410 billion GDP level, for example, $C + I_g$ totals $425 billion. This excess spending causes inventories to fall below their planned level, prompting firms to adjust production upward, toward the $470 billion output level. Once production reaches that level, it will be sustained there indefinitely unless there is some change in the location of the aggregate expenditures line.

Other Features of Equilibrium GDP

>> **LO11.4** Discuss two alternate ways to characterize the equilibrium level of real GDP in a private closed economy.

We have seen that $C + I_g =$ GDP at equilibrium in the private closed economy. A closer look at Table 11.2 reveals two more characteristics of equilibrium GDP:

- Saving and *planned* investment are equal ($S = I_g$).
- There are no *unplanned* changes in inventories.

Saving Equals Planned Investment

As row 6 in Table 11.2 shows, saving and planned investment are both $20 billion at the $470 billion equilibrium level of GDP.

leakage (1) A withdrawal of potential spending from the income-expenditures stream via *saving,* tax payments, or *imports;* (2) a withdrawal that reduces the lending potential of the banking system.

Saving is a **leakage,** or a withdrawal, of spending from the economy's circular flow of income and expenditures. Saving causes consumption to be less than total output or GDP. Because of saving, consumption by itself is insufficient to remove domestic output from the shelves, apparently setting the stage for a decline in total output.

injection An addition of spending into the income-expenditure stream: any increment to *consumption, investment, government purchases,* or *net exports.*

However, firms do not intend to sell their entire output to consumers. Some of that output will be capital goods sold to other businesses. Investment—that is, purchases of capital goods—is therefore an **injection** of spending into the income-expenditures stream. As an addition to consumption, investment is thus a potential replacement for the leakage of saving.

If the leakage of saving at a certain level of GDP exceeds the injection of investment, then $C + I_g$ will be less than GDP and that level of GDP cannot be sustained. Any GDP for which saving exceeds investment is an above-equilibrium GDP. Consider GDP of $510 billion (row 8 in Table 11.2). Households save $30 billion, but firms plan to invest only $20 billion. This $10 billion excess of saving over planned investment reduces total spending to $10 billion below the value of total output. Specifically, aggregate expenditures will be $500 billion while real GDP is $510 billion. This spending deficiency will reduce real GDP.

Conversely, if the injection of investment exceeds the leakage of saving, then $C + I_g$ will be greater than GDP and drive GDP upward. Any GDP for which investment exceeds saving is a below-equilibrium GDP. For example, at a GDP of $410 billion (row 3 in Table 11.2), households save only $5 billion, but firms invest $20 billion. So investment exceeds saving by $15 billion. The larger injection of investment spending more than compensates for this small leakage of saving at this relatively low GDP level.

Only where $S = I_g$—where the leakage of saving of $20 billion is exactly offset by the injection of planned investment of $20 billion—will aggregate expenditures ($C + I_g$) equal real output (GDP). That $C + I_g =$ GDP equality defines the equilibrium GDP.

No Unplanned Changes in Inventories

unplanned changes in inventories Changes in *inventories* that *firms* did not anticipate; changes in inventories that occur because of unexpected increases or decreases of aggregate spending (or of *aggregate expenditures*).

As part of their investment plans, firms may decide to increase or decrease their inventories. But as line 6 of Table 11.2 confirms, there are no **unplanned changes in inventories** at equilibrium GDP. This fact, along with $C + I_g =$ GDP, and $S = I_g$, characterizes equilibrium GDP in the private closed economy.

Unplanned changes in inventories play a major role in achieving equilibrium GDP. For example, consider the $490 billion *above-equilibrium* GDP shown in row 7 of Table 11.2. What happens if firms produce that output, thinking they can sell it? Households save $25 billion of their $490 billion DI, so consumption is only $465 billion. Planned investment—which includes planned changes in inventories—is $20 billion (column 5). So aggregate expenditures ($C + I_g$) are $485 billion, and sales fall short of production by $5 billion. Firms retain that extra $5 billion of goods as an unplanned increase in inventories (column 7). That unplanned increase in inventories results from the failure of total spending to remove all of total output from the shelves.

Because changes in inventories are a part of investment, we note that *actual investment* is $25 billion. It consists of $20 billion of planned investment *plus* the $5 billion unplanned increase in inventories. Actual investment equals the saving of $25 billion, even though saving exceeds planned investment by $5 billion. Because firms cannot earn profits by accumulating unwanted inventories, the $5 billion unplanned increase in inventories prompts them to cut back employment and production. GDP falls to its equilibrium level of $470 billion, at which unplanned changes in inventories are zero.

Now look at the *below-equilibrium* $450 billion output (row 5, Table 11.2). Because households save only $15 billion of their $450 billion DI, consumption is $435 billion. Planned investment by firms is $20 billion, so aggregate expenditures are $455 billion. Sales exceed production by $5 billion because a $5 billion unplanned decrease in business inventories has occurred. Firms must *disinvest* $5 billion in inventories (column 7). Note again that actual investment is $15 billion ($20 billion planned *minus* the $5 billion decline in inventories) and is equal to the saving of $15 billion, even though planned investment exceeds saving by $5 billion. The unplanned decline in inventories, resulting from the excess of sales over production, encourages firms to expand production. GDP rises to $470 billion, at which unplanned changes in inventories are zero.

When economists say differences between investment and saving can occur and bring about changes in equilibrium GDP, they are referring to planned investment and saving. Equilibrium occurs only when planned investment and saving are equal. But when unplanned changes in inventories are taken into account, investment and saving are always equal, regardless of the level of GDP. Why? Actual investment consists of planned investment *and* unplanned investment (unplanned changes in inventories). Unplanned changes in inventories act as a balancing item that equates the actual amounts saved and invested in any period.

Changes in Equilibrium GDP and the Multiplier

In Chapter 10, we established that an initial change in spending can cause a greater change in real output through the multiplier effect. In equation form,

$$\text{Multiplier} = \frac{\text{change in real GDP}}{\text{initial change in spending}}$$

Further, we discovered that the size of the multiplier depends on the size of the MPS in the economy:

$$\text{Multiplier} = \frac{1}{\text{MPS}}$$

We are about to apply those two versions of the multiplier to the aggregate expenditures model, but because the multiplier is such an important element of that model, we highly recommend that you quickly review Figure 10.7 **(Key Graph)** at this time.

Once you have reviewed Figure 10.7 **(Key Graph)**, note that in a private closed economy, $C + I_g = \text{GDP}$ when the economy is in equilibrium. So equilibrium GDP changes in response to changes in either the consumption schedule (C) or the investment schedule (I_g). Because changes in the investment schedule are the main sources of instability, we direct our attention toward them.

>> **LO11.5** Explain how the multiplier affects equilibrium real GDP.

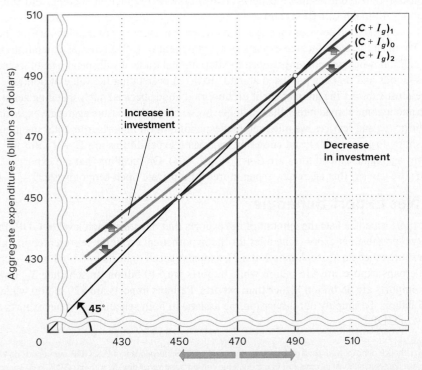

FIGURE 11.3
Changes in the aggregate expenditures schedule and the multiplier effect.

An upward shift of the aggregate expenditures schedule from $(C + I_g)_0$ to $(C + I_g)_1$ will increase the equilibrium GDP. Conversely, a downward shift from $(C + I_g)_0$ to $(C + I_g)_2$ will lower the equilibrium GDP. The extent of the changes in equilibrium GDP will depend on the size of the multiplier, which in this case is 4 (= 20/5). The multiplier is equal to 1/MPS (here, 4 = 1/.25).

Real domestic product, GDP (billions of dollars)

Figure 11.3 shows the effect of changes in investment spending on equilibrium real GDP. Suppose that the expected rate of return on investment rises or that the real interest rate falls such that investment spending increases by $5 billion. That would be shown as an upward shift of the investment schedule in Figure 11.1b. In Figure 11.3, the $5 billion increase of investment spending will increase aggregate expenditures from $(C + I_g)_0$ to $(C + I_g)_1$ and raise equilibrium real GDP from $470 billion to $490 billion.

If the expected rate of return on investment decreases or if the real interest rate rises, investment spending will decline by, say, $5 billion. That would be shown as a downward shift of the investment schedule in Figure 11.1b and a downward shift of the aggregate expenditures schedule from $(C + I_g)_0$ to $(C + I_g)_2$ in Figure 11.3. Equilibrium GDP will fall from $470 billion to $450 billion.

In our examples, a $5 billion change in investment spending leads to a $20 billion change in output and income. So the *multiplier* is 4 (= $20/$5). The MPS is 0.25, meaning that for every $1 billion of new income, $0.25 billion of new saving occurs. Therefore, $20 billion of new income is needed to generate $5 billion of new saving. Once that increase in income and saving occurs, the economy is back in equilibrium, with $C + I_g$ = GDP; saving equal to planned investment; and no unplanned changes in inventories. You can see, then, why the multiplier is equal to 1/MPS and that the multiplier process is an integral part of the aggregate expenditures model.

QUICK REVIEW

11.2

▶ In a private closed economy, equilibrium GDP occurs where aggregate expenditures equal real domestic output ($C + I_g$ = GDP).

▶ At equilibrium GDP, saving equals planned investment ($S = I_g$) and unplanned changes in inventories are zero.

▶ Actual investment consists of planned investment plus unplanned changes in inventories (+ or −) and is always equal to saving in a private closed economy.

▶ Through the multiplier effect, an initial change in investment spending can cause a magnified change in domestic output and income.

Adding International Trade

>> **LO11.6** Integrate the international sector into the aggregate expenditures model.

net exports (X_n) *Exports minus imports.*

We now move from a private closed economy to a private open economy that incorporates exports (X) and imports (M). We focus on **net exports** (exports minus imports), which may be either positive or negative.

Net Exports and Aggregate Expenditures

Like consumption and investment, exports create domestic production, income, and employment for a nation. Although U.S. goods and services produced for export are sent abroad, foreign spending on those goods and services increases production and creates jobs and incomes in the United States. We must therefore include exports as a component of U.S. aggregate expenditures.

In addition, when an economy is open to international trade, it will spend part of its income on imports—goods and services produced abroad. To avoid overstating the value of domestic production, we must subtract the amount spent on imported goods because such spending generates production and income abroad rather than at home. So, to correctly measure aggregate expenditures for domestic goods and services, we must subtract expenditures on imports from total spending.

In short, for a private closed economy, aggregate expenditures are $C + I_g$. But for an open economy, aggregate expenditures are $C + I_g + (X - M)$. Or, recalling that net exports (X_n) equal $(X - M)$, we can say that aggregate expenditures for a private open economy are $C + I_g + X_n$.

The Net Export Schedule

A net export schedule lists the amount of net exports that occurs at each level of GDP. Table 11.3 shows two possible net export schedules for the hypothetical economy represented in Table 11.2. In net export schedule X_{n1} (columns 1 and 2), exports exceed imports by $5 billion at each level of GDP. Perhaps exports are $15 billion while imports are $10 billion. In schedule X_{n2} (columns 1 and 3), imports are $5 billion higher than exports. Perhaps imports are $20 billion while exports are $15 billion. To simplify our discussion, we assume in both schedules that net exports are independent of GDP.[1]

---

[1]In reality, although our exports depend on foreign incomes and are thus independent of U.S. GDP, our imports do vary directly with our own domestic national income. Just as our domestic consumption varies directly with our GDP, so do our purchases of foreign goods. As our GDP rises, U.S. households buy not only more Cadillacs and Harleys, but also more Mercedes and Kawasakis. However, for now we will ignore the complications of the positive relationship between imports and U.S. GDP.

Figure 11.4a represents the two net export schedules in Table 11.3. Schedule X_{n1} is above the horizontal axis and depicts positive net exports of $5 billion at all levels of GDP. Schedule X_{n2}, which is below the horizontal axis, shows negative net exports of $5 billion at all levels of GDP.

Net Exports and Equilibrium GDP

The aggregate expenditures schedule labeled $C + I_g$ in Figure 11.4b reflects the private closed economy. It shows the combined consumption and gross investment expenditures occurring at each level of GDP. With no foreign sector, the equilibrium GDP is $470 billion.

But in the private open economy, net exports can be either positive or negative. Let's see how each of the net export schedules in Figure 11.4a affects equilibrium GDP.

TABLE 11.3
Two Net Export Schedules (in Billions)

(1) Level of GDP	(2) Net Exports, X_{n1} $(X > M)$	(3) Net Exports, X_{n2} $(X < M)$
$370	$+5	$−5
390	+5	−5
410	+5	−5
430	+5	−5
450	+5	−5
470	+5	−5
490	+5	−5
510	+5	−5
530	+5	−5
550	+5	−5

FIGURE 11.4
Net exports and equilibrium GDP.

(a) Net exports can be either positive, as shown by the net export schedule X_{n1} or negative, as depicted by net export schedule X_{n2}. (b) Positive net exports elevate the aggregate expenditure schedule from the closed-economy level of $C + I_g$ to the open-economy level of $C + I_g + X_{n1}$. Negative net exports lower the aggregate expenditures schedule from the closed-economy level of $C + I_g$ to the open-economy level of $C + I_g + X_{n2}$.

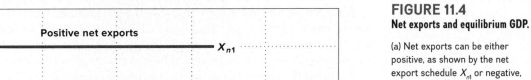

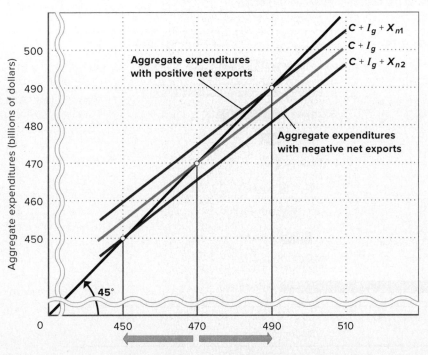

Real domestic product, GDP (billions of dollars)

(a)

Net export schedule, X_n

Real domestic product, GDP (billions of dollars)

(b)

Aggregate expenditures schedule

Positive Net Exports Suppose the net export schedule is X_{n1}. We account for the $5 billion of additional net export expenditures by the rest of the world by adding that $5 billion to the $C + I_g$ schedule in Figure 11.4b. Aggregate expenditures at each level of GDP are then $5 billion higher than $C + I_g$ alone. The aggregate expenditures schedule for the open economy thus becomes $C + I_g + X_{n1}$. As a result, the equilibrium shifts to where $C + I_g + X_{n1}$ intersects the 45-degree line. In this case, international trade increases equilibrium GDP from $470 billion in the private closed economy to $490 billion in the private open economy. Adding net exports of $5 billion has increased GDP by $20 billion, in this case implying a multiplier of 4.

Generalization: Other things equal, positive net exports increase aggregate expenditures and GDP beyond what they would be in a closed economy.

Negative Net Exports Next, suppose that net exports are a negative $5 billion, as shown by X_{n2} in Figure 11.4a. In that case, our hypothetical economy is importing $5 billion more of goods than it is exporting. The aggregate expenditures schedule shown as $C + I_g$ in Figure 11.4b therefore overstates the expenditures on domestic output at each level of GDP. We must reduce the sum of expenditures by the $5 billion net amount spent on imported goods. We do that by subtracting the $5 billion of net imports from $C + I_g$.

The relevant aggregate expenditures schedule in Figure 11.4b becomes $C + I_g + X_{n2}$ and equilibrium GDP falls from $470 billion to $450 billion. Again, a change in net exports of $5 billion has produced a fourfold change in GDP, reminding us that the multiplier in this example is 4.

We therefore have a corollary to our first generalization: Other things equal, negative net exports reduce aggregate expenditures and GDP below what they would be in a closed economy. When imports exceed exports, the contractionary effect of the larger amount of imports outweighs the expansionary effect of the smaller amount of exports, so equilibrium real GDP decreases.

As Global Perspective 11.1 shows, net exports vary greatly among the major industrial nations.

 GLOBAL PERSPECTIVE 11.1

NET EXPORTS OF GOODS, SELECTED NATIONS, 2020

Some nations, such as China and Germany, have positive net exports; other countries, such as the United States and France, have negative net exports. For several decades, China has been the country with the largest positive net exports while the United States has been the country with the largest negative net exports.

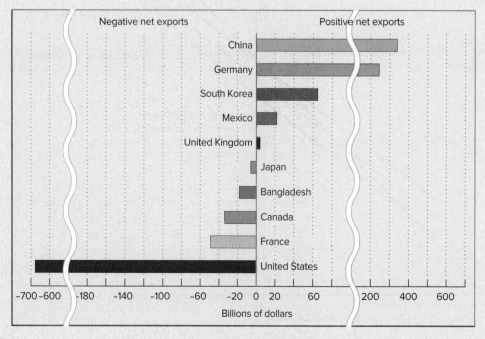

Source: The World Bank.

International Economic Linkages

Our analysis of net exports and real GDP suggests how circumstances or policies abroad can affect U.S. GDP.

Prosperity Abroad A rising level of real output and income among U.S. foreign trading partners enables the United States to sell more goods abroad, thus raising U.S. net exports and increasing U.S. real GDP (assuming initially there is excess capacity). There is good reason for Americans to be interested in our trading partners' prosperity. Their good fortune enables them to buy more U.S. exports, increasing our income and enabling us in turn to buy more foreign imports. These imported goods are the ultimate benefit of international trade. Trade transfers foreign prosperity to Americans.

Exchange Rates Depreciation (a decrease in the value) of the dollar relative to other currencies enables people abroad to obtain more dollars with each unit of their own currencies. The price of U.S. goods in terms of those currencies will fall, stimulating purchases of U.S. exports. Also, U.S. customers will find they need more dollars to buy foreign goods and, consequently, will reduce their spending on imports. If the economy has available capacity, the increased exports and decreased imports will increase U.S. net exports and expand the nation's GDP.

To check your understanding, think through the effects of an appreciation (increase in value) of the dollar on net exports and equilibrium GDP.

A Caution on Tariffs and Devaluations Because higher net exports increase real GDP, countries often look for ways to reduce imports and increase exports during recessions or depressions. Thus, a recession might tempt the U.S. federal government to increase tariffs and devalue the international value of the dollar (for instance, by supplying massive amounts of dollars in the foreign exchange market). Increasing net exports, the thinking goes, would expand domestic production, reduce domestic unemployment, and help the economy recover.

But this interventionist thinking is too simplistic. Suppose that the United States imposes high tariffs on foreign goods to reduce imports and thus increase our domestic production and employment. Our imports, however, are our trading partners' exports. So when we restrict our imports, we depress our trading partners' economies. They are likely to retaliate against us by imposing tariffs on our products. If they do so, our exports will decline, and our net exports may in fact fall. Thus imposing tariffs may decrease, not increase, our net exports.

That unfortunate possibility became a sad reality during the Great Depression of the 1930s, when various nations, including the United States, imposed trade barriers in an attempt to reduce their own domestic unemployment levels. The result was many rounds of retaliation that throttled world trade, worsened the depression, and increased domestic unemployment. Adding to the problem were some nations' attempts to increase their net exports by devaluing their currencies. Other nations then retaliated by devaluing their own currencies. The international exchange rate system collapsed, and world trade spiraled downward. Economic historians agree that tariffs and devaluations during the 1930s were huge policy mistakes.

▶ Positive net exports increase aggregate expenditures relative to the closed economy and, other things equal, increase equilibrium GDP.

▶ Negative net exports decrease aggregate expenditures relative to the closed economy and, other things equal, reduce equilibrium GDP.

▶ In the open economy, changes in (a) prosperity abroad, (b) tariffs, and (c) exchange rates can affect U.S. net exports and therefore U.S. aggregate expenditures and equilibrium GDP.

▶ Tariffs and deliberate currency depreciations are unlikely to increase net exports because other nations will retaliate.

**QUICK REVIEW
11.3**

Adding the Public Sector

Our final step in constructing the full aggregate expenditures model is to move the analysis from a private (no-government) open economy to an economy with a public sector (sometimes called a "mixed economy"). To do so, we must add government purchases and taxes to the model.

For simplicity, we assume that government purchases are independent of GDP and do not alter the consumption and investment schedules. Also, government's net tax revenues—total tax revenues less "negative taxes" in the form of transfer payments—are derived entirely from personal taxes. Finally, a fixed amount of taxes is collected regardless of the level of GDP.

>> **LO11.7** Integrate the public sector into the aggregate expenditures model.

TABLE 11.4 The Impact of Government Purchases on Equilibrium GDP

(1) Real Domestic Output and Income (GDP = DI), Billions	(2) Consumption (C), Billions	(3) Savings (S), Billions	(4) Investment (I_g), Billions	(5) Net Exports (X_n), Billions — Exports (X)	Imports (M)	(6) Government Purchases (G), Billions	(7) Aggregate Expenditures ($C + I_g + X_n + G$), Billions (2) + (4) + (5) + (6)
(1) $370	$375	$−5	$20	$10	$10	$20	$415
(2) 390	390	0	20	10	10	20	430
(3) 410	405	5	20	10	10	20	445
(4) 430	420	10	20	10	10	20	460
(5) 450	435	15	20	10	10	20	475
(6) 470	450	20	20	10	10	20	490
(7) 490	465	25	20	10	10	20	505
(8) 510	480	30	20	10	10	20	520
(9) 530	495	35	20	10	10	20	535
(10) **550**	**510**	**40**	**20**	**10**	**10**	**20**	**550**

Government Purchases and Equilibrium GDP

Suppose the government decides to purchase $20 billion of goods and services regardless of the level of GDP and tax collections.

Tabular Example Table 11.4 shows the impact of this purchase on the equilibrium GDP. Columns 1 through 4 are carried over from Table 11.2 for the private closed economy, in which the equilibrium GDP was $470 billion. The only new items are exports and imports in column 5 and government purchases in column 6. (Observe in column 5 that net exports are always zero.) As column 7 shows, the addition of government purchases to private spending ($C + I_g + X_n$) yields a new, higher level of aggregate expenditures ($C + I_g + X_n + G$). Comparing columns 1 and 7, we find that aggregate expenditures and real output are equal at a higher level of GDP. Without government purchases, equilibrium GDP was $470 billion (row 6); *with* government purchases, aggregate expenditures and real output are equal at $550 billion (row 10). Increases in public spending, like increases in private spending, shift the aggregate expenditures schedule upward and produce a higher equilibrium GDP.

Note, too, that government spending is subject to the multiplier. A $20 billion increase in government purchases has increased equilibrium GDP by $80 billion (from $470 billion to $550 billion). The multiplier in this example is 4.

Note that this $20 billion increase in government spending is *not* financed by increased taxes.

Graphical Analysis In Figure 11.5, we vertically add $20 billion of government purchases, G, to the level of private spending, $C + I_g + X_n$. That added $20 billion raises the aggregate expenditures schedule (private plus public) to $C + I_g + X_n + G$, resulting in an $80 billion increase in equilibrium GDP, from $470 to $550 billion.

A decline in government purchases G will lower the aggregate expenditures schedule in Figure 11.5 and result in a multiplied decline in the equilibrium GDP. Verify in Table 11.4 that if government purchases decline from $20 billion to $10 billion, the equilibrium GDP will fall by $40 billion.

Taxation and Equilibrium GDP

lump-sum tax A tax that collects a constant amount (the tax revenue of government is the same) at all levels of *GDP*.

The government not only spends but also collects taxes. Suppose it imposes a **lump-sum tax,** which is a tax of a constant amount or, more precisely, a tax yielding the same amount of tax revenue at each level of GDP. Let's assume this tax is $20 billion, so that the government obtains $20 billion of tax revenue at each level of GDP regardless of the level of government purchases.

Tabular Example In Table 11.5, which continues our example, we find taxes in column 2, and we see in column 3 that disposable (after-tax) income is lower than GDP (column 1) by the $20 billion amount of the tax. Because households use disposable income both to consume and to save,

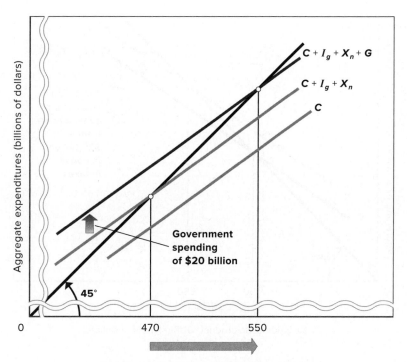

FIGURE 11.5
Government spending and equilibrium GDP.

The addition of government expenditures of G to our analysis raises the aggregate expenditures $(C + I_g + X_n + G)$ schedule and increases the equilibrium level of GDP, as would an increase in C, I_g, or X_n.

the tax lowers both consumption and saving. The MPC and MPS tell us how much consumption and saving will decline as a result of the $20 billion in taxes. Because the MPC is 0.75, the government tax collection of $20 billion will reduce consumption by $15 billion (= 0.75 × $20 billion). Because the MPS is 0.25, saving will drop by $5 billion (= 0.25 × $20 billion).

Columns 4 and 5 in Table 11.5 list the amounts of consumption and saving *at each level of GDP*. Note they are $15 billion and $5 billion smaller than those in Table 11.4. Taxes reduce disposable income relative to GDP by the amount of the taxes. This decline in DI reduces both consumption and saving at each level of GDP. The extent of the C and S reductions depends on the MPC and the MPS.

To find the effect of taxes on equilibrium GDP, we calculate aggregate expenditures again, as shown in column 9, Table 11.5. Aggregate spending is $15 billion less at each level of GDP than it

TABLE 11.5 Determination of the Equilibrium Levels of Employment, Output, and Income: Private and Public Sectors

(1) Real Domestic Output and Income (GDP = NI), Billions	(2) Taxes (T), Billions	(3) Disposable Income (DI), Billions (1) − (2)	(4) Consumption (Cₐ), Billions	(5) Savings (Sₐ), Billions (3) − (4)	(6) Investment (Iₘ), Billions	(7) Net Exports (Xₙ), Billions Exports (X)	Imports (M)	(8) Government Purchases (G), Billions	(9) Aggregate Expenditures (Cₐ + Iₘ + Xₙ + G), Billions (4)+(6)+(7)+(8)
(1) $370	$20	$350	$360	$−10	$20	$10	$10	$20	$400
(2) 390	20	370	375	−5	20	10	10	20	415
(3) 410	20	390	390	0	20	10	10	20	430
(4) 430	20	410	405	5	20	10	10	20	445
(5) 450	20	430	420	10	20	10	10	20	460
(6) 470	20	450	435	15	20	10	10	20	475
(7) 490	20	470	450	20	20	10	10	20	490
(8) 510	20	490	465	25	20	10	10	20	505
(9) 530	20	510	480	30	20	10	10	20	520
(10) 550	20	530	495	35	20	10	10	20	535

FIGURE 11.6
Taxes and equilibrium GDP.

If the MPC is 0.75, the $20 billion of taxes will lower the consumption schedule by $15 billion and cause a $60 billion decline in the equilibrium GDP. In the open economy with government, equilibrium GDP occurs where C_a(after-tax income) + $I_g + X_n + G$ = GDP. Here that equilibrium is $490 billion.

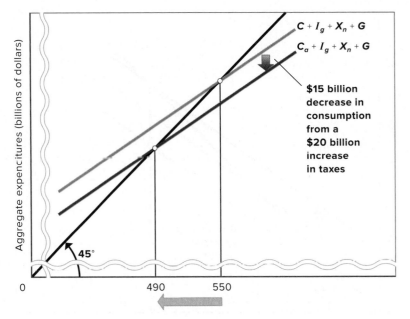

Real domestic product, GDP (billions of dollars)

was in Table 11.4. The reason is that after-tax consumption, designated by C_a, is $15 billion less at each level of GDP. A comparison of real output and aggregate expenditures in columns 1 and 9 shows that the aggregate amounts produced and purchased are equal only at $490 billion of GDP (row 7). The $20 billion lump-sum tax has reduced equilibrium GDP by $60 billion, from $550 billion (row 10, Table 11.4) to $490 billion (row 7, Table 11.5).

Graphical Analysis In Figure 11.6, the $20 billion increase in taxes shows up as a $15 (not $20) billion decline in the aggregate expenditures ($C_a + I_g + X_n + G$) schedule. This decline results solely from a decrease in the consumption C component of aggregate expenditures. Equilibrium GDP falls from $550 billion to $490 billion because of this tax-caused drop in consumption. With no change in government expenditures, tax increases lower the aggregate expenditures schedule relative to the 45° line and reduce equilibrium GDP.

In contrast, a *decrease* in existing taxes will raise the aggregate expenditures schedule in Figure 11.6 as a result of an increase in consumption at all GDP levels. You should confirm that a tax reduction of $10 billion (from the present $20 billion to $10 billion) will increase equilibrium GDP from $490 billion to $520 billion.

Injections, Leakages, and Unplanned Changes in Inventories In the full model, it is still the case that injections into the income-expenditures stream equal leakages from the income stream. For the private closed economy, $S = I_g$. For the expanded economy, imports and taxes are added leakages. Saving, importing, and paying taxes are all uses of income that subtract from potential consumption. Consumption will now be less than GDP—creating a potential spending gap—in the amount of after-tax saving (S_a), imports (M), and taxes (T). But exports (X), government purchases (G), and investment (I_g), are injections into the income-expenditures stream. At the equilibrium GDP, the sum of the leakages equals the sum of injections. In symbols:

$$S_a + M + T = I_g + X + G$$

You should use the data in Table 11.5 to confirm this equality between leakages and injections at the equilibrium GDP of $490 billion. Also, substantiate that a lack of such equality exists at all other possible levels of GDP.

Although not directly shown in Table 11.5, the equilibrium characteristic of "no unplanned changes in inventories" will also be fulfilled at the $490 billion GDP. Because aggregate expenditures equal GDP, all the goods and services produced will be purchased. There will be no unplanned increase in inventories, so firms will have no incentive to reduce their employment and production. Nor will they experience an unplanned decline in their inventories, which would prompt them to expand their employment and output to replenish their inventories.

Equilibrium versus Full-Employment GDP

In the aggregate expenditures model, equilibrium GDP need not equal the economy's full-employment GDP. In fact, Keynes specifically designed the model to explain situations like the Great Depression, in which the economy appeared to be trapped in a bad equilibrium in which real GDP was far below potential output.

The fact that equilibrium and potential GDP in the aggregate expenditures model need not match reveals critical insights about the causes of demand-pull inflation. We will first examine the "expenditure gaps" that give rise to differences between equilibrium and potential GDP. Then we will see how the model helps to explain the COVID-19 recession of 2020 and preview the policies that the federal government used to try to halt and reverse it.

>> LO11.8 Define equilibrium GDP, full-employment GDP, recessionary expenditure gaps, and inflationary expenditure gaps.

Recessionary Expenditure Gap

Suppose that in **Figure 11.7 (Key Graph),** panel (a), the full-employment level of GDP is $510 billion and the aggregate expenditures schedule is AE_1. (For simplicity, we now dispense with the $C_a + I_g + X_n + G$ labeling.) This schedule intersects the 45° line to the left of the economy's full-employment output, so the economy's equilibrium GDP of $490 billion is $20 billion short of its full-employment output of $510 billion.

According to columns 1 and 2 of row 8 in Table 11.2, total employment at the full-employment GDP of $510 billion would be 75 million workers. But columns 1 and 2 of row 7 indicate that the economy depicted in Figure 11.7a is employing only 70 million workers at the equilibrium GDP of $490 billion. So 5 million available workers are not employed, and the economy is sacrificing $20 billion of output.

A **recessionary expenditure gap** is the amount by which aggregate expenditures *at the full-employment level of GDP* fall short of the amount required to achieve the full-employment level of GDP. Insufficient total spending contracts or depresses the economy. Table 11.5 shows that at the full-employment level of $510 billion (column 1), the corresponding level of aggregate expenditures is only $505 billion (column 9). The recessionary expenditure gap is thus $5 billion, the amount by which the aggregate expenditures curve would have to shift upward to realize equilibrium at the full-employment GDP. Graphically, the recessionary expenditure gap is the *vertical* distance (measured at the full-employment GDP) by which the actual aggregate expenditures schedule AE_1 lies below the hypothetical full-employment aggregate expenditures schedule AE_0. In Figure 11.7a, this recessionary expenditure gap is $5 billion. Because the multiplier is 4, there is a $20 billion differential (the recessionary expenditure gap of $5 billion times the multiplier of 4) between the equilibrium GDP and the full-employment GDP. This $20 billion difference is a negative *GDP gap*.

recessionary expenditure gap The amount by which *aggregate expenditures* at the *full-employment level of GDP* fall short of the amount required to achieve the full-employment level of GDP. In the aggregate expenditures model, the amount by which the *aggregate expenditures schedule* must shift upward to increase *real GDP* to its full-employment, noninflationary level.

Keynes's Solution to a Recessionary Expenditure Gap Keynes pointed to two different policies that a government might pursue to close a recessionary expenditure gap and achieve full employment. The first is to increase government spending. The second is to lower taxes. Both work by increasing aggregate expenditures.

Look back at Figure 11.5, which shows how an increase in government expenditures G will increase overall aggregate expenditures and, consequently, the equilibrium real GDP. Applying this strategy to the situation in Figure 11.7a, government could completely close the $20 billion negative GDP gap if it increased spending by the $5 billion amount of the recessionary expenditure gap. Given the economy's multiplier of 4, the $5 billion increase in G would create a $20 billion increase in equilibrium real GDP, bringing the economy to full employment.

Government also could lower taxes to close the recessionary expenditure gap and thus eliminate the negative GDP gap. Look back at Figure 11.6, in which an increase in taxes results in lower after-tax consumption spending and a smaller equilibrium real GDP. Keynes suggested a reversal of this process: Because an increase in taxes lowers equilibrium real GDP, a decrease in taxes will raise equilibrium GDP. The decrease in taxes will leave consumers with higher after-tax income, which will lead to higher consumption expenditures and an increase in equilibrium real GDP.

By how much should the government cut taxes? The answer is: By exactly $6.67 billion, because the MPC is 0.75. The tax cut of $6.67 billion will increase consumers' after-tax income by $6.67 billion. They will then increase consumption spending by 0.75 of that amount, or $5 billion. Aggregate expenditures will increase by the $5 billion needed to close the recessionary expenditure gap. The economy's equilibrium real GDP will rise to its potential output of $510 billion.

But a big warning is needed here: As the economy moves closer to its potential output, it becomes harder to justify Keynes's assumption that prices are stuck. As the economy closes its negative GDP

..ıl KEY GRAPH

FIGURE 11.7 Recessionary and inflationary expenditure gaps.

The equilibrium and full-employment GDPs may not coincide. (a) A recessionary expenditure gap is the amount (vertical distance) by which aggregate expenditures at the full-employment GDP level fall short of those needed to achieve full-employment. Here, the $5 billion recessionary expenditure gap that exists at the full-employment GDP level of $510 billion causes a $20 billion negative GDP gap by shifting the equilibrium level of GDP from $510 billion (where AE_0 intersects the 45-degree line) to $490 billion (where AE_1 intersects the 45-degree line). (b) An inflationary expenditure gap is the amount (vertical distance) by which aggregate expenditures at the full-employment GDP level exceed those just sufficient to achieve full-employment. Here, the inflationary expenditure gap is $5 billion. This $5 billion shifts the equilibrium level of GDP from $510 billion (where AE_0 intersects the 45-degree line) to $530 billion (where AE_2 intersects the 45-degree line). This overspending produces demand-pull inflation.

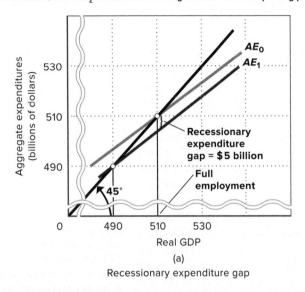

(a)
Recessionary expenditure gap

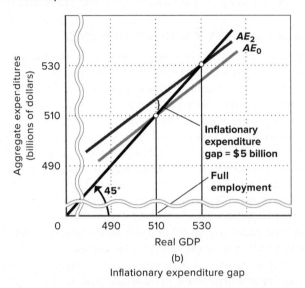

(b)
Inflationary expenditure gap

QUICK QUIZ FOR FIGURE 11.7

1. **In the economy depicted:**
   a. the MPS is 0.50.
   b. the MPC is 0.75.
   c. the full-employment level of real GDP is $530 billion.
   d. nominal GDP always equals real GDP.

2. **The inflationary expenditure gap depicted will cause:**
   a. demand-pull inflation.
   b. cost-push inflation.
   c. cyclical unemployment.
   d. frictional unemployment.

3. **The recessionary expenditure gap depicted will cause:**
   a. demand-pull inflation.
   b. cost-push inflation.
   c. cyclical unemployment.
   d. frictional unemployment.

4. **In the economy depicted, the $5 billion inflationary expenditure gap:**
   a. expands real GDP to $530 billion.
   b. leaves real GDP at $510 billion but causes inflation.
   c. could be remedied by equal $5 billion increases in taxes and government spending.
   d. implies that real GDP exceeds nominal GDP.

Answers: 1. b; 2. a; 3. c; 4. b

gap, nearly all workers are employed and nearly all factories are operating at or near full capacity. In that situation, there is no massive oversupply of productive resources to keep prices from rising. In fact, economists know from real-world experience that as GDP rises toward potential output, prices become increasingly flexible and inflationary in the medium run and the long run.

This fact is one of the major limitations of the aggregate expenditures model, and it is the reason we will develop the AD-AS model in the next chapter. That said, the aggregate expenditures model is still very useful because even an economy operating near full employment will show sticky or stuck prices in the short run. Over that shorter time horizon, the intuitions of the aggregate expenditures model will still hold true.

Inflationary Expenditure Gap

inflationary expenditure gap In the *aggregate-expenditures model*, the amount by which the *aggregate expenditures schedule* must shift downward to decrease the *nominal GDP* to its full-employment noninflationary level.

Economists use the term **inflationary expenditure gap** to describe the amount by which an economy's aggregate expenditures *at the full-employment level of GDP* exceed those just necessary to achieve the full-employment level of GDP. In Figure 11.7b, there is a $5 billion inflationary expenditure gap at the $510 billion full-employment GDP. This gap is shown by the vertical distance between the actual aggregate expenditures schedule AE_2 and the hypothetical schedule AE_0 that would be just sufficient to achieve the $510 billion full-employment GDP. Thus, the inflationary expenditure gap is the amount by which the aggregate expenditures schedule would have to shift downward to realize equilibrium at the full-employment level of GDP.

Why does the name "inflationary expenditure gap" contain the word *inflationary*? What does the situation depicted in Figure 11.7b have to do with inflation? The answer lies in the answer to a different question: *Can the economy achieve and maintain an equilibrium real GDP that is substantially above the full-employment output level?*

The unfortunate answer is no. If such a thing were possible, then the government could make real GDP as high as it wanted by simply increasing G to an arbitrarily high number. Graphically, it could raise the AE_2 curve in Figure 11.7b as far up as it wanted, thereby increasing equilibrium real GDP as high as it wanted. Living standards would skyrocket! But this outcome is not possible because, by definition, all the available workers in the economy are fully employed at the full-employment output level. Producing slightly more than the full-employment output level for a few months might be possible if employers can convince a sizable fraction of workers to work overtime day after day. But there simply is not enough labor for the economy to produce at much more than potential output for an extended period of time.

So what *does* happen in situations in which aggregate expenditures are so high that the model predicts an equilibrium level of GDP beyond potential output? The answer is twofold. First, the economy ends up producing either at potential output or just above potential output due to the limited supply of labor. Second, the economy experiences demand-pull inflation. With the supply of output limited by the supply of labor, high levels of aggregate expenditures drive up prices. Nominal GDP increases because of the higher price level, but real GDP does not. We will discuss this process in greater depth in the next chapter.

Application: The COVID Recession of 2020

In February 2020, the U.S. economy entered the shortest—but sharpest—recession on record as the COVID-19 pandemic prompted political leaders to impose lockdowns as a public health measure. We will defer discussion of the details of that recession until later chapters, but we can use the aggregate expenditures model to portray the ultimate effect of the crisis. We know that the AE_0 line in Figure 11.7a consists of the combined amount of after-tax consumption expenditures (C_a), gross investment expenditures (I_g), net export expenditures (X_n), and government purchases (G) planned at each level of real GDP. During the recession, both after-tax consumption and investment expenditures declined, with planned investment expenditures suffering the largest drop by far.

Aggregate expenditures thus declined, as from AE_0 to AE_1 in Figure 11.7a. The result was a multiple decline in real GDP, illustrated in the figure by the decline from $510 billion to $490 billion. In the language of the aggregate expenditures model, a recessionary expenditure gap produced one of the largest negative GDP gaps since the Great Depression. Employment nosedived by more than 22 million people, and the unemployment rate skyrocketed from 3.5 percent to almost 15 percent in just two months. As recessions go, it was a monster!

Policymakers undertook various macroeconomic stimulus policies to try to eliminate the recessionary expenditure gap as quickly as possible. The Federal Reserve lowered interest rates sharply to encourage investment and consumption while congress and the president passed several relief bills. The largest was the enormous, $2.2 trillion CARES Act that was designed to boost aggregate expenditures, reduce the recessionary expenditure gap, and, through the multiplier effect, increase real GDP and employment. Among other things, the CARES Act distributed $300 billion in one-time cash payments to individuals, funded $260 billion in increased unemployment benefits, lent or granted nearly $1 trillion to private businesses to keep them afloat, and distributed $340 billion to state and local governments whose tax collections were expected to collapse during the pandemic.

We defer discussion and further assessment of these stimulus attempts until Chapter 13, but Figure 11.7a clearly illuminates their purpose. If the government could drive up aggregate expenditures, such as from AE_1 to AE_0, the recession would come to an end and the recovery phase of the business cycle would begin.

Say's Law, the Great Depression, and Keynes

Aggregate Expenditure Theory Emerged as a Critique of Classical Economics and as a Response to the Great Depression.

Until the Great Depression of the 1930s, many prominent economists, including David Ricardo (1772–1823) and John Stuart Mill (1806–1873), believed that the market system would ensure full employment of an economy's resources. These so-called *classical economists* acknowledged that now and then abnormal circumstances such as wars, political upheavals, droughts, speculative crises, and gold rushes would occur, deflecting the economy from full-employment status. But they believed that when such deviations occurred, prices would automatically adjust so as to return the economy to full-employment output. For example, a slump in output and employment would result in lower prices, wages, and interest rates, which in turn would increase consumer spending, employment, and investment spending. Any excess supply of goods and workers would soon be eliminated.

Classical macroeconomists denied that the level of spending in an economy could be too low to bring about the purchase of the entire full-employment output. They based their denial of inadequate spending in part on *Say's law*, attributed to the nineteenth-century French economist J. B. Say (1767–1832). This law is the disarmingly simple idea that the very act of producing goods generates income equal to the value of the goods produced. The production of any output automatically provides the income needed to buy that output. In a nutshell, *supply creates its own demand*.

Say's law can best be understood in terms of a barter economy. A woodworker, for example, produces or supplies furniture as a means of buying or demanding the food and clothing produced by other workers. The woodworker's supply of furniture is the income that he will "spend" to satisfy his demand for other goods. The goods he buys (demands) will have a total value exactly equal to the goods he produces (supplies). And so it is for other producers and for the entire economy. Demand must be the same as supply!

Assuming that the composition of output is in accord with consumer preferences, all markets would be cleared of their outputs. It would seem that the only thing that firms need to do to sell the full-employment level of output is to produce that level of output. Say's law insists that there will be sufficient spending to purchase it all.

The Great Depression of the 1930s called Say's Law into question. In the United States, real GDP declined by 27 percent and the

Everett Historical/Shutterstock

unemployment rate rocketed to nearly 25 percent. Other nations experienced similar impacts. And cyclical unemployment lingered for a decade. An obvious inconsistency exists between a theory that says that unemployment is virtually impossible and the actual occurrence of a 10-year siege of substantial unemployment.

In 1936 British economist John Maynard Keynes (1883–1946) offered an explanation for cyclical unemployment and recessions. In his *General Theory of Employment, Interest, and Money*, Keynes attacked the foundations of classical theory and developed the ideas underlying the aggregate expenditures model. Keynes disputed Say's law, pointing out that income does not have to be spent in the same period that it is received. In fact, some income is always saved. In normal times, that saving is borrowed by businesses to buy capital goods—thereby boosting total spending in the economy. But if expectations about the future grow pessimistic, businesses will slash investment spending and a lot of that saving will not be put to use. The result will be insufficient total spending. Unsold goods will accumulate in producers' warehouses, and producers will respond by reducing their output and discharging workers. A recession or depression will result, and widespread cyclical unemployment will occur. Moreover, said Keynes, recessions are unlikely to be self-correcting. In contrast to the more laissez-faire view of the classical economists, Keynes argued that government should play an active role in stabilizing the economy.

QUICK REVIEW
11.4

▶ Government purchases shift the aggregate expenditures schedule upward and raise equilibrium GDP.

▶ Taxes reduce disposable income, lower consumption spending and saving, shift the aggregate expenditures schedule downward, and reduce equilibrium GDP.

▶ A recessionary expenditure gap is the amount by which an economy's aggregate expenditures schedule must shift upward to achieve the full-employment GDP; an inflationary expenditure gap is the amount by which the economy's aggregate expenditures schedule must shift downward to achieve full-employment GDP and eliminate demand-pull inflation.

Summary

LO11.1 Explain the role of sticky prices in the aggregate expenditures model.

The aggregate expenditures model views the total amount of spending in the economy as the primary factor determining the level of real GDP. The model assumes that the price level is fixed. Keynes made this assumption to reflect the general circumstances of the Great Depression, in which firms reduced output and employment, rather than prices, in response to a huge decline in their sales.

LO11.2 Derive an economy's investment schedule from the investment demand curve and an interest rate.

An investment schedule shows how much investment the firms in an economy are collectively planning to make at each possible level of GDP. In this chapter, we utilize a simple investment schedule in which investment is a constant value and therefore the same at all levels of GDP. That constant value is derived from the investment demand curve by determining what quantity of investment will be demanded at the economy's current real interest rate.

LO11.3 Combine consumption and investment to create an aggregate expenditures schedule for a private, closed economy and determine the economy's equilibrium level of output.

For a private closed economy, the equilibrium level of GDP occurs when aggregate expenditures and real output are equal or, graphically, where the $C + I_g$ line intersects the 45° line. At any GDP greater than equilibrium GDP, real output exceeds aggregate spending, resulting in unplanned investment in inventories and eventual declines in output and income (GDP). At any below-equilibrium GDP, aggregate expenditures will exceed real output, resulting in unplanned disinvestment in inventories and eventual increases in GDP.

LO11.4 Discuss two alternate ways to characterize the equilibrium level of real GDP in a private closed economy.

At equilibrium GDP, the amount households save (leakages) and the amount businesses plan to invest (injections) are equal. Any excess of saving over planned investment will lead to a shortfall of total spending, thus decreasing GDP. Any excess of planned investment over saving will cause an excess of total spending, thus increasing GDP. The change in GDP will in both cases correct the discrepancy between saving and planned investment.

At equilibrium GDP, there are no unplanned changes in inventories. When aggregate expenditures diverge from real GDP, an unplanned change in inventories occurs. Unplanned increases in inventories are followed by a cutback in production and a decline of real GDP. Unplanned decreases in inventories result in increased production and higher GDP.

Actual investment consists of planned investment plus unplanned changes in inventories and is always equal to saving.

LO11.5 Explain how the multiplier affects equilibrium real GDP.

A shift in the investment schedule (caused by changes in expected rates of return or changes in interest rates) shifts the aggregate expenditures curve and causes a new equilibrium level of real GDP changes by more than the amount of the initial change in investment. This multiplier effect (ΔGDP/ΔI_g) accompanies both

increases and decreases in aggregate expenditures and also applies to changes in net exports (X_n) and government purchases (G).

LO11.6 Integrate the international sector into the aggregate expenditures model.

The net export schedule in the model of the open economy relates net exports (exports minus imports) to equilibrium GDP. For simplicity, we assume that the level of net exports is the same at all levels of real GDP.

Positive net exports increase aggregate expenditures to a higher level than they would be if the economy were "closed" to international trade. Negative net exports decrease aggregate expenditures relative to those in a closed economy, decreasing equilibrium real GDP by a multiple of their amount. Increases in exports or decreases in imports have an expansionary effect on real GDP, while decreases in exports or increases in imports have a contractionary effect.

LO11.7 Integrate the public sector into the aggregate expenditures model.

Government purchases in the model of the mixed economy shift the aggregate expenditures schedule upward and raise GDP.

Taxation reduces disposable income, lowers consumption and saving, shifts the aggregate expenditures curve downward, and reduces equilibrium GDP.

In the complete aggregate expenditures model, equilibrium GDP occurs where $C_a + I_g + X_n + G =$ GDP. At the equilibrium GDP, *leakages* of after-tax saving (S_a), imports (M), and taxes (T) equal *injections* of investment (I_g), exports (X), and government purchases (G): $S_a + M + T = I_g + X_n + G$. Also, there are no unplanned changes in inventories.

LO11.8 Define equilibrium GDP, full-employment GDP, recessionary expenditure gaps, and inflationary expenditure gaps.

Equilibrium GDP and full-employment GDP may differ.

A recessionary expenditure gap is the amount by which aggregate expenditures at the full-employment GDP fall short of those needed to achieve the full-employment GDP. This gap produces a negative GDP gap (= actual GDP minus potential GDP). An inflationary expenditure gap is the amount by which aggregate expenditures at the full-employment GDP exceed those just sufficient to achieve the full-employment GDP. This gap causes demand-pull inflation.

Keynes suggested that the solution to the large negative GDP gap during the Great Depression was for government to increase aggregate expenditures. It could do so by increasing its own expenditures (G) or by lowering taxes (T) to increase after-tax consumption expenditures (C_a) by households. Because the economy had millions of unemployed workers and massive amounts of unused production capacity, government could boost aggregate expenditures without worrying about creating inflation.

The stuck-price assumption of the aggregate expenditures model is not credible when the economy approaches or attains its full-employment output. With unemployment low and excess production capacity small or nonexistent, an increase in aggregate expenditures will cause inflation along with any increase in real GDP.

Terms and Concepts

planned investment	leakage	lump-sum tax
investment schedule	injection	recessionary expenditure gap
aggregate expenditures schedule	unplanned changes in inventories	inflationary expenditure gap
equilibrium GDP	net exports	

Discussion Questions

1. What is an investment schedule, and how does it differ from an investment demand curve? **LO11.2**
2. Why does equilibrium real GDP occur where $C + I_g =$ GDP in a private closed economy? What happens to real GDP when $C + I_g$ exceeds GDP? When $C + I_g$ is less than GDP? What two expenditure components of real GDP are purposely excluded in a private closed economy? **LO11.3**
3. Why is saving called a *leakage*? Why is planned investment called an *injection*? Why must saving equal planned investment at equilibrium GDP in a private closed economy? Are unplanned changes in inventories positive, negative, or zero at equilibrium GDP? Explain. **LO11.4**
4. Other things equal, what effect will each of the following changes independently have on the equilibrium level of real GDP in a private closed economy? **LO11.5**
   a. A decline in the real interest rate.
   b. An overall decrease in the expected rate of return on investment.
   c. A sizable, sustained increase in stock prices.

5. Depict graphically the aggregate expenditures model for a private closed economy. Now show a decrease in the aggregate expenditures schedule and explain why the decline in real GDP in your diagram is greater than the decline in the aggregate expenditures schedule. What term is used for the ratio of a decline in real GDP to the initial drop in aggregate expenditures? **LO11.5**
6. Assuming the economy is operating below its potential output, how does an increase in net exports affect real GDP? Why is it difficult, perhaps even impossible, for a country to boost its net exports by increasing its tariffs during a global recession? **LO11.6**
7. What is a recessionary expenditure gap? An inflationary expenditure gap? Which is associated with a positive GDP gap? A negative GDP gap? **LO11.8**
8. **LAST WORD** What is Say's law? How does it relate to the view held by classical economists that the economy generally will operate at a position on its production possibilities curve (Chapter 1)? Use production possibilities analysis to demonstrate Keynes's view on this matter.

Review Questions

1. True or False: The aggregate expenditures model assumes flexible prices. **LO11.1**
2. If total spending is just sufficient to purchase an economy's output, then the economy is: **LO11.3**
   a. in equilibrium.
   b. in recession.
   c. in debt.
   d. in expansion.
3. True or False: If spending exceeds output, real GDP will decline as firms cut back on production. **LO11.3**
4. If inventories unexpectedly rise, then production _____ sales and firms will respond by _____ output. **LO11.3**
   a. trails; expanding
   b. trails; reducing
   c. exceeds; expanding
   d. exceeds; reducing
5. If the multiplier is 5 and investment increases by $3 billion, equilibrium real GDP will increase by: **LO11.5**
   a. $2 billion.
   b. $3 billion.
   c. $8 billion.
   d. $15 billion.
   e. none of the above.
6. A depression abroad will tend to _____ our exports, which in turn will _____ net exports, which in turn will _____ equilibrium real GDP. **LO11.6**
   a. reduce; reduce; reduce
   b. increase; increase; increase

   c. reduce; increase; increase
   d. increase; reduce; reduce
7. Explain graphically the determination of equilibrium GDP for a private economy through the aggregate expenditures model. Now add government purchases (any amount you choose) to your graph, showing their impact on equilibrium GDP. Finally, add taxation (any amount of lump-sum tax that you choose) to your graph and show its effect on equilibrium GDP. Looking at your graph, determine whether equilibrium GDP has increased, decreased, or stayed the same given the sizes of the government purchases and taxes that you selected. **LO11.7**
8. The economy's current level of equilibrium GDP is $780 billion. The full-employment level of GDP is $800 billion. The multiplier is 4. Given those facts, we know that the economy faces _____ expenditure gap of _____. **LO11.8**
   a. an inflationary; $5 billion
   b. an inflationary; $10 billion
   c. an inflationary; $20 billion
   d. a recessionary; $5 billion
   e. a recessionary; $10 billion
   f. a recessionary; $20 billion
9. If an economy has an inflationary expenditure gap, the government could attempt to bring the economy back toward the full-employment level of GDP by _____ taxes or _____ government expenditures. **LO11.8**
   a. increasing; increasing
   b. increasing; decreasing
   c. decreasing; increasing
   d. decreasing; decreasing

Problems

1. Assuming the level of investment is $16 billion and independent of the level of total output, complete the following table and determine the equilibrium levels of output and employment in this private closed economy. What are the values of the MPC and MPS? **LO11.3**

Possible Levels of Employment, Millions	Real Domestic Output (GDP = DI), Billions	Consumption, Billions	Saving, Billions
40	$240	$244	$ ____
45	260	260	____
50	280	276	____
55	300	292	____
60	320	308	____
65	340	324	____
70	360	340	____
75	380	356	____
80	400	372	____

2. Using the consumption and saving data in problem 1 and assuming investment is $16 billion, what are saving and planned investment at the $380 billion level of domestic output? What are saving and actual investment at that level? What are saving and planned investment at the $300 billion level of domestic output? What are the levels of saving and actual investment? In which direction and by what amount will unplanned investment change as the economy moves from the $380 billion level of GDP to the equilibrium level of real GDP? From the $300 billion level of real GDP to the equilibrium level of GDP? **LO11.4**

3. By how much will GDP change if firms increase their investment by $8 billion and the MPC is 0.80? If the MPC is 0.67? **LO11.5**

4. Suppose that a certain country has an MPC of 0.9 and a real GDP of $400 billion. If its investment spending decreases by $4 billion, what will be its new level of real GDP? **LO11.5**

5. The data in columns 1 and 2 in the table below are for a private closed economy. **LO11.6**
   a. Use columns 1 and 2 to determine the equilibrium GDP for this hypothetical economy.
   b. Now open up this economy to international trade by including the export and import figures of columns 3 and 4. Fill in columns 5 and 6 and determine the equilibrium GDP for the

open economy. What is the change in equilibrium GDP caused by the addition of net exports?
   c. Given the original $20 billion level of exports, what would be net exports and the equilibrium GDP if imports were $10 billion greater at each level of GDP?
   d. What is the multiplier in this example?

6. Assume that, without taxes, the consumption schedule of an economy is as follows. **LO11.7**

GDP, Billions	Consumption, Billions
$100	$120
200	200
300	280
400	360
500	440
600	520
700	600

   a. Graph this consumption schedule and determine the MPC.
   b. Assume now that a lump-sum tax is imposed such that the government collects $10 billion in taxes at all levels of GDP. Graph the resulting consumption schedule and compare the MPC and the multiplier with those of the pretax consumption schedule.

7. Refer to columns 1 and 6 in the table for problem 5. Incorporate government into the table by assuming that it plans to tax and spend $20 billion at each possible level of GDP. Also assume that the tax is a personal tax and that government spending does not induce a shift in the private aggregate expenditures schedule. What is the change in equilibrium GDP caused by the addition of government? **LO11.7**

8. **ADVANCED ANALYSIS** Assume that the consumption schedule for a private open economy is such that consumption $C = 50 + 0.8Y$. Assume further that planned investment I_g and net exports X_n are independent of the level of real GDP and constant at $I_g = 30$ and $X_n = 10$. Recall also that, in equilibrium, the real output produced (Y) is equal to aggregate expenditures: $Y = C + I_g + X_n$. **LO11.7**
   a. Calculate the equilibrium level of income or real GDP for this economy.
   b. What happens to equilibrium Y if I_g changes to 10? What does this outcome reveal about the size of the multiplier?

(1) Real Domestic Output (GDP = DI), Billions	(2) Aggregate Expenditures, Private Closed Economy, Billions	(3) Exports, Billions	(4) Imports, Billions	(5) Net Exports, Billions	(6) Aggregate Expenditures, Private Open Economy, Billions
$200	$240	$20	$30	$ ____	$ ____
250	280	20	30	____	____
300	320	20	30	____	____
350	360	20	30	____	____
400	400	20	30	____	____
450	440	20	30	____	____
500	480	20	30	____	____
550	520	20	30	____	____

9. Refer to the accompanying table in answering the questions that follow: **LO11.8**

(1) Possible Levels of Employment, Millions	(2) Real Domestic Output, Millions	(3) Aggregate Expenditures $(C_a + I_g + X_n + G)$, Millions
90	$500	$520
100	550	560
110	600	600
120	650	640
130	700	680

a. If full employment in this economy is 130 million, will there be an inflationary expenditure gap or a recessionary expenditure gap? What will be the consequence of this gap? By how much would aggregate expenditures in column 3 have to change at each level of GDP to eliminate the inflationary expenditure gap or the recessionary expenditure gap? What is the multiplier in this example?

b. Will there be an inflationary expenditure gap or a recessionary expenditure gap if the full-employment level of output is $500 billion? By how much would aggregate expenditures in column 3 have to change at each level of GDP to eliminate the gap? What is the multiplier in this example?

c. Assuming that investment, net exports, and government expenditures do not change with changes in real GDP, what are the values of the MPC, the MPS, and the multiplier?

10. Answer the following questions, which relate to the aggregate expenditures model: **LO11.8**

a. If C_a is $100, I_g is $50, X_n is −$10, and G is $30, what is the economy's equilibrium GDP?

b. If real GDP in an economy is currently $200, C_a is $100, I_g is $50, X_n is −$10, and G is $30, will the economy's real GDP rise, fall, or stay the same?

c. Suppose that full-employment (and full-capacity) output in an economy is $200. If C_a is $150, I_g is $50, X_n is −$10, and G is $30, what will be the macroeconomic result?

Aggregate Demand and Aggregate Supply

>> LEARNING OBJECTIVES

LO12.1 Define aggregate demand (AD) and explain how its downward slope is the result of the real-balances effect, the interest-rate effect, and the foreign purchases effect.

LO12.2 Explain the factors that shift AD.

LO12.3 Define aggregate supply (AS) and explain how it differs in the immediate short run, the short run, and the long run.

LO12.4 Explain the factors that shift AS.

LO12.5 Explain how AD and AS determine an economy's equilibrium price level and real GDP.

LO12.6 Use the AD–AS model to explain demand-pull inflation, cost-push inflation, and recessions.

LO12.7 (Appendix) Relate the aggregate demand curve to the aggregate expenditures model.

During the sharp and sudden COVID recession of 2020, the terms *aggregate demand* and *aggregate supply* moved from the obscurity of economic blogs to the spotlight of national newspapers, cable television, and social media.

The news media and the general public had many questions: How could the government prevent a total collapse of aggregate demand? What might be done to offset the highest unemployment rate since the Great Depression? Would the federal government's $2.2 trillion CARES Act increase aggregate demand and reduce unemployment, as intended? Could a resurgence of the pandemic derail an economic expansion?

Aggregate demand and aggregate supply are the key elements of the **aggregate demand–aggregate supply model (AD–AS model),** the focus of this chapter. The aggregate expenditures model of the previous chapter is an immediate-short-run model in which prices are assumed to be fixed. In contrast, the AD–AS model in this chapter is a "variable price" model that allows both the price level and real GDP to change.

aggregate demand–aggregate supply (AD–AS) model The macroeconomic model that uses *aggregate demand* and *aggregate supply* to determine and explain the *price level* and real *domestic output* (real *gross domestic product*).

Aggregate Demand

aggregate demand A schedule or curve that shows the total quantity of *goods* and *services* that would be demanded (purchased) at various *price levels*.

In Chapter 9, we saw that the overall level of prices in the economy can be measured with a *price index* that shows how the nominal price of a "market basket" of goods and services changes over time relative to its price in a specific base year.

Aggregate demand is a schedule or curve that shows the amount of a nation's output (real GDP) that buyers collectively desire to purchase at each possible price level. These buyers include the nation's households, businesses, and government along with households, businesses, and governments located in other nations.

There is an inverse, or negative, relationship between the economy's overall price level (as measured by the price index) and the amount of real GDP that is demanded by households, businesses, and governments: When the price level rises, the quantity of real GDP demanded decreases; when the price level falls, the quantity of real GDP demanded increases.

Aggregate Demand Curve

The inverse relationship between the price level and real GDP is shown in Figure 12.1, where the aggregate demand curve AD slopes downward, as does the demand curve for an individual product.

Why the downward slope? The explanation is *not* the same as the explanation for why the demand for a single product slopes downward. That explanation centered on the *income effect* and the *substitution effect:*

- When the price of an *individual* product falls, the consumer's (constant) nominal income allows a larger purchase of the product; that's the income effect.

- At the same time, the consumer will want to buy more of the individual product because it becomes less expensive relative to other goods, whose prices have not changed; that's the substitution effect.

These explanations do not work for aggregate demand:

- In Figure 12.1, when the economy moves down its aggregate demand curve, it moves to a lower general price level. But our circular flow model tells us that when consumers pay lower prices for goods and services, less nominal income flows to resource suppliers in the form of wages, rents, interest, and profits. As a result, a decline in the price level does not necessarily mean an increase in the nominal income of the economy as a whole. Thus, a decline in the price level need not produce an income effect (in which more output is purchased because lower nominal prices leave buyers with greater real income).

- For similar reasons, there is no overall substitution effect in Figure 12.1. That's because prices *in general* are falling as we move down the aggregate demand curve. Consequently, there is no tendency for the price of any individual product to become cheaper relative to other products. When prices as a group are all falling together, the rationale for the substitution effect evaporates.

real-balances effect The tendency for increases in the *price level* to lower the real value (or *purchasing power*) of financial *assets* with fixed *money* value and, as a result, to reduce total spending and real output, and conversely for decreases in the *price level*.

FIGURE 12.1

The aggregate demand curve.

The downsloping aggregate demand curve AD indicates an inverse (or negative) relationship between the price level and the amount of real output purchased.

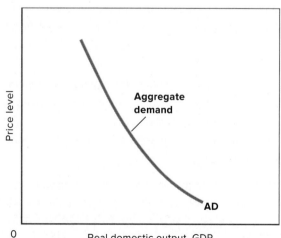

If the substitution and income effects do not explain the downward slope of the aggregate demand curve, what does? The explanation rests on three effects that follow from a price-level change.

Real-Balances Effect A change in the price level produces a **real-balances effect** in which consumer spending (*C*) varies inversely with changes in the price level. To understand how it works, begin by noting that when people refer to the "balances" in savings and other financial accounts, they are referring to *nominal balances*, which are simply the nominal dollar values in each account.

Because nominal balances are measured in money, they cannot by themselves tell us how much purchasing power a person possesses. That's because purchasing power also depends on prices. A nominal balance of $500 can purchase quite a bit if prices are low, but only a modest amount if prices are high.

The concept of real balances goes to the heart of the issue by using prevailing prices to convert nominal balances into real quantities. In particular, an individual's *real balances* are equal to the amount of real output that she could purchase at current prices if she liquidated (turned to cash) all of her assets and used the money to purchase goods and services. For any given amount of nominal balances, say $1,000, real balances will be higher if the price level falls and lower if the price level rises. For example, $1,000 will purchase more real output when prices are low than when they are high.

The fact that real balances (the purchasing power of nominal balances) vary inversely with the price level is the source of the real-balances effect. When the price level rises, real balances fall, purchasing power declines, and people demand less output. Conversely, when the price level falls, real balances increase, purchasing power rises, and people demand more output. So a higher price level means less consumption spending while a lower price level means more consumer spending.

Because consumer spending is a component of aggregate demand, the inverse relationship between the price level and consumption that is caused by the real-balances effect implies that the price level and aggregate demand must also be inversely related. As a result, the real-balances effect contributes to the downward slope of the AD curve.

Interest-Rate Effect The aggregate demand curve also slopes downward because of the **interest-rate effect,** under which an increase in the price level drives up the demand for money and thereby the interest rate, which in turn reduces investment spending (I) by businesses.

> **interest-rate effect** The tendency for increases in the *price level* to increase the demand for money, raise interest rates, and, as a result, reduce total spending and real output in the economy (and the reverse for *price-level* decreases).

The interest rate is the price that must be paid for the use of (borrowed) money. The interest rate is determined by the interaction of the demand for money with the supply of money. Given a fixed supply of money, any increase in money demand will drive up the interest rate.

When we draw an aggregate demand curve, we assume that the supply of money in the economy is fixed. But when the price level rises, consumers need more money for purchases and businesses need more money to meet their payrolls and to buy other resources. A $10 bill will do when the price of an item is $10, but a $10 bill plus a $1 bill is needed when the item costs $11. In short, a higher price level increases the demand for money. Given our assumption that the supply of money is fixed, that increase in the demand for money will cause an increase in the interest rate.

Higher interest rates curtail investment spending and interest-sensitive consumption spending. A firm that expects a 6 percent rate of return on a potential purchase of capital will find that investment potentially profitable when the interest rate is, say, 5 percent. But the investment will be unprofitable and will not be made when the interest rate has risen to 7 percent. Similarly, consumers may decide not to purchase a new house or new automobile when the interest rate on loans goes up. So, by increasing the demand for money and consequently the interest rate, a higher price level reduces the amount of real output demanded.

Foreign Purchases Effect The final reason why the aggregate demand curve slopes downward is the **foreign purchases effect,** under which an increase in the price level results in a decrease in net exports (X_n). When the U.S. price level rises relative to foreign price levels, people living abroad will tend to buy fewer U.S. goods and Americans will tend to buy more foreign goods. The strength of these tendencies will depend on whether exchange rates adjust quickly and completely. But the general tendency will be for U.S. exports to fall and U.S. imports to rise. In short, the increase in the domestic price level will tend to cause net exports to decline.

> **foreign purchases effect** The inverse relationship between the *net exports* of an economy and its *price level* relative to foreign price levels.

These three effects, of course, work in the opposite direction for a decline in the price level. A decline in the price level increases consumption through the real-balances effect and interest-rate effect; increases investment through the interest-rate effect; and raises net exports by increasing exports and decreasing imports through the foreign purchases effect.

Changes in Aggregate Demand

Other things equal, a change in the price level will change the amount of aggregate spending and therefore change the amount of real GDP demanded by the economy. Movements along a fixed aggregate demand curve represent changes in the amount of real GDP demanded that occur in response to a change in the price level. However, if one or more of those "other things" change,

> **>> LO12.2** Explain the factors that shift AD.

FIGURE 12.2 Changes in aggregate demand.

A change in one or more of the listed determinants of aggregate demand will shift the aggregate demand curve. The rightward shift from AD_1 to AD_2 represents an increase in aggregate demand; the leftward shift from AD_1 to AD_3 shows a decrease in aggregate demand. The horizontal distances between AD_1 and the dashed lines represent initial changes in spending. The multiplier effect magnifies those initial changes in spending to produce the full shifts out to, respectively, AD_2 and AD_3.

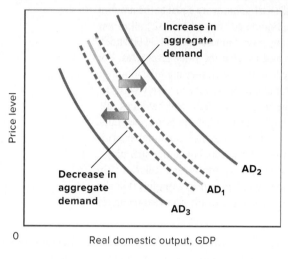

Determinants of Aggregate Demand: Factors That Shift the Aggregate Demand Curve

1. **Changes in consumer spending**
   a. Consumer wealth
   b. Consumer expectations
   c. Household borrowing
   d. Taxes

2. **Changes in investment spending**
   a. Interest rates
   b. Expected returns
      • Expected future business conditions
      • Technology
      • Degree of excess capacity
      • Business taxes

3. **Changes in government spending**

4. **Changes in net export spending**
   a. National income abroad
   b. Exchange rates

determinants of aggregate demand Factors such as consumption spending, *investment,* government spending, and *net exports* that, if they change, shift the aggregate demand curve.

the entire aggregate demand curve will shift. We refer to those other things as **determinants of aggregate demand** or, less formally, *aggregate demand shifters*. They are listed in Figure 12.2.

Changes (shifts) in aggregate demand can be broken down into two stages:

- A change in a determinant of aggregate demand that causes an initial change in the amount of real GDP demanded.

- A multiplier effect that magnifies that initial change in spending to produce a larger ultimate change in aggregate demand.

In Figure 12.2, the full rightward shift of the curve from AD_1 to AD_2 shows an increase in aggregate demand, separated into these two components.

The horizontal distance between AD_1 and the broken curve to its right illustrates an initial increase in spending—say, $5 billion of additional investment spending. If the economy's MPC is 0.75, then the simple multiplier is 4. So the aggregate demand curve shifts rightward from AD_1 to AD_2—four times the distance between AD_1 and the broken line. The multiplier process magnifies the $5 billion initial change in investment spending into successive rounds of additional consumption spending. After the shift, $20 billion (= $5 × 4) of additional real goods and services are demanded at each price level.

The leftward shift from AD_1 to AD_3 shows a decrease in aggregate demand, meaning that a smaller amount of real GDP is demanded at each price level. That shift begins with an initial decline in spending (shown as the horizontal distance between AD_1 and the dashed line to its left). That initial decline is then magnified by the multiplier effect into the full leftward shift, to AD_3.

Let's examine each determinant of aggregate demand listed in the table in Figure 12.2.

Consumer Spending

Even when the U.S. price level is constant, domestic consumers may alter their purchases of U.S.-produced real output. If those consumers decide to buy more output at each price level, the aggregate demand curve shifts to the right, as from AD_1 to AD_2 in Figure 12.2.

If they decide to buy less output, the aggregate demand curve shifts to the left, as from AD_1 to AD_3. Several factors other than a change in the price level may change consumer spending and therefore shift the aggregate demand curve. As Figure 12.2 shows, those factors are real consumer wealth, consumer expectations, household borrowing, and taxes.

Consumer Wealth Consumer wealth is the total dollar value of all assets owned by consumers less the dollar value of their liabilities (debts). Assets include stocks, bonds, and real estate. Liabilities include mortgages, student loans, and credit card balances.

Consumer wealth sometimes changes suddenly and unexpectedly due to surprising changes in asset values. An unforeseen increase in the stock market is a good example. The increase in wealth prompts pleasantly surprised consumers to save less and buy more. The resulting increase in consumer spending—the so-called *wealth effect*—shifts the aggregate demand curve to the right. In contrast, an unexpected decline in asset values causes an unanticipated reduction in consumer wealth at each price level. As consumers tighten their belts in response to the bad news, a "reverse wealth effect" sets in. Unpleasantly surprised consumers increase savings and reduce consumption, thereby shifting the aggregate demand curve to the left.

Consumer Expectations Changes in expectations about the future may alter consumer spending. When people expect their future real incomes to rise, they tend to spend more of their current incomes. Thus, current consumption spending increases (current saving falls), and the aggregate demand curve shifts to the right. Similarly, a widely held expectation of surging inflation in the near future may increase aggregate demand today because consumers will want to buy products before their prices escalate. Conversely, expectations of lower future income or lower future prices may reduce current consumption and shift the aggregate demand curve to the left.

Household Borrowing Consumers can increase their consumption spending by borrowing. Doing so shifts the aggregate demand curve to the right. By contrast, a decrease in borrowing for consumption purposes shifts the aggregate demand curve to the left. The aggregate demand curve also shifts to the left if consumers increase their savings to pay off their debts. With more money flowing to debt repayment, consumption expenditures decline, and the AD curve shifts left.

Personal Taxes A reduction in personal income tax rates raises take-home income and increases consumer purchases at each possible price level. Tax cuts shift the aggregate demand curve to the right. Tax increases reduce consumption spending and shift the aggregate demand curve to the left.

Investment Spending

Investment spending (the purchase of capital goods) is a second major determinant of aggregate demand. A decline in investment spending at each price level shifts the aggregate demand curve to the left. An increase in investment spending shifts it to the right. Investment spending depends on the real interest rate and the expected return from investment.

Real Interest Rates Other things equal, an increase in real interest rates will raise borrowing costs, lower investment spending, and reduce aggregate demand. We are not referring here to the "interest-rate effect" that results from a change in the price level. Instead, we are identifying a change in the real interest rate resulting from, say, a change in a nation's money supply. An increase in the money supply would lower the real interest rate, thereby increasing investment and aggregate demand. By contrast, a decrease in the money supply would raise the real interest rate, thereby reducing investment and decreasing aggregate demand.

Expected Returns Higher expected returns on investment projects increase the demand for capital goods and shift the aggregate demand curve to the right. Alternatively, declines in expected returns decrease investment and shift the aggregate demand curve to the left.

Expected returns are influenced by several factors:

- *Expectations about future business conditions* If firms are optimistic about future business conditions, they are more likely to forecast high rates of return on current investment and therefore may invest more today. If they think the economy will deteriorate in the future, they will forecast low rates of return and perhaps invest less today.

- *Technology* New and improved technologies enhance expected returns on investment and thus increase aggregate demand. For example, recent advances in gene-editing technology have motivated pharmaceutical companies to establish new labs and production facilities.

- *Degree of excess capacity* A rise in excess capacity—unused capital—reduces the expected return on new investment and hence decreases aggregate demand. Other things equal, firms operating factories at well below capacity have little incentive to build new factories. But when firms discover that their excess capacity is dwindling or has completely disappeared, their expected returns on new investment in factories and capital equipment rise. Thus, they increase their investment spending, and aggregate demand shifts to the right.

- *Business taxes* An increase in business taxes will reduce after-tax profits from capital investment and lower expected returns. As a result, investment and aggregate demand will decline. A decrease in business taxes has the opposite effects.

The variability of interest rates and expected returns makes investment highly volatile. Unlike consumption, investment spending rises and falls often, independent of changes in total income. Investment, in fact, is the least stable component of aggregate demand.

Government Spending

Government purchases are the third determinant of aggregate demand. An increase in government purchases (for example, more transportation projects) shifts the aggregate demand curve to the right, as long as tax collections and interest rates do not change as a result. In contrast, a reduction in government spending (for example, less military equipment) shifts the curve to the left.

Net Export Spending

The final determinant of aggregate demand is net export spending. Other things equal, higher U.S. *exports* mean an increased foreign demand for U.S. goods. So a rise in net exports (higher exports relative to imports) shifts the aggregate demand curve to the right. In contrast, a decrease in U.S. net exports shifts the aggregate demand curve to the left. (These changes in net exports are *not* those prompted by a change in the U.S. price level—those associated with the foreign purchases effect. The changes here are shifts of the AD curve, not movements along the AD curve.)

What might cause net exports to change, other than the price level? Two possibilities are changes in national income abroad and changes in exchange rates.

National Income Abroad Rising national income abroad encourages people living abroad to buy more products, some of which are made in the United States. U.S. net exports thus rise, and the U.S. aggregate demand curve shifts to the right. Declines in national income abroad do the opposite: They reduce U.S. net exports and shift the U.S. aggregate demand curve to the left.

Exchange Rates Changes in the dollar's exchange rate—the price of foreign currencies in terms of the U.S. dollar—may affect U.S. exports and therefore aggregate demand. Suppose the dollar depreciates in terms of the euro (meaning the euro appreciates in terms of the dollar). The new, relatively lower value of dollars and higher value of euros enables European consumers to obtain more dollars with each euro. From the perspective of Europeans, U.S. goods are now less expensive; it takes fewer euros to obtain them. So European consumers buy more U.S. goods, and U.S. exports rise. But U.S. consumers can now obtain fewer euros for each dollar. Because they must pay more dollars to buy European goods, Americans reduce their imports. U.S. exports rise, and U.S. imports fall. Conclusion: Dollar depreciation increases net exports (imports go down; exports go up) and therefore increases aggregate demand.

Dollar appreciation has the opposite effects: Net exports fall (imports go up; exports go down) and aggregate demand declines.

QUICK REVIEW
12.1

- Aggregate demand reflects an inverse relationship between the price level and the amount of real output demanded.

- Changes in the price level create real-balances, interest-rate, and foreign purchases effects that explain the downward slope of the aggregate demand curve.

- Changes in one or more of the determinants of aggregate demand (Figure 12.2) will shift the

aggregate demand curve by altering the amount of real GDP demanded at each price level.

- An increase in aggregate demand is shown as a rightward shift of the aggregate demand curve; a decrease, as a leftward shift of the curve.

- The multiplier effect magnifies initial changes in spending into larger changes in aggregate demand.

Aggregate Supply

Aggregate supply is a schedule or curve showing the relationship between a nation's price level and the amount of real domestic output that firms produce. This relationship varies depending on the time horizon and how quickly output prices and input prices can change. We will define three time horizons:

- In the *immediate short run*, both input prices and output prices are fixed.
- In the *short run*, input prices are fixed but output prices can vary.
- In the *long run*, both input prices and output prices can vary.

The relationship between the price level and total output is different in each of the three time horizons because input prices are stickier than output prices. Although both sets of prices become more flexible as time passes, output prices usually adjust more rapidly.

Aggregate Supply in the Immediate Short Run

Depending on the type of firm, the immediate short run can last anywhere from a few days to a few months. It lasts as long as *both* input prices and output prices stay fixed. Input prices are fixed in both the immediate short run and the short run by contractual agreements. In particular, 75 percent of the average firm's costs are wages and salaries—and these are almost always fixed by labor contracts for months or years at a time. As a result, they are usually fixed much longer than output prices, which can begin to change within a few days or a few months depending on the type of firm.

That said, output prices are also typically fixed in the immediate short run. Firms set fixed prices for their customers and then agree to supply whatever quantity demanded results at those fixed prices. For instance, once an appliance manufacturer sets its annual prices for refrigerators, stoves, and microwaves, it is obligated to supply as many appliances as customers want to buy at those prices. Similarly, a catalog company is obliged to sell however much customers want to buy of its products at the prices listed in its current catalog. And it is obligated to supply those quantities demanded until it sends out its next catalog.

With output prices fixed and firms selling however much customers want to purchase at those fixed prices, the **immediate-short-run aggregate supply curve** AS_{ISR} is a horizontal line, as Figure 12.3 shows. The AS_{ISR} curve is horizontal at the overall price level P_1, which is calculated from all of the individual prices set by the various firms in the economy. Its horizontal shape implies that the total amount of output supplied in the economy depends directly on the volume of spending that results at price level P_1. If total spending is low at price level P_1, firms will supply a small amount of output to match the low level of spending. If total spending is high at price level P_1, they will supply a high level of output to match the high level of spending. The resulting amount of output may be higher than or lower than the economy's full-employment output level Q_f.

Notice, however, that firms will respond in this manner to changes in total spending only as long as output prices remain fixed. As soon as firms can change their output prices, they will respond to changes in aggregate spending not only by increasing or decreasing output but also by raising or lowering prices. This situation leads to the upward sloping short-run aggregate supply curve that we discuss next.

Aggregate Supply in the Short Run

In macroeconomics, the short run begins after the immediate short run ends. More specifically, the short run is the period of time during which output prices are flexible but input prices are either totally fixed or highly inflexible.

>> **LO12.3** Define aggregate supply (AS) and explain how it differs in the immediate short run, the short run, and the long run.

aggregate supply A schedule or curve showing the total quantity of *goods* and *services* that would be supplied (produced) at various *price levels*.

immediate-short-run aggregate supply curve A horizontal *aggregate supply* curve that applies to time periods over which both input prices and output prices are fixed; an aggregate supply curve for which real output, but not the *price level*, changes when the *aggregate demand* curve shifts.

FIGURE 12.3
Aggregate supply in the immediate short run (ISR).

In the immediate short run, the aggregate supply curve AS_{ISR} is horizontal at the economy's current price level, P_1. With output prices fixed, firms collectively supply the level of output that is demanded at those prices. That level of output may differ from the economy's full-employment output level, Q_f.

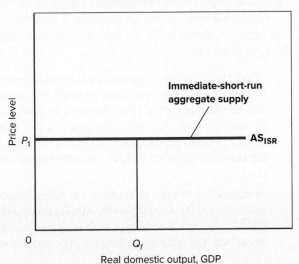

FIGURE 12.4

The aggregate supply curve (short run).

The upsloping aggregate supply curve AS indicates a direct (or positive) relationship between the price level and the amount of real output that firms will offer for sale. The AS curve is relatively flat below the full-employment output because unemployed resources and unused capacity allow firms to respond to price-level rises with large increases in real output. It is relatively steep beyond the full-employment output because resource shortages and capacity limitations make it difficult to expand real output as the price level rises.

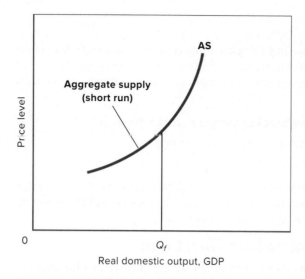

short-run aggregate supply curve An upward sloping *aggregate supply* curve relevant to time periods over which input prices are fixed but output prices are flexible; an aggregate supply curve for which real output and the price level both change when the *aggregate demand* curve shifts.

Some input prices are of course more flexible than others. Consider gasoline, which is an input for delivery firms like UPS. Because gasoline prices are quite flexible, UPS will have at least one very flexible input price. In contrast, wages at UPS are set by five-year labor contracts negotiated with its drivers' union, the Teamsters. Because wages are the firm's largest and most important input cost, UPS faces overall input prices that are inflexible for several years at a time. Thus, its "short run"—the period in which it can change its shipping prices but not its substantially fixed input prices—is actually quite long. Keep this example in mind as we derive the short-run aggregate supply for the entire economy. Its applicability does not depend on some arbitrary definition of how long the "short run" should be. Instead, the short run for which the model is relevant is any period of time during which output prices are flexible, but input prices are fixed or nearly fixed.

As Figure 12.4 shows, the **short-run aggregate supply curve** AS slopes upward because, with input prices fixed, changes in the price level will raise or lower firms' real profits. Consider an economy that has only a single multiproduct firm called Sahara whose owner must receive a real profit of $20 to produce the full-employment output of 100 units. Assume the owner's only input (aside from entrepreneurial talent) is 10 units of hired labor at $8 per worker, for a total wage cost of $80. Also assume that the 100 units of output sell for $1 per unit, so total revenue is $100. Sahara's nominal profit is $20 (= $100 − $80), and using the $1 price to designate the base-price index of 100, its real profit is also $20 (= $20/1.00). Well and good; the full-employment output is produced.

Next, consider what happens if the price of Sahara's output doubles. The doubling of the price level boosts total revenue from $100 to $200, but because we are discussing the short run during which input prices are fixed, the $8 nominal wage for each of the 10 workers remains unchanged so that total costs stay at $80. Nominal profit rises from $20 (= $100 − $80) to $120 (= $200 − $80). Dividing that $120 profit by the new price index of 200 (= 2.0 in hundredths), we find that Sahara's real profit is now $60. The rise in the real reward from $20 to $60 prompts the firm (economy) to produce more output. Conversely, price-level declines reduce real profits and cause the firm (economy) to reduce its output. So, in the short run, there is a direct, or positive, relationship between the price level and real output. When the price level rises, real output rises; and when the price level falls, real output falls. The result is an upward sloping short-run aggregate supply curve.

Notice, however, that the upward slope of the short-run aggregate supply curve is not constant. It is flatter at outputs below the full-employment output level Q_f and steeper at outputs above it. Why the difference?

- When the economy is operating below its full-employment output, it has large amounts of unused equipment and large numbers of unemployed workers. Firms can put these idle human and capital resources back to work with little upward pressure on per-unit production costs. And as output expands, few if any shortages of inputs will arise to raise per-unit production costs. Thus the slope of the short-run aggregate supply curve increases only slowly at output levels below the full-employment output level Q_f.

- In contrast, when the economy is operating beyond Q_f, the vast majority of its available resources are already employed. Adding more workers to a relatively fixed number of highly used capital resources such as plant and equipment creates congestion in the workplace and reduces the average efficiency of workers. Adding more capital, given the limited number of available workers, leaves equipment idle and reduces the efficiency of capital. Adding more land resources when capital and labor are highly constrained reduces the efficiency of land resources. Under these circumstances, total input costs rise more rapidly than total output. The result is rapidly rising per-unit production costs that give the short-run aggregate supply curve its rapidly increasing slope at output levels beyond Q_f.

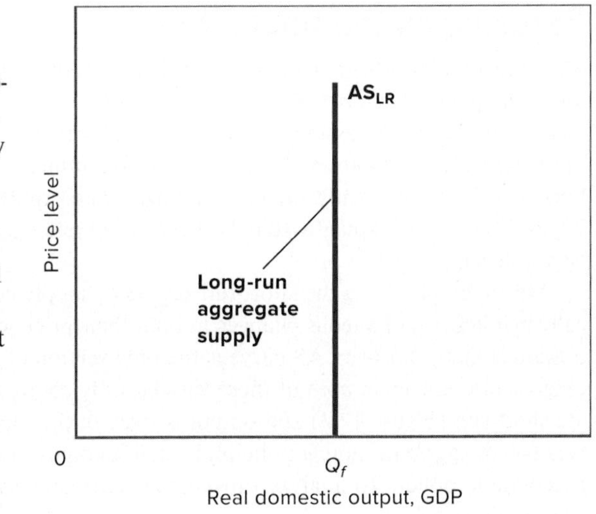

FIGURE 12.5
Aggregate supply in the long run.

The long-run aggregate supply curve AS$_{LR}$ is vertical at the full-employment level of real GDP (Q_f) because in the long run wages and other input prices rise and fall to match changes in the price level. So price-level changes do not affect firms' profits and thus they create no incentive for firms to alter their output.

Aggregate Supply in the Long Run

In macroeconomics, the long run is the time horizon over which both input prices and output prices are flexible. It begins after the short run ends. The long run may last from a couple of weeks to several years, depending on the industry. But for the economy as a whole, it is the time horizon over which all output and input prices—including wage rates—are fully flexible.

The **long-run aggregate supply curve** AS$_{LR}$ is vertical at the economy's full-employment output Q_f, as Figure 12.5 shows. The vertical curve means that in the long run the economy will produce the full-employment output level no matter what the price level is. How can this statement be true? Shouldn't higher prices cause firms to increase output? The explanation lies in the fact that in the long run, when both input prices and output prices are flexible, profit levels always adjust to give firms exactly the right profit incentive to produce exactly the full-employment output level, Q_f.

To see why, look back at the short-run aggregate supply curve AS in Figure 12.4. Suppose that the economy starts by producing at the full-employment output level Q_f and that the price level at that moment has an index value of $P = 100$. Now suppose that output prices double, so that the price index goes to $P = 200$. We previously demonstrated for our single-firm economy that this doubling of the price level will cause profits to rise in the short run and that the higher profits will motivate the firm to increase output.

This outcome, however, is dependent on the fact that input prices are fixed in the short run. Consider what will happen in the long run when they are free to change. Firms can produce beyond the full-employment output level only by running factories and businesses at extremely high rates. In doing so, they create a great deal of demand for the economy's limited supply of productive resources. In particular, labor is in great demand because the only way to produce beyond full employment is to have employees work overtime.

As time passes and input prices are free to change, the high level of resource demand will start to raise input prices. In particular, overworked employees will demand and receive raises as employers scramble to deal with the labor shortages that inevitably arise whenever the economy is producing above its full-employment output level. As input prices increase, firm profits begin to fall. As they decline, so does the motive that firms have to produce more than the full-employment output level.

This process of rising input prices and falling profits continues until the rise in input prices exactly matches the initial change in output prices (in our example, they both double). When that happens, firm profits in real terms return to their original level so that firms are once again motivated to produce at exactly the full-employment output level. This adjustment process means that in the long run, the economy will produce at full employment regardless of the price level (in our example, at either $P = 100$ or $P = 200$). Thus the long-run aggregate supply curve AS$_{LR}$ is vertical above the full-employment output level. Every possible price level on the vertical axis is associated with the economy producing at the full-employment output level in the long run.

long-run aggregate supply curve A vertical *aggregate supply* curve relevant to time periods over which input prices and output prices are both fully flexible; an aggregate supply curve for which the *price level*, but not real output, changes when the *aggregate demand* curve shifts; a vertical aggregate supply curve that implies fully flexible *prices*.

Focusing on the Short Run

The immediate-short-run aggregate supply curve, the short-run aggregate supply curve, and the long-run aggregate supply curve are all important. Each curve is appropriate to situations that match their respective assumptions about the flexibility of input and output prices. But our focus in the rest of this chapter and the chapters that immediately follow will be on the short-run time horizon and, consequently, on short-run aggregate supply curves, such as the AS curve shown in Figure 12.4. Unless explicitly stated otherwise, all references to "aggregate supply" are to short-run aggregate supply, AS.

We are emphasizing the short-run aggregate supply curve because real-world economies typically manifest simultaneous changes in both their price levels and their levels of real output. The upward sloping short-run AS curve is the only version of aggregate supply that can handle simultaneous movements in both of these variables. By contrast, the price level is fixed in the immediate short run (Figure 12.3) and output is fixed in the long run (Figure 12.5). This renders these versions of aggregate supply unhelpful when it comes to understanding business cycles and macroeconomic policy. To analyze those issues correctly, we must employ the short-run aggregate supply curve, AS.

**QUICK REVIEW
12.2**

▶ The immediate-short-run aggregate supply curve is horizontal: given fixed input and output prices, producers will supply whatever quantity of real output is demanded at the current price level.

▶ The short-run aggregate supply curve slopes upward: given fixed resource prices, higher output prices raise profits and encourage firms to increase their output levels.

▶ The long-run aggregate supply curve is vertical: given sufficient time, wages and other input prices rise or fall to match any change in the price level.

Changes in Aggregate Supply

>> LO12.4 Explain the factors that shift AS.

determinants of aggregate supply Factors such as input prices, *productivity*, and the legal-institutional environment that, if they change, shift the aggregate supply curve.

An aggregate supply curve identifies the relationship between the price level and real output, other things equal. But when one or more of those other things change, the curve shifts. The rightward shift of the curve from AS_1 to AS_2 in Figure 12.6 represents an increase in aggregate supply, indicating that firms are willing to produce and sell more real output at every price level. The leftward shift of the curve from AS_1 to AS_3 represents a decrease in aggregate supply. At each price level, firms produce less output than before.

Figure 12.6 lists the "other things" that shift the aggregate supply curve. Called the **determinants of aggregate supply** or *aggregate supply shifters*, they collectively position the aggregate supply

FIGURE 12.6 **Changes in aggregate supply.**

A change in one or more of the listed determinants of aggregate supply will shift the aggregate supply curve. The rightward shift of the aggregate supply curve from AS_1 to AS_2 represents an increase in aggregate supply; the leftward shift of the curve from AS_1 to AS_3 shows a decrease in aggregate supply.

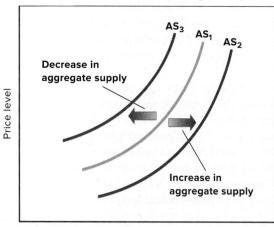

Determinants of Aggregate Supply: Factors That Shift the Aggregate Supply Curve

1. Changes in input prices
   a. Domestic resource prices
   b. Prices of imported resources

2. Changes in productivity

3. Changes in legal-institutional environment
   a. Business taxes and subsidies
   b. Government regulations

curve and shift the curve when they change. Changes in these determinants raise or lower per-unit production costs *at each price level*. These changes in per-unit production cost affect profits, leading firms to alter the amount of output they are willing to produce *at each price level*. Changes that increase profits cause firms to produce more, while changes that decrease profits cause firms to produce less.

As an example, firms may collectively offer $9 trillion of real output at a price level of 1.0 (100 in index value) when the supply shifters are all at particular values, but then only $8.8 trillion at that same price level if one or more of the supply shifters change. The point is that when one of the determinants listed in Figure 12.6 changes, the aggregate supply curve shifts to the right or left. Changes that reduce per-unit production costs shift the aggregate supply curve to the right, as from AS_1 to AS_2. Changes that increase per-unit production costs shift it to the left, as from AS_1 to AS_3.

The three aggregate supply determinants listed in Figure 12.6 require more discussion.

Input Prices

Input or resource prices—to be distinguished from the output prices that make up the price level— are a major ingredient of per-unit production costs and therefore a key determinant of aggregate supply. These resources can be either domestic or imported.

Domestic Resource Prices As stated earlier, wages and salaries make up about 75 percent of all business costs. Other things equal, decreases in wages increase profits by reducing per-unit production costs. So when wages fall, the aggregate supply curve shifts to the right. By contrast, increases in wages reduce profits by raising per-unit production costs. So when wages rise, the aggregate supply curve shifts to the left. Examples:

- Labor supply increases because of substantial immigration. Wages and per-unit production costs fall, shifting the AS curve to the right.

- Labor supply decreases because a rapid increase in pension income causes many older workers to opt for early retirement. Wage rates and per-unit production costs rise, shifting the AS curve to the left.

Similarly, the aggregate supply curve shifts when the prices of land or capital inputs change. Examples:

- The price of machinery and equipment falls because of declines in the prices of steel and electronic components. Per-unit production costs decline, and the AS curve shifts to the right.

- The supply of available land resources expands through discoveries of mineral deposits or technical innovations that transform "nonresources" (say, vast desert lands) into valuable resources (productive lands). The price of land declines, per-unit production costs fall, and the AS curve shifts to the right.

Prices of Imported Resources Resources imported from abroad (such as oil, tin, and copper) affect U.S. aggregate supply because added supplies of resources—whether domestic or imported— typically reduce resource prices and, consequently, per-unit production costs. Other things equal, a decrease in the price of imported resources will raise U.S. profits and increase U.S. aggregate supply. Conversely, an increase in the price of imported resources will lower U.S. profits and reduce U.S. aggregate supply, other things equal.

A good example of the major effect that changing resource prices can have on aggregate supply is the oil price hikes of the 1970s. At that time, the members of the Organization of Petroleum Exporting Countries (OPEC) worked in concert to decrease oil production and raise the price of oil. The tenfold increase in the price of oil that OPEC achieved during the 1970s drove per-unit production costs up and jolted the U.S. aggregate supply curve leftward.

Exchange-rate fluctuations may also alter the price of imported resources. Suppose that the dollar appreciates, enabling U.S. firms to obtain more foreign currency with each dollar. Domestic producers will now face a lower *dollar* price of imported resources. U.S. firms will respond by increasing their imports of foreign resources. By substituting cheap foreign resources for more expensive domestic resources, firms will lower their per-unit production costs at each level of output. Those falling per-unit production costs will shift the U.S. aggregate supply curve to the right.

A depreciation of the dollar has the opposite set of effects and shifts the aggregate supply curve to the left.

Productivity

productivity A measure of average output or real output per unit of input. For example, the productivity of labor is determined by dividing real output by hours of work.

The second major determinant of aggregate supply is **productivity,** which measures how much output can be produced from any given set of inputs. Mathematically, productivity is defined as average real output, or real output per unit of input:

$$\text{Productivity} = \frac{\text{total output}}{\text{total inputs}}$$

Higher productivity implies greater efficiency. An increase in productivity enables the economy to obtain more output from its limited resources.

An increase in productivity also implies a reduction in per-unit production costs. To see why that is true, let's work out an example of what productivity and per-unit production costs are before and after an increase in efficiency. Start by supposing that total output is 10 units, that 5 units of inputs are needed to produce that quantity, and that the price of each input unit is $2. Then,

$$\text{Productivity} = \frac{\text{total output}}{\text{total inputs}} = \frac{10}{5} = 2$$

meaning that we can produce two units of output for each unit of input. In addition, we see that:

$$\text{Productivity} = \frac{\text{total input cost}}{\text{total output}} = \frac{\$2 \times 5}{10} = \$1$$

which indicates that production costs are currently $1 per unit. (As an aside, note that we ascertained the total input cost by multiplying the per-unit input cost by the number of inputs used.)

Now suppose that productivity increases so that real output doubles to 20 units, while the price and quantity of input remain constant at $2 and 5 units, respectively. Using the above equations, we see that productivity rises from 2 to 4 and that the per-unit production cost of the output falls from $1 to $0.50. The doubled productivity has reduced the per-unit production cost by half.

By reducing per-unit production costs, an increase in productivity shifts the aggregate supply curve to the right. The main source of productivity advance is improved production technology, often embodied in new plant and equipment that replaces old plant and equipment. Other sources of productivity increases are a better-educated and better-trained workforce, improved forms of business enterprise, and the reallocation of labor resources from lower-productivity to higher-productivity uses.

Decreases in productivity are rare. But when they occur, they increase per-unit production costs and therefore reduce aggregate supply (shift the AS curve to the left).

Legal-Institutional Environment

Changes in the legal-institutional setting in which businesses operate are the final determinant of aggregate supply. Such changes may alter the per-unit costs of output and, in doing so, shift the aggregate supply curve. Two changes of this type are (1) changes in taxes and subsidies and (2) changes in the extent of regulation.

Business Taxes and Subsidies Higher business taxes, such as sales, excise, and payroll taxes, increase per-unit costs and reduce short-run aggregate supply. Higher business taxes shift aggregate supply to the left.

Similarly, a business subsidy—a payment or tax break by government to producers—lowers production costs and increases short-run aggregate supply. For example, the federal government subsidizes firms that blend ethanol (derived from corn) with gasoline to increase the U.S. gasoline supply. This reduces the per-unit production cost of making blended gasoline. To the extent that this and other subsidies are successful, the aggregate supply curve shifts rightward.

Government Regulation It is usually costly for businesses to comply with government regulations. More regulation therefore tends to increase per-unit production costs and shift the aggregate supply curve to the left. "Supply-side" proponents of deregulation of the economy have argued forcefully that, by increasing efficiency and reducing the paperwork associated with complex regulations, deregulation will reduce per-unit costs and shift the aggregate supply curve to the right. Other economists are less certain. Deregulation that results in accounting manipulations, monopolization, and business failures is likely to shift the AS curve to the left rather than to the right.

▶ Changes in one or more of the determinants of aggregate supply (Figure 12.6) will increase or decrease the aggregate amount of output supplied at each price level by either increasing or decreasing per-unit production costs.

▶ Decreases in per-unit production costs cause rightward shifts of the short-run aggregate supply curve while increases in per-unit production costs cause leftward shifts.

▶ Increases in productivity reduce per-unit production costs and shift the AS curve to the right, while decreases in productivity raise per-unit production costs and shift the AS curve to the left.

QUICK REVIEW

12.3

>> **LO12.5** Explain how AD and AS determine an economy's equilibrium price level and real GDP.

Equilibrium in the AD–AS Model

Of all the possible combinations of price levels and levels of real GDP, which combination will the economy gravitate toward, at least in the short run? **Figure 12.7 (Key Graph)** and its accompanying table provide the answer. Equilibrium occurs at the price level that equalizes the amounts of real output demanded and supplied. The intersection of the aggregate demand curve AD and the aggregate supply curve AS establishes the economy's **equilibrium price level** and **equilibrium real output**. Aggregate demand and aggregate supply *jointly* establish the price level and level of real GDP.

In Figure 12.7, the equilibrium price level and level of real output are 100 and $510 billion, respectively. To illustrate why those values constitute an equilibrium, suppose the price level is 92 rather than 100. We see from the table that the lower price level will encourage businesses to produce real output of $502 billion. This is shown by point *a* on the AS curve in the graph. But as revealed by the table and point *b* on the AD curve, buyers will want to purchase $514 billion of real output at price level 92. There will consequently be a $12 billion (= $514 billion demanded − $502 billion supplied) shortage of real output.

This shortage will not persist. Competition among buyers to purchase the limited ($502 billion) supply of real output will eliminate the shortage and drive the price level up from 92 to 100. The rise in the price level from 92 to 100 encourages producers to increase their real output from $502 billion to $510 billion and causes buyers to scale back their purchases from $514 billion to $510 billion. When equality occurs between the amounts of real output produced and purchased, as it does at price level 100, the economy will achieve equilibrium (here, at $510 billion of real GDP).

A final note: Although the equilibrium price level happens to be 100 in our example, nothing special is implied by that. Any price level can be an equilibrium price level.

equilibrium price level In the *aggregate demand–aggregate supply* (*AD–AS*) *model*, the *price level* at which *aggregate demand* equals *aggregate supply*; the price level at which the aggregate demand curve intersects the aggregate supply curve.

equilibrium real output (see *equilibrium real domestic output*) The *gross domestic product* at which the total quantity of *final goods* and final *services* purchased (*aggregate expenditures*) is equal to the total quantity of final goods and services produced (the *real domestic output*); the real domestic output at which the aggregate demand curve intersects the aggregate supply curve.

..ıll KEY GRAPH

FIGURE 12.7 The equilibrium price level and equilibrium real GDP.

The intersection of the aggregate demand curve and the aggregate supply curve determines the economy's equilibrium price level. At the equilibrium price level of 100 (in index-value terms), the $510 billion of real output demanded matches the $510 billion of real output supplied. So the equilibrium GDP is $510 billion.

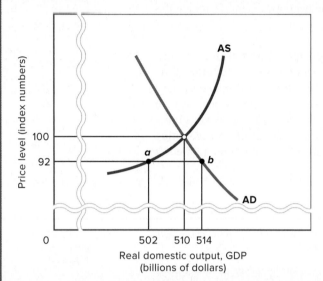

Real Output Demanded (Billions)	Price Level (Index Number)	Real Output Supplied (Billions)
$506	$108	$513
508	104	512
510	**100**	**510**
512	96	507
514	92	502

QUICK QUIZ FOR FIGURE 12.7

1. The AD curve slopes downward because:
a. per-unit production costs fall as real GDP increases.
b. the income and substitution effects are at work.
c. changes in the determinants of AD alter the amounts of real GDP demanded at each price level.
d. decreases in the price level give rise to real-balances effects, interest-rate effects, and foreign purchases effects that increase the amount of real GDP demanded.

2. The AS curve slopes upward because:
a. per-unit production costs rise as real GDP expands toward and beyond its full-employment level.
b. the income and substitution effects are at work.
c. changes in the determinants of AS alter the amounts of real GDP supplied at each price level.
d. increases in the price level give rise to real-balances effects, interest-rate effects, and foreign purchases effects that increase the amounts of real GDP supplied.

3. At price level 92:
a. a GDP surplus of $12 billion occurs that drives the price level up to 100.
b. a GDP shortage of $12 billion occurs that drives the price level up to 100.
c. the aggregate amount of real GDP demanded is less than the aggregate amount of real GDP supplied.
d. the economy is operating beyond its capacity to produce.

4. Suppose real output demanded rises by $4 billion at each price level. The new equilibrium price level will be:
a. 108.
b. 104.
c. 96.
d. 92.

Answers: 1. d; 2. a; 3. b; 4. b

Changes in Equilibrium

>> **LO12.6** Use the AD–AS model to explain demand-pull inflation, cost-push inflation, and recessions.

Now let's apply the AD–AS model to various situations. For simplicity, we will use P and Q symbols rather than actual numbers. Remember that these symbols represent, respectively, price index values and amounts of real GDP.

Increases in AD: Demand-Pull Inflation

Suppose the economy is operating at its full-employment output when businesses and government decide to increase their spending—actions that shift the aggregate demand curve to the right. Our list of determinants of aggregate demand (Figure 12.2) provides several reasons why this shift might occur. Perhaps firms boost their investment spending because they anticipate higher future profits from investments in new capital. And perhaps government increases spending to expand national defense.

As shown by the rise in the price level from P_1 to P_2 in Figure 12.8, the increase in aggregate demand beyond full-employment output causes inflation. This is demand-pull inflation because the price level is being pulled up by the increase in aggregate demand. Also observe that the increase in demand expands real output from the full-employment level Q_f to Q_1. The distance between Q_1 and Q_f is a positive, or "inflationary," GDP gap. Actual GDP exceeds potential GDP.

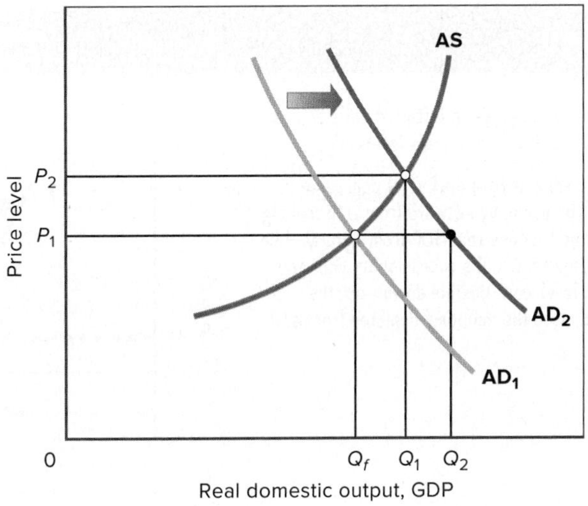

The classic American example of demand-pull inflation occurred in the late 1960s. The escalation of the war in Vietnam resulted in a 40 percent increase in defense spending between 1965 and 1967 and another 15 percent increase in 1968. The rise in government spending, on top of an already growing economy, shifted the economy's aggregate demand curve to the right, producing the worst inflation in two decades. Actual GDP exceeded potential GDP, thereby creating an inflationary GDP gap. Inflation jumped from 1.6 percent in 1965 to 5.7 percent by 1970.

Figure 12.8 reveals an interesting point concerning the multiplier effect. The increase in aggregate demand from AD_1 to AD_2 increases real output only to Q_1, not to Q_2, because part of the increase in aggregate demand is absorbed as inflation as the price level rises from P_1 to P_2. Had the price level remained at P_1, the shift of aggregate demand from AD_1 to AD_2 would have increased real output to Q_2. The full-strength multiplier effect would have occurred. But in Figure 12.8, inflation reduced the increase in real output—and thus the multiplier effect—by about one-half. Price-level flexibility weakens the realized multiplier effect.

FIGURE 12.8
An increase in aggregate demand that causes demand-pull inflation.

The increase of aggregate demand from AD_1 to AD_2 causes demand-pull inflation, shown as the rise in the price level from P_1 to P_2. It also causes an inflationary GDP gap of Q_1 minus Q_f. The rise of the price level reduces the size of the multiplier effect. If the price level had remained at P_1, the increase in aggregate demand from AD_1 to AD_2 would have increased output from Q_f to Q_2 and the multiplier would have been at full strength. But because of the increase in the price level, real output increases only from Q_f to Q_1 and the multiplier effect is reduced.

Decreases in AD: Recession and Cyclical Unemployment

Decreases in aggregate demand result in recession and cyclical unemployment. For example, in 2020, U.S. investment spending greatly declined because the onset of the COVID-19 pandemic caused businesspeople to assume sharply lower expected returns on investment. In particular, businesspeople were worried about poor future business conditions and high degrees of unused production capacity. **Figure 12.9 (Key Graph)** shows the resulting decline in aggregate demand as a leftward shift from AD_1 to AD_2.

If prices were flexible in Figure 12.9, the economy's equilibrium would adjust from point a to point c, implying both a recession (since Q_2 is less than Q_f) and a decline in the price level. But we now add an important twist to the analysis: *Deflation*—a decline in the price level—is not the norm in the American economy. The U.S. price level is downwardly *in*flexible. This is illustrated in Figure 12.9 by the broken horizontal line at the initial price level P_1 that prevailed before aggregate demand shifted to the left. The broken horizontal line indicates that prices are stuck (completely inflexible) at price level P_1.

With the price level stuck at P_1, the economy moves from a to b along the broken horizontal line rather than from a to c along the short-run aggregate supply curve. The outcome is a decline of real output from Q_f to Q_1, with *no* change in the price level. It is as if the aggregate supply curve in Figure 12.9 is horizontal at P_1, to the left of point a, as indicated by the dashed line.

The decline of real output from Q_f to Q_1 constitutes a *recession*, and because fewer workers are needed to produce the lower output, *cyclical unemployment* arises. The distance between Q_1 and Q_f is a negative, or "recessionary," GDP gap—the amount by which actual output falls short of potential output.

Figure 12.9 also reveals that without a fall in the price level, the multiplier is at full strength. With the price level stuck at P_1, real GDP decreases by $Q_f - Q_1$, which matches the full leftward

..ıll KEY GRAPH

FIGURE 12.9 **A recession resulting from a leftward shift of aggregate demand when the price level is downwardly inflexible.**

If the price level is downwardly inflexible at P_1, a decline of aggregate demand from AD_1 to AD_2 will move the economy leftward from a to b along the horizontal broken-line segment and reduce real GDP from Q_f to Q_1. Idle production capacity, cyclical unemployment, and a recessionary GDP gap (of $Q_1 - Q_f$) will result. If the price level were flexible downward, the decline in aggregate demand would move the economy depicted from a to c instead of from a to b.

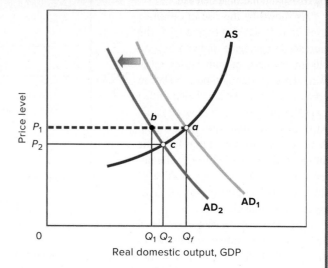

QUICK QUIZ FOR FIGURE 12.9

1. **If the price level remains stuck at P_1 and aggregate demand remains at AD_2, then:**
   a. the economy will be producing at full employment output.
   b. the price level will fall to P_2.
   c. the GDP gap will remain constant at $Q_1 - Q_f$.
   d. equilibrium will shift back to point a.

2. **Start from point b. If the price level becomes downwardly flexible, then:**
   a. the GDP gap will be reduced by the amount $Q_2 - Q_1$.
   b. the GDP gap will be reduced by the amount $Q_f - Q_1$.
   c. the GDP gap will be increased by the amount $Q_2 + Q_1$.
   d. the GDP gap will remain constant.

3. **Start from point b. For the economy to end up at point c would require:**
   a. upward price level flexibility.
   b. downward output flexibility.
   c. a downward shift of the AS curve.
   d. downward price flexibility.

4. **If prices were downwardly flexible, the equilibrium GDP and price level would be:**
   a. Q_f and P_1, respectively.
   b. Q_1 and P_1, respectively.
   c. Q_2 and P_1, respectively.
   d. Q_2 and P_2, respectively.

Answers: 1. c; 2. a; 3. d; 4. d

shift of the AD curve. The multiplier is at full strength because the reduction in aggregate demand occurs along what is, in effect, a horizontal segment of the AS curve. Because AS is effectively horizontal, none of the decrease in AD is dissipated as deflation, as some of it would be if prices were flexible and the economy shifted from a to c.

Note that this full-strength multiplier would also apply for an increase in aggregate demand from AD_2 to AD_1 along the broken line. The equilibrium would move from b to a, with GDP returning to Q_f and the price level remaining fixed at P_1. Thus, none of the increase in aggregate demand would be dissipated as inflation.

All recent recessions in the United States have generally mimicked the "GDP gap but no deflation" scenario shown in Figure 12.9. Consider the recession of 2007–2009, which resulted from chaos in the financial markets that quickly led to significant declines in spending by businesses and households. Aggregate demand declined dramatically, with actual GDP falling short of potential GDP by $1 trillion in 2009. At the same time, however, the price level barely budged, falling by only three-tenths of one percent in 2008 and in fact rising during 2009 as government stimulus efforts (lower taxes and higher spending) kicked in.

A similar thing happened during the pandemic recession of 2020. Actual GDP was 11 percent below potential GDP during the initial lockdown months, but the overall price level in the economy fell only slightly during those first few months before rising 1.3 percent over the entire year after government stimulus efforts kicked in.

GLOBAL PERSPECTIVE 12.1

SIZE OF GDP GAPS, SELECTED COUNTRIES, 2020

A country's GDP gap between potential output and actual output can be expressed as a percentage of potential output. In 2020, GDP gaps were negative in countries around the world, reflecting the fact that the COVID-19 pandemic was a worldwide phenomenon. Please note, however, that inflation was positive in each of the countries listed, reflecting the strength of downward price stickiness even during deep recessions.

Source: OECD Economic Outlook, Organisation for Economic Co-operation and Development (OECD).

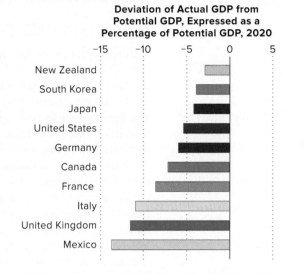

Deviation of Actual GDP from Potential GDP, Expressed as a Percentage of Potential GDP, 2020

Global Perspective 12.1 lists the 2020 GDP gaps of 10 countries. None of them experienced a deflation, even though all of them experienced negative GDP gaps as a result of the COVID-19 pandemic.

Decreases in AS: Cost-Push Inflation

Suppose that a major terrorist attack on oil facilities severely disrupts world oil supplies and drives up oil prices by, say, 300 percent. Higher energy prices will spread throughout the economy, driving up production and distribution costs on a wide variety of goods and services. The U.S. aggregate supply curve would shift to the left, say, from AS_1 to AS_2 in Figure 12.10. The resulting increase in the price level would generate *cost-push inflation*.

Consistent with the behavior of the U.S. economy, we are assuming in Figure 12.10 that the price level is flexible upward. So when aggregate supply shifts leftward from AS_1 to AS_2, the economy's equilibrium moves upward from point *a* to point *b*, with the price level rising from P_1 to P_2 and real output declining from Q_f to Q_1.

The effects of the leftward shift in aggregate supply are doubly bad. Along with the rising price level and cost-push inflation, a recession (and negative GDP gap) occurs. The oil-price shock of the early 1970s is the most famous example of this double whammy. The members of OPEC slowed their production rates to drive up the price of crude oil, which nearly quadrupled between October of 1973 and January of 1974. That dramatic increase in the price of oil increased per-unit production costs throughout the economy, pushing AS sharply to the left. The result was the 1973–1974 recession that saw real GDP decline by over 3 percent while inflation spiked to an annualized rate of 12 percent per year.

Back in the 1970s, oil expenditures were about 10 percent of U.S. GDP compared to only about 3 percent today. So the U.S. economy is nowadays substantially less vulnerable to cost-push inflation arising from

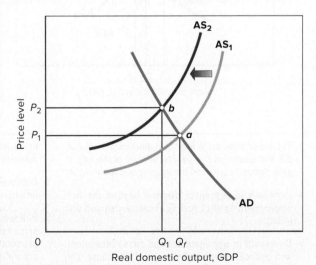

FIGURE 12.10
A decrease in aggregate supply that causes cost-push inflation.

A leftward shift of aggregate supply from AS_1 to AS_2 raises the price level from P_1 to P_2 and produces cost-push inflation. Real output declines and a recessionary GDP gap (of Q_1 minus Q_f) occurs.

oil shocks. That said, it is *not immune* from such shocks. A substantial supply shock caused by soaring oil prices would almost certainly cause U.S. aggregate supply to shift to the left by enough to again generate a decrease in output accompanied by significant cost-push inflation.

Increases in AS: Full Employment with Price-Level Stability

During the late 1990s, the United States experienced a combination of full employment, strong economic growth, and very low inflation. The unemployment rate fell to 4 percent and real GDP grew nearly 4 percent annually, *without igniting inflation*.

At first glance, this "macroeconomic bliss" seems to be incompatible with the AD–AS model. The aggregate supply curve suggests that increases in aggregate demand that strain the economy's production capacity will raise the price level (see Figure 12.8). Higher inflation, so it would seem, is the inevitable price paid for expanding output beyond the full-employment level.

But inflation remained very mild during the late 1990s. Figure 12.11 explains why. Thanks to the booming economy, aggregate demand increased from AD_1 to AD_2. Taken alone, that increase in aggregate demand would have moved the economy from *a* to *b*. Real output would have risen from full-employment output Q_1 to beyond-full-employment output Q_2. And the economy would have experienced significant inflation, shown by the increase in the price level from P_1 to P_3. Such inflation had in fact occurred during previous vigorous expansions of aggregate demand, including the expansion of the late 1980s.

Between 1990 and 2000, however, larger-than-usual increases in productivity occurred because of a burst of new technology relating to computers, the Internet, electronic commerce, and so on. In Figure 12.11, we represent this higher-than-usual productivity growth as the rightward shift from AS_1 to AS_2. The relevant aggregate demand and aggregate supply curves thus became AD_2 and AS_2, not AD_2 and AS_1. Instead of moving from *a* to *b*, the economy moved from *a* to *c*. Real output increased from Q_1 to Q_3, and the price level rose only modestly (from P_1 to P_2). The shift of the aggregate supply curve from AS_1 to AS_2 accommodated the rapid increase in aggregate demand and kept inflation mild.

But all good things come to an end. Aggregate demand eventually declined because of a substantial fall in investment spending, and in March 2001 the economy entered a recession. The terrorist attacks of September 11, 2001, further dampened private spending and prolonged the recession throughout 2001. The unemployment rate rose from 4.2 percent in January 2001 to 6.0 percent in December 2002. But consistent with downwardly flexible prices, the decline in aggregate demand did not cause a deflation. Inflation slowed, but remained positive. The price level did not fall.

The economy rebounded between 2002 and 2007, eventually re-achieving its earlier strong economic growth, low inflation, and low unemployment—until the housing bubble collapsed in 2006, and the so-called Great Recession started the following year.

FIGURE 12.11
Growth, full employment, and relative price stability.

Normally, an increase in aggregate demand from AD_1 to AD_2 would move the economy from *a* to *b* along AS_1. Real output would expand to Q_2, and inflation would result (P_1 to P_3). But in the late 1990s, significant increases in productivity shifted the aggregate supply curve, as from AS_1 to AS_2. The economy moved from *a* to *c* rather than from *a* to *b*. It experienced strong economic growth (Q_1 to Q_3), full employment, and only very mild inflation (P_1 to P_2) before receding in March 2001.

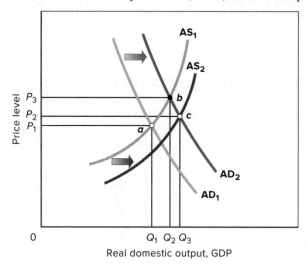

QUICK REVIEW

12.4

▶ The equilibrium price level and amount of real output are determined at the intersection of the aggregate demand curve and the aggregate supply curve.

▶ Increases in aggregate demand beyond the full-employment level of real GDP cause demand-pull inflation.

▶ Decreases in aggregate demand cause recessions and cyclical unemployment, partly because the price level and wages tend to be inflexible in a downward direction.

▶ Decreases in aggregate supply cause cost-push inflation.

▶ Full employment, high economic growth, and price stability are compatible with one another if productivity-driven increases in aggregate supply are sufficient to balance growing aggregate demand.

The COVID-19 Inflation

In 2021, Supply Chain Disruptions, Combined with Strong Aggregate Demand, Led to an Inflation Caused by Simultaneous Shifts in both AD *and* AS.

In 2021, inflation in the United States ran at a 7.0 percent annual rate as measured by the Consumer Price Index (CPI). That was the highest rate of inflation in the United States since 1981—when inflation was 10.3 percent—and it came as a surprise to both consumers and economic forecasters, who had been expecting inflation to be 2.5 percent or lower during 2021.

Surprising events often have surprising causes, and 2021's unexpected surge in inflation was no exception. Most bouts of inflation are caused either by aggregate demand shifting right while aggregate supply remains essentially stationary, *or* by aggregate supply shifting left while aggregate demand remains essentially stationary. The former is more common, with one famous example from U.S. history occurring in the late 1960s when the federal government's decision to simultaneously spend more on both social services (Medicare and Medicaid started in 1965) and the Vietnam War massively increased government spending and pushed aggregate demand to the right very rapidly. As illustrated by Figure 12.8, the resulting demand-pull inflation caused the price level to rise by 5.8 percent in 1970.

The most famous example of the other situation (in which aggregate supply shifts left while aggregate demand remains stationary or nearly stationary) began in October 1973 when several Arab countries that were major oil exporters slashed their production by 25 percent and placed an embargo against selling their oil to the United States and several other nations as a protest against those countries having provided military supplies to Israel after Israel had been sneak-attacked on the religious holiday of Yom Kippur by Egypt and Syria. Although the war itself lasted only three weeks, the oil embargo lasted until April 1974, by which time the world price of oil had quadrupled, from $2.90 per barrel to $11.65 per barrel. Since oil was a major productive input, the AS curve shifted left, thereby plunging the world into an inflationary recession, as illustrated in Figure 12.10.

The unexpected inflation of 2021 combined a rightward shift of AD and a leftward shift of AS. It consequently featured both cost-push inflation and demand-pull inflation operating simultaneously. The increase in aggregate demand came from the massive amount of government spending that congress and the president approved to fight the negative economic effects of the COVID-19 pandemic. The annualized rate of federal expenditures, including transfer payments, went from about $4.9 trillion per year just prior to the pandemic to a peak of about $9.1 trillion per year in mid-2020 before falling down to a still-high annualized rate of about $7.0 trillion per year during 2021. That surge of spending pushed the AD curve *sharply* to the right.

Norman Chan/Shutterstock

At the same time, a litany of supply chain disruptions shifted the AS curve to the left. These included everything from a shortage of computer chips to a dearth of unloading capacity at U.S. ports to factory shutdowns in various countries for various lengths of time due to anti-COVID lockdowns. All of those supply-reducing factors were augmented by labor shortages in the United States as older workers retired early and many younger workers decided to remain unemployed because they could make more collecting anti-pandemic unemployment benefits than they could working.

A key thing to keep in mind, however, was that real GDP had grown steadily throughout 2021, even after the various anti-pandemic stimulus programs had expired one by one. So as 2022 began, the focus was not on a threat of recession but rather on the high rate of inflation and what could be done to decrease it, especially because real wages had begun to decline due to the fact that consumer prices were going up faster than nominal wages.

As people looked to the future, supply chain problems were still apparent and the millions of older workers who had retired early seemed to be firm in their decision, implying that AS was not likely to start shifting rightward in any significant fashion any time soon. Consequently, prudence dictated that policymakers would have to be nimble if they wanted to return the economy to the mild inflation and steady growth witnessed in the late 2010s just prior to the pandemic. Any further leftward shifts of AS might have to be countered by rightward shifts of AD to prevent a recurrence of recession, but in a time of inflation, any rightward shifts of AD would only make the inflation problem worse.

Summary

LO12.1 Define aggregate demand (AD) and explain how its downward slope is the result of the real-balances effect, the interest-rate effect, and the foreign purchases effect.

The aggregate demand curve shows the level of real output that the economy demands at each price level.

The aggregate demand curve slopes downward because of the real-balances effect, the interest-rate effect, and the foreign purchases effect. The real-balances effect indicates that inflation reduces the real value or purchasing power of fixed-value financial assets held by households, causing cutbacks in consumer spending. The interest-rate effect means that, with a specific supply of money, a higher price level increases the demand for money, thereby raising the interest rate and reducing investment purchases. The foreign purchases effect suggests that an increase in one country's price level relative to other countries' price levels reduces the net export component of that nation's aggregate demand.

LO12.2 Explain the factors that shift AD.

The determinants of aggregate demand consist of spending by domestic consumers, by businesses, by government, and by foreign buyers. Changes in these groups' spending shift the aggregate demand curve. The extent of the shift is determined by the size of the initial change in spending and the strength of the economy's multiplier.

LO12.3 Define aggregate supply (AS) and explain how it differs in the immediate short run, the short run, and the long run.

The aggregate supply curve shows the levels of real output that businesses will produce at various possible price levels. The slope of the aggregate supply curve depends upon the flexibility of input and output prices.

The *immediate-short-run aggregate supply curve* assumes that both input prices and output prices are fixed. With output prices fixed, the aggregate supply curve is a horizontal line at the current price level. The *short-run aggregate supply curve* assumes nominal wages and other input prices remain fixed while output prices vary. The aggregate supply curve generally slopes upward because per-unit production costs, and hence the prices that firms receive, rise as real output expands. The aggregate supply curve is relatively steep to the right of the full-employment output level and relatively flat to the left of it.

The *long-run aggregate supply curve* assumes that nominal wages and other input prices fully match any change in the price level. The curve is vertical at the full-employment output level.

Because the short-run aggregate supply curve is the only version of aggregate supply that can handle simultaneous changes in the price level and real output, it serves well as the core aggregate supply curve for analyzing the business cycle and economic policy.

LO12.4 Explain the factors that shift AS.

The determinants of aggregate supply are input prices, productivity, and the legal-institutional environment. A change in any of these factors will change per-unit production costs at each output level and shift the aggregate supply curve.

LO12.5 Explain how AD and AS determine an economy's equilibrium price level and real GDP.

The intersection of the aggregate demand and aggregate supply curves determines an economy's equilibrium price level and real GDP. At the intersection, the quantity of real GDP demanded equals the quantity of real GDP supplied.

LO12.6 Use the AD–AS model to explain demand-pull inflation, cost-push inflation, and recessions.

Increases in aggregate demand to the right of the full-employment output cause inflation and positive GDP gaps (actual GDP exceeds potential GDP). An upward-sloping aggregate supply curve weakens the multiplier effect of an increase in AD because a portion of the increase in aggregate demand dissipates as inflation.

Shifts of the aggregate demand curve to the left of the full-employment output cause recession, negative GDP gaps, and cyclical unemployment. The price level may not fall during recessions because of downwardly inflexible prices and wages. When the price level is fixed, changes in aggregate demand produce full-strength multiplier effects.

Leftward shifts of the aggregate supply curve reflect increases in per-unit production costs and cause cost-push inflation, with accompanying negative GDP gaps. Rightward shifts of the aggregate supply curve, caused by large improvements in productivity, help explain the simultaneous achievement of full employment, economic growth, and price stability that occurred in the United States between 1996 and 2000.

Terms and Concepts

aggregate demand–aggregate supply (AD–AS) model

aggregate demand

real-balances effect

interest-rate effect

foreign purchases effect

determinants of aggregate demand

aggregate supply

immediate-short-run aggregate supply curve

short-run aggregate supply curve

long-run aggregate supply curve

determinants of aggregate supply

productivity

equilibrium price level

equilibrium real output

Discussion Questions

1. Why is the aggregate demand curve downsloping? Specify how your explanation differs from the explanation for the downsloping demand curve for a single product. What role does the multiplier play in shifts of the aggregate demand curve? **LO12.1**

2. Distinguish between "real-balances effect" and "wealth effect," as the terms are used in this chapter. How does each relate to the aggregate demand curve? **LO12.1**

3. What assumptions cause the immediate-short-run aggregate supply curve to be horizontal? Why is the long-run aggregate supply

curve vertical? Explain the shape of the short-run aggregate supply curve. Why is the short-run aggregate supply curve relatively flat to the left of the full-employment output and relatively steep to the right? **LO12.3**

4. Explain how an upsloping aggregate supply curve weakens the realized multiplier effect from an initial change in investment spending. **LO12.6**

5. Why does a reduction in aggregate demand in the actual economy reduce real output, rather than the price level? Why might a full-strength multiplier apply to a decrease in aggregate demand? **LO12.6**

6. Explain: "Unemployment can be caused by a decrease of aggregate demand or a decrease of aggregate supply." In each case, specify the price-level outcomes. **LO12.6**

7. Use shifts of the AD and AS curves to explain (a) the U.S. experience of strong economic growth, full employment, and price

stability in the late 1990s and early 2000s and (b) how a strong negative wealth effect from, say, a precipitous drop in house prices could cause a recession even though productivity is surging. **LO12.6**

8. In early 2020, the anti-pandemic lockdowns caused both consumption spending and the amount of labor employed by firms to sharply decline. Use AD–AS analysis to describe the two impacts on real GDP. **LO12.6**

9. **LAST WORD** What was so unusual about the bout of inflation that the United States experienced in 2021? Since real GDP kept on growing during 2021, what do we know about the relative sizes of the rightward shift of AD as compared with the leftward shift of AS? If AS had shifted further left, would it have been possible to offset that leftward shift of AS with a rightward shift in AD without further increasing the price level?

Review Questions

1. Which of the following help to explain why the aggregate demand curve slopes downward? **LO12.1**
   a. When the domestic price level rises, our goods and services become more expensive to people living abroad.
   b. When government spending rises, the price level falls.
   c. There is an inverse relationship between consumer expectations and personal taxes.
   d. When the price level rises, the real value of financial assets (like stocks, bonds, and savings account balances) declines.

2. Which of the following will shift the aggregate demand curve to the left? **LO12.2**
   a. The government reduces personal income taxes.
   b. Interest rates rise.
   c. The government raises corporate profit taxes.
   d. There is an economic boom overseas that raises the incomes of foreign households.

3. Label each of the following descriptions as being either an immediate-short-run aggregate supply curve, a short-run aggregate supply curve, or a long-run aggregate supply curve. **LO12.3**
   a. A vertical line.
   b. The price level is fixed.
   c. Output prices are flexible, but input prices are fixed.
   d. A horizontal line.
   e. An upsloping curve.
   f. Output is fixed.

4. Which of the following will shift the aggregate supply curve to the right? **LO12.4**
   a. A new networking technology increases productivity all over the economy.
   b. The price of oil rises substantially.
   c. Business taxes fall.
   d. The government passes a law doubling all manufacturing wages.

5. At the current price level, producers supply $375 billion of final goods and services while consumers purchase $355 billion of final goods and services. The price level is: **LO12.5**
   a. above equilibrium.
   b. at equilibrium.
   c. below equilibrium.
   d. more information is needed.

6. What effects would each of the following have on aggregate demand or aggregate supply, other things equal? In each case, use a diagram to show the expected effects on the equilibrium price level and the level of real output, assuming that the price level is flexible both upward and downward. **LO12.5**
   a. A widespread fear by consumers of an impending economic depression.
   b. A new national tax on producers based on the value added between the costs of the inputs and the revenue received from their output.
   c. A reduction in interest rates.
   d. A major increase in spending for health care by the federal government.
   e. The general expectation of coming rapid inflation.
   f. The complete disintegration of OPEC, causing oil prices to fall by one-half.
   g. A 10 percent across-the-board reduction in personal income tax rates.
   h. A sizable increase in labor productivity (with no change in nominal wages).
   i. A 12 percent increase in nominal wages (with no change in productivity).
   j. An increase in exports that exceeds an increase in imports (not due to tariffs).

7. True or False: Decreases in AD normally lead to decreases in both output and the price level. **LO12.6**

8. Assume that (a) the price level is flexible upward but not downward and (b) the economy is currently operating at its full-employment output. Other things equal, how will each of the following affect the equilibrium price level and equilibrium level of real output in the short run? **LO12.6**
   a. An increase in aggregate demand.
   b. A decrease in aggregate supply, with no change in aggregate demand.
   c. Equal increases in aggregate demand and aggregate supply.
   d. A decrease in aggregate demand.
   e. An increase in aggregate demand that exceeds an increase in aggregate supply.

9. True or False: If the price of oil suddenly increases by a large amount, AS will shift left, but the price level will not rise thanks to price inflexibility. **LO12.6**

Problems

1. Suppose that consumer spending initially rises by $5 billion for every 1 percent rise in household wealth and that investment spending initially rises by $20 billion for every 1 percentage point fall in the real interest rate. Also assume that the economy's multiplier is 4. If household wealth falls by 5 percent because of declining house values, and the real interest rate falls by 2 percentage points, in what direction and by how much will the aggregate demand curve initially shift at each price level? In what direction and by how much will it eventually shift? **LO12.2**

2. Answer the following questions on the basis of the following three sets of data for the country of North Vaudeville: **LO12.4**

(A)		(B)		(C)	
Price Level	Real GDP	Price Level	Real GDP	Price Level	Real GDP
110	275	100	200	110	225
100	250	100	225	100	225
95	225	100	250	95	225
90	200	100	275	90	225

   a. Which set of data illustrates aggregate supply in the immediate short run in North Vaudeville? The short run? The long run?

   b. Assuming no change in hours of work, if real output per hour of work increases by 10 percent, what will be the new levels of real GDP in the right column of A? Do the new data reflect an increase in aggregate supply or do they indicate a decrease in aggregate supply?

3. Suppose that the table presented below shows an economy's relationship between real output and the inputs needed to produce that output: **LO12.4**

Input Quantity	Real GDP
150.0	$400
112.5	300
75.0	200

   a. What is productivity in this economy?

   b. What is the per-unit cost of production if the price of each input unit is $2?

   c. Assume that the input price increases from $2 to $3 with no accompanying change in productivity. What is the new per-unit cost of production? In what direction would the $1 increase in input price push the economy's aggregate

supply curve? What effect would this shift of aggregate supply have on the price level and the level of real output?

   d. Suppose that the increase in input price does not occur but, instead, that productivity increases by 100 percent. What would be the new per-unit cost of production? What effect would this change in per-unit production cost have on the economy's aggregate supply curve? What effect would this shift of aggregate supply have on the price level and the level of real output?

4. Suppose that the aggregate demand and aggregate supply schedules for a hypothetical economy are as shown in the following table. **LO12.5**

Amount of Real GDP Demanded, Billions	Price Level (Price Index)	Amount of Real GDP Supplied, Billions
$100	300	$450
200	250	400
300	200	300
400	150	200
500	100	100

   a. Use the data above to graph the aggregate demand and aggregate supply curves. What are the equilibrium price level and the equilibrium level of real output in this hypothetical economy? Is the equilibrium real output also necessarily the full-employment real output?

   b. If the price level in this economy is 150, will quantity demanded equal, exceed, or fall short of quantity supplied? By what amount? If the price level is 250, will quantity demanded equal, exceed, or fall short of quantity supplied? By what amount?

   c. Suppose that buyers desire to purchase $200 billion of extra real output at each price level. Sketch in the new aggregate demand curve as AD_1. What are the new equilibrium price level and level of real output?

5. Refer to the data in the table that accompanies problem 2. Suppose that the present equilibrium price level and level of real GDP are 100 and $225, and that data set B represents the relevant aggregate supply schedule for the economy. **LO12.6**

   a. What must be the current amount of real output demanded at the 100 price level?

   b. If the amount of output demanded declined by $25 at the 100 price level shown in B, what would be the new equilibrium real GDP? In business cycle terminology, what would economists call this change in real GDP?

The Relationship of the AD Curve to the Aggregate Expenditures Model

LO12.7 Relate the aggregate demand curve to the aggregate expenditures model.

The aggregate demand curve of this chapter and the aggregate expenditures model of Chapter 11 are intricately related.

Deriving the AD Curve from the Aggregate Expenditures Model

We can directly connect the downward sloping AD curve to the aggregate expenditures model by relating various possible price levels to corresponding equilibrium GDPs. In Figure 1 we have stacked the aggregate expenditures model (Figure 1a) and the aggregate demand curve (Figure 1b) vertically. We can do so because the horizontal axes of both models measure real GDP. Now let's derive the AD curve in three distinct steps. (Throughout this discussion, keep in mind that price level P_1 is lower than price level P_2, which is lower than price level P_3.)

- First suppose that the economy's price level is P_1 and its aggregate expenditures schedule is AE_1, the top schedule in Figure 1a. The equilibrium GDP is then Q_1 at point 1. So, in Figure 1b, we can plot the equilibrium real output Q_2 and the corresponding price level P_1. Doing so gives us point 1′ in Figure 1b.

- Now assume the price level rises from P_1 to P_2. Other things equal, this higher price level will (1) decrease the value of real balances (wealth), decreasing consumption expenditures; (2) increase the interest rate, reducing investment and interest-sensitive consumption expenditures; and (3) increase imports and decrease exports, reducing net export expenditures. The aggregate expenditures schedule falls from AE_1 to AE_2 in Figure 1a, giving us equilibrium Q_2 at point 2. In Figure 1b we plot this new price-level–real-output combination, P_2 and Q_2, as point 2′.

- Finally, suppose the price level rises from P_2 to P_3. The value of real balances falls, the interest rate rises, exports fall, and imports rise. Consequently, the consumption, investment, and net export schedules fall, shifting the aggregate expenditures schedule downward from AE_2 to AE_3, which gives us equilibrium Q_3 at point 3. In Figure 1b, we plot point 3′, where the price level is P_3 and real output is Q_3.

FIGURE 1 Deriving the aggregate demand curve from the aggregate expenditures model.

(a) Rising price levels from P_1 to P_2 to P_3 shift the aggregate expenditures curve downward from AE_1 to AE_2 to AE_3 and reduce real GDP from Q_1 to Q_2 to Q_3. (b) The aggregate demand curve AD is derived by plotting the successively lower real GDPs from the upper graph against the P_1, P_2, and P_3 price levels.

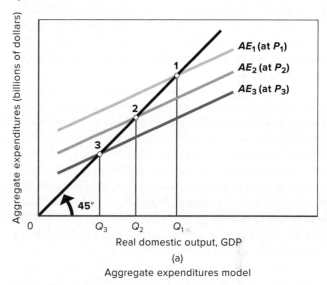

(a)
Aggregate expenditures model

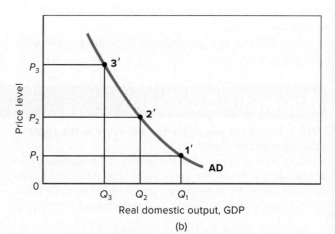

(b)
Aggregate demand–aggregate supply model

In summary, increases in the economy's price level successively shift its aggregate expenditures schedule downward and reduce real GDP. The resulting price-level–real-GDP combinations yield various points such as 1′, 2′, and 3′ in Figure 1b.

Together, such points locate the downward sloping aggregate demand curve for the economy.

Aggregate Demand Shifts and the Aggregate Expenditures Model

The determinants of aggregate demand listed in Figure 12.2 are the components of the aggregate expenditures model discussed in Chapter 11. When one of the determinants of aggregate demand changes, the aggregate expenditures schedule shifts upward or downward. We can easily link such shifts of the aggregate expenditures schedule to shifts of the AD curve.

Let's suppose that the price level is constant. In Figure 2 we begin with the aggregate expenditures schedule at AE_1 in the top diagram, yielding equilibrium real output Q_1. Assume now that investment increases in response to more optimistic business expectations, so the aggregate expenditures schedule rises from AE_1 to AE_2. (The notation "at P_1" reminds us that the price level is assumed constant.) The result will be a multiplied increase in equilibrium real output from Q_1 to Q_2.

In Figure 2b the increase in investment spending is reflected in the horizontal distance between AD_1 and the broken curve to its right. The immediate effect of the increase in investment is an increase in aggregate demand by the exact amount of the new spending. But then the multiplier process magnifies the initial increase in investment into successive rounds of consumption spending and an ultimate multiplied increase in aggregate demand from AD_1 to AD_2. Equilibrium real output rises from Q_1 to Q_2, the same multiplied increase in real GDP as that in the top graph. The initial increase in investment in the top graph has shifted the AD curve in the lower graph by a horizontal distance equal to the change in investment times the multiplier. This particular change in real GDP is still associated with the constant price level P_1. To generalize,

Shift of AD curve = initial change in spending × multiplier

FIGURE 2 Shifts of the aggregate expenditures schedule and of the aggregate demand curve.

(a) A change in some determinant of consumption, investment, or net exports (other than the price level) shifts the aggregate expenditures schedule upward from AE_1 to AE_2. The multiplier increases real output from Q_1 to Q_2. (b) The counterpart of this change is an initial rightward shift of the aggregate demand curve by the amount of initial new spending (from AD_1 to the broken curve). This leads to a multiplied rightward shift of the curve to AD_2, which is just sufficient to show the same increase of real output as that in the aggregate expenditures model.

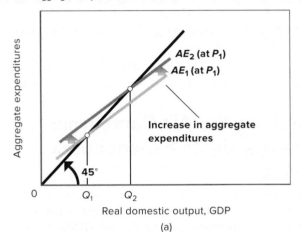

(a)
Aggregate expenditures model

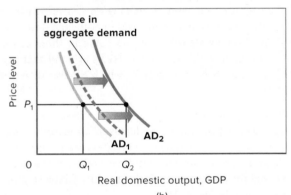

(b)
Aggregate demand–aggregate supply model

Appendix Summary

LO12.7 Relate the aggregate demand curve to the aggregate expenditures model.

A change in the price level alters the location of the aggregate expenditures schedule through the real-balances, interest-rate, and foreign purchases effects. We derive the AD curve from the aggregate expenditures model by allowing the price level to change and observing the effect on the aggregate expenditures schedule and thus on equilibrium GDP.

With the price level held constant, increases in consumption, investment, government, and net export expenditures shift the aggregate expenditures schedule upward and the AD curve to the right. Decreases in these spending components produce the opposite effects.

Appendix Discussion Questions

1. Explain carefully: "A change in the price level shifts the aggregate expenditures curve but not the aggregate demand curve." **LO12.7**
2. Suppose that the price level is constant and that investment decreases sharply. How would you show this decrease in the aggregate expenditures model? What is the outcome for real GDP? How would you show this fall in investment in the AD-AS model, assuming the economy is operating in what is, in effect, a horizontal section of the AS curve? **LO12.7**

Appendix Review Questions

1. True or False: A higher price level increases aggregate expenditures. **LO12.7**

2. If the government decreases expenditures, the *AE* curve will shift _____ and the AD curve will shift _____. **LO12.7**
   a. down; left
   b. down; right
   c. up; left
   d. up; right

Appendix Problems

1. Refer to Figures 1a and 1b in this Appendix. Assume that Q_1 is 300, Q_2 is 200, Q_3 is 100, P_3 is 120, P_2 is 100, and P_1 is 80. If the price level increases from P_1 to P_3 in Figure 1b, in what direction and by how much will real GDP change? If the slopes of the *AE* lines in Figure 1a are 0.8 and equal to the MPC, in what direction will the aggregate expenditures schedule in Figure 1a need to shift to produce the previously determined change in real GDP? What is the size of the multiplier in this example? **LO12.7**

2. Refer to Figure 2 in this Appendix and assume that Q_1 is $400 and Q_2 is $500, the price level is stuck at P_1, and the slopes of the *AE* lines in Figure 2a are 0.75 and equal to the MPC. In what direction and by how much does the aggregate expenditures schedule in Figure 2a need to shift to move the aggregate demand curve in Figure 2b from AD$_1$ to AD$_2$? What is the multiplier in this example? Given the multiplier, what must be the distance between AD$_1$ and the broken line to its right at P_1? **LO12.7**

Pavel Bobrovskiy/Shutterstock

USA CHAPTER
EURO **13**
ENGLAND

Fiscal Policy, Deficits, and Debt

>> LEARNING OBJECTIVES

LO13.1 Identify the purposes, tools, and limitations of fiscal policy.

LO13.2 Explain how built-in stabilizers moderate business cycles.

LO13.3 Describe how the cyclically adjusted budget reveals the status of U.S. fiscal policy.

LO13.4 Summarize recent U.S. fiscal policy.

LO13.5 Discuss the problems that governments may encounter in enacting and applying fiscal policy.

LO13.6 Discuss the size, composition, and consequences of the U.S. public debt.

fiscal policy Changes in government spending and tax collections designed to achieve full employment, price stability, and economic growth; also called *discretionary fiscal policy.*

In Chapter 11, we saw that an excessive increase in aggregate demand can cause demand-pull inflation and that a significant decline in aggregate demand can cause recession and cyclical unemployment. For these reasons, the federal government sometimes tries to "stimulate the economy" or "rein in inflation." Such countercyclical **fiscal policy** consists of deliberate changes in government spending and tax collections designed to achieve full employment, control inflation, and encourage economic growth. (The adjective "fiscal" simply means "financial.")

We begin this chapter by examining the logic behind fiscal policy, its current status, and its limitations. Then we examine a closely related topic: the U.S. public debt.

Fiscal Policy and the AD–AS Model

>> **LO13.1** Identify the purposes, tools, and limitations of fiscal policy.

Fiscal policy consists of changes in government spending and tax collections designed to achieve full employment, price stability, and economic growth. Fiscal policy can be either discretionary or nondiscretionary:

- **Discretionary fiscal policy** refers to changes in government spending and taxes that are *at the option of* the federal government. They do not occur automatically. The current congress must pass a discretionary spending or tax bill and the president must sign it into law.

- **Nondiscretionary fiscal policy** refers to changes in spending and taxes that occur automatically, or passively, without the need for current congressional action. They occur as the result of spending and tax provisions put into law by earlier congresses.

Council of Economic Advisers (CEA) A group of three persons that advises and assists the president of the United States on economic matters (including the preparation of the annual *Economic Report of the President*).

Discretionary fiscal policy is often initiated on the advice of the president's **Council of Economic Advisers (CEA),** a group of three economists who provide expertise and assistance on economic matters. Various congressional committees have final say, however, on the contents of any discretionary spending or tax bill that is sent to the president.

▂▃▅ KEY GRAPH

FIGURE 13.1 Expansionary fiscal policy with the multiplier effect.

If the price level is downwardly inflexible at P_1, a decrease of aggregate demand from AD_1 to AD_2 will reduce real GDP from $510 billion (full employment) to $490 billion. Expansionary fiscal policy (increases in government spending or decreases in taxes) can be used to push this economy out of recession. A $5 billion increase in government spending or a $6.67 billion decrease in personal taxes (producing a $5 billion initial increase in consumption) will shift aggregate demand rightward from AD_2 to the downward sloping dashed curve. Assuming an MPC of 0.75, this economy would have a multiplier of 4. So the initial $5 billion rightward shift provided by the government would be magnified into a total rightward shift of $20 billion (= 4 times $5 billion), returning aggregate demand back to AD_1 and real GDP back to $510 billion.

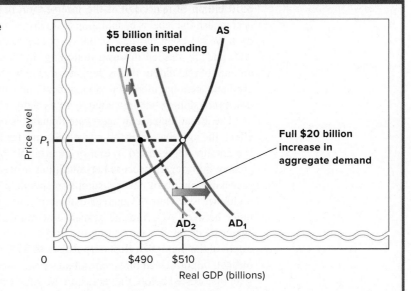

QUICK QUIZ FOR FIGURE 13.1

1. Suppose the government finds out too late that the MPC in the economy is 0.90 rather than 0.75, so that the multiplier is 10 instead of 4. The initial $5 billion stimulus would cause:
   a. the price level to rise higher than P_1.
   b. real GDP to fall short of $510 billion.
   c. the price level to fall below P_1.
   d. real GDP to fall short of $490 billion.

2. If the marginal propensity to save in the economy were 1, then the initial $5 government stimulus would result in a real GDP of:
   a. $460 billion.
   b. $485 billion.
   c. $490 billion.
   d. $495 billion.

3. Under the assumption that MPC = 0.75, an initial government stimulus of $7 billion (rather than $5 billion) would be:
   a. deflationary.
   b. recessionary.
   c. inflationary.
   d. discretionary.

4. Suppose that the government is expecting the aggregate supply curve AS to shift upward (left). If MPC = 0.75 and the government wishes to restore full employment output, then the government should provide an initial amount of stimulus that is:
   a. less than $5 billion.
   b. equal to $5 billion.
   c. greater than $5 billion.
   d. it depends on MPS.

Answers: 1. a; 2. d; 3. c; 4. c

Expansionary Fiscal Policy

When a recession occurs, the government may initiate an **expansionary fiscal policy** that is designed to increase aggregate demand and therefore raise real GDP. Consider **Figure 13.1 (Key Graph),** where lower profit expectations cause a sharp decline in investment spending that shifts the economy's aggregate demand curve to the left from AD_1 to AD_2. (Disregard the arrows and dashed downward sloping line for now.)

Suppose the economy's potential or full-employment output is $510 billion in Figure 13.1. If the price level is inflexible downward at P_1, the broken horizontal line becomes relevant to the analysis. The aggregate demand curve moves leftward and reduces real GDP from $510 billion to $490 billion. The result is a GDP gap of negative $20 billion (= $490 billion − $510 billion). Unemployment increases because fewer workers are needed to produce the reduced level of output. In short, the economy is suffering both recession and cyclical unemployment.

What fiscal policy should the federal government use to stimulate the economy? It has three main options: (1) increase government spending, (2) reduce taxes, or (3) use some combination of the two. If the federal budget is balanced at the outset, expansionary fiscal policy will create a government **budget deficit**—government spending in excess of tax revenues.

expansionary fiscal policy An increase in *government purchases* of *goods* and *services*, a decrease in *net taxes*, or some combination of the two for the purpose of increasing *aggregate demand* and expanding real output.

budget deficit The amount by which expenditures exceed revenues in any year.

Increased Government Spending As an overall strategy, the government will want to shift the aggregate demand curve back where it came from, thereby returning the economy to producing $510 billion of real GDP at the intersection of AD_1 and AS. One way for the government to accomplish that goal is by initiating $5 billion of new spending on highways, education, and health care. We represent this new $5 billion of government spending as the horizontal distance between AD_2 and the dashed downward sloping line immediately to its right. At each price level, the amount of real output that is demanded is now $5 billion greater than that demanded before government spending increased. So aggregate demand will shift rightward, from AD_2 to the dashed downward sloping line immediately to its right.

The initial increase in aggregate demand is not the end of the story. Through the multiplier effect, the aggregate demand curve will shift farther, all the way to AD_1, a distance that exceeds the amount represented by the originating $5 billion increase in government purchases. This greater shift occurs because the multiplier process magnifies the initial change in spending into successive rounds of new consumption spending. If the economy's MPC is 0.75, then the simple multiplier is 4. Thus the aggregate demand curve shifts rightward by four times the $5 billion distance between AD_2 and the dashed downward sloping line. Because this *particular* increase in aggregate demand occurs along the horizontal dashed-line segment, real output rises by the full extent of the multiplier. Real output rises to $510 billion, up $20 billion from its recessionary level of $490 billion. Unemployment falls as firms increase their employment to the full-employment level that existed before the recession. Mission accomplished.

Tax Reductions Alternatively, the government could reduce taxes to shift the aggregate demand curve rightward from AD_2 to AD_1. Suppose the government cuts personal income taxes by $6.67 billion, which increases disposable income by the same amount. Consumption will rise by $5 billion (= MPC of 0.75 × $6.67 billion), and saving will go up by $1.67 billion (= MPC of 0.25 × $6.67 billion). In this case, the horizontal distance between AD_2 and the dashed downward sloping line in Figure 13.1 represents only the $5 billion initial increase in consumption spending. Again, we call it "initial" consumption spending because the multiplier process yields successive rounds of increased consumption spending. The aggregate demand curve eventually shifts rightward by four times the $5 billion initial increase in consumption produced by the tax cut. Real GDP rises by $20 billion, from $490 billion to $510 billion, implying a multiplier of 4. Employment increases accordingly.

You may have noted that a tax cut must be somewhat larger than an increase in government spending to achieve the same amount of rightward shift in the aggregate demand curve. Why? Part of a tax reduction increases saving, rather than consumption. To increase initial consumption by a specific amount, the government must reduce taxes by more than that amount. When the MPC is 0.75, taxes must fall by $6.67 billion to increase consumption by $5 billion because $1.67 billion of the $6.67 billion tax reduction is saved (not consumed). The smaller the MPC, the greater the tax cut needed to accomplish a specific initial increase in consumption.

Combined Government Spending Increases and Tax Reductions The government may combine spending increases and tax cuts to produce the desired initial increase in spending and the eventual increase in aggregate demand and real GDP. For example, the government might increase its spending by $1.25 billion while reducing taxes by $5 billion. As an exercise, you should explain why this combination will produce the targeted $5 billion initial increase in new spending.

Contractionary Fiscal Policy

contractionary fiscal policy
A decrease in *government purchases* of *goods* and *services*, an increase in *net taxes*, or some combination of the two, for the purpose of decreasing *aggregate demand* and thus controlling *inflation*.

When demand-pull inflation occurs, a restrictive or **contractionary fiscal policy** may help control it. Look at Figure 13.2, where the full-employment level of real GDP is $510 billion. The economy starts at equilibrium at point *a*, where the initial aggregate demand curve AD_3 intersects aggregate supply curve AS. Suppose that after going through the multiplier process, a $5 billion initial increase in investment and net export spending shifts the aggregate demand curve to the right by $20 billion, from AD_3 to AD_4. (Ignore the downward sloping dashed line for now.) Given the upward sloping AS curve, the equilibrium GDP does not rise by the full $20 billion, however. It rises by only $12 billion, to $522 billion, thereby creating an inflationary GDP gap of $12 billion (= $522 billion − $510 billion). The upward slope of the AS curve means that some of the rightward movement of the AD curve ends up causing demand-pull inflation rather than increased output. The price level rises from P_1 to P_2, and the equilibrium moves to point *b*.

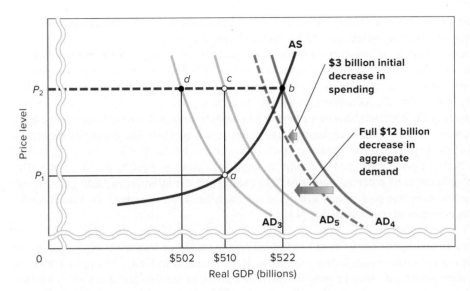

FIGURE 13.2
Contractionary fiscal policy.

Contractionary fiscal policy uses decreases in government spending, increases in taxes, or both, to reduce demand-pull inflation. Here, an increase in aggregate demand from AD_3 to AD_4 has driven the economy to point b and ratcheted the price level up to P_2, where it becomes inflexible downward. If the economy's MPC is 0.75 and the multiplier therefore is 4, the government can either reduce its spending by $3 billion or increase its taxes by $4 billion (which will decrease consumption by $3 billion) to eliminate the inflationary GDP gap of $12 billion (= $522 billion − $510 billion). Aggregate demand will shift leftward, first from AD_4 to the dashed downsloping curve to its left, and then to AD_5. With the price level remaining at P_2, the economy will move from point b to point c and the inflationary GDP gap will disappear.

Without a government response, the inflationary GDP gap will cause further inflation (as input prices rise in the long run to meet the increase in output prices). If the government looks to fiscal policy to eliminate the inflationary GDP gap, it can (1) decrease government spending, (2) raise taxes, or (3) use some combination of those two policies. When the economy faces demand-pull inflation, fiscal policy should move toward a government **budget surplus**—tax revenues in excess of government spending.

Decreased Government Spending To control demand-pull inflation, the government can decrease aggregate demand by reducing government spending. Look at Figure 13.2 and consider what would happen if the government attempted to design a spending-reduction policy to eliminate the inflationary GDP gap. Because the $12 billion gap was caused by the $20 billion rightward movement of the aggregate demand curve from AD_3 to AD_4, the government might naively think that it could solve the problem by causing a $20 billion leftward shift that would put the aggregate demand curve back in its original position. It could reduce government spending by $5 billion and then allow the multiplier effect to expand that initial decrease into a $20 billion decline in aggregate demand, thus shifting the aggregate demand curve leftward by $20 billion, putting it back at AD_3.

This policy would work fine if prices were flexible. The economy's equilibrium would move back from point b to point a, with equilibrium GDP returning to the full-employment level of $510 billion and the price level falling from P_2 back to P_1.

But this scenario is not what will actually happen. Instead, the price level is stuck at P_2, so that the dashed horizontal line at price level P_2 becomes important to the analysis. The fixed price level means that when the government reduces spending by $5 billion to shift the aggregate demand curve back to AD_3, it will actually cause a recession! The new equilibrium will not be at point a. It will be at point d, where aggregate demand curve AD_3 crosses the dashed horizontal line. At point d, real GDP is only $502 billion, $8 billion below the full-employment level of $510 billion.

The problem is that, with the price level downwardly inflexible at P_2, the $20 billion leftward shift of the aggregate demand curve causes a full $20 billion decline in real GDP. None of the change in aggregate demand can be dissipated as a decline in the price level. As a result, equilibrium GDP declines by the full $20 billion, falling from $522 billion to $502 billion, which is $8 billion below potential output. By failing to account for the inflexible price level, the government has overdone the decrease in government spending, replacing a $12 billion inflationary GDP gap with an $8 billion recessionary GDP gap. This was clearly not its goal.

Here's how it can avoid this scenario. The government first determines the size of the inflationary GDP gap. It is $12 billion. Second, it knows that with the price level fixed, the multiplier will be in full effect. Thus, it knows that any decline in government spending will be multiplied by a factor of 4. It then reasons that government spending will have to decline by only $3 billion rather than $5 billion. Why? Because the $3 billion initial decline in government spending will be

budget surplus The amount by which the revenues of the federal government exceed its expenditures in any year.

multiplied by 4, creating a $12 billion decline in aggregate demand. Under the circumstances, a $3 billion decline exactly offsets the $12 billion GDP gap.

Please note that the inflationary GDP gap is the problem that government wants to eliminate in Figure 13.2. To succeed, it doesn't have to undo the full $20 billion increase in aggregate demand that caused the inflation in the first place. With the price level stuck at P_2, the government only has to move the AD curve leftward by $12 billion.

Graphically, the horizontal distance between AD_4 and the dashed downward sloping line to its left represents the $3 billion decrease in government spending. Once the multiplier process is complete, this spending cut shifts the aggregate demand curve leftward by $12 billion, from AD_4 to AD_5. With the price level fixed at P_2, the economy will come to equilibrium at point c. The economy operates at its potential output of $510 billion, and the inflationary GDP gap is eliminated. Furthermore, the government will not accidentally push the economy into a recession by decreasing government spending by too much.

Increased Taxes Just as government can use tax cuts to increase consumption spending, it can use tax *increases* to *reduce* consumption spending. If the economy in Figure 13.2 has an MPC of 0.75, the government must raise taxes by $4 billion to achieve its fiscal policy objective. The $4 billion tax increase reduces saving by $1 billion (= the MPS of 0.25 × $4 billion). This $1 billion reduction in saving is, by definition, a reduction in savings, not spending. But the $4 billion tax increase also reduces consumption spending by $3 billion (= the MPC of 0.75 × $4 billion), as shown by the distance between AD_4 and the dashed downward sloping line to its left in Figure 13.2. After the multiplier process is complete, this initial $3 billion decline in consumption spending causes aggregate demand to shift leftward at each price level by $12 billion (= multiplier of 4 × $3 billion). With the economy moving to point c, the inflationary GDP gap is closed and the inflation is halted.

Combining Government Spending Decreases with Tax Increases The government may choose to combine spending decreases and tax increases in order to reduce aggregate demand and control inflation. To check your understanding, determine why a $1.5 billion decline in government spending combined with a $2 billion increase in taxes will shift the aggregate demand curve from AD_4 to AD_5.

QUICK REVIEW

13.1

▶ Discretionary fiscal policy is the purposeful change of government expenditures and tax collections by government to promote full employment, price stability, and economic growth.

▶ Expansionary fiscal policy consists of increases in government spending, reductions in taxes, or both, and is designed to expand real GDP by increasing aggregate demand.

▶ Contractionary fiscal policy entails decreases in government spending, increases in taxes, or both, and is designed to reduce aggregate demand and slow or halt demand-pull inflation.

▶ To be implemented correctly, contractionary fiscal policy must properly account for the ratchet effect and the fact that the price level will not fall as the government shifts the aggregate demand curve leftward.

Built-In Stability

Tax Collections and the Business Cycle

>> **LO13.2** Explain how built-in stabilizers moderate business cycles.

Under normal circumstances, government tax revenues change automatically over the course of the business cycle in ways that stabilize the economy. This automatic response, or built-in stability, constitutes what is commonly referred to as nondiscretionary (or "passive" or "automatic") budgetary policy. We did not include this built-in stability in the discussion about fiscal policy that we had in the last section because we implicitly assumed that the same amount of tax revenue was being collected at each level of GDP. But the actual U.S. tax system is such that *net tax revenues* vary directly with GDP. (Net taxes are tax revenues less transfers and subsidies. From here on, we will use "taxes" to mean "net taxes.")

Virtually any tax will yield more tax revenue as GDP rises. In particular, personal income taxes have progressive rates and thus generate more-than-proportionate increases in tax revenues as GDP expands. Furthermore, as GDP rises and more goods and services are purchased, revenues from corporate income taxes and from sales taxes and excise taxes also increase. And, similarly, revenues from payroll taxes rise as economic expansion creates more jobs. Conversely, when GDP declines, tax receipts from all these sources also decline.

Transfer payments (or "negative taxes") behave in the opposite way from tax revenues. Unemployment compensation payments and welfare payments decrease during economic expansion and increase during economic contraction.

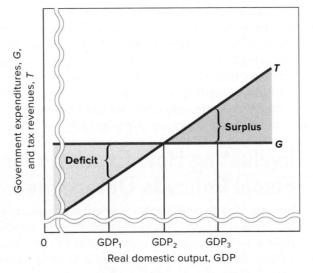

FIGURE 13.3
Built-in stability.

Tax revenues, *T*, vary directly with GDP, while government spending, *G*, is assumed to be independent of GDP. As GDP falls in a recession, deficits occur automatically and help alleviate the recession. As GDP rises during expansion, surpluses occur automatically and help offset possible inflation.

Automatic or Built-In Stabilizers

A **built-in stabilizer** is anything that increases the government's budget deficit (or reduces its budget surplus) during a recession and increases its budget surplus (or reduces its budget deficit) during an expansion without requiring explicit action by policymakers. As Figure 13.3 reveals, this is precisely what the U.S. tax system does. Government expenditures *G* are fixed and assumed to be independent of the level of GDP. Congress decides on a particular level of spending, but it does not determine the magnitude of tax revenues. Instead, it establishes tax rates, and the tax revenues then vary directly with the level of GDP that the economy achieves. Line *T* represents that direct relationship between tax revenues and GDP.

Economic Importance The economic importance of the direct relationship between tax receipts and GDP becomes apparent when we consider that:

- Taxes reduce spending and aggregate demand.
- Reductions in spending are desirable when the economy is moving toward inflation, whereas increases in spending are desirable when the economy is slumping.

As shown in Figure 13.3, tax revenues automatically increase as GDP rises during prosperity, and since taxes reduce household and business spending, they restrain the economic expansion. That is, as the economy moves toward a higher GDP, tax revenues automatically rise and move the budget from deficit toward surplus. In Figure 13.3, observe that the high and perhaps inflationary income level GDP_3 automatically generates a contractionary budget surplus.

Conversely, as GDP falls during recession, tax revenues automatically decline, increasing spending by households and businesses and thus cushioning the economic contraction. With a falling GDP, tax receipts decline and move the government's budget from surplus toward deficit. In Figure 13.3, the low level of income GDP_1 will automatically yield an expansionary budget deficit.

Tax Progressivity Figure 13.3 reveals that the size of the automatic budget deficits or surpluses—and therefore built-in stability—depends on the responsiveness of tax revenues to changes in GDP. If tax revenues change sharply as GDP changes, the slope of line *T* in the figure will be steep and the vertical distances between *T* and *G* (the deficits or surpluses) will be large. If tax revenues change very little when GDP changes, the slope will be gentle and built-in stability will be low.

The steepness of *T* in Figure 13.3 depends on the tax system itself:

- In a **progressive tax** system, the average tax rate (= tax revenue/GDP) rises with GDP.
- In a **proportional tax** system, the average tax rate remains constant as GDP rises.
- In a **regressive tax** system, the average tax rate falls as GDP rises.

The progressive tax system has the steepest tax line *T* of the three. However, tax revenues will rise with GDP under both the progressive and the proportional tax systems, and they may rise, fall, or stay the same under a regressive tax system. The main point is this: The more progressive the tax system, the greater the economy's built-in stability.

built-in stabilizer A mechanism that increases government's budget deficit (or reduces its surplus) during a recession and increases government's budget surplus (or reduces its deficit) during an expansion without any action by policymakers. The tax system is one such mechanism.

progressive tax At the individual level, a *tax* whose *average tax rate* increases as the taxpayer's *income* increases. At the national level, a *tax* for which the *average tax rate* (= tax revenue/*GDP*) rises with *GDP*.

proportional tax At the individual level, a *tax* whose *average tax rate* remains constant as the taxpayer's *income* increases or decreases. At the national level, a *tax* for which the *average tax rate* (= tax revenue/*GDP*) remains constant as *GDP* rises or falls.

regressive tax At the individual level, a *tax* whose *average tax rate* decreases as the taxpayer's *income* increases. At the national level, a *tax* for which the *average tax rate* (= tax revenue/*GDP*) falls as *GDP* rises.

The built-in stability provided by the U.S. tax system has reduced the severity of business fluctuations, perhaps by as much as 8 to 10 percent of the change in GDP that otherwise would have occurred.[1] In recession-year 2009, for example, revenues from the individual income tax fell by a staggering 22 percent. This decline helped keep household spending and real GDP from falling even more than they did. But built-in stabilizers can only dampen, not counteract, swings in real GDP. Discretionary fiscal policy (changes in tax rates and expenditures) or monetary policy (central bank–caused changes in interest rates) therefore may be needed to try to counter a recession or an inflation of any appreciable magnitude.

Evaluating How Expansionary or Contractionary Fiscal Policy Is Determined

>> **LO13.3** Describe how the cyclically adjusted budget reveals the status of U.S. fiscal policy.

How can we determine whether a government's discretionary fiscal policy is expansionary, neutral, or contractionary? We cannot simply examine the actual budget deficits or surpluses that take place under the current policy because they will necessarily include the automatic changes in tax revenues that accompany every change in GDP. In addition, the expansionary or contractionary strength of any change in discretionary fiscal policy depends not on its absolute size but on how large it is relative to the size of the economy. So, in evaluating the status of fiscal policy, we must adjust deficits and surpluses to eliminate automatic changes in tax revenues and also compare the sizes of the adjusted budget deficits and surpluses to the level of potential GDP.

Cyclically Adjusted Budget

cyclically adjusted budget The estimated annual budget deficit or surplus that would occur under existing tax rates and government spending levels if the economy were to operate at its *full-employment* level of GDP for a year; the *full-employment* budget deficit or surplus.

Economists use the **cyclically adjusted budget** (also called the *full-employment budget*) to adjust actual federal budget deficits and surpluses to account for the changes in tax revenues that happen automatically whenever GDP changes. The cyclically adjusted budget measures what the federal budget deficit or surplus would have been under existing tax rates and government spending levels if the economy had achieved its full-employment level of GDP (its potential output). The idea essentially is to compare *actual* government expenditures with the tax revenues *that would have occurred* if the economy had achieved full-employment GDP. That procedure removes budget deficits or surpluses that arise simply because of cyclical changes in GDP and thus tell us nothing about whether the government's current discretionary fiscal policy is fundamentally expansionary, contractionary, or neutral.

Consider Figure 13.4a, where line *G* represents government expenditures and line *T* represents tax revenues. In full-employment year 1, government expenditures of $500 billion equal tax revenues of $500 billion, as indicated by the intersection of lines *G* and *T* at point *a*. The cyclically adjusted budget deficit in year 1 is zero—government expenditures equal the tax revenues forthcoming at the full-employment output GDP_1. Obviously, the cyclically adjusted deficit *as a percentage of potential GDP* is also zero. The government's fiscal policy is neutral.

Now suppose that a recession occurs and GDP falls from GDP_1 to GDP_2, as shown in Figure 13.4a. Let's also assume that the government takes no discretionary action, so lines *G* and *T* remain as shown in the figure. Tax revenues automatically fall to $450 billion (point *c*) at GDP_2, while government spending remains unaltered at $500 billion (point *b*). A $50 billion budget deficit (represented by distance *bc*) arises. But this **cyclical deficit** is simply a by-product of the economy's slide into recession, not the result of discretionary fiscal actions by the government. We would be wrong to conclude from this deficit that the government is engaging in an expansionary fiscal policy. The government's fiscal policy has not changed. It is still neutral.

cyclical deficit Federal *budget deficit* that is caused by a recession and the consequent decline in tax revenues.

That fact is highlighted when we remove the cyclical part of the deficit and thus consider the cyclically adjusted budget deficit for year 2 in Figure 13.4a. The $500 billion of government expenditures in year 2 is shown by *b* on line *G*. And, as shown by *a* on line *T*, $500 billion of tax revenues would have occurred if the economy had achieved its full-employment GDP. Because both *b* and *a* represent $500 billion, the cyclically adjusted budget deficit in year 2 is zero, as is this deficit as a percentage of potential GDP. Since the cyclically adjusted deficits are zero in both years, we know that government did not change its discretionary fiscal policy, even though a recession occurred and an actual deficit of $50 billion resulted.

---

[1] Alan J. Auerbach and Daniel Feenberg, "The Significance of Federal Taxes as Automatic Stabilizers," *Journal of Economic Perspectives,* Summer 2000, p. 54.

FIGURE 13.4 Cyclically adjusted deficits.

(a) In the left-hand graph, the cyclically adjusted deficit is zero at the full-employment output GDP$_1$. But it is also zero at the recessionary output GDP$_2$ because the $500 billion of government expenditures at GDP$_2$ equals the $500 billion of tax revenues that would be forthcoming at the full-employment GDP$_1$. There has been no change in fiscal policy. (b) In the right-hand graph, discretionary fiscal policy, as reflected in the downward shift of the tax line from T_1 to T_2, has increased the cyclically adjusted budget deficit from zero in year 3 (before the tax cut) to $25 billion in year 4 (after the tax cut). This is found by comparing the $500 billion of government spending in year 4 with the $475 billion of taxes that would accrue at the full-employment GDP$_3$. Such a rise in the cyclically adjusted deficit (as a percentage of potential GDP) identifies an expansionary fiscal policy.

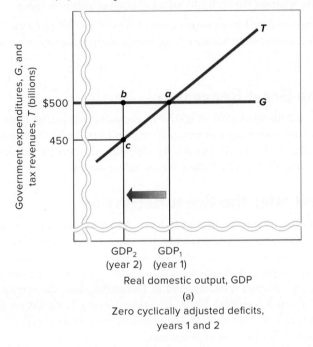

(a)

Zero cyclically adjusted deficits,
years 1 and 2

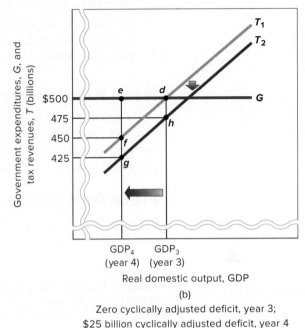

(b)

Zero cyclically adjusted deficit, year 3;
$25 billion cyclically adjusted deficit, year 4

Next, consider Figure 13.4b. Suppose that real output declined from full-employment GDP$_3$ in year 3 to GDP$_4$ in year 4. Also suppose that government responded to the recession by reducing tax rates in year 4, as represented by the downward shift of the tax line from T_1 to T_2. What will have happened to the size of the cyclically adjusted deficit?

Government expenditures in year 4 are $500 billion, as shown by e. Compare that amount of spending with the $475 billion of tax revenues that would occur if the economy achieved potential output level GDP$_1$. That is, compare the amount of spending at position e on line G with the amount of tax revenue that would be collected at position h if the economy were still operating at full employment. The $25 billion by which spending at e exceeds full-employment tax collections at h is the cyclically adjusted budget deficit for year 4.

As a percentage of potential GDP, the cyclically adjusted budget deficit has increased from zero in year 3 (before the tax-rate cut) to some positive percent [= ($25 billion/GDP$_3$) × 100] in year 4. This increase in the relative size of the full-employment deficit between the two years reveals that the new fiscal policy is *expansionary*.

In contrast, if we observed a cyclically adjusted deficit (as a percentage of potential GDP) of zero in one year, followed by a cyclically adjusted budget surplus in the next, we could conclude that fiscal policy has changed from being neutral to being contractionary. Because the cyclically adjusted budget adjusts for automatic changes in tax revenues, the increase in the cyclically adjusted budget surplus reveals that government either decreased its spending (G) or increased tax rates such that tax revenues (T) increased. These changes in G and T are precisely the discretionary actions that we have identified as elements of a *contractionary* fiscal policy.

► Automatic changes in net taxes (taxes minus transfers) add a degree of built-in stability to the economy.

► Cyclical deficits arise from declines in net tax revenues that automatically occur as the economy recedes and incomes and profits fall.

► The cyclically adjusted budget eliminates cyclical effects on net tax revenues; it compares actual levels of government spending to the projected levels of net taxes that would occur if the economy were achieving its full-employment output.

QUICK REVIEW

13.2

Recent and Projected U.S. Fiscal Policy

>> **LO13.4** Summarize recent U.S. fiscal policy.

Table 13.1 lists actual federal budget deficits and surpluses (column 2) as a percentage of actual GDP, and cyclically adjusted deficits and surpluses (column 3) as a percentage of potential GDP. Note that:

- Cyclically adjusted deficits are generally smaller than actual deficits because the actual deficits include cyclical deficits, whereas the cyclically adjusted deficits eliminate them.

- Only cyclically adjusted surpluses and deficits as percentages of potential GDP (column 3) provide the information needed to determine whether fiscal policy is expansionary, contractionary, or neutral.

Fiscal Policy before the Great Recession

Take a look at the data in Table 13.1 for the years 2005 to 2007. The economy reached full employment over those three years after taking several years to gradually recover from the 2001 recession that was precipitated by the September 11th terrorist attacks. By 2007, full employment had been restored, although a −1.2 percent cyclically adjusted budget deficit still remained.

Fiscal Policy during and after the Great Recession

In the summer of 2007, a crisis in the market for mortgage loans flared up and then quickly exploded through every part of the financial system. Banks went bankrupt, major corporations like General Motors hurtled toward bankruptcy, and the stock market fell almost 50 percent. As the crisis worsened, general pessimism spread beyond the financial markets to the overall economy. Businesses and households curtailed spending, and in December 2007, the economy entered what was later termed "the Great Recession." To simulate the economy, Congress passed a $152 billion economic stimulus package in 2008 that focused primarily on sending checks of up to $600 each to taxpayers, veterans, and Social Security recipients.

TABLE 13.1 Federal Deficits (−) and Surpluses (+) as Percentages of GDP, 2005–2021

(1) Year	(2) Actual Deficit − or Surplus +	(3) Cyclically Adjusted Deficit − or Surplus +*
2005	−2.5	−2.3
2006	−1.8	−1.9
2007	−1.1	−1.2
2008	−3.1	−2.9
2009	−9.3	−7.5
2010	−8.3	−6.4
2011	−8.1	−6.3
2012	−6.5	−5.1
2013	−4.0	−2.6
2014	−2.7	−1.7
2015	−2.4	−1.8
2016	−3.1	−2.6
2017	−3.4	−3.1
2018	−3.8	−3.9
2019	−4.7	−4.9
2020	−14.9	−14.3
2021	−12.4	−12.5

*As a percentage of potential GDP.

Source: Budget and Economic Data, Congressional Budget Office.

As a percentage of GDP, the *actual* federal budget deficit jumped from −1.1 percent in 2007 to −3.1 percent in 2008. This increase resulted from an automatic drop-off of tax revenues during the recession, along with the fiscal stimulus checks paid out in 2008. As Table 13.1 shows, the *cyclically adjusted* budget deficit rose from −1.2 percent of potential GDP in 2007 to −2.9 percent in 2008. This increase in the cyclically adjusted budget deficit reveals that fiscal policy in 2008 was in fact expansionary.

The government had hoped that those receiving checks would spend the money and thus boost consumption and aggregate demand. But households either saved the money or used it to pay down credit card loans. Spending remained low and the economy continued to founder.

In response, Congress enacted the American Recovery and Reinvestment Act of 2009. This gigantic $787 billion program consisted of tax rebates, plus large spending increases on infrastructure, education, and health care. The idea was to flood the economy with additional spending to try to boost aggregate demand and get people back to work.

Unlike the lump-sum stimulus checks of 2008, the 2009 tax rebates showed up as small increases in workers' monthly payroll checks. By giving workers smaller amounts per month rather than a single large check, the government hoped that people would spend rather than save the bulk of their enhanced income.

The recession officially ended during the summer of 2009, but the economy did not rebound vigorously. Unemployment remained high and tax collections were low due to a stagnant economy. As a result, policymakers decided to continue with large amounts of fiscal stimulus. Annual actual (not cyclically adjusted) budget deficits amounted to −4.0, −2.7, and −2.4 percent of GDP, respectively, in 2013, 2014, and 2015. The cyclically adjusted budget deficits for those years were, respectively, −2.6, −1.7, and −1.8 percent of potential GDP. Fiscal stimulus was diminishing, but remained noticeably stimulatory.

The final years of the 2010s saw a continued use of fiscal stimulus, as evidenced by the fact that the cyclically adjusted deficit rose to almost −5.0 percent in 2019 after tax cuts were paired with increased spending. These were, however, full-employment years. As a result, quite a few economists questioned whether the government should have been applying so much stimulus at a time when the economy's resources were fully employed. In their reckoning, that much stimulus would only lead to inflation. Other economists countered that strong fiscal stimulus was still needed to counter lingering problems in the financial sector.

Inflation was 2.1 percent in 2017, 2.4 percent in 2018, and 1.8 percent in 2019. Both groups of economists claimed that those figures supported their own position. The group worried about inflation pointed out that inflation was higher than the Federal Reserve's 2-percent inflation target in two out of those three years. To them, this indicated that the economy was overheating and inflation would accelerate. The other group argued that with inflation under 3 percent in all three years, overheating was unlikely.

Fiscal Policy during and after the Pandemic Recession of 2020

After enjoying several years of full employment at the end of the 2010s, the U.S. economy was hammered by the COVID-19 pandemic in the spring of 2020. The policymakers who imposed anti-pandemic lockdowns at the start of the crisis were acutely aware of the enormous economic damage likely to result from shutting down most private businesses for weeks or months. Thus, only two weeks after lockdowns started, Congress passed the $2.2 trillion Coronavirus Aid, Relief, and Economic Security, or CARES, Act to provide massive stimulus to both individuals and businesses.

That stimulus package and several subsequent stimulus bills caused the *actual* federal budget deficit to balloon to −14.9 percent of potential GDP, thereby bestowing on 2020 the distinction of having had the highest federal deficit ever recorded in peacetime. (Only the deficits of World War I and World War II were larger, with, for instance, 1943 witnessing a deficit of −26.8 percent of GDP as the United States battled Italy, Japan, and Germany simultaneously.)

An interesting fact, though, was that the cyclically adjusted deficit for 2020 was, at −14.3 percent, only slightly smaller than the actual deficit of −14.9 percent. That implied, accurately, that despite all of the economic chaos caused by COVID-19, the economy was, thanks to all the stimulus, operating relatively close to full employment. By the first quarter of 2021, the GDP gap was only negative 2.8 percent after plummeting as low as negative 10.7 percent during March 2020, the first month of lockdowns.

On the one hand, that small GDP gap as 2021 began indicated a success for the massive amounts of fiscal stimulus that had been applied during 2020. On the other hand, Congress had already approved various stimulus programs that would extend well into 2021. Speculation quickly ensued as to whether that massive amount of stimulus was going to turn out to be excessive. When inflation began to rise rapidly in the spring of 2021, that debate only intensified, with one side saying that it was too early to "take the foot off the gas" and the other arguing that the U.S. economy was starting to "speed out of control."

By March 2022, the inflation rate was running at 8.5 percent per year while the economy was operating near full employment. Thus, attention began to focus almost entirely on the high and rising inflation rate, since it was clear that there was no longer any need for additional stimulus. In addition, it was argued that the large deficit spending that was continuing to take place was very likely at least partly responsible for the high rate of inflation, since expansionary budget deficits are excessively stimulatory for economies operating near potential output.

Problems, Criticisms, and Complications of Implementing Fiscal Policy

>> **LO13.5** Discuss the problems that governments may encounter in enacting and applying fiscal policy.

Governments may encounter a number of significant problems in enacting and applying fiscal policy.

Problems of Timing

Several problems of timing may arise in connection with fiscal policy:

- *Recognition lag* is the time between the beginning of recession or inflation and the certain awareness that it is actually happening. This lag arises because the economy does not move smoothly through the business cycle. Even during good times, the economy has slow months interspersed with months of rapid growth and expansion. Recognizing a recession is difficult because several slow months will have to happen in succession before people can conclude with any confidence that the good times are over and a recession has begun.

  The same is true with inflation. Even periods of moderate inflation have months of high inflation—so that several high-inflation months must come in sequence before people can confidently conclude that inflation has moved to a higher level.

  Due to recognition lags, the economy is often 4 to 6 months into a recession or inflation before the situation is clearly discernible in the relevant statistics. As a result, the economic downslide or inflation may become more serious than it would have if the situation had been identified and acted on sooner.

- *Administrative lag* is the time between when policymakers recognize the need for a fiscal action and when that fiscal action is actually taken. The wheels of democratic government turn slowly. Following the terrorist attacks of September 11, 2001, the U.S. Congress was stalemated for five months before passing a compromise economic stimulus law in March 2002.

- *Operational lag* is the delay between the time fiscal action is ordered and the time that it actually begins to affect output, employment, or the price level. Tax changes have very short operational lags because they can be lowered instantly and have immediate impacts on household and business spending. By contrast, government spending on public works— new dams, interstate highways, and so on—requires long planning periods and even longer periods of construction. Such spending is of questionable use in offsetting short (for example, 6- to 12-month) periods of recession. Consequently, discretionary fiscal policy has increasingly relied on tax changes rather than on changes in spending so as to reduce or eliminate operational lag.

Please note that the fiscal policy response to the COVID-19 recession was highly unusual in that there was essentially zero recognition lag since policymakers understood that a recession would be an unavoidable side effect of imposing lockdowns. There was also almost zero administrative lag because congress finished debate over and approved the CARES Act less than two weeks after lockdowns were first imposed in mid-March of 2020. And the operational lag was also extremely short because relief money started flowing to individuals and businesses only about a month after the CARES Act was approved. But normal recessions are much harder to discern, and thus fiscal policy normally encounters substantial recognition, administrative, and operational lags.

Political Considerations

Fiscal policy is conducted in the political arena. That environment may not only slow the enactment of fiscal policy but also generate situations in which political considerations override economic considerations. Politicians are human—they want to get reelected. A strong economy at election time will certainly help them. So they may favor large tax cuts under the guise of expansionary fiscal policy even though that policy is economically inappropriate. Similarly, they may rationalize increased government spending on popular items such as farm subsidies, highways, education, and homeland security. At the extreme, elected officials and political parties might collectively "hijack" fiscal policy for political purposes, cause inappropriate changes in aggregate demand, and thereby cause (rather than avert) economic fluctuations. In short, elected officials may cause so-called **political business cycles**—swings in overall economic activity and real GDP resulting from election-motivated fiscal policy, rather than from a desire to offset volatility in the private sector. Political business cycles are difficult to document and prove, but there is little doubt that political considerations weigh heavily in the formulation of fiscal policy.

political business cycles
Fluctuations in the economy caused by the alleged tendency of Congress to destabilize the economy by reducing taxes and increasing government expenditures before elections and to raise taxes and lower expenditures after elections.

Future Policy Reversals

Fiscal policy may fail to achieve its objectives if households expect future reversals of policy. Consider a tax cut, for example. If taxpayers believe the tax reduction is temporary, they may save a large portion of their tax cut, reasoning that rates will return to their previous level in the future. They save more now so that they will be able to draw on their extra savings in the future when taxes rise again. So a tax reduction thought to be temporary may not increase present consumption spending and aggregate demand by as much as our simple model (Figure 13.1) suggests.

The opposite may be true for a tax increase. If taxpayers think it is temporary, they may reduce their saving to pay the tax while maintaining their present consumption. They may reason they can restore their saving when the tax rate again falls. So the tax increase may not reduce current consumption and aggregate demand by as much as policymakers intended.

To the extent that *consumption smoothing* occurs over time, fiscal policy will lose some of its strength.

Offsetting State and Local Finance

The fiscal policies of state and local governments are frequently *pro-cyclical*, meaning that they worsen rather than correct recession or inflation. Unlike the federal government, most state and local governments face constitutional or other legal requirements to balance their budgets. Like households and private businesses, state and local governments increase their expenditures during prosperity and cut them during recession.

During the Great Depression of the 1930s, most of the increase in federal spending was offset by decreases in state and local spending. During and immediately following the recession of 2001, many state and local governments offset lower tax revenues by raising tax rates, imposing new taxes, and reducing spending.

The $2.2 trillion CARES Act of 2020 made a special effort to reduce this problem by giving $340 billion to state and local governments. Because of that sizable federal aid, state and local governments did not have to increase taxes or reduce expenditure as much as they would have had to otherwise. Thus their collective fiscal actions did not offset the federal stimulus by nearly as much as would have been the case if states had not received the aid money.

Crowding-Out Effect

Another potential flaw of fiscal policy is the **crowding-out effect:** An expansionary fiscal policy (deficit spending) may increase the interest rate and reduce investment spending, thereby weakening or canceling the stimulus of the expansionary policy. The rising interest rate might also

crowding-out effect A rise in interest rates and a resulting decrease in *planned investment* caused by the federal government's increased borrowing to finance budget deficits and refinance debt.

potentially crowd out interest-sensitive consumption spending (such as purchasing automobiles on credit). But because investment is the most volatile component of GDP, the crowding-out effect focuses on investment and whether the stimulus provided by deficit spending may be partly or even fully neutralized by an offsetting reduction in investment spending.

To see the potential problem, realize that whenever the government borrows money (which it must do to engage in deficit spending), it increases the overall demand for money. If the monetary authorities are holding the money supply constant, this increase in demand will raise the price paid for borrowing money: the interest rate. Because investment spending varies inversely with the interest rate, some investment will be choked off or "crowded out."

Crowding out is likely to be less of a problem when the economy is in recession because investment demand tends to be weak. The reason: Output purchases slow during recessions, and therefore most businesses end up with substantial excess capacity. As a result, they do not have much incentive to add new machinery or build new factories. After all, why should they add capacity when some of their existing capacity is lying idle?

With investment demand weak during a recession, the crowding-out effect is likely to be very small. Simply put, there is not much investment for the government to crowd out. Even if deficit spending does increase the interest rate, the effect on investment may be fully offset by the improved investment prospects that businesses expect from the fiscal stimulus.

By contrast, when the economy is operating at or near full capacity, investment demand is likely to be quite strong, and crowding out will probably be a much more serious problem. When the economy is booming, factories will be running at or near full capacity, and firms will have high investment demand for two reasons. First, equipment running at full capacity wears out fast, so firms will be investing substantial amounts to replace worn-out machinery and equipment. Second, the economy is likely to be growing overall, so firms will be investing heavily in order to increase their production capacity and thereby take advantage of the economy's increasing demand for goods and services.

QUICK REVIEW

13.3

▸ The United States government ran the largest peacetime budget deficit in U.S. history—14.9 percent of GDP—as the result of the massive fiscal stimulus expended to offset the COVID-19 recession of 2020.

▸ Time lags, political problems, expectations, and state and local finances complicate fiscal policy.

▸ The crowding-out effect indicates that an expansionary fiscal policy may increase the interest rate and reduce investment spending.

The U.S. Public Debt

>> **LO13.6** Discuss the size, composition, and consequences of the U.S. public debt.

public debt The total amount owed by the federal government to the owners of government *securities;* equal to the sum of past government *budget deficits* less government *budget surpluses.*

The U.S. national debt, or **public debt,** is the accumulation of all past federal deficits and surpluses. The deficits have greatly exceeded the surpluses and have emerged mainly from war financing, recessions, and fiscal policy. As of January 2022, the total public debt was $29.7 trillion—$23.2 trillion held by the public, and $6.5 trillion held by federal agencies and the Federal Reserve.

To provide some historical perspective, please understand that the public debt was much smaller prior to the 2007–2009 recession. In 2006, it was $8.5 trillion. It then more than doubled, to $18.2 trillion by 2015, as large budget deficits were run to fight the Great Recession and aid the subsequent recovery.

The debt continued to rise during the late 2010s despite the economy returning to full employment in 2017. That ongoing rise despite full employment generated a large amount of consternation and concern that we will discuss and analyze in this section. As with much else in economics, the public debt brings with it both costs and benefits. Just before the COVID-19 pandemic hit in early 2020, the debt stood at $23.2 trillion. Over the next three months, as the CARES Act went into effect, it jumped to $26.5 trillion—which reflected $3.3 trillion of additional debt in just 90 days!

Ownership

U.S. government securities U.S. Treasury bills, notes, and *bonds* used to finance *budget deficits;* the components of the *public debt.*

The total public debt of over $29.7 trillion represents the total amount of money owed by the federal government to the holders of **U.S. government securities:** financial instruments issued by the federal government to borrow money to finance expenditures that exceed tax revenues. U.S. government securities (loan instruments) are of four types: *Treasury bills* (short-term securities), *Treasury notes* (medium-term securities), *Treasury bonds* (long-term securities), and *U.S. savings bonds* (long-term, nonmarketable bonds).

Figure 13.5 shows that the public, not including the Federal Reserve, held 58 percent of the federal debt in 2021 and that federal government agencies and the Federal Reserve held the remaining 42 percent. Citizens of foreign countries held about 26 percent of the total U.S. public debt in 2021, meaning that most of the U.S. public debt is held internally and not externally. Americans owed 74 percent of the public debt to Americans. Of the $7.7 trillion of debt held by foreigners, the top three holders were Japan, with 17 percent; China, with 14 percent; and the United Kingdom, with 8 percent.

A simple statement of the absolute size of the U.S. national debt ignores the fact that the wealth and productive ability of the U.S. economy is also vast. A wealthy, highly productive nation such as the United States can carry a large public debt much more easily than a low-income nation can. Thus, it is highly informative to examine the ratio of the public debt relative to GDP.

Figure 13.6 indicates that in 2021, the portion of the U.S. public debt that was held by the public (rather than by the Federal Reserve or government agencies) was 101 percent of that year's GDP.

Figure 13.6 also shows that the ratio of debt to GDP rose dramatically starting in 2008. That rapid increase occurred because of massive annual budget deficits that increased the ratio's

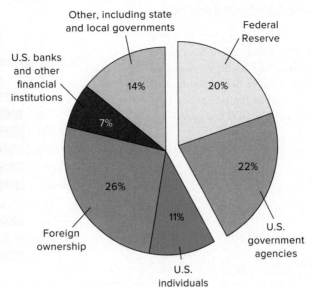

FIGURE 13.5
Ownership of U.S. public debt, 2021.

The $29.7 trillion of public debt owed by the United States federal government in 2021 can be divided into the 58 percent held by the public (excluding the Federal Reserve), and the proportion held by federal agencies and the Federal Reserve System (42 percent). Of the total debt, 26 percent is foreign-owned.

Sources: Economic Report of the President 2022 and Treasury Bulletin, April 2022, U.S. Treasury.

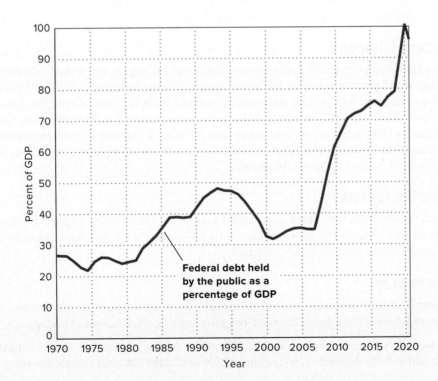

FIGURE 13.6
Federal debt held by the public, excluding the Federal Reserve, as a percentage of GDP, 1970–2021.

As a percentage of GDP, the federal debt held by the public increased steadily over the 1980–1995 period before declining significantly between 1995 and 2001. Since 2001, the percentage has gone up nearly every year, first jumping sharply after 2007–2009 recession and again in 2020 as the federal government borrowed sharply to fund anti-pandemic stimulus efforts. While the debt itself continued to rise in 2021, the debt-to-GDP ratio fell that year thanks to strong GDP growth.

Source: Federal Reserve Bank of St. Louis and U.S. Office of Management and Budget.

🌐 GLOBAL PERSPECTIVE 13.1

PUBLIC DEBT: INTERNATIONAL COMPARISONS

Although the United States has the world's largest public debt in absolute size, a number of other nations have public debts that are much larger fractions of their respective GDPs. In 2021, Venezuela had a public debt equal to over 300 percent of its annual GDP, while the U.S. public debt amounted to about 133 percent of U.S. GDP that year.

Public Sector Debt as Percentage of GDP, 2021

Venezuela	
Japan	
Greece	
Italy	
United States	
France	
Canada	
United Kingdom	
Brazil	
Germany	
Australia	
Mexico	

Source: IMF Datamapper, International Monetary Fund.

numerator (debt) faster than annual economic growth increased the ratio's denominator (GDP). The debt-to-GDP ratio then spiked dramatically in 2020 due to a simultaneous increase in the numerator (caused by massive borrowing to fund pandemic relief efforts) and decrease in the denominator (caused by GDP falling as a result of the pandemic). By contrast, the debt-to-GDP ratio fell in 2021 not because the debt declined in absolute terms but because strong GDP growth generated an increase in the denominator of the ratio that more than offset the increase in the numerator caused by that year's additional debt.

International Comparisons

It is not uncommon for countries to have sizable public debts. As Global Perspective 13.1 shows, the public debt as a percentage of real GDP in the United States is on the higher end for industrially advanced nations, but still below that of Japan, Italy, and Greece.

Interest Charges

Many economists conclude that the primary burden of the debt is the annual interest charge accruing on the government notes and bonds sold to finance the debt. In 2021, interest on the total public debt was $352 billion. Although this amount is sizable in absolute terms, it was only 1.5 percent of GDP for 2021. In other words, the federal government had to collect taxes equal to 1.5 percent of GDP to service the total public debt. This percentage was virtually unchanged from 2000 despite the much higher total public debt, mostly because the Federal Reserve kept interest rates low in the wake of the Great Recession.

False Concerns

You may wonder if the large public debt might bankrupt the United States or place a tremendous burden on your children and grandchildren. Fortunately, these are largely false concerns. People were wondering the same things 50 years ago!

Bankruptcy

The large U.S. public debt does not threaten to bankrupt the federal government or leave it unable to meet its financial obligations. There are two main reasons: refinancing and taxation.

Refinancing As long as lenders view the U.S. public debt as manageable and sustainable, the public debt is easily refinanced. As portions of the debt come due each month, the government does not cut expenditures or raise taxes to provide the funds required. Rather, it refinances the debt by selling new bonds and using the proceeds to pay off the maturing bonds. The new bonds are in strong demand because lenders obtain a tradable security that (unlike other assets such as stocks, corporate debt, and real estate) is considered nearly riskless since there is virtually zero chance that the U.S. government would default on its debt payments.

Of course, refinancing could become an issue with a high enough debt-to-GDP ratio. Some countries, including Greece, have encountered this problem. High and rising ratios in the United States might raise fears that the U.S. government might be unable to pay back loans as they come due. But this is a false concern for the United States, given the U.S. economy's strong long-term growth prospects and how modest the U.S. debt-to-GDP ratio is as compared with those of other countries (see Global Perspective 13.1).

Taxation Financially distressed private households and corporations cannot extract themselves from their financial difficulties by taxing the public. If their incomes or sales revenues fall short of their expenses, they can indeed go bankrupt. But the federal government *does* have the option of imposing new taxes or increase existing tax rates to finance its debt. Such tax hikes may be politically unpopular and may weaken incentives to work and invest, but they *are* a means of raising funds to finance the debt.

Burdening Future Generations

In 2021, public debt per capita was $83,885. Was each child born in 2021 handed a $83,885 bill from the federal government? Not really. The public debt does not impose as much of a burden on future generations because the United States owes a substantial portion of the public debt to itself. U.S. citizens and institutions (banks, businesses, insurance companies, governmental agencies, and trust funds) own about 73 percent of the U.S. government securities. Although that part of the public debt is a liability to Americans (as taxpayers), it is simultaneously an asset to Americans (as holders of Treasury bills, Treasury notes, Treasury bonds, and U.S. savings bonds).

To eliminate the American-owned part of the public debt would require a gigantic transfer payment from Americans to Americans. Taxpayers would pay higher taxes, and debt holders would receive an equal amount for their U.S. government securities. Purchasing power in the United States would not change. Only the repayment of the 27 percent of the public debt owned by foreigners would negatively impact U.S. purchasing power.

The public debt increased sharply during the Second World War. But the decision to finance military purchases through the sale of government bonds did not shift the economic burden of the war to future generations. The economic cost of the Second World War consisted of the civilian goods society had to forgo in shifting scarce resources to war goods production. Regardless of whether society financed this reallocation through higher taxes or through borrowing, the real economic burden of the war would have been the same. That burden was borne almost entirely by those who lived during the war. They were the ones who did without a multitude of consumer goods to enable the United States to arm itself and its allies.

The next generation inherited the debt from the war, but it also inherited an equal amount of government bonds that would pay them cash in future years. In addition, it inherited the enormous benefits from the victory—namely, preserved political and economic systems at home and the "export" of those systems to Germany, Italy, and Japan. Those outcomes enhanced postwar U.S. economic growth and helped raise the standard of living for future generations of Americans.

Substantive Issues

Although the preceding issues relating to the public debt are false concerns, several actual concerns do exist.

Income Distribution

The ownership of government securities is highly uneven. Some people own much more than the $83,885-per-person portion of government securities; other people own less or none at all. In general, the ownership of the public debt is concentrated among wealthier groups. While the overall federal tax system is progressive, interest payments on the public debt do mildly increase income inequality. Income is transferred from people who, on average, have lower incomes to the higher-income bondholders. If greater income equality is one of society's goals, then this redistribution is undesirable.

Incentives

The current public debt necessitates annual interest payments of $352 billion. With no increase in the size of the debt, that interest charge must be paid out of tax revenues. Higher taxes may dampen incentives to bear risk, to innovate, to invest, and to work. So, in this indirect way, a large public debt may impair economic growth and therefore impose a burden of reduced output (and income) on future generations.

Foreign-Owned Public Debt

external public debt
The portion of the public debt owed to foreign citizens, *firms,* and institutions.

The 26 percent of the U.S. debt held by foreign citizens, foreign businesses, and foreign governments (including foreign central banks) is an economic burden to Americans. Because we do not owe that portion of the debt "to ourselves," the payment of interest and principal on this **external public debt** enables foreigners to buy some of our output. In return for the benefits derived from the borrowed funds, the United States transfers goods and services to foreign lenders. However, Americans also own debt issued by foreign governments, so payment of principal and interest by those governments transfers some of their goods and services to Americans.

Crowding-Out Effect Revisited

A potentially more serious problem is the financing (and continual refinancing) of the large public debt, which can transfer a real economic burden to future generations by passing onto them a smaller stock of capital goods. This possibility involves the previously discussed crowding-out effect: the idea that public borrowing drives up real interest rates, thereby reducing private investment spending. If public borrowing happened only during recessions, crowding out would not likely be much of a problem. Because private investment demand tends to be weak during recessions, any increase in interest rates during a recession would at most cause only a small reduction in investment spending.

In contrast, the need to continuously finance a large public debt may be more troublesome. Continuous financing implies having to borrow large amounts of money when the economy is near or at full employment. Because private investment spending is strong near economic peaks, any increase in interest rates at or near a peak may result in a substantial decline in private investment spending. If the amount of current investment crowded out is extensive, future generations will inherit an economy with a smaller production capacity and, other things equal, a lower standard of living.

public investments
Government expenditures on public capital (such as roads, highways, bridges, mass-transit systems, and electric power facilities) and on *human capital* (such as education, training, and health).

Public Investments and Public-Private Complementarities But even with crowding out, two factors could partly or fully offset the net economic burden shifted to future generations. First, just as private expenditures may involve either consumption or investment, so it is with public goods. Part of the government spending enabled by the public debt is for public investment outlays (for example, highways, mass transit systems, and electric power facilities) and human capital (for example, investments in education, job training, and health). Like private expenditures on machinery and equipment, these **public investments** increase the economy's future production capacity by increasing the stock of public capital passed on to future generations. That greater stock of public capital may offset the diminished stock of private capital resulting from the crowding-out effect, thereby leaving the economy's overall production capacity unimpaired.

Public-private complementarities may also reduce the crowding-out effect. Some public and private investments are complementary. Thus, a public investment financed through debt could spur some private-sector investment by increasing its expected rate of return. For example, the presence of a newly built federal building in a particular city may encourage private investment in the form of nearby office buildings, shops, and restaurants. Through this complementary effect, government spending on public capital may shift the private investment

The Social Security and Medicare Time Bombs

As the Population Ages, Social Security and Medicare Face Gigantic Funding Shortfalls.

The percentage of the U.S. population age 62 or older will rise substantially over the next several decades. As a result, fewer workers will be paying taxes into the Social Security system (income during retirement) and the Medicare system (medical care during retirement). Simultaneously, however, the "greying of the population" will result in many more retirees. The number of workers per Social Security and Medicare beneficiary was roughly 5:1 in 1960. Today it is a little less than 3:1, and by 2040 it will be only 2:1. As that ratio continues to fall, it will become impossible at current tax rates to fulfill the benefits promised under current law. Either taxes must rise, or benefits must be cut.

The Social Security Shortfall Social Security is the major public retirement program in the United States. The program costs $1.2 trillion annually and is financed by a 12.4 percent tax on earnings up to a set level of earnings ($147,000 in 2022). Half the tax (6.2 percent) is paid by the worker; the other half by the employer. Social Security is largely an annual "pay-as-you-go" plan, meaning that most of the current revenues from the Social Security tax are paid to current Social Security retirees.

Until 2009, however, annual Social Security tax revenues exceeded annual Social Security retirement payouts. That excess annual inflow was used to buy U.S. Treasury securities that were credited to a government account called the Social Security Trust Fund. But starting in 2009, annual Social Security revenues fell below annual Social Security payouts and the system started shifting money from the trust fund to make up the difference. As a result, the trust fund is expected to be exhausted in 2034. For each year thereafter, annual tax revenues will cover only 75 percent of promised benefits.

The Medicare Shortfall The Medicare program is the U.S. health care program for people age 65 and older in the United States. The program costs $926 billion per year and has been growing at about 9 percent annually since 1980. Like Social Security, it also is a pay-as-you-go plan, meaning that current medical benefits for people age 65 or older are being funded by current tax revenues. Like the Social Security tax, half the Medicare earnings tax is paid by the employer (1.45 percent) and half by the employee (1.45 percent). Unlike Social Security, though, the Medicare tax is paid on all earnings, not just those up to an annual cap.

The financial status of Medicare is even worse than that of Social Security. To begin with, the Medicare Trust Fund will be depleted in 2026, 8 years before the Social Security Trust Fund is expected to be depleted. Then, in subsequent years, the percentage of scheduled Medicare benefits covered by the current Medicare tax will decline from 97 percent in 2025 to 72 percent in 2035 and 69 percent in 2080.

The Unpleasant Options To restore long-run balance to Social Security and Medicare, the federal government must either reduce benefits or increase revenues. It's as simple—and as complicated—as that! The Social Security Administration concludes that bringing projected Social Security revenues and payments into balance over the

Kim Reinick/123RF

next 75 years would require a 16 percent permanent reduction in Social Security benefits, a 13 percent permanent increase in tax revenues, or some combination of the two. To bring projected Medicare revenues and expenses into long-run balance would require an increase in the Medicare payroll tax by 122 percent, a 51 percent reduction of Medicare payments from their projected levels, or some combination of each.

The options for closing all or part of the Social Security and Medicare funding gaps involve difficult economic trade-offs and dangerous political risks. Here are just a few examples:

- Increasing the retirement age for collecting Social Security or Medicare benefits will upset preretirement workers, who will start collecting benefits at older ages.

- Subjecting a larger portion of total earnings to the Social Security tax would constitute a gigantic tax increase on the earnings of the country's highest trained and educated individuals. This might reduce the incentive for younger people to obtain education and advance in their careers.

- Disqualifying wealthy individuals from receiving Social Security and Medicare benefits would tilt the programs toward becoming redistribution programs, rather than insurance programs. This would undermine the broad existing political support for the programs.

- Redirecting legal immigration toward high-skilled, high-earning entrants and away from low-skilled, low-earning immigrants to raise Social Security and Medicare revenues would also raise the ire of some native-born high-skilled workers and the proponents of immigration based on family reunification.

- Placing the payroll tax revenues into accounts that individuals, not the government, would own, maintain, and bequeath would transform the Social Security and Medicare programs from guaranteed "defined benefit plans" into much riskier "defined contribution plans." The high short-run volatility of the stock market might leave some unlucky people destitute in old age.

The problem is huge and will not go away. The federal government and the American people will eventually have to face up to the overpromising-underfunding problem and find ways to resolve it.

demand curve to the right. Even if the government borrowing needed to build the new federal building boosts the interest rate, total private investment need not fall. However, the increase in private investment might be smaller than anticipated. If it is, then the crowding-out effect will not be fully offset.

QUICK REVIEW
13.4

▶ The U.S. public debt—$29.7 trillion in 2021—is the total accumulation of all past federal budget deficits and surpluses; about 26 percent of the U.S. public debt is held by foreigners.

▶ The U.S. public debt held by the public (excluding the Federal Reserve) was 101 percent of GDP in 2021, up from 33 percent in 2000.

▶ The federal government is in no danger of going bankrupt because it needs only to refinance (not

retire) the public debt and it can raise revenues, if needed, through higher taxes.

▶ The borrowing and interest payments associated with the public debt may (a) increase income inequality; (b) require higher taxes, which may dampen incentives; and (c) impede the growth of the nation's stock of capital through crowding out of private investment.

Summary

LO13.1 Identify the purposes, tools, and limitations of fiscal policy.

Fiscal policy consists of deliberate changes in government spending, taxes, or both to promote full employment, price-level stability, and economic growth. Fiscal policy requires increases in government spending, decreases in taxes, or both (a budget deficit) to increase aggregate demand and push an economy from a recession. Decreases in government spending, increases in taxes, or both (a budget surplus) are appropriate fiscal policy for decreasing aggregate demand to try to slow or halt demand-pull inflation.

LO13.2 Explain how built-in stabilizers moderate business cycles.

Built-in stability arises from net tax revenues, which vary directly with the level of GDP. During recession, the federal budget automatically moves toward a stabilizing deficit; during expansion, the budget automatically moves toward an anti-inflationary surplus. Built-in stability lessens, but does not fully correct, undesired changes in real GDP.

LO13.3 Describe how the cyclically adjusted budget reveals the status of U.S. fiscal policy.

Actual federal budget deficits can go up or down because of changes in GDP, changes in fiscal policy, or both. Deficits caused by changes in GDP are called cyclical deficits. The cyclically adjusted budget removes cyclical deficits from the budget and therefore measures the budget deficit or surplus that would occur if the economy operated at its full-employment output throughout the year. Changes in the cyclical budget deficit or surplus provide meaningful information as to whether the government's fiscal policy is expansionary, neutral, or contractionary. Changes in the actual budget deficit or surplus do not, because such deficits or surpluses can include cyclical deficits or surpluses.

LO13.4 Summarize recent U.S. fiscal policy.

The final years of the 2010s saw significant cyclically adjusted budget deficits of around 4 to 5 percent of GDP despite the U.S. economy operating at full employment. The amount of fiscal stimulus then multiplied in response to the COVID-19 pandemic, with the cyclically adjusted budget deficit peaking in 2020 at −14.3 percent of potential GDP.

LO13.5 Discuss the problems that governments may encounter in enacting and applying fiscal policy.

Certain problems complicate the enactment and implementation of fiscal policy. They include (a) timing problems associated with recognition, administrative, and operational lags; (b) the potential for misuse of fiscal policy for political rather than economic purposes; (c) the fact that state and local finances tend to be pro-cyclical; (d) potential ineffectiveness if households expect future policy reversals; and (e) the possibility of fiscal policy crowding out private investment.

LO13.6 Discuss the size, composition, and consequences of the U.S. public debt.

The public debt is the total accumulation of all past federal government deficits and surpluses. In 2021 the U.S. public debt was $29.7 trillion, or $83,885 per person. The public holds 58 percent of that federal debt; the Federal Reserve and federal agencies hold the other 42 percent. Foreigners hold 26 percent of the federal debt. Interest payments as a percentage of GDP were about 1.5 percent in 2021.

Because of large annual deficits, the U.S. public debt more than tripled between 2008 and 2021, rising from $9.2 trillion in 2008 to $27.9 trillion in 2021. The concern that a large public debt may bankrupt the U.S. government is generally a false worry because (a) the debt needs only to be refinanced rather than retired and (b) the federal government has the power to increase taxes to make interest payments on the debt.

In general, the public debt is not a vehicle for shifting economic burdens to future generations. Americans inherit not only most of the public debt (a liability) but also most of the U.S. government securities (an asset) that finance the debt.

More substantive problems associated with public debt include the following: (a) Payment of interest on the debt may increase income inequality. (b) Interest payments on the debt require higher taxes, which may impair incentives. (c) Paying interest or principal on the portion of the debt held by foreign nationals means a transfer of real output abroad. (d) Government borrowing to refinance or pay interest on the debt may increase interest rates and crowd out private investment spending, leaving future generations with a smaller stock of capital than they would have had otherwise.

The increase in investment in public capital that may result from debt financing may partly or wholly offset the crowding-out effect of the public debt on private investment. Also, the added public investment may stimulate private investment, where the two are complements.

Terms and Concepts

fiscal policy

Council of Economic Advisers (CEA)

expansionary fiscal policy

budget deficit

contractionary fiscal policy

budget surplus

built-in stabilizer

progressive tax

proportional tax

regressive tax

cyclically adjusted budget

cyclical deficit

political business cycles

crowding-out effect

public debt

U.S. government securities

external public debt

public investments

Discussion Questions

1. What is the role of the Council of Economic Advisers (CEA) as it relates to fiscal policy? Use an Internet search to find the names and university affiliations of the present members of the CEA. **LO13.1**

2. What are government's fiscal policy options for ending severe demand-pull inflation? **LO13.1**

3. (For students who were assigned Chapter 11) Use the aggregate expenditures model to show how government fiscal policy could eliminate either a recessionary expenditure gap or an inflationary expenditure gap (Figure 11.7). Explain how equal-size increases in G and T could eliminate a recessionary gap and how equal-size decreases in G and T could eliminate an inflationary gap. **LO13.1**

4. Some politicians have suggested that the United States enact a constitutional amendment requiring that the federal government balance its budget annually. Explain why such an amendment, if strictly enforced, would force the government to enact a contractionary fiscal policy whenever the economy experiences a severe recession. **LO13.1**

5. Explain how built-in (automatic) stabilizers work. What are the differences between proportional, progressive, and regressive tax systems as they relate to an economy's built-in stability? **LO13.2**

6. Define the cyclically adjusted budget, explain its significance, and state why it may differ from the actual budget. Suppose the full-employment, noninflationary level of real output is GDP$_3$ (not GDP$_2$) in the economy depicted in Figure 13.3. If the economy is operating at GDP$_2$ instead of GDP$_3$, what is the status of its cyclically adjusted budget? The status of its current fiscal policy? What change in fiscal policy would you recommend? How would you accomplish that in terms of the G and T lines in the figure? **LO13.3**

7. Briefly state and evaluate the problem of time lags in enacting and applying fiscal policy. Explain the idea of a political business cycle. How might expectations of a near-term policy reversal weaken fiscal policy based on changes in tax rates? What is

the crowding-out effect, and why might it be relevant to fiscal policy? **LO13.5**

8. How do economists distinguish between the absolute and relative sizes of the public debt? Why is the distinction important? Distinguish between refinancing the debt and retiring (repaying) the debt. How does an internally held public debt differ from an externally held public debt? Contrast the effects of retiring an internally held debt and retiring an externally held debt. **LO13.6**

9. True or false? If false, explain why. **LO13.6**
   a. The total public debt is more relevant to an economy than the public debt as a percentage of GDP.
   b. An internally held public debt is like a debt of the left hand owed to the right hand.
   c. The Federal Reserve and federal government agencies hold more than three-fourths of the public debt.
   d. As a percentage of GDP, the total U.S. public debt is the highest such debt among the world's advanced industrial nations.

10. Why might economists be quite concerned if the annual interest payments on the U.S. public debt sharply increased as a percentage of GDP? **LO13.6**

11. Trace the cause-and-effect chain through which financing and refinancing of the public debt might affect real interest rates, private investment, the capital stock, and economic growth. How might investment in public capital and public-private complementarities alter the outcome of the cause-effect chain? **LO13.6**

12. **LAST WORD** What do economists mean when they say Social Security and Medicare are "pay-as-you-go" plans? What are the Social Security and Medicare trust funds, and how long will they have money left in them? What is the key long-run problem of both Social Security and Medicare? To fix the problem, do you favor increasing taxes or do you prefer reducing benefits?

Review Questions

1. Which of the following would help a government reduce an inflationary output gap? **LO13.1**
   a. Raising taxes.
   b. Lowering taxes.
   c. Increasing government spending.
   d. Decreasing government spending.

2. The economy is in a recession. A congresswoman suggests increasing spending to stimulate aggregate demand and raising

taxes simultaneously to pay for the increased spending. Her suggestion to combine higher government expenditures with higher taxes is: **LO13.1**
   a. the worst possible combination of tax and expenditure changes.
   b. the best possible combination of tax and expenditure changes.
   c. a mediocre and contradictory combination of tax and expenditure changes.

3. During the recession of 2007–2009, the U.S. federal government's tax collections fell from about $2.6 trillion down to about $2.1 trillion while GDP declined by about 4 percent. Does the U.S. tax system appear to have built-in stabilizers? **LO13.2**
   a. Yes
   b. No
4. Last year, while a hypothetical economy was in a recession, government spending was $595 billion, and government revenue was $505 billion. Economists estimate that if the economy had been at its full-employment level of GDP last year, government spending would have been $555 billion and government revenue would have been $550 billion. Which of the following statements about this government's fiscal situation are true? **LO13.3**
   a. The government has a non–cyclically adjusted budget deficit of $595 billion.
   b. The government has a non–cyclically adjusted budget deficit of $90 billion.
   c. The government has a non–cyclically adjusted budget surplus of $90 billion.
   d. The government has a cyclically adjusted budget deficit of $555 billion.
   e. The government has a cyclically adjusted budget deficit of $5 billion.
   f. The government has a cyclically adjusted budget surplus of $5 billion.

5. Label each of the following scenarios as an example of a recognition lag, administrative lag, or operational lag. **LO13.5**
   a. To fight a recession, congress has passed a bill to increase infrastructure spending—but the legally required environmental-impact statement for each new project will take at least two years to complete before any building can begin.
   b. Distracted by a war that is going badly, politicians take no notice until inflation reaches 8 percent.
   c. Politicians recognize a sudden recession, but it takes many months of political deal making before they finally approve a stimulus bill.
   d. To fight a recession, the president orders federal agencies to get rid of petty regulations that burden private businesses—but the federal agencies begin by spending a year developing a set of regulations on how to remove petty regulations.
6. In January, the interest rate is 5 percent and firms borrow $50 billion per month for investment projects. In February, the federal government doubles its monthly borrowing from $25 billion to $50 billion, driving the interest rate up to 7 percent. As a result, firms cut back their borrowing to only $30 billion per month. Which of the following is true? **LO13.6**
   a. There is no crowding-out effect because the government's increase in borrowing exceeds firms' decrease in borrowing.
   b. There is a crowding-out effect of $20 billion.
   c. There is no crowding-out effect because both the government and firms are still borrowing a lot.
   d. There is a crowding-out effect of $25 billion.

Problems

1. Assume that a hypothetical economy with an MPC of .8 is experiencing a severe recession. By how much would government spending have to rise to shift the aggregate demand curve rightward by $25 billion? How large a tax cut would be needed to achieve the same increase in aggregate demand? Determine one possible combination of a government spending increase and a simultaneous tax increase that would accomplish the same goal. **LO13.1**
2. Refer back to the table in Figure 12.7 in the previous chapter. Suppose that aggregate demand increases such that the amount of real output demanded rises by $7 billion at each price level. By what percentage will the price level increase? Will this inflation be demand-pull inflation, or will it be cost-push inflation? If potential real GDP (that is, full-employment GDP) is $510 billion, what will be the size of the positive GDP gap after the change in aggregate demand? If government wants to use fiscal policy to counter the resulting inflation without changing tax rates, would it increase government spending or decrease it? **LO13.1**
3. (For students who were assigned Chapter 11) Assume that, without taxes, the consumption schedule for an economy is as shown below: **LO13.2**

GDP, Billions	Consumption, Billions
$100	$120
200	200
300	280
400	360
500	440
600	520
700	600

a. Graph this consumption schedule. What is the size of the MPC?
b. Assume that a lump-sum (regressive) tax of $10 billion is imposed at all levels of GDP. Calculate the tax rate at each level of GDP. Graph the resulting consumption schedule and compare the MPC and the multiplier with those of the pretax consumption schedule.
c. Now suppose a proportional tax with a 10 percent tax rate is imposed instead of the regressive tax. Calculate and graph the new consumption schedule, and calculate the MPC and the multiplier.
d. Finally, impose a progressive tax such that the tax rate is 0 percent when GDP is $100, 5 percent at $200, 10 percent at $300, 15 percent at $400, and so forth. Determine and graph the new consumption schedule, noting the effect of this tax system on the MPC and the multiplier.
e. Use a graph similar to Figure 13.3 to show why proportional and progressive taxes contribute to greater economic stability, while a regressive tax does not.
4. Refer to the following table for Waxwania: **LO13.2**

Government Expenditures, G	Tax Revenues, T	Real GDP
$160	$100	$500
160	120	600
160	140	700
160	160	800
160	180	900

What is the marginal tax rate in Waxwania? The average tax rate? Which of the following describes the tax system: proportional, progressive, or regressive?

5. Refer to the table for Waxwania in problem 4. Suppose that Waxwania is producing $600 of real GDP, whereas the potential real GDP (or full-employment real GDP) is $700. How large is its budget deficit? Its cyclically adjusted budget deficit? Its cyclically adjusted budget deficit as a percentage of potential real GDP? Is Waxwania's fiscal policy expansionary, or is it contractionary? **LO13.3**

6. Suppose that a country has no public debt in year 1 but experiences a budget deficit of $40 billion in year 2, a budget surplus of $10 billion in year 3, and a budget deficit of $2 billion in year 4.

What is the absolute size of its public debt in year 4? If its real GDP in year 4 is $104 billion, what is this country's public debt as a percentage of real GDP in year 4? **LO13.6**

7. Suppose that the investment demand curve in a certain economy is such that investment declines by $100 billion for every 1 percentage point increase in the real interest rate. Also, suppose that the investment demand curve shifts rightward by $150 billion at each real interest rate for every 1 percentage point increase in the expected rate of return from investment. If stimulus spending (an expansionary fiscal policy) by government increases the real interest rate by 2 percentage points, but also raises the expected rate of return on investment by 1 percentage point, how much investment, if any, will be crowded out? **LO13.6**

PART 5

CHAPTER

14

isak55/Shutterstock

Money, the Federal Reserve, and Interest Rates

>> **LEARNING OBJECTIVES**

LO14.1 Explain the functions of money.

LO14.2 Describe the components of the U.S. money supply.

LO14.3 Describe what "backs" the money supply.

LO14.4 Discuss the structure of the Federal Reserve.

LO14.5 Identify the functions and responsibilities of the Federal Reserve.

LO14.6 Explain the fractional reserve system used by U.S. banks and why the Fed might wish to influence their creation of checkable-deposit money.

LO14.7 Explain how the equilibrium interest rate is determined and why interest rates and bond prices vary inversely.

Money is a fascinating aspect of the economy:

> Money bewitches people. They fret for it, and they sweat for it. They devise most ingenious ways to get it, and most ingenuous ways to get rid of it. Money is the only commodity that is good for nothing but to be gotten rid of. It will not feed you, clothe you, shelter you, or amuse you unless you spend it or invest it. It imparts value only in parting. People will do almost anything for money, and money will do almost anything for people. Money is a captivating, circulating, masquerading puzzle.[1]

In this chapter and the next, we unmask the critical role of money in the economy. A well-operating monetary system helps the economy achieve both full employment and the efficient use of resources. A malfunctioning monetary system distorts the allocation of resources and creates severe fluctuations in output, employment, and prices.

>> **LO14.1** Explain the functions of money.

medium of exchange Any item sellers generally accept and buyers generally use to pay for a *good* or *service; money;* a convenient means of exchanging goods and *services* without engaging in *barter.*

The Functions of Money

What exactly is money? There is an old saying that "money *is* what money *does*." Generally, anything that performs the functions of money is money. Here are those functions:

- *Medium of exchange* First and foremost, money is a **medium of exchange** that is used for buying and selling goods and services. A bakery worker does not want to be paid 200 bagels per week. Nor does the bakery owner want to receive, say, halibut in exchange for bagels. Money

[1] *Creeping Inflation: The Pickpocket Prosperity.* Federal Reserve Bank of Philadelphia, 1957.

is a social invention with which resource suppliers and producers can be paid, and it can be used to buy any item in the marketplace. As a medium of exchange, money allows society to escape the complications of barter. And because it provides a convenient way of exchanging goods, money enables society to gain the advantages of geographic and human specialization.

- *Unit of account* Money is also a **unit of account.** Society uses monetary units—dollars, in the United States—to measure the relative worth of a wide variety of goods, services, and resources. Just as we measure distance in miles or kilometers, we gauge the value of goods in dollars.

  With money as an acceptable unit of account, the price of each item needs to be stated only in terms of the monetary unit. We need not state the price of cows in terms of corn, crayons, and cranberries. Money aids rational decision making by enabling buyers and sellers to easily compare the relative values of goods, services, and resources by simply examining their respective money prices. It also permits us to define debt obligations, determine taxes owed, and calculate the nation's GDP.

- *Store of value* Money also serves as a **store of value** that enables people to transfer purchasing power from the present to the future. People normally do not spend their entire paychecks on the day they receive them. To buy things later, they store some of their wealth as money. The money you place in a safe or a checking account will still be available to you a few weeks or months from now. When inflation is nonexistent or mild, holding money is a relatively risk-free way to store your wealth.

unit of account A standard unit in which *prices* can be stated and the value of *goods* and *services* can be compared; one of the three functions of *money.*

store of value An asset set aside for future use; one of the three functions of *money.*

People can choose to hold some or all of their wealth in a wide variety of assets besides money. These assets include real estate, stocks, bonds, precious metals such as gold, and even collectible items like fine art or comic books. But a key advantage that money has over all other assets is its *liquidity*, or spendability.

An asset's **liquidity** is the ease with which it can be converted quickly with little or no loss of purchasing power into either physical cash (bills and coins) or cash balances held in electronic systems like PayPay and Venmo that transfer cash around electronically. The more liquid an asset is, the more quickly it can be converted into physical or electronic cash and used to purchase goods, services, and other assets.

Levels of liquidity vary greatly. By definition, cash is perfectly liquid. By contrast, a house is highly illiquid for two reasons. First, it may take several months before a willing buyer is found and a sale negotiated. Second, there is a loss of purchasing power when the house is sold because numerous fees must be paid to real estate agents and other individuals to complete the sale.

As we are about to discuss, our economy uses several different types of money including cash, coins, checking account deposits, savings account deposits, and even more exotic things like deposits in money market mutual funds. As we describe the various forms of money in detail, take the time to compare their relative levels of liquidity—both with each other and as compared to other assets like stocks, bonds, and real estate. Cash is perfectly liquid. Other forms of money are highly liquid, but less liquid than cash.

liquidity The degree to which an asset can be converted quickly into cash with little or no loss of purchasing power. *Money* is said to be perfectly liquid, whereas other assets have lesser degrees of liquidity.

The Components of the Money Supply

Societies have used many items as money, including whales' teeth, circular stones, elephant-tail bristles, gold coins, furs, and pieces of paper. Anything that is widely accepted as a medium of exchange can serve as money. In the United States, currency (cash) is not the only form of money. For example, certain debts of government and financial institutions also are used as money. Thus, the total quantity, or stock, of money depends upon what forms of money (cash, checkable deposits, etc.) are included in the tally.

In the United States, the two best-known tallies are known as $M1$ and $M2$. $M1$ contains the most immediately spendable (liquid) categories of money. $M2$ includes all the categories in $M1$ *plus* two additional categories of slightly less spendable money.

>> **LO14.2** Describe the components of the U.S. money supply.

Money Definition *M1*

The narrowest definition of the U.S. money supply is called *M1.* It consists of three components:

- *Currency* (coins and paper money) in the hands of the public.
- *Checkable deposits at commercial banks,* on which checks of any size can be drawn, at any time and as often as desired.

M1 The most narrowly defined money supply, equal to *currency* in the hands of the public, *checkable deposits*, and *savings deposits* held at *commercial banks* and thrifts.

FIGURE 14.1

Components of money supply *M*1 and money supply *M*2, in the United States.

(a) *M*1 is a narrow definition of the money supply that includes currency (in circulation) and checkable deposits. (b) *M*2 is a broader definition that includes *M*1 along with two other categories of relatively liquid account balances, retail money market funds and small-denominated time deposits.

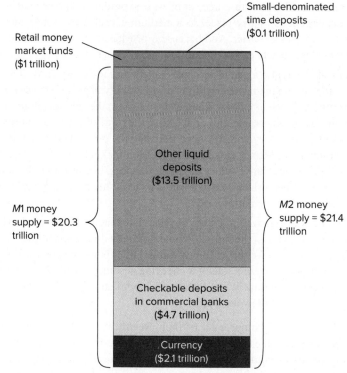

Source: Board of Governors of the Federal Reserve System.

- *Other liquid deposits*, including checkable deposits held at credit unions and other so-called thrift institutions *plus* savings deposits held at either commercial banks or thrift institutions.[2]

The supplies of coins and paper money are determined by the U.S. Department of the Treasury and the Federal Reserve System (the U.S. *central bank*). Commercial banks ("banks") and savings institutions ("thrifts") provide checkable deposits. Figure 14.1 shows that in November 2021, *M*1 was $20.3 trillion and *M*2 was $21.4 trillion. Thus, *M*2 was only $1.1 trillion, or about 5 percent, larger than *M*1.

Federal Reserve Note
Paper money issued by the *Federal Reserve Banks.*

Currency: Coins + Paper Money   U.S. currency consists of metal coins and paper money. The metal coins are issued by the U.S. Treasury while the paper money consists of **Federal Reserve Notes** issued by the Federal Reserve System. The coins are minted by the U.S. Mint, while the paper money is printed on behalf of the Federal Reserve by the Bureau of Engraving and Printing. Both the U.S. Mint and the Bureau of Engraving and Printing are part of the U.S. Department of the Treasury.

token money   Bills or coins for which the amount printed on the *currency* bears no relationship to the value of the paper or metal embodied within it; for currency still circulating, *money* for which the face value exceeds the commodity value.

As with the currencies of other countries, the currency of the United States is **token money.** That is, the face value of any piece of currency is unrelated to its *intrinsic value*—the value of the physical material (metal or paper and ink) from which that piece of currency is constructed. Governments make sure that face values exceed intrinsic values to discourage people from deconstructing coins and bills in order to resell the material that they are made out of as scrap metal or scrap paper. For instance, if 50-cent pieces each contained 75 cents' worth of metal, then it would be profitable to melt them down and sell the metal. Fifty-cent pieces would disappear from circulation very quickly!

Figure 14.1 shows that currency (coins and paper money) represents about 10.3 percent of *M*1 and about 9.8 percent of *M*2.

checkable deposit   Any deposit in a *commercial bank* or *thrift institution* against which a check may be written.

Checkable Deposits   The safety and convenience of checks has made **checkable deposits** a large component of the *M*1 money supply. You would not think of stuffing a large amount of currency—say, $2,396 in bills—into an envelope and then dropping that envelope into a mailbox to pay a debt. But writing and mailing a check for a large sum is commonplace, as is swiping, tapping, or inserting a "debit card" that automatically pulls money out of a checking account to make a payment.

---

[2]Prior to May 2020, the "savings deposits held at either commercial banks or thrift institutions" component of the money supply was excluded from *M*1 but included in *M*2. As a result, *M*1 used to be substantially smaller and the non-*M*1 parts of *M*2 substantially larger.

In terms of checks, the person cashing a check must endorse it (sign it on the reverse side); the writer of the check subsequently receives a record of the cashed check as a receipt. Similarly, because you must sign your checks, the theft or loss of your checkbook is not nearly as calamitous as losing a large amount of currency. Finally, it is more convenient to swipe a debit card or write a check than to transport and count out large sums of currency. For all these reasons, checkable deposits are a large component of the money stock in the United States. About 23 percent of $M1$ and 22 percent of $M2$ are in the form of checkable deposits, on which checks can be drawn and debit card payments processed.

It might seem strange that checking account balances are regarded as part of the money supply. But the reason is clear: Checks and debit card payments are simply a way to transfer the ownership of bank deposits, and they are generally acceptable as a medium of exchange. Although checks are less generally accepted than currency or debit card payments for many small purchases, most sellers willingly accept checks as payment for major purchases. Moreover, people can convert checkable deposits into paper money and coins on demand; checks drawn on those deposits are thus the equivalent of currency.

In addition, cash-transfer systems like PayPal and Venmo are often set up to be able to draw money out of checking accounts. Thus, another reason that checkable deposits are considered money is because they can be converted almost instantaneously into spendable electronic cash balances in systems like PayPal and Venmo.

To summarize:

Money, $M1$ = currency + checkable deposits at commercial banks + other liquid deposits.

Institutions That Offer Checkable Deposits   In the United States, a variety of financial institutions allow customers to write checks on the funds they have deposited. **Commercial banks** are the primary depository institutions. They accept the deposits of households and businesses, keep the money safe until it is withdrawn via checks or debit card activity, and in the meantime use it to make a wide variety of loans. Commercial bank loans provide short-term financial capital to businesses, and they finance consumer purchases of automobiles and other durable goods.

> **commercial bank** A *firm that engages in the business of banking (accepts deposits, offers checking accounts, and makes loans).*

Savings and loan associations (S&Ls), mutual savings banks, and credit unions supplement the commercial banks. Collectively, these institutions are called **thrift institutions,** or simply "thrifts." *Savings and loan associations* and *mutual savings banks* accept the deposits of households and businesses and then use the funds to finance home mortgages and to provide other loans. *Credit unions* accept deposits from and lend to "members," who usually are a group of people who work for the same company.

> **thrift institution** A *savings and loan association, mutual savings bank, or credit union.*

The checkable deposits of banks and thrifts are known variously as demand deposits, NOW (negotiable order of withdrawal) accounts, ATS (automatic transfer service) accounts, and share draft accounts. Depositors can write checks on all of these accounts whenever, and in whatever amount, they choose.

Two Qualifications   We must qualify our discussion in two important ways. First, currency held by the U.S. Treasury, the Federal Reserve banks, commercial banks, and thrift institutions is excluded from $M1$ and other measures of the money supply. A paper dollar or four quarters in the wallet of, say, Emma Buck obviously constitutes just $1 of the money supply. But if we counted currency held by banks as part of the money supply, the same $1 would count for $2 of money supply if Emma deposited the currency into her checking account. By excluding currency held by banks when determining the total money supply, we avoid this problem of double counting.

> **near-money** Financial *assets that are not themselves a medium of exchange but that have extremely high liquidity and thus can be readily converted into money.* Includes noncheckable *savings accounts, time deposits,* and short-term *U.S. government securities* plus savings bonds.

Also *excluded* from the money supply are any checkable deposits of the government (specifically, the U.S. Treasury) or the Federal Reserve that are held by commercial banks or thrift institutions. This exclusion enables a better assessment of the amount of money available *to the private sector* for potential spending. The amount of money available to households and businesses is of keen interest to the Federal Reserve in conducting its monetary policy (which we discuss in Chapter 15).

Money Definition *M2*

A second and broader definition of money includes all the categories of highly spendable money contained in $M1$ plus two near-monies. **Near-monies** are certain highly liquid financial assets that do not function directly or fully as a medium of exchange but can be readily converted into currency or checkable deposits. The $M2$ definition of money includes two categories of near-monies.

> **M2** A more broadly defined *money supply,* equal to $M1$ plus small *time deposits* (of less than $100,000) and individual *money market mutual fund* balances.

time deposit An interest-earning deposit in a *commercial bank* or *thrift institution* that the depositor can withdraw without penalty after the end of a specified period.

- *Small-denominated (less than $100,000) time deposits* Funds from **time deposits** become available at their maturity. For example, a person can convert a 6-month time deposit (usually referred to as a *certificate of deposit*, or CD) to currency without penalty 6 months or more after depositing it. In return for this withdrawal limitation, financial institutions pay a higher interest rate on time deposits than on ordinary checking or savings deposits (which can be withdrawn at any time without penalty). Note that while CD holders can in fact "cash in" CDs before their maturity dates, they would have to bear severe penalties if they did so. Because those early-withdrawal penalties discourage CD holders from spending their CD balances as readily as they would spend currency or checking account balances, funds held in time deposits are excluded from $M1$.

money market mutual funds (MMMFs) *Mutual funds* that invest in short-term *securities*. Depositors can write checks in minimum amounts or more against their accounts.

- *Retail money market funds (i.e., money market mutual funds held by individuals)* By making a telephone call, using the Internet, or writing a check for $500 or more, a depositor can redeem shares in a **money market mutual fund (MMMF)** offered by a mutual fund company. Such companies use the combined funds of individual shareholders to buy interest-bearing short-term credit instruments such as CDs and U.S. government securities. By holding those interest-earning assets, the funds can in turn offer interest payments on the balances held by shareholders in their MMMF accounts. The MMMFs in $M2$ include only the MMMF accounts held by individuals; those held by businesses and other institutions are excluded. The fact that MMMF checks must be for $500 or more (rather than for any amount) is why MMMFs are not included in $M1$.

Note that $M2$ is defined such that it encompasses the immediate medium-of-exchange items (currency and checkable deposits) that constitute $M1$ plus two near-monies that can be easily converted into currency and checkable deposits. $M2$ is, consequently, a measure of the portion of the money supply that is highly spendable.

In equation form:

$$\text{Money, } M2 = M1 + \text{small-denominated time deposits} + \text{MMMFs held by individuals}$$

In Figure 14.1, we see that the addition of the two categories that are unique to $M2$ implies a measure of money supply that is only slightly larger than the narrower $M1$ money supply. The nearby Consider This story explains why credit cards payments are not money.

CONSIDER THIS . . .

Are Credit Cards Money?

You may wonder why we have ignored credit cards such as Visa and Master-Card in our discussion of how the money supply is defined. After all, credit cards are a convenient way to buy things and account for about 27 percent of the dollar value of all transactions in the United States. The answer is that a credit card is not money. Rather, it is a convenient means of obtaining a short-term loan from the financial institution that issued the card.

What happens when you purchase an item with a credit card? The bank that issued the card will reimburse the seller by making a money payment and charging the establishment a transaction fee. Then, later, you will reimburse the bank for its loan to you by also making a money payment. Rather than reduce your cash or checking account balance with each purchase, you bunch your payments once a month (i.e., when your credit card bill comes due). You may have to pay an annual

Adam Crowley/Getty Images

fee for the services provided, and if you pay the bank in installments, you will pay a sizable interest charge on the loan. Credit cards are merely a means of deferring or postponing payment for a short period. Your checking account balance that you use to pay your credit card bill *is* money; the credit card is *not* money.*

Although credit cards are not money, they allow individuals and businesses to "economize" in the use of money. Credit cards enable people to hold less currency in their billfolds and, prior to payment due dates, fewer checkable deposits in their bank accounts. Credit cards also help people coordinate the timing of their expenditures with their receipt of income.

---

*A bank debit card, however, is very similar to a check in your checkbook. Unlike a purchase with a credit card, a purchase with a debit card creates a direct "debit" (a subtraction) from your checking account balance. That checking account balance is money—it is part of $M1$.

▶ Money serves as a medium of exchange, a unit of account, and a store of value.

▶ The *M1* definition of money includes currency held by the public, checkable deposits in commercial banks, and other liquid deposits, including savings deposits and checkable deposits held at thrifts.

▶ Thrift institutions, as well as commercial banks, offer accounts on which checks can be written.

▶ The *M2* definition of money includes *M1* plus small-denominated (less than $100,000) time deposits and money market mutual fund balances held by individuals.

What "Backs" the Money Supply?

The money supply in the United States essentially is "backed" (guaranteed) by the government's ability to keep the value of money relatively stable. Nothing more!

>> **LO14.3** Describe what "backs" the money supply.

Money as Debt

The major components of the money supply—paper money and checkable deposits—are debts, or promises to pay. In the United States, paper money is the circulating debt of the Federal Reserve Banks. Checkable deposits are the debts of commercial banks and thrift institutions.

Paper currency and checkable deposits have no intrinsic value. A $5 bill is just an inscribed piece of paper. A checkable deposit is merely a bookkeeping entry. And coins, we know, have less intrinsic value than their face value. Nor will government redeem the paper money you hold for anything tangible, such as gold.

To many people, it seems shady that the government does not back its currency with anything tangible. But the decision not to back the currency with anything tangible was made for a very good reason. If the government backed the currency with something tangible like gold, then the money supply would vary with the availability of gold. By not backing the currency, the government grants itself the freedom to provide as much or as little money as may be needed to best suit the country's economic needs. By choosing not to back the currency, the government gives itself the ability to freely "manage" the nation's money supply. Its monetary authorities are free to provide whatever amount of money is needed to promote full employment, price-level stability, and economic growth.

Value of Money

So why are currency and checkable deposits money, whereas, say, Monopoly (the game) money is not? What gives a $20 bill or a $100 check its value? The answer to these questions has three parts.

Acceptability Currency and checkable deposits are money because people accept them as money. By virtue of long-standing business practice, currency and checkable deposits perform the most essential function of money: They are acceptable as a medium of exchange. We accept paper money and checkable deposits because we are confident that they can be exchanged for goods, services, and resources.

Legal Tender Our confidence in the acceptability of paper money is strengthened because the government has designated currency as **legal tender.** Specifically, each bill contains the statement, "This note is legal tender for all debts, public and private." In other words, paper money is a valid and legal means of paying any debt that was contracted in dollars.

Note, however, that payments for goods and services are not payments of debts. Thus, private firms are under no legal obligation to accept cash in exchange for goods and services. It is perfectly legal for them to require customers to pay for products in noncash forms, such as cashier's checks or money orders. People selling goods and services can also legally refuse to take small coins or large bills.

The general acceptance of paper currency by society is more important than the government's decree that it serve as legal tender. This can be understood by the fact that checks function as money despite never having been designated as legal tender by the government. That being said, the Federal Deposit Insurance Corporation (FDIC) and the National Credit Union Administration (NCUA) enhance our willingness to use checks as a medium of exchange by insuring checking account deposits held at, respectively, commercial banks and thrifts.

legal tender Any form of *currency* that by law must be accepted by creditors (lenders) for the settlement of a financial debt; a nation's official currency is legal tender within its own borders.

Relative Scarcity The value of money, like the economic value of anything else, depends on its supply and demand. Money derives its value from its scarcity relative to its *utility* (its want-satisfying power). The utility of money lies in its capacity to be exchanged for goods and services, now or in the future. The economy's demand for money thus depends on the total dollar volume of transactions in any period plus the amount of money that individuals and businesses want to hold for future transactions. With a reasonably constant demand for money, the supply of money provided by the monetary authorities will determine the domestic value or "purchasing power" of the monetary unit (dollar, yen, euro, and so forth).

Money and Prices

The purchasing power of money is the amount of goods and services a unit of money will buy.

The Purchasing Power of the Dollar The amount a dollar will buy varies inversely with the price level. That is, a reciprocal relationship exists between the general price level and the dollar's purchasing power. When the consumer price index or "cost-of-living" index goes up, the value of the dollar goes down, and vice versa. Higher prices decrease the dollar's value because people need more dollars to buy a particular amount of goods, services, or resources. For example, if the price level doubles, the value of the dollar declines by one-half, or 50 percent.

Conversely, lower prices increase the dollar's purchasing power because people need fewer dollars to obtain a specific quantity of goods and services. If the price level falls by, say, 50 percent, then the purchasing power of the dollar doubles.

In equation form, the relationship looks like this:

$$\$V = 1/P$$

To find the value of the dollar, $\$V$, divide 1 by the price level P expressed as an index number (in hundredths). If the price level is 1, then the value of the dollar is 1. If the price level rises to, say, 1.20, $\$V$ falls to $1/1.2 = 0.833$; thus, a 20 percent increase in the price level reduces the value of the dollar by 16.67 percent. Check your understanding of this reciprocal relationship by determining the value of $\$V$ and its percentage rise when P falls by 20 percent, from 1 to 0.80.

Inflation and Acceptability In Chapter 9, we noted situations in which a nation's currency becomes worthless and unacceptable in exchange. These instances of runaway inflation, or *hyperinflation*, happen when a government issues so many pieces of paper currency that the purchasing power of each of those units of money becomes almost totally undermined. The infamous post-World War I hyperinflation in Germany is an example. In December 1919, there were about 50 billion marks in circulation. Four years later, there were 496,585,345,900 billion marks in circulation! The result? The German mark in 1923 was worth an infinitesimal fraction of its 1919 value.

Runaway inflation may significantly depreciate the value of money between the time it is received and the time it is spent. Rapid declines in the value of a currency may cause it to cease being used as a medium of exchange. Businesses and households may refuse to accept paper money in exchange because they do not want to bear the loss in its value that will occur while it is in their possession. (All this despite the fact that the government says that paper currency is legal tender!) Without an acceptable domestic medium of exchange, the economy may simply revert to barter. Alternatively, more stable currencies such as the U.S. dollar or European euro may come into widespread use. At the extreme, a country may adopt a foreign currency as its own official currency as a way to end its economy's dependence on a hyperinflating local currency.

Similarly, people will use money as a store of value only as long as there is no sizable deterioration in the value of that money because of inflation. An economy can effectively employ money as a unit of account only when its purchasing power is relatively stable. A monetary "yardstick" that has shrunk to some length shorter than a yard (in terms of purchasing power) does not permit buyers and sellers to establish the terms of trade clearly. When the value of money is declining rapidly, sellers do not know what to charge and buyers do not know what to pay.

Stabilizing Money's Purchasing Power

Rapidly rising price levels (rapid inflation)—and the consequent erosion of money's purchasing power—typically result from imprudent economic policies, especially rapid increases in the money supply.

Because money's purchasing power varies inversely with the price level, stabilizing the purchasing power of a nation's money requires stabilizing the nation's price level. Such price-level stability (2 to 3 percent annual inflation) can be achieved through intelligent management of the nation's money supply and interest rates (*monetary policy*). It also requires appropriate *fiscal policy* that supports the efforts of the nation's monetary authorities to hold down inflation.

In the United States, a combination of legislation, government policy, and social practice tends to inhibit imprudent expansions of the money supply. The critical role of U.S. monetary authorities in maintaining the dollar's purchasing power is the subject of Chapter 16. For now, simply note that the monetary authorities make available a particular quantity of money, such as *M*2 in Figure 14.1, and can change that amount through their policy tools.

▶ In the United States, money consists of the debts of government, commercial banks, and thrift institutions.

▶ These debts efficiently perform the functions of money as long as their value, or purchasing power, is relatively stable.

▶ The value of money is rooted not in specified quantities of precious metals such as gold, but in the amounts of goods, services, and resources that money will purchase.

▶ The value of the dollar (its domestic purchasing power) is inversely related to the price level.

▶ Stabilizing the purchasing power of the monetary unit calls for (a) effective control over the supply of money by the monetary authorities and (b) the application of appropriate fiscal policies by the president and congress.

The Federal Reserve and the Banking System

In the United States, the "monetary authorities" are the members of the Board of Governors of the **Federal Reserve System** (the "Fed"). As Figure 14.2 shows, the Board directs the activities of the 12 Federal Reserve Banks, which in turn control the lending activity of the nation's banks and thrift institutions. The Fed's major goal is to control the money supply. Because checkable deposits in banks and thrifts are such a large part of the money supply, its duties also involve ensuring the stability of the banking system, including not only commercial banks but also savings and loans associations, mutual savings banks, and credit unions.

Historical Background

Early in the twentieth century, Congress decided that centralization and public control were essential for an efficient banking system. Decentralized, unregulated banking had fostered the inconvenience and confusion of numerous private bank notes being used as currency. It also had

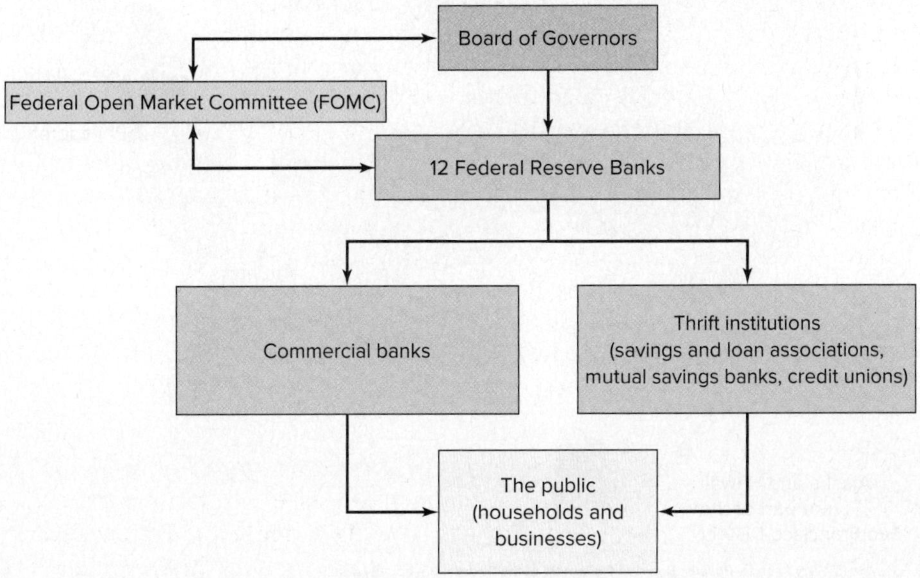

>> **LO14.4** Discuss the structure of the Federal Reserve.

Federal Reserve System The U.S. central bank, consisting of the *Board of Governors* of the Federal Reserve and the 12 *Federal Reserve Banks*, which controls the lending activity of the nation's banks and thrifts and thus the *money supply;* commonly referred to as the "Fed."

FIGURE 14.2
Framework of the Federal Reserve System and its relationship to the public.

The Board of Governors makes the basic policy decisions that provide monetary control of the U.S. money and banking systems. The 12 Federal Reserve Banks implement these decisions. Both the Board of Governors and the 12 Federal Reserve Banks are aided by the Federal Open Market Committee (FOMC).

resulted in occasional episodes of monetary mismanagement such that the money supply was inappropriate to the economy's needs. Sometimes "too much" money precipitated rapid inflation; other times "too little money" stunted the economy's growth by hindering the production and exchange of goods and services.

Furthermore, acute problems in the banking system occasionally erupted when banks either closed down or insisted on immediate repayment of loans to prevent their own failure. At such times, a banking crisis could emerge, with individuals and businesses that had lost confidence in their banks attempting to withdraw all of their money simultaneously—thereby further weakening the banks.

An unusually acute banking crisis in 1907 motivated Congress to create a National Monetary Commission to study the economy's monetary and banking problems and to propose a course of action for Congress. The result was the Federal Reserve Act of 1913.

Let's examine the various parts of the Federal Reserve System and their relationship to one another.

Board of Governors

> **Board of Governors** The seven-member group that supervises and controls the money and banking system of the United States; the Board of Governors of the *Federal Reserve System;* the Federal Reserve Board.

The central authority of the U.S. money and banking system is the **Board of Governors** of the Federal Reserve System. The U.S. president, with the confirmation of the Senate, appoints the seven Board members. Terms are 14 years and staggered so that one member is replaced every 2 years. In addition, new members are appointed when resignations occur. The president selects the chairperson and vice chairperson of the Board from among the members. Those officers serve 4-year terms and can be reappointed to new 4-year terms by the president. The long-term appointments provide the Board with continuity, experienced membership, and independence from political pressures that could result in inflation.

The 12 Federal Reserve Banks

> **Federal Reserve Banks** The 12 banks chartered by the U.S. government that collectively act as the *central bank* of the United States. They set monetary policy and regulate the private banking system under the direction of the *Board of Governors* and the *Federal Open Market Committee.* Each of the 12 is a *quasi-public bank* and acts as a *banker's bank* in its designated geographic region.

The 12 **Federal Reserve Banks,** which blend private and public control, collectively serve as the U.S. "central bank." They also serve as "bankers' banks."

Central Bank Most nations have a single central bank—for example, the United Kingdom's Bank of England or Japan's Bank of Japan. The U.S. central bank consists of 12 banks whose policies are coordinated by the Fed's Board of Governors. The 12 Federal Reserve Banks accommodate the geographic size and economic diversity of the United States as well as the large number of commercial banks and thrifts that are spread across the country.

Figure 14.3 shows the location of the 12 Federal Reserve Banks and the district that each serves. These banks implement the Board of Governors' basic policies.

FIGURE 14.3
The 12 Federal Reserve Districts.

The Federal Reserve System divides the United States into 12 districts, each having one central bank and, in some instances, one or more branches of the central bank.

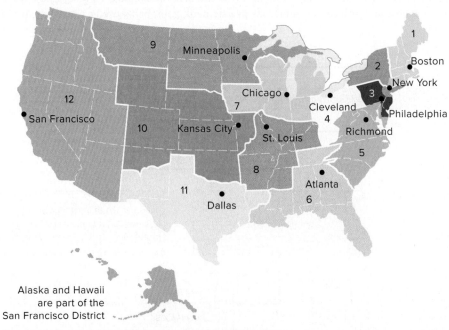

Alaska and Hawaii are part of the San Francisco District

Source: Federal Reserve Bulletin, Board of Governors of the Federal Reserve System.

Quasi-Public Banks The 12 Federal Reserve Banks are quasi-public banks that blend private ownership and public control. Each Federal Reserve Bank is owned by the private commercial banks in its district. (Federally chartered banks are required to purchase shares of stock in the Federal Reserve Bank in their district.) But the Board of Governors, a government body, sets the basic policies that the Federal Reserve Banks pursue.

Despite their private ownership, the Federal Reserve Banks are in practice public institutions. Unlike private firms, they are not motivated by profit. The policies they follow are designed by the Board of Governors to promote the well-being of the economy as a whole. Thus, the Fed's activities are frequently at odds with the profit motive. Also, the Federal Reserve Banks do not compete with commercial banks. In general, they do not deal with the public. Rather, they interact with the government on the one hand and commercial banks and thrifts on the other.

Bankers' Banks The Federal Reserve Banks are "bankers' banks" that perform essentially the same functions for banks and thrifts as those institutions perform for the public. Just as banks and thrifts accept deposits from, and make loans to, the public, so the central banks accept the deposits of, and make loans to, banks and thrifts. The funds that commercial banks and thrifts keep on deposit with the Fed are known as **reserve balances,** which is why the Fed's full name—the Federal Reserve Bank—contains the word "reserve."

In noncrisis situations, the vast majority of reserve balances are the result of ongoing commercial bank and thrift operations, including taking deposits from individuals and businesses and receiving funds as borrowers repay loans. On those normal, noncrisis days, less than $150 million of reserve balances are the result of banks or thrifts borrowing from the Fed. But during financial crises, when the Fed acts as the "lender of last resort" to the banking system, the Federal Reserve Banks can lend out as much money as is needed to ensure that commercial banks and thrifts can meet their cash payment obligations.

Those emergency loans come in the form of reserve balances that the Fed deposits into the Federal reserve accounts of the banks and thrifts receiving emergency loans. During the initial lockdown phase of the COVID-19 pandemic in the spring of 2020, for example, the Fed lent $129 billion of reserve balances to banks and thrifts in just three weeks in order to make sure that the panicky mood that was evident on both Wall Street and Main Street did not precipitate a nationwide banking crisis.

The Federal Reserve Banks also have a third function, which banks and thrifts do not perform: They issue currency. In particular, Congress has authorized the Federal Reserve Banks to create and put into circulation Federal Reserve Notes, which constitute the U.S. economy's paper money supply.

reserve balances Funds that *commercial banks* and *thrift institutions* hold on deposit at the *central bank*.

FOMC

The **Federal Open Market Committee (FOMC)** aids the Board of Governors in conducting monetary policy. The FOMC is made up of 12 individuals:

- The seven members of the Board of Governors.
- The president of the New York Federal Reserve Bank.
- Four presidents selected from the remaining Federal Reserve Banks, each serving on a one-year rotating basis.

The FOMC meets regularly to direct the purchase and sale of government securities (bills, notes, bonds) in the "open market" in which such securities are bought and sold daily. The FOMC also makes decisions about the extent to which the Fed borrows and lends government securities in the open market. These *open-market operations* that help to control the nation's money supply and interest rates are conducted mostly by Federal Reserve Bank of New York, which is located in the heart of New York City's financial district, just a couple of blocks from Wall Street.

Federal Open Market Committee (FOMC) The 12-member group within the *Federal Reserve System* that decides U.S. *monetary policy* and how it is executed through *open-market operations* (in which the Fed buys and sells U.S. government securities to adjust the *money supply*).

Commercial Banks and Thrifts

There are about 4,300 commercial banks in the United States. All of these banks are private corporations. They are, however, sometimes mistaken for being government entities because each of these banks can be categorized as being either a "state" bank, or as a "national" or "federal" bank.

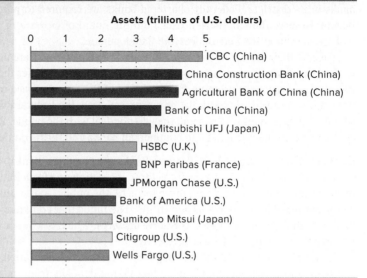

THE WORLD'S 12 LARGEST COMMERCIAL BANKS, 2021

The world's 12 largest private sector banks are headquartered in just five countries: China, France, Japan, the United Kingdom, and the United States.

Source: "The World's Largest Public Companies 2021," *Forbes.*

Those terms are correct, but refer to whether a bank has a state or a federal charter, not whether it is owned or controlled by a state government or the federal government.

- Roughly three-fourths of the 4,300 commercial banks are state banks. These private banks are chartered (authorized) by individual states to operate within their respective borders.
- The remaining one-fourth of commercial banks are chartered by the federal government to operate nationally; these private banks are referred to as national, or federal, banks.

Some of the national banks are very large, ranking among the world's largest financial institutions (see Global Perspective 14.1).

The 7,000 or so thrift institutions—most of which are credit unions—are regulated by agencies separate and apart from the Board of Governors and the Federal Reserve Banks. The financial operations of credit unions are, for example, closely monitored by the National Credit Union Administration (NCUA).

That being said, thrift institutions are just as subject to monetary control by the Federal Reserve System as commercial banks, as is illustrated in Figure 14.2. Decisions concerning monetary policy affect thrifts as well as commercial banks.

Fed Functions, Responsibilities, and Independence

>> LO14.5 Identify the functions and responsibilities of the Federal Reserve.

The Fed performs several functions:

- *Issuing currency* The Federal Reserve Banks issue Federal Reserve Notes, the paper currency used in the United States. (The Federal Reserve Bank that issued a particular bill is identified in black in the upper left of new bills. "A1," for example, identifies the Boston bank, "B2" the New York bank, and so on.)
- *Holding reserves and setting reserve requirements* The Federal Reserve System is a banker's bank that allows commercial banks and thrifts to deposit currency with the Fed. Those deposits are known as *reserve balances* and the Fed has the legal power to set *reserve requirements,* which are percentages of individual checking account balances that banks and thrifts may be required to maintain as *bank reserves* to facilitate withdrawals by customers.[3]

---

[3]Please note that the Fed eliminated reserve requirements in 2020 and has stated that it has no intention of bringing them back. Whereas in previous decades the Fed viewed reserve requirements as a sensible way to help ensure the financial stability of the banking system, its current policy is to rely instead on bank capital requirements, which provide for financial stability by requiring bank and thrift shareholders to provide large enough reserves of financial capital to carry those institutions through all but the most extreme financial crises.

- *Lending to financial institutions and serving as an emergency lender of last resort* The Federal Reserve makes routine short-term loans to banks and thrifts and charges them an interest rate called the *discount rate*. During financial emergencies, the Fed also serves as the lender of last resort for not only banks and thrifts but also other sorts of financial firms (like insurance companies and money market funds) whose stability is considered essential to the health of the U.S. economy.

- *Providing for check collection* The Fed provides the banking system with a means for collecting on checks. If Suzannah writes a check on her Miami bank to Jobohán, who deposits it in his Dallas bank, how does the Dallas bank collect the money represented by the check drawn against the Miami bank? The Fed solves the problem ("clears checks") by adjusting the reserves (deposits) that the two banks hold at the Fed. In this example, the Miami bank's reserves are decreased by the amount of Suzannah's check while the Dallas bank's reserves are increased by the amount of Suzannah's check. The Dallas bank can then transfer that money into Jobohán's account.

- *Acting as the federal government's fiscal agent* The Fed acts as the fiscal agent (provider of financial services) for the federal government, which collects huge sums through taxation, spends equally large amounts on goods and services, and both sells and redeems its own bonds. To carry out those activities, the federal government employs the Federal Reserve.

- *Supervising banks* The Fed supervises the operations of banks. It periodically assesses bank profitability, ensures that banks perform according to the regulations, and seeks to uncover questionable practices or fraud.

- *Controlling the money supply* The Fed's most famous responsibility is to manage the money supply (and thus interest rates) according to the economy's needs. The Fed's goal is to make an amount of money available that is consistent with (1) full employment in the labor markets and (2) a stable price level. While most of the Fed's other functions are routine, managing the nation's money supply requires policy decisions that must be made when and if needed, and tailored as necessary to meet the circumstances, which sometimes include major financial and economic crises, such as dealing with the COVID-19 pandemic. (We will discuss how the Fed handles decisions about the money supply and interest rates in detail in Chapter 15.)

Federal Reserve Independence

Congress purposely established the Federal Reserve System as an independent agency of the federal government. The objective was to protect the Fed from political pressures so that it could effectively control the money supply and maintain price stability. Political pressures on Congress and the executive branch may at times result in inflationary fiscal policies, including tax cuts and special-interest spending. If Congress and the executive branch also controlled the nation's monetary policy, citizens and lobbying groups would undoubtedly pressure elected officials to keep interest rates low even though at times high interest rates are necessary to reduce aggregate demand and thus control inflation. An independent monetary authority (the Fed) can take actions to increase interest rates when higher rates are needed to stem inflation. Studies show that countries that have independent central banks like the Fed have lower rates of inflation, on average, than countries that have little or no central bank independence.

▶ The U.S. banking system consists of (a) the Board of Governors of the Federal Reserve System, (b) the 12 Federal Reserve Banks, and (c) some 4,300 commercial banks and 7,000 thrift institutions (mainly credit unions).

▶ The 12 Federal Reserve Banks are simultaneously (a) central banks, (b) quasi-public banks, and (c) bankers' banks.

▶ The major functions of the Fed are to (a) issue Federal Reserve Notes, (b) set reserve requirements, (c) lend money to financial institutions and serve as the lender of last resort in national financial emergencies, (d) provide for the rapid collection of checks, (e) act as the fiscal agent for the federal government, (f) supervise the operations of the banks, and (g) regulate the supply of money in the best interests of the economy.

QUICK REVIEW

14.3

Fractional Reserve Banking and the Money Supply

>> LO14.6 Explain the fractional reserve system used by U.S. banks and why the Fed might wish to influence their creation of checkable-deposit money.

As noted earlier, *M*1 and *M*2 include both currency (coins and Federal Reserve Notes) as well as checkable deposits. As mentioned earlier, the U.S. Mint produces the coins and the U.S. Bureau of Engraving and Printing creates the Federal Reserve Notes.

But who creates the checkable deposits that are also part of *M*1 and *M*2? Surprisingly, it is loan officers!

Although that may sound like something a congressional committee should investigate, the monetary authorities are well aware that banks and thrifts create checkable deposits. In fact, the Federal Reserve relies *entirely* on banks and thrifts to create this vital component of the nation's money supply.

The Fractional Reserve Banking System

fractional reserve banking system A system in which *commercial banks* and *thrift institutions* hold less than 100 percent of their checkable-deposit liabilities as reserves of *currency* held in bank vaults or as deposits at the *central bank*.

The ability of loan officers at banks and thrifts to create checkable-deposit money is the result of the United States having a **fractional reserve banking system** in which only a portion (fraction) of checkable deposits are backed by reserves of currency either (1) stored on-site in the vaults of commercial bank and thrifts or (2) kept as *reserve balances* on deposit at the central bank. Our goal is to explain this system, which is used by nearly every country in the world, and show how commercial banks and thrifts create checkable deposits by issuing loans.

Illustrating the Idea: The Goldsmiths Here is the history behind the idea of the fractional reserve system.

When early traders began to use gold in making transactions, they soon realized that it was both unsafe and inconvenient to carry gold and to have it weighed and assayed (judged for purity) every time they negotiated a transaction. So by the sixteenth century they had begun to deposit their gold with goldsmiths, who would store it in vaults for a fee. On receiving a gold deposit, the goldsmith would issue a receipt to the depositor. Soon people were paying for goods with goldsmiths' receipts, which served as one of the first types of paper money.

At this point the goldsmiths—embryonic bankers—used a 100 percent reserve system; they backed their circulating paper money receipts fully with the gold that they held "in reserve" in their vaults. But because of the public's acceptance of the goldsmiths' receipts as paper money, the goldsmiths soon realized that owners rarely redeemed the gold they had in storage. In fact, the goldsmiths observed that the amount of gold being deposited with them in any week or month was likely to exceed the amount that was being withdrawn.

Then some clever goldsmith hit on the idea that their circulating paper money receipts could be issued in excess of the amount of gold held. Goldsmiths would put these receipts, which were redeemable in gold, into circulation by making interest-earning loans to merchants, manufacturers, and even governments. A borrower might, for instance, borrow $10,000 worth of gold receipts today with the promise to repay $10,500 worth of gold receipts in one year (a 5 percent interest rate). Borrowers were willing to accept loans in the form of gold receipts because the receipts were accepted as a medium of exchange in the marketplace.

This was the beginning of the fractional reserve system of banking, in which reserves in bank vaults are a fraction of the total money supply. If, for example, the goldsmith issued $1 million in receipts for actual gold in storage and another $1 million in receipts as loans, then the total value of paper money in circulation would be $2 million—twice the value of the gold. Gold reserves would be a fraction (one-half) of outstanding paper money.

Significant Characteristics of Fractional Reserve Banking The goldsmith story highlights two significant characteristics of fractional reserve banking. First, banks can create money through lending. In fact, goldsmiths created money when they made loans that were not fully backed by gold reserves. The quantity of such money goldsmiths could create depended on the amount of reserves they deemed prudent to have available. The smaller the amount of reserves thought necessary, the larger the amount of paper money the goldsmiths could create. Today, gold is no longer used as bank reserves. Instead, currency itself serves as bank reserves so that the creation of checkable-deposit money by banks (via their lending) is limited by the amount of currency reserves (either cash in vaults or *reserve balances* at the Fed) that the banks feel prudent, or are required by law, to keep. As we will see in the next chapter, one way that the Fed can influence bank lending—and, thus, the total volume of checkable-deposit money in the economy—is by changing the total amount of currency reserves in the banking system through what are referred to as "open-market" purchases and sales of government bonds. The more reserves banks have, the more likely they are to lend, all other things equal.

A second reality is that banks operating on the basis of fractional reserves are vulnerable to "panics" or "runs." A goldsmith who issued paper money equal to twice the value of his gold reserves would be unable to convert all that paper money into gold in the event that all the holders of that money appeared at his door at the same time demanding their gold. In fact, many European and U.S. banks were once ruined by this unfortunate circumstance. However, a bank panic is highly unlikely if the banker's reserve and lending policies are prudent. Indeed, one reason why banking systems are highly regulated industries is to prevent runs on banks.

This is also why the United States has the system of deposit insurance that we mentioned earlier. By guaranteeing deposits, deposit insurance helps to prevent the sort of bank runs that used to happen so often before deposit insurance was available. In those situations, rumors would spread that a bank was about to go bankrupt and that it only had a small amount of reserves left in its vaults. Bank runs are called "bank runs" because depositors would literally run to the bank trying to be one of the lucky few to withdraw their money while the bank had any reserves left. The rumors were usually totally unfounded. But, unfortunately, a bank could still go bankrupt even if it began the day with its normal amount of reserves. With so many customers withdrawing money simultaneously, it would run out of reserves and be forced to default on its obligations to its remaining depositors. By guaranteeing depositors that they will always get their money back, deposit insurance removes the incentive to try to withdraw one's deposit before anyone else can. It thus forestalls most bank runs.

Finally, it should be noted that while the making of new loans creates checkable-deposit money, the repayment of old loans destroys checkable-deposit money. Thus, *the overall volume of checkable-deposit money circulating in the economy depends upon the total outstanding volume of loans that have been extended by banks and thrifts at any point in time.*

Fed Influence over Lending and the Money Supply

Because bank and thrift loan officers create money through lending, the Federal Reserve is extremely attentive to the incentives and restrictions that it places on banks and thrifts with regard to their lending decisions. By modulating those incentives and restrictions, the Fed has at its disposal a powerful mechanism for altering the money supply and, as a result, influencing interest rates and economic activity.

In the next chapter, we will provide a detailed description of the various tools that the Fed uses to influence bank lending behavior. For now, just understand that from the perspective of individuals and businesses, Fed policy changes that prompt banks to increase their lending will result in easier access to credit, both in terms of the sheer volume of loans made available to the public as well as those loans being made available at lower interest rates. Both can spur spending in the economy, in particular greater investment spending on the part of businesses and increased consumption spending on the part of households and consumers.

The opposite is also true. If the Fed institutes policy changes that prompt banks to decrease their lending, individuals and firms will have a harder time accessing credit, both in terms of a lesser volume of loans made available to them and in terms of those loans charging higher interest rates. Both will tend to reduce spending in the economy, with firms borrowing and spending less on investment goods and individuals and households spending less on housing, automobiles, and other forms of consumption for which borrowing is common.

Thus, any decision by the Fed that influences bank lending will tend to change: (1) the total amount of checkable-deposit money in the economy; (2) the overall money supply; (3) interest rates; and (4) overall economic activity. It is for that reason that the Fed was established by congress as the primary supervisor of the banking system in addition to being the primary supervisor of the overall U.S. monetary system. The Fed would be far less effective at managing the money supply, interest rates, and economic activity if it were not also the nation's central bank and thus in a position to directly influence bank and thrift lending.

▶ Under the fractional reserve banking system, only a portion (fraction) of checkable deposits are backed by currency, which makes the system vulnerable to banking panics.

▶ Loan officers create checkable-deposit money any time they extend a loan.

▶ The overall volume of checkable-deposit money circulating in the economy depends upon the total outstanding volume of loans.

▶ The Fed can alter the money supply and thereby affect interest rates and economic activity by altering the incentives and restrictions that it places on bank lending and bank money creation.

Interest Rates

>> **LO14.7** Explain how the equilibrium interest rate is determined and why interest rates and bond prices vary inversely.

interest The payment made for the use of (borrowed) *money.*

The Fed influences the economy primarily through its ability to change the money supply (*M*1 and *M*2) and therefore affect interest rates and economic activity. **Interest** is the price paid for the use of money. It is the price that borrowers must pay lenders for transferring purchasing power to the future, the price that borrowers must pay lenders to compensate them for not being able to use their money until it is repaid, and the price that borrowers must pay to use $1 for 1 year. Although there are many different interest rates, we will simply speak of *the* interest rate unless we state otherwise.

Let's see how the interest rate is determined. Because it is a price, we again turn to demand-and-supply analysis for the answer.

The Demand for Money

The public wants to hold some of its wealth as money for two main reasons:

- To facilitate purchases (transactions).
- To hold as an asset (store of value).

These two sources of money demand are named, respectively, the transactions demand for money and the asset demand for money. Let's discuss them in sequence.

transactions demand for money The amount of money people want to hold for use as a *medium of exchange* (to make payments); varies directly with *nominal GDP.*

Transactions Demand, D_t The first reason people hold money is because it is convenient for purchasing goods and services. Households usually are paid once a week, every 2 weeks, or monthly, but their expenditures are less predictable and typically more frequent. Thus households must have enough money on hand to buy groceries and pay mortgage and utility bills. Businesses, too, need to have money available to pay for labor, materials, and other inputs. The demand for money as a medium of exchange is called the **transactions demand for money.**

Nominal GDP is the main determinant of the amount of money demanded for transactions. The larger the total money value of all the goods, services, and resources exchanged in the economy, the larger the amount of money needed to facilitate those transactions. The transactions demand for money varies directly with nominal GDP. We specify *nominal* GDP because households, firms, and financial institutions will want more money for transactions if prices rise or if real output increases. In both instances, a larger dollar volume is needed to accomplish the desired transactions.

In **Figure 14.4a (Key Graph),** we graph the quantity of money demanded for transactions against the interest rate. For simplicity, we assume that the quantity demanded depends exclusively on nominal GDP and is therefore independent of the interest rate. Our simplifying assumption allows us to graph the transactions demand D_t as a vertical line. This demand curve is positioned at $100 billion, on the assumption that nominal GDP is $300 billion and each dollar held for transactions purposes is spent an average of three times per year. Thus the public needs $100 billion (= $300 billion/3) to purchase that amount of nominal GDP.

asset demand for money The amount of *money* people want to hold as a *store of value;* this amount varies inversely with the *interest rate.*

Asset Demand, D_a The second reason for holding money derives from money's function as a store of value. People may hold their wealth either in tangible assets like real estate or in a variety of financial assets, including stocks, bonds, and money. To the extent they want to hold money as an asset, there is an **asset demand for money.**

To understand why people have an asset demand for money, you must compare money with other financial assets, such as bonds. Bonds make regular, substantial interest payments, while

...ıl KEY GRAPH

FIGURE 14.4 The demand for money, the supply of money, and the equilibrium interest rate in the market for money.

The total demand for money D_m is determined by horizontally adding the transactions demand for money D_t to the asset demand for money D_a. The transactions demand is vertical because it is assumed to depend on nominal GDP rather than on the interest rate. The asset demand varies inversely with the interest rate because of the opportunity cost involved in holding currency and checkable deposits that pay no interest or very low interest. Combining the money supply (stock) S_m with the total money demand D_m portrays the market for money and determines the equilibrium interest rate i_e.

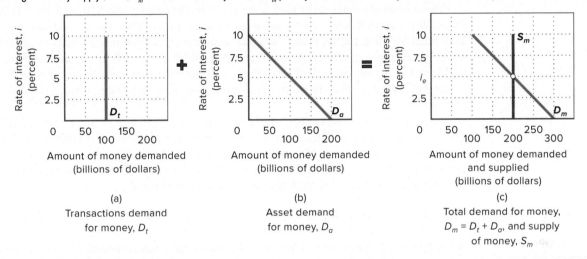

(a)
Transactions demand
for money, D_t

(b)
Asset demand
for money, D_a

(c)
Total demand for money,
$D_m = D_t + D_a$, and supply
of money, S_m

QUICK QUIZ FOR FIGURE 14.4

1. **In this graph, at the interest rate i_e (5 percent):**
   a. the amount of money demanded as an asset is $50 billion.
   b. the amount of money demanded for transactions is $200 billion.
   c. bond prices will decline.
   d. $100 billion is demanded for transactions, $100 billion is demanded as an asset, and the money supply is $200 billion.

2. **In this graph, at an interest rate of 10 percent:**
   a. no money will be demanded as an asset.
   b. total money demanded will be $200 billion.
   c. the Federal Reserve will supply $100 billion of money.
   d. there will be a $100 billion shortage of money.

3. **Curve D_a slopes downward because:**
   a. lower interest rates increase the opportunity cost of holding money.
   b. lower interest rates reduce the opportunity cost of holding money.

   c. the asset demand for money varies directly (positively) with the interest rate.
   d. the transactions-demand-for-money curve is perfectly vertical.

4. **Suppose the supply of money declines to $100 billion. The equilibrium interest rate would:**
   a. fall, the amount of money demanded for transactions would rise, and the amount of money demanded as an asset would decline.
   b. rise, while the amounts of money demanded both for transactions and as an asset would fall.
   c. fall, while the amounts of money demanded both for transactions and as an asset would increase.
   d. rise, the amount of money demanded for transactions would be unchanged, and the amount of money demanded as an asset would decline.

Answers: 1. d; 2. a; 3. b; 4. d

money earns either zero interest (currency) or extremely low interest (checking account deposits). Thus, from that perspective, bonds are a more attractive financial asset.

But that's not the end of the story. Bonds, stocks, and other financial assets are also riskier than money. Bond prices, for example, sometimes fall, generating *capital losses* for their owners. By contrast, the value of money is quite steady unless inflation is strong. So while money pays zero interest, it holds its value much better than bonds and other financial assets under normal circumstances. This gives people a reason to demand money as an asset.

Another reason that people demand money as an asset is because money can be used to purchase other assets when good "buying opportunities" arise. Money will hold its value when the stock market crashes 20 percent; so anyone holding money can jump in and buy stocks at low, post-crash prices. The only way to "buy the dips" is to have money on hand when the prices of other assets decline.

Knowing these advantages and disadvantages, the public must decide how much of its financial assets to hold as money. Their decision depends primarily on the interest rate. When a household or business holds money, it incurs the opportunity cost of the interest it could have received if it had used that money to purchase bonds. If bonds pay 6 percent interest, for example, then holding $100 as cash or in a noninterest checking account would cost $6 per year of forgone income.

The amount of money demanded as an asset therefore varies inversely with the interest rate (which is the opportunity cost of holding money as an asset). When the interest rate rises, being liquid and avoiding capital losses becomes more costly. So the public reacts by reducing its quantity demanded of money. By contrast, when the interest rate falls, the cost of being liquid and avoiding capital losses declines. The public therefore increases the quantity of financial assets that it wants to hold as money. This inverse relationship just described is shown by D_a in Figure 14.4b.

Also note that when we speak of the "public" here, we mean anyone and everyone outside the Federal Reserve. That includes businesses, the government, and financial institutions, including banks. Thus, the asset demand for money also includes the demand that banks and thrifts have for currency held as reserves against loan losses and withdrawals. The higher the interest rate, the less money banks want to hold as bank reserves, all other things equal.

total demand for money
The sum of the *transactions demand for money* and the *asset demand for money.*

Total Money Demand, D_m As Figure 14.4 shows, we find the **total demand for money,** D_m, by horizontally adding the asset demand for money to the transactions demand for money. The result is the downward sloping line in Figure 14.4c, which represents the total amount of money the public wants to hold, both for transactions and as an asset, at each possible interest rate.

Recall that the transactions demand for money depends on nominal GDP. A change in nominal GDP will, consequently, shift the total demand for money curve D_m by altering the transactions demand for money. Consider an increase in nominal GDP. That will increase the transactions demand for money, and that extra transactions demand will shift the total money demand curve to the right. In contrast, a decline in nominal GDP shifts the total money demand curve to the left. As an example, suppose nominal GDP increases from $300 billion to $450 billion, and the average dollar held for transactions is still spent three times per year. Then the transactions demand curve will shift from $100 billion (= $300 billion/3) to $150 billion (= $450 billion/3). The total money demand curve will then lie $50 billion farther to the right at each possible interest rate.

The Equilibrium Interest Rate

We can combine the demand for money with the supply of money to determine the equilibrium interest rate. In Figure 14.4c, the vertical line S_m represents the money supply. It is a vertical line because the monetary authorities and financial institutions have provided the economy with some particular stock of money. Here, it is $200 billion.

Just as in a product market or a resource market, the intersection of demand and supply determines the equilibrium price in the market for money. In Figure 14.4, this equilibrium price is the equilibrium interest rate, i_e. At this interest rate, the quantity of money demanded (= $200 billion) equals the quantity of money supplied (= $200 billion).

As you have just seen, changes in the demand for money, the supply of money, or both can change the equilibrium interest rate. We are, however, most interested in changes in the money supply since the Fed can affect the money supply. To that end, please remember this important generalization: *An increase in the money supply will lower the equilibrium interest rate, while a decrease in the money supply will raise the equilibrium interest rate.*

Interest Rates and Bond Prices

Interest rates and bond prices are inversely related. When the interest rate increases, bond prices fall; when the interest rate decreases, bond prices rise. Why?

First understand that bonds are bought and sold in financial markets, with the price of bonds being determined by the interaction of bond demand with bond supply. As an example, suppose

Cryptocurrencies

The Blockchain Technology Behind Bitcoin Allows Private Citizens to Issue Digital "Cryptocurrencies."
But Will Central Bank Digital Currencies Eventually Dominate?

In 2008, a secretive computer programmer who used the name Satoshi Nakamoto as an alias began recruiting other programmers to help him develop the "blockchain" technology that now underpins all of the world's digital currencies, including the two most popular, Bitcoin and Ether.

A blockchain is a sequence, or chain, of updates made to an electronic document known as a distributed ledger. Each updated version of the ledger is referred to as a block and the key insight developed by Nakamoto was that a blockchain could be used to keep track of property rights, including the ownership of digital money.

A key problem, historically, with any system of property rights is figuring out with certainty who owns what. Consider a 2-acre plot of land that you find for sale just north of Las Vegas, Nevada. There may be several people who will tell you that they own all or part of that plot—but what if only one of them says it's for sale?

Would you dare to buy the plot from that guy? And would anybody else recognize you as the rightful owner if you paid him his asking price?

The solution, traditionally, to these sorts of "who owns what" problems has been for the government to maintain centralized records of property ownership. Thus, for instance, there are official government records about who owns every square inch of land in and around Las Vegas. Anyone interested in buying property in Las Vegas can consult those records to see who owns what land and thus who has the right to sell any particular piece of land to someone else.

What Satoshi Nakamoto realized was that blockchain technology would allow private individuals, rather than the government, to maintain records about property rights that everybody involved would agree were both accurate and up-to-date. That is accomplished by a "consensus mechanism" by which any update to a blockchain has to be agreed upon by a majority of users. That certification system is almost perfectly secure against tampering because the resources that would be needed to fake a majority vote would cost billions of dollars on a large blockchain like Bitcoin. In addition, any rigged vote would be discovered quickly and almost immediately undone by a subsequent (non-rigged) vote.

One of the things that a blockchain can keep track of is the ownership of digital currencies, such as Bitcoin or Ether, which at their most fundamental levels are just strings of serial numbers recorded on a blockchain. Thus, for example, if you wanted to pay me a bitcoin for a used car, we would record that transaction on the Bitcoin blockchain by updating it so that the ownership of that particular bitcoin passed from your name to my name.

Blockchain-based digital currencies like Bitcoin and Ether are often referred to as **cryptocurrencies** because part of their consensus mechanism involves the use of cryptography, which is the branch of mathematics that studies how to create secure records and communication.

Travis Wolfe/Shutterstock

As of late 2022, there were over 21,000 cryptocurrencies trading in the world with a combined market value of just under $1 trillion. But it was also the case that no cryptocurrency had yet become widely used as a method of payment for goods and services. For that, official government-issued currencies were still overwhelmingly dominant throughout the world.

At the same time, 10 national central banks—including those of China, Nigeria, and Jamaica—had by late 2022 issued their own blockchain-based digital currencies in parallel with their respective traditional (paper) currencies. More than forty other central banks have indicated that they might also follow suit and issue their own CBDC, or central bank digital currency.

Thus, one possibility for the future of digital payments is that private cryptocurrencies like Bitcoin and Ether may never become very popular for transactions, with people instead using central bank digital currencies to pay for most goods and services. If that turns out to be the case, CBDCs could also revolutionize monetary and fiscal policy because when a recession happens, a government or central bank could choose to stimulate the economy by simply gifting additional currency units into the "cryptowallets" of each and every citizen, thereby providing them with more money to save, spend, or invest.

Satoshi Nakamoto's goal was to create digital money that was independent of government control. But it may turn out to be national governments and their central banks that have the last laugh when it comes to popularizing digital money.

---

cryptocurrency A digital money that uses blockchain technology to keep track of the ownership of particular pieces of digital currency.

that a bond with no expiration date pays a fixed $50 annual interest payment and is selling for its face value of $1,000. The "interest yield" on this bond is 5 percent:

$$\frac{\$50}{\$1,000} = 5\% \text{ interest yield}$$

Now suppose that the interest rate in the economy rises to $7\frac{1}{2}$ percent from 5 percent. Newly issued bonds will pay $75 per $1,000 loaned. Older bonds paying only $50 will not be sellable at their $1,000 face value. To compete with the $7\frac{1}{2}$ percent bond, the price of those older bonds must fall to $667 to remain competitive. The $50 fixed annual interest payment will then yield $7\frac{1}{2}$ percent to whoever buys the bond:

$$\frac{\$50}{\$667} = 7\frac{1}{2}\%$$

Next, suppose that the interest rate falls to $2\frac{1}{2}$ percent from the original 5 percent. Newly issued bonds will pay $25 on $1,000 loaned. A bond paying $50 will be highly attractive. Bond buyers will bid up its price to $2,000, where the yield will equal $2\frac{1}{2}$ percent:

$$\frac{\$50}{\$2,000} = 2\frac{1}{2}\%$$

These three examples demonstrate that bond prices fall when the interest rate rises and rise when the interest rate falls. *There is an inverse relationship between the interest rate and bond prices.*

If you are a visual learner, there is a simple image that captures this inverse relationship. Imagine two friends at a park riding a seesaw. At one end is Mr. Bond, and at the other is his friend, Mr. Rate. When Mr. Bond goes up, Mr. Rate goes down, and vice versa.

Another way of understanding why bond prices and interest rates move in opposite directions is to look back at the three examples above and notice that the annual payment is always fixed at $50. So the more you pay for the right to receive that $50 payment, the lower your rate of return (yield). Here are a few other examples to drive that point home.

- Pay $100 for the bond, and your rate of return is 50 percent ($= \$50/\$100 \times 100$)
- Pay $500 for the bond, and your rate of return is 10 percent ($= \$50/\$500 \times 100$)
- Pay $5,000 for the bond, and your rate of return is 1 percent ($= \$50/\$5000 \times 100$)

The more you pay today for a fixed future amount, the lower your percentage return. Test yourself by calculating what the yield would be on this bond at a price of $900 and at a price of $1,250. Verify that the higher price generates a lower yield.

▶ The total demand for money is the sum of the transactions demand for money and the asset demand for money.

▶ The equilibrium interest rate is determined where total money demand intersects money supply.

▶ Interest rates and bond prices are inversely related.

Summary

LO14.1 Explain the functions of money.
Money is anything that serves simultaneously as (*a*) a medium of exchange, (*b*) a unit of monetary account, and (*c*) a store of value.

LO14.2 Describe the components of the U.S. money supply.
There are two major definitions of the money supply, $M1$ and $M2$.

$M1$ consists of currency, checkable deposits at banks, and other liquid deposits, such as savings deposits at banks and checkable deposits held at thrifts.

$M2$ consists of $M1$ *plus* small-denominated (less than $100,000) time deposits and money market mutual fund balances held by individuals.

LO14.3 Describe what "backs" the money supply.
The money supply in the United States is "backed" (guaranteed) by the government's ability to keep the value of money relatively stable, which in turn depends largely on the government's effectiveness in managing the money supply.

LO14.4 Discuss the structure of the Federal Reserve
The U.S. banking system consists of (*a*) the Board of Governors of the Federal Reserve System, (*b*) the 12 Federal Reserve Banks, and (*c*) some 4,600 commercial banks and 7,000 thrift institutions (mainly credit unions). The Board of Governors is the basic policy-making body for the entire banking system. The directives of the Board and the Federal Open Market Committee (FOMC) are

implemented through the 12 Federal Reserve Banks, which are simultaneously (a) central banks, (b) quasi-public banks, and (c) bankers' banks.

LO14.5 Identify the functions and responsibilities of the Federal Reserve.

The major functions of the Fed are to (a) issue Federal Reserve Notes, (b) hold reserves deposited by banks and thrifts (and set reserve requirements, if any), (c) lend money to financial institutions and serve as the lender of last resort in national financial emergencies, (d) provide for the rapid collection of checks, (e) act as the fiscal agent for the federal government, (f) supervise the operations of the banks, and (g) regulate the supply of money in the economy's best interests.

The Fed is essentially an independent institution, controlled neither by the president nor by Congress. This independence shields the Fed from political pressure and allows it to raise and lower interest rates (via changes in the money supply) as needed to promote full employment, price stability, and economic growth.

LO14.6 Explain the fractional reserve system used by U.S. banks and why the Fed might wish to influence their creation of checkable-deposit money.

Under a fractional reserve banking system, only a portion (fraction) of checkable deposits are backed by currency. That fractional backing implies that a U.S. banks are vulnerable to bank panics. To mitigate that risk, the U.S. banking system employs deposit insurance. The Fed also stands ready to make emergency loans to banks experiencing bank runs.

Under a fractional reserve system, banks and thrifts create checkable-deposit money any time they extend a loan. Contrariwise, checkable-deposit money is destroyed (ceases to exist) whenever a bank or thrift loan is repaid.

The Fed can alter the money supply and affect interest rates and economic activity by altering the incentives and restrictions that it places on bank lending and bank money creation. Any decision by the Fed that influences bank lending will tend to change: the total amount of checkable-deposit money, the overall money supply, the total volume of lending, interest rates, and overall economic activity.

LO14.7 Explain how the equilibrium interest rate is determined and why interest rates and bond prices vary inversely.

The total demand for money consists of the transactions demand for money plus the asset demand for money. The amount of money demanded for transactions varies directly with nominal GDP; the amount of money demanded as an asset varies inversely with the interest rate. The market for money combines the total demand for money (= transaction demand + asset demand) with money supply to determine equilibrium interest rates.

The Fed can alter the interest rate by increasing or decreasing the money supply. When it does so, it affects some interest rates more than others. Those that are more (less) strongly affected are those paid on loans of low (high) risk and short (long) duration.

Interest rates and bond prices are inversely related.

Terms and Concepts

medium of exchange
unit of account
store of value
liquidity
M1
Federal Reserve Notes
token money
checkable deposits
commercial bank

thrift institution
near-money
M2
time deposits
money market mutual fund (MMMF)
legal tender
Federal Reserve System
Board of Governors
Federal Reserve Banks

reserve balances
Federal Open Market Committee (FOMC)
fractional reserve banking system
interest
transactions demand for money
asset demand for money
total demand for money
cryptocurrency

Discussion Questions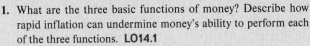

1. What are the three basic functions of money? Describe how rapid inflation can undermine money's ability to perform each of the three functions. **LO14.1**
2. Which two of the following financial institutions offer checkable deposits included within the M1 money supply: mutual fund companies; insurance companies; commercial banks; securities firms; thrift institutions? Which of the following items is *not* included in either M1 or M2: currency held by the public; checkable deposits; money market mutual fund balances; small-denominated (less than $100,000) time deposits; currency held by banks; savings deposits? **LO14.2**
3. What are the components of the M1 money supply? What is the largest component? Which of the components of M1 is legal

tender? Why is the face value of a coin greater than its intrinsic value? What near-monies are included in the M2 money supply? **LO14.2**
4. Explain and evaluate the following statements: **LO14.2**
   a. The invention of money is one of the great achievements of humanity, for without it the enrichment that comes from broadening trade would have been impossible.
   b. Money is whatever society says it is.
   c. In the United States, the debts of government and commercial banks are used as money.
   d. People often say they would like to have more money, but what they usually mean is that they would like to have more goods and services.

e. When the price of everything goes up, it is not because every-thing is worth more but because the currency is worth less.

f. Any central bank can create money; the trick is to create enough, but not too much, of it.

5. What "backs" the money supply in the United States? What determines the value (domestic purchasing power) of money? How does the purchasing power of money relate to the price level? In the United States, who is responsible for maintaining money's purchasing power? **LO14.3**

6. How is the chairperson of the Federal Reserve System selected? Describe the relationship between the Board of Governors of the Federal Reserve System and the 12 Federal Reserve Banks. What is the purpose of the Federal Open Market Committee (FOMC)? What is its makeup? **LO14.4**

7. The following are two hypothetical ways in which the Federal Reserve Board might be appointed. Would you favor either of these two methods over the present method? Why or why not? **LO14.4**

a. Upon taking office, the U.S. president appoints seven people to the Federal Reserve Board, including a chair. Each appointee must be confirmed by a majority vote of the Senate, and each serves the same 4-year term as the president.

b. Congress selects seven members from its ranks (four from the House of Representatives and three from the Senate) to serve at congressional pleasure as the Board of Governors of the Federal Reserve System.

8. What do economists mean when they say that the Federal Reserve Banks are central banks, quasi-public banks, and bankers' banks? **LO14.4**

9. Why do economists nearly uniformly support an independent Fed rather than one beholden directly to either the president or Congress? **LO14.5**

10. Identify three functions of the Federal Reserve, other than its main role of controlling the supply of money. **LO14.5**

11. Explain why merchants accepted gold receipts as a means of payment even though the receipts were issued by goldsmiths, not the government. What risk did goldsmiths introduce into the payments system by issuing loans in the form of gold receipts? **LO14.6**

12. Why is the banking system in the United States referred to as a fractional reserve banking system? What is the role of deposit insurance in a fractional reserve system? **LO14.6**

13. What is the basic determinant of (*a*) the transactions demand and (*b*) the asset demand for money? Explain how to combine these two demands graphically to determine total money demand. How is the equilibrium interest rate in the money market determined? Use a graph to show how an increase in the total demand for money affects the equilibrium interest rate (no change in money supply). Use your general knowledge of equilibrium prices to explain why the previous interest rate is no longer sustainable. **LO14.7**

14. **LAST WORD** What is a blockchain and how can it be used to keep track of property rights? Have any cryptocurrencies become popular with consumers for buying goods and services? How could a central bank use its CBDC to apply fiscal stimulus during a recession?

Review Questions

1. The three functions of money are: **LO14.1**
   a. liquidity, store of value, and gifting.
   b. medium of exchange, unit of account, and liquidity.
   c. liquidity, unit of account, and gifting.
   d. medium of exchange, unit of account, and store of value.

2. Suppose that a small country currently has $4 million of currency in circulation, $6 million of checkable deposits, $200 million of savings deposits, $40 million of small-denominated time deposits, and $30 million of money market mutual fund deposits. From these numbers we see that this small country's *M*1 money supply is _____, while its *M*2 money supply is _____. **LO14.2**
   a. $10 million; $280 million
   b. $10 million; $270 million
   c. $210 million; $280 million
   d. $250 million; $270 million

3. Recall the formula that states that $V = 1/P$, where V is the value of the dollar and P is the price level. If the price level falls from 1 to 0.75, what will happen to the value of the dollar? **LO14.3**
   a. It will rise by a third (33.3 percent).
   b. It will rise by a quarter (25 percent).
   c. It will fall by a quarter (−25 percent).
   d. It will fall by a third (−33.3 percent).

4. Which group votes on the open-market operations that are used to control the U.S. money supply and interest rates? **LO14.4**
   a. Federal Reserve System
   b. The 12 Federal Reserve Banks
   c. Board of Governors of the Federal Reserve System
   d. Federal Open Market Committee (FOMC)

5. An important reason why members of the Federal Reserve's Board of Governors are each given extremely long, 14-year terms is to: **LO14.4**
   a. insulate members from political pressures that could result in inflation.
   b. help older members avoid job searches before retiring.
   c. attract younger people with lots of time left in their careers.
   d. avoid the trouble of constantly having to deal with new members.

6. Which of the following is *not* a function of the Fed? **LO14.5**
   a. Setting reserve requirements for banks
   b. Advising Congress on fiscal policy
   c. Regulating the supply of money
   d. Serving as a lender of last resort

7. A goldsmith has $2 million of gold in his vaults. He issues $5 million in gold receipts. His gold holdings are what fraction of the paper money (gold receipts) he has issued? **LO14.6**
   a. 1/10
   b. 1/5
   c. 2/5
   d. 5/5

8. Suppose that last year $30 billion in new loans were extended by banks while $50 billion in old loans were paid off by borrowers. What happened to the money supply? **LO14.6**
   a. Increased
   b. Decreased
   c. Stayed the same

9. When bond prices go up, interest rates go _____. **LO14.7**
   a. up
   b. down
   c. nowhere

10. If nominal GDP increases and the money supply remains fixed, the interest rate will, other things equal, go _____. **LO14.7**
    a. up
    b. down
    c. nowhere

11. If the asset demand for money increases at the same time that the money supply decreases, the interest rate will _____, other things held equal. **LO14.7**
    a. rise
    b. fall
    c. remain unchanged

Problems

1. Assume that the following asset values (in millions of dollars) exist in Ironmania: Federal Reserve Notes in circulation = $700; Money market mutual funds (MMMFs) held by individuals = $400; Corporate bonds = $300; Iron ore deposits = $50; Currency in commercial banks = $100; Savings deposits = $140; Checkable deposits = $1,500; Small-denominated (less than $100,000) time deposits = $100; Coins in circulation = $40. **LO14.2**
    a. What is $M1$ in Ironmania?
    b. What is $M2$ in Ironmania?

2. Assume that Jimmy Cash has $2,000 in his checking account at Folsom Bank and uses his checking account debit card to withdraw $200 of cash from the bank's ATM machine. By what dollar amount did the $M1$ money supply change as a result of this single, isolated transaction? **LO14.2**

3. Suppose the price level and value of the U.S. dollar in year 1 are 1 and $1, respectively. If the price level rises to 1.25 in year 2, what is the new value of the dollar? If, instead, the price level falls to 0.50, what is the value of the dollar? **LO14.3**

4. Assume that the following data characterize the hypothetical economy of Trance: money supply = $200 billion; quantity of money demanded for transactions = $150 billion; quantity of money demanded as an asset = $10 billion at 12 percent

interest, increasing by $10 billion for each 2-percentage-point fall in the interest rate. **LO14.7**
    a. What is the equilibrium interest rate in Trance?
    b. At the equilibrium interest rate, what are the quantity of money supplied, the quantity of money demanded, the amount of money demanded for transactions, and the amount of money demanded as an asset in Trance?

5. Suppose a bond with no expiration date has a face value of $10,000 and annually pays $800 in fixed interest. In the table provided below, calculate and enter either the interest rate that the bond would yield to a bond buyer at each of the bond prices listed or the bond price at each of the interest yields shown. What generalization can you draw from the completed table? **LO14.7**

Bond Price	Interest Yield, %
$ 8,000	_____
_____	8.9
$10,000	_____
$11,000	_____
_____	6.2

Monetary Policy, GDP, and the Price Level

>> LEARNING OBJECTIVES

LO15.1 Explain the tools of monetary policy, including open-market operations, forward guidance, and the administered rates.

LO15.2 Relate how the Fed's tools and strategies have evolved over the past several decades.

LO15.3 Define the Fed's dual mandate and explain how conflicts can arise between meeting the inflation target and the unemployment target.

LO15.4 Explain how monetary policy affects real GDP and the price level.

LO15.5 Explain the advantages and shortcomings of monetary policy.

LO15.6 Describe how the various components of macroeconomic theory and stabilization policy fit together.

LO15.7 (Appendix) State the Taylor Rule and explain how it balances the two parts of the Fed's dual mandate.

monetary policy Actions or communications by a *central bank* intended to help it achieve its macroeconomic policy objectives, which for the U.S. *Federal Reserve* are full employment of the labor force and a stable *price level.*

Some newspaper commentators have stated that the chair of the Federal Reserve Board (Jerome Powell in 2022) is the second most powerful person in the United States, after the President. That statement is an exaggeration, but there is no doubt about the chair's influence, nor about the importance of the Federal Reserve and the **monetary policy** that it conducts. Such policy consists of deliberate changes in the money supply to influence interest rates and thus the total level of spending in the economy. The goal of monetary policy is to achieve and maintain price-level stability, full employment, and economic growth. The chair has some big responsibilities!

Tools of Monetary Policy

>> **LO15.1** Explain the tools of monetary policy, including open-market operations, forward guidance, and the administered rates.

The Federal Reserve employs a wide variety of "monetary policy tools" to help it manage the U.S. money supply and thereby affect interest rates and economic activity.

Open-Market Operations

The Fed has the legal right to buy and sell financial assets as part of its efforts to manage the money supply and interest rates. The only assets that the Fed normally buys or sells are U.S. government bonds (issued by the U.S. Treasury to finance the federal debt) or bonds issued by various federal agencies (like the Federal National Mortgage Association, which issues bonds to help finance home mortgages). There are major public markets in which these types of bonds are purchased and sold. Because these markets are said to be "open" to the public, the Fed's transactions in these markets are known as **open-market operations.**

The Fed's purchases and sales of bonds are made in large quantities so as to influence the equilibrium price of bonds and, consequently, their interest rates. In addition, the Fed's purchases and sales also affect the supply of money in the hands of the public, which is why the Fed's policy actions are referred to as monetary policy.

Buying Bonds to Decrease an Interest Rate As a concrete example of how open-market operations affect interest rates and the money supply, suppose that the Fed wishes to decrease the interest rate on 20-year U.S. Treasury bonds.

As we explained in the last chapter, a bond's price and its interest rate are inversely related; thus, when a bond's price goes up, its interest rate goes down, and vice versa. The Fed uses that inverse relationship to decide whether to purchase or sell a particular type of bond. Since the Fed wants, in this example, to decrease the interest rate on 20-year government bonds, it will know that it will have to increase their price. Thus, it will buy lots of 20-year Treasury bonds, knowing that the increase in demand generated by its purchases will raise the equilibrium price of those bonds and therefore decrease their equilibrium interest rate.

That purchase of bonds by the Fed will also automatically increase the money supply because the Fed will pay for those bonds by creating new money, which it hands over to the sellers of the bonds to pay them for the bonds that they just sold to the Fed.

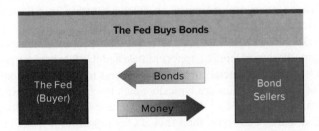

Selling Bonds to Increase an Interest Rate The Fed could also reverse the transactions just described if it wanted to achieve the opposite result, a higher interest rate on 20-year government bonds. In that case, the Fed would know that it would need to decrease the price of those bonds (since a lower bond price will imply a higher interest rate). To accomplish that goal, the Fed will go into its inventory of bonds (that it has built up over the years by purchasing bonds in the open markets) and find some 20-year Treasury bonds to sell. It will then sell those bonds on the open market, thereby increasing the supply of 20-year Treasury bonds and lowering their equilibrium price. That price decrease will automatically raise their interest rate while also decreasing the economy's money supply, since all the money paid by the buyers of those bonds to the Fed will be taken out of circulation by the Fed once the Fed receives those funds.

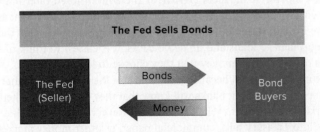

Table 15.1 summarizes the effects that open-market bond purchases and sales have on bond interest rates and the money supply.

Administered Rates

The Federal Reserve has three **administered rates,** or interest rates that are set (administered) by the Fed to influence the lending and borrowing decisions of financial institutions. The key point about these rates is that they are directly controlled by the Federal Reserve and, thus, not a

open-market operations The purchases and sales of U.S. government *securities* that the *Federal Reserve System* undertakes in order to influence *interest rates* and the *money supply;* one method by which the *Federal Reserve* implements *monetary policy.*

administered rate An *interest rate* set by a *central bank* to help it manage market-determined *interest rates.*

TABLE 15.1 The Effects of Open-Market Operations on the Money Supply, Bond Prices, and Interest Rates

Fed Action	Effect on Money Supply	Effect on Bond Price	Effect on Bond Interest Rate
The Fed buys bonds	The money supply increases because the Fed creates new money to pay for the bonds.	Fed buying increases bond *demand,* driving up the equilibrium bond price.	Bond interest rate decreases as equilibrium bond price increases.
The Fed sells bonds	The money supply decreases because the Fed removes from circulation the money that it receives for the bonds.	Fed selling increases bond *supply,* driving down the equilibrium bond price.	Bond interest rate increases as equilibrium bond price decreases.

product of market forces. That is very useful because their independence from market forces implies that they can serve as decisive outside influences on a wide variety of market equilibrium interest rates.

Two of the administered rates—the *interest rate on reserve balances* and the *overnight reverse repo rate*—are set, or administered, by the Fed to influence market equilibrium interest rates in the so-called money market. The term **money market** is an umbrella term that refers to a wide variety of short-term lending markets that involve commercial and financial loans that range in duration from overnight to 1 year. The money market includes the markets for U.S. Treasury bills, bank certificates of deposit, commercial paper (short-term promissory notes, or IOUs, issued by businesses), interbank loans (loans between banks and thrifts), money market mutual funds, and lending-and-repurchase agreements, or "repos," in which a valuable financial asset (usually a U.S. Treasury bond) serves as collateral.

money market The financial *markets* in which short-term, low-risk debt *securities* are traded, including U.S. Treasury bills, overnight loans of bank reserves, and commercial paper.

The money market offers those with funds to lend—banks, money managers, and individual investors—safe, liquid, short-term lending opportunities, and it offers borrowers—banks, securities dealers, hedge funds, and nonfinancial corporations—access to low-interest loans since the interest rates on low-risk/short-term loans are typically much lower than the interest rates on higher-risk/longer-term loans due to the fact that lenders demand less compensation (lower interest rates) for short-term loans of low risk than they do for longer-term loans of higher risk. The money market is very important because it accounts for about one-third of all lending and credit in the U.S. economy.

The Interest Rate on Reserve Balances (IORB) In 2020, the Fed ended its previous practice of requiring each bank (and thrift) to keep a minimum amount of currency reserves on deposit at their regional Federal Reserve Bank. Since that time, banks have been legally free to decide for themselves how big their reserves against withdrawals and bank runs will be. They have also been free to decide how large a fraction of those reserves they will keep in the form of currency as opposed to investments in highly liquid short-term debt assets (like Treasury bills and commercial paper) that can be sold almost instantly in the money market to raise cash to fund withdrawals or to fend off bank runs.

interest rate on reserve balances (IORB) The *interest rate* that the Federal Reserve pays *banks* and thrifts on any money that they deposit at (loan to) a Federal Reserve Bank on an overnight basis; one of the three *administered rates* set by the Federal Reserve.

The **interest rate on reserve balances (IORB)** is the administered rate that the Fed offers to commercial banks on any currency that they choose to keep on deposit overnight as reserve balances at one of the twelve Federal Reserve Banks. Since any such deposits are paid the IORB rate, they are functionally equivalent to loans and, in some cases, it is easiest to think of the IORB rate as the rate that banks receive for any money that they choose to lend to the Fed.

The IORB rate is very powerful because if the Fed sets the IORB rate higher than the interest rates available in the money market, banks will know that they can earn a higher interest rate (the IORB rate) by parking currency at their local Federal Reserve Bank than they can by investing their reserve funds into Treasury bills, commercial paper, or other money market loans.

That ability to modulate the willingness of banks to lend money into the money market gives the Fed substantial control over equilibrium interest rates in the money market. As a concrete example, suppose that the Fed sets the IORB rate at 2 percent. In that case, banks will not be interested in any money market investment opportunities that pay less than 2 percent since they could obviously do better by keeping their funds on deposit overnight at the Fed and receiving the 2-percent IORB rate. To compete for the attention of banks, those other lending opportunities will have to offer interest rates of at least 2 percent per year. Thus, by setting the IORB rate at 2 percent, the Fed has the ability to nudge money market interest rates into being near to or above 2 percent, as well.

In actual practice, some money market rates will remain a bit lower, since there are other lenders in the money markets besides banks. But by being able to control the interest rate at which banks are willing to lend into the money markets, the Fed can in large measure control money-market interest rates and thus all the business and financial activity in the economy that is affected by money-market rates.

Finally, please note that changes in the IORB rate also affect the size of the economy's overall money supply and thus influence the overall level of interest rates in the economy, too, as per Figure 14.4. That is true because whatever amount of money is lent by banks to the Fed at the IORB rate is money that sits in the Fed's vaults rather than circulating through the economy. Thus, when the Fed raises the IORB rate, it decreases the overall money supply and puts upward pressure on interest rates in general (not just on money-market interest rates).

The Overnight Reverse Repo Rate (ON RRP)   The **overnight reverse repo rate (ON RRP)** is the administered rate that the Fed offers to nonbank financial companies on any currency that they choose to lend to the Fed on an overnight basis. Those loans are transacted by means of a reverse version of a "lending and repurchase," or "repo," agreement. Under such a "reverse repo" transaction, the Fed sells a U.S. Treasury security to a lender at a price just below the bond's current market price while also promising to buy the bond back the next morning at the full market price. This "sell then buy back" arrangement is equivalent to an overnight loan from the lender to the Fed in which the bond serves as collateral in the case of default. That is true because if the Fed were to fail to buy the bond back the next morning as promised, the lender could sell the bond at full value to get their money back. On the other hand, if the Fed does buy the bond back the next morning as promised, then the difference between the slightly-below-market price at which the Fed sold the bond to the lender and the full market price at which the Fed buys the bond back will provide a monetary gain to the lender that is functionally equivalent to interest.

The Fed administers the *overnight reverse repo rate* separately from the *interest rate on reserve balances* for two reasons. First, the Fed is only legally allowed to pay interest on reserve balances to banks and other depository institutions that take checkable deposits. Thus, only depository institutions can receive the IORB rate on money that they leave on deposit overnight at the Fed. That matters because depository institutions are not the only financial firms that participate in the money market. Thus, if the Fed is to have even stronger control over money-market interest rates, it needs a way to influence the behavior of the nonbanks that operate in the money market. The *overnight reverse repo rate* satisfies that need because it allows the Fed to offer nonbanks an alternative to money market investments. Just as the availability of the IORB rate implies that banks will not want to invest in the money market at any rate below the IORB rate, the availability of the ON RRP rate ensures that nonbanks will not want to invest in the money market at any rate below the ON RRP rate.

Thus, between the IORB rate offered to depository institutions like banks and the ON RRP rate offered to nondepository financial firms like money market mutual funds, the Fed has strong control over money-market interest rates. In fact, one way to think about the IORB and ON RRP rates is that they give the Fed the ability to "put a floor" under money-market rates, meaning a level below which money-market rates are unlikely to go. As an example, suppose that the Fed sets the IORB rate at 1.75 percent and the ON RRP rate at 1.65 percent. Then there would be hardly any participants in the money market that would lend money for less than 1.65 percent per year. The banks will not lend for anything less than the 1.75 percent IORB rate that they can get by loaning money to the Fed, and the nonbanks will not lend for anything less than the 1.65 percent ON RRP rate that they can get for loaning money to the Fed. Thus, it is highly likely that nearly every interest rate in the money market will end up being near to or above 1.65 percent.

The Fed has consistently set the ON RRP rate about 0.10 percentage points below the IORB rate rather than, for instance, setting them at equal rates. That gap allows the Fed to manage the money-market lending behavior of banks and nonbanks independently of each other, rather than give both groups of financial firms exactly the same incentives with regard to lending to the Fed or lending into the money market (as would be the case if the Fed set the ON RRP and IORB rates at equal levels).

Finally, please note that changes in the ON RRP rate also affect the size of the economy's overall money supply and thus influence the overall level of interest rates in the economy, as well, as per Figure 14.4. That is true because whatever amount of money is lent by nonbanks to the Fed

overnight reverse repo rate (ON RRP)   The *interest rate* that the Federal Reserve pays eligible nonbank financial firms for any money that they loan to a Federal Reserve Bank overnight using a reverse *repo* transaction; one of the three *administered rates* set by the *Federal Reserve.*

at the ON RRP rate is money that sits in the Fed's vaults rather than circulating in the economy. Thus, when the Fed raises the ON RRP rate, it decreases the overall money supply and puts upward pressure on interest rates in general (not just on money-market interest rates).

The Discount Rate The so-called *discount rate* is the third and final of the Fed's three administered interest rates. Unlike the IORB and ON RRP rates, which are both rates at which financial institutions can lend money *to* the Fed, the **discount rate** is an interest rate at which depository institutions can borrow money *from* the Fed. Any such loans must be collateralized, meaning that the Fed will loan a bank money at the discount rate but only if the bank posts U.S. Treasury securities or other low-risk bonds as collateral that the Fed will get to keep if the bank does not repay the loan.

> **discount rate** The interest rate that the *Federal Reserve Banks* charge on the loans they make to *commercial banks* and *thrifts;* one of the three *administered rates* set by the *Federal Reserve.*

The point of the discount rate is to give banks a backup source of low-cost (that is, low-interest-rate) liquidity if they are unable to obtain funds in the money market. Normally that is not an issue, but if a specific bank is hit with a bank run, then it may not be able to find anyone in the money market willing to lend it the money that it needs to calm the bank run by demonstrating that it has the ability to fulfill each and every request from depositors to withdraw funds. In such a situation, the bank can go to the Fed and borrow the currency it needs to calm the panic. The rate that it will pay on that loan is the discount rate, and the currency that is borrowed from the Fed will come in the form of newly created reserve balances that the Fed will deposit into the bank's account at the Fed.

Another situation in which the discount rate is useful is during major financial crises. During such crises, part or all of the money market may freeze up, so that even the highest quality borrowers with perfect credit ratings cannot borrow money. That happened during the financial crisis in 2008, but the banking system was not hit with any widespread bank runs because people knew that even if a bank panic started, the banks involved could borrow whatever money they might need to pay depositors and calm the panic from the Fed at the discount rate.

The Fed always sets the discount rate higher than the IORB rate because if the discount rate (at which banks can borrow *from* the Fed) were lower than the IORB rate (at which banks can lend *to* the Fed), banks would have access to an infinitely large and totally unearned profit opportunity, since they could, for instance, borrow some money at, say, 1.5 percent from the Fed and then turn right around and lend that money back to the Fed at a higher interest rate, like 2.5 percent. To prevent that sort of *arbitrage* situation from ever arising, the Fed always sets the discount rate higher than the IORB rate.

Table 15.2 summarizes the three administered rates and gives their respective values in January 2020, before the COVID-19 pandemic, and January 2022, after the Fed had aggressively lowered the administered rates to help fight the negative economic consequences of the pandemic.

The Fed's Ability to Enforce the Administered Rates A key point about the three administered rates is that the Fed has 100 percent credibility in enforcing them, due to the Fed's ability to create as much new money as it wants, any time it wants.

TABLE 15.2 The Federal Reserve's Three Administered Interest Rates, January 2020 and January 2022

Name	Eligible Entities	Description	Purpose	Percentage Rate in January 2020	Percentage Rate in January 2022
Discount rate	Depository institutions (banks and thrifts)	Interest rate paid *to* the Fed for currency reserves borrowed against collateral	Low-cost emergency liquidity for depository institutions	2.25	0.25
Interest on reserve balances (IORB)	Depository institutions (banks and thrifts)	Interest rate paid *by* the Fed on currency deposits held at Federal Reserve Banks	Control of money-market interest rates	1.55	0.15
Overnight reverse repo rate (ON RRP)	Select nondepository financial firms, including money market funds	Interest rate paid *by* the Fed on collateralized loans	Control of money-market interest rates	1.45	0.05

Consider the two rates that the Fed uses to control interest rates in the money market. The IORB and ON RRP rates involve the Fed paying interest on money that is loaned to it overnight by, respectively, banks and nonbanks. The Fed's promise to pay interest on those loans is fully credible because the Fed can create the money necessary to pay that interest any time it wants and in any amount it wants. Thus, nobody on Wall Street ever doubts the ability of the Fed to use IORB and ON RRP to incentivize banks and nonbanks to lend to the Fed at those rates rather than into the money market at lower rates.

Similarly, consider the money that banks are eligible to borrow from the Fed at the discount rate. That lending facility is intended to calm financial markets if there is a bank run or a financial crisis. It is fully credible in those situations because the Fed can create however much money as may be needed to satisfy every single request that the Fed may receive from banks to borrow at the discount rate. Thus, the Fed's ability to use the discount rate to calm bank panics is also unlimited.

Forward Guidance

Another powerful tool that the Fed has at its disposal is **forward guidance,** or intentionally and clearly communicating to the public exactly how the Federal Reserve sees the state of the economy and, on that basis, how the Fed intends to conduct monetary policy going forward. Those communications are influential because individuals and businesses will use what the Fed says to help shape their own spending and investment decisions. In fact, forward guidance may be strong enough to alter the economy's macroeconomic trajectory just by itself.

If, for example, the Fed says that the economy seems to be slipping into a recession and, as a result, it plans to lower interest rates over the following six months to stimulate the economy, businesses that might have otherwise decided to cut back on investment spending (because they feared a deep recession and collapsing sales) may now decide to go ahead and invest in new plant and equipment (because they can see that the Fed shares their fears and is going to take strong steps to try to partly preclude—or even fully avert—the looming recession). Thus, as long as the Fed has credibility with the public, its ability to shape public expectations with forward guidance is itself a powerful monetary policy tool that can be used in conjunction with the Fed's other monetary policy tools.

Along those lines, it should be noted that forward guidance can affect the economy's overall money supply. That is true because, as you will recall from the previous chapter, part of the economy's money supply is *checkable deposits* held at banks and thrifts. That is important to remember with respect to forward guidance because when banks and thrifts issue new loans, they do so by creating new checkable-deposit money that gets deposited into borrowers' checking accounts.

- If the Fed's forward guidance is optimistic, or "positive," about the economy's prospects, then loan officers and potential borrowers will likely feel more positive about the economy's prospects, too, and thus more likely to want to borrow and lend. If the dollar volume of new loans being granted exceeds the dollar value of old loans being paid off, the total amount of checkable-deposit money will increase, thereby increasing the overall size of the money supply, all other things equal.
- Contrariwise, if the Fed's forward guidance is pessimistic, or "negative," about the economy's prospects, then it will be likely that fewer loans will be demanded and granted. If the dollar volume of new loans being granted ends up being less than the dollar value of old loans being paid off, the total amount of checkable-deposit money will decrease, thereby reducing the overall size of the money supply, all other things equal.

The Federal Funds Rate Many central banks have a **policy rate** that they use as part of their forward guidance efforts. The policy rate helps to communicate to the public, in a very brief and easy to understand format, the bank's **monetary policy stance,** that is, whether the bank's current outlook with respect to monetary policy is expansionary, restrictive, or neutral.

The Federal Reserve's policy rate is known as the **federal funds rate,** and, like all policy rates, it is an interest rate on a specific type of short-term, low-risk loan. In some countries, the policy rate is the interest rate on overnight loans of currency that are negotiated between commercial

forward guidance Public communications made by a *central bank* to describe (1) how it perceives the state of the *economy* and (2) how it intends to manage *monetary policy.*

policy rate A short-term *interest rate* that a *central bank* manages to help communicate the stance of *monetary policy* as well as to achieve its *monetary policy* goals.

monetary policy stance A *central bank's* disposition regarding how it sees the current and future state of the economy and, thus, whether its current monetary policy actions will be consistent with an *expansionary monetary policy,* a *restrictive monetary policy,* or a *neutral monetary policy.*

federal funds rate The *interest rate* that U.S. banks and other nonbank financial firms charge one another on overnight loans of *currency* held on deposit at one of the twelve *Federal Reserve Banks;* the Federal Reserve's *policy rate.*

banks. In the United States, the policy rate is the overnight lending rate that large financial firms and government agencies charge each other to borrow currency held on deposit at one of the Federal Reserve Banks. That *federal funds rate* is determined in the **federal funds market,** whose participants include U.S. commercial banks and thrifts, U.S. branches of foreign banks, savings and loan organizations, and government-sponsored enterprises, such as the Federal National Mortgage Association (Fannie Mae), as well as securities firms and agencies of the federal government.

It should be noted, however, that while the *federal funds market* is indeed a competitive market in which supply and demand determine an equilibrium price, it is nevertheless a highly constrained and aggressively managed market. At any moment in time, the Fed sets a **federal funds target range** for the federal funds rate. This target range is usually only a quarter-of-a-percent wide. Thus, for example, the upper limit of the federal funds target range may be set at 2.00 percent per year while the bottom limit is set at 1.75 percent per year. At other times, the target range may be set so that the upper limit is 0.25 percent per year while the bottom limit is 0.00 percent per year. In almost all cases, the gap between the upper and lower limits is exactly 0.25 percent.

The Fed then adjusts the IORB rate available to depository institutions and the ON RRP rate available to nondepository financial firms to ensure that the equilibrium interest rate in the federal funds market—the **effective federal funds rate**—always ends up being within the *federal funds target range*. That level of control over the equilibrium interest rate in the federal funds market is possible because the federal funds market is part of the overall money market and, as you know, the Fed can guide all of the interest rates within the money market by adjusting the IORB rate and the ON RRP rate either higher or lower. If the Fed wants the equilibrium *effective federal funds rate* to fall, it will lower the IORB and ON RRP rates. And if the Fed wants the equilibrium *effective federal funds rate* to rise, it will raise the IORB and ON RRP rates.

One of the great benefits to the Fed of publicly announcing the federal funds target range is simplicity. The general public is largely unaware of the existence of the administered rates, how open-market operations work, or that the Fed is constantly taking steps to guide short-term interest rates by influencing the money market. But the Fed is able to convey in an uncomplicated fashion the overall stance of monetary policy by simply announcing the current target range for the federal funds rate and whether it expects to raise or lower the target range in the future based on current and projected macroeconomic conditions. Individuals and businesses can then gather most of what they need to know from simple headlines, such as, "The Fed Raises Target Range to Fight Inflation" or "Fearing Recession, FOMC Lowers Federal Funds Target Range."

Finally, please note that changing the federal funds target range and then using IORB and ON RRP to guide the effective federal funds rate into the target range changes the economy's money supply because, as we mentioned above, changes in IORB and ON RRP directly alter the amount of money in the hands of the public. When the IORB and ON RRP interest rates are increased, financial firms lend more money to the Fed, thereby reducing the amount of money held by the public outside the Fed. And contrariwise, when the IORB and ON RRP interest rates are decreased, financial firms lend less money to the Fed, thereby increasing the amount of money held by the public outside the Fed. Those changes in the economy's overall money supply in turn affect the overall level of interest rates in the economy, as per Figure 14.4.

QUICK REVIEW

15.1

▶ The Fed has three main tools of monetary control: (a) open-market operations, (b) changing the administered interest rates, and (c) forward guidance.

▶ The three administered interest rates are the interest rate on reserve balances (IORB) at which banks and other depository institutions can loan money to the Fed; the overnight reverse repo rate (ON RRP) at which nondepository financial institutions can loan money to the Fed;

and the discount rate at which banks and other depository institutions can borrow money from the Fed.

▶ The Fed uses the federal funds target range to signal its monetary policy stance to the public.

▶ Open-market operations, changes in the administered rates, and forward guidance alter the money supply.

The Evolution of the Fed's Tools and Strategies

A good way to understand how the Federal Reserve System uses its current set of monetary policy tools to influence the macroeconomy is to study how its set of tools, and its strategies for employing those tools, have evolved over the past 30 years, mostly as a result of the major challenges the Fed faced during the financial crisis of 2007–2008.

>> LO15.2 Relate how the Fed's tools and strategies have evolved over the past several decades.

From Conventional to Unconventional

Before the extremely severe financial crisis of 2007–2008, the Fed employed a smaller collection of monetary policy tools. It was not yet, for example, paying IORB or ON RRP, and thus could not use them to control the effective federal funds rate or other money-market interest rates.

The Fed did, however, set targets for the federal funds rate back then just as it does today. But the way that the Fed achieved those targets was not by adjusting the IORB or ON RRP rates (which did not yet exist). Instead, the Fed used open-market operations to guide the effective federal funds rate toward its target.

To do that, the Fed would first announce a change in its target for the federal funds rate and then buy or sell short-term U.S. Treasury securities from banks to alter the amounts of money (in the form of *reserve balances*) that the banks held at the Fed. Those changes in the amounts of money held by banks would cause those institutions to lend more or less money in the federal funds market and thus alter the equilibrium federal funds rate that is determined in that market.

The financial crisis of 2007–2008 was so severe, however, that the Fed felt it necessary to slash the federal funds rate from 5.25 percent in July 2007 down to nearly zero percent in December 2008. That was deeply problematic because, as the federal funds rate approached zero, the Fed appeared to be "out of ammunition" with respect to being able to apply further stimulus to an economy that was experiencing its worst recession since the Great Depression of the 1930s.

That pessimism was based on the fact that, up to that point in time, the Fed's primary way of stimulating the U.S. economy when it was experiencing a business downturn was to stimulate investment spending by lowering the federal funds rate and thereby guiding other interest rates lower, too. Money-market rates invariably fell when the federal funds rate fell, and longer-term interest rates would also typically decline at least somewhat when the federal funds rate was reduced. But with the effective federal funds rate already reduced to just 0.16 percent in late 2008, there appeared to be no way for the Fed to generate any further monetary policy stimulus since it didn't seem possible for the Fed to reduce the federal funds rate by any substantial additional amount since doing so would result in a negative interest rate. If zero was the limit, the Fed's ability to simulate the economy was maxed out.

The Zero Lower Bound By cutting the effective federal funds rate to nearly zero, the Fed had been forced to confront the **zero lower bound problem,** which refers to the fact that once short-term interest rates are at zero percent, any further rate cuts will probably cause more harm than good. To understand why, first note that further rate cuts are indeed possible. That may sound strange, but the Fed is very much capable of forcing short-term interest rates below zero, into negative territory.

As an example, consider a 1-year bond that will pay its owner $103 in a year. If you bought that bond today for $100 and held it for a year, you would get a positive 3 percent return since you would, in a year's time, receive three dollars more than the $100 that you paid today. But suppose the Fed buys so many of this type of bond that its price today rises to $105. Then if you bought it today for $105 and held it for a year, you would end up with a *negative* rate of return because what you would get for it in a year ($103) would be less than what you are paying for it today ($105).

From this example, it is clear that the Fed could always, if it wanted to, drive bond prices up high enough to cause their interest rates to turn negative. Indeed, the Fed's legal authority to print money guarantees it the ability to drive bond prices up however high it would like and thus generate negative interest rates to whatever degree it might like.

zero lower bound problem The constraint placed on the ability of a *central bank* to stimulate the economy through lower short-term *interest rates* by the fact that short-term *interest rates* cannot be driven lower than zero without causing depositors to withdraw funds from the banking system.

The Fed, however, has never seen fit to follow such a strategy. That is because negative interest rates might discourage, rather than encourage, spending in the economy. In particular, if the Fed were to force the federal funds rate into negative territory, then interest rates on checking accounts and money-market funds would likely go negative, too. That is a big problem because many people who hold checking accounts and money-market accounts would withdraw all of their money from those accounts in favor of cash, which by definition has neither a positive nor a negative interest rate. That is, they would prefer getting zero interest on physical cash as compared with negative rates on deposit accounts (whose balances, due to those negative rates, would necessarily shrink over time as the negative rates ate away at their value).

Those withdrawals would amount to a slow-motion bank panic that would drain loanable funds from the banking system. In addition, the overall rate of consumption spending might also decline due to the fact that we live in the age of e-commerce, in which so much economic activity is transacted electronically. If a negative interest rate caused people to convert checking account balances that are easily accessed electronically into physical cash that cannot be spent online, there might be less economic activity overall, all other things equal.

On the other hand, some economists have conjectured that negative interest rates might possibly stimulate economic activity, their hypothesis being that negative interest rates on checking account balances might cause people to try to spend their money more rapidly, before the negative rates reduced the spending power of those balances.

After considering the various theoretical conjectures that economists were making about the possible economic effects of negative interest rates, the Fed concluded that negative interest rates were too risky to try, since nobody actually knew if negative rates would make the economy's recessionary situation better or worse. But with negative rates being a "no go," the Fed needed to figure out some other way to try to stimulate the economy.

Quantitative Easing The Fed's pre-crisis strategy of focusing almost entirely on the federal funds rate and other short-term interest rates had been the standard, or "conventional," approach to monetary policy for many decades. But with further reductions of short-term rates not being an option during the 2007–2009 financial crisis due to the zero lower bound problem, the Fed needed to come up with a new, "unconventional" approach that could be used to apply additional stimulus after it had already slashed the federal funds rate down to nearly zero. The Fed's solution was to keep the federal funds rate and other short-term interest rates at a low level (through the use of IORB and ON RRP) while pioneering the use of open-market operations that would lower the longer-term interest rates that drive many business investment decisions.

As background, please understand that economists believe that most decisions by businesses about whether to invest in new capital equipment or spend money on R&D depend on long-term interest rates. That is because businesses wish to synchronize the monetary returns that they hope will be generated by those investments with the debt payments needed to repay the loans that were used to fund those investments. As a simple example, consider a farmer who wishes to plant a new grove of orange trees. It will take at least five years before those trees are mature enough to generate full harvests. Thus, if the farmer is investigating various loan options to fund the planting of those trees, he will prefer a long-term loan that won't be due or require monthly payments for at least five years. That way, by the time he has to make loan payments, the trees will be mature and producing not only fruit but also revenue, some of which can be used to pay back the loan.

Many business investments take at least a year or two to start generating revenue. Certain ones, like R&D for innovative new medicines, may not pay off for ten or twenty years. Thus, when it comes to influencing business investment decisions, longer-term interest rates are very important. It was with that in mind that the Fed initiated the program that would end up being called *quantitative easing,* or QE.

The Fed put this new strategy into effect by purchasing hundreds of billions of dollars' worth of 10-year and 20-year U.S. Treasury bonds as well as equally large amounts of long-duration bonds issued by federal agencies. Those purchases raised the prices of those particular long-duration federally issued bonds, thereby reducing their interest rates. But the Fed was aiming for wider effects because it knew that by lowering the interest rates on longer-duration government bonds, it would also tend to lower the interest rates on the longer-duration bonds that private companies issue to fund investment spending. Those spillover effects were expected to occur because bonds of similar duration compete with each other for the economy's limited supply of loanable funds. By lowering the interest rates on longer-term *federally issued* debt, the Fed would be able to put downward pressure on longer-term *privately issued* debt, much of which is used, as we just mentioned, to fund business investment spending.

This strategy of using open-market bond purchases to try to drive down all sorts of longer-term interest rates came to be known as **quantitative easing, or QE,** because the Fed would always pre-announce the *quantity* of money that it was going to create and spend on a particular round of bond buying in order to generate an *easing* of the borrowing conditions (interest rates) facing companies that wished to borrow by issuing longer-term bonds.

The Fed's first round of quantitative easing started in November 2008 when the Fed pre-announced that it was going to buy $800 billion of mortgage-backed securities from federal agencies like the Federal Home Loan Mortgage Corporation (Freddie Mac). Later rounds of quantitative easing included a pre-announced commitment to buy $600 billion of U.S. Treasury bonds by June 30, 2011, as well as a pre-announced commitment that the Fed would, starting in December of 2012, purchase $85 billion per month of various types of long-term Treasury and agency bonds until it felt that the economy had recovered enough that such purchases were no longer needed.

Forward Guidance Another key innovation after the financial crisis was the Fed's expanded use of forward guidance. As just mentioned, during the financial crisis, the Fed started to pre-announce each round of quantitative easing. It did so to indicate to the public not only that it was concerned about the lingering effects of the 2007–2009 recession but that, in addition to lowering short-term interest rates down to extremely low levels, it was going to take an additional concrete step—quantitative easing—to help the economy recover as quickly as possible.

The Fed also put more emphasis on making clear statements about the federal funds target range and making it crystal clear to the public just how the FOMC members felt at any point in time about the current state of the economy and its future prospects. This was done by issuing an official statement after each FOMC meeting that summarized exactly how the FOMC members saw the current macroeconomic situation and what current and future actions they anticipated taking.

All of this forward guidance was done deliberately to help instill a feeling of confidence on the part of the public. The Fed's message was: "Hey, everybody! We are *not* out of ammunition. Short-term interest rates may be near zero, but we have innovative new ways to stimulate the economy, including trillions of dollars' worth of quantitative easing that will put downward pressure on longer-term interest rates."

quantitative easing (QE)
An *open-market operation* in which a *central bank* pre-announces that it will spend a fixed quantity of *money* purchasing long-term bonds so as to lower long-term *interest rates* and thereby ease *credit* conditions for long-horizon investors, such as *businesses* borrowing to purchase *capital goods*.

CONSIDER THIS . . .

Picking Winners

It might have occurred to you to wonder why the Fed limits its open-market operations to purchases and sales of government debt. If the Fed's goal is to affect economic activity, why shouldn't it also purchase a wider variety of financial assets, such as corporate bonds, corporate stock, real estate, or even industrial commodities like oil and lumber?

The simplest answer is that purchasing most of those assets would be illegal because congress has not yet passed a law that would allow the Fed to buy or sell those assets. More important, however, is *why* congress has not given the Fed that latitude.

Congress does not want the Fed creating favoritism or inefficiencies in the private sector. If the Fed, for instance,

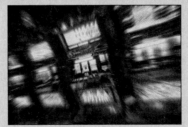
Design Pics

announced that it would be purchasing a lot of Tesla bonds and thereby lowering the interest rate at which Tesla corporation can borrow, it would give Tesla a competitive advantage over its auto-making competitors whose bonds the Fed would not be buying. And if the Fed regularly purchased or sold industrial commodities like oil, copper, and aluminum, the equilibrium quantities and prices in those markets would not reflect the social optimum where MB = MC. Instead, the Fed would likely cause over- or under-production that would generate deadweight *efficiency losses* to society.

To avoid those sorts of problems, the Fed sticks to government bonds.

Evaluating the New Normal

By the mid-2010s, the economy had recovered enough that the Fed began to taper down its quantitative-easing efforts. A couple of years later, as the economy recovered even more, the Fed began to reverse QE with a policy that came to be known as **quantitative tightening, or QT.** Instead of buying long-term government bonds to lower their interest rates, the Fed began to sell them in order to raise their interest rates. That made good sense because a robustly growing economy clearly did not need the stimulus provided by artificially low long-term interest rates.

An open question, however, was whether the Fed should (1) return to the conventional monetary policy it had practiced before the financial crisis or (2) treat the unconventional monetary policy that it had developed during the crisis as the "new normal."

One argument in favor of making unconventional monetary policy the new normal was that it seemed to have worked pretty well during and after the financial crisis. A second Great Depression had been averted, and by the late 2010s the economy was enjoying full employment and low inflation. Thus, many asked whether there would be any benefit to going back to the old ways of doing things. Had not the old ways been incapable of dealing with the zero lower bound? And how much worse might the crisis have been if the Fed had not been willing to innovate?

Along those lines, proponents of the new normal asked rhetorical questions like: Wasn't it a good thing that the Fed had learned to control short-term interest rates with IORB and ON RRP rather than open-market operations? Wasn't it good that the Fed had started doing QE and QT so that it could affect long-term interest rates as well as short-term interest rates and thereby allow itself the opportunity to add further stimulus to the economy even when short-term interest rates were up against the zero lower bound? And, in addition to all that, wasn't it a positive thing that the Fed could now control short-term and long-term interest rates independently of one another?

One counterargument was that the artificially low long-term interest rates created by QE may have encouraged congress to run larger budget deficits than it otherwise would have, thereby making it more likely that, to repay that additional debt, some future congress would feel compelled to impose sharply higher tax rates that would then slow economic growth by removing from the private sector trillions of dollars that would otherwise have gone toward consumer spending or business investment.

Another fear was that the trillions of dollars of reserves that the Fed had created to finance its QE bond purchases might end up generating a huge inflation if those massive quantities of bank reserves were ever used to vastly increase bank lending and the amount of checkable account deposit money that was circulating in the economy. A notable fact about IORB and ON RRP, however, is that they can be used to mitigate that inflationary threat.

That is true because whenever the Fed raises the IORB and ON RRP rates, it encourages banks and other financial firms to lend reserves to the Fed rather than using them to back new loans and thereby create new checkable deposit money. The higher the IORB and ON RRP rates, the greater the quantity of reserves that banks will lend to the Fed, thereby reducing their ability to create new checkable deposit money, all other things equal.

Figuratively speaking, IORB and ON RRP transform the Fed's own vaults into a giant "money sponge" that the Fed can use to reduce the overall money supply, thereby reducing inflationary pressures, all other things equal. It was indeed the case that when inflation unexpectedly shot up to 7.0 percent per year in 2021, one of the Fed's first policy moves was to signal that it would begin raising the IORB and ON RRP rates as part of its efforts to try to get inflation back under control.

These debates will continue. But for the time being, the Fed has announced that unconventional monetary policy is the new normal, and that it will continue to make use of the tools and strategies that it developed during the financial crisis.

---

quantitative tightening (QT) The opposite of *quantitative easing.* An *open-market operation* in which a *central bank* pre-announces that it will sell a fixed quantity of long-term bonds so as to raise long-term *interest rates* and thereby tighten *credit* conditions for long-horizon investors, such as *businesses* borrowing to purchase *capital goods.*

QUICK REVIEW

15.2

▶ The severity of the 2007–2008 financial crisis caused the Fed to slash short-term interest rates down to nearly zero.

▶ To get around the zero lower bound problem, the Fed introduced several unconventional monetary policies, including the use of quantitative easing, or

QE, to lower the longer-term interest rates that have the greatest effect on business investment and R&D spending.

▶ The Fed also increased its use of forward guidance and began using the IORB and ON RRP rates to control short-term interest rates.

The Dual Mandate

Now that you understand the Fed's monetary policy tools, it's time to study how the Fed uses those tools to comply with the dual mandate given to it by congress in 1977.

The **dual mandate** states that the Fed's two highest objectives should be full employment and stable prices. To that end, the Fed has set itself two concrete targets that it pursues simultaneously:

1. Achieving the *full-employment rate of unemployment,* which is currently around 3 to 4 percent of the labor force.
2. Achieving the Fed's *target rate of inflation,* which is currently set at 2 percent per year.

The Fed's Unemployment Target

The **full-employment rate of unemployment,** or *natural rate of unemployment*, is the unemployment rate that exists in an economy when it is producing at potential output (full employment). At full employment, every person who wants a job is employed, so that there is zero *cyclical unemployment.* Structural and frictional unemployment do remain, however, as there will still be some people either between jobs (*frictional unemployment*) or in need of retraining after their old jobs were eliminated due to changes in consumer preferences, evolving production technologies, or offshoring (*structural unemployment*). Thus, the full-employment rate of unemployment is not zero unemployment, but, rather, a modest positive number that reflects frictional and structural unemployment.

The full-employment rate of unemployment also reflects changes in government industrial policy and labor force regulations, the size of labor force growth relative to the growth rate of the demand for labor, and a wide variety of other factors that affect how much labor is necessary to produce the full-employment level of output, how much labor is available to produce it, and how quickly the frictionally and structurally unemployed return to work. These factors change over time, thereby causing the full-employment rate of unemployment to change over time, too.

The full-employment rate of unemployment is currently estimated to lie somewhere between 3 and 4 percent of the labor force. In December 2021, for example, the median estimate made by Federal Reserve board members and Federal Reserve bank presidents was 3.5 percent. In practice, this estimate serves as the FOMC's **target rate of unemployment.**

- If the actual unemployment rate rises appreciably higher than 3.5 percent, the Fed will be inclined, other things equal, toward assuming that the economy is decelerating and consequently in need of an **expansionary monetary policy** (or "easy money" policy) under which the Fed would increase the money supply and lower interest rates to encourage investment and consumption spending.
- Contrariwise, if the actual unemployment rate falls appreciably below 3.5 percent, the Fed will be inclined, other things equal, toward assuming that the economy will soon experience a burst of inflation as firms bid up resource prices in an attempt to produce more than the full-employment level of output. That presumption will suggest a **restrictive monetary policy** (or "tight money" policy) under which the Fed would reduce the money supply and increase interest rates to restrain investment and consumption spending.
- Finally, if the actual unemployment rate is exactly at, or very close to, 3.5 percent, the Fed would be inclined toward a **neutral monetary policy** under which the Fed would leave the money supply and interest rates alone unless the economy were experiencing a significant inflation or deflation, in which case the Fed might adjust the money supply and interest rates to deal with those price-level problems.

The Fed's Inflation Target

As just indicated, the unemployment rate cannot *by itself* determine whether monetary policy should be expansionary, restrictive, or neutral. The Fed must also consider whether inflation is above or below the Fed's **target rate of inflation,** which has been set at 2 percent per year since 2012.[1]

---

[1] Prior to 2012, the Fed had a general, but unspecific, goal with respect to inflation, which was to "maintain price stability." Setting a specific inflation target in 2012 was an example of the Fed using forward guidance to try to help the public understand what the Fed's motivations were and thus what the Fed would be likely to do with respect to its monetary policy stance at any point in the future.

>> **LO15.3** Define the Fed's dual mandate and explain how conflicts can arise between meeting the inflation target and the unemployment target.

dual mandate The 1977 congressional directive that the Federal Reserve System's highest priorities should be *full employment* and price level stability. In practice, the Fed aims for the *full-employment rate of unemployment* and an *inflation rate* of 2 percent per year.

full-employment rate of unemployment The *unemployment rate* at which there is no *cyclical unemployment* of the *labor force;* equal to around 4 percent (rather than zero percent) in the United States because *frictional* and *structural unemployment* are unavoidable.

target rate of unemployment The Fed's desired *unemployment rate,* equal to the *full-employment rate of unemployment,* which is estimated to be between 4 and 5 percent for the U.S. economy.

expansionary monetary policy *Central bank* actions to increase the *money supply,* lower *interest rates,* and expand *real GDP.* Implemented when the economy is operating below *potential output.* Also known as an "easy money" policy.

restrictive monetary policy *Central bank* actions to reduce the *money supply,* increase *interest rates,* and reduce *inflation.* Implemented when the economy is operating above *potential output.* Also known as a "tight money" policy.

neutral monetary policy
A *monetary policy* in which the *money supply* and *interest rates* are left as they are by the *central bank* because the economy appears to be operating at *potential output,* with stable *prices* and a low level of *unemployment.* Compare with *expansionary monetary policy* and *restrictive monetary policy.*

target rate of inflation The publicly announced annual *inflation* rate that a *central bank* attempts to achieve through *monetary policy* actions if it is following an *inflation-targeting* monetary policy.

Why 2 Percent? There are several reasons why 2 percent was selected as the Fed's inflation target, rather than, say, 10 percent or zero percent.

Compensating for Upward Measurement Bias There is a consensus among economists that the *Consumer Price Index* (CPI) and other measures of inflation have an upward bias, meaning that they tend to say that inflation is higher than it actually is.

The upward bias in inflation measurement is estimated to be around half a percent, or 0.5 percent, per year. That fact implies that it would be dangerous for the Fed to have an inflation target of less than 0.5 percent. To see why, imagine that the Fed sets an inflation target of zero and then uses contractionary monetary policy to guide measured inflation down to that target rate. In that situation, the fact that measured inflation has a half-percent upward bias will imply that actual (unbiased) inflation will be about a half a percent lower, or negative 0.5 percent. That is deeply problematic because deflations (periods of negative inflation) usually only happen if the economy is in a severe recession, like the Great Depression of the 1930s or the severe recession of 2007–2009. Thus, to avoid accidentally putting the economy into a recession by conducting an overly contractionary monetary policy, the Fed must set an inflation target of *at least* positive 0.5 percent.

Protecting Savers On the other hand, the Fed does not want to set too high an inflation target because it will want to avoid any substantial loss of purchasing power on the part of savers, creditors, and people on fixed incomes who fail to anticipate the inflation created by the Fed. An inflation rate of 10 percent or even 5 percent would cause noticeable harm to those who are caught unaware. It is also the case that individuals and businesses begin to complain about inflation when it reaches 4 or 5 percent per year. Knowing these facts, the Fed has opted for a 2-percent inflation target as a way of balancing the need to have a target greater than 0.5 percent with the need to not let inflation get uncomfortably high.

Assisting Downward Wage Flexibility A low but positive rate of inflation also helps to overcome the downward inflexibility of real wages by giving firms the ability to lower real wages by simply keeping nominal wages fixed as the 2-percent rate of inflation chips away at the purchasing power of those fixed nominal wages. This matters because it is *real* (inflation-adjusted) wages that determine real labor costs and, thus, the willingness of employers to hire additional employees. By making it easier for real wages to decline, the Fed makes it more likely that when a recession strikes and millions are unemployed, real wages can adjust downward and thereby increase the number of workers that firms want to hire. (See the Consider This piece in Chapter 9 for details.)

Avoiding the Zero Lower Bound A target rate of 2 percent should also help the Fed avoid the *zero lower bound problem* in which any nominal interest rate lower than zero will cause people to withdraw money from their checking accounts, thereby putting contractionary pressure on the economy because (1) banks will have a reduced ability to extend loans and (2) people who've switched to cash may spend less than they did back when they previously had ready access to electronic payments drawn from checking account balances.

inflationary expectations
The public's forecast about likely future *inflation* rates; influenceable by central bank policy actions, including a credible *target rate of inflation.*

The 2-percent target rate helps to avoid those problems by helping the public form its **inflationary expectations.** Just as long as the Fed is believed to be credible in its pronouncements, people will believe that it will use its control over the money supply to correct any deviation away from its 2-percent inflation target. That, in turn, will ensure that the nominal interest rates facing businesses and consumers should normally be at least 3 or 4 percent per year.

We know that such should be the case because of the equation presented in Chapter 9 that tells us that *the nominal interest rate = real interest rate + expected inflation.* If people believe that the Fed will always follow through on its commitment to maintaining an inflation rate at or near its target rate of 2 percent, then expected inflation on the right-hand side of that equation will be 2 percent. That will mean that the left-hand side, the nominal interest rate, will also have to be at least 2 percent. In fact, it should be even higher by the amount of the real interest rate (on the right-hand side of the equation) that lenders demand as compensation for the use of their money. Since that real rate of interest is likely to be at least 1 to 2 percent, the nominal interest rate should be at least 3 or 4 percent, which is high enough that if the economy were to enter into a recession, the Fed would have plenty of room to cut interest rates and stimulate the economy before having to worry about the zero lower bound problem.

Balancing Inflation and Unemployment Other things equal, the Fed will be more inclined toward a restrictive monetary policy if the actual rate of inflation is above the target rate of inflation, and more inclined toward an expansionary monetary policy if the actual rate of inflation is

.ıll KEY GRAPH

FIGURE 15.1 The dual-mandate bullseye chart.

The Federal Reserve's 2-percent inflation target and 3.5-percent unemployment target provide the "crosshairs" that define the center of the dual-mandate bullseye. For comparison, the red dot indicates where actual unemployment and actual inflation were in January 2022. The closer the Fed can get to hitting the center of the bullseye, the closer it is to achieving its dual mandate.

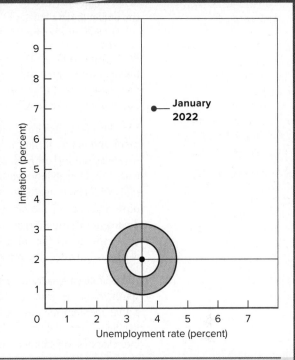

QUICK QUIZ FOR FIGURE 15.1

1. **In the figure, the Fed's dual-mandate target is illustrated by:**
   a. the red dot.
   b. the vertical cross-hairs line.
   c. the origin point where the vertical and horizontal axes intersect.
   d. the black dot.

2. **Points that lie northwest (up and to the left) of the center of the bullseye indicate that the Fed should:**
   a. definitely tighten monetary policy.
   b. definitely loosen monetary policy.
   c. definitely be neutral with monetary policy and make no changes.
   d. reflect on the mixed signals that it is receiving.

3. **If the Fed's inflation target increased from 2 percent to 3 percent and its unemployment target increased from 3.5 percent to 5 percent, then:**
   a. the red dot would move up and to the right.
   b. the black dot would move up and to the right.
   c. both crosshairs would move down and to the left.
   d. the red dot would move down and to the left.

4. **Points that lie northeast (up and to the right) of the center of the bullseye indicate that the Fed should:**
   a. raise its inflation target and increase its unemployment target.
   b. reflect on the mixed signals that it is receiving.
   c. definitely loosen monetary policy.
   d. definitely tighten monetary policy.

Answers: 1. d; 2. a; 3. b; 4. b

below the target rate of inflation. But it must also consider whether the unemployment rate is above or below the full-employment rate of unemployment. The two parts of the dual mandate must be pursued in tandem.

The Bullseye Chart

To help you visualize how the Fed pursues the dual mandate, consider **Figure 15.1 (Key Graph),** which presents the Federal Reserve's dual-mandate "bullseye chart" as of January 2022. The red dot indicates where the actual unemployment rate and actual inflation rate stood in January 2022. By contrast, the center of the bullseye plots the Fed's two target rates.

The position of the red dot relative to the center of the bullseye indicates the amounts by which actual unemployment and actual inflation differed from the Fed's target rates for unemployment and inflation in January 2022. As an exercise, look up the current unemployment and inflation rates and plot the spot that represents them. Is that spot close to the center of the bullseye? And in what direction does it lie relative to the center of the bullseye? To the northwest? Directly south? To the southeast? Keep that relative position in mind as you read the next section.

Adjusting Policy to Target the Bullseye

What should the Fed do when actual inflation and actual unemployment differ from the center of the dual-mandate bullseye?

It depends on where the red dot lies relative to the center of the bullseye.

Northwest and Southeast: No Conflicts If the red dot that plots actual inflation and unemployment is located to the northwest or southeast of the center of the bullseye, the Fed will have no confusion as to the stance of monetary policy. In those two quadrants, the actual inflation and unemployment rates will both suggest the same policy stance.

The Northwest Quadrant—Restrictive Policy Required If the current combination of actual employment and actual inflation is to the northwest of the center of the bullseye (that is, at any point where actual inflation exceeds 2 percent and actual unemployment is less than 3.5 percent), the economy is probably overheating and a restrictive monetary policy is in order. Higher interest rates will reduce aggregate demand, thereby putting downward pressure on prices while simultaneously cooling off the labor market. The actual inflation rate should fall downward, toward the 2-percent inflation target. The actual unemployment rate should rise upward, toward the 3.5 percent estimate of the full-employment rate of unemployment. If the restrictive monetary policy works as intended, the red dot will migrate toward the black dot at the center of the bullseye.

The Southeast Quadrant—Expansionary Policy Needed Now consider the situation for points to the southeast of the center of the bullseye. For those points, actual inflation is less than 2 percent while actual unemployment is higher than 3.5 percent. Any such combination suggests an economy operating below potential output. For these points, an expansionary monetary policy is appropriate. Lower interest rates will stimulate aggregate demand, thereby reducing the unemployment rate down toward the 3.5 percent estimate of the full-employment rate of unemployment while simultaneously raising the inflation rate up toward the Fed's 2-percent target. If the expansionary monetary policy works as intended, the red dot will migrate toward the black dot at the center of the bullseye.

Southwest and Northeast: Conflicts Things are not clear-cut in the other two quadrants. As you are about to see, the Fed will not easily know what to do in those locations because the inflation rate and unemployment rate will be suggesting *opposite* policy stances.

The Southwest Quadrant—Conflicting Signals To the southwest of the center of the bullseye (actual inflation less than 2 percent, actual unemployment less than 3.5 percent), the Fed will have a policy predicament. The fact that the actual unemployment rate is below the full-employment rate of unemployment will suggest that the Fed should be inclined toward a restrictive monetary policy. But the fact that the inflation rate is below 2 percent will suggest that an expansionary policy is in order.

The Northeast Quadrant—Conflicting Signals The opposite problem exists in the northeast quadrant (actual inflation greater than 2 percent, actual unemployment higher than 3.5 percent). There, the unemployment rate will be suggesting an expansionary monetary policy (to reduce the unemployment rate down to the 3.5 percent target) while the inflation rate will be suggesting a contractionary monetary policy (to reduce the inflation rate down to the 2-percent inflation target).

Putting Policy Weights on Inflation and Unemployment Complicating matters even further is the fact that very few policymakers are likely to give equal weight to inflation and unemployment. Indeed, if inflation remains mild, there may not be much harm if it exceeds the 2-percent target. By contrast, every bit of cyclical unemployment represents not only personal misery for those left unemployed but also permanently foregone output that cannot be recovered. Thus, most economists assume that FOMC members will give more weight to meeting the full-employment target.

One famous macroeconomic model, the so-called *Taylor rule*, goes so far as to assume that the FOMC will care *twice* as much about achieving the full-employment rate of unemployment as it will about meeting the 2-percent inflation target. Because this model has at times made accurate predictions about the FOMC's behavior with regard to setting an expansionary or restrictive monetary policy, its assumption that the FOMC cares twice as much about unemployment may be roughly correct. That being said, the FOMC is free to set monetary policy however it wishes, and has no allegiance to the Taylor Rule or any other system that tries to suggest how the Fed should weigh the trade-offs that may arise in specific situations between meeting one target or the other. The point of Figure 15.1 is not to predict exactly what the Fed will do in any given situation but rather to point out how its commitment to the dual mandate will tend to influence its decisions.

▶ The dual mandate states that the Fed's top two goals should be full employment and stable prices.

▶ In pursuing the dual mandate, the Fed aims for an inflation rate of 2 percent and an unemployment rate equal to its best estimate of the full-employment rate of unemployment. In the early 2020s, Fed officials believed that value to be around 3.5 percent of the labor force.

▶ The actual unemployment and inflation rates may give the Fed conflicting signals about whether monetary policy should be expansionary, restrictive, or neutral.

Monetary Policy, Real GDP, and the Price Level

We have identified and explained the tools of expansionary and restrictive monetary policy. We now want to explain how monetary policy affects investment, aggregate demand, real GDP, and the price level.

>> **LO15.4** Explain how monetary policy affects real GDP and the price level.

Cause-Effect Chain

The four diagrams in **Figure 15.2 (Key Graph)** will help you understand how monetary policy works toward achieving its goals.

The Market for Money Figure 15.2a represents the "market for money" that we studied in Chapter 14.[2] It brings together the demand curve for money D_m as well as three supply curves for money: S_{m1}, S_{m2}, and S_{m3}.

Recall from the previous chapter that the total demand for money is composed of the transactions demand for money plus the asset demand for money. Demand curve D_m represents that sum.

Each of the three money supply curves is represented by a vertical line. That's because each line represents a different amount of money supply determined by the Fed. Since the Fed can set whatever supply of money it wants independently of the interest rate, each money supply curve plots as a vertical line (indicating that the quantity of money is independent of the interest rate).

The equilibrium interest rate is the rate at which the amount of money demanded equals the amount supplied. If the supply of money is $125 billion ($S_{m1}$), the equilibrium interest rate is 10 percent. With a money supply of $150 billion ($S_{m2}$), the equilibrium interest rate is 8 percent; with a money supply of $175 billion ($S_{m3}$), the equilibrium interest rate is 6 percent.

You know from Chapter 10 that the real (rather than the nominal) interest rate is critical for investment decisions. So here we assume that Figure 15.2a portrays the real interest rate.

Investment These 10, 8, and 6 percent real interest rates are carried rightward to the investment demand curve in Figure 15.2b. This curve shows the inverse relationship between the interest rate—the cost of borrowing to invest—and the amount of investment spending. At the 10 percent interest rate, it will be profitable for the nation's businesses to invest $15 billion; at 8 percent, $20 billion; at 6 percent, $25 billion.

Changes in the interest rate mainly affect the investment component of total spending, although they also affect spending on durable consumer goods (such as autos) that are purchased on credit. Changes in the real interest rate greatly affect investment spending because of the large cost and long-term nature of capital purchases. Capital equipment, factory buildings, and warehouses are tremendously expensive. In absolute terms, interest charges on funds borrowed for these purchases are considerable. So the lower the interest rate, the more firms are willing to invest.

Similarly, the interest cost on a house purchased with a home mortgage loan is quite large. A 0.5 percent increase in the interest rate could amount to tens of thousands of dollars over the duration of the loan.

In brief, the impact of changing interest rates is mainly on investment (and, through that, on aggregate demand, output, employment, and the price level). Moreover, as Figure 15.2b shows, investment spending varies inversely with the real interest rate, so that if the real interest rate increases, investment spending declines, and vice versa.

Equilibrium GDP Figure 15.2c shows the impact that our three real interest rates (and their corresponding levels of investment spending) have on aggregate demand. Aggregate demand curve AD_1 is associated with the $15 billion level of investment spending, AD_2 with the $20 billion level

---

[2]Please note that this "market for money" in which the demand for and supply of money determine an equilibrium interest rate has nothing at all to do with the wide variety of short-term lending markets for business and government loans that are collectively referred to as "the money market."

.ıll KEY GRAPH

FIGURE 15.2 Monetary policy and equilibrium GDP.

An expansionary monetary policy that shifts the money supply curve rightward from S_{m1} to S_{m2} in (a) lowers the interest rate from 10 to 8 percent in (b). As a result, investment spending increases from $15 billion to $20 billion, shifting the aggregate demand curve rightward from AD_1 to AD_2 in (c) so that real output rises from the recessionary level of $880 billion to the full-employment level $Q_f = $900 billion along the horizontal dashed line. In (d), the economy at point *a* has an inflationary output gap of $10 billion because it is producing at $910 billion, which is $10 billion above the full-employment output level. A restrictive monetary policy that shifts the money supply curve leftward in (a) from $S_{m0} = $175 billion to $162.5 billion will increase the interest rate from 6 percent to 7 percent. Investment spending thus falls by $2.5 billion, from $25 billion to $22.5 billion in (b). This initial decline is multiplied by 4 by the multiplier process so that the aggregate demand curve shifts leftward in (d) by $10 billion from AD_3 to AD_4, moving the economy along the horizontal dashed line to equilibrium *b*. This returns the economy to full-employment output and eliminates the inflationary output gap.

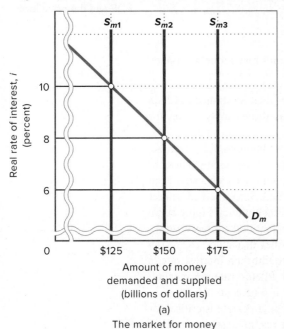

(a)
The market for money

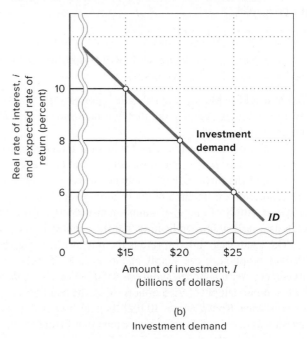

(b)
Investment demand

QUICK QUIZ FOR FIGURE 15.2

1. **The ultimate objective of an expansionary monetary policy is depicted by:**
   a. an increase in the price level from P_2 to P_3.
   b. a reduction of the interest rate from 8 to 6 percent.

   c. an increase in investment from $20 billion to $25 billion.
   d. an increase in real GDP from Q_1 to Q_f.

of investment spending, and AD_3 with the $25 billion level of investment spending. Other things equal, higher investment spending shifts the aggregate demand curve to the right.

Suppose the money supply in Figure 15.2a is $150 billion ($S_{m2}$), producing an equilibrium interest rate of 8 percent. In Figure 15.2b, we see that this 8 percent interest rate will bring about $20 billion of investment spending. This $20 billion of investment spending joins with consumption spending, net exports, and government spending to yield aggregate demand curve AD_2 in Figure 15.2c. The equilibrium levels of real output and prices are $Q_f = $900 billion and P_2, as determined by the intersection of AD_2 and the aggregate supply curve AS.

To test your understanding of these relationships, explain why each of the other two levels of money supply in Figure 15.2a results in a different interest rate, level of investment, aggregate demand curve, and equilibrium real output.

Effects of an Expansionary Monetary Policy

Recall that real-world price levels tend to be downwardly inflexible. Thus, with our economy starting from the initial equilibrium where AD_2 intersects AS, the price level will be downwardly inflexible at P_2 so that aggregate supply will be horizontal for values of real output to the left of Q_f. Thus,

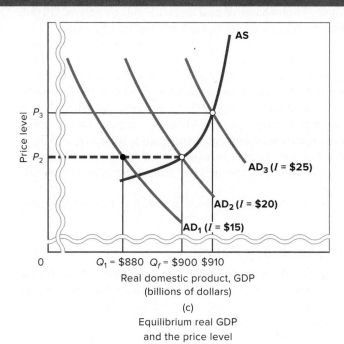

(c)
Equilibrium real GDP
and the price level

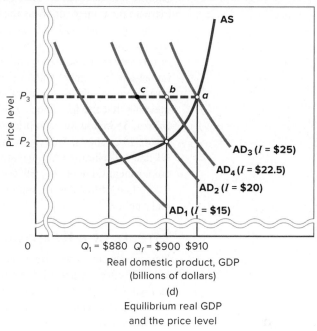

(d)
Equilibrium real GDP
and the price level

2. A successful restrictive monetary policy is evidenced by a shift in the money supply curve from:
a. S_{m3} to a point halfway between S_{m2} and S_{m3}, a decrease in investment from $25 billion to $22.5 billion, and a decline in aggregate demand from AD_3 to AD_4.
b. S_{m1} to S_{m2}, an increase in investment from $20 billion to $25 billion, and an increase in real GDP from Q_1 to Q_f.
c. S_{m3} to S_{m2}, a decrease in investment from $25 billion to $20 billion, and a decline in the price level from P_3 to P_2.
d. S_{m3} to S_{m2}, a decrease in investment from $25 billion to $20 billion, and an increase in aggregate demand from AD_2 to AD_3.

3. The Federal Reserve could increase the money supply from S_{m1} to S_{m2} by:
a. increasing the discount rate.
b. reducing taxes.
c. purchasing bonds as part of quantitative easing (QE).
d. selling bonds as part of quantitative tightening (QT).

4. If the spending-income multiplier is 4 in the economy depicted, an increase in the money supply from $125 billion to $150 billion will:
a. shift the aggregate demand curve rightward by $20 billion.
b. increase real GDP by $25 billion.
c. increase real GDP by $100 billion.
d. shift the aggregate demand curve leftward by $5 billion.

Answers: 1. d; 2. a; 3. c; 4. a

if aggregate demand decreases, the economy's equilibrium moves leftward along the dashed horizontal line shown in Figure 15.2c.

Such a decline would happen if the money supply fell to $125 billion ($S_{m1}$), shifting the aggregate demand curve leftward to AD_1 in Figure 15.2b. The result is a real output of $880 billion, $20 billion less than the economy's full-employment output level of $900 billion. The economy will be experiencing recession, a negative GDP gap, and substantial unemployment. The Fed therefore should institute an expansionary monetary policy.

The FOMC will take some combination of the following expansionary monetary policy actions: (1) utilize positive forward guidance by announcing a lower federal funds target range; (2) lower the IORB and ON RRP rates as necessary to guide the effective federal funds rate down into the new federal funds target range; and/or (3) engage in quantitative easing by purchasing longer-term government bonds. The intended outcome is lower short-term and long-term interest rates that will increase investment, aggregate demand, and equilibrium GDP.

Those lower rates can be achieved by the Fed because its expansionary monetary policy actions will all tend to expand the money supply: (1) Positive forward guidance backed by a lower effective federal funds rate will cause an increase in checkable-deposit money as more loans are extended by depository institutions due to increased optimism about future economic prospects;

(2) the lower IORB and ON RRP rates will increase the amount of money circulating in the economy outside the Fed's vaults as financial firms react to the lower IORB and ON RRP rates by lending less reserves to the Fed; and (3) purchases of government bonds as part of QE will increase the money supply as the Fed creates new money to pay for those bond purchases.

Suppose that the Fed's expansionary actions increase the money supply from \$125 billion to \$150 billion (S_{m1} to S_{m2}). That reduces the interest rate from 10 to 8 percent in Figure 15.2a, which in turn boosts investment spending from \$15 billion to \$20 billion in Figure 15.2b. This \$5 billion increase in investment shifts the aggregate demand curve rightward by more than the increase in investment because of the multiplier effect. If the economy's MPC is 0.75, the multiplier will be 4, meaning that the \$5 billion increase in investment shifts the AD curve rightward by \$20 billion ($= 4 \times \$5$ billion) at each price level. Specifically, aggregate demand shifts from AD_1 to AD_2, as Figure 15.2c shows. This rightward shift in the aggregate demand curve along the dashed horizontal line will eliminate the negative GDP gap by increasing GDP from \$880 billion to the full-employment GDP of $Q_f = \$900$ billion.[3]

Column 1 in Table 15.3 summarizes the chain of events associated with an expansionary monetary policy.

Effects of a Restrictive Monetary Policy

Next we consider restrictive monetary policy. We will use graphs *a*, *b*, and *d* of Figure 15.2 to demonstrate the effects of a restrictive monetary policy. Figure 15.2d represents exactly the same economy as Figure 15.2c but adds some extra curves that relate only to restrictive monetary policy. You should consequently ignore Figure 15.2c as we go through this section.

To see how restrictive monetary policy works, first consider a situation in which the economy moves from operating at a full-employment equilibrium to operating at more than full employment, so that inflation is a problem and restrictive monetary policy is appropriate. Assume that the economy begins at the full-employment equilibrium where AD_2 and AS intersect. At this equilibrium, $Q_f = \$900$ billion, and the price level is P_2.

Next, assume that the money supply expands from \$150 billion to \$175 billion (S_{m3}) in Figure 15.2a. The result is an interest rate of 6 percent, investment spending of \$25 billion rather than \$20 billion, and aggregate demand AD_3. As the AD curve shifts to the right from AD_2 to AD_3 in Figure 15.2d, the economy moves along the upward sloping AS curve until it reaches an equilibrium at point *a*, where AD_3 intersects AS. At the new equilibrium, the price level has risen to P_3 and the equilibrium level of real GDP has increased to \$910 billion, indicating an inflationary GDP gap of \$10 billion ($= \$910$ billion $- \$900$ billion). Aggregate demand AD_3 is excessive relative to the economy's full-employment level of real output $Q_f = \$900$ billion. To rein in spending, the Fed will institute a restrictive monetary policy.

TABLE 15.3 Monetary Policies for Recession and Inflation

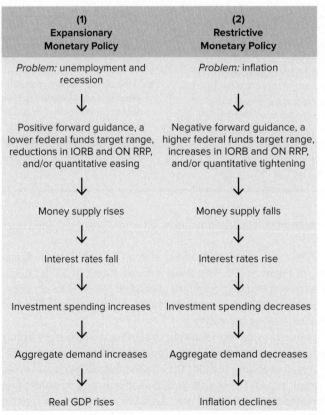

(1) Expansionary Monetary Policy	(2) Restrictive Monetary Policy
Problem: unemployment and recession	*Problem:* inflation
↓	↓
Positive forward guidance, a lower federal funds target range, reductions in IORB and ON RRP, and/or quantitative easing	Negative forward guidance, a higher federal funds target range, increases in IORB and ON RRP, and/or quantitative tightening
↓	↓
Money supply rises	Money supply falls
↓	↓
Interest rates fall	Interest rates rise
↓	↓
Investment spending increases	Investment spending decreases
↓	↓
Aggregate demand increases	Aggregate demand decreases
↓	↓
Real GDP rises	Inflation declines

---

[3]To keep things simple, we are assuming that the increase in real GDP does not increase the demand for money. In reality, the transactions demand for money would rise along with real GDP, thereby slightly increasing interest rates in the economy and slightly offsetting the decline of the interest rate from 8 to 6 percent that was engineered by the Fed.

The FOMC will undertake some combination of the following restrictive monetary policy actions: (1) utilize negative forward guidance by announcing a higher federal funds target range; (2) raise the IORB and ON RRP rates as necessary to guide the effective federal funds rate up into the new federal funds target range; and/or (3) engage in quantitative tightening by selling longer-term government bonds. The intended outcome is higher short-term and long-term interest rates that will decrease investment, aggregate demand, and equilibrium GDP.

Those higher rates can be achieved by the Fed because its restrictive monetary policy actions will all tend to decrease the money supply: (1) Negative forward guidance backed by a higher effective federal funds rate will cause a decrease in the total amount of checkable-deposit money as fewer new loans are extended due to decreased optimism about future economic prospects; (2) the higher IORB and ON RRP rates will increase the amount of money locked away in the Fed's vaults as financial firms react to the higher IORB and ON RRP rates by lending more reserves to the Fed; and (3) sales of longer-term government bonds as part of QT will decrease the money supply as the Fed stores away in its vaults, completely out of public circulation, all of the money paid to it by the purchasers of those bonds.

The Fed must be careful, though, about just *how much* to decrease the money supply. The problem is that prices are inflexible at price level P_3. As a result, the dashed horizontal line to the left of point a in Figure 15.2d becomes relevant, and the Fed cannot simply lower the money supply to S_{m2} in Figure 15.2a. If it were to do that, investment demand would fall to $20 billion in Figure 15.2b, and the AD curve would shift to the left from AD_3 back to AD_2. But because of inflexible prices, the economy's equilibrium would move to point c, where AD_2 intersects the horizontal dashed line that represents aggregate supply to the left of point a. This would put the economy into a recession, with equilibrium output below the full-employment output level $Q_f = $900 billion.

What the Fed needs to do to achieve full employment is to move the AD curve back only from AD_3 to AD_4, so that the economy will come to equilibrium at point b. This will require a $10 billion decrease in aggregate demand, so that equilibrium output falls from $910 billion at point a to $Q_f = $900 billion at point b. The Fed can achieve this shift by setting the supply of money in Figure 15.2a at $162.5 billion.

To see how this works, draw in a vertical money supply curve in Figure 15.2a at $162.5 billion and label it as S_{m4}. It will be exactly halfway between money supply curves S_{m2} and S_{m3}. Notice that the intersection of S_{m4} with the money demand curve D_m results in a 7 percent interest rate. In Figure 15.2b, this 7 percent interest rate results in investment spending of $22.5 billion (halfway between $20 billion and $25 billion). Thus, by setting the money supply at $162.5 billion, the Fed can reduce investment spending by $2.5 billion, lowering it from the $25 billion associated with AD_3 down to only $22.5 billion. This decline in investment spending initially shifts the AD curve only $2.5 billion to the left of AD_3. But then the multiplier process works its magic. Because the multiplier is 4 in our model, the AD curve ends up moving by a full $10 billion ($= 4 \times $2.5 billion) to the left, to AD_4. This shift moves the economy to equilibrium b, returning output to the full-employment level and eliminating the inflationary GDP gap.[4]

Column 2 in Table 15.3 summarizes the cause-effect chain of a restrictive money policy.

QUICK REVIEW

15.4

▶ The Fed engages in an expansionary monetary policy when it increases the money supply to reduce interest rates and increase investment spending and real GDP.

▶ The Fed engages in a restrictive monetary policy when it reduces the money supply to increase interest rates and reduce investment spending and inflation.

▶ When pursuing a restrictive monetary policy, the Fed must be careful to take into account downward price stickiness and its effect on the size of the multiplier.

Monetary Policy: Evaluation and Issues

Monetary policy has become the dominant component of U.S. national stabilization policy. It has two key advantages over fiscal policy:

- Speed and flexibility.
- Isolation from political pressure.

>> **LO15.5** Explain the advantages and shortcomings of monetary policy.

---

[4]Again, we assume for simplicity that the decrease in GDP does not feed back to reduce the demand for money and thus the interest rate. In reality, this would occur, slightly offsetting the increase in the interest rate that was engineered by the Fed.

Compared with fiscal policy, monetary policy can be quickly altered. Recall that congressional deliberations may delay the application of fiscal policy for months. In contrast, the FOMC is free to update monetary policy on a daily basis if necessary.

Also, because the members of the Board of Governors serve 14-year terms, they are relatively isolated from political lobbying and need not worry about retaining their popularity with voters. Thus, the Board, more readily than congress, can engage in politically unpopular policies (such as higher interest rates) that may be necessary for the economy's long-term health.

In addition, monetary policy is subtler and more politically neutral than fiscal policy. Changes in government spending and taxes directly affect the allocation of resources, and are sometimes so narrowly targeted that they bring benefits only to a single firm or a single congressional district. By contrast, because monetary policy works broadly and indirectly, it is more politically palatable.

Recent U.S. Monetary Policy

The Federal Reserve has been very busy over the last two decades.

The Mortgage Default Crisis The 2007–2008 financial crisis was precipitated by a huge wave of home-mortgage defaults that began in 2006. The Fed responded with several actions as the crisis became severe in the summer of 2007. In August 2007, it lowered the discount rate by half a percentage point. Then, between September 2007 and April 2008, it lowered the effective federal funds rate from 5.25 percent to 2.00 percent. The Fed also took a series of extraordinary actions to prevent the failure of key financial firms that would otherwise have been overwhelmed by withdrawal requests on the part of depositors and investors.

By late 2008, it was clear that the U.S. economy faced a crisis unequaled since the Great Depression of the 1930s. The Fed responded with a series of innovative monetary policy initiatives.

zero interest rate policy (ZIRP) A *monetary policy* in which a *central bank* sets *nominal interest rates* at or near zero percent per year in order to stimulate the economy.

The Fed began by moving toward a **zero interest rate policy,** or **ZIRP,** in December 2008. Under ZIRP, the Fed aimed to keep short-term interest rates near zero to stimulate the economy. It lowered the federal funds target range to just zero to 0.25 percent and acted aggressively as a lender of last resort, lending freely at the discount rate. The Fed also took the highly unusual step of acting as a "buyer of last resort," purchasing debt securities from financial firms at pre-crisis prices so that those firms would not have to sell those assets at the low, panic prices then prevailing in the bond markets.

The crisis was resolved by late 2009, after which the Fed no longer had to act as a lender or buyer of last resort. But with the unemployment rate rising toward 10 percent, the Fed had to figure out a way to continue stimulating the economy even though ZIRP meant that short-term interest rates were as low as they could go without encountering the zero lower bound problem.

As explained earlier, the Fed's solution was to keep short-term interest rates low with IORB and ON RRP while initiating its first quantitative easing, or QE, program to lower longer-term interest rates.

The 2010s Recovery By the close of 2015, the Fed felt that various economic indicators were signaling that monetary stimulus could end. For example, the unemployment rate had fallen back to just 5 percent in 2015, which was well below its 2009 peak of 10 percent. On that basis, the FOMC decided that the Fed could abandon ZIRP and QE while raising interest rates back up toward normal levels using forward guidance, a higher federal funds target range, increases in IORB and ON RRP, and quantitative tightening. Over the next five years, interest rates gradually increased and the economy continued to improve.

By early 2020, the U.S. economy was operating at full employment, with a 3.5-percent unemployment rate that exactly equaled the Fed's unemployment target and a 2.3-percent inflation rate that was only slightly higher than the Fed's inflation target. Given that the economy was operating almost exactly at the center of the Fed's bullseye target, it seemed that the Fed might have very little to do for the next few years.

The 2020 COVID Recession When COVID-19 struck in the spring of 2020 and governments all over the world ordered lockdowns, it was clear that the economic damage might be severe. The Fed responded with every tool at its disposal. It used forward guidance to make it clear to the public that it understood that the crisis was severe and needed an aggressive response. It lowered the federal funds target range down to the lowest possible non-negative range, 0 to 0.25 percent. It used the administered rates to not only get the effective federal funds rate into the new target range but to also guide all of the other money-market rates to very low levels. And it reinitiated QE by purchasing $3 trillion of longer-term bonds to lower longer-term interest rates.

Thanks in large part to the Fed's aggressive actions, the COVID recession was the shortest on record and the economy was back to producing at potential output by the fall of 2021, just 18 months after lockdowns were initiated in March 2020.

Problems and Complications

U.S. monetary policy faces both limitations and complications.

Recognition and Operational Lags Recall from Chapter 13 that fiscal policy is hindered by three delays, or lags—a recognition lag, an administrative lag, and an operational lag. By contrast, while monetary policy also usually faces a recognition lag and an operational lag, the FOMC's ability to alter its monetary policy stance on a daily, or even hourly, basis implies that monetary policy is *not* subject to an administrative lag.

With respect to the Fed's recognition lag, the COVID pandemic was perhaps the only instance in U.S. history where monetary policy was *not* subject to a recognition lag. That was true because the implementation of lockdowns and workplace closures made it obvious to everyone that a recession was going to happen. Under more typical circumstances, however, monetary policy *does* face a recognition lag because the many random fluctuations in economic activity and the rate of inflation that occur over the course of the business cycle make it difficult for the Fed to quickly recognize when the economy is *truly* starting to recede or when inflation is *really* starting to taking off.

With respect to the Fed's operational lag, changes in interest rates typically involve an operational lag of at least 3 to 6 months because that much time is required for interest-rate changes to have any substantial impacts on investment, aggregate demand, real GDP, or the price level. By contrast, the effects of forward guidance on individual and firm behavior can be nearly instantaneous. The same is true of the Fed's ability to calm a financial panic by showing that it will act as a lender of last resort.

Cyclical Asymmetry and the Liquidity Trap As a general matter, monetary policy may be highly effective in slowing expansions and controlling inflation but much less reliable in pulling the economy out of a severe recession. As a result, economists sometimes say that monetary policy is subject to a **cyclical asymmetry.** The metaphor of "pushing on a string" is often invoked to capture this dichotomy, or difference.

To understand the metaphor, imagine that the FOMC is standing on the left-hand side of Figure 15.2c, holding one end of a monetary-policy string. And then imagine that the other end of the monetary-policy string is tied to the AD curve. Because the string would go taut if pulled on, monetary policy may be useful in pulling aggregate demand to the left. But because the string would go limp if pushed on, monetary policy will be ineffective at pushing aggregate demand to the right.

The reason for this asymmetry, or difference, is the asymmetric way in which people act in response to higher interest rates. If pursued vigorously, a restrictive monetary policy can, for example, make banks feel that the extension of new business loans is very unattractive compared to other lending options made available by the Fed. Why, for example, would a bank want to extend risky businesses loans at 5 percent if the Fed, via IORB, is offering them a risk-free rate of 5.5 percent? The result is less lending, less investment, and reduced aggregate demand. Consequently, the Fed can almost certainly achieve a restrictive goal with the policy tools at its disposal.

By contrast, the Fed cannot be certain of achieving an expansionary goal by lowering interest rates. That's because it may encounter a **liquidity trap,** in which the lower interest rates and larger amounts of bank reserves (liquidity) that the Fed provides to fight a recession have little or no effect on lending, borrowing, investment, or aggregate demand. For example, the Fed's response to the 2007–2009 financial crisis involved lowering short-term rates to nearly zero and purchasing so many government bonds from the public that the perfectly liquid reserve balances held by banks and thrifts soared from just $44 billion before the crisis to over $1.1 trillion in 2009.

cyclical asymmetry The idea that *monetary policy* may be more successful in slowing expansions and controlling *inflation* than in extracting the economy from severe recession.

liquidity trap A situation in a severe *recession* in which the *central bank's* injection of additional currency (liquidity) into the financial system has little or no additional positive impact on lending, borrowing, *investment,* or *aggregate demand.*

A New Inflationary Era?

As the Fed Decided How Aggressively to Raise Interest Rates to Fight the Post-Pandemic Inflation, It Had to Consider Whether the World Economy Had Permanently Transitioned to a More Inflationary Era.

When inflation spiked after the COVID-19 pandemic, both Wall Street and Main Street wondered how, exactly, the Fed would react, both in the short run and in the long run. A crucial consideration was whether the U.S. economy—and indeed the entire world economy—had shifted from an era during which inflation fighting was easy to one in which inflation fighting would be more difficult due to permanent changes in resource supplies and production processes.

Consider labor force growth. The U.S. labor force grew rapidly starting in the 1960s as the very large Baby Boom generation entered the labor force, as the U.S. massively expanded legal immigration, and as legal and cultural changes facilitated women's entering the labor force in huge numbers for the first time.

As a result of those massive and ongoing increases in the supply of labor, wage growth was suppressed relative to what it would have been had the labor force not grown as rapidly. From the perspective of employers, labor was relatively inexpensive, which in turn pushed the aggregate supply curve rightward relative to where it would have been if labor costs had been higher.

The net effect was downward pressure on the price level, all other things equal. And that meant that the Fed was operating in an economic environment that enjoyed constant downward price pressures due to strong labor force growth.

That all started to change after the 2007–2008 recession as immigration to the United States slowed. The change accelerated sharply when over a million older workers decided to retire early during the COVID pandemic. And it was kicked up yet another notch when over a million prime-age workers did not return to employment after the pandemic ended. The net result was a U.S. labor force that was about 2.5 million workers smaller at the end of 2022 than it would have been had pre-pandemic labor-force growth trends continued.

That smaller pool of available workers generated widespread labor shortages across many industries, thereby driving up the cost of labor and shifting the aggregate supply curve leftward. And because the U.S. birth rate plunged during the pandemic, it became more likely that the long-run growth rate of the U.S. labor force might fall significantly over the coming decades, even after accounting for future immigration. Such a scenario would, all other things equal, generate higher labor costs and, thus, higher inflationary pressures.

A second economywide factor that could be permanently inflationary is the reversal of globalization that was observed in the aftermath of the pandemic. After international supply chains were repeatedly snarled during the pandemic, many corporate managers reacted by reorganizing their production processes so as to have components and inputs produced less far away. That, though, drives up costs because "on-shoring" and "near-shoring" almost always involve the use of suppliers who are more expensive, sometimes significantly so. If that trend continues and becomes permanent, it will put upward pressure on inflation that did not exist when components

Michael Vi/Shutterstock

and raw materials were sourced to the very cheapest producer anywhere in the world.

A third factor that suggests that the world economy may be permanently moving into a higher-cost, more inflationary era is the fact that energy costs look likely to rise going forward for both geopolitical and environmental reasons. In terms of geopolitics, sanctions against Russia for invading the Ukraine in early 2022 meant less Russian oil and natural gas being sold onto the world energy market, driving up their price. In addition, many governments are passing laws to move away from lower-cost but more-polluting energy sources like coal and oil toward wind, solar, and renewables. Unfortunately, many of those "green energy" sources come with higher price tags, either for dealing with their intermittency (the sun does not shine at night; the wind often fails to blow) or for having to build out a lot of new infrastructure (such as for delivering more electricity across electrical grids if all vehicles switch from gasoline and diesel to electric). The net result may be higher energy prices throughout the economy and thus constant inflationary pressures that central banks will have to deal with.

For central bankers, several possibilities are raised by the prospect of a new era that has stronger inflationary pressures. If such an era is indeed upon us, central banks might, for example, have to raise interest rates more aggressively than they did before the pandemic to keep inflation equally under control. Alternatively, perhaps it might be better to not try very hard to fight the new inflationary trends if doing so would generate high unemployment. If that were the eventual consensus, then the Fed might settle for, say, a 4-percent inflation target rather than a 2-percent inflation target and only raise interest rates aggressively if inflation rose appreciably higher than 4 percent. Time will tell.

Nevertheless, despite all of that liquidity, commercial bank lending fell by 25 percent during the recession and remained weak over the following five years. Banks were fearful that loans would not be paid back. So they opted to make fewer loans. The result was low investment spending and low aggregate demand despite the much lower interest rates and much greater liquidity that had been engineered by the Fed.

Finally, it should be pointed out that the Fed has continued to maintain high amounts of liquidity in the banking system by purchasing massive amounts of government bonds from the public through various forms of open-market operations, including QE and reverse-repo transactions. The Fed refers to that high-liquidity policy as the "ample reserves regime" and has stated that it intends to continue with an ample reserves regime for the foreseeable future. As a result, bank and thrift reserve balances are expected to remain at very high levels, and indeed totaled over $3.8 trillion at the start of 2022.

Other Issues and Concerns The liquidity trap scenario demonstrates that the Fed is not omnipotent. An expansionary monetary policy can suffer from a "you can lead a horse to water, but you can't make it drink" problem. As we just explained, the Fed can lower interest rates, but it cannot guarantee that banks will want to make additional loans. Households and businesses can frustrate the Fed, too, by not wanting to borrow. And when the Fed buys securities from the public, the sellers may save the money they receive from the Fed, rather than increasing their spending on goods and services.

The liquidity trap that occurred during the 2007–2009 crisis was a primary reason why congress acted so forcefully with respect to *fiscal* policy in the spring of 2009. With monetary policy maxed out, Congress approved the gargantuan American Recovery and Redevelopment Act, which authorized the infusion of $787 billion of tax cuts and government spending in 2009 and 2010. This spending helped to ensure a rightward shift of AD even after interest rates had fallen toward zero and banks were sitting on reserves rather than lending.

Fiscal policy was also used aggressively during the COVID-19 crisis, since it was not clear that banks would lend or that borrowers would borrow despite the Fed's herculean efforts to lower both short-term and long-term interest rates. The Paycheck Protection Program and the CARES Act got cash directly into the hands of unemployed workers and struggling businesses. The result was a highly potent dose of fiscal stimulus at a time when monetary policy was very likely "maxed out" and hobbled by a liquidity trap.

The fiscal stimulus was in fact so effective and so long lasting that it contributed significantly to the jump in the U.S. inflation rate from 1.4 percent in the first year of the pandemic, 2020, to 7.0 percent the next year. As you know, that extremely large increase in the inflation rate occurred because the massive fiscal stimulus enacted by congress to fight the pandemic combined with supply chain problems caused by the pandemic to simultaneously shift AD to the right and AS to the left, thereby generating the highest U.S. inflation rate since 1981.

QUICK REVIEW
15.5

▸ Monetary policy has several major advantages over fiscal policy, including isolation from political pressures and the absence of an administrative lag.

▸ To help stimulate the economy after the Great Recession, the Federal Reserve implemented the zero interest rate policy (ZIRP) and quantitative easing (QE).

▸ The main weaknesses of monetary policy are cyclical asymmetry, the liquidity trap, and the recognition and operational lags.

The "Big Picture"

Figure 15.3 (Key Graph) brings together the analytical and policy aspects of macroeconomics discussed in this and the seven preceding chapters. This "big picture" shows how the many concepts and principles that we have covered relate to one another and how they constitute a coherent theory of the price level and real output in a market economy.

Study this diagram and you will see that the price level, output, employment, and income all result from the interaction of aggregate supply and aggregate demand. The items shown in red relate to public policy.

>> **LO15.6** Describe how the various components of macroeconomic theory and stabilization policy fit together.

..Il KEY GRAPH

FIGURE 15.3   The AD–AS theory of the price level, real output, and stabilization policy.

This figure integrates the various components of macroeconomic theory and stabilization policy. Components that either constitute public policy or are strongly influenced by public policy are shown in red.

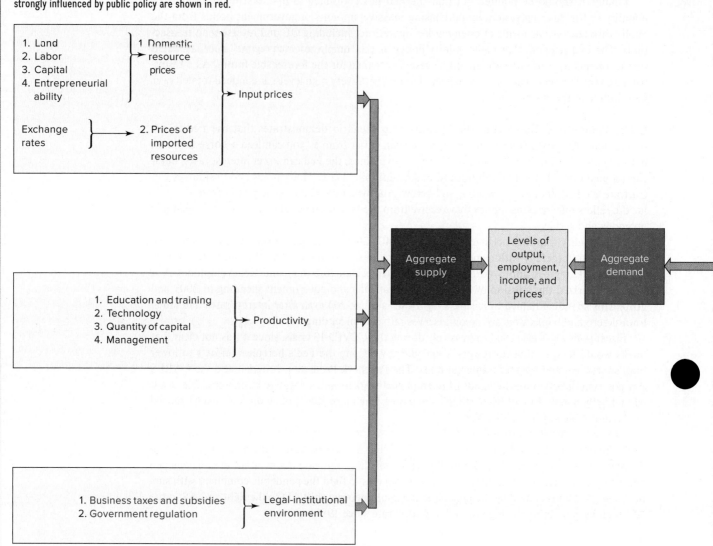

QUICK QUIZ FOR FIGURE 15.3

1. **All else equal, an increase in domestic resource availability will:**
   a. increase input prices, reduce aggregate supply, and increase real output.
   b. raise labor productivity, reduce interest rates, and lower the international value of the dollar.
   c. increase net exports, increase investment, and reduce aggregate demand.
   d. reduce input prices, increase aggregate supply, and increase real output.

2. **All else equal, an expansionary monetary policy during a recession will:**
   a. lower the interest rate, increase investment, and reduce net exports.
   b. lower the interest rate, increase investment, and increase aggregate demand.
   c. increase the interest rate, increase investment, and reduce net exports.
   d. reduce productivity, aggregate supply, and real output.

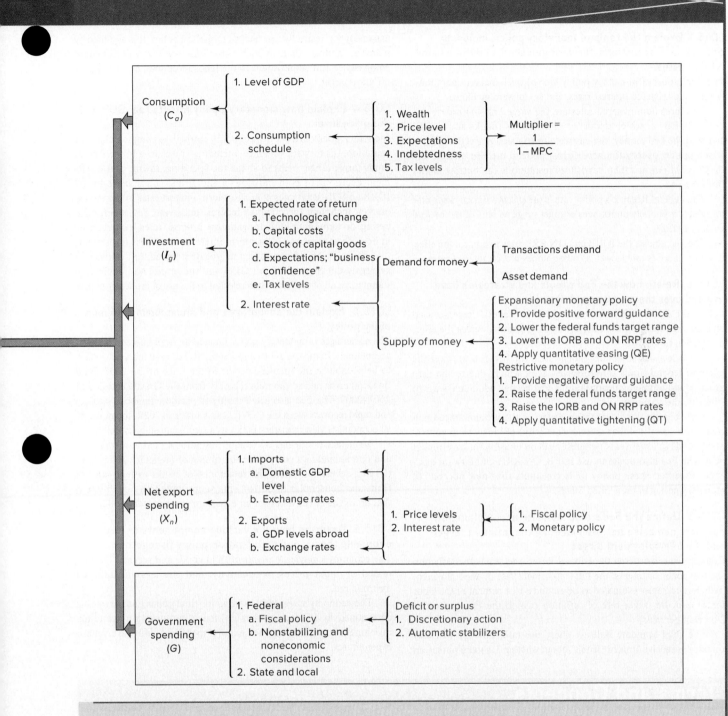

3. A personal income tax cut, combined with a reduction in corporate income and excise taxes, would:
   a. increase consumption, investment, aggregate demand, and aggregate supply.
   b. reduce productivity, raise input prices, and reduce aggregate supply.
   c. increase government spending, reduce net exports, and increase aggregate demand.
   d. increase the supply of money, reduce interest rates, increase investment, and expand real output.

4. An appreciation of the dollar would:
   a. reduce the price of imported resources, lower input prices, and increase aggregate supply.
   b. increase net exports and aggregate demand.
   c. increase aggregate supply and aggregate demand.
   d. reduce consumption, investment, net export spending, and government spending.

Answers: 1. d; 2. b; 3. a; 4. a

Summary

LO15.1 Explain the tools of monetary policy, including open-market operations, forward guidance, and the administered rates.

The main tools of monetary policy are (*a*) open-market operations, (*b*) the administered interest rates, and (*c*) forward guidance.

The three administered rates are the *interest rate on reserve balances* (IORB) at which depository institutions (banks and thrifts) can lend the Fed money; the *overnight reverse repo rate* (ON RRP) at which nondepository financial firms can lend the Fed money; and the *discount rate* at which depository institutions can borrow money from the Fed.

The Federal Reserve's policy rate is the *effective federal funds rate*, for which it publicly announces a target range as part of its forward guidance efforts.

The Fed adjusts the IORB and ON RRP rates to control the effective federal funds rate as well as other money market interest rates.

LO15.2 Relate how the Fed's tools and strategies have evolved over the past several decades.

Before the 2007–2008 financial crisis, the Federal Reserve used open-market operations exclusively for raising and lowering the effective federal funds rate.

The crisis was so severe, though, that the Fed had to lower the effective federal funds rate to nearly zero, which, due to the zero lower bound problem, meant that the Fed needed additional ways to stimulate the economy.

One solution was quantitative easing, or the pre-announced purchase of a specific dollar amount (quantity) of longer-term government bonds to lower (ease) interest rates on longer-term government debt. The Fed also began to use IORB, ON RRP, and forward guidance. Together, these policy tools constitute the "new normal" of monetary policy in the United States.

LO15.3 Define the Fed's dual mandate and explain how conflicts can arise between meeting the inflation target and the unemployment target.

Congress has instructed the Federal Reserve to simultaneously pursue two goals, or targets: the full-employment rate of unemployment (which is currently estimated to be around 3 to 4 percent of the labor force) and the target rate of inflation (which the Fed has set at 2 percent per year).

The Dual Mandate Bullseye chart illustrates how the Fed may sometimes receive "mixed signals" about whether it should pursue an expansionary, restrictive, or neutral monetary policy. It is assumed by many economists that, in such situations, the Fed will put more emphasis on full employment in the labor force than on meeting its inflation target.

LO15.4 Explain how monetary policy affects real GDP and the price level.

Monetary policy affects the economy through a complex chain of causation: (*a*) forward guidance, including any change to the federal funds target range, helps to shape the spending, saving, and investment decisions of both individuals and firms; (*b*) changes to the IORB and ON RRP rates alter short-term interest rates in the money market, including the effective federal funds rate; (*c*) quantitative easing or tightening shift longer-term interest rates; (*d*) changes in both short-term and longer-term interest rates affect investment; (*e*) changes in investment affect aggregate demand; (*f*) changes in aggregate demand affect real GDP and the price level. Table 15.3 summarizes all of the basic ideas relevant to the use of monetary policy.

LO15.5 Explain the advantages and shortcomings of monetary policy.

The advantages of monetary policy include its flexibility and political acceptability. In the late 2000s and 2010s, the Fed used monetary policy to help stabilize the financial sector in the wake of the 2007–2009 financial crisis and to promote recovery from the Great Recession of 2007–2009. The Fed also acted swiftly to promote financial stability and rapid recovery when the COVID crisis struck in 2020. Today, nearly all economists view monetary policy as a significant stabilization tool.

Monetary policy has two major limitations: (1) the recognition and operational lags complicate the timing of monetary policy; and (2) in a severe recession, the reluctance of banks to lend—and of firms and households to borrow—may contribute to a liquidity trap that limits the effectiveness of an expansionary monetary policy.

LO15.6 Describe how the various components of macroeconomic theory and stabilization policy fit together.

The economy's *aggregate supply* of final goods and services is determined by input prices, productivity, and the legal-institutional environment.

The economy's *aggregate demand* for final goods and services is determined by the factors that influence consumption spending, investment expenditures, net export spending, and government expenditures.

Terms and Concepts

monetary policy	federal funds rate	expansionary monetary policy
open-market operations	federal funds market	restrictive monetary policy
administered rate	federal funds target range	neutral monetary policy
money market	effective federal funds rate	target rate of inflation
interest rate on reserve balances (IORB)	zero lower bound problem	inflationary expectations
overnight reverse repo rate (ON RRP)	quantitative easing (QE)	zero interest rate policy (ZIRP)
discount rate	quantitative tightening (QT)	cyclical asymmetry
forward guidance	dual mandate	liquidity trap
policy rate	full-employment rate of unemployment	
monetary policy stance	target rate of unemployment	

Discussion Questions

1. What are open-market operations, and how do they affect interest rates and the money supply? **LO15.1**
2. What are the Federal Reserve's three administered rates and which of them involve the Fed borrowing as opposed to lending? Which one is most important in terms of helping to mitigate or avoid bank runs? **LO15.1**
3. Why does the Fed employ forward guidance? How does the federal funds target range relate to the Fed's forward-guidance efforts? **LO15.1**
4. What is the zero lower bound? What bad things might happen if the Fed lowered short-term interest rates below zero? **LO15.2**
5. What is the difference between quantitative tightening and quantitative easing? Why did the Fed feel that it was necessary to start using quantitative easing for the first time during the financial crisis? **LO15.2**
6. What are the two parts of the Fed's dual mandate? How does the dual mandate relate to the bullseye chart? Which quadrants of the bullseye chart give conflicting signals to the Fed and what is the source of the confusion in each case? **LO15.3**
7. How does the Fed's 2-percent inflation target help with downward wage flexibility? **LO15.3**
8. Explain the links between changes in a nation's money supply, interest rate, investment spending, aggregate demand, real GDP, and price level. **LO15.4**

9. Suppose that the FOMC chair makes an official public statement that (1) substantially increases investor expectations for faster economic growth but which (2) does *not* change the administered rates or what the Fed has been doing with respect to quantitative easing, open-market operations, and other monetary policy actions. What will be the effect on the investment demand curve? (Hint: Recall the difference between a movement along a curve and a shift of a curve.) **LO15.4**
10. Why was the Fed designed to be insulated from political pressure? What might go wrong with monetary policy if it were not insulated from political pressure? Explain. **LO15.5**
11. What do economists mean when they say that monetary policy can exhibit cyclical asymmetry? How does the idea of a liquidity trap relate to cyclical asymmetry? Why is the possibility of a liquidity trap significant to policymakers? **LO15.5**
12. What component of aggregate demand is influenced by technological change? What about for aggregate supply? How would improvements in productivity affect investment spending? Other things equal, how would improvements in the productivity of capital affect the interest rate? **LO15.6**
13. **LAST WORD** Why would slower growth of the labor force put upward pressure on inflation? What are "on-shoring" and "near-shoring" and how do they affect inflationary pressures in the economy? How might the Fed react to an era of higher inflationary pressures? Explain.

Review Questions

1. If the effective federal funds rate is 2.14 percent, which of the following is most likely to be the Fed's target range for the federal funds rate? **LO15.1**
   a. 0.00 to 0.25 percent
   b. 1.00 to 1.25 percent
   c. 2.00 to 2.25 percent
   d. none of the above
2. If the IORB rate is 4.25 percent, the effective federal funds rate is 4.18 percent, and the ON RRP rate is 4.00 percent, which group might lend money in the federal funds market? **LO15.1**
   a. Commercial banks
   b. Nonbank financial companies
   c. The Federal Reserve
3. A commercial bank sells a Treasury bond to the Federal Reserve for $100,000. The money supply: **LO15.1**
   a. increases by $100,000.
   b. decreases by $100,000.
   c. is unaffected by the transaction.
4. How did the Federal Reserve control the federal funds rate before the 2007–2009 financial crisis? **LO15.2**
   a. Quantitative easing
   b. Open-market operations
   c. Forward guidance
   d. All of the above
5. Which policy would be the most helpful in lowering long-term interest rates? **LO15.2**
   a. Numerical neutrality
   b. Quantitative easing
   c. Raising the administered rates
   d. Lowering the federal funds target range

6. The dual mandate tells the Fed that its two highest priorities should be stable prices and _____. **LO15.3**
   a. economic growth
   b. high wages
   c. low inequality
   d. low unemployment
7. Which combination would give the FOMC conflicting signals about the stance of monetary policy? **LO15.3**
   a. Inflation and unemployment both below target
   b. Inflation and unemployment both on target
   c. Inflation above target and unemployment below target
   d. Inflation below target and unemployment above target
8. In which situation does the Fed have to worry most about downward price stickiness? **LO15.4**
   a. When applying expansionary monetary policy
   b. When applying restrictive monetary policy
   c. When continuing a neutral monetary policy
   d. All of the above
9. Other things equal, a lower real interest rate will cause: **LO15.4**
   a. the AS curve to shift left.
   b. the AD curve to shift right.
   c. the AS curve to shift right.
   d. the AD curve to shift left.
10. The metaphor most commonly invoked to capture the idea that an expansionary monetary policy might not work due to borrowers not wanting to borrow or lenders not wanting to lend is: **LO15.5**
    a. pulling on a rope.
    b. hovering over a slope.
    c. pushing on a string.
    d. pouring through a sieve.

11. True or False: A liquidity trap occurs when expansionary monetary policy fails to work because a decrease in interest rates does not cause an increase in lending and borrowing. **LO15.5**

12. True or False: In the United States, monetary policy has two key advantages over fiscal policy: (1) isolation from political pressure and (2) speed and flexibility. **LO15.5**

Problems

Mc Graw Hill connect

1. Draw two separate demand and supply diagrams that illustrate, respectively, bond purchases and bond sales by the Fed. In each figure, the price of bonds is the vertical axis variable while the quantity of bonds demanded or supplied is the horizontal axis variable. In each of the two figures, show the initial equilibrium before the Fed action and the new equilibrium after the Fed has (1) increased the demand for bonds in the first figure and (2) increased the supply of bonds in the second figure. Note which way the equilibrium bond price moves in each figure, and then use the fact that "bond prices and interest rates move inversely" to infer in which direction interest rates move in each situation. **LO15.1**

2. Draw and label your own Dual-Mandate Bullseye chart. First draw and label the two axes. Then draw in the crosshairs and the bullseye, indicating with tick marks and descriptive labels the numerical values of the inflation target and the unemployment target. Then label the four quadrants by their compass positions (Northeast, Southeast, Southwest, Northwest). Next, for each quadrant, write whether points in that quadrant are above or below each target value (for instance, the labels for the Northeast would be: "inflation > 2-percent target," and, "unemployment > 3.5 percent target"). Then add a label to each quadrant that indicates whether the Fed is getting "consistent signals" or "inconsistent signals" about whether to engage in either a restrictive, expansionary, or neutral monetary policy. Next, for any quadrant where the Fed is getting *consistent signals*, write down what the Fed's monetary policy stance should be for that quadrant (i.e., restrictive, expansionary, or neutral). **LO15.3**

3. Examine the nearby Dual-Mandate Bullseye chart that shows where the U.S. economy was exactly one year before the COVID-19 lockdowns began. Write a brief essay of just a paragraph or two explaining how an FOMC member might have reacted to this information, including whether the Fed was getting mixed signals and what policies they might have recommended to move the red dot toward the center of the bullseye. (Note that at that time, the Fed believed the full-employment rate of unemployment to be about 4.2 percent of the labor force.) **LO15.3**

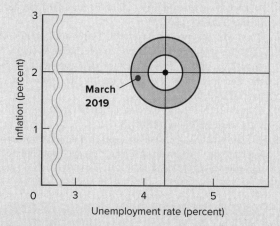

4. Refer to the table for Moola below to answer the following questions. What is the equilibrium interest rate in Moola? What is the level of investment at the equilibrium interest rate? Is there either a recessionary output gap (negative GDP gap) or an inflationary output gap (positive GDP gap) at the equilibrium interest rate and, if either, what is the amount? Given money demand, by how much would the Moola central bank need to change the money supply to close the output gap? What is the expenditure multiplier in Moola? **LO15.4**

Money Supply	Money Demand	Interest Rate	Investment at Interest (Rate Shown)	Potential Real GDP	Actual Real GDP at Interest (Rate Shown)
$500	$800	2%	$50	$350	$390
500	700	3	40	350	370
500	600	4	30	350	350
500	500	5	20	350	330
500	400	6	10	350	310

The Taylor Rule

LO15.7 State the Taylor Rule and explain how it balances the two parts of the Fed's dual mandate.

Weighing Unemployment against Inflation

When deciding whether monetary policy should be expansionary, restrictive, or neutral at any given point in time, the Federal Open Market Committee (FOMC) has to do its best to abide by the dual mandate's requirement that the Fed attempt to maintain full employment and stable prices simultaneously. As the monetary policy bullseye chart makes clear, however, the Fed may end up receiving conflicting signals from the unemployment rate and the inflation rate as to whether monetary policy should be expansionary, contractionary, or neutral and, thus, whether interest rates may have to be raised, lowered, or left alone.

As economists have attempted to model the Fed's decision making with regard to setting interest rates, they have done their best to take that dilemma into account. The most famous such model, the so-called *Taylor rule*, does so by assuming that the FOMC will care more about meeting the unemployment part of the dual mandate than the inflation part of the dual mandate.

The Taylor Rule

The stance of monetary policy is a matter of policy discretion by the members of the FOMC. At each of their meetings, committee members assess whether the current monetary policy stance—expansionary, restrictive, or neutral—remains appropriate for achieving the twin goals of stable prices and full employment. If the majority of FOMC members conclude that a change is needed, the FOMC adjusts how it is handling the monetary policy tools at its disposal.

A rule of thumb suggested by economist John Taylor roughly matches the FOMC's actual policy decisions about the *effective federal funds rate* during many time periods. It is based on economists' widely held belief that central bankers are willing to tolerate above-target inflation if doing so helps to achieve full employment.

To capture that preference, the **Taylor rule** takes into account both the Fed's 2-percent inflation target as well as its 3.5-percent unemployment rate target. It does so by assuming

that the two major components of the Fed's interest-rate targeting decisions will be:

- The **inflation gap** (= current actual inflation rate − 2 percent target inflation rate)
- The **unemployment gap** (= current actual unemployment rate − 3.5 percent target unemployment rate)

There are several ways to express the Taylor rule mathematically.[1] The most intuitive version is:

$$\text{Fed target interest rate} = \text{real risk-free interest rate} \\ + \text{current actual inflation rate} \\ + 0.5 \times (\text{inflation gap}) \\ - 1.0 \times (\text{unemployment gap})$$

The real risk-free interest rate is the minimum real rate of return that lenders demand for the use of their money. Based on historical data, the real risk-free interest rate is normally about 2 percent per year. Substituting that value into the Taylor rule gives us:

$$\text{Fed target interest rate} = 2 + \text{current actual inflation rate} \\ + 0.5 \times (\text{inflation gap}) \\ - 1.0 \times (\text{unemployment gap})$$

Predicting Fed Policy with the Taylor Rule

We can use the Taylor rule to predict the Fed's interest rate target for the effective federal funds rate and, thus, whether it will pursue an expansionary monetary policy (by lowering the effective federal funds rate from its current level) or a restrictive monetary policy (by raising the effective federal funds rate from its current level).

- Suppose, for example, that the current actual inflation rate is 3 percent and the current actual unemployment rate is 2.5 percent. Then the inflation gap is 1 percent (= 3 percent actual inflation − 2 percent target inflation) and the unemployment gap is negative 1 percent

inflation gap The difference between the current actual rate of *inflation* and the central bank's *target rate of inflation;* a key component of the *Taylor Rule.*

unemployment gap The difference between the actual rate of *unemployment* and the *full-employment rate of unemployment,* which is believed to be between 3 and 4 percent for the U.S. economy; a key component of the *Taylor rule.*

Taylor rule A *monetary rule* proposed by economist John Taylor that would stipulate exactly how much the *Federal Reserve System* should change *real interest rates* in response to divergences of *real GDP* from potential GDP and divergences of actual rates of *inflation* from a target rate of inflation.

[1]The version of the Taylor rule that we present uses Okun's law to convert deviations of actual GDP from full-employment GDP into deviations of the actual unemployment rate from the full-employment rate of unemployment.

(= 2.5 percent actual unemployment rate − 3.5 percent target unemployment rate). Substituting those values into our equation, we find that the Fed's target interest rate will be 6.5 percent [= 2 percent real risk-free rate + 3 percent current actual inflation rate + 0.5 × inflation gap of 1 percent − 1.0 × unemployment gap of minus 1 percent].

- Similarly, let's suppose that the Fed is hitting the dual-mandate bullseye dead center. In that case, actual inflation is equal to the target rate of 2 percent and actual unemployment is equal to the target rate of 3.5 percent. Substituting those values into the Taylor rule tells us that when the economy is operating at the Fed's dual-mandate sweet spot, the Fed will want to target an interest rate of 4 percent [= 2 percent real-risk free rate + 2 percent current actual inflation rate + 0.5 × inflation gap of zero − 1.0 × unemployment gap of zero].

Favoring the Unemployment Gap over the Inflation Gap

Note that in the Taylor rule equation, the coefficient on the inflation gap is 0.5 while the coefficient on the unemployment gap is 1.0. This reflects the fact that policymakers are assumed to care more about the unemployment gap than about the inflation gap. In fact, they are assumed to care precisely twice as much about the unemployment gap because the unemployment gap's coefficient of 1.0 is twice as large as the inflation gap's coefficient of 0.5.

Those differing weights give us a hint as to how the real-world FOMC may deal with situations in which the economy is operating in either the southwest or northeast quadrants of the bullseye chart. Those are the quadrants in which inflation and unemployment give contradictory signals about monetary policy. The Taylor rule's coefficient weights on the unemployment gap and the inflation gap tell us that the Fed will resolve the contradictory signals by targeting an effective federal funds rate that puts twice as much weight on closing the unemployment gap as it does on closing the inflation gap.

The Taylor Rule and Quantitative Easing

One of the ways that the Taylor rule is of great interest is because it can be used to demonstrate why the Fed felt it necessary to initiate quantitative easing to help the economy recover from the Great Recession of 2007–2009.

Consider the economic situation in 2009. Actual inflation was −0.36 percent and actual unemployment was 10.0 percent. If we assume an inflation target of 2.0 percent and a natural rate of unemployment of 3.5 percent, then the effective federal funds rate suggested by the Taylor Rule turns out to be *negative* 6.04 percent [= 2 − 0.36 + 0.5 × (−0.36 − 2.0) − 1.0 × (10.0 − 3.5)].

That's a nice suggestion, but it's also a dangerous suggestion because the zero lower bound problem implies that any negative interest rate would very likely end up generating more harm than help. Long before the Fed could even get to negative 2.0 percent—let alone negative 6.04 percent!—people would begin removing deposits from the banking system in order to convert their money into cash that would not be subject to a negative rate of return. That conversion could, in turn, cause all sorts of economic problems, including decreased spending by consumers.

What the Fed's then-chair Ben Bernanke understood at the time was that the recession of 2007–2009 was so severe that the Fed was in uncharted territory. Whereas all of the downturns between the Great Depression of the 1930s and the Great Recession of 2007–2009 had been mild enough that they could be handled with reductions in short-term interest rates, getting out of the Great Recession would have required reductions in longer-term interest rates, too. The result was quantitative easing and the Fed's decision to purchase large amounts of longer-term government bonds in order to lower longer-term interest rates and thereby provide additional economic stimulus after the Fed had already lowered short-term interest rates down to nearly zero.

Appendix Summary

LO15.7 State the Taylor Rule and explain how it balances the two parts of the Fed's dual mandate.
The Taylor rule attempts to model how the Federal Reserve and other central banks will set their policy rates if they feel that there is a trade-off between meeting their goals with respect to inflation on the one hand and employment on the other hand.

When applied to the U.S. economy, the Taylor rule suggests that the Federal Reserve's target for its policy rate, the effective federal funds rate, will equal the sum of the real risk-free interest rate of 2 percent + the current rate of inflation + 1/2 times the inflation gap − 1.0 times the unemployment gap.

Appendix Terms and Concepts

Taylor rule   inflation gap   unemployment gap

Appendix Discussion Questions

1. Does the Taylor Rule put a higher weight on resolving the unemployment gap or the inflation gap? Explain. **LO15.7**

Appendix Review Questions

1. The Taylor Rule puts _____ as much weight on closing the unemployment gap as it does on closing the inflation gap. **LO15.7**
   a. just
   b. twice
   c. half
   d. ten times

2. In 2020, near the start of the COVID crisis, the annualized inflation rate briefly hit −5.9 percent while the unemployment rate briefly soared to 14.7 percent. If the target inflation rate was 2.0 percent and the full-employment rate of unemployment was 3.5 percent, what value does the Taylor Rule predict for the Fed's target interest rate back then? Would that rate have been possible given the zero lower bound problem? **LO15.7**
   a. Negative 3.35 percent; not possible.
   b. Positive 1.95 percent; possible.
   c. Negative 19.5 percent; not possible.
   d. Positive 3.35; possible.

Appendix Problems

1. In 1980, the U.S. inflation rate was 13.5 percent and the unemployment rate reached 7.8 percent. Suppose that the target rate of inflation was 3 percent back then and that the full-employment rate of unemployment was 6 percent at that time. What value does the Taylor rule predict for the Fed's target interest rate? Would you be surprised to learn that the effective federal funds rate reached 18.9 percent in December 1980? Explain why or why not. **LO15.7**

2. Suppose that actual inflation is 3 percentage points, the Fed's inflation target is 2 percentage points, and unemployment is 1 percentage point below the Fed's unemployment target. According to the Taylor rule, what value will the Fed want to set for its target interest rate? **LO15.7**

Financial Economics

isak55/Shutterstock

>> LEARNING OBJECTIVES

LO16.1 Distinguish between economic investment and financial investment.

LO16.2 Explain the time value of money and calculate the present value of money.

LO16.3 Distinguish among the most common financial investments: stocks, bonds, and mutual funds.

LO16.4 Explain how percentage rates of return provide a common framework for comparing assets.

LO16.5 Define arbitrage.

LO16.6 Define risk and distinguish between diversifiable and nondiversifiable risk.

LO16.7 Explain the factors that determine investment decisions.

LO16.8 Explain why arbitrage will tend to move all investments onto the Security Market Line.

Financial economics studies investor preferences and how they affect the trading and pricing of financial assets like stocks, bonds, and real estate. The two most important investor preferences are a desire for high rates of return and a dislike of risk and uncertainty. This chapter explains how these preferences interact to produce a strong positive relationship between risk and return: The riskier an investment, the higher its rate of return. This positive relationship compensates investors for bearing risk.

Financial Investment

>> **LO16.1** Distinguish between economic investment and financial investment.

economic investment
Spending for the production and accumulation of *capital*, additions to *inventories*, or the research and development of new goods or services, including funds spent on the creation of new works of music, literature, or software. Compare with *financial investment*.

Financial economics focuses on the investments that individuals and firms make in the wide variety of assets available to them in our modern economy. Before proceeding, it is important for you to understand the difference between economic investment and financial investment.

Economic investment refers either to paying for *new* additions to the capital stock or for *new* replacements for capital stock that has worn out. Thus, *new* factories, houses, retail stores, construction equipment, and wireless networks are all good examples of economic investments. So are purchases of office computers to replace computers that have become obsolete as well as purchases of new commercial airplanes to replace planes that have served out their useful lives. Economic investment also includes research and development spending and spending to produce new intellectual assets like books, films, and music. Economic investment pays for things that will increase the economy's ability to produce desired goods and services.

Financial investment is a far broader, much more inclusive concept. It includes economic investment and a whole lot more. **Financial investment** refers to either buying or building an asset with the expectation of financial gain. It does not distinguish between *new* assets and *old* assets. Purchasing an old house or an old factory is just as much a financial investment as purchasing a new house or a new factory. For financial investment, it does not matter if the purchase of an asset adds to the capital stock, replaces the capital stock, or does neither.

Investing in old comic books is just as much a financial investment as building a new oil refinery. Finally, unlike economic investment, financial investment can involve either *financial assets* (such as stocks, bonds, and futures contracts) or *real assets* (such as land, factories, and retail buildings).

When bankers, entrepreneurs, corporate executives, retirement planners, and ordinary people use the word investment, they almost always mean financial investment. In fact, the ordinary meaning of the word investment *is* financial investment. So, for this chapter, we use the word investment in its ordinary sense of "financial investment" rather than in the far narrower sense of "economic investment," which we have used throughout most of the rest of this book. In addition, much of our focus will be on tradable financial assets like stocks and bonds that are collectively known as **securities** under U.S. law.

financial investment The purchase of a financial asset (such as a *stock, bond,* or *mutual fund*) or real asset (such as a house, land, or factories) in the expectation of financial gain. Compare with economic investment.

securities Financial assets such as stocks and bonds that are tradable in organized financial markets, such as the New York Stock Exchange (NYSE).

Present Value

Because a specific amount of money is more valuable to a person the sooner it is received, people are going to want to be compensated if you ask them to wait to receive it. The amount that you must compensate them for having to wait is the *time value of money* (also known as the time value of delay).

The time value of money underlies one of the fundamental ideas in financial economics: **present value,** which is the present-day value of returns or costs that are expected to arrive in the future. Present value is especially useful when investors wish to determine the proper current price to pay for an asset. In fact, the proper current price for any risk-free investment *is* the present value of its expected future returns. And while some adjustments have to be made when determining the proper price of a risky investment, the process is entirely based on the logic of present value. Thus we begin our study of finance by explaining present value and how we use it to price risk-free assets. Next, we turn our attention to risk and how the financial markets determine the prices of risky assets by taking into account investor preferences regarding the trade-off between potential return and potential risk.

>> **LO16.2** Explain the time value of money and calculate the present value of money.

present value Today's value of some amount of *money* that is to be received at a particular future date.

Compound Interest

The best way to understand present value is by first understanding compound interest. **Compound interest** explains how quickly an investment increases in value when interest is paid, or *compounded,* not only on the original amount invested but also on all interest payments that have been previously made.

As an example of compound interest in action, consider Table 16.1, which shows the amount of money that $100 invested today becomes if it increases, or compounds, at an 8 percent annual interest rate, i, for various numbers of years. *To simplify, we will express annual interest rates as decimals.* So the 8 percent annual interest rate can be expressed as $i = 0.08$. The key to understanding compound interest is to realize that 1 year's worth of growth at interest rate i will always result in $(1 + i)$ times as much money at the end of a year as there was at the beginning of the year. Consequently, if the first year begins with $100 and if $i = 0.08$, then $(1 + 0.08)$ or 1.08 times as much money—$108—will be available at the end of the year.

compound interest *Interest* that is paid both on an original sum of money and on interest that has already been paid on that sum.

We show the computation for the first year in column 2 of Table 16.1 and display the $108 outcome in column 3. The same logic also applies to other initial amounts. If a year begins with $500, there will be 1.08 times more money after 1 year, or $540. Algebraically, let X_0 denote the amount of money at the start of the first year and X_1 the amount after 1 year's worth of growth.

Then we see that any given number of dollars X_0 at the start of the first year grows into $X_1 = (1 + i)X_0$ dollars after 1 year's worth of growth.

Next, consider what happens if the initial investment of $100 that grew into $108 after 1 year continues to grow at 8 percent interest for a second year. The $108 available at the beginning of the second year will grow into an amount of

(1) Years of Compounding	(2) Compounding Computation	(3) Value at Year's End
1	$100 (1.08)	$108.00
2	100 (1.08)^2	116.64
3	100 (1.08)^3	125.97
4	100 (1.08)^4	136.05
5	100 (1.08)^5	146.93
17	100 (1.08)^{17}	370.00

TABLE 16.1
Compounding: $100 at 8 Percent Interest

money that is 1.08 times larger by the end of the second year. That amount, as shown in Table 16.1, is $116.64. Notice that we make the computation in the table by multiplying the initial $100 by $(1.08)^2$. We do so because the original $100 is compounded by 1.08 into $108, and then the $108 is again compounded by 1.08. More generally, the second year begins with $(1 + i)X_0$ dollars, which will grow to $(1 + i)(1 + i)X_0 = (1 + i)^2 X_0$ dollars by the end of the second year.

Similar reasoning shows that the amount of money at the end of 3 years has to be $(1 + i)^3 X_0$ because the amount of money at the beginning of the third year, $(1 + i)^2 X_0$, gets multiplied by $(1 + i)$ to convert it into the amount of money at the end of the third year. In terms of Table 16.1, that amount is $125.97, which is $(1.08)^3 \$100$.

As you can see, we now have a fixed pattern. The $100 that is invested at the beginning of the first year becomes $(1 + i)\$100$ after 1 year, $(1 + i)^2\$100$ after 2 years, $(1 + i)^3\$100$ after 3 years, and so on. It therefore is clear that the amount of money after t years will be $(1 + i)^t\$100$. This pattern always holds true, regardless of the size of the initial investment. Thus, investors know that if they invest X_0 dollars today and earn compound interest at the rate i, then X_0 dollars will grow into exactly $(1 + i)^t X_0$ dollars after t years. Economists express that fact with the following formula:

$$X_t = (1 + i)^t X_0 \tag{1}$$

Equation 1 captures the idea that if investors have the opportunity to invest X_0 dollars today at interest rate i, then they have the ability to transform X_0 dollars today into $(1 + i)^t X_0$ dollars in t years.

But notice that the logic of the equality also works in reverse, in that it also shows that $(1 + i)^t X_0$ dollars in t years can be transformed into X_0 dollars today. That may seem very odd, but it is exactly what happens when people take out loans. For instance, consider a situation in which an investor named Roberto takes out a loan for $100 today, a loan that will accumulate interest at 8 percent per year for 5 years. Under such an arrangement, the amount Roberto owes will grow with compound interest into $(1.08)^5\$100 = \$146.93$ in 5 years. This means that Roberto can convert $146.93 in 5 years (the amount required to pay off the loan) into $100 today (the amount he borrows today).

Consequently, the compound interest formula given in equation 1 defines not only the rate at which present amounts of money can be converted to future amounts of money but also the rate at which future amounts of money can be converted into present amounts of money.

The Present Value Model

The present value model simply rearranges equation 1 to make it easier to transform future amounts of money into present amounts of money. To derive the formula used to calculate the present value of a future amount of money, we divide both sides of equation 1 by $(1 + i)^t$ to obtain

$$\frac{X_t}{(1 + i)^t} = X_0 \tag{2}$$

The logic of equation 2 is identical to that of equation 1. Both allow investors to convert present amounts of money into future amounts of money and vice versa. However, equation 2 makes it much easier to convert a given number of dollars in the future into their present-day equivalent. In fact, it says that X_t dollars in t years converts into exactly $X_t/(1 + i)^t$ dollars today. This may not seem important, but it is actually very powerful because it allows investors to easily calculate how much they should pay for any particular asset.

To understand why, realize that an asset's owner obtains the right to receive one or more future payments. If an investor is considering buying an asset, her problem is to try to determine how much she should pay today to buy the asset and receive those future payments. Equation 2 makes this task very easy. If she knows how large a future payment will be (X_t dollars), when it will arrive (in t years), and what the interest rate is (i), then she can apply equation 2 to determine the payment's present value: that is, its value in present-day dollars. If she does this for each of the future payments that the asset in question is expected to make, she will be able to calculate the overall present value of all of the asset's future payments by simply summing together the present values of each of those individual payments. This will allow her to determine the price she should pay for the asset. *The asset's current price should exactly equal the sum of the present values of all of the asset's future payments.*

As a simple example, suppose that Cecilia has the chance to buy an asset that is guaranteed to return a single payment of exactly $370.00 in 17 years. Again let's assume the interest rate is 8 percent per year. Then Cecelia can use equation 2 to determine the present value of that future payment: $370.00/(1 + 0.8)^{17} = $370.00/(1.08)^{17} = $100 today. This is confirmed in the row for year 17 in Table 16.1.

To see why Cecilia should be willing to pay a price that is *exactly* equal to the $100 present value of the asset's single future payment of $370.00 in 17 years, consider the following thought experiment. What would happen if she were to invest $100 today in an alternative investment that guarantees to compound her money for 17 years at 8 percent per year? How large would her investment in this alternative become? Equation 1 and Table 16.1 tell us that the answer is exactly $370.00.

This is very important because it shows that Cecilia and other investors have two different ways of purchasing the right to receive $370.00 in 17 years. They can either:

- Purchase the asset in question for $100.
- Invest $100 in the alternative asset that pays 8 percent per year.

Because either investment will deliver the same future benefit, both investments are in fact identical. Consequently, they should have identical prices. Each should cost precisely $100 today.

A good way to understand why this must be the case is to consider how the presence of the alternative investment affects the behavior of both the potential buyers and the potential sellers of the asset in question. First, notice that Cecilia and other potential buyers would never pay more than $100 for the asset in question because they know that they can get the same future return of $370.00 in 17 years by investing $100 in the alternative asset. At the same time, the people selling the asset in question would not sell it to Cecilia or other potential buyers for anything less than $100 since they know that the only other way for Cecilia and other potential investors to get a future return of $370.00 in 17 years is by paying $100 for the alternative investment. Since Cecilia and the other potential buyers will not pay more than $100 for the asset in question and its sellers will not accept less than $100 for the asset in question, the result will be that the asset in question and the alternative investment will have exactly the same price of $100 today.

QUICK REVIEW 16.1

- Financial investment refers to buying an asset with the hope of financial gain.
- The time-value of money is the idea that a specific amount of money is more valuable to a person the sooner it is received because of the potential for compound interest.
- Compound interest is the payment of interest not only on the original amount invested but also on any interest payments previously made; X_0 dollars today growing at interest rate i will become $(1 + i)^t X_0$ dollars in t years.
- The present value formula facilitates transforming future amounts of money into present-day amounts of money; X_t dollars in t years converts into exactly $X_t/(1 + i)^t$ dollars today.
- An investment's proper current price is equal to the sum of the present values of all the future payments that it is expected to make.

Applications

Present value has many everyday applications. Let's examine two of them.

Take the Money and Run? The winners of state lotteries typically receive their winnings in equal installments spread out over 20 years. For instance, suppose that Zoe gets lucky and wins a $100 million jackpot. She will not receive $100 million all at once. Rather, she will receive $5 million per year for 20 years, for a total of $100 million.

Zoe may object to this installment payment system for a variety of reasons. For one thing, she may be very old, so that she is not likely to live long enough to collect all of the payments. Therefore, she might prefer to receive her winnings immediately so that she can make large immediate donations to her favorite charities or large immediate investments in a business project. And, of course, she may just be impatient and want to buy a lot of really expensive consumption goods sooner rather than later.

Fortunately for Zoe, if she does wish to receive her winnings sooner rather than later, several private financial companies are ready and willing to help her. They do so by arranging swaps. Lottery winners sell the right to receive their installment payments in exchange for a single lump sum that they get immediately. The people who hand over the lump sum receive the right to collect the installment payments.

Present value is crucial to arranging these swaps because the financial companies use it to determine the value of the lump sum that lottery winners like Zoe will receive in exchange for giving up their installment payments. The lump sum is equal to the sum of the present values of each of the future payments. Assuming an interest rate of 5 percent per year, the sum of the present values of each of Zoe's 20 installment payments of $5 million is $62,311,051.71. So, depending on her preferences, Zoe can either receive that amount immediately or $100 million spread out over 20 years.

Salary Caps and Deferred Compensation Another example of present value comes directly from the sporting news. Many professional sports leagues worry that richer teams, if not held in check, will outbid poorer teams for the best players. The result would be a situation in which only the richer teams have any real chance of doing well and winning championships.

To prevent that outcome from happening, many leagues have instituted salary caps. These are upper limits on the total amount of money that each team can spend on salaries during a given season. For instance, one popular basketball league has a salary cap of about $120 million per season, which means that each team's total wage bill for all its players has to be no more than $120 million each year.

Typically, however, the salary contracts that are negotiated between individual players and their teams are for multiple seasons. So, during negotiations, players are often asked to help their team stay under the current season's salary cap by agreeing to receive more compensation in later years. For instance, suppose that a team's current payroll is $100 million, and it would like to add a superstar named HiTop to a two-year contract. HiTop, however, is used to earning $30 million per year. This is a major problem for the team because the $120 million salary cap means that the most that the team can pay HiTop for the current season is $20 million.

A common solution is for HiTop to agree to receive only $20 million the first season in order to help the team stay under the salary cap. In exchange for this concession, the team agrees to pay HiTop more than the $30 million he would normally demand for the second season. The team uses the present-value formula to figure out how large his second-season salary should be. HiTop, too, can use the present-value formula to figure out that if the interest rate is 8 percent per year, he should be paid a total of $40.8 million during his second season, because this amount will equal the $30 million he wants for the second season plus $10.8 million to make up for the $10 million reduction in his salary during the first season. That is, the present value of the $10.8 million of delayed compensation that he will receive during the second season precisely equals the $10 million that he agrees to give up during the first season.

Some Popular Investments

>> **LO16.3** Distinguish among the most common financial investments: stocks, bonds, and mutual funds.

The number and types of financial "instruments" in which one can invest are numerous, amazingly creative, and highly varied. Most are much more complicated than the investments we used to explain compounding and present value. But, fortunately, all investments share three features:

- They require that investors pay some price—determined in the market—to acquire them.
- They give their owners the chance to receive future payments.
- The future payments are typically risky.

These features allow us to treat all assets in a unified way. Three of the most popular investments are stocks, bonds, and mutual funds. In 2019, the median value of stock holdings for U.S. families that held stocks was $25,000; the median value for bonds was $121,000; and the median value for "pooled funds" (mainly mutual funds) was $110,000.[1]

Stocks

stock (corporate) An ownership share in a corporation.

Recall that **stocks** are ownership shares in a corporation. If an investor owns 1 percent of a corporation's shares, she gets 1 percent of the votes at the annual shareholders' meeting that selects the company's managers, and she is also entitled to 1 percent of any future profit distributions. There is no guarantee, however, that a company will be profitable.

---

[1]Federal Reserve, "Changes in U.S. Family Finances from 2016 to 2019; Evidence from the Survey of Consumer Finances," p. 16.

Firms often lose money and sometimes even go **bankrupt,** meaning that they are unable to make timely payments on their debts. In the event of a bankruptcy, control of a corporation's assets goes to a bankruptcy judge, whose job is to enforce the legal rights of the people who loaned money to the company. The judge will try to ensure that the company's debtors are repaid. Typically, repaying debtors involves selling off the corporation's assets (factories, real estate, patents, and so on) to raise money to pay off the company's debts.

The money raised by selling the firm's assets may be greater than or less than the amount of the firm's debts. If it is greater than the value of the firm's debts, any remaining money is divided equally among shareholders. If it is less than the firm's debts, the shareholders get nothing at all while the lenders have to accept less than what they are owed. If, for instance, they are collectively owed $100 million but the bankruptcy court's "fire sale" yields only $80 million, then each lender will get back only 80 cents for each dollar they were owed by the firm. In Wall Street slang, the lenders "have to take a haircut."

The maximum amount of money that shareholders can lose is what they pay for their shares. If the company goes bankrupt owing more than the value of the firm's assets, shareholders do not have to make up the difference. This **limited liability rule** limits the risk involved in investing in corporations by capping investors' potential losses at the amount that they paid for their shares. Investors can lose money, but no more than what they paid to purchase their shares.

When firms are profitable, however, investors can look forward to gaining financially in either or both of two possible ways. The first is through **capital gains,** meaning that they sell their shares for more money than they paid for them. The second is by receiving **dividends,** which are equal shares of any current or future profits that are paid out by a company to its shareholders. As we will soon explain, a corporation's current share price is determined by the size of the capital gains and dividends that investors expect the corporation to generate in the future.

Bonds

Bonds are debt contracts that are issued most frequently by governments and corporations. They typically work as follows: An initial investor lends the government or the corporation a certain amount of money, say $1,000, for a certain period of time, say 10 years. In exchange, the government or corporation promises to make a series of semiannual payments in addition to returning the $1,000 at the end of the 10 years. The semiannual payments constitute interest on the loan. For instance, the bond agreement may specify that the borrower will pay $30 every six months. The bond therefore generates $60 per year in payments, which is equal to a 6 percent interest rate on the initial $1,000 loan.

The initial investor is free to sell the bond at any time to other investors, who then gain the right to receive any of the remaining semiannual payments as well as the final $1,000 payment when the bond comes due after 10 years. As we will soon demonstrate, the price at which the bond sells to another investor depends on the current rates of return available on other investments offering a similar stream of future payments and facing a similar level of risk.

The primary risk a bondholder faces is the possibility that the corporation or government that issues the bond will **default** on, or fail to make, the bond's promised payments. This risk is much greater for corporations, but default risk is also possible with respect to local and state governments. They sometimes default when (1) they cannot raise enough tax revenue to make their bond payments or (2) when defaulting on bond payments is politically easier than making budget cuts. The U.S. federal government, however, has never defaulted on its bond payments and is very unlikely to ever default because it has access to huge amounts of current and potential tax revenue and can sell U.S. securities to the Fed as a way to obtain money.

Bonds are much more predictable than stocks. Unless a bond goes into default, its owner knows the size of its future payments and exactly when they will arrive. By contrast, stock prices and dividends are highly volatile because they depend on profits, which vary greatly depending on the overall business cycle and on factors specific to individual firms and industries—things such as changing consumer preferences, variations in the costs of inputs, and changes in the tax code. The fact that bonds are typically more predictable (and thus less risky) than stocks explains why they generate lower average rates of return than stocks. Indeed, this difference in rates of return has been very large historically. From 1926 to 2021, stocks on average returned about 10 percent per year worldwide, while bonds on average returned only roughly 6 percent per year worldwide.

bankrupt A legal situation in which an individual or *firm* finds that it cannot make timely interest payments on money it has borrowed. In such cases, a bankruptcy judge can order the individual or firm to liquidate (turn into cash) its assets in order to pay lenders at least some portion of the amount they are owed.

limited liability rule A law that limits the potential losses that an investor in a *corporation* may suffer to the amount that she paid for her shares in the corporation. Encourages *financial investment* by limiting risk.

capital gain The gain realized when *securities* other *assets* are sold for a *price* greater than the price paid for them.

dividends Payments by a corporation of all or part of its profit to its stockholders (the corporate owners).

bond A financial contract that obligates a borrower to make coupon (interest) payments for a specified period of time before also paying back the principal amount that was initially borrowed.

defaults Situations in which borrowers stop making loan payments or do not pay back loans that they took out and are now due.

mutual funds Investment companies that pool money from numerous individual investors in order to purchase *portfolios* of *stocks* or *bonds;* includes both *index funds* as well as *actively managed funds.*

portfolio A specific collection of *stocks, bonds,* or other *financial investments* held by an individual or a *mutual fund.*

index funds *Mutual funds* whose *portfolios* exactly match a stock or bond index (a collection of *stocks* or *bonds* meant to capture the overall behavior of a particular category of investments) such as the Standard & Poor's 500 Index or the Russell 3000 Index.

actively managed funds *Mutual funds* that have portfolio managers who constantly buy and sell *assets* in an attempt to generate high returns.

passively managed funds *Mutual funds* whose *portfolios* are not regularly updated by a fund manager attempting to generate high returns. Rather, once an initial portfolio is selected, it is left unchanged so that investors receive whatever return that unchanging portfolio subsequently generates. *Index funds* are a type of passively managed fund.

TABLE 16.2 The 10 Largest Mutual Funds, October 2021

Fund Name*	Assets under Management, Billions
Vanguard 500 Index Admiral Shares	$411.0
SPDR S&P 500 ETF	386.4
Fidelity 500 Index Fund	350.3
Vanguard Total Stock Index Admiral Shares	315.5
iShares Core S&P 500	287.0
Vanguard Total Stock Index Institutional Plus	269.7
Vanguard Total Stock Market Index ETF	263.0
Vanguard 500 Index ETF	247.0
Vanguard Total Stock Market Index Institutional	230.8
Fidelity Government Cash Reserves	210.0

Source: "The 25 Largest Mutual Funds," MarketWatch.com.

Mutual Funds

A **mutual fund** is a company that maintains a professionally managed **portfolio,** or collection, of either stocks or bonds. The company purchases the portfolio by pooling the money of many investors. Because these investors provide the money to purchase the portfolio, they own it, and any gains or losses generated by the portfolio flow directly to them. Table 16.2 lists the 10 largest U.S. mutual funds based on their assets under management.

Most of the more than 9,300 mutual funds currently operating in the United States choose to maintain portfolios that invest in specific categories of bonds or stocks. For instance, some fill their portfolios exclusively with the stocks of small tech companies, while others buy only bonds issued by certain state or local governments. In addition, there are **index funds** whose portfolios exactly match a stock index or bond index. Stock and bond indexes follow the performance of a particular group of stocks or bonds to gauge how well a particular category of investments is doing. For instance, the Standard & Poor's 500 Index contains the 500 largest stocks trading in the United States to capture how the stocks of large corporations vary over time.

There is an important distinction between actively managed and passively managed mutual funds. **Actively managed funds** have portfolio managers who constantly buy and sell assets in an attempt to generate high returns. By contrast, index funds are **passively managed funds** because the assets in their portfolios are chosen to exactly match whatever stocks or bonds are contained in their respective underlying indexes.

Later in this chapter, we discuss the relative merits of actively managed funds and index funds, but for now we point out that both types are very popular and that, overall, U.S. households held $34.4 trillion in mutual funds and corporate equities at the end of 2020. By way of comparison, U.S. GDP in 2020 was $20.9 trillion, and the estimated value of all the financial assets held by households in 2020 (including everything from individual stocks and bonds to checking account deposits) was about $100.7 trillion.

QUICK REVIEW

16.2

▶ Three popular forms of financial investments are stocks, bonds, and mutual funds.

▶ Stocks are ownership shares in corporations and bestow upon their owners a proportional share of any future profit.

▶ Bonds are debt contracts that promise to pay a fixed series of payments in the future.

▶ Mutual funds are pools of investor money used to buy portfolios of stocks or bonds.

Calculating Investment Returns

>> **LO16.4** Explain how percentage rates of return provide a common framework for comparing assets.

Investors buy assets to obtain one or more future payments. The simplest case is purchasing an asset for resale. For instance, an investor may buy a house for $300,000 with the hope of selling it for $360,000 one year later. On the other hand, she could also rent out the house for $3,000 per month and thereby receive a stream of future payments. Or she could do a little of both, paying

$300,000 for the house now, renting it out for five years, and then selling it. In that case, she is expecting a stream of smaller payments followed by a large one.

Percentage Rates of Return

Economists have developed a common framework for evaluating the gains or losses of assets that make only one future payment as well as those that make many future payments. They state the gain or loss as a **percentage rate of return,** by which they mean the percentage gain or loss (relative to the buying price) over a given period of time, typically a year. For instance, if Noelle buys a rare comic book today for $100 and sells it in 1 year for $125, she makes a 25 percent per year rate of return. She determines this rate of return by dividing the gain of $25 by the purchase price of $100. By contrast, if she sold the comic book for only $92, then she would make a loss of 8 percent per year (which she calculates by dividing the $8 loss by the purchase price of $100).

A similar calculation is made for assets that deliver a series of payments. For instance, an investor who buys a house for $300,000 and expects to rent it out for $3,000 per month is expecting to make a 12 percent per year rate of return because he divides his $36,000 per year of rent collections by the $300,000 purchase price of the house.

percentage rate of return
The percentage gain or loss, relative to the buying *price,* of an *economic investment* or *financial investment* over some period of time.

The Inverse Relationship between Asset Prices and Rates of Return

A fundamental concept in financial economics is that, other things equal, *an investment's rate of return is inversely related to its price. The higher the price paid for an asset, the lower its rate of return will be, all other things equal.* To understand why, consider a bond that pays $24,000 of interest each year. If an investor pays $100,000 for the bond, he will earn a 24 percent per year rate of return (the $24,000 annual interest payment divided by the $100,000 purchase price of the bond).

But suppose that the purchase price of the bond rises to $200,000. In that case, the investor will earn only a 12 percent per year rate of return, because the $24,000 annual interest payment is divided by the much larger purchase price of $200,000. Consequently, as the price of the bond goes up, the rate of return from buying it goes down.

The same relationship holds for other investments, such as rental property. The higher the price of a rental property, given its monthly rent, the lower the rate of return. The underlying cause of this general relationship is the fact that the future payments are held constant while one varies the current price. The fact that the future payments are held constant implies that there is an upper limit to the financial rewards of owning the asset. As a result, the more an investor pays for the asset now, the smaller those future payments will be relative to the amount paid to obtain them. Thus, higher asset prices imply lower rates of return.

CONSIDER THIS . . .

Corporate Ownership

The rise of mutual funds has radically changed the way corporations are controlled. Before the 1970s, corporations knew that the vast majority of their shares were owned by individuals, the large majority of whom were interested in holding their shares for the long run. Those long-run individual investors paid close attention to what corporate officers were doing and would reprimand bad decisions at annual shareholder meetings.

By contrast, neither actively nor passively managed funds have much incentive to care about the long-run success of the companies whose shares they buy and sell. Consider actively managed funds. Their managers lack an incentive to care about long-term

Chris Stein/Stone/Getty Images

performance because they are paid bonuses that depend almost entirely on quarterly performance rather than long-term performance. At the same time, the managers of passively managed funds have no incentive to care about corporate management or policy initiatives because they simply buy whatever stocks are included in their funds' respective underlying indexes.

Critics worry that the decline of close scrutiny by individual shareholders has helped to exacerbate a variety of problems, including corporate managers being paid excessive salaries and CEOs being overly focused on accounting gimmicks that offer a short-run boost to company share prices rather than good management decisions that will pay off only after many years have passed.

Arbitrage

>> LO16.5 Define arbitrage.

arbitrage The activity of selling one asset and buying an identical or nearly identical asset to benefit from temporary differences in *prices* or *rates of return;* the practice that equalizes prices or returns on similar financial instruments and thus eliminates further opportunities for riskless financial gains.

Arbitrage is the term that financial economists use for the buying and selling process that leads profit-seeking investors to equalize the average expected rates of return generated by identical or nearly identical assets. Arbitrage happens when investors try to profit from situations where two identical or nearly identical assets have different rates of return. They do so by simultaneously selling the asset with the lower rate of return and buying the asset with the higher rate of return. For instance, consider what will happen in a case where two very similar t-shirt companies start with different rates of return despite the fact that they are equally profitable and have equally good future prospects. To make things concrete, suppose that a company called T4me starts out with a rate of return of 10 percent per year while TSTG (T-Shirts to Go) starts out with a rate of return of 15 percent per year.

Because both companies are basically identical and have equally good prospects, investors in T4me will want to shift over to TSTG, which offers higher rates of return for the same amount of risk. As they begin to shift over, however, the prices of the two companies' stocks will change—and with them, the two companies' rates of return. Because so many investors will be selling the shares of the lower-return company, T4me, the supply of its shares trading on the stock market will increase, thereby causing T4me's share price to decline. But because asset prices and rates of return are inversely related, the lower share price will cause T4me's rate of return to rise.

At the same time, the rate of return on the higher-return company, TSTG, will begin to fall. As investors switch from T4me to TSTG, the increased demand for TSTG's shares will drive up their price. And as the price of TSTG goes up, its rate of return must fall.

This arbitrage process will continue—with the rate of return on the higher-return company falling and the rate of return on the lower-return company rising—until both companies have the same rate of return. This convergence happens because as long as the rates of return on the two companies are not identical, there will always be some investors who will want to sell the shares of the lower-return company so they can buy the shares of the higher-return company. As a result, arbitrage will continue until the rates of return are equal.

Generally, only a very short period of time is needed for prices to equalize. In fact, for highly traded assets like stocks and bonds, arbitrage often forces the rates of return on identical or nearly identical investments to converge within a matter of minutes or sometimes even within a matter of seconds. This convergence is very helpful to small investors who do not have a large amount of time to study the thousands of potential investment opportunities available in the financial markets. Thanks to arbitrage, they can invest with the confidence that assets with similar characteristics will have similar rates of return.

QUICK REVIEW

16.3

▶ Stating gains or losses as percentage rates of return provides a common framework for comparing different assets.

▶ Asset prices and percentage rates of return are inversely related.

▶ Arbitrage refers to the buying and selling that takes place to equalize the percentage rates of return on identical or nearly identical assets.

Risk

>> LO16.6 Define risk and distinguish between diversifiable and nondiversifiable risk.

risk The uncertainty as to the future returns of a particular *financial investment* or *economic investment.*

Investors purchase assets to obtain one or more future payments. As used by financial economists, the word **risk** refers to investors' uncertainty regarding the eventual size of those future payments.

The underlying problem is that the future is uncertain. Many factors affect an investment's future payments, and each of these may turn out better or worse than expected. As a simple example, consider buying a farm. Suppose that in an average year, the farm will generate a profit of $100,000. But if a freak hailstorm damages the crops, the profit will fall to only $60,000. If weather conditions turn out to be perfect, the farm's profit will rise to $120,000. Because there is no way to tell in advance what will happen, investing in the farm is risky.

When financial economists use the word *risk*, they do not use it in the casual way that refers only to potentially bad outcomes (as in, "there is a risk that this experimental medicine may kill you"). In financial economics, the word *risk* means that an outcome—good or bad, major or minor, likely or unlikely—lacks certainty. Some outcome will occur, but you cannot be sure what it will be. For instance, suppose that you are given a raffle ticket that will pay you either $10, $100, or $1,000 when a drawing is made in one month. There are no bad outcomes in this particular case, only good ones. But because you do not know with certainty which outcome will occur, the situation is, by our definition, risky. However, the word *risk* in financial economics certainly does not preclude negative outcomes. If you buy shares of common stock in some company, your stock may go up in value. But the company could also go bankrupt, in which case you may lose your entire investment.

Diversification

Investors have many options regarding their portfolios, or collections of investments. For example, they can choose to concentrate their wealth in just one or two investments or spread it out over a large number of investments. **Diversification** is the strategy of investing in a large number of investments to reduce the overall risk to the entire portfolio. It is the process of not putting all of your eggs in one basket.

Diversification generally succeeds in reducing risk. If an investor's portfolio consists of only one investment—say, one stock—then if anything awful happens to that stock, the investor's entire portfolio will suffer greatly. By contrast, if the investor spreads his wealth over many stocks, then a bad outcome for any one particular stock will cause only a small amount of damage to the overall portfolio. In addition, it is typically the case that if something bad is happening to one part of the portfolio, something good will be happening to another part of the portfolio, and the two effects will tend to offset each other. Thus, diversification reduces the risk to the overall portfolio.

Even though diversification can reduce a portfolio's risks, it cannot eliminate them entirely. Even if an investor has placed each of his eggs into different baskets, all of the eggs may still end up broken if all of the different baskets get dropped simultaneously. That is, even if an investor has created a well-diversified portfolio, all of the investments still have a chance to do badly simultaneously. As an example, consider the COVID-19 recession of 2020. With economic activity declining and consumer spending falling, nearly all companies faced reduced sales and lowered profits, a fact that caused their stock prices to decline simultaneously. Consequently, even if investors had diversified their portfolios across numerous stocks, their portfolios still declined in value because nearly all of their investments performed poorly simultaneously.

Financial economists divide an individual investment's overall risk into two components, diversifiable risk and nondiversifiable risk. **Diversifiable risk** (or *idiosyncratic risk*) is the risk that is specific to a given investment and that can be eliminated by diversification. For instance, a soda pop maker faces the risk that the demand for its product may suddenly decline because people want to drink mineral water instead of soda pop. But this risk does not matter to an investor if she has a diversified portfolio that contains stock in the soda pop maker as well as stock in a mineral water company. While the stock price of the soda pop maker falls due to the change in consumer preferences, the stock price of the mineral water company is going up—so that, as far as the overall portfolio is concerned, the two effects will offset each other.

By contrast, **nondiversifiable risk** (or *systemic risk*) pushes all investments in the same direction at the same time so that there is no possibility of using good effects to offset bad effects. The best example of a nondiversifiable risk is the business cycle. If the economy does well, then corporate profits rise and nearly every stock does well. But if the economy does badly, then corporate profits fall and nearly every stock does badly. As a result, even if one builds a well-diversified portfolio, the business cycle will still affect that portfolio because nearly every asset in the portfolio will move in the same direction at the same time whenever the economy improves or worsens.

That said, creating a diversified portfolio is still an investor's best strategy because doing so at least eliminates diversifiable risk. Indeed, for investors who have successfully created diversified portfolios, all diversifiable risks will be eliminated, so that the only remaining source of risk is nondiversifiable risk.

Thus, when investors consider whether to add a particular investment to a portfolio that is already diversified, they can ignore the investment's diversifiable risk. They can ignore it because, as part of a diversified portfolio, the investment's diversifiable risk will be "diversified away." Indeed, the only risk left is the amount of nondiversifiable risk that the investment carries. Investors can therefore base their decisions about whether to add a potential new investment to their portfolios by comparing the potential investment's level of nondiversifiable risk with its potential returns. If they find this trade-off attractive, they will add the investment, whereas if it seems unattractive, they will not.

Global Perspective 16.1 shows that investment risk varies significantly across countries due to underlying differences in political, economic, and financial risks.

diversification The strategy of investing in a large number of investments in order to reduce the overall risk to an entire investment *portfolio.*

diversifiable risk Investment *risk* that investors can reduce via *diversification;* also called idiosyncratic risk.

nondiversifiable risk Investment *risk* that investors are unable to reduce via *diversification;* also called systemic risk.

GLOBAL PERSPECTIVE 16.1

INTERNATIONAL DIFFERENCES IN RISK

The International Country Risk Guide attempts to distill the political, economic, and financial risks facing 140 countries into a single "composite risk rating" for each country, with higher numbers indicating less risk. The table below presents the ranks and rating numbers for 15 countries, including the three least risky (ranked 1 through 3) and the three most risky (ranked 138 through 140). Risk ratings numbers above 80 are considered *very low risk;* 70–80 are considered *low risk;* 60–70 *moderate risk;* 50–60 *high risk;* and below 50 *very high risk.*

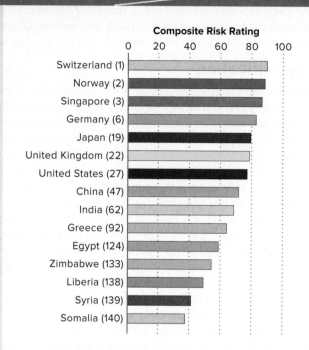

Composite Risk Rating

Source: "International Country Risk Guide," PRS Group.

QUICK REVIEW

16.4

▶ An asset is risky if its future payments are uncertain.

▶ Diversification is an investment strategy in which savers invest in a large number of different investments in order to reduce the overall risk to their entire portfolio.

▶ Risks that can be canceled out by diversification are called diversifiable risks; risks that cannot be canceled out by diversification are called nondiversifiable risks.

Comparing Risky Investments

>> LO16.7 Explain the factors that determine investment decisions.

Economists believe that the two most important factors affecting investment decisions are returns and risks—specifically nondiversifiable risks. But for investors to compare different investments on the basis of returns and risks, they need ways to measure returns and risks. The two standard measures are, respectively, the average expected rate of return and the beta statistic.

Average Expected Rate of Return

average expected rate of return The *probability-weighted average* of an investment's possible future returns.

probability-weighted average Each of the possible future rates of return from an investment multiplied by its respective probability (expressed as a decimal) of happening.

Each investment's **average expected rate of return** is the probability-weighted average of the investment's possible future rates of return. The term **probability-weighted average** simply means that each of the possible future rates of return is multiplied by its probability expressed as a decimal (so that a 50 percent probability is 0.50 and a 23 percent probability is 0.23) before being added together to obtain the average. For instance, if an investment has a 75 percent probability of generating 11 percent per year and a 25 percent probability of generating 15 percent per year, then its average expected rate of return will be 12 percent = (0.75 × 11 percent) + (0.25 × 15 percent). By weighting each possible outcome by its probability, this process ensures that the resulting average gives more weight to outcomes that are more likely to happen (unlike the normal averaging process, which would treat every outcome the same).

Once investors have calculated the average expected rates of return for all the assets they are interested in, there will naturally be some impulse to simply invest in those assets with the highest rates of return. But while that strategy might satisfy investor cravings for high rates of return, it would not take proper account of the fact that investors dislike risk and uncertainty. To quantify their dislike, investors require a statistic that measures each investment's risk level.

Beta

One popular statistic that measures risk is called beta. **Beta** is a *relative* measure of nondiversifiable risk. It measures how the nondiversifiable risk of a given asset or portfolio of assets compares with that of the **market portfolio,** which is the name given to a portfolio that contains every asset available in the financial markets. The market portfolio is a useful standard of comparison because it is as diversified as possible. In fact, because it contains every possible asset, each and every diversifiable risk will be diversified away. As a result, the market portfolio's risk and volatility must be due entirely to nondiversifiable risk. Consequently, the market portfolio can serve as a useful benchmark against which to measure any particular asset's level of nondiversifiable risk.

Such comparisons are very simple because the beta statistic is standardized such that the market portfolio's level of nondiversifiable risk is set equal to 1.0. Consequently, an asset with beta = 0.5 has a level of nondiversifiable risk that is one-half of that possessed by the market portfolio, while an asset with beta = 2.0 has twice as much nondiversifiable risk as the market portfolio. In addition, investors can use beta numbers to compare various assets. For instance, an asset with beta = 2.0 has four times more exposure to nondiversifiable risk than an asset with beta = 0.5.

Beta can be calculated not only for individual assets but also for portfolios. Indeed, it can be calculated for portfolios no matter how many or how few assets they contain and no matter what those assets are. Thus mutual fund investors can use beta to quickly see how the nondiversifiable risk of any given fund's portfolio compares with that of other potential investments that they may be considering.

In summary: The beta statistic is used along with average expected rates of return to give investors standard measures of risk and return that allow them to sensibly compare different investment opportunities.

beta A relative measure of *nondiversifiable risk* that measures how the nondiversifiable risk of a given *asset* or *portfolio* compares with that of the *market portfolio* (the portfolio that contains every asset available in the financial markets).

market portfolio The portfolio consisting of every financial asset (including every *stock* and *bond*) traded in the financial markets. Used to calculate *beta* (a measure of the degree of riskiness) for specific stocks, bonds, and mutual funds.

Relationship between Risk and Average Expected Rate of Return

The fact that investors dislike risk has a profound effect on asset prices and average expected rates of return. In particular, their dislike of risk and uncertainty causes investors to pay higher prices for less-risky assets and lower prices for more-risky assets. But because asset prices and average expected rates of return are inversely related, less-risky assets will have lower average expected rates of return than more-risky assets.

Stated another way: *Risk levels and average expected rates of return are positively related*. The more risky an investment is, the higher its average expected rate of return will be. A great way to understand this relationship is to think of higher average expected rates of return as a form of compensation. Because investors dislike risk, they demand higher levels of compensation the more risky an asset is. The higher levels of compensation come in the form of higher average expected rates of return.

Be sure to note that this phenomenon affects all assets. Regardless of whether the assets are stocks, bonds, real estate, or anything else, assets with higher levels of risk always end up with higher average expected rates of return to compensate investors for the higher levels of risk involved. No matter what the investment opportunity is, investors examine its possible future payments, determine how risky they are, and then select a price that reflects those risks. Because less-risky investments command higher prices, they end up with lower rates of return, whereas more-risky investments end up with lower prices and, consequently, higher rates of return.

The Risk-Free Rate of Return

We have just demonstrated that there is a positive relationship between risk and returns, with higher returns compensating investors for higher levels of risk. One investment, however, is considered to be risk-free for all intents and purposes. That investment is short-term U.S. government bonds.

These bonds are short-term loans to the U.S. government, with the duration of the loans ranging from 4 weeks to 26 weeks. They are essentially risk-free because there is almost no chance that the U.S. government will not be able to repay these loans on time and in full. To pay its debt, it can shift funds within its enormous budget, raise taxes, or borrow newly created money from the Fed. Although it is true that the U.S. government may eventually be destroyed or disabled to such an extent that it will not be able to repay some of its loans, the chances of such a calamity happening within 4 or even 26 weeks are essentially zero. Consequently, because it is a near certainty that the bonds will be repaid in full and on time, investors think of them as risk-free.

This leads us to another consideration. Because higher levels of risk lead to higher rates of return, and vice versa, a person might be tempted to assume—incorrectly—that because government bonds are risk-free, they should earn a zero percent rate of return. The problem with this line of thinking is that it mistakenly assumes that risk is the only thing that rates of return compensate for. The truth is, however, that rates of return compensate not only for risk but also for something else that economists call *time preference*.

time preference The human tendency, because of impatience, to prefer to spend and consume in the present rather than save and wait to spend and consume in the future; this inclination varies in strength among individuals.

Time preference refers to the fact that because people tend to be impatient, they typically prefer to consume things in the present rather than in the future. For example, most people, if given the choice between a serving of their favorite dessert immediately or a serving of their favorite dessert in five years, will choose to consume the serving immediately.

This time preference for consuming sooner rather than later affects the financial markets because people want to be compensated for delayed consumption. In particular, if Dave asks Oprah to lend him $1 million for one year, he is implicitly asking Oprah to delay consumption for a year because if she lends Dave the $1 million, she will not be able to spend that money herself for at least a year. If Oprah is like most people and prefers to spend her $1 million sooner rather than later, the only way Dave will be able to convince Oprah to loan him $1 million is to offer her some form of compensation. The compensation comes in the form of an interest payment that will allow Oprah to consume more in the future than she can now. For instance, Dave can offer to pay Oprah $1.1 million in one year in exchange for $1 million today. That is, Oprah will get back the $1 million she lends to Dave today as well as an extra $100,000 to compensate her for being patient.

Notice that this type of interest payment has nothing to do with risk. It is purely compensation for being patient and must be paid even if there is no risk involved and 100 percent certainty that Dave will fulfill his promise to repay.

Because short-term U.S. government bonds are for all intents and purposes completely risk-free and 100 percent likely to repay as promised, their rates of return are *purely* compensation for time preference and the fact that people must be compensated for delaying their own consumption opportunities when they lend money to the government. Therefore, the rate of return earned by short-term U.S. government bonds is often called the **risk-free interest rate**, or i^f, to indicate that their rate of return is not in any way a compensation for risk.

risk-free interest rate The *interest rate* earned on short-term U.S. government bonds.

Keep in mind, however, that the Fed has the power to change the risk-free interest rate generated by short-term U.S. government bonds. As discussed in Chapter 15, the Fed can use open-market operations to lower or raise interest rates by making large purchases or sales of U.S. securities in the bond market. These open-market operations affect the money supply, which affects all interest rates, including the rates on short-term U.S. government bonds. Thus the Fed indirectly determines the risk-free interest rate and, consequently, the compensation that investors receive for being patient.

QUICK REVIEW

16.5

▶ The average expected rate of return is the probability-weighted average of an investment's possible future returns.

▶ Beta measures the nondiversifiable risk of an investment relative to the amount of nondiversifiable risk facing the market portfolio, which is the portfolio containing every asset available in the financial markets.

▶ Because investors dislike risk, riskier investments must offer higher rates of return to compensate investors for bearing more risk.

▶ Average expected rates of return compensate investors for both risk and time preference, which is the preference most people have to consume sooner rather than later.

The Security Market Line

>> **LO16.8** Explain why arbitrage will tend to move all investments onto the Security Market Line.

Security Market Line (SML) A line that shows the *average expected rate of return* of all *financial investments* at each level of *nondiversifiable risk,* the latter measured by *beta.*

Investors must be compensated for time preference as well as for the amount of nondiversifiable risk that an investment carries with it. This section introduces a simple model called the **Security Market Line,** which indicates how this compensation is determined for tradable financial assets (securities) no matter what their respective risk levels happen to be.

The underlying logic of the model is this: Any investment's average expected rate of return has to be the sum of two parts—one that compensates for time preference and another that compensates for risk. That is,

$$\text{Average expected} = \text{rate that compensates for}$$
$$\text{rate of return} \quad \text{time preference}$$
$$+ \text{rate that compensates for risk}$$

As noted earlier, the compensation for time preference is equal to the risk-free interest rate, i^f, that is paid on short-term government bonds. As a result, this equation can be simplified to

$$\text{Average expected rate of return} = i^f + \text{rate that compensates for risk}$$

Finally, because economists typically refer to the rate that compensates for risk as the **risk premium,** this equation can be simplified even further to

$$\text{Average expected rate of return} = i^f + \text{risk premium}$$

risk premium The rate of return in excess of the *risk-free interest rate* that compensates a lender or investor for *risk.*

Naturally, the size of the risk premium that compensates for risk will vary depending on how risky an investment happens to be. In particular, it will depend on how big or small the investment's beta is. Investments with large betas and lots of nondiversifiable risk will require larger risk premiums than investments that have small betas and low levels of nondiversifiable risk. And, in the most extreme case, risk-free assets that have betas equal to zero will require no compensation for risk at all since they have no risk to compensate for.

This logic is translated into Figure 16.1. The horizontal axis of Figure 16.1 measures risk levels using beta; the vertical axis measures average expected rates of return. As a result, any investment can be plotted on Figure 16.1 just as long as we know its beta and its average expected rate of return. We have plotted two investments in Figure 16.1. The first is a risk-free short-term U.S. government bond, which is indicated by the lower-left dot in the figure. The second is the market portfolio, which is indicated by the dot in the middle of the figure.

The lower dot is located where it is because every risk-free asset has a beta = 0 and an expected return equal to i^f. These values place the lower dot i^f percentage points up the vertical axis, as shown in Figure 16.1. Note that this location conveys the logic that because this asset has no risk, its average expected rate of return only has to compensate investors for time preference—which is why its average expected rate of return is equal to precisely i^f and no more.

The market portfolio, by contrast, is risky, so that its average expected rate of return must compensate investors not only for time preference but also for the level of risk to which the market portfolio is exposed, which by definition is beta = 1.0. This implies that the vertical distance from the horizontal axis to the upper dot is equal to the sum of i^f and the market portfolio's risk premium.

The straight line connecting the risk-free asset's lower dot and the market portfolio's upper dot is called the Security Market Line, or SML. The SML is extremely important because it defines the relationship between average expected rates of return and risk levels that must hold for all assets and all portfolios trading in the financial markets. The SML illustrates the idea that every asset's average expected rate of return is the sum of a rate of return that compensates for time preference and a rate of return that compensates for risk.

As we explained earlier, the precise location of the intercept at any given time is determined by the Federal Reserve's monetary policy and how it affects the rate of return on short-term U.S. government bonds. The slope of the SML, however, is determined by investors' feelings about risk and how much compensation they require for dealing with it. If investors greatly dislike risk, then the SML will have to be very steep, so that any given increase in risk on the horizontal axis will result in a very large increase in compensation as measured by average expected rates of return on the vertical axis. On the other hand, if investors dislike risk only moderately, then the SML will be relatively flat since any given increase in risk on the horizontal axis would require only a moderate increase in compensation as measured by average expected rates of return on the vertical axis.

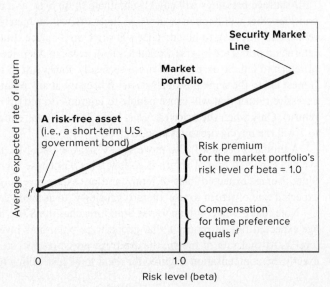

FIGURE 16.1
The Security Market Line.

The Security Market Line shows the relationship between average expected rates of return and risk levels that must hold for every asset or portfolio trading in the financial markets. Each investment's average expected rate of return is the sum of the risk-free interest rate that compensates for time preference as well as a risk premium that compensates for the investment's level of risk. The Security Market Line's upward slope reflects the fact that investors must be compensated for higher levels of risk with higher average expected rates of return.

FIGURE 16.2

Risk levels determine average expected rates of return.

The Security Market Line can be used to determine an investment's average expected rate of return based on its risk level. In this figure, investments having a risk level of beta = X will have an average expected rate of return of Y percent per year. This average expected rate of return will compensate investors for time preference in addition to providing them exactly the right-sized risk premium to compensate them for dealing with a risk level of beta = X.

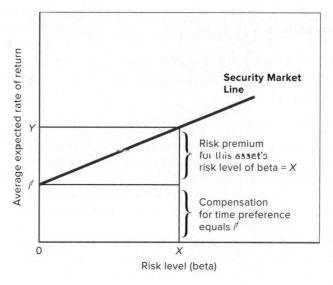

FIGURE 16.3

Arbitrage and the Security Market Line.

Arbitrage pressures will tend to move any asset or portfolio that lies off the Security Market Line back onto the line. Since asset A, for instance, begins with a rate of return higher than the rate Y which is sufficient to compensate investors for risk level X, investors will buy asset A eagerly, driving up its price and decreasing its average expected rate of return. And they will continue to do so until asset A moves down vertically to point B on the SML and earns exactly the rate of return Y that is necessary to compensate investors for risk level X. The opposite happens with asset C, whose initial rate of return is not enough to compensate investors for risk level X. Investors will sell asset C and cause its price to fall until its rate of return rises up to Y on the SML. Therefore, all assets with risk level X end up on the Security Market Line at point B.

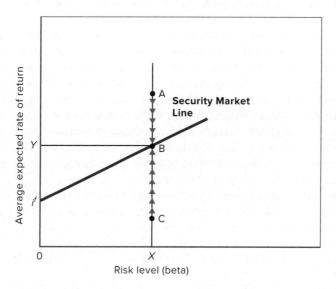

It is important to realize that once investor preferences about risk have determined the slope of the SML and monetary policy has determined its vertical intercept, *the SML plots out the precise relationship between risk levels and average expected rates of return that should hold for every asset.* Consider Figure 16.2, where there is an asset whose risk level on the horizontal axis is beta = X. The SML tells us that every asset with that risk level should have an average expected rate of return equal to Y on the vertical axis. This average expected rate of return exactly compensates for both time preference and the fact that the asset in question is exposed to a risk level of beta = X.

Finally, it should be pointed out that arbitrage will ensure that all investments having an identical level of risk also will have an identical rate of return—the return given by the SML. This is illustrated in Figure 16.3, where the three assets A, B, and C all share the same risk level of beta = X but initially have three different average expected rates of return. Since asset B lies on the SML, it has the average expected rate of return Y that precisely compensates investors for time preference and risk level X. Asset A, however, has a higher average expected rate of return that overcompensates investors for risk level X while asset C has a lower average expected rate of return that undercompensates investors for risk level X.

Arbitrage pressures will quickly eliminate these over- and under-compensations. For instance, consider what will happen to asset A. Investors will be hugely attracted to its overly high rate of return and will rush to buy it. That will drive up its price. But because average expected rates of return and prices are inversely related, the increase in A's price will cause its average expected rate of return to fall. So asset A will move vertically downward in Figure 16.3 until it reaches point B. It must fall to the same position as asset B because at any point higher than B, asset A will earn an excessive return that will cause people to continue to bid up its price (and thus lower its rate of return). Only when the price of A has been driven up far enough such that its rate of return falls to Y will the buying pressures stop.

A similar process will also move asset C back to the SML. Investors will dislike the fact that its average expected rate of return is so low. This will cause them to sell it, driving down its price. Since average expected rates of return and prices are inversely related, this will cause its average expected rate of return to rise, thereby causing C to ascend vertically in Figure 16.3.

Note that C will continue to rise until it reaches the SML, since only then will it have the average expected rate of return Y that properly compensates investors for time preference and risk level X. At that rate of return, the arbitrage pressures will stop since investors will be receiving exactly the compensation required for them to be just willing to own asset C.

Security Market Line: Applications

The SML analysis is highly useful in clarifying why investors scrutinize the intentions and actions of the Federal Reserve and change their behaviors during financial crises.

An Increase in the Risk-Free Rate by the Fed We have just explained how the position of the Security Market Line is fixed by two factors. The vertical intercept is set by the risk-free interest rate while the slope is determined by the amount of compensation investors demand for bearing nondiversifiable risk. As a result, changes in either factor can shift the SML and thereby cause large changes in both average expected rates of return and asset prices.

As an example, consider what happens to the SML if the Federal Reserve changes policy and uses open-market operations (described in Chapter 15) to increase the risk-free interest rate that is paid on short-term government bonds. Since the risk-free interest rate is the SML's vertical intercept, the Fed's action will move the SML's vertical intercept upward, as illustrated in Figure 16.4. The result is a parallel upward shift of the SML from SML_1 to SML_2. (The shift is parallel because nothing has happened that would affect the SML's slope, which is determined by the amount of compensation that investors demand for bearing risk.)

Notice what this upward shift implies. Not only does the rate of return on short-term U.S. government bonds increase when the Federal Reserve changes policy, but the rate of return on risky assets increases as well. For instance, consider asset A, which originally has rate of return Y_1. After the SML shifts upward, asset A ends up with the higher rate of return Y_2. There is a simple intuition behind this increase. Risky assets must compete with risk-free assets for investor money. When the Federal Reserve increases the rate of return on risk-free short-term U.S. government bonds, they become more attractive to investors. But to get the money to buy more risk-free bonds, investors have to sell risky assets. This drives down their prices and—because prices and average expected rates of return are inversely related—causes their average expected rates of return to increase. The result is that asset A moves up vertically in Figure 16.4, its average expected rate of return increasing from Y_1 to Y_2 as investors reallocate their wealth from risky assets like asset A to risk-free bonds.

This process explains why investors are so watchful of the Federal Reserve and keenly interested in its policies. Any increase in the risk-free interest rate leads to a decrease in asset prices that directly reduces investors' wealth.

The Fed's power to change asset prices through monetary policy stems entirely from the fact that changes in the risk-free rate shift the SML and thus totally redefine the investment opportunities available in the economy. As the set of options changes, investors modify their portfolios to obtain the best possible combination of risk and returns from the new set of investment options. In doing so, they engage in massive amounts of buying and selling to get rid of assets they no longer want and acquire assets that they now desire. These massive changes in supply and demand for financial assets are what cause their prices to change so drastically when the Federal Reserve alters the risk-free interest rate.

The Security Market Line during the COVID Pandemic The premium demanded by investors to take on risk may vary from one period to another depending upon economic circumstances. The special circumstances of the financial markets during the early days of the COVID-19 recession of 2020 provide an excellent illustration of so-called *time-varying risk premiums* and thus the impact that Federal Reserve actions had during the crisis.

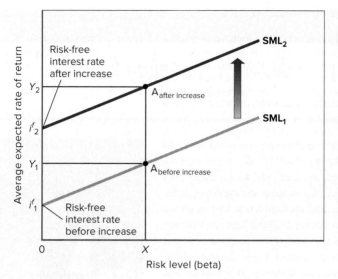

FIGURE 16.4
An increase in risk-free interest rates causes the SML to shift up vertically.

The risk-free interest rate set by the Federal Reserve is the Security Market Line's vertical intercept. Consequently, if the Federal Reserve increases the risk-free interest rate, the Security Market Line's vertical intercept will move up. This rise in the risk-free interest rate will result in a decline in all asset prices and thus an increase in the average expected rate of return on all assets. So the Security Market Line will shift up parallel from SML_1 to SML_2. Here, asset A with risk level beta = X sees its average expected rate of return rise from Y_1 to Y_2.

LAST WORD

Index Funds versus Actively Managed Funds

Do Actively Managed Funds Outperform Index Funds?

It might seem obvious to you that actively managed funds would generate higher rates of return than index funds. After all, active fund managers are paid to "beat the market," while an index fund manager does virtually nothing, his portfolio earning whatever the underlying index earns. Surprisingly, however, the exact opposite is true. Once costs are taken into account, index funds trounce managed funds by well over 1 percent per year. Now, 1 percent per year may not sound like a lot, but the compound interest formula of equation 1 near the start of this chapter shows that $10,000 growing for 30 years at 10 percent per year becomes $170,449.40, whereas that same amount of money growing at 11 percent for 30 years becomes $220,892.30. For anyone saving for retirement, an extra 1 percent per year is a very big deal.

Why do actively managed funds do so much worse than index funds? The answer is twofold. First, arbitrage makes it virtually impossible for actively managed funds to select portfolios that will do any better than index funds that have similar levels of risk. As a result, *before taking costs into account,* actively managed funds and index funds produce very similar returns. Second, actively managed funds charge their investors much higher fees than do passively managed funds. So, *after taking costs into account,* actively managed funds do worse by about 1 percent per year.

Let's discuss each of these factors in more detail. The reason that actively managed funds cannot do better than index funds before taking costs into account has to do with the power of arbitrage to ensure that investments having equal levels of risk also have equal average expected rates of return. As we explained above with respect to Figure 16.3, investments that deviate from the Security Market Line (SML) are very quickly forced back onto the SML by arbitrage so that investments with equal levels of risk have equal average expected rates of return. This implies that index funds and actively managed funds with equal levels of risk will end up with identical average expected rates of return despite the best efforts of actively managed funds to produce superior returns.

The reason actively managed funds charge much higher fees than index funds is because they run up much higher costs while

Sirtravelalot/Shutterstock

trying to produce superior returns. Not only do they have to pay large salaries to active managers, but they also have to pay for the massive amounts of trading that those managers engage in. The costs of running an index fund are, by contrast, very small since changes are made to an index fund's portfolio only on the rare occasions when the fund's underlying index changes. As a result, trading costs are low and there is no need to pay for an active manager. The overall result is that while the largest and most popular index fund currently charges its investors only 0.04 percent per year for its services, the typical actively managed fund charges about 0.71 percent per year.

So why are actively managed funds still in business? The answer may well be that index funds are boring. Because they are set up to mimic indexes that are in turn designed to show what average performance levels are, index funds are by definition stuck with average rates of return and absolutely no chance of exceeding average rates of return. For investors who want to try to beat the average, actively managed funds are the only way to go.

When the pandemic hit and the economy slowed dramatically due to lockdowns, the Federal Reserve used expansionary monetary policy to lower interest rates, including the interest rates of short-term U.S. government bonds. Because the risk-free interest rate earned by these securities determines the vertical intercept of the Securities Market Line, the actual SML for the economy shifted downward from that shown in Figure 16.1 as short-term U.S. government bond rates fell. This decline would be portrayed as the opposite of the upward shift shown in Figure 16.4.

But wouldn't we expect stock market prices to rise when the risk-free rate of return falls? That certainly did *not* happen during the short but sharp recession. Yes, stock market prices normally rise when the risk-free interest rate falls. But during this unusual period, investors became very fearful about losses from investments in general and began to look for any place of financial safety. As their appetite for risk decreased, they demanded a much higher rate of compensation for taking on any particular level of risk. In terms of Figure 16.4, the slope of the SML greatly increased. Thus, between the Fed's deliberate reduction of the risk-free rate and investors' diminished appetite for risk, two things happened at once to the SML: (1) Its intercept (the risk-free rate) fell but (2) the SML became much steeper. In Figure 16.1, these two effects would be shown by a much steeper SML emanating from a lower point on the vertical axis.

The increase in the slope of the SML overwhelmed the decline in the intercept. Investors sold off stocks, which greatly reduced stock prices, even though the risk-free interest rate fell simultaneously. The net effect was a stock market crash during the first month of the pandemic.

But when it became clear after a few weeks that the pandemic would be less awful than initially feared, investors' appetite for risk began to grow again, implying that the slope of the SML started to flatten. The Fed was still holding the risk-free interest rate very low, but the increasingly flat slope of the SML drove up stock prices steadily, so that major stock market indexes like the S&P 500 had regained their pre-COVID peaks within six months of the "COVID crash."

▶ The Security Market Line (SML) is a straight, upsloping line showing how the average expected rates of return on investments vary with their respective levels of nondiversifiable risk as measured by beta.

▶ Arbitrage ensures that every asset in the economy should plot onto the SML.

▶ The positive slope of the SML reflects the fact that investors dislike nondiversifiable risk; the greater their dislike, the steeper the slope.

▶ The Fed can shift the entire SML upward or downward by using monetary policy to change the risk-free interest rate on short-term U.S. government bonds.

QUICK REVIEW

16.6

Summary

LO16.1 Distinguish between economic investment and financial investment.

Financial economics focuses on investor preferences and how they affect the trading and pricing of the wide variety of financial assets available in the modern economy, including stocks, bonds, and real estate.

LO16.2 Explain the time value of money and calculate the present value of money.

The compound-interest formula states that if X_0 dollars are invested today at interest rate i and allowed to grow for t years, the original investment will become $(1 + i)^t X_0$ dollars in t years. The present-value formula rearranges the compound-interest formula. It tells investors the current number of dollars that they have to invest today to receive X_t dollars in t years. A risk-free investment's proper current price is the sum of the present values of each of the investment's expected future payments.

LO16.3 Distinguish among the most common financial investments: stocks, bonds, and mutual funds.

Stocks give shareholders the right to share in any future profits that corporations may generate. Bonds provide bondholders with the right to receive a fixed stream of future payments that serve to repay a loan. Mutual funds own and manage portfolios of bonds and stocks; fund investors get the returns generated by those portfolios.

LO16.4 Explain how percentage rates of return provide a common framework for comparing assets.

Investors can use percentage rates of return as a common framework for comparing different assets, even when those various assets have a wide variety of current prices and a large diversity of future payment amounts. The percentage rate of return generated by an asset is inversely related to its price.

LO16.5 Define arbitrage.

Arbitrage is the process whereby investors equalize the average expected rates of return generated by identical or nearly identical assets. If two identical assets have different rates of return, investors will sell the asset with the lower rate of return and buy the asset with the higher rate of return. Because investment prices and investment returns move inversely, the returns of the higher-returning asset will fall while the returns of the lower-returning asset will rise. This will continue until the rates of return on the two assets have been equalized.

LO16.6 Define risk and distinguish between diversifiable and nondiversifiable risk.

An asset is risky if its future payments are uncertain. Risks that can be canceled out by diversification are called diversifiable risks. Risks that cannot be canceled out by diversification are called nondiversifiable risks.

LO16.7 Explain the factors that determine investment decisions.

Investors can estimate a risky investment's proper current value by calculating its average expected rate of return, which uses a probability-weighted average to place more weight on outcomes that are more likely to happen.

Beta measures the nondiversifiable risk of an investment relative to the amount of nondiversifiable risk facing the market portfolio, which, by definition, has a beta equal to 1.0.

Investors must be compensated for the delayed use of their money (time preference) and risk. Because a well-diversified portfolio has zero diversifiable risk, investors need to be compensated only for the portfolio's nondiversifiable risk.

An asset's average expected rate of return is the sum of the return that compensates for delay (time preference) plus the return that compensates for nondiversifiable risk.

LO16.8 Explain why arbitrage will tend to move all investments onto the Security Market Line.

The Security Market Line (SML) is a straight upsloping line showing how the average expected rates of return on assets and portfolios in the economy vary with their respective levels of nondiversifiable risk as measured by beta. Arbitrage ensures that every asset in the economy should plot onto the SML.

The slope of the SML reflects the investors' dislike for nondiversifiable risk, with steeper slopes reflecting greater dislike for that risk. The vertical intercept of the SML equals the risk-free interest rate that compensates for delay (time preference).

Terms and Concepts

economic investment	defaults	nondiversifiable risk
financial investment	mutual funds	average expected rate of return
securities	portfolio	probability-weighted average
present value	index funds	beta
compound interest	actively managed funds	market portfolio
stock	passively managed funds	time preference
bankrupt	percentage rate of return	risk-free interest rate
limited liability rule	arbitrage	Security Market Line
capital gain	risk	risk premium
dividends	diversification	
bond	diversifiable risk	

Discussion Questions

1. Suppose that the city of New York issues bonds to raise money to pay for a new tunnel linking New Jersey and Manhattan. An investor named Susan buys one of the bonds on the same day that the city of New York pays a contractor for completing the first stage of construction. Is Susan making an economic or a financial investment? What about the city of New York? **LO16.1**

2. What is compound interest? How does it relate to the formula $X_t = (1 + i)^t X_0$? What is present value? How does it relate to the formula $X_t/(1 + i)^t = X_0$? **LO16.2**

3. How do stocks and bonds differ in terms of the future payments that they are expected to make? Which type of investment (stocks or bonds) is considered to be more risky? Given what you know, which investment (stocks or bonds) do you think commonly goes by the nickname "fixed income"? **LO16.3**

4. What are mutual funds? What different types of mutual funds are there? And why do you think they are so popular with investors? **LO16.3**

5. Corporations often distribute profits to their shareholders in the form of dividends, which are quarterly payments sent to shareholders. Suppose that you have the chance to buy a share in a fashion company called Rogue Designs for $35 and that the company will pay dividends of $2 per year on that share. What is the annual percentage rate of return? Next, suppose that you and other investors could get a 12 percent per year rate of return on the stocks of other very similar fashion companies. If investors care only about rates of return, what should happen to the share price of Rogue Designs? (Hint: This is an arbitrage situation.) **LO16.5**

6. Why is it reasonable to ignore diversifiable risk and care only about nondiversifiable risk? What about investors who put all their money into only a single risky stock? Can they properly ignore diversifiable risk? **LO16.6**

7. If we compare the betas of various investment opportunities, why do the assets that have higher betas also have higher average expected rates of return? **LO16.7**

8. The U.S. government issues longer-term bonds with horizons of up to 30 years. Why do 20-year bonds issued by the U.S. government have lower rates of return than 20-year bonds issued by corporations? And which do you think has the higher rate of return, longer-term U.S. government bonds or short-term U.S. government bonds? Explain. **LO16.7**

9. What determines the vertical intercept of the Security Market Line (SML)? What determines its slope? And what will happen to an asset's price if it initially plots onto a point above the SML? **LO16.8**

10. Suppose that the Federal Reserve thinks that a stock market bubble is occurring and wants to reduce stock prices. What should it do to interest rates? **LO16.8**

11. Consider another situation involving the SML. Suppose that the risk-free interest rate stays the same, but that investors' dislike of risk grows more intense. Given this change, will average expected rates of return rise or fall? Next, compare what will happen to the rates of return on low-risk and high-risk investments. Which will have a larger increase in average expected rates of return, investments with high betas or investments with low betas? And will high-beta or low-beta investments show larger percentage changes in their prices? **LO16.8**

12. **LAST WORD** Why is it so hard for actively managed funds to generate higher rates of return than passively managed index funds having similar levels of risk? Is there a simple way for an actively managed fund to increase its average expected rate of return?

Review Questions

1. Identify each of the following investments as either an economic investment or a financial investment. **LO16.1**
   a. A company builds a new factory.
   b. A pension plan buys some Space X stock.
   c. A mining company sets up a new gold mine.
   d. A merchant buys a 100-year-old farmhouse in the countryside.
   e. A bus driver buys a newly built home in the city.
   f. A company buys an old factory.

2. It is a fact that $(1 + 0.12)^3 = 1.40$. Knowing that to be true, what is the present value of $140 received in three years if the annual interest rate is 12 percent? **LO16.2**
   a. $1.40
   b. $12
   c. $100
   d. $112

3. Asset X is expected to deliver 3 future payments. They have present values of, respectively, $1,000, $2,000, and $7,000. Asset Y is expected to deliver 10 future payments, each having a present value of $1,000. Which of the following statements correctly describes the relationship between the current price of Asset X and the current price of Asset Y? **LO16.2**
   a. Asset X and Asset Y should have the same current price.
   b. Asset X should have a higher current price than Asset Y.
   c. Asset X should have a lower current price than Asset Y.

4. Tamar can buy an asset this year for $1,000. She is expecting to sell it next year for $1,050. What is the asset's anticipated percentage rate of return? **LO16.4**
   a. 0 percent
   b. 5 percent
   c. 10 percent
   d. 15 percent

5. Sammy buys stock in a suntan-lotion maker and also stock in an umbrella maker. One stock does well when the weather is good; the other does well when the weather is bad. Sammy's portfolio indicates that "weather risk" is a _____ risk. **LO16.6**
   a. diversifiable
   b. nondiversifiable
   c. automatic

6. An investment has a 50 percent chance of generating a 10 percent return and a 50 percent chance of generating a 16 percent return. What is the investment's average expected rate of return? **LO16.7**
   a. 10 percent
   b. 11 percent
   c. 12 percent
   d. 13 percent
   e. 14 percent
   f. 15 percent
   g. 16 percent

7. If an investment has 35 percent more nondiversifiable risk than the market portfolio, its beta will be: **LO16.7**
   a. 35
   b. 1.35
   c. 0.35

8. The interest rate on short-term U.S. government bonds is 4 percent. The risk premium for any asset with a beta = 1.0 is 6 percent. What is the average expected rate of return on the market portfolio? **LO16.8**
   a. 0 percent
   b. 4 percent
   c. 6 percent
   d. 10 percent

9. Suppose that an SML indicates that assets with a beta = 1.15 should have an average expected rate of return of 12 percent per year. If a particular stock with a beta = 1.15 currently has an average expected rate of return of 15 percent, what should we expect to happen to its price? **LO16.8**
   a. Rise.
   b. Fall.
   c. Stay the same.

10. If the Fed increases interest rates, the SML will shift _____ and asset prices will _____. **LO16.8**
    a. down; rise
    b. down; fall
    c. up; rise
    d. up; fall

Problems

1. Suppose that you invest $100 today in a risk-free investment and let the 4 percent annual interest rate compound. Rounded to full dollars, what will be the value of your investment 4 years from now? **LO16.2**

2. Suppose that you desire to get a lump-sum payment of $100,000 two years from now. Rounded to full dollars, how many current dollars will you have to invest today at 10 percent interest to accomplish your goal? **LO16.2**

3. Suppose that a risk-free investment will make three future payments of $100 in 1 year, $100 in 2 years, and $100 in 3 years. If the Federal Reserve has set the risk-free interest rate at 8 percent, what is the proper current price of this investment? What is the price of this investment if the Federal Reserve raises the risk-free interest rate to 10 percent? **LO16.2**

4. Suppose initially that two assets, A and B, will each make a single guaranteed payment of $100 in 1 year. But asset A has a current price of $80 while asset B has a current price of $90. **LO16.5**
   a. What are the rates of return of assets A and B at their current prices? Given these rates of return, which asset should investors buy and which asset should they sell?
   b. Assume that arbitrage continues until A and B have the same expected rate of return. When arbitrage ends, will A and B have the same price?
   Next, consider another pair of assets, C and D. Asset C will make a single payment of $150 in one year, while D will make a single payment of $200 in one year. Assume that the current price of C is $120 and that the current price of D is $180.

c. What are the rates of return of assets C and D at their current prices? Given these rates of return, which asset should investors buy and which asset should they sell?

d. Assume that arbitrage continues until C and D have the same expected rate of return. When arbitrage ends, will C and D have the same price?

Compare your answers to questions *a* through *d* before answering question *e*.

e. We know that arbitrage will equalize rates of return. Does it also guarantee to equalize prices? In what situations will it equalize prices?

5. Consider an asset that costs $120 today. You are going to hold it for 1 year and then sell it. Suppose that there is a 25 percent chance that it will be worth $100 in a year, a 25 percent chance that it will be worth $115 in a year, and a 50 percent chance that it will be worth $140 in a year. What is its average expected rate of return? Next, figure out what the investment's average expected rate of return would be if its current price were $130 today. Does the increase in the current price increase or decrease the asset's average expected rate of return? At what price would the asset have a zero average expected rate of return? **LO16.7**

6. **ADVANCED ANALYSIS** Suppose that the equation for the SML is $Y = 0.05 + 0.04X$, where Y is the average expected rate of return, 0.05 is the vertical intercept, 0.04 is the slope, and X is the risk level as measured by beta. What is the risk-free interest rate for this SML? What is the average expected rate of return at a beta of 1.5? What is the value of beta at an average expected rate of return of 7 percent? **LO16.8**

Extending the Analysis of Aggregate Supply

>> LEARNING OBJECTIVES

LO17.1 Explain the relationship between short-run aggregate supply and long-run aggregate supply.

LO17.2 Apply the extended (short-run/long-run) AD–AS model to inflation, recessions, and economic growth.

LO17.3 Explain the short-run trade-off between inflation and unemployment (the Phillips Curve).

LO17.4 Explain why there is no long-run trade-off between inflation and unemployment.

LO17.5 Explain the relationships among tax rates, tax revenues, and aggregate supply.

During the early years of the Great Depression, many economists suggested that the economy would correct itself in the *long run* without government intervention. Economist John Maynard Keynes responded, "In the long run we are all dead!"

For several decades following the Great Depression, macroeconomists understandably focused on refining fiscal policy and monetary policy to smooth business cycles and address the problems of unemployment and inflation. The main emphasis was on short-run problems and policies associated with the business cycle.

But over people's lifetimes, and from generation to generation, the long run is tremendously important for economic well-being. For that reason, macroeconomists have refocused attention on long-run macroeconomic adjustments, processes, and outcomes. The renewed emphasis on the long run has produced significant insights about aggregate supply, economic growth, and economic development. We will also see in the next chapter that it has renewed historical debates over the causes of macro instability and the effectiveness of stabilization policy.

Our goals in this chapter are to extend the analysis of aggregate supply to the long run, examine the inflation-unemployment relationship, and evaluate the effect of taxes on aggregate supply. The latter is a key concern of so-called *supply-side economics*.

From Short Run to Long Run

In Chapter 12, we noted that in macroeconomics the flexibility of input prices defines the difference between the **short run** and the **long run.** Input prices are inflexible or even totally fixed in the short run but fully flexible in the long run. By contrast, output prices are flexible in both the short run and the long run.

The assumption that input prices are flexible only in the long run leads to large differences in the shape and position of the short-run aggregate supply curve and the long-run aggregate supply curve. As Chapter 12 explained, the short-run aggregate supply curve is an upward sloping line, whereas the long-run aggregate supply curve is a vertical line at the economy's full-employment output level, Q_f.

We will begin this chapter by discussing how aggregate supply transitions from the short run to the long run. Once that is done, we will combine the long-run and short-run aggregate supply curves with the aggregate demand curve to form a single model that can provide insights into how the economy adjusts to economic shocks as well as changes in monetary and fiscal policy in both the short run and the long run. That will lead us to discuss how economic growth relates to long-run aggregate supply and how inflation and aggregate supply are related in the long run and the short run. We will conclude with a discussion of a particular set of economic policies that may help increase both short-run aggregate supply and long-run aggregate supply.

Short-Run Aggregate Supply

Our immediate objective is to demonstrate the relationship between short-run aggregate supply and long-run aggregate supply. We begin by briefly reviewing short-run aggregate supply.

Consider the short-run aggregate supply curve AS_1 in Figure 17.1a. This curve is based on three assumptions: (1) The initial price level is P_1, (2) firms and workers have established nominal wages on the expectation that this price level will persist, and (3) the price level is flexible both upward and downward. Observe from point a_1 that at price level P_1 the economy is operating at its full-employment output Q_f. This output is the real production forthcoming when the economy is operating at its natural rate of unemployment (or potential output).

Now let's review the short-run effects of a change in the price level, say, from P_1 to P_2 in Figure 17.1a. The higher output prices associated with price level P_2 increase firms' revenues, and because their nominal wages and other input prices remain unchanged, their profits rise. Those higher profits

FIGURE 17.1 Short-run and long-run aggregate supply.

(a) In the short run, nominal wages and other input prices do not respond to price-level changes and are based on the expectation that price level P_1 will continue. An increase in the price level from P_1 to P_2 increases profits and output, moving the economy from a_1 to a_2; a decrease in the price level from P_1 to P_3 reduces profits and real output, moving the economy from a_1 to a_3. The short-run aggregate supply curve therefore slopes upward. (b) In the long run, a rise in the price level results in higher nominal wages and other input prices and thus shifts the short-run aggregate supply curve to the left. Conversely, a decrease in the price level reduces nominal wages and shifts the short-run aggregate supply curve to the right. After such adjustments, the economy obtains equilibrium at points such as b_1 and c_1. Thus, the long-run aggregate supply curve is vertical at the full-employment output.

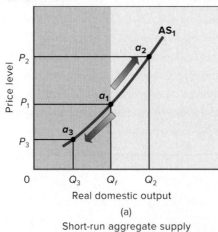

(a)
Short-run aggregate supply

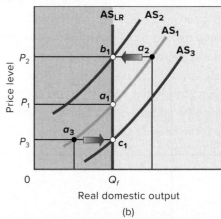

(b)
Long-run aggregate supply

lead firms to increase their output from Q_f to Q_2, and the economy moves from a_1 to a_2 on aggregate supply AS_1. At output Q_2 the economy is operating beyond its full-employment output. The firms make this possible by extending the work hours of part-time and full-time workers, enticing new workers such as homemakers and retirees into the labor force, and hiring and training the structurally unemployed. Thus, the nation's unemployment rate declines below its natural rate.

How will the firms respond when the price level *falls*, say, from P_1 to P_3 in Figure 17.1a? Because the prices they receive for their products are lower while workers' nominal wages remain unchanged, firms discover that their revenues and profits have diminished or disappeared. They reduce their production and employment, and, as shown by the movement from a_1 to a_3, real output falls to Q_3. A higher unemployment rate accompanies the decline in real output. At output Q_3 the unemployment rate is greater than the natural rate of unemployment associated with output Q_f.

Long-Run Aggregate Supply

The outcomes are different in the long run. To explain why, we need to account for changes in nominal wages that occur in response to changes in the price level. Doing so allows us to derive the economy's long-run aggregate supply curve.

We illustrate the implications for aggregate supply in Figure 17.1b. Again, suppose that the economy is initially at point a_1 (P_1 and Q_f). As we've seen, an increase in the price level from P_1 to P_2 will move the economy from point a_1 to point a_2 along the short-run aggregate supply curve AS_1. At a_2, the economy is producing more than its potential output. The demand for productive inputs is very high, so input prices will begin to rise. In particular, the high demand for labor will drive up nominal wages, which will increase per-unit production costs. That increase in marginal production costs will squeeze profit margins. Producers will respond by producing less. So the short-run supply curve will shift leftward from AS_1 to AS_2, which now reflects the higher price level P_2 and the new expectation that P_2, not P_1, will continue. The leftward shift in the short-run aggregate supply curve to AS_2 moves the economy from a_2 to b_1. Real output falls back to its full-employment level Q_f, and unemployment rises to its natural rate.

What is the long-run outcome of a *decrease* in the price level? Assuming eventual downward wage flexibility, a decline in the price level from P_1 to P_3 in Figure 17.1b works in the opposite way from a price-level increase. At first the economy moves from point a_1 to a_3 on AS_1. Profits are squeezed or eliminated because prices have fallen but nominal wages and other input costs have not. But this movement along AS_1 is the short-run supply response that results only while input prices remain constant. As time passes, input prices will begin to fall because the economy is producing below its full-employment output level. With so little output being produced, the demand for inputs will be low, and their prices will begin to decline. In particular, the low demand for labor will drive down nominal wages, reduce per-unit production costs, and raise profit margins. Lower nominal wages therefore shift the short-run aggregate supply curve rightward from AS_1 to AS_3 because at any given price level P, firms will want to produce more units of output. After short-run aggregate supply shifts to AS_3, real output returns to its full-employment level of Q_f at point c_1.

By tracing a line between the long-run equilibrium points b_1, a_1, and c_1, we obtain a long-run aggregate supply curve. Observe that it is vertical at the full-employment level of real GDP. After long-run adjustments in nominal wages and other nominal input prices have been completed, real output is Q_f regardless of the specific price level.

Long-Run Equilibrium in the AD–AS Model

Figure 17.2 helps us understand long-run equilibrium in the AD–AS model, which we just extended to encompass both short-run and long-run aggregate supply. (Hereafter, we refer to this model as the extended AD–AS model, with "extended" referring to the inclusion of both the short-run and the long-run aggregate supply curves.)

In the short run, equilibrium occurs where the downward sloping aggregate demand curve and upward sloping short-run aggregate supply

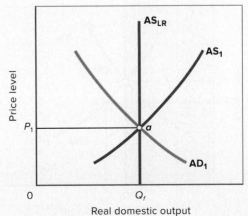

FIGURE 17.2
Equilibrium in the long-run AD–AS model.

The long-run equilibrium price level P_1 and level of real output Q_f occur at the intersection of the aggregate demand curve AD_1, the long-run aggregate supply curve AS_{LR}, and the short-run aggregate supply curve AS_1.

curve intersect. Equilibrium can occur at any level of output, not only the full-employment level. Either a negative GDP gap or a positive GDP gap is possible in the short run.

In the long run, however, the short-run aggregate supply curve adjusts as we just described. After those adjustments, long-run equilibrium occurs where the aggregate demand curve, vertical long-run aggregate supply curve, and short-run aggregate supply curve all intersect. Figure 17.2 shows the long-run outcome. Equilibrium occurs at point a, where AD_1 intersects both AS_{LR} and AS_1, and the economy achieves its full-employment (or potential) output, Q_f. At long-run equilibrium price level P_1 and output level Q_f, neither a negative GDP gap nor a positive GDP gap occurs. The economy's *natural rate of unemployment* prevails, meaning that the economy achieves full employment.

In the United States, output Q_f in Figure 17.2 implies a 4 to 5 percent unemployment rate. The natural rate of unemployment can vary from one time period to another and can differ between countries. But whatever the rate happens to be, it defines the level of potential output and establishes the location of the long-run AS curve.

▶ The short-run aggregate supply curve slopes upward because nominal wages and other input prices are fixed in the short run while output prices change, thereby increasing (as output prices rise) or decreasing (as output prices fall) firm profits and the incentive to produce output.

▶ The long-run aggregate supply curve is vertical because input prices eventually rise in response to changes in output prices.

▶ The long-run equilibrium GDP and price level occur at the intersection of the aggregate demand curve, the long-run aggregate supply curve, and the short-run aggregate supply curve.

▶ In long-run equilibrium, the economy achieves its natural rate of unemployment and its full-potential real output.

Applying the Extended AD–AS Model

>> **LO17.2** Apply the extended (short-run/long-run) AD–AS model to inflation, recessions, and economic growth.

The extended AD–AS model helps clarify the long-run aspects of demand-pull inflation, cost-push inflation, and recession.

Demand-Pull Inflation in the Extended AD–AS Model

Recall that demand-pull inflation occurs when an increase in aggregate demand pulls up the price level. Earlier, we depicted this inflation by shifting an aggregate demand curve rightward along a stable aggregate supply curve (see Figure 12.8).

In our extended AD–AS model, an increase in the price level that is associated with GDP exceeding the full employment level eventually leads to an increase in nominal wages and thus a leftward shift of the short-run aggregate supply curve. In Figure 17.3, we initially suppose the price level is P_1 at the intersection of aggregate demand curve AD_1, short-run supply curve AS_1, and long-run aggregate supply curve AS_{LR}. The economy is achieving its full-employment real output Q_f at point a.

Now consider the effects of an increase in aggregate demand as represented by the rightward shift from AD_1 to AD_2. This shift might result from any one of a number of factors, including an increase in investment spending or a rise in net exports. Whatever its cause, the increase in aggregate demand boosts the price level from P_1 to P_2 and expands real output from Q_f to Q_2 at point b. There, a positive GDP gap of $Q_2 - Q_f$ occurs.

FIGURE 17.3
Demand-pull inflation in the extended AD–AS model.

An increase in aggregate demand from AD_1 to AD_2 drives up the price level and increases real output in the short run. But in the long run, nominal wages rise and the short-run aggregate supply curve shifts leftward, as from AS_1 to AS_2. Real output then returns to its prior level, and the price level rises even more. In this scenario, the economy moves from a to b and then eventually to c.

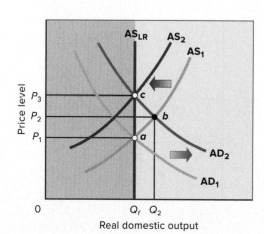

So far, none of this is new to you. But now the distinction between short-run aggregate supply and long-run aggregate supply becomes important. With the economy producing above potential output, inputs will be in high demand. Input prices including nominal wages will rise. As they do, the short-run aggregate supply curve will ultimately shift leftward such that it intersects long-run aggregate supply at point c. There, the economy has reestablished a long-run equilibrium, with the price level and real output now P_3 and Q_f, respectively. Only at point c does the new aggregate demand curve AD_2 intersect both the short-run aggregate supply curve AS_2 and the long-run aggregate supply curve AS_{LR}.

In the short run, demand-pull inflation drives up the price level and increases real output. In the long run, only the price level rises. In the long run, the initial increase in aggregate demand moves the economy along its vertical aggregate supply curve AS_{LR}. For a while, an economy can operate beyond its full-employment level of output. But the demand-pull inflation eventually causes adjustments of nominal wages that return the economy to its full-employment output Q_f.

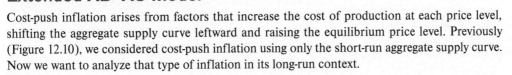

Cost-Push Inflation in the Extended AD–AS Model

Cost-push inflation arises from factors that increase the cost of production at each price level, shifting the aggregate supply curve leftward and raising the equilibrium price level. Previously (Figure 12.10), we considered cost-push inflation using only the short-run aggregate supply curve. Now we want to analyze that type of inflation in its long-run context.

Analysis Look at Figure 17.4, in which we again assume that the economy is initially operating at price level P_1 and output level Q_f (point *a*). Suppose that international oil producers agree to reduce the supply of oil to boost its price by, say, 100 percent. As a result, the per-unit production cost of producing and transporting goods and services rises substantially in the economy represented by Figure 17.4. This increase in per-unit production costs shifts the short-run aggregate supply curve to the left, as from AS_1 to AS_2, and the price level rises from P_1 to P_2 (as seen by comparing points *a* and *b*). In this case, the leftward shift of the aggregate supply curve is not a *response* to a price-level increase, as it was in our previous discussions of demand-pull inflation. Rather, it is the *cause* of the price-level increase.

Policy Dilemma Cost-push inflation creates a dilemma for policymakers. Without some expansionary stabilization policy, aggregate demand in Figure 17.4 remains in place at AD_1 and real output declines from Q_f to Q_2. Government can counter this recession, negative GDP gap, and high unemployment by using fiscal policy and monetary policy to increase aggregate demand to AD_2. But there is a potential policy trap here: An increase in aggregate demand to AD_2 will further raise inflation by increasing the price level from P_2 to P_3 (a move from point *b* to point *c*).

Suppose the government recognizes this policy trap and decides not to increase aggregate demand from AD_1 to AD_2 (you can now disregard the dashed AD_2 curve) and instead decides to allow a cost-push-created recession to run its course. How will that happen? Widespread layoffs, plant shutdowns, and business failures eventually occur. At some point the demand for oil, labor, and other inputs will decline so much that oil prices, nominal wages, and other input prices will decline. When that happens, the initial leftward shift of the short-run aggregate supply curve will reverse itself. That is, the declining per-unit production costs caused by the recession shift the short-run aggregate supply curve rightward from AS_2 to AS_1. The price level returns to P_1, and the full-employment level of output is restored at Q_f (point *a* on the long-run aggregate supply curve AS_{LR}).

This analysis yields two generalizations:

- If the government attempts to maintain full employment when there is cost-push inflation, even more inflation will occur.

- If the government takes a hands-off approach to cost-push inflation, the recession will linger. Although falling input prices will eventually undo the initial rise in per-unit production costs, the economy in the meantime will experience high unemployment and a loss of real output. There will also be a deflation as the economy adjusts back from *b* to *a*.

The nearby Consider This feature discusses how supply shocks contributed to the COVID-19 inflation.

FIGURE 17.4
Cost-push inflation in the extended AD–AS model.

Cost-push inflation occurs when the short-run aggregate supply curve shifts leftward, as from AS_1 to AS_2. If government counters the decline in real output by increasing aggregate demand to the broken line, the price level rises even more. That is, the economy moves in steps from *a* to *b* to *c*. In contrast, if government allows a recession to occur, nominal wages eventually fall and the aggregate supply curve shifts back rightward to its original location. The economy moves from *a* to *b* and eventually back to *a*.

CONSIDER THIS . . .

Cost-Push Contagion

In late 2019, the U.S. economy was enjoying rapid, noninflationary growth. The unemployment rate was just 3.5 percent, real GDP was growing robustly at 2.6 percent per year, and inflation was muted at just 1.8 percent per year. Even better, all forecasts were for the strong growth and low inflation to continue.

But then the COVID-19 virus spread worldwide, causing governments around the world to impose strict lockdowns during the spring of 2020 for at least a month or two, with various lesser restrictions, such as social distancing, continuing through the next two years.

The lockdowns acted as a major negative supply shock since tens of millions of people were prevented from going

Andrey_Popov/Shutterstock

to work. The general slowdown in spending—despite massive fiscal stimulus by the Federal government—also caused tens of thousands of businesses to go bankrupt, especially in the food service and hospitality industries. Those reductions in productive capacity shifted aggregated supply even further leftward. The result was a sharp initial decrease in real GDP in the spring of 2020 followed over the next year by steadily increasing consumer prices, so that by the summer of 2021 inflation was running at a 5.4 percent annual rate. COVID-19 had infected the economy as well as human beings. Cost-push inflation had arrived and looked ready to stay a while. By the summer of 2022, inflation was running at 9.1 percent per year.

A Controversy: Recessions and Stimulus in the Extended AD–AS Model

By far the most controversial application of the extended AD–AS model is its application to recession (or depression) caused by decreases in aggregate demand. We will look at this controversy in detail in Chapter 18; here we simply identify the key point of contention.

Suppose in Figure 17.5 that aggregate demand initially is AD_1 and that the short-run and long-run aggregate supply curves are AS_1 and AS_{LR}, respectively. Therefore, as shown by point a, the price level is P_1 and output is Q_f. Now suppose that investment spending declines dramatically, reducing aggregate demand to AD_2. Observe that real output declines from Q_f to Q_1, indicating that a recession has occurred. But if we make the controversial assumption that prices and nominal wages are flexible downward, the price level falls from P_1 to P_2. With the economy producing below potential output at point b, demand for inputs will be low. Eventually, nominal wages and input prices fall; when that happens, the short-run aggregate supply curve shifts rightward from AS_1 to AS_2. The negative GDP gap evaporates without the need for expansionary fiscal or monetary policy since real output expands from Q_1 (point b) back to Q_f (point c). The economy is again located on its long-run aggregate supply curve AS_{LR}, but now at lower price level P_3.

There is much disagreement about this hypothetical scenario. The key point of dispute revolves around the degree to which both input and output prices may be downwardly inflexible and how long it would take in the actual economy for the necessary downward price and wage adjustments to occur to regain the full-employment level of output. For now, suffice it to say that most economists believe that if such adjustments are forthcoming, they will occur only after the economy has experienced a relatively long-lasting recession with its accompanying high unemployment and large loss of output. The severity and length of the major recession of 2007–2009 has strengthened this view. Therefore, economists recommend active monetary policy, and perhaps fiscal policy, to counteract recessions.

Economic Growth with Ongoing Inflation

We have seen how demand and supply shocks can cause, respectively, demand-pull inflation and cost-push inflation. In these previous cases, the extent of the inflation was *finite* because the

FIGURE 17.5
Recession in the extended AD–AS model.

A recession occurs when aggregate demand shifts leftward, as from AD_1 to AD_2. If prices are downwardly flexible, the price level falls from P_1 to P_2 as the economy moves from point a to point b. With the economy in recession at point b, nominal wages will fall, shifting the aggregate supply curve from AS_1 to AS_2. The price level declines to P_3, and real output returns to Q_f. The economy moves from a to b to c.

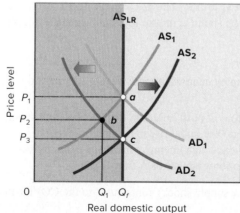

size of the initial movement in either the AD curve or the AS curve was *limited*. For instance, in Figure 17.3, the aggregate demand curve shifts right by a limited amount, from AD_1 to AD_2. As the economy's equilibrium moves from *a* to *b* to *c*, the price level rises from P_1 to P_2 to P_3. During this transition, inflation obviously occurs because the price level is rising. But once the economy reaches its new equilibrium at point *c*, the price level remains constant at P_3 and no further inflation takes place. That is, the limited movement in aggregate demand causes a limited amount of inflation that ends when the economy returns to full employment.

But the modern economy almost always experiences continuous, but usually mild, positive rates of inflation. That can happen only with ongoing shifts in either the aggregate demand or long-run aggregate supply curve because any single, finite shift will cause inflation of limited magnitude and duration. This insight is crucial to understanding why modern economies usually experience ongoing inflation while achieving economic growth. Both aggregate demand and long-run aggregate supply increase over time in the actual economy. The ongoing, positive, and mild rates of inflation that we observe in the actual economy happen because the increases in aggregate demand generally exceed the increases in long-run aggregate supply. It will be helpful to examine this point graphically.

Increases in Long-Run Aggregate Supply As discussed in Chapter 8, economic growth is driven by supply factors such as improved technologies and access to more or better resources. Economists illustrate economic growth as either an outward shift of an economy's production possibilities curve or as a rightward shift of its long-run aggregate supply curve. As Figure 17.6 shows, the outward shift of the production possibilities curve from *AB* to *CD* in graph *a* is equivalent to the rightward shift of the economy's long-run aggregate supply curve from AS_{LR1} to AS_{LR2} in graph *b*.

Let's simply transfer this rightward shift of the economy's long-run aggregate supply curve to Figure 17.7, which depicts U.S. economic growth in the context of the extended aggregate demand–aggregate supply model. Suppose the economy's long-run aggregate supply curve initially is AS_{LR1}, while its aggregate demand curve and short-run aggregate supply curve are AD_1 and AS_1, as shown. The equilibrium price level is P_1 and the equilibrium level of real output is Q_1.

Now let's assume that economic growth driven by changes in supply factors (quantity and quality of resources and technology) shifts the long-run aggregate supply curve rightward from AS_{LR1} to AS_{LR2} while the economy's aggregate demand curve remains at AD_1. Also, suppose that product and resource prices are flexible downward. The economy's potential output will expand, as reflected by the increase of available real output from Q_1 to Q_2. With aggregate demand constant at AD_1, the

FIGURE 17.6 Production possibilities and long-run aggregate supply.

(a) Economic growth driven by supply factors (such as improved technologies or the use of more or better resources) shifts an economy's production possibilities curve outward, as from *AB* to *CD*. (b) The same factors shift the economy's long-run aggregate supply curve to the right, as from AS_{LR1} to AS_{LR2}.

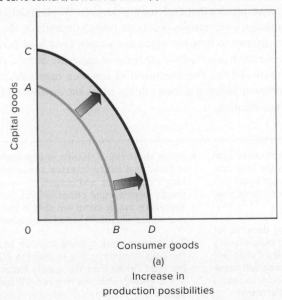

(a)
Increase in
production possibilities

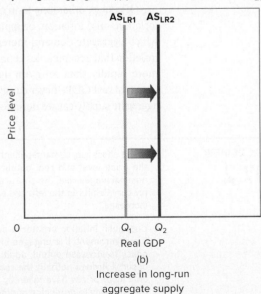

(b)
Increase in long-run
aggregate supply

FIGURE 17.7
Depicting U.S. growth via the extended AD–AS model.

Long-run aggregate supply and short-run aggregate supply have increased over time, as from AS_{LR1} to AS_{LR2} and AS_1 to AS_2. Simultaneously, aggregate demand has shifted rightward, as from AD_1 to AD_2. The actual outcome of these combined shifts has been economic growth, shown as the increase in real output from Q_1 to Q_2, accompanied by mild inflation, shown as the rise in the price level from P_1 to P_2.

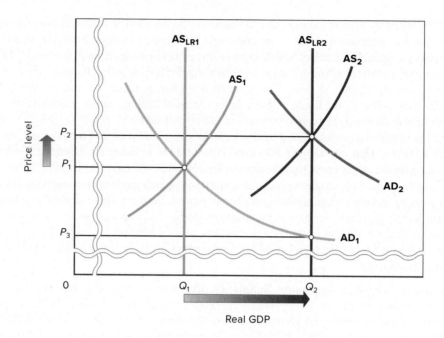

rightward shift of the long-run aggregate supply curve will lower the price level from P_1 to P_3. *Taken alone, expansions of long-run aggregate supply in the economy are deflationary.*

Increases in Aggregate Demand and Inflation But a decline in the price level, such as the one from P_1 to P_3 in Figure 17.7, is not part of the long-run U.S. growth experience. Why not? Because the U.S. central bank—the Federal Reserve—engineers ongoing increases in the nation's money supply to create rightward shifts of the aggregate demand curve. These increases in aggregate demand would be highly inflationary without the increases in long-run aggregate supply. But because the Fed usually ensures that the inflationary rightward shifts of the aggregate demand curve proceed only slightly faster than the deflationary rightward shifts of the aggregate supply curve, only mild inflation occurs along with economic growth.

We illustrate this outcome in Figure 17.7, where aggregate demand shifts to the right from AD_1 to AD_2 at the same time long-run aggregate supply shifts rightward from AS_{LR1} to AS_{LR2}. Real output expands from Q_1 to Q_2 and the price level increases from P_1 to P_2. At the higher price level P_2, the economy confronts a new short-run aggregate supply curve AS_2. Figure 17.7 describes the actual U.S. experience: economic growth, accompanied by mild inflation. Since the early 1980s, real output has increased on average at about 2.5 percent annually while inflation has averaged roughly 2.6 percent a year.

Of course, other long-term outcomes besides that depicted are possible. Whether deflation, zero inflation, mild inflation, or rapid inflation accompanies economic growth depends on the extent to which aggregate demand increases relative to long-run aggregate supply. Over long periods, any inflation that accompanies economic growth is exclusively the result of aggregate demand increasing more rapidly than long-run aggregate supply. The expansion of long-run aggregate supply—of potential real GDP—never causes inflation. Holding all other things equal, the expansion of long-run aggregate supply causes deflation, not inflation.

QUICK REVIEW

17.2

▶ In the short run, demand-pull inflation raises both the price level and real output. In the long run, nominal wages rise, the short-run aggregate supply curve shifts to the left, and only the price level increases.

▶ Cost-push inflation creates a policy dilemma for the government: If it engages in an expansionary policy to increase output, additional inflation will occur; if it does nothing, the recession will linger until input prices have fallen by enough to return the economy to producing at potential output.

▶ In the short run, a decline in aggregate demand reduces real output (creates a recession). In the long run, if input and output prices are downwardly flexible, input prices will fall, the short-run aggregate supply curve will shift to the right, and real output will return to its full-employment level.

▶ The economy has ongoing inflation because the Fed uses monetary policy to shift the AD curve to the right faster than the supply factors of economic growth shift the long-run AS curve to the right.

The Inflation-Unemployment Relationship

We have just seen that the Fed can determine how much inflation occurs in the economy by how much it causes aggregate demand to shift relative to aggregate supply. Given that low inflation and low unemployment rates are the Fed's major economic goals, its ability to control inflation brings up at least two interesting policy questions: Are low unemployment and low inflation compatible goals or conflicting goals? How do we explain situations in which high unemployment and high inflation coexist?

The extended AD-AS model supports three significant generalizations relating to these questions:

- Under normal circumstances, there is a short-run trade-off between the inflation rate and the unemployment rate.

- Aggregate supply shocks can cause both higher inflation rates and higher unemployment rates.

- There is no significant trade-off between inflation and unemployment over long periods of time.

Let's examine each of these generalizations.

The Phillips Curve

We can demonstrate the short-run trade-off between the inflation rate and the unemployment rate through the **short-run downward sloping Phillips Curve,** named after A. W. Phillips, who developed the idea in Great Britain. This curve, shown in Figure 17.8a, suggests an inverse relationship between the inflation rate and the unemployment rate. Lower unemployment rates (measured as leftward movements on the horizontal axis) are associated with higher rates of inflation (measured as upward movements on the vertical axis).

The underlying rationale of the Phillips Curve becomes apparent when we view the short-run aggregate supply curve in Figure 17.9 and perform a simple mental experiment. Suppose that in some short-run period aggregate demand expands from AD_0 to AD_2, either because firms decide to buy more capital goods or because the government decides to increase its expenditures. Whatever the cause, the short-run price level rises from P_0 to P_2 and real output rises from Q_0 to Q_2. As real output rises, the unemployment rate falls.

Now let's compare what would have happened if the increase in aggregate demand had been larger, say, from AD_0 to AD_3. The equilibrium at P_3 and Q_3 indicates that the amount of inflation and the growth of real output would both have been greater (and that the unemployment rate would have been lower). Similarly, suppose aggregate demand during the year had increased only modestly, from AD_0 to AD_1. Compared with our shift from AD_0 to AD_2, the amount of inflation and the growth of real output would have been smaller (and the unemployment rate higher).

>> **LO17.3** Explain the short-run trade-off between inflation and unemployment (the Phillips Curve).

short-run downward sloping Phillips Curve A downward sloping line illustrating the inverse relationship that A.W. Phillips theorized should exist between the *unemployment rate* (on the horizontal axis) and the *inflation rate* (on the vertical axis). Believed by many mainstream economists to hold in the *short run* but not in the *long run.*

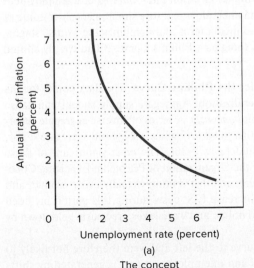

(a)
The concept

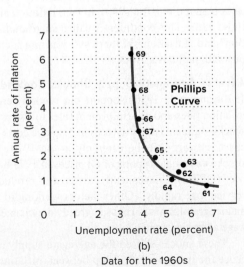

(b)
Data for the 1960s

FIGURE 17.8
The Phillips Curve: concept and empirical data.

(a) The Phillips Curve relates annual rates of inflation and annual rates of unemployment for a series of years. Because this is an inverse relationship, there presumably is a trade-off between unemployment and inflation. (b) Data points for the 1960s seemed to confirm the Phillips Curve concept. (Note: The unemployment rates are annual averages and the inflation rates are on a December-to-December basis.)

FIGURE 17.9
The short-run effect of changes in aggregate demand on real output and the price level.

Comparing the effects of various possible increases in aggregate demand leads to the conclusion that the larger the increase in aggregate demand, the higher the rate of inflation and the greater the increase in real output. Because real output and the unemployment rate move in opposite directions, we can generalize that, given short-run aggregate supply, high rates of inflation should be accompanied by low rates of unemployment.

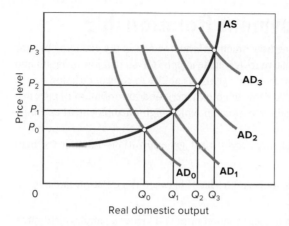

The generalization we draw from this mental experiment is this: *Assuming a constant short-run aggregate supply curve*, high inflation rates are accompanied by low unemployment rates, and low inflation rates are accompanied by high unemployment rates. Other things equal, the expected relationship should look something like Figure 17.8a

Figure 17.8b reveals that the annual values for U.S. inflation and unemployment during the 1960s fit the theory nicely. On the basis of that evidence and evidence from other countries, most economists working at the end of the 1960s concluded there was a stable, predictable trade-off between unemployment and inflation. Moreover, U.S. macroeconomic policy was built on that supposed trade-off. Economists believed that it was impossible to achieve "full employment without inflation." Manipulation of aggregate demand through fiscal and monetary measures would move the economy along the Phillips Curve. An expansionary fiscal and monetary policy that boosted aggregate demand and lowered the unemployment rate would simultaneously increase inflation. The government could use a restrictive fiscal and monetary policy to reduce the inflation rate, but only at the cost of a higher unemployment rate and more forgone production. Society had to choose between the incompatible goals of price stability and full employment; it had to decide where to locate on its Phillips Curve.

For reasons that we will soon explain, today's economists reject the idea of a stable, unmoving Phillips Curve. Nevertheless, they agree there is a short-run trade-off between unemployment and inflation: *Given short-run aggregate supply, increases in aggregate demand increase real output and reduce the unemployment rate.* As the unemployment rate dips below the natural rate, a demand-pull inflation will be generated. Conversely, when recession sets in and the unemployment rate increases, the weak aggregate demand that caused the recession also leads to lower inflation rates.

Periods of time during which we see both exceptionally low unemployment *and* exceptionally low inflation do occur, but only under special sets of economic circumstances. One such period was the late 1990s, when faster productivity growth increased aggregate supply and fully blunted the inflationary impact of rapidly rising aggregate demand (review Figure 12.11).

Aggregate Supply Shocks and the Phillips Curve

The unemployment-inflation experience of the 1970s and early 1980s demolished the idea of an always-stable Phillips Curve. In Figure 17.10, we show the Phillips Curve for the 1960s in blue and then add the data points for 1970 through 2015. Observe that in most of the years of the 1970s and early 1980s, the economy experienced both higher inflation rates *and* higher unemployment rates than it did in the 1960s. In fact, inflation and unemployment rose simultaneously in some of those years. This condition is called **stagflation**—a media term that combines the words "stagnation" and "inflation." If there still was any such thing as a Phillips Curve, it had clearly shifted outward, perhaps as shown.

stagflation *Inflation* accompanied by stagnation in the rate of growth of output and an increase in *unemployment* in the economy; simultaneous increases in the *inflation* rate and the *unemployment* rate.

aggregate supply shocks Sudden, large changes in resource costs that shift an economy's aggregate supply curve.

Adverse Aggregate Supply Shocks Contradict the Phillips Curve The data points for the 1970s and early 1980s support our second generalization: Aggregate supply shocks can cause inflation rates and unemployment rates to rise *simultaneously*. A series of adverse **aggregate supply shocks**—sudden, large increases in resource costs that jolt an economy's short-run aggregate supply curve leftward—hit the economy in the 1970s and early 1980s. The most significant of these shocks was a quadrupling of oil prices in 1973 by the Organization of Petroleum Exporting Countries (OPEC). Consequently, the cost of producing and distributing virtually every product and service rose rapidly. (Other factors working to increase U.S. costs during this period included major agricultural shortfalls, a greatly depreciated dollar, and wage hikes previously held down by wage and price controls.)

These shocks shifted the aggregate supply curve to the left and were therefore not likely to cause the inverse relationship between inflation and unemployment that is generated by shifts

FIGURE 17.10 Inflation rates and unemployment rates, 1960–2021.

A series of aggregate supply shocks in the 1970s resulted in higher rates of inflation *and* higher rates of unemployment. So data points for the 1970s and 1980s tended to be above and to the right of the blue Phillips Curve for the 1960s. In the 1990s, the inflation-unemployment data points slowly moved back (down and to the left) toward the position of the 1960s Phillips Curve; so the points for the late 1990s and 2000s are somewhat similar to those from the 1960s. However, the data point for 2009 (9.3 percent unemployment, −0.34 percent inflation) was located dramatically lower and much farther to the right relative to the data point for 2008 (5.8 percent unemployment, 3.8 percent inflation). That movement reflected negative inflation accompanied by much higher unemployment during 2009. As the economy slowly mended after the Great Recession, the data points for 2011 through 2016 (highlighted in blue) showed inflation and unemployment falling simultaneously—a pattern inconsistent with moving along a single fixed Philips curve.

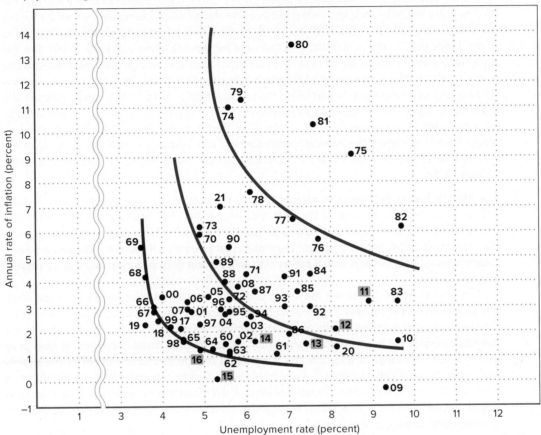

Source: U.S. Bureau of Labor Statistics.

of the AD curve along a fixed AS curve (as in Figure 17.9). Indeed, the cost-push inflation model shown in Figure 17.4 tells us that we should expect to see exactly the opposite relationship between inflation and unemployment when a supply shock shifts the AS curve to the left. That's because a leftward shift of the short-run aggregate supply curve in Figure 17.4 increases the price level and reduces real output, thereby increasing the unemployment rate at the same time inflation is also increasing.

This scenario, say most economists, is what happened during two periods in the 1970s. The U.S. unemployment rate shot up from 4.9 percent in 1973 to 8.5 percent in 1975, reflecting a significant decline in real GDP. In the same period, the U.S. price level rose by 21 percent. The stagflation scenario recurred in 1978, when OPEC increased oil prices by more than 100 percent. The U.S. price level rose by 26 percent over the 1978–1980 period, while unemployment increased from 6.1 to 7.2 percent.

Stagflation's Demise in the 1980s Another look at Figure 17.10 reveals a generally inward movement of the inflation-unemployment points between 1982 and 1989. One precursor to this favorable trend of lower unemployment accompanied by lower inflation was the deep recession of 1981–1982, largely caused by a restrictive monetary policy aimed at reducing double-digit inflation. Other factors were at work, too. Foreign competition throughout this period held down wage and price hikes in several basic industries such as automobiles and steel. Deregulation of the airline and trucking industries also resulted in wage reductions. A significant decline in OPEC's monopoly power and a greatly reduced reliance on oil in the production process produced a stunning fall in the price of oil and its derivative products, such as gasoline.

All these factors combined to reduce per-unit production costs and to shift the short-run aggregate supply curve rightward (as from AS_2 to AS_1 in Figure 17.4). By 1989, inflation had decreased from a peak of 13.4 percent down to 4.8 percent while the unemployment rate had fallen from a peak of 9.7 percent down to 5.3 percent. Stagflation was at an end.

Post–Great Recession Evidence against a Stable Phillips Curve It also appeared for a while that the Phillips curve might be making a comeback because the inflation-unemployment points for the late 1990s and 2000s in Figure 17.10 are closer to the points associated with the Phillips Curve of the 1960s than to the points that plot the data for the late 1970s and early 1980s. But the severe recession of 2007–2009 led to shifts in unemployment and inflation that were inconsistent with a stable Phillips curve along which there was a predictable inverse relationship between inflation and unemployment. In particular, the points for 2011 through 2016 moved substantially down and to the left as the economy experienced an ongoing pattern of falling inflation coinciding with falling unemployment as it recovered from the Great Recession. That movement represented a positive relationship between unemployment and inflation, exactly the opposite of the inverse relationship between those two variables that you would expect to find along a stable Phillips Curve.

The Misery Index The media sometimes express the sum of the unemployment rate and the inflation rate as a rough gauge of the economic discomfort that inflation and unemployment jointly impose on an economy in a particular year. The sum of the two rates is the *misery index*. For example, a nation with a 5 percent unemployment rate and a 5 percent inflation rate has a misery index number of 10, as does a nation with an 8 percent unemployment rate and a 2 percent inflation rate.

Global Perspective 17.1 shows the misery index for several nations between 2010 and 2021. The U.S. misery index number has been neither exceptionally low nor exceptionally high relative to the misery index numbers for the other major economies shown. However, economists do not put much stock in the misery index because they do not view the national discomfort associated with a 1 percent change in inflation and a 1 percent change in unemployment as necessarily equivalent. In particular, the misery index can greatly disguise the extent of hardship during a recession. The rise in the unemployment rate in these circumstances causes a huge loss of national output and income (and a great increase in misery!), even if lower inflation partially or fully offsets the higher unemployment rate.

GLOBAL PERSPECTIVE 17.1

THE MISERY INDEX, SELECTED NATIONS, 2010–2021

The U.S. misery index number (the sum of its unemployment rate and inflation rate) has generally been in the midrange of such numbers relative to other major economies in recent years.

Source: The World Bank (data.worldbank.org) and International Labour Organization (ilo.org). Inflation rates and unemployment rates are both on an average annual basis.

The Long-Run Phillips Curve

The overall set of data points in Figure 17.10 supports our third generalization relating to the inflation-unemployment relationship: There is no apparent *long-run* trade-off between inflation and unemployment. Economists point out that when decades (as opposed to a few years) are considered, any rate of inflation is consistent with the natural rate of unemployment. We know from Chapter 9 that the natural rate of unemployment is the unemployment rate that occurs when cyclical unemployment is zero; it is the full-employment rate, or the rate of unemployment when the economy achieves its potential output.

Why is there a short-run inflation-unemployment trade-off but not a long-run trade-off? Figure 17.11 provides an answer.

>> **LO17.4** Explain why there is no long-run trade-off between inflation and unemployment.

Short-Run Phillips Curve

Consider Phillips Curve PC_1 in Figure 17.11. Suppose the economy initially is experiencing a 3 percent inflation rate and a 5 percent natural rate of unemployment. Such short-term curves as PC_1, PC_2, and PC_3 (drawn as straight lines for simplicity) exist because the actual inflation rate is not always the same as the expected rate.

Establishing an additional point on Phillips Curve PC_1 will clarify this conclusion. We begin at a_1, where we assume nominal wages are set on the assumption that the 3 percent inflation rate will continue. That is, because workers expect output prices to rise by 3 percent per year, they negotiate wage contracts that feature 3 percent per year increases in nominal wages so that their nominal wage increases exactly offset the expected increase in prices and thereby keep their real wages the same.

But suppose that the inflation rate rises to 6 percent, perhaps because the Fed has decided to move the AD curve to the right even faster than it had been moving it before. With a nominal wage rate set on the expectation of a 3 percent inflation rate, the higher product prices raise business profits. Firms respond to the higher profits by hiring more workers and increasing output. In the short run, the economy moves to b_1, which, unlike a_1, involves a lower unemployment rate (4 percent) and a higher inflation rate (6 percent). The move from a_1 to b_1 is consistent both with an upward sloping aggregate supply curve and with the inflation-unemployment trade-off implied by the Phillips Curve. But this short-run Phillips Curve simply is a manifestation of the following principle: *When the actual inflation rate is higher than expected, profits temporarily rise and the unemployment rate temporarily falls.*

Long-Run Vertical Phillips Curve

Point b_1 is not a stable equilibrium. Workers will recognize that their nominal wages have not increased as fast as inflation and will therefore renegotiate their labor contracts, demanding faster increases in nominal wages. These faster increases in nominal wages make up for the higher inflation rate and restore the workers' lost purchasing power. As these new labor contracts kick in, business profits fall to their prior level. The reduction in profits means that the original motivation to employ more workers and increase output has disappeared.

Unemployment then returns to its natural level at point a_2. Note, however, that the economy now faces both a higher actual inflation rate as well as a higher expected inflation rate—6 percent rather than 3 percent. Because wages are a production cost, the 6 percent increase in wage rates that was negotiated in response to inflation rising from 3 to 6 percent implies faster future increases in output prices as firms are forced to raise prices more rapidly (6 percent per year rather than 3 percent per year) to

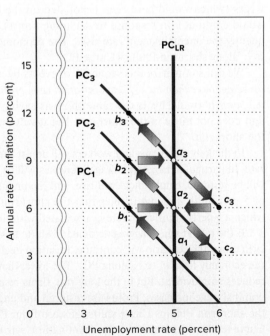

FIGURE 17.11
The long-run vertical Phillips Curve.

Increases in aggregate demand beyond those consistent with full-employment output may temporarily boost profits, output, and employment (as from a_1 to b_1). But nominal wages eventually will catch up so as to sustain real wages. When they do, profits will fall, negating the previous short-run stimulus to production and employment (the economy now moves from b_1 to a_2). Consequently, there is no trade-off between the rates of inflation and unemployment in the long run; that is, the long-run Phillips Curve is roughly a vertical line at the economy's natural rate of unemployment.

make up for the 6 percent rate of wage growth that was just negotiated. In other words, the initial increase in inflation will become *persistent* because it leads to renegotiated labor contracts that perpetuate the increase in the inflation rate from 3 percent to 6 percent. In addition, because the new labor contracts are public, the higher inflation rates that they cause will be *expected* by everyone rather than being a surprise.

In view of the higher 6 percent expected inflation rate, the short-run Phillips Curve shifts upward from PC_1 to PC_2 in Figure 17.11. An "along-the-Phillips-Curve" kind of movement—as from a_1 to b_1 on PC_1—is merely a short-run or transient occurrence. In the long run, after nominal wage contracts catch up with increases in the inflation rate, unemployment returns to its natural rate at a_2, and there is a new short-run Phillips Curve PC_2 that has the higher expected inflation rate (6 percent) at the natural rate of unemployment (5 percent).

The scenario repeats if aggregate demand continues to increase more rapidly than expected. Prices rise momentarily ahead of nominal wages, profits expand, and employment and output increase (as with the movement from a_2 to b_2 along PC_2). But in time, the rate at which nominal wages increase accelerates to match the higher (9 percent) rate of inflation at b_2. Profits then fall to their original level, pushing unemployment back to its natural rate at a_3. The economy's "reward" for temporarily lowering the unemployment rate below the natural rate is to lock in a still-higher (9 percent) inflation rate.

Movements along a given short-run Phillips curve that lead to higher inflation and a below-natural rate of unemployment (such as the movement from a_1 to b_1 on PC_1) cause the short-run curve to shift rightward, to a less favorable position (such as PC_2) at which the expected and actual inflation rates are higher. A stable Phillips Curve with a consistent, inverse relationship between the unemployment rate and the inflation rate simply does not exist in the long run. Instead, the economy is characterized in the long run by the **long-run vertical Phillips Curve,** defined in Figure 17.11 by the vertical line (PC_{LR}) that runs through a_1, a_2, and a_3. Along that vertical long-run Phillips Curve, *any* rate of inflation is consistent with the 5 percent natural rate of unemployment. Thus, the thinking goes, society ought to choose a low inflation rate rather than a high one.

Disinflation

The distinction between the short-run Phillips Curve and the long-run Phillips Curve also helps to explain **disinflation**—by which we mean reductions in the rate of inflation. Suppose that in Figure 17.11 the economy starts at a_3, where the inflation rate is 9 percent. And suppose that a decline in the rate at which aggregate demand shifts to the right faster than aggregate supply (as happened during the 1981–1982 recession) reduces inflation below the 9 percent expected rate, say, to 6 percent. Business profits fall because output prices are rising less rapidly than nominal wages (which would have been negotiated on the assumption that the 9 percent inflation rate would continue). In response to declining profits, firms reduce their employment, and consequently the unemployment rate rises. The economy temporarily slides downward from point a_3 to c_3 along short-run Phillips Curve PC_3.

We can summarize this sequence of events by noting that *when the actual inflation rate ends up being lower than the expected inflation rate, profits temporarily fall and the unemployment rate temporarily rises.* This is the same thing as saying that a stable short-run Phillips curve exists and does not move in the short run. But it will only exist and remain fixed in one location in the short run.

In the long run, firms and workers will adjust their expectations to the new 6 percent inflation rate. In particular, negotiated wage increases will be set at 6 percent rather than 9 percent. Profits will be restored, employment will rise, and the unemployment rate will fall back to its natural rate of 5 percent at a_2. That implies that the short-run Phillips curve shifts leftward to PC_2, along which a 6-percent inflation rate is associated with the 5-percent natural rate of unemployment.

If the rate at which aggregate demand shifts to the right faster than aggregate supply declines even more, the scenario will continue. Inflation declines from 6 percent to, say, 3 percent, moving the economy from a_2 to c_2 along PC_2. The lower-than-expected inflation rate squeezes profits and reduces employment. But in the long run, firms respond to the lower profits by negotiating lower nominal wage increases. Profits are restored and unemployment returns to its natural rate at a_1 as the short-run Phillips Curve shifts leftward from PC_2 to PC_1. Meanwhile, the long-run Phillips Curve remains vertical at the 5-percent natural rate of unemployment.

long-run vertical Phillips Curve The *Phillips Curve* after all *nominal wages* and other input prices have adjusted to changes in the rate of *inflation;* a line emanating straight upward at the economy's *natural rate of unemployment.*

disinflation A reduction in the rate of *inflation.*

▶ As implied by the upward sloping short-run aggregate supply curve, there may be a short-run trade-off between the inflation rate and the unemployment rate. This trade-off is reflected in the Phillips Curve.

▶ Aggregate supply shocks that produce severe cost-push inflation can cause stagflation—a simultaneous increase in the inflation rate and the unemployment rate. Such stagflation occurred from 1973 to 1975 and from 1978 to 1980, producing Phillips Curve data points above and to the right of the Phillips Curve for the 1960s.

▶ After all nominal wage adjustments responding to increases and decreases in the inflation rate have occurred, the economy ends up back at its full-employment level of output and its natural rate of unemployment. The long-run Phillips Curve therefore is vertical at the natural rate of unemployment.

Taxation and Aggregate Supply

A final topic in our discussion of aggregate supply is taxation, a key aspect of **supply-side economics.** "Supply-side economists" or "supply-siders" stress that changes in aggregate supply are an active force in determining the levels of inflation, unemployment, and economic growth. Government policies can either impede or promote rightward shifts of the short-run and long-run aggregate supply curves shown in Figure 17.2. One such policy is taxation.

These economists argue that the enlargement of the U.S. tax system has impaired incentives to work, save, and invest. In this view, high tax rates impede productivity growth and hence slow the expansion of long-run aggregate supply. By reducing the after-tax rewards of workers and producers, high tax rates reduce the financial attractiveness of working, saving, and investing.

Taxes and Incentives to Work, Save, and Invest

Supply-siders focus their attention on *marginal tax rates*—the rates on extra dollars of income—because those rates affect the benefits from working, saving, or investing more. In 2021, marginal federal income tax rates varied from 10 to 37 percent.

Supply-siders believe that lower marginal tax rates cause people to work more, thereby increasing aggregate inputs of labor. In particular, lower marginal tax rates increase the after-tax wage rate, making leisure more expensive and work more attractive. So lower income tax rates should increase the supply of labor and, along with it, GDP.

Saving, remember, is the prerequisite of investment and the returns that come from investment. Thus, supply-side economists recommend lower marginal tax rates on investments as a way of encouraging saving and investing. They argue that higher investment is desirable because it will equip workers with more and technologically superior machinery and equipment. Labor productivity will rise. Long-run aggregate supply will shift to the right at a faster pace. Unemployment and inflation should both decrease.

The Laffer Curve

According to supply-siders, reductions in marginal tax rates increase the nation's aggregate supply and can leave the nation's tax revenues unchanged or even enlarge them. Thus, tax cuts need not produce federal budget deficits.

This conclusion is based on the **Laffer Curve,** named after Arthur Laffer, the economist who popularized it. The Laffer Curve in Figure 17.12 depicts the relationship between tax rates and tax revenues. As tax rates increase from 0 to 100 percent, tax revenues increase from zero to some maximum level (at *m*) and then fall to zero. Tax revenues decline beyond some point because higher tax rates discourage economic activity, thereby shrinking the tax base (domestic output and income). This outcome is easiest to see at the extreme, where the tax rate is 100 percent. Tax revenues here are, in theory, reduced to zero because the 100 percent confiscatory tax rate has halted production. A 100 percent tax rate applied to a tax base of zero yields no revenue.

>> LO17.5 Explain the relationships among tax rates, tax revenues, and aggregate supply.

supply-side economics A view of *macroeconomics* that emphasizes the role of costs and *aggregate supply* in explaining *inflation, unemployment,* and *economic growth.*

Laffer Curve A curve relating government tax rates and tax revenues and on which a particular tax rate (between zero and 100 percent) maximizes tax revenues.

FIGURE 17.12
The Laffer Curve.

The Laffer Curve suggests that up to point *m* higher tax rates will result in larger tax revenues. But tax rates higher than *m* will adversely affect incentives to work and produce, reducing the size of the tax base (output and income) to the extent that tax revenues will decline. It follows that if tax rates are above *m*, reductions in tax rates will produce increases in tax revenues.

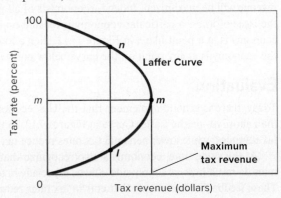

In the early 1980s, Laffer suggested that the United States was at a point such as *n* on the curve in Figure 17.12. At *n*, tax rates are so high that production is discouraged to the extent that tax revenues are below the maximum at *m*. If the economy is at *n*, then reducing the tax rate can increase tax revenues or leave them unchanged. For example, lowering the tax rate from point *n* to point *m* will increase tax revenues, while lowering the tax rate further, to point *l*, will bring in the same total tax revenue as before at point *n*.

Laffer's reasoning was that lower tax rates stimulate incentives to work, save and invest, innovate, and accept business risks, thus triggering an expansion of real output and income. That enlarged tax base sustains tax revenues even though tax rates are lowered. Indeed, between points *n* and *m*, a lower tax rate results in *increased* tax revenue.

Also, when taxes are lowered, tax avoidance (which is legal) and tax evasion (which is not) decline. High marginal tax rates prompt taxpayers to avoid taxes through various legal tax shelters, such as buying municipal bonds, on which the interest earned is legally tax-free. High rates also encourage some taxpayers to illegally evade income taxes by hiding income from the Internal Revenue Service. Supply-siders note that lower tax rates reduce the inclination to engage in either tax avoidance or tax evasion.

The Laffer curve also implies that for any amount of tax revenue that the government can possibly collect, there will be both a high tax rate at which that amount of revenue can be collected as well as a low tax rate at which that amount of revenue can be collected. As an example, compare points *n* an *l* in Figure 17.12. Point *n* has a high tax rate and point *l* has a low tax rate, but they both collect the same amount of tax revenue. So if the government's major goal when setting tax rates is simply to collect a particular total amount of tax revenue, Laffer argued that the government should always opt for the lower tax rate. By doing so, the government will collect the revenue it desires while impinging as little as possible on the private economy.

Criticisms of the Laffer Curve

The Laffer Curve and its supply-side implications have been subject to severe criticism.

Taxes, Incentives, and Time A fundamental criticism concerns the sensitivity of economic incentives to changes in tax rates. Skeptics say ample empirical evidence shows that a tax cut's impact on incentives is small, of uncertain direction, and relatively slow to emerge. For example, studies indicate that decreases in tax rates lead some people to work more but lead others to work less. Those who work more are enticed by the higher after-tax pay; they substitute work for leisure because the opportunity cost of leisure has increased. But other people work less because the higher after-tax pay enables them to "buy more leisure." With the tax cut, they can earn the same level of after-tax income while working fewer hours.

Inflation or Higher Real Interest Rates Most economists think that the demand-side effects of a tax cut are more immediate and certain than longer-term supply-side effects. Thus, tax cuts undertaken when the economy is at or near full employment may produce increases in aggregate demand that overwhelm any increase in aggregate supply. The likely result is inflation or a restrictive monetary policy to prevent inflation. If the latter occurs, real interest rates will rise and investment will decline, which defeats the purpose of the supply-side tax cuts.

Position on the Curve Some skeptics argue that the Laffer Curve is merely a logical necessity. They agree with Laffer that there must be *some* tax rate between 0 and 100 percent at which tax revenue will be maximized. Indeed, economists of all persuasions agree with that conclusion. But the issue of *where* a particular economy is located on its Laffer Curve is not at all obvious. If the economy is at a point like *n* in Figure 17.12, then a lower tax rate will *increase* tax revenue. But if the economy is at any point on the curve below point *m,* a tax cut will *reduce* tax revenue.

Evaluation

Today, there is general agreement that the U.S. economy is operating at a point below *m*—rather than above *m*—on the Laffer Curve in Figure 17.12. In this zone, higher personal tax rates increase tax revenues, while lower personal tax rates reduce tax revenues.

At the same time, economists also recognize that, other things being equal, changes in tax rates do result in *some* supply-side effects, especially in terms of altering certain taxpayers' behavior. These feedback effects imply that cuts in tax rates reduce tax revenues in percentage terms by less

Do Tax Increases Reduce Real GDP?*

Determining the Relationship between Changes in Taxes and Changes in GDP Is Fraught with Complexity. Christina Romer and David Romer Devised a Novel Way to Approach the Topic. Their Findings Suggest that Tax Increases Reduce Real GDP.

How do changes in the level of taxation affect the level of economic activity? The simple positive correlation between taxation and economic activity shows that, on average, when economic activity rises more rapidly, tax revenues also rise more rapidly. But this correlation almost surely does not reflect a positive effect of tax increases on output. Rather, under our tax system, any positive shock to output raises tax revenues by increasing income.

In "The Macroeconomic Effects of Tax Changes: Estimates Based on a New Measure of Fiscal Shocks," Christina Romer and David Romer observe that this difficulty is just one of many manifestations of a more general problem. Changes in taxes occur for many reasons. And because the factors that give rise to tax changes often are correlated with other developments in the economy, disentangling the effects of tax changes from the effects of those other factors is inherently difficult.

To address this problem, Romer and Romer use the narrative record—presidential speeches, executive branch documents, congressional reports, and so on—to identify the size, timing, and principal motivation for all major tax policy actions in the post–World War II United States. This narrative analysis allows them to separate revenue changes resulting from legislation from changes occurring for other reasons. It also allows them to classify legislated changes according to their primary motivation.

Romer and Romer find that despite the complexity of the legislative process, significant tax changes have been motivated by one of four factors: counteracting other influences in the economy; paying for increases in government spending; addressing inherited budget deficits; or promoting long-run growth.

They then argue that tax changes that were legislated to counteract other influences on the economy, or to pay for increases in government spending, are very likely to be correlated with other factors affecting the economy. As a result, these observations are likely to lead to unreliable estimates of the effects of tax changes.

But tax changes that are made to promote long-run growth, or to reduce an inherited budget deficit, are undertaken for reasons essentially unrelated to other factors influencing output. Thus, examining the behavior of output following these sorts of tax changes is likely to provide reliable estimates of the output effects of tax changes. The results of this more reliable test indicate that tax changes have very large effects: a tax increase equal to 1 percent of real GDP lowers real GDP by roughly 2 to 3 percent.

Thinkstock/Stockbyte/Getty Images

Romer and Romer also find that the output effect of a tax change is much more closely tied to actual changes in tax policy as opposed to news or gossip about potential future tax changes. Investment, in particular, falls sharply in response to actual tax changes. Indeed, the strong response of investment helps to explain why the output consequences of tax increases are so large.

Romer and Romer additionally find suggestive evidence that tax increases that were legislated to reduce an inherited budget deficit have much smaller output costs than other tax increases. This is consistent with the idea that deficit-driven tax increases may have important expansionary effects through improved expectations, lower long-term interest rates, or improved confidence regarding the economy's prospects.

than the tax-rate reductions themselves. Similarly, tax-rate increases do not raise tax revenues by as much in percentage terms as the tax-rate increases. These effects are driven by the fact that changes in marginal tax rates alter taxpayer behavior and thus affect taxable income. Although these effects seem to be relatively modest, they need to be considered in designing tax policy—and, in fact, the federal government's Office of Tax Policy created a special division in 2007 devoted to estimating the magnitude of such effects for proposed changes in U.S. tax laws.

As discussed in this chapter's Last Word, this new division's forecasting challenges are made even more difficult by the fact that the effects of a tax-rate change appear to depend not only on how large the rate change happens to be but also on *why* the tax rate is being modified.

QUICK REVIEW
17.4

▸ Supply-side economists focus their attention on government policies, such as high taxation, that may impede the expansion of aggregate supply.

▸ The Laffer Curve relates tax rates to levels of tax revenue and suggests that, under some circumstances, cuts in tax rates will expand the tax base (output and income) and increase tax revenues.

▸ Most economists believe that the United States is currently operating along the portion of the Laffer Curve where tax rates and tax revenues move in the same, not opposite, directions.

▸ Today's economists recognize the importance of considering supply-side effects in designing optimal fiscal policy.

Summary

LO17.1 Explain the relationship between short-run aggregate supply and long-run aggregate supply.

In macroeconomics, the short run is the period in which nominal wages do not respond to changes in the price level. The long run is the period in which nominal wages fully respond to changes in the price level.

The short-run aggregate supply curve slopes upward. Because nominal wages are unresponsive to price-level changes, increases in the price level (prices received by firms) increase profits and real output. Conversely, decreases in the price level reduce profits and real output. However, the long-run aggregate supply curve is vertical. With sufficient time for adjustment, nominal wages rise and fall with the price level, moving the macroeconomic equilibrium up and down along the vertical long-run aggregate supply curve at the economy's full-employment output level.

LO17.2 Apply the extended (short-run/long-run) AD–AS model to inflation, recessions, and economic growth.

In the short run, demand-pull inflation raises the price level and real output. Once nominal wages rise to match the increase in the price level, the temporary increase in real output is reversed.

In the short run, cost-push inflation raises the price level and lowers real output. Unless the government expands aggregate demand, nominal wages eventually decline under conditions of recession, and the short-run aggregate supply curve shifts back to its initial location. Prices and real output eventually return to their original levels.

If prices and wages are flexible downward, a decline in aggregate demand lowers output and the price level. The decline in the price level eventually lowers nominal wages and shifts the short-run aggregate supply curve rightward. Full-employment output is thus restored.

One-time changes in aggregate demand (AD) and aggregate supply (AS) can cause only limited bouts of inflation. Ongoing mild inflation occurs because the Fed purposely increases AD slightly faster than the expansion of long-run AS that is driven by the supply factors of economic growth.

LO17.3 Explain the short-run trade-off between inflation and unemployment (the Phillips Curve).

Assuming a stable, upward sloping short-run aggregate supply curve, rightward shifts of the aggregate demand curve yield the generalization that higher inflation rates are associated with lower unemployment rates, and vice versa. This inverse relationship is known as the Phillips Curve, and empirical data for the 1960s were consistent with it. Since the 1960s, however, the data have only sometimes been consistent with an inverse relationship between unemployment and inflation. So while there is evidence supporting an inverse relationship in the short run during certain periods of time, no stable long-run relationship between inflation and unemployment seems to exist.

LO17.4 Explain why there is no long-run trade-off between inflation and unemployment.

Although there may be a short-run trade-off between inflation and unemployment, there is no long-run trade-off. Workers adapt their expectations to new inflation realities, and when they do, the unemployment rate returns to the natural rate. So the long-run Phillips Curve is vertical at the natural rate, meaning that higher rates of inflation do not permanently "buy" the economy less unemployment.

LO17.5 Explain the relationships among tax rates, tax revenues, and aggregate supply.

Supply-side economists focus attention on government policies, such as high taxation, that impede the expansion of aggregate supply. The Laffer Curve relates tax rates to levels of tax revenue and suggests that under some circumstances, cuts in tax rates will expand the tax base (output and income) and increase tax revenues. Most economists believe that the United States is currently operating in the range of the Laffer Curve where tax rates and tax revenues move in the same, not opposite, direction. However, today's economists do recognize the importance of considering supply-side effects in designing optimal fiscal policy.

Terms and Concepts

short run

long run

short-run downward sloping Phillips Curve

stagflation

aggregate supply shocks

long-run vertical Phillips Curve

disinflation

supply-side economics

Laffer Curve

Discussion Questions

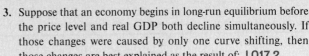

1. Distinguish between the short run and the long run as they relate to macroeconomics. Why is the distinction important? **LO17.1**
2. Which of the following statements are true? Which are false? Explain why the false statements are untrue. **LO17.1**
   a. Short-run aggregate supply curves reflect an inverse relationship between the price level and the level of real output.
   b. The long-run aggregate supply curve assumes that nominal wages are fixed.
   c. In the long run, an increase in the price level will result in an increase in nominal wages.
3. Suppose the government misjudges the natural rate of unemployment to be much lower than it actually is, and thus undertakes expansionary fiscal and monetary policies to lower it. Use the concept of the short-run Phillips Curve to explain why these policies might at first succeed. Use the concept of the long-run Phillips Curve to explain these policies' long-run outcome. **LO17.4**

4. What do the distinctions between short-run aggregate supply and long-run aggregate supply have in common with the distinction between the short-run Phillips Curve and the long-run Phillips Curve? Explain. **LO17.4**
5. What is the Laffer Curve, and how does it relate to supply-side economics? Why is determining the economy's location on the curve so important in assessing tax policy? **LO17.5**
6. Why might one person work more, earn more, and pay more income tax when his or her tax rate is cut, while another person will work less, earn less, and pay less income tax under the same circumstance? **LO17.5**
7. **LAST WORD** On average, does an increase in taxes raise or lower real GDP? If taxes as a percentage of GDP go up by 1 percent, by how much does real GDP typically change? Are the decreases in real GDP caused by tax increases temporary or permanent? Does the intention of a tax increase matter?

Review Questions

1. Suppose the full-employment level of real output (Q) for a hypothetical economy is $250 and the price level (P) initially is 100. Use the short-run aggregate supply schedules below to answer the questions that follow: **LO17.1**

AS (P_{100})		AS (P_{125})		AS (P_{75})	
P	Q	P	Q	P	Q
125	$280	125	$250	125	$310
100	250	100	220	100	280
75	220	75	190	75	250

   a. What is the level of real output in the short run if the price level unexpectedly rises from 100 to 125 because of an increase in aggregate demand? What happens if the price level unexpectedly falls from 100 to 75 because of a decrease in aggregate demand? Explain each situation, using numbers from the table.
   b. What is the level of real output in the long run when the price level rises from 100 to 125? When it falls from 100 to 75? Explain each situation.
   c. Illustrate the circumstances described in parts *a* and *b* on graph paper, and derive the long-run aggregate supply curve.
2. Suppose that AD and AS intersect at an output level that is higher than the full-employment output level. After the economy adjusts back to equilibrium in the long run, the price level will be _____. **LO17.2**
   a. higher than it is now
   b. lower than it is now
   c. the same as it is now

3. Suppose that an economy begins in long-run equilibrium before the price level and real GDP both decline simultaneously. If those changes were caused by only one curve shifting, then those changes are best explained as the result of: **LO17.2**
   a. the AD curve shifting right.
   b. the AS curve shifting right.
   c. the AD curve shifting left.
   d. the AS curve shifting left.
4. Identify the two descriptions below as being the result of either cost-push inflation or demand-pull inflation. **LO17.2**
   a. Real GDP is below the full-employment level and prices have risen recently.
   b. Real GDP is above the full-employment level and prices have risen recently.
5. Use graphical analysis to show how each of the following will affect the economy, first in the short run and then in the long run. Assume that the United States is initially operating at its full-employment level of output, that prices and wages are eventually flexible both upward and downward, and that there is no counteracting fiscal or monetary policy. **LO17.2**
   a. Because of a war abroad, the oil supply to the United States is disrupted, sending oil prices rocketing upward.
   b. Construction spending on new homes rises dramatically, greatly increasing total U.S. investment spending.
   c. Economic recession occurs abroad, significantly reducing foreign purchases of U.S. exports.
6. Between 2000 and 2020, the U.S. price level rose by about 50 percent while real output increased by about 42 percent. Use the aggregate demand–aggregate supply model to illustrate these outcomes graphically. **LO17.2**

7. Assume there is a particular short-run aggregate supply curve for an economy and the curve is relevant for several years. Use AD–AS analysis to show graphically why higher rates of inflation over this period will be associated with lower rates of unemployment, and vice versa. What is this inverse relationship called? **LO17.3**

8. Aggregate supply shocks can cause _____ inflation rates that are accompanied by _____ unemployment rates. **LO17.3**
   a. higher; higher
   b. higher; lower
   c. lower; higher
   d. lower; lower

9. Suppose that firms are expecting 6 percent inflation while workers are expecting 9 percent inflation. How much of a pay raise will workers demand if their goal is to maintain the purchasing power of their incomes? **LO17.4**
   a. 3 percent
   b. 6 percent
   c. 9 percent
   d. 12 percent

10. Suppose that firms were expecting inflation to be 3 percent, but it actually turned out to be 7 percent. Other things equal, firm profits will be: **LO17.4**
    a. smaller than expected.
    b. larger than expected.

Problems

Mc Graw Hill **connect**

1. Use the nearby figure to answer the following questions. Assume that the economy initially is operating at price level 120 and real output level $870. This output level is the economy's potential (full-employment) level of output. Next, suppose that the price level rises from 120 to 130. By how much will real output increase in the short run? In the long run? Instead, now assume that the price level drops from 120 to 110. Assuming flexible product and resource prices, by how much will real output fall in the short run? In the long run? What is the long-run level of output at each of the three price levels shown? **LO17.1**

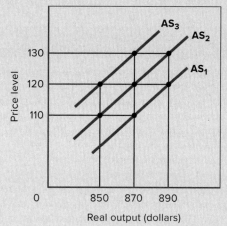

2. **ADVANCED ANALYSIS** Suppose that the equation for a particular short-run AS curve is $P = 20 + 0.5Q$, where P is the price level and Q is real output in dollar terms. What is Q if the price level is 120? Suppose that the Q in your answer is the full-employment level of output. By how much will Q increase *in the short run* if the price level unexpectedly rises from 120 to 132? By how much will Q increase *in the long run* due to the price-level increase? **LO17.1**

3. Suppose that over a 30-year period Buskerville's price level increased from 72 to 138, while its real GDP rose from $1.2 trillion to $2.1 trillion. Did economic growth occur in Buskerville? If so, by what average yearly rate in percentage terms (rounded to one decimal place)? Did Buskerville experience inflation? If so, by what average yearly rate in percentage terms (rounded to one decimal place)? Which shifted rightward faster in Buskerville: its long-run aggregate supply curve (AS_{LR}) or its aggregate demand curve (AD)? **LO17.2**

4. Suppose that for years East Confetti's short-run Phillips Curve was such that each 1 percentage point increase in its unemployment rate was associated with a 2 percentage point decline in its inflation rate. Then, during several recent years, the short-run pattern changed such that its inflation rate rose by 3 percentage points for every 1 percentage point drop in its unemployment rate. Graphically, did East Confetti's Phillips Curve shift upward or did it shift downward? Explain. **LO17.3**

Current Issues in Macro Theory and Policy

>> LEARNING OBJECTIVES

LO18.1 Describe alternative perspectives on the causes of macroeconomic instability.

LO18.2 Explain why new classical economists believe the economy will self-correct from aggregate demand and aggregate supply shocks.

LO18.3 Describe the rules versus discretion debate regarding stabilization policy.

As any academic discipline evolves, it naturally evokes a number of internal disagreements. Economics is no exception. In this chapter, we examine a few alternative perspectives on macro theory and policy. We focus on the disagreements regarding three interrelated questions: (1) What causes instability in the economy? (2) Is the economy self-correcting? (3) Should government adhere to *rules* or use *discretion* in setting economic policy?

What Causes Macro Instability?

Capitalist economies experienced considerable instability during the twentieth century. The United States, for example, experienced the Great Depression, numerous recessions, inflation, and deflation. Instability has continued in the twenty-first century, with the U.S. experiencing a tech-bubble recession in 2001, a real-estate financial-crisis recession from 2007 to 2009, and a pandemic recession in 2020.

>> **LO18.1** Describe alternative perspectives on the causes of macroeconomic instability.

Economists have different perspectives about the causes of macroeconomic instability.

Mainstream View

For simplicity, we will use the term "mainstream view" to characterize the prevailing macroeconomic perspective of the majority of economists. According to the mainstream view, instability arises from two sources: (1) price stickiness and (2) unexpected shocks to either aggregate demand or aggregate supply.

As we explained in Chapter 17, in the long run, when input prices and output prices are fully flexible and have time to adjust to changes in aggregate demand or short-run aggregate supply, the economy always returns to producing at potential output. In the shorter run, however, stickiness in either input or output prices means that any shock to either aggregate demand or aggregate supply will result in changes in output and employment.

Changes in Aggregate Demand Mainstream macroeconomics focuses on aggregate spending and its components. Recall that the basic equation underlying aggregate expenditures is

$$C_a + I_g + X_n + G = \text{GDP}$$

That is, the aggregate amount of after-tax consumption, gross investment, net exports, and government spending determines the total amount of goods and services produced and sold. In equilibrium, $C_a + I_g + X_n + G$ (aggregate expenditures) equals GDP (real output). A decrease in the price level increases equilibrium GDP and thus allows us to trace out a downward sloping aggregate demand curve for the economy (see the Chapter 12 appendix). Any change in one of the spending components in the aggregate expenditures equation shifts the aggregate demand curve. The result is a change in equilibrium real output, the price level, or both.

Investment spending in particular is subject to wide "booms" and "busts." Significant increases in investment spending are multiplied into even greater increases in aggregate demand and thus can produce demand-pull inflation. Significant declines in investment spending are multiplied into even greater decreases in aggregate demand and thus can cause recessions.

Adverse Aggregate Supply Shocks In the mainstream view, the second source of macroeconomic instability arises on the supply side. Occasionally, such external events as wars or an artificial supply restriction of a key resource can boost resource prices and significantly raise per-unit production costs. The result is a sizable decline in a nation's aggregate supply, which destabilizes the economy by simultaneously causing cost-push inflation and recession.

Monetarist View

monetarism The macroeconomic view that the main cause of changes in aggregate output and the *price level* is fluctuations in the *money supply;* espoused by advocates of a *monetary rule.*

Monetarism (1) focuses on the money supply, (2) holds that markets are highly competitive, and (3) says that a competitive market system gives the economy a high degree of macroeconomic stability. Monetarists argue that the price and wage flexibility provided by competitive markets should cause fluctuations in aggregate demand to alter product and resource prices rather than output and employment. Thus, monetarists say, the market system would provide substantial macroeconomic stability *were it not for government interference in the economy.*

The problem, as monetarists see it, is that government is to blame for downward wage and price inflexibility because government has implemented minimum-wage laws, pro-union legislation, guaranteed prices for certain farm products, and pro-business monopoly legislation. They argue that government interference has undermined the market's natural ability to provide macroeconomic stability. Moreover, monetarists believe that the Fed's attempts to use monetary policy to mitigate business cycles have backfired, so that its monetary policy actions intensify (rather than dampen) the business cycle.

equation of exchange $MV = PQ$, in which M is the supply of *money, V* is the *velocity* of money, P is the *price level,* and Q is the physical volume of *final goods* and final *services* produced.

velocity The number of times per year that the average dollar in the *money supply* is spent for *final goods* and final *services; nominal gross domestic product (GDP)* divided by the *money supply.*

Equation of Exchange The fundamental equation of monetarism is the **equation of exchange:**

$$MV = PQ$$

where M is the supply of money; V is the **velocity** of money, that is, the average number of times per year a dollar is spent on final goods and services; P is the price level or, more specifically, the average price at which each unit of physical output is sold; and Q is the physical volume of all goods and services produced.

The left side of the equation of exchange, MV, represents the total amount spent by purchasers of output, while the right side, PQ, represents the total amount received by sellers of that output. The nation's money supply (M) multiplied by the number of times it is spent each year (V) must equal the nation's nominal GDP ($= P \times Q$). The dollar value of total spending must equal the dollar value of total output.

Stable Velocity Official statistics show that the velocity of money changes over time. Monetarists argue that these changes in velocity are mostly gradual, which they say is to be expected because the underlying factors that affect velocity are themselves slow to change, so that changes in velocity from one year to the next can be readily anticipated. Monetarists also hold that velocity does not change in response to changes in the money supply itself. Instead, people have a stable desire to hold money relative to holding other financial assets, holding real assets, and buying current output. The factors that determine the amount of money the public wants to hold depend mainly on the level of nominal GDP, and those factors in turn determine money velocity.

Example: Assume that when nominal GDP is $400 billion, the public desires $100 billion of money to purchase that output. That means that V is 4 (= $400 billion of nominal GDP/$100 billion of money). If we further assume that the actual money supply is $100 billion, the economy will be in equilibrium with respect to money because the actual amount of money supplied ($100 billion) will equal the amount the public wants to hold ($100 billion).

If velocity is stable, the equation of exchange suggests that there is a predictable relationship between the money supply and nominal GDP ($= PQ$). An increase in the money supply of, say, $10 billion will upset equilibrium in our example because the public will find itself holding more money or liquidity than it wants. That is, the actual amount of money held ($110 billion) will exceed the amount of holdings desired ($100 billion). In that case, the reaction of the public (households and businesses) is to restore its desired balance of money relative to other items, such as stocks and bonds, factories and equipment, houses and automobiles, and clothing and toys. But the spending of money by individual households and businesses will leave more cash in the checkable deposits or billfolds of other households and firms. And they too will try to "spend down" their excess cash balances. But, overall, the $110 billion money supply cannot be spent down because a dollar spent is a dollar received.

Instead, the collective attempt to reduce cash balances will increase aggregate demand, thereby boosting nominal GDP. Because velocity in our example is 4—that is, each dollar is spent, on average, four times per year—nominal GDP rises from $400 billion to $440 billion. At that higher nominal GDP, the money supply of $110 billion equals the amount of money desired ($440 billion/4 = $110 billion), so that equilibrium is reestablished.

The $10 billion increase in the money supply thus eventually increases nominal GDP by $40 billion. Spending on goods, services, and assets expands until nominal GDP has gone up enough to restore the original 4-to-1 equilibrium relationship between nominal GDP and the money supply.

Note that the relationship GDP/M defines V. So a stable relationship between nominal GDP and M implies a stable value for V, and vice versa. With V stable, any change in M will cause a proportionate change in nominal GDP. Thus, monetarists say that changes in the money supply have a predictable effect on nominal GDP ($= P \times Q$). An increase in M increases P or Q, or some combination of both. A decrease in M reduces P or Q, or some combination of both.

Monetary Causes of Instability Monetarists say that inappropriate monetary policy is the single most important cause of macroeconomic instability. An increase in the money supply directly increases aggregate demand. Under conditions of full employment, that increase in aggregate demand raises the price level. For a time, higher prices cause firms to increase their real output, and the unemployment rate falls below its natural rate. But after nominal wages rise to reflect the higher prices and thus to restore real wages, real output moves back to its full-employment level and the unemployment rate returns to its natural rate. The inappropriate increase in the money supply leads to inflation, together with instability of real output and employment.

Conversely, a decrease in the money supply reduces aggregate demand. Real output temporarily falls, and the unemployment rate rises above its natural rate. Eventually, nominal wages fall and real output returns to its full-employment level. The inappropriate decline in the money supply leads to deflation, together with instability of real GDP and employment.

Here, the contrast between mainstream macroeconomists and monetarists comes into sharp focus. Mainstream macroeconomists view the instability of investment as the main cause of macroeconomic instability, and they consider monetary policy to be a stabilizing factor because changes in the money supply can be used to raise or lower interest rates as needed, thereby smoothing out the swings in investment that drive macroeconomic instability. In contrast, monetarists view changes in the money supply as the main cause of instability in the economy. For example, they say that the Great Depression occurred largely because the Fed allowed the money supply to fall by roughly one-third during that period. Monetarists acknowledge that investment *did* collapse during the Great Depression, but they view that decline as an effect of bad monetary policy rather than as one of the driving factors behind the downturn.

Real-Business-Cycle View

A third view holds that business cycles are caused by real factors that affect aggregate supply, rather than by monetary, or spending, factors that cause fluctuations in aggregate demand. In **real-business-cycle theory,** business fluctuations result from significant changes in technology and resource availability. Those changes affect productivity and thus the long-run growth trend of aggregate supply.

An example focusing on recession will clarify this thinking. Suppose productivity (output per worker) declines sharply because of a large increase in oil prices, which makes it prohibitively expensive to operate certain types of machinery. That decline in productivity implies a reduction

real-business-cycle theory
A theory that *business cycles* result from changes in *technology* and *resource* availability, which affect *productivity* and thus increase or decrease long-run *aggregate supply.*

FIGURE 18.1
Real-business-cycle theory.

In real-business-cycle theory, a decline in resource availability shifts the nation's long-run aggregate supply curve to the left from AS_{LR1} to AS_{LR2}. The decline in real output from Q_1 to Q_2, in turn, reduces money demand (less is needed) and money supply (fewer loans are taken out) such that aggregate demand shifts leftward from AD_1 to AD_2. The result is a recession in which the price level remains constant.

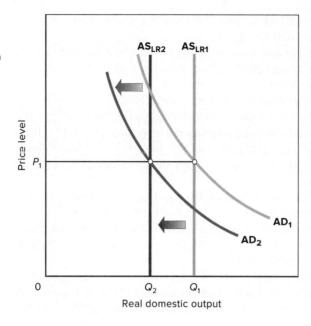

in the economy's ability to produce real output. The result will be a decrease in the economy's long-run aggregate supply curve, as represented by the leftward shift from AS_{LR1} to AS_{LR2} in Figure 18.1.

As real output falls from Q_1 to Q_2, the public needs less money to buy the reduced volume of goods and services. So the demand for money falls. Moreover, the slowdown in business activity means that businesses need to borrow less from banks, reducing the part of the money supply that banks create through their lending. Thus, the supply of money also falls. In this controversial scenario, changes in the supply of money respond to changes in the demand for money. The decline in the money supply then reduces aggregate demand, as from AD_1 to AD_2 in Figure 18.1. The outcome is a decline in real output from Q_1 to Q_2, with no change in the price level.

Conversely, a large increase in aggregate supply (not shown) caused by, say, major innovations in the production process will shift the long-run aggregate supply curve rightward. Real output will increase, and so will money demand and money supply. Aggregate demand will shift rightward by an amount equal to the rightward shift of long-run aggregate supply. Real output will increase without driving up the price level.

Conclusion: In real-business-cycle theory, macro instability arises on the aggregate supply side of the economy. That stands in sharp contrast to the belief held by both mainstream economists and monetarists that aggregate demand fluctuations are responsible for most business cycle fluctuations.

The nearby Consider This story explains why the Great Recession of 2007–2009 is better explained by the mainstream view than by real-business-cycle theory.

CONSIDER THIS . . .

Too Much Money?

The severe recession of 2007–2009 fits the mainstream view that recessions are caused by AD shocks rather than the real-business-cycle view that they are caused by AS shocks. In particular, the recession began with an unexpected financial crisis that caused significant reductions in investment and consumption that significantly reduced aggregate demand. Additionally, the price level was sticky downward, with the leftward shift of the aggregate demand curve generating mostly declines in output and income rather than lower prices and deflation.

Economists with monetarist leanings, however, cite monetary factors as the main cause of the financial crisis that led to the initial declines in aggregate demand. They argue that the Federal Reserve flooded the economy with too much money and held interest rates too low for too long in promoting recovery from the 2001

Baron Wolman/The Image Bank/ Getty Images

recession. In this line of reasoning, the excess money and low interest rates contributed to the pre-recession price bubble in the housing market. When that bubble burst, the resulting mortgage defaults set in motion the forces that produced the decline in AD and therefore the recession.

All economists agree that the bursting of the housing bubble led to the recession. And too-loose monetary policy may have contributed to the bubble. But mainstream economists also cite the role of the very large international flows of foreign savings into the United States during this period. These inflows drove down interest rates and helped to fuel the housing bubble. Other factors such as "pass-the-risk" lending practices, government policies promoting home ownership, and poorly designed and enforced financial regulations certainly came into play. The mainstream view is that causes of the financial crisis and recession were numerous and complex.

Coordination Failures

A fourth and final view of macroeconomic instability relates to **coordination failures,** which occur when people fail to reach a mutually beneficial equilibrium because they lack a way to coordinate their actions.

As an example, let's consider a recession. Suppose that individual firms and households expect other firms and consumers to cut back on investment and consumption. As a result, each firm and household will anticipate a reduction of aggregate demand. Firms therefore reduce their own investment spending because they anticipate that their future production capacity will become excessive. Households also reduce their own consumption spending because they antici-pate that they will experience reduced work hours, possible layoffs, and falling incomes in the future.

Aggregate demand will indeed decline and the economy will indeed experience a recession in response to what amounts to a self-fulfilling prophecy. Moreover, the economy will stay at a below-full-employment level of output because, once there, producers and households have no individual incentive to increase spending. If all producers and all households could agree to increase their investment and consumption spending simultaneously, then aggregate demand would rise, and real output and real income would increase. Each producer and each consumer would be better off. However, this outcome will not occur because there is no mechanism for firms and house-holds to agree on such a joint spending increase.

In this case, the economy is stuck in an *unemployment equilibrium* because of a coordination failure. With a different set of expectations, a coordination failure might leave the economy in an *inflation equilibrium*. The economy therefore has a number of such potential equilibrium posi-tions, some good and some bad, depending on people's mix of expectations. Macroeconomic instability, then, reflects the economy's movement from one such equilibrium position to another as expectations change.

> **coordination failure** A situation in which people do not reach a mutually beneficial outcome because they lack some way to jointly coordinate their actions; a possible cause of macroeconomic instability.

QUICK REVIEW

18.1

▸ Mainstream economists say that macroeconomic instability usually stems from swings in investment spending and, occasionally, from adverse aggre-gate supply shocks.

▸ Monetarists view the economy through the equa-tion of exchange ($MV = PQ$). If velocity V is stable, changes in the money supply M lead directly to changes in nominal GDP ($= P \times Q$). For monetar-ists, changes in M caused by inappropriate mone-tary policy are the single most important cause of macroeconomic instability.

▸ In the real-business-cycle theory, significant changes in "real" factors such as technology, resource availability, and productivity change the economy's long-run aggregate supply, causing macroeconomic instability.

▸ Macroeconomic instability can result from coordina-tion failures—less-than-optimal equilibrium positions that occur because businesses and households lack a way to coordinate their actions.

Does the Economy "Self-Correct"?

Just as there are disputes over the causes of macroeconomic instability, there are disputes over whether or not the economy will correct itself when instability does occur. Economists also dis-agree on how long it will take for any such self-correction to take place. The points of disagree-ment can be understood by examining how *new classical economics* approaches macroeconomic self-correction.

New Classical View of Self-Correction

New classical economists tend to be either monetarists or adherents of **rational expectations theory,** which assumes that people will do their logical (rational) best to correctly anticipate future events as much as possible so as to minimize the likelihood of ever being caught off guard. To the degree that they are able to understand and anticipate future events or the future consequences of current events, they will be able to make better current decisions with respect to maximizing both personal utility and business profits. Examples: (1) Before driving up into the mountains, you check the weather news hourly so you can develop an accurate sense about likely weather hazards. (2) You study macroeconomics so that you will know the best places to invest your money if the Fed decides to loosen monetary policy. (3) Knowing how bad this year's flu virus is, you wash your hands several times per day in order to reduce your chances of becoming infected.

> **>> LO18.2** Explain why new classical economists believe the economy will self-correct from aggregate demand and aggregate supply shocks.

> **rational expectations theory** A hypothesis that assumes that people develop logical (rational) models that attempt to correctly antici-pate future events (expecta-tions) as much as possible so as to make better cur-rent decisions given what is likely to happen in the fu-ture. Can cause individuals and firms to take actions that offset monetary and fiscal policy initiatives.

FIGURE 18.2 The new classical view of self-correction.

(a) An *unanticipated* increase in aggregate demand from AD₁ to AD₂ first moves the economy from *a* to *b,* and the economy then self-corrects to *c.* By contrast, an *anticipated* increase in aggregate demand from AD₁ to AD₂ moves the economy directly from *a* to *c.* (b) An *unanticipated* decrease in aggregate demand from AD₁ to AD₃ moves the economy from *a* to *d,* and the economy then self-corrects to *e.* By contrast, an anticipated decrease in aggregate demand from AD₁ to AD₃ moves the economy directly from *a* to *e.* (Mainstream economists, however, say that if the price level remains at P_1, the economy will move from *a* to *f,* and even if the price level falls to P_4, the economy may remain at *d* because of downward wage inflexibility.)

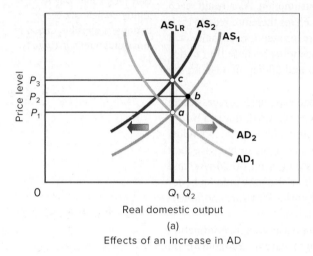

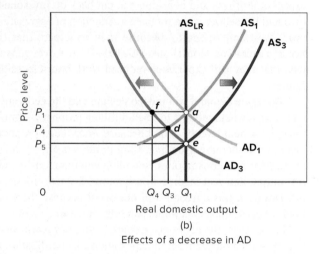

(a)

Effects of an increase in AD

(b)

Effects of a decrease in AD

new classical economics
The theory that, although unanticipated *price-level* changes may create macroeconomic instability in the short run, the economy will return to and stabilize at the full-employment level of domestic output in the long run because *prices* and *wages* adjust automatically to correct movements away from the full-employment output level.

New classical economics contends that when the economy diverges from its full-employment output, internal mechanisms within the economy automatically move it back to that output. So policymakers should stand back and let the automatic correction occur, rather than engage in active fiscal and monetary policy. This perspective is often associated with the vertical long-run Phillips Curve, which we discussed in Chapter 17. But we will analyze it here using the extended AD–AS model that was also developed in Chapter 17.

Examples of Macroeconomic Self-Correction Figure 18.2a demonstrates the new classical idea that the economy is capable of self-correction. Specifically, an increase in aggregate demand, say, from AD₁ to AD₂, moves the economy upward along its short-run aggregate supply curve AS₁ from *a* to *b.* The price level rises and real output increases. With the economy producing beyond potential output, high resource demand drives up the prices of labor and other productive inputs. Per-unit production costs increase and the short-run aggregate supply curve shifts leftward, eventually from AS₁ to AS₂. The economy moves from *b* to *c,* and real output returns to its full-employment level, Q_1. This level of output dictates the position of the economy's vertical long-run aggregate supply curve, AS_LR.

Conversely, a decrease in aggregate demand from AD₁ to AD₃ in Figure 18.2b first moves the economy downward along its short-run aggregate supply curve AS₁ from point *a* to *d.* The price level declines, as does the level of real output. With the economy producing below potential output, low resource demand drives down the prices of labor and other productive inputs. When that happens, per-unit production costs decline and the short-run aggregate supply curve shifts to the right, eventually from AS₁ to AS₃. The economy moves to *e,* where it again achieves its full-employment level, Q_1. As in Figure 18.2a, the economy in Figure 18.2b has automatically self-corrected to its full-employment output and its natural rate of unemployment.

Rational Expectations Theory and the Speed of Self-Correcting Adjustments There is some disagreement among new classical economists on how long it will take for self-correction to occur. Monetarists usually hold the *adaptive expectations* view that people form their expectations by extrapolating from present and past conditions. As a result, they only gradually change their expectations as experience unfolds, which means that the shifts in the short-run aggregate supply curves shown in Figure 18.2 may not occur for two or three years, or even longer, if people are assumed to have adaptive expectations. By contrast, other new classical economists believe that people have *rational expectations*, meaning that they are forward looking and do their best to rationally and accurately anticipate future outcomes. Under the assumption of rational expectations, price-level changes that are fully anticipated will be changes that people adjust to quickly, or even instantaneously.

Although many areas of economics (including finance and game theory) have incorporated rational expectations theory, our interest here is with the new classical version of rational expectations theory as it relates to macroeconomic adjustments. This application of rational expectations theory (hereafter, RET) is based on two assumptions:

- People behave rationally, gathering and intelligently processing information to form expectations about things that are economically important to them. They adjust those expectations quickly as new developments affecting future economic outcomes occur. Where there is adequate information, people's beliefs about future economic outcomes will accurately reflect the likelihood that those outcomes will occur. For example, if it is clear that a certain policy will cause inflation, people will recognize that fact and adjust their economic behavior in anticipation of inflation.

- RET economists assume that all product and resource markets are highly competitive and that prices and wages are flexible both upward and downward. But the RET economists go further, assuming that new information is quickly (in some cases, instantaneously) taken into account in market demand and supply curves. The upshot is that equilibrium prices and quantities should adjust *rapidly* to unforeseen events like unexpected technological advances or unexpected aggregate supply shocks. And they adjust *instantaneously* to events that have known outcomes—for example, changes in fiscal or monetary policy.

Unanticipated Price-Level Changes RET implies not only that the economy is self-correcting but also that self-correction occurs quickly even in response to unexpected macroeconomic shocks. According to RET, unanticipated changes in the price level—called **price-level surprises**—*do* cause temporary changes in real output. As an example, suppose that an unanticipated increase in foreign demand for U.S. goods increases U.S. aggregate demand from AD_1 to AD_2 in Figure 18.2a. The immediate result that we actually observe is an unexpected increase in the price level from P_1 to P_2 and an unexpected increase in GDP to a level higher than full employment.

price-level surprises
Unanticipated changes in the *price level.*

But now an interesting question arises. If wages and prices are fully flexible, as assumed in RET, why doesn't the higher price level cause wages and other input prices to rise *immediately*? If they did rise immediately, the aggregate supply curve would instantaneously shift leftward from AS_1 to AS_2, so that any increase in real output would last only a brief moment or two. The economy would jump almost directly from point *a* to point *c*.

As we have already noted, the macroeconomic adjustments that we actually observe after a positive demand shock like the movement from AD_1 to AD_2 don't move anywhere nearly as rapidly as that. So RET proponents need to provide us with an explanation as to why the economy moves first (as it does) from point *a* to *b* along AS_1 before having to wait months or even years for aggregate supply to shift left so as to return the economy to full employment at point *c*. If firms have rational expectations, they should know that they are going to end up back at point *c*, producing no more output than they did at point *a*. So why would they as rational agents ever bother increasing their output levels above full employment?

The RET explanation is that firms increase output from Q_1 to Q_2 because of misperceptions about the rising prices that they observe for their own products. They mistakenly confuse the general increase in the price level that is actually taking place across the entire economy for a specific increase in the price of their own product. They mistakenly think that their own selling price is increasing *relative to* the prices of other products. That makes them think that their profit margins are going to increase, which in turn spurs them to increase output beyond the full-employment level.

The truth, of course, is that *all* prices, including the price of labor (nominal wages), are going to rise in response to the unexpected demand shock. Once firms see that *all* prices and wages are rising, they will decrease their production to previous levels. But that will only happen once they realize their mistake about confusing the general increase in the price level for a specific increase in the price of their own product. That realization could take a while. And so RET theorists have an explanation for why the economy only slowly adjusts from *a* to *b* to *c* even when people are assumed to utilize rational expectations.

The same analysis in reverse applies to an unanticipated price-level decrease. In Figure 18.2b, firms at first misunderstand why the prices of their own products are falling from *a* to *b* after aggregate demand unexpectedly shifts left from AD_1 to AD_3. They mistakenly believe that their own respective prices are falling due to decreases in the demand for their own products relative to the demand for other products. Not understanding that aggregate demand has decreased all across the economy, they mistakenly anticipate declines in their own respective profits and consequently cut production. The collective result of those individual reductions is a decrease in real output that will persist until firms see what is really happening with aggregate demand. Once firms see what is really happening—that *all* prices and wages are dropping, not just their own—they will increase their respective outputs. When they do, the short-run aggregate supply curve in Figure 18.2b will shift rightward from AS_1 to AS_3, and the economy will "self-correct" by moving from *d* to *e*.

Fully Anticipated Price-Level Changes In RET, *fully anticipated* price-level changes do not change real output, even for short periods. In Figure 18.2a, again consider the increase in aggregate demand from AD_1 to AD_2. Businesses immediately recognize that the higher prices being paid for their products are part of the inflation they had anticipated. They also understand that the same forces that are causing the inflation will result in higher nominal wages, leaving their profits unchanged. The economy therefore moves directly from *a* to *c*. The price level rises as expected, and output remains at its full-employment level Q_1, also as expected.

Similarly, a *fully anticipated* price-level decrease will leave real output unchanged. Firms anticipate that nominal wages will decline by the same percentage amount as the declining price level, leaving profits unchanged. The economy represented by Figure 18.2b therefore moves directly from *a* to *e*. Deflation occurs, but the economy continues to produce its full-employment output Q_1. The anticipated decline in aggregate demand causes no change in real output.

Mainstream View of Self-Correction

While mainstream economists have incorporated some aspects of RET into their own models, most economists strongly disagree with RET on the question of downward price and wage flexibility. While the stock market, foreign exchange market, and certain commodity markets experience day-to-day or minute-to-minute price changes, including price declines, the same is not true of many product markets and most labor markets. There is ample evidence, say mainstream economists, that many prices and wages are inflexible downward for long periods. As a result, it may take years for the economy to move from recession back to full-employment output, unless it gets help from fiscal and monetary policy.

Downward Wage Inflexibility There are several reasons why firms may not be able to, or may not want to, lower nominal wages. Firms may not be able to cut wages because of wage contracts and the legal minimum wage. And firms may not want to lower wages if they fear potential problems with morale, effort, and efficiency.

efficiency wage An above-market (above-equilibrium) *wage* that minimizes wage costs per unit of output by encouraging greater effort or reducing turnover.

Efficiency Wage Theory An **efficiency wage** is an above-market-equilibrium wage that minimizes a firm's labor cost per unit of output. Normally, we would think that the market wage is the efficiency wage because it is the lowest wage at which a firm can obtain a particular type of labor. But where the cost of supervising workers is high or where worker turnover is great, firms may discover that paying more than the market wage lowers their wage cost per unit of output.

Example: Suppose a firm's workers, on average, produce 8 units of output at a $9 market wage but 10 units of output at a $10 above-market wage. The efficiency wage is $10, not the $9 market wage. At the $10 wage, the labor cost per unit of output is only $1 (= $10 wage/10 units of output), compared with $1.12 (= $9 wage/8 units of output) at the $9 wage.

How can a higher wage result in greater efficiency?

- *Greater work effort* The above-market wage raises the cost to workers of losing their jobs as a result of poor performance. Because workers have a strong incentive to retain their relatively high-paying jobs, they are more likely to provide greater work effort. In other words, workers are more reluctant to shirk (neglect or avoid work) because the higher wage makes job loss more costly to them. Consequently, the above-market wage can be the efficient wage; it can enhance worker productivity so much that the higher wage more than pays for itself.

- *Lower supervision costs* With less incentive among workers to shirk, the firm needs fewer supervisory personnel to monitor work performance. Lower supervisory costs, too, can lower the firm's overall wage cost per unit of output.

- *Reduced job turnover* The above-market pay discourages workers from voluntarily leaving their jobs. The lower turnover rate in turn reduces the firm's cost of hiring and training workers. It also gives the firm a more experienced, more productive workforce.

The key implication for macroeconomic instability is that efficiency wages add to the downward inflexibility of wages. Firms that pay efficiency wages will be reluctant to cut wages when aggregate demand declines, because such cuts may encourage shirking, require more supervisory personnel, and increase turnover. In other words, wage cuts that reduce productivity and raise per-unit labor costs are self-defeating.

QUICK REVIEW 18.2

▸ New classical economists believe that the economy "self-corrects" when unanticipated events divert it from its full-employment level of real output.

▸ In rational expectations theory (RET), unanticipated price-level changes cause changes in real output in the short run but not in the long run.

▸ According to RET, market participants immediately change their actions in response to anticipated price-level changes such that no change in real output occurs.

▸ Mainstream economists say that the economy can get mired in recession for several months or more because of downward price and wage inflexibility. Sources of downward wage inflexibility include minimum wages, labor contracts, and efficiency wages.

Rules or Discretion?

The different views on the causes of instability and on the speed of self-correction have led to vigorous debate. Should the government adhere to policy rules that prohibit it from causing instability in an economy that is otherwise stable? Or should it use discretionary fiscal and monetary policy, when needed, to stabilize a sometimes-unstable economy?

>> **LO18.3** Describe the rules versus discretion debate regarding stabilization policy.

In Support of Policy Rules

Monetarists and other new classical economists believe that policy rules will reduce instability in the economy. They believe that such rules will prevent government from trying to "manage" aggregate demand. That outcome is desirable because, in their view, such management is likely to *cause* more instability than it cures.

Monetary Rules Because inappropriate monetary policy is the major source of macroeconomic instability, say monetarists, the enactment of a **monetary rule** would make sense. One such rule would be a requirement that the Fed expand the money supply each year at the same annual rate as the typical growth rate of the economy's productive capacity. That fixed-rate expansion of the money supply would occur whatever the state of the economy. The Fed's sole monetary role would be to use its tools (open-market operations, the discount rate, interest on reserves, and reserve requirements) to ensure that the nation's money supply grew steadily by, say, 3 to 5 percent a year. According to Milton Friedman, a prominent monetarist,

> Such a rule . . . would eliminate . . . the major cause of instability in the economy—the capricious and unpredictable impact of countercyclical monetary policy. As long as the money supply grows at a constant rate each year, be it 3, 4, or 5 percent, any decline into recession will be temporary. The liquidity provided by a constantly growing money supply will cause aggregate demand to expand. Similarly, if the supply of money does not rise at a more than average rate, any inflationary increase in spending will burn itself out for lack of fuel.[1]

Figure 18.3 illustrates the rationale for a monetary rule. Suppose the economy represented there is operating at its full-employment real output, Q_1. Also suppose the nation's long-run aggregate supply curve shifts rightward, as from AS_{LR1} to AS_{LR2}, each year, signifying the average annual increase in potential real output. As you know, such annual increases in "potential GDP" result from added resources, improved resources, and improved technology.

Monetarists argue that a monetary rule would tie increases in the money supply to the typical rightward shift of long-run aggregate supply. Due to the direct link between changes in the money supply and aggregate demand, the monetary rule would ensure that the AD curve shifts rightward, as from AD_1 to AD_2, each year. As a result, while GDP increases from Q_1 to Q_2, the price level will remain constant at P_1. A monetary rule, in short, will promote steady growth of real output along with price stability.

monetary rule (1) A set of guidelines to be followed by a *central bank* that wishes to adjust monetary policy over time to achieve goals such as promoting *economic growth,* encouraging *full employment,* and maintaining a stable *price level.* (2) The guidelines for conducting monetary policy suggested by *monetarism.* As traditionally formulated, the *money supply* should be expanded each year at the same annual rate as the potential rate of growth of *real gross domestic product;* the supply of money should be increased steadily between 3 and 5 percent per year. (Also see *Taylor rule.*)

---

[1]Lawrence S. Ritter and William L. Silber, *Money* (Basic Books, 1984).

FIGURE 18.3
Rationale for a monetary rule.

A monetary rule that required the Fed to increase the money supply at an annual rate linked to the long-run increase in potential GDP would shift aggregate demand rightward, as from AD_1 to AD_2, at the same pace as the shift in long-run aggregate supply, here, AS_{LR1} to AS_{LR2}. Thus the economy would experience growth without inflation or deflation.

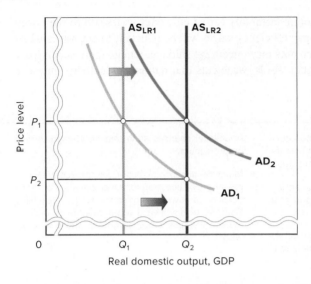

Generally, rational expectations economists also support a monetary rule. They conclude that an expansionary or restrictive monetary policy will alter the inflation rate but not real output. Suppose, for example, the Fed implements an easy money policy to reduce interest rates, expand investment spending, and boost real GDP. On the basis of past experience and economic knowledge, the public will anticipate that this policy is inflationary and will take protective actions. Workers will press for higher nominal wages; firms will raise their product prices; and lenders will increase their nominal interest rates on loans.

All these responses are designed to prevent inflation from having adverse effects on the real income of workers, businesses, and lenders. But collectively they would immediately raise wage and price levels. So the increase in aggregate demand brought about by the expansionary monetary policy would be completely dissipated in higher prices and wages. Real output and employment would not be increased by the easy money policy. Only higher prices and inflation would result.

In this view, the combination of rational expectations and instantaneous market adjustments dooms discretionary monetary policy to ineffectiveness. If discretionary monetary policy produces only inflation (or deflation), say the RET economists, then it makes sense to limit the Fed's discretion and to require that Congress enact a monetary rule consistent with either price-level stability or inflation-rate stability.

Inflation Targeting In recent decades, the call for a Friedman-type monetary rule has faded. In 2012, the Fed did, however, adopt a flexible version of another type of monetary rule. Under **inflation targeting**, the Fed commits to adjusting monetary policy as necessary to achieve a publicly announced inflation rate. The Fed's choice for its **target rate of inflation** was 2 percent per year, in line with the target rates chosen around the same time by the European Central Bank and the Bank of Japan.

Strictly interpreted, inflation targeting would focus the Fed's attention nearly exclusively on controlling inflation and deflation, rather than on counteracting business fluctuations. Proponents of strict inflation targeting generally believe the economy will have fewer, shorter, and less severe business cycles if the Fed adheres to the rule "Set a known inflation goal and achieve it." The Fed, however, reserves the right to use monetary policy as necessary to smooth the business cycle even if doing so might cause inflation to deviate from the target rate of 2 percent.

Global Perspective 18.1 lists the inflation targets of several national and regional central banks. Some countries, like Mexico, have a target *range* for inflation—such as 2 percent to 4 percent per year—rather than a single target number. In those cases, the middle value of the target range is presented.

inflation targeting The declaration by a *central bank* of a goal for a specific range of *inflation* in a future year, coupled with *monetary policy* designed to achieve the goal.

target rate of inflation The publicly announced annual *inflation* rate that a *central bank* attempts to achieve through *monetary policy* actions if it is following an *inflation targeting* monetary policy.

Balanced Budget Monetarists and new classical economists also question the effectiveness of *fiscal* policy. At the extreme, a few of them favor a constitutional amendment requiring the federal government to balance its budget annually. Others suggest that government adopt a "passive" fiscal policy, not intentionally creating budget deficits or surpluses. They believe that deficits and surpluses caused by recession or inflationary expansion will eventually correct themselves as the economy self-corrects to its full-employment output level.

Monetarists are particularly strong in their opposition to expansionary fiscal policy. They believe that the deficit spending accompanying such a policy has a strong tendency to "crowd out" private investment. Suppose government runs a budget deficit by printing and selling U.S. securities— that is, by borrowing from the public. By engaging in such borrowing, the government is competing with private businesses for funds. The borrowing increases the demand for money, which then raises the interest rate and crowds out a substantial amount of private investment that would otherwise have been profitable. The net effect of a budget deficit on aggregate demand therefore is unpredictable and, at best, modest.

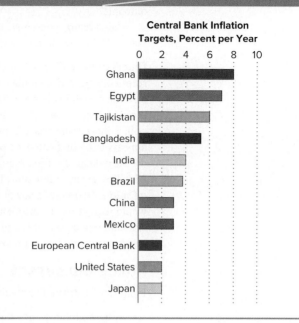

CENTRAL BANK INFLATION TARGETS, SELECTED CENTRAL BANKS, 2021

Not all central banks use inflation targets. But among those that do, the target rates vary substantially. Areas that have enjoyed low inflation rates over the past few decades usually have target rates of 2 percent—as is the case for Japan and the United States. By contrast, countries that have experienced high rates of inflation in recent decades typically have higher inflation targets. Those higher targets are often part of a long-term strategy to use a series of incremental reductions of the target rate, spread out over many years, to gradually squeeze inflation down to a low level like 2 percent.

Source: Various central bank websites.

Central Bank Inflation Targets, Percent per Year

Ghana
Egypt
Tajikistan
Bangladesh
India
Brazil
China
Mexico
European Central Bank
United States
Japan

RET economists reject discretionary fiscal policy for the same reason they reject active monetary policy: They don't think it can work. Business and labor will immediately adjust their behavior in anticipation of the price-level effects of a change in fiscal policy. The economy will move directly to the anticipated new price level. Like monetary policy, say the RET theorists, fiscal policy can move the economy along its vertical long-run aggregate supply curve. But because its effects on inflation are fully anticipated, fiscal policy cannot alter real GDP even in the short run. The best course of action for government is to balance its budget.

In Defense of Discretionary Stabilization Policy

Mainstream economists oppose both a strict, Friedman-style monetary rule and a balanced-budget requirement. They believe that monetary policy and fiscal policy are important tools for achieving and maintaining full employment, price stability, and economic growth.

Discretionary Monetary Policy In supporting discretionary monetary policy, mainstream economists argue that the rationale for the Friedman monetary rule is flawed. While there is indeed a close relationship between the money supply and nominal GDP over long periods, over shorter periods the relationship breaks down. The reason is that the velocity of money has proved to be more variable and unpredictable than monetarists contend. Arguing that velocity is variable both cyclically and over time, mainstream economists contend that a constant annual rate of increase in the money supply might not eliminate fluctuations in aggregate demand. In terms of the equation of exchange, a steady rise of M does not guarantee a steady expansion of aggregate demand because V–the rate at which money is spent–can change.

Look again at Figure 18.3, in which we demonstrated the Friedman-style monetary rule that the Fed should expand the money supply annually by a fixed percentage, regardless of the state of the economy. During the period in question, optimistic business expectations might create a boom in investment spending and thus shift the aggregate demand curve to some location to the right of AD_2. (You may want to pencil in a new AD curve, labeling it AD_3.) The price level will then rise above P_1; that is, demand-pull inflation will occur. In this case, the monetary rule will not accomplish its goal of maintaining price stability. Mainstream economists say that the Fed can use a restrictive monetary policy to reduce the excessive investment spending and thereby hold the rightward shift of aggregate demand to AD_2, thus avoiding inflation.

Now suppose instead that investment declines because of pessimistic business expectations. Aggregate demand will then increase by some amount less than the increase from AD_1 to AD_2 in Figure 18.3. Again, the monetary rule fails the stability test: The price level sinks below P_1 (deflation occurs). Or if the price level is inflexible downward at P_1, the economy will not achieve its full-employment output (unemployment rises). An expansionary monetary policy can help avoid each outcome.

Mainstream economists quip that the trouble with the monetary rule is that it tells the policy-maker, "Don't do something; just stand there."

Discretionary Fiscal Policy Mainstream economists support the use of fiscal policy to keep recessions from deepening or to keep mild inflation from becoming severe inflation. They recognize the possibility of crowding out but do not think it is a serious problem when business borrowing is depressed, which is usually the case in a recession. Because politicians can abuse fiscal policy, most economists feel that it should be held in reserve for situations where monetary policy appears to be ineffective or working too slowly.

As indicated earlier, mainstream economists oppose requirements to balance the budget annually. Tax revenues fall sharply during recessions and rise briskly during periods of demand-pull inflation. Therefore, a law or a constitutional amendment mandating an annually balanced budget would require the government to increase tax rates and reduce government spending during recession and reduce tax rates and increase government spending during economic booms. The first set of actions would worsen recession, and the second set would fuel inflation.

Policy Successes

Finally, mainstream economists point out several specific policy successes in the past four decades:

- A tight money policy dropped inflation from 13.5 percent in 1980 to 3.2 percent in 1983.
- An expansionary fiscal policy reduced the unemployment rate from 9.7 percent in 1982 to 5.5 percent in 1988.
- An easy money policy helped the economy recover from the 1990–1991 recession.
- Judicious tightening of monetary policy in the mid-1990s, and then again in the late 1990s, helped the economy remain on a noninflationary, full-employment growth path.
- In late 2001 and 2002, expansionary fiscal and monetary policy helped the economy recover from a series of economic blows, including the collapse of numerous Internet startup firms; a severe decline in investment spending; the impacts of the terrorist attacks of September 11, 2001; and a precipitous decline in stock values.
- In 2007 the Fed vigorously responded to a crisis in the mortgage market by ensuring monetary liquidity in the banking system. Besides aggressively lowering the federal funds rate from 5.25 percent in the summer of 2007 to just 2 percent in April 2008, the Fed greatly increased the reserves of the banking system. It also undertook other lender-of-last-resort actions to unfreeze credit and prevent a possible collapse of the entire financial system. During the Great Recession of 2007–2009, the Fed lowered the federal funds rate further, holding it in the 0 to 0.25 percent range to break the economy's downward slide and to promote economic recovery.
- To help prevent the world economy from sliding into a financial crisis when the COVID-19 pandemic began to bite, the Fed injected nearly $4 trillion of liquidity (cash) into the world financial system between February and June 2020 through either asset purchases (mostly government bonds) or by making dollar loans to major financial institutions and other central banks. The Fed also lowered the Federal funds rate very aggressively, from 1.59 percent to just 0.05 percent, between March 3 and April 3 of 2020. Those decisive actions resulted in the shortest U.S. recession on record (just two months) and a quick return to a positive outlook among business-people and investors, with, for example, the stock market regaining its pre-pandemic highs by mid-August of 2020, just six months after the crisis began to affect financial markets.

QUICK REVIEW

18.3

▸ Mainstream economists disagree with monetarists and rational expectations economists as to whether the Fed should use monetary rules or discretion.

▸ Monetarist and rational expectations economists oppose discretion because they believe that discretion adds more instability to the business cycle than it cures.

▸ Mainstream economists oppose strict monetary rules and defend both monetary and fiscal policy discretion because they believe that both theory and evidence suggest that discretionary policies are helpful in achieving full employment, price stability, and economic growth.

Market Monetarism

Market Monetarists Call for a New Monetary Rule That Would Institutionalize Fed Policy Responses to Changes in Real Output and Inflation.

In the aftermath of the Great Recession of 2007–2008, a new breed of "market monetarists" suggested that the Fed and other central banks should use prediction markets to adjust monetary policy.

In prediction markets, people can place bets on how likely it is that a particular political or financial outcome will end up happening. There are, for example, many commodities futures markets where people can bet on things like the price of corn next January or the price of oil in five years.

Extensive studies have shown that prediction markets make by far the most accurate predictions about the future—much better than those made by individual experts or even groups of experts attempting to pool their many decades of expertise. The superior prognosticating performance of prediction markets appears to be due to the fact that they incorporate the knowledge and insights of everyone who participates. As a result, even information that is only known to a few nonexperts can improve the prediction.

Prediction markets are not perfect. They do make mistakes—for instance predicting the wrong candidate to win the presidential election or predicting that the price of oil will be $46 per barrel in July whereas the actual price ends up being $53 per barrel. But because prediction markets are the best available tool for predicting future outcomes, market monetarists want to piggyback on their predictive accuracy to help the Fed set monetary policy. In particular, they argue that the Fed should set up a prediction market for nominal GDP and then use the predictions generated by that market to adjust monetary policy.

As you know, nominal GDP can grow for two reasons: inflation or increases in real GDP. Market monetarists point out that if you look back over many decades of data, nominal GDP growth in the United States has averaged about 5 percent per year. Of that amount, about 3 percent per year has on average been due to real GDP growth while the remaining 2 percent has been caused by inflation.

The Fed's goal would be for the prediction market to always be predicting 5 percent growth in nominal GDP. If the prediction ever deviated from that 5 percent target, the Fed would loosen or tighten monetary policy in whatever direction would be needed for the prediction to adjust back to 5 percent.

To see how this monetary rule would work, suppose that the prediction market for nominal GDP is forecasting only 4 percent nominal GDP growth next year (rather than the desired rate of 5 percent). Because prediction markets make the most accurate forecasts, this 4 percent prediction will be our best available information on what is likely to happen with the economy next year. And since what is likely to happen is less than the target rate of 5 percent, stimulus will

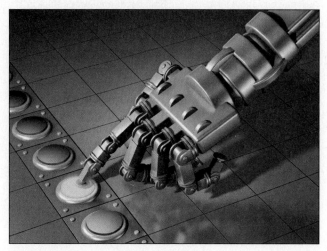

Matthias Kulka/The Image Bank/Getty Images

be called for. Market monetarists would want the Fed to loosen monetary policy and stimulate the economy until the participants in the nominal GDP prediction market are "voting with their pocketbooks" that nominal GDP will grow by 5 percent next year. When the predicted growth rate reaches 5 percent, the Fed can stop stimulating.

On the flip side, if the prediction market were forecasting 7 percent nominal GDP growth next year rather than the desired 5 percent, market monetarists would want the Fed to tighten monetary policy until the market's prediction fell back down to the 5 percent target rate. That way, contractionary monetary policy would only be applied if and when the prediction market is indicating that the economy is overheating (relative to the 5 percent target growth rate for nominal GDP). Once the prediction market is indicating that the economy is on target again, contractionary actions can end and the Fed can switch to a neutral policy stance (i.e., neither expansionary nor contractionary).

Market monetarism has prompted a vigorous debate. Some opponents argue that "targeting the forecast" would overly constrain the Fed's discretion when reacting to severe crises while others point out that a 5 percent target for nominal GDP growth would prevent real GDP growth from ever exceeding 5 percent per year. So while market monetarism has garnered several prominent proponents, including Nobel Laureate Paul Krugman and former Council of Economic Advisors Chair Christina Romer, the debate over an optimal monetary policy rule will continue.

TABLE 18.1 Summary of Alternative Macroeconomic Views

Issue	Mainstream Macroeconomics	New Classical Economics	
		Monetarism	Rational Expectations
View of the private economy	Potentially unstable	Stable in long run at natural rate of unemployment	Stable in long run at natural rate of unemployment
Cause of the observed instability of the private economy	Investment plans unequal to saving plans (changes in AD); AS shocks	Inappropriate monetary policy	Unanticipated AD and AS shocks in the short run
Assumptions about short-run price and wage stickiness	Both prices and wages stuck in the immediate short run; in the short run, wages sticky while prices inflexible downward but flexible upward	Prices flexible upward and downward in the short run; wages sticky in the short run	Prices and wages flexible both upward and downward in the short run
Appropriate macro policies	Active fiscal and monetary policy	Monetary rule	Monetary rule
How changes in the money supply affect the economy	By changing the interest rate, which changes investment and real GDP	By directly changing AD, which changes GDP	No effect on output because price-level changes are anticipated
View of the velocity of money	Unstable	Stable	No consensus
How fiscal policy affects the economy	Changes AD and GDP via the multiplier process	No effect unless money supply changes	No effect because price-level changes are anticipated
View of cost-push inflation	Possible (AS shock)	Impossible in the long run in the absence of excessive money supply growth	Impossible in the long run in the absence of excessive money supply growth

Summary of Alternative Views

Table 18.1 summarizes the fundamental ideas and policy implications of the three schools of macroeconomic theory that we have discussed: mainstream macroeconomics, monetarism, and rational expectations.

These different perspectives have obliged mainstream economists to rethink some of their fundamental principles and to revise many of their positions. Although considerable disagreement remains, mainstream macroeconomists agree with monetarists that "money matters" and that excessive growth of the money supply is the major cause of long-lasting, rapid inflation. They also agree with RET proponents and advocates for coordination failures that expectations matter. If government can create expectations of price stability, full employment, and economic growth, households and firms will tend to act in ways to make them happen.

In closing this chapter, let us note that it is thanks to ongoing challenges to conventional wisdom that macroeconomics continues to evolve. Do not presume that any of these schools of thought will have the last laugh. Much remains to be discovered.

Summary

LO18.1 Describe alternative perspectives on the causes of macroeconomic instability.

The mainstream view holds that macro instability is caused by a combination of price stickiness and shocks to aggregate demand or aggregate supply. With prices inflexible in the short run, changes in aggregate demand or short-run aggregate supply result in changes in output and employment. In the long run when input prices and output prices are fully flexible, the economy will produce at potential output.

Monetarism focuses on the equation of exchange: $MV = PQ$. Because velocity V is thought to be stable, changes in M (the money supply) create changes in nominal GDP ($= PQ$). Monetarists believe that the most significant cause of macroeconomic instability has

been inappropriate monetary policy. Rapid increases in M cause inflation; insufficient growth of M causes recession.

Real-business-cycle theory identifies changes in resource availability and technology (real factors), which alter productivity, as the main causes of macroeconomic instability. In this theory, shifts of the economy's long-run aggregate supply curve change real output.

A coordination failure occurs when people lack a way to coordinate their actions in order to achieve a mutually beneficial equilibrium. Depending on people's expectations, the economy can come to rest at either a good equilibrium (noninflationary full-employment output) or a bad equilibrium (less-than-full-employment output or demand-pull inflation).

Rational expectations theory rests on two assumptions: (1) With sufficient information, people's beliefs about future economic outcomes accurately reflect the likelihood that those outcomes will occur; and (2) markets are highly competitive, and prices and wages are flexible both upward and downward.

LO18.2 Explain why new classical economists believe the economy will self-correct from aggregate demand and aggregate supply shocks.

New classical economists (monetarists and rational expectations theorists) see the economy as automatically correcting itself when disturbed from its full-employment level of real output. In RET, unanticipated changes in aggregate demand change the price level, which in the short run leads firms to change output. But once the firms realize that all prices are changing (including nominal wages) as part of general inflation or deflation, they restore their output to the previous level. By contrast, anticipated changes in aggregate demand produce only changes in the price level, not changes in real output.

Mainstream economists reject the new classical view that all prices and wages are flexible downward. They contend that nominal wages, in particular, are inflexible downward because of several factors, including minimum-wage laws, labor contracts, and efficiency wages. Thus declines in aggregate demand lower real output, not only wages and prices.

LO18.3 Describe the rules versus discretion debate regarding stabilization policy.

Monetarist and rational expectations economists say the Fed should adhere to some form of policy rule, rather than rely exclusively on discretion. The Friedman rule would direct the Fed to increase the money supply at a fixed annual rate equal to the long-run growth of potential GDP. In 2012, the Fed took another path, however, and adopted an inflation target of 2 percent per year, thereby committing itself to adjusting monetary policy to reach that goal except in extreme cases where a different inflation rate might be necessary to smooth the business cycle.

Monetarists and rational expectations theorists also support maintaining a "neutral" fiscal policy, as opposed to using discretionary fiscal policy to create budget deficits or budget surpluses. A few monetarists and rational expectations economists favor a constitutional amendment requiring the federal government to balance its budget annually.

Mainstream economists oppose strict, Friedman-style monetary rules and a balanced-budget requirement, and they defend discretionary monetary and fiscal policies. They say that both theory and evidence suggest that such policies are helpful in achieving full employment, price stability, and economic growth.

Terms and Concepts

monetarism	coordination failure	efficiency wage
equation of exchange	rational expectations theory	monetary rule
velocity	new classical economics	inflation targeting
real-business-cycle theory	price-level surprises	target rate of inflation

Discussion Questions

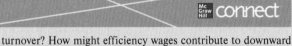

1. According to mainstream economists, what is the usual cause of macroeconomic instability? What role does the spending-income multiplier play in creating instability? How might adverse aggregate supply factors cause instability, according to mainstream economists? **LO18.1**

2. Briefly describe the difference between a so-called real business cycle and a more traditional "spending" business cycle. **LO18.1**

3. Craig and Kris were walking directly toward each other in a congested store aisle. Craig moved to his left to avoid Kris, and at the same time Kris moved to his right to avoid Craig. They bumped into each other. What concept does this example illustrate? How does this idea relate to macroeconomic instability? **LO18.1**

4. State and explain the basic equation of monetarism. What is the major cause of macroeconomic instability, as viewed by monetarists? **LO18.1**

5. Use the equation of exchange to explain the rationale for a monetary rule. Why will such a rule run into trouble if V unexpectedly falls because of, say, a drop in investment spending by businesses? **LO18.1**

6. What is an efficiency wage? How might payment of an above-market wage reduce shirking by employees and reduce worker turnover? How might efficiency wages contribute to downward wage inflexibility, at least for a time, when aggregate demand declines? **LO18.2**

7. Explain the difference between "active" discretionary fiscal policy advocated by mainstream economists and "passive" fiscal policy advocated by new classical economists. Explain: "The problem with a balanced-budget amendment is that it would, in a sense, require active fiscal policy—but in the wrong direction—as the economy slides into recession." **LO18.3**

8. You have just been elected president of the United States, and the present chair of the Federal Reserve Board has resigned. You need to appoint a new person to this position, as well as a person to chair your Council of Economic Advisers. Using Table 18.1 and your knowledge of macroeconomics, identify the views on macro theory and policy you would want your appointees to hold. Remember, the economic health of the entire nation—and your chances for reelection—may depend on your selection. **LO18.3**

9. **LAST WORD** Compare and contrast the market monetarist 5-percent target for nominal GDP growth with the older, simpler monetary rule advocated by Milton Friedman.

Review Questions

1. If prices are sticky and the number of dollars of gross investment unexpectedly increases, the _____ curve will shift _____. **LO18.1**
   a. AD; right
   b. AD; left
   c. AS; right
   d. AS; left

2. First, imagine that both input prices and output prices are fixed in the economy. What does the aggregate supply curve look like? If AD decreases in this situation, what will happen to equilibrium output and the price level? Next, imagine that input prices are fixed, but output prices are flexible. What does the aggregate supply curve look like? In this case, if AD decreases, what will happen to equilibrium output and the price level? Finally, if both input prices and output prices are fully flexible, what does the aggregate supply curve look like? In this case, if AD decreases, what will happen to equilibrium output and the price level? (To check your answers, review Figures 12.3, 12.4, and 12.5 in Chapter 12.) **LO18.1**

3. Suppose that the money supply is $1 trillion and money velocity is 4. Then the equation of exchange would predict nominal GDP to be: **LO18.1**
   a. $1 trillion.   c. $5 trillion.
   b. $4 trillion.   d. $8 trillion.

4. If the money supply fell by 10 percent, a monetarist would expect nominal GDP to _____. **LO18.1**
   a. rise
   b. fall
   c. stay the same

5. An economy is producing at full employment when AD unexpectedly shifts to the left. A new classical economist would assume that as the economy adjusts back to producing at full employment, the price level will _____. **LO18.2**
   a. increase
   b. decrease
   c. stay the same

6. Use an AD-AS graph to demonstrate and explain the price-level and real-output outcome of an anticipated decline in aggregate demand, as viewed by RET economists. (Assume that the economy initially is operating at its full-employment level of output.) Then demonstrate and explain on the same graph the outcome as viewed by mainstream economists. **LO18.2**

7. Place "MON," "RET," or "MAIN" beside the statements that most closely reflect monetarist, rational expectations, or mainstream views, respectively: **LO18.3**
   a. Anticipated changes in aggregate demand affect only the price level; they have no effect on real output.
   b. Downward wage inflexibility means that declines in aggregate demand can cause long-lasting recession.
   c. Changes in the money supply M increase PQ; at first only Q rises, because nominal wages are fixed, but once workers adapt their expectations to new realities, P rises and Q returns to its former level.
   d. Fiscal and monetary policies smooth out the business cycle.
   e. The Fed should increase the money supply at a fixed annual rate.

Problems

1. Suppose that the money supply and the nominal GDP for a hypothetical economy are $96 billion and $336 billion, respectively. What is the velocity of money? How will households and businesses react if the central bank reduces the money supply by $20 billion? By how much will nominal GDP have to fall to restore equilibrium, according to the monetarist perspective? **LO18.1**

2. Assume the following information for a hypothetical economy in year 1: money supply = $400 billion; the long-term average annual growth rate of potential GDP = 3 percent; velocity = 4. Assume that the banking system initially has no excess reserves

and that the reserve requirement is 10 percent. Also suppose that velocity is constant and that the economy initially is operating at its full-employment real output. **LO18.3**
   a. What is the level of nominal GDP in year 1?
   b. Suppose the Fed adheres to a monetary rule that says that the money supply should grow at the same rate as potential GDP. How big will the money supply have to be in year 2 to meet its monetary rule? And by how much will the money supply have to increase between year 1 and year 2 to meet its monetary rule?

PART 7

International Trade

Andrew F. Kazmierski/Shutterstock

>> **LEARNING OBJECTIVES**

LO19.1 List several key facts about international trade.

LO19.2 Define comparative advantage and explain how specialization and trade add to a nation's output.

LO19.3 Explain why differences between world prices and domestic prices lead to exports and imports.

LO19.4 Analyze the economic effects of tariffs and quotas.

LO19.5 Critique the most frequently presented arguments for protectionism.

LO19.6 Explain the objectives of the WTO, EU, NAFTA, and USMCA, and discuss offshoring and trade adjustment assistance.

Backpackers in the wilderness like to think they are "leaving the world behind," but, like Atlas, they carry the world on their shoulders. Much of their equipment is imported—knives from Switzerland, rain gear from South Korea, cameras from Japan, aluminum pots from England, sleeping bags from China, and compasses from Finland.

International trade and the global economy affect all of us daily, whether we are hiking in the wilderness, driving our cars, buying groceries, or working at our jobs. We cannot "leave the world behind." We are enmeshed in a global web of economic relationships.

This chapter focuses on the trading of goods and services. In later chapters, we examine the U.S. balance of payments, exchange rates, U.S. trade deficits, and the economics of developing nations.

Some Key Trade Facts

The following are important facts relating to international trade.

>> **LO19.1** List several key facts about international trade.

- U.S. exports and imports have more than doubled as percentages of GDP since 1980.

- A *trade deficit* occurs when imports exceed exports. The United States has a trade deficit in goods. In 2021, U.S. imports of goods exceeded U.S. exports of goods by $1,091 billion.

- A *trade surplus* occurs when exports exceed imports. The United States has a trade surplus in services (such as air transportation services and financial services). In 2021, U.S. exports of services exceeded U.S. imports of services by $230 billion.

- Principal U.S. exports include chemicals, agricultural products, consumer durables, aircraft, and computer software and services (think Microsoft and Google).

- The United States is also a large exporter of educational services since all the money spent on tuition at U.S. schools by foreign students counts as a U.S. service export. During the 2019/2020 academic year the U.S. hosted over one million foreign students and reported $41 billion in education exports.

GLOBAL PERSPECTIVE 19.1

EXPORTS AS A SHARE OF GDP, SELECTED NATIONS, 2021

Some countries engage in much more international trade than other countries. The dollar value of exports exceeds 80 percent of the dollar value of GDP in Belgium and the Netherlands, which are both small European countries that do a lot of trade with large neighboring countries like France and Germany that have tens of millions of eager consumers ready to purchase Belgian and Dutch products. By contrast, exports are only 16 percent of GDP in Japan and just 10 percent in the United States, reflecting the fact that both of those countries have huge populations that are capable of consuming the large majority of output produced by domestic firms.

Source: Organisation for Economic Co-operation and Development (OECD).

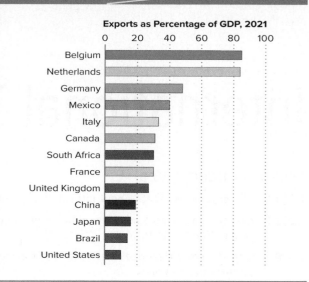

Exports as Percentage of GDP, 2021

- Principal U.S. imports include petroleum, automobiles, metals, household appliances, and computers.
- Like other advanced industrial nations, the United States imports many goods that are in the same categories as the goods that it exports. Examples include automobiles, computers, chemicals, semiconductors, and petroleum.
- Canada is the United States' most important trading partner as measured by the dollar value of trade. In 2021, about 12 percent of U.S. exported goods and services were sold to Canadians, who in turn provided 11 percent of imported U.S. goods and services.
- The United States has a sizable trade deficit in goods with China. In 2021 it was $355 billion.
- Starting in 2012, the hydraulic fracking boom greatly reduced U.S. dependence on foreign oil. In 2018, the U.S. become a net exporter of oil for the first time in 75 years as well as the world's largest producer of oil, ahead of Russia and Saudi Arabia.
- The United States leads the world in the combined volume of exports and imports, as measured in dollars.
- China, the United States, Germany, Japan, and the United Kingdom (in that order) were the top five exporters by dollars in 2020.
- Currently, the United States provides about 9.5 percent of the world's exports.
- Exports of goods and services make up about 10 percent of total U.S. output. That percentage is much lower than the percentage in many other nations, including Belgium, the Netherlands, Germany, Mexico, Canada, South Africa, and Brazil. (See Global Perspective 19.1.)
- China has become a major international trader, with an estimated $2.7 trillion of exports in 2020. Other Asian economies—including South Korea, Taiwan, and Singapore—are also active in international trade. Their combined exports exceed those of France, Britain, or Italy.
- International trade links the world's economies together. Through trade, changes in economic conditions in one place on the globe can quickly affect other places.
- International trade is often at the center of debates over economic policy, both within the United States and internationally.

With this information in mind, let's turn to the economics of international trade.

The Economic Basis for Trade

The simple answer to the question "Why do nations **trade**?" is "They trade because it is beneficial." The benefits that emerge relate to three underlying facts:

- The distribution of natural, human, and capital resources among nations is uneven; nations differ in their endowments of economic resources.

- Efficient production of various goods requires different technologies, and not all nations have the same level of technological expertise.

- Products are differentiated as to quality and other attributes, and some people may prefer certain goods imported from abroad rather than similar goods produced domestically.

To understand the interaction of these three facts, think of China, which has an abundance of inexpensive labor. As a result, China can produce efficiently (at low cost of other goods forgone) a variety of **labor-intensive goods,** such as textiles, electronics, apparel, toys, and sporting goods.

In contrast, Australia has vast amounts of land with which it can inexpensively produce such **land-intensive goods** as beef, wool, and meat. Mexico, meanwhile, has the soil, tropical climate, rainfall, and ready supply of unskilled labor that allow for the low-cost production of vegetables. And industrially advanced economies such as the United States and Germany that have relatively large amounts of capital can inexpensively produce **capital-intensive goods** such as airplanes, automobiles, agricultural equipment, machinery, and chemicals.

Also, regardless of their resource intensities, nations can develop individual products that are in demand worldwide because of their special qualities. Examples: fashions from Italy, chocolates from Belgium, software from the United States, and watches from Switzerland.

The distribution of resources, technology, and product distinctiveness among nations is relatively stable over short time periods but can change dramatically over longer time periods. When that distribution changes, the relative efficiency and success that nations have in producing and selling goods also change. As national economies evolve, the size and quality of their labor forces may change, the volume and composition of their capital stocks may shift, new technologies may develop, and even the quality of land and the quantity of natural resources may change. In short, as economists say, comparative advantage can change.

Comparative Advantage

If a country's borders are open to international trade, that country is said to have an open economy. By contrast, when a country's borders are closed to international trade, a country is said to have a closed economy.

When a country has an open economy, it will produce more of certain goods (exports) and fewer of other goods (imports) than it would if its borders were closed to international trade. That happens because an open economy will shift the use of its labor and other productive resources toward export industries and away from import industries. For example, in the presence of international trade, the United States uses more resources to make commercial aircraft and to grow wheat, and fewer resources to make television sets and to sew clothes. So we ask: Do such shifts of resources make economic sense? Do they enhance the U.S. standard of living?

The answers are affirmative. International trade and specialization increase the productivity of U.S. resources and allow the United States to obtain greater total output than otherwise would be possible. These benefits are the result of exploiting both *absolute advantage* and *comparative advantage*.

Because these concepts are often confused, let's take a moment to explain that the key difference between *absolute advantage* and *comparative advantage* lies in how a person conceptualizes what the word "efficiency" means and thus what it means for a country to be "efficient" at producing a specific product. Pay close attention in what follows to the fact that one definition has to do with inputs, while the other has to do with outputs.

>> **LO19.2** Define comparative advantage and explain how specialization and trade add to a nation's output.

trade The voluntary exchange of goods, services, or assets between two or more parties.

labor-intensive goods Products requiring relatively large amounts of *labor* to produce.

land-intensive goods Products requiring relatively large amounts of land to produce.

capital-intensive goods Products that require relatively large amounts of *capital* to produce.

- One way to think about efficiency is the way that an engineer does, in terms of how much of the product the country can make from a given amount of resource *inputs*.

- The other is to think of efficiency the way an economist does, in terms of how much of other types of *output* must be foregone to produce one unit of the product in question.

Let's use steel as an example.

absolute advantage A situation in which a person or country can produce more of a particular product from a specific quantity of resource inputs than some other person or country.

comparative advantage A situation in which a person or country can produce a specific product at a lower *opportunity cost* in terms of other types of *output* foregone than some other person or country; the basis for specialization and trade.

- A country is said to have an **absolute advantage** over other countries in the production of steel if it can produce more steel than any other country from an identical set of resource inputs.

- By contrast, a country is said to have a **comparative advantage** over other countries in the production of steel if it can produce steel at a lower *opportunity cost* in terms of alternative types of output (for instance, hamburgers or yoga lessons) that must be foregone in order to free up the resources necessary to produce one unit of steel.

In 1776, Adam Smith used the concept of absolute advantage to argue for international specialization and trade. He noted that nations will be better off if each specializes in the production of those products in which it has an absolute advantage and is therefore the most efficient producer in the engineering sense:

> It is the maxim of every prudent master of a family, never to attempt to make at home what it will cost him more to make than to buy. The taylor does not attempt to make his own shoes, but buys them of the shoemaker. The shoemaker does not attempt to make his own clothes, but employs a taylor. The farmer attempts to make neither the one nor the other, but employs those different artificers. . . .
>
> What is prudence in the conduct of every private family, can scarce be folly in that of a great kingdom. If a foreign country can supply us with a commodity cheaper than we can make it, better buy it of them with some part of the produce of our own industry, employed in a way in which we have some advantage.[1]

Adam Smith's invocation of absolute advantage as the basis of international trade struck everyone as decidedly reasonable because it lined up with engineering efficiency: each country would specialize in whatever it could produce at the lowest cost in terms of resource inputs.

But several decades later, David Ricardo realized that what matters isn't a product's cost measured in terms of the amount of inputs needed to make it but, rather, in terms of alternative products foregone to make it. If the whole purpose of production is to produce goods and services that people want to consume, then the correct way to think about the opportunity cost of producing 10 tons of steel is not "How much labor, coal, and iron ore are required to produce 10 tons of steel?" but, rather, "What other valuable consumption products have to be foregone in order to produce 10 tons of steel?" That is, the correct way to think about the opportunity cost of 10 tons of steel is not to measure the raw materials that went into producing it but, rather, all of the other products that could have been made from those same inputs.

As Ricardo pointed out, this "foregone-consumption perspective" implies that a nation does not need Smith's absolute advantage (i.e., total superiority in the engineering efficiency with which it produces products) to benefit from specialization and trade. It only needs a comparative advantage, meaning the ability to produce a product at a lower opportunity cost in terms of other consumption goods and services forgone.

Ricardo also demonstrated an even more startling fact about international trade. He showed that it is also advantageous for a country to specialize and trade with other countries even if it is *less* productive (in the engineering sense) in *all* economic activities relative to other nations. A nation with an absolute *dis*advantage in all products does not have to despair. It can also benefit from trade just as long as it has a comparative advantage in at least one product (which in practice is always the case).

The nearby Consider This story (A CPA and a House Painter) provides a simple, two-person illustration of Ricardo's principle of comparative advantage. Be sure to read it now because it will greatly help you understand the graphical analysis that follows.

---

[1] Adam Smith, *The Wealth of Nations* (originally published, 1776; New York: Modern Library, 1937), p. 424.

CONSIDER THIS . . .

A CPA and a House Painter

Suppose that Madison, a certified public accountant (CPA), is a swifter painter than Mason, the professional painter she is thinking of hiring. Also assume that Madison can earn $50 per hour as an accountant but would have to pay Mason $15 per hour. And suppose that Madison would need 30 hours to paint her house but Mason would need 40 hours.

Should Madison take time away from her accounting to paint her own house, or should she hire the painter? Madison's opportunity cost of painting her house is $1,500 (= 30 hours of sacrificed CPA time × $50 per CPA hour). The cost of hiring Mason is only $600 (= 40 hours of painting × $15 per hour of painting). Although Madison is better at both accounting and painting, she will get her house painted at lower cost by specializing in accounting

Kim Steele/Digital Vision/Getty Images

and using some of her earnings from accounting to hire a house painter.

Similarly, Mason can reduce his cost of obtaining accounting services by specializing in painting and using some of his income to hire Madison to prepare his income tax forms. Suppose Mason would need 10 hours to prepare his tax return, while Madison could handle the task in 2 hours. Mason would sacrifice $150 of income (= 10 hours of painting time × $15 per hour) to do something he could hire Madison to do for $100 (= 2 hours of CPA time × $50 per CPA hour). By specializing in painting and hiring Madison to prepare his tax return, Mason lowers the cost of getting his tax return prepared.

We will see that what is true for our CPA and house painter is also true for nations. Specializing on the basis of comparative advantage enables nations to reduce the cost of obtaining the goods and services they desire.

▶ International trade enables nations to specialize, increase productivity, and increase the amount of output available for consumption.

▶ A country is said to have an *absolute advantage* over the other producers of a product if it can produce the product more efficiently, by which we mean that it can produce more of the product from any given amount of resource inputs than can any other producer.

▶ A country is said to have a *comparative advantage* over the other producers of a product if it can produce the product at a lower opportunity cost, by which we mean that it must forgo less of the output of alternative products when allocating resources to producing the product in question.

QUICK REVIEW
19.1

Two Isolated Nations

Our goal is to place the idea of comparative advantage into the context of trading nations. Our method is to build a simple model that relies on the familiar concept of the production possibilities curve. Suppose the world consists of just two nations, the United States and Mexico. For simplicity, suppose that the labor forces in the United States and Mexico are of equal size. Each nation can produce both beef and raw (unprocessed) vegetables but at different levels of economic efficiency. Suppose the U.S. and Mexican domestic production possibilities curves for beef and vegetables are those shown in Figure 19.1a and Figure 19.1b. Note three realities relating to the production possibilities curves in the two graphs:

- *Constant costs* The curves derive from the data in Table 19.1 and are drawn as straight lines, in contrast to the bowed-outward production possibilities frontiers we examined in Chapter 1. We have therefore replaced the law of increasing opportunity costs with the assumption of constant costs. This substitution simplifies our discussion but does not impair the validity of our analysis and conclusions.

- *Different costs* The production possibilities curves of the United States and Mexico reflect different resource mixes and differing levels of technology. Specifically, the differing slopes of the two curves reflect the numbers in the figures and reveal that the opportunity costs of producing beef and vegetables differ between the two nations.

FIGURE 19.1
Production possibilities for the United States and Mexico.

The two production possibilities curves show the combinations of vegetables and beef that the United States and Mexico can produce domestically. The curves for both countries are straight lines because we are assuming constant opportunity costs. (a) As reflected by the slope of *VB* in the left graph, the opportunity-cost ratio in the United States is 1 vegetable ≡ 1 beef. (b) The production possibilities curve *vb* in the right graph has a steeper slope, reflecting the different opportunity-cost ratio in Mexico of 2 vegetables ≡ 1 beef. The difference in the opportunity-cost ratios between the two countries defines their comparative advantages and is the basis for specialization and international trade.

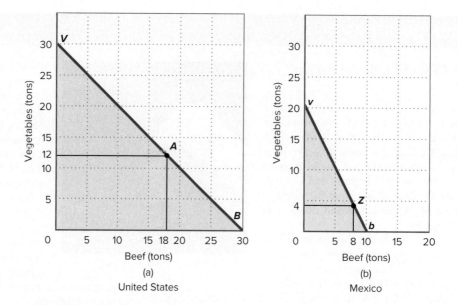

(a) United States

(b) Mexico

- *U.S. absolute advantage in both products* A producer (an individual, firm, or country) has an absolute advantage over another producer if it can produce more of a product than the other producer using the same amount of resources. Because of our convenient assumption that the U.S. and Mexican labor forces are the same size, the two production possibilities curves show that the United States has an absolute advantage in producing both products. If the United States and Mexico use their entire (equal-size) labor forces to produce either vegetables or beef, the United States can produce more of either than Mexico can. The United States, using the same number of workers as Mexico, has greater production possibilities. Output per worker—labor productivity—in the United States exceeds that in Mexico in producing both products.

Opportunity-Cost Ratio in the United States In Figure 19.1a, with full employment, the United States will operate at some point on its production possibilities curve. On that curve, it can increase its output of beef from 0 tons to 30 tons by forgoing 30 tons of vegetables. The *absolute value* of the slope of the production possibilities curve is 1 (= 30 vegetables/30 beef), meaning that the United States must sacrifice 1 ton of vegetables for each extra ton of beef. In the United States, the **opportunity-cost ratio** (domestic exchange ratio) for the two products is 1 ton of vegetables (*V*) for 1 ton of beef (*B*), or

opportunity-cost ratio An equivalency showing the number of units of two products that can be produced with the same *resources;* the equivalency 1 corn ≡ 3 olives shows that the resources required to produce 3 units of olives must be shifted to corn production to produce 1 unit of corn.

United States: 1*V* ≡ 1*B* (The "≡" sign simply means "equivalent to")

Within its borders, the United States can "exchange" a ton of vegetables for a ton of beef. Our constant-cost assumption means that this exchange or opportunity-cost relationship prevails for all possible moves from one point to another along the U.S. production possibilities curve.

Opportunity-Cost Ratio in Mexico Mexico's production possibilities curve in Figure 19.1b represents a different full-employment opportunity-cost ratio. Mexico must give up 20 tons of

TABLE 19.1 International Specialization According to Comparative Advantage and the Gains from Trade

Country	(1) Outputs before Specialization	(2) Outputs after Specialization	(3) Amounts Exported (−) and Imported (+)	(4) Outputs Available after Trade	(5) Gains from Specialization and Trade (4) − (1)
United States	18 beef	30 beef	−10 beef	20 beef	2 beef
	12 vegetables	0 vegetables	+15 vegetables	15 vegetables	3 vegetables
Mexico	8 beef	0 beef	+10 beef	10 beef	2 beef
	4 vegetables	20 vegetables	−15 vegetables	5 vegetables	1 vegetables

vegetables to obtain 10 tons of beef. The absolute value of the slope of the production possibilities curve is 2 (= 20 vegetables/10 beef). So, in Mexico, the opportunity-cost ratio for the two goods is 2 tons of vegetables for 1 ton of beef, or

$$\text{Mexico: } 2V \equiv 1B$$

Self-Sufficiency Output Mix If the United States and Mexico are isolated and self-sufficient, then each country must choose an output mix on its own production possibilities curve. Each will select the mix that provides it with the greatest total utility or satisfaction. Let's assume that point *A* in Figure 19.1a is the optimal mix in the United States. That is, society deems the combination of 18 tons of beef and 12 tons of vegetables preferable to any other combination of the goods available along the production possibilities curve. Mexico's optimal product mix is 8 tons of beef and 4 tons of vegetables, as indicated by point *Z* in Figure 19.1b. The two countries' choices are reflected in column 1 of Table 19.1.

Specializing Based on Comparative Advantage

A producer (an individual, firm, or nation) has a *comparative advantage* in producing a particular product if it can produce that product at a lower opportunity cost than other producers. Comparative advantage is the key determinant in whether or not nations can gain from specialization and trade. In fact, absolute advantage turns out to be irrelevant.

In our example, for instance, the United States has an absolute advantage over Mexico in producing both vegetables and beef. Still, the United States can gain from specialization and trade with Mexico because what actually matters is whether the opportunity costs of producing the two products (beef and vegetables) differ in the two countries. If they do, then each nation will enjoy a comparative advantage in one of the products. As a result, total output can increase if each country specializes in the production of the good in which it has the lower opportunity cost.

The **principle of comparative advantage** says that total output will be greatest when each good is produced by the nation that has the lowest domestic opportunity cost for producing that good. In our two-nation illustration, the United States has the lower domestic opportunity cost for beef. The United States must forgo only 1 ton of vegetables to produce 1 ton of beef, whereas Mexico must forgo 2 tons of vegetables for 1 ton of beef. The United States has a comparative (opportunity cost) advantage in beef and should specialize in beef production. The "world" (that is, the United States and Mexico) in our example would clearly not be economizing in the use of its resources if a high-cost producer (Mexico) produced a specific product (beef) when a low-cost producer (the United States) could have produced it. Having Mexico produce beef means that the world economy would have to give up more vegetables than is necessary to obtain a ton of beef.

Mexico has the lower domestic opportunity cost for vegetables. It must sacrifice only $\frac{1}{2}$ ton of beef to produce 1 ton of vegetables, while the United States must forgo 1 ton of beef to produce 1 ton of vegetables. Mexico has a comparative advantage in vegetables and should specialize in vegetable production. Again, the world would not be employing its resources economically if vegetables were produced by a high-cost producer (the United States) rather than by a low-cost producer (Mexico). If the United States produced vegetables, the world would be giving up more beef than necessary to obtain each ton of vegetables. Table 19.2 summarizes the situation.

A comparison of columns 1 and 2 in Table 19.1 verifies that specialized production enables the world to obtain more output from its fixed amount of resources. By specializing completely in beef, the United States can produce 30 tons of beef and no vegetables. Mexico, by specializing

principle of comparative advantage The proposition that an individual, region, or nation will benefit if it specializes in producing goods for which its own *opportunity costs* are lower than the opportunity costs of a trading partner, and then exchanging some of the products in which it specializes for other desired products produced by others.

TABLE 19.2 Comparative-Advantage Example: A Summary

Beef	Vegetables
Mexico: Must give up 2 tons of vegetables to get 1 ton of beef.	*Mexico:* Must give up $\frac{1}{2}$ ton of beef to get 1 ton of vegetables.
United States: Must give up 1 ton of vegetables to get 1 ton of beef.	*United States:* Must give up 1 ton of beef to get 1 ton of vegetables.
Comparative advantage: United States	*Comparative advantage:* Mexico

completely in vegetables, can produce 20 tons of vegetables and no beef. These figures exceed the yields generated without specialization: 26 tons of beef (= 18 in the United States + 8 in Mexico) and 16 tons of vegetables (= 12 in the United States + 4 in Mexico) As a result, the world ends up with 4 more tons of beef (= 30 tons − 26 tons) and 4 more tons of vegetables (= 20 tons − 16 tons) than it would with self-sufficiency and unspecialized production.

Terms of Trade

terms of trade The rate at which units of one product can be exchanged for units of another product; the *price* of a *good* or *service;* the amount of one good or service that must be given up to obtain 1 unit of another good or service.

We have just seen that specialization in production will allow the largest possible amounts of both beef and vegetables to be produced. But with each country specializing in the production of only one item, how will the vegetables produced by Mexico and the beef produced by the United States be divided between consumers in the two countries? The key turns out to be the **terms of trade,** the exchange ratio at which the United States and Mexico trade beef and vegetables.

Crucially, the terms of trade also establish whether each country will find it worthwhile to bother specializing at all. Why? The terms of trade determine whether each country can "get a better deal" by specializing and trading than it could if it opted instead for self-sufficiency. For example, note that because $1B \equiv 1V (= 1V \equiv 1B)$ in the United States, it must get more than 1 ton of vegetables for each 1 ton of beef exported; otherwise, it will not benefit from exporting beef in exchange for Mexican vegetables. The United States must get a better "price" (more vegetables) for its beef through international trade than it can get domestically. Otherwise, no gain from trade exists and such trade will not occur.

Similarly, because $1B \equiv 2V (= 2V \equiv 1B)$ in Mexico, Mexico must obtain 1 ton of beef by exporting less than 2 tons of vegetables to get it. Mexico must be able to pay a lower "price" for beef in the world market than it must pay domestically. Otherwise, it will not want to trade. The international exchange ratio or terms of trade must therefore lie somewhere between

$$1B \equiv 1V (\text{United States' cost conditions})$$

and

$$1B \equiv 2V (\text{Mexico's cost conditions})$$

Where between these limits will the exchange ratio fall? The United States will prefer a rate close to $1B \equiv 2V$, say, $1B \equiv 1\frac{3}{4}V$. The United States wants to obtain as many vegetables as possible for each 1 ton of beef it exports. Mexico wants a rate near $1B \equiv 1V$, say, $1B \equiv 1\frac{1}{4}V$ because Mexico wants to export as few vegetables as possible for each 1 ton of beef it receives in exchange.

The actual exchange ratio (= terms of trade) depends on world supply and demand for the two products. If overall world demand for vegetables is weak relative to its supply and if the demand for beef is strong relative to its supply, the price of vegetables will be lower and the price of beef will be higher. The exchange ratio will settle nearer the $1B \equiv 2V$ terms that the United States prefers. If overall world demand for vegetables is great relative to their supply and if the demand for beef is weak relative to its supply, the ratio will settle nearer the $1B \equiv 1V$ level favorable to Mexico.

Gains from Trade

trading possibilities line A line that shows the different combinations of two products that an economy is able to obtain (consume) when it specializes in the production of one product and trades (exports) it to obtain the other product.

Suppose the international terms of trade are $1B \equiv 1\frac{1}{2}V$. The possibility of trading on these terms permits each nation to augment its domestic production possibilities curve with a trading possibilities line (or curve), as shown in **Figure 19.2 (Key Graph).** Just as a production possibilities curve shows the amounts of these products that a full-employment economy can obtain by shifting resources from one to the other, a **trading possibilities line** shows the amounts of the two products that a nation can obtain by specializing in one product and trading for the other. The trading possibilities lines in Figure 19.2 reflect the assumption that both nations specialize on the basis of comparative advantage: The United States specializes completely in beef (at point B in Figure 19.2a), and Mexico specializes completely in vegetables (at point v in Figure 19.2b).

Improved Alternatives With specialization and trade, the United States is no longer constrained by its domestic production possibilities line, which requires it to give up 1 ton of beef for every

..ıll KEY GRAPH

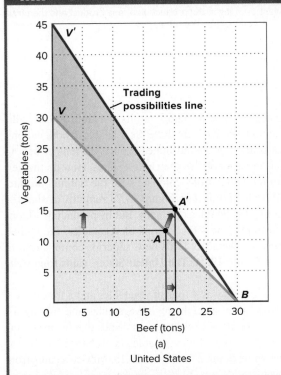

(a)
United States

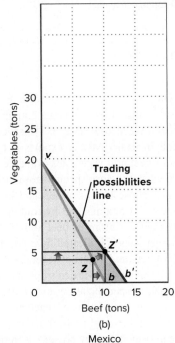

(b)
Mexico

FIGURE 19.2 Trading possibilities lines and the gains from trade.

As a result of specialization and trade, both the United States and Mexico can have higher levels of output than the levels attainable on their domestic production possibilities curves. (a) The United States can move from point *A* on its domestic production possibilities curve to, say, *A'* on its trading possibilities line. (b) Mexico can move from *Z* to *Z'*.

QUICK QUIZ FOR FIGURE 19.2

1. The production possibilities curves in graphs (a) and (b) imply:
a. increasing domestic opportunity costs.
b. decreasing domestic opportunity costs.
c. constant domestic opportunity costs.
d. first decreasing, then increasing domestic opportunity costs.

2. Before specialization, the domestic opportunity cost of producing 1 unit of beef is:
a. 1 unit of vegetables in both the United States and Mexico.
b. 1 unit of vegetables in the United States and 2 units of vegetables in Mexico.
c. 2 units of vegetables in the United States and 1 unit of vegetables in Mexico.
d. 1 unit of vegetables in the United States and $\frac{1}{2}$ unit of vegetables in Mexico.

3. After specialization and international trade, the world output of beef and vegetables is:
a. 20 tons of beef and 20 tons of vegetables.
b. 45 tons of beef and 15 tons of vegetables.
c. 30 tons of beef and 20 tons of vegetables.
d. 10 tons of beef and 30 tons of vegetables.

4. After specialization and international trade:
a. the United States can obtain units of vegetables at less cost than it could before trade.
b. Mexico can obtain more than 20 tons of vegetables, if it so chooses.
c. the United States no longer has a comparative advantage in producing beef.
d. Mexico can benefit by prohibiting vegetables imports from the United States.

Answers: 1. c; 2. b; 3. c; 4. a

---

1 ton of vegetables. Instead, through trade with Mexico, the United States can get $1\frac{1}{2}$ tons of vegetables for every ton of beef that it exports to Mexico, as long as Mexico has vegetables to export. Trading possibilities line *BV'* thus represents the $1B \equiv 1\frac{1}{2}V$ trading ratio.

Similarly, Mexico no longer has to move down its domestic production possibilities curve, giving up 2 tons of vegetables for each ton of beef. It can now export just $1\frac{1}{2}$ tons of vegetables for each 1 ton of beef that it wants by moving down its trading possibilities line *vb'*.

Specialization and trade create a new exchange ratio between beef and vegetables, and each nation's trading possibilities line reflects that ratio. For both nations, this exchange ratio is superior to the unspecialized (domestic only) exchange ratio embodied in their respective production possibilities curves. In both countries, self-sufficiency is inefficient and therefore undesirable.

▶ The principle of comparative advantage says that total world output will be greatest when each good is produced by the nation that has the lowest domestic opportunity cost.

▶ The rate at which countries can trade units of one product for units of another product is referred to as the terms of trade.

▶ A trading possibilities line shows the amounts of two products that a nation can obtain by specializing in the production of one product and then trading for the other.

Greater Output Specialization according to comparative advantage results in a more efficient allocation of world resources, and larger outputs of both products are therefore available to both nations.

Suppose that at the $1B \equiv 1\frac{1}{2}V$ terms of trade, the United States exports 10 tons of beef to Mexico and, in return, Mexico exports 15 tons of vegetables to the United States. How do the new quantities of beef and vegetables available to the two nations compare with the optimal product mixes that existed before specialization and trade? Point A in Figure 19.2a reminds us that the United States chose 18 tons of beef and 12 tons of vegetables originally. But by producing 30 tons of beef and no vegetables and by trading 10 tons of beef for 15 tons of vegetables, the United States can obtain 20 tons of beef and 15 tons of vegetables. This new, superior combination of beef and vegetables is indicated by point A' in Figure 19.2a. The United States' **gains from trade** are 2 tons of beef *and* 3 tons of vegetables.

gains from trade The extra output that trading partners obtain through specialization of production and exchange of *goods* and *services*.

Similarly, recall that Mexico's optimal product mix was 4 tons of vegetables and 8 tons of beef (point Z) before specialization and trade. Now, after specializing in vegetables and trading for beef, Mexico can have 5 tons of vegetables and 10 tons of beef. It accomplishes that by producing 20 tons of vegetables and no beef and exporting 15 tons of its vegetables in exchange for 10 tons of American beef. This new position is indicated by point Z' in Figure 19.2b. Mexico's gains from trade are 1 ton of vegetables *and* 2 tons of beef.

Points A' and Z' in Figure 19.2 are superior economic positions to points A and Z. This fact is enormously important! We know that a nation can expand its production possibilities boundary either by (1) expanding the quantity and improving the quality of its resources or by (2) implementing technological improvements. We have now established that international trade enables a nation to circumvent the output constraint illustrated by its production possibilities curve. An economy can grow by expanding international trade. The outcome of international specialization and trade is equivalent to having more and better resources or discovering and implementing improved production techniques.

Table 19.1 summarizes the transactions and outcomes in our analysis. Please give it one final careful review.

Trade with Increasing Opportunity Costs

To explain the basic principles underlying international trade, we simplified our analysis in several ways. For example, we limited discussion to two products and two nations. But multiproduct and multinational analysis yield the same conclusions. We also assumed constant opportunity costs (linear production possibilities curves), which is a more substantive simplification. Let's consider the effect of allowing increasing opportunity costs (concave-to-the-origin production possibilities curves) to enter the picture.

Suppose that the United States and Mexico are initially at positions on their concave production possibilities curves where their domestic cost ratios are $1B \equiv 1V$ and $1B \equiv 2V$, as they were in our constant-cost analysis. As before, comparative advantage indicates that the United States should specialize in beef and Mexico in vegetables. But now, as the United States begins to expand beef production, its cost of beef will rise; it will have to sacrifice more than 1 ton of vegetables to get 1 additional ton of beef. Resources are no longer perfectly substitutable between alternative uses, as the constant-cost assumption implied. Resources less and less suitable to beef production must be allocated to the U.S. beef industry in expanding beef output, and that means increasing costs—the sacrifice of larger and larger amounts of vegetables for each additional ton of beef.

Similarly, suppose that Mexico expands vegetable production starting from its $1B \equiv 2V$ cost ratio position. As production increases, it will find that its $1B \equiv 2V$ cost ratio begins to rise. Sacrificing 1 ton of beef will free resources that are capable of producing only something less than 2 tons of vegetables because those transferred resources are less suitable to vegetable production.

As the U.S. cost ratio falls from $1B \equiv 1V$ and the Mexican ratio rises from $1B \equiv 2V$, a point will be reached where the cost ratios are equal in the two nations, perhaps at $1B \equiv 1\frac{3}{4}V$. At this point, the underlying basis for further specialization and trade—differing cost ratios—has disappeared, and further specialization is therefore uneconomical. And, most important, this point of equal cost ratios may be reached while the United States is still producing some vegetables along with its beef and Mexico is still producing some beef along with its vegetables. The primary effect of increasing opportunity costs is less-than-complete specialization. For this reason, we often find domestically produced products competing directly against identical or similar imported products within a particular economy.

The Case for Free Trade

The case for free trade can be reduced to one compelling argument: Through free trade based on the principle of comparative advantage, the world economy can achieve a more efficient allocation of resources and a higher level of material well-being than it can without free trade.

Because the resource mixes and technological knowledge of the world's nations are all somewhat different, each nation can produce particular commodities at different opportunity costs. Each nation should produce goods for which its domestic opportunity costs are lower than the domestic opportunity costs of other nations, and it should exchange those goods for products for which its domestic opportunity costs are higher than those of other nations. If every nation follows this guideline, the world will realize the advantages of geographic and human specialization. The world and each free-trading nation will obtain a larger real income from its fixed supplies of resources.

Government trade barriers lessen or eliminate gains from specialization. If nations cannot trade freely, they must shift resources from efficient (low-cost) to inefficient (high-cost) uses to satisfy their diverse wants. A recent study estimates household income in the United States to be about $18,000 per year higher than it would otherwise be thanks to the massive decline in tariff rates since the end of World War II.[2] To put that figure in perspective, note that median household income in the United States in 2020 was a little under $70,000 per year. Thus, around a quarter of today's median household income can be attributed to falling tariff rates and the benefits that derive from international specialization and trade.

One side benefit of free trade is that it promotes competition and deters monopoly. The increased competition from foreign firms forces domestic firms to find and use the lowest-cost production techniques. It also compels them to be innovative with respect to both product quality and production methods, thereby contributing to economic growth. In addition, free trade gives consumers a wider range of product choices. Finally, free trade links national interests and breaks down national animosities. Confronted with political disagreements, trading partners tend to negotiate rather than make war.

▶ International trade enables nations to specialize, increase productivity, and increase output available for consumption.

▶ Comparative advantage means total world output will be greatest when each good is produced by the nation that has the lowest domestic opportunity cost.

▶ Specialization is less than complete among nations because opportunity costs normally rise as any specific nation produces more of a particular good.

QUICK REVIEW

19.3

Supply and Demand Analysis of Exports and Imports

Supply and demand analysis reveals how equilibrium prices and quantities of exports and imports are determined. The amount of a good or a service that a nation will export or import depends on differences between the equilibrium world price and the equilibrium domestic price. The interaction of *world* supply and demand determines the equilibrium **world price**—the price that equates the quantities supplied and demanded globally through international trade. By contrast, the interaction of *domestic* supply and demand determines the equilibrium **domestic price**—the price that would prevail in a closed economy that does not engage in international trade. The domestic price equates quantity supplied and quantity demanded domestically.

In the absence of trade, the domestic prices in a closed economy may or may not equal the world equilibrium prices. When economies are opened for international trade, differences between

>> **LO19.3** Explain why differences between world prices and domestic prices lead to exports and imports.

world price The international market *price* of a *good* or *service*, determined by world demand and supply.

domestic price The *price* of a *good* or *service* within a country, determined by domestic demand and supply.

---

[2]Gary Clyde Hufbauer and Zhiyao (Lucy) Lu, "The Payoff to America from Globalization: A Fresh Look with a Focus on Costs to Workers," Peterson Institute for International Economics, *Policy Brief 17-16,* May 2017 (updated).

world and domestic prices encourage exports or imports. To understand why, consider the international effects of price differences in a simple two-nation world, consisting of the United States and Canada, which are both producing aluminum. We assume there are no trade barriers, such as tariffs and quotas, and no international transportation costs.

Supply and Demand in the United States

Figure 19.3a shows the domestic supply curve S_d and the domestic demand curve D_d for aluminum in the United States, which for now is a closed economy. The intersection of S_d and D_d determines the equilibrium domestic price of $1 per pound and the equilibrium domestic quantity of 100 million pounds. Domestic suppliers produce 100 million pounds and sell them all at $1 a pound. There are no domestic surpluses or shortages of aluminum. But what would happen if the U.S. economy is opened to trade and the world price of aluminum is above or below this $1 domestic price?

U.S. Export Supply If the aluminum price in the rest of the world (that is, Canada) exceeds $1, U.S. firms will produce more than 100 million pounds and will export the excess domestic output. First, consider a world price of $1.25. We see from the supply curve S_d that U.S. aluminum firms will produce 125 million pounds of aluminum at that price. The demand curve D_d tells us that U.S. consumers will purchase only 75 million pounds at $1.25. The outcome is a domestic surplus of 50 million pounds of aluminum. U.S. producers will export those 50 million pounds at the $1.25 world price.

What if the world price is $1.50? The supply curve shows that U.S. firms will produce 150 million pounds of aluminum, while the demand curve tells us that domestic consumers will buy only 50 million pounds. So U.S. producers will export the domestic surplus of 100 million pounds.

In the upper half of Figure 19.3b, we plot the domestic surpluses—the U.S. exports—that occur at world prices above the $1 domestic equilibrium price. When the world and domestic prices are equal (= $1), the quantity of exports supplied is zero (point a) because there is no surplus of domestic output available to export at that price. When the world price is $1.25, U.S. firms export 50 million pounds of surplus aluminum (point b). At a $1.50 world price, the domestic surplus of 100 million pounds is exported (point c).

FIGURE 19.3 **U.S. export supply and import demand.**

(a) Domestic supply S_d and demand D_d set the domestic equilibrium price of aluminum at $1 per pound. At world prices above $1, there are domestic surpluses of aluminum. At prices below $1, there are domestic shortages. (b) Surpluses are exported (top curve), and shortages are met by importing aluminum (lower curve). The export supply curve shows the direct relationship between world prices and U.S. exports; the import demand curve portrays the inverse relationship between world prices and U.S. imports.

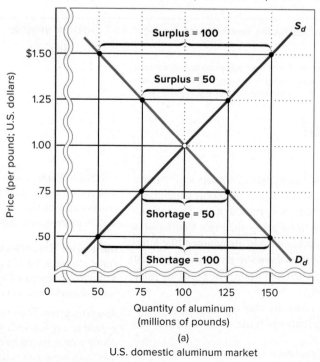

(a)
U.S. domestic aluminum market

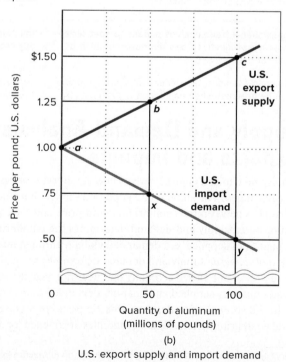

(b)
U.S. export supply and import demand

The U.S. **export supply curve,** found by connecting points *a*, *b*, and *c*, shows the amount of aluminum that U.S. producers will export at each world price above $1. This curve *slopes upward*, indicating a direct or positive relationship between the world price and the amount of U.S. exports. As world prices increase relative to domestic prices, U.S. exports rise.

U.S. Import Demand If the world price is below the domestic $1 price, the United States will import aluminum. Consider a $0.75 world price. The supply curve in Figure 19.3a reveals that at that price U.S. firms produce only 75 million pounds of aluminum. But the demand curve shows that the United States wants to buy 125 million pounds at that price. The result is a domestic shortage of 50 million pounds. To satisfy that shortage, the United States will import 50 million pounds of aluminum.

At an even lower world price, $0.50, U.S. producers will supply only 50 million pounds. Because U.S. consumers want to buy 150 million pounds at that price, there is a domestic shortage of 100 million pounds. Imports will flow to the United States to make up the difference. That is, at a $0.50 world price U.S. firms will supply 50 million pounds, and 100 million pounds will be imported.

In the lower half of Figure 19.3b, we plot the U.S. **import demand curve** from these data. This *downward sloping curve* shows the amounts of aluminum that the United States will import at world prices below the $1 U.S. domestic price. The relationship between world prices and imported amounts is inverse or negative. At a world price of $1, domestic output will satisfy U.S. demand; imports will be zero (point *a*). At $0.75, the United States will import 50 million pounds of aluminum (point *x*); at $0.50, the United States will import 100 million pounds (point *y*). Connecting points *a*, *x*, and *y* yields the *downward sloping* U.S. import demand curve. It reveals that as world prices fall relative to U.S. domestic prices, U.S. imports increase.

Supply and Demand in Canada

We repeat our analysis in Figure 19.4, this time from Canada's viewpoint. (We have converted Canadian dollar prices to U.S. dollar prices via the exchange rate.) Note that the domestic supply curve S_d and the domestic demand curve D_d for aluminum in Canada yield a domestic price of $0.75, which is $0.25 lower than the $1 U.S. domestic price.

export supply curve An upward sloping curve that shows the amount of a product that domestic *firms* will export at each *world price* that is above the *domestic price*.

import demand curve A downsloping curve showing the amount of a product that an economy will import at each *world price* below the *domestic price*.

FIGURE 19.4 **Canadian export supply and import demand.**

(a) At world prices above the $0.75 domestic price, production in Canada exceeds domestic consumption. At world prices below $0.75, domestic shortages occur. (b) Surpluses result in exports, and shortages result in imports. The Canadian export supply curve and import demand curve depict the relationships between world prices and exports or imports.

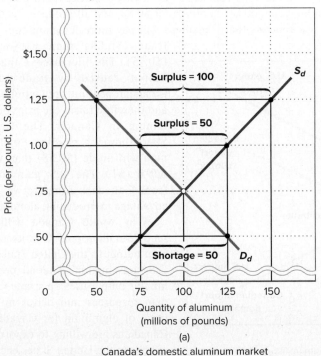

(a)
Canada's domestic aluminum market

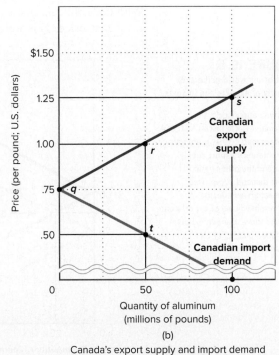

(b)
Canada's export supply and import demand

The analysis proceeds exactly as above except that the domestic price is now the Canadian price. If the world price is $0.75, Canadians will neither export nor import aluminum (giving us point q in Figure 19.4b). At world prices above $0.75, Canadian firms will produce more aluminum than Canadian consumers will buy. Canadian firms will export the surplus. When the world price is $1, Figure 19.4b tells us that Canada will have (and will export) a domestic surplus of 50 million pounds (yielding point r). At $1.25, it will have (and will export) a domestic surplus of 100 million pounds (point s). Connecting these points yields the upward sloping Canadian export supply curve, which reflects the domestic surpluses (and hence the exports) that occur when the world price exceeds the $0.75 Canadian domestic price.

At world prices below $0.75, domestic shortages occur in Canada. When the world price is $0.50, Figure 19.4a shows that Canadian consumers want to buy 125 million pounds of aluminum, but Canadian firms will produce only 75 million pounds. The shortage will bring 50 million pounds of imports to Canada (point t in Figure 19.4b). The Canadian import demand curve in that figure shows the Canadian imports that will occur at all world aluminum prices below the $0.75 Canadian domestic price.

Equilibrium World Price, Exports, and Imports

equilibrium world price
The *price* of an internationally traded product that equates the quantity of the product demanded by importers with the quantity of the product supplied by exporters; the price determined at the intersection of the export supply curve and the import demand curve.

We now have the tools for determining the **equilibrium world price** of aluminum and the equilibrium world levels of exports and imports when the world is opened to trade. Figure 19.5 combines the U.S. export supply curve and import demand curve shown in Figure 19.3b with the Canadian export supply curve and import demand curve that we derived in Figure 19.4b. The two U.S. curves proceed rightward from the $1 U.S. domestic price; the two Canadian curves proceed rightward from the $0.75 Canadian domestic price.

International equilibrium occurs in this two-nation model where one nation's import demand curve intersects another nation's export supply curve. In this case, the U.S. import demand curve intersects Canada's export supply curve at e. There, the world price of aluminum is $0.88. The Canadian export supply curve indicates that Canada will export 25 million pounds of aluminum at this price. Also at this price the United States will import 25 million pounds from Canada, indicated by the U.S. import demand curve. The $0.88 world price equates the quantity of imports demanded and the quantity of exports supplied (25 million pounds). Thus, there will be world trade of 25 million pounds of aluminum at $0.88 per pound.

After trade, the single $0.88 world price will prevail in both Canada and the United States. Only one price for a standardized commodity can persist in a highly competitive world market. With trade, all consumers can buy a pound of aluminum for $0.88, and all producers can sell it for that price. This world price means that Canadians will pay more for aluminum with trade ($0.88) than without it ($0.75). The increased Canadian output caused by trade raises Canadian per-unit production costs and therefore raises the price of aluminum in Canada. The United States, however, pays less for aluminum with trade ($0.88) than without it ($1). The U.S. gain comes from Canada's comparative cost advantage in producing aluminum.

Why would Canada willingly send 25 million pounds of its aluminum output to the United States for U.S. consumption? After all, producing this output uses up scarce Canadian resources and drives up the price of aluminum for Canadians. Canadians are willing to export aluminum to the United States because

FIGURE 19.5
Equilibrium world price and quantity of exports and imports.

In a two-nation world, the equilibrium world price (= $0.88) is determined by the intersection of one nation's export supply curve and the other nation's import demand curve. This intersection also decides the equilibrium volume of exports and imports. Here, Canada exports 25 million pounds of aluminum to the United States.

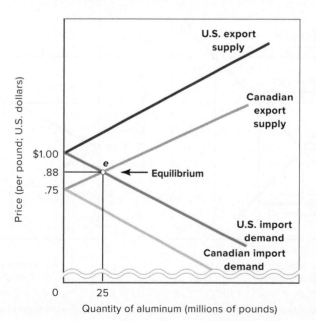

Canadians gain the means—the U.S. dollars—to import other goods, say, computer software, from the United States. Canadian exports enable Canadians to acquire imports that have greater value to Canadians than the exported aluminum. Canadian exports to the United States finance Canadian imports from the United States.

> A nation will export a particular product if the world price exceeds the domestic price; it will import the product if the world price is less than the domestic price.

> In a two-country world model, equilibrium world prices and equilibrium quantities of exports and imports occur where one nation's export supply curve intersects the other nation's import demand curve.

QUICK REVIEW
19.4

Trade Barriers and Export Subsidies

While a nation as a whole gains from trade, trade may harm particular domestic industries and their workers. Those industries might seek to preserve their economic positions by persuading their respective governments to protect them from imports—perhaps through tariffs, import quotas, or other trade barriers.

Indeed, the public may be won over by the apparent plausibility ("Cut imports and prevent domestic unemployment") and the patriotic ring ("Buy American!") of the arguments. The alleged benefits of tariffs are immediate and clear-cut to the public, but the adverse effects cited by economists are obscure and dispersed over the entire economy. When political deal-making is added in—"You back tariffs for the apparel industry in *my* state, and I'll back tariffs for the auto industry in *your* state"—the outcome can be a politically robust network of trade barriers. These impediments to free international trade can take several forms.

Tariffs are excise taxes or "duties" on the dollar values or physical quantities of imported goods. They may be imposed to obtain revenue or to protect domestic firms. A **revenue tariff** is usually applied to a product that is not being produced domestically, for example, tin, coffee, or bananas in the case of the United States. Revenue tariffs are designed to provide the federal government with revenue, and their rates tend to be modest. A **protective tariff** is implemented to shield domestic producers from foreign competition. These tariffs impede free trade by increasing the prices of imported goods and therefore shifting sales toward domestic producers. Although protective tariffs are usually not high enough to stop the importation of foreign goods, they put foreign producers at a competitive disadvantage. A tariff on imported auto tires, for example, will make domestically produced tires more attractive to consumers.

An **import quota** is a government-imposed limit on the quantities or total values of specific items that are imported in some period. Once a quota is filled, further imports of that product are prohibited. Import quotas are more effective than tariffs in impeding international trade. With a tariff, a product can go on being imported in large quantities. But with an import quota, all imports are prohibited once the quota is filled.

A **voluntary export restriction (VER)** is a trade barrier by which foreign firms "voluntarily" limit the amount of their exports to a particular country. VERs have the same effect as import quotas. Exporters agree to them to avoid more stringent tariffs or quotas. In the late 1990s, for example, Canadian producers of softwood lumber (fir, spruce, cedar, pine) agreed to a VER on exports to the United States under the threat of a permanently higher U.S. tariff.

Nontariff barriers (NTBs) include onerous licensing requirements, unreasonable standards pertaining to product quality, or simply bureaucratic hurdles and delays in customs procedures. Some nations require importers of foreign goods to obtain licenses and then restrict the number of licenses issued. Japan and several European countries require domestic importers of several types of foreign goods to obtain licenses. By restricting the number of licenses, governments can limit imports.

An **export subsidy** is a government payment to a domestic producer of export goods designed to aid that producer in attracting foreign buyers for its output. By offsetting some of a firm's production costs, the subsidies enable the domestic firm to charge a lower price and thus to sell more exports in world markets. For example, the United States and other nations have subsidized domestic farmers to boost the domestic food supply. These subsidies have artificially lowered the export prices of U.S. agricultural exports.

>> **LO19.4** Analyze the economic effects of tariffs and quotas.

tariff A *tax* imposed by a nation on an imported good.

revenue tariff A *tariff* designed to produce *income* for the federal government.

protective tariff A *tariff* designed to shield domestic producers of a *good* or *service* from the competition of foreign producers.

import quota A limit imposed by a nation on the quantity (or total value) of a good that may be imported during some period of time.

voluntary export restrictions (VER) Voluntary limitations by countries or *firms* of their exports to a particular foreign nation; undertaken to avoid the enactment of formal trade barriers by the foreign nation.

nontariff barriers (NTBs) All barriers other than *protective tariffs* that nations erect to impede international trade, including *import quotas,* licensing requirements, unreasonable product-quality standards, unnecessary bureaucratic detail in customs procedures, and so on.

export subsidy A government payment to a domestic producer to enable the *firm* to reduce the *price* of a *good* or *service* to foreign buyers.

..ıl KEY GRAPH

FIGURE 19.6 The economic effects of protective tariffs and import quotas.

This economy is initially closed to international trade, so that the equilibrium price and quantity are determined by the intersection of domestic demand D_d and domestic supply S_d. When the economy is opened to trade, the domestic price falls to the world price P_w, with domestic consumers purchasing d units and domestic suppliers producing a units. A tariff that increases the price of the product from P_w to P_t will reduce domestic consumption from d to c. Domestic producers will be able to sell more output (b rather than a) at a higher price (P_t rather than P_w). Foreign exporters are injured because they sell less output (bc rather than ad). The yellow area indicates the amount of tariff paid by domestic consumers. An import quota of $Q = bc$ units causes the supply curve to shift right by bc units to $S_d + Q$, thereby shifting the equilibrium to where domestic demand D_d intersects $S_d + Q$. The import quota of bc units has the same effects as the tariff, with one exception: The amount represented by the yellow area will go to foreign producers rather than to the domestic government.

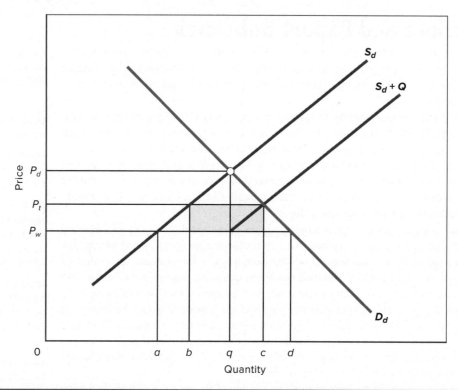

QUICK QUIZ FOR FIGURE 19.6

1. **If the government set the import quota at *ad* units instead of *bc* units, the supply curve $S_d + Q$ would intersect domestic demand D_d at:**
    a. the domestic price P_d, and imports would equal zero.
    b. the tariff price P_t, and imports would equal *bc*.
    c. the tariff price P_t, and imports would equal *ad*.
    d. the world price P_w, and imports would equal *ad* units.

2. **If the government set an import quota greater than zero but less than *bc*, the price would be:**
    a. higher than P_d.
    b. between P_t and P_d.
    c. between P_w and P_t.
    d. less than P_w.

3. **If the government cuts the tariff in half, domestic producers will see their sales:**
    a. increase
    b. decrease.
    c. fall by half.
    d. double.

4. **If the government sets the tariff equal to $P_d - P_w$ dollars, the trade deficit will:**
    a. increase to *ab*.
    b. decrease to zero
    c. increase to $P_d - P_t$.
    d. remain steady at *bc*.

Economic Impact of Tariffs

We will confine our in-depth analysis of the effects of trade barriers to the two most common types of trade barriers: tariffs and quotas. Once again, we turn to supply-and-demand analysis for help. Curves D_d and S_d in **Figure 19.6 (Key Graph)** show domestic demand and supply for a product in which a nation, say, the United States, does *not* have a comparative advantage—for example, smartphones. (Disregard curve $S_d + Q$ for now.) Without world trade, the domestic price and output will be P_d and q, respectively.

Assume now that the domestic economy is opened to world trade and that China, which *does* have a comparative advantage in smartphones, begins to sell its smartphones in the United States. We assume that with free trade the domestic price cannot differ from the world price, which here is P_w. At P_w, domestic consumption is d and domestic production is a. The horizontal distance between the domestic supply and demand curves at P_w represents imports of ad. Thus far, our analysis is similar to the analysis of world prices in Figure 19.3.

Direct Effects Suppose now that the United States imposes a tariff on each imported smartphone. The tariff, which raises the price of imported smartphones from P_w to P_t, has four effects:

- *Decline in consumption* Consumption of smartphones in the United States declines from d to c as the higher price moves buyers up and to the left along their demand curve. The tariff prompts consumers to buy fewer smartphones and reallocate a portion of their expenditures to less-desired substitute products. U.S. consumers are clearly injured by the tariff, because they pay $P_t - P_w$ more for each of the c units they buy at price P_t.

- *Increased domestic production* U.S. producers—which are not subject to the tariff—receive the higher price P_t per unit. Because this new price is higher than the pretariff world price P_w, the domestic smartphone industry moves up and to the right along its supply curve S_d, increasing domestic output from a to b. Domestic producers thus enjoy both a higher price *and* expanded sales, which explains why domestic producers lobby for protective tariffs. From a social point of view, however, the increase in domestic production from a to b means that the tariff permits domestic producers of smartphones to bid resources away from other, more efficient, U.S. industries.

- *Decline in imports* Chinese producers are hurt. Although the sales price of each smartphone that they sell in the United States is higher by $P_t - P_w$, that amount accrues to the U.S. government, not to Chinese producers. The after-tariff world price, or the per-unit revenue to Chinese producers, remains at P_w, but the volume of U.S. imports (Chinese exports) falls from ad to bc.

- *Tariff revenue* The yellow rectangle represents the amount of revenue the tariff yields. Total revenue from the tariff is determined by multiplying the tariff, $P_t - P_w$ per unit, by the number of smartphones imported, bc. This tariff revenue is a transfer of income from consumers to government and does not represent any net change in the nation's economic well-being. The result is that government gains this portion of what consumers lose by paying more for smartphones.

Indirect Effect Tariffs have a subtle effect beyond what our supply and demand diagram can show. Because China sells fewer smartphones in the United States, it earns fewer dollars and so must buy fewer U.S. exports. U.S. export industries must then cut production and release resources. These are highly efficient industries, as we know from their comparative advantage and their ability to sell goods in world markets.

Tariffs directly promote the expansion of inefficient industries that do not have a comparative advantage. They also indirectly cause the contraction of relatively efficient industries that do have a comparative advantage. Put bluntly, tariffs shift resources in the wrong direction—and that is not surprising. We know that specialization and world trade lead to more efficient use of world resources and greater world output. But protective tariffs reduce world trade. Therefore, tariffs also reduce efficiency and the world's real output.

Economic Impact of Quotas

Quotas have the same economic impact as a tariff, with one big difference: While tariffs generate revenue for the domestic government, a quota transfers that revenue to foreign producers.

Suppose in Figure 19.6 that, instead of imposing a tariff, the United States prohibits any imports of Chinese smartphones in excess of bc units. In other words, an import quota of bc smartphones is imposed on China. We deliberately chose the size of this quota to be the same amount as imports would be under a $P_t - P_w$ tariff so that we can compare "equivalent" situations. As a consequence of the quota, the supply of smartphones is $S_d + Q$ in the United States. This supply consists of the domestic supply plus the fixed amount bc ($= Q$) that importers will provide at each domestic price. The supply curve $S_d + Q$ does not extend below price P_w because Chinese producers will not export any smartphones to the United States at any price below P_w. Instead, they would sell them to other countries at the world market price of P_w.

Most of the economic results are the same as those with a tariff. Prices of smartphones are higher (P_t instead of P_w) because imports have been reduced from ad to bc. Domestic consumption of smartphones is down from d to c. U.S. producers enjoy both a higher price (P_t rather than P_w) and increased sales (b rather than a).

The difference between tariffs and quotas is that the price increase of $P_t - P_w$ paid by U.S. consumers on imports of bc—the yellow area—no longer goes to the U.S. Treasury as tariff (tax) revenue but flows to the Chinese firms that have acquired the quota rights to sell smartphones in the United States. For consumers in the United States, a tariff produces a better economic outcome than a quota, other things being the same. A tariff generates government revenue that can be used to cut other taxes or to finance public goods and services that benefit the United States. In contrast, the higher price created by quotas results in additional revenue for foreign producers.

▶ A tariff on a product increases its price, reduces its consumption, increases its domestic production, reduces its imports, and generates tariff revenue for the government.

▶ An import quota does the same, except a quota generates revenue for foreign producers rather than for the government imposing the quota.

Net Costs of Tariffs and Quotas

Study after study finds that the costs of tariffs and quotas to consumers substantially exceed the gains to producers and government. A sizable net cost or efficiency loss to society arises from trade protection. Furthermore, industries employ large amounts of economic resources to influence Congress to pass and maintain protectionist laws. Because these rent-seeking efforts divert resources away from more socially desirable purposes, trade restrictions impose these additional costs on society as well.

Conclusion: The gains that U.S. trade barriers create for protected industries and their workers come at the expense of much greater losses for the entire economy. The result is economic inefficiency, reduced consumption, and lower standards of living.

The Case for Protection: A Critical Review

>> **LO19.5** Critique the most frequently presented arguments for protectionism.

Despite the logic of specialization and trade, protectionists still exist in some union halls, corporate boardrooms, and political conference rooms. What arguments do protectionists make to justify trade barriers? How valid are those arguments?

Military Self-Sufficiency Argument

The argument here is not economic but political-military: Protective tariffs can preserve or strengthen industries that produce the materials essential for national defense. In an uncertain world, political-military objectives (self-sufficiency) sometimes must take precedence over economic goals (efficiency in the use of world resources).

Unfortunately, it is difficult to measure and compare the benefit of increased national security against the cost of economic inefficiency when protective tariffs are imposed. Economists can only point out that when a nation levies tariffs to increase military self-sufficiency, it incurs economic costs.

All people in the United States would agree that relying on hostile nations for necessary military equipment is not a good idea, yet the self-sufficiency argument is open to serious abuse. Nearly every industry can claim that it makes direct or indirect contributions to national security and hence deserves protection from imports.

Diversification-for-Stability Argument

Highly specialized economies such as Saudi Arabia (based on oil) and Cuba (based on sugar) are dependent on international markets for their income. In these economies, wars, international political developments, recessions abroad, and random fluctuations in world supply and demand for one or two particular goods can cause deep declines in export revenues and therefore in domestic income. Tariff and quota protections are allegedly needed in such nations to enable greater industrial diversification and greater domestic stability.

There is some truth in this diversification-for-stability argument. But the argument has little or no relevance to the United States and other advanced economies with highly diversified economies.

Infant Industry Argument

The infant industry argument contends that protective tariffs can allow new domestic industries to establish themselves. Temporarily shielding young domestic firms from the severe competition of more mature and more efficient foreign firms gives infant industries a chance to develop and become efficient producers. Tariff protection for such infant industries will correct for a misallocation of world resources that was caused by historically different levels of economic development between domestic and foreign industries.

There are some logical problems with the infant industry argument. For instance, it is difficult to determine which infant industries are capable of achieving economic maturity and therefore deserve protection. Also, protective tariffs may persist even after industrial maturity has been realized.

Most economists believe that if infant industries are to be subsidized, there are better means than tariffs for doing so. Direct subsidies, for example, have the advantage of making explicit which industries are being aided and to what degree.

Protection-Against-Dumping Argument

The protection-against-dumping argument contends that tariffs can protect domestic firms from "dumping" by foreign producers. **Dumping** is the sale of a product in a foreign country at prices either below cost or below the prices commonly charged at home. Foreign companies may dump their goods to drive their competitors out of business. If that company is a monopoly in the home country, it may dump its good for a lower price in foreign countries in order to achieve the per-unit cost savings associated with large-scale production.

Because dumping is an "unfair trade practice," most nations prohibit it. For example, where dumping is shown to injure U.S. firms, the federal government imposes tariffs called *antidumping duties* on the goods in question. But relatively few documented cases of dumping occur each year, and specific instances of unfair trade do not justify widespread, permanent tariffs. Moreover, antidumping duties can be abused. Often, what is alleged to be dumping is simply comparative advantage at work.

> **dumping** The sale of a product in a foreign country at *prices* either below cost or below the prices commonly charged at home.

Increased Domestic Employment Argument

Arguing for a tariff to "save U.S. jobs" becomes fashionable when the economy encounters a recession. In an economy that engages in international trade, exports involve residents of foreign countries spending their money to purchase domestically produced output, while imports reflect domestic residents spending their money to obtain output produced in foreign countries. So, according to this argument, reducing imports will divert spending that is currently being used to purchase another nation's output toward purchases of domestically produced output. Thus, domestic output and employment will rise.

This "increased domestic employment" argument has several shortcomings. First, while imports may eliminate some U.S. jobs, they create others. Thus, while imports have indeed eliminated the jobs of some U.S. steel and textile workers in recent decades, other workers have gained jobs unloading ships, flying imported aircraft, and selling imported electronic equipment. Import restrictions alter the composition of employment, but they may have little or no effect on the overall volume of employment.

Smoot-Hawley Tariff Act Legislation passed in 1930 that established very high *tariffs*. Its objective was to reduce *imports* and stimulate the domestic economy, but it resulted only in retaliatory tariffs by other nations.

Second, nations adversely affected by tariffs and quotas are likely to retaliate, causing a "trade war" (more precisely, a *trade barrier war*) that chokes off trade and makes all nations worse off. The **Smoot-Hawley Tariff Act** of 1930 is a classic example. Although that act was meant to reduce imports and stimulate U.S. production, its high tariffs prompted adversely affected nations to retaliate with their own equally high tariffs. International trade fell, lowering the output and income of all nations. Economic historians generally agree that the Smoot-Hawley Tariff Act contributed to both the length and severity of the Great Depression.

Finally, forcing an excess of exports over imports cannot succeed in raising domestic employment over the long run. It is through U.S. imports that foreign nations earn dollars to buy U.S. exports. In the long run, a nation must import in order to export. The long-run impact of tariffs is not an increase in domestic employment but, at best, a reallocation of workers away from export industries and toward protected domestic industries. This shift implies a less efficient allocation of resources.

Cheap Foreign Labor Argument

The cheap foreign labor argument says that domestic firms and workers must be shielded from the ruinous competition of countries where wages are low. If protection is not provided, cheap imports will flood U.S. markets, and the prices of U.S. goods—along with the wages of U.S. workers—will be pulled down. That is, domestic living standards in the United States will be reduced.

The cheap foreign labor argument suggests that, to maintain its standard of living, the United States should not trade with low-wage Mexico. But what would actually happen if the United States did not trade with Mexico? Would wages and living standards actually rise in the United States as a result? No. To obtain vegetables, the United States will have to reallocate a portion of its labor from its relatively more-efficient beef industry to its relatively less-efficient vegetable industry. As a result, the average productivity of U.S. labor will fall, as will real wages and living standards. Both countries' labor forces will have diminished standards of living because without specialization and trade they will have less output available to them. Compare column 4 with column 1 in Table 19.1 or points A' and Z' with A and Z in Figure 19.2 to confirm this point.

The cheap foreign labor argument incorrectly focuses on labor costs *per hour*. As an example, suppose that a U.S. factory pays its workers $20 per hour while a factory in a developing country pays its workers $4 per hour. The proponents of the cheap foreign labor argument look at these numbers and conclude—incorrectly—that it is impossible for the U.S. factory to compete with the factory in the developing country. But this conclusion fails to take into account two crucial facts:

- What actually matters are labor costs *per unit of output*, not labor costs *per hour of work*.
- Differences in productivity typically mean that labor costs *per unit of output* are often nearly identical between high-wage and low-wage countries despite huge differences in hourly wage rates.

To see why these points matter, let's take the productivity of the two factories into account. Because the U.S. factory uses much more sophisticated technology, better-trained workers, and much more capital per worker, one worker in one hour can produce 20 units of output. Because the U.S. workers get paid $20 per hour, the U.S. factory's labor cost per unit of output is $1. The factory in the developing country is much less productive because it uses less efficient technology, and its relatively untrained workers have much less machinery and equipment to work with. A worker there produces only 4 units per hour. Given the foreign wage of $4 per hour, the labor cost per unit of output at the factory in the developing country is also $1. Thus, the lower wage rate per hour at the factory in the developing country does not translate into lower labor costs per unit— meaning that it won't be able to undersell its U.S. competitor just because its workers get paid lower wages per hour.

In short, firms in developing countries only *sometimes* have an advantage in terms of labor costs per unit of output. Whether they do in any specific situation varies by industry and firm and depends on differences in productivity as well as differences in labor costs per hour. For many goods, labor productivity in high-wage countries like the United States is so much higher than labor productivity in low-wage countries that it is actually cheaper *per unit of output* to manufacture those goods in high-wage countries. That is why, for instance, Intel still makes microchips in the United States and why most automobiles are still produced in the United States, Japan, and Europe rather than in low-wage countries.

▶ Most rationales for trade protections are special-interest requests that, if followed, would create gains for protected industries and their workers at the expense of greater losses for the economy.

▶ The cheap foreign labor argument against international trade fails because its proponents forget to take into account differences in productivity between high-wage and low-wage countries.

QUICK REVIEW
19.6

Multilateral Trade Agreements and Free-Trade Zones

Aware of the detrimental effects of trade wars and the general weaknesses of arguments for trade protections, nations have worked to lower tariffs worldwide.

>> **LO19.6** Explain the objectives of the WTO, EU, NAFTA, and USMCA, and discuss offshoring and trade adjustment assistance.

General Agreement on Tariffs and Trade

In 1947, 23 nations, including the United States, signed the **General Agreement on Tariffs and Trade (GATT).** GATT was based on three principles: (1) equal, nondiscriminatory trade treatment for all member nations; (2) the reduction of tariffs by multilateral negotiation; and (3) the elimination of import quotas. Basically, GATT provided a forum for the multilateral negotiation of reduced trade barriers.

Since the Second World War, member nations have completed eight "rounds" of GATT negotiations to reduce trade barriers. The eighth round of negotiations began in Uruguay in 1986. After seven years of complex discussions, in 1993 a new agreement was reached by GATT's 128 member nations. The Uruguay Round agreement took effect on January 1, 1995, and its provisions were phased in through 2005.

Under this agreement, tariffs on thousands of products were eliminated or reduced, with overall tariffs dropping by 33 percent. The agreement also liberalized government rules that in the past impeded a global market for services such as advertising, accounting, legal services, tourist services, and financial services. Quotas on imported textiles and apparel were phased out and replaced with tariffs. Other provisions reduced agricultural subsidies paid to farmers and protected intellectual property (patents, trademarks, and copyrights) against piracy.

General Agreement on Tariffs and Trade (GATT) The international agreement reached in 1947 in which 23 nations agreed to eliminate *import quotas*, negotiate reductions in *tariff* rates, and give each other equal and nondiscriminatory treatment. It now includes most nations and has become the *World Trade Organization*.

World Trade Organization

The Uruguay Round agreement established the **World Trade Organization (WTO)** as GATT's successor. Some 164 nations belonged to the WTO in 2021. The WTO oversees trade agreements reached by its member nations, and it rules on trade disputes between members. It also provides forums for further rounds of trade negotiations. The ninth and latest round of negotiations—the **Doha Development Agenda**—was launched in Doha, Qatar, in late 2001. (The trade rounds occur over several years in several venues but are named after the city or country of origination.) The negotiations are aimed at further reducing tariffs and quotas, as well as agricultural subsidies that distort trade.

GATT and the WTO have been positive forces in the trend toward liberalized world trade. The trade rules agreed upon by the member nations provide a strong bulwark against the protectionism called for by the special-interest groups in the various member nations.

The WTO is quite controversial. Critics are concerned that rules crafted to expand international trade and investment enable firms to circumvent national laws that protect workers and the environment. Critics ask: What good are minimum-wage laws, worker-safety laws, collective-bargaining rights, and environmental laws if firms can easily shift their production to nations that have weaker laws or if consumers can buy goods produced in those countries?

Proponents of the WTO respond that labor and environmental protections should be pursued directly by the nations so affected, and via international organizations other than the WTO. These

World Trade Organization (WTO) An organization of 164 nations (as of 2021) that oversees the provisions of the current world trade agreement, resolves trade disputes stemming from it, and holds forums for further rounds of trade negotiations.

Doha Development Agenda The latest, uncompleted (as of late 2021) sequence of trade negotiations by members of the *World Trade Organization;* named after Doha, Qatar, where the set of negotiations began. Also called the Doha Round.

issues should not be linked to the process of trade liberalization, which confers widespread economic benefits across nations. Moreover, say WTO proponents, many environmental and labor concerns are greatly overblown. Most world trade is among advanced industrial countries, not between them and countries with lower environmental and labor standards. Moreover, the free flow of goods and resources raises output and income in the developing nations. Historically, such increases in living standards have eventually resulted in stronger, not weaker, protections for the environment and for workers.

The European Union

European Union (EU) An association of 28 European nations (as of mid-2019) that has eliminated tariffs and quotas among them, established common tariffs for imported goods from outside the member nations, eliminated barriers to the free movement of capital, and created other common economic policies.

Countries have also sought to reduce tariffs by creating regional free-trade zones. The most prominent example is the **European Union (EU).** Initiated in 1958 as the Common Market, the EU was initially composed of just six European nations. As of 2021, it had 27 members.

The EU has abolished tariffs and import quotas on nearly all products traded among the participating nations and established a common system of tariffs applicable to all goods received from nations outside the EU. It has also liberalized the movement of capital and labor within the EU and has created common policies in other economic matters of joint concern, such as agriculture, transportation, and business practices.

EU integration has achieved for Europe what the U.S. constitutional prohibition on tariffs by individual states has achieved for the United States: increased regional specialization, greater productivity, greater output, and faster economic growth. The free flow of goods and services has created large markets for EU industries. The resulting economies of large-scale production have enabled these industries to achieve much lower costs than they could have achieved in their small, single-nation markets.

eurozone The 19 nations (as of 2019) of the 28-member (as of 2019) *European Union* that use the *euro* as their common *currency*. The eurozone countries are Austria, Belgium, Cyprus, Estonia, Finland, France, Germany, Greece, Ireland, Italy, Luxembourg, Malta, the Netherlands, Portugal, Slovakia, Slovenia, and Spain.

One of the most significant accomplishments of the EU was the establishment of the so-called **eurozone** or euro area in the early 2000s. As of 2018, 19 members of the EU (Austria, Belgium, Cyprus, Estonia, Finland, France, Germany, Greece, Ireland, Italy, Latvia, Lithuania, Luxembourg, Malta, the Netherlands, Portugal, Slovenia, Slovakia, and Spain) use the euro as a common currency. But the United Kingdom, Denmark, and Sweden have opted not to use the common currency, at least for now.

Economists believe that the adoption of the euro raised the standard of living in eurozone nations. By ending the inconvenience and expense of exchanging currencies, the euro has enhanced the free flow of goods, services, and resources among eurozone members. Companies that previously sold products in only one or two European nations have found it easier to price and sell their products in all 19 eurozone countries. The euro has also allowed consumers and businesses to more easily comparison shop for outputs and inputs, which has increased competition, reduced prices, and lowered costs.

North American Free Trade Agreement

North American Free Trade Agreement (NAFTA) The 1993 treaty that established an international free-trade zone composed of Canada, Mexico, and the United States.

In 1993 Canada, Mexico, and the United States created a major free-trade zone. The **North American Free Trade Agreement (NAFTA)** established a free-trade area that has about the same combined output as the EU but encompasses a much larger geographic area. NAFTA has eliminated tariffs and other trade barriers among Canada, Mexico, and the United States for most goods and services.

Critics of NAFTA feared that it would cause a massive loss of U.S. jobs as firms moved to Mexico to take advantage of lower wages and weaker regulations on pollution and workplace safety. Also, they were concerned that Japan and South Korea would build plants in Mexico and transport goods tariff-free to the United States, further hurting U.S. firms and workers.

In retrospect, critics were much too pessimistic. Since the passage of NAFTA in 1993, employment in the United States has increased by more than 38 million workers. NAFTA has increased trade among Canada, Mexico, and the United States and has enhanced the standard of living in all three countries.

In late 2018, negotiations were completed for a trade treaty that is intended to be the successor to NAFTA. Known as the United States-Mexico-Canada Agreement (or USMCA), the treaty cannot go into effect until after it is ratified by the governments of all three countries. The document leaves most elements of NAFTA in place but calls for stronger environmental and labor protections while also insisting on higher minimum wages in Mexican export industries as well as additional protections for intellectual property.

Trade Adjustment Assistance

The **Trade Adjustment Assistance Act** of 2002 introduced some innovative policies to help those hurt by shifts in international trade patterns. The law provides cash assistance (beyond unemployment insurance) for up to 78 weeks for workers displaced by imports or the relocation of U.S. manufacturing plants to other countries. To obtain the assistance, workers must participate in job searches, training programs, or vocational education. Also provided are relocation allowances to help displaced workers move to new jobs within the United States. Refundable tax credits for health insurance help workers maintain their insurance coverage during the retraining and job-search period. Workers who are 50 years of age or older are eligible for "wage insurance," which replaces some of the difference in pay (if any) between their old and new jobs. Many economists support trade adjustment assistance because it not only helps workers hurt by international trade but also helps create the political support necessary to reduce trade barriers and export subsidies.

However, not all economists favor trade adjustment assistance. Loss of jobs from imports, sending work abroad, and plant relocations to other countries account for only a small fraction (about 4 percent in recent years) of total job losses in the economy each year. Many workers also lose their jobs because of changing patterns of demand, changing technology, bad management, and other dynamic aspects of a market economy. Some critics ask, "What makes losing one's job to international trade worthy of such treatment, compared to losing one's job to, say, technological change or domestic competition?"

Offshoring of Jobs

Some U.S. jobs lost because of international trade are lost because of the ongoing globalization of resource markets, especially the market for labor. In recent years, U.S. firms have found the outsourcing of work abroad to be increasingly profitable. Economists call this business activity **offshoring**—shifting work previously done by U.S. workers to workers located in other nations. Offshoring is not a new practice, but traditionally it involved components for U.S. manufacturing goods. For example, Boeing has long offshored the production of major airplane parts for its "American" aircraft.

Recent advances in computer and communications technology have enabled U.S. firms to offshore service jobs such as data entry, book composition, software coding, call-center operations, medical transcription, and claims processing to countries such as India and the Philippines. Where offshoring occurs, some of the value added in the production process accrues to foreign countries rather than to the United States. Therefore part of the income generated from the production of U.S. goods is paid to foreigners, not to American workers.

Offshoring is a wrenching experience for many Americans who lose their jobs, but it is not necessarily bad for the overall economy. Offshoring simply reflects growing specialization and international trade in services or "tasks." As with trade in goods, trade in services reflects comparative advantage and is beneficial to both trading parties. Moreover, the United States has a sizable trade surplus with other nations in services. The United States gains by specializing in high-valued services such as transportation services, accounting services, legal services, and advertising services, where it maintains a comparative advantage. It then "trades" to obtain lower-valued services such as call-center and data-entry work, for which comparative advantage lies abroad.

Offshoring also increases the demand for complementary jobs in the United States. Jobs that are close substitutes for existing U.S. jobs are lost, but the number of complementary jobs in the United States grows. For example, the lower price of writing software code in India may mean a lower cost of software sold in the United States and abroad. That lower cost, in turn, may create more jobs for U.S.-based workers such as software designers, marketers, and distributors. Moreover, offshoring may encourage domestic investment and the expansion of firms in the United States by reducing their production costs and keeping them competitive worldwide. In some instances, "offshoring jobs" may equate to "importing competitiveness." Entire firms that might otherwise disappear abroad may remain profitable in the United States only because they can offshore some of their work.

Trade Adjustment Assistance Act A U.S. law passed in 2002 that provides cash assistance, education and training benefits, health care subsidies, and *wage* subsidies (for persons age 50 or older) to workers displaced by *imports* or relocations of U.S. *plants* to other countries.

offshoring The practice of shifting work previously done by domestic workers to workers located abroad.

Petition of the Candlemakers, 1845

French Economist Frédéric Bastiat (1801–1850) Devastated the Proponents of Protectionism by Satirically Extending Their Reasoning to Its Logical and Absurd Conclusions.

Petition of the Manufacturers of Candles, Waxlights, Lamps, Candlesticks, Street Lamps, Snuffers, Extinguishers, and of the Producers of Oil Tallow, Rosin, Alcohol, and, Generally, of Everything Connected with Lighting.

TO MESSIEURS THE MEMBERS OF THE CHAMBER OF DEPUTIES.

Gentlemen—You are on the right road. You reject abstract theories, and have little consideration for cheapness and plenty. Your chief care is the interest of the producer. You desire to emancipate him from external competition, and reserve the national market for national industry.

We are about to offer you an admirable opportunity of applying your—what shall we call it? your theory? No; nothing is more deceptive than theory; your doctrine? your system? your principle? but you dislike doctrines, you abhor systems, and as for principles, you deny that there are any in social economy: we shall say, then, your practice, your practice without theory and without principle.

We are suffering from the intolerable competition of a foreign rival, placed, it would seem, in a condition so far superior to ours for the production of light, that he absolutely inundates our national market with it at a price fabulously reduced. The moment he shows himself, our trade leaves us—all consumers apply to him; and a branch of native industry, having countless ramifications, is all at once rendered completely stagnant. This rival . . . is no other than the Sun.

What we pray for is, that it may please you to pass a law ordering the shutting up of all windows, skylights, dormer windows, outside and inside shutters, curtains, blinds, bull's-eyes; in a word, of all openings, holes, chinks, clefts, and fissures, by or through which the light of the sun has been in use to enter houses, to the prejudice of the meritorious manufacturers with which we flatter ourselves we have accommodated our country—a country which, in gratitude, ought not to abandon us now to a strife so unequal.

If you shut up as much as possible all access to natural light, and create a demand for artificial light, which of our French

Malcolm Fife/Pixtal/age fotostock

manufacturers will not be encouraged by it? If more tallow is consumed, then there must be more oxen and sheep; and, consequently, we shall behold the multiplication of artificial meadows, meat, wool, hides, and, above all, manure, which is the basis and foundation of all agricultural wealth.

The same remark applies to navigation. Thousands of vessels will proceed to the whale fishery; and, in a short time, we shall possess a navy capable of maintaining the honor of France, and gratifying the patriotic aspirations of your petitioners, the undersigned candlemakers and others.

Only have the goodness to reflect, Gentlemen, and you will be convinced that there is, perhaps, no Frenchman, from the wealthy coalmaster to the humblest vender of lucifer matches, whose lot will not be ameliorated by the success of this our petition.

Source: Frédéric Bastiat, *Economic Sophisms* (The Foundation for Economic Education, 1996).

QUICK REVIEW

19.7

▶ The General Agreement on Tariffs and Trade (GATT) of 1947 reduced tariffs and quotas and established a process for numerous subsequent rounds of multinational trade negotiations.

▶ The World Trade Organization (WTO)—GATT's current successor—rules on trade disputes.

▶ The European Union (EU) and the North American Free Trade Agreement (NAFTA) established multinational free-trade zones.

▶ The offshoring of jobs has prompted programs like trade adjustment assistance to help displaced workers transition to new jobs.

Summary

LO19.1 List several key facts about international trade.
The United States leads the world in the combined volume of exports and imports. Other major trading nations are Germany, Japan, the western European nations, and the Asian economies of China, South Korea, Taiwan, and Singapore. The United States' principal exports include chemicals, agricultural products, consumer durables, aircraft, and computer software and services; its principal imports include petroleum, automobiles, metals, household appliances, and computers.

LO19.2 Define comparative advantage and explain how specialization and trade add to a nation's output.
World trade is based on three considerations: the uneven distribution of economic resources among nations, the fact that efficient production of various goods requires particular techniques or combinations of resources, and the differentiated products produced among nations.

Mutually advantageous specialization and trade are possible between any two nations if they have different domestic opportunity-cost ratios for any two products. By specializing on the basis of comparative advantage, nations can obtain larger real incomes with fixed amounts of resources. The terms of trade determine how the trading nations share this increase in world output.

LO19.3 Explain why differences between world prices and domestic prices lead to exports and imports.
A nation's export supply curve shows the quantities of a product the nation will export at world prices that exceed the domestic price (the price in a closed, no-international-trade economy). A nation's import demand curve reveals the quantities of a product it will import at world prices below the domestic price.

In a two-nation model, the equilibrium world price and the equilibrium quantities of exports and imports occur where one nation's export supply curve intersects the other nation's import demand curve. A nation will export a particular product if the world price exceeds the domestic price; it will import the product if the world price is less than the domestic price. The country with the lower costs of production will be the exporter and the country with the higher costs of production will be the importer.

LO19.4 Analyze the economic effects of tariffs and quotas.
Trade barriers take the form of protective tariffs, quotas, nontariff barriers, and voluntary export restrictions. Export subsidies also distort international trade. Supply-and-demand analysis demonstrates that protective tariffs and quotas increase the prices and reduce the quantities demanded of the affected goods. Sales by foreign exporters diminish; domestic producers, however, gain higher prices and more sales. Consumer losses from trade restrictions greatly exceed producer and government gains, creating an efficiency loss to society.

LO19.5 Critique the most frequently presented arguments for protectionism.
The strongest arguments for protection are the infant industry and military self-sufficiency arguments. Most other arguments for protection are interest-group appeals or reasoning fallacies that emphasize producer interests over consumer interests or stress the immediate effects of trade barriers while ignoring long-run consequences. The cheap foreign labor argument for protection fails because it focuses on labor costs per hour rather than on what really matters: labor costs per unit of output.

LO19.6 Explain the objectives of the WTO, EU, NAFTA, and USMCA, and discuss offshoring and trade adjustment assistance.
In 1947 the General Agreement on Tariffs and Trade (GATT) was formed to encourage nondiscriminatory treatment for all member nations, to reduce tariffs, and to eliminate import quotas.

GATT's successor, the World Trade Organization (WTO), had 164 member nations in 2021. It implements trade agreements, rules on trade disputes between members, and provides forums for continued discussions on trade liberalization.

Free-trade zones liberalize trade within regions. Two examples of free-trade arrangements are the 27-member European Union (EU) and the North American Free Trade Agreement (NAFTA), comprising Canada, Mexico, and the United States.

The Trade Adjustment Assistance Act of 2002 provides cash assistance, education and training benefits, health care subsidies, and wage subsidies to qualified workers displaced by imports or relocations of plants from the United States to abroad.

Offshoring is the practice of shifting work previously done by Americans in the United States to workers located in other nations. Although offshoring eliminates some U.S. jobs, it lowers production costs and expands sales, and it therefore may create other U.S. jobs. Less than 4 percent of all job losses in the United States each year are caused by imports, offshoring, or plant relocations abroad.

Terms and Concepts

trade

labor-intensive goods

land-intensive goods

capital-intensive goods

absolute advantage

comparative advantage

opportunity-cost ratio

principle of comparative advantage

terms of trade

trading possibilities line

gains from trade

world price

domestic price

export supply curve

import demand curve

equilibrium world price

tariff

revenue tariff

protective tariff

import quota

voluntary export restriction (VER)

nontariff barrier (NTB)

export subsidy

dumping

Smoot-Hawley Tariff Act

General Agreement on Tariffs and Trade (GATT)

World Trade Organization (WTO)

Doha Development Agenda

European Union (EU)

eurozone

North American Free Trade Agreement (NAFTA)

Trade Adjustment Assistance Act

offshoring

Discussion Questions

1. Quantitatively, how important is international trade to the United States relative to the importance of trade to other nations? What country is the United States' most important trading partner, quantitatively? With what country does the United States have the largest trade deficit? **LO19.1**

2. Distinguish among land-, labor-, and capital-intensive goods, citing an example of each without resorting to the examples in the text. How do these distinctions relate to international trade? How do distinctive products, unrelated to resource intensity, relate to international trade? **LO19.2**

3. Explain: "The United States can make certain toys with greater productive efficiency than China can. Yet we import those toys from China." Relate your answer to the ideas of Adam Smith and David Ricardo. **LO19.2**

4. Suppose Big Country can produce 80 units of X by using all its resources to produce X or 60 units of Y by devoting all its resources to Y. Comparable figures for Small Nation are 60 units of X and 60 units of Y. Assuming constant costs, in which product should each nation specialize? Explain why. What are the limits of the terms of trade between these two countries? **LO19.2**

5. What is an export supply curve? What is an import demand curve? How do such curves relate to the determination of the equilibrium world price of a tradable good? **LO19.3**

6. Why is a quota more detrimental to an economy than a tariff that results in the same level of imports as the quota? What is the net outcome of either tariffs or quotas for the world economy? **LO19.4**

7. "The potentially valid arguments for tariff protection—military self-sufficiency, infant industry protection, and diversification for stability—are also the most easily abused." Why are these arguments susceptible to abuse? **LO19.4**

8. Evaluate the effectiveness of artificial trade barriers, such as tariffs and import quotas, as a way to achieve and maintain full employment throughout the U.S. economy. How might such policies reduce unemployment in one U.S. industry but increase it in another U.S. industry? **LO19.4**

9. In 2018, manufacturing workers in the United States earned average compensation of $21.86 per hour. That same year, manufacturing workers in Mexico earned average compensation of $3.20 per hour. How can U.S. manufacturers possibly compete? Why isn't all manufacturing done in Mexico and other low-wage countries? **LO19.4**

10. How might protective tariffs reduce both the imports and the exports of the nation that levies tariffs? How might import competition lead to quality improvements and cost reductions by U.S. firms? **LO19.4**

11. Identify and state the significance of each of the following trade-related entities: (*a*) the WTO, (*b*) the EU, (*c*) the eurozone, and (*d*) NAFTA. **LO19.6**

12. What form does trade adjustment assistance take in the United States? How does such assistance promote political support for free-trade agreements? Do you think workers who lose their jobs because of changes in trade laws deserve special treatment relative to workers who lose their jobs because of other changes in the economy, say, changes in patterns of government spending? **LO19.6**

13. What is offshoring of white-collar service jobs, and how does it relate to international trade? Why has offshoring increased over the past few decades? Give an example (other than that in the text) of how offshoring can eliminate some U.S. jobs while creating other U.S. jobs. **LO19.6**

14. **LAST WORD** What central point was Bastiat trying to make in his fictional petition of the candlemakers?

Review Questions

1. In Country A, a worker can make 5 bicycles per hour. In Country B, a worker can make 7 bicycles per hour. Which country has an absolute advantage in making bicycles? **LO19.2**
   a. Country A
   b. Country B

2. In Country A, the production of 1 bicycle requires using resources that could otherwise be used to produce 11 lamps. In Country B, the production of 1 bicycle requires using resources that could otherwise be used to produce 15 lamps. Which country has a comparative advantage in making bicycles? **LO19.2**
   a. Country A
   b. Country B

3. True or False: If Country B has an absolute advantage over Country A in producing bicycles, it will also have a comparative advantage over Country A in producing bicycles. **LO19.2**

4. Suppose that the opportunity-cost ratio for sugar and almonds is $4S \equiv 1A$ in Hawaii but $1S \equiv 2A$ in California. Which state has the comparative advantage in producing almonds? **LO19.2**
   a. Hawaii
   b. California
   c. Neither

5. Suppose that the opportunity-cost ratio for fish and lumber is $1F \equiv 1L$ in Canada but $2F \equiv 1L$ in Iceland. Then _____ should specialize in producing fish while _____ should specialize in producing lumber. **LO19.2**
   a. Canada; Iceland
   b. Iceland; Canada

6. Suppose that the opportunity-cost ratio for watches and cheese is $1C \equiv 1W$ in Switzerland but $1C \equiv 4W$ in Japan. At which of the following international exchange ratios (terms of trade) will

Switzerland and Japan be willing to specialize and engage in trade with each other? **LO19.2**

*Select **one or more** answers from the choices shown.*
a. $1C \equiv 3W$
b. $1C \equiv \frac{1}{2}W$
c. $1C \equiv 5W$
d. $\frac{1}{2}C \equiv 1W$
e. $2C \equiv 1W$

7. Which of the following are benefits of international trade? **LO19.2**

*Choose **one or more** answers from the choices shown.*
a. A more efficient allocation of resources
b. A higher level of material well-being
c. Gains from specialization
d. Promoting competition
e. Deterring monopoly
f. Reducing the threat of war

8. We see quite a bit of international trade in the real world. And trade is driven by specialization. So why don't we see full specialization—for instance, all cars in the world being made in South Korea, or all the mobile phones in the world being made in China? Choose the best answer from among the following choices. **LO19.2**
a. High tariffs
b. Extensive import quotas
c. Increasing opportunity costs
d. Increasing returns

9. True or False: If a country is open to international trade, the domestic price of a product can differ from the international price of that product. **LO19.3**

10. Suppose that the current international price of wheat is $6 per bushel and that the United States is currently exporting

30 million bushels per year. If the United States suddenly became a closed economy with respect to wheat, would the domestic price of wheat in the United States end up higher or lower than $6? **LO19.3**
a. Higher
b. Lower
c. It will stay the same.

11. Suppose that if Iceland and Japan were both closed economies, the domestic price of fish would be $100 per ton in Iceland and $90 per ton in Japan. If the two countries decided to open up to international trade with each other, which of the following could be the equilibrium international price of fish once they begin trading? **LO19.3**
a. $75
b. $85
c. $95
d. $105

12. Draw a domestic supply-and-demand diagram for a product in which the United States does not have a comparative advantage. What impact do foreign imports have on domestic price and quantity? On your diagram show a protective tariff that eliminates approximately one-half of the assumed imports. What are the price-quantity effects of this tariff on (*a*) domestic consumers, (*b*) domestic producers, and (*c*) foreign exporters? How would the effects of a quota that creates the same amount of imports differ? **LO19.4**

13. American apparelmakers complain to Congress about competition from China. Congress decides to impose either a tariff or a quota on apparel imports from China. Which policy would Chinese apparel manufacturers prefer? **LO19.4**
a. Tariff
b. Quota

Problems

1. Assume that the comparative-cost ratios of two products—baby formula and tuna fish—are as follows in the nations of Canswicki and Tunata:

Canswicki: 1 can baby formula $\equiv$ 2 cans tuna fish
Tunata: 1 can baby formula $\equiv$ 4 cans tuna fish

In what product should each nation specialize? Which of the following terms of trade would be acceptable to both nations: (a) 1 can baby formula $\equiv 2\frac{1}{2}$ cans tuna fish; (b) 1 can baby formula $\equiv$ 1 can tuna fish; (c) 1 can baby formula $\equiv$ 5 cans tuna fish? **LO19.2**

2. The accompanying hypothetical production possibilities tables are for New Zealand and Spain. Each country can produce apples and plums. Plot the production possibilities data for each of the two countries separately. Referring to your graphs, answer the following: **LO19.2**

New Zealand's Production Possibilities Table (Millions of Bushels)

Product	Production Alternatives			
	A	B	C	D
Apples	0	20	40	60
Plums	15	10	5	0

Spain's Production Possibilities Table (Millions of Bushels)

Product	Production Alternatives			
	R	S	T	U
Apples	0	20	40	60
Plums	60	40	20	0

a. What is each country's opportunity cost ratio of producing plums and apples?
b. Which nation should specialize in each product?
c. Show the trading possibilities lines for each nation if the actual terms of trade are 1 plum for 2 apples. (Plot these lines on your graph.)
d. Suppose the optimum product mixes before specialization and trade were alternative B in New Zealand and alternative S in Spain. What would be the gains from specialization and trade?

3. The following hypothetical production possibilities tables are for China and the United States. Assume that before specialization and trade, the optimal product mix for China is alternative B and for the United States is alternative U. **LO19.2**
a. Are comparative-cost conditions such that the two countries should specialize? If so, what product should each produce?

b. What is the total gain in apparel and chemical output that would result from such specialization?

c. What are the limits of the terms of trade? Suppose that the *actual* terms of trade are 1 unit of apparel for 1.5 tons of chemicals and that the *actual* amount traded is 4 units of apparel for 6 tons of chemicals. What are the gains from specialization and trade for each nation?

China Production Possibilities						
Product	A	B	C	D	E	F
Apparel (in thousands)	30	24	18	12	6	0
Chemicals (in tons)	0	6	12	18	24	30

U.S. Production Possibilities						
Product	R	S	T	U	V	W
Apparel (in thousands)	10	8	6	4	2	0
Chemicals (in tons)	0	4	8	12	16	20

4. Refer to Figure 3.6. Assume that the graph depicts the U.S. domestic market for corn. How many bushels of corn, if any, will the United States export or import at a world price of $1, $2, $3, $4, and $5? Use this information to construct the U.S. export supply curve and import demand curve for corn. Suppose that the only other corn-producing nation is France, where the domestic price is $4. Which country will export corn, and which country will import it? **LO19.3**

CHAPTER

20

The Balance of Payments, Exchange Rates, and Trade Deficits

>> LEARNING OBJECTIVES

LO20.1 Explain the two types of international financial transactions.

LO20.2 Define and explain the two components of the balance of payments: the current account and the capital and financial account.

LO20.3 Explain how exchange rates are determined.

LO20.4 Distinguish between flexible and fixed exchange rates.

LO20.5 Explain the current system of managed floating exchange rates.

LO20.6 Identify the causes and consequences of recent U.S. trade deficits.

LO20.7 (Appendix) Explain how exchange rates worked under the gold standard and Bretton Woods.

On May 6, 2022, 1 U.S. dollar could buy 1.41 Australian dollars, 0.81 British pounds, 1.29 Canadian dollars, 0.95 European euros, 130.57 Japanese yen, or 20.18 Mexican pesos. What explains this seemingly haphazard array of exchange rates?

In Chapter 19 we examined comparative advantage as the underlying economic basis of world trade. Now we introduce and explain the highly important monetary and financial aspects of international trade.

International Financial Transactions

International financial transactions fall into two broad categories:

- **International trade** encompasses all cross-border purchases and sales of currently produced goods and services. Examples include an Egyptian firm exporting cotton to the United States and a U.S. company hiring an Indian call center to answer its phones.

- **International asset transactions** include all cross-border purchases and sales of real or financial assets in which the property rights to those assets are transferred from a citizen of one country to a citizen of another country. International asset transactions include selling a business to foreign investors and purchasing a vacation home in another country from a local citizen.

>> **LO20.1** Explain the two types of international financial transactions.

international trade The exchange (trade) of goods and services across international borders.

international asset transactions The sale, trade, or transfer of ownership rights to either real or financial assets, including currency, across international borders.

These two categories of international financial transactions reflect the fact that whether they live in different countries or the same country, individuals and firms can only exchange two things: currently produced goods and services or assets.

Money is by far the most commonly exchanged asset. Money flows from the buyers of the goods, services, or assets to the sellers of the goods, services, or assets. Importers are buyers and exporters are sellers. As a result, *imports cause outflows of money while exports cause inflows of money.*

When the buyers and sellers are both from places that use the same currency, there is no confusion about what type of money to use. Americans from California and Wisconsin will use their common currency, the dollar. People from France and Germany will use their common currency, the euro. However, when the buyers and sellers are from places that use different currencies, an *intermediate* asset transaction has to take place: The buyers must convert their own currency into the currency that the sellers use and accept.

Consider the case of an English software company that wants to buy an artificial intelligence supercomputer made by a U.S. company. The U.S. company sells these high-powered machines for $300,000. To pay for the machine, the English company has to convert some of its money (British pounds) into the money that the U.S. company will accept (U.S. dollars). This process is not difficult. As we will soon explain, there are many easy-to-use foreign exchange markets in which those who need to sell pounds and buy dollars can interact with people who want to do just the opposite (buy pounds and sell dollars). The demand and supply created by these two groups will determine the equilibrium exchange rate between the two currencies. That exchange rate will, in turn, determine how many pounds the English company must pay for the supercomputer. For instance, if the exchange rate is £1 = $2, then the English company will have to convert £150,000 to obtain the $300,000 necessary to purchase the computer.

QUICK REVIEW
20.1

▶ International financial transactions involve trade either in currently produced goods and services or assets.

▶ While imports of goods, services, and assets cause outflows of money, exports of goods, services, and assets create inflows of money.

▶ If buyers and sellers use different currencies, then foreign exchange transactions take place so that the seller (exporter) can be paid in its own currency.

The Balance of Payments

>> **LO20.2** Define and explain the two components of the balance of payments: the current account and the capital and financial account.

balance of payments A summary of all the financial transactions that take place between the individuals, *firms,* and governmental units of one nation and those of all other nations during a year.

A nation's **balance of payments** is the sum of all the financial transactions that take place between its residents and the residents of foreign nations. Most of these transactions fall into the two main categories that we just discussed: international trade and international asset transactions. But the balance of payments also includes international transactions that fall into other categories. They include expenditures made by tourists, interest and dividends received or paid abroad, debt forgiveness, and remittances made by immigrants to their relatives back home.

The Bureau of Economic Analysis at the U.S. Department of Commerce compiles a balance-of-payments statement each year. This statement summarizes all of the billions of payments that U.S. individuals and firms receive from foreigners as well as all of the billions of payments that U.S. individuals and firms make to foreigners. It shows inward flows of money *to* the United States and outward flows of money *from* the United States. For convenience, all of these money payments are stated in U.S. dollars, even though many of the payments were made using foreign currencies.

Table 20.1 is a simplified balance-of-payments statement for the United States in 2021. It is organized into two broad categories: the *current account* and the *capital and financial account.*

current account The section in a nation's *international balance of payments* that records its exports and imports of *goods* and *services,* its net *investment income,* and its *net transfers.*

Current Account

The top portion of Table 20.1 is called the **current account.** It mainly summarizes U.S. trade in currently produced goods and services. Items 1 and 2 show U.S. exports and imports of goods in 2021. U.S. exports have a *plus* (+) sign because they generate flows of money into the United States. U.S. imports have a *minus* (−) sign because they cause flows of money out of the United States.

TABLE 20.1 The U.S. Balance of Payments, 2021 (in Billions)

CURRENT ACCOUNT	
(1) U.S. goods exports	$+1,762
(2) U.S. goods imports	−2,853
(3) *Balance on goods*	$−1,091
(4) U.S. exports of services	+771
(5) U.S. imports of services	−541
(6) *Balance on services*	+230
(7) *Balance on goods and services*	−861
(8) Net investment income	+174*
(9) Net transfers	−135
(10) **Balance on current account**	−822
CAPITAL AND FINANCIAL ACCOUNT	
Capital account	
(11) *Balance on capital account*	−2
Financial account	
(12) Foreign purchases of assets located in the United States	+1,948†
(13) U.S. purchases of assets located abroad	−1,124†
(14) *Balance on financial account*	+824
(15) **Balance on capital and financial account**	+822
	$ 0

*Includes other, less significant, categories of income.
†Includes one-half of a $137 billion statistical discrepancy as well as one-half of $42 billion in net financial derivatives transactions.

Source: Bureau of Economic Analysis, U.S. Department of Commerce. Preliminary 2021 data. The export and import data are on a "balance-of-payment basis" and usually vary from the data on exports and imports reported in the National Income and Product Accounts.

Balance on Goods Items 1 and 2 in Table 20.1 reveal that in 2021, U.S. goods exports of $1,762 billion were less than U.S. goods imports of $2,853 billion. A country's *balance of trade on goods* is the difference between its exports and its imports of goods. If exports exceed imports, the result is a trade surplus on the balance of goods. If imports exceed exports, the result is a trade deficit on the balance of goods. We note in item 3 that, in 2021, the United States incurred a trade deficit on goods of $1,091 billion.

Balance on Services The United States exports not only goods, such as airplanes and oil, but also services, such as insurance contracting, business consulting, air travel, and investment advice. Item 4 in Table 20.1 shows that these service "exports" totaled $771 billion in 2021. These exports generated flows of money into the United States, thus the + sign. Item 5 indicates that the United States also imports services from foreigners. Those service imports totaled $541 billion in 2021, and because they generate flows of money out of the United States, they carry a − sign. Summed together, items 4 and 5 indicate that the balance on services (item 6) in 2021 was $230 billion.

The **balance on goods and services** shown as item 7 is the difference between U.S. exports of goods and services (items 1 and 4) and U.S. imports of goods and services (items 2 and 5). In 2021, U.S. imports of goods and services exceeded U.S. exports of goods and services by $861 billion. So a **trade deficit** of that amount is said to have occurred on the U.S. balance of goods and services. In contrast, a **trade surplus** on the balance of goods and services will occur whenever exports of goods and services exceed imports of goods and services.

Item 7, the overall U.S. trade balance, is equal to the sum of the trade deficits or trade surpluses that the United States has with each country in the world. To give you a sense of how large those surpluses and deficits are, and by how much they vary from country to country, Global Perspective 20.1 indicates the size of the U.S. trade deficit or surplus with particular nations. The U.S. trade deficit with China is particularly large.

Balance on Current Account Items 8 and 9 do not relate directly to international trade in goods and services. They are listed as part of the current account because they are international financial flows that account for certain international financial transactions that *look like* international trade in goods or services. For instance, item 8, *net investment income*, represents the

balance on goods and services The exports of *goods* and *services* of a nation less its imports of goods and services in a year.

trade deficit The amount by which a nation's *imports* of goods (or goods and *services*) exceed its *exports* of goods (or goods and *services*).

trade surplus The amount by which a nation's *exports* of goods (or goods and *services*) exceed its *imports* of goods (or goods and *services*).

GLOBAL PERSPECTIVE 20.1

U.S. TRADE BALANCES IN GOODS AND SERVICES, SELECTED NATIONS, 2021

The United States has large trade deficits in goods and services with several nations, in particular, China, Mexico, Germany, and Japan.

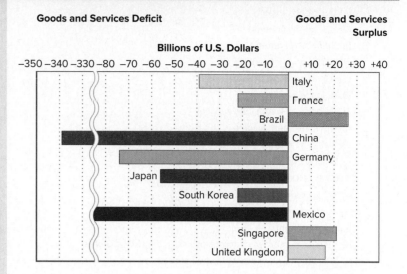

Source: Bureau of Economic Analysis.

difference between (a) the interest and dividend payments that foreigners pay to U.S. citizens and companies for the services provided by U.S. capital invested abroad ("exported" capital) and (b) the interest and dividends that U.S. citizens and companies pay to foreigners for the services provided by foreign capital invested here ("imported" capital). In 2021, U.S. net investment income was a positive $174 billion.

Item 9 shows net transfers, both public and private, between the United States and the rest of the world. Included here are foreign aid, pensions paid to U.S. citizens living abroad, and remittances by immigrants to relatives abroad. These $135 billion of transfers are net U.S. outpayments (and therefore listed as a negative number in Table 20.1). They are listed as part of the current account because they can be considered the financial flows that accompany the granting of gifts and the importing of "thank you notes."

balance on current account The exports of *goods* and *services* of a nation less its imports of goods and services plus its *net investment income* and *net transfers* in a year.

By adding all of the transactions in the current account, we obtain the **balance on current account** shown in item 10. In 2021 the United States had a current account deficit of $822 billion. In other words, U.S. current account transactions generated more money flows out of the United States than money flows into the United States.

Capital and Financial Account

The bottom portion of Table 20.1 summarizes U.S. international asset transactions. It is called the **capital and financial account** and consists of two separate accounts: the *capital account* and the *financial account*.

capital and financial account The section of a nation's *international balance of payments* that records (1) debt forgiveness by and to foreigners and (2) foreign purchases of assets in the United States and U.S. purchases of assets abroad.

Capital Account The capital account mainly measures debt forgiveness—which is an asset transaction because the person forgiving a debt essentially hands the IOU back to the borrower. It is a "net" account (one that can be either + or −). The negative $2 billion listed in line 11 tells us that in 2021 U.S. citizens forgave $2 billion more of debt owed to them by foreigners than foreigners forgave debt owed to them by Americans. The − sign indicates a debit; it is an "on-paper" outpayment (asset transfer) equal to the net amount of debt forgiven.

Financial Account The financial account summarizes international asset transactions, that is, international purchases and sales of real or financial assets. Line 12 lists the amount of foreign purchases of assets in the United States. It has a + sign because any purchase of a U.S.-owned asset by a foreigner generates a flow of money toward the American who sells the asset. Line 13 lists U.S. purchases of assets abroad. This item has a − sign because such purchases generate a flow of money from the Americans who buy foreign assets toward the foreigners who sell them those assets.

Items 12 and 13, added together, yield a positive $824 billion balance on the financial account for 2021 (line 14). In 2021 the United States "exported" $1,948 billion of ownership of its real and financial assets and "imported" $1,124 billion. In other words, this surplus in the financial account brought in income of $824 billion to the United States. The **balance on capital and financial account** (line 15) is $822 billion. It is the sum of the $2 billion debit on the capital account and the $824 billion surplus on the financial account.

Observe that the $822 billion surplus in the capital and financial account equals the $822 billion deficit in the current account. In fact, the two numbers always equal—or "balance." Let's see why.

balance on capital and financial account The sum of the *capital account balance* and the *financial account balance.*

Why the Balance?

The balance on the current account and the balance on the capital and financial account must always sum to zero because any deficit or surplus in the current account automatically creates an offsetting entry in the capital and financial account. People can trade only two things: currently produced goods and services or preexisting assets (including money). Therefore, if trading partners have an imbalance in their trade of currently produced goods and services, the only way to make up for that imbalance is with a net transfer of assets from one party to the other.

To understand why, suppose that Finley (a U.S. citizen) makes shoes and Henri (a Swiss citizen) makes watches and that the two trade only with each other. Assume that their financial assets consist entirely of money, with each beginning the year with $1,000 in their own bank account. Suppose that this year Finley exports $300 of shoes to Henri and imports $500 of watches from Henri. Finley therefore ends the year with a $200 goods deficit with Henri.

However, Finley and Henri's goods transactions also result in asset exchanges that cause a net transfer of assets from Finley to Henri that are exactly equal in value to Finley's $200 goods deficit with Henri. Why? Henri pays Finley $300 for her shoes while Finley pays Henri $500 for his watches. The *net* result of these opposite-direction asset movements is that $200 of Finley's initial assets of $1,000 are transferred to Henri. This transfer is unavoidable because the $300 that Finley receives from her exports of shoes pays for only the first $300 of her $500 of imports of watches. The only way for Finley to pay for the remaining $200 of watch imports is for her to transfer $200 of her initial asset holdings to Henri. Consequently, Finley's assets decline by $200, from $1,000 to $800, while Henri's assets rise by $200, from $1,000 to $1,200.

Consider how the transaction between Finley and Henri affects the U.S. balance-of-payments statement (Table 20.1), other things equal. Finley's $200 goods deficit with Henri shows up in the U.S. current account as a −$200 entry in the balance on goods account (line 3) and carries down to a −$200 entry in the balance on current account (line 10).

In the capital and financial account, this $200 is recorded as +$200 in the account labeled *foreign purchases of assets located in the United States* (line 12). This +$200 then carries down to the balance on capital and financial account (line 15).

For a slightly different perspective, consider the entries this way: Henri has used $200 worth of watches to purchase $200 of Finley's initial $1,000 of assets. The +$200 entry in line 12 simply recognizes this fact. This +$200 entry exactly offsets the −$200 in the current account.

Thus, the balance of payments always balances. Any current account deficit or surplus in the top half of the statement automatically generates an offsetting international asset transfer that shows up in the capital and financial account in the bottom half of the statement. That is, current account deficits generate transfers of assets *to* foreigners, while current account surpluses generate transfers of assets *from* foreigners.

▶ A nation's balance-of-payments statement summarizes all of the international financial transactions that take place between its residents and the residents of all foreign nations. It includes the current account balance and the capital and financial account balance.

▶ The current account balance is a nation's exports of goods and services less its imports of goods and services plus its net investment income and net transfers.

▶ The capital and financial account balance includes the net amount of the nation's debt forgiveness as well as the nation's sale of real and financial assets to people living abroad less its purchases of real and financial assets from foreigners.

▶ The current account balance and the capital and financial account balance always sum to zero because any current account imbalance automatically generates an offsetting international asset transfer.

QUICK REVIEW

20.2

Flexible Exchange Rates

>> LO20.3 Explain how exchange rates are determined.

flexible exchange rate A *rate of exchange* that is determined by the international demand for and supply of a nation's money and that is consequently free to rise or fall because it is not subject to *currency interventions*. Also referred to as a "floating exchange rate."

Exchange-rate systems come in two varieties:

- In a **flexible- or floating-exchange-rate** system, demand and supply determine exchange rates without government intervention.

- In a **fixed-exchange-rate** system, a government sets the exchange rates for its currency and adjusts monetary and fiscal policy as necessary to maintain those rates.

We begin by looking at flexible exchange rates. Let's examine the rate, or price, at which U.S. dollars might be exchanged for British pounds in the market for foreign currency. In **Figure 20.1 (Key Graph)** we show demand D_1 and supply S_1 of pounds. Note that both the demand for and supply of pounds are expressed in terms of U.S. dollars. They interact to determine the equilibrium price for pounds, which is expressed in terms of how many dollars are required to purchase one pound.

The *demand-for-pounds curve* D_1 slopes downward because all British goods and services will be cheaper to Americans if pounds become less expensive. That is, at lower dollar prices for pounds, Americans can obtain more pounds and therefore more British goods and services per dollar. To buy those cheaper British goods, U.S. consumers will increase the quantity of pounds they demand.

..ıl KEY GRAPH

FIGURE 20.1 **The market for foreign currency (pounds).**

The intersection of the demand-for-pounds curve D_1 and the supply-of-pounds curve S_1 determines the equilibrium dollar price of pounds, here, $2. That means that the exchange rate is $2 = £1. Not shown: An increase in demand for pounds or a decrease in supply of pounds will increase the dollar price of pounds and thus cause the pound to appreciate. Also not shown: A decrease in the demand for pounds or an increase in the supply of pounds will reduce the dollar price of pounds, meaning that the pound has depreciated.

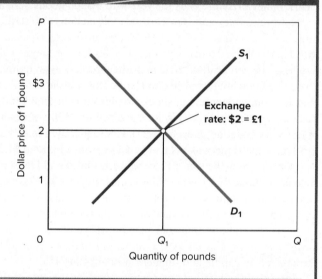

QUICK QUIZ FOR FIGURE 20.1

1. **Which of the following statements is true?**
   a. The quantity of pounds demanded falls when the dollar appreciates.
   b. The quantity of pounds supplied declines as the dollar price of the pound rises.
   c. At the equilibrium exchange rate, the pound price of $1 is £$\frac{1}{2}$.
   d. The dollar appreciates if the demand for pounds increases.

2. **At the price of $2 for £1 in this figure:**
   a. the dollar-pound exchange rate is unstable.
   b. the quantity of pounds supplied equals the quantity demanded.
   c. the dollar price of £1 equals the pound price of $1.
   d. U.S. goods exports to Britain must equal U.S. goods imports from Britain.

3. **Other things equal, a leftward shift of the demand curve in this figure:**
   a. would depreciate the dollar.
   b. would create a shortage of pounds at the previous price of $2 for £1.

   c. might be caused by a major recession in the United States.
   d. might be caused by a significant rise of real interest rates in Britain.

4. **Other things equal, a rightward shift of the supply curve in this figure would:**
   a. depreciate the dollar and might be caused by a significant rise of real interest rates in Britain.
   b. depreciate the dollar and might be caused by a significant fall of real interest rates in Britain.
   c. appreciate the dollar and might be caused by a significant rise of real interest rates in the United States.
   d. appreciate the dollar and might be caused by a significant fall of real interest rates in the United States.

As a concrete example, suppose that you are a U.S. citizen on vacation in London. If it takes only 50 cents to buy 1 pound, you will end up wanting to purchase many more souvenirs than if it cost $1.50 to buy 1 pound. The lower the dollar price of purchasing a pound, the less expensive British goods and services appear to you and the more dollars you want to sell for pounds in order to buy "cheap" British products. So the demand curve for pounds slopes downward.

The *supply-of-pounds curve* S_1 slopes upward because the British will purchase more U.S. goods as the dollar price of a pound rises (that is, as the pound price of a dollar falls). The more dollars the British can get in exchange for £1, the less expensive U.S. products will look to them and, hence, the more pounds they will want to supply so as to get the dollars they need to purchase "cheap" U.S. products.

The intersection of the supply curve and the demand curve determine the dollar price of pounds. In Figure 20.1, that price (exchange rate) is $2 for £1. At this exchange rate, the quantities of pounds supplied and demanded are equal; neither a shortage nor a surplus of pounds occurs.

fixed exchange rate A *rate of exchange* that is pegged by a government or central bank at a particular ratio (for instance, $1 = 6 yuan) rather than being allowed to vary with changes in demand and supply.

Depreciation and Appreciation

An exchange rate determined by market forces can, and often does, change constantly, just as stock and bond prices do.

- When the dollar price of pounds *rises*, for example, from $2 = £1 to $3 = £1, the dollar has *depreciated* relative to the pound (and the pound has appreciated relative to the dollar). When a currency depreciates, more units of it (dollars) are needed to buy a single unit of the other currency (the pound).
- When the dollar price of pounds *falls*, for example, from $2 = £1 to $1 = £1, the dollar has *appreciated* relative to the pound (and the pound has depreciated relative to the dollar). When a currency appreciates, fewer units of it (dollars) are needed to buy a single unit of the other currency (pounds).

Note that a depreciation of the dollar implies an appreciation of the pound, and vice versa. When the dollar price of a pound jumps from $2 = £1 to $3 = £1, the pound has appreciated relative to the dollar because it takes fewer pounds to buy $1. At $2 = £1, it took £$\frac{1}{2}$ to buy $1; at $3 = £1, it takes only £$\frac{1}{3}$ to buy $1. Conversely, when the dollar appreciates relative to the pound, the pound depreciates relative to the dollar. More pounds are needed to buy a dollar.

In general, the relevant terminology and relationships between the U.S. dollar and another currency are as follows (where the "≡" sign means "is equivalent to").

- Dollar price of foreign currency *increases* ≡ dollar depreciates relative to the foreign currency ≡ foreign currency price of dollar decreases ≡ foreign currency appreciates relative to the dollar.
- Dollar price of foreign currency *decreases* ≡ dollar appreciates relative to the foreign currency ≡ foreign currency price of dollar increases ≡ foreign currency depreciates relative to the dollar.

Determinants of Flexible Exchange Rates

What factors cause a nation's currency to appreciate or depreciate in the market for foreign exchange? Here are three generalizations:

- If the demand for a nation's currency increases, that currency will appreciate. If the demand declines, that currency will depreciate.
- If the supply of a nation's currency increases, that currency will depreciate. If the supply decreases, that currency will appreciate.
- If a nation's currency appreciates, some foreign currency depreciates relative to it.

With these generalizations in mind, let's examine the determinants of exchange rates—the factors that shift the demand or supply curve for a certain currency. As we do so, keep in mind that the other-things-equal assumption is always in force.

Changes in Tastes Any change in consumer tastes or preferences for the products of a foreign country may alter the demand for that nation's currency and change its exchange rate. If technological advances in U.S. aircraft make them more attractive to British consumers and businesses, then the British will supply more pounds in the exchange market to purchase more U.S. airplanes. The supply-of-pounds curve shifts to the right, causing the pound to depreciate and the dollar to appreciate.

In contrast, the U.S. demand-for-pounds curve shifts to the right if British woolen apparel becomes more fashionable in the United States. The pound will appreciate and the dollar will depreciate.

Relative Income Changes A nation's currency is likely to depreciate if its growth of national income is more rapid than that of other countries. Here's why: A country's imports vary directly with its income level. As national income rises in the United States, Americans will buy both more domestic goods and more foreign goods. If the U.S. economy is expanding rapidly and the British economy is stagnant, U.S. imports of British goods, and therefore U.S. demands for pounds, will increase. The dollar price of pounds will rise, so the dollar will depreciate.

Relative Inflation Rate Changes Other things equal, changes in the relative inflation rates of two nations change their relative price levels and alter the exchange rate between their currencies. The currency of the nation with the higher inflation rate—the more rapidly rising price level—tends to depreciate. Suppose, for example, that inflation is zero percent in Great Britain and 5 percent in the United States so that prices, on average, are rising by 5 percent per year in the United States while, on average, prices remain unchanged in Great Britain. U.S. consumers will seek out more of the now relatively lower-priced British goods, increasing the demand for pounds. British consumers will purchase less of the now relatively higher-priced U.S. goods, reducing the supply of pounds. This combination of increased demand for pounds and reduced supply of pounds causes the pound to appreciate and the dollar to depreciate.

According to **purchasing-power-parity theory**, exchange rates should eventually adjust such that they equate the purchasing power of various currencies. If a certain market basket of identical products costs $10,000 in the United States and £5,000 in Great Britain, the exchange rate should move to $2 = £1. That way, a dollar spent in the United States will buy exactly as much output as it would if it were first converted to pounds (at the $2 = £1 exchange rate) and then used to buy output in Great Britain.

In terms of our example, 5 percent inflation in the United States will increase the price of the market basket from $10,000 to $10,500, while the zero percent inflation in Great Britain will leave the market basket priced at £5,000. For purchasing power parity to hold, the exchange rate would have to move from $2 = £1 to $2.10 = £1. That means the dollar would depreciate and the pound would appreciate. In practice, however, exchange rates are often very slow to adjust to equate the purchasing power of various currencies and thereby achieve "purchasing power parity," even over long periods.

Relative Interest Rates Changes in relative interest rates between two countries may alter their exchange rate. Suppose that real interest rates rise in the United States but stay constant in Great Britain. British citizens will then find the United States a more attractive place in which to loan money directly or loan money indirectly by buying bonds. To make these loans, they have to supply pounds in the foreign exchange market to obtain dollars. The increase in the supply of pounds results in depreciation of the pound and appreciation of the dollar.

Changes in Relative Expected Returns on Stocks, Real Estate, and Production Facilities International investing extends beyond buying foreign bonds. It also includes international investments in stocks and real estate as well as foreign purchases of factories and production facilities. Other things equal, the extent of this foreign investment depends on relative expected returns. To make the investments, investors in one country must sell their own local currency to purchase the foreign currencies needed for their foreign investments.

For instance, suppose that investing in England suddenly becomes more popular due to a more positive outlook regarding expected returns on English stocks, real estate, and production facilities. U.S. investors therefore will sell U.S. assets to buy more assets in England. The U.S. assets will be sold for dollars, which will then be brought to the foreign exchange market and exchanged for pounds, which will in turn be used to purchase British assets. The increased demand for pounds in the foreign exchange market will cause the pound to appreciate and therefore the dollar to depreciate relative to the pound.

purchasing-power-parity theory The idea that if countries have *flexible exchange rates* (rather than *fixed exchange rates*), the exchange rates between national currencies will adjust to equate the purchasing power of various currencies. In particular, the exchange rate between any two national currencies will adjust to reflect the *price-level* differences between the two countries.

TABLE 20.2 Determinants of Exchange Rates: Factors That Change the Demand for or the Supply of a Particular Currency and Thus Alter the Exchange Rate

Determinant	Examples
Change in tastes	Japanese electronic equipment declines in popularity in the United States (Japanese yen depreciates; U.S. dollar appreciates).
	European tourists reduce visits to the United States (U.S. dollar depreciates; European euro appreciates).
Change in relative incomes	England encounters a recession, reducing its imports, while U.S. real output and real income surge, increasing U.S. imports (British pound appreciates; U.S. dollar depreciates).
Change in relative inflation rates	Switzerland experiences a 1% inflation rate compared to Canada's 5% rate (Swiss franc appreciates; Canadian dollar depreciates).
Change in relative real interest rates	The Federal Reserve drives up interest rates in the United States, while the Bank of England takes no such action (U.S. dollar appreciates; British pound depreciates).
Changes in relative expected returns on stocks, real estate, or production facilities	Corporate tax cuts in the United States raise expected after-tax investment returns in the United States relative to those in Europe (U.S. dollar appreciates; the euro depreciates).
Speculation	Currency traders believe South Korea will have much greater inflation than Taiwan (South Korean won depreciates; Taiwanese dollar appreciates).
	Currency traders think Norway's interest rates will plummet relative to Denmark's rates (Norway's krone depreciates; Denmark's krone appreciates).

Speculation *Currency speculators* buy and sell currencies with an eye toward reselling or repurchasing them at a profit. Suppose speculators expect the U.S. economy to (1) grow more rapidly than the British economy and (2) experience more rapid inflation than Britain. These expectations translate into an anticipation that the pound will appreciate and the dollar will depreciate. Speculators who are holding dollars will therefore try to convert them into pounds. This effort will increase the demand for pounds and cause the dollar price of pounds to rise (that is, cause the dollar to depreciate). A self-fulfilling prophecy occurs: The pound appreciates and the dollar depreciates because speculators act on the belief that these changes will in fact take place. In this way, speculation can cause changes in exchange rates.

Table 20.2 provides additional examples of the determinants of exchange rates; the table is worth careful study.

Disadvantages of Flexible Exchange Rates

Flexible exchange rates may cause several significant problems, all related to the fact that flexible exchange rates are often volatile and can change by a large amount in just a few weeks or months. In addition, they often take substantial swings that can last several years or more.

Uncertainty and Diminished Trade The risks and uncertainties associated with flexible exchange rates may discourage the flow of trade. Suppose a U.S. automobile dealer contracts to purchase 10 British cars for £150,000. At the current exchange rate of, say, $2 for £1, the U.S. importer expects to pay $300,000 for these automobiles. But if during the 3-month delivery period the exchange rate shifts to $3 for £1, the £150,000 payment contracted by the U.S. importer will become $450,000.

That increase in the dollar price of pounds may thus turn the U.S. importer's anticipated profit into a substantial loss. Aware of the possibly adverse change in the exchange rate, the U.S. importer may not be willing to assume the risks involved. The U.S. firm may confine its operations to domestic automobiles, thereby reducing the volume of international trade.

The same thing can happen with investments. Assume that when the exchange rate is $3 to £1, a U.S. firm invests $30,000 (or £10,000) in a British enterprise. It estimates a return of 10 percent; that is, it anticipates annual earnings of $3,000, or £1,000. Suppose these expectations prove correct in that the British firm earns £1,000 in the first year on the £10,000 investment. But suppose that during the year, the value of the dollar appreciates to $2 = £1. The absolute return is now only $2,000 (rather than $3,000), and the rate of return falls from the anticipated 10 percent to only $6\frac{2}{3}$ percent (= $2,000/$30,000).

Investment is always risky. But the risk of changing exchange rates affects only international investments, not domestic investments. That added risk may persuade the U.S. investor not to venture overseas.

Terms-of-Trade Changes A decline in the international value of its currency will worsen a nation's terms of trade. For example, an increase in the dollar price of a pound will mean that the United States must export more goods and services to finance a specific level of imports from Britain.

Instability Flexible exchange rates may destabilize the domestic economy because wide fluctuations in the exchange rate may stimulate and then depress domestic industries that produce exported goods. If the U.S. economy is operating at full employment and its currency depreciates, the results will be inflationary, for two reasons. (1) Foreign demand for U.S. goods may rise, increasing total spending and pulling up U.S. prices. Also, the prices of all U.S. imports will increase. (2) Conversely, appreciation of the dollar will lower U.S. exports and increase imports, possibly causing unemployment.

Flexible or floating exchange rates also may complicate the use of domestic stabilization policies that seek full employment and price stability, especially in nations whose exports and imports are large relative to their total domestic output.

QUICK REVIEW

20.3

▶ Under a flexible exchange rate system, exchange rates are determined by the demand for, and supply of, individual national currencies in the foreign exchange market.

▶ Determinants of flexible exchange rates (factors that shift currency supply and demand curves) include (a) changes in tastes; (b) relative national incomes; (c) relative inflation rates; (d) real interest rates; (e) relative expected returns on stocks, real estate, and production facilities; and (f) speculation.

▶ The volatility of flexible exchange rates may have several negative consequences, including discouraging international trade, worsening a nation's terms of trade, and destabilizing a nation's domestic economy by depressing export industries.

Fixed Exchange Rates

>> **LO20.4** Distinguish between flexible and fixed exchange rates.

To circumvent the disadvantages of flexible exchange rates, governments have at times fixed or "pegged" their exchange rates. Under a fixed exchange rate, the government stands ready to buy or sell as much of its own currency as is demanded or supplied at the constant (fixed) exchange rate that it announces.

Suppose that the U.S. government decides to fix the dollar-pound exchange rate at $2 = £1. To enforce that peg, the U.S. government must stand ready to exchange both pounds for dollars as well as dollars for pounds at the fixed ratio of $2 = £1. If Americans want to exchange $20 billion for pounds, the U.S. government will need to come up with 10 billion pounds (= the required number of pounds at the $2 = £1 exchange rate). And if Britons wish to exchange £6 billion for dollars, the U.S. government will have to come up with 12 billion dollars (= required number of dollars at the $2 = £1 exchange rate).

Foreign Exchange Market Replaced by Government Peg

As long as the U.S. government is able to come up with the necessary amounts of both dollars (to satisfy exchange requests for pounds) and pounds (to satisfy exchange requests for dollars), the fixed exchange rate will preempt the foreign exchange market. All buying and selling of pounds for dollars or dollars for pounds will take place with the U.S. government. The U.S. government will *become* the dollar-pound foreign exchange market.

There will be no other dollar-pound market because, as long as the U.S. government can maintain the peg, there will be no other exchange rate that buyers and sellers will both simultaneously prefer, and thus no possibility of a given buyer and a given seller ever voluntarily agreeing to exchange dollars for pounds at any other exchange rate. To understand why, consider an exchange rate like $3 = £1. British citizens wishing to convert pounds to dollars will prefer $3 = £1 to the $2 = £1 exchange rate being offered by the U.S. government because each of their pounds would convert into $3 rather than $2. But will British citizens be able to find anyone willing to take the opposite end of the deal and exchange dollars for pounds at a $3 = £1 exchange rate? The answer is no, because anyone wishing to convert dollars to pounds can go to the U.S. government and exchange money at the rate of $2 = £1, under which they will have to give up only $2 (rather than $3) to buy £1. So while British citizens prefer any exchange rate that gives them more dollars per pound than the $2 = £1 rate being offered by the U.S. government, they are not going to find anybody willing to exchange money at those rates. Thus anybody who wants to exchange pounds for dollars will end up dealing with the U.S. government and exchanging money at the $2 = £1 fixed rate.

You should take a moment to convince yourself that the reverse is also true: While Americans would prefer an exchange rate that requires them to give up less than $2 for each £1, no British citizen would willingly accept a rate lower than $2 = £1 because doing so would mean receiving fewer dollars for their pounds than if they exchanged their pounds at the $2 = £1 exchange rate being offered by the U.S. government. So everyone wishing to exchange dollars for pounds will also end up dealing with the U.S. government and exchanging money at the $2 = £1 fixed exchange rate.

Note, however, that if the U.S. government ever stops honoring its pledge to exchange dollars for pounds and pounds for dollars at the $2 = £1 exchange rate, a private market for foreign exchange will instantly pop back into existence to connect the buyers and sellers of dollars and pounds. Because the exchange rate will be determined by supply and demand once again, it may end up at an equilibrium value that is substantially different from the fixed exchange rate that the government abandoned.

Official Reserves

A government that opts for a fixed exchange rate typically places its central bank in charge of day-to-day operations. It thus becomes the central bank's task to exchange as much local currency for foreign currency and as much foreign currency for local currency as is necessary each day to maintain the peg.

Satisfying requests to exchange foreign currency for local currency is easy, as the central bank has the legal right to print as much local currency as it wants. But to satisfy requests to exchange local currency for foreign currency, the central bank must maintain a stock (inventory) of foreign currency because it can't legally create additional units of any other country's money.

The stock of the particular foreign currency that is used to maintain the fixed exchange rate is just one component of the **official reserves** that the central bank will maintain for the government. The official reserves will consist not only of stockpiles of various foreign currencies but also stockpiles of bonds issued by foreign governments, gold reserves, and special reserves held at the International Monetary Fund. The stockpiles of foreign currencies are called **foreign-exchange reserves,** or, less formally, FX reserves.

official reserves Foreign *currencies* owned by the central bank of a nation.

foreign-exchange reserves Stockpiles of foreign currencies maintained by a nation's *central bank.* Obtained when the *central bank* sells local currency in exchange for foreign currency in the *foreign exchange market.*

Defending a Peg by Altering Demand or Supply

Because a central bank that sets a fixed exchange rate must stand ready to buy and sell as much domestic and foreign currency as is demanded each day, it is possible that a central bank will run out of FX reserves. If that happens, the central bank will have to abandon its peg unless it (1) can get an emergency loan of foreign currency from the International Monetary Fund or (2) take drastic steps to alter or limit the quantities of currency demanded and supplied each day. Those drastic steps fall into three categories.

Trade Policies A nation that is pursuing a fixed exchange rate can undertake policies that alter the volume of international trade and finance as a way of helping to maintain a peg. The United States could try, for instance, to maintain the $2 = £1 exchange rate in the face of a shortage of pounds by discouraging imports (thereby reducing the demand for pounds) and encouraging exports (thus increasing the supply of pounds). Imports could be reduced by means of new tariffs or import quotas; special taxes could be levied on the interest and dividends U.S. financial investors receive from foreign investments. Also, the U.S. government could subsidize certain U.S. exports to increase the supply of pounds.

The fundamental problem is that these policies reduce the volume of world trade and change its makeup from what is economically desirable. When nations impose tariffs, quotas, and the like, they lose some of the economic benefits of a free flow of world trade. That loss should not be underestimated: Trade barriers by one nation lead to retaliatory responses from other nations, multiplying the loss.

exchange controls Restrictions that a government may impose over the quantity of foreign currency demand by its citizens and *firms* and over the *rate of exchange* as a way to limit the nation's quantity of *outpayments* relative to its quantity of *inpayments* (in order to eliminate a *payments deficit*).

Exchange Controls and Rationing Another option is to adopt rationing via exchange controls (which are also sometimes referred to as capital controls). Under **exchange controls,** the U.S.

government could handle the problem of a pound shortage by requiring that all pounds obtained by U.S. exporters be sold to the federal government. Then the government would allocate or ration this limited supply of pounds among various U.S. importers. This policy would restrict the value of U.S. imports to the amount of foreign exchange earned by U.S. exports. Assuming balance in the capital and financial account, there would then be no balance-of-payments deficit.

There are major objections to exchange controls:

- *Distorted trade* Like *trade controls* (tariffs, quotas, and export subsidies), exchange controls will distort the pattern of international trade away from the pattern suggested by comparative advantage.

- *Favoritism* The process of rationing scarce foreign exchange might lead to government favoritism toward selected importers (big contributors to reelection campaigns, for example).

- *Restricted choice* Controls will limit freedom of consumer choice. The U.S. consumers who prefer Volkswagens might have to buy Chevrolets. The business opportunities for some U.S. importers might be impaired if the government decides to limit imports.

- *Black markets* Enforcement problems are likely under exchange controls. U.S. importers might want foreign exchange badly enough to pay more than the $2 = £1$ official rate, setting the stage for black-market dealings between importers and illegal sellers of foreign exchange.

Domestic Macroeconomic Adjustments A final way to help maintain a fixed exchange rate is to use domestic stabilization policies (monetary policy and fiscal policy) to eliminate a shortage of foreign currency. Tax hikes, reductions in government spending, and a high-interest-rate policy will reduce total spending in the U.S. economy and, consequently, domestic income. Because the volume of imports varies directly with domestic income, demand for British goods, and therefore for pounds, will be restrained.

If these "contractionary" policies reduce the domestic price level relative to Britain's, U.S. buyers of consumer and capital goods will divert their demands from British goods to U.S. goods, reducing the demand for pounds. Moreover, the high-interest-rate policy will lift U.S. interest rates relative to those in Britain.

Lower prices on U.S. goods and higher U.S. interest rates will increase British imports of U.S. goods and increase British financial investment in the United States. Both developments will increase the supply of pounds. The combination of a decrease in the demand for and an increase in the supply of pounds will reduce or eliminate the original U.S. balance-of-payments deficit.

Maintaining fixed exchange rates by such means is hardly appealing. The "price" of exchange-rate stability for the United States will be a decline in output, employment, and price levels—in other words, a recession. Maintaining a peg and achieving domestic stability are both important national economic goals, but to sacrifice macroeconomic stability simply to defend a currency peg would be to let the tail wag the dog.

This chapter's Last Word discusses these concerns in the context of the so-called exchange rate trilemma, which points out that governments have to make hard choices when it comes to choosing an exchange rate policy.

▶ To circumvent the disadvantages of flexible exchange rates, at times nations have fixed or "pegged" their exchange rates.

▶ Under a system of fixed exchange rates, nations set their exchange rates and then maintain them by buying or selling official reserves of currencies, establishing trade barriers, employing exchange controls, or incurring inflation or recession.

▶ Under a fixed exchange rate, any increase (decrease) in foreign exchange reserves will automatically generate an accompanying increase (decrease) in the domestic money supply that can cause inflation (deflation) unless it is offset by other policy actions.

The Current Exchange Rate System: The Managed Float

>> LO20.5 Explain the current system of managed floating exchange rates.

Over the past 140 years, the world's nations have used three different exchange-rate systems. From 1879 to 1934, most nations used a gold standard, which implicitly created fixed exchange rates. From 1944 to 1971, most countries participated in the Bretton Woods system, which was a fixed-exchange-rate system indirectly tied to gold. Since 1971, most countries have mixed mostly flexible exchange rates with occasional **currency interventions** during which a government buys or sells foreign exchange in order to stabilize short-term changes in exchange rates or to correct exchange rate imbalances that are negatively affecting the world economy.

Because the current exchange-rate system mixes mostly flexible exchange rates with occasional government intervention, it is thought of as generating **managed floating exchange rates.** Under this system, the major currencies such as dollars, euros, pounds, and yen fluctuate in response to changes in supply and demand. At the same time, some developing nations like China peg their currency to the U.S. dollar, and then allow their currency to fluctuate with it against other currencies. Also, some nations peg the value of their currencies to a "basket" or group of other currencies.

How well does the managed float work? It has both proponents and critics.

In Support of the Managed Float Proponents of the managed-float system argue that it has functioned far better than many experts anticipated. Skeptics had predicted that fluctuating exchange rates would reduce world trade and finance. But in real terms, world trade under the managed float has grown tremendously over the past several decades. Moreover, as supporters are quick to point out, currency crises, such as those in Turkey and Lebanon in 2021, were not the result of the floating-exchange-rate system itself. Rather, the abrupt currency devaluations and depreciations resulted from internal problems in those nations.

Proponents also point out that the managed float has weathered severe economic turbulence that might have caused a fixed-rate system to break down. Events including the OPEC oil embargoes of 1970s, major national recessions in the 1980s, and the collapse of the Soviet Bloc in the 1990s all caused substantial imbalances in international trade and finance, as did soaring U.S. budget deficits in the 2000s, the Great Recession of 2007–2009, and the European Debt Crisis of the mid-2010s. Flexible rates enabled the system to adjust to all these events, whereas the same events would have put unbearable pressure on a fixed-rate system.

Concerns with the Managed Float There is still much sentiment in favor of greater exchange-rate stability. Those favoring more stable exchange rates see problems with the current system. They argue that the excessive volatility of exchange rates under the managed float threatens the prosperity of economies that rely heavily on exports. Several financial crises in individual nations (including Mexico, South Korea, Indonesia, Thailand, Russia, and Brazil) were exacerbated by abrupt changes in exchange rates. These crises led to massive "bailouts" of those economies via loans from the International Monetary Fund (IMF). But the availability of IMF bailouts may spur moral hazard. Nations may undertake risky and inappropriate economic policies because they expect the IMF to bail them out if problems arise. Moreover, some exchange-rate volatility has occurred even when underlying economic and financial conditions were relatively stable, suggesting that speculation plays too large a role in determining exchange rates.

Skeptics say the managed float is basically a "nonsystem" because the guidelines as to what each nation may or may not do with its exchange rates are not specific enough to keep the system working in the long run. Nations inevitably will be tempted to intervene in the foreign exchange market, not merely to smooth out short-term fluctuations in exchange rates but also to prop up their currency if it is chronically weak, manipulate the exchange rate to achieve domestic stabilization goals, or utilize an artificially depreciated currency to give its exporters an unfair advantage in international trade.

So what are we to conclude? Flexible exchange rates have not worked perfectly, but they have not failed miserably. Thus far they have survived, and no doubt have eased, several major shocks to the international trading system. Meanwhile, the "managed" part of the float has given nations some sense of control over their collective economic destinies. On balance, most economists favor continuation of the present system of "almost" flexible exchange rates.

---

currency intervention
A government's buying and selling of its own currency or foreign currencies to alter international exchange rates.

managed floating exchange rate An *exchange rate* that is allowed to change (float) as a result of changes in *currency* supply and demand but at times is altered (managed) by governments via their buying and selling of particular currencies.

▶ The managed floating system of exchange rates (1971–present) relies on foreign exchange markets to establish equilibrium exchange rates.

▶ Under the system, nations can buy and sell official reserves of foreign currency to stabilize short-term changes in exchange rates or to correct exchange-rate imbalances that are negatively affecting the world economy.

▶ Proponents point out that international trade and investment have grown tremendously under the system. Critics say that it is a "nonsystem" and argue that the exchange rate volatility allowed under the managed float discourages international trade and investment. That is, trade and investment would be even larger if exchange rates were more stable.

QUICK REVIEW
20.5

Recent U.S. Trade Deficits

>> **LO20.6** Identify the causes and consequences of recent U.S. trade deficits.

As Figure 20.2a shows, the United States has experienced large and persistent trade deficits in recent decades. These deficits rose rapidly in the early 2000s, with the trade deficit on goods and services peaking at $764 billion in 2006. The trade deficit on goods and services then declined precipitously to just $395 billion in 2009 as consumers and businesses greatly curtailed their purchases of imports during the Great Recession of 2007–2009. As the economy recovered from that recession, the trade deficit on goods and services began rising again and reached $555 billion in 2011 before a series of annual deficits that ranged between $447 billion and $581 billion through 2019.

The strong stimulus spending enacted to fight the COVID-19 pandemic in 2020 and the strong rebound in U.S. economic growth during 2021 caused cash-rich U.S. consumers to increase their purchases of imports at the same time that many foreign consumers cut back on their purchases of U.S. exports (because their countries were experiencing slower recoveries from the COVID-19 recession than the United States was). The result was a massive $861 billion trade deficit in goods and services for the United States in 2021.

The current account deficit (Figure 20.2b) reached a then-record high of $817 billion in 2006, equivalent to about 6.0 percent of that year's GDP. The current account deficit subsequently declined to $380 billion—2.6 percent of GDP—in the recession year 2009. After the 2007–2009 recession ended, the current account deficit fluctuated but generally tended to increase, reaching $472 billion in 2019, or about 2.2 percent of that year's GDP. In 2021, however, the current account deficit soared to $822 billion, thereby exceeding 2006's previous record of $817 billion. But because U.S. GDP had grown 66 percent larger between 2006 and 2021, the $822 billion current account deficit of 2021 was only about 3.6 percent of that year's GDP, meaning that it was, as a percentage of GDP, substantially less than the $817 billion current account deficit recorded in 2006.

Causes of the Trade Deficits

The large U.S. trade deficits have had several causes. First, the U.S. economy expanded more rapidly between 2002 and 2007 than the economies of several U.S. trading partners. The strong U.S. income growth that accompanied that economic growth enabled Americans to greatly increase their purchases of imported products. In contrast, Japan and some European nations suffered recession or experienced relatively slow income growth over that same period. So consumers in those countries increased their purchases of U.S. exports much less rapidly than Americans increased their purchases of foreign imports.

FIGURE 20.2 **U.S. trade deficits, 2005–2021.**

(a) The United States experienced large deficits in *goods* and in *goods and services* between 2005 and 2021. (b) The U.S. current account, generally reflecting the goods and services deficit, was also in substantial deficit. The large current account and trade deficits are expected to continue for many years to come.

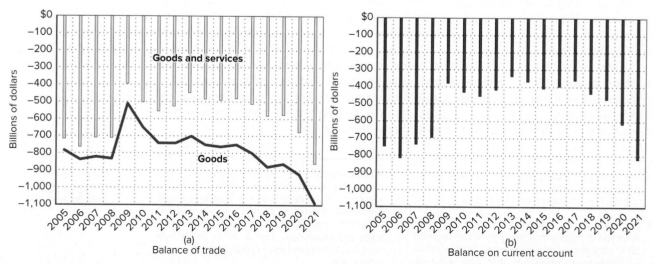

(a)
Balance of trade

(b)
Balance on current account

Source: Bureau of Economic Analysis.

Another factor explaining the large trade deficits is the enormous U.S. trade imbalance with China. In 2021 the United States imported $355 billion more of goods and services from China than it exported to China. Even in the recession year 2009, the trade deficit with China was $220 billion. The 2021 deficit with China was 50 percent larger than the combined deficits with Mexico ($108 billion), Germany ($70 billion), and Japan ($60 billion). The United States is China's largest export market, and although China has greatly increased its imports from the United States, its standard of living has not yet risen sufficiently for its households to afford large quantities of U.S. products. Adding to the problem, China's government has fixed the exchange rate of its currency, the yuan, to a basket of currencies that includes the U.S. dollar. Therefore, China's large trade surpluses with the United States have not caused the yuan to appreciate much against the U.S. dollar. Greater appreciation of the yuan would have made Chinese goods more expensive in the United States and reduced U.S. imports from China. In China, a stronger yuan would have reduced the dollar price of U.S. goods and increased Chinese purchases of U.S. exports. That combination—reduced U.S. imports from China and increased U.S. exports to China—would have reduced the large U.S. trade imbalance.

A declining U.S. saving rate (= saving/total income) also contributed to the large U.S. trade deficits. Up until the recession of 2007–2009, the U.S. saving rate declined substantially, while its investment rate (= investment/total income) increased. The gap between U.S. investment and U.S. saving was filled by foreign purchases of U.S. real and financial assets, which created a large surplus on the U.S. capital and financial account. Because foreign savers were willing to finance a large part of U.S. investment, Americans were able to save less and consume more. Part of that added consumption spending was on imported goods.

Finally, many foreigners simply view U.S. assets favorably because of the relatively high risk-adjusted rates of return they provide. The purchase of those assets provides foreign currency to Americans that enables them to finance their strong appetite for imported goods. The capital account surpluses, therefore, may partially cause the high U.S. trade deficits, not just result from those high deficits.

Implications of U.S. Trade Deficits

The prerecession U.S. trade deficits were the largest ever run by a major industrial nation. Whether the large trade deficits should be of significant concern to the United States and the rest of the world is debatable. Most economists see both benefits and costs to trade deficits.

Increased Current Consumption At the time a trade deficit or a current account deficit is occurring, American consumers benefit. A trade deficit means that the United States is receiving more goods and services as imports from abroad than it is sending out as exports. Taken alone, a trade deficit allows the United States to consume outside its production possibilities curve. It augments the domestic standard of living. But there is a catch: The gain in present consumption may come at the expense of reduced future consumption. When and if the current account deficit declines, Americans may have to consume less than before and perhaps even less than they produce.

Increased U.S. Indebtedness A trade deficit is considered unfavorable because it must be financed by borrowing from the rest of the world, selling off assets, or dipping into official reserves. Recall that current account deficits are financed by surpluses in the capital and financial accounts. Such surpluses require a net inflow of dollars to buy U.S. assets, including debt issued by Americans. Therefore, when U.S. exports are insufficient to finance U.S. imports, the United States increases both its debt to people abroad and the value of foreign claims against assets in the United States. Financing of the U.S. trade deficit has resulted in a larger foreign accumulation of claims against U.S. financial and real assets than the U.S. claim against foreign assets. In 2021, foreigners owned about $18 trillion more of U.S. assets (corporations, land, stocks, bonds, loan notes) than U.S. citizens and institutions owned of foreign assets.

If the United States wants to regain ownership of these domestic assets, at some future time it will have to export more than it imports. At that time, domestic consumption will be lower because the United States will need to send more of its output abroad than it receives as imports. Therefore, the current consumption gains delivered by U.S. current account deficits may mean permanent debt, permanent foreign ownership, or large sacrifices of future consumption.

We say "may mean" because the foreign lending to U.S. firms and foreign investment in the United States increases the U.S. capital stock. U.S. production capacity therefore might increase

LAST WORD

The Exchange Rate Trilemma

Countries Cannot Achieve All Three of the Most Coveted Goals of Exchange Rate Policy Simultaneously. The Best They Can Do is "Two Out of Three."

Countries must choose between three possible Exchange Rate Policies. This three-way choice—or "trilemma"—is made more difficult by the fact that each Policy can achieve only two out three desirable Goals. Countries would love to be able to achieve all three goals at once. But only two out of three can be obtained at a time—which means that policymakers have to think very carefully about which two Goals they care about the most and, thus, which Policy they need to select in order to achieve those two Goals.

In the nearby triangular figure, each corner represents one of the three Goals.

- Goal A is *Exchange-Rate Stability*, meaning that a country's exchange rate with other currencies will remain stable (or even perfectly constant) over time.

- Goal B is *Free Financial and Trade Flows*, meaning that anyone can buy or sell as much of the country's currency as they would like in order to buy or sell assets anywhere in the world or to import or export goods to whatever extent they please.

- Goal C is an *Independent Monetary Policy* that can always be directed toward setting interest rates and monetary policy so as to best suit the needs of the country's own domestic economy and its own unique business cycle (rather than having to focus on other factors).

As we mentioned above, it is only possible for countries to achieve two out of the three Goals at a time. But countries do not choose exchange rate Goals; they choose exchange-rate Policies. As it turns out, there are exactly three exchange-rate Policies to choose from. In the figure, the three Policies are represented by the three sides of the triangle, with each side connecting the two Goals that it can achieve.

- Policy #1 is Exchange Controls, meaning rules set by the central bank as to how much money individuals and businesses can exchange per day or per month if there is a fixed exchange rate or a highly constrained dirty float. If a country opts for Policy #1 (Exchange Controls), then it can achieve Goal A (*Exchange Rate Stability)* and Goal C (an *Independent Monetary Policy*) but not Goal B (*Free Financial and Trade Flows*).

- By contrast, if a country opts for Policy #2 (a Fixed Exchange Rate), then it can achieve Goal A (*Exchange Rate Stability*) and Goal B (*Free Financial and Trade Flows*) but not Goal C (an *Independent Monetary Policy*).

- Finally, if a country opts for Policy #3 (a Floating Exchange Rate), then it can achieve Goal B (*Free Financial and Trade Flows*) and Goal C (an *Independent Monetary Policy*) but not Goal A (*Exchange Rate Stability*).

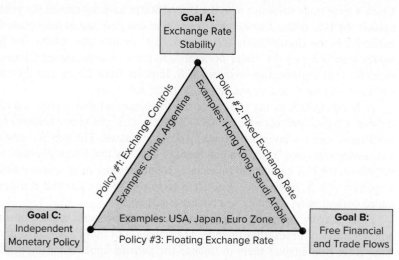

Note again that the side of the triangle that represents a particular Policy connects to the two Goals that that Policy can achieve. Also note that the side of the triangle that represents a particular policy lies *opposite* to the Goal that it cannot achieve. So, for example, the side of the triangle that is labeled Policy #2 (Fixed Exchange Rate) connects to the two goals that it can achieve (Goals A and B) while lying opposite to the goal that it cannot achieve (Goal C).

Let's give you some intuition about why countries can only achieve two out of the three Goals when they select a particular exchange-rate Policy. Consider Hong Kong, which uses Policy #2 (a Fixed Exchange Rate). In pursuing that Policy, Hong Kong must exchange as much or as little of its own currency as is necessary each day to maintain its fixed exchange rate with the U.S. dollar. But that means that its monetary policy is entirely devoted to maintaining its fixed exchange rate and thus cannot be used for expansive or restrictive monetary policy. By choosing to maintain a fixed exchange rate, Hong Kong loses the ability to maintain an *Independent Monetary Policy* (Goal C). Yet, at the same time, its choice of a Fixed Exchange Rate does ensure that it will achieve *Exchange Rate Stability* (Goal A) and *Free Financial and Trade Flows* (Goal B) since a fixed-exchange rate is by definition stable and the willingness of the Hong Kong central bank to exchange as much or as little of its own currency as is necessary to preserve its exchange rate peg means that there will always be as many Hong Kong dollars as people may want for international trade or international asset transactions.

To test yourself, see if you can explain why Policy #1 precludes Goal B and why Policy #3 precludes Goal A.

more rapidly than otherwise because of a large surplus on the capital and financial account. Faster increases in production capacity and real GDP enhance the economy's ability to service foreign debt and buy back real capital, if that is desired.

Trade deficits therefore are a mixed blessing. The long-term impacts of the record-high U.S. trade deficits are largely unknown. That "unknown" worries some economists, who are concerned that foreigners will lose financial confidence in the United States. If that happens, those foreigners will restrict their lending to American households and businesses and also reduce their purchases of U.S. assets. Both actions will decrease the demand for U.S. dollars in the foreign exchange market and cause the U.S. dollar to depreciate. A sudden, large depreciation of the U.S. dollar might disrupt world trade and negatively affect economic growth worldwide. Other economists, however, downplay this scenario. Because any decline in the U.S. capital and financial account surplus is automatically met with a decline in the current account deficit, U.S. net exports would rise and the overall impact on the American economy would be slight.

**QUICK REVIEW
20.6**

▶ The United States has had large trade deficits in recent decades.

▶ Causes include (a) more rapid income growth in the United States than in Japan and some European nations, resulting in expanding U.S. imports relative to exports; (b) the emergence of a large trade deficit with China; (c) continuing large trade deficits with oil-exporting nations; and (d) a large surplus in the capital and financial account, which enabled Americans to reduce their saving and buy more imports.

▶ The severe recession of 2007–2009 in the United States substantially lowered the U.S. trade deficit by reducing American spending on imports.

▶ U.S. trade deficits have produced current increases in the living standards of U.S. consumers but the accompanying surpluses on the capital and financial account have increased U.S. debt to the rest of the world and increased foreign ownership of assets in the United States.

Summary

LO20.1 Explain the two types of international financial transactions.

International financial transactions involve trade either in currently produced goods and services or in preexisting assets. Exports of goods, services, and assets create inflows of money, while imports cause outflows of money. If buyers and sellers use different currencies, then foreign exchange transactions take place so that exporters can be paid in their own currency.

LO20.2 Define and explain the two components of the balance of payments: the current account and the capital and financial account.

The balance of payments records all international trade and financial transactions taking place between a given nation and the rest of the world. The balance on goods and services (the trade balance) compares exports and imports of both goods and services. The current account balance includes not only goods and services transactions but also net investment income and net transfers.

The capital and financial account includes (*a*) the net amount of the nation's debt forgiveness and (*b*) the nation's sale of real and financial assets to people living abroad less its purchases of real and financial assets from foreigners.

The current account and the capital and financial account always sum to zero. A deficit in the current account is always offset by a surplus in the capital and financial account. Conversely, a surplus in the current account is always offset by a deficit in the capital and financial account.

LO20.3 Explain how exchange rates are determined.

Flexible or floating exchange rates between international currencies are determined by the demand for and supply of those currencies. Under flexible rates, a currency will depreciate or appreciate as a result of changes in tastes, relative income changes, relative changes in inflation rates, relative changes in real interest rates, and speculation. The exchange-rate fluctuations that occur under a flexible exchange rate system introduce uncertainty that can reduce the volume of international trade and destabilize the local economy.

LO20.4 Distinguish between flexible and fixed exchange rates.

Some countries have their central banks fix, or peg, their exchange rates to a particular value in order to eliminate the uncertainty about future exchange rates that arises under a floating exchange rate system. Because foreign currencies must be bought and sold to maintain a fixed exchange rate, the central bank will maintain reserves (stockpiles) of various foreign currencies. Those foreign exchange (FX) reserves are a subset of a nation's overall collection of official reserves, which can include gold, foreign bonds, and special reserves held with the International Monetary Fund in addition to its holdings of FX reserves.

To maintain a fixed exchange rate, a central bank will simultaneously stand ready to sell as much foreign currency as buyers demand at the fixed exchange rate and buy as much foreign currency as sellers wish to supply at the fixed exchange rate. If FX reserves fall continuously, they may become exhausted. In such situations, and assuming the country wishes to continue the peg, the country will have to invoke protectionist trade policies, engage in exchange controls, or endure undesirable domestic macroeconomic adjustments.

LO20.5 Explain the current system of managed floating exchange rates.

Since 1971, most of the world's major economies have used a system of managed floating exchange rates. Under a managed float, market forces generally set rates, although governments intervene with varying frequency to alter their exchange rates.

LO20.6 Identify the causes and consequences of recent U.S. trade deficits.

Between 1997 and 2007, the United States had large and rising trade deficits, which are projected to last well into the future. Causes of the trade deficits include (*a*) more rapid income growth in the United States than in Japan and some European nations, resulting in expanding U.S. imports relative to exports, (*b*) the emergence of a large trade deficit with China, and (*c*) a large surplus in the capital and financial account, which enabled Americans to reduce their saving and buy more imports.

U.S. trade deficits have produced current increases in the living standards of U.S. consumers. The accompanying surpluses on the capital and financial account have increased U.S, debt to the rest of the world and increased foreign ownership of assets in the United States. This greater foreign investment in the United States, however, has undoubtedly increased U.S. production possibilities.

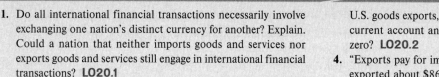

Terms and Concepts

international trade	trade surplus	purchasing-power-parity theory
international asset transactions	balance on current account	official reserves
balance of payments	capital and financial account	foreign-exchange reserves
current account	balance on capital and financial account	exchange controls
balance on goods and services	flexible- or floating-exchange-rate system	currency interventions
trade deficit	fixed-exchange-rate system	managed floating exchange rates

Discussion Questions

1. Do all international financial transactions necessarily involve exchanging one nation's distinct currency for another? Explain. Could a nation that neither imports goods and services nor exports goods and services still engage in international financial transactions? **LO20.1**

2. Explain: "U.S. exports earn supplies of foreign currencies that Americans can use to finance imports." Indicate whether each of the following creates a demand for or a supply of European euros in foreign exchange markets: **LO20.1**
   a. A U.S. airline firm purchases several Airbus planes assembled in France.
   b. A German automobile firm decides to build an assembly plant in South Carolina.
   c. A U.S. college student decides to spend a year studying at the Sorbonne in Paris.
   d. An Italian manufacturer ships machinery from one Italian port to another on a Liberian freighter.
   e. The U.S. economy grows faster than the French economy.
   f. A U.S. government bond held by a Spanish citizen matures, and the loan amount is paid back to that person.
   g. It is widely expected that the euro will depreciate in the near future.

3. What do the plus signs and negative signs signify in the U.S. balance-of-payments statement? Which of the following items appear in the current account and which appear in the capital and financial account: U.S. purchases of assets abroad, U.S. services imports, foreign purchases of assets in the United States,

U.S. goods exports, U.S. net investment income? Why must the current account and the capital and financial account sum to zero? **LO20.2**

4. "Exports pay for imports. Yet in 2021 the nations of the world exported about $861 billion more of goods and services to the United States than they imported from the United States." Resolve the apparent inconsistency of these two statements. **LO20.2**

5. Generally speaking, how is the dollar price of euros determined? Cite a factor that might increase the dollar price of euros. Cite a different factor that might decrease the dollar price of euros. Explain: "A rise in the dollar price of euros necessarily means a fall in the euro price of dollars." Illustrate and elaborate: "The dollar-euro exchange rate provides a direct link between the prices of goods and services produced in the eurozone and in the United States." Explain the purchasing-power-parity theory of exchange rates, using the euro-dollar exchange rate as an illustration. **LO20.3**

6. Suppose that a Swiss watchmaker imports watch components from Sweden and exports watches to the United States. Also suppose the dollar depreciates, and the Swedish krona appreciates, relative to the Swiss franc. Speculate as to how each would hurt the Swiss watchmaker. **LO20.3**

7. Explain why the U.S. demand for Mexican pesos slopes downward and the supply of pesos to Americans slopes upward. Assuming a system of flexible exchange rates between Mexico and the United States, indicate whether each of the following

will cause the Mexican peso to appreciate or depreciate, other things equal: **LO20.3**

  a. The United States unilaterally reduces tariffs on Mexican products.

  b. Mexico encounters severe inflation.

  c. Deteriorating political relations reduce American tourism in Mexico.

  d. The U.S. economy moves into a severe recession.

  e. The United States engages in a high-interest-rate monetary policy.

  f. Mexican products become more fashionable to U.S. consumers.

  g. The Mexican government encourages U.S. firms to invest in Mexican oil fields.

  h. The rate of productivity growth in the United States diminishes sharply.

8. Explain why you agree or disagree with the following statements. Assume other things equal. **LO20.3**

  a. A country that grows faster than its major trading partners can expect the international value of its currency to depreciate.

  b. A nation whose interest rate is rising more rapidly than interest rates in other nations can expect the international value of its currency to appreciate.

  c. A country's currency will appreciate if its inflation rate is less than that of the rest of the world.

9. Is it accurate to think of a fixed exchange rate as a simultaneous price ceiling and price floor? Explain. **LO20.4**

10. What have been the major causes of the large U.S. trade deficits in recent years? What are the major benefits and costs associated with trade deficits? Explain: "A trade deficit means that a nation is receiving more goods and services from abroad than it is sending abroad." How can that situation be considered "unfavorable"? **LO20.6**

11. **LAST WORD** Explain why Policy #1 precludes the achievement of Goal B while promoting the success of Goals A and C. Then explain why Policy #3 makes it impossible for a country to achieve Goal A while simultaneously helping it to achieve Goals C and B.

Review Questions

1. An American company wants to buy a television from a Chinese company. The Chinese company sells its TVs for 1,200 yuan each. The current exchange rate between the U.S. dollar and the Chinese yuan is $1 = 6 yuan. How many dollars will the American company have to convert into yuan to pay for the television? **LO20.1**

  a. $7,200

  b. $1,200

  c. $200

  d. $100

2. Suppose that a country has a trade surplus of $50 billion, a balance on the capital account of $10 billion, and a balance on the current account of −$200 billion. The balance on the capital and financial account is: **LO20.2**

  a. $10 billion.

  b. $50 billion.

  c. $200 billion.

  d. −$200 billion.

3. The exchange rate between the U.S. dollar and the British pound starts at $1 = £0.5. It then changes to $1 = £0.75. Given this change, we would say that the U.S. dollar has _____ while the British pound has _____. **LO20.3**

  a. depreciated; appreciated

  b. depreciated; depreciated

  c. appreciated; depreciated

  d. appreciated; appreciated

4. A meal at a McDonald's restaurant in New York costs $8. The identical meal at a McDonald's restaurant in London costs £4. According to the purchasing-power-parity theory of exchange rates, the exchange rate between U.S. dollars and British pounds should tend to move toward: **LO20.3**

  a. $2 = £1.

  b. $1 = £2.

  c. $4 = £1.

  d. $1 = £4.

5. Suppose that the Fed is fixing the dollar-pound exchange rate at $2.50 = £1. If the Fed's reserve of pounds falls by £500 million, by how much would the supply of dollars increase, all other things equal? **LO20.4**

6. Suppose that the government of China is currently fixing the exchange rate between the U.S. dollar and the Chinese yuan at a rate of $1 = 6 yuan. Also suppose that at this exchange rate, the people who want to convert dollars to yuan are asking to convert $10 billion per day of dollars into yuan, while the people who want to convert yuan into dollars are asking to convert 36 billion yuan per day into dollars. What will happen to the size of China's official reserves of dollars? **LO20.4**

  a. They will increase.

  b. They will decrease.

  c. They will stay the same.

7. Suppose that a country follows a managed-float policy but that its exchange rate is currently floating freely. In addition, suppose that it has a massive current account deficit. Other things equal, are its official reserves increasing, decreasing, or staying the same? If it decides to engage in a currency intervention to reduce the size of its current account deficit, will it buy or sell its own currency? As it does so, will its official reserves of foreign currencies get larger or smaller? **LO20.5**

8. If the economy booms in the United States while going into recession in other countries, the U.S. trade deficit will tend to _____. **LO20.6**

  a. increase

  b. decrease

  c. remain the same

9. Other things equal, if the United States continually runs trade deficits, foreigners will own _____ U.S. assets. **LO20.6**

  a. more and more

  b. less and less

  c. the same amount of

Problems

1. Alpha's balance-of-payments data for 2020 are shown below. All figures are in billions of dollars. What are the (*a*) balance on goods, (*b*) balance on goods and services, (*c*) balance on current account, and (*d*) balance on capital and financial account? **LO20.2**

Goods exports	$+40
Goods imports	−30
Service exports	+15
Service imports	−10
Net investment income	−5
Net transfers	+10
Balance on capital account	0
Foreign purchases of Alpha assets	+20
Alpha purchases of assets abroad	−40

2. China had a $49.1 billion overall current account surplus in 2018. Assuming that China's net debt forgiveness was zero in 2018 (its capital account balance was zero), by how much did Chinese purchases of financial and real assets abroad exceed foreign purchases of Chinese financial and real assets? **LO20.2**

3. Refer to the following table, in which Q_d is the quantity of loonies demanded, P is the dollar price of loonies, Q_s is the quantity of loonies supplied in year 1, and Q_s' is the quantity of loonies supplied in year 2. All quantities are in billions and the dollar-loonie exchange rate is fully flexible. **LO20.3**

Q_d	P	Q_s	Q_s'
10	125	30	20
15	120	25	15
20	115	20	10
25	110	15	5

a. What is the equilibrium dollar price of loonies in year 1?
b. What is the equilibrium dollar price of loonies in year 2?
c. Did the loonie appreciate or did it depreciate relative to the dollar between years 1 and 2?
d. Did the dollar appreciate or did it depreciate relative to the loonie between years 1 and 2?
e. Which one of the following could have caused the change in relative values of the dollar (used in the United States) and the loonie (used in Canada) between years 1 and 2: (1) More rapid inflation in the United States than in Canada, (2) an increase in the real interest rate in the United States but not in Canada, or (3) faster income growth in the United States than in Canada?

4. Suppose that the current Canadian dollar (CAD) to U.S. dollar exchange rate is $0.85 CAD = $1 US and that the U.S. dollar price of an iPhone is $300. What is the Canadian dollar price of an iPhone? Next, suppose that the CAD to U.S. dollar exchange rate moves to $0.96 CAD = $1 US. What is the new Canadian dollar price of an iPhone? Other things equal, would you expect Canada to import more or fewer iPhones at the new exchange rate? Explain. **LO20.3**

5. **ADVANCED ANALYSIS** Return to problem 3 and assume that the exchange rate is fixed at 110. In year 1, what is the minimum initial size of the U.S. reserve of loonies such that the United States can maintain the peg throughout the year? What is the minimum initial size that is necessary at the start of year 2? Next, consider only the data for year 1. What peg should the United States set if it wants the fixed exchange rate to increase the domestic money supply by $1.2 trillion? **LO20.4**

Previous International Exchange-Rate Systems

LO20.7 Explain how exchange rates worked under the gold standard and Bretton Woods.

This chapter explained the current system of managed floating exchange rates. But before this system began in 1971, the world had previously used two other exchange rate systems: the gold standard, which implicitly created fixed exchange rates, and the Bretton Woods system, which was an explicit fixed-rate system indirectly tied to gold. Because the features and problems of these two systems help explain why we have the current system, they are well worth knowing more about.

The Gold Standard: Fixed Exchange Rates

Between 1879 and 1934 the world's major nations adhered to a fixed-rate system called the **gold standard.** Under this system, each nation had to:

- Define its currency in terms of a quantity of gold.
- Maintain a fixed relationship between its stock of gold and its money supply.
- Allow gold to be freely exported and imported.

When each nation defines its currency in terms of gold, the various national currencies have fixed relationships with one another. For example, if the United States defines $1 as worth 25 grains of gold, and Britain defines £1 as worth 50 grains of gold, then a British pound is worth 2×25 grains, or $2. This exchange rate was fixed under the gold standard. The exchange rate did not change in response to changes in currency demand and supply.

Gold Flows If we ignore the costs of packing, insuring, and shipping gold between countries, under the gold standard the rate of exchange would not vary from this $2 = £1 rate. No one in the United States would pay more than $2 = £1 because 50 grains of gold could always be bought for $2 in the United States and sold for £1 in Britain. Nor would the British pay more than £1 for $2. Why should they when they could buy 50 grains of gold in Britain for £1 and sell it in the United States for $2?

Under the gold standard, the potential free flow of gold between nations resulted in fixed exchange rates.

Domestic Macroeconomic Adjustments When currency demand or supply changes, the gold standard requires domestic macroeconomic adjustments to maintain the fixed

---

gold standard A historical system of fixed exchange rates in which nations defined their currencies in terms of gold, maintained fixed relationships between their stocks of gold and their money supplies, and allowed gold to be freely exported and imported.

---

exchange rate. To understand why, suppose that U.S. tastes change such that U.S. consumers want to buy more British goods. The resulting increase in the demand for pounds creates a shortage of pounds in the United States, implying a U.S. balance-of-payments deficit.

What will happen? Remember that the rules of the gold standard prohibit the exchange rate from moving from the fixed $2 = £1 rate. The rate cannot move to, say, a new equilibrium at $3 = £1 to correct the imbalance. Instead, gold will flow from the United States to Britain to correct the payments imbalance.

But recall that the gold standard requires participants to maintain a fixed relationship between their domestic money supplies and their quantities of gold. The flow of gold from the United States to Britain will require a reduction of the money supply in the United States. Other things equal, that outflow will reduce total spending in the United States and lower U.S. real domestic output, employment, income, and, perhaps, prices. Also, the decline in the money supply will boost U.S. interest rates.

The opposite will occur in Britain. The inflow of gold will increase the money supply, which will increase total spending in Britain. Domestic output, employment, income, and, perhaps, prices will rise. The British interest rate will fall.

Declining U.S. incomes and prices will reduce the U.S. demand for British goods and therefore reduce the U.S. demand for pounds. Lower interest rates in Britain will make it less attractive for U.S. investors to make financial investments there, also lessening the demand for pounds. For all these reasons, the demand for pounds in the United States will decline. In Britain, higher incomes, prices, and interest rates will make U.S. imports and U.S. financial investments more attractive. In buying these imports and making these financial investments, British citizens will supply more pounds in the exchange market.

In short, domestic macroeconomic adjustments in the United States and Britain, triggered by the international flow of gold, will produce new demand and supply conditions for pounds such that the $2 = £1 exchange rate is maintained. After all the adjustments are made, the United States will not have a payments deficit and Britain will not have a payments surplus.

Thus the gold standard has the advantage of maintaining stable exchange rates and correcting balance-of-payments deficits and surpluses automatically. However, its critical drawback is that nations must accept domestic adjustments in such distasteful forms as unemployment and falling incomes on the one hand, or inflation on the other hand. Under the gold standard, a nation's money supply is altered by changes in supply and demand in currency markets, and nations cannot establish their own monetary policy in their own national interest. If the United States, for example, were to experience declining output and income, the loss of gold under the gold standard would reduce the U.S. money supply. A reduced money supply would increase interest rates, decrease borrowing and spending, and produce further declines in output and income.

Collapse of the Gold Standard

The gold standard collapsed under the weight of the worldwide Depression of the 1930s. As domestic output and employment fell worldwide, the restoration of prosperity became the primary goal of afflicted nations. They responded by enacting protectionist measures to reduce imports. The idea was to get their economies moving again by promoting consumption of domestically produced goods. To make their exports less expensive abroad, many nations redefined their currencies at lower levels in terms of gold. For example, a country that had previously defined the value of its currency at 1 unit = 25 grains of gold might redefine it as 1 unit = 10 grains of gold. Such redefining is an example of **devaluation**—a deliberate action by a government to reduce the international value of its currency. A series of such devaluations in the 1930s meant that exchange rates were no longer fixed. The lack of fixed exchange rates violated a major tenet of the gold standard, and the system broke down.

The Bretton Woods System

The Great Depression and the Second World War left world trade and the world monetary system in shambles. To lay the groundwork for a new international monetary system, in 1944, the major nations held an international conference at Bretton Woods, New Hampshire. The conference produced a commitment to a modified fixed-exchange-rate system called an *adjustable-peg system,* or, simply, the **Bretton Woods system**. The new system sought to capture the advantages of the old gold standard (fixed exchange rate) while avoiding its disadvantages (painful domestic macroeconomic adjustments).

Furthermore, the conference created the **International Monetary Fund (IMF)** to make the new exchange-rate system feasible and workable. The new international monetary system managed through the IMF prevailed with modifications until 1971. (The IMF still plays a basic role in international finance; in recent decades it has performed a major role in providing loans to developing countries, nations experiencing financial crises, and nations making the transition from communism to capitalism.)

---

devaluation A decrease in the governmentally defined value of a currency.

Bretton Woods system The international monetary system developed after the Second World War in which *adjustable pegs* were employed, the *International Monetary Fund* helped stabilize foreign exchange rates, and gold and the dollar were used as *international monetary reserves.*

International Monetary Fund (IMF) The international association of nations that was formed after the Second World War to make loans of foreign monies to nations with temporary *balance of payments deficits* and, until the early 1970s, manage the international system of pegged exchange rates agreed upon at the Bretton Woods conference. It now mainly makes loans to nations facing possible defaults on private and government loans.

IMF and Pegged Exchange Rates

How did the adjustable-peg system of exchange rates work? First, as with the gold standard, each IMF member had to define its currency in terms of gold (or dollars), thus establishing rates of exchange between its currency and the currencies of all other members. In addition, each nation was obligated to keep its exchange rate stable with respect to every other currency. To do so, nations would have to use their official currency reserves to intervene in foreign exchange markets.

Assume again that the U.S. dollar and the British pound are "pegged" to each other at $2 = £1. And suppose again that the demand for pounds temporarily increases so that a shortage of pounds occurs in the United States (the United States has a balance-of-payments deficit). How can the United States keep its pledge to maintain a $2 = £1 exchange rate when the new equilibrium rate is, say, $3 = £1? As we noted previously, the United States can supply additional pounds to the exchange market, increasing the supply of pounds such that the equilibrium exchange rate falls back to $2 = £1.

Under the Bretton Woods system, there were three main sources of the needed pounds:

- *Official reserves* The United States might currently possess pounds in its official reserves as the result of past actions against a payments surplus.
- *Gold sales* The U.S. government might sell some of its gold to Britain for pounds. The proceeds would then be offered in the exchange market to augment the supply of pounds.
- *IMF borrowing* The needed pounds might be borrowed from the IMF. Nations participating in the Bretton Woods system were required to make contributions to the IMF based on the size of their national income, population, and trade volume. If necessary, the United States could borrow pounds on a short-term basis from the IMF by supplying its own currency as collateral.

Fundamental Imbalances: Adjusting the Peg

The Bretton Woods system recognized that from time to time a nation may be confronted with persistent and sizable balance-of-payments problems that cannot be corrected through the means listed above. In such cases, the nation would eventually run out of official reserves and be unable to maintain its current fixed exchange rate. The Bretton Woods remedy was correction by devaluation, that is, by an "orderly" reduction of the nation's pegged exchange rate. Also, the IMF allowed each member nation to alter the value of its currency by 10 percent, on its own, to correct a so-called fundamental (persistent and continuing) balance-of-payments deficit. Larger exchange-rate changes required the permission of the Fund's board of directors.

By requiring approval of significant rate changes, the Fund guarded against arbitrary and competitive currency devaluations by nations seeking only to boost output in their own countries at other countries' expense. In our example, devaluation of the dollar would increase U.S. exports and lower U.S. imports, helping to correct the United States' persistent payments deficit.

Demise of the Bretton Woods System

Under this adjustable-peg system, nations came to accept gold and the dollar as international reserves. The acceptability of gold as an international medium of exchange derived from its earlier use under the gold standard. Other nations accepted the dollar as international money because the United States had accumulated large quantities of gold, and between 1934 and 1971 it maintained a policy of buying gold from, and selling gold to, foreign governments at a fixed price of $35 per ounce. The dollar was convertible into gold on demand, so the dollar came to be regarded as a substitute for gold, or "as good as gold." The discovery of new gold was limited, but a growing volume of dollars helped facilitate the expanding volume of world trade during this period.

But a major problem arose. The United States had persistent payments deficits throughout the 1950s and 1960s. Those deficits were financed in part by U.S. gold reserves but mostly by payment of U.S. dollars. As the number of dollars held by foreigners soared and the U.S. gold reserves dwindled, other nations began to question whether the dollar was really "as good as gold." The ability of the United States to continue to convert dollars into gold at $35 per ounce became increasingly doubtful, as did the role of dollars as international monetary reserves. Thus the dilemma was: To maintain the dollar as a reserve medium, the U.S. payments deficit had to be eliminated. But elimination of the payments deficit would remove the source of additional dollar reserves and thus limit the growth of international trade and finance.

The problem culminated in 1971 when the United States ended its 37-year-old policy of exchanging gold for dollars at $35 per ounce. It severed the link between gold and the international value of the dollar, thereby "floating" the dollar and letting market forces determine its value. The floating of the dollar withdrew U.S. support from the Bretton Woods system of fixed exchange rates and effectively ended the system. Nearly all major currencies began to float. The result has been the current regime of "managed floating exchange rates" described earlier in this chapter.

Appendix Summary

LO20.7 Explain how exchange rates worked under the gold standard and Bretton Woods.

Between 1879 and 1934, most major trading nations were on the gold standard, in which each nation fixed an exchange rate between its currency and gold. With each nation's currency fixed to gold, the system also implicitly set fixed exchange rates between different national currencies.

Any balance-of-payments imbalance would automatically lead to offsetting international flows of gold. These gold flows, in turn, led to automatically occurring domestic macroeconomic adjustments as the country exporting gold automatically encountered a decrease in its money supply while the country importing gold automatically experienced an increase in its money supply. When the Great Depression hit, many countries found these automatic adjustments too hard to bear, and they abandoned the gold standard.

The Bretton Woods system was implemented after the end of the Second World War and lasted until 1971. Under this system, the United States fixed the value of the U.S. dollar to gold at a rate of $35 per ounce. Other countries then set fixed exchange rates with the dollar so that their currencies were indirectly fixed to gold through the dollar.

The International Monetary Fund was created to administer the Bretton Woods system, which allowed countries some flexibility in adjusting their exchange rates to help offset balance-of-payments imbalances.

As the United States encountered increasingly large balance-of-payments imbalances in the 1960s and early 1970s, its ability to maintain its gold peg of $35 per ounce lost credibility. The United States abandoned the gold standard in 1971, thereby ending the Bretton Woods system. All major currencies then began the current regime of managed floating exchange rates.

Appendix Terms and Concepts

gold standard   devaluation   Bretton Woods system   International Monetary Fund (IMF)

Appendix Discussion Questions

1. Compare and contrast the Bretton Woods system of exchange rates with that of the gold standard. What caused the collapse of the gold standard? What caused the demise of the Bretton Woods system? **LO20.7**

Appendix Review Questions

1. Think back to the gold standard period. If the United States suffered a recession, to what degree could it engage in expansionary monetary policy? **LO20.7**

Appendix Problems

1. Suppose Zeeland pegs its currency, the zee, at 1 zee = 36 grains of gold. Aeeland pegs its currency, the aeellar, at 1 aeellar = 10 grains of gold. **LO20.7**
   a. What is the exchange rate between the zee and the aeellar?
   b. How many aeellars could you get for 7 zees?
   c. In terms of gold, would you rather have 14.5 zees or 53 aeellars?

CHAPTER
21

The Economics of Developing Countries

>> LEARNING OBJECTIVES

LO21.1 Distinguish between industrially advanced countries and developing countries.

LO21.2 List the obstacles to economic development.

LO21.3 Explain the vicious circle of poverty that afflicts low-income nations.

LO21.4 Describe the role of government in promoting economic development.

LO21.5 Explain how industrial nations attempt to aid low-income countries.

It is difficult for those of us in the United States, where per capita GDP in 2020 was about $63,544, to grasp the fact that about 700 million people, or about 10 percent of the world's population, live on $1.90 or less a day. Hunger and disease are the norm in many nations of the world.

In this chapter we identify the developing countries, discuss their characteristics, and explore the obstacles that impede their growth. We also examine the appropriate roles of the private sector and government in economic development. Finally, we look at policies that might help developing countries increase their growth rates.

The Rich and the Poor

>> **LO21.1** Distinguish between industrially advanced countries and developing countries.

Just as there is considerable income inequality among families within a nation, so too is there great income inequality among nations. According to the United Nations, the richest 20 percent of the world's population receives more than 75 percent of the world's income; the poorest 20 percent receives less than 2 percent. The poorest 60 percent receives less than 6 percent of the world's income.

Classifications

industrially advanced countries High-income countries such as the United States, Canada, Japan, and the nations of western Europe that have highly developed *market economies* based on large stocks of technologically advanced *capital goods* and skilled labor forces.

The World Bank classifies countries into four income categories—high-income, upper-middle-income, lower-middle-income, and low-income—on the basis of national income per capita, as Figure 21.1 shows. The *high-income nations*, shown in dark green, are known as the **industrially advanced countries (IACs).** They include the United States, Japan, Canada, Australia, New Zealand, and most of western Europe. In general, these nations have well-developed market economies based on large stocks of capital goods, advanced production technologies, and well-educated workers. In 2020 this group of economies had an average per capita income of $46,036.

FIGURE 21.1 Groups of economies.

The world's nations are grouped into industrially advanced countries (IACs) and developing countries (DVCs). The IACs (shown in dark green) are high-income countries. The DVCs are upper-middle-income, lower-middle-income, and low-income countries (shown respectively in light green, yellow, and orange).

Low ($1,045 or less)　Lower middle ($1,046–$4,095)　Upper middle ($4,096–$12,695)　High ($12,696 or more)　No data

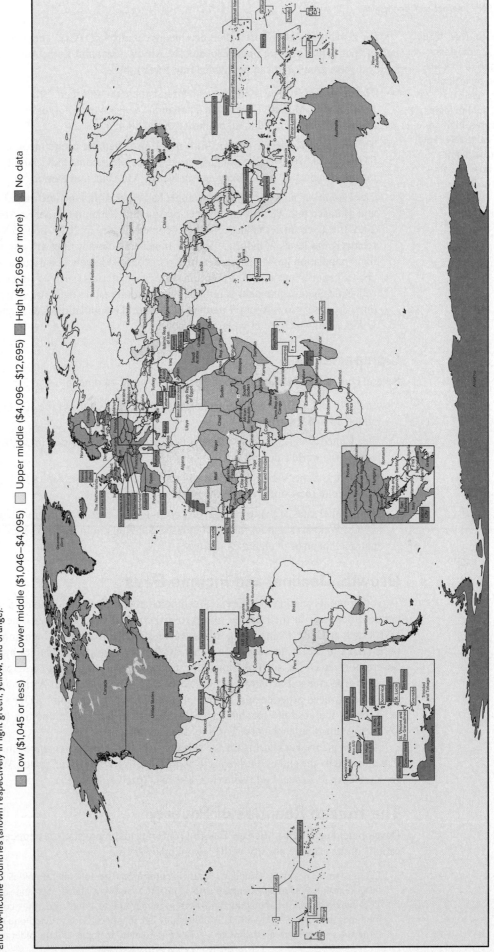

Source: The World Bank. Note that national income per capita is converted to U.S. dollars using the World Bank's Atlas Method, which adjusts national amounts to U.S. dollars using 3-year exchange rate averages.

developing countries Many countries of Africa, Asia, and Latin America that are characterized by lack of capital goods, use of nonadvanced technologies, low literacy rates, high unemployment, relatively rapid population growth, and labor forces heavily committed to agriculture.

The remaining nations are called **developing countries (DVCs).** They have wide variations of income per capita and are mainly located in Africa, Asia, and Latin America. The DVCs are a highly diverse group that can be divided into three groups:

- The *upper-middle-income nations*, shown in light green in Figure 21.1, include Brazil, Iraq, South Africa, Mexico, China, and Thailand. The per capita output of these nations ranged from $4,220 to $12,570 in 2020 and averaged $9,426.

- The *lower-middle-income nations*, shown in yellow, had per capita incomes ranging from $1,060 to $4,070 in 2020 with an average per capita income of $2,201. This category includes Tajikistan, India, Bangladesh, Kenya, Vietnam, and Samoa.

- The *low-income nations*, shown in orange, had a per capita income of $1,045 or less in 2020 and averaged only $811 of income per person. Sub-Saharan nations in Africa represented 23 of the 27 countries falling into this income category in 2020. Low-income DVCs have relatively low levels of industrialization. In general, literacy rates are low, unemployment is high, population growth is rapid, and exports consist largely of agricultural produce (such as cocoa, bananas, sugar, and raw cotton) and raw materials (such as copper, iron ore, natural rubber). Capital equipment is minimal, production technologies are simple, and labor productivity is very low. About 9 percent of the world's population lives in these low-income DVCs, all of which suffer widespread poverty.

Comparisons

Several comparisons will bring the differences in world income into sharper focus:

- In 2020, U.S. GDP was $20.9 trillion. The combined GDPs of the 125 DVCs in that year added up to $31.0 trillion.

- The United States, with only 4.2 percent of the world's population in 2020, produced 24.7 percent of the world's output.

- In 2020, U.S. per capita GDP was 117 times greater than per capita GDP in the Democratic Republic of the Congo, one of the world's poorest nations.

- The annual sales of the world's largest corporations exceed the national incomes of many DVCs. Walmart's annual world revenues of $559 billion in 2020 were greater than the national incomes of all but 21 nations.

Growth, Decline, and Income Gaps

Two other points relating to Figure 21.1 should be noted. First, nations have demonstrated considerable differences in their ability to improve their circumstances over time. On the one hand, DVCs such as Chile, China, India, Malaysia, and Thailand achieved high annual growth rates in their GDPs in recent decades. Consequently, their real output per capita increased severalfold. Several former DVCs, such as Singapore, Greece, and Hong Kong (now part of China), have achieved IAC status. In contrast, a number of DVCs in sub-Saharan Africa and the Middle East have recently been experiencing stagnant or even declining per capita GDPs.

Second, the absolute income gap between rich and poor nations has been widening. The DVCs must grow faster than the IACs for the gap to be narrowed.

A quick glance back at Figure 8.1 will confirm the "great divergence" in standards of living that emerged by the end of the twentieth century between the United States, Western Europe, and Japan relative to Africa, Latin America, and Asia (excluding Japan).

The Human Realities of Poverty

Development economist Michael Todaro points out that mere statistics conceal the human implications of the extreme poverty in the low-income DVCs:

> Let us examine a typical "extended" family in rural Asia. The Asian household is likely to comprise ten or more people, including parents, five to seven children, two grandparents, and some aunts and uncles. They have a combined annual income, both in money and in "kind" (i.e., they consume a share of the food they grow), of $250 to $300. Together they live in a poorly constructed one-room house as tenant farmers on a large agricultural estate. . . . The father, mother, uncle, and the older children must work all

TABLE 21.1 Selected Socioeconomic Indicators of Development

Country	(1) Per Capita Income, 2020*	(2) Life Expectancy at Birth, 2019	(3) Under-5 Mortality, Rate per 1,000, 2019	(4) Adult Illiteracy Rate, Percent, 2018	(5) Regular Internet Users, percent, 2020	(6) Per Capita Energy Consumption, 2018**
United States	$63,544	79	7	1	89	310
Japan	42,197	84	3	1	93	151
China	17,312	77	8	3	71	103
Brazil	14,836	76	14	7	74	61
India	6,454	70	34	26	41	23
Mauritania	5,257	65	73	47	21	12
Ethiopia	2,423	67	51	48	25	3
Mozambique	1,967	61	74	39	15	8

*Purchasing power parity basis (see World Bank website for definition and methodology).
**Millions of British Thermal Units (BTUs) per person per year.

Source: The World Bank's *World Development Indicators* (data.worldbank.org) and United States Energy Information Agency (eia.gov).

day on the land. None of the adults can read or write. . . . There is only one meal a day. . . . The house has no electricity, sanitation, or fresh water supply. There is much sickness, but qualified doctors and medical practitioners are far away in the cities attending to the needs of wealthier families. The work is hard, the sun is hot and aspirations for a better life are constantly being snuffed out. In this part of the world the only relief from the daily struggle for physical survival lies in the spiritual traditions of the people.[1]

Table 21.1 contrasts various socioeconomic indicators for selected DVCs with those for the United States and Japan.

Obstacles to Economic Development

The paths to economic development are essentially the same for developing countries and industrially advanced economies:

>> LO21.2 List the obstacles to economic development.

- The DVCs must use their existing supplies of resources more efficiently. In other words, they must eliminate unemployment and underemployment, and they must combine labor and capital resources in a way that achieves lowest-cost production. They must also direct their scarce resources so that they will achieve allocative efficiency.

- The DVCs must expand the quantity and quality of their resources. By achieving greater supplies of raw materials, capital equipment, and productive labor, and by advancing their technological knowledge and human capital, DVCs can push their production possibilities curves outward.

All DVCs are aware of these two paths to economic development. Why, then, have some of them traveled those paths while others have lagged far behind? The differences lie in the nations' physical, human, and socioeconomic environments.

Natural Resources

The distribution of natural resources among the DVCs is extremely uneven. Some DVCs have valuable deposits of bauxite, tin, copper, tungsten, nitrates, and petroleum, and they have used their natural resource endowments to achieve rapid growth. For example, several members of the Organization of Petroleum Exporting Countries (OPEC), including Kuwait, have used oil experts to grow their economies. In other cases, multinational corporations of industrially advanced countries own or control a DVC's natural resources, often diverting much of the economic benefits of these resources abroad. Furthermore, world markets for many of the farm products and raw materials that the DVCs export are subject to large price fluctuations that contribute to the DVCs' instability.

---

[1]Michael P. Todaro, *Economic Development* (Pearson Education, 2000).

Other DVCs lack mineral deposits, have little arable land, and have few sources of power. Moreover, most of the low-income countries are situated in Central and South America, Africa, the Indian subcontinent, and southeast Asia, where tropical climates prevail. The heat and humidity hinder productive labor; human, crop, and livestock diseases are widespread; and weed and insect infestations plague agriculture.

A weak resource base can be a serious obstacle to growth. Real capital can be accumulated and the quality of the labor force improved through education and training. But it is not as easy to augment the natural resource base. It may be unrealistic for many of the DVCs to envision an economic destiny comparable with that of, say, the United States or Canada—both of which were endowed by nature with thick forests, rich soils, plenty of oil, and rich mineral deposits. But we must be careful in generalizing: Japan, for example, has achieved a high standard of living despite limited natural resources. It simply imports the large quantities of natural resources that it needs to produce goods for consumption at home and for export abroad.

Human Resources

Three statements describe many of the poorest DVCs with respect to human resources:

- Populations are large.
- Unemployment and underemployment are widespread.
- Educational levels and labor productivity are low.

Large Populations As equation (1) demonstrates, a nation's standard of living or real income per capita depends on the size of its total output (or income) relative to its total population:

$$\text{Standard of living} = \frac{\text{Total output (or income)}}{\text{Population}} \quad\quad (1)$$

Some of the DVCs with the most meager natural and capital resources have not only low total incomes but also large populations. These large populations often produce high population densities (population per square mile). In column 2 of Table 21.2, note the high population densities of the selected DVCs relative to the lower densities of the United States and the world.

The high population densities of many DVCs have resulted from decades of higher rates of population growth than most IACs. Column 3 of Table 21.2 shows the varying rates of population growth in selected countries over a recent period: 2019–2020. Although *total fertility rates*—the number of children per biological female's lifetime—are dramatically declining in most DVCs, the population growth rates of the DVCs remain considerably higher than those of the IACs. Between 2019 and 2020, the annual population growth rate was 2.7 percent for the low-income DVCs, 1.4 percent for the lower-middle income DVCS, and 1.0 for the upper-middle income DVCs. Those numbers are substantially higher than the 0.4 percent rate of population growth found in the IACs (with much of that being due to immigration into IACs; indeed, the total fertility rate in the large majority of IACs is now substantially less than the replacement rate necessary to keep their populations stable over time).

Because a large percentage of the world's population lives in DVCs, their population growth is the most significant component of worldwide population growth. Over the next 15 years, 9 out of every 10 people added to the world population are projected to be born in developing nations.

TABLE 21.2
Population Statistics, Selected Countries

(1) Country	(2) Population per Square Kilometer, 2020*	(3) Annual Rate of Population Increase, 2019–2020
United States	36	0.4
Pakistan	287	2.0
Bangladesh	1,265	1.0
Nigeria	226	2.5
India	464	1.0
China	149	0.3
Kenya	94	2.3
Philippines	368	1.3
Yemen	54	2.3
World	**60**	**1.0**

*1 square kilometer (km) = 0.386 square mile.

Source: World Development Indicators 2021, The World Bank (data.worldbank.org).

In some of the poorest DVCs, rapid population growth strains the levels of income growth so severely that per capita income remains stagnant or even falls toward subsistence levels. In the worst instances, death rates rise sharply as war, drought, and natural disasters cause severe malnutrition and disease.

Boosting the standard of living in countries that have subsistence or near-subsistence levels of income is a daunting task. When a DVC is just starting to modernize its economy, initial increases in real income can for a time increase population and short-circuit the process. If population increases are sufficiently large, they simply spread the higher level of total income among more people such that the original gain in per capita income disappears.

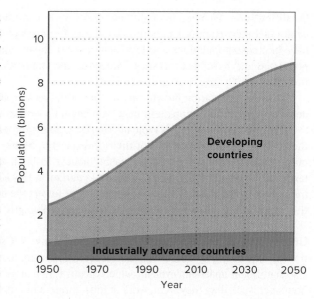

FIGURE 21.2
Population growth in developing countries and advanced industrial countries, 1950–2050.

The majority of the world's population lives in the developing nations, and those nations will account for most of the increase in population through the middle of the twenty-first century.

Source: United Nations.

The Demographic Transition Why might income gains in the poorest DVCs increase population growth, at least for a while? The answer is the **demographic transition,** or the period of several decades during which the population expands because it takes time to transition from a situation of high birth and death rates to a situation of low birth and death rates.

Before the Industrial Revolution and modern medicines and technology, the entire world was one in which both death rates and birthrates were high. There were no antibiotics to treat disease, no understanding of preventing diseases through immunization, and no understanding of food- and water-borne illnesses caused by bacteria and viruses. Given the high death rates that resulted from that ignorance, most families opted to have six or more children so that two or three might survive to adulthood. Thus, high birthrates accompanied high death rates.

When modern medicine and sanitation arrive in a country, death rates plunge quite rapidly. But people who are accustomed to high death rates will continue for several decades to have large families, thinking, out of habit, that large families are necessary for having at least a couple of children survive to adulthood. As people become used to lower death rates, they adjust downward the number of children they are having. That creates the situation of low death rates accompanied by low birth rates that is found today in almost every high income and middle income nation—that is, the nations that have already completed the demographic transition. But many poorer DVCs are still in the intermediate period where death rates have fallen while birthrates are yet to fall. Thus, their populations are growing quite rapidly because they experience many more births than deaths each year.

Most experts see birth control as a key strategy for hastening the demographic transition. But low literacy rates make it difficult to disseminate information about contraceptive devices. In addition, large families are a major source of labor in poor agricultural areas. Adults may also regard having many children as a kind of informal social security system: the more children they have, the greater the probability of having a relative to care for them in old age.

Chinese authorities took a harsh stance on fertility choices in 1980, when they instituted a "one child per family" law that imposed fines, removed social benefits, and in some cases forced abortions on any family that had, or attempted to have, more than one child. The law was widely credited with assisting in the dramatic increase in living standards that accompanied China's subsequent economic boom. But the policy may have been too effective over the long run because, by 2012, China's labor force was declining and the government faced a situation in which too few workers would be paying taxes to support too many retirees. As a result, the one child per family law was eliminated in late 2015 in hopes of encouraging Chinese families to have more children. In 2021, the Chinese government announced that it was going to begin encouraging families to have up to three children.

demographic transition The massive decline in birthrates that occurs once a developing country achieves higher standards of living because the perceived marginal cost of additional children begins to exceed the perceived marginal benefit.

Qualifications We need to qualify our focus on population growth as a major cause of low per-capita incomes. High population density does not consign a nation to poverty. China and India have immense populations and low incomes, but Japan, Singapore, and Hong Kong are densely populated and have high incomes. Moreover, the standard of living in many parts of China and India has rapidly increased in recent years.

Also, the population growth rate for the DVCs as a group has declined significantly in recent decades. The world's population may even begin to decline toward the later part of this century.

Development economists typically suggest a dual approach to development. The surest way for the poorest DVCs to break out of their poverty, they argue, is to implement policies that expand output and income while also increasing access to birth control information and methods. In terms of the standard of living equation (1) earlier in this section, a set of policies that raises the numerator (total income) and holds constant or lowers the denominator (population) will provide the biggest lift to a developing nation's standard of living.

Unemployment and Underemployment For many DVCs, employment-related data are either nonexistent or highly unreliable. But observation suggests that unemployment is high. There is also significant **underemployment,** which means that a large number of people are employed fewer hours per week than they want, work at jobs unrelated to their training, or spend much of the time on their jobs unproductively.

underemployment A situation in which workers are employed in positions requiring less education and skill than they have.

Many economists contend that unemployment may be as high as 15 to 20 percent in the rapidly growing urban areas of the DVCs. There has been substantial migration in most developing countries from rural to urban areas, motivated by the expectation of finding jobs with higher wage rates than are available in agricultural and other rural employment. But this huge migration to the cities reduces a migrant's chance of obtaining a job. In many cases, migration to the cities has greatly exceeded the growth of urban job opportunities, resulting in very high urban unemployment rates. Thus, rapid rural-urban migration has given rise to urban unemployment rates that are two or three times higher than rural rates.

In many of the poorer DVCs, rural agricultural labor is so abundant relative to capital and natural resources that a significant percentage of the labor contributes little or nothing to agricultural output. Similarly, many DVC workers are self-employed as proprietors of small shops, in handicrafts, or as street vendors. Unfortunately, however, many of them must endure long stretches of idle time at work due to a lack of demand. While they are not unemployed, they are clearly underemployed.

Some perspective is needed, however. The nearby Consider This story explains that, despite the unemployment problems that challenge DVCs, extreme poverty has fallen dramatically around the world in recent decades. This is good news, but much more could be done to increase employment opportunities—and thus living standards—in poorer countries.

CONSIDER THIS . . .

Faster, Please

The World Bank defines extreme poverty as an income of $1.90 per day or less, adjusted to local currency and accounting for differences in the cost of living and inflation. Under that definition, extreme poverty has plummeted in recent decades.

Between 1990 and 2017, the number of people living in extreme poverty declined from 1.9 billion to 698 million. That decline of about 1.2 billion people living in extreme poverty is especially impressive because the world's population increased from 5.3 billion to 7.5 billion over the

John Wollwerth/Shutterstock

same time horizon. If you work out the percentages, you will find that the extreme poverty rate fell from 35.9 percent of the world's population in 1990 to 9.3 percent in 2017.

That sharp decline in extreme poverty represents a massive decrease in human suffering. That is because people living in extreme poverty are typically unable to provide for basic human needs, such as sufficient food, safe drinking water, adequate sanitation facilities, proper health care, sturdy shelter, and education.

Low Labor Productivity DVCs have found it difficult to invest in physical capital. As a result, their workers are poorly equipped with machinery and tools and therefore are relatively unproductive. Remember that rapid population growth tends to reduce the amount of physical capital available per worker, and that reduction erodes labor productivity and decreases real per capita incomes.

Moreover, most poor countries have not been able to invest adequately in their human capital (see Table 21.1, columns 3 and 4). Consequently, expenditures on health and education have been meager. Low levels of literacy, high levels of malnutrition, lack of proper medical care, and insufficient educational facilities all contribute to populations that are ill equipped for industrialization and economic expansion. Also, a number of the poorest DVCs forgo vast amounts of productive human capital by denying or restricting educational and work opportunities to women.

Particularly vital is the absence of a vigorous entrepreneurial class willing to bear risks, accumulate capital, and provide the organizational requisites essential to economic growth. Closely related is the lack of labor trained to handle the routine supervisory functions basic to any program of development. Ironically, the higher-education systems of some DVCs emphasize the humanities and offer relatively few courses in business, engineering, and the sciences. Some DVCs are ruled by repressive governments, which create an environment hostile to thinking independently, taking initiatives, and assuming economic risks.

While migration from the DVCs to other countries has modestly offset rapid population growth, it has also deprived some DVCs of highly productive workers. Often the best-trained and most highly motivated workers, such as physicians, engineers, teachers, and nurses, leave the DVCs to better their circumstances in the IACs. This so-called "brain drain" contributes to the deterioration in the overall skill level and productivity of the labor force.

Capital Accumulation

The accumulation of capital goods is an important focal point of economic development. All DVCs have a relative lack of capital goods such as factories, machinery, equipment, and public utilities. Better-equipped labor forces would greatly enhance productivity and would help boost per capita output. There is a close relationship between output per worker (labor productivity) and real income per worker. A nation must produce more goods and services per worker as output to enjoy more goods and services per worker as income. One way of increasing labor productivity is to provide each worker with more tools and equipment.

Once initiated, the process of capital accumulation may be cumulative. If capital accumulation increases output faster than population growth, a margin of saving may arise that permits further capital formation. In a sense, capital accumulation feeds on itself.

Let's look more closely at domestic capital accumulation.

Domestic Capital Formation Like any other nation, a developing nation accumulates capital through saving and investing. A nation must save (refrain from consumption) to free some of its resources from the production of consumer goods. Investment spending must then absorb those released resources in the production of capital goods. But impediments to saving and investing are much greater in a low-income nation than they are in an advanced economy.

Savings Potential Consider first the savings side of the picture. Some of the lowest-income countries, such as Burundi, Chad, Ghana, Guinea, Liberia, Madagascar, Mozambique, and Sierra Leone, have negative saving or save only 0 to 7 percent of their GDPs. Their people are simply too poor to save a significant portion of their incomes. Interestingly, however, some middle-income countries save a larger percentage of their domestic outputs than do advanced industrial countries. In 2019 India and China saved 30 and 44 percent of their domestic outputs, respectively, compared to 27 percent for Japan, 28 percent for Germany, and 19 percent for the United States. The problem is that the DVCs' domestic outputs are so low that even when saving rates are larger than those of advanced nations, the total volume of saving is not large.

Capital Flight Some of the developing countries have suffered **capital flight,** the transfer of private DVC savings to accounts held in the IACs. (In this usage, "capital" is simply "money," "money capital," or "financial capital.") Many wealthy citizens of DVCs have used their savings to invest in the more economically advanced nations, enabling them to avoid high investment risks at home, which include the loss of savings or real capital from government expropriation, abrupt changes in taxation, potential hyperinflation, or high volatility of exchange rates. If a DVC's political climate is

capital flight The transfer of savings from *developing countries* to *industrially advanced countries* to avoid government expropriation, taxation, or higher rates of *inflation,* or simply to realize greater returns on *financial investments.*

unsettled, savers may shift their funds overseas to a "safe haven" in fear that a new government might confiscate their wealth. Rapid or skyrocketing inflation in a DVC will have similar detrimental effects. Transferring savings overseas may also be a means of evading high domestic taxes on interest income or capital gains. Finally, investors may send their money capital to the IACs to achieve higher interest rates or to take advantage of a greater variety of investment opportunities.

Whatever the motivation, the amount of capital flight from some DVCs is significant and offsets much of the IACs' lending and granting of financial aid to developing nations.

infrastructure The interconnected network of large-scale *capital goods* (such as roads, sewers, electrical grids, railways, ports, and the Internet) needed to operate a technologically advanced economy.

Investment Obstacles The infrastructure (stock of public capital goods) in many DVCs is insufficient to enable private firms to achieve adequate returns on their investments. Poor roads and bridges, inadequate railways, little gas and electricity production, poor communications, unsatisfactory housing, and inadequate educational and public health facilities create an inhospitable environment for private investment. A substantial portion of any new private investment would have to be used to create the infrastructure needed by all firms. Rarely can firms provide an investment in infrastructure themselves and still earn a positive return on their overall investment.

How, then, can developing nations build up their infrastructure? The higher-income DVCs may be able to do so through taxation and public spending. But, in the lowest-income DVCs, there is little income to tax. Nevertheless, a poor DVC can accumulate capital by transferring surplus agricultural labor to the improvement of the infrastructure. If each agricultural village allocated its surplus labor to the construction of irrigation canals, wells, schools, sanitary facilities, and roads, significant amounts of capital might be accumulated at no significant sacrifice of consumer goods production. Such investment bypasses the problems inherent in the financial aspects of capital accumulation. It does not require consumers to save portions of their money income, nor does it presume the presence of an entrepreneurial class eager to invest. When leadership and cooperative spirit are present, this "in-kind" investment is a promising avenue for accumulating basic capital goods.

In some developing nations, the major obstacle to investment is the lack of entrepreneurs who are willing to assume the risks associated with investment. In addition, the incentive to invest may be weak even in the presence of substantial savings and a large number of willing entrepreneurs. Several factors may combine in a DVC to reduce investment incentives, including political instability, high inflation rates, and lack of economies of scale. A related problem in many countries is the high cost of legally registering a new business. As Global Perspective 21.1 indicates, those costs are prohibitive in many countries, amounting to more than twice what an average person makes in a year!

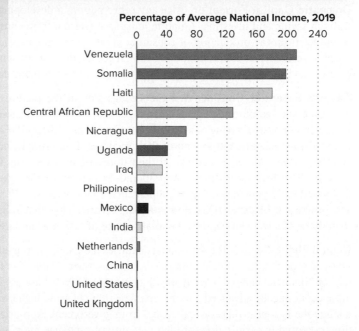

GLOBAL PERSPECTIVE 21.1

COST OF BUSINESS START-UP PROCEDURES AS A PERCENTAGE OF AVERAGE INCOME, 2019

In every country in the world, entrepreneurs have to complete paperwork and pay fees to register a new business with the local government. For each country, the World Bank's Doing Business Project publishes those costs as a percentage of average national income. Those percentages are startlingly high in several low-income countries, including Venezuela, Somalia, and Haiti. By contrast they are quite low in several developing nations, such as India and China, as well as in every industrially advanced country. In the United Kingdom, for instance, it costs just £12 (or about $17 dollars) to register a new business with the government.

Source: World Bank's Doing Business Project, The World Bank, doingbusiness.org.

Technological Advance

Given the rudimentary state of technology in the DVCs, they are far from the frontiers of technological advance. But the IACs have accumulated an enormous body of technological knowledge that the developing countries might adopt and apply without expensive research. Crop rotation and contour plowing require no additional capital equipment and would contribute significantly to productivity. By raising grain storage bins a few inches above ground, farmers could avoid a large amount of grain spoilage. Although such changes may sound trivial to people who live in advanced nations, the resulting gains in productivity might mean the difference between subsistence and starvation in some poverty-ridden nations.

The application of either existing or new technological knowledge often requires the use of new and different capital goods. But, within limits, a nation can obtain at least part of that capital without an increase in the rate of capital formation. If a DVC channels the annual flow of replacement investment from technologically inferior to technologically superior capital equipment, it can increase productivity even with a constant level of investment spending. Indeed, it can achieve some advances through **capital-saving technology** rather than **capital-using technology.** A new fertilizer, better adapted to a nation's topography and climate, might be cheaper than the fertilizer currently being used. A seemingly high-priced metal plow that lasts 10 years may be cheaper in the long run than an inexpensive but technologically inferior wooden plow that has to be replaced every year.

To what extent have DVCs adopted and effectively used available IAC technological knowledge? The picture is mixed. Such technological borrowing has been instrumental in the rapid growth of such Pacific Rim countries as Japan, South Korea, Taiwan, and Singapore. Similarly, the OPEC nations have benefited significantly from IAC knowledge of oil exploration, production, and refining.

Still, the transfer of advanced technologies to the poorest DVCs is not an easy matter. In IACs, technological advances usually depend on the availability of highly skilled labor and abundant capital. Such advances tend to be capital-using or, to put it another way, labor-saving. Developing economies require technologies appropriate to quite different resource endowments: abundant unskilled labor and very limited quantities of capital goods. Although labor-using and capital-saving technologies are appropriate to DVCs, much of the IACs' highly advanced technology is inappropriate for them. They must develop their own appropriate technologies. However, because technological change that fails may well mean hunger and malnutrition, there is a strong tendency to retain traditional production techniques.

capital-saving technology An improvement in *technology* that permits a greater quantity of a product to be produced with a specific amount of *capital* (or permits the same amount of the product to be produced with a smaller amount of capital).

capital-using technology An improvement in *technology* that requires the use of a greater amount of *capital* to produce a specific quantity of a product.

Sociocultural and Institutional Factors

Economic considerations alone do not explain why an economy does or does not grow. Substantial sociocultural and institutional readjustments are usually an integral part of the growth process. Economic development means not only changes in a nation's physical environment (new transportation and communications facilities, new schools, new housing, new plants and equipment) but also changes in the way people think, behave, and associate with one another. An openness to break from custom and tradition is frequently a prerequisite of economic development. A critical but intangible ingredient in that development is the **will to develop.** Economic growth may hinge on what individuals within DVCs want for themselves and their children. Do they want more material abundance? If so, are they willing to make the necessary changes in their institutions and ways of doing things?

will to develop The mental state of wanting *economic growth* strongly enough to change from old to new ways of doing things.

Sociocultural Obstacles Sociocultural impediments to growth are numerous and varied. In some DVCs, tribal and ethnic allegiances take precedence over national allegiance. Each tribe confines its economic activity to the tribal unit, eliminating any possibility for production-increasing specialization and trade. The desperate economic circumstances in Somalia, Sudan, Libya, Syria, and Afghanistan are due in no small measure to military and political conflicts among rival groups.

In countries with a formal or informal caste system, labor is allocated to occupations on the basis of status or tradition rather than on the basis of skill or merit. The result is a misallocation of human resources.

Religious beliefs and observances may seriously restrict the length of the workday and divert to ceremonial uses resources that might have been used for investment. Some religious and

capricious-universe view The view held by some people that fate and outside events, rather than hard work and enterprise, will determine their economic destinies

land reform Policy changes aimed at creating a more efficient distribution of land ownership in developing countries. Can involve everything from government purchasing large land estates and dividing the land into smaller farms to consolidating tiny plots of land into larger, more efficient private farms.

philosophical beliefs are dominated by the view that the universe is capricious, the idea that there is little or no correlation between an individual's activities and endeavors and that person's outcomes or experiences. The **capricious-universe view** leads to a fatalistic attitude. If "providence" rather than hard work, saving, and investing is the cause of one's lot in life, why save, work hard, and invest? Why engage in family planning? Why innovate?

Other attitudes and cultural factors may impede economic activity and growth: emphasis on the performance of duties rather than on individual initiative; focus on the group rather than on individual achievement; and the belief in reincarnation, which reduces the importance of one's current life.

Institutional Obstacles Political corruption and bribery are common in many DVCs. School systems and public service agencies are often ineptly administered, and petty politics frequently impairs their functioning. Tax systems are arbitrary, unjust, cumbersome, and detrimental to incentives to work and invest.

Because of the predominance of farming in DVCs, the problem of achieving an optimal institutional environment in agriculture is a vital consideration in any growth program. Specifically, the institutional problem of **land reform** demands attention in many DVCs. But the necessary reform may vary tremendously from nation to nation. In some DVCs the problem is excessive concentration of land ownership in the hands of a few wealthy families. This situation is demoralizing for tenants, weakens their incentive to produce, and typically does not promote capital improvements. At the other extreme is the situation in which each family owns and farms a piece of land far too small for the use of modern agricultural technology.

An important complication is that political considerations sometimes push reform in the direction of farms that are too small to achieve economies of scale.

Examples: Land reform in South Korea weakened the political control of the landed aristocracy and opened the way for the emergence of strong commercial and industrial middle classes, all to the benefit of the country's economic development. In contrast, the prolonged dominance of the landed aristocracy in the Philippines may have stifled economic development there.

QUICK REVIEW
21.1

▶ About 9 percent of the world's population lives in the low-income DVCs, which typically are characterized by scarce natural resources, inhospitable climates, large populations, high unemployment and underemployment, low education levels, and low labor productivity.

▶ For DVCs just beginning to modernize, high birthrates caused by improved medical care and sanitation can increase population faster than income growth, leading to lower living standards; but as

development continues, the opportunity costs of having children rise and population growth typically slows.

▶ Low saving rates, capital flight, weak infrastructures, and lack of investors impair capital accumulation in many DVCs.

▶ Sociocultural and institutional factors are often serious impediments to economic growth in DVCs.

The Vicious Circle

>> **LO21.3** Explain the vicious circle of poverty that afflicts low-income nations.

vicious circle of poverty A problem common in some *developing countries* in which their low *per capita incomes* are an obstacle to realizing the levels of *savings* and *investment* needed to achieve rates of growth of output that exceed their rates of population growth.

Many DVCs are caught in a **vicious circle of poverty.** They stay poor because they are poor! Consider Figure 21.3. Common to most DVCs is low per capita income. A family that is poor has little ability or incentive to save. Furthermore, low incomes mean low levels of product demand. Thus, there are few available resources, on the one hand, and no strong incentives, on the other hand, for investment in physical or human capital. Consequently, labor productivity is low. And because output per person is real income per person, it follows that per capita income is low.

Many economists think that the key to breaking out of this vicious circle is to increase the rate of capital accumulation, to achieve an investment level of, say, 10 percent of national income. But Figure 21.3 reminds us that rapid population growth may partially or entirely undo the potentially beneficial effects of a higher rate of capital accumulation. Suppose that initially a DVC is realizing no growth in its real GDP but somehow manages to increase saving and investment to 10 percent of its GDP. As a result, real GDP begins to grow at, say, 2.5 percent per year. With a stable population, real GDP per capita will also grow at 2.5 percent per year. If that growth persists, the standard of living will double in about 28 years. But what if population also grows at the rate of 2.5 percent per year, as it does in parts of the Middle East, northern Africa, and sub-Saharan Africa? Then real income per person will remain unchanged and the vicious circle will persist.

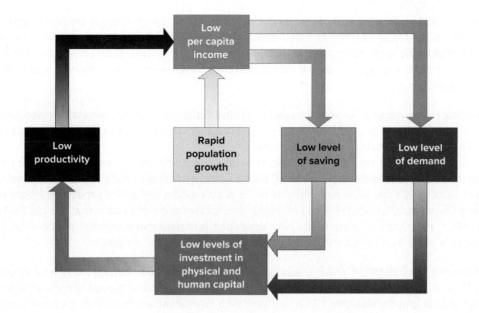

FIGURE 21.3
The vicious circle of poverty.

Low per capita incomes make it difficult for poor nations to save and invest, a condition that perpetuates low productivity and low incomes. Furthermore, rapid population growth may quickly absorb increases in per capita real income and thereby destroy the possibility of breaking out of the poverty circle.

But if population can be kept constant or limited to some growth rate significantly below 2.5 percent, real income per person will rise. Then the possibility arises of further enlargement of the flows of saving and investment, continuing advances in productivity, and the continued growth of per capita real income. If a nation can achieve a process of self-sustaining expansion of income, saving, investment, and productivity, then it can transform the self-perpetuating vicious circle of poverty into a self-regenerating, beneficent circle of economic progress. The challenge is to create effective policies and strategies that accomplish that transition.

The Role of Government

Economists suggest that developing nations have several avenues for fostering economic growth and improving their standards of living. Much of this is possible only if, however, a government has a sufficient amount of **state capacity**, meaning that a government has the ability to accomplish specific policy goals, such as providing public goods, enforcing property rights, and maintaining a monopoly on the legal use of force within its territory.

>> LO21.4 Describe the role of government in promoting economic development.

state capacity The ability of a government to achieve specific policy goals.

Unfortunately, some of the world's poorest countries lack state capacity because they are plagued by banditry and intertribal warfare that divert attention and resources from the task of development. A strong, stable national government is needed to establish domestic law and order and to achieve peace and unity. Research demonstrates that political instability (as measured by the number of revolutions and coups per decade) and slow economic growth go hand in hand.

A government that lacks state capacity is referred to as a fragile state or **failed state** and in such instances the practical power of the government to provide even basic government services such as elementary education, basic sanitation, and effective levels of law enforcement may be close to zero. In 2021, failed states included Yemen, Somalia, Syria, and South Sudan. Thus, our list of avenues that DVC governments have for fostering economic development begins with the achievement and maintenance of state capacity itself.

failed state A nation whose government lacks the *state capacity* to maintain even basic government functions like law enforcement and the provision of basic services like education and sanitation.

A Positive Role

Fortunately, most DVCs have significant amounts of state capacity that can be directed toward fostering economic development. But economists generally agree that as soon as sufficient state capacity has been achieved, government efforts must support private efforts, not substitute for them. That is not always the case in practice, however.

Establishing the Rule of Law Clearly defined and strictly enforced property rights bolster economic growth by ensuring that individuals receive and retain the fruits of their labor.

Because legal protections reduce investment risk, the rule of law encourages direct investments by firms in the IACs. Government itself must live by the law. The presence of corruption in the government sanctions criminality throughout the economic system. Such criminality discourages the growth of output because it lowers the returns available to honest workers and honest businesspeople.

Building Infrastructure Government is the only institution that is in a position to provide public infrastructure. But it need not do all the work through government entities. It can contract out much of the work to private enterprises.

Recall that DVCs (or *follower countries*) can adopt technologies that were developed at high cost in the more technologically advanced leader countries without paying any of those development costs. DVCs can often jump directly to the most modern and highly productive infrastructure without going through the long process of development and replacement that was required in the IACs. For example, many DVCs have developed Internet-capable wireless phone networks instead of using their scarce resources to build and expand landline systems.

Embracing Globalization Other things equal, open economies that participate in international trade grow faster than closed economies. Also, DVCs that welcome foreign direct investment enjoy greater growth rates than DVCs that view such investment suspiciously or even as exploitation and therefore put severe obstacles in its way.

Realistic exchange-rate policies by government also help. Exchange rates that are fixed at unrealistic levels invite balance-of-payments problems and speculative trading in currencies. Often, such trading forces a nation into an abrupt devaluation of its currency, sending shock waves throughout its economy. More flexible exchange rates enable more gradual adjustments and thus less susceptibility to major currency shocks and the domestic disruption they cause.

Building Human Capital Government programs that encourage literacy, education, and labor-market skills enhance economic growth by building human capital. In particular, policies that close the education gap between women and men spur economic growth in developing countries. Promoting the education of women pays off in terms of reduced fertility, greater productivity, and greater emphasis on educating children.

Promoting Entrepreneurship The lack of a sizable and vigorous entrepreneurial class in some DVCs means that private enterprise is not capable of spearheading the growth process. Government may have to take the lead, at least at first. But many DVCs would benefit by converting some of their state enterprises into private firms. State enterprises often are inefficient, more concerned with providing maximum employment than with introducing modern technology and delivering goods and services at minimum per-unit cost. Moreover, state enterprises are poor "incubators" for developing profit-focused, entrepreneurial persons who leave the firm to set up their own businesses.

microcredit Anti-poverty programs that lend small amounts of money to poor entrepreneurs.

Developing Credit Systems Banking systems in some of the poorest DVCs are nearly nonexistent, which makes it difficult for domestic savers and international lenders to lend money to DVC borrowers, who in turn wish to create capital goods. A first step toward developing effective credit systems is **microcredit,** in which groups of people pool their money and make small loans to budding entrepreneurs and owners of small businesses. People from the IACs can offer microcredit loans to entrepreneurs in DVCs, helping nurture the spirit of enterprise. The benefits of micro-lending accrue not only to the entrepreneurs receiving the micro loans but also to their nations as a whole because the micro loans that are invested successfully create jobs, expand output, and raise the standard of living.

Avoiding High Rates of Inflation At the national level, DVC governments must guard against excessive money creation and the high inflation that it brings. High inflation rates simply are not conducive to economic investment and growth because inflation lowers the real returns generated by investments. DVCs can help keep inflation in check by establishing independent central banks to maintain proper control over their money supplies. Studies indicate that DVCs that control inflation enjoy higher growth rates than those that do not.

Controlling Population Growth Government can provide information about birth control options. Families with fewer children consume less and save more; they also free up time for women to receive an education and participate in the labor market. As women participate in the labor market, they tend to reduce their fertility rate, which further helps to control population growth.

Making Peace with Neighbors Countries at war or in fear of war with neighboring nations divert scarce resources to armaments, rather than to private capital or public infrastructure. Sustained peace among neighboring nations eventually leads to economic cooperation and integration, broadened markets, and stronger economic growth.

Public-Sector Problems

Although the public sector can positively influence economic development, serious problems can and do arise with government-directed initiatives. Indeed, development experts are less enthusiastic about the role of government in the growth process than they were a few decades ago. Unfortunately, government misadministration and **corruption** are common in many DVCs, and government officials sometimes line their own pockets with foreign-aid funds. Moreover, political leaders often confer monopoly privileges on relatives, friends, and political supporters and grant exclusive rights to relatives or friends to produce, import, or export certain products. Such monopoly privileges lead to higher domestic prices and diminish the DVC's ability to compete in world markets.

Similarly, managers of state-owned enterprises are often appointed on the basis of cronyism rather than competence. Many DVC governments, particularly in Africa, have created "marketing boards" as the sole purchaser of agricultural products from local farmers. The boards buy farm products at artificially low prices and sell them at higher world prices; the "profit" ends up in the pockets of government officials. In recent years, the perception of government has shifted from that of catalyst and promoter of growth to that of a potential impediment to development. According to a recent ranking of 180 nations based on perceived corruption, the 40 nations at the bottom of the list (most corrupt) were DVCs. Global Perspective 21.2 shows the corruption scores for 16 selected nations, including the two least corrupt (New Zealand and Denmark) and the two most corrupt (South Sudan and Somalia).

corruption The misuse of government power, with which one has been entrusted or assigned, to obtain private gain; includes payments from individuals or companies to secure advantages in obtaining government contracts, avoiding government regulations, or obtaining inside knowledge about forthcoming policy changes.

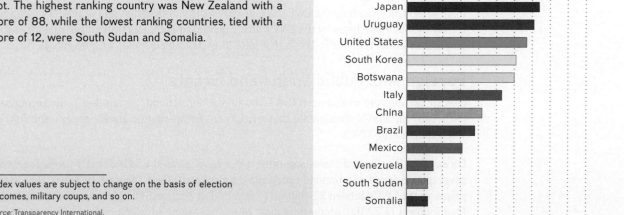

GLOBAL PERSPECTIVE 21.2

THE CORRUPTION PERCEPTIONS INDEX, SELECTED NATIONS, 2020*

The corruption perceptions index measures the degree of corruption existing among public officials and politicians as seen by businesspeople, risk analysts, and the general public. An index value of 100 is highly clean and 0 is highly corrupt. The highest ranking country was New Zealand with a score of 88, while the lowest ranking countries, tied with a score of 12, were South Sudan and Somalia.

Corruption Index Value, 2020

0 10 20 30 40 50 60 70 80 90 100

New Zealand
Denmark
Finland
Germany
Japan
Uruguay
United States
South Korea
Botswana
Italy
China
Brazil
Mexico
Venezuela
South Sudan
Somalia

*Index values are subject to change on the basis of election outcomes, military coups, and so on.

Source: Transparency International.

The Role of Advanced Nations

>> **LO21.5** Explain how industrial nations attempt to aid low-income countries.

How can the IACs help developing countries in their pursuit of economic growth? To what degree have IACs provided assistance?

Expanding Trade

Some authorities maintain that the simplest and most effective way for the industrially advanced nations to aid DVCs is to lower international trade barriers. Such action would enable DVCs to elevate their national incomes through increased trade. Trade barriers instituted by the IACs are often highest for labor-intensive manufactured goods, such as textiles, clothing, footwear, and processed agricultural products. These are precisely the sorts of products for which the DVCs have a comparative advantage. Also, many IACs' tariffs rise as the degree of product processing increases; for example, tariffs on chocolates are higher than those on cocoa. Tariffs therefore discourage DVCs from developing processing industries of their own.

Additionally, large agricultural subsidies in the IACs encourage excessive production of food and fiber in the IACs. The overproduction flows into world markets, where it depresses agricultural prices. DVCs, which typically do not subsidize farmers, therefore face artificially low prices for their farm exports. The IACs could greatly help DVCs by reducing farm subsidies along with tariffs.

But lowering trade barriers is certainly not a panacea. Some poor nations need only large foreign markets for their raw materials to achieve growth. But the problem for many poor nations is not to obtain markets in which to sell existing products or relatively abundant raw materials but rather to get the capital and technical assistance they need to produce products for domestic consumption.

Also, close trade ties with advanced nations entail certain disadvantages. Dependence by the DVCs on exports to the IACs leaves the DVCs highly vulnerable to recessions in the IACs. As firms cut back production in the IACs, the demand for DVC resources declines; and as income in the IACs declines, the demand for DVC-produced goods declines. By reducing the demand for DVC exports, recessions in the IACs can severely reduce the prices of raw materials exported by the DVCs. For example, during the recession of 2007–2009, the world price of zinc fell from $2.02 per pound to $0.49 per pound, and the world price of copper fell from $4.05 per pound to $1.40 per pound. These sorts of price declines severely reduce DVC export earnings when recessions strike IACs.

Admitting Temporary Workers

Some economists recommend that the IACs help the DVCs by accepting more seasonal or other temporary workers from the DVCs. Temporary migration provides an outlet for surplus DVC labor. Moreover, migrant remittances to families in the home country serve as a sorely needed source of income. The problem is that some temporary workers do not leave when their visas or work permits expire, which may not be in the IACs' long-run best interest.

Discouraging Arms Sales

Finally, the IACs can help the DVCs as a group by discouraging the sale of military equipment to the DVCs. Such purchases by the DVCs divert public expenditures from infrastructure and education and heighten tensions in DVCs that have long-standing disputes with neighbors.

Foreign Aid: Public Loans and Grants

Official development assistance (ODA), or simply "foreign aid," is another route through which IACs can help DVCs. Foreign aid that strengthens infrastructure could enhance the flow of private capital to the DVCs.

Direct Aid The United States and other IACs have assisted DVCs directly through a variety of programs designed to stimulate economic development. Over the past 10 years, U.S. loans and grants to the DVCs totaled $21 billion to $36 billion per year. The U.S. Agency for International Development (USAID) administers most of this aid, some of which consists of grants of surplus food under the Food for Peace program. Other advanced nations also have substantial foreign aid

GLOBAL PERSPECTIVE 21.3

OFFICIAL DEVELOPMENT ASSISTANCE AS A PERCENTAGE OF GDP, SELECTED NATIONS

The United States is the world's largest provider of official development assistance (ODA). In 2020, the United States provided $35.5 billion of ODA out of a worldwide total of $161.1 billion. But many industrialized nations contribute a larger percentage of their national incomes to development assistance than does the United States, as indicated by the bar chart.

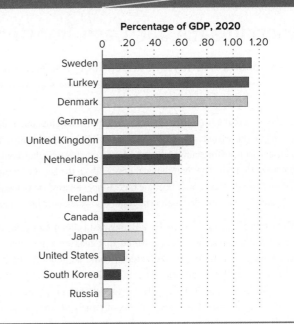

Percentage of GDP, 2020

Source: Organisation for Economic Co-operation and Development (OECD).

programs. In 2020 foreign aid from the IACs to the developing nations totaled $161.1 billion, or about one-fourth of 1 percent of the IACs' collective GDP that year. Global Perspective 21.3 illustrates that countries differ widely in how much development aid ("official development assistance") they award as a percentage of their respective GDPs.

A large portion of foreign aid is distributed on the basis of political and military considerations rather than strictly economic considerations. Egypt, Iraq, Israel, and Pakistan, for example, are major recipients of U.S. aid. Asian, Latin American, and African nations with lower standards of living receive less.

Only one-fourth of foreign aid goes to the 10 countries in which 70 percent of the world's poorest people live. The most affluent 40 percent of the DVC population receives over twice as much aid as the poorest 40 percent. Many economists argue that the IACs should shift foreign aid away from the middle-income DVCs and toward the poorest DVCs.

Some of the world's poorest nations do receive large amounts of foreign aid relative to their meager GDPs. For example, in 2019 foreign aid relative to GDP was 56 percent in Tuvalu, 38 percent in Somalia, 22 percent in Afghanistan, 20 percent in Tonga, and 16 percent in South Sudan.

These and many other low-income DVCs also receive large amounts of support from private donors in the IACs. In fact, in recent years the private giving to the DVCs by private U.S. universities, foundations (such as the Gates Foundation), voluntary organizations, and religious organizations has exceeded the foreign aid provided by the U.S. government.

The large accumulated debts of some of the poorest DVCs have become a severe roadblock to their growth. Therefore, some of the recent direct assistance by the IACs to the DVCs has taken the form of forgiving parts of the past IAC-government loans to low-income DVCs. In 2005 the G8 nations canceled $55 billion of debt owed by developing countries to the World Bank, the International Monetary Fund, and the African Development Bank. Of course, debt forgiveness creates a *moral hazard problem*. If current debt forgiveness creates an expectation of later debt forgiveness, a country has little incentive against running up a new debt. Therefore, future loans by the IACs must be extended cautiously in the future to nations that currently receive debt forgiveness.

By contrast, there were few worries about moral hazard when the G20 nations chose, in April 2020, to suspend the collection of debt payments owed by 73 developing countries to help them through the COVID-19 pandemic. Because those debt payments were suspended temporarily, rather than being forgiven permanently, the G20 action was expected to provide little to no temptation for any developing government to fall prey to moral hazard and borrow excessively in the hope of future debt forgiveness.

Microfinance and Cash Transfers

Development Efforts Have Increasingly Focused on Lending, Granting, or Gifting Money to Individuals.

For the most of the twentieth century, international development efforts focused on infrastructure projects, such as building roads, bridges, and electrical grids. Efforts aimed directly at individuals were relatively rare and poorly funded. That has changed drastically in the last few decades as development efforts have become increasingly focused on delivering cash directly to poor individuals. The results, however, have been mixed.

Microcredit In the mid-1970s, a Bangladeshi economics professor named Muhammad Yunus discovered that making small loans to poor villagers in his native Bangladesh could sometimes facilitate economic growth and advancement at the individual level. A group of women could, for instance, start a modest but profitable textile company if they could borrow amounts of money as small as $10 or $20 to purchase looms and other equipment.

The even more startling part was that these small loans, or *microcredit*, were nearly always paid back. Whereas the poor had often been thought of by development experts as being too uneducated or inexperienced to help themselves out of poverty, Yunus showed that the poor often had good business sense and were in some cases constrained not by ignorance but by a lack of capital.

In 1983, Yunus established the Grameen Bank (literally the "Village Bank") to provide microcredit throughout Bangladesh. The Grameen Bank later expanded beyond microcredit into banking and insurance services for the poor, a set of activities that came to be referred to as **microfinance.** Its individual-focused approach to development spawned hundreds of imitators in scores of nations and earned Yunus the 2006 Nobel Peace Prize.

Tim Gerard Barker/Lonely Planet Images/Getty Images

Unfortunately, development economists have found that microfinance does not offer a consistent way out of poverty by itself. Randomized experiments show that, on average, the households and individuals receiving microcredit usually do no better than nonrecipients on economic, health, and social outcomes such as family income, the total number of calories consumed, and rates of school attendance.

---

microfinance The provision of small loans and other financial services to low-income *entrepreneurs* and small-business owners in *developing countries*.

World Bank A bank that lends (and guarantees loans) to *developing countries* to assist them in increasing their *capital stock* and thus in achieving *economic growth*.

The World Bank Group The United States and other IACs also support the DVCs by participating in the **World Bank,** whose major objective is helping DVCs achieve economic growth by lending DVC governments the money that they need to complete specific development projects.

The World Bank was established in 1945, along with the International Monetary Fund (IMF). Supported by 189 member nations, the World Bank not only lends out of its capital funds but also sells bonds, lends the proceeds, and guarantees and insures private loans:

- The World Bank is a "last-resort" lending agency; its loans are limited to economic projects for which private funds are not readily available.

- The majority of World Bank loans are "hard loans" that are only issued to projects that are judged to be capable of generating returns sufficient to pay off them off.

- Many World Bank loans have been for basic development projects—dams, irrigation projects, health and sanitation programs, communications, and transportation facilities. The Bank has helped finance the infrastructure needed to encourage the flow of private capital.

- The Bank has provided technical assistance to the DVCs by helping them determine what avenues of growth seem appropriate for their economic development.

Two divisions of the World Bank focus on lending to the private sector and on concessional loans that function more like grants than the hard loans that the World Bank typically issues. The

Conditional cash transfers Conditional cash transfer programs provide poor families with transfers (grants) of cash if they send their children to school and participate in preventive health programs. As just one example, the Mexican government's *Oportunidades* program gives bi-weekly cash grants to poor families who keep their kids in school and participate in health screenings and nutritional programs.

Conditional cash transfer programs have been in place since the early 1990s, which makes them old enough for us to be able to draw some conclusions about their effectiveness. Some very positive outcomes are apparent. The programs have been shown to increase school enrollment by up to 30 percent and to improve health and nutrition so much that rates of illness among young children fall by more than 10 percent. Children enrolled in conditional cash transfer programs also end up taller than children who are not enrolled.

Unfortunately, the effectiveness of conditional cash transfers in relieving poverty in developing countries is limited by other factors. As just one example, school enrollment goes up but test scores stay the same, probably because the schools themselves are poorly funded and often ineffective. Similarly, the wages earned by the students who stay in school longer don't seem to be much higher than those of the students who dropped out earlier, probably because of the low quality of many schools as well as high rates of unemployment in many local labor markets.

Unconditional cash transfers The newest antipoverty initiatives targeted at individuals are known as **unconditional cash transfers** because they simply hand cash to poor adults with no conditions attached. They operate under the theory that many poor people are held back by a lack of either physical or human capital, and that if you were to give them no-strings-attached cash, they would use the money to pay for tools and training.

That assumption has proven true in early testing. As an example, a randomized study in Uganda that started in 2008 offered the chance to receive unconditional cash transfers to young people who were willing to submit essays detailing what they planned to do with any money received. Half of the participants were then randomly selected to receive the money, with it being made explicitly clear that nobody would be following up to see if the recipients actually spent the money on what they had written in their essays (which, for the most part, indicated a desire to spend cash transfers on vocational training and business equipment).

The researchers running the study found that the half who were randomly selected to receive unconditional cash transfers ended up "65 percent more likely to practice a skilled trade such as carpentry, metalworking, tailoring, or hairstyling" than those who did not receive unconditional cash transfers. Even better, the results were long lasting, with recipients earning salaries that were 41 percent higher four years later.

Because unconditional cash transfer programs are quite new, however, it is not yet clear whether their early promise can be replicated in other places or even why granting cash unconditionally seems to work better than either conditional cash transfers or microfinance. Experiments are under way to find out.

---

conditional cash transfers Anti-poverty programs in which households receive regular cash transfers (grants) as long as they keep their children in school and participate in preventative health care programs.

unconditional cash transfers Anti-poverty programs that give cash transfers (grants) to poor individuals with no strings attached in the hope that the recipients will improve their economic prospects by spending the money on either education or physical capital.

International Finance Corporation (IFC) loans money to private enterprises within DVCs. The *International Development Association (IDA)* grants money that does not have to be paid back to the poorest DVC governments in addition to issuing them "soft loans" that have generously low interest rates and extended payout periods.

Foreign Harm? The foreign-aid approach to helping DVCs has met with several criticisms.

Dependency and Incentives A basic criticism is that foreign aid may promote dependency rather than self-sustaining growth. Critics argue that injections of funds from the IACs encourage the DVCs to ignore the painful economic decisions, the institutional and cultural reforms, and the changes in attitudes toward thrift, industry, hard work, and self-reliance that are needed for economic growth. They say that, after some five decades of foreign aid, the DVCs' demand for foreign aid has increased rather than decreased. These aid programs should have withered away if they had been successful in promoting sustainable growth.

Bureaucracy and Centralized Government IAC aid is given to the governments of the DVCs, not to their residents or businesses. The consequence is that the aid typically generates massive, ineffective government bureaucracies and centralizes government power over the economy. The stagnation and collapse of the Soviet Union and communist countries of eastern Europe is evidence that highly bureaucratized economies are not very conducive to economic growth and development.

Furthermore, the bureaucratization of the DVCs often shifts the nation's focus from producing more output to bickering over how unearned "income" should be distributed.

Corruption and Misuse Some estimates suggest that from 10 to 20 percent of foreign aid is "diverted" to the private bank accounts of local government officials. Also, IAC-based aid consultants and multinational corporations are major beneficiaries of aid programs. Some economists contend that as much as one-fourth of each year's aid is spent on expert consultants. Furthermore, because IAC corporations manage many of the aid projects, they are major beneficiaries of, and lobbyists for, foreign aid.

Flows of Private Capital

foreign direct investment
Financial investments made to obtain a lasting ownership interest in *firms* operating outside the economy of the investor; may involve purchasing existing assets or building new production facilities.

The total flow of private capital to DVCs was $616 billion in 2020. The main private investors and lenders are now private IAC firms and individuals, not commercial banks. Also, more of the flow is in the form of **foreign direct investment** in DVCs, rather than loans to DVC governments. For example, General Motors or Ford might finance the construction of plants in Mexico or Brazil to assemble autos or produce auto parts. JPMorgan Chase or Bank of America might make loans to private firms operating in Argentina or China or to the governments of Thailand and Malaysia.

Whereas some DVCs once viewed foreign direct investment as "exploitation," many of them now seek out foreign direct investment as a way to expand their capital stock and improve their citizens' job opportunities and wages. Those wages are often very low by IAC standards but high by DVC standards. Another benefit of direct investment in DVCs is that management skills and technological knowledge often accompany the capital.

Unfortunately for the low-income DVCs, the strong flow of private capital to the DVCs has been very selective. The vast majority of IAC investment and lending has been directed toward China, India, Mexico, and other middle-income DVCs, with only small amounts flowing toward such extremely impoverished DVCs as those in Africa.

In fact, as we have indicated, many of the lowest-income countries face staggering debt burdens from previous government and private loans. Payment of interest and principal on this external debt is diverting expenditures away from maintenance of infrastructure, new infrastructure, education, and private investment.

Further, the flows of private capital to both the middle-income and low-income DVCs fell after the COVID-19 pandemic began in early 2020. It may be several years before foreign direct investment regains its momentum.

**QUICK REVIEW
21.2**

▶ The IACs can assist the DVCs through expanded trade, foreign aid, and flows of private capital.

▶ Many of the poorest DVCs have large external debts that pose an additional obstacle to economic growth.

▶ The worldwide COVID-19 recession reduced direct investment by IACs in DVCs.

Summary

LO21.1 Distinguish between industrially advanced countries and developing countries.
The majority of the world's nations are developing countries (low- and middle-income nations). While some DVCs have been realizing rapid growth rates in recent years, others have experienced little or no growth.

LO21.2 List the obstacles to economic development.
Scarcities of natural resources make it more challenging, but not impossible, for a nation to develop.

The large and rapidly growing populations in many DVCs contribute to low per capita incomes. Increases in per capita incomes frequently induce greater population growth, often reducing per capita incomes to near-subsistence levels. The demographic transition view, however, suggests that rising living standards must precede declining birthrates.

Most DVCs suffer from unemployment and underemployment. Labor productivity is low because of insufficient investment in physical and human capital.

In many DVCs, formidable obstacles impede both saving and investment. In some of the poorest DVCs, the savings potential is very low, and many savers transfer their funds to the IACs rather than invest them domestically. The lack of a vigorous entrepreneurial class and the weakness of investment incentives also impede capital accumulation.

Appropriate social and institutional changes and, in particular, the presence of the will to develop are essential ingredients in economic development.

LO21.3 Explain the vicious circle of poverty that afflicts low-income nations.

The vicious circle of poverty brings together many of the obstacles to growth, supporting the view that poor countries stay poor because of their poverty. Low incomes inhibit saving and the accumulation of physical and human capital, making it difficult to increase productivity and incomes. Overly rapid population growth may offset promising attempts to break the vicious circle.

LO21.4 Describe the role of government in promoting economic development.

The obstacles to growth—the absence of an entrepreneurial class, the dearth of infrastructure, the saving-investment dilemma, and the presence of social-institutional obstacles to growth—suggest that government should play a major role in initiating growth. Economists suggest that DVCs that have achieved basic levels of state capacity and the rule of law can make further development progress through such policies as building infrastructure, opening their economies to international trade, setting realistic exchange rates, encouraging foreign direct investment, building human capital, encouraging entrepreneurship, controlling population growth, and making peace with neighbors. However, the corruption and maladministration that are common to the public sectors of many DVCs suggest that government may not be very effective in instigating growth.

LO21.5 Explain how industrial nations attempt to aid low-income countries.

Advanced nations can encourage development in the DVCs by reducing IAC trade barriers and by directing foreign aid (official development assistance) to the neediest nations, providing debt forgiveness to the poorest DVCs, allowing temporary low-skilled immigration from the DVCs, and discouraging arms sales to the DVCs. Critics of foreign aid, however, say that it (a) creates DVC dependency, (b) contributes to the growth of bureaucracies and centralized economic control, and (c) is rendered ineffective by corruption and mismanagement.

In recent years the IACs have reduced foreign aid to the DVCs but have increased direct investment and other private capital flows to the DVCs. Little of the foreign direct investment, however, has gone to the poorest DVCs. Also, foreign direct investment plummeted during the worldwide recession of 2007–2009.

Terms and Concepts

industrially advanced countries (IACs)

developing countries (DVCs)

demographic transition

underemployment

capital flight

infrastructure

capital-saving technology

capital-using technology

will to develop

capricious universe view

land reform

vicious circle of poverty

state capacity

failed state

microcredit

corruption

World Bank

foreign direct investment

microfinance

conditional cash transfers

unconditional cash transfers

Discussion Questions

1. What are the four categories used by the World Bank to classify nations on the basis of national income per capita? Identify any two nations of your choice for each of the four categories. **LO21.1**
2. Explain how the absolute per capita income gap between rich and poor nations might increase, even though per capita income (or output) is growing faster in DVCs than in IACs. **LO21.1**
3. Explain how each of the following can be obstacles to the growth of income per capita in the DVCs: lack of natural resources, large populations, low labor productivity, poor infrastructure, and capital flight. **LO21.2**
4. What is the demographic transition? Contrast the demographic transition view of population growth with the traditional view that slower population growth is a prerequisite for rising living standards in the DVCs. **LO21.2**
5. As it relates to the vicious circle of poverty, what is meant by the saying "Some DVCs stay poor because they are poor"? Change the box labels as necessary in Figure 21.3 to explain rapid economic growth in countries such as South Korea and Chile. What factors other than those contained in the figure might contribute to that growth? **LO21.3**

6. Because real capital is supposed to earn a higher return where it is scarce, how do you explain the fact that most international investment flows to the IACs (where capital is relatively abundant) rather than to the DVCs (where capital is very scarce)? **LO21.3**
7. What factors cause failed states? List and discuss five policies that DVC governments might undertake to promote economic development and expansion of income per capita in their countries. **LO21.4**
8. Do you think that the problems the DVCs face require a government-directed or a private-sector-directed development process? Explain your reasoning. **LO21.4**
9. Why do you think there is so much government corruption in some developing countries? **LO21.4**
10. What types of products do the DVCs typically export? How do those exports relate to the law of comparative advantage? How do tariffs by IACs reduce DVCs' standard of living? **LO21.5**
11. Do you favor debt forgiveness to all DVCs, just the poorest ones, or none at all? What incentive problem might debt relief create? Would you be willing to pay $20 a year more in personal income taxes for debt forgiveness? How about $200? How about $2,000? **LO21.5**

12. Do you think that IACs such as the United States should open their doors wider to the immigration of low-skilled DVC workers as a way to help DVCs develop? Do you think that it is appropriate for students from DVC nations to stay in IAC nations to work and build careers? **LO21.5**

13. **LAST WORD** Explain the differences among microcredit, conditional cash transfers, and unconditional cash transfers. Then explain how effective each policy has been.

Review Questions

1. True or False: The term *developing country* (DVC) is applied to rich nations like the United States and Germany because their economies are always growing quickly by developing new technologies. **LO21.1**

2. True or False: A DVC that has little in the way of natural resources is destined to remain poor. **LO21.2**

3. Suppose a country's total output is growing 10 percent per year, but its population is growing 11 percent per year. What will happen to living standards? **LO21.2**
   a. They will rise.
   b. They will fall.
   c. They will remain the same.

4. A DVC's population is growing 2 percent per year and its output is growing 3 percent per year. If the government wants to improve living standards over the coming decades, which of the following would probably be the best savings rate for the economy? **LO21.2**
   a. 0 percent
   b. 2 percent
   c. 5 percent
   d. 10 percent

5. Compare a hypothetical DVC with a hypothetical IAC. In the DVC, average per capita income is $500 per year. In the IAC, average per capita income is $40,000 per year. If both countries have a savings rate of 10 percent per year, the amount of savings per capita in the DVC will be _____ per person per year, while in the IAC it will be _____ per person per year. **LO21.3**
   a. $50; $4,000
   b. $5; $400
   c. $450; $36,000
   d. None of the above

6. Which of the following policies would economists consider to be actions by a DVC government that will *improve* growth prospects? **LO21.4**
   *Choose **one or more** answers from the choices shown.*
   a. Helping to extend the banking system to the rural poor.
   b. Passing high tariffs against foreign products.
   c. Constructing better ports, roads, and Internet networks.
   d. Charging high fees for public elementary schools.

7. True or False: Economists are unanimous that foreign aid greatly helps DVCs. **LO21.5**

8. True or False: Some economists argue that the single best thing that IACs could do for DVCs in terms of economic growth is to eliminate trade barriers between IACs and DVCs. **LO21.5**

Problems

1. Assume a DVC and an IAC currently have real per capita outputs of $500 and $50,000, respectively. If both nations have a 3 percent increase in their real per capita outputs, by how much will the per capita output gap change? **LO21.1**

2. Assume that a very tiny and very poor DVC has income per capita of $300 and total national income of $3 million. How large is its population? If its population grows by 2 percent in some year while its total income grows by 3 percent, what will be its new income per capita rounded to full dollars? If the population had not grown during the year, what would have been its income per capita? **LO21.2**

Glossary

Note: Terms set in *italic type* are defined separately in this glossary.

45° (degree) line The reference line in a two-dimensional graph that shows equality between the variable measured on the *horizontal axis* and the variable measured on the *vertical axis*. In the *aggregate expenditures model,* the line along which the value of output (measured horizontally) is equal to the value of *aggregate expenditures* (measured vertically).

ability-to-pay principle The idea that those who have greater *income* (or *wealth*) should pay a greater proportion of it as taxes than those who have less income (or wealth).

absolute advantage A situation in which a person or country can produce more of a particular product from a specific quantity of resource inputs than some other person or country.

absolute value The magnitude of a number without regard to its sign. For any number x, the absolute value of x is denoted $|x|$, and $|x| = +x$ no matter whether x itself is a positive or negative number. Thus, $|-3| = +3$ and $|+3| = +3$.

accounting profit The *total revenue* of a *firm* less its *explicit costs;* the profit (or net income) that appears on accounting statements and that is reported to the government for tax purposes.

acreage allotments A pre-1996 government program that limited the total number of acres to be used in producing (reduced amounts of) various food and fiber products and allocated these acres among individual farmers. These farmers had to limit their plantings to the allotted number of acres to obtain *price supports* for their crops.

actively managed funds *Mutual funds* that have portfolio managers who constantly buy and sell *assets* in an attempt to generate high returns.

administered rate An *interest rate* set by a *central bank* to help it manage market-determined *interest rates.*

adverse selection problem A problem arising when information known to one party to a contract or agreement is not known to the other party, causing the latter to incur major costs. Example: Individuals who have the poorest health are most likely to buy health insurance.

Affordable Care Act (ACA) A major health care law passed by the federal government in 2010. Major provisions include an individual health insurance mandate, a ban on insurers refusing to accept patients with preexisting conditions, and federal (rather than state) regulation of health insurance policies.

AFL-CIO An acronym for the American Federation of Labor–Congress of Industrial Organizations; the largest federation of *labor unions* in the United States.

agency shop A place of employment where the employer may hire either *labor union* members or nonmembers but where those employees who do not join the union must either pay union dues or donate an equivalent amount of money to a charity.

aggregate A collection of specific economic units treated as if they were one unit.

aggregate demand A schedule or curve that shows the total quantity of *goods* and *services* that would be demanded (purchased) at various *price levels.*

aggregate demand–aggregate supply (AD-AS) model The macroeconomic model that uses *aggregate demand* and *aggregate supply* to determine and explain the *price level* and real domestic output (*real gross domestic product*).

aggregate expenditures schedule A table of numbers showing the total amount spent on *final goods* and final *services* at different levels of *real gross domestic product* (*real GDP*).

aggregate supply A schedule or curve showing the total quantity of *goods* and *services* that would be supplied (produced) at various *price levels.*

aggregate supply shocks Sudden, large changes in resource costs that shift an economy's aggregate supply curve.

agribusiness The portion of the agricultural and food product industries that is dominated by large corporations.

Agricultural Act of 2018 The 2018 act that made minor changes to programs and policies of the Agricultural Act of 2014.

agricultural risk coverage A form of crop insurance that pays out if the total revenue generated by all the farmers planting a given crop in a given county falls below a predetermined value.

Alcoa case A 1945 case in which the courts ruled that the possession of monopoly power, no matter how reasonably that power had been used, was a violation of the antitrust laws; temporarily overturned the *rule of reason* applied in the *U.S. Steel case.*

allocative efficiency The apportionment of resources among *firms* and industries to obtain the production of the products most wanted by society (consumers); the output of each product at which its *marginal cost* and *marginal benefit* are equal, and at which the sum of *consumer surplus* and *producer surplus* is maximized.

AT&T case A major antitrust case decided in 1984 that broke up the American Telephone and Telegraph company (AT&T), which had run a domestic telephone monopoly across the entire United States for many decades, into 22 regional telephone operating companies.

anchoring The tendency people have to unconsciously base, or "anchor," the valuation of an item they are currently thinking about on recently considered but logically irrelevant information.

anticipated inflation Increases in the *price level* (*inflation*) that occur at the expected rate.

antitrust laws Legislation (including the *Sherman Act* and *Clayton Act*) that prohibits anticompetitive business activities such as *price fixing,* bid rigging, monopolization, and *tying contracts.*

antitrust policy The use of the *antitrust laws* to promote *competition* and *economic efficiency.*

aquaculture The cultivation of aquatic animals and plants for food.

arbitrage The activity of selling one *asset* and buying an identical or nearly identical asset to benefit from temporary differences in *prices* or *rates of return;* the practice that equalizes prices or returns on similar financial instruments and thus eliminates further opportunities for riskless financial gains.

asset demand for money The amount of *money* people want to hold as a *store of value;* this amount varies inversely with the *interest rate.*

asymmetric information A situation where one party to a market transaction has more information about a product or service than the other. The result may be an under- or overallocation of resources.

average expected rate of return The *probability-weighted average* of an investment's possible future returns.

average fixed cost (AFC) A *firm's* total *fixed cost* divided by output (the quantity of product produced).

average product (AP) The total output produced per unit of a *resource* employed; equal to *total product* divided by the quantity of the employed resource.

average propensity to consume (APC) Fraction (or percentage) of *disposable income* that *households* spend on *consumer goods;* consumption divided by *disposable income.*

average propensity to save (APS) Fraction (or percentage) of *disposable income* that *households* save; *saving* divided by *disposable income.*

average revenue Total revenue from the sale of a product divided by the quantity of the product sold (demanded); equal to the *price* at which the product is sold when all units of the product are sold at the same price.

average tax rate Total tax paid divided by total *taxable income* or some other base (such as total income) against which to compare the amount of tax paid. Expressed as a percentage.

average total cost (ATC) A firm's *total cost* divided by output (the quantity of product produced); equal to *average fixed cost* plus *average variable cost.*

average variable cost (AVC) A firm's total *variable cost* divided by output (the quantity of product produced).

backflows The return of workers to the countries from which they originally emigrated.

balance of payments A summary of all the financial transactions that take place between the individuals, *firms,* and governmental units of one nation and those of all other nations during a year.

balance on capital and financial account The sum of the *capital account balance* and the *financial account balance.*

balance on current account The exports of *goods* and *services* of a nation less its imports of goods and services plus its *net investment income* and *net transfers* in a year.

balance on goods and services The exports of *goods* and *services* of a nation less its imports of goods and services in a year.

bankrupt A legal situation in which an individual or *firm* finds that it cannot make timely interest payments on money it has borrowed. In such cases, a bankruptcy judge can order the individual or firm to liquidate (turn into cash) its assets in order to pay lenders at least some portion of the amount they are owed.

barrier to entry Anything that artificially prevents the entry of *firms* into an *industry.*

barter The direct exchange of one *good* or *service* for another good or service.

base year The year with which other years are compared when an index is constructed; for example, the base year for a *price index.*

beaten paths Migration routes taken previously by family, relatives, friends, and other migrants.

behavioral economics The branch of economic theory that combines insights from economics, psychology, and biology to make more accurate predictions about human behavior than conventional *neoclassical economics,* which is hampered by its core assumptions that people are fundamentally *rational* and almost entirely self-interested. Behavioral economics can explain *framing effects, anchoring, mental accounting,* the *endowment effect, status quo bias, time inconsistency,* and *loss aversion.*

behavioral remedy A directive imposed by a regulator on an offending *monopoly* firm that seeks to resolve the firm's illegal monopoly behavior by requiring different actions be taken by the firm in the future, such as not engaging in price fixing or refraining from using tying contracts.

benefits-received principle The idea that those who receive the benefits of *goods* and *services* provided by government should pay the taxes required to finance them.

beta A relative measure of *nondiversifiable risk* that measures how the nondiversifiable risk of a given *asset* or *portfolio* compares with that of the *market portfolio* (the portfolio that contains every asset available in the financial markets).

bilateral monopoly A market in which there is a single seller (*monopoly*) and a single buyer (*monopsony*).

Board of Governors The seven-member group that supervises and controls the money and banking system of the United States; the Board of Governors of the *Federal Reserve System;* the Federal Reserve Board.

bond A financial contract that obligates a borrower to make coupon (interest) payments for a specified period of time before also paying back the principal amount that was initially borrowed.

brain drains The exit or *emigration* of highly educated, highly skilled workers from a country.

break-even income The level of *disposable income* at which *households* plan to consume (spend) all their income and to save none of it.

break-even point An output at which a *firm* makes a *normal profit* (*total revenue = total cost*) but not an *economic profit.*

Bretton Woods system The international monetary system developed after the Second World War in which *adjustable pegs* were employed, the *International Monetary Fund* helped stabilize foreign exchange rates, and gold and the dollar were used as *international monetary reserves.*

British thermal unit (BTU) The amount of energy required to raise the temperature of 1 pound of water by 1 degree Fahrenheit.

budget constraint The limit that the size of a consumer's income (and the *prices* that must be paid for *goods* and *services*) imposes on the ability of that consumer to obtain goods and services.

budget deficit The amount by which expenditures exceed revenues in any year.

budget line A line that shows the different combinations of two products a consumer can purchase with a specific money income, given the products' *prices.*

budget surplus The amount by which the revenues of the federal government exceed its expenditures in any year.

built-in stabilizer A mechanism that increases government's budget deficit (or reduces its surplus) during a recession and increases government's budget surplus (or reduces its deficit) during an expansion without any action by policymakers. The tax system is one such mechanism.

business cycle Recurring increases and decreases in the level of economic activity over periods of years; consists of peak, recession, trough, and expansion phases.

businesses Economic entities (*firms*) that purchase resources and provide *goods* and *services* to the economy.

capital Man-made physical objects (factories, roads) and intangible ideas (the recipe for cement) that do not directly satisfy human wants but which help to produce *goods* and *services* that do satisfy human wants. One of the four *economic resources.*

capital and financial account The section of a nation's *international balance of payments* that records (1) debt forgiveness by and to foreigners and (2) foreign purchases of assets in the United States and U.S. purchases of assets abroad.

capital flight The transfer of savings from *developing countries* to *industrially advanced countries* to avoid government expropriation, taxation, or higher rates of *inflation,* or simply to realize greater returns on *financial investments.*

capital gain The gain realized when *securities* other *assets* are sold for a *price* greater than the price paid for them.

capital-intensive goods Products that require relatively large amounts of *capital* to produce.

capital-saving technology An improvement in *technology* that permits a greater quantity of a product to be produced with a specific amount of *capital* (or permits the same amount of the product to be produced with a smaller amount of capital).

capital-using technology An improvement in *technology* that requires the use of a greater amount of *capital* to produce a specific quantity of a product.

capricious-universe view The view held by some people that fate and outside events, rather than hard work and enterprise, will determine their economic destinies.

cartel A formal agreement among *firms* (or countries) in an *industry* to set the *price* of a product and establish the outputs of the individual firms (or countries) or to divide the market for the product geographically.

catch-up growth The rapid increases in real GDP per capita that can be achieved when a poor *follower country* adopts, rather than reinvents, cutting edge technologies that took *leader countries* decades to invent and implement.

cease-and-desist order An order from a court or government agency to a corporation or individual to stop engaging in a specified practice.

Celler-Kefauver Act The federal law of 1950 that amended the *Clayton Act* by prohibiting the acquisition of the assets of one *firm* by another firm when the effect would be less competition.

change in demand A movement of an entire *demand curve* (or of the numerical entries in a demand schedule) such that the *quantity demanded* changes at every particular *price;* caused by a change in one or more of the *determinants of demand.*

change in quantity demanded A change in the *quantity demanded* along a fixed *demand curve* (or within a fixed demand schedule) as a result of a change in the *price* of the product.

change in quantity supplied A change in the *quantity supplied* of a product along a fixed *supply curve* (or within a fixed supply schedule) as a result of a change in the product's *price.*

change in supply A movement of an entire *supply curve* (or of the numerical entries in a schedule) such that the *quantity supplied* changes at every particular *price;* caused by a change in one or more of the *determinants of supply.*

checkable deposit Any deposit in a *commercial bank* or *thrift institution* against which a check may be written.

circular flow diagram An illustration showing the flow of *resources* from *households* to *firms* and of products from firms to households. These flows are accompanied by reverse flows of *money* from firms to households and from households to firms.

Clayton Act The federal antitrust law of 1914 that strengthened the *Sherman Act* by making it illegal for *firms* to engage in certain specified practices including *tying contracts, interlocking directorates,* and certain forms of *price discrimination.*

closed shop A place of employment where only workers who are already members of a labor union may be hired.

Coase theorem The idea, first stated by economist Ronald Coase, that some *externalities* can be resolved through private negotiations among the affected parties.

cognitive biases Misperceptions or misunderstandings that cause *systematic errors.* Most result either (1) from *heuristics* that are prone to *systematic errors* or (2) because the brain is attempting to solve a type of problem (such as a calculus problem) for which it was not evolutionarily evolved and for which it has little innate capability.

coinsurance The percentage of (say, health care) costs that an insured individual pays while the insurer pays the remainder.

collective bargaining The negotiation of labor contracts between *labor unions* and *firms* or government entities.

collective demand for a public good A schedule or a curve showing the collective willingness to pay of consumers for a public good. Can be found by vertically adding individual demand curves, which is equivalent to adding the respective maximum prices that individual consumers are willing to pay for the last unit of the public good at each possible quantity demanded.

collective-action problem The difficulty of getting a large group of voters to organize against a policy when the costs of that policy are widely dispersed (so that none of them individually has much of a personal incentive to take action).

collusion Cooperation or conspiracy in which *firms* act together (collude) to fix *prices,* divide a market, or otherwise restrict competition. Most collusion is illegal.

command system A method of organizing an economy in which property resources are publicly owned and government uses *central economic planning* to direct and coordinate economic activities; *socialism;* communism. Compare with *market system.*

commercial bank A *firm* that engages in the business of banking (accepts deposits, offers checking accounts, and makes loans).

comparative advantage A situation in which a person or country can produce a specific product at a lower *opportunity cost* in terms of other types of *output* foregone than some other person or country; the basis for specialization and trade.

compensating wage differences Differences in the *wages* received by workers in different jobs to compensate for the nonmonetary differences between the jobs.

competition The effort and striving between two or more independent rivals to secure the business of one or more third parties by offering the best possible terms.

complementary goods Products and *services* that are used together. When the *price* of one falls, the demand for the other increases (and conversely).

complementary resources Productive inputs that are used jointly with other inputs in the production process; resources for which a decrease in the *price* of one leads to an increase in the demand for the other.

compound interest *Interest* that is paid both on an original sum of money and on interest that has already been paid on that sum.

conditional cash transfers Anti-poverty programs in which households receive regular cash transfers (grants) as long as they keep their children in school and participate in preventative health care programs.

conflict minerals   Minerals (especially gold, tin, tantalum, and tungsten) that are minded and sold by combatants in war zones in Africa as a way to help finance their military activities.

conglomerate merger   The merger of two *firms* operating in separate industries or separate geographic areas so that neither firm is a supplier, customer, or competitor of the other; any merger that is neither a *horizontal merger* nor a *vertical merger*.

constant returns to scale   The situation when a firm's *average total cost* of producing a product remains unchanged in the *long run* as the firm varies the size of its *plant* (and, hence, its output).

constant-cost industry   An *industry* in which the entry and exit of *firms* have no effect on the *prices* that firms in the industry must pay for resources and thus no effect on production costs.

consumer equilibrium   In marginal utility theory, the combination of goods purchased that maximizes *total utility* by applying the *utility-maximizing rule*.

consumer goods   Products and *services* that satisfy human wants directly.

Consumer Price Index (CPI)   An index that measures the *prices* of a fixed "market basket" of some 300 *goods* and *services* bought by a "typical" consumer.

consumer sovereignty   The determination by consumers of the types and quantities of *goods* and *services* that will be produced with the scarce resources of the economy; consumers' direction of production through their *dollar votes*.

consumer surplus   The difference between the maximum *price* a consumer is (or consumers are) willing to pay for an additional unit of a product and its market price; the triangular area below the demand curve and above the market price.

consumption of fixed capital   An estimate of the amount of *capital* worn out or used up (consumed) in producing the *gross domestic product;* also called depreciation.

consumption schedule   A table of numbers showing the amounts *households* plan to spend for *consumer goods* at different levels of *disposable income*.

contestable industries   Industries in which even dominant firms have to worry about competition because new entrants and existing competitors are able to compete successfully for market share and users.

contractionary fiscal policy   A decrease in *government purchases* of *goods* and *services,* an increase in *net taxes,* or some combination of the two, for the purpose of decreasing *aggregate demand* and thus controlling *inflation*.

coordination failure   A situation in which people do not reach a mutually beneficial outcome because they lack some way to jointly coordinate their actions; a possible cause of macroeconomic instability.

coordination problem   The chronic failure of command economies to harmonize the economic activities of producers so as to efficiently satisfy consumer demands; caused by command economies eschewing economic coordination via markets, prices, and profits in favor of central planning.

copayment   A fixed amount (such as $25 per office visit) that the insured individual must pay even after the annual deductible has been passed.

core inflation   The underlying increases in the *price level* after volatile food and energy *prices* are removed.

corporate income tax   A tax levied on the net income (accounting profit) of corporations.

corruption   The misuse of government power, with which one has been entrusted or assigned, to obtain private gain; includes payments from individuals or companies to secure advantages in obtaining government contracts, avoiding government regulations, or obtaining inside knowledge about forthcoming policy changes.

cost-benefit analysis   A method for deciding whether or not to provide a public good that involves a comparison of the total cost of providing that public good with its collective benefit (measured by collective willingness to pay).

cost-of-living adjustment (COLA)   An automatic increase in the incomes (*wages*) of workers when *inflation* occurs; often included in *collective bargaining* agreements between *firms* and *unions*. Cost-of-living adjustments are also guaranteed by law for *Social Security* benefits and certain other government *transfer payments*.

cost-push inflation   Increases in the *price level* (*inflation*) resulting from an increase in resource costs (for example, raw-material prices) and hence in *per-unit production costs;* inflation caused by reductions in *aggregate supply*.

Council of Economic Advisers (CEA)   A group of three persons that advises and assists the president of the United States on economic matters (including the preparation of the annual *Economic Report of the President*).

countercyclical payments (CCPs)   Cash *subsidies* paid to farmers when market *prices* for certain crops drop below targeted prices. Payments are based on previous production and are received regardless of the current crop grown.

creative destruction   The hypothesis that the creation of new products and production methods destroys the market power of firms committed to existing products and older ways of doing business.

credible threat   In a *sequential game* with two players, a statement made by Player 1 that truthfully (credibly) threatens a penalizing action against Player 2 if Player 2 does something that Player 1 does not want Player 2 to do. Opposite of *empty threat*.

crop insurance   Insurance that farmers can purchase that will pay out if crop selling prices or crop revenues fall below predetermined values.

cross elasticity of demand   The ratio of the percentage change in *quantity demanded* of one good to the percentage change in the *price* of some other good. A positive coefficient indicates the two products are *substitute goods;* a negative coefficient indicates they are *complementary goods*.

crowding-out effect   A rise in interest rates and a resulting decrease in *planned investment* caused by the federal government's increased borrowing to finance budget deficits and refinance debt.

currency intervention   A government's buying and selling of its own currency or foreign currencies to alter international exchange rates.

current account   The section in a nation's *international balance of payments* that records its exports and imports of *goods* and *services,* its net *investment income,* and its *net transfers*.

cyclical asymmetry   The idea that *monetary policy* may be more successful in slowing expansions and controlling *inflation* than in extracting the economy from severe recession.

cyclical deficit   Federal *budget deficit* that is caused by a recession and the consequent decline in tax revenues.

cyclical unemployment   A type of *unemployment* caused by insufficient total spending (insufficient *aggregate demand*) and which typically begins in the *recession* phase of the *business cycle*.

cyclically adjusted budget The estimated annual budget deficit or surplus that would occur under existing tax rates and government spending levels if the economy were to operate at its *full-employment* level of GDP for a year; the *full-employment* budget deficit or surplus.

deadweight loss A reduction in the total net benefit that society can obtain from its limited supply of resources. Caused by an underallocation or overallocation of resources to the production of a particular *good* or *service*. Also called *efficiency loss*.

decreasing-cost industry An *industry* in which expansion through the entry of *firms* lowers the *prices* that firms in the industry must pay for resources and therefore decreases their production costs.

deductible The dollar sum of (for example, health care) costs that an insured individual must pay before the insurer begins to pay.

defaults Situations in which borrowers stop making loan payments or do not pay back loans that they took out and are now due.

defensive medicine The recommendation by physicians of more tests and procedures than are warranted medically or economically as a way of protecting themselves against later malpractice suits.

deflation A decline in the general level of *prices* in an economy; a decline in an economy's *price level*.

demand A schedule or curve that shows the various amounts of a product that consumers are willing and able to purchase at each of a series of possible *prices* during a specified period of time.

demand curve A curve that illustrates the *demand* for a product by showing how each possible *price* (on the *vertical axis*) is associated with a specific *quantity demanded* (on the *horizontal axis*).

demand factor (in growth) The requirement that *aggregate demand* increase as fast as *potential output* if *economic growth* is to proceed as quickly as possible.

demand schedule A table of numbers showing the amounts of a *good* or *service* buyers are willing and able to purchase at various *prices* over a specified period of time.

demand shocks Sudden, unexpected changes in demand.

demand-pull inflation Increases in the *price level* (*inflation*) resulting from increases in *aggregate demand*.

demand-side market failures Underallocations of resources that occur when private demand curves understate consumers' full willingness to pay for a *good* or *service*.

demographers Scientists who study the characteristics of human populations.

demographic transition The massive decline in birthrates that occurs once a developing country achieves higher standards of living because the perceived marginal cost of additional children begins to exceed the perceived marginal benefit.

dependent variable A variable that changes as a consequence of a change in some other (independent) variable; the "effect" or outcome.

deregulation The removal of most or even all of the government regulation and laws designed to supervise an industry. Sometimes undertaken to combat *regulatory capture*.

derived demand The demand for a resource that depends on the demand for the products it helps to produce.

determinants of aggregate demand Factors such as consumption spending, *investment*, government spending, and *net exports* that, if they change, shift the aggregate demand curve.

determinants of aggregate supply Factors such as input prices, *productivity*, and the legal-institutional environment that, if they change, shift the aggregate supply curve.

determinants of demand Factors other than *price* that determine the quantities demanded of a *good* or *service*. Also referred to as "demand shifters" because changes in the determinants of demand will cause the *demand curve* to shift either right or left.

determinants of supply Factors other than *price* that determine the quantities supplied of a *good* or *service*. Also referred to as "supply shifters" because changes in the determinants of supply will cause the *supply curve* to shift either right or left.

devaluation A decrease in the governmentally defined value of a currency.

developing countries Many countries of Africa, Asia, and Latin America that are characterized by lack of capital goods, use of nonadvanced technologies, low literacy rates, high unemployment, relatively rapid population growth, and labor forces heavily committed to agriculture.

diagnosis-related group (DRG) system Payments to doctors and hospitals under *Medicare* based on which of hundreds of carefully detailed diagnostic categories best characterize each patient's condition and needs.

dictator game A mutually anonymous behavioral economics game in which one person ("the dictator") unilaterally determines how to split an amount of money with the second player.

differentiated oligopoly An *oligopoly* in which *firms* produce a *differentiated product*.

diffusion The spread of an *innovation* through its widespread imitation.

digital platform An *Internet* website or software application (app) that facilitates interactions between two or more distinct but interdependent sets of users.

dilemma of regulation The trade-off faced by a *regulatory agency* in setting the maximum legal *price* a monopolist may charge: The *socially optimal price* is below *average total cost* (and either bankrupts the *firm* or requires that it be subsidized), while the higher, *fair-return price* does not produce *allocative efficiency*.

diminishing marginal utility The principle that as a consumer increases the consumption of a *good* or *service*, the *marginal utility* obtained from each additional unit of the good or service decreases.

direct controls Government policies that directly constrain activities that generate *negative externalities*. Examples include maximum emissions limits for factory smokestacks and laws mandating the proper disposal of toxic wastes.

direct network effect A *network effect* that involves only a single network of users connected to a *digital platform*. Compare with *indirect network effect*.

direct payments Cash subsidies paid to farmers based on past production levels; a permanent transfer payment unaffected by current crop *prices* and current production.

direct relationship The relationship between two variables that change in the same direction, for example, product *price* and quantity supplied; a positive relationship.

discount rate The interest rate that the *Federal Reserve Banks* charge on the loans they make to *commercial banks* and *thrifts;* one of the three *administered rates* set by the *Federal Reserve*.

discouraged workers Employees who have left the *labor force* because they have not been able to find employment.

discrimination The practice of according individuals or groups inferior treatment in hiring, occupational access, education and training, promotion, wage rates, or working conditions even though they have the same abilities, education, skills, and work experience as other workers.

discrimination coefficient A measure of the cost or disutility of prejudice; the monetary amount an employer is willing to pay to hire a preferred worker rather than a nonpreferred worker of the same ability.

diseconomies of scale The situation when a firm's *average total cost* of producing a product increases in the *long run* as the firm increases the size of its *plant* (and, hence, its output).

disinflation A reduction in the rate of *inflation.*

disposable income (DI) *Personal income* less personal taxes; income available for *personal consumption expenditures* and *personal saving.*

diversifiable risk Investment *risk* that investors can reduce via *diversification;* also called idiosyncratic risk.

diversification The strategy of investing in a large number of investments in order to reduce the overall risk to an entire investment *portfolio.*

dividends Payments by a corporation of all or part of its profit to its stockholders (the corporate owners).

division of labor The separation of the work required to produce a product into a number of different tasks that are performed by different workers; *specialization* of workers.

Doha Development Agenda The latest, uncompleted (as of late 2021) sequence of trade negotiations by members of the *World Trade Organization;* named after Doha, Qatar, where the set of negotiations began. Also called the Doha Round.

dollar votes The "votes" that consumers cast for the production of preferred products when they purchase those products rather than the alternatives that were also available.

domestic price The *price* of a *good* or *service* within a country, determined by domestic demand and supply.

dominant strategy In a strategic interaction (*game*) between two or more players, a course of action (strategy) that a player will wish to undertake no matter what the other players choose to do.

dual mandate The 1977 congressional directive that the Federal Reserve System's highest priorities should be *full employment* and price level stability. In practice, the Fed aims for the *full-employment rate of unemployment* and an *inflation rate* of 2 percent per year.

dumping The sale of a product in a foreign country at *prices* either below cost or below the prices commonly charged at home.

DuPont cellophane case The antitrust case brought against DuPont in which the U.S. Supreme Court ruled (in 1956) that while DuPont had a monopoly in the narrowly defined market for cellophane, it did not monopolize the more broadly defined market for flexible packaging materials. It was thus not guilty of violating the *Sherman Act.*

durable good A consumer good with an expected life (use) of three or more years.

earmarks Narrow, specially designated spending authorizations placed in broad legislation by senators and representatives for the purpose of providing benefits to *firms* and organizations within their constituencies. Earmarked projects are exempt from competitive bidding and normal evaluation procedures.

earned-income tax credit (EITC) A refundable federal *tax credit* for low-income working people designed to reduce poverty and encourage labor-force participation.

economic cost A payment that must be made to obtain and retain the *services* of a *resource;* the income a *firm* must provide to a resource supplier to attract the resource away from an alternative use; equal to the quantity of other products that cannot be produced when resources are instead used to make a particular product.

economic growth (1) An outward shift in the *production possibilities curve* that results from an increase in resource supplies or quality or an improvement in *technology;* (2) an increase of real output (*gross domestic product*) or real output per capita.

economic immigrants International migrants who have moved from one country to another to obtain economic gains such as better employment opportunities.

economic investment Spending for the production and accumulation of *capital,* additions to *inventories,* or the research and development of new goods or services, including funds spent on the creation of new works of music, literature, or software. Compare with *financial investment.*

economic perspective A viewpoint that envisions individuals and institutions making rational decisions by comparing the *marginal benefits* and *marginal costs* associated with their actions.

economic principle A widely accepted generalization about the economic behavior of individuals or institutions.

economic profit The return flowing to those who provide the economy with the *economic resource* of *entrepreneurial ability;* the total revenue of a *firm* less its *economic costs* (which include both *explicit costs* and *implicit costs*); also called "pure profit" and "above-normal profit."

economic rent Any payment to a resource provider or seller of output in excess of the *economic cost* (opportunity cost) of providing that resource or output.

economic resources The *land, labor, capital,* and *entrepreneurial ability* that are used to produce *goods* and *services.* Also known as the *factors of production.*

economic system A particular set of institutional arrangements and a coordinating mechanism for solving the *economizing problem;* a method of organizing an economy, of which the *market system* and the *command system* are the two general types.

economic, or pure, profit The return flowing to those who provide the economy with the *economic resource* of *entrepreneurial ability;* the total revenue of a *firm* less its *economic costs* (which include both *explicit costs* and *implicit costs*); also called "above-normal profit."

economics The social science concerned with how individuals, institutions, and society make optimal (best) choices under conditions of scarcity.

economies of scale The situation when a firm's *average total cost* of producing a product decreases in the *long run* as the firm increases the size of its *plant* (and, hence, its output).

economizing problem The choices necessitated because society's economic wants for *goods* and *services* are unlimited but the resources available to satisfy these wants are limited (scarce).

effective federal funds rate The equilibrium *interest rate* determined in the *federal funds market;* the interest rate that U.S. banks and other depository institutions charge one another for overnight loans of currency held on deposit at one of the twelve *Federal Reserve Banks.*

efficiency factor (in growth) The capacity of an economy to achieve *allocative* and *productive efficiency* and thereby fulfill the potential for growth that the *supply factors* (*of growth*) make possible; the capacity of an economy to achieve *economic efficiency* and thereby reach the optimal point on its *production possibilities curve.*

efficiency gains from migration   The increases in total worldwide output that take place if the additions to output from *immigration* in the destination nation exceed the loss of output from *emigration* in the origin nation.

efficiency loss   Reductions in combined consumer and producer surplus caused by an underallocation or overallocation of resources to the production of a *good* or *service*. Also called *deadweight loss.*

efficiency loss of a tax   The loss of *net benefits* to society because a tax reduces the production and consumption of a taxed good below the level of *allocative efficiency.* Also called the *deadweight loss* of the tax.

efficiency wage   An above-market (above-equilibrium) *wage* that minimizes wage costs per unit of output by encouraging greater effort or reducing turnover.

elastic demand   Product or resource demand whose *price elasticity of demand* is greater than 1, so that any given percentage change in *price* leads to a larger percentage change in *quantity demanded.* As a result, quantity demanded is relatively sensitive to (elastic with respect to) price.

elasticity of resource demand   A measure of the responsiveness of *firms* to a change in the *price* of a particular *resource* they employ or use; the percentage change in the quantity demanded of the *resource* divided by the percentage change in its *price.*

employer mandate   The requirement under the *Patient Protection and Affordable Care Act* (*PPACA*) of 2010 that firms with 50 or more employees pay for insurance policies for their employees or face a fine of $2,000 per employee per year. Firms with fewer than 50 employees are exempt.

empty threat   In a *sequential game* with two players, a noncredible (bluffing) statement made by Player 1 that threatens a penalizing action against Player 2 if Player 2 does something that Player 1 does not want Player 2 to do. Opposite of *credible threat.*

endowment effect   The tendency people have to place higher valuations on items they possess (are endowed with) than on identical items that they do not possess; perhaps caused by *loss aversion.*

entitlement programs   Government programs such as *social insurance, Medicare,* and *Medicaid* that guarantee (entitle) particular levels of transfer payments or noncash benefits to all who fit the programs' criteria.

entrepreneurial ability   The human resource that combines the other *economic resources* of *land, labor,* and *capital* to produce new products or make innovations in the production of existing products; provided by *entrepreneurs.*

entrepreneurs   Individuals who provide *entrepreneurial ability* to *firms* by setting strategy, advancing innovations, and bearing the financial risk if their firms do poorly.

equality-efficiency trade-off   The decrease in *economic efficiency* that may accompany a decrease in *income inequality;* the presumption that some income inequality is required to achieve economic efficiency.

equation of exchange $MV = PQ$, in which M is the supply of *money,* V is the *velocity* of money, P is the *price level,* and Q is the physical volume of *final goods* and final *services* produced.

equilibrium GDP   The gross domestic product at which the total quantity of final goods and final services purchased (aggregate expenditures) is equal to the total quantity of final goods services produced (the real domestic output); the real domestic output at which the aggregate demand curve intersects the aggregate supply curve. Also known as *equilibrium real output.*

equilibrium position   In the indifference curve model, the combination of two goods at which a consumer maximizes his or her *utility* (reaches the highest attainable *indifference curve*), given a limited amount to spend (a *budget constraint*).

equilibrium price   The *price* in a competitive market at which the *quantity demanded* and the *quantity supplied* are equal, there is neither a shortage nor a surplus, and there is no tendency for price to rise or fall.

equilibrium price level   In the *aggregate demand–aggregate supply* (*AD-AS*) *model,* the *price level* at which *aggregate demand* equals *aggregate supply;* the price level at which the aggregate demand curve intersects the aggregate supply curve.

equilibrium quantity   (1) The quantity at which the intentions of buyers and sellers in a particular market match at a particular *price* such that the *quantity demanded* and the *quantity supplied* are equal; (2) the profit-maximizing output of a *firm.*

equilibrium real output   (see *equilibrium real domestic output*) The *gross domestic product* at which the total quantity of *final goods* and final *services* purchased (*aggregate expenditures*) is equal to the total quantity of final goods and services produced (the real domestic output); the real domestic output at which the aggregate demand curve intersects the aggregate supply curve.

equilibrium world price   The *price* of an internationally traded product that equates the quantity of the product demanded by importers with the quantity of the product supplied by exporters; the price determined at the intersection of the export supply curve and the import demand curve.

European Union (EU)   An association of 28 European nations (as of mid-2019) that has eliminated tariffs and quotas among them, established common tariffs for imported goods from outside the member nations, eliminated barriers to the free movement of capital, and created other common economic policies.

eurozone   The 19 nations (as of 2019) of the 28-member (as of 2019) *European Union* that use the *euro* as their common *currency.* The eurozone countries are Austria, Belgium, Cyprus, Estonia, Finland, France, Germany, Greece, Ireland, Italy, Luxembourg, Malta, the Netherlands, Portugal, Slovakia, Slovenia, and Spain.

excess capacity   *Plant* resources that are underused when imperfectly competitive *firms* produce less output than that associated with achieving minimum *average total cost.*

exchange controls   Restrictions that a government may impose over the quantity of foreign currency demand by its citizens and *firms* and over the *rate of exchange* as a way to limit the nation's quantity of *outpayments* relative to its quantity of *inpayments* (in order to eliminate a *payments deficit*).

excise tax   A tax levied on the production of a specific product or on the quantity of the product purchased.

excludability   The characteristic displayed by those goods and services for which sellers are able to prevent nonbuyers from obtaining benefits.

exclusive unionism   The policy, pursued by many *craft unions,* in which a *union* first gets employers to agree to hire only union workers and then excludes many workers from joining the union so as to restrict the supply of labor and drive up wages. Compare with *inclusive unionism.* The policies typically employed by a *craft union.*

exit mechanism   The method of resolving workplace dissatisfaction by quitting one's job and searching for another.

expansion   The phase of the *business cycle* in which *real GDP, income,* and employment rise.

expansionary fiscal policy An increase in *government purchases* of *goods* and *services,* a decrease in *net taxes,* or some combination of the two for the purpose of increasing *aggregate demand* and expanding real output.

expansionary monetary policy *Central bank* actions to increase the *money supply,* lower *interest rates,* and expand *real GDP.* Implemented when the economy is operating below *potential output.* Also known as an "easy money" policy.

expectations The anticipations of consumers, *firms,* and others about future economic conditions.

expected rate of return The increase in profit a *firm* anticipates it will obtain by purchasing capital or engaging in research and development (*R&D*); expressed as a percentage of the total cost of the investment (or R&D) activity.

expected-rate-of-return curve As it relates to research and development (*R&D*), a curve showing the anticipated gain in *profit,* as a percentage of R&D expenditure, from an additional dollar spent on R&D.

expenditures approach The method that adds all expenditures made for *final goods* and final *services* to measure the *gross domestic product.*

explicit cost The monetary payment made by a *firm* to an outsider to obtain a *resource.*

export subsidy A government payment to a domestic producer to enable the *firm* to reduce the *price* of a *good* or *service* to foreign buyers.

export supply curve An upward sloping curve that shows the amount of a product that domestic *firms* will export at each *world price* that is above the *domestic price.*

external public debt The portion of the public debt owed to foreign citizens, *firms,* and institutions.

externality A cost or benefit from production or consumption that accrues to someone other than the immediate buyers and sellers of the product being produced or consumed (see *negative externality* and *positive externality*).

extraction cost All costs associated with extracting a natural resource and readying it for sale.

factors of production The four *economic resources: land, labor, capital,* and *entrepreneurial ability.*

failed state A nation whose government lacks the *state capacity* to maintain even basic government functions like law enforcement and the provision of basic services like education and sanitation.

fair-return price For *natural monopolies* subject to rate (*price*) regulation, the price that would allow the regulated monopoly to earn a *normal profit;* a price equal to *average total cost.*

fairness A person's opinion as to whether a price, wage, or allocation is considered morally or ethically acceptable.

fallacy of composition The false notion that what is true for the individual (or part) is necessarily true for the group (or whole).

farm commodities Agricultural products such as grains, milk, cattle, fruits, and vegetables that are usually sold to processors, who use the products as inputs in creating *food products.*

fast-second strategy An approach by a dominant *firm* in which it allows other firms in its *industry* to bear the risk of innovation and then quickly becomes the second firm to offer any successful new product or adopt any improved production process.

federal funds market The financial *market* in which *banks* and other financial firms negotiate overnight loans of *currency* ("federal funds") held on deposit at one of the twelve *Federal Reserve Banks.*

federal funds rate The *interest rate* that U.S. banks and other non-bank financial firms charge one another on overnight loans of *currency* held on deposit at one of the twelve *Federal Reserve Banks;* the Federal Reserve's *policy rate.*

federal funds target range The 0.25-percent-wide range within which the *Federal Reserve* guides its *policy rate,* the *effective federal funds rate.* Also a key part of the Federal Reserve's *forward guidance* communications.

Federal Open Market Committee (FOMC) The 12-member group within the *Federal Reserve System* that decides U.S. *monetary policy* and how it is executed through *open-market operations* (in which the Fed buys and sells U.S. government securities to adjust the *money supply*).

Federal Reserve Banks The 12 banks chartered by the U.S. government that collectively act as the *central bank* of the United States. They set monetary policy and regulate the private banking system under the direction of the *Board of Governors* and the *Federal Open Market Committee.* Each of the 12 is a *quasi-public bank* and acts as a *banker's bank* in its designated geographic region.

Federal Reserve Note Paper money issued by the *Federal Reserve Banks.*

Federal Reserve System The U.S. central bank, consisting of the *Board of Governors* of the Federal Reserve and the 12 *Federal Reserve Banks,* which controls the lending activity of the nation's banks and thrifts and thus the *money supply;* commonly referred to as the "Fed."

Federal Trade Commission Act The federal law of 1914 that established the *Federal Trade Commission.*

fee for service In the health care *industry,* payment to physicians for each visit made or procedure performed.

final goods and services Products that have been purchased for final use (rather than for resale or further processing or manufacturing).

financial investment The purchase of a financial asset (such as a *stock, bond,* or *mutual fund*) or real asset (such as a house, land, or factories) in the expectation of financial gain. Compare with economic investment.

first-mover advantage In *game theory,* the benefit obtained by the party that moves first in a *sequential game.* A situation that occurs in a *sequential game* if the player who gets to move first has an advantage in terms of final outcomes over the player(s) who move subsequently.

fiscal policy Changes in government spending and tax collections designed to achieve full employment, price stability, and economic growth; also called *discretionary fiscal policy.*

fishery A stock of fish or other marine animal that is composed of a distinct group, for example, New England cod, Pacific tuna, or Alaskan crab.

fishery collapse A rapid decline in a *fishery*'s population because its fish are being harvested faster than they can reproduce.

fixed cost Any cost that in total does not change when the *firm* changes its output.

fixed exchange rate A *rate of exchange* that is pegged by a government or central bank at a particular ratio (for instance, $1 = 6 yuan) rather than being allowed to vary with changes in demand and supply.

flexible exchange rate A *rate of exchange* that is determined by the international demand for and supply of a nation's money and that is consequently free to rise or fall because it is not subject to *currency interventions.* Also referred to as a "floating exchange rate."

flexible prices Product *prices* that freely move upward or downward when product demand or supply changes.

follower countries As it relates to *economic growth,* countries that adopt advanced technologies that previously were developed and used by *leader countries.*

food products Processed *farm commodities* sold through grocery stores and restaurants. Examples: bread, meat, fish, chicken, pork, lettuce, peanut butter, and breakfast cereal.

foreign direct investment *Financial investments* made to obtain a lasting ownership interest in *firms* operating outside the economy of the investor; may involve purchasing existing assets or building new production facilities.

foreign purchases effect The inverse relationship between the *net exports* of an economy and its *price level* relative to foreign price levels.

foreign-exchange reserves Stockpiles of foreign currencies maintained by a nation's *central bank.* Obtained when the *central bank* sells local currency in exchange for foreign currency in the *foreign exchange market.*

forward guidance Public communications made by a *central bank* to describe (1) how it perceives the state of the *economy* and (2) how it intends to manage *monetary policy.*

four-firm concentration ratio The percentage of total *industry* sales accounted for by the top four *firms* in an industry.

fractional reserve banking system A system in which *commercial banks* and *thrift institutions* hold less than 100 percent of their checkable-deposit liabilities as reserves of *currency* held in bank vaults or as deposits at the *central bank.*

framing effects In *prospect theory,* changes in people's decision making caused by new information that alters the context, or "frame of reference," that they use to judge whether options are viewed as gains or losses relative to the *status quo.*

free-rider problem The inability of potential providers of an economically desirable *good* or *service* to obtain payment from those who benefit, because of *nonexcludability.*

freedom of choice The freedom of owners of property resources to employ or dispose of them as they see fit, of workers to enter any line of work for which they are qualified, and of consumers to spend their incomes in the manner that they prefer.

freedom of enterprise The freedom of *firms* to obtain economic resources, to use those resources to produce products of the firms' own choosing, and to sell their products in markets of their choice.

Freedom to Farm Act A law passed in 1996 that revamped 60 years of U.S. farm policy by ending *price supports* and *acreage allotments* for wheat, corn, barley, oats, sorghum, rye, cotton, and rice.

freemium pricing A pricing strategy in which an Internet business offers its core product for free but charges users for upgrades and special features that some users may be willing to pay for.

frictional unemployment A type of unemployment caused by workers voluntarily changing jobs and by temporary layoffs; unemployed workers between jobs.

full-employment rate of unemployment The *unemployment rate* at which there is no *cyclical unemployment* of the *labor force;* equal to around 4 percent (rather than zero percent) in the United States because *frictional* and *structural unemployment* are unavoidable.

future value The amount to which some current amount of *money* will grow if *interest* earned on the amount is left to compound over time. (*See compound interest.*)

gains from trade The extra output that trading partners obtain through specialization of production and exchange of *goods* and *services.*

game theory The study of how people behave in strategic situations in which individuals must take into account not only their own possible actions but also the possible reactions of others. Originally developed to analyze the best ways to play games like poker and chess.

GDP gap Actual *gross domestic product* minus *potential output;* may be either a positive amount (a *positive GDP gap*) or a negative amount (a *negative GDP gap*).

General Agreement on Tariffs and Trade (GATT) The international agreement reached in 1947 in which 23 nations agreed to eliminate *import quotas,* negotiate reductions in *tariff* rates, and give each other equal and nondiscriminatory treatment. It now includes most nations and has become the *World Trade Organization.*

Gini ratio A numerical measure of the overall dispersion of income among *households,* families, or individuals; found graphically by dividing the area between the diagonal line and the *Lorenz curve* by the entire area below the diagonal line.

gold standard A historical system of fixed exchange rates in which nations defined their currencies in terms of gold, maintained fixed relationships between their stocks of gold and their money supplies, and allowed gold to be freely exported and imported.

government failure Inefficiencies in resource allocation caused by problems in the operation of the *public sector* (government). Specific examples include the *principal-agent problem,* the *special-interest effect,* the *collective-action problem, rent seeking,* and *political corruption.*

government purchases (G) Expenditures by government for *goods* and *services* that government consumes in providing public services as well as expenditures for publicly owned capital that has a long lifetime; the expenditures of all governments in the economy for those *final goods* and final *services.*

gross domestic product (GDP) The total market value of all *final goods* and *services* produced annually within the boundaries of a nation.

gross output (GO) The dollar value of the economic activity taking place at every stage of production and distribution. By contrast, *gross domestic product* (GDP) only accounts for the value of final output.

gross private domestic investment (I_g) Expenditures that increase the nation's stock of capital, which is the collection of physical objects and intangible ideas that help to produce goods and services. Includes spending on final purchases of plant, machinery, and equipment by business enterprises; residential construction; changes in *inventories*; expenditures on the *research and development (R&D)* of new productive technologies; and money spent on the creation of new works of art, music, writing, film, and software.

growth accounting The bookkeeping of the supply-side elements such as productivity and labor inputs that contribute to changes in *real GDP* over some specific time period.

H1-B provision A provision of the U.S. immigration law that allows the annual entry of 65,000 high-skilled workers in "specialty occupations" such as science, *R&D,* and computer programming to work legally and continuously in the United States for six years.

health maintenance organizations (HMOs) Health care providers that contract with employers, insurance companies, labor unions, or government units to provide health care for their workers or others who are insured.

health savings accounts (HSAs) Tax-free savings accounts into which people with high-deductible health insurance plans can place funds each year. Accumulated funds can be used to pay out-of-pocket medical expenses such as *deductibles* and *copayments*. Unused funds accumulate from year to year and can be used after retirement to supplement *Medicare*.

Herfindahl index A measure of the concentration and competitiveness of an *industry*; calculated as the sum of the squared percentage market shares of the individual *firms* in the industry.

heuristics The brain's low-energy mental shortcuts for making decisions. They are "fast and frugal" and work well in most situations but in other situations result in *systematic errors*.

homogeneous oligopoly An *oligopoly* in which *firms* produce a *standardized product*.

horizontal axis The "left-right" or "west-east" measurement line on a graph or grid.

horizontal merger The merger into a single *firm* of two firms producing the same product and selling it in the same geographic market.

households Economic entities (of one or more persons occupying a housing unit) that provide *resources* to the economy and use the *income* received to purchase *goods* and *services* that satisfy economic wants.

human capital The knowledge and skills that make a person productive.

hyperinflation An extremely high rate of *inflation*, usually defined as an inflation rate in excess of 50 percent per month.

imitation problem The potential for a *firm's* rivals to produce a close variation of (imitate) a firm's new product or process, greatly reducing the originator's profit from *R&D* and *innovation*.

immediate market period The length of time during which the producers of a product are unable to change the quantity supplied in response to a change in price and in which there is a *perfectly inelastic supply*.

immediate-short-run aggregate supply curve A horizontal *aggregate supply* curve that applies to time periods over which both input prices and output prices are fixed; an aggregate supply curve for which real output, but not the *price level*, changes when the *aggregate demand* curve shifts.

imperfect competition All *market structures* except *pure competition*; includes *monopoly, monopolistic competition,* and *oligopoly*.

implicit cost The monetary income a *firm* sacrifices when it uses a *resource* it owns rather than supplying the resource in the market; equal to what the resource could have earned in the best-paying alternative employment; includes a *normal profit*.

import competition The competition that domestic *firms* encounter from the products and *services* of foreign producers.

import demand curve A downsloping curve showing the amount of a product that an economy will import at each *world price* below the *domestic price*.

import quota A limit imposed by a nation on the quantity (or total value) of a good that may be imported during some period of time.

in-app purchases A pricing strategy in which an internet business (that may or may not give away its core product for free) charges users of its application software ("app") for items that enhance the user experience within the application.

incentive function The inducement that an increase in the price of a commodity gives to sellers to make more of it available (and conversely for a decrease in *price*), and the inducement that an increase in price offers to buyers to purchase smaller quantities (and conversely for a decrease in price).

incentive pay plan A compensation structure that ties worker pay directly to performance. Such plans include piece rates, bonuses, *stock options,* commissions, and *profit-sharing plans*.

incentive problem The difficulty common to command economies wherein the numerical production targets set by central planning boards cause managers to produce substandard or unwanted output.

inclusive unionism The policy, pursued by *industrial unions,* in which a *union* attempts to include every worker in a given *industry* so as to be able to restrict the entire industry's labor supply and thereby raise wages. Compare with *exclusive unionism*.

income approach The method that adds all the *income* generated by the production of *final goods* and final *services* to measure the *gross domestic product*.

income effect A change in the quantity demanded of a product that results from the change in *real income (purchasing power)* caused by a change in the product's *price*.

income elasticity of demand The ratio of the percentage change in the *quantity demanded* of a good to a percentage change in consumer *income;* measures the responsiveness of consumer purchases to income changes.

income inequality The unequal distribution of an economy's total *income* among *households* or families.

income mobility The extent to which *income* receivers move from one part of the income distribution to another over some period of time.

increasing returns An increase in a *firm's* output by a larger percentage than the percentage increase in its inputs.

increasing-cost industry An *industry* in which expansion through the entry of new *firms* raises the *prices* that firms in the industry must pay for *resources* and therefore increases their production costs.

independent unions U.S. unions that are not affiliated with the *AFL-CIO* or *Strategic Organizing Center*.

independent variable The variable causing a change in some other (dependent) variable.

index funds *Mutual funds* whose *portfolios* exactly match a stock or bond index (a collection of *stocks* or *bonds* meant to capture the overall behavior of a particular category of investments) such as the Standard & Poor's 500 Index or the Russell 3000 Index.

indifference curve A curve showing the different combinations of two products that yield the same satisfaction or *utility* to a consumer.

indifference map A set of *indifference curves,* each representing a different level of *utility,* that together show the preferences of a consumer.

indirect network effect A *network effect* involving two or more *networks* connected by a *digital platform,* in which a change in the number of users within one network causes changes felt by the users of a different network which in turn boomerang back to the original network of users to affect the value of their network. Compare with *direct network effect*.

individual transferable quotas (ITQs) Limits (quotas) set by a government or a fisheries commission on the total number or total weight of a species that an individual fisher can harvest during some particular time period; fishers can sell (transfer) the right to use all or part of their respective individual quotas to other fishers.

industrial regulation   The older and more traditional type of business or commercial regulation in which government is concerned with the *prices* charged and the *services* provided to the public in specific *industries*. Differs from *social regulation*.

industrially advanced countries   High-income countries such as the United States, Canada, Japan, and the nations of western Europe that have highly developed *market economies* based on large stocks of technologically advanced *capital goods* and skilled labor forces.

inelastic demand   Product or resource demand for which the *price elasticity of demand* is less than 1, so that any given percentage change in *price* leads to a smaller percentage change in *quantity demanded*. As a result, quantity demanded is relatively insensitive to (inelastic with respect to) price.

inferior good   A *good* or *service* whose consumption declines as *income* rises, other things equal.

inflation   A rise in the general level of *prices* in an economy; an increase in an economy's *price level*.

inflation gap   The difference between the current actual rate of *inflation* and the central bank's *target rate of inflation*; a key component of the *Taylor Rule*.

inflation targeting   The declaration by a *central bank* of a goal for a specific range of *inflation* in a future year, coupled with *monetary policy* designed to achieve the goal.

inflationary expectations   The public's forecast about likely future *inflation* rates; influenceable by central bank policy actions, including a credible *target rate of inflation*.

inflationary expenditure gap   In the *aggregate-expenditures model*, the amount by which the *aggregate expenditures schedule* must shift downward to decrease the *nominal GDP* to its full-employment noninflationary level.

inflexible prices   Product *prices* that remain in place (at least for a while) even though *supply* or *demand* has changed; stuck prices or sticky prices.

information technology   New and more efficient methods of delivering and receiving information through the use of computers, wi-fi networks, wireless phones, and the Internet.

infrastructure   The interconnected network of large-scale *capital goods* (such as roads, sewers, electrical grids, railways, ports, and the Internet) needed to operate a technologically advanced economy.

injection   An addition of spending into the income-expenditure stream: any increment to *consumption, investment, government purchases,* or *net exports*.

innovation   The first commercially successful introduction of a new product, use of a new method of production, or creation of a new form of business organization.

insurable risk   An eventuality for which both the frequency and magnitude of potential losses can be estimated with considerable accuracy. Insurance companies are willing to sell insurance against such risks.

insurance exchanges   Government-regulated markets for health insurance in which individuals seeking to purchase health insurance to comply with the *personal mandate* of the *Patient Protection and Affordable Care Act* (*PPACA*) of 2010 will be able to comparison shop among insurance policies approved by regulators. Each state will have its own exchange.

interest   The payment made for the use of (borrowed) *money*.

interest income   The *income* received by the owners of *capital* for supplying capital to *businesses*.

interest rate on reserve balances (IORB)   The *interest rate* that the Federal Reserve pays *banks* and thrifts on any money that they deposit at (loan to) a Federal Reserve Bank on an overnight basis; one of the three *administered rates* set by the Federal Reserve.

interest-rate cost-of-funds curve   As it relates to research and development (*R&D*), a curve showing the *interest rate* a *firm* must pay to obtain any particular amount of funds to finance R&D.

interest-rate effect   The tendency for increases in the *price level* to increase the demand for money, raise interest rates, and, as a result, reduce total spending and real output in the economy (and the reverse for *price-level* decreases).

interindustry competition   The competition for sales between the products of one *industry* and the products of another industry.

interlocking directorate   A situation where one or more members of the board of directors of a *corporation* are also on the board of directors of a competing corporation; illegal under the *Clayton Act*.

intermediate goods and services   Products that are purchased for resale or further processing or manufacturing.

international asset transactions   The sale, trade, or transfer of ownership rights to either real or financial assets, including currency, across international borders.

International Monetary Fund (IMF)   The international association of nations that was formed after the Second World War to make loans of foreign monies to nations with temporary *balance of payments deficits* and, until the early 1970s, manage the international system of pegged exchange rates agreed upon at the Bretton Woods conference. It now mainly makes loans to nations facing possible defaults on private and government loans.

international trade   The exchange (trade) of goods and services across international borders.

Internet   The world-wide *network* of interconnected computers that can communicate and share data; also known as the world wide web, or www.

invention   The conception of a new product or process combined with the first proof that it will work.

inventories   Goods that have been produced but remain unsold.

inverse relationship   The relationship between two variables that change in opposite directions, for example, product *price* and quantity demanded; a negative relationship.

inverted-U theory   The idea that, other things equal, *R&D* expenditures as a percentage of sales rise with *industry* concentration, reach a peak at a *four-firm concentration ratio* of about 50 percent, and then fall as the ratio further increases.

investment   Expenditures that increase the volume of physical *capital* (roads, factories, wireless networks) and intangible ideas (formulas, processes, algorithms) that help to produce goods and services. Also known as *economic investment*. Not to be confused with *financial investment*.

investment demand curve   A curve that shows the amounts of *investment* demanded by an economy at a series of *real interest rates*.

investment schedule   A curve or schedule that shows the amounts that firms plan to invest at various possible values of *real gross domestic product* (real GDP).

invisible hand   The tendency of *competition* to cause individuals and firms to unintentionally but quite effectively promote the interests of society even when each individual or firm is only attempting to pursue its own interests.

kinked-demand curve A *demand curve* that has a flatter slope above the current *price* than below the current price. Applies to a *noncollusive oligopoly* firm if its rivals will match any price decrease but ignore any price increase.

labor Any mental or physical exertion on the part of a human being that is used in the production of a *good* or *service*. One of the four *economic resources*.

labor force Persons 16 years of age and older who are not in institutions and who are employed or are unemployed and seeking work.

labor productivity Total output (GDP) divided by the quantity of labor (hours of work) employed to produce it; the *average product* of labor, or output per hour of work.

labor-force participation rate The percentage of the working-age population that is actually in the *labor force*.

labor-intensive goods Products requiring relatively large amounts of *labor* to produce.

Laffer Curve A curve relating government tax rates and tax revenues and on which a particular tax rate (between zero and 100 percent) maximizes tax revenues.

laissez-faire capitalism A hypothetical *economic system* in which the government's economic role is limited to protecting private property and establishing a legal environment appropriate to the operation of *markets* in which only mutually agreeable transactions take place between buyers and sellers; sometimes referred to as "pure capitalism."

land In addition to the part of the earth's surface not covered by water, this term refers to any and all natural resources ("free gifts of nature") that are used to produce *goods* and *services*. Thus, it includes the oceans, sunshine, coal deposits, forests, the electromagnetic spectrum, and *fisheries*. Note that land is one of the four *economic resources*.

land reform Policy changes aimed at creating a more efficient distribution of land ownership in developing countries. Can involve everything from government purchasing large land estates and dividing the land into smaller farms to consolidating tiny plots of land into larger, more efficient private farms.

land-intensive goods Products requiring relatively large amounts of land to produce.

law of demand The principle that, other things equal, an increase in a product's *price* will reduce the quantity of it demanded, and conversely for a decrease in price.

law of diminishing marginal utility The principle that as a consumer increases the consumption of a *good* or *service*, the *marginal utility* obtained from each additional unit of the good or service decreases.

law of diminishing returns The principle that as successive increments of a variable *resource* are added to a fixed resource, the *marginal product* of the variable resource will eventually decrease.

law of increasing opportunity costs The principle that as the production of a good increases, the *opportunity cost* of producing an additional unit rises.

law of supply The principle that, other things equal, an increase in the *price* of a product will increase the quantity of it supplied, and conversely for a price decrease.

leader countries As it relates to *economic growth*, countries that develop and use the most advanced technologies, which then become available to *follower countries*.

leakage (1) A withdrawal of potential spending from the income-expenditures stream via *saving*, tax payments, or *imports*; (2) a withdrawal that reduces the lending potential of the banking system.

learning by doing Achieving greater *productivity* and lower *average total cost* through gains in knowledge and skill that accompany repetition of a task; a source of *economies of scale*.

least-cost combination of resources The quantity of each *resource* that a *firm* must employ in order to produce a particular output at the lowest total cost; the combination at which the ratio of the *marginal product* of a resource to its *marginal resource cost* (to its *price* if the resource is employed in a competitive market) is the same for the last dollar spent on each of the resources employed.

legal immigrant A person who lawfully enters a country for the purpose of residing there.

legal tender Any form of *currency* that by law must be accepted by creditors (lenders) for the settlement of a financial debt; a nation's official currency is legal tender within its own borders.

limited liability rule A law that limits the potential losses that an investor in a *corporation* may suffer to the amount that she paid for her shares in the corporation. Encourages *financial investment* by limiting risk.

liquidity The degree to which an asset can be converted quickly into cash with little or no loss of purchasing power. *Money* is said to be perfectly liquid, whereas other assets have lesser degrees of liquidity.

liquidity trap A situation in a severe *recession* in which the *central bank's* injection of additional currency (liquidity) into the financial system has little or no additional positive impact on lending, borrowing, *investment,* or *aggregate demand*.

loanable funds theory of interest The concept that the supply of and demand for *loanable funds* determine the equilibrium rate of *interest*.

lockout A negotiating tactic in which a *firm* forbids its unionized workers to return to work until a new *collective bargaining* agreement is signed; a means of imposing costs (lost wages) on union workers.

logrolling The trading of votes by legislators to secure favorable outcomes on decisions concerning the provision of *public goods* and *quasi-public goods*.

long run In *microeconomics,* a period of time long enough to enable producers of a product to change the quantities of all the resources they employ, so that all resources and costs are variable and no resources or costs are fixed.

long run (macroeconomics) In *macroeconomics,* a period of time sufficiently long for *nominal wages* and other input *prices* to change in response to a change in a nation's *price level*.

long-run aggregate supply curve A vertical *aggregate supply* curve relevant to time periods over which input prices and output prices are both fully flexible; an aggregate supply curve for which the *price level,* but not real output, changes when the *aggregate demand* curve shifts; a vertical aggregate supply curve that implies fully flexible *prices*.

long-run supply A schedule or curve showing the prices at which a purely competitive industry will make various quantities of its product available in the *long run*.

long-run vertical Phillips Curve The *Phillips Curve* after all *nominal wages* and other input prices have adjusted to changes in the rate of *inflation*; a line emanating straight upward at the economy's *natural rate of unemployment*.

Lorenz curve A curve showing the distribution of income in an economy. The cumulated percentage of families (income receivers) is measured along the horizontal axis and the cumulated percentage of income is measured along the vertical axis.

loss aversion In *prospect theory,* the property of most people's preferences that the pain generated by losses feels substantially more intense than the pleasure generated by gains.

lump-sum tax A tax that collects a constant amount (the tax revenue of government is the same) at all levels of *GDP.*

M1 The most narrowly defined money supply, equal to *currency* in the hands of the public, *checkable deposits,* and *savings deposits* held at *commercial banks* and thrifts.

M2 A more broadly defined *money supply,* equal to *M1* plus small *time deposits* (of less than $100,000) and individual *money market mutual fund* balances.

macroeconomics The part of *economics* concerned with the performance and behavior of the economy as a whole. Focuses on *economic growth,* the *business cycle, interest rates, inflation,* and the behavior of major economic *aggregates* such as the household, business, and government sectors.

managed floating exchange rate An *exchange rate* that is allowed to change (float) as a result of changes in *currency* supply and demand but at times is altered (managed) by governments via their buying and selling of particular currencies.

marginal analysis The comparison of *marginal* ("extra" or "additional") *benefits* and *marginal costs,* usually for decision making.

marginal cost (MC) The extra (additional) cost of producing 1 more unit of output; equal to the change in *total cost* divided by the change in output (and, in the short run, to the change in total *variable cost* divided by the change in output).

marginal cost-marginal benefit rule As it applies to *cost-benefit analysis,* the tenet that a government project or program should be expanded to the point where the *marginal cost* and *marginal benefit* of additional expenditures are equal.

marginal product (MP) The additional output produced when 1 additional unit of a resource is employed (the quantity of all other resources employed remaining constant); equal to the change in *total product* divided by the change in the quantity of a resource employed.

marginal productivity theory of income distribution The hypothesis that the *wage* rate paid to *labor* will tend to equal the *marginal revenue product* of labor.

marginal propensity to consume (MPC) The fraction of any change in *disposable income* spent for *consumer goods;* equal to the change in consumption divided by the change in disposable income.

marginal propensity to save (MPS) The fraction of any change in *disposable income* that *households* save; equal to the change in *saving* divided by the change in disposable income.

marginal rate of substitution (MRS) The rate at which a consumer is willing to substitute one good for another (from a given combination of goods) and remain equally satisfied (have the same *total utility*); equal to the slope of a consumer's *indifference curve* at each point on the curve.

marginal resource cost (MRC) The amount by which the total cost of employing a *resource* increases when a *firm* employs 1 additional unit of the resource (the quantity of all other resources employed remaining constant); equal to the change in the *total cost* of the resource divided by the change in the quantity of the resource employed.

marginal revenue The change in *total revenue* that results from the sale of 1 additional unit of a *firm*'s product; equal to the change in total revenue divided by the change in the quantity of the product sold.

marginal revenue product (MRP) The change in a firm's *total revenue* when it employs 1 additional unit of a *resource* (the quantity of all other resources employed remaining constant); equal to the change in *total revenue* divided by the change in the quantity of the resource employed.

marginal tax rate The *tax* rate paid on an additional dollar of *income.*

marginal utility The extra *utility* a consumer obtains from the consumption of 1 additional unit of a *good* or *service;* equal to the change in *total utility* divided by the change in the quantity consumed.

market Any institution or mechanism that brings together buyers (demanders) and sellers (suppliers) of a particular *good* or *service.*

market failure The inability of a *market* to bring about the allocation of *resources* that best satisfies the wants of society; in particular, the overallocation or underallocation of resources to the production of a particular *good* or *service* because of *externalities* or *asymmetric information,* or because markets fail to provide desired *public goods.*

market portfolio The portfolio consisting of every financial asset (including every *stock* and *bond*) traded in the financial markets. Used to calculate *beta* (a measure of the degree of riskiness) for specific stocks, bonds, and mutual funds.

market structure The characteristics of an *industry* that define the likely behavior and performance of its *firms.* The primary characteristics are the number of firms in the industry, whether they are selling a *differentiated product,* the ease of entry, and how much control firms have over output prices. The most commonly discussed market structures are *pure competition, monopolistic competition, oligopoly,* pure *monopoly,* and *monopsony.*

market system (1) An *economic system* in which individuals own most *economic resources* and in which *markets* and *prices* serve as the dominant coordinating mechanism used to allocate those resources; *capitalism.* Compare with *command system.* (2) All the product and resource markets of a *market economy* and the relationships among them.

marketing loan program A federal farm subsidy under which certain farmers can receive a loan (on a per-unit-of-output basis) to plant a crop and then, depending on the harvest *price* of the crop, either pay back the loan with interest or keep the loan proceeds while forfeiting their harvested crop to the lender.

mechanism design The part of *game theory* concerned with designing the rules of a *game* so as to maximize the likelihood of players reaching a socially optimal outcome.

median-voter model The theory that under majority rule the median (middle) voter will be in the dominant position to determine the outcome of an election.

Medicaid A federal program that helps finance the medical expenses of individuals covered by the *Supplemental Security Income* (*SSI*) and *Temporary Assistance for Needy Families* (*TANF*) programs.

Medicare A federal program that provides for (1) compulsory hospital insurance for senior citizens, (2) low-cost voluntary insurance to help older Americans pay physicians' fees, and (3) subsidized insurance to buy prescription drugs. Financed by *payroll taxes.*

medium of exchange Any item sellers generally accept and buyers generally use to pay for a *good* or *service; money;* a convenient means of exchanging goods and *services* without engaging in *barter.*

mental accounting The tendency people have to create separate "mental boxes" (or "accounts") in which they deal with particular financial transactions in isolation, rather than dealing with them as part of an overall decision-making process that would consider how to best allocate their limited budgets across all possible options by using the *utility-maximizing rule.*

microcredit Anti-poverty programs that lend small amounts of money to poor entrepreneurs.

microeconomics The part of economics concerned with (1) decision making by individual units such as a *household,* a *firm,* or an *industry* and (2) individual markets, specific *goods* and *services,* and product and resource *prices.*

microfinance The provision of small loans and other financial services to low-income *entrepreneurs* and small-business owners in *developing countries.*

Microsoft case A 2002 antitrust case in which Microsoft was found guilty of violating the *Sherman Act* by engaging in a series of unlawful activities designed to maintain its *monopoly* in operating systems for personal computers; as a remedy the company was prohibited from engaging in a set of specific anticompetitive business practices.

midpoint formula A method for calculating *price elasticity of demand* or *price elasticity of supply* that averages the starting and ending *prices* and quantities when computing percentages.

minimum efficient scale (MES) The lowest level of output at which a *firm* can minimize long-run *average total cost.*

minimum wage The lowest *wage* that employers may legally pay for an hour of work.

modern economic growth The historically recent phenomenon in which nations for the first time have experienced sustained increases in *real GDP per capita.*

monetarism The macroeconomic view that the main cause of changes in aggregate output and the *price level* is fluctuations in the *money supply;* espoused by advocates of a *monetary rule.*

monetary policy Actions or communications by a *central bank* intended to help it achieve its macroeconomic policy objectives, which for the U.S. *Federal Reserve* are full employment of the labor force and a stable *price level.*

monetary policy stance A *central bank's* disposition regarding how it sees the current and future state of the economy and, thus, whether its current monetary policy actions will be consistent with an *expansionary monetary policy,* a *restrictive monetary policy,* or a *neutral monetary policy.*

monetary rule (1) A set of guidelines to be followed by a *central bank* that wishes to adjust monetary policy over time to achieve goals such as promoting *economic growth,* encouraging *full employment,* and maintaining a stable *price level.* (2) The guidelines for conducting monetary policy suggested by *monetarism.* As traditionally formulated, the *money supply* should be expanded each year at the same annual rate as the potential rate of growth of *real gross domestic product;* the supply of money should be increased steadily between 3 and 5 percent per year. (Also see *Taylor rule.*)

money Any item that is generally acceptable to sellers in exchange for *goods* and *services.*

money market The financial *markets* in which short-term, low-risk debt *securities* are traded, including U.S. Treasury bills, overnight loans of bank reserves, and commercial paper.

money market mutual funds (MMMFs) *Mutual funds* that invest in short-term *securities.* Depositors can write checks in minimum amounts or more against their accounts.

monopolistic competition A *market structure* in which many *firms* sell a *differentiated product,* entry is relatively easy, each firm has some control over its product *price,* and there is considerable *non-price competition.*

monopsony A *market structure* in which there is only a single buyer of a good, *service,* or *resource.*

moral hazard problem The possibility that individuals or institutions will behave more recklessly after they obtain insurance or similar contracts that shift the financial burden of bad outcomes onto others. Example: A bank whose deposits are insured against losses may make riskier loans and investments.

MR = MC rule The principle that a *firm* will maximize its profit (or minimize its loss) by producing the output at which *marginal revenue* and *marginal cost* are equal, provided product *price* is equal to or greater than *average variable cost.*

MRP = MRC rule The principle that to maximize profit (or minimize losses), a *firm* should employ the quantity of a resource at which its *marginal revenue product* (MRP) is equal to its *marginal resource cost* (MRC), the latter being the wage rate in a purely competitive labor market.

multi-homing The phenomenon that occurs when consumers use one or more competing Internet products simultaneously. Also called *multi-tenanting.*

multiple counting Wrongly including the value of *intermediate goods* in the *gross domestic product;* counting the same *good* or *service* more than once.

multiplier The ratio of a change in *equilibrium GDP* to the change in *investment* or in any other component of *aggregate expenditures* or *aggregate demand;* the number by which a change in any such component must be multiplied to find the resulting change in equilibrium GDP.

mutual funds Investment companies that pool money from numerous individual investors in order to purchase *portfolios* of *stocks* or *bonds;* includes both *index funds* as well as *actively managed funds.*

mutual interdependence A situation in which a change in *price* strategy (or in some other strategy) by one *firm* will affect the sales and profits of another firm (or other firms). Any firm that makes such a change can expect its rivals to react to the change.

myopia Refers to the difficulty human beings have with conceptualizing the more distant future. Leads to decisions that overly favor present and near-term options at the expense of more distant future possibilities.

Nash equilibrium The situation that occurs in some *simultaneous games* wherein every player is playing his or her *dominant strategy* at the same time and thus no player has any reason to change behavior.

national health insurance A program in which a nation's government provides a basic package of health care to all citizens at no direct charge or at a low cost-sharing level. Financing is out of general *tax* revenues.

national income Total *income* earned by *resource* suppliers for their contributions to *gross domestic product* plus *taxes on production and imports;* the sum of wages and salaries, *rent, interest, profit, proprietors' income,* and such taxes.

national income accounting The techniques used to measure the overall production of a country's economy as well as other related variables.

National Labor Relations Act (NLRA) The basic labor-relations law in the United States. Defines the legal rights of unions and management and identifies unfair union and management labor practices; established the *National Labor Relations Board.* Often referred to as the Wagner Act, after the legislation's sponsor, New York Senator Robert F. Wagner.

National Labor Relations Board (NLRB)   The board established by the *National Labor Relations Act* of 1935 to investigate unfair labor practices, issue *cease-and-desist orders,* and conduct elections among employees to determine if they wish to be represented by a *labor union.*

natural monopoly   An *industry* in which *economies of scale* are so great that a single *firm* can produce the industry's product at a lower average total cost than would be possible if more than one firm produced the product.

natural rate of unemployment (NRU)   The *full-employment rate of unemployment;* the *unemployment rate* occurring when there is no cyclical unemployment and the economy is achieving its *potential output;* the unemployment rate at which actual *inflation* equals expected inflation.

near-money   Financial *assets* that are not themselves a *medium of exchange* but that have extremely high *liquidity* and thus can be readily converted into *money.* Includes noncheckable *savings accounts, time deposits,* and short-term *U.S. government securities* plus savings bonds.

negative externality   A cost imposed without compensation on third parties by the production or consumption of sellers or buyers. Example: A manufacturer dumps toxic chemicals into a river, killing fish prized by sports fishers. Also known as an external cost or a spillover cost.

negative network effect   The phenomenon observed when the value of a *network* decreases as the size of a network (number of users) increases. Also referred to as a negative network *externality.*

negative self-selection   As it relates to international migration, the idea that those who choose to move to another country have poorer *wage* opportunities in the origin country than those with similar skills who choose not to *emigrate.*

negative-sum game   A strategic interaction (game) between two or more parties (players) in which the winners' gains are less than the losers' losses so that the gains and losses sum to a negative number.

neoclassical economics   The dominant and conventional branch of economic theory that attempts to predict human behavior by building economic models based on simplifying assumptions about people's motives and capabilities. These include that people are fundamentally *rational;* motivated almost entirely by *self-interest;* good at math; and unaffected by *heuristics, time inconsistency,* and *self-control problems.*

net benefits   The total benefits of some activity or policy less the total costs of that activity or policy.

net domestic product (NDP)   *Gross domestic product* less the part of the year's output that is needed to replace the *capital goods* worn out in producing the output; the nation's total output available for consumption or additions to the *capital stock.*

net exports (X_n)   *Exports* minus *imports.*

net private domestic investment   *Gross private domestic investment* less *consumption of fixed capital;* the addition to the nation's stock of *capital* during a year.

network   In *economics,* a group of people or objects that are connected to each other by a *service* or piece of *infrastructure* that facilitates flows of *goods,* services, or information.

network congestion   A *negative network effect* that occurs when a network's capacity limits are approached or exceeded and the quality of the network's services declines as a result.

network effect   The phenomenon whereby the value of a *network* depends on the size of the network (number of users).

network effects   Increases in the value of a product to each user, including existing users, as the total number of users rises.

network pollution   A *negative network effect* that occurs on social networks when the presence of too many connected users degrades the average quality of the information that users obtain from the network.

network switching cost   The cost that a user will have to incur in order to switch from one *network* product to a competing *network* product.

neutral monetary policy   A *monetary policy* in which the *money supply* and *interest rates* are left as they are by the *central bank* because the economy appears to be operating at *potential output,* with stable prices and a low level of *unemployment.* Compare with *expansionary monetary policy* and *restrictive monetary policy.*

new classical economics   The theory that, although unanticipated *price-level* changes may create macroeconomic instability in the short run, the economy will return to and stabilize at the full-employment level of domestic output in the long run because *prices* and *wages* adjust automatically to correct movements away from the full-employment output level.

nominal gross domestic product (GDP)   *GDP* measured in terms of the *price level* at the time of measurement; *GDP* not adjusted for *inflation.* Compare with *real gross domestic product* (*real GDP*).

nominal income   The number of dollars received by an individual or group for its *resources* during some period of time.

nominal interest rate   The *interest rate* expressed in terms of annual amounts currently charged for *interest* and not adjusted for *inflation.*

nominal wage   The amount of *money* received by a worker per unit of time (hour, day, etc.); money wage.

noncash transfer   A *government transfer payment* in the form of *goods* and *services* rather than *money,* for example, food stamps, housing assistance, and job training; also called *in-kind transfers.*

noncompeting groups   Collections of workers who do not compete with each other for employment because the skill and training of the workers in one group are substantially different from those of the workers in other groups.

nondiversifiable risk   Investment *risk* that investors are unable to reduce via *diversification;* also called systemic risk.

nondurable good   A *consumer good* with an expected life (use) of less than three years.

nonexcludability   The inability to keep nonpayers (free riders) from obtaining benefits from a certain good; a characteristic of a *public good.*

nonprice competition   Competition based on distinguishing one's product by means of *product differentiation* and then *advertising* the distinguished product to consumers.

nonrenewable natural resource   Things such as oil, natural gas, and metals, that are either in actual fixed supply or that renew so slowly as to be in virtual fixed supply when viewed from a human time perspective.

nonrivalry   The idea that one person's benefit from a certain *good* does not reduce the benefit available to others; a characteristic of a *public good.*

nontariff barriers (NTBs) All barriers other than *protective tariffs* that nations erect to impede international trade, including *import quotas,* licensing requirements, unreasonable product-quality standards, unnecessary bureaucratic detail in customs procedures, and so on.

normal good A *good* or *service* whose consumption increases when *income* increases and falls when income decreases, other things equal.

normal profit The payment made by a *firm* to obtain and retain *entrepreneurial ability*; the minimum *income* that entrepreneurial ability must receive to induce *entrepreneurs* to provide their entrepreneurial ability to a firm; the level of *accounting profit* at which a firm generates an *economic profit* of zero after paying for entrepreneurial ability.

normative economics The part of economics involving value judgments about what the economy should be like; focused on which economic goals and policies should be implemented; policy economics.

North American Free Trade Agreement (NAFTA) The 1993 treaty that established an international free-trade zone composed of Canada, Mexico, and the United States.

occupational licensing The laws of state or local governments that require that a worker satisfy certain specified requirements and obtain a license from a licensing board before engaging in a particular occupation.

occupational segregation The crowding of women or minorities into less desirable, lower-paying occupations.

official reserves Foreign *currencies* owned by the central bank of a nation.

offshoring The practice of shifting work previously done by domestic workers to workers located abroad.

Okun's law The generalization that any 1-percentage-point rise in the *unemployment rate* above the *full-employment rate of unemployment* is associated with a rise in the *negative GDP gap* by 2 percent of *potential output* (potential *GDP*).

oligopoly A *market structure* in which a few *firms* sell either a *standardized* or *differentiated product,* into which entry is difficult, in which the firm has limited control over product *price* because of *mutual interdependence* (except when there is collusion among firms), and in which there is typically *nonprice competition.*

one-time game A strategic interaction (*game*) between two or more parties (players) that all parties know will take place only once.

open shop A place of employment in which the employer may hire nonunion workers and in which the workers need not become members of a *labor union.*

open-market operations The purchases and sales of U.S. government *securities* that the *Federal Reserve System* undertakes in order to influence *interest rates* and the *money supply;* one method by which the *Federal Reserve* implements *monetary policy.*

opportunity cost The amount of other products that must be forgone or sacrificed to produce a unit of a given product.

opportunity-cost ratio An equivalency showing the number of units of two products that can be produced with the same *resources;* the equivalency 1 corn ≡ 3 olives shows that the resources required to produce 3 units of olives must be shifted to corn production to produce 1 unit of corn.

optimal amount of R&D The level of *R&D* at which the *marginal benefit* and *marginal cost* of R&D expenditures are equal.

optimal reduction of an externality The reduction of a *negative externality* such as pollution to the level at which the *marginal benefit* and *marginal cost* of reduction (abatement) are equal.

other-things-equal assumption The assumption that factors other than those being considered are held constant. Also known as the *ceteris paribus* assumption.

output effect The possibility that when the *price* of the first of a pair of *substitute resources* falls, the *quantity demanded* of both resources will rise because the reduction in the price of the first resource so greatly reduces production costs that the volume of output created with the two resources increases by so much that the quantity demanded of the second resource increases even after accounting for the *substitution effect.* (See the second definition listed in the entry for *substitution effect.*)

overnight reverse repo rate (ON RRP) The *interest rate* that the Federal Reserve pays eligible nonbank financial firms for any money that they loan to a Federal Reserve Bank overnight using a reverse *repo* transaction; one of the three *administered rates* set by the *Federal Reserve.*

paradox of thrift The possibility that households trying to protect themselves against a recession by saving more may inadvertently worsen the recession and hurt themselves by reducing overall consumption and economic activity.

paradox of voting A situation where paired-choice voting by majority rule fails to provide a consistent ranking of society's preferences for *public goods* or *public services.*

parity concept The idea that year after year the sale of a specific output of a farm product should enable a farmer to purchase a constant amount of nonagricultural *goods* and *services.*

parity ratio The ratio of the *price* received by farmers from the sale of an agricultural commodity to the prices of other goods paid by them; usually expressed as a percentage; used as a rationale for *price supports.*

passively managed funds *Mutual funds* whose *portfolios* are not regularly updated by a fund manager attempting to generate high returns. Rather, once an initial portfolio is selected, it is left unchanged so that investors receive whatever return that unchanging portfolio subsequently generates. *Index funds* are a type of passively managed fund.

patent An exclusive right given to inventors to produce and sell a new product or machine for 20 years from the time of patent application.

payroll tax A *tax* levied on employers of labor equal to a percentage of all or part of the *wages* and salaries paid by them and on employees equal to a percentage of all or part of the wages and salaries received by them.

peak The point in a *business cycle* at which business activity has reached a temporary maximum; the point at which an *expansion* ends and a *recession* begins. At the peak, the economy is near or at *full employment* and the level of real output is at or very close to the economy's capacity.

per se violations Collusive actions, such as attempts by *firms* to fix *prices* or divide a market, that are violations of the *antitrust laws,* even if the actions themselves are unsuccessful.

per-unit production cost The average production cost of a particular level of output; total input cost divided by units of output.

percentage rate of return The percentage gain or loss, relative to the buying *price,* of an *economic investment* or *financial investment* over some period of time.

perfectly elastic demand Product or *resource* demand in which *quantity demanded* can be of any amount at a particular product or resource *price;* graphs as a horizontal *demand curve.*

perfectly inelastic demand Product or *resource* demand in which *price* can be of any amount at a particular quantity of the product or resource that is demanded; when the *quantity demanded* does not respond to a change in price; graphs as a vertical *demand curve.*

personal consumption expenditures (C) The expenditures of *households* for both durable and nondurable *consumer goods.*

personal income (PI) The earned and unearned *income* available to resource suppliers and others before the payment of personal *taxes.*

personal income tax A *tax* levied on the taxable income of individuals, *households,* and unincorporated *firms.*

personal mandate The requirement under the *Patient Protection and Affordable Care Act* (*PPACA*) of 2010 that all U.S. citizens and legal residents purchase health insurance unless they are already covered by employer-sponsored health insurance or government-sponsored health insurance (*Medicaid* or *Medicare*).

Pigovian tax A *tax* or charge levied on the production of a product that generates *negative externalities.* If set correctly, the tax will precisely offset the overallocation (overproduction) generated by the negative externality.

planned investment The amount that *firms* plan or intend to invest.

policy rate A short-term *interest rate* that a *central bank* manages to help communicate the stance of *monetary policy* as well as to achieve its *monetary policy* goals.

political business cycles Fluctuations in the economy caused by the alleged tendency of Congress to destabilize the economy by reducing taxes and increasing government expenditures before elections and to raise taxes and lower expenditures after elections.

political corruption The unlawful misdirection of government resources, or actions that occur when government officials abuse their entrusted powers for personal gain. (Also see *corruption.*)

portfolio A specific collection of *stocks, bonds,* or other *financial investments* held by an individual or a *mutual fund.*

positive economics The analysis of facts or data to establish scientific generalizations about economic behavior.

positive externality A benefit obtained without compensation by third parties from the production or consumption of sellers or buyers. Example: A beekeeper benefits when a neighboring farmer plants clover. Also known as an *external benefit* or a spillover benefit.

positive network effect The phenomenon observed when the value of a *network* increases as the size of the network (number of users) increases. Also called a positive network *externality.*

positive-sum game A strategic interaction (game) between two or more parties (players) in which the winners' gains exceed the losers' losses so that the gains and losses sum to something positive.

potential output The real output (*GDP*) an economy can produce when it fully employs its available resources.

poverty rate The percentage of the population with incomes below the official poverty income levels that are established by the federal government.

precommittments Actions taken ahead of time that make it difficult for the future self to avoid doing what the present self desires. See *time inconsistency* and *self-control problems.*

preferred provider organization (PPO) An arrangement in which doctors and hospitals agree to provide health care to insured individuals at rates negotiated with an insurer.

present value Today's value of some amount of *money* that is to be received at a particular future date.

price ceiling A legally established maximum *price* for a *good,* or *service.* Normally set at a price below the *equilibrium price.*

price discrimination The selling of a product to different buyers at different *prices* when the price differences are not justified by differences in cost.

price elasticity of demand The ratio of the percentage change in *quantity demanded* of a product or *resource* to the percentage change in its *price;* a measure of the responsiveness of buyers to a change in the price of a product or resource.

price elasticity of supply The ratio of the percentage change in *quantity supplied* of a product or *resource* to the percentage change in its *price;* a measure of the responsiveness of producers to a change in the price of a product or resource.

price floor A legally established minimum *price* for a *good,* or service. Normally set at a price above the *equilibrium price.*

price index An index number that shows how the weighted-average *price* of a "market basket" of goods changes over time relative to its price in a specific *base year.*

price leadership An informal method that *firms* in an *oligopoly* may employ to set the *price* of their product: One firm (the leader) is the first to announce a change in price, and the other firms (the followers) soon announce identical or similar changes.

price loss coverage A form of crop insurance that pays participating farmers if the market price of their output falls below a predetermined value.

price supports The term used to refer to *price floors* applied to *farm commodities;* the minimum *price* that the government allows farmers to receive for farm commodities like wheat or corn.

price taker A seller (or buyer) that is unable to affect the *price* at which a product or *resource* sells by changing the amount it sells (or buys).

price war Successive, competitive, and continued decreases in the *prices* charged by *firms* in an oligopolistic *industry.* At each stage of the price war, one *firm* lowers its price below its rivals' price, hoping to increase its sales and revenues at its rivals' expense. The war ends when the price decreases cease.

price-level surprises Unanticipated changes in the *price level.*

pricing power The ability of a firm to raise *price* without substantially reducing *quantity demanded;* increases as *demand* becomes increasingly *inelastic.*

principal-agent problem (1) At a *firm,* a conflict of interest that occurs when agents (workers or managers) pursue their own objectives to the detriment of the principals' (stockholders') goals. (2) In *public choice theory,* a conflict of interest that arises when elected officials (who are the agents of the people) pursue policies that are in their own interests rather than policies that would be in the better interests of the public (the principals).

principle of comparative advantage The proposition that an individual, region, or nation will benefit if it specializes in producing goods for which its own *opportunity costs* are lower than the opportunity costs of a trading partner, and then exchanging some of the products in which it specializes for other desired products produced by others.

prisoner's dilemma A famous *game* analyzed in *game theory* in which two players who could have reached a mutually beneficial outcome through cooperation will instead end up at a mutually inferior outcome as they pursue their own respective interests (instead of cooperating). Helps to explain why collusion can be difficult for *oligopoly* firms to achieve or maintain.

private good A *good* or *service* that is individually consumed and that can be profitably provided by privately owned *firms* because they can exclude nonpayers from receiving the benefits.

private information Facts known by one party to a market transaction but hidden from others; results in *asymmetric information*.

private property The right of private persons and *firms* to obtain, own, control, employ, dispose of, and bequeath *land, capital,* and other property.

probability weighted average Each of the possible future rates of return from an investment multiplied by its respective probability (expressed as a decimal) of happening.

process innovation The development and use of new or improved production or distribution methods.

producer surplus The difference between the actual *price* a producer receives (or producers receive) and the minimum acceptable price; the triangular area above the *supply curve* and below the market price.

product differentiation A strategy in which one *firm*'s product is distinguished from competing products by means of its design, related *services,* quality, location, or other attributes (except *price*).

product innovation The development and sale of a new or improved product (or service).

product market A market in which products are sold by *firms* and bought by *households*.

production possibilities curve A curve showing the different combinations of two goods or *services* that can be produced in a *full-employment, full-production* economy where the available supplies of *resources* and technology are fixed.

productive efficiency The production of a *good* in the least costly way; occurs when production takes place at the output level at which per-unit production costs are minimized.

productivity A measure of average output or real output per unit of input. For example, the productivity of labor is determined by dividing real output by hours of work.

profit-maximizing combination of resources The quantity of each *resource* a *firm* must employ to maximize its *profit* or minimize its loss; the combination of resource inputs at which the *marginal revenue product* of each resource is equal to its *marginal resource cost* (to its *price* if the resource is employed in a competitive market).

progressive tax At the individual level, a *tax* whose *average tax rate* increases as the taxpayer's *income* increases. At the national level, a *tax* for which the *average tax rate* (= tax revenue/*GDP*) rises with *GDP*.

property tax A *tax* on the value of property (*capital, land, stocks and bonds,* and other *assets*) owned by *firms* and *households*.

proportional tax At the individual level, a *tax* whose *average tax rate* remains constant as the taxpayer's *income* increases or decreases. At the national level, a *tax* for which the *average tax rate* (= tax revenue/*GDP*) remains constant as *GDP* rises or falls.

prospect theory A *behavioral economics* theory of preferences having three main features: (1) people evaluate options on the basis of whether they generate gains or losses relative to the *status quo;* (2) gains are subject to *diminishing marginal utility,* while losses are subject to diminishing marginal disutility; and (3) people are prone to *loss aversion.*

protective tariff A *tariff* designed to shield domestic producers of a *good* or *service* from the competition of foreign producers.

public assistance programs Government programs that pay benefits to those who are unable to earn *income* (because of permanent disabilities or because they have very low income and dependent children); financed by general *tax* revenues and viewed as public charity (rather than earned rights).

public choice theory The economic analysis of government decision making, politics, and elections.

public debt The total amount owed by the federal government to the owners of government *securities;* equal to the sum of past government *budget deficits* less government *budget surpluses.*

public good A *good* or *service* that is characterized by *nonrivalry* and *nonexcludability.* These characteristics typically imply that no private *firm* can break even when attempting to provide such products. As a result, they are often provided by governments, who pay for them using general *tax* revenues.

public interest theory of regulation The presumption that the purpose of the regulation of an *industry* is to protect the public (consumers) from abuse of the power possessed by *natural monopolies.*

public investments Government expenditures on public capital (such as roads, highways, bridges, mass-transit systems, and electric power facilities) and on *human capital* (such as education, training, and health).

purchasing-power-parity theory The idea that if countries have *flexible exchange rates* (rather than *fixed exchange rates*), the exchange rates between national currencies will adjust to equate the purchasing power of various currencies. In particular, the exchange rate between any two national currencies will adjust to reflect the *price-level* differences between the two countries.

pure monopoly A *market structure* in which one *firm* sells a unique product, into which entry is blocked, in which the single firm has considerable control over product *price,* and in which *nonprice competition* may or may not be found.

pure rate of interest The hypothetical *interest rate* that is completely *risk*-free and only compensates investors for their willingness to patiently forego alternative consumption and investment opportunities until their money is repaid.

pure, or perfect, competition A *market structure* in which a very large number of *firms* sells a *standardized product,* into which entry is very easy, in which the individual seller has no control over the product *price,* and in which there is no nonprice competition; a market characterized by a very large number of buyers and sellers.

purely competitive labor market A *resource market* in which many *firms* compete with one another in hiring a specific kind of *labor,* numerous equally qualified workers supply that labor, and no one controls the market *wage rate.*

quadratic voting system A majority voting system in which voters can express strength of preference by purchasing as many votes as they like at a price equal to the square of the number of votes purchased. Quadratic voting is more likely (but not guaranteed) to result in economically efficient decisions than traditional one-person-one-vote (1p1v) majority voting systems.

quantitative easing (QE) An *open-market operation* in which a *central bank* pre-announces that it will spend a fixed quantity of *money* purchasing long-term bonds so as to lower long-term *interest rates* and thereby ease *credit* conditions for long-horizon investors, such as *businesses* borrowing to purchase *capital goods.*

quantitative tightening (QT) The opposite of *quantitative easing.* An *open-market operation* in which a *central bank* pre-announces that it will sell a fixed quantity of long-term bonds so as to raise long-term *interest rates* and thereby tighten *credit* conditions for long-horizon investors, such as *businesses* borrowing to purchase *capital goods.*

quasi-public good A *good* or *service* to which *excludability* could apply but that has such a large *positive externality* that government sponsors its production to prevent an underallocation of resources.

rational Behaviors and decisions that maximize a person's chances of achieving their goals. See *rational behavior*.

rational behavior Human behavior based on comparison of *marginal costs* and *marginal benefits;* behavior designed to maximize *total utility*. See *rational*.

rational expectations theory A hypothesis that assumes that people develop logical (rational) models that attempt to correctly anticipate future events (expectations) as much as possible so as to make better current decisions given what is likely to happen in the future. Can cause individuals and firms to take actions that offset monetary and fiscal policy initiatives.

real GDP *Gross domestic product* adjusted for *inflation;* gross domestic product in a year divided by the GDP *price index* for that year, the index expressed as a decimal. Compare with *nominal GDP*.

real GDP per capita *Inflation*-adjusted output per person; *real GDP*/population.

real gross domestic product (GDP) *Gross domestic product* adjusted for *inflation;* gross domestic product in a year divided by the GDP *price index* for that year, the index expressed as a decimal. Compare with *nominal GDP*.

real income The amount of *goods* and *services* that can be purchased with *nominal income* during some period of time; nominal income adjusted for *inflation*.

real interest rate The *interest rate* expressed in dollars of constant value (adjusted for *inflation*) and equal to the *nominal interest rate* less the expected rate of inflation.

real wage The amount of *goods* and *services* a worker can purchase with his or her *nominal wage;* the *purchasing power* of the *nominal wage*.

real-balances effect The tendency for increases in the *price level* to lower the real value (or *purchasing power*) of financial *assets* with fixed *money* value and, as a result, to reduce total spending and real output, and conversely for decreases in the *price level*.

real-business-cycle theory A theory that *business cycles* result from changes in *technology* and *resource* availability, which affect *productivity* and thus increase or decrease long-run *aggregate supply*.

recession A period of declining *real GDP*, accompanied by lower *real income* and higher *unemployment*.

recessionary expenditure gap The amount by which *aggregate expenditures* at the *full-employment level of GDP* fall short of the amount required to achieve the full-employment level of GDP. In the aggregate expenditures model, the amount by which the *aggregate expenditures schedule* must shift upward to increase *real GDP* to its full-employment, noninflationary level.

regressive tax At the individual level, a *tax* whose *average tax rate* decreases as the taxpayer's *income* increases. At the national level, a *tax* for which the *average tax rate* (= tax revenue/*GDP*) falls as *GDP* rises.

regulatory agency An agency, commission, or board established by the federal government or a state government to control the *prices* charged and the *services* offered by a *natural monopoly* or *public utility*.

regulatory capture The situation that occurs when a governmental *regulatory agency* ends up being controlled by the industry that it is supposed to be regulating.

remittances Payments by *immigrants* to family members and others located in the immigrants' home countries.

renewable natural resources Things such as forests, water in reservoirs, and wildlife that are capable of growing back or building back up (renewing themselves) if they are harvested at moderate rates.

rent control A law that sets a maximum price on the rents that a landlord can legally charge tenants for renting an apartment or a house.

rent-seeking behavior Attempts by individuals, firms, or unions to use political influence to receive payments in excess of the minimum amount they would normally be willing to accept to provide a particular good or service.

repeated game A strategic interaction (*game*) between two or more parties (players) that all parties know will take place repeatedly.

replacement rate The *total fertility rate* necessary to offset deaths in a country and thereby keep the size of its population constant (without relying on immigration). For most countries, a total fertility rate of about 2.1 births per woman per lifetime.

reserve balances Funds that *commercial banks* and *thrift institutions* hold on deposit at the *central bank*.

residual claimant In a market system, the economic agent who receives (is claimant to) whatever profit or loss remains (is residual) at a firm after all other *input* providers have been paid. The residual is compensation for providing the economic input of *entrepreneurial ability* and flows to the firm's owners.

resource market A market in which *households* sell and *firms* buy *resources* or the services of resources.

restrictive monetary policy *Central bank* actions to reduce the *money supply*, increase *interest rates*, and reduce *inflation*. Implemented when the economy is operating above *potential output*. Also known as a "tight money" policy.

revenue tariff A *tariff* designed to produce *income* for the federal government.

right-to-work law A state law that makes it illegal to require that a worker join a *labor union* in order to retain his or her job; laws that make *union shops* and *agency shops* illegal.

risk The uncertainty as to the future returns of a particular *financial investment* or *economic investment*.

risk premium The rate of return in excess of the *risk-free interest rate* that compensates a lender or investor for *risk*.

risk-free interest rate The *interest rate* earned on short-term U.S. government *bonds*.

rivalry The characteristic displayed by certain goods and services that consumption by one person precludes consumption by others.

rule of 70 A method for determining the number of years it will take for some measure to double, given its annual percentage increase. Example: To determine the number of years it will take for the *price level* to double, divide 70 by the annual rate of *inflation*.

rule of reason The rule stated and applied in the *U.S. Steel* case that only combinations and contracts unreasonably restraining trade are subject to actions under the antitrust laws and that size and possession of *monopoly* power are not by themselves illegal. Compare with *per se violation*.

sales tax A *tax* levied on the cost (at retail) of a broad group of products.

saving The flow of money that is generated when *personal consumption expenditures* are less than *disposable income*. Compare with *savings*.

saving schedule A table of numbers that shows the amounts *households* plan to save (plan not to spend for *consumer goods*), at different levels of *disposable income*.

scarcity The limits placed on the amounts and types of *goods* and *services* available for consumption as the result of there being only limited *economic resources* from which to produce output; the fundamental economic constraint that creates *opportunity costs* and that necessitates the use of *marginal analysis* (*cost-benefit analysis*) to make optimal choices.

scientific method The procedure for the systematic pursuit of knowledge involving the observation of facts and the formulation and testing of hypotheses to obtain theories, principles, and laws.

securities Financial assets such as stocks and bonds that are tradable in organized financial markets, such as the New York Stock Exchange (NYSE).

Security Market Line (SML) A line that shows the *average expected rate of return* of all *financial investments* at each level of *nondiversifiable risk*, the latter measured by *beta*.

self-control problems Refers to the difficulty people have in sticking with earlier plans and avoiding suboptimal decisions when finally confronted with a particular decision-making situation. A manifestation of *time inconsistency* and potentially avoidable by using *precommitments*.

self-interest That which each *firm*, property owner, worker, and consumer believes is best for itself and seeks to obtain.

self-selection As it relates to international migration, the idea that those who choose to move to a new country tend to have greater motivation for economic gain or greater willingness to sacrifice current consumption for future consumption than those with similar skills who choose to remain at home.

sequential game A strategic interaction (*game*) between two or more parties (players) in which each party moves (makes a decision) in a predetermined order (sequence).

service An (intangible) act or use for which a consumer, *firm*, or government is willing to pay.

Sherman Act The federal antitrust law of 1890 that makes *monopoly* and conspiracies to restrain trade criminal offenses.

shocks Sudden, unexpected changes in *demand* (or *aggregate demand*) or supply (or *aggregate supply*).

short run In *microeconomics*, a period of time in which producers are able to change the quantities of some but not all of the *resources* they employ; a period in which some resources (usually *plant*) are fixed and some are variable.

short run (macroeconomics) In *macroeconomics*, the relatively short period of time (typically, weeks to months) in which *nominal wages* and other input *prices* do not change in response to a change in a nation's *price level*.

short-run aggregate supply curve An upward sloping *aggregate supply* curve relevant to time periods over which input prices are fixed but output prices are flexible; an aggregate supply curve for which real output and the price level both change when the *aggregate demand* curve shifts.

short-run downward sloping Phillips Curve A downward sloping line illustrating the inverse relationship that A.W. Phillips theorized should exist between the *unemployment rate* (on the horizontal axis) and the *inflation rate* (on the vertical axis). Believed by many mainstream economists to hold in the *short run* but not in the *long run*.

short-run supply curve A *supply curve* that shows the quantity of a product a *firm* in a purely competitive *industry* will offer to sell at various *prices* in the *short run*; the portion of the firm's short-run *marginal cost curve* that lies above its *average-variable-cost* curve.

shortage The amount by which the *quantity demanded* of a product exceeds the *quantity supplied* at a particular (below-equilibrium) *price*.

simultaneous consumption The same-time derivation of *utility* from some product by a large number of consumers.

simultaneous game A strategic interaction (*game*) between two or more parties (players) in which every player moves (makes a decision) at the same time.

skill transferability The ease with which people can shift their work talents from one job, region, or country to another job, region, or country.

slope of a straight line The ratio of the vertical change (the rise or fall) to the horizontal change (the run) between any two points on a straight line. The slope of an upward-sloping line is positive, reflecting a direct relationship between two variables; the slope of a downward-sloping line is negative, reflecting an inverse relationship between two variables.

Smoot-Hawley Tariff Act Legislation passed in 1930 that established very high *tariffs*. Its objective was to reduce *imports* and stimulate the domestic economy, but it resulted only in retaliatory tariffs by other nations.

social insurance programs Programs that replace the earnings lost when people retire or are temporarily unemployed, that are financed by payroll *taxes*, and that are viewed as earned rights (rather than charity).

social regulation Regulation in which government is concerned with the conditions under which *goods* and *services* are produced, their physical characteristics, and the impact of their production on society. Differs from *industrial regulation*.

Social Security The social insurance program in the United States financed by federal *payroll taxes* on employers and employees and designed to replace a portion of the earnings lost when workers become disabled, retire, or die.

socially optimal price The *price* of a product that results in the most efficient allocation of an economy's *resources* and that is equal to the *marginal cost* of the product.

special-interest effect Any political outcome in which a small group ("special interest") gains substantially at the expense of a much larger number of persons who each individually suffers a small loss.

specialization The use of the *resources* of an individual, a *firm*, a region, or a nation to concentrate production on one or a small number of *goods* and *services*.

stagflation *Inflation* accompanied by stagnation in the rate of growth of output and an increase in *unemployment* in the economy; simultaneous increases in the *inflation rate* and the *unemployment rate*.

Standard Oil case A 1911 antitrust case in which Standard Oil was found guilty of violating the *Sherman Act* by illegally monopolizing the petroleum *industry*. As a remedy the company was divided into several competing *firms*.

start-up firm A new *firm* focused on creating and introducing a particular new product or employing a specific new production or distribution method.

startups Newly formed firms that are attempting to pioneer a new product or production method.

state capacity The ability of a government to achieve specific policy goals.

statistical discrimination The practice of judging an individual on the basis of the average characteristics of the group to which he or she belongs rather than on his or her own personal characteristics.

status quo The existing state of affairs; in *prospect theory,* the current situation from which gains and losses are calculated.

status quo bias The tendency most people have when making choices to select any option that is presented as the default (*status quo*) option. Explainable by *prospect theory* and *loss aversion.*

stock (corporate) An ownership share in a corporation.

store of value An *asset* set aside for future use; one of the three functions of *money.*

strategic behavior Self-interested economic actions that take into account the expected reactions of others.

Strategic Organizing Center (SOC) A loose federation of American unions that includes the Service Workers and Teamsters unions; the second largest union federation after the *AFL-CIO.*

strike The withholding of *labor* services by an organized group of workers (a *labor union*).

structural remedy A directive imposed by a regulator on an offending monopoly firm that seeks to resolve the firm's illegal monopoly behavior by changing the structure of the offending business, for instance by breaking it up into multiple competing firms.

structural unemployment *Unemployment* of workers whose skills are not demanded by employers, who lack sufficient skill to obtain employment, or who cannot easily move to locations where jobs are available.

substitute goods Products or *services* that can be used in place of each other. When the *price* of one falls, the *demand* for the other product falls; conversely, when the price of one product rises, the demand for the other product rises.

substitute resources Productive inputs that can be used instead of other inputs in the production process; resources for which an increase in the *price* of one leads to an increase in the demand for the other.

substitution effect (1) A change in the quantity demanded of a *consumer good* that results from a change in its relative expensiveness caused by a change in the good's own *price.* (2) The reduction in the *quantity demanded* of the second of a pair of *substitute resources* that occurs when the price of the first resource falls and causes *firms* that employ both resources to switch to using more of the first resource (whose price has fallen) and less of the second resource (whose price has remained the same).

subtractive versioning A pricing strategy in which an internet business offers customers the option of paying to remove an annoying feature (such as advertising) from its base offering.

Supplemental Nutrition Assistance Program (SNAP) A government program that provides food money to low-income recipients by depositing electronic money onto *Electronic Benefit Transfer (EBT) cards.* Formerly known as the food-stamp program.

Supplemental Security Income (SSI) A federally financed and administered program that provides a uniform nationwide minimum *income* for the aged, blind, and disabled who do not qualify for benefits under *Social Security* in the United States.

supply A schedule or curve that shows the various amounts of a product that producers are willing and able to make available for sale at each of a series of possible *prices* during a specified period of time.

supply curve A curve that illustrates the *supply* for a product by showing how each possible *price* (on the *vertical axis*) is associated with a specific *quantity supplied* (on the *horizontal axis*).

supply factors (in growth) The four determinants of an economy's physical ability to achieve *economic growth* by increasing *potential output* and shifting out the *production possibilities curve.* The four determinants are improvements in technology plus increases in the quantity and quality of natural resources, human resources, and the stock of capital goods.

supply schedule A table of numbers showing the amounts of a *good* or *service* producers are willing and able to make available for sale at each of a series of possible *prices* during a specified period of time.

supply shocks Sudden, unexpected changes in *aggregate supply.*

supply-side economics A view of *macroeconomics* that emphasizes the role of costs and *aggregate supply* in explaining *inflation, unemployment,* and *economic growth.*

surplus The amount by which the *quantity supplied* of a product exceeds the *quantity demanded* at a specific (above-equilibrium) *price.*

systematic errors Suboptimal choices that (1) are not *rational* because they do not maximize a person's chances of achieving his or her goals and (2) occur routinely, repeatedly, and predictably.

target rate of inflation The publicly announced annual *inflation* rate that a *central bank* attempts to achieve through *monetary policy* actions if it is following an *inflation targeting* monetary policy.

target rate of unemployment The Fed's desired *unemployment rate,* equal to the *full-employment rate of unemployment,* which is estimated to be between 4 and 5 percent for the U.S. economy.

tariff A *tax* imposed by a nation on an imported good.

taste-for-discrimination model A theory that views discrimination as a preference for which an employer is willing to pay.

tax incidence The degree to which a *tax* falls on a particular person or group.

tax subsidy A grant in the form of reduced *taxes* through favorable *tax* treatment. For example, employer-paid health insurance is exempt from federal *income taxes* and *payroll taxes.*

taxes on production and imports A *national income accounting* category that includes such taxes as *sales, excise,* business property taxes, and *tariffs* that *firms* treat as costs of producing a product and pass on (in whole or in part) to buyers by charging a higher *price.*

Taylor rule A *monetary rule* proposed by economist John Taylor that would stipulate exactly how much the *Federal Reserve System* should change *real interest rates* in response to divergences of *real GDP* from potential GDP and divergences of actual rates of *inflation* from a target rate of inflation.

technological advance (1) An improvement in the quality of existing products, the invention of entirely new products, or the creation of new or better ways of producing or distributing products. (2) Any improvement in the methods by which resources are combined such that the same quantity of inputs can be made to yield a combination of outputs that is preferred to any combination of outputs that was previously possible.

technological lock-in The unwillingness of users to switch to a better product or technology because so many people are already using an older technology that enjoys *positive network effects.*

Temporary Assistance for Needy Families (TANF) A state-administered and partly federally funded program in the United States that provides financial aid to poor families; the basic welfare program for low-income families in the United States; contains time limits and work requirements.

terms of trade The rate at which units of one product can be exchanged for units of another product; the *price* of a *good* or *service;* the amount of one good or service that must be given up to obtain 1 unit of another good or service.

The Agricultural Act of 2014 The agricultural law enacted in the United States in 2014 that eliminated *direct payments* and *countercyclical payments* in favor of two types of *crop insurance–price loss coverage* and *agricultural risk coverage.*

thrift institution A *savings and loan association, mutual savings bank,* or *credit union.*

time deposit An interest-earning deposit in a *commercial bank* or *thrift institution* that the depositor can withdraw without penalty after the end of a specified period.

time inconsistency The human tendency to systematically misjudge at the present time what will actually end up being desired at a future time.

time preference The human tendency, because of impatience, to prefer to spend and consume in the present rather than save and wait to spend and consume in the future; this inclination varies in strength among individuals.

time-value of money The idea that a specific amount of *money* is more valuable to a person the sooner it is received because the money can be placed in a financial account or *investment* and earn *compound interest* over time; the *opportunity cost* of receiving a sum of money later rather than earlier.

tipping point The size of a *network* beyond which further network growth becomes self-sustaining (due to the network's sheer size creating large enough *positive network effects* to attract additional users, whose participation further increases the size of the network's positive network effects, thereby attracting even more users, and so on).

token money Bills or coins for which the amount printed on the *currency* bears no relationship to the value of the paper or metal embodied within it; for currency still circulating, *money* for which the face value exceeds the commodity value.

total allowable catch (TAC) The overall limit set by a government or a fisheries commission on the total number of fish or tonnage of fish that fishers collectively can harvest during some particular time period. Used to set the fishing limits for *individual transferable quotas (ITQs).*

total cost The sum of *fixed cost* and *variable cost.*

total demand for money The sum of the *transactions demand for money* and the *asset demand for money.*

total fertility rate The average number of children per lifetime birthed by a nation's women.

total product (TP) The total output of a particular *good* or *service* produced by a *firm* (or a group of firms or the entire economy).

total revenue (TR) The total number of dollars received by a *firm* (or firms) from the sale of a product; equal to the total expenditures for the product produced by the firm (or firms); equal to the quantity sold (demanded) multiplied by the *price* at which it is sold.

total surplus The sum of consumer surplus and producer surplus; a measure of social welfare; also known as social surplus.

total utility The total amount of satisfaction derived from the consumption of a single product or a combination of products.

total-revenue test A test to determine *elasticity of demand.* Demand is elastic if *total revenue* moves in the opposite direction from a *price* change; it is inelastic when it moves in the same direction as a price change; and it is of unitary elasticity when it does not change when price changes.

trade The voluntary exchange of goods, services, or assets between two or more parties.

Trade Adjustment Assistance Act A U.S. law passed in 2002 that provides cash assistance, education and training benefits, health care subsidies, and *wage* subsidies (for persons age 50 or older) to workers displaced by *imports* or relocations of U.S. *plants* to other countries.

trade deficit The amount by which a nation's *imports* of goods (or goods and *services*) exceed its *exports* of goods (or goods and *services*).

trade surplus The amount by which a nation's *exports* of goods (or goods and *services*) exceed its *imports* of goods (or goods and *services*).

trading possibilities line A line that shows the different combinations of two products that an economy is able to obtain (consume) when it specializes in the production of one product and trades (exports) it to obtain the other product.

tragedy of the commons The tendency for commonly owned *natural resources* to be overused, neglected, or degraded because their common ownership gives nobody an incentive to maintain or improve them.

transactions demand for money The amount of money people want to hold for use as a *medium of exchange* (to make payments); varies directly with *nominal GDP.*

transfer payment A payment of *money* (or *goods* and *services*) by a government to a *household* or *firm* for which the payer receives no *good* or *service* directly in return.

trough The point in a *business cycle* at which business activity has reached a temporary minimum; the point at which a *recession* ends and an *expansion* (recovery) begins. At the trough, the economy experiences substantial *unemployment* and *real GDP* is less than *potential output.*

tying contract A requirement imposed by a seller that a buyer purchase another (or other) of its products as a condition for buying a desired product; a practice forbidden by the *Clayton Act.*

U.S. government securities U.S. Treasury bills, notes, and *bonds* used to finance *budget deficits;* the components of the *public debt.*

U.S. Steel case The antitrust action brought by the federal government against the U.S. Steel Corporation in which the courts ruled (in 1920) that only unreasonable restraints of trade were illegal and that size and the possession of monopoly power were not by themselves violations of the *antitrust laws.*

ultimatum game A *behavioral economics* game in which a mutually anonymous pair of players interact to determine how an amount of money is to be split. The first player suggests a division. The second player either accepts that proposal (in which case the split is made accordingly) or rejects it (in which case neither player gets anything).

unanticipated inflation An increase of the *price level* (*inflation*) at a rate greater than expected.

unauthorized immigrants   People who have entered a country unlawfully to reside there; also called undocumented workers, unauthorized workers, and illegal aliens.

unconditional cash transfers   Anti-poverty programs that give cash transfers (grants) to poor individuals with no strings attached in the hope that the recipients will improve their economic prospects by spending the money on either education or physical capital.

underemployment   A situation in which workers are employed in positions requiring less education and skill than they have.

unemployment   The failure to use all available *economic resources* to produce desired *goods* and *services;* the failure of the economy to fully employ its *labor force.*

unemployment gap   The difference between the actual rate of *unemployment* and the *full-employment rate of unemployment,* which is believed to be between 3 and 4 percent for the U.S. economy; a key component of the *Taylor rule.*

unemployment insurance   The social insurance program that in the United States is financed by state *payroll taxes* on employers and makes *income* available to workers who become unemployed and are unable to find jobs.

unemployment rate   The percentage of the *labor force* unemployed at any time.

uninsurable risk   An eventuality for which the frequency or magnitude of potential losses is unpredictable or unknowable. Insurance companies are not willing to sell insurance against such risks.

union shop   A place of employment where the employer may hire either *labor union* members or nonmembers but where nonmembers must become members within a specified period of time or lose their jobs.

unionization rate   The percentage of a particular population of workers that belongs to *labor unions;* alternatively, the percentage of a population of workers that is represented by one union or another in *collective bargaining.*

unit elasticity   *Demand* or *supply* for which the *elasticity coefficient* is equal to 1; means that the percentage change in the *quantity demanded* or *quantity supplied* is equal to the percentage change in *price.*

unit of account   A standard unit in which *prices* can be stated and the value of *goods* and *services* can be compared; one of the three functions of *money.*

unplanned changes in inventories   Changes in *inventories* that *firms* did not anticipate; changes in inventories that occur because of unexpected increases or decreases of aggregate spending (or of *aggregate expenditures*).

user cost   The *opportunity cost* of extracting and selling a *nonrenewable natural resource* today rather than waiting to extract and sell the resource in the future; the *present value* of the decline in future revenue that will occur because a nonrenewable natural resource is extracted and sold today rather than being extracted and sold in the future.

utility   The want-satisfying power of a *good* or *service;* the satisfaction or pleasure a consumer obtains from the consumption of a good or service (or from the consumption of a collection of *goods* and *services*).

utility-maximizing rule   The principle that to obtain the greatest *total utility,* a consumer should allocate *money income* so that the last dollar spent on each *good* or *service* yields the same *marginal utility* (MU). For two goods X and Y, with prices P_x and P_y, total utility will be maximized by purchasing the amounts of X and Y such that $MU_x/P_x = MU_y/P_y$ for the last dollar spent on each good.

value added   The value of a product sold by a *firm* less the value of the products (materials) purchased and used by the firm to produce that product.

variable cost   A cost that increases when the *firm* increases its output and decreases when the firm reduces its output.

velocity   The number of times per year that the average dollar in the *money supply* is spent for *final goods* and final *services; nominal gross domestic product* (*GDP*) divided by the *money supply.*

venture capital   That part of household *savings* used to finance high-risk business enterprises in exchange for *stock* (and thus a share of any *profit* if the enterprises are successful).

vertical axis   The "up-down" or "north-south" measurement line on a graph or grid.

vertical intercept   The point at which a line meets the vertical axis of a graph.

vertical merger   The merger of one or more *firms* engaged in different stages of the production of a particular *final good.*

very long run   In microeconomics, a period of time long enough that *technology* can change and *firms* can introduce new products.

vicious circle of poverty   A problem common in some *developing countries* in which their low *per capita incomes* are an obstacle to realizing the levels of *savings* and *investment* needed to achieve rates of growth of output that exceed their rates of population growth.

voice mechanism   Communication by workers through their *union* to resolve grievances with an employer.

voluntary export restrictions (VER)   Voluntary limitations by countries or *firms* of their exports to a particular foreign nation; undertaken to avoid the enactment of formal trade barriers by the foreign nation.

wage   The *price* paid for the use or *services* of *labor* per unit of time (per hour, per day, and so on).

wage differential   The difference between the *wage* received by one worker or group of workers and that received by another worker or group of workers.

wealth effect   The tendency for people to increase their consumption spending when the value of their financial and real *assets* rises and to decrease their consumption spending when the value of those assets falls.

Wheeler-Lea Act   The federal law of 1938 that amended the *Federal Trade Commission Act* by prohibiting unfair and deceptive acts or practices of commerce (such as false and misleading advertising and the misrepresentation of products).

will to develop   The mental state of wanting *economic growth* strongly enough to change from old to new ways of doing things.

winner-take-all industries   Industries in which factors such as *economies of scale* and *positive network effects* might be expected to lead to *pure monopoly.*

World Bank   A bank that lends (and guarantees loans) to *developing countries* to assist them in increasing their *capital stock* and thus in achieving *economic growth.*

world price   The international market *price* of a *good* or *service,* determined by world demand and supply.

World Trade Organization (WTO)   An organization of 164 nations (as of 2021) that oversees the provisions of the current world trade agreement, resolves trade disputes stemming from it, and holds forums for further rounds of trade negotiations.

X-inefficiency   The production of output, whatever its level, at a higher average (and total) cost than is necessary for producing that level of output.

zero interest rate policy (ZIRP)   A *monetary policy* in which a *central bank* sets *nominal interest rates* at or near zero percent per year in order to stimulate the economy.

zero lower bound problem   The constraint placed on the ability of a *central bank* to stimulate the economy through lower short-term *interest rates* by the fact that short-term *interest rates* cannot be driven lower than zero without causing depositors to withdraw funds from the banking system.

zero-sum game   A strategic interaction (game) between two or more parties (players) in which the winners' gains exactly offset the losers' losses so that the gains and losses sum to zero.

Historical Economic
Data Tables

Selected Economics Statistics for Various Years, 1929–1993

Statistics in rows 1–5 are in billions of dollars in the year specified. Numbers may not add to totals because of rounding.

GDP AND INCOME DATA	1929	1933	1940	1942	1944	1946	1950	1960	1970	1972
1 Gross domestic product (billions of nominal dollars)	104.6	57.2	102.9	166.0	224.4	227.5	299.8	542.4	1,073.3	1,279.1
1A Personal consumption expenditures	77.4	45.9	71.3	89.0	108.6	144.2	192.0	331.2	646.7	768.2
1B Gross private domestic investment	17.2	2.3	14.6	11.8	9.2	33.1	56.5	86.5	170.0	228.1
1C Government purchases	9.6	8.9	15.6	65.4	108.6	43.0	50.5	120.5	252.6	286.2
1D Net exports of goods and services	0.4	0.1	1.5	−0.3	−2.0	7.2	0.7	4.2	3.9	−3.4
2 Net domestic product	94.1	49.1	92.3	151.0	203.1	201.8	266.4	474.5	936.5	1,118.1
3 National income	94.2	48.9	91.5	152.4	200.9	201.3	266.6	478.9	937.5	1,119.5
3A Wages and salaries	51.4	29.8	52.7	88.0	124.3	122.5	158.3	301.3	623.3	731.3
3B Rent	6.1	2.9	3.8	5.5	6.3	6.9	8.8	16.5	20.7	22.7
3C Interest	4.6	4.0	3.3	3.2	2.4	1.8	3.1	10.3	39.5	48.0
3D Profits	10.8	−0.2	9.9	20.8	25.0	18.2	36.1	54.7	86.2	117.2
3E Proprietor's income	14.0	5.3	12.2	23.3	29.3	35.7	37.5	50.6	77.8	95.1
3F Taxes on production and imports*	7.3	7.1	9.6	11.6	13.6	16.2	22.8	45.5	90.0	105.2
4 Personal income	85.3	47.2	79.4	126.7	169.7	182.5	233.7	422.1	865.0	1,024.5
5 Disposable income	83.6	46.4	77.7	121.8	152.1	165.3	214.8	376.1	762.0	900.8
6 Disposable income per capita	686	369	588	903	1,099	1,169	1,416	2,080	3,715	4,291
7 Personal saving as a percent of disposable income	4.7	−0.7	6.8	26.2	27.9	11.8	9.3	10.1	12.8	12.4

OTHER STATISTICS	1929	1933	1940	1942	1944	1946	1950	1960	1970	1972
8 Real GDP (billions of 2012 dollars)	1,110.2	817.8	1,331.1	1,862.8	2,353.2	2,059.8	2,291.1	3,262.1	4,954.4	5,386.7
9 Economic growth rate (percent change in real GDP)	—	−1.2	8.8	18.9	8.0	−11.6	8.7	2.6	0.2	5.3
10 Consumer price index (1982–1984 = 100)	17.1	13.0	14.0	16.3	17.6	19.5	25.0	29.8	39.8	42.5
11 Rate of inflation (percent change in CPI)	0.0	−5.1	0.7	10.9	1.7	8.3	5.8	1.4	5.6	3.4
12 Money supply, M2 (billions of $)	—	—	—	—	—	—	—	312.4	626.5	802.3
13 Effective federal funds interest rate (%)	—	—	—	—	—	—	—	3.21	7.17	4.44
14 Prime interest rate (%)	5.50	1.50	1.50	1.50	1.50	1.50	2.07	4.82	7.90	5.25
15 Population (millions)	121.9	125.7	132.1	134.9	138.4	141.4	151.7	180.8	205.1	209.9
16 Real GDP per capita (in 2012 dollars)	9,107	6,506	10,076	13,809	17,003	14,567	15,103	18,043	24,156	25,663
17 Growth rate of real GDP per capita (%)	—	−1.8	7.9	17.6	6.7	−12.5	6.9	0.5	−1.0	4.1
18 Civilian labor force (millions)	49.2	51.6	55.6	56.4	54.6	57.5	62.1	69.7	82.8	87.0
18A Employment (millions)	47.6	38.8	47.5	53.8	54.0	55.3	58.9	65.8	78.7	82.1
18B Unemployment (millions)	1.6	12.8	8.1	2.7	0.7	2.3	3.2	3.9	4.1	4.9
19 Unemployment rate (%)	3.2	24.9	14.6	4.7	1.2	3.9	5.3	5.5	4.9	5.6
20 Productivity growth, business sector (%)	—	—	—	—	—	—	8.2	1.8	2.0	3.2
21 After-tax manufacturing profit per dollar of sales (cents)	—	—	—	—	—	—	7.1	4.4	4.5	4.4
22 Price of crude oil (U.S. average, dollars per barrel)	1.27	0.67	1.02	1.19	1.21	1.41	2.51	2.88	3.18	3.39
23 Federal budget surplus (+) or deficit (−) (billions of dollars)	0.7	−2.6	−2.9	−20.5	−47.6	−15.9	−3.1	0.3	−2.8	−23.4
24 Federal budget surplus (+) or deficit (−) as a percent of GDP	0.7	−4.5	−2.8	−12.4	−21.2	−7.0	−1.0	0.1	−0.3	−1.8
25 Public debt (billions of dollars)	16.9	22.5	50.7	79.2	204.1	271.0	256.9	290.5	389.2	448.5
26 Public debt as a percent of GDP	16.2	39.3	49.3	47.7	91.0	119.1	85.7	53.6	36.3	35.1
27 Balance on current account (billions of dollars)	—	—	—	—	—	4.9	−1.8	2.8	2.3	−5.8

*Combines items from smaller accounts.

1974	1976	1978	1980	1982	1984	1986	1988	1990	1991	1992	1993
1,545.2	1,873.4	2,351.6	2,857.3	3,343.8	4,037.6	4,579.6	5,236.4	5,963.1	6,158.1	6,520.3	6,858.6
930.2	1,147.7	1,422.3	1,750.7	2,071.3	2,492.3	2,886.3	3,330.0	3,809.0	3,943.4	4,197.6	4,452.0
274.5	323.2	478.4	530.1	581.0	820.1	849.1	937.0	993.4	944.3	1,013.0	1,106.8
341.4	404.2	476.3	589.6	711.5	827.9	976.1	1,078.9	1,238.6	1,299.0	1,344.5	1,364.9
−0.8	−1.6	−25.4	−13.1	−20.0	−102.7	−131.9	−109.4	−77.9	−28.6	−34.7	−65.2
1,338.3	1,613.2	2,024.4	2,428.9	2,806.8	3,439.2	3,894.3	4,451.9	5,074.6	5,225.7	5,560.1	5,855.1
1,346.4	1,609.4	2,022.7	2,418.6	2,834.5	3,433.9	3,831.2	4,471.6	5,013.8	5,164.4	5,475.2	5,730.3
887.7	1,048.3	1,316.8	1,622.2	1,893.0	2,215.9	2,542.1	2,948.0	3,340.4	3,450.5	3,668.2	3,817.3
23.2	20.3	16.5	19.0	23.8	24.7	18.3	22.5	28.2	38.6	60.6	90.1
71.7	87.4	114.8	182.2	274.8	330.2	353.1	377.9	433.4	391.8	365.6	353.1
125.7	174.3	238.6	223.6	229.9	337.9	324.4	414.5	417.7	452.6	477.2	524.6
112.2	131.0	166.0	171.6	171.2	228.2	256.5	325.5	353.2	354.2	400.2	428.0
125.9	148.1	170.0	200.0	241.8	297.0	336.8	383.2	440.9	476.7	503.4	517.2
1,251.8	1,502.6	1,863.7	2,323.6	2,791.6	3,292.7	3,733.1	4,283.4	4,913.8	5,084.9	5,420.9	5,657.9
1,100.8	1,330.0	1,634.1	2,024.1	2,436.9	2,914.8	3,295.3	3,777.5	4,319.1	4,496.0	4,808.1	5,009.2
5,146	6,098	7,340	8,888	10,494	12,330	13,691	15,414	17,264	17,734	18,714	19,245
13.3	11.6	10.7	11.1	12.0	11.3	8.8	8.5	8.4	8.8	9.4	7.9

1974	1976	1978	1980	1982	1984	1986	1988	1990	1991	1992	1993
5,660.1	5,952.8	6,572.8	6,763.5	6,810.1	7,637.7	8,231.7	8,872.2	9,371.5	9,361.3	9,691.1	9,957.7
−0.5	5.4	5.5	−0.3	−1.8	7.2	3.5	4.2	1.9	−0.1	3.5	2.8
51.9	58.4	67.9	86.4	97.7	105.5	110.8	120.7	134.2	138.2	142.3	146.3
12.1	5.0	9.0	12.4	3.8	4.0	1.2	4.4	6.3	3.0	3.0	2.8
902.1	1,152.0	1,366.0	1,599.8	1,905.9	2,306.4	2,728.0	2,988.2	3,271.8	3,372.2	3,424.7	3,474.5
10.51	5.05	7.94	13.35	12.24	10.23	6.80	7.57	8.10	5.69	3.52	3.02
10.80	6.84	9.05	15.28	14.85	12.06	8.32	9.32	10.01	8.46	6.25	6.00
213.9	218.1	222.6	227.7	232.2	236.4	240.7	245.1	250.2	253.5	256.9	260.3
26,461	27,294	29,527	29,704	29,329	32,308	34,199	36,198	37,456	36,928	37,723	38,255
−1.5	4.4	4.4	−1.4	−2.7	6.3	2.5	3.2	0.7	−1.4	2.2	1.4
92.0	96.2	102.2	107.0	110.2	113.5	117.8	121.7	125.9	126.4	128.1	129.2
86.8	88.8	96.0	99.3	99.5	105.0	109.6	115.0	118.8	117.7	118.5	120.3
5.2	7.4	6.2	7.7	10.7	8.5	8.2	6.7	7.1	8.6	9.6	8.9
5.6	7.7	6.1	7.1	9.7	7.5	7.0	5.5	5.6	6.8	7.5	6.9
−1.7	3.2	1.1	−0.2	−0.8	2.7	2.9	1.5	1.0	3.3	4.4	−0.6
6.4	5.5	5.3	5.6	4.4	4.8	4.6	6.6	4.8	4.1	3.1	3.7
6.87	8.19	9.00	21.59	28.52	25.88	12.51	12.58	20.03	16.54	15.99	14.25
−6.1	−73.7	−59.2	−73.8	−128.0	−185.4	−221.2	−155.2	−221.0	−269.2	−290.3	−255.1
−0.4	−3.9	−2.5	−2.6	−3.8	−4.6	−4.8	−3.0	−3.7	−4.4	−4.5	−3.7
492.7	653.5	789.2	930.2	1,197.1	1,663.0	2,214.8	2,684.4	3,364.8	3,801.7	4,177.0	4,535.7
31.9	34.9	33.6	32.6	35.8	41.2	48.4	51.3	56.4	61.7	64.1	66.1
2.0	4.3	−15.1	2.3	−5.5	−94.3	−147.2	−121.2	−79.0	2.9	−51.6	−84.8

Sources: Bureau of Economic Analysis; Bureau of Labor Statistics; Federal Reserve System; *Economic Report of the President 2022;* and U.S. Energy Information Administration.

Selected Economics Statistics for Various Years, 1994–2021

Statistics in rows 1–5 are in billions of dollars in the year specified. Numbers may not add to totals because of rounding.

GDP AND INCOME DATA	1994	1995	1996	1997	1998	1999	2000	2001	2002	2003	2004	2005	2006
1 Gross domestic product (billions of nominal dollars)	7,287.2	7,639.7	8,073.1	8,577.6	9,062.8	9,631.2	10,251.0	10,581.9	10,929.1	11,456.5	12,217.2	13,039.2	13,815.6
1A Personal consumption expenditures	4,721.0	4,962.6	5,244.6	5,536.8	5,877.2	6,283.8	6,767.2	7,073.8	7,348.9	7,740.7	8,232.0	8,769.1	9,277.2
1B Gross private domestic investment	1,256.5	1,317.5	1,432.1	1,595.6	1,736.7	1,887.1	2,038.4	1,934.8	1,930.4	2,027.1	2,281.3	2,534.7	2,701.0
1C Government purchases	1,402.3	1,449.4	1,492.8	1,547.1	1,611.6	1,719.9	1,826.4	1,950.0	2,089.5	2,210.6	2,338.1	2,475.3	2,623.8
1D Net exports of goods and services	−92.5	−89.8	−96.4	−102.0	−162.7	−259.6	−381.1	−376.7	−439.7	−522.0	−634.1	−739.9	−786.5
2 Net domestic product	6,231.6	6,517.4	6,897.8	7,338.2	7,753.1	8,232.2	8,739.7	8,982.4	9,271.1	9,737.4	10,395.4	11,068.2	11,691.5
3 National income	6,114.6	6,452.3	6,870.6	7,349.9	7,825.7	8,291.5	8,872.4	9,146.6	9,394.2	9,815.8	10,495.8	11,195.5	11,942.3
3A Wages and salaries	4,006.2	4,198.1	4,416.9	4,708.8	5,071.1	5,402.7	5,847.1	6,038.3	6,135.1	6,353.6	6,719.5	7,066.1	7,479.7
3B Rent	113.7	124.9	142.5	147.1	165.2	178.5	183.5	202.4	208.4	227.1	242.8	221.1	181.1
3C Interest	347.3	357.4	361.9	394.4	456.7	466.0	542.1	542.2	462.0	443.6	377.3	471.8	564.8
3D Profits	624.8	706.2	789.5	869.7	808.5	834.9	786.6	758.7	911.7	1,056.3	1,289.3	1,488.6	1,646.3
3E Proprietor's income	456.6	481.2	543.8	584.0	640.2	696.4	753.9	831.0	870.0	897.5	962.9	979.1	1,050.9
3F Taxes on production and imports*	566.0	584.5	616.0	645.9	684.0	713.0	759.2	774.0	807.0	837.7	904.0	968.8	1,019.5
4 Personal income	5,947.1	6,291.4	6,678.5	7,092.5	7,606.7	8,006.8	8,655.9	9,012.8	9,160.9	9,498.5	10,044.3	10,604.9	11,384.7
5 Disposable income	5,254.0	5,543.0	5,841.4	6,160.7	6,574.2	6,894.9	7,419.6	7,773.8	8,108.8	8,495.0	8,995.5	9,392.5	10,027.7
6 Disposable income per capita	19,943	20,792	21,658	22,570	23,806	24,684	26,274	27,255	28,160	29,230	30,674	31,732	33,558
7 Personal saving as a percent of disposable income	6.9	7.0	6.5	6.3	6.8	5.0	4.7	4.9	5.7	5.4	5.0	2.9	3.6

OTHER STATISTICS	1994	1995	1996	1997	1998	1999	2000	2001	2002	2003	2004	2005	2006
8 Real GDP (billions of 2012 dollars)	10,358.9	10,637.0	11,038.3	11,529.2	12,045.8	12,623.4	13,138.0	13,263.4	13,488.4	13,865.5	14,399.7	14,901.3	15,315.9
9 Economic growth rate (percent change in real GDP)	4.0	2.7	3.8	4.4	4.5	4.8	4.1	1.0	1.7	2.8	3.9	3.5	2.8
10 Consumer price index (1982–1984 = 100)	150.1	153.9	159.1	161.8	164.4	168.8	174.6	177.4	181.8	185.5	191.7	198.1	203.1
11 Rate of inflation (percent change in CPI)	2.6	2.5	3.4	1.7	1.6	2.7	3.4	1.6	2.5	2.0	3.3	3.3	2.5
12 Money supply, M2 (billions of $)	3,486.4	3,629.5	3,818.6	4,032.9	4,375.2	4,638.0	4,924.7	5,432.7	5,770.9	6,065.9	6,417.2	6,680.1	7,069.5
13 Effective federal funds interest rate (%)	4.21	5.83	5.30	5.46	5.35	4.97	6.24	3.88	1.67	1.13	1.35	3.22	4.97
14 Prime interest rate (%)	7.14	8.83	8.27	8.44	8.36	8.00	9.24	6.94	4.68	4.12	4.34	6.19	7.96
15 Population (millions)	263.5	266.6	269.7	273.0	276.2	279.3	282.4	285.2	288.0	290.6	293.3	296.0	298.8
16 Real GDP per capita (in 2012 dollars)	39,313	39,899	40,928	42,232	43,613	45,197	46,523	46,506	46,835	47,713	49,095	50,342	51,258
17 Growth rate of real GDP per capita (%)	2.8	1.5	2.6	3.2	3.3	3.6	2.9	0.0	0.7	1.9	2.9	2.5	1.8
18 Civilian labor force (millions)	131.0	132.3	134.0	136.3	137.7	139.4	142.6	143.8	144.9	146.5	147.4	149.3	151.4
18A Employment (millions)	123.1	124.9	126.7	129.6	131.5	133.5	136.9	136.9	136.5	137.7	139.2	141.7	144.4
18B Unemployment (millions)	8.0	7.4	7.2	6.7	6.2	5.9	5.7	6.8	8.4	8.8	8.1	7.6	7.0
19 Unemployment rate (%)	6.1	5.6	5.4	4.9	4.5	4.2	4.0	4.7	5.8	6.0	5.5	5.1	4.6
20 Productivity growth, business sector (%)	0.9	1.1	2.1	2.7	3.3	4.2	3.0	3.2	3.1	5.7	1.6	1.8	1.2
21 After-tax manufacturing profit per dollar of sales (cents)	5.5	6.0	6.5	6.7	6.0	6.4	6.9	0.8	3.2	5.4	7.1	7.4	8.1
22 Price of crude oil (U.S. average, dollars per barrel)	13.19	14.62	18.46	17.23	10.87	15.56	26.72	21.84	22.51	27.56	36.77	50.28	59.69
23 Federal budget surplus (+) or deficit (−) (billions of dollars)	−203.2	−164.0	−107.4	−21.9	69.3	125.6	236.2	128.2	−157.8	−377.6	−412.7	−318.3	−248.2
24 Federal budget surplus (+) or deficit (−) as a percent of GDP	−2.8	−2.1	−1.3	−0.3	0.8	1.3	2.3	1.2	−1.4	−3.3	−3.4	−2.4	−1.8
25 Public debt (billions of dollars)	4,800.2	4,988.7	5,323.2	5,502.4	5,614.2	5,776.1	5,662.2	5,943.4	6,405.7	6,998.0	7,596.1	8,170.4	8,680.2
26 Public debt as a percent of GDP	65.9	65.3	65.9	64.1	61.9	60.0	55.2	56.2	58.6	61.1	62.2	62.7	62.8
27 Balance on current account (billions of dollars)	−121.6	−113.6	−124.8	−140.7	−215.1	−286.6	−401.9	−394.1	−456.1	−522.3	−635.9	−749.2	−816.7

*Combines items from smaller accounts.

2007	2008	2009	2010	2011	2012	2013	2014	2015	2016	2017	2018	2019	2020	2021**
14,474.2	14,769.9	14,478.1	15,049.0	15,599.7	16,254.0	16,843.2	17,550.7	18,206.0	18,695.1	19,479.6	20,527.2	21,372.6	20,893.7	22,996.1
9,746.6	10,050.1	9,891.2	10,260.3	10,698.9	11,047.4	11,363.5	11,847.7	12,263.5	12,693.3	13,239.1	13,913.5	14,428.7	14,047.6	15,741.6
2,673.0	2,477.6	1,929.7	2,165.5	2,332.6	2,621.8	2,826.0	3,044.2	3,237.2	3,205.0	3,381.4	3,637.8	3,826.3	3,637.8	4,120.0
2,790.6	2,983.0	3,076.3	3,155.6	3,147.9	3,136.5	3,133.0	3,168.8	3,231.6	3,303.1	3,399.1	3,572.0	3,713.9	3,859.5	4,052.7
−735.9	−740.9	−419.2	−532.3	−579.6	−551.6	−479.4	−510.0	−526.2	−506.3	−539.9	−596.2	−596.3	−651.2	−918.2
12,221.4	12,411.0	12,106.6	12,658.0	13,125.3	13,678.0	14,162.0	14,735.7	15,294.6	15,708.0	16,361.5	17,253.7	17,937.0	17,317.8	19,148.2
12,297.3	12,359.3	12,054.8	12,781.1	13,375.5	14,099.6	14,507.1	15,228.1	15,749.5	16,033.4	16,774.9	17,673.3	18,273.1	17,710.7	19,920.2
7,878.5	8,056.8	7,759.0	7,925.4	8,226.2	8,567.4	8,835.0	9,250.2	9,699.4	9,966.1	10,426.1	10,959.5	11,447.7	11,572.2	12,580.9
186.3	290.3	347.6	433.7	506.5	534.5	577.4	602.7	609.5	626.6	652.7	681.9	692.1	711.6	726.4
637.3	673.4	544.7	471.0	449.6	494.0	459.2	504.8	591.1	567.3	612.5	598.7	558.2	618.8	686.1
1,533.2	1,285.8	1,386.8	1,728.7	1,809.8	1,997.4	2,010.7	2,120.2	2,060.5	2,037.7	2,128.9	2,305.0	2,367.8	2,243.8	2,805.8
995.5	959.7	937.6	1,107.3	1,227.4	1,346.4	1,402.2	1,445.6	1,420.8	1,423.3	1,505.8	1,580.4	1,598.9	1,650.0	1,821.9
1,066.5	1,093.3	1,079.1	1,115.0	1,156.0	1,159.9	1,222.6	1,304.6	1,368.2	1,412.4	1,448.9	1,547.8	1,608.4	914.3	1,299.1
12,021.4	12,477.6	12,080.4	12,594.5	13,339.3	14,014.3	14,193.6	14,976.6	15,685.2	16,096.9	16,850.2	17,706.0	18,424.4	19,627.6	21,077.2
10,528.9	10,970.1	10,928.0	11,356.9	11,885.6	12,504.8	12,517.3	13,192.0	13,745.3	14,138.7	14,801.2	15,629.7	16,219.3	17,432.0	18,494.5
34,899	36,021	35,568	36,654	38,059	39,732	39,474	41,276	42,672	43,556	45,283	47,536	49,073	52,544	55,671
3.3	4.6	5.9	6.2	6.8	8.6	6.1	7.1	7.5	7.0	7.3	7.6	7.6	16.6	12.3

2007	2008	2009	2010	2011	2012	2013	2014	2015	2016	2017	2018	2019	2020	2021**
15,623.9	15,643.0	15,236.3	15,649.0	15,891.5	16,254.0	16,553.3	16,932.1	17,390.3	17,680.3	18,079.1	18,606.8	19,032.7	18,384.7	19,427.3
2.0	0.1	−2.6	2.7	1.5	2.3	1.8	2.3	2.7	1.7	2.3	2.9	2.3	−3.4	5.7
211.4	211.4	217.3	220.5	227.2	231.2	234.7	236.3	237.8	242.6	247.8	252.6	258.3	261.6	280.1
4.1	0.0	2.8	1.4	3.1	1.8	1.5	0.7	0.6	2.1	2.1	1.9	2.3	1.3	7.1
7,469.4	8,189.7	8,493.1	8,799.4	9,657.7	10,457.0	11,026.1	11,678.7	12,341.0	13,210.6	13,853.0	14,376.9	15,337.9	19,154.9	21,553.1
5.02	1.92	0.16	0.18	0.10	0.14	0.11	0.09	0.13	0.39	1.00	1.83	2.16	0.37	0.08
8.05	5.07	3.25	3.25	3.25	3.25	3.25	3.25	3.26	3.51	4.10	4.90	5.29	3.53	3.25
301.7	304.5	307.2	309.8	312.3	314.7	317.1	319.6	322.1	324.6	326.9	328.8	330.5	331.8	332.2
51,786	51,373	49,597	50,513	50,885	51,649	52,202	52,979	53,990	54,468	55,305	56,590	57,588	55,409	58,481
1.0	−0.8	−3.5	1.8	0.7	1.5	1.1	1.5	1.9	0.9	1.5	2.3	1.8	−3.8	5.4
153.1	154.3	154.2	153.9	153.6	155.0	155.4	155.9	157.1	159.2	160.3	162.1	163.5	160.8	161.2
146.1	145.4	139.9	139.1	139.9	142.5	143.9	146.3	148.8	151.4	153.3	155.8	157.5	147.8	152.6
7.1	8.9	14.3	14.8	13.7	12.5	11.5	9.6	8.3	7.8	7.0	6.3	6.0	12.9	8.6
4.6	5.8	9.3	9.6	8.9	8.1	7.4	6.2	5.3	4.9	4.4	3.9	3.7	8.1	5.4
2.5	−0.1	6.1	1.7	−0.2	0.3	1.5	0.6	0.6	1.3	1.1	1.5	2.1	2.4	1.9
7.3	4.2	5.6	8.3	9.2	8.5	8.9	8.8	7.9	8.7	8.4	9.1	8.5	6.9	13.8
66.52	94.04	56.35	74.71	95.73	94.52	95.99	87.39	44.39	38.29	48.05	61.40	55.59	36.86	65.90
−160.7	−458.6	−1,412.7	−1,294.4	−1,299.6	−1,087.0	−680.0	−485.0	−439.0	−584.7	−665.4	−779.0	−983.6	−3,132.4	−2,775.3
−1.1	−3.1	−9.8	−8.6	−8.3	−6.7	−4.0	−2.8	−2.4	−3.1	−3.4	−3.8	−4.6	−15.0	−12.1
9,229.2	10,699.8	12,311.3	14,025.2	15,222.9	16,432.7	17,156.1	18,141.4	18,922.2	19,976.8	20,492.7	21,974.1	23,201.4	27,747.8	29,617.2
63.8	72.4	85.0	93.2	97.6	101.1	101.9	103.4	103.9	106.9	105.2	107.0	108.6	132.8	128.8
−736.6	−696.5	−379.7	−432.0	−455.3	−418.1	−339.5	−370.0	−408.9	−397.6	−361.7	−438.2	−472.2	−616.1	−821.6

**Data for 2021 and the years immediately prior are subject to change because of subsequent government data revisions.

Sources: Bureau of Economic Analysis; Bureau of Labor Statistics; Federal Reserve System; Economic Report of the President 2022; and U.S. Energy Information Administration.

Index